CIVIL LIBERTIES AND HUMAN RIGHTS
IN ENGLAND AND WALES

CIVIL LIBERTIES AND HUMAN RIGHTS IN ENGLAND AND WALES

Second Edition

DAVID FELDMAN

OXFORD

UNIVERSITY PRESS

OXFORD
UNIVERSITY PRESS

Great Clarendon Street, Oxford OX2 6DP

Oxford University Press is a department of the University of Oxford.
It furthers the University's objective of excellence in research, scholarship,
and education by publishing worldwide in

Oxford New York

Auckland Bangkok Buenos Aires Cape Town Chennai
Dar es Salaam Delhi Hong Kong Istanbul Karachi Kolkata
Kuala Lumpur Madrid Melbourne Mexico City Mumbai Nairobi
São Paulo Shanghai Singapore Taipei Tokyo Toronto

and an associated company in Berlin

Oxford is a registered trade mark of Oxford University Press
in the UK and in certain other countries

Published in the United States
by Oxford University Press Inc., New York

A catalogue record for this book is available from the British Library

Library of Congress Cataloging in Publication Data
ISBN 0–19–876559–2
ISBN 0–19–876503–7 (pbk.)

Typeset in Adobe Minion
by RefineCatch Limited, Bungay, Suffolk
Printed in Great Britain
on acid-free paper by
Biddles Ltd
Guildford and King's Lynn

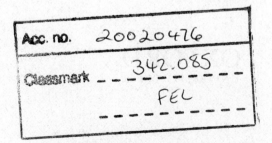

In memory of Alec Feldman, FRIBA
1910–1976

OUTLINE CONTENTS

DETAILED CONTENTS

PART I PUTTING VALUES INTO PRACTICE: THE NATURE OF CIVIL LIBERTIES AND HUMAN RIGHTS

PART III PRIVACY

PREFACE TO THE SECOND EDITION

Since the first edition of this book appeared in 1993, the law in the UK has been transformed. There is now, for the first time, a law of human rights in England and Wales, the Convention rights under the Human Rights Act 1998 complementing and to some extent subsuming the law of civil liberties. In some ways, this has made the task of preparing a new edition less troublesome: an author on the subject no longer has to struggle to impose a rights-based structure without national legal authority on a diffuse mass of public and private law. It is no longer considered eccentric to explain and evaluate the law in terms of its compliance with, or capacity to advance, international human rights. On the other hand, the law is no less diffuse, and the volume of material emanating from Strasbourg, Westminster, and national courts has grown virtually unmanageably. What is more, as the 1998 Act has started to bite, the novelties of the new statutory structure seem to have multiplied the uncertainties.

The new shape of the book reflects this. Every chapter has been substantially rewritten. There is now a full treatment of the principles and machinery of the 1998 Act in Chapter 2. Chapter 3, on dignity and equality, is largely new; the complex interweaving of standards derived from Community law and international law with those of national law has made the treatment of discrimination larger, if not necessarily clearer. The discussion of rights to life and physical integrity in Chapters 4 and 5 may be almost unrecognizable to those who were familiar with the first edition: the caselaw of the European Court of Human Rights on the positive obligations of the state under Articles 2 and 3 of the European Convention on Human Rights has altered the picture radically. Extensive changes to procedural rules concerning criminal investigation and procedure (particularly the Regulation of Investigatory Powers Act 2000) and immigration and asylum adjudication have resulted in substantial amendments and additions to Chapters 6 and 8, while some growth in sensitivity to the needs and rights of prisoners has necessitated extensive changes to Chapter 7. The changes to the chapters on aspects of privacy and freedom of expression have generally been less fundamental, but they have been revised to take account of the impact of developing caselaw and of the Human Rights Act 1998 on, for example, the relationship between privacy-related rights and freedom of expression, of the Data Protection Act 1998 and the Freedom of Information Act 2000, and of a continuing proliferation of judicial decisions on aspects of contempt of court. Chapter 18, on protest and assembly, has been substantially revised in the light of a growing literature on the subject (some of which has been critical of the treatment of the subject in the first edition and all of which has been illuminating) and a mixture of relatively liberal judicial decisions with relatively illiberal legislation. The discussion of social rights, including rights to equality and health care, has been taken from the penultimate chapter of the first edition, distributed through the remainder of the book as it became relevant, and brought up to date. My main regret about this new edition is that it has proved impossible to find room for discussion of the rights to education (which had a place in the first edition, albeit a small one) or freedom of religion (which remains a notable omission). Perhaps they can be included in a subsequent edition, should there be a call for one (although it might require advances in the bookbinder's art, which the size of this edition already taxes severely).

For all that has changed, the aim is the same as it was in 1993: to provide an accessible account of the law, illustrating its operation in a (perhaps idiosyncratically chosen) range of contexts. I hope that readers will be drawn to look behind the technicalities at the values which shape the law and the policies which the law advances. The shape, scope, and meaning of the rights and liberties are always contested, and it behoves us to contribute thoughtfully to the debate. In coming years, society's commitment to liberty will probably be subject to special strains as the free world takes steps to protect itself against appalling acts of terrorism of the kind that caused horrific loss of life in the destruction of the World Trade Centre in New York and elsewhere earlier this week. It is important to ensure that the response, including any restriction of liberty, is proportionate to the great aim of countering a grave threat to the enjoyment of human rights and civil liberties. Our attachment to our liberties should not obscure the fact that many of them have instrumental rather than intrinsic worth. Preserving them intact would be a Pyrrhic victory if it makes it unreasonably easy for a few people to commit unspeakable atrocities which threaten the social and economic infrastructure which makes it possible to enjoy a free and worthwhile life. On the other hand, lawyers have a special responsibility to try to ensure that we do not lose sight of the purpose of any restriction, or of a sense of proportion.

In preparing this new edition, I have incurred many new debts of gratitude. I am grateful to the Faculty and School of Law in the University of Birmingham for funding the appointment of research assistants and associates who have helped me at various times. I have been very fortunate in the high quality of the people who held those positions and of the support which they provided: Florence Campbell helped greatly with Chapters 1 and 2, while David Green and Emma Maynard provided a mass of material relating to aspects of criminal investigation which now informs Chapters 4, 5, and 6. I have benefited hugely from the opportunity to learn from many people at the University, and especially from stimulating and informative discussions and exchanges of information and ideas with Tony Arnull, Sophie Boyron, Catherine Dupré, Evelyn Ellis, Adrian Hunt, Jules Lonbay, Bernadette Lynch, Jeremy McBride, John Miller, Liz Wicks, Gordon Woodman, and Moira Wright, and students taking numerous undergraduate and postgraduate courses.

Outside the University, the reviewers of the first edition were very constructive. Where I have failed to take their criticisms on board in preparing the new edition, it is usually not so much because I disagree with them as because I lack the necessary knowledge and ability to take the sensible steps which they suggested. I am grateful to Stephen Cretney, Christine Gray and Christopher McCrudden, who have pointed out various errors and offered new insights; I hope this edition reflects their help. Lord Lester of Herne Hill QC has offered many ideas and much information and support. I have learned a great deal from people participating in the various seminars in which I have taken part. Those organized by the Judicial Studies Board were particularly illuminating, and I am especially indebted to Dame Brenda Hale, Sir Anthony Hooper, Sir John Laws, Judge David Pearl, and Sir Stephen Sedley. My colleagues serving the two Houses of Parliament, and the members of the Joint Committee on Human Rights, have helped (perhaps more than they realised) by raising novel issues and suggesting ways of dealing with them. I owe special debts to the Chair of the Committee, Jean Corston MP, and to Andrew Makower and David Doig who were the first Clerks to the Joint Committee on Human Rights. I am grateful to the Clerk of the Parliaments for permission to publish this new edition; needless to say the views contained in it are personal to me, and do not reflect the views of any Member, Officer, or member of staff of either House or of the Houses corporately.

At Oxford University Press, I appreciate the skill of Chris Rycroft, Michaela Coulthard, Miranda Vernon, Jane Kavanagh, and Sophie Rogers, who applied enough pressure to ensure that a typescript finally appeared, while being flexible enough to allow me to do a reasonably thorough job. Without their diplomacy, there would have been no second edition. I am also grateful to Joy Ruskin-Tompkins for dealing so efficiently and speedily with the proofreading, and to all the other people who contributed during the process of editing and production to the task of converting a typescript into a real book.

My final and most significant debts are to my friends and family. In particular, Frank Meisel threw himself selflessly into the role of Deputy Head of the School of Law at the University of Birmingham when I was Dean and Head of School between 1997 and 2000, while Sarah Taylor was an outstandingly supportive PA, a role taken over by Michelle Sampson and Yasmin Muthy in the Committee Office of the House of Lords from 2000. Without their friendship and practical support, this project would have been impossible. No words can express my gratitude to and admiration for my family. Jill, Rebecca, and Jonathan got on very successfully with their own lives, offered encouragement when it was needed, tolerated my long absences in the room above the garage which now serves as my study, and (more difficult) put up with my foul moods when I was in the house. We are still together, and by my reckoning reasonably sane: perhaps no more need be said. Winnie, the dog who sat with me while most of the first edition was written, is no more, and is still missed; her successors, Hosta and Chloe, are neither as scholarly nor as patient, and sensibly left me to get on with writing alone, as did the two cats, the three sheep, and the horse. I am grateful to all the animals for not making a mess of the drafts.

All these people (and animals), and many others whom I have no space to mention individually, can claim credit for any good qualities which this book has. I am wholly responsible for its shortcomings.

It is time for me to let go of the book. It is dedicated to my father, the best sort of liberal. If you, the readers, find it useful, or even interesting, his efforts in raising me will have been worthwhile.

David Feldman
Yieldingtree, 14 September 2001

TABLE OF UNITED KINGDOM CASES

TABLE OF CASES FROM
OTHER JURISDICTIONS

EUROPEAN COURT OF JUSTICE

TABLE OF UNITED KINGDOM LEGISLATION

TABLE OF LEGISLATION FROM
OTHER JURISDICTIONS

TABLE OF INTERNATIONAL
INSTRUMENTS

PART I

PUTTING VALUES INTO PRACTICE: THE NATURE OF CIVIL LIBERTIES AND HUMAN RIGHTS

1

SOME BASIC VALUES: CIVIL LIBERTIES, HUMAN RIGHTS, AND AUTONOMY

The drive to protect civil liberties presupposes that freedom is worth fostering. Yet the seemingly simple notion that those who live in a free society are more fortunate than those who live under less liberal conditions is problematic. This study of civil liberties therefore begins by examining the various meanings of freedom, the ways in which people can be free or unfree, and the kinds of reasons which may justify treating liberty as a good which individuals and society should pursue. Is the exercise of free choice and action a good in itself, as some liberal individualists would argue? If so, it requires us to limit the power of the state to interfere with individual autonomy, even to the extent of restricting the state's capacity to advance collective goals. Does the exercise of individual freedoms tend to produce the greatest good, as utilitarian liberals suggest? If so, does this mean that a freedom can legitimately be abridged in order to secure advantages for some which outweigh the benefits, in the aggregate, which flow from the exercise of the freedom in question? These are issues which have a practical importance for lawyers and politicians, as they affect both the range of rights which societies are prepared to acknowledge that their members have, and the principles determining the limits of the rights when they collide either with other rights or with important social interests, such as the relief of hunger or the maintenance of democracy. Some assertions of rights, and some methods of protecting them, may not always be compatible with other ideals. In order to clarify some basic issues, this chapter examines the philosophical background to civil liberties and rights, and the relationship between models of rights, models of democracy, and constitutional structures, in order to explain the position from which the discussion of concrete rights and liberties proceeds in the rest of the book.

1.1 LIBERTY, LIBERTIES, CIVIL LIBERTIES, FUNDAMENTAL LIBERTIES, AND HUMAN RIGHTS

As Professor Keith Ewing and Professor Conor Gearty have observed, the first edition of this book failed to 'address the question of where human rights end and civil liberties begin'.[1] One needs to distinguish between five ideas: liberty; liberties; civil

---

[1] K. D. Ewing and C. A. Gearty, *The Struggle for Civil Liberties: Political Freedom and the Rule of Law in Britain, 1914–1945* (Oxford: Oxford University Press, 2000), 3.

liberties; fundamental liberties; and human rights. The notion that it is good for people to enjoy 'liberty', or freedom, is basic to political liberalism. In its simplest and most general sense, liberty entails non-interference by others with one's freedom of choice and action. It supports personal autonomy. It can never be absolute, because protection against interference is valuable only when one is with other people who might wish to interfere, and in such a situation those people also have an expectation of liberty which restrict one's own. Furthermore, it would be wrong to overrate the value of autonomy. An autonomous person displays certain character-istics: a degree of reflectiveness, self-awareness, and social awareness which allows him or her to form plans and understand their impact on everyone in the immediate social group. It is linked to dignity, as the use one makes of autonomy contributes to dignity, self-respect, and the esteem of one's peers. However, it is only one of many personal and social aptitudes, and it is not determinative of a person's entitlement to respect.[2]

To allow clashes of liberty to be resolved, one's liberty must be policed by law or some other form of social regulation. When the state makes itself responsible for this, it may set about its task by establishing certain aspects of liberty as being particularly valuable, and identifying these as distinct areas of liberty, or 'liberties'. These may be regarded as particularly valuable for a variety of reasons. Sometimes they protect people's physical or moral integrity, as in the case of freedom from violence or enforced experimentation. Other liberties protect human dignity, advance democratic politics, foster fair public decision-making, safeguard one's ability to enter into social relationships for fun, business, or more intimate purposes, or perform other socially worthwhile roles. Differentiating between liberties allows their relative weights to be assessed, and balanced against each other or against public-interest grounds which may be asserted for interfering with them. The state need not differentiate systematic-ally between liberties in this way. As we shall see, the traditional approach in the UK was to treat liberty as an undifferentiated whole, leaving the state (particularly Parlia-ment) a very wide discretion to decide for itself how to balance aspects of liberty against each other or against public interests in different settings. But where liberties are distinguished from each other, it makes possible a more principled treatment of conflicts between them than would otherwise be possible.

There is no generally agreed way of separating civil liberties from other liberties, but the word 'civil' is taken for present purposes to refer to the way in which the liberty contributes to the relationship between the individual and the state in civil society. Civil liberties are those which people enjoy by virtue of being citizens of a state, rather than by reason of being merely members of human society. To say that something is a civil liberty implies that (a) the liberty is particularly significant in allowing people to participate as a citizen in the functioning of the state, such as freedom of political expression, or (b) the liberty is particularly significant in defining the relationship between the state and its citizens, such as freedom from arbitrary or discriminatory treatment. In either case, describing something as a civil liberty

---

[2] G. Dworkin, *The Theory and Practice of Autonomy* (Cambridge: Cambridge University Press, 1988), chs 1 and 2; T. E. Hill, *Autonomy and Self-Respect* (Cambridge: Cambridge University Press, 1991), chs 1 and 2.

indicates that one thinks that the state has a special obligation to protect one against interference with it, either as a matter of political morality or as a matter of law.

This marks a step beyond simple liberties, which are essentially rights not to be interfered with, or 'negative rights', as they are sometimes called. Civil liberties, however, impose positive obligations on the state to assist people in protecting or exercising the liberties. They can thus be seen as being connected to positive rights, people's claims on the state for help. The nature and extent of the state's positive obligations will vary. Where this obligation is more than usually powerful, the liberty in question can be described as 'fundamental', and where a state's constitution gives special status to some liberties, these can be said to be constitutional rights or liberties.

The term 'human rights' is used here in a technical sense. It would be possible to use it to refer to rights which people have merely by reason of being part of a human society. It would then be necessary to consider what rights, if any, people have intrinsically as human beings.[3] To avoid the need for this, 'human rights' will be treated as a legal term of art, referring to those rights which have been enshrined in international human rights treaties, particularly in the period since the end of World War II. Such treaties have made states subject to legal obligations, in public international law, to guarantee certain rights to all who find themselves within their jurisdiction. Such rights may be both negative and positive, and go beyond the scope of civil liberties, not least because they apply to everyone subject to a state's jurisdiction, not only to citizens of that state.

1.2 THE NOTION OF LIBERTY AS A GOOD

Since the entire structure of civil liberties presupposes that liberty is worth fostering, it is useful to start by briefly examining two questions. First, why and under what conditions is liberty a good? Secondly, what types of positive rights may be needed in order to protect whatever sort of liberty is thought to merit protection?

(1) WHY IS FREEDOM A GOOD?

Two questions arise here. First, is liberty generally, or a particular liberty, a good in itself, or does it derive its value from its capacity to advance ulterior goods? These alternatives may be called respectively the *deontological* and the *teleological*. The *deontological* approach seeks to explain liberty as something to be sought whether or not it advances any ulterior purpose. The *teleological* approach associates the value of freedom with some further good which the exercise of freedom advances. This may be an advantage for society as a whole, as in the case of John Stuart Mill's utilitarian defence of liberty,[4] or the critical social theory of Roberto Unger which has been

---

[3] See, e.g. C. S. Nino, *The Ethics of Human Rights* (Oxford: Clarendon Press, 1991), chs 1 and 5.

[4] J. S. Mill, *On Liberty*, in M. Warnock (ed.), *Utilitarianism* (London: Fontana, 1962), 126–250. Mill's views are discussed below.

called 'super-liberalism'.[5] Alternatively, it may be an advantage for an individual or group, such as the right of minorities to follow their particular religious practices. Teleological reasoning limits access to goods. They will be available only where making them available, to particular people and in particular circumstances, advances the desired ulterior object. Teleological theories therefore require principles controlling the distribution of goods, and objectives by reference to which any pattern of distribution may be evaluated. Deontological theories, on the other hand, are non-distributive. Once something has been identified as a good, it must *prima facie* be made available to all, without differentiating by reference to preferred outcomes.

However, at a certain point the distinction between deontological and teleological theories of freedom collapses, since any idea of liberty must necessarily depend ultimately on an evaluation of the proper ends of human beings in the light of a vision of the human condition.[6] This may be based in part on experience; indeed, it would be a poor theory of rights which left experience of human aspirations out of account. Yet experience takes us only so far. If anthropologists tour the world and find that there is a virtually universal taboo on the taking of life, this may suggest that life is important and is universally valued, but it does not require us to hold that people have a right to live, still less that all people always have a right to live. Ultimately, a commitment to any right must be based on a belief about the range of aspirations which it is proper or desirable for people to pursue.[7] This requires an evaluative assessment which is additional to, and may even supplant, observation of existing practices. However, the fact that it involves an element of moral subjectivity does not make the judgment less valuable, so long as one accepts the persuasiveness of the outcome.[8]

Secondly, do liberties and rights derive their worth from their value to individuals only, or does it depend also on their value to society? Historically, liberty and rights have usually been espoused by individualists, and viewed with suspicion by socialists as hurdles to achieving social goals. However, as suggested above, rights represent a balance between potentially conflicting interests, some individual, some social. We will see in Chapter 3 and subsequently how particular human rights encapsulate a political judgment about the extent to which and the circumstances in which a right may be restricted for social or individual purposes, and the kinds of justification for such a limitation which will be acceptable. It would be simplistic to present rights and liberties as anti-social to the extent that they advance individuals' interests. Before protecting rights or liberties by law, a state, and the society it protects, will want to be satisfied that they are likely to foster a good society, not merely to make individuals better off. Recognizing and protecting someone's right or liberty, and tolerating their exercise of it, involves a potential cost to other individuals and to society generally. It is

---

[5] R. M. Unger, *Law and Modern Society: Toward a Criticism of Social Theory* (New York: Free Press, 1976), 192–223, 238–42; R. M. Unger, 'The Critical Legal Studies Movement', 96 *Harv. LR* 563–675 (1983); W. Ewald, 'Unger's Philosophy: A Critical Legal Study', 97 *Yale LJ* 665–756 (1988) at 733*ff*; R. F. Devlin, 'On the Road to Radical Reform: A Critical View of Unger's Politics' (1990) 28 *Osgoode Hall LJ* 641–721.

[6] This point is explained later in this section, and in s. 1(2) below.

[7] For this reason, the anthropological school of natural rights writing, typified by M. Mead, 'Some Anthropological Considerations Concerning Natural Law' (1961) 6 *Natural Law Forum* 51–64, is wanting.

[8] See J. Mackie, *Ethics: Inventing Right and Wrong* (London: Penguin, 1990).

proper for societies to give more weight to liberties and rights when they are exercised in ways which produce most social benefit, or impose the least social cost. Even privacy-related rights, at first sight entirely individualistic, confer social benefits by making possible social relationships and family life, and may be limited to secure other social benefits, as Article 8 of the European Convention on Human Rights demonstrates (see Chapter 9 below).

This does not mean that individual interests are unimportant in justifying the protection of liberties and rights. For many liberal theorists, liberalism is fundamentally the belief that discovering and pursuing one's own conception of the Good is the highest purpose of human life. Respecting individuals' conceptions of the Good maximizes each individual's moral autonomy. Freedom to identify one's own idea of the Good, and to develop a plan for life accordingly, should be constrained only to the extent necessary to protect the similar liberties of other people, and maintain a society in which such choice is possible. The law should protect at least the basic liberties, that is, those necessary to the pursuit of any socially acceptable conception of the good life. This is the approach which John Rawls adopts in *A Theory of Justice*.[9] It requires that basic liberties be given considerable respect, and that they should have priority over the pursuit of social goods (such as economic development) perhaps even to the extent of giving them the status of entrenched, constitutional rights, in order to shield them from challenge in the day-to-day rough and tumble of political contention.[10]

Seeing individual choice of goods as the highest human good, and the priority of liberty over other values, are highly controversial ideas. Socialist and communitarian theorists have challenged any political theory which places the individual and his or her choices somehow outside society. People's values and choices are shaped by society, and liberty is possible only if nurtured by society.[11] Communitarians therefore argue against elevating individual autonomy over social goods, and reject the priority of liberty. These are not conclusive arguments against a Rawlsian form of liberalism, as it is implicit in Rawls's writing that liberty can be secured only through social co-operation, and that the priority of liberty needs justification by reference to social conditions.[12] It is for this reason that Rawls, while treating the distribution of liberty in society as an essential part of a theory of social justice, speaks of society as 'a system of fair co-operation over time'.[13] The gulf between Rawls and the communitarians is much smaller than that between both of them and individualist libertarians such as Robert Nozick, who insist on the subordination of social organization to individual

[9] J. Rawls, *A Theory of Justice*, revised edn. (Oxford: Clarendon Press, 1999), 78–81, 112–8, 358–65. Associated with this notion may be an idea that the driving force behind a person's choice of goods is, or should be, the search for self-improvement and self-fulfilment, which gives a distinctive moral justification for nurturing individual freedom of choice. Rawls made this the basis of the psychology which underpins his theory. He called it the 'Aristotelian principle': ibid., 372–80. As will be seen, however, this is not a necessary part of liberal theory.

[10] This underlies the idea of rights as 'trumps' which in case of conflict will defeat other interests which do not amount to rights: R. Dworkin, *Taking Rights Seriously* (London: Duckworth, 1976), esp. ch. 7.

[11] S. Mulhall and A. Swift, *Liberals and Communitarians* (Oxford: Basil Blackwell, 1996), 13–18.

[12] J. Rawls, *Political Liberalism* (New York: Columbia University Press, 1993), 320–3.

[13] J. Rawls, *Political Liberalism*, 15; R. Alejandro, 'Rawls's Communitarianism' (1993) 23 *Canadian Journal of Philosophy* 75–100; S. A. Schwarzenbach, 'Rawls, Hegel and Communitarianism' (1991) 19 *Political Theory* 539–71.

autonomy. (More will be said about Nozick's theory below.) Within the liberal tradition, H. L. A. Hart argued that it is rational to prefer basic freedoms to an improvement in material conditions (at least in a society where there is limited abundance of
wealth and resources) only if one harbours the ideal of 'a public-spirited citizen who
prizes political activity and service to others as among the chief goods of life and
could not contemplate as tolerable an exchange of the opportunities for such activity
for mere material goods or contentment'.[14] In *Political Liberalism*, Rawls makes it clear
that the free citizen's willingness to subordinate personal interests to social goods
when participating in public decision-making is a political choice, not a presupposition about human nature, but one must still accept that it is proper for people to wish
to behave in this way.[15]

A moral argument for the propriety of taking account of social goals in justifying
individuals' choices is provided by Professor Joseph Raz in *The Morality of Freedom*.[16]
Raz argues that the freedom of autonomous moral actors to make their own decisions
is valuable partly because it advances social ends. The identification of basic liberties
therefore depends, in part at least, on governmental notions of the public good. In
respect of rights to freedom of expression, privacy, freedom of religion, and freedom
from discrimination, for example, 'one reason for affording special protection to
individual interests is that thereby one also protects a collective good, an aspect of a
public culture'.[17] At the same time, certain social goods are needed if freedom is to
have value. Freedom is useful only if the social and economic structure of society
provides a sufficient range of choices to allow people's capacity for choice to be
exercised. Accordingly, freedom is seen as a collective as much as an individual good.[18]
For individuals, Raz argues, autonomy contributes to a person's well-being only if it
leads one to pursue things which are objectively valuable and worthy of choice.[19] It
seems that this may constrain the range of permitted freedoms and the purposes to
which they may morally be put: a decision to make a freedom into a constitutional
right is an expression of the collective political culture of a community. Individuals
acting collectively must only maintain a social commitment to the idea of the moral
significance of individual choice if that choice is to have moral value. Individual
freedom of choice is contingent on social arrangements.

The belief in human beings as social individuals, beings for whom both sociability
and individuality are essential parts of their make-up, is ultimately a deontological
belief. This is liable to leave one open to charges of subjectiveness, and one's theory to
the accusation that it represents no more than a personal preference. However, beliefs
of this sort may be objectively assessed as being more or less rational, according to

---

[14] H. L. A. Hart, 'Rawls on Liberty and its Priority', in N. Daniels (ed.), *Reading Rawls: Critical Studies of A Theory of Justice* (Oxford: Basil Blackwell, 1975), 230–52 at 252 (reproduced in H. L. A. Hart, *Essays in Jurisprudence and Philosophy* (Oxford: Clarendon Press, 1983), 223–47).

[15] See Rawls, *A Theory of Justice*, revised edn., 373–4.

[16] Oxford: Clarendon Press, 1986.

[17] Ibid., 256.

[18] Ibid., 255–60.

[19] J. Raz, *Ethics in the Public Domain: Essays in the Morality of Law and Politics* (Oxford: Clarendon Press, 1994), ch. 4, esp. at 104–5.

how well they fit people's observable behaviour and psychologies, and people normally function most healthily as members of social groups. Professor John Finnis provides an instructive example of this approach. He grounds his view of humanity in two principles: the idea that certain objects of desire are self-evidently good, and so are not chosen merely through subjective preference; and the claim that one of these self-evident goods is practical reasonableness, which helps one to identify the other self-evident goods.[20] Although Finnis argues that the self-evident desirability of certain goods means their selection is not subjective, his claim is just as fully grounded in an idea of the human condition as any other. The importance of the idea of self-evidence is that it combines, on the one hand, a recognition of the deontological nature of ideas about the values which make life worth living with, on the other hand, an assertion that deontological beliefs (despite not being logically verifiable or falsifiable) need be no less rational than teleological ones.

This is a convincing position (even if one does not accept that Finnis's self-evident goods are as self-evident as Finnis believes them to be), because any teleological position which is morally valuable ultimately rests on a deontological claim. For example, utilitarianism at first sight appears to avoid deontology by adopting an apparently scientific principle for maximizing happiness (or minimizing pain). John Stuart Mill, in justifying liberty, assumed that liberty would make available new ways of looking at the world, and that this would be more likely than censorship to lead to a better-understood and better-ordered world. The benefits of allowing freedom of thought and expression, therefore, would tend to outweigh any short-term disadvantages, as long as certain limits are imposed to prevent freedoms from being used so as to precipitate actual harm to other people.[21] This way of measuring advantages and disadvantages, however, depends on certain assumptions. One is that everyone is sufficiently alike, feeling pleasure and pain in the same way and to the same extent, for their responses to be commensurable. This idea, expressed by Bentham in the maxim that each person is to count for one, and nobody is to count for more than one,[22] is fundamental to democratic as well as utilitarian theory, but it reflects a value judgment which cannot be scientifically tested and which rests on metaphysical assumptions. Another of Mill's presuppositions is that the pains of being subjected to offence are less weighty, but the pain of physical harm is weightier, than the benefits which flow from advancing knowledge. This again rests on an act of faith rather than logical derivation from some other value, and so is properly regarded as deontological. Behind every teleological justification lurks a deontological belief.

The set of beliefs which best serves to justify rights and liberties seems to me to be that which forms the foundation for Raz's thesis: a belief that freedom of will and a capacity for self-directed action within a social environment are the most important of human characteristics. In order to respect each other's capacity for independent

---

[20] J. Finnis, *Natural Law and Natural Rights* (Oxford: Clarendon Press, 1980), chs 3, 4, and 5.

[21] J. S. Mill, *On Liberty*, ch. 4, in M. Warnock (ed.), *Utilitarianism* (London: Fontana, 1962), 126–250 at 205–25.

[22] J. Bentham, Introduction to *Constitutional Code*, in J. Bowring (ed.), *Works of Jeremy Bentham* (Edinburgh: William Tait, 1843), ix. 5–8; J. S. Mill, *Utilitarianism*, in Warnock (ed.), *Utilitarianism*, 251–321 at 319.

decision-making and action, where one's will is not overborne by coercion but operates within a set of social relationships, we must be given room to experiment with
different ideas and aims, to select our favoured goals, to decide on the best way of
achieving them, and to give effect to that decision. If one has such a view of human
beings, then freedom is essential; freedom is a good for all, deriving its value as much
from its social importance as from its contribution to individual autonomy.[23]
Furthermore, because the idea is based on what is assumed to be human nature, there
is an underlying idea that people are equally entitled to any goods that are going, or
(where the goods are in limited supply) to an equal opportunity to compete for them.
This leads both to a presumption in favour of sharing out goods on a *per capita* basis,
and to a presumption that the *per capita* share should be equal unless there are
reasonable grounds, related to the nature of the good in question, for distinguishing
between people.[24]

(2) WHAT SORT OF RIGHTS AND FREEDOMS DOES THIS CONCEPTION DEMAND?

It might seem that the idea of autonomy implies merely that people should be free
from interference by others. If so, it would be satisfied by rights to non-interference
(liberties), calling for no right to assistance from, or imposition of any positive duty
on, others (what one might call, following Hohfeld, claim-rights).[25] But a right to
freedom from interference will not necessarily guarantee the conditions necessary for
individuals to exercise autonomy, for two reasons. First, some vulnerable people need
support if they are to be able to exercise autonomy. Society has responsibilities, discharged through performance of duties, towards those who are not capable of living a
life of full moral autonomy on their own resources. For instance, a legal system might
not recognize children or people with a mental disability as fully autonomous, but
despite (or because of) this might regard them as being the beneficiaries of duties
owed to them for their benefit by parents, doctors, or governmental bodies.[26] These
people have claim-rights, which focus on what other people can do for the right-
holder rather than on what right-holders can do for themselves. Secondly, even fully
competent adults may be free from interference with their wish to participate in

[23] See J. Rawls, *Theory of Justice*; J. Raz, *Morality of Freedom*; R. Nozick, *Anarchy, State and Utopia* (Oxford: Basil Blackwell, 1974); Sir Isaiah Berlin, *Four Essays on Liberty* (Oxford: Clarendon Press, 1969), 121–31. This approach is different from that of C. Kukathas and P. Pettit, *Rawls, A Theory of Justice and its Critics* (Cambridge: Polity Press, 1990), who argue that community solidarity has value because of its importance to individuals, and can therefore be weighed against other individual goods rather than being an independent source of moral value.

[24] P. Westen, *Speaking of Equality: An Analysis of the Rhetorical Force of 'Equality' in Moral and Legal Discourse* (Princeton, NJ: Princeton University Press, 1991), 146–62, offers the most comprehensive analysis in the literature to date of the moral foundations of claims to equal *per capita* distributions.

[25] W. N. Hohfeld, *Fundamental Legal Conceptions as Applied in Judicial Reasoning* (New Haven, Conn.: Yale University Press, 1923).

[26] The idea that those whose interests are served by the performance of duties have rights is known as the 'interest' or 'benefit' theory of rights, and is distinguished from the 'will' theory according to which capacity to hold a right depends on being able to exercise the will to assert or give effect to the right. See J. Waldron, *Theories of Rights* (Oxford: Oxford University Press, 1984), 9–12.

political discourse, but may be unable to exercise that freedom effectively unless society provides systems for communication and political organization. The real value of people's liberties in practice depends on the extent to which a society recognizes a responsibility to provide the infrastructure which allows individuals to participate and maximize the fulfilment of their choices. Autonomy is worthless unless one has the ability to live according to one's autonomous moral judgments.[27]

The way in which a society selects and balances claim-rights and negative freedoms depends on the respective places of individualism and collective responsibility in the dominant political culture. If the stress is laid on individual autonomy, the guaranteed rights are likely to be predominantly of the liberty type, with only such guaranteed claim-rights as are necessary to give substance to the liberties. If more emphasis is placed on responsibilities for other people's welfare, a greater range of claim-rights will result (such as rights to public provision of health and welfare services or education), perhaps with a view to ensuring that all guaranteed liberties have at least a certain minimum value to all people, but the range of guaranteed liberties may have to be reduced to allow the interference with autonomy required to enforce the claim-rights of all. This is likely, because claim-rights, once recognized, may by their nature allow or require liberties to be restricted to the extent necessary to secure the claim-rights.

The attitude which dominated Britain for most of the twentieth century valued individual freedom, but within a coercive framework designed to provide an orderly society. Particularly from the 1940s, there was a strong communitarian element on which the welfare state was founded. On the other hand, moral paternalism, which had been responsible (for example) for extensive censorship and control of life-style, was eased progressively from the late 1950s. In the 1980s, the Conservative government embedded a view of society which was more liberal in economic matters while being more repressive in other fields. There was an attempt to move towards what Robert Nozick approvingly describes as a 'minimal state': one which provides security from internal and external threats, but performs no other functions.[28] The rights which citizens enjoy in such a state can be described as negative liberties: freedoms from harm, rather than rights to goods.[29] According to these radical liberals, the state has no responsibility for taking positive steps to ensure that people are able to take advantage of liberties, but only to prevent other people from improperly interfering with the liberties. On this view, the only illegitimate interference with autonomy consists in what other people do to you.[30] Yet even radical individualists like Nozick and Friedrich Hayek accepted that the state has certain responsibilities in respect of freedom, the main one being to create or foster conditions in which freedoms may be protected.[31] There must therefore be a legal system and a police force available to

---

[27] G. Dworkin, *The Theory and Practice of Autonomy* (Cambridge: Cambridge University Press, 1988), 41.

[28] *Anarchy, State and Utopia*, 26–8, 333–4.

[29] Berlin, *Four Essays on Liberty*, 122–3.

[30] For further discussion, see J. Gray, *Hayek on Liberty*, 2nd edn. (Oxford: Basil Blackwell, 1986), 67–71, 125–9; J. Paul (ed.), *Reading Nozick* (Oxford: Basil Blackwell, 1982).

[31] F. A. Hayek, *The Constitution of Liberty* (London: Routledge Kegan Paul, 1960), ch. 15, esp. 223; Nozick, *Anarchy, State and Utopia*, chs 5 and 6.

remedy attempts by one person to infringe or prevent the exercise of another's freedoms. The state must provide this.

But even this does not go far enough if one takes autonomy seriously. Liberties are useful only to the extent to which they can be enjoyed, and are contingent on a fair opportunity to take advantage of such liberties as one wishes to exercise, so the value of any liberty will be seriously curtailed if there is no opportunity to make use of it.[32] Where there are serious inequalities of wealth and opportunity, the negative freedoms which the state guarantees are most valuable to those who can best afford to exploit them, and may have no value at all to people who live at or below subsistence level and have no time or money to spare from the vital task of surviving. To say that such people are free is true (if at all) only in terms of legal theory. Descriptively, in reality, they are to some degree unfree. On this view, freedom of the press is not a valuable liberty unless everyone has a reasonable opportunity to use the press as a medium of communication and to read the resulting publications. Similarly, freedom of movement is valueless unless people have adequate resources of money and leisure to enable them to travel. If this has to be earned, freedom to work is essential; but the latter freedom is worthless unless all people have access to an education system which is sufficient to enable them to do the work which is available, a health-care system adequate to keep them (as far as possible) fit enough to work, and economic conditions which provide sufficient employment opportunities. Transfers of wealth may be needed for socially useful purposes, such as to provide grants for educating those who cannot afford to educate themselves by their own assets. And so on. The negative liberties guaranteed by a minimal state mean less to some citizens than to others, and the differentiation is imposed by the social or economic structure of society without regard to any rational moral criteria. On this view, the state ought to act to create the conditions in which everyone's autonomy has an opportunity to flourish. This means that people should be guaranteed a basic standard of living, so that all have a real chance to make and exploit additional opportunities for themselves.

This leads to an extended notion of freedom, under which a person is unfree if the range of his or her choices is constrained *either* by human interference *or* by shortage of resources or physical capacity. On this view it becomes possible to argue that liberties are of value only if supported by claim-rights which obligate other members of society to make available the resources which each person needs to give effect to his or her choices. This in turn opens the way to a broadened theory of individual rights and civil liberties in which negative freedom is complemented and at the same time limited by positive social or economic rights. These rights are very different from classical liberties, but are justified on the basis that they are needed in order to make negative liberty equally valuable to all. In other words, they seek to create a bridge between the value of liberty and the different values of equality and social justice.

---

[32] Thus, Raz instances a man in a pit with some food, whose only choice is whether or not to eat, and a lone woman on a desert island whose entire attention is consumed by the need to avoid being caught by a fierce carnivorous animal, and argues that: 'Neither the Man in the Pit nor the Hounded Woman enjoys an autonomous life.' Raz, *Morality of Freedom*, at 373–4. See also N. McCormick, *Legal Right and Social Democracy: Essays in Legal and Political Philosophy* (Oxford: Clarendon Press, 1982), 42–3.

This model of rights has implications for the content and scope of negative freedoms. For example, all negative freedoms may have to be restricted in order to secure the economic rights which enable all citizens to have access to a similar range of freedoms. It is important to remember, when assessing claims to rights based on this sort of argument, that one right is not being restricted in favour of another of the same logical type; rather, the *availability* of one freedom is restricted in order to enhance the *practical value* to others of a different freedom. There is, therefore, a distinction between: (a) rights which maximize the range of freedoms; and (b) rights which maximize the utility of those freedoms.

This is the source of the notion of positive rights, mainly social and economic in nature. The rights to a minimum wage, to health care, to housing, to support when unemployed or raising a family, are all designed, first, to ensure that people do not need to starve, and, secondly, to enable them to devote additional earnings to purposes of their choice (the so-called 'poverty trap', in which people whose income increases lose a corresponding or even greater sum in welfare benefits, is one way in which the second objective may be frustrated).[33] These rights correlate with duties, not of forbearance, but of active assistance, which society is expected to discharge through the medium of the state. Thus, positive economic or social rights envisage that the role of the state is take active steps to improve the lot of the worst-off groups in society. This may require transfer payments through taxation and the distribution of welfare benefits, or provision of services and facilities, or a degree of regulation of market activities, all of which must be paid for by taxing better-off members of society.

One's reaction to this will depend in part on one's view of the market. If it is seen as a natural forum for allocating resources, regulation looks like an attempt to use a human artefact—the state redistribution system—to interfere with the natural order of the world. On the other hand, if one sees the market itself as a human artefact, there may be no reason to deny ourselves the opportunity to modify its operation by means of another artefact when the uncontrolled functioning of market mechanisms produces results which seem to us to be antisocial or unfair.

The political and legal implications can be illustrated by considering possible legal and governmental responses to discrimination. If it turns out that some groups are systematically disadvantaged in education, for example because prejudice against their colour makes them vulnerable to low pay and this limits the educational opportunities which are available to them or their children, there are three possible responses. One, the liberal freedom-based response, is to ask whether members of such groups have a right to be free from discrimination on the ground of colour. If the answer is 'yes', Parliament makes laws to forbid (and provide remedies for) discrimination by individuals on that ground. This is essentially the approach adopted in Britain in the Race Relations Act 1976,[34] which treats discrimination as being as much

---

[33] F. Field, M. Meacher, and C. Pond, *To Him Who Hath: A Study of Poverty and Taxation* (Harmondsworth: Penguin, 1976), 56; Institute for Fiscal Studies, *The Structure and Reform of Direct Taxation: Report of a Committee Chaired by Professor J. E. Meade* (London: George Allen and Unwin, 1978), 82–7.

[34] See ch. 3 below.

a matter of individual responsibility as a social evil. On the other hand, the social rights approach would be to make laws which required members of those groups to be given advantages in education and employment (and perhaps other relevant fields) until they no longer stood at a disadvantage as compared with members of other groups. This latter approach (sometimes called 'affirmative action') involves positive action by the state which goes beyond merely policing negative freedoms. Finally, there is an intermediate approach (elements of which are incorporated within the UK legislation), making a state agency (here, the Commission for Racial Equality) responsible for fostering awareness of the legal and social obligations on employers, educators, and others, to avoid discriminating, and for assisting victims of unlawful discrimination to enforce their rights.

However, the social rights approach is attacked by some liberals precisely because it involves extensive state intervention in private lives and negative freedoms. It is argued that it is improper for the state to make people pay for other people's welfare if, unlike the position in relation to provision of policing and security services, the payers receive no benefit in return for their contribution. To take someone's hard-earned pay in order to provide an advantage for someone else is, according to Nozick, tantamount to the state imposing forced labour on the taxpayer.[35] This claim deserves attention, because, if supportable, it defeats all assertions of positive economic and social rights. It depends on the root idea that nobody has a right to interfere with property once the right to that property has vested in the right-holder. Indeed, it is sometimes said that the institution of property arises before society, and it is the primary aim of people in coming together in civil society to protect their property.[36] The Irish State, for instance, in Article 43 of its Constitution, acknowledges that 'man, in virtue of his rational being, has the natural right, antecedent to positive law, to the private ownership of external goods', and 'accordingly guarantees to pass no law attempting to abolish the right of private ownership or the general right to transfer, bequeath, and inherit property'. At the same time, the state recognizes that these rights 'ought, in civil society, to be regulated by the principles of social justice', and accordingly retains the right 'to delimit the exercise of the said rights with a view to reconciling their exercise with the exigencies of the common good'.[37]

Nozick's argument, like Article 43, gives property rights the same status as rights to personal integrity, such as the freedoms from enslavement and attack. However, unlike Article 43, Nozick denies the right of the state to regulate property rights according to principles of social justice. It is not clear what supports Nozick's

[35] Nozick, *Anarchy, State and Utopia*, 169–72.

[36] J. Locke, *Two Treatises of Government*, II, s. 1, described people coming together to protect their property, that being therefore one of the fundamental obligations of the civil magistracy, but as A. Ryan, *Property and Political Theory* (Oxford: Basil Blackwell, 1984), 15, 24, points out, this may have been part of Locke's attempt to show that the jurisdiction of the civil power is entirely secular, in opposition to the divine-right theories of Filmer. Whether or not this is a correct interpretation of Locke, the idea was influential in *Entick v. Carrington* (1765) 19 St. Tr. 1029 at col. 1066, where Lord Camden CJ observed, 'The great end for which men entered into civil society, was to secure their property. That right is preserved sacred and incommunicable in all instances, where it has not been taken away or abridged by some public law for the good of the whole'. This curiously anticipates the formulation in the French Declaration of the Rights of Man, 1791.

[37] See also European Convention on Human Rights, Protocol No. 1, Art. 1.

assertion of such a privileged status for property rights.[38] The main argument is a negative one, denying the justice or effectiveness of interfering with property rights merely to advance a programme of achieving greater fairness in the distribution of social or economic goods. It is said that achieving and maintaining any pattern of distribution which could be called fair requires continuous redistribution by the state; as unfairnesses creep in as soon as uncontrolled competition occurs, a single redistribution will be insufficient to achieve long-term fairness of what Nozick calls the 'patterned' type. This redistribution will be unproductive or counter-productive for either of two reasons: it will not work, and it will not be fair.

First, according to Hayek, no person or government has sufficient knowledge about the complex interactions of causes and effects in the economy to be able to predict what the results of conscious interference with the historical processes of the market will be. It is therefore safest to leave market processes to determine the best distribution of benefits and burdens in society.[39] Secondly, according to Nozick, government redistributions of goods will fail to do justice to people's 'historical' entitlements, that is, to the benefits which they accumulated in the past and expected to be free to enjoy under the rules in force at the time of their acquisition. Redistribution to achieve a just 'patterned distribution' is tantamount to retrospective legislation, because it infringes historical entitlements. As such, it is said to infringe a basic principle of the rule of law forbidding retrospective legislation in most circumstances. On this view, the only achievable form of justice of distribution is that which results from the fair application and enforcement of existing rules on property acquisition and devolution in a market economy: the 'hidden hand' of market forces produces a result, which cannot be adjudged unjust while respecting historical entitlements.[40]

These arguments presuppose either that the rules of acquisition themselves are fair, or that they are unchallengeable. This, however, would make it illegitimate for the rules ever to be amended. Such a limitation on the legislative authority of the state should not readily be accepted, particularly where the state legislatures are democratically accountable, as the restriction would severely circumscribe the scope of the law-making powers of representative legislatures.[41] The basis of the presupposition needs to be examined. On the historical entitlements theory, the result of exchanges, acquisitions, and disposals according to the existing legal rules can be treated as just only if the historically first acquisition was itself just. The rule most often relied on is that a person who expends time and energy in cultivating or improving land, or drawing from the land a naturally occurring substance, thereby becomes entitled to treat the land or resulting produce and profit as his own property. Were this not so, it is said, there would be no reason for anyone to improve the lot of society as a whole by

---

[38] See A. Halpin, *Rights & Law, Analysis & Theory* (Oxford: Hart Publishing, 1997), 241–50.

[39] F. A. Hayek, *Law, Legislation and Liberty* (Routledge & Kegan Paul, 1981), i. 8–54; Gray, *Hayek on Liberty*, chs 1 and 2.

[40] Nozick, *Anarchy, State and Utopia*, 180.

[41] For the idea that some such limits are implicit in the notion of the rule of law, see Hayek, *Law, Legislation and Liberty*, iii esp. ch. 18; G. de Q. Walker, *The Rule of Law: Foundation of Constitutional Democracy* (St. Lucia: Queensland University Press, 1989).

cultivating or producing more than he needs for his own subsistence and making the excess available through the market or charitable donation.[42]

This general right of original acquisition by labour is not absolute, however. Locke recognized some limits on the extent to which individuals may legitimately annex things for their own benefit. The main one is that the right to acquire land by applying one's labour to it operates only so far as enough land remains for others who want or need it, and the remainder is of as good quality as that which is taken.[43] This has been developed by Waldron, who has argued that exclusive rights of property are morally justifiable only if everyone is able to exercise actual dominion of the same extent over at least some other assets of the same kind.[44] If this is not possible, the right to property is not genuinely open to all, as not all enjoy the conditions necessary to exercise it, and so property rights fail to comply with the liberal justification of being equally available to all.

A further limitation, which Locke imposed on property acquisition, is that property, once acquired, must not be allowed to go to waste.[45] This is related to the idea that the needy have a right to the surplus property of others which the needy require in order to survive. This right is not dependent on charity: Locke considered that the needy owned the surplus property of others for this purpose.[46] It follows that, for Locke, if the resource is vital to life and, after acquisition, it becomes scarce (as where land which has been enclosed by someone includes a waterhole which, in a drought, becomes the sole source of drinking water in the area, or there is a shortage of clothing in cold weather), the person who acquired the property is obligated to make it available to all who need it, rather than leaving them to die of thirst or profiteering from the natural calamity which has dried up other sources of water.

Nozick seems to accept that a model for the original acquisition of property would be morally unacceptable if such conditions are not included, even though he ultimately balks at admitting them as legal limitations in modern capitalist conditions.[47] Even in the liberal model of property rights, therefore, original entitlements are justified and restricted instrumentally in order to advance some social values.[48] That being so, it would be odd to claim that these conditions ceased to bind those who acquire property further along the historical chain of entitlements. To be consistent, liberals such as Nozick should accept that the obligation on individuals to allow enough good quality resources for all when appropriating resources for themselves constitutes a condition on their moral right to hold property at all.

---

[42] This prudential justification is brought out most clearly in Nozick, *Anarchy, State and Utopia*, 265–8; Locke, *Two Treatises of Government*, II, s. 34.

[43] Locke, *Two Treatises of Government*, II, s. 48.

[44] J. Waldron, *The Right to Private Property* (Oxford: Clarendon Press, 1988), ch. 12.

[45] Locke, *Two Treatises of Government*, II, s. 47. For thorough discussion of the theories by which Locke and Nozick justified rights to property, see Waldron, *The Right to Private Property*, chs 6 and 7.

[46] Ryan, *Property and Political Theory*, 34.

[47] *Anarchy, State and Utopia*, 178–82. See the discussions in Paul (ed.), *Reading Nozick*, by O. O'Neill, 'Nozick's Entitlements', at 305–22, and C. C. Ryan, 'Yours, Mine, and Ours: Property Rights and Individual Liberty', at 323–43.

[48] Rawls, *Theory of Justice*, does exactly this, leading to the suggestion that he is a 'covert utilitarian': Halpin, *Rights & Law, Analysis & Theory*, 235–41.

However, this may impose an obligation on the state to regulate markets, limiting some liberties in the process. If, under the influence of the 'hidden hand' in a market economy, private individuals cannot judge how much of a given resource is available to all in society, and lack the instrumentalities for ensuring that all have their share, the job must perforce be done by the state. In redistributing shares in this way through taxation and welfare benefits, the state is not interfering with property rights properly vested in the people who held the property immediately before the redistribution; it is giving effect to the essential conditions for allowing people to enjoy property rights at all. After all, the rules which allow acquisition of property by applying one's labour to a commodity are social rules. Society adopted them in the first place, and it is proper for society through its authorized agency, the state, to enforce the rules if people are unable or unwilling to observe the conditions contained within the rules.[49] Were this not so, it would have been irrational for any society to have adopted rules which allowed the acquisition of more than small amounts of personal property. It would have been more rational to hold, first, that the labourer might acquire a right to no more (but no less) than the profits which flow from his work (rather than complete freedom to deal with the capital asset), and, secondly, that users have a duty to manage the land and other profit-making resources for the benefit of the community as a whole.

The claim that property rights have some special status therefore breaks down, so that interference by the state for the purpose of securing the survival and security of members of the community and enhancing their enjoyment of their liberties may be legitimate. This might, for example, justify taxation to provide some welfare benefits and health care. Whether taxation may legitimately go beyond this is a matter of political judgment for each society. If the rules which permit the holding of private property are social rules, not eternally valid and unchallengeable divine law, then the conditions for holding property, the permissible extent of holdings, and the accept-able justifications for interfering with holdings, are also social rules, and are legitim-ately liable to be changed in order to give effect to a democratically approved social plan. Protections for property rights are needed, but they may be no greater (though, perhaps, no less) than the protections given to other liberties, such as freedom of speech or freedom from arbitrary arrest and detention.

It follows that there is nothing in democratic liberal theory which necessarily excludes legal protection for positive social and economic rights. People who depre-cate attempts to enforce such rights (for example, those on the political Right who consider that the European Social Charter does not deserve to be considered as con-ferring rights on anyone or imposing duties on governments) are articulating a

---

[49] This is a form of what is sometimes called a 'concession' theory of property, because it presents property as a concession by the state and accordingly subject to conditions imposed by the state from time to time. Concession theories have been bedevilled by those who seek to distinguish them from 'contract' theories, which treat property as arising naturally from (rather than being a necessary condition for) agreements (express or implied) between free individuals. It should therefore be made clear that the argument advanced in the text does not depend on the idea that property is, or should be, a special privilege of a limited class (quite the reverse), nor on the notion that it consists of a limitation on any general principle of common ownership in law or morality.

personal preference for one type of political or economic programme over others. Their claims, when analysed, do not turn out to have an irrebuttable philosophical foundation.

If an idea of rights as including a right to enjoy freedoms which are theoretically available to all can be defended against extreme liberals such as Hayek and Nozick, the whole idea of individual rights needs to be defended against a socialist critique. Some radical critics of liberal individualism, such as Marx, have accepted that individual rights are necessarily individualistic and reject them as symptomatic of the alienation and egoism of people under capitalism, which must be replaced by an emancipated and united society. In socialist states, notably in the USSR before its break-up, constitutions do not give a high priority to individual rights. The Constitution of the USSR actually contained an impressive list of individual rights guaranteed to its citizens, but their exercise was stated to be legitimate only so far as it was consistent with the supreme goal of the state, defined in the Preamble as 'the building of a classless communist society in which there will be public, communist self-government'. Teleology reigned supreme, and the steps needed to achieve the goal, as defined by the executive, took precedence over individual liberties and theories of rights.[50]

In such a system, it is often thought, there is no room for individual democratic or other rights. However, this may be unnecessarily pessimistic. It may be possible to reconcile socialist teleology with individual freedom.[51] The definition of rights and liberties is not wholly selfish. It is part of a process whereby people attempt to fashion the conditions in which co-operation becomes possible, protecting the freedom which we need if we are to fulfil our social responsibilities towards other people as well as to advance our own interests. This reflects the mixed character, what has been called the 'unsocial sociability', of human society, rather than simply generalized alienation.[52] It should, therefore, not surprise anyone that the Constitution of the USSR acknowledged rights, but that they were socialist rather than individual rights, required to serve social goals. In the event of conflict between the goals and the socialist rights as formally expressed in the Constitution, the goals had to prevail.

(3) POLITICAL RIGHTS

Another type of right now needs to be introduced, which is not designed to increase either the availability or utility of moral autonomy to individuals, but which enables individuals to participate in political decisions. We can call these *political rights*, and they are essential to a developed notion of citizenship in a liberal society. They presuppose both the need for coercive state action and the legitimacy of coercive limits on liberties. However, political rights stipulate the methods of selecting the people

[50] A. Erh-Soon Tay, 'Marxism, Socialism and Human Rights', in E. Kamenka and A. Erh-Soon Tay (eds.), *Human Rights* (London: Edward Arnold, 1978), 104–12.

[51] For attempts to achieve such a reconciliation, see, e.g. T. Campbell, *The Left and Rights* (London: Routledge & Kegan Paul, 1983); C. Sypnowich, *The Concept of Socialist Law* (Oxford: Clarendon Press, 1990).

[52] A. I. Melden, *Rights and Persons* (Oxford: Oxford University Press, 1977), 234–5.

who are to settle the limits of liberties and the terms on which they are to act. For example, in a representative democracy citizens will have rights in the selection of representative members of a legislature; coercive limits to liberties may be said to be legitimate if (perhaps only if) imposed by a given number of the elected representatives. In a direct democracy citizens will have rights to vote in, and even initiate, referenda on particular issues; coercion is then justified if approved by a given majority of voters. In either case, the legislative authority may be required by constitutional arrangements to act within limits to its coercive powers, to refrain from infringing certain rights, or to advance specified interests; these conditions may or may not be legally enforceable.

Political rights must not be confused with negative liberties. Political rights may, if exercised in different ways, result in the scope of individual liberties (such as freedom of speech) being maintained, increased, or diminished. However, as Sir Isaiah Berlin observed, they are primarily concerned to control the types of body to which, and the conditions under which, citizens surrender their individual autonomy, rather than protecting the freedom of each citizen to give effect to his or her plan for life.[53] Political rights are essentially procedural: they define an individual's power to influence the coercive processes of the state; they do not guarantee that the combined effect of all exercises of individuals' political rights will be to maintain liberties. Even democracy may produce illiberal results, and any state organization requires citizens to recognize that they may sometimes legitimately be coerced and their liberties restricted against their wills.

Some theorists argue that if one has agreed (expressly or by implication) to abide by a form of political organization, or even if one should rationally have agreed to it (whether or not one has done so in fact), the restrictions on one's liberty which that organization imposes should properly be regarded as emanations of one's own will and not coercive at all. Locke, Kant, Hegel, Rousseau, Bentham, and Marx, amongst many others, have argued that 'true' freedom comes only through subjecting one's desires to the common good, to rationality, or to some other ideal which effectively withdraws the individual's capacity for self-direction. This idea is evident in theories of democracy according to which citizens submit to the will of the community expressed through the ballot-box in exchange for a right to participate, to have one's voice counted, in the ballot. Here the right to self-determination is treated as an aspect of liberty.

This is not liberty as we have understood it so far, however. It replaces the will of the individual with an external assessor's view of what is good for the individual, a form of paternalism, or (even less individualistically) it substitutes the good of the community for the good of the individual. This does not lead to individual self-fulfilment unless the individual is trained (or brainwashed) always and only to want what is considered by the external decision-maker to be good for the community. Only then will the 'true' (or rational) desires of the individual be identical with the result of the collective decision-making process.

---

[53] Sir Isaiah Berlin, 'Two Concepts of Liberty', in *Four Essays on Liberty*, 118–72 at 129–31; see also the Introduction at xliii *et seq.*

Even then, the resulting deemed satisfaction of individual wants will not advance individual autonomy, as liberties do. While collective self-determination may require certain political rights for individuals, it is the autonomy of the group, rather than that of individual members of it, which self-determination advances. Although the desire for self-fulfilment may perhaps sometimes be satisfied by identifying myself with the interests of the community, this is as likely to lead to self-abnegation as to the realization of actual (as contrasted with hypothetical, idealized, or metaphysical) desires.

The power of a group to determine how its members shall act does not entail any necessary protection for the liberties of individuals within it. As Sir Isaiah Berlin and others have observed, individual members may prefer to be subject to autocratic government by other members of the group rather than benefit from the paternalism of a well-meaning colonial power, but this form of *positive* liberty is a claim to be recognized and respected as a member of a particular group, rather than a freedom to pursue one's individual goals. A negative right which seems to advance individual freedom, such as freedom of religion, may involve individual adherents to a religion in a choice which entails the surrender of much of their moral autonomy. Democracy, self-determination, and liberty are different values which may conflict;[54] they are not necessarily capable of being contained within a coherent moral framework. We will return to this point in section 1.4.

1.3 NATURAL AND POSITIVE RIGHTS[55]

So far, we have introduced the relationship between autonomy, freedom, and a number of kinds of liberties and rights, and have seen some of the implications of each. We now turn to look at the systems of reasoning and justification which support those values. Are normative, or ought-based, structures needed to make it possible to assert particular rights or liberties, and to assess claims to particular liberties in specified circumstances? This section examines two broad traditions of thought which have influenced the ways in which rights and liberties are formulated in western societies. These are the *natural rights* tradition and the *positive rights* tradition. As will be seen, they do not always lead to the same results. Each is powerful, but any practically useful theory of liberties is likely to attempt a degree of synthesis between them. To complicate the matter further, the traditions are not atomic; each is comprised of a number of different elements. The brief discussion of them which follows is intended to do no more than indicate some of the elements, illustrate their relationship, and suggest some of their consequences.

---

[54] Berlin, *Four Essays on Liberty*, at 167 *et seq.*; R. Rorty, *Contingency, Irony and Solidarity* (Cambridge: Cambridge University Press, 1989), chs 1–3.

[55] See generally Halpin, *Rights & Law, Analysis & Theory*, chs 8 and 9.

(1) THE NATURAL RIGHTS TRADITION

The natural rights tradition arises out of classical natural-law theories, although it was not originally a major part of them: most early natural lawyers were more concerned with duties owed by citizens to God, the state, or society, than with any citizen's rights which might correlate with duties on God, the state, or society.[56] Nevertheless, a number of societies have displayed a strong tradition of respect for and pride in freedom which forms part of their fundamental social values. The idea that it is important for people to be able to say that they are free of arbitrary government, and that the state has a fundamental responsibility (either social or legal) to maintain that freedom against internal or external threats, is sometimes derived from divine law as interpreted by the major religions. It was significant in shaping the social characteristics of ancient Israel, Athens, and Rome, and of the Netherlands in the seventeenth century.[57] Appeals to divine law could, however, have the effect of merely legitimating a regime which was absolutist rather than liberal. The use made of the doctrine of the 'Divine Right of Kings' asserted by the early Stuart monarchs in seventeenth-century England exemplifies the absolutist tendencies of divine law, particularly in a state with an established church.

This led some liberals to turn away from reliance on divine revelation and attempt instead to discover natural laws from the observable state of the world and human behaviour. The idea that people could profitably employ their rationality for such important matters, instead of relying on divine revelation, was not entirely new. The thirteenth-century conception of natural law embraced by St Thomas Aquinas and Duns Scotus had recognized an interpretative role for human rationality in elucidating the divine will.[58] However, the eighteenth century saw the emergence of a particularly optimistic view of human nature and potential. Jean-Jacques Rousseau's influential view of man as innately noble and free, but corrupted by conventional civilisation,[59] contrasted starkly with the traditional Christian view of man as innately corrupt and needing to be saved by religion. By putting the individual in the centre of the moral universe, Rousseau created an individualistic philosophy which concentrated on the importance of man's moral and intellectual independence. Self-discipline was the foundation of moral improvement.[60]

[56] See generally A. P. d'Entrèves, *Natural Law: An Introduction to Legal Philosophy*, 2nd edn. (London: Hutchinson, 1970), ch. 4; R. Tuck, *Natural Rights Theories: Their Origin and Development* (Cambridge: Cambridge University Press, 1979), *passim*; J. J. Shestack, 'The Jurisprudence of Human Rights', in T. Meron (ed.), *Human Rights in International Law: Legal and Policy Issues* (Oxford: Clarendon Press, 1984), ch. 3.

[57] See S. Schama, *The Embarrassment of Riches* (London: Collins, 1987), ch. 2 on the significance of Old Testament parallels in Dutch culture.

[58] Thomas Aquinas, *Summa Theologica*, Qu. XCIII, Art. 3, and Qu. XCIV, Arts. 2–4. Duns Scotus used rationality principles to argue that ownership of property (*dominium*) was incompatible with natural law, because in a state of innocence the optimal arrangement is common use of assets: *Questiones in Librum Sententiarum* 15.2, in *Opera Omnia* (Paris, 1894), xviii. 256–7. For discussion, see Tuck, *Natural Rights Theories: Their Origin and Development*, 21; d'Entrèves, *Natural Law: An Introduction to Legal Philosophy*, ch. 3.

[59] Jean-Jacques Rousseau, *Du Contrat Social* (1762), Book I, translated in Sir Ernest Barker (ed.), *Social Contract: Essays by Locke, Hume, Rousseau* (London: Oxford University Press, 1971), 167–307.

[60] For analysis, see J. Plamenatz, *Man and Society: A Critical Examination of Some Important Social and Political Theories from Machiavelli to Marx*, 2nd edn., rev. M. E. Plamenatz and R. Wokler (London: Longman, 1992), ii, ch. 4.

In such a theory, rights, and particularly individual freedoms, needed to be protected against interference by society and the state in the name of social morality or
propriety. In Rousseau's vision, this was to be done by laws to which all citizens were
to contribute—the laws would reflect the 'general will'—and to which all would be
required to maintain allegiance on pain of banishment or death.[61] This distinctly
illiberal conclusion of the theory disappoints many liberals, but it provides the basis
for the legal protection of liberties: the laws which will help to hold elements of
society in a slightly uneasy equilibrium are themselves required to respect the liberties
which underpin the legitimacy of society.

The trust which Rousseau had in human nature and self-discipline was not
rational. It was an act of faith. However, any rational speculation about the good
society or the good life must begin with a set of beliefs about the ends of human life
and the objects of societies. The eighteenth-century rationalists were often prepared
to allow considerable scope for enlightened despotism on the part of rulers, without
limiting it by reference to the general will. On a less optimistic view than Rousseau's
of human nature, this is not an irrational course: one needs to have means to control
the effects of people's baser instincts in order to secure co-operation. Thomas Hobbes's advocacy of Leviathan, the state to which all owe obedience, is an example of the
way in which a form of secular natural law can have a tendency towards absolutism.[62]
Natural law on its own, therefore, does not guarantee rights, because the use to which
it is put will depend on the political aspirations of those who invoke it.

In France and the United States of America, the meritorious objective of limiting
governmental power was institutionalized through secular, rather than religious, political theory in the eighteenth and nineteenth centuries, and natural law was driven by
revolutionary objectives.[63] When it became clear after the French Revolution, in the
wake of the Terror which Robespierre unleashed, that populist governments could
disregard human freedom and rationalism as much as aristocratic ones, the pressure
for human rights grew. Activists like Tom Paine used the notion of human rights as a
way of translating the ideal of individual freedom into action. Human rights formed
both a reason for action and a blueprint for the post-revolutionary regulation of
government. It is in this role that natural rights appear in the United States' Declaration of Independence and the French Declaration of the Rights of Man, specifying
the basic beliefs of the founding fathers as to the values which were to guide the
politics of the new states.[64]

Across much of the world since then, the idea of liberties, derived from secular

[61] *Du Contrat Social*, Book I, s. 7; Book II, s. 3–6; Book IV, *passim*.

[62] Thomas Hobbes, *Leviathan* (1651; ed. J. Plamenatz, London: Fontana, 1962), chs 13, 14, 15, 18, 20, 21;
G. S. Kavka, *Hobbesian Moral and Political Theory* (Princeton, NJ: Princeton University Press, 1986), 245.

[63] The link between secular philosophy and rights theories is noted by E. J. Hobsbawm, *The Age of
Revolution 1789–1848* (London: Sphere Books, 1973), who observes at 270 that Thomas Paine 'is as famous
for having written the first book to demonstrate in popular language that the Bible is not the word of God
(*The Age of Reason*, 1794), as for his *Rights of Man* (1791)'. He goes on (at 288) to note the link between free
enterprise and a natural right to liberty.

[64] On France, see G. Rudé, *The French Revolution* (London: Weidenfeld & Nicolson, 1988), 59–60; S.
Schama, *Citizens* (London: Viking Penguin, 1989), 746–847. On the USA, see L. Levy, *Constitutional Opinions:
Aspects of the Bill of Rights* (New York: Oxford University Press, 1986), 124–5.

natural-law reasoning, has exercised a compellingly powerful hold on popular imaginations. In England, by contrast, we will see that the law has developed by throwing off the conservative aspects of natural law without replacing it with anything which rests explicitly on natural-law foundations; yet it will be argued that natural law presuppositions of a rationalist type underlie much of English positivism.

In what rational, secular sense is a commitment to freedom 'natural'? There are several ways in which it has been argued that law, freedom, or rights, or some particular laws or freedoms, are ordained by nature. Law may be natural because human nature makes it essential for people to be constrained by rules in order to survive or achieve some purpose which is thought to constitute a natural goal of humanity. To this, it has been objected that rules, duties, and rights are not natural facts but 'ought statements', or, as philosophers say, are normative. As a matter of logic, one cannot derive an 'ought' from an 'is' statement, but only from another 'ought'. As a matter of formal logic, this is no doubt correct. It is a fact that dead people cannot vote, but it does not necessarily follow, as a matter of logic, that democracy entails a right to life. However, natural rights arguments are not attempts to derive values directly from facts.[65] They aim instead to derive rights indirectly, by way of layers of normative argument or assumptions which are sometimes explicit but are often tacit.

A relatively sophisticated natural rights argument can be represented in the following propositions.[66]

1   One of the features typical of human nature is that people commonly consider that it is worth their while to try to construct a picture of their relationship with things outside themselves. This is thought to be worthwhile for its own sake, irrespective of any practical advantage which might accrue: it is a natural facet of human curiosity and a certain cast of mind which seeks order in apparent chaos.
2   If such activities are thought to be independently valuable, they are likely to be important to people's assessments of the quality of their lives.
3   One of the proper functions of society is to enable people to optimize the quality of their lives as far as possible.
4   People have a right to intellectual freedom.

These propositions are linked, but they do not follow logically from one another. The fundamental proposition is (3), a statement of values, not fact. Proposition (4), in form a statement of social fact (the recognition in a society of a right) but one which involves the acceptance of certain values, follows from (3) only under the conditions specified in (1) and (2), which are wholly factual hypotheses. In other words, natural rights are logically derived from values, not facts. The factual propositions supporting the rights merely specify the conditions which make a freedom particularly valuable and under which it will be possible to say that in a given society, with a particular view of the human condition, at a specified time, people are entitled to that freedom. Like the conditions, the techniques for establishing propositions (1) to (3) are culturally

---

[65] Finnis, *Natural Law and Natural Rights*, 33–48.

[66] This paragraph and the one following are heavily influenced by Finnis, *Natural Law and Natural Rights*, chs 3, 4, 5, and 6, although they do not purport to be an account of Finnis's theory.

specific. In societies where the prevailing intellectual ethos is rationalist, people are likely to adopt a mix of empirical and reflective methods which make up what Finnis calls 'practical reasonableness'.[67] The test of last resort for particular rights or freedoms may be the political process or a judicial process or a combination of the two. In other societies, such questions may not be open to speculation, being finally disposed of by statements of absolute and final authority. The authoritative statements may emanate from a human autarch, from express agreement of individuals or states party to international conventions, or may stem from a deity and be manifested through oracular techniques or techniques of textual interpretation which may include elements of practical reasonableness.

This theory of natural rights will surprise some readers because of the modesty of the claims made for the rights under it. They are not seen as eternal, unchanging, or universal, and it is not necessary to see any rights as absolute (although neither is it necessary to argue that there are *no* absolute rights).[68] They derive their authority from present conditions and beliefs. It is a mistake to see natural rights or natural law as any more uniform and unchanging than nature (human or other) is. To say that a right is natural is to assert only that it springs from a given society's view of human nature and the aspirations and responsibilities of members of that society. Societies change, and the nature of the changes is controlled by a multiplicity of factors. It may be that the rights which seem to flow naturally from capitalist forms of social organization will not be seen as natural in a post-capitalist society (whatever form that may take), and that is to take account of only one of the possible variables (economic structure). Other factors which affect the perceived naturalness of kinds of rights include differing understandings of what count as justifying arguments for rights, differing epistemologies which determine how one can seek to establish the existence of the conditions for particular rights, and differing political arrangements for settling disputes about rights.

Practical natural rights theories are thus founded on a mixture of moral and political analysis, social psychology, and practical reason. Natural rights do not float in a Platonic heaven of ideal, eternal concepts, despite the assumptions of many of their critics.[69] They are as tough, real, variable, and elusive as nature itself. 'Natural' rights should be understood not in contradistinction to 'human' or 'social' rights—society is after all a natural aspect of most human conditions—but as advancing values which are good in themselves, rather than being justified by reference to consequentialist arguments.

[67] *Natural Law and Natural Rights*, 88 ('being able to bring one's own intelligence to bear effectively . . . on the problems of choosing one's actions and lifestyle and shaping one's own character').

[68] For argument supporting the view that there are absolute rights, see A. Gewirth, 'Are there any Absolute Rights?' in J. Waldron (ed.), *Theories of Rights* (Oxford: Oxford University Press, 1984), 91–109.

[69] For the most famous critique, see J. Bentham, *Anarchical Fallacies*, in J. Bowring (ed.), *The Works of Jeremy Bentham*, ii. 491 ff. For a balanced, rationalist approach from a natural lawyer, see d'Entrèves, *Natural Law: An Introduction to Legal Philosophy*, ch. 4. A thorough discussion of the historical foundations of natural rights theories is provided by Tuck, *Natural Rights Theories: Their Origin and Development, passim*. For a shorter account, see E. Kamenka, 'The Anatomy of an Idea', in E. Kamenka and A. Erh-Soon Tay (eds.), *Human Rights* (London: Edward Arnold, 1978), 1–12.

(2) POSITIVE RIGHTS, UTILITARIANISM, AND LEGAL POSITIVISM

The positive rights tradition is closely linked to legal positivism, just as the natural rights tradition is linked to natural-law theories. Historically, legal positivism in Britain is rooted in rationalist, reforming thought of the late eighteenth and early nineteenth centuries. In particular, it is a child of utilitarianism,[70] and developed as a reaction against what Jeremy Bentham saw as the conservative tendencies of the common lawyers who called in aid natural law to discourage the use of legislation for social reform, while perpetuating an inhuman, inconsistent, and inefficient system of positive law.[71] As part of the process of making reforming legislation respectable, Bentham attacked the idea of natural rights, which (as he saw it) acted sometimes as illegitimate constraints on reform, and at other times precipitated a breakdown of the lawful authority on which systematic reform depended, as when the Declaration of the Rights of Man and the Citizen helped to cement the French Revolution of 1789.[72] For Bentham, legitimate, enforceable rights came not from nature but from laws duly passed by the supreme political authority of the state, the sovereign legislature. The scope of freedoms is always to be established first by way of the political and then through the legal process, and justified by consequentialist arguments of utility.

Bentham's positivism had a liberating political influence, in that it enabled law, as a system of rules posited and so open to amendment by a politically sovereign body, to become a tool in the hands of social reformers. At the same time the felicific calculus, the system for aggregating pleasures and pains in order to determine marginal utility which Bentham advocated as the most rational way of assessing the desirability of laws, is capable of taking into account many of the factors which would lead a natural rights theorist to assert an entitlement to a freedom. The evaluation of pleasure according to its intensity, duration, and so on is as applicable to pleasure derived from an activity which is a good in itself as it is to one which brings pleasure indirectly and consequentially.

However, scientific utilitarians face two problems. The first is to show that units of measurement for pleasure and pain can be applied equally to different types of pleasure and pain. One way of resolving this problem is to find a way of assigning an economic value to all pleasures and pains, based on the sums which a rational person would think it worth paying to obtain or avoid them. This attempt lies at the heart of the discipline of welfare economics. But it leads on to the second problem: the felicific calculus and welfare economics, in their crude forms, can each be accused of failing to take liberties (or rights) sufficiently seriously. This is because it is essential to the method of the felicific calculus that the pleasure derived from exercising a freedom, and thus the justification for allowing that freedom, can at any time be outweighed by a countervailing pain to others from allowing the exercise of the freedom. Whilst the pleasure which I derive from freedom to write this chapter is to be taken into account in deciding whether or not I should continue to be allowed to write it, classical

---

[70] H. L. A. Hart, *Essays on Bentham* (Oxford: Clarendon Press, 1982), ch. 4; E. Halévy, *The Growth of Philosophical Radicalism* (London: Faber & Faber, 1972), 155–81.

[71] See G. Postema, *Bentham and the Common Law Tradition* (Oxford: Clarendon Press, 1986), ch. 8.

[72] H. L. A. Hart, *Essays in Jurisprudence and Legal Philosophy* (Oxford: Clarendon Press, 1983), chs 8 and 9.

utilitarianism does not give that pleasure any greater weight or importance than the pleasure which might flow to others from denying me that freedom, nor does it attempt to distinguish between good and bad *reasons* for wanting to deny me that freedom. In quantifying pleasure and pain it takes no account of the moral significance of freedoms and of interference with them. It provides no framework for the moral evaluation of freedoms unless one considers that the maximization of pleasure and the minimization of pain together form an exhaustive catalogue of important moral values. Few people would be prepared to accept that.

The risk of losing rights which even utilitarians regard as having fundamental importance has led some people to qualify classical utilitarianism to give added protection to such rights against a simple balance of pain or preference. As no right can sensibly be allowed absolute protection, in order to establish a shield for liberties it was necessary to define both the scope of the protected interests and the grounds on which interference with liberty was to be permitted. Only in assessing whether those grounds had been sufficiently made out in a particular case were the balance of pleasures and pains to be taken into account. The most notable attempt to amend utilitarianism in this way was made by John Stuart Mill in his essay *On Liberty*, published in 1859. He asserted the primacy of freedom, and argued that individuals or society could legitimately exercise coercion and control over other individuals only for the purpose of self-protection. In defending this thesis he relied on consequentialist arguments, while allowing that rights had a 'special utility'. Freedom of thought and discussion were to be protected because when suppressing views one could never know whether they were true or false. The risk of losing a truth is too serious to be justifiable on utilitarian grounds; even if the suppressed opinion is false, it is valuable because, by demonstrating its falsity, the truth can be reinforced. Individuality is valuable because variety maximizes the chances of valuable inventions and innovations being made; intellectual and market freedoms expand the range of options available to everyone. As a correlative of this libertarian individualism, the role of the state is to be reduced; sometimes activities should be left to the private sector even if it is likely that they would be done better by government agencies, because trying to do the job will broaden people's experience and stimulate them to new efforts, with a consequential benefit for them and (perhaps) for society as a whole.[73]

This is a paternalist form of liberalism. It makes it clear that utility is not about what people want but about what is (or is thought to be) good for them. They must take responsibility even if they would rather not have it, because, even if they suffer extreme pain as a result of their failure, they will be better people, and deemed to have enjoyed extra pleasure, for having made the attempt. Underlying the individualism is a deep distrust of popular democracy as a process for settling where the balance of utility lies. In itself, that would be neither suprising nor unusual: similar expressions of distrust are to be found in earlier writers from Plato to John Austin and later writers from Lenin to Schumpeter and Dahl. It is more perturbing, however, to note that Mill's defence of liberty succeeds if and only if one accepts that the social disbenefits of interfering with freedom of expression are as compellingly serious as he

---

[73] J. S. Mill, *On Liberty*, chs 2 and 4.

supposed. Such dis-benefits are speculative rather than immediate, and the argument based on them invites a response which simply gives greater weight to the protection of society against equally speculative harm, supposedly flowing from abuse of the liberty. Sir Patrick (later Lord) Devlin gave just such a response in arguing that it is proper, and sometimes even necessary, to impose coercive limits on freedom of the person in order to defend society against the 'harm' inflicted by homosexuality. In his exchange with Professor H. L. A. Hart, Devlin was playing the utilitarians at their own game, demonstrating that utilitarianism offers no reliable defence for liberties against the operation of the felicific calculus.[74]

The positivist conception of liberties and rights was developed at a time when democratic processes were relatively undeveloped. There was no approach to universal suffrage in Britain until nearly 130 years after the first publication of Bentham's *Introduction to the Principles of Morals and Legislation* in 1789. Bentham himself died in the year of the 1832 Reform Act. At such a time, the felicific calculus was in the relatively safe hands of scientific philosophers (as they regarded themselves). Burgeoning democracy threatened to substitute real preferences for the scientific balance of pleasure and pain; latter-day utilitarians viewed the prospect without enthusiasm, and like Mill moved to entrench certain liberties, or at least provide for a presumption in favour of maintaining liberty, putting a heavy burden on those who advocated restrictions. This, however, could not be justified from within utilitarian theory itself, unless (like Mill, but unlike Bentham) one were to stipulate a special utilitarian value in protecting rights.[75]

Legal positivism, then, is not necessarily incompatible with guaranteeing protection of specified liberties and rights. If the constitutional law of a particular jurisdiction permits it, legislation can be passed protecting specified liberties, and can be entrenched. English positivists, however, have faced particular problems in relation to the entrenchment of rights. There are two reasons for this. First, the constitutional law of England, and perhaps also of Scotland and Northern Ireland, until recently, recognized no limitations on the legislative competence of the UK Parliament. One of the paradoxical consequences of this extreme version of parliamentary sovereignty was that Parliament could not, in theory, limit its own power, even by restricting the conditions under which it would forthwith be capable of interfering with fundamental liberties or rights. This doctrine has recently become less significant in the light of the subjection of UK law to the supra-national legal order of the EC, but it retains some significance in fields which are not yet covered by Community law.[76]

Secondly, British democratic theory has been dominated, as has its legal complement in positivist theory, by the idea of the importance of political judgments of the

[74] See H. L. A. Hart, *Law, Liberty, and Morality* (Oxford: Oxford University Press, 1963); P. Devlin, *The Enforcement of Morals* (Oxford: Oxford University Press, 1965). For a more recent liberal approach to the problem, see J. Feinberg, *Harmless Wrongdoing: The Moral Limits of the Criminal Law* (Oxford: Clarendon Press, 1988).

[75] D. Lyons, *Rights, Welfare, and Mill's Moral Theory* (Oxford: Oxford University Press, 1994), chs 1 and 6.

[76] See J. Jaconelli, *Enacting a Bill of Rights* (Oxford: Clarendon Press, 1980). This matter is discussed further in ch. 2 below.

electorate through the ballot-box as the ultimate source of legislative legitimacy.[77] Entrenching rights is seen as anti-democratic, in that it restricts the power of the citizens at the ballot-box and the legislative power of their elected representatives in the House of Commons, the dominant part of Parliament, often increasing the power of judges. These judges are, in the UK, not electorally accountable, and are unlikely to have available either the information needed to decide the social questions which arise in adjudication about fundamental rights, or the procedures for obtaining that information.[78] These considerations bring us face to face with the political aspect of civil liberties and human rights claims.

(3) THE RELATIONSHIP BETWEEN NATURAL AND POSITIVE RIGHTS

This section concludes the examination of natural rights and positive rights theories as the basis for human rights and civil liberties law, by drawing attention to the relationship between the theories and some of the implications. Both natural and positive theories of rights have strengths, but neither can operate effectively on its own. If rights can be identified only by reference to moral values, a natural law element (within the meaning ascribed to natural law above) is a necessary background to provide substance for the scheme of human rights law. On the other hand, identifying specially important moral values will do little good unless people respect them. The rights produced by a natural law approach will be of little practical use unless society is unusually committed to the morality which produced the rights or can be coerced into respecting them. A system of politics is needed to give social recognition and authority to the scheme of rights and translate them into positive law. Legal positivism alone cannot suffice to identify the interests which should be protected by rights, because positivism, aiming to be neutral between different sets of non-legal values, serves merely to show how such values may be converted into legal rules; but the paraphernalia of positive law and legal institutions are important aids to securing respect for rights, performing educational, coercive, and symbolic roles according to circumstances.

It seems, then, that certain natural law and positivist approaches to rights are complementary rather than in conflict. Indeed, those parts of positive law which consist of statements of proper or desired behaviour, backed by a reward or sanction, presuppose the rightness of those forms of behaviour. Such ideas of rightness can be derived only from a system of social or moral values operating independently of law.[79]

[77] P. P. Craig, 'Bentham, Public Law and Democracy' [1987] *PL* 407–27; P. P. Craig, *Public Law and Democracy in the United Kingdom and the United States of America* (Oxford: Clarendon Press, 1991), ch. 2.
[78] J. A. G. Griffith, 'The Political Constitution' (1979) 42 *MLR* 1–21, esp. at 16; Craig, *Public Law and Democracy in the United Kingdom and the United States of America*, ch. 7. Courts in the UK have a restrictive attitude to class actions and representative plaintiffs, and no equivalent of the American Brandeis brief. For discussion of the implications, see D. Feldman, 'Public Interest Litigation and Constitutional Theory in Comparative Perspective' (1992) 55 *MLR* 44–73.
[79] The importance of this intimate connection between legal rule-making and moral standards is developed in R. Dworkin, *Taking Rights Seriously* (London: Duckworth, 1977), and the same author's *Law's Empire* (London: Fontana, 1986). See also C. Palley, *The United Kingdom and Human Rights* (London: Sweet & Maxwell, 1991), ch. 1.

Despite Bentham's imprecations against natural law,[80] every law reformer must start with a supra-legal objective or standard and move to implement it in positive law through the medium of politics. Bentham's attack, properly understood, was on the petrification of natural law by Blackstone, who regarded natural law as a definitive and unchanging set of rules embodied in the common law, rather than on the natural-law approach described in this chapter.[81] Natural law, seen as a method of argument and justification rather than as a collection of immutable truths, is always necessary.

On the other hand, the loss of the cosmic dimension to natural law and natural rights means that they require careful analysis, and may (probably will) be influenced by attitudes and needs which are specific to particular cultures, societies, and economic systems. It will be impossible to identify values which are regarded as equally fundamental in every society, although if people in different societies produced a list of their 'top ten' rights or freedoms some rights would probably appear on most lists. What sort of rights would these be?

H. L. A. Hart suggested that, if there are such things as natural rights at all, they must encompass a right to liberty, as other rights are valuable only to the extent that one has a right to the freedom necessary to exercise them.[82] This attractive view is fundamental to much liberal thinking, but it depends on a number of variable factors. This section concludes its examination of natural and positive rights by raising four such factors.

(i) The sort of rights being discussed

The idea of a right to liberty helps to explain negative rights, such as freedom of speech and freedom from arbitrary arrest. Unless there is a claim-right to support such freedoms, they become unenforceable in law. However, the right to liberty is neither a necessary nor a sufficient condition for the recognition of positive rights. The enjoyment of a positive right, such as a right to be free from hunger, does not depend on an exercise of freedom, and it makes no sense to speak of some social and economic rights being exercised. Instead, they impose duties on others to act to benefit those who hold the rights. The social and economic rights themselves are seen as preconditions to the proper enjoyment of those negative rights which are the stuff of classical liberal theory. Thus, a right to liberty may be seen as a condition, together with economic or social rights, for the universal opportunity to exercise negative (freedom of choice) rights.

(ii) Assumptions about the content of other natural rights

Hart's idea of a right to liberty seems to assume that the negative rights which a right to liberty would underpin make up the central, if not the only, kind of right which would be produced by applying natural rights reasoning. Despite its apparent value-neutrality and generalizability, Hart's right to liberty is itself a product of liberal

---

[80] The best-known example is in his *Anarchical Fallacies*, above, n. 56.

[81] See Postema, *Bentham and the Common Law Tradition*, 328–36.

[82] H. L. A. Hart, 'Are there any Natural Rights?' (1955) **64** *Philosophical Rev.* 175–91, reprinted in A. Quinton (ed.), *Political Philosophy* (Oxford: Oxford University Press, 1967), 53–66.

theory. If one's view of natural rights stems from a socialist tradition, allowing for economic and social rights as 'natural', the right to liberty would provide an inadequate foundation, and one would have to find a different fundamental natural right.

(iii) Rights and the contingent nature of social organization

This in turn suggests that one's conception of natural rights is conditional on a particular set of political values. Indeed, rights-talk may be seen as a way of expressing a vision of the world in such a way as to give extra rhetorical force to such political values. An idea of this sort has been powerfully developed by Richard Rorty, through ideas which he calls 'contingency' and 'irony'.[83]

The ironic approach to freedom portrays the human condition and human values as contingent, rather than inevitable, developments. People see things as they do because of an accidental confluence of contingencies, which they seek to explain in language which makes sense of it for their purposes at that particular time. The ironist, however, maintains radical and continuing doubts about the vocabulary currently in use to describe values and the world, and does not look to this vocabulary to resolve these doubts, but instead tries out other ways of describing things and values ('languages') to see whether they seem to do the job better.[84] This approach eschews the language of self-evident goods and the essential nature of humanity or society. On this view,[85] it is unhelpful to ask, or to try to answer, questions about the essential nature of beings, about the nature of truth, or the nature of morality. People can mould the world by redescribing it in new language, and the advantage of a liberal community over an illiberal one is that it allows more freedom to develop new languages, and more opportunity for people to choose the form of language which best advances their purposes.[86] The idea of openness to new visions differs from the arguments advanced by Mill, in that whereas Mill assumed that the availability of new ways of looking at the world would necessarily lead to a better-understood and better-ordered world, Rorty suggests only that it may perhaps lead to a differently understood and differently organized world which may for some purposes be better (but may equally be worse for others).

According to Rorty, the advantage of his view of liberty and liberal society lies in its capacity to accommodate an account of liberty which suits the prevailing ethic of moral pluralism better than other available candidates. It frees one to decide (within the limits imposed by language) how to formulate freedoms so as to reflect one's understanding of the best resolution of competing moral imperatives. This is undoubtedly an advantage in that it frees us to construct a system of liberties from scratch. Of course, irony itself does not help us to choose a system, and so to choose the purposes for which we want to restate our visions of the world. However, it usefully emphasizes the importance of social or institutional acceptance to any

---

[83] R. Rorty, *Contingency, Irony and Solidarity* (Cambridge: Cambridge University Press, 1989).
[84] Ibid., 73.
[85] Ibid., chs 2 and 3.
[86] Ibid., ch. 1.

conception of rights. The rhetorical usefulness of rights-talk will be very limited unless everyone who matters accepts the language of rights in the same way.

(iv) Constitutional and political culture

This latter aspect of Rorty's ideas highlights another characteristic of ideas of rights already noted in relation to Hart's notion of a right to liberty. Both the rights people have and the ways in which they can be protected and enforced arise out of a constitutional and political culture which dictates the language in which rights-talk is conducted. It thereby tends to reinforce the existing arrangements, and limits the range of alternatives which are likely to be taken seriously by people—or by those who matter—in that society. Nevertheless, in a pluralist society such as that which obtains in the UK, the political system has to accommodate many different cultures, each with a distinctive attitude to rights. We live in a society characterized by disagreement about the proper use of rights-talk. Conceptions of rights are controversial, as this chapter has shown.

The traditionally dominant conception of rights in the legal cultures of the UK has been based on liberal theory. Liberties have predominated over claim-rights. Nevertheless, being part of an international legal community which has increasingly developed the language of claim-rights against the state created a tension between the language and tradition of English and Scots law and the language and culture of international human rights law to which the nation and the government subscribe, albeit sometimes reluctantly.[87] The Human Rights Act 1998, which is discussed in Chapter 2, narrows the gap between international human-rights law and municipal law in the UK, and is an important step in the process of resolving this linguistic and institutional tension.

1.4 RIGHTS, DEMOCRACY, AND THE RULE OF LAW

The final issue which this chapter addresses briefly is the relationship between rights, democracy, and the rule of law. By recognizing freedoms on the ground of moral autonomy, however one defines it, the state is committed to accepting that certain matters are, for the time being, properly to be regarded as lying in the private rather than the public sphere of decision-making. This distinction between the public and private spheres of life is thought by many to be a fundamental dichotomy in liberal society and legal systems.[88] It does not imply that the state or society has no legitimate interest in the matters in question. Rather, it suggests that the individual's choice should normally outrank social preferences in relation to matters lying within the private sphere. Once the boundaries have been set, and appropriate legal rules have

[87] For governmental disapproval of the terminology employed in the European Convention on Human Rights and Fundamental Freedoms in 1950, see A. Lester, 'Fundamental Rights: The United Kingdom Isolated' [1984] *PL* 46–72.

[88] See the discussion by E. Sparer, 'Fundamental Human Rights, Legal Entitlements, and the Social Struggle: A Friendly Critique of the Critical Legal Studies Movement' (1984) **36** *Stanford LR* 509–74 at 515–52.

been made and promulgated, the doctrine of the rule of law means that it is the job of the courts to ensure that people are able to exercise their freedoms and that the boundaries between the public and private spheres are not overstepped (particularly by the state).

This might be thought to introduce a tension between freedom and democracy, in that the creation of a sphere of private autonomy, and the work of the courts in policing it, prevents normal democratic decision-making processes from operating in that area. This is especially worrying to democrats in countries which have constitutionally entrenched and judicially enforceable Bills of Rights. For example, the First Amendment to the US Constitution prevents Congress from legislating to abridge press freedom. This places a restriction on the power of the democratically accountable representatives of the people. Furthermore, because the rule of law imposes a duty on politically independent judges to determine issues of constitutional law, the meaning and reach of the rights, and hence the scope of the restriction on democratic accountability, fall to be determined by judges who are not generally democratically accountable. However, the clash between freedoms or rights on the one hand and democracy on the other is not as stark as it might appear, for two reasons.

First, the delimitation of the private and public spheres remains a matter for public debate and, ultimately, decision. This is the case even where individual rights are constitutionally defined and protected against amendment by ordinary legislation, since every constitution has procedures whereby it may be amended. The need for constitutional amendment to change the scope of a freedom gives some freedoms a privileged place in political discussion, but does not remove them from the political stage. They may remain highly controversial. Even the judges who have to determine the scope of constitutional protections for the rights are likely to be influenced by public debate on the issues. This is the reason why the method of appointing new Justices to the US Supreme Court, taking account of their known political views, becomes so important in a democratic state. It provoked the extended political debates in the Senate Judiciary Committee which resulted in the Senate's rejection of Judge Bork, nominated by President Reagan,[89] and the eventual (somewhat grudging) confirmation of Judge Clarence Thomas, nominated to replace Justice Thurgood Marshall in 1991.

Secondly, citizens must have certain guaranteed rights if an effective democratic structure is to be put in place and maintained. It is impossible to imagine a properly functioning democracy in a country where people by and large are not guaranteed freedom of expression, a free press, a right to vote, a right to petition Parliament, freedom of protest, and freedom from arbitrary arrest and detention by government agencies. Such rights are fundamental to the notion of democracy, and to the development of the very idea of citizenship.[90] They could not be abrogated by democratic

---

[89] For discussion, see P. Bobbitt, *Constitutional Interpretation* (Oxford: Basil Blackwell, 1991), 83–108.

[90] T. Janoski, *Citizenship and Civil Society* (Cambridge: Cambridge University Press, 1998), ch. 2; Sir John Laws, 'Law and Democracy' [1995] *PL* 72–93; Jeffrey Jowell QC, 'Beyond the Rule of Law: Towards Constitutional Judicial Review' [2000] *PL* 671–83.

decision-makers in the public sphere without undermining the very democracy which is said to legitimize public decision-making. However these rights are formulated, and whatever means (constitutional law or political convention) may be used to protect them, it would be perverse to argue that there is anything undemocratic about a restriction on the capacity of decision-makers to interfere with the rights which are fundamental to democracy itself.

2

WAYS OF IDENTIFYING AND
PROTECTING RIGHTS AND LIBERTIES

This chapter first looks at the protection of human rights in international law generally, under the International Covenant on Civil and Political Rights, and under the European Convention on Human Rights. It then looks at a variety of ways in which rights may be protected in municipal law, depending on the constitutional structure and social values of different societies and legal systems. Next, the chapter examines the new regime adopted in the UK under the Human Rights Act 1998.

2.1 INTERNATIONAL HUMAN RIGHTS LAW

This section examines the general nature of human rights and the rights of peoples in international law.[1]

(1) INTERNATIONAL HUMAN RIGHTS LAW AS THE SYNTHESIS OF NATURAL AND POSITIVE RIGHTS

Throughout the world, in international relations and international law, discourse is increasingly being conducted in the language of human rights. This trend represents the significant inroads which are being made by the international community of nations on the notion of state sovereignty.[2] Until relatively recently, attempts by one nation to tell another how to treat the latter's citizens on its territory would have been dismissed as a blatant attempt to interfere in the internal affairs of a sovereign state. Now, however, it is recognized that humanity has a common interest in the treatment of people by governments, wherever they may be.

As explained in Chapter 1, the idea at the root of human rights thinking is that there are certain rights which are so fundamental to society's well-being and to people's

---

[1] Good general introductions are provided by P. Sieghart, *The Lawful Rights of Mankind* (Oxford: Clarendon Press, 1986), S. Davidson, *Human Rights* (Buckingham: Open University Press, 1993), and A. H. Robertson and J. G. Merrills, *Human Rights in the World: An Introduction to the Study of the International Protection of Human Rights*, 4th edn. (Manchester: Manchester University Press, 1996). On the theory of international human rights law, see C. Palley, *The United Kingdom and Human Rights* (London: Sweet & Maxwell, 1991).

[2] For an illuminating analysis of the significance of varying conceptions of state sovereignty, see E. Wicks, 'State Sovereignty—Towards a Refined Legal Conceptualization' (2000) **29** *Anglo-American Law Rev.* 282–314.

chance of leading a fulfilling life that governments are obligated to respect them, and the international order has to protect them. The identification of the human rights which are to be protected is, generally, the result of discussion between states' representatives in the course of negotiating multilateral treaties. Each state must decide what it wants from others, and what it is prepared to concede itself while safeguarding its most significant interests. The actual drafting of the treaties is largely in the hands of lawyers, and the final drafts are the result of attempts to encapsulate those rights on which agreement can be reached in language which is acceptable to all the States Parties. The form of rights enshrined in international human rights instruments is, therefore, a compromise between the objectives of the various states, influenced by approaches to human rights in different legal, moral, political, and economic cultures, and then reduced to legal language with as much precision as can be achieved given the pressure to find a form of words which will be acceptable to all.

A state which undertakes international obligations in relation to the treatment of its own citizens accepts a certain limitation of its national sovereignty over its internal affairs. Other states acquire an interest in the ways in which a state is treating people within its jurisdiction. That interest can be pursued not only through international diplomacy, but also through international law. For example, in *Ireland v. United King-dom*,[3] Ireland took action against the UK under the European Convention on Human Rights in respect of the treatment meted out to suspected terrorists by the British army in Ulster. Even if the states concerned are not parties to a justiciable treaty, there may be formalized mechanisms for pursuing a human-rights issue between them through diplomacy. In Europe, a non-judicial forum for exerting such diplomatic pressure was established under the Helsinki Final Act (1975), in the shape of the Conference on Security and Co-operation in Europe (CSCE).[4]

Governments will not normally allow their national sovereignty to be compromised in this way unless either (a) there are compelling reasons for doing so, in the shape of balancing advantages to be gained, or (b) they are cynical or complacent enough to believe that they will not need to take any steps to bring their law and practice into line with their new obligations. Calls for the protection of human rights in international law have been most persuasive and effective when prompted by serious disregard for humanitarian values. For example, nineteenth-century concern over the slave-trade seems to have generated the first international human-rights treaties, which made the slave-trade illegal, and required states to take action against it. Humanitarian law, particularly to protect combatants and non-combatants in war-time, followed. Next came treaties to protect minority population groups, including religious minorities, in the newly created or reformed countries which arose after the

---

[3] Eur. Ct. HR Series A, No. 25, Judgment of 18 Jan. 1978.

[4] Part VII of the Final Act is a declaration of intent on the part of the participating states to respect 'human rights and fundamental freedoms, including the freedom of thought, conscience, religion or belief, for all without distinction as to race, sex, language or religion'. For brief commentary, see Robertson and Merrills, *Human Rights in the World*, 179–90. A very good selection of materials on subsequent developments in the Helsinki process, with a valuable introduction, is provided by A. Bloed (ed.), *From Helsinki to Vienna: Basic Documents of the Helsinki Process* (Dordrecht: Martinus Nijhoff, 1990).

First World War, by virtue of the Treaty of Versailles.[5] In the UK, these have been given legal effect by a series of statutes and executive actions. For example, slavery had been held to be incompatible with English common law in *Somersett*'s case,[6] but stamping out the slave-trade required governments to co-operate in stopping and searching slaving ships as they crossed the Atlantic. In international law, any of the powers would have been justified in regarding as illegal the search of a vessel flying its flag by a ship of another power. Treaties were accordingly entered into between the UK and France (1831 and 1833) and Spain (1835), allowing each country's navy to search ships flying the others' flags, which led to British cruisers capturing more than one hundred vessels, flying the Spanish flag but equipped to carry slaves, between 1835 and 1840.[7] The searches were a source of conflict with the USA, with whom there was no treaty, until after the American Civil War, and action had to be taken against American slaving vessels. This was held by the English courts to be protected as an act of state.[8] Other treaties, requiring domestic legislation to introduce criminal penalties and extend the jurisdiction of the UK courts over acts committed elsewhere, concerned matters including genocide, torture, and crimes against the laws of war.[9]

But it was the public revelation, with the defeat of Hitler's Germany in 1945, of the inhumanity which people acting in the name of their states could inflict on others, which sparked a huge explosion in the range and number of human rights instruments. In the aftermath of the nationalist-inspired racial slaughter in Germany under the Third Reich, the General Assembly of the United Nations on 10 December 1948 adopted a Universal Declaration of Human Rights, noting in its Preamble that 'disregard and contempt for human rights have resulted in barbarous acts which have outraged the conscience of mankind, and the advent of a world in which human beings shall enjoy freedom of speech and belief and freedom from fear and want has been proclaimed as the highest aspiration of the common people'.[10] The Universal Declaration was not intended to impose binding obligations, as a matter of law, on the Member States of the United Nations, but has formed the basis for a large number of binding international human rights instruments, and is incorporated by reference in others.[11] These other instruments, including regional ones open to states in the

---

[5] On this background, see Robertson and Merrills, *Human Rights in the World*, 14–23; M. D. Evans, *Religious Liberty and International Law in Europe* (Cambridge: Cambridge University Press, 1997).

[6] *Somersett v. Stewart* (1772) 20 St. Tr. 1, where Lord Mansfield held that a slave brought to England was legally free, even though slavery was lawful in the country from which he had been brought.

[7] Sir Llewellyn Woodward, *The Age of Reform 1815–1870*, 2nd edn. (Oxford: Clarendon Press, 1962), 240–1, 370.

[8] *Buron v. Denman* (1848) 2 Ex. 167.

[9] See Genocide Act 1969, incorporating Art. II of the Convention on the Prevention and Punishment of the Crime of Genocide (approved by UN General Assembly, 1948) in the Schedule; Criminal Justice Act 1988, s. 134, creating a crime of torture, defined in accordance with the UN Convention against Torture and Other Cruel, Inhuman or Degrading Treatment or Punishment (1984); and the War Crimes Act 1991, controversially passed by the use of the Parliament Acts 1911 and 1949 after twice being rejected by the House of Lords.

[10] UN Doc. A/811.

[11] See, e.g. the International Covenant on Civil and Political Rights (1966); various regional instruments, including the European Convention for the Protection of Human Rights and Fundamental Freedoms (1950), the American Convention on Human Rights (1969, which also derives from the American Declaration of the

Americas, Africa, and Europe, are expressed in different terms, protecting rights defined in different ways, with a variety of monitoring and adjudication procedures. Nevertheless, there are common threads linking them, and it has been suggested that there is a gradual convergence of standards.[12]

The UK is party to, *inter alia*, the International Covenant on Civil and Political Rights, and the European Convention on the Protection of Human Rights and Fundamental Freedoms. Both these instruments are legally binding in international law, and have implementation procedures which will be examined later in this chapter. The rights guaranteed by the states which ratified these instruments are a mixture of individual rights (as in the European Convention on Human Rights) and social and economic rights (as, for example, under the International Covenant on Economic, Social and Cultural Rights, 1966, the various Conventions drafted by the International Labour Organisation,[13] and the European Social Charter, 1961). International law thus seeks to protect rights of many different types.

All these various rights are turned from what, in Chapter 1, were described as natural rights claims into positive legal rights by their adoption or recognition as legally binding on states in international law. The range of these rights is still increasing, and now takes in the collective right of peoples to self-determination, unknown in times of imperial expansion, during which western ideas of rights and individualism established an hegemony. Interestingly, this right is included, as Article 1, in both the International Covenant on Civil and Political Rights and the International Covenant on Economic, Social and Cultural Rights, yet the nature of self-determination is controversial, particularly in relation to groups which form a minority population within a sovereign state.[14] Cultural groups which, though temporarily submerged, survived, now seek to reassert their group identities. Peoples which have deployed arguments based on these rights include the Jews in relation to the establishment of the state of Israel in 1948, the claims of Palestinians to a national homeland at present, and the claims of indigenous peoples in the USA, Australia, New Zealand, Canada, and elsewhere.[15] Pressure for aboriginal rights and concern for the plight of

Rights and Duties of Man, 1948), and the African Charter on Human and Peoples' Rights (1981); and the agreement to abide by the provisions of the UN Charter and Universal Declaration in s.VII of the Final Act of the Helsinki Conference (1975).

[12] C. Scott, 'The Independence and Permeability of Human Rights Norms: Towards a Partial Fusion of the International Covenants on Human Rights' (1989) 27 *Osgoode Hall LJ* 769–878.

[13] The ILO is one of the specialized agencies which were brought into a special relationship with the United Nations under Arts. 57 and 63 of the UN Charter. See M. N. Shaw, *International Law*, 4th edn. (Cambridge: Cambridge University Press, 1997), 249–52; F. Wolf, 'Human Rights and the International Labour Organization', in T. Meron (ed.), *Human Rights in International Law: Legal and Policy Issues* (Oxford: Clarendon Press, 1984), ch. 7.

[14] See I. Brownlie, 'The Rights of Peoples in Modern International Law', in J. Crawford (ed.), *The Rights of Peoples* (Oxford: Clarendon Press, 1988); R. L. Barsh, 'Indigenous Peoples and the Right to Self-Determination in International Law', in B. Hocking (ed.), *International Law and Aboriginal Human Rights* (Sydney: Law Book Co., 1988), 68–82.

[15] There is a massive literature on these subjects. For a good introduction, see R. Schaffer, 'International Law and Sovereign Rights of Indigenous Peoples', in Hocking (ed.), *Aboriginal Rights*, 19–42. For a discussion of the rights of Australian aborigines, see P. Bailey, *Human Rights: Australia in an International Context* (Sydney: Butterworths, 1990), 192–206.

aboriginals developed in Australia parallel to similar concerns in other parts of the world, helped by the influence of international conventions outlawing genocide and guaranteeing the rights of peoples.[16] The combination of international law with domestic and international political pressure has finally forced the governments of the Australian Commonwealth and states to address the problem of accommodating the legal rights of the aboriginal people to the commercial interests of the Australian economy.[17]

Such rights, although encapsulated in positive international law, remain controversial, both because the scope and implications of (for example) the rights of a people to self-determination are uncertain,[18] and because the effects which a state will be willing to attribute to such rights will depend largely on the background political and philosophical attitudes towards rights.[19] Nevertheless, the idea that human rights are uncertain or vague, and for that reason are otiose or unenforceable, is a misconception. Once embodied in a legally binding international instrument, they are no less certain or more vague than most domestic law statutes. They can be construed like the legal texts which they are. 'Accordingly, the need for standards founded on systems of divine or natural law has disappeared, and with it the need for the legal positivist to object to them.'[20] English lawyers, therefore, need not fear that they will be incapable of interpreting international human rights instruments; they have the necessary techniques and experience readily to hand.

The charge of vagueness or uncertainty is more fairly levelled at rights under customary international law,[21] which, being a reflection of the practice of states, is subject to change and difficulties of definition. Nevertheless, there is growing acceptance that certain rights, originally protected only by treaty, have, by reason of acceptance in the practice of states, become part of customary international law, and so are capable of binding even those states which have been reluctant to sign human rights conventions. The International Court of Justice has recognized several such rights in the course of its decisions, influenced by the fact that they form fundamental principles enunciated in the UN Charter and the Universal Declaration of Human Rights.[22] The rights include freedom from wrongful deprivation of freedom in conditions of hardship, and (it has been suggested) the right not to be subjected to torture or cruel, inhuman or degrading treatment or punishment and the right to liberty and

[16] For summaries, see I. Brownlie, *Principles of Public International Law* (Oxford: Clarendon Press, 1990) 595–8.

[17] The way in which this is being done is outside the scope of this book. See P. H. Bailey, *Human Rights: Australia in an International Context* (Sydney: Butterworths, 1990), 192–213; *Mabo v. Queensland* (1992) 66 ALJR 408, HC of Australia.

[18] For consideration of these questions by the ICJ, see *The South West Africa Cases* (Preliminary Objections) [1962] ICJ Rep. 319; see also *The South West Africa Cases* (Second Phase) [1966] ICJ Reports 6.

[19] See Brownlie, *Public International Law*, 595–8.

[20] P. Sieghart, *The International Law of Human Rights* (Oxford: Clarendon Press, 1983), 15. See also Sieghart, *The Lawful Rights of Mankind*, 40–41.

[21] Full discussion is provided by T. Meron, *Human Rights and Humanitarian Norms as Customary Law* (Oxford: Clarendon Press, 1989).

[22] *The Tehran Hostages Case* [1980] ICJ 3; N. S. Rodley, 'Human Rights and Humanitarian Intervention: The Case Law of the World Court' (1989) **38** *ICLQ* 321–33; Meron, *Human Rights and Humanitarian Norms*, 106–14.

security of the person,[23] and may well go much further, including rights of peoples to self-determination. However, following the ICJ's judgment in *Military Activities in Nicaragua*[24] concerning the military support given by the United States to the Contra rebels in Nicaragua, it seems that all the human rights recognized in customary international law can be traced to some international instrument, such as the UN Charter or the Universal Declaration of Human Rights. It also seems that, where the rights are contained in an instrument such as the International Covenant on Civil and Political Rights or the European Convention on Human Rights, and the parties to a dispute are also parties to that instrument, the appropriate means of settling the matter is that laid down under the instrument in question. It appears to follow that the acceptance of human rights as part of customary law extends the range of parties bound to respect the rights beyond those states which are parties to the relevant international instruments, but does not alter the substance of the obligations on those states which, like the UK, are parties. If the range of recognized rights were to increase, to take in some which are in instruments to which the UK is not currently a party, it is possible that the scope of the UK's international law obligations would be increased. However, it is likely that the UK would have become a party to any such instrument before the rights in it had received sufficient acceptance by states to be regarded as part of customary international law.

2.2 INTERNATIONAL LAW: THE UNITED NATIONS, AND THE INTERNATIONAL COVENANT ON CIVIL AND POLITICAL RIGHTS

(1) THE UNITED NATIONS AND HUMAN RIGHTS

A number of instruments operating under the umbrella of the United Nations in the realm of international law affect individuals' human rights and offer a route to redress.[25] The Charter of the United Nations (1945) contains references to human rights,[26] and Article 1 specifies, as one of the purposes of the organization, promoting respect for human rights and fundamental freedoms. The Economic and Social Council (ECOSOC), established under Article 7 of the UN Charter, was permitted to make recommendations for that purpose, and to prepare draft conventions.[27] Under Article 68, ECOSOC established a Commission on Human Rights, which was to have, as one of its first tasks, the drafting of an international Bill of Rights. The first step was to draft a declaration, which was considered by ECOSOC and adopted (as the Universal Declaration of Human Rights) by the UN General Assembly in 1948. The next step was for the Commission to draft what turned out to be two Covenants which

---

[23] Rodley, 'Human Rights and Humanitarian Intervention', at 327; N. S. Rodley, *The Treatment of Prisoners in International Law*, 2nd edn. (Oxford: Clarendon Press, 1999), 62–74.

[24] [1986] ICJ 14, discussed in Rodley, 'Human Rights and Humanitarian Intervention', at 327ff.

[25] For a general survey, see Robertson and Merrills, *Human Rights in the World*, chs 2, 3, and 8.

[26] Preamble; Arts. 1, 13, 55, 62, 68, 76.

[27] Art. 62.

were to be open to signature by states which were members of the UN or of one of its specialized agencies, any State Party to the Statute of the International Court of Justice, and any other state invited by the General Assembly to become a party to the Covenants.[28] This gave the Covenants a potentially wider reach than the UN Declaration, which had been in the form of a proclamation by members of the UN General Assembly. As treaties, the Covenants were binding on those who ratified them. The drafting of the Covenants proved a longer and more contentious task than that of the Declaration. Political and ideological differences came to the fore. It was 1966 before the International Covenant on Civil and Political Rights (ICCPR) and the International Covenant on Economic, Social and Cultural Rights (ICESCR) were adopted by the General Assembly and opened for signature, and 1976 before they were in force.

The decision to embody the two sets of rights in separate instruments was a way of allowing states to accept obligations in respect of one type of rights if they were not prepared to accept both. This was a pragmatic response to the deep philosophical and political differences of opinion as to the 'true' meaning of freedom, noted in Chapter 1. It also enabled different enforcement and monitoring procedures to be adopted in respect of each. The rights contained in ICESCR are heavily dependent on the economic conditions prevailing in different parts of the world, and on the state of the economies of each State Party to the Covenant. The rights in ICCPR are less dependent, and generally speaking protect individuals' freedoms rather than positive rights to state assistance or intervention.[29] It was therefore possible for the UN Commission on Human Rights to include, and the General Assembly to adopt, a procedure for implementing ICCPR which included some element of evaluation of the performance of States Parties in giving effect to the Convention, as well as the usual role of maintaining communication with states.

Between 1945 and 1966, however, the Secretary-General of the UN received very large numbers of communications alleging human rights infringements. Where these came from individuals or non-governmental organizations,[30] the UN Commission on Human Rights took the view that they could not be considered in an international forum, as entertaining communications from people or bodies other than states would amount to unjustified 'intervention in matters which are essentially within the domestic jurisdiction of States', contrary to Article 2(7) of the UN Charter. However, as the number of members of the UN grew, a different view developed. In 1966, the General Assembly passed Resolution 2144(XX), encouraging ECOSOC to find ways of improving the capacity of the UN to stop human rights violations wherever they occurred. In 1970, ECOSOC responded by authorizing the UN Commission on

---

[28] International Covenant on Civil and Political Rights, Art. 48; International Covenant on Economic, Social and Cultural Rights, Art. 26.

[29] The major exception is that Art. 1, identical in ICCPR and ICESCR, provides for the right of all peoples to self-determination. For reasons considered in ch. 1, this is outside the scope of a book on civil liberties. See D. McGoldrick, *The Human Rights Committee: Its Role in the Development of the International Covenant on Civil and Political Rights* (Oxford: Clarendon Press, 1991), 14–16 and ch. 5.

[30] On the latter, see D. Weissbrodt, 'The Contribution of International Non-Governmental Organizations to the Protection of Human Rights', in Meron (ed.), *Human Rights in International Law*, ch. 11.

Human Rights, by ECOSOC Resolution 1503, to consider 'communications, together with replies of governments, if any, which appear to reveal a consistent pattern of gross and reliably attested violations of human rights and fundamental freedoms within the terms of reference of the Sub-Commission'.[31]

The Resolution 1503 procedure, as it is known, is conducted by a five-member Working Group of the Sub-Commission on the Prevention of Discrimination and Protection of Minorities. The Working Group considers communications and the governments' replies to them. It identifies cases which disclose a 'consistent pattern of gross and reliably attested violations' involving many people over an extended period. It refers these to the Sub-Commission. The proceedings are confidential, but summaries of communications and developments in relation to them are supplied to representatives of all states on the UN Commission on Human Rights. In rare cases, where a country's responses to a communication are unsatisfactory, the communication is passed by the Sub-Commission, via the Commission, to ECOSOC, at which point ECOSOC may make it public. The system works through pressure rather than adjudication, and allows the UN to examine matters which are not otherwise open to review by any authority outside the country which is the subject of the communication.[32]

Alongside the Resolution 1503 procedure, the UN Commission on Human Rights and the Sub-Commission from time to time undertake comprehensive investigations of the human rights position in particular countries, and thematic investigations of the status of particular rights in all Member States. In the case of the thematic investigations, they work through specially appointed working groups or individual rapporteurs.[33] Apart from this, there are also specialist expert committees, which are set up under treaties and are independent of the UN, charged with the implementation of particular human rights treaties, including the Convention on the Elimination of All Forms of Racial Discrimination (1965), the Convention on the Elimination of All Forms of Discrimination against Women (1979), the Convention against Torture and Other Cruel, Inhuman or Degrading Treatment (1984), and the Convention on the Rights of the Child (1989).[34] In December 1993, a new body was established: the UN High Commissioner for Human Rights has the challenging tasks of raising the profile of human rights in international decision-making, providing guidance and assistance to states in building democratic institutions and ensuring that existing institutions function in accordance with human rights principles, and co-ordinating the activities of the various UN human rights organizations.[35]

---

[31] Resolution 1503, para. 1.

[32] Robertson and Merrills, *Human Rights in the World*, 78–83. See M. Banton, 'Decision-taking in the Committee on the Elimination of Racial Discrimination', in P. Alston and J. Crawford (eds.), *The Future of UN Human Rights Treaty Monitoring* (Cambridge: Cambridge University Press, 2000), 55–78; M. R. Bustelo, 'The Committee on the Elimination of Discrimination against Women at the Crossroads', ibid., 79–111; G. Lansdown, 'The Reporting Process under the Convention on the Rights of the Child', ibid., 113–28; S. Leckie, 'The Committee on Economic, Social and Cultural Rights: Catalyst for Change in a System Needing Reform', ibid., 129–44; R. Bank, 'Country-oriented Procedures under the Convention against Torture: Towards a New Dynamism', ibid., 145–74; and A. Clapham, 'UN Human Rights Reporting Procedures: an NGO Perspective', ibid., 175–98.

[33] Robertson and Merrills, *Human Rights in the World*, 83–95.

[34] Ibid., 95–112.

[35] General Assembly Resolution 48/141; Robertson and Merrills, *Human Rights in the World*, 112–14.

(2) THE OPERATION OF THE ICCPR

The body set up under Article 28 of ICCPR to implement the Covenant is the Human Rights Committee (HRC).[36] This is made up of eighteen people, 'of high moral character and recognized competence in the field of human rights',[37] elected by representatives of the States Parties, from a list of people nominated by the States Parties,[38] for a period of four years.[39] The Committee may not include more than one national of the same state.[40] Those elected serve in their personal capacity, not as representatives of their states.[41] The HRC makes an annual report on its activities to the UN General Assembly,[42] and although it is not formally accountable to it, being established under a separate Covenant, the HRC is dependent on the UN for its secretariat and resources.[43] It has three main functions.

(i) Studying reports from States Parties

The HRC studies reports received from States Parties, under Article 40(1), on the measures which the States Parties have taken to give effect to the rights recognized in ICCPR and the progress made in the enjoyment of those rights. These reports are to be submitted by a State Party within one year of the time when the Covenant enters into force for that State Party, and thereafter when the HRC requests. In practice, the reports are often late and sometimes not very informative; States Parties tend to paint a bland, rosy picture, rather than highlighting difficulties which they may be facing. The HRC therefore interviews the representative of the State Party concerned, and sometimes requests a supplementary report in order to illuminate matters of concern. The HRC then has to transmit its reports, and such comments as it considers appropriate, to the State Parties, and may also transmit them to ECOSOC.[44] The HRC has taken a robust view of its functions, using evidence derived from sources other than the often anodyne reports received from States Parties, and making searching evaluations and suggestions. This monitoring function is intended to be constructive, and to assist the States Parties in what is assumed to be their endeavour to improve respect for human rights in their jurisdictions.

It has certainly proved possible to exert some moral pressure through this reporting procedure, establishing dialogue with states and conducting it in a probing and not uncritical manner, without allowing meetings to become unduly confrontational. However, the success of this process depends heavily on the willingness of states to participate in it. In practice, there is generally a reasonable level of co-operation. This makes it possible for Professor McGoldrick to conclude that, despite some deficien-

---

[36] McGoldrick, *The Human Rights Committee*, provides a comprehensive account of HRC and its work, to which the following brief sketch is deeply indebted.

[37] ICCPR, Art. 28(1), (2).

[38] Ibid., Art. 29(1).

[39] Ibid., Art. 32.

[40] Ibid., Art. 31(1).

[41] Ibid., Art. 28(3).

[42] Ibid., Art. 45.

[43] McGoldrick, *The Human Rights Committee*, 52–3, 97–8.

[44] ICCPR, Art. 40(4).

cies, 'the reporting procedure has been developed into a much more useful procedure of international implementation (in the broad sense) than might confidently have been predicted when the Covenant was adopted in 1966'.[45]

(ii) Receiving communications from States Parties

The second function of the HRC is to receive communications under Article 41 to the effect that a State Party is not fulfilling its obligations under ICCPR. Such communications can be considered only if both the State Party making the allegation and that against whom it is made have made declarations recognizing the competence of the HRC to receive and consider them. In addition, the HRC must normally have ascertained that all available domestic remedies have been exhausted, unless the application of the remedies is unreasonably prolonged. The HRC may then make available its good offices to try to achieve a friendly solution. If this fails, the HRC will prepare a report on the facts and submissions of the States Parties, and may, with the prior consent of the States Parties concerned, appoint an *ad hoc* Conciliation Commission, which attempts to achieve a friendly solution in accordance with respect for human rights. If this proves impossible, the Conciliation Commission will report to the HRC, setting out its findings on relevant facts and its views on the possibility of an amicable solution,[46] and the HRC will include its account of the matter in its next annual report, which is considered by the Third Committee of the General Assembly. At that point, the available procedures run out. It is a long drawn out, cumbersome procedure, and holds out little prospect of success. It seems, therefore, unsurprising that this procedure has not, so far, proved popular.[47]

(iii) Receiving communications from individuals

The third function of the HRC arises under the Optional Protocol to ICCPR. Any State Party which signs the Optional Protocol recognizes the competence of the HRC to receive and consider communications from any individual who is subject to the jurisdiction of the State Party and who claims to be a victim of violation by that State Party of any of the rights set forth in ICCPR.[48] Communications which are anonymous, or which the HRC considers to be an abuse of the right to submit communications or to be incompatible with the Covenant, are inadmissible.[49] Before considering an admissible communication, the HRC must ascertain that the matter is not being considered under any other procedure of international investigation or settlement,

---

[45] McGoldrick, *The Human Rights Committee*, 102. Others take a less sanguine view. See J. Crawford, 'The UN Human Rights Treaty System: A System in Crisis', in Alston and Crawford (eds.), *The Future of UN Human Rights Treaty Monitoring*, 1–12, pointing out the difficulties caused by a large backlog of reporting and constraints on resources within the UN. For concluding observations on the UK's fifth periodic report, see CCPR/CO/73/UK, 05/11/2001.

[46] ICCPR, Art. 42.

[47] McGoldrick, *The Human Rights Committee*, 50.

[48] Optional Protocol, Art. 1. Communications may be submitted by an individual on behalf of another who is prevented by the state in question from communicating directly, and the HRC may then require the state to permit the victim to communicate directly with the HRC. On this, and the refusal to extend *locus standi* to organizations, see McGoldrick, *The Human Rights Committee*, 132–4, 169–77.

[49] Optional Protocol, Art. 3.

and that the individual has exhausted available domestic remedies (unless the application of those remedies is unreasonably prolonged).[50] The State Party concerned has six months to submit written explanations or statements clarifying the matter and setting out any remedial action which the state may have taken.[51] The HRC considers the matter at closed meetings, and then forwards its views to the individual and the state concerned.[52]

The HRC has developed a substantial case-load under the Optional Protocol, and has taken a robust approach to states which try to avoid co-operating with its deliberations.[53] For example, if a state merely offers a blanket denial of the individual's claim, without any detailed rebuttal of the facts alleged in the communication, the HRC has treated the unsupported denial as insufficient to counter the allegations, and has taken the view that the individual's claim is made out.[54] When that view is reached, and is notified to the individual and state concerned, the HRC has more or less exhausted its powers. Its effectiveness depends on the willingness of the state to comply, or on the publicity (at present very weak) which it can muster for its view in order to bring pressure to bear on the state. While the state concerned sometimes takes action to rectify any deficiency which the HRC identifies, the record on co-operation and compliance with the HRC's considerations is patchy, and a majority of States Parties to the Covenant (including the UK) have not signed the Optional Protocol. The summary which is included in the HRC's annual report to the General Assembly,[55] and consideration by the Third Committee of the General Assembly, does not unduly worry states unless they have unusually thin skins in relation to their international reputations. In Professor McGoldrick's balanced assessment of the Optional Protocol, its significance lies, first, in the effect which it may have over a period of decades in encouraging progress in the international protection of human rights, and, secondly, in the enhanced status which it gives to individuals in international law; but 'it is of little comfort to victims of human rights violations'.[56] Furthermore, there is no necessary connection between the adjudication of individual complaints and the overall level of human rights compliance in states.[57]

---

[50] Optional Protocol, Art. 5.

[51] Ibid., Art. 4.

[52] Ibid., Art. 5(3), (4).

[53] Two excellent selections of decisions are published as: Human Rights Committee, *Selected Decisions Under the Optional Protocol (Second to Sixteenth Sessions)* (New York: UN, 1985); *Selected Decisions of the Human Rights Committee Under the Optional Protocol*, ii. *Seventeenth to Thirty-second Sessions* (New York: UN, 1990).

[54] See, e.g. *J. L. Massera and Others v. Uruguay*, Annual Report of the HRC, 1979, UN Doc. A/34/40, p. 124; Human Rights Committee, *Selected Decisions under the Optional Protocol*, i. p. 40; McGoldrick, *The Human Rights Committee*, 147–9.

[55] Optional Protocol, Art. 6.

[56] McGoldrick, *The Human Rights Committee*, 204; M. G. Schmidt, 'Individual Human Rights Complaints Procedures based on United Nations Treaties and the Need for Reform' (1992) 41 *ICLQ* 645–59.

[57] H. J. Steiner, 'Individual Claims in a World of Massive Violations: What Role for the Human Rights Committee?', in Alston and Crawford (eds.), *The Future of UN Human Rights Monitoring*, 15–53.

2.3 INTERNATIONAL LAW: THE COUNCIL OF EUROPE AND THE EUROPEAN CONVENTION ON HUMAN RIGHTS

(1) BACKGROUND

The European Convention on Human Rights was drafted in the late 1940s under the aegis of the Council of Europe.[58] The Convention was signed by the High Contracting Parties in 1950, and entered into force in 1953. It was the first international human rights instrument to provide means for its own interpretation and enforcement: it established a Commission to receive and examine complaints about infringements of rights by the States Parties, and a Court to adjudicate finally on complaints in the light of its authoritative interpretation of the Convention. It also gave the Committee of Ministers of the Council of Europe both an adjudicative role and a monitoring role in relation to compliance by states. Still more importantly, Article 25 of the Convention enabled any State Party to recognize the jurisdiction of the Commission to examine petitions from victims (including individuals or organizations) of breaches of the Convention by that state. This was unusual, in that only sovereign states normally have standing in international law, but it was an important provision for those people who did not have another state taking an interest in their rights, and has been copied in other instruments (such as the International Covenant on Civil and Political Rights, as explained above).

Not until 14 January 1966 did the UK make a declaration under Article 25 recognizing the right of individual petition in respect of events occurring after that time. The declaration was originally made for a period of only five years, but was renewed every five years, save that petitions relating to the Isle of Man have been excluded since 1976 (following Manx concerns at the petition in *Tyrer*, a case concerning judicial birching in the Isle of Man).[59] In 1981, the declaration gave the Commission jurisdiction to receive individual petitions concerning violations in the UK's remaining overseas territories, other than Hong Kong. Since the Eleventh Protocol to the ECHR entered into force on 1 November 1998, extensively amending the procedures under the Convention, Article 34 has made it impossible for the High Contracting Parties to exclude the right of individual application.

The Eleventh Protocol made other extensive changes to address serious delays which had developed in dealing with cases as a result of a vast expansion in the number of applications, exacerbated by the accession of former Soviet bloc nations to the Council of Europe. To streamline the Convention procedure, the Commission was

---

[58] For general background, see Robertson and Merrills, *Human Rights in the World*, 102–5. For a more detailed account, ending before the important Eleventh Protocol, see A. H. Robertson and J. G. Merrills, *Human Rights in Europe*, 3rd edn. (Manchester: Manchester University Press, 1993), 1–24.

[59] The case reached the European Court of Human Rights: *Tyrer v. United Kingdom*, Eur. Ct. HR, Series A, No. 26, Judgment of 25 April 1978. This case is discussed further in ch. 4 below. Because individual petitions concerning the Isle of Man are now excluded, it will not be possible (for example) for any individual to challenge the continued criminalization there of homosexual acts between consenting adults. *Cp. Dudgeon v. United Kingdom*, Eur. Ct. HR, Series A, No. 45, Judgment of 22 October 1981.

abolished, the politicized Committee of Ministers was removed from the adjudicative process, and a more flexible Court structure took over responsibility for the whole of the process up to the point of delivering a final judgment. However, this may turn out to be only a short-term measure. By 2000, there were 41 Member States of the Council of Europe, all of whom had ratified the Convention. This gave direct access to the Court to their 800 million or so residents, plus an unlimited number of others who have dealings with the states. The ten thousand or more applications now being received annually are once again outstripping the capacity of the reformed procedure, and there is already talk of further procedural reform through a possible Thirteenth Protocol, which might allow the Court to be more selective in the cases with which it decides to deal. The Court is the victim of its own success in providing a procedure for human-rights adjudication which both nation-states and individuals are prepared to trust.

Alongside the Court, the Council of Europe established a new office, that of the Commissioner for Human Rights, in 1999. The first Commissioner, Mr. Alvaro Gil-Robles, has the task of promoting human rights in Member States of the Council of Europe, and identifying shortcomings in the protection of human rights. The Commissioner cannot entertain individual complaints, but can take up general issues on his own initiative, pursue them in co-operation with national institutions, and report on them.

In what follows, the main focus will be on arrangements to provide remedies for individual violations of the ECHR.

(2) PROCEDURE

The procedure is currently as follows.[60] Any High Contracting Party, or a person who claims to be a victim of a violation of a right guaranteed under the Convention, may address an application to the European Court of Human Rights.[61] The application must be made in writing, and signed by the applicant or his or her representative.[62] An application by an individual must include (*inter alia*) the applicant's personal details (although the President of the Chamber of the Court which deals with the case may authorize anonymity 'in exceptional and duly justified cases', so they need not be made public if there are reasons for avoiding disclosure), and details of any representative; the High Contracting Party or Parties against which the application is made; a succinct statement of the facts, the alleged violations with relevant arguments, the applicant's compliance with conditions for admissibility of the application, and the relief which is sought; and all relevant documents.[63]

The admissibility of the application will then be considered. A three-judge committee of the Court may unanimously decide that it is inadmissible or strike the case out

---

[60] See K. Starmer, *European Human Rights Law: The Human Rights Act 1998 and the European Convention on Human Rights* (London: Legal Action Group, 1999), ch. 30.

[61] European Convention on Human Rights, Arts. 33 (inter-state cases), 34 (individual applications).

[62] Rules of the European Court of Human Rights, r. 45.

[63] Ibid., r. 47.

of the list where no further examination is needed.[64] A Judge Rapporteur will be appointed to report on the case, and the report will be considered by the Committee. If it does not unanimously decide that the application is inadmissible or should be struck out of the list, the case will be referred to a seven-judge Chamber of the Court (which always includes the judge appointed in respect of the High Contracting Party against which the application is brought).[65] This Chamber first considers the admissibility of the application. To be admissible, it must satisfy five tests. First, the application must not be anonymous or substantially the same as a matter which has already been considered by the Court or submitted to another international body for settlement or arbitration.[66] Secondly, before applying, the applicant must first have exhausted his domestic remedies.[67] In practice, this means that the applicant has to have taken all reasonable steps to obtain a remedy through available legal or administrative procedures. It is not usually necessary to take steps if one has received well-founded legal advice that they would be pointless.[68] The Court will take account of practical realities, and will not insist on people attempting to take advantage of national remedies which are theoretically available but which offer the applicant no real prospect of proper redress. For example, the applicant might belong to a group which has been subject either to systematic discrimination or to a campaign of murder and 'disappearance'.[69] Thirdly, the application must have been presented within six months of the date of the final decision in the domestic forum.[70] Fourthly, the application must not be incompatible with the provisions of the Convention, an abuse of the right of petition, or manifestly ill-founded.[71] These are not only threshold tests: the Court must reject an application which, at any stage of the proceedings, it finds to have failed any of them.[72] Fifthly, the applicant must be a 'person, non-governmental organization or group of individuals claiming to be the victim of a violation by one of the High Contracting Parties' of a Convention right.[73] This test for standing is very broad in some ways. Bodies corporate may apply, as long as the right which they are asserting is one which can be enjoyed by such a body. The applicant must be directly affected by the alleged violation or at risk of suffering a violation in the future.[74] The act or omission need not be aimed at the applicant if he or she suffers as a direct result: where people are denied permission to enter and remain in a country, members

---

[64] ECHR, Art. 28.

[65] ECHR, Art. 29; Rules of Court, r. 54.

[66] ECHR, Art. 35(2).

[67] Ibid., Art. 35(1).

[68] *Donnelly v. United Kingdom* (1972) 4 D&R 4, 72, Eur. Commn. HR; *Hilton v. United Kingdom* (1976) 4 D&R 177, Eur. Ct. HR (persistent refusal by prison authorities to allow prisoner access to legal advice); *Cremieux v. France* (1989) 62 D&R 67, 80, Eur. Commn. HR; *Vernillo v. France* (1991) 13 EHRR 880, para. 27, Eur. Commn. HR.

[69] *Akdivar v. Turkey* (1997) 23 EHRR 143, Eur. Ct. HR.

[70] ECHR, Art. 35(1).

[71] Ibid., Art. 35(3).

[72] Ibid., Art. 35(4).

[73] Ibid., Art. 34.

[74] See, e.g. *Norris v. Ireland* (1988) 13 EHRR 186, where the Court accepted that the applicant was a victim. He was a homosexual man complaining that the criminalization of homosexual acts in Ireland violated his Art. 8 right to respect for his private life, although he accepted that the risk of being prosecuted was remote.

of their families who already live there may suffer a violation of the right to respect for their private lives under Article 8 of the Convention.[75] Similarly, where a person is killed, his or her spouse can claim to be a victim of any violation of Article 2.[76] A person may cease to be a victim if the state remedies the violation later, but only if the steps taken by the state amount to a recognition of the violation and provide adequate redress.[77] If an applicant dies while the case is being considered by the Court, the application may be continued by a spouse or close relative with a legitimate interest in the proceedings.[78]

If the application is admissible, the Court examines the case in confidence, conducting an investigation if necessary. The parties exchange their views on the application with the Court, and the respondent High Contracting Party is required to furnish all necessary facilities for the purpose of establishing the facts. The Court also places itself (through the agency of its Registrar) 'at the disposal of the parties concerned with a view to securing a friendly settlement of the matter on the basis of respect for human rights as defined in the Convention and the protocols thereto'.[79] If the Court is satisfied that such a settlement has been achieved, it will strike the case out of its list.[80] It is then for the states concerned to take any steps agreed in the friendly settlement.

If, however, it proves impossible to reach a friendly settlement, the Court decides the case on its merits. It has power to appoint its own fact-finding delegation to investigate the case and to hear witnesses and experts,[81] although it is far more usual to rely on the evidence submitted to it by the parties in writing. There may be a hearing at which the parties' representatives make short oral submissions. The President of the Chamber may permit third-party interventions in the proceedings,[82] which can be helpful in providing the Court with independent evidence or analysis of relevant municipal law. If the case 'raises a serious question affecting the interpretation of the Convention or the protocols thereto, or where the resolution of a question before the Chamber might have a result inconsistent with a judgment previously delivered by the Court, the Chamber may, at any time before it has rendered its judgment, relinquish jurisdiction in favour of the Grand Chamber, unless one of the parties to the case objects.'[83] The case will then be heard by a Grand Chamber of seventeen judges, including the judge elected in respect of the State Party concerned.[84]

[75] *Abdulaziz, Cabales and Balkandali v. United Kingdom* (1985) 7 EHRR 471.
[76] *McCann v. United Kingdom* (1995) 21 EHRR 97.
[77] In *Amuur v. France* (1996) 22 EHRR 533, an asylum seeker had been held in breach of Art. 5(1), and had been deported to Syria before receiving any remedy in France. The Court held that the remedy was inadequate in those circumstances; the applicant remained a victim. See also *Dalban v. Romania* App. No. 28114/95, Judgment of 28 September 1999.
[78] See, e.g. *Lukanov v. Bulgaria* (1997) 24 EHRR 121 (the wife of a man who had been wrongfully detained); *Dalban v. Romania* App. No. 28114/95, Judgment of 28 September 1999.
[79] ECHR, Art. 38; Rules of Court, r. 62.
[80] ECHR, Art. 39.
[81] Rules of Court, rr. 42, 65–9.
[82] ECHR, Art. 36; Rules of Court, r. 61.
[83] ECHR, Art. 30.
[84] Ibid., Art. 27.

In due course, the judgment is given in writing, according to a prescribed format.[85] Within three months of judgment being given by a Chamber, any party to the case may, 'in exceptional cases', request that the case be referred to the Grand Chamber of seventeen judges. A panel of five judges of the Grand Chamber considers such a request, and may accept the case 'if the case raises a serious question affecting the interpretation or application of the Convention or the protocols thereto, or a serious issue of general importance'. If the Grand Chamber accepts the case, it decides it by means of a judgment.[86] This judgment is final.[87] If the Grand Chamber does not accept the case, or the parties declare that they will not request a referral to the Grand Chamber, or three months after the judgment of the Chamber if no party has requested referral before that time, the judgment of the Chamber becomes final, and in any case the final judgment is published.[88]

Where the Court has held that there has been a violation which cannot be fully remedied under national law, it 'shall, if necessary, afford just satisfaction to the injured party'.[89] The meaning of 'just satisfaction' is nowhere explained. It does not necessarily entail monetary compensation. Some violations give rise to moral or physical harms, rather than financial loss. Where the injury affects money or other property, and can be assessed in pecuniary terms, for example in relation to the right to property under Article 1 of the First Protocol, the Court uses available evidence to assess the loss, which forms the basis for an award of damages. In relation to physical injury and detention, compensation is harder to assess, and there no clear principles emerge from the Strasbourg caselaw, although some advocates are beginning to rely on English tariffs of damages before the Court. It is particularly hard to put a price on interference with family life and other moral harms. The Court often decides that it would be inappropriate to award damages, holding that the judgment itself, that a violation has been committed, constitutes just satisfaction in itself for such harms. The process certainly does not make people rich, although it helps to restore the wealth of those who have been deprived of it.[90]

The effect of a final judgment holding that a High Contracting Party has violated the Convention is to impose an obligation on the Party in international law to amend its domestic law to bring it into line with the Convention, to compensate the victim if ordered to do so, and to take such other steps as may be required of it by the Court.[91] The process is therefore doubly valuable: it may well secure 'just satisfaction' for a victim where domestic law has failed to provide an adequate remedy, and lead to a change in that law so that other people do not in future have their rights under the

---

[85] Rules of Court, Chapter VIII.
[86] ECHR, Art. 43.
[87] Ibid., Art. 44(1).
[88] Ibid., Art. 44(2), (3).
[89] ECHR, Art. 41.
[90] See D. Shelton, *Remedies in International Human Rights Law* (Oxford: Oxford University Press, 1999), Part III; and for a comprehensive study of the Strasbourg caselaw on damages, see Law Commission Report No. 266 and Scottish Law Commission Report No. 180, *Damages under the Human Rights Act 1998*, Cm. 4853, SE/200/182 (London and Edinburgh: The Stationery Office, 2000).
[91] ECHR, Art. 46(1).

Convention violated. The Committee of Ministers of the Council of Europe is responsible for overseeing the execution of the judgment, monitoring compliance by the state concerned.[92]

(3) THE PRINCIPLES APPLIED BY THE COURT

The Court (and, in earlier days, the Commission) have developed important and distinctive principles to guide them in applying the Convention. Initially, the Court's authority relied entirely on the consent of the High Contracting Parties, signified through their acts of signing and ratifying the Convention under which the institutions were established. However, thereafter the Commission and Court quickly decided that the continuing legitimacy of the Convention depended on their success in making the rights which it guaranteed real and effective by means of a procedure which was demonstrably fair and gave appropriate weight both to the rights and to the dignity of the states, which, under Article 1 of the Convention, had the primary responsibility for securing the rights.[93] These considerations have led to the adoption of the following general principles.

(a) The ECHR is taken to encapsulate minimum standards of human-rights protection capable of applying to all forty-one Member States of the Council of Europe. It is not part of the Court's job to set aspirational targets. For this reason, the Court sometimes waits for signs of a developing consensus between European States before extending an interpretation of a right. For example, the Court has been very cautious in responding to arguments that the right to respect for private and family life requires states to recognize, for all legal purposes, the reassigned gender of a post-operative transsexual, in the absence of a clear European consensus on the right approach to the issue.[94]

(b) The Convention rights are to be made effective and real, not theoretical or merely illusory.[95] This may, for example, require under Article 6 that free legal assistance be available to a litigant where this is indispensable to his ability to allowing him to pursue an effective remedy for a violation of a civil right.[96]

(c) In order to make rights real and effective, some of the rights impose positive obligations on the state to take action to help to protect rights, not merely to refrain from interfering with them.[97] This is considered further below.

(d) The Court treats the Convention as a living instrument, and recognizes that ideas about the proper scope and content of fundamental freedoms are

[92] ECHR, Art. 46(2).
[93] See D. Feldman, 'Human Rights Treaties, Nation States, and Conflicting Moralities', (1995) 1 *Contemporary Issues in Law* 61–85; D. Feldman, 'Establishing the Legitimacy of Judicial Procedures for Protecting Human Rights', (2001) 13 *REDP/ERPL* 139–79.
[94] See below, Ch. 12.
[95] See particularly the preamble to the Convention and Articles 1 and 13, which are not among the Convention rights for the purposes of the Human Rights Act 1998, s. 1 and Sch. 1, but may be used to help interpretation of the Act.
[96] *Airey v. Ireland*, Eur. Ct. HR, Series A, No. 32, Judgment of 9 October 1979.
[97] See Art. 1 of the ECHR, which is not one of the Convention rights under the 1998 Act.

dynamic and constantly developing in reaction to events in the world, other international treaties, changing moral and social structures and beliefs, and scientific and medical developments.[98] As the Court wrote in *Tyrer v. United Kingdom*,[99] in relation to whether birching as a judicial punishment should be regarded as degrading within the meaning of Article 2:

> 'The Court must also recall that the Convention is a living instrument which ... must be interpreted in the light of present-day conditions. In the case now before it the Court cannot but be influenced by the developments and commonly accepted standards in the penal policy of the Member States of the Council of Europe in this field.'

(e) This means that the doctrine of precedent does not operate in the way in which *stare decisis* operates in common-law jurisdictions. Instead, the Court regards its previous decisions as a starting-point rather than as binding precedents, and there is no strict distinction between *ratio decidendi* and *obiter dictum*: any part of the judgment may provide guidance for the interpretation of the Convention in later cases.[100] However, the Court values consistency and reasonable predictability, which are aspects of the Rule of Law on which the Court has built in interpreting terms such as 'lawful', 'in accordance with the law', and 'prescribed by law' in the Convention. This is why Article 30 allows a Chamber to relinquish a case to the Grand Chamber of the Court 'where the resolution of a question before the Chamber might have a result inconsistent with a judgment previously delivered by the Court'.

(f) Many of the terms of the treaty are treated as having an 'autonomous meaning', independent of the meaning which they have in national law, and are interpreted without regard to the original intentions of the drafters of or the parties to the ECHR. The object is to ensure that, so far as possible, terms in the Convention have a consistent meaning when applied to any of the High Contracting Parties, and to prevent states denying the protection of the Convention to people within their jurisdictions by categorizing issues in such a way that the rights do not arise. More is said of this below.

(g) The Court has great respect for the principles of human dignity, equality, and democracy (which includes, as the Court has often said,[101] a commitment to the values of tolerance, pluralism, and broad-mindedness without which democracy would be impossible). In this, the Court follows the Preamble to the Charter of the United Nations (1948), which declared the determination 'to reaffirm faith in fundamental human rights, in the dignity and worth of the

---

[98] See, e.g. *Tyrer v. United Kingdom*, Eur. Ct. HR, Series A, No. 31, Judgment of 25 April 1978; P. van Dijk and G. J. H. van Hoof, *Theory and Practice of the European Convention on Human Rights*, 3rd edn. (The Hague: Kluwer, 1998), 77–80.

[99] Series A, No. 26, Judgment of 25 April 1978.

[100] See S. Grosz, J. Beatson, and P. Duffy QC, *Human Rights: The 1998 Act and the European Convention* (London: Sweet & Maxwell, 1999), 24–27; D. Feldman, 'Precedent and the European Court of Human Rights', in Law Commission Consultation Paper No. 157, *Criminal Law—Bail and the Human Rights Act 1998* (London: The Stationery Office, 1999), Appendix C, 112–124.

[101] For example, in *Handyside v. United Kingdom* (1976) 1 EHRR 737.

human person, in the equal rights of men and women and of nations large and small'. The Preamble to the Universal Declaration of Human Rights, referring to that, recognized 'the inherent dignity and . . . the equal and inalienable rights of all members of the human family' as 'the foundation of freedom, justice and peace in the world', while Article 1 recognized that 'All human beings are born free and equal in dignity and rights . . .' In the Preamble to the ECHR, the signatory states referred to the Universal Declaration on Human Rights, but gave the same message a more collectivist slant, highlighting the importance of democracy,

'Reaffirming their profound belief in those fundamental freedoms which are the foundation of justice and peace in the world and are best maintained on the one hand by an effective political democracy and on the other by a common understanding and observance of the human rights on which they depend.'

Equality is a particularly pervasive value in the approach to the Convention. The right to equal enjoyment of rights is expressly protected by Article 14. Although Article 14 appears to confer only a right not to be discriminated against in the enjoyment of other Convention rights,[102] the Strasbourg organs have drawn attention to the fact that Article 14 imposes a positive as well as negative obligation on states as to the way in which the enjoyment of Convention rights is secured.[103]

(4) THE USE OF THE NOTIONS OF 'AUTONOMOUS CONCEPTS' AND 'POSITIVE OBLIGATIONS' WHEN INTERPRETING CONVENTION RIGHTS

As noted above, the Court and Commission have used the notions of autonomous concepts and positive obligations when interpreting the scope of Convention rights. What do these terms mean?

(i) Autonomous concepts

The Court has held that some of the terms used in the Convention have a meaning which is different from that which the same or similar terms have in the municipal law of any State Party.[104] This is sometimes called the 'autonomous meaning' of the Convention terms, and the terms are said to refer to 'autonomous concepts'. The object, as noted above, is to ensure that, states cannot dictate the meaning of the terms to the Court. Thus states cannot unilaterally reduce their obligations under the Convention in public international law by giving restricted or extended meanings to the terms in municipal law. For example:

---

[102] When Protocol No. 12 comes into force, it will create a free-standing right to be free of discrimination on a wide variety of grounds.

[103] See the Report of the Commission in the *Belgian Linguistic* case, Series B, No. 3 (1967), 24 June 1965, 305–306. For further discussion of equality and Art. 14, see ch. 3, below.

[104] See, e.g. Van Dijk and Van Hoof, 77; *Engel v. The Netherlands*, Eur. Ct. HR, Series A, No. 22, Judgment of 8 June 1976.

(a) In Article 6 (fair-trial rights in the determination of criminal charges and civil rights and obligations), the concepts of 'determination', 'criminal charge', 'civil right', and 'civil obligation' have autonomous meanings, so a state cannot exclude the operation of Article 6 in a particular context by treating a matter as non-criminal, or defining a right or obligation as public rather than civil, for the purposes of municipal law.

(b) Similarly in Article 7 (*nulla poena sine lege*), the concept of 'criminal offence' has an autonomous meaning.

(c) In Article 8 (right to respect for private and family life, home and correspondence), 'private life', 'family life', 'home', and 'correspondence' all have autonomous meanings.

These autonomous meanings will be explored further as and when they become relevant in relation to substantive rights.

(ii) Positive obligations

Most of the rights under the Convention are negative rights, or rights to freedom from interference. However, a few rights impose obligations on the state to take positive action to protect people. Some of these positive obligations are imposed expressly by the text of the Convention. Others have been implied by the Court or Commission from the text.

The first source of express positive obligations is Article 1, which requires the High Contracting Parties (i.e. the states) to 'secure to everyone within their jurisdiction' the Convention rights. Article 14 demands that the Convention rights should be secured without discrimination. These provisions impose an obligation on the state to establish appropriate legal rules and procedures for those purposes. Article 13, by giving people a right to an effective remedy for violations of Convention rights, imposes an obligation on the state to ensure that it has appropriate rules and institutions in place to provide such a remedy. Article 2(1), by providing for everyone's right to life to be protected by law, requires the state to have appropriate legal rules and procedures in place to provide that protection.[105] Article 5(1) requires the state to provide legal rules and procedures to govern the circumstances in which people may lawfully be deprived of their liberty. Article 5(2)–(5) imposes obligations in respect of the treatment of people who have been lawfully deprived of their freedom, and imposes an obligation to compensate people for detentions which do not comply with the requirements of the Article. Article 6(1) requires the state to provide legal rules and procedures to permit fair trials and to comply with the positive obligations set out in Article 6 in relation to the conduct of hearings. Article 12 requires the state to provide legal rules to permit people to change their civil status through marriage.

A more extensive and less clearly defined set of positive obligations are those which the Commission and Court implied by interpreting the text of the Convention in the light of its underlying values and purposes. The following list is not exhaustive, and new positive obligations may be created by further dynamic interpretation.

[105] *McCann and others v. United Kingdom*, Eur. Ct. HR (1995) 21 EHRR 97.

- The right to life under Article 2 has been interpreted as imposing obligations on the state to protect people against threats to their lives in certain circumstances, to lay down procedures to ensure that proper care is taken when assessing the absolute necessity for taking life, and to ensure that there is an effective investigation of allegations of killing.[106]

- The right to be free of torture and inhuman or degrading treatment or punishment under Article 3 is interpreted as imposing a duty on the state to take adequate steps to protect people effectively against such treatment at the hands of private as well as public bodies and persons, including a possibility of successfully prosecuting suspected offenders.[107]

- The right to respect for private, etc., life under Article 8(1) carries with it positive obligations, since the idea of 'respect' is not a passive one. For example, the appropriate state bodies may have an obligation under Article 8 to use environmental and planning law to control polluters whose activities make it difficult or unhealthy for people to live in their homes in affected areas,[108] or to provide information about environmental hazards.[109] Article 8 has been applied to the ability to obtain information about one's own background and history when one has been in the care of a public authority.[110] States also have obligations in respect of the storage of information about people.[111] This has implications for the use which can be made of information about people's criminal past activities, for example by circulating information about the predilections of convicted shoplifters or paedophiles. The idea of family life has been given an extended meaning under Article 8 to take account of the value of mutual enjoyment of a wide range of *de facto* relationships of personal intimacy and genetic closeness.[112] As well as including the mutual enjoyment by parent and child of each other's company,[113] family life includes relationships between members of the extended family, such as uncle and nephew;[114] the relationship between a man and his child, conceived when the man and the mother were unmarried but living

---

[106] *McCann and others v. United Kingdom*, Eur. Ct. HR (1996) 21 EHRR 97.

[107] See, e.g. *A. v. United Kingdom*, Eur. Ct. HR, 27 EHRR 611, Judgment of 23 September 1998.

[108] See *López Ostra v. Spain*, Series A, No. 303-C, Judgment of 9 December 1994, where the level of harm caused was insufficient to amount to a breach of Art. 3 but the failure of the state to control it was nevertheless a violation of Art. 8; *Hatton v. United Kingdom*, App. No. 36022/97, Judgment of 2 Oct. 2001 (duty to make proper assessment of risk to local residents from night flying at Heathrow).

[109] See *Guerra v. Italy* (1998) 26 EHRR 357 at para 35 of the Judgment.

[110] *Gaskin v. United Kingdom*, Series A, No. 160, Judgment of 7 July 1989. For an account of the international arrangements in relation to this, see J. Michael, *Privacy and Human Rights*, in C. McCrudden and G. Chambers, *Individual Rights and the Law in Britain* (Oxford: Clarendon Press, 1994) ch. 9. For the English law, as influenced by the European Community Data Protection Directive, see Data Protection Act 1998, which will have to be (re-)interpreted in the light of the Human Rights Act 1998, s. 3.

[111] *Leander v. Sweden*, Series A, No. 116, Judgment of 26 March 1987.

[112] *Marckx v. Belgium* (1979) 2 EHRR 330; *Berrehab v. The Netherlands*, Series A, No. 138, Judgment of 21 June 1988.

[113] *Andersson v. Sweden*, Series A, No. 226, Judgment of 25 February 1992.

[114] *Boyle v. United Kingdom*, Series A, No. 282-B, Judgment of 28 February 1994 (uncle denied contact with child in care following abuse allegations, without legal process to determine issue—friendly settlement following determination on merits by Commission).

together, following the break-up of the relationship;[115] the relationship between a man and the child conceived during an extra-marital affair between the mother and the man.[116] The test is the *de facto* closeness of the tie of emotion and dependence between people who share a relationship of a family kind, not the biological link or the definition of 'family' in municipal law. Furthermore, the right to respect for family life has been held to require fair procedural protections provided by law for parents when their children are in danger of being taken into care: the Court has held that an interference with family life, in order to be justifiable, must be regulated by procedures adequate to ensure that the various interests are taken fairly into account.[117] There is thus an overlap between this aspect of Article 8 and aspects of Article 6. Even when a child is in care, public authorities must not normally place the children and manage their contacts so as to make a restoration of family relationships unlikely.[118]

- The right to freedom of assembly under Article 11 imposes an obligation on the state to take appropriate steps to ensure that counter-demonstrators do not make it impossible for demonstrators to assemble and protest peacefully.

It can thus be seen that the dynamic interpretation of the Convention in the light of changing social and moral assumptions is capable of producing more extensive obligations on states than are immediately obvious from a superficial perusal of the text.

(5) INTERPRETING PERMITTED RESTRICTIONS ON CONVENTION RIGHTS

When a state seeks to justify interfering with a right, and it is a right which admits of qualification, the state must satisfy the Court that the conditions for justifying the interference have been met. These conditions are either set out expressly in the text of the relevant Article or are implied by the Court. For the sake of simplicity, we can concentrate on a right which expressly allows for interference to be justified and sets out criteria for assessing the legality of the justification which the state asserts: the right to freedom of expression under Article 10. The structure of the legal analysis which must be followed under Article 10 applies also to Articles 8, 9, and 11 under their express terms. Similar principles have been applied to some other Articles by implication. Article 10 provides:

'1.   Everyone has the right to freedom of expression. This right shall include freedom to hold opinions and to receive and impart information and ideas without interference by public authority and regardless of frontiers. This Article shall not prevent states from requiring the licensing of broadcasting, television or cinema enterprises.

---

[115] *Keegan v. Ireland*, Series A, No. 290, Judgment of 26 May 1994 (adoption of child without father's consent violated father's Art. 8 rights).

[116] *Kroon v. The Netherlands*, Series A, No. 297-C, Judgment of 27 October 1994 (legal assumption of the child's legitimacy, preventing real father from legally recognizing the child as his own, violated rights under Art. 8; law of state must enable family ties to be developed, and legally recognized and safeguarded).

[117] *W. v. United Kingdom*, Series A, No. 121-A, Judgment of 8 July 1987, introducing due-process values to a range of decision-making functions which might not fall naturally within Art. 6(1).

[118] *Olsson v. Sweden*, Series A, No. 130, Judgment of 24 March 1988; *Hokkanen v. Finland*, A/299-A.

2.   The exercise of these freedoms, since it carries with it duties and responsibilities, may be subject to such formalities, conditions, restrictions or penalties as are prescribed by law and are necessary in a democratic society, in the interests of national security, territorial integrity or public safety, for the prevention of disorder or crime, for the protection of health or morals, for the protection of the reputation or rights of others, for preventing the disclosure of information received in confidence, or for maintaining the authority and impartiality of the judiciary.'

The first step is to establish whether an interest of the applicant protected by Article 10(1) has been interfered with. If it has, the Court decides whether the responsibility of the state is engaged in respect of that interference. If it is engaged, attention turns to Article 10(2), to see whether the state can establish a justification for the interference. There are essentially three elements that the state must establish under Article 10(2): first, that the interference was prescribed by law; secondly, that the interference had a legitimate aim, in the sense of having been undertaken for one of the purposes listed in that paragraph; and thirdly, that the interference was necessary in a democratic society in pursuit of the legitimate aim. Each of these elements has been given an autonomous meaning by the Court.

To be '*prescribed by law*' or '*in accordance with the law*', an interference must be shown to be **both** (i) not unlawful in municipal law **and** (ii) complying with European standards of legality, which require that

- there must be a sound foundation in positive municipal law for the states inter-ference with the right, so that the interference can be said to be regulated by law in the jurisdiction concerned;[119]

- the system of regulation must be adequate to ensure that the rights of all those people affected are taken into account (importing at least some Article 6 standards);[120] and

- the relevant positive law must be sufficiently clear and accessible to people to allow them to predict with reasonable certainty when and how their rights will be affected.[121]

When assessing what is '*necessary in a democratic society*' *for one of the permitted purposes* (which will generally be exhaustively defined in the relevant Article), the Court works according to a 'rich' model of democracy, which is different from mere majority rule. In a democracy which respects Convention rights, minorities must be adequately protected against unfair treatment and the abuse by the major-ity of a dominant position.[122] An interference with a right must be shown to have been

---

[119] *Malone v. United Kingdom*, Eur. Ct. HR, Series A, No. 82, (1984) 7 EHRR 14; *Halford v. United Kingdom*, Eur. Ct. HR, RJD 1997-III, No. 39, Judgment of 25 June 1997; 24 EHRR 523.

[120] See, e.g. *W. v. United Kingdom*, Series A, No. 121-A, Judgment of 8 July 1987.

[121] *Malone*, n. 119 above.

[122] *Handyside v. United Kingdom* (1976) 1 EHRR 737 at para. 49 of the judgment; *Chassagnou v. France*, Judgment of 29 April 1999 at para. 112.

- a response to a pressing social need to act for that purpose, and
- a proportionate response to that purpose.[123]

Proportionality is assessed mainly by asking whether the interference with the right is more extensive than is justified by the legitimate aim. This involves balancing the seriousness of the interference against the seriousness of the threat to the interests which are protected within the purposes for which it is legitimate to interfere with the right. Part of that balancing exercise requires the Court to consider whether the extent of the interference is greater than is reasonably necessary to achieve the legitimate aim. In a democratic society, there must also be proper safeguards against arbitrariness.

The principle of proportionality is a vehicle for conducting a balancing exercise.[124] It does not directly balance the right against the reason for interfering with it. Instead, it balances the nature and extent of the interference against the reasons for interfering. The court or tribunal must take into account a number of factors, including:

(i) whether it would have been possible to achieve the legitimate aim by a less intrusive means; whether the interference is such as to deprive the right-holder of the very essence of the right; whether the right is of sufficient importance in the circumstances to warrant particularly strong reasons being required to justify any interference;

(ii) whether the interference causes harm to the right-holder which is serious enough to outweigh any benefit which that interference might achieve through furthering a legitimate aim.

A *'margin of appreciation', or area of discretionary judgment,* is allowed to states when making judgments about the existence of a pressing social need and the nature of an appropriate response. The notion of the 'margin of appreciation' is based on the fact that national authorities are in a better position than an international tribunal to judge what is necessary under local conditions. In public international law, it offers a way of mediating the tension between the claims of state sovereignty in relation to international institutions and the need to universalize human-rights standards so far as possible in international law. However, it is a controversial doctrine, because it tends to undermine the universalizability of human-rights standards, and it has come under challenge within as well as outside the Court.

---

[123] See, e.g. on Art. 10(2), *Sunday Times v. United Kingdom* (the Thalidomide case), Series A, No. 30, Judgment of 26 April 1979; *Handyside v. United Kingdom* (the *Little Red Schoolbook* case), Series A, No. 24, Judgment of 7 December 1976; *Observer and Guardian v. United Kingdom and Sunday Times v. United Kingdom (No. 2)* (the *Spycatcher* cases), Series A, Nos. 216 and 217 respectively, Judgments of 26 November 1991; *Wingrove v. United Kingdom,* Reports 1996-V, No. 33, Judgment of 25 November 1996; and on Art. 8(2), *Malone v. United Kingdom,* Series A, No. 82, Judgment of 2 August 1984; *Kruslin v. France,* Series A, No. 176-A, Judgment of 24 April 1990; *Halford v. United Kingdom,* n. 119 above.

[124] See Van Dijk and Van Hoof, 80–2; J. McBride, 'Proportionality and the European Convention on Human Rights', in E. Ellis (ed.), *The Principle of Proportionality in the Laws of Europe* (Oxford: Hart Publishing, 1999), 23–35.

2.4 APPROACHES TO PROTECTING RIGHTS IN
MUNICIPAL LEGAL SYSTEMS

When one thinks of ways of protecting rights, judicial enforcement often leaps to mind. However, a range of techniques can be used. This section examines the main ones, and briefly introduces the institutions which support each in the UK.

Municipal judicial protection may provide a remedy where the right is enshrined in municipal law and is regarded as being justiciable or remediable by courts. For example, the courts may be able to develop the ordinary law to protect fundamental freedoms. In the past in the UK, legal remedies protecting civil liberties were tied closely to private law causes of action. Freedom from restraint was guaranteed by the action for false imprisonment or trespass to the person. Freedom from unauthorized searches and seizures was secured by actions for trespass to property, or, where search warrants had been unlawfully obtained, by the tort of abuse of process.[125] This left certain rights unprotected. For example, there is no tort remedy for interference with freedom of speech or of association. Nor, in some people's view, was there a remedy for infringement of any right to privacy as such, unless the means of interference constituted a trespass to person or property or a breach of confidence (although a different view is now emerging).[126] To some extent the courts have been able to circumvent these problems. Where statutes have imposed duties on public bodies to provide services, it is sometimes possible to bring actions for breach of statutory duty as a way of securing compensation for failure to comply with the duty, effectively coupling the statutory duty with a private right.[127] The existence of a statutory duty may also create a sufficiently proximate relationship between the provider of services and the client to enable the courts to impose a duty of care, breach of which will sound in damages for negligence, although the scope for developing tort rights for citizens from statutory duties on public bodies, which was expanding after 1977, has been much reduced recently.[128]

The judges have sometimes deployed new or previously underdeveloped torts, such as misfeasance in a public office, offering a way of obtaining compensation where a public official knowingly acts in disregard of a legal duty, knowing that it was likely to cause damage to the victim.[129] However, in English common law there is no tort of causing loss or injury by the unlawful administrative action of a public authority. To obtain compensation, a plaintiff must show not merely that the authority acted

---

[125] See R. Clayton and H. Tomlinson, *Civil Actions Against the Police*, 2nd edn. (London: Sweet & Maxwell, 1992), *passim*.

[126] *Malone v. Metropolitan Police Commissioner* [1979] Ch. 344; [1979] 2 All ER 620; *Kaye v. Robertson* [1991] FSR 62, CA, where the court regretted the absence of a remedy for invasion of privacy by journalists (the case did not concern actions of officials). For more recent developments, see *Douglas v. Hello! Ltd.* [2001] 2 WLR 992, CA, considered in ch. 9, below.

[127] K. M. Stanton, *Breach of Statutory Duty* (London: Sweet & Maxwell, 1986).

[128] *Anns v. Merton LBC* [1978] AC 728, HL, overruled in *Murphy v. Brentwood DC* [1990] 2 All ER 908, HL.

[129] *Bourgoin SA v. Ministry of Agriculture, Fisheries and Food* [1986] QB 716, [1985] 3 All ER 585, CA.

unlawfully, but also that the act breached a duty owed to the plaintiff as a matter of private law.

If the breach of a legal duty does not amount to a tort or breach of contract, the only legal remedy will be judicial review of the impugned act, leading to an order quashing it or a declaration of invalidity, together perhaps with a mandatory order requiring the authority to comply with its legal obligations. Judicial review is an important forum for protecting (for example) the rights of parents and children against local authorities' child-care decision-making processes, the rights of prisoners, and those of immigrants. Nevertheless, there are procedural disadvantages which a person claiming judicial review must overcome, as compared with the position of a plaintiff in a tort action. The judicial review claimant requires the permission of the court to proceed; does not get discovery as of right, but must show a strongly arguable case of unlawfulness and show that discovery is likely to be necessary to the fair disposal of the proceedings; and is not normally entitled to cross-examine witnesses, as the hearings are usually conducted on the basis of written affidavits.

On the other hand, one feature which used to limit the effectiveness of judicial protection for civil liberties and human rights has been removed by an important judicial decision. Until recently, the courts did not grant coercive relief against representatives of the Crown, who were regarded as covered by the privilege of the Crown in litigation,[130] except where EC law required injunctive relief in order to provide an effective remedy.[131] This was not too serious a problem in relation to the final judgment, because the court could make a declaration of the duties of the Crown and this declaration was, by convention, honoured. There was, however, a real difficulty over pre-trial relief: the Crown could not be required to refrain, pending trial, from further action which might infringe the citizen's rights. The courts have no power to grant an interim declaration, and interim injunctions were not generally available against the Crown any more than final ones are. However, the position changed in *M. v. Home Office*.[132] The applicant was a Zairean asylum seeker who claimed that he had been tortured there. His application for asylum was rejected, and he applied for judicial review of the decision on the day when he was due to be deported to Zaire on a flight via Paris. An undertaking was given on behalf of the Home Secretary to the judge that M would not be deported until the case had been decided. The Home Secretary, Kenneth Baker, subsequently received legal advice that he was not bound by the undertaking, enforcement of which would be equivalent to enforcing an injunction against the Crown. M was deported, and the Home Secretary took no steps to have him brought back when the aeroplane landed at Paris. M's legal advisers brought proceedings against the Home Office and the Secretary of State for contempt of court in breaching the undertaking. The House of Lords, affirming the decision of a majority of the Court of Appeal, unanimously held that an officer of the Crown could be subject to coercive court orders, that they could be enforced against that officer by way

---

[130] *R. v. Secretary of State for Transport, ex parte Factortame Ltd.* [1990] 2 AC 85, HL.

[131] Case C-213/89, *R. v. Secretary of State for Transport, ex parte Factortame Ltd. (No. 2)* [1991] 1 AC 603, CJEC and HL.

[132] [1994] 1 AC 377, HL.

of proceedings for contempt, and that the Home Secretary had committed contempt by breaching the undertaking given to the court on his behalf. It would only rarely be necessary to issue an injunction against the Crown, but it was important to reiterate that, as a matter of constitutional law, officers of the Crown are subject to the law, and do not comply with it merely as a matter of grace. The decision ensures that people have the same remedial rights against the Crown in proceedings under national law as they have when European Community law is involved.

In many other jurisdictions, where some rights have constitutionally protected status, these may be judicially enforceable in a way which leads to substantive legal restrictions on the power of the legislature, with judicial review of the constitutionality of legislation. This is commonplace in many countries.

Where there are express constitutional limitations on the powers of a legislature, courts in the USA,[133] Australia,[134]and elsewhere, have concluded that the doctrines of the separation of powers and the rule of law require them to act as the final arbiters of the constitutionality of legislation. It is not normally considered necessary for the constitution to have made express provision for judicial remedies in such cases, although sometimes (as for Canada under the Constitution Act 1982, section 24) a constitution will do so. In the UK, a power of judicial review of primary parliamentary legislation has been thrust on our judges by the demands of European Community law, which, when directly effective and (in the case of regulations) directly applicable, has primacy over inconsistent municipal law, including Acts of Parliament.[135]

This review role is controversial under constitutions like those of the UK, the USA, and Australia, which (unlike that of Canada) do not expressly provide for judicial review of legislation, or lay down limits to it, because it gives courts the capacity to frustrate even a democratically approved legislative programme. But in countries where judicial review is a well-entrenched part of the constitutional heritage, such as the USA, most of the controversy concerns the principles of constitutional interpretation which should guide the exercise of the review power, rather than the existence of the power.[136]

Even when acting within any formal limits on legislative power, the legislature may find that the law offers a measure of special protection to some rights. Under classical Westminster constitutions, with legislatures which, within their limits, are said to be sovereign (in the Diceyan sense of all-powerful), the common law may impose some restrictions on what Parliament can do, or on the methods which must be adopted to produce particular results. There are two ways of achieving this. One is to develop

---

[133] *Marbury v. Madison*, 1 Cranch. 137 (1803).

[134] G. Lindell, 'Duty to Exercise Review', in L. Zines (ed.), *Commentaries on the Australian Constitution* (Sydney: Butterworths, 1977), 150–90; B. Galligan, *The Politics of the High Court* (St Lucia, Qld: Univ. of Queensland Press, 1987), ch. 2.

[135] Case C-213/89, *Factortame Ltd. v. Secretary of State for Transport (No. 2)* [1991] 1 All ER 70, CJEC and HL.

[136] See the discussion of methods of interpretation on review in P. Bobbitt, *Constitutional Fate: Theory of the Constitution* (New York: Oxford University Press, 1982); P. Bobbitt, *Constitutional Interpretation* (Oxford: Basil Blackwell, 1991).

presumptions which will apply when interpreting statutes, allowing judges to resolve any ambiguities in statutes in such a way as to minimize the impact of the statute on any principles or rights which they regard as particularly important elements of the common law. This is a relatively weak protection for special rights, as it can be overridden by express words or necessary implication.

The other approach is more direct, and represents an explicit common-law limitation on legislative power. Here, judges identify certain standards as fundamental to the historical common law, and deny that Parliament has the power to abrogate them. This is an approach which was suggested by Sir Robin (later Lord) Cooke, then President of the Court of Appeal in New Zealand, as a possible corrective to a constitution which appears on its face to place vast legislative power in a Parliament dominated by an executive over which there are few, if any, effective checks between elections.[137]

This is not as radical as it sounds. As Mr. T. R. S. Allan has pointed out, in the UK the judges exercise some control over what Parliament can legislate for effectively, through the way in which they interpret legislation. A number of presumptions operate in the absence of evidence of a contrary legislative intent. These include the presumption that legislation is not intended to be retroactive, is not intended to interfere with vested property rights, and (most significantly for administrative law) is not intended to oust the jurisdiction of the courts.[138] These presumptions protect some of the rights of which Sir Robin Cooke was speaking, although he also included the right to a fair hearing before an unbiased tribunal and the right to be free of torture (very much the sorts of rights protected under the main human rights instruments in international law, and which, if part of customary international law, would be automatically incorporated into domestic law in the absence of inconsistent domestic provisions).

The idea of the special constitutional status of the common law was central to the permeating influence of English common law abroad. In the days of the British Empire, the English common law was carried round the world on shipboard, and colonial legislatures, which were in this respect (and in others) legally inferior to the Westminster Parliament, were initially unable to amend it save in so far as it was inappropriate to local conditions. Even when freed from that fetter, the colonial judges often presumed, as a principle of statutory interpretation, that their local legislatures did not intend to change the common law as received into the colony. This made it necessary, ultimately, for the Westminster Parliament to make it clear that the local legislatures had power to modify the common law, by passing the Colonial Laws Validity Act 1865. In more recent times, the Privy Council, on appeal from common-law jurisdictions, has treated some common-law rights as fundamental, and still

---

[137] *New Zealand Drivers' Association v. New Zealand Road Carriers* [1982] 1 NZLR 374 at 390; *Fraser v. State Services Commission* [1984] 1 NZLR 116 at 121; *Taylor v. New Zealand Poultry Board* [1984] 1 NZLR 394 at 398. See J. Caldwell, 'Judicial Sovereignty: A New View' [1984] *NZULJ* 357–9; P. A. Joseph, 'Beyond Parliamentary Sovereignty' (1989) 18 *Anglo-Amer. LR* 91–123.

[138] *Anisminic Ltd. v. Foreign Compensation Commission* [1969] 2 AC 147, HL. See T. R. S. Allan, 'Legislative Supremacy and the Rule of Law: Democracy and Constitutionalism' [1985] *CLJ* 111–43; T. R. S. Allan, 'Constitutional Rights and Common Law' (1991) 11 *Oxf. J. Legal Studies* 453–80.

sometimes seems to apply what has been called an 'Imperial common law' which limits the scope for common-law variations between jurisdictions and partially protects certain fundamental common-law rights (i.e. those rights which are fundamental to the common law, rather than fundamental to the people subject to it).[139] Where there is political resistance to enacting a code of fundamental rights, judges sometimes feel the need to adopt this sort of approach. Sir John Laws has argued that there are fundamental common-law rights, including the right of access to courts, and that they could and should be protected by way of judicial review, perhaps even against Act of Parliament.[140]

There have been clear signs that such thinking is developing into, at least, presumptions of interpretation of statutes and principles of common-law development. It has been held that there are some rights which Parliament can override only by express and unambiguous language in a statute. While these rights have not yet been enumerated, examples seem to include: the right to challenge official decisions by legal action without interference;[141] a right to equality of access to the courts without excessive burdens being imposed by way of court fees;[142] a right for offenders to be treated fairly when the Home Secretary exercised a discretion, conferred by statute, to set a minimum term of imprisonment for an individual inmate;[143] and a right for a prisoner to bring his case to the attention of investigative journalists with a view to challenging the correctness of his conviction.[144] In addition, some judges who were reluctant to go along with the implications of fundamental common-law rights nevertheless advocated incorporation of the European Convention on Human Rights into municipal law.[145]

But these presumptions are not always sufficiently weighty to protect rights, as UK decisions allowing a retrospective operation to certain social security legislation show.[146] The presumptions are not in themselves common-law rights. Rather, they

[139] J. W. Harris, 'Privy Council and Common Law' (1990) 106 *LQR* 574–600.

[140] Sir John Laws, 'Is the High Court the Guardian of Fundamental Constitutional Rights?' [1993] *PL* 59–79; Sir John Laws, 'Law and Democracy' [1995] *PL* 72–93; Sir John Laws, 'The Constitution: Morals and Rights' [1996] *PL* 622–35; Sir John Laws, 'The Limitations of Human Rights' [1998] *PL* 254–65. See also Sir Stephen Sedley, 'Human Rights: A Twenty-First Century Agenda' [1995] *PL* 386–400; Lord Woolf, 'Droit Public—English Style' [1995] *PL* 57–71, esp. at 67–71. For a limited dissent, see Lord Irvine of Lairg QC, 'Judges and Decision-Makers: The Theory and Practice of *Wednesbury* Review' [1996] *PL* 59–78.

[141] See, e.g. *Anisminic Ltd. v. Foreign Compensation Commission* [1969] 2 AC 147, HL, interpreting a statutory provision, which purported to oust the jurisdiction of the High Court to review the legality of a decision of the Commission, in such a way as to deprive the provision of any real effect; *Raymond v. Honey* [1983] 1 AC 1, HL, holding that a prison governor who interfered with a prisoner's letter to the court thereby committed contempt of court, despite apparent authorization in secondary legislation for the interception.

[142] *R. v. Lord Chancellor, ex parte Witham* [1998] QB 575, DC.

[143] See, e.g. *R. v. Secretary of State for the Home Department, ex parte Venables and Thompson* [1998] AC 407, HL, on the effect of popular opinion on minimum sentences set for two children convicted of murder; *R. v. Secretary of State for the Home Department, ex parte Pierson* [1998] AC 539, HL, especially *per* Lord Steyn at 575*ff*, arguing for a substantive content to be given to the principle or spirit of legality.

[144] *R. v. Secretary of State for the Home Department, ex parte Simms* [1999] 3 WLR 328, HL.

[145] Sir Thomas Bingham, 'The European Convention on Human Rights: Time to Incorporate' (1993) 109 *LQR* 390–400; Lord Woolf, 'Droit Public—English Style' [1995] *PL* 57–71, esp. at 67–71; Lord Steyn, 'The Weakest and Least Dangerous Branch of Government' [1997] *PL* 84–95.

[146] *R. v. Secretary of State for Social Security, ex parte Britnell* [1991] 1 WLR 198, HL; *Secretary of State for Social Security v. Tunnicliffe* [1991] 2 All ER 712, CA.

give limited protection to people's legitimate expectations. If the courts are to be active in creating a set of common-law fundamental rights, capable of restricting the effect of legislation, they will have to do it directly, by finding guarantees of rights embedded immovably in the common-law system.[147] It would not be easy to justify such a move in a democracy, but it might be done, and the scope of the rights might be usefully delimited, if the judges concentrated on enforcing only those rights which are essential to a democratic society. Such a limited set of common law fundamental rights has recently been embraced by the High Court of Australia in *Australian Capital Television Pty. Ltd. v. The Commonwealth*, enabling the court to strike down parliamentary legislation which had attempted to restrict political advertising before elections and referendums.[148] It would derive support from those theories of judicial review which see review as legitimate if directed to securing and enforcing the conditions for democratic politics as carried on in the society in question, although these theories are not uncontroversial and may not be easily transplanted from the context of the US Constitution in which they were grown.[149]

However, judicial creativity in the field of fundamental rights must be kept within certain bounds. If judges start to act as legislators rather than adjudicators, they may undermine the legitimacy of their decisions, because they would not be acting within their constitutional domain. Politicians are particularly concerned to protect their freedom to give effect to a democratic mandate without interference by judges on the basis of supposedly fundamental but uncodified and unlegislated rights.[150] It remains to be seen whether the idea of fundamental common-law rights remains significant now that many of the rights under the ECHR have been incorporated in the Human Rights Act 1998.

In any case, the legal enforcement of rights is not the only, or necessarily the most valuable, system for advancing respect for them. Judicial techniques are at their most effective when providing a remedy for infringements which have already occurred, although by clarifying the law and proclaiming the impropriety of certain conduct the courts may well incidentally reinforce respect for rights and prevent future infringements. Other methods are often better at making rights a normal part of planning and decision-making by public authorities. To these we now turn.

---

[147] This is, in effect, what Coke CJ did, *obiter*, in *Dr. Bonham*'s case (1610) 8 Co. Rep. 114 at 118, suggesting that a statute making someone a judge in his own cause would be void. However, as S. de Smith and R. Brazier, *Constitutional and Administrative Law*, 6th edn. (Harmondsworth: Penguin, 1989) observe at 71 n.34, in his *Institutes*, book 4, 32, Coke seems to accept the absolute sovereignty of Parliament. See further J. W. Gough, *Fundamental Law in English Constitutional History* (Oxford: Clarendon Press, 1955), ch. 3.

[148] (1992) 66 ALJR 695, HC of Australia.

[149] See J. Hart Ely, *Democracy and Distrust: A Theory of Judicial Review* (Cambridge, Mass.: Harvard University Press, 1980); D. Feldman, 'Democracy, the Rule of Law and Judicial Review' (1990) 19 *Federal LR* 1–30. For critiques of the approach, see, e.g. D. J. Galligan, 'Judicial Review and Democratic Principles: Two Theories' (1983) 57 *ALJ* 69–79; R. Dworkin, *A Matter of Principle* (Oxford: Clarendon Press, 1986), 57–69; L. H. Tribe, *Constitutional Choices* (Cambridge, Mass.: Harvard University Press, 1985), 3–20; M. Tushnet, *Red, White, and Blue: A Critical Analysis of Constitutional Law* (Cambridge, Mass.: Harvard University Press, 1988); P. P. Craig, *Public Law and Democracy in the United Kingdom and the United States of America* (Oxford: Clarendon Press, 1990), 106–13.

[150] See Lord Irvine of Lairg QC, 'Judges and Decision-Makers: The Theory and Practice of *Wednesbury* Review' [1996] *PL* 59–78.

Regulatory protection and enforcement may be offered to some rights. Special bodies may be set up to monitor compliance with right-conferring rules, with powers to make recommendations and reports to Parliament (e.g. the Human Rights and Equal Opportunities Commission in Australia,[151] and the Parliamentary Commissioner for Administration in the UK[152]), or to make efforts to secure settlement of disputes or initiate or support legal action in support of rights. Examples in the UK include the Commission for Racial Equality established under the Race Relations Act 1976, the Equal Opportunities Commission created by the Sex Discrimination Act 1975, and the Disability Rights Commission, established under the Disability Rights Commission Act 1999 to oversee the implementation of the Disability Discrimination Act 1995. The Northern Ireland Act 1998 established an Equality Commission for Northern Ireland (bringing together two Northern Ireland commissions: the Fair Employment Commission, which had previously provided protection against religious discrimination in employment, and the Commission for Racial Equality) and a Human Rights Commission for Northern Ireland. It has been suggested that a Human Rights Commission should be established for the whole of the UK, perhaps with a similar Commission for the devolved jurisdictions of Scotland and Wales.[153] Some people have argued that it would be best to have a single, overarching Commission.[154] Others have suggested a unified Equality Commission operating alongside a separate Human Rights Commission.[155] As yet, the government is not persuaded of the need for a UK Human Rights Commission, or that it would offer value for money.[156] Each of the Commissions which has so far been created in the UK has power to attempt to conciliate between parties to disputes and to support legal action against those who are alleged to have breached rights, but the main system for enforcing the rights under the legislation is for aggrieved citizens to bring actions claiming compensation in an appropriate tribunal or court in proceedings which may be supported by the relevant Commission. The Equal Opportunities Commission has also been held to have standing in its own name to challenge government-made regulations on the avail-

---

[151] On the latter, see Bailey, *Human Rights: Australia,* n. 17 above, at 106–246.

[152] On the work of the PCA, see R. Rawlings, 'The MP's Complaints Service' (1990) 53 *MLR* 22–42, 249–69; G. Drewry and C. Harlow, 'A "Cutting Edge"? The Parliamentary Commissioner and MPs' (1990) 53 *MLR* 745–69. The PCA deals with complaints against central government departments. A parallel body, the Commission for Local Administration, deals with local government, but has no direct access to Parliament.

[153] S. Spencer and I. Bynoe, *A Human Rights Commission: the Options for Britain and Northern Ireland* (London: IPPR, 1998).

[154] See, e.g. S. Spencer and I. Bynoe, *A Human Rights Commission: The Options for Britain and Northern Ireland* (London: IPPR, 1998), 108–28.

[155] See, e.g. B. Hepple QC, M. Coussey, and T. Choudhury, *Equality: A New Framework. Report of the Independent Review of the Enforcement of UK Anti-Discrimination Legislation* (Oxford: Hart Publishing, 2000), 51–5.

[156] See *Rights Brought Home: The Human Rights Bill,* Cm. 3728, paras. 3.9–3.11; Lord Irvine of Lairg LC and Lord Williams of Mostyn (then Parliamentary Under-Secretary of State at the Home Office) during Second Reading in the House of Lords, *Official Report, House of Lords,* 3 November 1997, vol. 582, cols. 1233 and 1309 respectively; Lord Williams of Mostyn during the Committee Stage, *Official Report, House of Lords,* 24 November 1997, vol. 583, cols. 849–851 and 27 November 1997, vol. 583, col. 1153; Mr. Mike O'Brien MP, Parliamentary Under-Secretary of State at the Home Department, during the Committee Stage in the House of Commons, *Official Report, House of Commons,* 24 June 1998, vol. 314, cols. 1087–1088.

ability of unfair-dismissal and redundancy payments for part-time workers, on the ground that restrictions indirectly discriminated against women workers.[157] However, the main role of the Commissions is to monitor developments and to educate the public, seeking to encourage good race or sex relations, rather than enforce rights aggressively. Where a right is new, and social attitudes have to change to accommodate it, a coercive attitude on the part of the Commissions could be counter-productive. The present approach is to try to improve public awareness by drawing up and promulgating codes of practice and offering advice. Yet these steps are not always effective, and the Commissions have been accused of being oversensitive to the dangers of coercion. When dealing with discrimination in employment, for example, it is always difficult to judge when best to change from a strategy of co-operation to one of coercion. This is particularly likely to be applied to service provision, most typically the subject of economic and social rights, and is often a convenient and effective way of encouraging compliance.

Thus, as a way of enforcing rights it suffers from potential weaknesses. The emphasis placed by some (though not all) regulators on accommodation and friendly settlement may lead to rights being compromised rather than just satisfaction being secured for breaches.[158] Indeed, the fact that the rights have been put in the care of a regulator rather than a court may lead courts to regard those rights as less important than others, and treat the regulator as if it was an emanation of the state interfering with rights rather than as a protector. Some commentators feel that this has been the fate of the Commission for Racial Equality in the UK.[159]

Regulators face a further difficulty in that they are required to play a dual role: they must try to change attitudes in the long term, as well as provide short-term remedies for individual victims of unlawfulness. In such an enterprise, adopting a confrontational attitude may be counter-productive. Regulators have to continue to work with offenders, and there are well-documented tendencies to identify with their problems to the point where the agency ceases to be effective as a regulator.

During the 1990s in the UK successive governments sought other ways of protecting rights to public provision which did not depend on law. Some of these relied only peripherally on regulation. The *Citizen's Charter* programme,[160] including specialized Charters for different areas of public-service provision, forms part of a move to improve the responsiveness and accountability of public services. Successive governments have sought to secure standards of performance by monitoring and regulation, and wherever possible relieving people of the need to depend on the state. For example, the *Patient's Charter* encourages people to provide feedback to the health providers about the quality of service received, waiting times, and so on. It exhorts people not to be put off by the notion that they will be victimized by doctors for

---

[157] *R. v. Secretary of State for Employment, ex parte Equal Opportunities Commission* [1995] 1 AC 1, HL.

[158] B. M. Hutter, *The Reasonable Arm of the Law: The Law Enforcement Procedures of Environmental Health Officers* (Oxford: Clarendon Press, 1988).

[159] R. Baldwin and C. McCrudden, *Regulation and Public Law* (London: Weidenfeld & Nicolson, 1987), chs 4 and 11.

[160] Cm. 1599 (London: HMSO, 1991).

making a complaint.[161] At the same time, the Charters make clear the responsibilities of the recipients of services to contribute to the efficiency of the service: the *Patient's Charter* points to the inefficiency which results from people failing to turn up to appointments without warning staff, and the *Parent's Charter*[162] emphasizes the responsibility which parents share with teachers for their children's education.

There is no doubt that such procedures are important in improving the quality of the service delivered, and that there is room for them to supply remedies for service users which are not otherwise available, so long as the procedures are administered properly and are advertised.[163] However, it is not clear that, without more, this is an adequate way of protecting, or enhancing the value of, rights. A level of independence is needed. The dangers of lack of rigour in reviewing the work of colleagues, failure to adopt adequate procedures or to publicize them properly, and public reluctance to take complaints to the departments which are the subject of the complaints, all emphasize the importance of having outside scrutiny of, and ideally control over, the complaints process, particularly when the complainants are likely to belong to a vulnerable group, such as prisoners, sick patients, or children in care.[164] An externally operated ombudsman scheme forms a useful backup to internal procedures, but, as ombudsmen are typically concerned with maladministration rather than rights, they may not always be able to remedy injustices which flow from infringements of rights.

A rather different approach is to reduce the role of public authorities in providing services, by encouraging people to seek private landlords, by privatizing public services such as refuse collection and delivery of electricity and other main services, and by bringing commercial undertakings and public institutions into partnership through programmes such as the Private Finance Initiative. Standards are then maintained through complaints procedures, the market, and commercial pressures. This represents a move from allowing people a voice in public services to facilitating their exit from reliance on public services. Accordingly, it denies people legal rights in the services in question. Instead, it offers choice between potential service providers: doctors, schools, landlords. This right to choose is intended to keep providers responsive, because their incomes will depend on their performance; dissatisfied customers will move elsewhere.

It remains to be seen how effectively this approach will protect rights. The market will not operate properly unless people have enforceable rights and know how to enforce them. It does not provide rights. This is implicitly recognized in the *Charter*, which accepts that regulation is needed where the providers of services enjoy a sub-

---

[161] Dept. of Health, *The Patient's Charter* (London: HMSO, 1991), 18.

[162] Dept. of Education, *The Updated Parent's Charter* (London: HMSO, 1995).

[163] N. Lewis, S. Cracknell, and M. Seneviratne, *Complaints Procedures in Local Government* (Sheffield: University of Sheffield, 1987), provides a valuable study of attitudes to complaints process in one area of the public service. For comments, see C. Crawford, 'Complaints, Codes and Ombudsmen in Local Government' [1988] *PL* 246–67. Support for internal review and appeal procedures comes from a US study, which is not blind to the potential drawbacks (although arguably underestimates their importance): J. L. Mashaw, *Bureaucratic Justice: Managing Social Security Disability Claims* (New Haven, Conn.: Yale University Press, 1983).

[164] M. J. Lindsay, 'Complaints Procedures and Their Limitations in the Light of the "Pindown" Inquiry' [1991] *JSWFL* 432–41.

stantial monopoly, as is the case in relation to gas, electricity, and water services within a region. Here the right to choose is an inadequate protection for service quality, because there is no competing provider for a person to turn to if dissatisfied with the current one. If, as seems possible, the range of competitors is reduced in a recession, market forces will tend to produce monopolies or oligopolies in a range of services. Rights which are entirely dependent on market forces are, at best, very weak rights. The *Citizen's Charter* approach to rights is a long way from conferring rights in economic and social programmes, or creating what Charles Reich called 'the new property'[165] from rights to public assets and public support.

Using government's commercial muscle may be successful in persuading people or bodies in a client relationship to government to observe rights. For example, government agencies can make it a condition of placing orders for goods or services with particular firms that they should meet criteria, set by government, for the proportion of employees who are to be women or members of ethnic minorities. This method of advancing the rights of under-privileged citizens, known as 'contract compliance', has been more widely used in the USA than in the UK, although it is less favoured by Republican administrations than by Democratic ones.[166] It depends heavily on the commitment of government to particular rights, and is sensitive to changes of political direction, as it involves a conscious exercise of the economic muscle of government (that which Daintith has called the *dominium* as opposed to the *imperium* power of the state).[167]

Parliamentary techniques place the responsibility for protecting rights squarely on the legislature itself. There are various self-policing steps which a parliament can take to try to ensure that it does not infringe rights, or does not do so without due consideration.[168] One is to have a standing committee which scrutinizes all legislation to check for human rights or civil liberties implications. In the Australian Commonwealth Parliament, the Senate Scrutiny of Bills Committee performs this function in relation to Bills, and the Senate Regulations and Ordinances Committee deals with subordinate legislation which has to be laid before Parliament. Both committees are advised by independent legal advisers of acknowledged independence and expertise (so far they have been academic lawyers of high repute), and have small dedicated secretariats staffed by parliamentary public servants. They seek explanations for any apparent breaches of rights from the department responsible for the legislation, and if an explanation is not forthcoming or is unsatisfactory the committees report to that effect to the Senate. The Regulations and Ordinances Committee can also move for disallowance of subordinate legislation. The committees are heavily dependent on the

---

[165] C. Reich, 'The New Property' (1964) 73 *Yale LJ* 733–87.

[166] For an excellent review, see P. E. Morris, 'Legal Regulation of Contract Compliance: An Anglo-American Comparison' (1990) 19 *Anglo-Amer. LR* 87–144.

[167] T. Daintith, 'The Executive Power Today: Bargaining and Economic Control', in J. Jowell and D. Oliver, *The Changing Constitution*, 2nd edn. (Oxford: Clarendon Press, 1989), 193–218 (the essay does not appear in the 4th edn., 2000).

[168] A thorough and very influential analysis, advocating such developments in the UK, is that by D. Kinley, *The European Convention on Human Rights: Compliance without Incorporation* (Aldershot: Dartmouth Publishing Co., 1993), chs 5–8.

goodwill and respect of both the Senate and the government. The Committees have succeeded in achieving a remarkable success rate in inducing drafting changes, helped by operating in a multi-party Senate in which the government often does not command a majority. Both committees work on a cross-party basis, avoiding controversy by reviewing only on grounds on which there is consensus and avoiding any discussion of the policy objectives of the legislation.

Another model is the New Zealand Parliament's Select Committee on Legislation. This subjects each Bill to a public hearing at which objections on human rights grounds can be voiced, and reports back to the Parliament. The effectiveness of this committee depends even more than the Australian Senate committees on the goodwill of the government, which normally has a clear majority in New Zealand's unicameral assembly and exercises tight party control. The role of all these committees is deliberative rather than adjudicative; that is to say, they have no power to disallow legislation, but can only report to the full legislative body which may decide to allow legislation to proceed despite a committee's reservations.

A third approach merges legislative and adjudicative techniques. It allows a special tribunal to adjudicate authoritatively on the constitutionality of legislation during its parliamentary passage. In France, for instance, Article 61 of the Constitution of the Fifth Republic makes provision for a special body to do this. The ordinary courts in France, including the *tribunaux administratives* headed by the *Conseil d'État*, do not have authority to declare primary legislation in the form of *lois* to be unconstitutional.[169] However, if in the course of the deliberations on a proposed measure in the National Assembly sixty deputies or sixty senators insist on it, the measure is referred to the *Conseil constitutionnel*, a court of nine members who are appointed, three each, by the President of the Republic, the President of the Senate, and the President of the National Assembly, for a period of nine years. This body examines the proposed legislation, and decides whether it is constitutional and what restrictions are to be imposed on its scope to bring it into line with the written constitution and with certain general principles of law and constitutional principles derived from (*inter alia*) the 1789 Declaration of the Rights of Man.[170] The judgment of the *Conseil constitutionnel* is binding. This is not a judicial review process, because it operates on the proposed *loi* at a formative stage; the members of the *Conseil* need not be lawyers, although their approach to constitutional questions has been influenced by that of the lawyers of the *Conseil d'État* to the constitutionality of subordinate legislation in the form of *ordonnances*. In fact, the process is seen as a stage in the political contest over the legislation; it has been used increasingly by opposition parties to delay or restrict government proposals, and it can offer a useful bargaining counter to the opposition.

---

[169] However, the *Conseil d'État* will disapply under Art. 55 of the Constitution a *loi* which conflicts with treaty obligations, including rights or obligations having direct effect under EC law: see, e.g. *Nicolo*, Decision of 20 October 1989, noted by R. Errera [1990] *PL* 134–6, who points out the possible impact on French law of international human rights instruments as a result of the decision; *Palazzi*, Decision of 8 July 1991, and the commentary by R. Errera [1991] *PL* 614–16.

[170] See A. Stone, 'In the Shadow of the Constitutional Council: The "Juridicisation" of the Legislative Process in France' (1989) 12(2) *West European Politics* 12–34; J. Bell, *French Constitutional Law* (Oxford: Clarendon Press, 1992), 29–56.

Nevertheless, the *Conseil* has shown itself to be an independent voice in the legislative process, taking its adjudicative and constitutional role seriously, and has restricted legislative programmes on a number of occasions to protect rights.[171]

In the UK, Parliament has the primary responsibility for protecting rights, both positively by legislating for new rights, and negatively by refraining from legislating in a way which abridges existing rights. It has traditionally been the responsibility of individual members to bring to the attention of Parliament any threat to rights in proposed legislation, and several important new rights have been conferred by private Members' Bills. However, in the wake of the Human Rights Act 1998, Parliament has established new machinery to provide a focus for its responsibilities in relation to human rights. A Joint Committee on Human Rights was established in January 2001 to exercise a combination of functions relating to the conduct of inquiries and the scrutiny of legislation in connection with matters relating to human rights in the UK (excluding consideration of individual cases). Its work complements that of other scrutiny committees, such as the new House of Lords Constitution Committee (established in February 2001) which scrutinizes all Bills for any constitutional implications.

In relation to scrutiny of EU legislation, the House of Commons has a Select Committee on European Legislation, and the House of Lords has a European Union Select Committee with a sub-committee which also scrutinizes law emanating from the Community to consider whether it raises questions of legal or political importance.[172] As the European Union commits itself steadily to greater respect for rights, through the caselaw of the Court of Justice, Article 6(2) of the Treaty on European Union, and the EU Charter of Fundamental Rights, human rights questions have taken on a higher profile in the activities of these committees.

In relation to delegated legislation, the House of Lords has a powerful committee, the Delegated Powers and Regulatory Reform Committee, which scrutinizes provisions in Bills which would delegate legislative powers to executive bodies, and makes proposals to ensure that delegated legislation is not permitted in matters which would be inappropriate and that a proper level of scrutiny is required for such instruments, taking account of their human rights implications among other considerations. For scrutiny of subordinate legislation, the House of Commons and the House of Lords have a Joint Select Committee on Statutory Instruments, which examines instruments to check that they do not infringe constitutional proprieties and that standards of drafting are maintained.[173] The Committee examines instruments for compatibility

[171] B. Nicholas, 'Fundamental Rights and Judicial Review in France' [1978] *PL* 82–101, 155–77; B. Neuborne, 'Judicial Review and Separation of Powers in France and the United States' (1982) 57 *New York University LR* 363–442, especially at 377–410; M. H. Davis, 'The Law/Politics Distinction, the French Conseil Constitutionnel, and the US Supreme Court' (1986) 34 *Amer. J. Comparative Law* 45–92; J. Bell, 'Equality in the Caselaw of the *Conseil Constitutionnel*' [1987] *PL* 426–46; C. Vroom, 'Constitutional Protection of Individual Liberties in France: The *Conseil Constitutionnel* since 1971' (1988) 63 *Tulane LR* 265–334; T. Prosser, 'Constitutions and Political Economy: The Privatization of Public Enterprises in France and Great Britain' (1990) 53 *MLR* 304–20.

[172] See J. A. G. Griffith and M. Ryle, *Parliament: Functions, Practice and Procedures* (London: Sweet & Maxwell, 1989), 436–8.

[173] Ibid., 444–5. The House of Commons has a separate Select Committee on Statutory Instruments to scrutinize those instruments which deal with matters which fall within the exclusive privilege of the Commons, such as appropriation and supply.

with Convention rights under the Human Rights Act 1998, as this is a condition for the validity of most of them. Additional protection for rights could be given if the committees took active steps to monitor delegated legislation for infringements of rights guaranteed under other human rights treaties which bind the state, as the Australian Senate's Regulations and Ordinances Committee does.

Finally, *managerial* techniques may be a valuable way of advancing rights within an organization. They allow the organization to police its own performance, formulating guidance and promulgating it to staff, and setting up mechanisms for monitoring the behaviour of staff through peer review, supervision, and appraisal systems. Sometimes a special office will be set up within an organization to oversee the process. For example, in the USA, it has been realized that the anti-discrimination provisions of the Civil Rights Act 1964 have not yet resulted in equalizing the opportunities for members of ethnic minorities and women to rise to senior positions in organizations in numbers proportional to their representation in the population as a whole. Some organizations, such as universities, have responded by appointing 'affirmative action officers' to attempt to improve the position. The holders of these imaginative appointments have a necessarily limited scope for action, usually needing to act in an accommodating rather than an authoritarian way, and may be subject to conflicting loyalties where their affirmative action objectives go against the wider business interests of the organization.[174]

2.5 THE CHANGING APPROACH TO RIGHTS AND LIBERTIES IN LAW IN THE UK

(1) THE DOMESTIC TRADITION OF LIBERTY RATHER THAN LIBERTIES

Until recently, the general approach to protecting rights in the UK was to think in terms, not of liberties or freedoms, but liberty or freedom. The dominant idea has been that of an undifferentiated mass of liberty. By virtue of the doctrine of parliamentary sovereignty, Parliament could encroach on freedom without legal constraint. No entrenched constitution or bill of rights restricted Parliament's power to interfere with freedom. People relied on their elected representatives in Parliament to ensure that any encroachment was authorized only in clearly particularized ways and for specified and democratically justifiable purposes. Enumerating and giving special protection to certain fundamental freedoms was seen as unnecessary, and as potentially endangering freedoms which were not so specified.

There are, of course, instruments which seem to protect important rights and have attracted great respect. Examples include Magna Carta, the first version of which was imposed on King John by his barons in 1215, and the Bill of Rights 1689, which William, Prince of Orange and his wife Mary accepted when offered the English

---

[174] See R. J. Townshend-Smith, 'The Role of Affirmative Action Officers in North American Universities' (1990) 19 *Anglo-Amer. LR* 325–44.

throne in 1688. Even when they were promulgated, those instruments had little impact on the well-being of the average subject. They merely protected the interests of some subjects (generally the more powerful ones) against a recurrence of abuses of monarchical power. The rights were largely assertions of the interests of powerful groups.

Magna Carta and the 1689 Bill of Rights can be repealed or amended by statute, without even the need for express words. Except in relation to the protection of property against unauthorized taxation,[175] the Bill of Rights has been restrictively interpreted, for example denying a remedy to prisoners under the clause forbidding cruel and unusual punishment unless the punishment could be shown to be both cruel and unusual.[176] Furthermore, the gradual extension of the state in the nineteenth century, through the Factory Acts and other social legislation, and the increasing role of inspectorates and local boards of works, meant that some of the old negative liberties were chipped away in order to secure improved quality of life (economic and social rights) for the worst off groups in society.[177] As the process continued in the twentieth century, the protective function of the courts for negative freedoms was increasingly displaced by new tribunals, which were established to implement new social rights rather than to protect liberties.

Once the traditional liberal certainties were called into question, and the assumption that negative freedoms were more important and deserving of respect than social engineering was contested, the nature of the rights which people should have could more easily be debated.[178] Throughout the twentieth century, doubt about the capacity of political controls to protect domestic rights grew, partly because of scepticism over the will of Parliament to restrain the growing power of the executive. Party control over MPs, which allowed a party in government largely to avoid effective challenge in the House of Commons, militated against Parliament's ability to protect freedom against really determined governmental assaults on liberty, particularly at times of war or national emergency.[179] These doubts have gone hand in hand with criticisms of the UK's political system, which many people consider to be inadequately representative of the range of opinion in the country, having developed little since the UK took the first steps towards democracy during the nineteenth century. In that situation, attention began to turn from respect for liberty, protected principally by the good sense of the legislature, to controversy over particular liberties and rights, especially when they were seen to conflict. During the second half of the twentieth century, the many international human-rights instruments to which the UK became a party stimulated debate over the scope of particular rights and freedoms, and the best means of protecting them. Decisions of the European Court of Human Rights have ensured that the issues are kept in clear focus.

---

[175] *Congreve v. Home Office* [1976] QB 629.

[176] *Williams v. Home Office (No. 2)* [1981] 1 All ER 1211; *R. (Bancoult) v. Secretary of State for Foreign and Commonwealth Affairs* [2001] 2 WLR 1219, DC.

[177] D. Fraser, *The Evolution of the British Welfare State*, 2nd edn. (London: Macmillan, 1984), 1–145.

[178] For an account of this process, see C. Harlow and R. Rawlings, *Law and Administration* 2nd edn. (London: Butterworths, 1997), chs 1–5.

[179] See K. D. Ewing and C. A. Gearty, *The Struggle for Civil Liberties: Political Freedom and the Rule of Law in Britain, 1914–1945* (Oxford: Oxford University Press, 2000), *passim*.

New rights were recognized after World War II, as the central state began to take on positive responsibilities for supporting and caring for people who had previously depended either on local government bodies or charity. The state began to treat needy people as having a *right* to support, enabling us to speak of 'welfare rights' and the other rights to commercial and domestic assistance from the state which Charles Reich dubbed 'the new property'.[180] Yet the period since Mrs. Thatcher became Prime Minister in 1979, which has seen concerted attempts to reduce the responsibilities of the state and to emphasize people's responsibility for their own welfare, has demonstrated that these rights are not quite as well-rooted in the system as classic liberties.

The structure of the welfare state reflected a belief that problems of poverty, homelessness, ignorance, and sickness were too pervasive and intractable to be left to charity. It was also thought to be wrong that the *value* of freedom to individuals should vary wildly because of their hugely different resources: to paraphrase Anatole France, the freedom to contract for a night's board and lodging at a comfortable hotel is worth nothing to a homeless person without the means to pay for it.

This gradual development of rights-consciousness, as distinct from liberty-consciousness, has been influenced by the UK's closer association with European institutions. Those European nations which came under the influence of the French Declaration of the Rights of Man and the Citizen during the Napoleonic period have tended to have a closer attachment to human rights than the UK had. However, during the second half of the twentieth century, the institutions of the Council of Europe and, to a lesser extent, of the European Communities and Union, had a gradual but fundamental impact on the place of rights in legal and political thought in the UK.

(2) THE COUNCIL OF EUROPE

The UK's accession to the European Convention on Human Rights, by which it has been bound since it entered into force in 1953, was an important step towards increasing the influence of human rights thinking in the UK, although it has been shown that the British government took the step only reluctantly and suspiciously (despite having been closely concerned in the drafting of the Convention),[181] and probably signed the Convention only because they expected never to be challengeable under it.[182] Initially, the government insured against challenge by refusing to make a declaration accepting the right of victims to petition the Commission under the optional terms of Article 25 of the Convention. Once the Labour government made a declaration under Article 25 with effect from 1966, the UK regularly had to defend itself against charges of

---

[180] C. Reich, 'The New Property' (1964) 73 *Yale LJ* 733–87.

[181] A. Lester, 'Fundamental Rights: The United Kingdom Isolated' [1984] *PL* 46–72; E. Wicks, 'The United Kingdom Government's Perceptions of the European Convention on Human Rights at the Time of Entry' [2000] *PL* 438–55; G. Marston, 'The UK's Part in the Preparation of the ECHR' (1993) 24 ICLQ 796–826.

[182] R. Kerridge, 'Incorporation of the European Convention on Human Rights into United Kingdom Domestic Law', in M. P. Furmston, R. Kerridge, and B. E. Sufrin (eds.), *The Effect on English Domestic Law of Membership of the European Communities and Ratification of the European Convention on Human Rights* (The Hague: Martinus Nijhoff, 1983), 247–82.

infringing Convention rights, and has often changed domestic law to give effect to decisions of the European Commission and Court of Human Rights.

However, the Convention has no direct effect on English law, because it is a treaty. The UK adopts a 'dualist' approach to the relationship between national law and international treaties, which do not form part of municipal law unless and to the extent[183] that legislation is passed making the rights and obligations under the treaty part of municipal law. Accordingly, people in the UK were unable to obtain a remedy from a national court for violation of a Convention right, unless the infringement also gave rise to an independent cause of action in municipal law. Where there was no such cause of action, they had to turn to the European Commission of Human Rights in Strasbourg.[184]

Nevertheless, the Convention had an indirect impact on municipal law. Lord Bingham MR in his maiden speech to the House of Lords identified six ways in which the ECHR and its jurisprudence were of relevance:[185]

'First, . . . where a United Kingdom statute is capable of two interpretations . . . the courts will presume that Parliament intended to legislate in conformity with the convention and not in conflict with it . . . Secondly, if the common law is uncertain, unclear or incomplete, the courts have to make a choice; . . . they will rule, wherever possible, in a manner which conforms with the convention and does not conflict with it . . . Thirdly, when the courts are called upon to construe a domestic statute enacted to fulfil a convention obligation, the courts will ordinarily assume that the statute was intended to be effective to that end . . . Fourthly, where the courts have a discretion to exercise . . . they seek to act in a way which does not violate the convention . . . Fifthly, when . . . courts are called upon to decide what, in a given situation, public policy demands, it has been held to be legitimate that we shall have regard to our international obligations enshrined in the convention as a source of guidance on what British public policy requires. Sixthly and lastly, matters covered by the law of the European Community . . . on occasion give effect to matters covered by convention law. The Court of Justice takes the view that on matters subject to Community law, the law common to the Member States is part of the law which applies. All Member States are parties to the convention and it so happens from time to time that laws derived from the convention are incorporated as part of the law of the Community. That of course is a law which the courts in this country must apply since we are bound by Act of Parliament to do so, and that is a means by which, indirectly, convention rights find their way into domestic law.'

---

[183] There may be problems in establishing how far a convention has been adopted by legislation. For example, the Geneva Conventions Act 1957 gave the British courts criminal jurisdiction in respect of 'grave' breaches of the Geneva Conventions of 12 August 1949 on humanitarian protection of people in times of armed conflict. This was all that was required by the Convention. However, the Act included in its Schedules the full texts of all four conventions. It has been suggested that this amounts to recognition in domestic law having the effect of giving the UK courts jurisdiction in respect of all breaches of the Conventions, not only in respect of grave breaches of them: see F. Hampson, 'The Geneva Conventions and the Detention of Civilians and Alleged Prisoners of War' [1991] *PL* 507–22 at 517–19.

[184] Compare, e.g. *Malone v. Metropolitan Police Commissioner* [1979] Ch. 344, [1979] 2 All ER 620 with *Malone v. United Kingdom*, Eur. Ct. HR, Series A, No. 82, Judgment of 2 August 1984, 5 EHRR 385; or *Weeks v. United Kingdom*, Eur. Ct. HR, Series A, No. 145, Judgment of 5 October 1988, 10 EHRR 293, with *R. v. Secretary of State for the Home Department, ex parte Weeks*, The Times, 15 March 1988. On the status of the Convention in the states, see A. Z. Drzemczewski, *The European Human Rights Convention in Domestic Law* (Oxford: Clarendon Press, 1982).

[185] HL Debs, 3 July 1996, vol. 573, cols. 1465–1467.

Furthermore, it can be argued that the Convention engenders a legitimate expectation that decision-makers will at least properly consider rights guaranteed under it when making decisions which affect people's rights.[186] There was thus scope for Convention-based reasoning even before the Human Rights Act 1998 made most of the rights under the Convention part of municipal law in the UK.[187] The same applied to other human-rights instruments to which the UK was a party, although they were cited in court far less often than the ECHR. However, the courts refused to give remedies for breaches of the Convention (or any other treaty) which were not related to directly effective Community rights and which did not give rise to a cause of action in English law. They would not grant a declaration that there had or had not been an infringement of the Convention.[188] Nor would English courts usually entertain applications for judicial review of administrative actions merely on the ground that they were said to breach the Convention. It did not amount to illegality or unreasonableness for a public authority to refuse to consider himself bound by a provision in the Convention, although the more significant the right infringed, and the greater the interference with it, the weightier would be the reasons which the authority would have to establish in order to avoid the imputation of having acted unreasonably and hence unlawfully.[189]

(3) THE EUROPEAN COMMUNITIES AND HUMAN RIGHTS

Since 1973, the UK has been a Member State of the European Community. In Member States, rights having direct effect under Community law can be relied on in domestic courts, which have an obligation to provide adequate remedies for breach. This may include disapplying an otherwise valid statute,[190] and providing compensation to those who suffered loss through the implementation of national law which is incompatible with Community law.[191] The courts' obligation arises by virtue of a supranational, rather than international, legal order, and one which became part of municipal law in the UK by virtue of the European Communities Act 1972, section 2. However, there was originally no provision in Community law requiring Community

[186] *Minister for Immigration and Ethnic Affairs v. Teoh* (1995) 183 CLR 273, HC of Australia; *R. v. Secretary of State for the Home Department, ex parte Ahmed and Patel* [1998] INLR 570; P. Bayne, 'Administrative Law, Human Rights and International Humanitarian Law' (1990) 64 *ALJ* 203–8; Lord Lester, 'Government Compliance with International Human Rights Law: A New Year's Legitimate Expectation' [1996] *PL* 187.

[187] For a good account, see M. J. Beloff QC and H. Mountfield, 'Unconventional Behaviour? Judicial Uses of the European Convention in England and Wales' [1996] EHRLR 467.

[188] *Malone v. Metropolitan Police Commissioner* [1979] Ch. 344, [1979] 2 All ER 620.

[189] *Bugdaycay v. Secretary of State for the Home Department* [1987] AC 514, HL; *R. v. Secretary of State for the Home Department, ex parte Brind* [1991] 1 AC 696, HL; *R. v. Ministry of Defence, ex parte Smith* [1996] QB 517, CA. For discussion, see F. Donson, 'Civil Liberties and Judicial Review: Can the Common Law Really Protect Rights?', in P. Leyland and T. Woods (eds.), *Administrative Law Facing the Future: Old Constraints and New Horizons* (London: Blackstone Press, 1997), 347–73.

[190] See, e.g. Case C-213/89, *Factortame Ltd. v. Secretary of State for Transport (No. 2)* [1991] 1 All ER 70, CJEC and HL.

[191] Joined Cases C-46/93 and C-48/93, *Brasserie de Pêcheur SA v. Federal Republic of Germany* [1996] QB 404, CJEC; *R. v. Secretary of State for Transport, ex parte Factortame Ltd. (No. 5)* [1999] 3 WLR 1062, HL.

institutions, or the institutions of Member States when implementing Community law and policy, to respect human rights.

In some Member States, the primacy of Community law was therefore seen as a potential threat to hard-won constitutional guarantees of rights. Faced with a conflict between Community law and the protections for fundamental rights under the German *Grundgesetz* (Basic Law, or constitution), the *Bundesverfassungsgericht* (Federal Constitutional Court) decided that it would reserve to itself the right to apply German constitutional human-rights law in preference to conflicting Community law until such time as the Communities had a directly elected Parliament and guaranteed protection for human rights at least equivalent to that which was available under the *Grundgesetz*.[192] This challenge could have undermined much of the structure which the Court of Justice had developed to allow for harmonized implementation of Community law in Member States. The Court of Justice responded by developing earlier *dicta* into a principle that Community law protected, as general principles of law, the fundamental rights derived from the common constitutional traditions of Member States and international instruments to which they had contributed or were parties.[193] However, the Court still insisted that Community law had to take precedence over national law, even fundamental rights in constitutional law, in order to facilitate the consistent application of Community law as between Member States.[194] This caused considerable disquiet in Germany, where the *Bundesverfassungsgericht*, in the first of the so-called '*Solange*' ('so long as') cases, stated that it would not apply Community law in a manner which violated fundamental rights under the German *Grundgesetz*.[195] In response, the Court of Justice accepted that it, and national courts interpreting Community law, would have regard to the fundamental rights forming general principles of Community law when they become relevant to a question of Community law, either as grounds for judicial review of the action of Community institutions or as guides to the interpretation of Community law.[196]

In practice, there is no guarantee that the Court of Justice will interpret rights in ways which protect them as extensively as national constitutional courts or the European Court of Human Rights.[197] The Court of Justice has not been as dynamic in its development of human rights as the European Court of Human Rights. In a number of cases, the Court of Justice has adopted a less extensive interpretation of a right, or permitted a more intrusive interference with it, than would have found favour with

---

[192] *Internationale Handelsgesellschaft mbH v. Einfuhr- und Vorratstelle für Getreide und Futtermittel* [1974] 2 CMLR 540, BvfG of Germany.

[193] E.g. Case 29/69, *Stauder v. City of Ulm* [1969] ECR 419, CJEC, at para. 7 of the judgment; Case 11/70 *Internationale Handelsgesellschaft mbH v. Einfuhr- und Vorratstelle für Getreide und Futtermittel* [1970] ECR 1125, at paras. 3–4 of the judgment.

[194] Case 11/70, *Internationale Handelsgesellschaft mbH v. Einfuhr- und Vorratstelle für Getreide und Futtermittel* [1970] ECR 1125.

[195] *Internationale Handelsgesellschaft mbH v. Einfuhr- und Vorratstelle für Getreide und Futtermittel* [1974] 2 CMLR 540.

[196] E.g. Case 4/73, *Nold v. Commission of the European Communities* [1974] ECR 491, CJEC; Case 36/75, *Rutili v. Minister for the Interior* [1975] ECR 1219.

[197] See D. Spielmann, 'Human Rights Case Law in the Strasbourg and Luxembourg Courts: Conflicts, Inconsistencies, and Complementarities', in P. Alston, with M. Bustelo, and J. Heenan, (eds.), *The EU and Human Rights* (Oxford: Oxford University Press, 1999), 757–80.

the European Court of Human Rights. The rights have been most fully implemented in Community law in the field of employment disputes with the Community institutions as employers, although even there restrictions on rights may be permitted which would not be allowed in national or public international law.[198] The Court of Justice has rarely struck down a legislative or executive act by a Community institution on the ground of an incompatibility with a Convention right: the general principles have had their main impact in cases brought against institutions by members of staff, and have not restricted the competence of Community institutions in relation to Member States or ordinary citizens. This leaves a gap in the protection for rights at Community level which is causing increasing concern,[199] particularly since the Court of Justice ruled, in an advisory opinion, that the Community lacks the competence to become party to the European Convention on Human Rights.[200] The German *Bundesverfassungsgericht* has made conciliatory noises in the light of the Court of Justice's development of a rhetoric of respect for fundamental rights, saying that it will maintain effective protection of rights for people in Germany but will do so in a co-operative rather than confrontational relationship with the Court of Justice.[201] None the less, it is not surprising that German courts have continued to assert their ultimate right to refuse to enforce Community measures which violate basic rights.[202]

The human-rights standards recognized by the Court of Justice were finally given expression in the Treaties at Maastricht, in what is now (post-Amsterdam) Art. 6(2) of the Amsterdam Treaty.[203] Maastricht also saw the incorporation into the Treaties of a Social Chapter, giving additional rights in employment and certain other rights, to which the UK acceded at the time of the Treaty of Amsterdam. But there are reckoned to be some serious gaps in the protection offered to rights through the CJEC, including (i) the lack of any clear statement of what rights are protected, and (ii) the lack of any clear enumeration of the grounds on which and conditions under which Community institutions or Member States may legitimately interfere with rights. The first, but not the second, of these gaps may be filled (at least in part) by the EU Charter of Fundamental Rights, which was formally proclaimed at the EU summit in Nice in December 2000.[203a]

If these developments stimulate practical improvements in the way in which human rights are protected against Community institutions, they may have a substantial, though indirect, impact on UK domestic law in cases concerning Community law

[198] See, e.g. Case C-404/92P, *X. v. Commission* [1994] ECR I-4737.

[199] See, e.g. P. Alston and J. H. H. Weiler, 'An "Ever Closer Union" in Need of a Human Rights Policy: The European Union and Human Rights', in Alston *et al.* (ed.), *The EU and Human Rights*, 3–66; G. Gaja, 'New Instruments and Institutions for Enhancing the Protection of Human Rights in Europe?', ibid., 781–800.

[200] Opinion 2/94 [1996] ECR I-1759, CJEC.

[201] *Re the Application of Wünsche Handelsgesellschaft* [1987] 3 CMLR 225, BvfG.

[202] U. Everling, 'Will Europe Slip on Bananas? The Bananas Judgment of the Court of Justice and National Courts' (1996) 33 *CMLR* 401; L. Betten and N. Grief, *EU Law and Human Rights* (London: Longman, 1998), 64–70.

[203] Formerly Art. F2 of the Maastricht Treaty.

[203a] E. Wicks, 'Declaratory of Existing Rights: the UK's role in drafting a European Bill of Rights, Mark II' [2001] *PL* 527–41.

having direct effect without the need for implementing domestic legislation.[204] How-ever, if the Court of Justice fails to apply even the minimum standards acceptable to civilized European society (as established by the European Court of Human Rights) to bear on the activities of Community institutions and Member States implementing Community law and policy, there will be further conflict between the Court of Justice and Member States over the primacy of Community law. For example, under section 3 of the Human Rights Act 1998, courts in the UK are obliged to interpret the European Communities Act 1972, section 2, in a manner compatible with Convention rights. This might generate significant limitations on the power of public authorities in the UK to implement EU Directives in ways which do not comply with Convention rights. As a source of protection for human rights, the EU still has unrealized potential.

(4) THE LEAD-UP TO THE UK'S CONSTITUTIONAL LEGISLATION OF 1998

The earlier parts of this section have shown how, by the mid-1990s, the UK was becoming more rights-conscious than it had traditionally been. Under the influence of the ECHR and of developments elsewhere in the common-law world, judges in the UK were feeling their way slowly towards recognizing Convention rights, and some were even talking about the courts as guardians of fundamental common-law rights. The EU was giving a higher profile to fundamental rights in ways which had the capacity to affect national law directly. This resulted in certain rights-based incursions on the Diceyan doctrine of parliamentary sovereignty. Statutes could be disapplied to the extent of an incompatibility with Community law. The courts had developed a principle of interpretation that Parliament did not intend to legislate inconsistently with fundamental, common-law rights, so government needed to draft legislation which was intended to interfere with such rights, or to authorize subordinate legisla-tion interfering with them, in wholly unequivocal and unambiguous terms.

In this atmosphere, it was only a matter of time before the position of fundamental freedoms and human rights would have to be formalized in UK law. This move would have twin benefits. It would help to plug the gaps which were becoming evident in the ability of municipal law to protect individuals' rights (a weakness which became more obvious once the UK granted the right of individuals to apply to the Strasbourg institutions under the ECHR). It would also reduce the threat of unconstrained judicial interference with the executive and Parliament. There were two possible ways of approaching this: either to bring into municipal law some or all of the rights which, under treaties in international law, the UK was already bound to respect; or to attempt to fashion a full-scale, home-grown bill of rights for the UK, perhaps based on, but going beyond, the terms of the ECHR.

[204] See L. Betten and N. Grief, *EU Law and Human Rights* (London: Longman, 1998), chs 3 and 4; B. de Witte, 'The Past and Future Role of the European Court of Justice in the Protection of Human Rights', in P. Alston, M. Bustelo, and J. Heenan (eds.), *The EU and Human Rights* (Oxford: Oxford University Press, 1999), 859–97; J. T. Lang, 'The Sphere in which Member States are Obliged to Comply with General Principles of Law and Community Fundamental Rights Principles', 1991/2 *Legal Issues in European Integration* 23–35; T. Tridimas, *General Principles of EU Law* (Oxford: Clarendon Press, 1999).

The campaign to achieve formal recognition of rights has a long history.[205] In his 1974 Hamlyn Lectures,[206] Sir Leslie (later Lord) Scarman argued for a Bill of Rights, which, he thought, would be particularly pressing if devolution were to become a reality, and which could have protected people in Northern Ireland against methods of interrogating suspected terrorists which, the European Court of Human Rights was later to hold,[207] amounted to inhuman or degrading treatment which violated Article 3 of the ECHR. In 1975, Alan Beith, a Liberal MP, introduced a Bill of Rights Bill to the House of Commons, and in March 1976 Lord Wade introduced a bill to incorporate the ECHR in the House of Lords. At this stage, there was significant support, among leading figures in all the main political parties, for improving human-rights protection. Lord Hailsham, who had been Lord Chancellor in the Conservative government which had lost power in the 1974 General Election and who was to be Lord Chancellor again under Mrs. Thatcher from 1979, was won over to the cause of a bill of rights (at least while in opposition). Lord Wade's Bill was instrumental in encouraging the House of Lords to establish a Select Committee on the subject in 1977. The Committee reported in 1978.[208] The Committee split six–five on the question of whether there should be a Bill of Rights (with the narrow majority in favour), but unanimously thought that, if there were to be one, it should be based on the ECHR. Thereafter the impetus for change seemed to dissipate somewhat in Parliament, but academic attention increasingly concentrated on the arguments about the merits of enacting a bill of rights, and the means by which such a bill might be adopted in the light of the UK's constitutional traditions.[209]

Incorporation was and remained the policy of the Liberal Party and the Liberal Democrat Party, but lost ground among the Conservative Party during the long period of Conservative government between 1979 and 1997. Incorporation became official Labour Party policy only in September 1993,[210] when it was in opposition and its leadership was seeking to modernize the party. There were regular parliamentary debates, and bills were regularly but unsuccessfully introduced to incorporate the ECHR, for example by Lord Broxbourne (formerly the Conservative MP Derek Walker-Smith QC) in 1985.

[205] See M. Zander, *A Bill of Rights?*, 4th edn. (London: Sweet & Maxwell, 1997), ch. 1.

[206] Sir Leslie Scarman, *English Law—The New Dimension* (London: Sweet & Maxwell, 1974).

[207] *Ireland v. United Kingdom*, Series A, No. 25, Judgment of 18 January 1978 (the Court disagreed with the Commission, which had held that the treatment amounted to torture: Series B, No. 23-I, Decision of 25 January 1976; but found a violation of Art. 3 none the less).

[208] HL No. 176 of 1977–78.

[209] P. Wallington and J. McBride, *Civil Liberties and a Bill of Rights* (London: Cobden Trust, 1976); Lord Lloyd of Hampstead, 'Do We Need a Bill of Rights?' (1976) 39 *MLR* 121–9; A. J. M. Milne, 'Should We Have a Bill of Rights?' (1977) 40 *MLR* 389–96; *Report of the Select Committee on a Bill of Rights*, HL Paper No. 176 of 1976–77 (London: HMSO, 1977); J. Jaconelli, *Enacting a Bill of Rights* (Oxford: Clarendon Press, 1980); C. Campbell (ed.), *Do We Need a Bill of Rights?* (London: Temple Smith, 1980); J. Jaconelli, *Enacting a Bill of Rights* (Oxford: Clarendon Press, 1980); M. Zander, *A Bill of Rights?*, 4th edn. (London: Sweet and Maxwell, 1997); Advisory Committee to the Constitutional Commission, *Report: Individual and Democratic Rights* (Canberra: Commonwealth of Australia, 1987); K. D. Ewing and C. A. Gearty, *Freedom Under Thatcher: Civil Liberties in Modern Britain* (Oxford: Clarendon Press, 1990), ch. 9; P. P. Craig, *Public Law and Democracy in the United Kingdom and the United States of America* (Oxford: Clarendon Press, 1990), ch. 7.

[210] *A New Agenda for Democracy: Labour's Proposals for Constitutional Reform* (London: Labour Party, 1993), following a speech by Labour leader John Smith MP in March 1993.

Several non-governmental organizations published reports which included draft bills of rights for the UK in the early 1990s.[211] Back in Parliament, two very influential bills were introduced to the House of Lords by the Liberal Democrat peer, Lord Lester of Herne Hill QC, in the 1994–95 and 1996–97 sessions. They gained support in the House of Lords but did not pass the House of Commons.[212] However, things were shifting within the Labour Party. In December 1996, the Labour Party issued a policy discussion document[213] written by Paul Boateng and Jack Straw, setting out proposals for incorporation in significant detail, and incorporation formed part of the Labour Party manifesto for the 1997 General Election. In October 1997, the new Labour government published a White Paper, *Rights Brought Home*,[214] and introduced the Human Rights Bill to the House of Lords. It received the Royal Assent on 9 November 1998, and came fully into force on 2 October 2000, after a major programme of preparation by government departments and the judiciary.[215]

In the meantime, the Scotland Act 1998, Government of Wales Act 1998, and Northern Ireland Act 1998 had been passed. Each Act restricted the legislative and executive competences of the respective devolved legislatures and executives by providing that their powers did not extend to legislating or acting in a manner incompatible with a Convention right, as defined in the Human Rights Act 1998. The rights thus became legally enforceable in Scotland, Wales, and Northern Ireland against the respective legislatures and executives, in relation to devolved matters, once the respective devolved bodies began to operate. As the rights took effect in relation to the powers of the devolved legislatures and executives, their scope gave rise to 'devolution issues' in the courts, on which a final appeal lies to the Judicial Committee of the Privy Council. Scottish courts, in particular, had developed a significant jurisprudence on the Convention rights before the Human Rights Act 1998 came into force.

The Human Rights Act 1998 was thus not so much a sea-change as a legislative endorsement of a long-running politico-legal trend. The form of the Act was influenced by the preceding debates, both within Parliament and among lawyers, academics, and non-governmental organizations, such as Liberty/NCCL, JUSTICE, Charter 88, the Institute for Public Policy Research, the Incorporation Project at King's College London, and the Constitution Unit at University College London. Only time will tell whether this is merely the first step towards a full-scale Bill of Rights for the UK. At the moment, it is a compromise which falls short of that, a partial incorporation of most but not all of the rights contained in the ECHR without direct reference to the

---

[211] See, e.g. Institute of Public Policy Research, *The Constitution of the United Kingdom* (London: IPPR, 1991); Liberty, *A People's Charter: Liberty's Bill of Rights* (London: Liberty, 1991).

[212] See Lord Lester, 'The Mouse that Roared: the Human Rights Bill 1995' [1995] *PL* 198; Lord Lester of Herne Hill QC, 'First Steps Towards a Constitutional Bill of Rights' [1997] *EHRLR* 124–31.

[213] Jack Straw and Paul Boateng, *Bringing Rights Home: Labour's Plans to Incorporate the European Convention on Human Rights into UK Law* (London: Labour Party, 1996), reprinted in [1997] *EHRLR* 71–80.

[214] Home Office, *Rights Brought Home: The Human Rights Bill*, Cm. 3782 (London: The Stationery Office, 1997).

[215] For a panoramic view of the factors underlying the passage of the Bill and the implementation of the Act, see F. Klug, *Values for a Godless Age: the Story of the United Kingdom's New Bill of Rights* (London: Penguin Books, 2000).

rights which bind the UK under other treaties to which the state is a party. The next section provides an outline of the effect of the Act.

2.6 THE HUMAN RIGHTS ACT 1998[216]

There are four main elements in the scheme of the Act.

First, the Act identifies the rights under the ECHR which are to form part of municipal law, and makes provision for the significance which the caselaw of the Strasbourg institutions will have for the interpretation of the Convention rights under the Act.

Secondly, the Act introduces a principle of statutory interpretation which requires that all legislation (whether primary or subordinate, and whenever enacted or made) is to be read and given effect in a manner compatible with Convention rights so far as it is possible to do so.

Thirdly, the incorporation of rights does not formally affect parliamentary sovereignty. Parliament remains free to legislate in a manner incompatible with the Convention rights which become part of municipal law under the Act. The Act is not entrenched, and is, in theory, liable to amendment in the usual way. However, it is probable that the Act has special status in two respects, because of the nature of its subject-matter and the way in which our courts already approach fundamental human rights. First, it is very unlikely that any provision of the Act will be subject to implied repeal in subsequent legislation. Secondly, it is clear that the enactment of subsequent legislation incompatible with Convention rights will not have the effect of either impliedly repealing or limiting the scope of the Convention rights in Schedule 1 to the 1998 Act. The Act can thus be regarded as having a status superior to other legislation in these respects.[217] Nevertheless, the courts cannot strike down or disapply a provision in primary legislation on the ground that it is incompatible with a Convention right, although they may grant a declaration of incompatibility. Public authorities must perform their duties under primary legislation, even if the legislation requires them to act in a manner incompatible with Convention rights.

Fourthly, subject to that, the Act imposes a legal duty on public authorities (a term which is not fully defined, but includes courts and tribunals) to act in a manner compatible with Convention rights, and entitles the victim of a violation of such a right to a remedy. Subordinate legislation which is incompatible with a Convention

---

[216] The Act has generated a large literature. For books combining authoritative introductions with excellent treatment of detailed aspects, see Lord Lester of Herne Hill QC and D. Pannick QC, *Human Rights Law and Practice* (London: Butterworths, 1999, with 1st Supplement 2000); K. Starmer, *European Human Rights Law* (London: Legal Action Group, 1999); S. Grosz, J. Beatson QC, and the late P. Duffy QC, *Human Rights: The 1998 Act and the European Convention* (London: Sweet and Maxwell, 1999); J. Wadham and H. Mountfield, *Blackstone's Guide to the Human Rights Act 1998* (London: Blackstone Press, 1999; 2nd edn., 2000); R. Clayton and H. Tomlinson, *The Law of Human Rights* (Oxford: Oxford University Press, 2000).

[217] See D. Feldman, 'The Human Rights Act 1998 and Constitutional Principles' (1999) 19 *Legal Studies* 165–206.

right is liable to be quashed or declared invalid, unless it could not have been drafted to be compatible with the right because of the demands of primary legislation.

Each of these elements will be considered in turn.

(1) THE CONVENTION RIGHTS

Section 1 of, and Schedule 1 to, the Act set out those rights under the ECHR which are to be part of municipal law ('the Convention rights'). Section 1(1) defines the term 'Convention rights' as the rights and fundamental freedoms set out in the various articles of 'the Convention', which is defined in turn in section 21(1) as the ECHR 'as it has effect for the time being in relation to the UK'. This makes it clear that the rights are those which operate in international law in relation to the UK. Schedule 1 to the Act reproduces the English-language version of these rights, but as the Convention rights are those operating under the ECHR the French-language version of them is equally authentic and authoritative. The current list of rights is as follows:

(i) the right to legal protection for life, and to legal limitations on circumstances in which intentional deprivation of life is permissible (Article 2);

(ii) the right to be free of torture and inhuman or degrading treatment or punishment (Article 3);

(iii) the right to be free of slavery, servitude, and forced or compulsory labour (Article 4);

(iv) the right not to be deprived of liberty and security of the person except in accordance with a procedure prescribed by law and with various safeguards (Article 5);

(v) the right to a fair and public hearing within a reasonable time by an independent and impartial tribunal established by law in determination of civil rights and obligations and criminal charges, with special procedural safeguards in criminal cases (Article 6);

(vi) the right not to be punished for an action which did not constitute an offence under national or international law at the time of its commission (Article 7);

(vii) the right to respect for private and family life, home and correspondence (Article 8);

(viii) the right to freedom of thought, conscience, and religion (Article 9);

(ix) the right to freedom of expression, including receiving information, without interference by a public authority and regardless of frontiers (Article 10);

(x) the right to freedom of peaceful assembly and association, including the right to form and join a trade union (Article 11);

(xi) the right to marry and found a family (Article 12);

(xii) the right to have the other rights secured without discrimination (Article 14);

(xiii) the entitlement to peaceful enjoyment of possessions, and limitations on deprivation of property (Protocol 1, Article 1);

(xiv) the right to education, in relation to which the state is to respect the right of parents to ensure that children receive education in conformity with their religious and philosophical convictions (Protocol 1, Article 2);

(xv) the right to free elections by secret ballot at reasonable intervals (Protocol 1, Article 3);

(xvi) the right not to be sentenced to death save in respect of acts committed in time of war or of imminent threat of war (Protocol 6, Articles 1 and 2).

Section 1(1) and 1(2) provide that these rights have effect subject to:

(i) Article 16 of the ECHR, which provides that the rights of aliens to freedom of expression, freedom of peaceful assembly and association, and freedom from discrimination may be restricted by the state, as long as other rights are respected;

(ii) Article 17, providing that nothing in the ECHR permits any state, group, or person to engage in any activity or perform any act aimed at the destruction of any of the rights and freedoms under the ECHR or at their limitation to a greater extent than is provided for in the ECHR itself;

(iii) Article 18, which stipulates that restrictions to rights and freedoms which are permitted under the ECHR must not be applied for any purpose other than those for which they have been prescribed;

(iv) any designated derogation (the derogation in respect of Article 5, which was originally contained in Part I of Schedule 3 to the Act, having been repealed with effect from 1 April 2001 under the Human Rights Act 1998 (Amendment) Order 2001, SI 2001 No. 1216, a new derogation took effect on 13 November 2001 under the Human Rights Act 1998 (Designated Derogation) Order 2001, SI 2001 No. 3644); and

(v) any designated reservation (currently the UK's reservation to parents' right to have their children taught in conformity with their own religious and philosophical convictions).

Articles 16 to 18 are set out in Schedule 1 to the Act. The designated derogation and reservation are set out in Schedule 3 to the Act. Section 1(4)–(6) provides that Schedules 1 and 3 may be amended by statutory instrument for certain purposes. For example, if the UK were to ratify Protocol Nos. 4, 7, or 12, containing rights which the UK has not yet accepted, it would not be necessary to pass primary legislation in order to amend the Act to include the new rights as 'Convention rights'.

One right which already binds the UK in international law under the ECHR is omitted from the list of 'Convention rights' under the Act. The government declined to include Article 13, the right to an effective remedy before a national authority for a violation of another Convention right, both because they thought that the remedial arrangements under the Act were sufficient to meet the requirements of Article 13 without a separate right to a remedy, and because of concern that the judges might exploit such a right to develop new and unexpected types of remedies against public authorities (the mutual inconsistency of these two justifications will be immediately obvious). It remains to be seen whether this proves to be a significant lacuna in the Act.

As the Convention rights are, in principle, those which bind the UK under the text of the ECHR, it is not surprising to find that section 2(1) requires courts and tribunals which have to interpret the articles to 'take into account' any relevant decision of the Strasbourg institutions, which for practical purposes means the Commission and the Court. This means that the caselaw of those institutions is persuasive but not binding on our courts. There is no doctrine of *stare decisis* in the Strasbourg institutions, which (as noted earlier) treat the ECHR as a dynamic instrument, not a static one. It would have been strange had the Strasbourg caselaw been more authoritative in the UK than it is in Strasbourg. Nevertheless, courts and tribunals in the UK should follow rulings by the Court regarding the scope or content of rights under the ECHR, to the extent of treating the Court's definition of a right as setting the minimum scope which that right should be allowed in domestic law. If national courts do not do so, it will undermine one of the purposes of the Human Rights Act 1998, which is to ensure that people in the UK can obtain effective remedies in national law for violations of Convention rights.

On the other hand, to the extent that the Court is often reluctant to extend the scope of Convention rights beyond the bounds of a current European consensus on social, scientific, and moral issues because of the need to maintain international acceptance of its authority, national courts should be prepared to consider extending the scope of rights beyond that so far required by the Court. There is no reason for national courts to resort to considerations of international comity to limit the rights of people in the UK, because the authority of national courts does not depend on maintaining international consensus. Furthermore, the dynamic potential of the ECHR would be impaired if national authorities felt bound to adopt a static approach to implementing rights, based on the most recent decision of the Court, as international consensus on the content of rights would never move on. National courts interpreting Convention rights under the Human Rights Act 1998 should therefore be free to adopt a more liberal interpretation of Convention rights than the Court, but should not be free to adopt a more restrictive interpretation of a right than that adopted by the Court. The same applies to the Court's view of what constitutes an interference with a right: national courts should hold behaviour to be an interference if it would be treated as such by the Strasbourg organs, but may in some circumstances wish, and should allow themselves, to treat as an interference behaviour which the Court has held not to interfere with a right.

When one turns from the scope of rights to justifications for interfering with rights, the position is similar in principle. National courts should not allow interference by public authorities with Convention rights to be more extensive than that which is permitted by the Strasbourg organs, and should feel free to be more rigorous than the Court in reviewing and rejecting some purported justifications for interference. The purposes for which it is permitted to interfere with Convention rights (for example, under Article 8(2), 'in the interests of national security, public safety or the economic well-being of the country, for the prevention of disorder or crime, for the protection of health or morals, or for the protection of the rights and freedoms of others') should not be interpreted to allow public authorities more grounds for interfering with

Convention rights than would have been allowed by the Court to states.[218] For example, it would be inappropriate to allow lack of international consensus as to the recognition of the reassigned gender of transsexuals to affect the interpretation of their rights to recognition in national, as against international, law. In the same way, where the Court has used the notion of the 'margin of appreciation' to hold that a state's interference with a right is not unlawful, the judgment on that point will be of no authority in municipal law, since the margin of appreciation is entirely and peculiarly a creature of international, not national, law. As Lord Hope of Craighead said in *R. v. Director of Public Prosecutions, ex parte Kebilene*,[219] the idea of the 'margin of appreciation' is premised on the greater ability of national than international authorities to make judgments about where there is a pressing social need and what is a proportionate response to it in the circumstances which obtain in a particular state. Courts which are national authorities cannot duck the issue in that way, although (as in current administrative law) courts may respect what Lord Lester and David Pannick have called a 'discretionary area of judgment' of decision-makers who are specially well qualified to make particular judgments or, in relation to political judgments, who are democratically accountable for their decisions.[220]

Courts remain free to refer to international instruments which are binding on the UK but are not among the Convention rights when interpreting Convention rights, in the same way that they made use of the body of the ECHR itself before incorporation. Such instruments include Article 13 of the ECHR, the International Covenant on Civil and Political Rights, the UN Convention on the Rights of the Child, and a range of conventions dealing with discrimination and some social rights. They are used by the Court in Strasbourg as an aid to interpreting rights under the ECHR, and can be used by our courts and tribunals for the same purpose. These instruments may also be used when interpreting ambiguous municipal legislation, developing the common law, or exercising discretion as to the grant of remedies.

Courts and tribunals in the various jurisdictions in the UK have been prepared to have regard to each other's decisions on the interpretation of Convention rights and the 1998 Act more generally. They may also look to the decisions of courts in other common-law countries which already have a wealth of experience of interpreting constitutional or quasi-constitutional bills of rights. These decisions may be of considerable assistance when considering whether particular activities fall within the scope of Convention rights, or when deciding whether a specific type of interference with a right is 'necessary in a democratic society' for a legitimate purpose. Decisions of the Canadian Supreme Court on the Charter of Rights and Freedoms, those of the

---

[218] See generally Sir Anthony Hooper, 'The Impact of the Human Rights Act on Judicial Decision-making' [1998] *EHRLR* 676–86 at 682–3; D. Pannick QC, 'Principles of Interpretation of the Human Rights Act and the Discretionary Area of Judgment' [1998] *PL* 545; R. A. Edwards, 'Generosity and the Human Rights Act: the Right Interpretation?' [1999] *PL* 400–5; Lord Irvine of Lairg LC, 'Activism and Restraint: Human Rights and the Interpretative Process' [1999] *EHRLR* 350–72; D. Feldman, 'Precedent and the European Court of Human Rights', in Law Commission Consultation Paper No. 157, *Criminal Law: Bail and the Human Rights Act 1998*, Appendix C, pp. 112–24.

[219] [1999] 3 WLR 972, HL, at 993–4 *per* Lord Hope of Craighead.

[220] Lord Lester of Herne Hill QC and D. Pannick QC, *Human Rights Law and Practice* (London: Butterworths, 1999), 74, para. 3.21.

Court of Appeal of New Zealand on the New Zealand Bill of Rights Act 1990, and those of the South African Constitutional Court on the rights under South Africa's 1993 and 1996 Constitutions, may all contain useful insights. If one wants to undertake comparative study, the South African Constitutional Court's judgments are particularly helpful to comparative lawyers, as the Constitution expressly requires the court to interpret rights taking account of international human-rights treaties and expressly permits it to take account of the caselaw of other national courts. The judgments therefore often contain valuable accounts of the decisions of international tribunals and of particularly important national courts on relevant human-rights issues. The decisions of courts in other Council of Europe states on constitutional and international human-rights issues may also be very helpful. There is a small but growing English-language literature on fundamental rights in other European jurisdictions.[221]

However, our courts should ensure that they understand the constitutional and legal background to decisions of foreign courts before making use of their judgments, in order to minimize the twin risks of counsel 'cherry-picking' among authorities, and misusing for one purpose ideas developed for a different context or purpose. For example, the caselaw of the United States Supreme Court is often likely to be unhelpful, in view of the very considerable differences between the constitutional structure and heritage of the USA and those of the UK. Again, unlike the UK, many European countries have a monist (rather than dualist) approach to the relationship between municipal and international law, and this can significantly affect the way in which they give effect to human rights, making their reasoning and assumptions inapplicable in the UK. Even when examining decisions from other UK jurisdictions, it will be important to bear in mind that (for example) a decision made in the context of a 'devolution issue' under the Scotland Act 1998, the Northern Ireland Act 1998, or the Government of Wales Act 1998, establishing the legislative competence of a devolved legislature or executive, may not be directly applicable to a case arising out of an alleged violation of a Convention right by an ordinary administrative body or a limited-purpose public authority. This will apply particularly to assessing justifications for interfering with rights, for example under Article 8(2).

(2) THE INTERPRETATION OF LEGISLATION

Section 3 of the Act provides:

'(1)   So far as it is possible to do so, primary legislation and subordinate legislation must be read and given effect in a way which is compatible with the Convention rights.
  (2)   This section—

  (a) applies to primary legislation and secondary legislation whenever enacted;

---

[221] See, e.g. C. Gearty (ed.), *European Civil Liberties and the European Convention on Human Rights: A Comparative Study* (The Hague: Martinus Nijhoff, 1997).

(b) does not affect the validity, continuing operation or enforcement of any incompatible primary legislation; and

(c) does not affect the validity, continuing operation or enforcement of any incompatible subordinate legislation if (disregarding any possibility of revocation) primary legislation prevents removal of the incompatibility.'

In the light of this, it is clear that we cannot now assume there is a single 'right answer' to the question, 'What does a provision in legislation mean?' Instead, there is a range of possible answers, and only those which are not incompatible with Convention rights may normally be adopted.[222] This recognizes the indeterminate nature of language in a more explicit way than has usually been the case, except in relation to EU law. While it will not be proper to treat 'black' as meaning 'white' in order to secure compatibility, a real effort will have to be made to find a tenable interpretation of, or a way of applying, legislation, which is compatible with Convention rights.

This means that the process of interpreting statutes will involve an extra step. After interpreting it according to ordinary principles, the court or tribunal will have to ask whether the result produced is compatible with the Convention rights. If the result is incompatible, it will be necessary to try to re-interpret it to achieve compatibility. The desirability of achieving compatibility will outweigh purposive principles of interpretation. It will not be permissible to use parliamentary debates on a Bill[223] in order to argue against a Convention-compatible interpretation. Purposive interpretation will be permitted only when choosing between meanings which are compatible with the Convention rights. The interpretative duty of courts and tribunals under section 3 is not based on either the presumed intention of the legislature or a need to resolve a textual ambiguity in the legislation. Encouraging courts to be creative in the interpretation and application of Convention rights and legislation which affects them, the 1998 Act may lead to an interpretation of legislation which is directly contrary to that intended by the promoters and drafters of other Acts. Parliament itself has decreed that judges should behave in this way.

It is not yet clear how far courts will be prepared to stretch the natural meaning of statutory language, as distinct from purposive considerations, in order to achieve compatibility. The suggestions which follow should be seen as indicative of possible approaches, rather than as predictions.

---

[222] On this, see Lord Irvine of Lairg LC, 'The Development of Human Rights in Britain' [1998] PL 221–36 at 228; G. Marshall, 'Interpreting Interpretation in the Human Rights Bill' [1998] PL 167–70; M. J. Beloff, 'What Does It All Mean?', in L. Betten (ed.), The Human Rights Act 1998—What It Means (The Hague: Kluwer, 1999), 11–56; Lord Lester of Herne Hill QC, 'The Art of the Possible: Interpreting Statutes under the Human Rights Act' [1998] EHRLR 665; Sir Anthony Hooper, 'The Impact of the Human Rights Act on Judicial Decision-making' [1998] EHRLR 676–86 at 682–3, on reading in words of qualification to other statutes; Sir William Wade QC, 'Human Rights and the Judiciary' [1998] EHRLR 520; G. Marshall, 'Two Kinds of Compatibility: More about Section 3 of the Human Rights Act 1998' [1999] PL 377–83; N. Bamforth, 'The Application of the Human Rights Act 1998 to Public Authorities and Private Bodies' [1999] CLJ 159–70 at 168–70; F. Bennion, 'What Interpretation is "Possible" under Section 3(1) of the Human Rights Act 1998?' [2000] PL 77–91; R. A. Edwards, 'Reading Down Legislation under the Human Rights Act' (2000) 20 LS 353–71.

[223] Pepper v. Hart [1993] AC 593, HL.

First, it is likely that provisions will be 'read down' where necessary to narrow the scope of apparently broadly-expressed powers so as to make them compatible with Convention rights, as in US and Canadian constitutional jurisprudence. *Secondly*, courts are willing to read words into or out of legislation in order to make it comply, as long as it does not involve the court in legislative rather than interpretative activity (the boundary between the two being uncertain at present). The courts already do this in relation to subordinate legislation which would otherwise be incompatible with EU law.[224] *Thirdly*, section 19 of the Human Rights Act 1998 requires a Minister introducing a bill to either House of Parliament to make a statement either that, in the Minister's opinion, the bill is compatible with the Convention rights, or that it is not but the government wishes the House to consider it none the less. Where a court is dealing with an Act of Parliament in relation to which the responsible Minister made a statement of compatibility, it should start from an assumption that the legislation can be interpreted compatible with all Convention rights, in order to give effect to the intention evinced by the statement of compatibility. For this purpose, courts and tribunals should regard themselves as having a wide scope for creative interpretation. This will be a special application of the *Pepper v. Hart* technique.[225] *Fourthly*, the obligation is to 'read and give effect to' the legislation in a compatible manner. In a case where it is not possible to 'read' it in a manner which will guarantee compatibility in all circumstances, one may still be able to 'give effect to' it in order to avoid incompatibility in individual cases. For example, one might use judicial discretion to deploy the available remedies in such a way as to avoid incompatible outcomes whenever possible, even if the words are such as to make it impossible to guarantee that this can always be achieved. This may be useful, in view of the notorious difficulty of predicting how legislation (or interpretations of it) will operate in unforeseen circumstances.

The Convention rights must be applied to pre-Human Rights Act legislation, changing the interpretation of that legislation where necessary. In relation to the judicial interpretation of primary and subordinate legislation, the combination of the interpretation under section 3 of the Act and the principles to be applied in interpreting the Convention rights in the light of Strasbourg caselaw means that all previous decisions are liable to be reconsidered. If a court or tribunal follows earlier authority

---

[224] On the general principles, see R. A. Edwards, 'Reading Down Legislation under the Human Rights Act' (2000) 20 *LS* 353–71; *Poplar Housing and Regeneration Community Association Ltd. v. Donoghue* [2001] 3 WLR 183, CA, at 204–5, paras. 75–7. For practical applications, see *R. v. A. (No. 2)* [2001] 2 WLR 1546, HL, on making protection for complainants in sex cases against humiliating cross-examination under Youth Justice and Criminal Evidence Act 1999, s. 41, compatible with the right to a fair trial under ECHR Art. 6(1); *R. v. Lambert* [2001] 3 WLR 206, HL, holding that it is possible to construe Misuse of Drugs Act 1971, s. 28(2) and (3), as imposing only an evidential burden on defendants to produce evidence that they did not know, suspect, or have reason to suspect that material in their possession was a controlled drug; *R. (Daly) v. Secretary of State for the Home Department* [2001] 2 WLR 1622, HL, on Prison Rules purporting to authorize searches of material subject to legal privilege. On the approach under EC law, see *Pickstone v. Freemans plc* [1989] AC 66, HL (implying words into a statutory instrument) and *Litster v. Forth Dry Dock & Engineering Co. Ltd.* [1990] 1 AC 546, HL (creatively interpreting apparently clear words). Both these cases were decided before *R. v. Secretary of State for Transport, ex parte Factortame Ltd. (No. 2)* [1991] 1 AC 603, CJEC and HL.

[225] For the organized text of the parliamentary debates on the Human Rights Bill, see J. Cooper and A. Marshall Williams, *Legislating for Human Rights: The Parliamentary Debates on the Human Rights Bill* (Oxford: Hart Publishing, 2000).

which produces a Convention-incompatible interpretation of the legislation when it would have been possible to interpret it compatibly, it acts unlawfully. This produces a certain level of instability in the structure of statute law and the operation of *stare decisis*. The caselaw on particular statutes will probably re-stabilize fairly quickly. However, it will always be necessary to keep in mind the possibility that an interpretation initially held to be compatible with a Convention right might subsequently become incompatible because of the dynamic interpretation of Convention rights. If that occurs, later courts will once again come under an obligation to depart from the earlier interpretation. A degree of stability might be retained if the Court of Appeal or House of Lords decides that such reconsideration can be conducted only in courts or tribunals not bound by the first authoritative interpretations under the Act, i.e. subject to normal rules of precedent. However, it is equally possible that such a rule might be incompatible with the evolving Convention rights and so unlawful.[226]

(3) THE IMPACT OF THE ACT ON THE VALIDITY OF LEGISLATION AND ON PARLIAMENTARY SOVEREIGNTY

(i) The validity of primary legislation

The Act protects parliamentary sovereignty by providing that a Convention right 'does not affect the validity, continuing operation or enforcement of any incompatible primary legislation'.[227] It gives a very wide meaning to 'primary legislation', to include, as well as all public general, local and personal, and private Acts of the Westminster Parliament, any Measure of the Church Assembly or the General Synod of the Church of England, any Order in Council made under the Northern Ireland Constitution Act 1973, section 38(1)(a) or section 58(1) of the Northern Ireland Act 1998 relating to council elections, any Order in Council made under the royal prerogative, any Order in Council which amends an Act of Parliament (including some remedial orders made under the Human Rights Act itself), and any order or other instrument which brings primary legislation into force (commencement orders).[228] The Scotland Act 1998, section 29(2), the Government of Wales Act 1998, section 107, and the Northern Ireland Act 1998, section 6(2), provide that the legislative competence of the Scottish Parliament and the Assemblies of Wales and Northern Ireland respectively does not extend to legislation which is incompatible with Convention rights under the Human Rights Act 1998.

The inclusion of Orders in Council made under the royal prerogative in the protected category of 'primary legislation' is comprehensible, in that the power to make them has not been delegated by higher authority. However, in the hierarchy of legal

---

[226] See Sir Anthony Hooper, 'The Impact of the Human Rights Act on Judicial Decision-making' [1998] *EHRLR* 676–86 at 682–3.

[227] Human Rights Act 1998, s.3(2), which similarly protects incompatible subordinate legislation 'if (disregarding any possibility of revocation) primary legislation prevents removal of the incompatibility'.

[228] Human Rights Act 1998, s.21(1). Some remedial orders will amend primary legislation which is not an Act of Parliament, such as Orders in Council under the Royal Prerogative or Orders made under the Northern Ireland legislation, and so will not themselves be primary legislation within the meaning of the Act: *cp.* ss.10 and 6(6)(b).

norms, Orders in Council made under the prerogative rank below Acts of Parliament, despite having an independent source of legal authority. Prerogative powers must not be exercised in ways which are incompatible with the provisions of Acts of Parliament (even those which have not been brought into force).[229] The subordination of pre-rogative law-making powers buttresses the constitutional doctrine of the supremacy of Parliament over the executive, and gives legal expression to an aspect of the consti-tutional convention of the accountability of the executive to Parliament. So far as it is possible to make valid and effective law which defies Convention rights without parliamentary authority and which is immune to judicial review, effective parlia-mentary sovereignty is compromised, rather than protected, by the Act.

Not only should the executive be subordinate to Parliament; the principle of legal-ity, which forms part of the Rule of Law, requires that the executive should be accountable to the courts for the legality of its use of prerogative powers. The subjec-tion of the executive to law, which has been a recurring theme of constitutional thinking since Bracton, was enshrined in the speeches in *R. v Minister for the Civil Service, ex parte Council of Civil Service Unions*,[230] where it was held that the exercise of prerogative powers was to be regarded, for the purposes of judicial review, as being on the same footing as the exercise of delegated powers, subject to the operation of the doctrine of justiciability. The Human Rights Act 1998, by treating prerogative law-making powers as giving rise to primary legislation, denies the beneficial effect of that decision to people whose Convention rights are violated by an exercise of such a power. The House of Lords' decision will continue to apply in other litigation, such as judicial review and collateral challenges in criminal courts, where the ground of attack is not incompatible with a Convention right. It is hard to see why legislation made under the prerogative should be liable to be quashed on judicial review, save only where its unlawfulness consists of the violation of a Convention right. It is even more absurd to treat as primary legislation statutory instruments made under the authority of the Northern Ireland Constitution Act 1973, section 38(1)(a) and section 58(1) of the Northern Ireland Act 1998. These instruments are not in any real sense 'primary'. When legislation by the Northern Ireland Assembly counts as subordinate legislation for the purposes of the Human Rights Act 1998,[231] it looks odd for statutory instru-ments made for Northern Ireland by the Secretary of State to be treated as primary legislation especially as they were intended to allow the Secretary of State to protect minorities against gerrymandering.

(ii) The validity of subordinate legislation

Although the Act does not say so expressly, subordinate legislation, as defined in section 21(1) of the Act, is invalid and ineffective to the extent that it cannot be inter-preted so as to be compatible with any Convention right, unless primary legislation

---

[229] *R. v. Secretary of State for the Home Department, ex parte Fire Brigades Union* [1995] 2 All ER 244, HL (Lords Browne-Wilkinson, Lloyd, and Nicholls; Lords Keith and Mustill dissenting). On the implications of the wide meaning of 'primary legislation' in the Human Rights Act 1998, see P. Billings and B. Pontin, 'Prerogative Powers and the Human Rights Act: Elevating the Status of Orders in Council' [2001] *PL* 21–7.

[230] [1985] AC 374, HL.

[231] See sub-paras. (c)–(e) of the definition of 'subordinate legislation' in the Human Rights Act 1998, s. 21(1).

makes removal of the incompatibility impossible. This is clear from section 3(2)(c), which provides that the duty to read and give effect to legislation in a way which is compatible with Convention rights

'does not affect the validity, continuing operation or enforcement of any incompatible subordinate legislation if (disregarding any possibility of revocation) primary legislation prevents the removal of the incompatibility.'

It is also clear that a public authority making a piece of subordinate legislation which is incompatible with a Convention right acts unlawfully by virtue of section 6(1). For this reason, it is possible for section 10(4) to refer to a 'provision . . . in subordinate legislation' which 'has been quashed, or declared invalid, by reason of incompatibility with a Convention right'. This does not mean that officials and others who act in good faith in reliance on an apparently valid piece of subordinate legislation will be liable in damages to people affected by their actions if the provision is later held to be invalid because of an incompatibility with a Convention right. There is doubt about the extent to which a person may be entitled to protection when relying on a law which appears on its face to be valid but turns out to be vitiated by an underlying flaw. The importance of upholding Convention rights might be expected to cause courts to lean towards more or less absolute liability (at least on public authorities) to compensate victims of violations in these circumstances. In the past the courts have not categorically ruled out the possibility that invalid laws might nevertheless have some capacity to immunize people against liability for acting in reliance on them. For example, in *Percy v. Hall*[232] the Court of Appeal held that officers who had arrested a person in the reasonable belief that she had committed an offence under a bye-law which turned out to be invalid were not liable to pay damages for false arrest. On the other hand, the basic common-law principle is that a person whose rights are infringed by a public authority is entitled to compensation, unless the authority can establish a lawful justification. Where a detention extends beyond the period authorized, and there is no express court order for continued detention which protects the detainor, the prisoner has a right to compensation for false imprisonment.[233] This is particularly important where the liberty of the subject is at stake, but the principle applies more generally.[234] The application of the principle in the context of the Human Rights Act issue will probably have to be established at an early stage.

(iii) Declarations of incompatibility, adverse rulings in Strasbourg, and remedial orders

Although the judiciary has no power to strike down primary legislation which cannot be interpreted so as to be compatible with the Convention rights, a superior court

---

[232] [1997] QB 924, CA. See also *Olotu v. Home Office* [1997] 1 WLR 328, CA (custody time limit expired, but prison governor who continued to detain person pending a court order for release was acting lawfully in reliance on previous court order authorizing detention).

[233] *R. v. Governor of Brockhill Prison, ex parte Evans (No. 2)* [2000] 3 WLR 843, HL.

[234] *Eshugbayi Eleko v. Officer Administering the Government of Nigeria* [1931] AC 662, PC, at 670 *per* Lord Atkin; *Boddington v. British Transport Police* [1999] 2 AC 143, esp. at 173 *per* Lord Steyn. See generally A. W. Bradley, R. Allen QC, and P. Sales, 'The Impact of the Human Rights Act 1998 upon Subordinate Legislation Promulgated before October 2, 2000' [2000] *PL* 358–67.

which concludes that the legislation is incompatible may grant a declaration of incompatibility, after inviting the Crown (in the person of the responsible Minister, Department, or executive) to intervene in the proceedings.[235] This entails a certain element of judicial review of an Act of Parliament, albeit lacking real remedial teeth.[236]

The capacity to grant a declaration of incompatibility subtly alters the allocation of powers. For the first time, Parliament has invited the judges to tell it that it has acted wrongly by legislating incompatibly with a Convention right. The wrong which a court declares in a declaration of incompatibility relating to an Act of Parliament appears to be a non-legal wrong. Making such a declaration takes the judges into a new field. The standards which they will apply (the Convention rights) are part of national law, but judges will not be behaving straightforwardly as adjudicators of legal wrongs.

Where a court makes a declaration of incompatibility, it operates as a formal invitation to the relevant Minister and Parliament to reconsider the incompatible legislation. The Minister may do nothing, probably triggering an application to the European Court of Human Rights. The incompatible primary legislation may be amended, by introducing a Bill to Parliament if it is in the form of an Act, or by other means if it takes another form, with or without compensation for earlier victims of the violation. Alternatively, in limited circumstances, the Minister may make a 'remedial order' under section 10 of and Schedule 2 to the Act, except in respect of a Measure of the Church Assembly or General Synod of the Church of England.[237] Such so-called 'Henry VIII' provisions are constitutionally questionable, because of the oddity of a legislative instrument being amended by another instrument which ranks lower in the hierarchy of legal norms. They allow the executive to usurp the legislative authority of Parliament and turn it against Parliament, weakening the democratic protection for people's rights. Remedial orders under the Human Rights Act do not represent a major threat, since the power is capable of being invoked only to protect rights, not to interfere with them.[238] The provisions of the Act limit the risk that Ministers will use them for improper ends, and maximize the opportunity for parliamentary scrutiny. A Minister may make such an order only when any available appeal against the declaration of incompatibility has been concluded or abandoned, and the Minister considers that there are compelling reasons for making a remedial order rather than introducing a Bill to Parliament.[239] The procedure was envisaged as a fast-track method of rectifying a violation.[240] However, except in cases of urgency, the process of making a remedial order is long drawn out and ensures that Parliament has the opportunity to scrutinize fully the draft Order and the reasons for making it.

[235] Human Rights Act 1998, ss. 4, 5.

[236] On the impact on parliamentary sovereignty and the effectiveness of a declaration of incompatibility as a remedy, see D. Feldman, 'The Human Rights Act 1998 and Constitutional Principles' (1999) 19 *Legal Studies* at 186–7; I. Leigh and L. Lustgarten, 'Making Rights Real: The Courts, Remedies and the Human Rights Act' [1999] *CLJ* 509–45, esp. at 536–42.

[237] Human Rights Act 1998, s. 10(6).

[238] See Lord Irvine, introducing the Second Reading debate in the House of Lords *Official Report*, 3 November 1997, vol. 582, col. 1231.

[239] Human Rights Act 1998, s. 10(2).

[240] *Rights Brought Home*, para. 2.18.

Initially, a document must be laid before Parliament containing an explanation of the incompatibility which the draft Order seeks to remove; details of the relevant declaration of incompatibility or finding of the European Court of Human Rights; a statement of the reasons for seeking to make a remedial order and for adopting the terms proposed for the Order; and a draft of the proposed Order.[241] After sixty days from the day on which the document was first laid, the Minister must lay a draft of the Order before Parliament. If representations were made (including any relevant parliamentary report or resolution,[242] such as a report from the Joint Committee on Statutory Instruments or the Joint Human Rights Committee) in relation to the original document, the draft Order must be accompanied by a summary of the representations, and a statement of any changes introduced to the draft as a result.[243] The order may not be made unless the draft has first been approved by resolution of each House within sixty days of having been laid.

In urgent cases, the Order may be made immediately if it declares that 'it appears to the person making it that, because of the urgency of the matter, it is necessary to make the order without a draft being so approved'.[244] The Order must then be laid before Parliament, together with the information which in ordinary cases is required to be laid sixty days before laying a draft Order. If, within sixty days of laying the Order before Parliament, representations are received, the person who made the Order must (after the end of the sixty day period) lay before Parliament a statement summarizing the representations and giving details of any changes which he or she proposes to make to the Order as a result of them. If there are such changes, the person must make a new remedial order and lay the replacement Order before Parliament. The original and any replacement Order cease to have effect unless approved by a resolution of each House within 120 days beginning with the day on which the original order was made.[245]

In view of these constraints, remedial orders following declarations of incompatibility are likely to be very rare. The first proposal for a draft remedial order was laid before Parliament in July 2001 to amend sections 72 and 73 of the Mental Health Act 1998 following a declaration granted on 28 March 2001 in *R. (H.) v. Mental Health Review Tribunal North and East London Region (Secretary of State for Health intervening)*[245a] that placing the burden on a patient to establish that the conditions for detention were no longer fulfilled was incompatible with ECHR Article 5. It will usually be possible for courts to avoid making a declaration of incompatibility by interpreting the legislation compatibly with Convention rights, pursuant to the duty imposed by section 3 of the 1998 Act. If that proves impossible, and a declaration of incompatibility is made, the government will usually find it quicker and simpler to amend the offending legislation by way of a single-clause Bill than to embark on the complex and time-consuming process of making a remedial order. For these reasons, remedial orders are most likely

---

[241] Human Rights Act 1998, Sch. 2, paras. 3(1)(a) and 5.
[242] Human Right Act 1998, Sch. 2, para. 5.
[243] Ibid., Sch. 2, paras. 2(a), 3(2).
[244] Ibid., Sch. 2, para. 2(b).
[245] Ibid., Sch. 2, para. 4.
[245a] [2001] 3 WLR 512, CA.

to be used to amend Acts of Parliament where, for example, the liberty of the individual is at stake, so that the urgent procedure can be used.

There is another situation in which a Minister may make a remedial order. Where the European Court of Human Rights has made a decision in proceedings against the UK in the light of which it appears that a legislative provision 'is incompatible with an obligation of the United Kingdom arising from the Convention',[246] a remedial order can be made. In this case, the order need not relate to an incompatibility with one of the Convention rights which is included in the 1998 Act, or to an interpretation of the Convention right which has been accepted by a court in the UK. For example, the remedial order may amend an Act of Parliament in order to remove an incompatibility with Article 13 of the Convention (the right to an effective remedy from a national authority for violations of other Convention rights), which binds the UK in international law but is not one of the rights incorporated in the 1998 Act. Alternatively, it may amend the law to remove a violation of a substantive right (such as the right to respect for private life under Article 8) as interpreted by the Strasbourg court, which would not amount to a violation of the right as interpreted by national courts. This use of a remedial order to amend a statute in order to give effect to an obligation of the state in international law, which goes beyond its obligations in national law, is a novel constitutional step outside the context of European Community law.[247]

(iv) Making legislation: the duties of Ministers and Parliament

Because primary legislation is valid notwithstanding any incompatibility with a Convention right, legislators have a heavy responsibility to give proper consideration to issues of compatibility. In relation to a Bill introduced to Parliament, section 19 of the 1998 Act requires the Minister in charge of the Bill to state either that in his view the Bill is compatible with the Convention rights (a 'statement of compatibility' under section 19(1)(a)), or that he is unable to make a statement of compatibility but that nevertheless the government (not the individual Minister) wishes the House to proceed with the Bill (under section 19(1)(b)). The statement must be in writing, and must be published 'in such manner as the Minister making it considers appropriate'. The method which is employed is to include the statement on the front cover of the printed version of every Bill. This focuses the Minister's and the drafter's minds, and Parliament's attention, on Convention rights. Where (in the light of appropriate advice) it is impossible to make a statement of compatibility, section 19(1) makes it clear that the government is collectively responsible for the serious step of inviting the House to proceed with a Bill which probably violates a Convention right. The statement may also guide courts or tribunals which have to decide how strenuously to seek an interpretation of the provisions which is compatible with Convention rights. A more rights-centred interpretation will be justified where the Minister has made a statement of compatibility than where Parliament has proceeded having recognized the likelihood of incompatibility, although the court need not accept the correctness of the Minister's view.

---

[246] Ibid., s. 10(1)(b).

[247] In relation to EC law, see the power granted by European Communities Act 1972, s. 2(2) and (4), and Sch. 2.

Parliament has established a new Joint Select Committee, which has taken responsibility for reviewing Bills for compatibility with the Convention and for reporting to
both Houses in time for its views to be taken into account, as contemplated in the White
Paper, *Rights Brought Home*.[248] In the Second Reading debate in the House of Lords the
Lord Chancellor said that the government had 'given very positive thought to' and was
'attracted to the idea of a parliamentary committee on human rights, whether a separate committee of each House or a joint committee of both Houses' which could keep
the protection of human rights under review, contribute to public education and
promoting a human rights culture, receive written submissions and hold meetings
across the country. This was preferred to the establishment of a Human Rights Commission.[249] It could also keep under review the effectiveness of the remedies provided
under section 8 of the Act.[250] The government also promised improved procedures
for pre-vetting legislation in draft, and new guidelines to Departments.[251] Since then,
the government has also agreed that Ministers will make statements in relation to the
Convention-rights compatibility of statutory instruments which are subject to the
affirmative resolution procedure. This informal arrangement does not apply systematically to private Members' Bills and private Bills. (The latter lacuna offered a ground
for some MPs to block all private Bills during the 1999–2000 session.) However, a
compromise has been worked out whereby the Minister whose departmental responsibilities are closest to the subject-matter of the Bill will make a statement, at a convenient
time, giving a view as to the compatibility of the Bill with Convention rights.

There is a particularly pressing need to improve the pre-legislative and legislative
scrutiny of other measures which count as primary legislation for the purposes of the
1998 Act, since they are all valid notwithstanding any incompatibility with a Convention right: Orders in Council under the royal prerogative, Measures of the Church
Assembly and the General Synod of the Church of England, Orders in Council made
under the Northern Ireland Constitution Act 1973, section 38(1)(a) and equivalent
provisions under the Northern Ireland Act 1998, commencement orders, and orders
made under 'Henry VIII' clauses other than remedial orders made under the Human
Rights Act itself (which are dealt with under Schedule 2).

(4) DUTIES AND REMEDIES[252]

This section is concerned with the scope of duties and remedies under the Human
Rights Act 1998. It considers (i) the range of people who are subject to duties under the

---

[248] Paras. 3.6–3.7.

[249] House of Lords *Official Report*, 3 November 1997, vol. 582, col. 1234. There is, however, a Human
Rights Commission for Northern Ireland, established under the Northern Ireland Act 1998, and the Scottish
Parliament may soon establish one.

[250] House of Lords *Official Report*, 18 November 1997, vol. 583, col. 476, Lord Irvine during the committee
stage. On its early work, see D. Feldman, 'Whitehall, Westminster and Human Rights' (2001) 21(3) *Pub.
Money & Management*, 19–24.

[251] *Rights Brought Home*, paras. 3.4–3.5.

[252] See I. Leigh and L. Lustgarten, 'Making Rights Real: the Courts, Remedies, and the Human Rights Act'
[1999] *CLJ* 509–45; D. Feldman, 'Remedies for Violations of Convention Rights under the Human Rights
Act' [1998] *EHRLR* 691–711; D. McGoldrick, 'The United Kingdom's Human Rights Act 1998 in Theory
and Practice' (2001) 50 *ICLQ*, 901–53.

Act, (ii) those who can enforce rights under the Act, (iii) the scope for intervention by third parties to litigation involving Convention rights, (iv) the circumstances in which the rights can be asserted, and (v) the types of remedies for which the Act provides.

(i) Those subject to Convention rights: 'public authorities'

Under the Act, the primary focus of the Convention rights is on public authorities. Section 6(1) provides:

'It is unlawful for a public authority to act in a way which is incompatible with a Convention right.'

However, section 6(2) provides that it is not unlawful for a public authority to act incompatibly with a Convention right if '(a) as the result of one or more provisions of primary legislation, the authority could not have acted differently; or (b) in the case of one or more provisions of, or made under, primary legislation which cannot be read or given effect in a way which is compatible with the Convention rights, the authority was acting so as to give effect to or enforce those provisions'. This protects parliamentary sovereignty, and particularly the capacity of Parliament to legislate to violate Convention rights so long as it does so clearly and unambiguously. If it is possible to exercise a discretion in a manner compatible with Convention rights, it is unlawful to choose a way of exercising it which is incompatible in its effect. Only if primary legislation, which cannot be interpreted under section 3 to allow compatible action, prevents any other outcome will it be lawful to act incompatibly.

By virtue of section 6(6), 'act' normally includes 'omission' for the purpose of the duty under section 6(1). However, it was desired to protect parliamentary sovereignty by avoiding the imposition of a legally enforceable duty to make or amend primary legislation. Section 6(6) therefore provides that 'a failure to (a) introduce in, or lay before, Parliament a proposal for legislation; or (b) make any primary legislation or remedial order' is not an unlawful act for the purpose of grounding liability under section 6(1).

As section 6(1) imposes legal duties only on a 'public authority', it is important to know which people or bodies fall into that category. However, the Act does not define the term exhaustively. Indeed, during the Bill's passage through Parliament, the government successfully opposed amendments seeking to include an exhaustive definition. Instead, the Act works on the assumption that some bodies are so clearly public authorities that they do not need to be identified, and nothing is said about them. It is reasonable to suppose that such bodies include, for example, government departments, local authorities, the police, Inland Revenue Commissioners, and Customs and Excise Commissioners, which have no private rights or functions. Ignoring them, the Act contents itself with making special provision for three kinds of bodies. *First*, section 6(3)(a) specifies that every court or tribunal is a public authority. They are therefore subject to all the duties which flow from section 6(1), with consequences of uncertain effect, some of which are discussed below. *Secondly*, there are people and bodies which do not obviously fall into the category of public authorities, but which have a mix of public functions and private concerns. Under section 6(3)(b), as limited by section 6(5), these are public authorities, and so subject to the duty to comply with

Convention rights, but not in relation to acts of a private nature. *Thirdly*, in order to protect both parliamentary privilege and parliamentary sovereignty, sub-sections (3) and (4) of section 6 provide that the two Houses of Parliament, and persons exercising functions in connection with proceedings in Parliament, despite being archetypally public in their nature and functions, are not public authorities for the purpose of section 6, other than the House of Lords acting in a judicial capacity.

The term 'public authority' will have to be settled by judicial decisions on a case-by-case basis. During the committee stage in the House of Lords, Lord Irvine LC and Lord Lester appeared to think that the caselaw on judicial review would not be directly in point, but that courts would build up principles on a case-by-case basis as they had already done in relation to judicial review.[253] In the House of Commons, the Home Secretary, Mr. Straw, took the view that the Strasbourg caselaw would provide a minimum line, and other bodies which are subject to judicial review in the UK on the principles established in cases such as *R. v. Panel on Take-overs and Mergers, ex parte Datafin plc*[254] would also be subject to the obligation to comply with Convention rights. In practice, the Strasbourg caselaw on this point is unlikely to be very helpful. Before the Strasbourg organs, the only possible respondent is the state. Even when a state is held to have a positive obligation to protect somebody's Convention right by compelling someone else to act in a certain way, the issue is whether the responsibility of the state is engaged, not whether a particular person or body within the state is bound by the right. In relation to the caselaw on judicial review, Mr. Straw said, 'It is not easily summarized and could not have been simply written into the Bill, but the concepts are reasonably clear and I think that we can build on them'.[255] This is probably true. In addition, the caselaw of the Court of Justice of the European Community developing the doctrine in Case C188/89 *Foster v. British Gas plc*,[256] imposing liability on 'emanations of the state' for non-compliance with unimplemented Directives, is likely to be useful.

The 'limited-purpose' public authorities under section 6(3)(b) may encompass people and institutions which are not subject to judicial review, such as religious groups and private schools, if they are held to exercise public functions. The Court of Appeal has held that a private housing association is exercising public functions, and so is a public authority for the purposes of the 1998 Act, when it operates under an arrangement with a local authority under which it effectively stands in the shoes of the authority, although in its other functions it would not be a public authority. Being a charity does not make a body a public authority; there must be something about a particular function which puts a public stamp on the activity, as in relation to the question whether a body is amenable to judicial review.[257] Indicators of publicness

---

[253] House of Lords *Official Report*, 24 November 1997, vol. 583, cols. 784 and 796 (Lord Irvine) and 792–3 (Lord Lester).

[254] [1987] QB 815, CA.

[255] House of Commons *Official Report*, 17 June 1998, vol. 314, cols. 406–9.

[256] [1991] 1 QB 405, CJEC, [1991] 2 AC 306, HL.

[257] *Poplar Housing and Regeneration Community Association Ltd. v. Donoghue* [2001] 3 WLR 183, CA, at 198–202, paras. 55–66. *Cp. R. (Heather) v. Leonard Cheshire Foundation and AG* [2001] EWHC Admin 429. See N. Bamforth, 'The Application of the Human Rights Act 1998 to Public Authorities and Private Bodies' [1999] *CLJ* 159–70; D. Oliver, 'The Frontiers of the State: Public Authorities and Public Functions under the Human Rights Act' [2000] *PL* 476–93.

might include being established under statute or royal charter, receiving money from public funds, having activities controlled (or perhaps merely monitored) by state bodies, and providing services which allow clients or customers to secure their legal (including Convention) rights. It is hard to predict how far this will extend, but any solution is likely to raise tricky problems, as a few examples will demonstrate.

- Private schools might be held to exercise public functions in respect of the education of their pupils, as in the classroom they are substituting for the state's function in securing to everyone the right to education which arises both under Protocol 1, Article 2 of the ECHR and under statute. While the schools will have private functions as well (for example, in relation to their contractual relations with parents), and all or most of a school's funds might come from private sources, the education delivered will have to meet standards provided by a statutory regime, and schools may be subject to requirements for registration and regulation. On balance, will this make private schools limited-purpose public authorities, bound to respect pupils' Convention rights, for instance in respect of disciplinary matters and free expression?

- Are universities public authorities? They discharge functions in relation to education. Most of them receive public funds, although some receive less than half their income in that way. They are established under royal charter or statute and are extensively regulated and monitored by the state. On the other hand, they have many students who are not funded by the state at all, derive a very large proportion of their income from commercial sources, enter into contracts with their students, provide a range of services (including accommodation, leisure, and catering facilities) on something approaching a commercial basis, and exercise no authority over anyone except when conferring degrees and maintaining student and staff discipline. It seems that they should be limited-purpose public authorities, but how easy will it be to distinguish their public functions from their private acts?

- Is the BBC a public authority? It is established under royal charter, and is funded largely from the licence fee, which is a form of tax. It is structurally independent of government, but its Governors are appointed by government. It is generally less regulated under statute than the commercial broadcasters, but has no commercial or private interests of its own. It looks like a public authority, either all-purpose or limited-purpose, making it directly subject to all the Convention rights, including freedom of expression and the right to respect for private life.

- Is Independent Television News (ITN) a public authority? It is a commercial organization, with shareholders and a profit motive. On the other hand, the grant of licences to commercial broadcasters is subject to extensive statutory controls in the public interest, and is performed by regulatory bodies (the Independent Television Commission and the Radio Authority) which apply statutory criteria going beyond the purely commercial when assessing bids and evaluating performance. It would be strange if the BBC is a public authority, and subject to privacy-related rights under the Human Rights Act 1998, but ITN is not. Does one's right against the news media depend on which arm of the media happens to be invading one's privacy?

- Are the proprietors of newspapers public authorities, bound by Convention rights? At first sight they look private and commercial, receiving little or no public funding and being subject to little or no state control. However, the press has regularly claimed special status because of its role in fostering free speech and providing the conditions necessary for democracy. It has even established a right to a qualified legal privilege against liability for defamation on this basis.[258] Would it be consistent for courts to accept that the private press is performing functions of such public importance as to justify giving them legal privileges denied to others when informing the public and investigating allegations of sleaze in public life, yet treat them as wholly private bodies when it comes to the application of Convention rights? In order to treat the press consistently, recognize their public importance, and avoid a situation in which it is possible for someone to assert a privacy-related right against the BBC under the Act but see a newspaper publish the offending material with impunity, it would make a great deal of sense to treat all the media of public information and opinion as being at least limited-purpose public authorities.

- Turning to courts and tribunals, which are certainly all-purpose public authorities, we face problems about the scope of the duties which flow from their status. They certainly have a duty under section 3 of the Act to re-interpret legislation if necessary so as to read and give effect to it in a Convention-compatible manner so far as possible. They also clearly have a duty to apply the Convention rights to other public authorities in the course of litigation. But how far are they obliged to ensure that their acts and omissions are Convention-compatible in litigation between two private parties? If they are required to do so, the legal relations between private parties will be affected by Convention rights, not because the parties themselves are bound by them, but because one or both of the parties have Convention rights against the court or tribunal which indirectly influence the outcome of the litigation. Yet the general scheme of the Act, imposing duties primarily on public authorities, is to make the rights operate 'vertically', governing relationships between bodies performing state functions and private persons. To what extent will the recognition that courts and tribunals are public authorities, and so bound by the Convention rights, allow the rights to operate between private persons, having what is known as 'horizontal effect'? This matter is considered further below, in sub-section (iv).

Only time will give us answers to these questions.

(ii) Who may rely on the Convention rights?

Section 7 of the Act provides that only a person claiming to the *victim* of a violation will be entitled to claim that a public authority has acted, or is about to act, unlawfully (within the meaning of section 6(1) of the Act) by reason of the violation in any

---

[258] *Reynolds v. Times Newspapers Ltd.* [1999] 3 WLR 1010, HL; *R. v. Secretary of State for the Home Department, ex parte Simms* [2000] AC 115, HL; *McCartan Turkington Breen (a firm) v. Times Newspapers Ltd. (Northern Ireland)* [2000] 3 WLR 1670, HL.

proceedings in which this is relevant. By virtue of section 7(1), (3), (4), and (7), 'victim' has a special meaning. A person is a victim only if he or she would be so regarded under the ECHR, Article 34, so as to be able to initiate proceedings in Strasbourg. The scope of standing under Article 34 has been described above, in section 2.3. The standing rules are a rare example of a matter in the caselaw of the Strasbourg organs dictating domestic law under the Act, rather than merely having to be taken into account by our courts. The rules on standing in Strasbourg are relatively generous in allowing indirect victims, prospective victims, non-governmental organizations and unincorporated associations and groups to bring proceedings as long as they are or would be prejudicially affected by the alleged violation. However, a person or body who or which has not suffered or been under threat of injury as a result of the alleged violation is not entitled to apply under Article 34. It follows that an interest group which is not itself a victim is not permitted to litigate alleged violations of Convention rights. In this respect, the 'victim' test is more restrictive than the test for standing to claim judicial review under CPR Part 54, where the requirement for the applicant to have a 'sufficient interest in the matter to which the application relates' under section 31 of the Supreme Court Act 1981 has been interpreted as allowing representative and interest-group litigation in suitable cases. This may prevent important human-rights issues being litigated, where the victim is not in a position to litigate effectively because of poverty, lack of legal aid, ignorance, or economic or social pressure brought to bear by those responsible for violations.[259]

(iii) Third-party interventions

Although the 'victim' test prevents non-victims from instituting litigation to vindicate other people's Convention rights, Part 54, rule 17 of the Civil Procedure Rules now makes express provision for third-party interventions in judicial review proceedings, including issues relating to Convention rights, which have been properly commenced by a victim. Nothing similar applies in other proceedings (civil or criminal) in which Convention rights issues arise. There is also provision in section 5 of the Act for the Crown to intervene in any proceedings where a court is considering making a declaration of incompatibility. The Court must inform the Attorney-General, and allow time for him to decide whether or not to make submissions.

(iv) When and how may the Convention rights be used? Offence, defence, and horizontal effect

Whenever litigation depends on the interpretation of legislation, the court's duty to read or give effect to it, so far as possible, in a manner compatible with Convention rights will make the rights a relevant consideration, even in private proceedings. It might be argued that the court's interpretative duty should not be invoked where neither party is entitled to rely on the Convention rights against another party. However, this would have the chaotic result that legislation would mean one thing in

---

[259] See J. Marriott and D. Nicol, 'The Human Rights Act, Representative Standing and the Victim Culture' [1998] *EHRLR* 730–41; J. Miles, 'Standing under the Human Rights Act 1998: Theories of Rights Enforcement and the Nature of Public Law Adjudication' [2000] *CLJ* 133–67.

litigation involving a public authority and a victim, and something different in other litigation. Courts should not allow a situation to develop in which people's rights and obligations under legislation vary according to the type of party with whom they are dealing, or (worse) the type of litigation in which one might become engaged to protect those rights.

Furthermore, section 3(2) makes it clear that the interpretative provisions of the Act apply to primary and subordinate legislation whether enacted or made before or after 2 October 2000. As a result, some subordinate legislation which was perfectly valid up until that date, but which is incompatible with a Convention right, became invalid on that date.

The Convention rights took effect to restrict the legislative competence of the Scottish Parliament, the Northern Ireland Assembly, and the Welsh Assembly, and the powers of the Northern Ireland and Scottish Executives, from the time at which they began to operate, despite the fact that this was well before the Act comes into force.[260] A majority of the House of Lords held in *R. v. Lambert*[260a] that a person lawfully convicted of an offence before the Human Rights Act 1998 came into force could not rely on a Convention right to impugn the conviction in an appeal heard after the Act came into force. This is a pragmatically convenient answer, although (as Lord Steyn pointed out in his dissenting speech) it is hard to reconcile with the clear words of the statute and the obligation on the courts, as public authorities, to act compatibly with Convention rights after 2 October 2000 unless compelled by clear words in primary legislation to do otherwise.

In other contexts, a person's ability to rely on a Convention right depends on whether it is relied on as a sword or a shield. Section 7(1)(a) provides a cause of action to victims in respect of acts committed on or after 2 October 2000 which are unlawful by reason of an incompatibility with a Convention right. Sections 7(1)(b) and 22(4) allow a violation by a public authority of a Convention right to be used as a defence in litigation (civil or criminal) instigated by a public authority, 'whenever the act in question took place'. This allows the defendant to argue that a decision, rule, or action made or taken by a public authority, which forms the basis for a prosecution or civil action, is unlawful by virtue of section 6(1) of the Act, thus undermining the proceedings, even if it was made or taken, and the proceedings commenced, before the Act comes into force. Where a litigant intends to use the Convention rights as a sword rather than a shield, section 7(5) requires that the proceedings must be commenced within one year (if no shorter time limit is otherwise specified for those proceedings), although the court or tribunal may allow a longer period if it considers it 'just and equitable having regard to all the circumstances'. The one-year time limit for ordinary civil litigation to assert Convention rights is longer than the six months permitted for applicants to commence proceedings in Strasbourg, and the three months allowed to applicants for judicial review, but significantly shorter than the normal limitation periods of three, six, and twelve years for litigation in tort, contract, and real property

---

[260] See Scotland Act 1998, ss. 29(2), 57, Northern Ireland Act 1998, ss. 6, 24, and Government of Wales Act 1998, s. 107.

[260a] [2001] 3 WLR 206, HL. See also *Pearce v. Governing Body of Mayfield School, The Times*, 9 October 2001, CA.

matters respectively. The period of a year was arrived at as a compromise between the importance of Convention rights and the public interest in certainty and finality in the work of public authorities.

The question was raised earlier of the capacity of the Convention rights to affect legal relationships between purely private parties, having what is sometimes called 'horizontal effect'. This might stem from the duty of courts and tribunals under section 6(1), as public authorities, to act in a manner compatible with Convention rights. For instance, it might be argued that the obligation of the court or tribunal as a public authority to respect the party's private life under Article 8 requires it to give a remedy for invasion of privacy as such against another private party, perhaps by developing liability for private nuisance beyond its current scope as a protection for property interests, notwithstanding the fact that the other private party does not act unlawfully by virtue of section 6 of the Act in invading the first party's privacy. For example, the right to respect for private life and the home under Article 8 of the ECHR might be held to demand adequate protection from public authorities against harassment. If this cannot be done under the law of trespass or nuisance as it is currently formulated, it might make it necessary to develop private law to provide the appropriate level of legal protection. For this purpose, courts might have to reconsider the majority decision of the House of Lords in *Hunter v. Canary Wharf Ltd.*[261] that the law of private nuisance protects only people whose property rights are infringed, not the rights of mere licensees to quiet occupation of their homes. It is strongly arguable that this violates the Article 8 rights of those who are licensees of their homes and suffer harassment for which the law provides inadequate redress.

However, the idea that Convention rights have such an effect on private law is controversial. It is clear that the rights do not directly bind private persons and bodies, a process known in German law as '*drittwirkung*'. The Act itself makes it clear that the rights are to have some effects on private relationships, both by way of the court's interpretative duty under section 3 and as a result of the detailed provisions of section 12 concerning remedies in cases involving the press. Beyond that, it has been suggested that the duty of courts in private proceedings is limited to securing due-process rights such as those under Articles 5, 6, and 7 of the ECHR.[262] But this is hard to sustain. Section 6 of the Act, in making courts and tribunals public authorities, does not restrict the Convention rights with which they must act compatibly. Accordingly, Professor Sir William Wade has argued[263] that courts must give effect to all rights in all proceedings (unless otherwise provided by primary legislation which cannot be interpreted so as to allow compatible action). This would produce very wide horizontal effect. On the other hand, it has been powerfully argued that the rights should not be applied systematically to private parties in private proceedings. Sir Richard Buxton[264] has pointed out that the rights in the ECHR bind only states in international law, and

[261] [1997] AC 665, HL, overruling *Khorasandjian v. Bush* [1993] QB 727, CA.

[262] S. Kentridge QC, 'The Incorporation of the European Convention on Human Rights', in University of Cambridge Centre for Public Law (ed.), *Constitutional Reform in the United Kingdom: Practice and Principles* (Oxford: Hart Publishing, 1998), 69–71.

[263] Sir William Wade QC, 'Human Rights and the Judiciary' [1998] *EHRLR* 520–533 at 524 ff.

[264] Sir Richard Buxton, 'The Human Rights Act and Private Law' (2000) 116 *LQR* 48–65.

argues that applying them against private individuals in municipal law would alter the content of the rights in a way for which the Act gives no authorization. He suggests that the duty of courts under section 6 of the Act is only to give effect to rights against parties who would be regarded in Strasbourg as falling within the responsibility of the state, i.e. public authorities. However, this seems to assume that the nature of the obligation and the person or body subject to it are inseparably interdependent. While the nature of a body will influence the rights which it can have and the obligations to which it is subject, the nature of the body and the substance of the rights are conceptually distinct.

These positions lie at opposite ends of a spectrum of views. Other authors occupy the middle ground, often on the basis of extensive comparative research.[265] One plausible view is that the substantive law will be relatively unaffected, not least because it will be difficult, if not impossible, to frame a claim against a private person in terms of the duty owed by the court at trial, rather than basing it on breach of a legal duty owed by the defendant. On the other hand, a court which is considering granting a remedy in any case might well be required to ensure that any order it makes respects the Convention rights of the parties, producing a type of 'remedial horizontality'.[266] If the Convention rights have an effect on substantive private law, it may be most marked where the Article concerned is interpreted as giving rise to positive obligations on the state to assist people seeking to protect the right. The obligation on the court, as a public authority, is likely to be more far-reaching in such circumstances than where the ECHR imposes merely a negative obligation on the state to refrain from interfering with someone's freedom. Whether this makes it possible for courts to develop a private-law tort of invasion of privacy on the back of Article 8 of the ECHR, as some have suggested,[267] and whether it would in any event be desirable, remains open to argument.[268]

(v) Remedies: section 8 of the Act

Article 13 of the ECHR confers a right to an effective remedy before a national authority for a violation of a Convention right. This is not one of the Convention rights listed in section 1 of the Act. However, the Lord Chancellor explained during the Committee stage in the House of Lords that one reason for the omission is that the remedial provisions of the Act, particularly section 8, meet the requirements of Article 13, allowing courts to provide effective remedies for violations of the Convention rights.[269] Section 8(1) provides:

[265] For an excellent comparative study, see M. Hunt, 'The "Horizontal Effect" of the Human Rights Act' [1998] *PL* 423–43.

[266] See I. Leigh, 'Horizontal Rights, the Human Rights Act and Privacy: Lessons from the Commonwealth?' (1999) **48** *ICLQ* 57–87.

[267] See R. Singh, 'Privacy and the Media after the Human Rights Act' [1998] *EHRLR* 712–29; cp. Leigh, *op. cit.*, n. 266 above; G. Phillipson and H. Fenwick, 'Breach of Confidence as a Privacy Remedy in the Human Rights Act Era' (2000) **63** *MLR* 660–93.

[268] See the discussions in N. Bamforth, 'The Application of the Human Rights Act 1998 to Public Authorities and Private Bodies' [1999] *CLJ* 159–70; D. Feldman, 'The Human Rights Act and Constitutional Principles' (1999) **19** *Legal Studies* 165–206 at 199–203; G. Phillipson, 'The Human Rights Act, "Horizontal Effect" and the Common Law: a Bang or a Whimper?' (1999) **62** *MLR* 824–49, and Ch. 9 below.

[269] See *House of Lords Official Report*, 18, November 1997, vol. 583, col. 475.

'(1) In relation to any act (or proposed act) of a public authority which the court finds is (or would be) unlawful, it may grant such relief or remedy, or make such order, within its powers as it considers just and appropriate.'

Damages may be awarded for a violation of a Convention right only if the court or tribunal already has 'power to award damages, or to order the payment of compensation, in civil proceedings'.[270] Furthermore, the court has to be satisfied that it is necessary to award compensation, on top of any other relief or remedy granted, 'to afford just satisfaction' to the victim (section 8(3)). 'Just satisfaction' is a Strasbourg term of art: Article 41 of the ECHR empowers the Court to afford just satisfaction to a victim, and section 8(4) of the Act requires a court or tribunal in the UK to 'take into account the principles applied by the European Court of Human Rights in relation to the award of compensation under Article 41. Unfortunately, as the Law Commission has recently explained in a comprehensive survey of the subject,[271] the Court does not yet seem to work according to principles. One can only say that:

- the Court often decides that the giving of a judgment in favour of the applicant constitutes just satisfaction without the need for monetary compensation;
- when compensation is awarded for non-pecuniary loss, the levels of compensation tend to be on the low side compared with what people could expect to receive for pain and suffering in the UK;
- when pecuniary losses are alleged, they must be proved in detail if they are to be recoverable; and
- the Court does not seem to make any awards of exemplary or punitive damages against states.

If, as is likely, damages under the Act will usually be limited in scope and quantum, it is important to bear in mind section 11 of the Act, which provides:

'A person's reliance on a Convention right does not restrict—

(a) any other right or freedom conferred on him by or under any law having effect in any part of the UK; or

(b) his right to make any claim or bring any proceedings which he could make or bring apart from sections 7 to 9.'

There will therefore often be tactical advantages in relying on ordinary torts, etc., which may attract damages as of right and in larger measure than will a cause of action under section 8 of the Act.

In the light of this, the major impact of the Convention rights on remedies is likely

---

[270] Human Rights Act 1998, s. 8(2). It is likely that the damages will be regarded as being tortious, for breach of the statutory duty under s. 6(1) of the 1998 Act, as are damages for breach of EC law contrary to the European Communities Act 1972: *R. v. Secretary of State for Transport, ex parte Factortame (No. 7)* [2001] 1 WLR 942.

[271] Law Commission and Scottish Law Commission, Report Nos. 266 and 180 respectively, *Damages under the Human Rights Act 1998* (London: The Stationery Office, 2000). See also M. Amos, 'Damages for Breach of the Human Rights Act 1998' [1999] *EHRL Rev.* 178–94.

to be in the field of judicial review. The Act will require the courts to develop substantive grounds of review consistent with the Convention, and will make violation of Convention rights a head of unlawfulness rather than something relevant only to the question of irrationality.[272] This reverses the effect of the decision in *Brind v. Secretary of State for the Home Department.*[273] Furthermore, reference to Strasbourg caselaw in accordance with section 2 of the Act involves the courts in developing a proportionality-based approach to alleged violations of rights in many cases.

(vi) The effect of section 12 of the Human Rights Act 1998 on remedies

This section was the result of agitation by and on behalf of the press and the Press Complaints Commission (PCC) during the passage of the Bill. A wholly unsatisfactory clause was inserted in the House of Lords, and the present section 12 was substituted by government amendment in the House of Commons. It does not protect the PCC or extend the substantive rights of the press. However, it extends the effect of Article 10 (freedom of expression) in several ways.

First, it applies to any relief which is sought from a court 'which, if granted, might affect the exercise of the Convention right to freedom of expression' (section 12(1)), so that it applies not only in cases brought by or against public authorities but to all actions for defamation and breach of confidence.

Secondly, it imposes strict limits on the circumstances in which *ex parte* injunctions can be granted, especially those which restrain publication, in such cases (section 12(2), (3)), which alters the normal principles on the grant of interim injunctions.

Thirdly, in relation to any remedy in any proceedings the court 'must have particular regard to the importance of' freedom of expression whoever the parties are (section 12(4)).

Fourthly, where the case relates to journalistic, literary, or artistic material, the court must have particular regard to the extent to which the material is already, or is about to be, in the public domain, and the extent to which publication would be in the public interest, together with any relevant privacy code such as those promulgated by the Press Complaints Commission and the Broadcasting Standards Commission (section 12(4)).

The result could be significant in relation to remedies against journalists and others in a wide range of cases. For instance, the fourth point could well have led to a different result in the interlocutory stages of the *Spycatcher* litigation[274] in relation to orders restraining reports of legal proceedings, and is likely to improve the lot of the media significantly in such cases. 'Having particular regard to' a right does not tell us what is to be done with it, but it at least strongly implies that we should give it greater weight than competing rights (except, perhaps, those under Article 9: compare section 13 of the Act). These matters are considered in section 2.7 and Chapters 13 to 18 below.

---

[272] D. Feldman, 'The Human Rights Act 1998 and Substantive Ultra Vires', in C. Forsyth (ed.), *Judicial Review and the Constitution* (Oxford: Hart Publishing, 2000), 245–68.

[273] [1991] 1 AC 696, HL.

[274] *Attorney-General v. Guardian Newspapers Ltd.* [1987] 1 WLR 1248, HL.

2.7 CONCLUSION: VALUES, THE COMMUNITY, AND
THE INDIVIDUAL

The fundamental rules of the UK's constitution were, in the past, almost entirely procedural. They were concerned almost entirely with *how* laws could be made. They told us little about the objectives or values which might justify particular rules or outcomes. The UK prided itself on adhering to a form of representative democracy. Some fundamental values are intrinsic to representative democracy, which gives rise to 'the demands of pluralism, tolerance and broadmindedness without which there is no "democratic society" '.[275] Nevertheless, few of these values, or other fundamental social values, found constitutional expression. This was not too serious a problem when there was a political consensus that individualism could properly be restrained to further communal goods. However, that belief was eroded in the 1980s and 1990s by belief in the market as the supreme arbiter of value. Public-choice theory marginalized both Parliament and traditional government as channels for legitimate policy-making.[276] Private industry, which typically has no public-service ethos or political accountability, took over many formerly public functions. Patchy regulation and uneven democratic scrutiny left many important values (including communal solidarity, human dignity, and democracy itself) vulnerable.

The Human Rights Act 1998 helps to re-inject such values into the UK's political structure. If they are internalized by administrators and legislators, it will contribute to a sound ethical base for political and constitutional decision-making. The Convention rights affect two sets of values. First, there are general legal values which, Professor Dawn Oliver has argued, span both public and private law: autonomy, dignity, respect, status, and security.[277] These are predominantly individualistic (although, as I have argued elsewhere, their capacity to contribute to worthwhile social life is one of the factors which gives them value).[278] Secondly, there are distinctively public values: representative democracy, creating an accountable political elite, and the free press which helps to maintain the conditions for democracy; principles such as the Rule of Law and associated supervisory systems designed to control abuse of power; transparency in decision-making and (to a lesser extent) freedom of information and principled consistency in decision-making, which can underpin other constitutional aspirations; and the expertise of a professional executive class working to advance

[275] *Handyside v. United Kingdom*, Series A, No 24, Judgment of 7 December 1976, para. 49 of the judgment. On the use made of the idea of democracy by the European Court of Human Rights, see A. Mowbray, 'The Role of the European Court of Human Rights in the Promotion of Democracy' [1999] *PL* 703–25.

[276] Something similar happened in Canada under the liberal-conservative Prime Minister Brian Mulroney, although a higher level of political pluralism was maintained: see W. A. Bogart, *Courts and Country: The Limits of Litigation and the Social and Political Life of Canada* (Toronto: Oxford University Press, 1994), 6–8.

[277] D. Oliver, 'The Underlying Values of Public and Private Law', in M. Taggart (ed.), *The Province of Administrative Law* (Oxford: Hart Publishing, 1997), ch. 11.

[278] D. Feldman, 'Privacy-related Rights and their Social Value', in P. Birks (ed.), *Privacy and Loyalty* (Oxford: Clarendon Press, 1997), ch. 2; D. Feldman 'Content Neutrality', in I. Loveland (ed.), *Importing the First Amendment: Freedom of Expression in American, English and European Law* (Oxford: Hart Publishing, 1998), ch. 8.

public welfare.[279] The values of autonomy, dignity, respect, status, and security have, on the whole, been part of our law for a long time. The Convention rights, which are firmly founded on them, can only assist the law to protect them. Articles 2, 3, 4, 5, 8, 9, 10, 11, and 12, and Articles 2 and 3 of the First Protocol, are founded on and help to provide the conditions necessary for autonomy, dignity, and respect. Articles 5, 6, 7 and 8, Article 1 of the First Protocol, and the Sixth Protocol are particularly concerned with security, especially legal security. Articles 4 and 14 are specially concerned with status, particularly equality. The Convention rights thus provide a more systematic basis for protecting these values, and for justifying judicial remedies for interference with them, than we have at present (as is shown by the chaotic state of the law relating to privacy and personal dignity in England and Wales if one compares it with that available in, to take one instance, Germany).[280] For example, the need to provide a secure footing for rule-making or judicial decisions which balance rights against each other leads to the inclusion in Article 17 of an abuse of power doctrine: nobody may do any act 'aimed at the destruction of any of the rights and freedoms set forth herein or at their limitation to a greater extent than is provided for in the Convention'. This makes possible fairly intrusive restrictions by public authorities on people's freedom to use rights where they conflict with the rights of others (a situation where the state must act as arbiter). At a collective level, it may also permit restrictions on people's freedom to advance political programmes which, if implemented, would undermine the political freedom or other human rights of others.

Convention rights are unlikely to operate in a purely liberal and individualistic way. A strong element of collectivism is already an important part of the Convention rights, a fact which contributes to the perception that there are tensions within the structure of the ECHR.[281] This is reflected in two ways. First, several rights have an obvious collectivist aspect, particularly if one takes account of the way in which they have been interpreted by the Strasbourg Commission and Court. This is most obvious if one focuses attention not on values shared by public and private law, but on the distinctively public-law values of democracy, accountability, controlled elitism, and public welfare. The caselaw of the European Court of Human Rights in respect of freedom of expression under Article 10 gives more weight to political expression than to other forms of expression, by reason of the importance of democratic society in the text of the Convention rights. For this reason, the concerns of the press and of the Press Complaints Commission which led Lord Wakeham, its chairman, to seek amendments to the Bill in the House of Lords were misconceived.[282] He was worried about the possible impact on the press of the right to respect for private and family

---

[279] On the role of these values in the decision-making of the House of Lords in the 1980s, see D. Feldman, 'Public Law Values in the House of Lords' (1990) 106 *LQR* 246–76.

[280] See B. S. Markesinis and N. Nolte, 'Some Comparative Reflections on the Right of Privacy of Public Figures in Public Places', in P. Birks (ed.), *Privacy and Loyalty*, ch. 5; B. Markesinis, 'Privacy, Freedom of Expression and the Human Rights Bill: Lessons from Germany' (1999) 115 *LQR* 47–88.

[281] For an acute exploration of this, see A. McHarg, 'Reconciling Human Rights and the Public Interest: Conceptual Problems and Doctrinal Uncertainty in the Jurisprudence of the European Court of Human Rights' (1999) 62 *MLR* 671–96.

[282] See, e.g. his speech towards the end of the third reading debate, House of Lords *Official Report*, 5 February 1998, vol. 585, cols. 830–3.

life, home and correspondence under Article 8. He failed to appreciate that, under the caselaw of the Strasbourg organs, Article 8 rights had always to be balanced against the right to freedom of expression under Article 10, in respect of which the value of a free press has always been given great weight.[283] Nevertheless, the Lord Chancellor promised a dialogue on the issue,[284] and in the House of Commons the government responded to Lord Wakeham's concerns by introducing what is now section 12 of the Act. Courts and tribunals considering whether to grant relief which might affect the exercise of the Convention right to freedom of expression must have particular regard to the importance of that right. In relation to journalistic, literary or artistic material or conduct, the court or tribunal must take account of the extent to which the material is or is about to be available to the public, and of the public interest in publication, together with the terms of any relevant privacy code such as that promulgated by the Press Complaints Commission. Relief may not be given against a person who is neither present nor represented in court unless the court is satisfied that the applicant has taken all reasonable steps to notify the person or that there are compelling reasons for not notifying him. Finally, no interim order restraining publication is to be granted unless the court is satisfied that the applicant is likely to establish at trial that publication should not be allowed. This entirely changes the footing on which the courts approach applications for interim relief in cases such as *Spycatcher*[285] and for orders restraining reports of legal proceedings. It is likely to be beneficial, but should not produce results very different from those which would have followed from a loyal application of the Strasbourg caselaw under Article 10.

The respect shown by the Strasbourg organs for the judgment of an electorally accountable political elite, including particularly the legislature, is another manifestation of concern for democratic processes. The weight which the Court attaches to the considered view of the executive authority of a state as to what is necessary in a democratic society (i.e. a proportionate response to a pressing social need) in order to pursue one of the public-interest objectives which, under the Convention, can justify an interference with certain rights, is another sign of that respect. Similarly, weight is given to the judgment of the political elite in a state when assessing whether a derogation from a Convention right is justified by a public emergency threatening the life of the nation, and whether the extent of the derogation is strictly required by the exigencies of a situation, within the meaning of Article 15 of the Convention. Maintaining and strengthening democracy and national security as collective values is a central theme of the Convention and its caselaw.

Collective, public-interest considerations are not limited to rights or limitations of rights with an obviously collectivist aspect. Even apparently liberal, individualist rights have a collective significance which has been reflected in the decisions of the Strasbourg organs. The debate over the position of religious institutions provides an

---

[283] This point was made by the Lord Chancellor: House of Lords, *Official Report*, 3 November 1997, vol. 582, cols. 1229–30. See R. Singh, 'Privacy and the Media after the Human Rights Act' [1998] *EHRLR* 712–29.

[284] Lord Irvine LC, House of Lords *Official Report*, 5 February 1998, vol. 585, col. 841.

[285] *Attorney-General v. Guardian Newspapers Ltd.* [1987] 1 WLR 1248, HL.

example of this. In the House of Lords, amendments to the Bill were proposed[286] to
prevent the rights under Articles 8 and 12 forcing religious leaders to solemnize
marriages which would not be in accordance with their religious laws (for example,
marrying same-sex couples),[287] or prohibiting them from seeking to appoint to positions in religious schools only people who would be sympathetic to the religious ethos
of the institution. Yet the rights under Articles 8 and 12 would have to be weighed
against the right of the religious group to freedom of religion under Article 9, and the
right of parents to ensure such education and teaching in conformity with their own
religious and philosophical convictions under Article 2 of Protocol No. 1. Nevertheless, the amendments were passed. In the House of Commons, the government used
its majority to replace the amendments with a minor concession. Section 13 now
provides that a court or tribunal, when deciding a question which might affect the
exercise by a religious organization of its Convention right to freedom of thought,
conscience, and religion under Article 9, 'must have particular regard to the importance of that right'. This seems to provide a statutory basis for giving greater weight to
rights under Article 9 than to other rights when they conflict. Article 9, in the contexts
which caused concern during the debate, protects the collective interests of religious
groups as much as individual rights, so section 13 provides another example of
the importance of collective interests to the scheme of the Convention rights under
the Act.

   The right to a fair trial under Article 6 is also social as much as individual in nature.
The rights to freedom of conscience and belief under Article 9, to freedom of expression in Article 10, and to freedom of peaceful assembly and association in Article 11,
all gain added importance because of the way in which they contribute to the conditions for maintaining a vigorously functioning democracy, which ultimately is a social
rather than an individual good. Even the rights to respect for private and family life
and to marry and found a family under Articles 8 and 12 respectively are not simply
individualistic. The right to found a family is concerned with approved forms of social
organization as much as individual choice. The right to respect for private life and the
home gains added value from the contribution it makes to enabling people to form
worthwhile social groupings and pursue activities which make them more useful
members of society, while the obligations which states have as a result include obligations to secure people's homes against toxic pollution and to preserve as far as possible family relationships. Furthermore, Article 16 allows states to restrict the political
activity of aliens, this being an aspect of the right of states in international law to
protect national security and national self-determination.

   The second respect in which the Convention rights contain a collectivist element is
that, even where a Convention right is being asserted individualistically, the individual
interest must nearly always be balanced against a limited range of approved social
interests when deciding whether it is possible to justify an interference with the right.

[286] Baroness Young, supported by the Bishop of Ripon, on third reading in the House of Lords: House of
Lords *Official Report*, 5 February 1998, vol. 585, cols. 770–773, and see also col. 790.
[287] For concern about this, see, e.g. Baroness Young during the committee stage, House of Lords *Official
Report*, 24 November 1997, vol. 583, col. 801.

Most of the rights are subject to exceptions which allow public interests to be taken into account. Of those contained in Schedule 1, only the rights to be free of torture and inhuman or degrading treatment or punishment (Article 3), to a fair trial (Article 6), to be free of punishment for conduct which at the time was not an offence (Article 7), to marry and found a family (Article 12), and to be free of discrimination in respect of the securing of other rights (Article 14) are not expressly subject to public-interest exceptions. Typical conditions for justifiable interference are those provided in Article 8(2): the interference is permitted if it is 'in accordance with the law and necessary in a democratic society' (phrases to which judicial interpretation has attached special meanings under the Convention) for one of a list of purposes set out in the Article itself. The judiciary is the final arbiter of whether or not a particular interference satisfies these criteria. Even where the right appears to be absolute, the scope for interpretation leaves open the possibility of injecting public-interest considerations. They play a part, for example, when deciding what is meant by 'degrading' in Article 3 (the term has both subjective and social elements);[288] what the incidents of a fair trial are, and how soon it must take place in order to be within a reasonable time, for the purposes of Article 6(1); how certain the law governing an offence must be in order for it to be established under national law at a particular time for the purposes of Article 7(1); and what is meant by 'marry ... according to the national laws governing the exercise of this right' for the purposes of Article 12.

There are other ways in which the UK is justified in interfering with Convention rights to further communal interests. Under Article 57, at the time of signature or ratification a state may enter reservations in respect of any particular provision 'to the extent that any law then in force in its territory is not in conformity with the provision', refusing to accept an obligations to modify the law of the state.[289] On signing the First Protocol to the ECHR in 1952, the UK entered a reservation to Article 2 of the Protocol to the effect that the right of parents to ensure education and teaching in accordance with their religious and philosophical convictions was accepted by the UK 'only so far as it is compatible with the provision of efficient instruction and training, and the avoidance of unreasonable public expenditure'. Under the Human Rights Act 1998, Article 2 of the First Protocol is to be read subject to this 'designated reservation',[290] which clearly gives priority to general welfare over individual rights in relation to educational choice. Furthermore, where a particular treaty permits, a state may derogate from certain provisions. The ECHR permits derogation 'in time of war or other public emergency threatening the life of the nation ... to the extent strictly required by the exigencies of the situation, provided that such measures are not

---

[288] See *Tyrer v. United Kingdom*, Eur. Ct. HR, Series A, No. 26, Judgment of 25 April 1978; *Costello-Roberts v. United Kingdom*, Eur. Ct. HR, Series A, No. 247-C, Judgment of 25 March 1993.

[289] Art. 57 was originally Art. 64. On reservations under the ECHR, see van Dijk and van Hoof, *op cit.*, n. 18 above, 773–84. On reservations in respect of treaties generally in international law, see the Vienna Convention on the Law of Treaties, 1969, Arts 19–23; I. Brownlie QC, *Principles of Public International Law*, 4th edn. (Oxford: Clarendon Press, 1990), 608–11; M. Shaw, *International Law*, 4th edn. (Cambridge: Cambridge University Press, 1997), 641–9, especially at 647–8; D. W. Greig, 'Reservations: Equity as a Balancing Factor?' (1995) 16 *Australian Year Book of International Law* 21–172.

[290] Human Rights Act 1998, ss. 1(2) and 15 and Sch. 3, Part II.

inconsistent with its other obligations under international law'. No derogation is permitted from Articles 2 (except in respect of lawful acts of war), 3, 4(1), or 7.[291] In 1988 the Court held in *Brogan v. United Kingdom*[292] that the detention of terrorist suspects for up to seven days on the authorization of the Secretary of State violated the right of detainees to be brought promptly before a judicial officer as required by Article 5(3). The government decided, having regard to the conditions created by terrorism connected with the affairs of Northern Ireland, that it needed to continue to exercise that power of detention without judicial oversight. A derogation from Article 5(3) was accordingly entered under Article 15 of the Convention so far as those powers[293] were inconsistent with the obligations imposed by Article 5. The Court subsequently upheld the validity of this derogation in *Brannigan and McBride v. United Kingdom.*[294] That derogation was withdrawn in 2001, but has now been replaced by one to permit detention without trial under the Anti-terrorism, Crime and Security Act 2001.[295] Again, this allows collective interests to trump individual rights for particularly pressing purposes.

All this shows that the Convention rights are not founded on a notion of liberal individualism in the classic form espoused by Adam Smith or Robert Nozick. The whole structure of the Convention and each of its rights requires a balance between the interests of the community and the interests of individuals conceived of as members of the community rather than as being isolated from it or from each other. This essentially communitarian approach sets the Convention sharply apart from the more individualistic approach to fundamental rights adopted, for example, under the Constitution of the USA. The Convention's approach is far more closely in tune with the essentially collectivist cultural heritage which forms part of the bedrock on which the constitution of the UK developed and must build than with American-style liberal individualism.

This does not mean that the Act will fail to protect individual rights. The Convention rights can help to control the process by which public authorities balance collective against individual interests. Under Article 18, restrictions imposed on rights for a prescribed purpose must not be used for a non-prescribed purpose. This new source of substantive and procedural values constraining arbitrariness in the use of public power will represent a major contribution to the values of the UK's constitution. In the past there has been no principled and systematic control over the balancing process, and therefore no criteria for deciding what kinds of arguments or considerations offer adequate and legitimate grounds for interfering with an individual right or liberty. Under the Act, by contrast, the permitted grounds for interfering with Convention rights are set out. By combining the text of Schedules 1 and 3 with the caselaw of the Strasbourg organs and what will doubtless be a burgeoning national jurisprudence, the limits to the power of public authorities to interfere with Conven-

---

[291] Art. 15(1), (2).

[292] Series A, No. 145, (1988) 11 EHRR 117.

[293] The powers were contained in Prevention of Terrorism (Temporary Provisions) Act 1989, s.14 (as amended) and Sch. 5, para. 6, repeated by the Terrorism Act 2000.

[294] Series A, No. 258-B (1993).

[295] Human Rights Act 1998 (Designated Derogation) Order 2001, SI 2001, No. 3644.

tion rights will be more or less exhaustively established. It will help to provide principled standards for assessing use of public power.

On the other hand, the Convention rights are by no means a comprehensive basis for a modern system of protection for these values. As Sir Sydney Kentridge has said:[296]

'The European Convention on Human Rights is a mid-century bill of rights, designed to accommodate a number of countries with a variety of legal systems and political histories. There can be no doubt that a new, home-grown, British Bill of Rights would have looked rather different.'

Kentridge is almost certainly correct to say that there would have been more extensive reference to the duties and responsibilities towards the community, consistently with the belief in social order and the concern for public welfare which are hallmarks of traditional collectivist constitutionalism. On the other hand, it is hard to imagine that highly pragmatic UK politicians would have been prepared to sacrifice the flexibility of the system to any great extent. The approach adopted in the ECHR, which accepts that it is legitimate to interfere with different rights to different extents and in different circumstances, has attractions.

In any case, it is not easy to predict what additional rights would have been included in a home-grown bill of rights. The extra rights contained in the ICCPR might have been included. For example, the right to freedom of expression under Article 19 is rather more far-reaching than that under Article 10 of the ECHR, and is subject to fewer exceptions. The ICCPR has a free-standing right to be free of discrimination, whereas that under the ECHR only forbids discrimination in relation to the protection and enjoyment of other Convention rights. The ICCPR also contains, in Article 20, a provision requiring the state to legislate to outlaw propaganda for war and racial, etc. hatred, which would help to clarify the scope of legitimate freedom of expression and its accompanying duties and responsibilities under Article 10 of the ECHR.

By contrast, in view of the attack which successive governments have launched on trial by jury, the right of silence, and the traditional belief that the prosecution must prove its case without help from the accused, it seems less likely that those rights would today be included in a home-grown bill of rights. Such rights are more likely to be protected by judicial interpretation of Convention rights than by principled self-control on the part of legislators. When one turns from classical, liberal rights and freedoms to social rights of the kind recognized in the Universal Declaration of Human Rights and legally protected in international law under treaties, to which the UK is party, such as the International Covenant on Economic, Social and Cultural Rights and the European Social Charter, the prospect of incorporation in a home-grown bill of rights is even more remote. It is unlikely that such rights as a right to a job or to a basic standard of living would be acceptable to government as part of a bill of rights. Even if they were to be included, there would be difficulties relating to their

---

[296] S. Kentridge QC, 'The Incorporation of the European Convention on Human Rights', in University of Cambridge Centre for Public Law (ed.), *Constitutional Reform in the United Kingdom*, ch. 7, at 69.

justiciability. The Constitutional Court of South Africa had to face this problem in *Minister of Public Works and others v. Kyalami Ridge Environmental Association and another*[296a] where flooding had left many people homeless and it was argued that the government had acted unconstitutionally in applying land for use as temporary housing without lawful authority or consultation with residents near the land whose interests were affected, in a way that prejudiced environmental concerns. The court held that the flood victims' constitutional right to housing, the government's power to deal with emergencies and its rights as landowner provided a legal basis for the government's decision, and accepted that the court should not interfere with the government's assessment of the competing rights and interests as long as the government acted lawfully in discharging its constitutional obligations. Such constrained deference to government in relation to social rights has parallels elsewhere in the world, and is inevitable where such matters are given constitutional status.

It may, therefore, be over-optimistic to see the 1998 Act as initiating a process of institutionalizing a growing range of fundamental rights. British suspicion of rights, even of the classical, liberal variety, runs deep, because of their capacity to derail important social values. A generation or so of acclimatization is likely to be needed before any serious extension to the range of rights will be contemplated. Sir Sydney Kentridge QC has pointed out:[297]

'Unlike the Bills of Rights in the German or South African Constitutions [the Act] does not represent a break with an abhorrent past nor is its object to address great social problems such as those which have faced the United States Supreme Court in the second half of this century.'

The Act's ability to inject values which could fill the ethical vacuum at the heart of public life depends on the perceived legitimacy of the Convention rights, which in turn depends on their capacity to accommodate the most important elements of the UK's constitutional heritage. In the absence of popular enthusiasm for root-and-branch constitutional change, the new values in the Act will have to interact with existing institutions. Change will result, but continuity will be observable: we will experience development, not revolution.

[296a] Case CCT 55/00, Judgment of 29 May 2001, unreported. K. D. Ewing, 'Constitutional Reform and Human Rights: Unfinished Business' (2001) 5 *Edinburgh LR* 1–28, argues for social rights to be incorporated in domestic law alongside Convention rights.

[297] *Loc. cit.*, n. 296 above.

3

EQUALITY AND DIGNITY

This chapter examines two of the important values underpinning human rights and civil liberties in international and municipal law. In Chapter 1, most attention was paid to the idea of autonomy. Here, we concentrate on two other values which supplement that of autonomy in the law of civil liberties and human rights: human dignity and equality. In relation to each value, we consider the illuminating yet complex ideas which they reflect, and the legal measures adopted in municipal and international law to advance their protection. Legal efforts to enhance human dignity and equality have often had a social rather than individualist focus. Individual autonomy is one of the hallmarks of a dignified existence, and equal respect for the autonomy of others is one of the elements of equality, but autonomy is not a sufficient condition for either equality or dignity. The chapter therefore begins by considering the contribution which international law has made to identifying the social conditions for a dignified life in conditions of equality, before examining the ideas of dignity and equality in more detail.

3.1 SOCIAL AND ECONOMIC RIGHTS ADVANCING DIGNITY AND EQUALITY IN INTERNATIONAL LAW

Social and economic rights are important in providing the conditions for the pursuit of human dignity and equal opportunities. In the struggle to achieve a society in which everyone has the opportunity to make good use of their freedoms and opportunities, the acknowledgment and pursuit of social and economic rights can be a useful weapon, alongside the individual freedoms which classical liberal theory espouses. Although the idea of rights attaching to groups within society by reason of their distinctive needs is sometimes hard to reconcile with individual rights for members of those groups and outsiders,[1] some element of concern for people's social positions can be seen to be a possible component of a commitment to individual freedom. The recognition of individual freedom by the state implies that the state should do its best to produce the social and economic conditions in which people can

---

[1] See the illuminating analysis by M. Malik, 'Communal Goods as Human Rights', in C. Gearty and A. Tomkins (eds.), *Understanding Human Rights* (London: Mansell Publishing, 1996), 138–69.

exercise choice and pursue the chosen ends or values. In the UK, this need for fairness is broadly understood by politicians.

Nevertheless, conflicts between political theories as to the notion of social justice have made it difficult to achieve consensus within or between states as to the identity, scope, and enforcement of such rights. In an effort to maintain the widest possible agreement, social rights have generally been drawn in international instruments so as to limit the impact of economic and social inequalities on individuals' capacities to take advantage of liberty, rather than to impose a single notion of what is meant by equality or social justice. Within the UK, even basic values are subject to political processes, and divisions of opinion on the best approach reflect political battle lines. On the whole, socialists have favoured a commitment to equality in the form of common ownership of as much of the economically productive property in society as possible. It was traditionally envisaged that this would be achieved through state ownership of key industries, and that the state would be responsible for guaranteeing to everyone access to the services which were seen as vital for full personal develop-ment and participation in the benefits which society offers. For much of the second half of the twentieth century, this was pursued by means of state funding for and provision of services under the banner of the welfare state, including the National Health Service, state education, and systems of public sector housing and social secur-ity benefits to protect the poorest members of society from starvation, homelessness, and the worst forms of degradation.

Few would regard it as improper for the state to provide a safety net for the weakest and poorest members of society. However, there has been increasing disagreement as to the extent to which provision of the safety net should be regarded as a responsibil-ity of the state rather than private provision. Furthermore, free-marketeers in the UK have traditionally rejected socialist plans for state ownership, preferring to rely on the operation of the market to spread ownership of the economic base widely through society. Between 1979 and 1997, the Conservative government embarked on an exten-sive programme of selling off key strategic enterprises which previous Labour gov-ernments had nationalized. The Labour government has not reversed the process since 1997, and seem inclined to extend it through privatization and partnerships between the public and private sectors in key areas of education, health, and transport. This is not the place to try to evaluate these programmes, but it should be noted that they represent attempts to achieve a similar goal to those of traditional socialism—namely the widest possible distribution of wealth and control over social assets—while limiting the intervention of the state.

This section therefore examines the development of social and economic rights in international law, without losing sight of their contested character.

(1) THE UNITED NATIONS AND THE INTERNATIONAL LABOUR ORGANIZATION

In international law, social and economic rights have grown in importance in recent years as international instruments recognizing such rights have proliferated. The Pre-amble to the Charter of the United Nations refers to the determination of the Member States to promote social progress and better standards of life, and for those ends 'to employ international machinery for the promotion of the economic and social advancement of all peoples', and Article 55 committed the organization to promoting (among other objectives) 'higher standards of living, full employment, and conditions of economic and social progress and development'. Responsibility for pursuing these objectives was vested by Article 60 in the Economic and Social Council under the General Assembly, while Articles 57 to 59 contemplated that some of the work would be done by specialized agencies, of which the most significant for this purpose has been the International Labour Organization (ILO).[2]

The ILO originated in 1919, in the aftermath of the First World War, and its mission is to advance social justice, in the belief (as stated in the Preamble to its Constitution) that 'universal and lasting peace can be established only if it is based upon social justice'. To this end, in 1944 the ILO General Conference adopted a Declaration of Aims and Purposes[3] which are to inspire the policy of its members. The Declaration contains a lengthy credo: labour is not to be regarded as a commodity; freedom of expression and association are essential to sustained progress; poverty anywhere constitutes a danger to prosperity everywhere; and the war against want must be carried on with unrelenting vigour within each nation and by means of concerted international efforts. All human beings have the right to pursue both material well-being and spiritual development in conditions of freedom and dignity, economic security, and equal opportunity, without discrimination on the ground of race, creed, or sex. To advance these aims, the ILO has an obligation to further programmes which will achieve (*inter alia*) full employment, rising standards of living, worker satisfaction, a minimum living wage, a basic income for all in need, and a just share in the fruits of progress for all, recognition of rights to free collective bargaining, adequate protection for the life and health of all workers, child welfare and maternity protection, and provision of adequate nutrition, housing, and facilities for recreation and culture. The list ends with an assurance of equality of educational and vocational opportunity.

In performing its obligations, the ILO has adopted a number of Conventions on matters including forced labour (1930); the right of workers and employers to establish organizations (1948); collective bargaining (1949); equal remuneration for work of equal value without discrimination on the ground of sex (1951); and discrimination in employment or occupation (1958). The general thrust of these Conventions, and of the work of the ILO generally, is towards a raising of standards everywhere towards minimum acceptable conditions. The form of social justice which is favoured is not, therefore, the utopian ideal of universal equality, but a rather more limited notion of justice according to which needs are catered for, while further benefits of social activity are open to competition. The competition must, however, be socially

---

[2] A. H. Robertson and J. G. Merrills, *Human Rights in the World: An Introduction to the Study of the International Protection of Human Rights*, 4th edn. (Manchester: Manchester University Press, 1996), 282–8; F. Wolf, 'Human Rights and the International Labour Organization', in T. Meron (ed.), *Human Rights in International Law: Legal and Policy Issues* (Oxford: Clarendon Press, 1984), 273–305.

[3] For text, see I. Brownlie, *Basic Documents on Human Rights*, 3rd edn. (Oxford: Clarendon Press, 1992), 243–5.

just, which means that it must be accessible to all nationals under conditions of fair equality of opportunity. In other words, the various Conventions seek to establish (i) a safety net for all, and (ii) a level playing field on which competition for the fruits of economic and social progress will be played out. The rights to organize and bargain collectively, and to be free from discrimination, are aspects of the arrangements for a level playing field. Another aspect is the right to equal educational opportunities. This is advanced by the work of the United Nations Educational, Scientific, and Cultural Organization (UNESCO), another specialized agency related to the United Nations, which adopted the Convention against Discrimination in Education in 1960.

To put this model of social justice and social rights in perspective, it is instructive to compare it with the influential model of justice advanced by John Rawls in *A Theory of Justice*.[4] Rawls's general principle of justice proposes that an equal distribution of goods is just, unless an unequal distribution works to the advantage of the least favoured group in society. Similarly, the ILO principles contemplate redistribution of goods, by means of mechanisms such as taxation and social security payments, without regard to principles of equality save in respect of the equal application of the criterion of need. However, once a society has advanced to a point where basic needs are catered for, Rawls contemplates the surplus being distributed in accordance with a different set of principles (the 'special conception' of justice). These respect people's individual basic rights, which (as outlined in Chapter 1 above) are largely concerned with political and personal fulfilment. Once everyone's basic needs (however they may be defined) are met, additional income or wealth may be distributed unequally. A distribution is not to be regarded as unjust merely because it results in substantial inequality of wealth above the level of basic need. Rawls insists that positions of social, economic, and political privilege must be open to all under conditions of fair equality of opportunity. This, too, is in tune with the principles in ILO and UNESCO Conventions. However, in two respects Rawls's approach and that of the UN's specialized agencies seem to diverge. First, Rawls gives specially protected status only to basic individual liberties, not to social and economic rights. This difference is partly cancelled out by the second: Rawls expressly insists, unlike the ILO Conventions, that unequal distributions of social and economic goods above the baseline of need are justifiable if and only if the effect is to benefit the least favoured group. The effect is to permit net inequalities of wealth and power to exist, and even to widen, but only if a share of the fruits of them is made available to all. Whether this share of the fruits of progress is fair, as required by the ILO Declaration of Aims and Purposes, is a matter of judgment.

The essential work of the ILO, and other specialist agencies of the UN, such as UNESCO, in the field of human rights, is thus to encourage the universal satisfaction of basic needs and the fair distribution of the fruits of progress both within states and internationally, and to promote equality of opportunity by restraining discrimination in the provision of education, training, employment opportunities, terms and conditions of employment, and social security benefits.

---

[4] J. Rawls, *A Theory of Justice* (Oxford: Clarendon Press, 1972; revised edn., 1999).

The UN also provided the framework for developing a codification of collective rights in the International Covenant on Economic, Social and Cultural Rights (ICESC).[5] This was the sister Covenant to the International Covenant on Civil and Political Rights, and was similarly derived from the Universal Declaration of Human Rights. Concluded in 1966, it is a treaty imposing obligations on States Parties to it to recognize the importance of certain rights, including those to the self-determination of peoples, equality, work, trade union representation, social security, protection for families, an adequate standard of living, the best possible standard of health, education, and participation in the cultural life of society and the benefits of scientific progress. It is overseen by the Economic and Social Council (ECOSOC), which receives periodic reports from States Parties on their compliance with the Covenant, and submits reports and recommendations to the UN Commission on Human Rights, General Assembly and other UN organs. The main work of scrutiny is carried out by the Committee on Economic, Social and Cultural Rights, established in 1985 by ECOSOC resolution 1985/17. The Committee has eighteen members who are experts in human rights, serving in their personal rather than representative capacity. They scrutinize the periodic reports from States Parties, give guidance on the interpretation of the treaty in the form of General Comments on its provisions, and 'assist' ECOSOC in performing its functions by reporting to it.[6] The effectiveness of the Committee's scrutiny depends heavily on the work of non-governmental organizations providing information about the true state of affairs in the territories of states, which can provide a basis for evaluating States Parties' own reports. The Committee can report that a state has violated rights. This is made difficult by diplomatic concerns, and also by the programmatic nature of most of the rights: states' obligations are generally to take appropriate positive action to advance enjoyment of the rights through social or economic programmes, rather than a right to have a specific standard of living now. Nevertheless, where positive state action has blatantly violated rights, such as the expulsion of families from their homes in the Dominican Republic and Panama, the Committee felt able to report that the states had failed to respect the right to housing.[7] There are signs that the Committee is slowly but steadily giving some teeth to economic and social rights, although by their nature it is not easy to supervise them or judge compliance with them in absolute terms.

(2) THE COUNCIL OF EUROPE AND THE EUROPEAN COMMUNITY

At a European level, the Council of Europe and the European Community have been moving parallel to the ILO.

---

[5] See M. Craven, *The International Covenant on Economic, Social and Cultural Rights: A Perspective on its Development* (Oxford: Clarendon Press, 1995).

[6] Craven, *The International Covenant*, ch. 2.

[7] See S. Leckie, 'The Committee on Economic, Social and Cultural Rights: A Catalyst for Change in a System Needing Reform', in P. Alston and J. Crawford (eds.), *The Future of UN Human Rights Treaty Monitoring* (Cambridge: Cambridge University Press, 2000), 129–44 at 133–5.

(i) The Council of Europe and the European Social Charter

In 1961, the Member States of the Council of Europe signed the European Social Charter (ESC),[8] which came into force in 1965. The Contracting Parties which were signatories to the Charter intended to complement the European Convention on Human Rights by providing for the enjoyment of social rights by nationals of Contracting Parties resident or working regularly within their territory, and refugees.[9] Among the rights contained in the Charter are rights in respect of employment: a right to work, and to do so under fair and safe conditions, for fair remuneration, and with the right to organize and bargain collectively. Alongside these provisions are rights to special protection for women, children, and young people in employment; rights to education, and to vocational training and guidance; rights to provision for health care, social security, welfare services, and care for disabled people; and rights to protection for the family, and particularly for mothers and children. The contracting parties are to secure the rights (in the words of the Preamble) 'without discrimination on grounds of race, colour, sex, religion, political opinion, national extraction or social origin', in order to 'make every effort in common to improve the standard of living and to promote the social well-being of both their urban and rural populations by means of appropriate institutions and action'. However, states need not accept obligations in respect of all the rights. As Professor Harris puts it, 'The ESC is unusual in that it permits states to ratify it on an *á la carte* basis. They are required to accept at least ten of the nineteen articles of the ESC or forty-five of its seventy-two paragraphs'.[10]

There is no enforcement mechanism equivalent to that under the European Convention on Human Rights. Instead, each state is to submit to the Secretary-General of the Council of Europe biennial reports on developments in relation to rights under provisions which that state has accepted, and occasional reports (as requested by the Committee of Ministers) as to the provisions in Part II of the Charter, giving specific rights, which the state concerned has not accepted.[11] Reports are examined by a Committee of Experts appointed by the Committee of Ministers from a list of 'independent experts of the highest integrity and recognized competence in international social questions, nominated by the Contracting Parties'.[12] The Committee of Experts decides whether states have violated rights guaranteed under the Charter. To facilitate consistency between the work of the Council of Europe and that of the ILO, Article 26 of the Charter provides that the ILO is to be invited to nominate a representative to participate in a consultative capacity in the deliberations of the Committee of Experts. The reports from states, and the conclusions of the Committee of Experts, are considered by a Sub-Committee of the Governmental Social Committee of the Council of Europe, on which each of the Contracting Parties is represented. This body

---

[8] For commentary, see D. J. Harris, *The European Social Charter* (Charlottesville, Va.: University of Virginia Press, 1984); Robertson and Merrills, *Human Rights in the World*, 245–55.

[9] Appendix to the European Social Charter, paras. 1 and 2.

[10] D. J. Harris, 'Lessons from the Reporting System of the European Social Charter', in Alston and Crawford (eds.), *The Future of UN Human Rights Treaty Monitoring*, 347–60 at 347, n. 3.

[11] European Social Charter, Arts. 21 and 22.

[12] Ibid., Arts. 24, 25.

presents reports, which often consist largely of opinions as to whether violations of the Charter found by the Committee of Experts have in fact occurred, to the Committee of Ministers. The Committee of Ministers also receives views from the Consultative Assembly of the Council of Europe. The Committee of Ministers may then make necessary recommendations to each Contracting Party, but recommendations require to be approved by a two-thirds majority of the members of the Council of Europe (not all of whom are Contracting Parties to the Charter).[13]

Until recently, this regime had not been particularly effective in influencing the development of law and policy in the UK, or (generally) elsewhere in Europe. The Charter, like the various ILO conventions, imposes obligations on the state which take effect in international law, but does not confer enforceable rights on individuals. Individuals, collective groups, and non-governmental organizations (other than the ILO) do not have standing to participate in the regime of regular reports and reviews of progress to which states are subject. The central position of the Governmental Social Committee has meant that the operation of the Charter has depended heavily on the political will of the Contracting Parties to give the Charter a dynamic function. In a geographical area where a fairly high measure of economic prosperity has been achieved by applying predominantly liberal, capitalist politico-economic theories, this political will has predictably been lacking. However, matters changed dramatically with the collapse of the 'Iron Curtain' between eastern and western Europe. When former eastern bloc countries started to apply for membership of the Council of Europe, the Charter was seen as a valuable instrument for evaluating the performance of those countries in protecting and enhancing social and economic rights as they moved from command economies to market economies.

In the 1980s and 1990s, the potential for development of social and economic rights through European Community institutions, together with the eastern European developments, spurred Member States of the Council of Europe to take steps to improve the effectiveness of the Charter. First, the Director-General of the Council of Europe decided to transfer responsibility for the operation of the Charter to the Council's Directorate of Human Rights. This Directorate had always been responsible for the operation of the European Convention on Human Rights, and had been instrumental in raising its profile and encouraging its dynamic development, but the Charter had never been part of its remit. Secondly, the Committee of Ministers established an *ad hoc* committee, consisting of nominated experts, to make proposals for improving the effectiveness of the Charter and its supervisory machinery. The committee's report led to an Amending Protocol to the Charter being opened for signature in 1991. When it enters into force the Protocol will significantly change the supervisory arrangements. After nearly ten years, it still lacks ratification by six of the states (including the UK[14]) which must accept it before it can enter into force. The principal changes are as follows.[15]

[13] Arts. 27, 28, 29. See Harris, 'Lessons from the Reporting System of the Social Charter'.

[14] The UK signed the Protocol on the day it was opened for signature, 21 October 1991, but has not yet ratified it.

[15] For authoritative discussion, see D. J. Harris, 'A Fresh Impetus for the European Social Charter' (1992) 41 *ICLQ* 659–76.

First, responsibility for authoritatively interpreting the Charter will move from the Governmental Social Committee to the Committee of Experts. The main function of the Governmental Committee will become that of advising the Committee of Ministers on the circumstances in which it should exercise its power to make recommendations to Contracting Parties. This will reduce the direct influence of governments over the interpretation of the rights under the Charter. Secondly, the membership of the Committee of Experts will be increased, to take account of its increased workload, and the Committee will have power to hold oral hearings at which to seek additional information and clarification of reports from Contracting Parties. Thirdly, the Parliamentary Assembly will change its role, from being consulted by the Committee of Ministers to conducting independent debates on the report of the Committee of Experts. Eliminating the Assembly from the formal supervisory process will speed it up and simplify it.

Finally, a new version of the Charter, the European Social Charter (Revised), was opened for signature in 1996, and entered into force in 1999. This incorporates the obligations of states which had ratified an Additional Protocol to the 1961 Charter which was opened for signature in 1988 (not yet signed by the UK), making available a system of adjudication on collective complaints by employers' and trade union organizations in respect of alleged breaches of the Charter by states. The UK signed the Revised Charter in 1997, but has not yet ratified it, and so is not yet bound by it. Even if it ratifies the Revised Charter in the future, the UK need not be bound by the provisions for adjudication of collective complaints, since Articles C and D in Part IV of the Revised Charter make it clear that the collective complaints provisions bind only those states which had already ratified the Additional Protocol of 1988, unless other states accept those enhanced supervision arrangements on ratifying the Revised Charter or subsequently.

(ii) The protection of social and economic rights through Community law

At the same time, the Social Chapter of the treaty establishing the European Community[16] assumed greater importance, being expanded in scope by an Agreement between eleven of the twelve Member States (excluding the UK) as part of the Final Act at the Maastricht summit conference in 1991 which became part of the Treaty of European Union 1992, entering into force in November 1993. This committed the Community and Member States to the objectives of promoting high employment, improved living and working conditions, social protection, equal pay for equal work, dialogue between management and labour, and the development of human resources. It empowered the EC Council of Ministers to adopt Directives setting minimum standards for gradual implementation, and made the Commission responsible for promoting the objectives. The UK, alone among the fifteen Member States, did not become a party to the Social Chapter, because it believed that implementing it would involve an incursion on domestic sovereignty by Community authorities, and would make British industry less competitive. The Labour government which took office in 1997 reversed this policy, and accepted the Social Chapter, which enabled its provi-

---

[16] Arts. 117–22 of the Treaty of Rome, as amended.

sions to be brought within the body of the Treaty establishing the European Communities by the Amsterdam Treaty of 1997.

The EC Social Chapter was a significant step towards converting the aspirational standards of the European Social Charter into 'hard law' applicable in national courts. Further progress was made in the amendments made to the Treaty of European Union by the Treaty of Amsterdam in 1997. The Member States added a recital to the preamble to the Treaty of European Union: 'Confirming their attachment to fundamental rights as defined in the European Social Charter . . . and the 1989 Community Charter of the Fundamental Social Rights of Workers'. Both these Charters are also mentioned in the amended version of what is now Article 136 (formerly Article 117) of the Treaty of Rome which established the European Communities. The Amsterdam Treaty extended the jurisdiction of the Court of Justice in respect of violations of human rights to various matters relating to co-operation between Member States in justice and home affairs, and introduced what is now Article 13 of the consolidated Treaty establishing the European Community allowing the Council of Ministers, acting unanimously on a recommendation from the Commission, to 'take appropriate action to combat discrimination based on sex, racial or ethnic origin, religion or belief, age or sexual orientation'.[17] As we shall see, the scope of European anti-discrimination law has already been greatly enlarged as a result.

It follows that what started as a free trade community has acquired, over the years, considerable ability to make law which is binding in Member States to give effect to at least some social rights.[18] This presents a number of problems, including that of maintaining social rights in the face of a basic ethos favouring free-market capitalism.[19] It suggests that social rights, like civil and political rights before them, are likely to present issues relating to the consistency of standards applied under the regime of the EU with those operating through the Council of Europe, and the European Social Charter in particular, not to mention the further layers of standards in international treaties and 'soft law' relating to social rights at a global (or, at any rate, supra-European) level.[20] This relationship has acquired a further layer of complexity with the proclamation in December 2000 of the EU Charter of Fundamental Rights, which includes a range of social rights alongside civil and political rights. The interplay of these sets of standards is likely to provide a focus for the work of human rights lawyers in the coming decade.

[17] P. Craig and G. de Búrca, *EU Law Text, Cases and Materials*, 2nd edn. (Oxford: Oxford University Press, 1998), 32–48 provide a very good, concise explanation of the changes made by the Treaty of Amsterdam.

[18] See L. Betten and N. Grief, *EU Law and Human Rights* (London: Longman, 1998), chs 3, 6, and 7.

[19] For discussion, see M. Poiares Maduro, 'Striking the Elusive Balance between Economic Freedom and Social Rights in the EU', in P. Alston, M. Buştelo, and J. Heenan (eds.), *The EU and Human Rights* (Oxford: Oxford University Press, 1999), 449–72.

[20] See S. Sciarra, 'From Strasbourg to Amsterdam: Prospects for the Convergence of European Social Rights Policy', in Alston *et al.* (eds), *The EU and Human Rights*, 473–501.

(3) IMPLEMENTING SOCIAL AND ECONOMIC RIGHTS IN DOMESTIC LAW:
PRACTICE AND POTENTIAL

Because the UK adopts a dualist view of international law, in which treaty obligations
are not automatically incorporated into domestic law, the European Social Charter
and the other conventions dealing with economic and social rights do not have direct
effect in English law, and are not justiciable in our courts. Indeed, it would often be
hard for a court to apply them, since they are in form generally exhortatory rather
than prescriptive, and leave a great deal of leeway to states which have to implement
them. For instance, judges could not easily fashion remedies which respected the
difference between the functions of the judiciary and the executive, or the need for
flexibility allowing the pursuit of different political programmes, when addressing
provisions such as the following, taken from the ILO Social Policy (Basic Aims and
Standards) Convention (1962):

'All policies shall be primarily directed to the well-being and development of the population
and to the promotion of its desire for social progress.' (Article 1, paragraph 1)

'The improvement of standards of living shall be regarded as the principal objective in the
planning of economic development.' (Article 2)

'All practicable measures shall be taken in the planning of economic development to
harmonize such development with the healthy evolution of the communities concerned.'
(Article 3, paragraph 1)

The need to regard the obligations on states as variable, to take account of their
different economic and social circumstances, is expressly recognized by, for example,
Article 2, paragraph 1 of the ICESC as follows:

1.   'Each State Party to the present Covenant undertakes to take steps, individually and
through international assistance and co-operation, especially economic and technical, to the
maximum of its available resources, with a view to achieving progressively the full realization of the rights recognized in the present Covenant by all appropriate means, including
particularly the adoption of legislative measures.'

On the other hand, some obligations would be much more easily justiciable. In
relation to the right to safe and healthy working conditions, the parties to Article 3 of
the European Social Charter undertake: (1) to issue safety and health regulations; (2)
to provide for the enforcement of such regulations by measures of supervision; (3) to
consult, as appropriate, employers' and workers' organizations on measures intended
to improve industrial safety and health. There is no reason why any of these provisions should be regarded as non-justiciable. Adjudicating on the obligations which
they impose would not involve judges in assessing social or economic policy, or in
evaluating unusually intractable forms of evidence. Similarly, paragraphs 2 and 3 of
Article 2 of the International Covenant on Economic, Social and Cultural Rights
shows how such instruments can set out obligations which are in principle justiciable,
while defining the limited field within which states are to enjoy what might be called,
as in the caselaw of the European Court of Human Rights, a 'margin of appreciation'
within which their discretion is largely unfettered:

'2. States Parties to the present Covenant undertake to guarantee that the rights enunciated in the present Covenant will be exercised without discrimination of any kind as to race, colour, sex, language, religion, political or other opinion, national or social origin, property, birth or other status.

3. Developing countries, with due regard to human rights and their national economy, may determine to what extent they would guarantee the economic rights recognized in the present Covenant to non-nationals.'

At national level, the desire to recognize such rights together with a fear of judicial entanglement in a political mire has produced some interesting compromises. Article 45.1 of the 1937 Constitution of Ireland contains a rule of imperfect obligation. It requires the state to 'strive to promote the welfare of the whole people by securing and protecting as effectively as it may a social order in which justice and charity shall inform all the institutions of the national life'. In particular, this is to be done by directing its policy towards securing a range of Directive Principles of Social Policy enumerated in Article 45.2. As one might expect, the opening words of Article 45 state that these are 'for the general guidance of the Oireachtas [Parliament] . . . and shall not be cognizable by any Court under any of the provisions of this Constitution'. Yet even rights which are too vague to be judicially enforceable, or which are necessarily subject to a governmental discretion to act pragmatically in the light of prevailing circumstances, may still not be entirely beyond judicial notice. The framers of the 1947 Constitution of the Union of India were influenced by Ireland in formulating Directive Principles of State Policy in Part IV of the Constitution.[21] These set out broad policy objectives, requiring the state to direct its policy towards securing social objectives which include an adequate means of livelihood for all citizens, equal pay for equal work for men and women, and the protection and improvement of the environment. The state is said to have a duty to comply with the Directive Principles, which are, however, not to be enforceable by any court.[22] The Indian Supreme Court has none the less been prepared to exercise judicial review of executive or legislative acts to ensure that the Directive Principles are taken into account as relevant considerations,[23] and the express rights are to be interpreted harmoniously with the Directive Principles.[24] A contrasting approach is adopted in the 1996 Constitution of South Africa, where the Bill of Rights includes rights to environmental protection (section 24), state measures within available resources to foster equitable access to land (section 25(5)), adequate housing (section 26), access to health care, water, food,

[21] G. Austin, *The Indian Constitution: Cornerstone of a Nation* (New-Delhi: Oxford University Press, 1999), 76.

[22] Indian Constitution, Art. 37. A similar model has been adopted in South Africa's 1996 Constitution, as a compromise between denying constitutional status to social and economic rights and attempting to make them fully justiciable.

[23] *Pandey v. State of West Bengal* [1988] LRC (Const) 241; P. P. Craig and S. L. Deshpande, 'Rights, Autonomy and Process: Public Interest Litigation in India' (1989) 9 *Oxford J. of Legal Studies* 356–73.

[24] In *Krishnan v. State of Andhra Pradesh* [1993] 4 LRC 234, SC of India, this produced a right to set up an educational establishment. In *Delhi Development Horticulture Employees' Union v. Delhi Administration, Delhi and others* [1993] 4 LRC 182, 189–90, it was held that at some future time it might possibly enable the express constitutional right to life to be interpreted as giving rise to a right to a livelihood, although that could not happen until economic conditions made practicable the enforcement of such a right.

and social security (section 27), and education (section 29). These are not formally differentiated from civil and political rights, but the sections make it clear that the duty lying on the state is limited to what it is reasonable to do in the light of available resources, and usually seeking a progressive improvement rather than immediate achievement of a set standard. The practical effect is not very different from that of India's Directive Principles.

The willingness of courts to take such steps depends heavily on local political conditions, particularly on the way in which judges see such obligations and their willingness to risk conflict with government. In Ireland, courts have been far less willing than judges in India to make even limited use of the Directive Principles, perhaps because Article 45 of the Constitution of Ireland provides that the Principles 'shall not be cognizable by any Court', in contrast to the Indian Constitution's 'shall not be enforceable'. Nevertheless, it is conceivable that courts might be prepared to treat those policy objectives which form part of treaty obligations and which are not expressly stated to be non-cognizable as relevant considerations, so that executive decisions taken without considering them might be subject to judicial review. It would be by no means unreasonable, at a time when international co-operation is of growing importance in all fields, for courts to hold that the international obligations which the UK government has voluntarily undertaken form at least a relevant consideration to be taken into account by government on ordinary judicial review principles.

The principal remaining possibility for making a set of social and economic rights enforceable in English law derives from the combination of the EC Social Chapter and the EU Charter of Fundamental Rights, which were mentioned above. These may in time produce effects on the law in the UK. In the short term, accepting the Social Chapter will make little impact on English law. It does not give rise immediately to enforceable community rights: the Agreement merely permits the Council to adopt Directives laying down 'minimum requirements for gradual implementation, having regard to the conditions and technical rules obtaining in each of the Member States'.[25] In the long term, the Social Chapter will ultimately lead to a set of enforceable social and economic rights. However, these will cover a fairly small field, related principally to employment matters. Although the enforcement measures available are more effective than those available under the European Social Charter, the rights under the Agreement are nowhere near as comprehensive as those guaranteed, if the government has the commitment to them, under the Charter. There will therefore continue to be a role for the Charter even if the government ultimately signs the Agreement. In addition, the EU Charter of Fundamental Rights, which includes a range of social and economic rights, provides a set of background values by reference to which Community law will be interpreted.

[25] Arts. 136–43 EC.

3.2 THE IDEA OF HUMAN DIGNITY

(1) THE VARIOUS MEANINGS OF HUMAN DIGNITY

Many modern constitutions, reacting to appalling assaults on the essence of human-ity, have included a right to human dignity in a bill of rights, or have referred to human dignity as one of the fundamental values underpinning the constitution. Article 1(1) of Germany's *Grundgesetz* (Basic Law) of 1949 provides, 'The dignity of man shall be inviolable. To respect and protect it shall be the duty of all state author-ity'. Section 10 of South Africa's 1996 Constitution states, 'Everyone has inherent dignity and the right to have their dignity respected an protected'. Courts have founded significant jurisprudential developments on these provisions, such as the decision of the Constitutional Court of South Africa that capital punishment was unconstitutional because it was incompatible with human dignity.[26]

Human dignity is undoubtedly an intuitively attractive idea, but it is more complex than it appears at first sight.[27] It operates on three levels: the dignity attaching to the whole human species; the dignity of groups within the human species; and the dignity of human individuals. The legal implications are slightly different at each level. The dignity of the species as a whole requires rules which differentiate between humans and other species, and which protect the special status and integrity of humans. This might be done, for example, by legal regimes designed to prevent or regulate artificial interfer-ence with both the process of human reproduction and the naturalness of the genetic constitution of the human race (a regime administered in the UK by the Human Fertilisation and Embryology Authority under the Human Fertilisation and Embry-ology Act 1990). In France, the *Conseil constitutionnel* treated the dignity of the species as a fundamental constitutional principle when considering the constitutional validity of two laws to regulate the use of body parts and body products, medically assisted procreation, and prenatal diagnostic techniques. As a result, the constitutionality of the laws was assessed partly by reference to the effect of the provisions on human dignity. The laws would have infringed human dignity had they given rights of ownership over the human body or body parts, or instituted a system of bioethics which failed to safeguard the genetic integrity of the human species. But the laws in question respected the dignity of the human body and species in those respects, and so were held to be constitutional.[28] This is the sense in which human dignity may influence changes to

[26] *S. v. Makwanyane* 1995 (3) SA 391, CC. See also Israel's Basic Law: Human Dignity and Liberty (1992, as amended in 1994), ss.1(a), 2, 4, and 8, and the application of the right to protection for dignity which led the Supreme Court of Israel to hold that a range of methods used by the Israeli security forces to interrogate terrorist suspects were unlawful in *Public Committee Against Torture in Israel and others v. The State of Israel and others*, Judgment of 6 September 1999.

[27] For fuller discussion, see D. Feldman, 'Human Dignity as a Legal Value', Part I [1999] *PL* 682–702; Part II [2000] *PL* 61–76.

[28] Conseil constitutionnel, décision de 27 juillet 1994, nos. 94–343–344, DC: relative au respect du corps humain et à l'utilisation des éléments et produits du corps human, à l'assistance médicale à la procréation et au diagnostique prénatal (lois no. 94–653 and no. 94–654 du 29 juillet 1994), Dalloz, 1995 jurisprudence, 237; Dalloz, 1995 sommaire, 299. See S. Wheatley, 'Human Rights and Human Dignity in the Resolution of Certain Ethical Questions in Biomedicine' [2001] *EHRLR* 312–25.

the law regulating research on human embryos, even if one does not accept that an individual embryo is properly described as a person before birth. The law on cloning illustrates this. When the High Court held that the law did not control cloning of humans, emergency legislation was passed within two weeks to fill the gap.[28a]

The second level of dignity, that of groups within the species, excludes discrimination between groups on irrelevant grounds, and allows them to assert rights to exist and to continue their traditions. Rules against genocide, apartheid, and incitement to racial hatred fall in this category, as do arrangements for giving remedies for group libels. Treating a person with respect for their dignity is incompatible with discrimination on grounds which are morally irrelevant, providing a link between the values of dignity and equality.

The third level is that of individuals. At this level, dignity requires the right to make one's own decisions, and to contribute to decisions made by others which affect one's life. For example, the law generally forbids medical treatment without the patient's consent; while the principles of fairness and natural justice confer a right to have one's voice heard in matters which touch one's interests. But we may be required to respect the dignity of people who lack freedom of choice, such as those in a permanent vegetative state. Such cases present difficult questions about the relationship between dignity and autonomy, and between different kinds of dignity.

In respect of classic liberal rights, the dignity of the species and the dignity of the individual tend to work together. For example, when the Constitutional Court of South Africa decided in *S. v. Makwanyane*[29] that capital punishment was incompatible with human dignity, it reflected a sense that in certain circumstances it degrades both the individual and the whole of humanity to treat people in such a way. But the idea of dignity is not inextricably linked to a liberal-individualist view of human beings as people whose life choices deserve respect. If the state takes a particular view on what is required for people to live dignified lives, it may introduce regulations to restrict the freedom which people have to make choices which, in the state's view, interfere with the dignity of the individual, a social group, or the human race as a whole. Restrictions on assisting suicide and on the capacity to give legally effective consent to certain practices or procedures (discussed more fully in Chapters 4 and 5, below) provide examples of this. The quest for human dignity may subvert rather than enhance choice, and in some circumstances may limit rather than extend the scope of traditional 'first-generation' human rights and fundamental freedoms. Once it becomes a tool in the hands of law-makers and judges, the concept of human dignity is a two-edged sword.

French law illustrates the capacity of dignity both to support social rights and to undermine individual rights. When considering the constitutionality of a law amending the arrangements for providing and paying for public housing for homeless people, the *Conseil constitutionnel* decided that the legislature had power to authorize provision for homeless people, as well as winter shelter for travellers, in view of the statement in the Preamble to the 1946 Constitution of the importance of protecting

---

[28a] *R. (Quintaville, on behalf of Pro-Life Alliance) v. Secretary of State for Health*, unreported, 15 November 2001, Admin. Ct. (Crane J); Human Reproductive Cloning Act 2001.
[29]   1995 (3) SA 391, CC.

the dignity of the human person against all forms of degradation.[30] This took the notion of human dignity well beyond the historical sense in which it was used in the 1946 Constitution (subsequently superseded by the 1958 Constitution), where it related to the immediate post-war concern with Nazi atrocities. In effect, the *Conseil's* approach allows all social rights to be seen as advancing human dignity.[31] It recognized that protecting human dignity as an ideal in French constitutional law could give rise to a positive duty to provide the conditions in which dignity could flourish, as well as a duty to protect individuals against assaults on their human dignity.

French courts have also shown that human dignity can be used paternalistically to restrict freedom of choice, enabling the state to impose on individuals its own view of the good life in preference to theirs. In the '*lancer des nains*' case, the *Conseil d'État* upheld orders banning dwarf-throwing competitions in their areas. The spectacles were organized by Fun Productions, a company which employed a dwarf, Manuel Wackenheim, as the projectile to be thrown by hopeful contestants. Mr. Wackenheim was willing to undertake the task, which he saw as a source of financial security and even fame in a world where many careers (including policing) were barred to him because of his size. His employers ensured that he had proper protective clothing and that appropriate precautions were taken to protect his health. The *Conseil d'Etat* held that it was an affront to human dignity to put on a spectacle devoted to allowing spectators to throw a person selected by reason of his suffering from a physical handicap, and that the police had power to stop such spectacles to protect the security of the dwarf and of spectators, notwithstanding Mr. Wackenheim's keenness to take part and his rights and those of the company to freedom of occupation, of commerce, and of industry, it had been justifiable to ban the events (and indeed to fine Fun Productions for organizing them).[32] This puts human dignity, approached at the levels of the group (people with a growth handicap) and the species, above the freedom of an individual member of the group to choose how to exploit his or her physical form or to engage in an occupation of choice.

Furthermore, at the levels of the social group and the individual human dignity has two aspects, subjective and objective. The subjective aspect is concerned with one's sense of self-worth, which is usually associated with forms of behaviour which communicate that sense to others. The objective aspect is concerned with the state's and other people's attitudes to an individual or group, usually in the light of social norms or expectations. It is in this sense that people who lack the capacity to cultivate the subjective aspect of dignity can nevertheless be said to have a type of dignity which demands respect. For example, very young children and patients in a persistent vegetative state can be regarded as having intrinsic human dignity in this objective sense, in that responsible beings owe a moral, and often a legal, duty to have regard to their interests and rights when making decisions affecting their welfare. A description of

[30] Conseil constitutionnel, décision no. 94–359, DC: loi relative à la diversité de l'habitat, 19 janvier 1995, Actualité juridique de droit administratif, 1995, 455.

[31] Ibid., at 457.

[32] CE, ass., 27 octobre 1995, *Cne de Morsang-sur-Orge*, Dalloz Jur. 1995, 257; C.E., ass., 27 octobre 1995, *Ville d'Aix-en-Provence, Rec. CE*, 372; Dalloz Jur., 1996, 177, with annotation by G. Leberton.

people as showing dignity relates to their behaviour and personalities in terms of social values which identify that sort of behaviour or personality as good or worthwhile. In this way, ideas about descriptions of dignity are linked to beliefs about what is involved in living a good life, and to ideas of the Good more generally. As Alasdair Macintyre has shown, such ideas are culturally specific, so that ideas of dignity will vary between cultures and societies. It will also be difficult to retain consensus in relation to them within a single pluralist society.[33] In relation to the subjective aspect of dignity, the law of human rights will typically be concerned to prevent treatment which damages a person's self-respect and physical or moral integrity. With regard to the objective aspect, the law will usually have to go further, imposing positive duties on people to act in ways which optimize the conditions for social respect and dignity.

It seems, then, that speaking of human dignity is a way of expressing a set of moral problems rather than a technique for resolving them (in hard cases at any rate). The law can at best provide a circumscribing circle of rights which, in some of their effects, help to preserve the field for a dignified life. Yet treaties and constitutions have been drafted, and tribunals have framed their decisions, in terms of human dignity, so we will now examine the legal meaning and impact of using the term in those contexts.

(2) THE PLACE OF DIGNITY IN INTERNATIONAL HUMAN-RIGHTS LAW

The desire to promote human dignity underlies many of the rights under post-World-War-II international human-rights instruments, even if the notion has been more often deployed than analysed. The Preamble to the Charter of the United Nations (1945) states:

'We the peoples of the United Nations determined to save succeeding generations from the scourge of war, which twice in our lifetime has brought untold sorrow to mankind, and to reaffirm faith in fundamental human rights, in the dignity and worth of the human person, in the equal rights of men and women and of nations large and small, . . . have resolved to combine our efforts to accomplish these aims.'

The Preamble to the Universal Declaration on Human Rights (United Nations, 1948) also refers to the dignity and worth of the human person.

The Preambles to both the International Covenant on Economic, Social and Cultural Rights and the International Covenant on Civil and Political Rights (1966) include declarations 'that, in accordance with the principles in the Charter of the United Nations, recognition of the inherent dignity and of the equal and inalienable rights of all members of the human family is the foundation of freedom, justice and peace in the world' and 'that these rights derive from the inherent dignity of the human person'. Similar reliance on the dignity of the human person as a justification for enforcing human rights appears from many other instruments, including the ECHR, which refers in its Preamble to the UN Declaration on Human Rights and in respect of which the Strasbourg organs have frequently referred to human dignity as

---

[33] A. Macintyre, *After Virtue: a Study in Moral Theory*, 2nd edn. (London: Duckworth, 1985), esp. ch. 16.

one of the values underpinning the rights. In the context of EU law, the acceptance by the European Court of Justice that fundamental rights gave rise to general principles of Community law[34] helped to give support to human dignity in people's dealings with Community organs. Article 6(2) of the Treaty of European Community, as amended at Amsterdam, requires the Community to respect fundamental rights. Most recently, the EU Charter of Fundamental Rights was proclaimed at Nice in December 2000. Its preamble identifies 'the indivisible, universal values of human dignity, freedom, equality and solidarity', together with the principles of democracy and the rule of law, as the foundations of the Union. Article 1 states, 'Human dignity is inviolable. It must be respected and protected'. Unlike the treaty provisions which have been mentioned, the Charter does not directly give rise to legally enforceable rights; it is a form of 'soft law'. Nevertheless, it is very likely to influence the interpretation of EU treaty provisions and other sources of EU law, raising the profile of the notion of human dignity with all its opportunities and drawbacks.

Relying on 'the inherent dignity of the human person' as a foundation for rights is different from conferring a right to dignity. It was suggested above that dignity is a quality or characteristic of human beings, so that an individual cannot have a right to it. On the other hand, one clearly has an interest in having one's human dignity respected, and this may support more specific rights. The fundamental, shared quality of human beings gives rise automatically to an irrebuttable presumption of human dignity, which attaches to individuals by virtue of their membership of the human species. An umbrella of rights may be justified as preventing interference with this general human dignity. Subordinate forms of dignity, derived from an individual's personal qualities and behaviour, may for some purposes also be sufficiently valuable to justify a right to protection. Such protective rights could be termed 'rights to dignity' in so far as they have the object of upholding dignity indirectly.

However, even in this limited form the right to human dignity appears in human-rights instruments only in certain circumstances. One occasionally comes across an express right to dignity in international human-rights law. For example, the American Convention on Human Rights, Article 11(1) provides, 'Everyone has the right to have his honor respected and his dignity recognized'. The Inter-American Commission has concluded that the vaginal search and inspection of members of a prisoner's family as a condition of allowing them to visit him violated the family members' rights to honour and dignity, because 'it involves a particularly intimate aspect of a woman's private life' and the procedure 'is likely to provoke intense feelings of shame and anguish in almost all persons subjected to it. In addition, subjecting a 13 year old child to such a procedure could result in serious psychological damage that is difficult to evaluate'.[35] This express provision for a right to respect for dignity does not actually include a right to dignity as such, and even in the form of an express right to respect for dignity it is unusual, being specifically mentioned as a right mainly in relation to situations which are particularly likely to lead to an assault on dignity.

The primary situations in which there is an express right to dignity are those where

---

[34] Case 29/69, *Stauder v. City of Ulm* [1969] ECR 419, CJEC.
[35] Report No. 38/96 of 15 October 1996, Case 10,506 v. Argentina, paras. 93–4.

people have lost their liberty, whether for their own good, the protection of the public, or pursuant to criminal proceedings. For example, the International Covenant on Civil and Political Rights (1966), Article 10(1) provides, 'All persons deprived of their liberty shall be treated with humanity and with respect for the inherent dignity of the human person', and the remainder of Article 10 makes particular provision for detained suspects and convicted prisoners. The UN Convention on the Rights of the Child (1989), Article 37(c) provides that, where children are deprived of their liberty they have the right to be treated 'with humanity and respect for the inherent dignity of the human person, and in a manner which takes into account the needs of persons of their age', and 'shall be separated from adults unless it is considered to be in the child's best interests not to do so . . . ' Article 28(2) of the 1989 Convention requires States Parties to 'take all appropriate measures to ensure that school discipline is administered in a manner consistent with the child's human dignity . . . ', although this is part of a progressive programme rather than an immediate right.

These are special cases. Generally, instead of giving a right to dignity to every adult, international human-rights instruments require institutional (including legal) arrangements in states to respect people's inherent human dignity. International human rights provide a framework of side-constraints which restrict the freedom of public authorities and, sometimes, others to violate human dignity in specified ways. In this way, the desirability of upholding human dignity becomes one of a number of important background considerations in the light of which specific human rights fall to be interpreted.

In view of the wide-ranging significance of human dignity as a justification for conferring and protecting human rights, there is arguably no human right which is unconnected to human dignity. Nevertheless, some rights seem to have a particularly prominent role in upholding human dignity. These include the right to be free of inhuman or degrading treatment, the right to respect for private and family life, the right to freedom of conscience and belief, the right to freedom of association, the right to marry and found a family, and the right to be free of discriminatory treatment. Apart from freedom from inhuman and degrading treatment (which is concerned with both dignity and physical integrity), these are not principally directed to protecting dignity. Family life, conscience, association, marriage, and non-discrimination are more directly geared to protecting the interests in autonomy, equality, and respect. Nevertheless, autonomy, equal respect, and self-respect are important in providing circumstances in which dignity can flourish, and rights which protect them usefully, if indirectly, buttress dignity. There are also social and economic rights, such as the right of those unable to provide for themselves to receive by way of social assistance at least the support (including money and accommodation) necessary to maintain life in ways reasonably conducive to minimum levels of human dignity. Other rights which recognize the importance of dignity and may, in some circumstances, contribute to its maintenance include the right to life, the right to be free of arbitrary arrest and detention, the right to due process in legal proceedings, and the right to freedom of expression.

Many of these rights are considered in subsequent chapters, so the discussion here is limited to pointing out the relationship between dignity and other values which the rights support. There is a theory according to which one of the reasons (if not the main or only one) for conferring due-process rights on people is to mark the importance to people's dignity and sense of worth of involving them in the process of making decisions which affect them. On this view, due-process rights such as those provided under Article 6 and, to a lesser extent, Article 5 of the ECHR are dignitary rights. Against this, one can set the views of those such as Professor Denis Galligan who argue that the sole or main reason for protecting due process is that it tends to improve the quality of decision-making and the accuracy of outcomes.[36] Whichever view is taken of the *purpose* of the rights, it cannot be sensibly denied that at least one *effect* of due-process rights is to respect the dignity of the people involved in the litigation. The same it true of many other rights. There is probably no right which exclusively protects dignity, but they all or nearly all help to guarantee the conditions under which people may live dignified lives.

(3) DIGNITY IN CONSTITUTIONAL LAW

Human dignity is given a significant role in some constitutional bills of rights. In particular, it is a common feature of new constitutions in states which are trying to shake off a legacy of disregard for the human dignity of some, at least, of its citizens. It thus figures significantly in the German *Grundgesetz*, where Article 1 provides: '(1) The dignity of man shall be inviolable. To respect and protect it shall be the duty of all state authority'. In private law, this was used by the *Bundesgerichthof* to develop a right to personality, aided by Article 2(1) ('Everyone shall have the right to the free development of his personality in so far as he does not violate the rights of others or offend against the constitutional order or against morality') in the *Schacht* case[37] (a process which was subsequently approved by the *Bundesverfassungsgericht* in the *Soraya* case[38]) and, arising out of that, a right of privacy.

Human dignity has also been an important influence on the post-apartheid constitutions of South Africa. Section 1(a) of the 1996 Constitution identifies human dignity as one of the values on which the sovereign democratic state of South Africa is founded. Section 7(1) proclaims that the Bill of Rights, forming Chapter 2 of the Constitution, 'affirms the democratic values of dignity, equality and freedom'. As already noted, section 10 states, 'Every person has inherent dignity and the right to have their dignity respected and protected'. This right is non-derogable.[39] Dignity also forms an important value in interpreting both the Bill of Rights and other legislation, and for developing common and customary law.[40] In this setting, emphasizing dignity serves to concentrate attention on the importance of ensuring that some people are not treated as less than human or as inferior to others.

However, a right to dignity invites judges to give effect to a value which is to some

---

[36] See the discussion in D. Galligan, *Due Process and Fair Procedures* (Oxford: Clarendon Press, 1996), ch. 4.

[37] BGH May 25 1954, BGHZ 13, 334.

[38] BVerfGE 34, 269 (1973).

[39] Constitution of South Africa, s. 37(5), Table.

[40] Ibid., s. 39(1), (2).

degree culturally determined. It may restrict freedom, acting as a screen behind which paternalism or moralism reign. Its value depends on the attitudes of those who enforce it.

(4) INDIRECT PROTECTION OF DIGNITY IN ENGLISH LAW

Although human dignity is increasingly significant in the constitutional settings examined in the previous section, it does not yet have a developed role in the constitution of the UK. Although Professor Dawn Oliver has suggested that it is one of the values underlying both public and private law in the UK, together with autonomy, respect, status, and security,[41] the constitutional significance of dignity seems less fundamental in practice than, for example, effectiveness of government, account-ability, and representativeness (around which are designed the institutions of parlia-mentary democracy). Even among the values which Professor Oliver identifies, dignity would appear, from its concrete effects in law, to rank below autonomy and security, on which legal institutions such as property are founded.

English law recognizes that dignity is an important value which may generate duties on public authorities to provide assistance to those who would otherwise be left destitute. This gives rise to something in the nature of a social or economic right, which extends at least as far as is necessary to maintain life and a minimum level of dignity. It may also lead to the development of principles and remedies in public law. As Simon Brown LJ pointed out in *R. v. Secretary of State for Social Security, ex parte Joint Council for the Welfare of Immigrants*,[42] this is essential if other rights which people have are to be given reality. Where regulations purported to withdraw benefits from people wishing to exercise their right to seek asylum in the UK, his Lordship held that the regulations would either render the right nugatory by making it impos-sible for asylum-seekers to remain in the UK, or 'necessarily contemplate for some a life so destitute that no civilised nation can tolerate it'. The latter would violate a common-law obligation to maintain poor immigrants stated by Lord Ellenborough CJ as early as 1803: 'the law of humanity, which is anterior to all positive laws, obliges us to afford them relief, to save them from starving'.[43] Respect for human dignity may require the state to take positive action to assist those who are unable to provide for themselves. The Court of Appeal in *Ex parte Joint Council for the Welfare of Immigrants* held that only clear words in an Act of Parliament could authorize the making of regulations which would have the effect of violating that obligation or depriving people of the opportunity to exercise their statutory right to seek asylum. The link to dignity is clear (unfortunately Parliament promptly legislated in clear words to permit the regulations to be made).

---

[41] See D. Oliver, 'The Underlying Values of Public and Private Law', in M. Taggart (ed.), *The Province of Administrative Law* (Oxford: Hart Publishing, 1997), ch. 11; D. Oliver, *Common Values and the Public-Private Divide* (London: Butterworths, 1999), ch. 3.

[42] [1996] 4 All ER 385, CA, at 401.

[43] *R. v. Eastbourne (Inhabitants)* (1803) 4 East 103 at 107, 102 ER 769 at 770 *per* Lord Ellenborough CJ.

(5) CONCLUSION

Human dignity is already an important background value for human-rights law and constitutional development in international law and in a growing number of national jurisdictions. Because of its place among the values underpinning the ECHR, it is likely to become increasingly significant in the UK under the Human Rights Act 1998, when interpreting both Convention rights and other legislation. On the other hand, the content of dignity's central core is not clear, making it an uncertain guide. The nature of dignity, culturally and contextually specific as it is, and dependent as much on the viewpoint of the observer as on the aspirations of the protagonists, may sometimes need to be treated with cautious awareness of its limitations as well as its strengths. It can never be more than one of a number of values, principles, and policies which pull decision-makers in different directions. Giving weight to dignity adds a new value to the legal system which changes the way in which questions are asked and answered, allowing a wider range of interests to be taken into account, but not thereby making intractable moral and legal issues any easier.

3.3 EQUALITY AND SOCIAL JUSTICE

' . . . We hold these truths to be self-evident, that all men are created equal, that they are endowed by their Creator with certain unalienable Rights, that among these are Life, Liberty and the pursuit of Happiness . . . ' [Unanimous Declaration of Independence by the thirteen United States of America, 4 July 1776.]

The notion that everyone is, in some fundamental sense, equal is an important element in the history of ideas. The principle that like cases should be treated alike and different cases differently is rooted in the belief that equal treatment is morally better than unequal treatment where relevantly similar conditions obtain. As Professor Jeffrey Jowell has argued, this idea is so basic to legal systems under the rule of law that equality can properly be regarded as a fundamental constitutional principle, even in the context of the UK's notoriously non-prescriptive constitution, injecting a non-discrimination principle into a field as unpromising as review of administrative action for unreasonableness in administrative law.[44]

Equality is not, however, an easy notion to apply in practice. Unlike some other qualities, such as colour, it is virtually impossible to conceive of equality in the abstract. The only field in which an entirely abstract notion of equality can be maintained is that of mathematics, where the characteristic of equality relates to numbers, which are artificial entities operating in only one dimension. Numbers can be said to be equal or unequal because they are defined artificially so that their numerical value is their only significant feature. In relation to entities which have more than one significant quality, it is not possible to speak of the entities themselves being globally equal or unequal. They might be equal in respect of one characteristic, and unequal in

[44] J. Jowell, 'Is Equality a Constitutional Principle?' (1994) 47(2) *Current Legal Problems* 1–18.

respect of others. In social life, numbers normally have no moral, political, or legal significance in themselves (although they may be morally or politically significant when applied to people, as in the context of majoritarian democracy). People, unlike numbers, have characteristics besides our numerical value which we may consider to be important for different purposes: reliability, kindness, rationality, honesty, status, intelligence, sex, race, ethnicity, and so on. It is our non-numerical characteristics in combination which define our social standing, the way we are seen by others, and (often) the way we see ourselves. Apart from their common status as human beings, people can be said to be equal either by reference to some particular, measurable quality (such as intelligence), or by reference to their standing under some rule prescribing their entitlements or responsibilities. There is no other sense in which two people can be said to be equal.

This has implications for the use of the idea of equality as a criterion of social justice. First, to speak of equality one needs to define the criterion in respect of which equality is sought. For that particular type of equality to be morally relevant to solving a problem, there must be a moral rule or principle establishing that criterion as a morally significant one in relation to the issue in question. Equality has no moral value independently of the moral value of the good, characteristic, or value in respect of which equality falls to be assessed. Secondly, two people may be equal or unequal under a rule in a number of senses. They may be entitled:

(a) to be treated equally by others (regardless of whether that leaves them in similar positions afterwards);

(b) to be placed in a similar position (regardless of whether that involves unequal treatment);

(c) to be equally free to exploit whatever abilities or property they may have without interference (which is very likely to lead to different results for each person); or

(d) to be assisted (unequally) so that they have an equal opportunity to exploit their different talents, etc.

Each of these senses of equality is related to a different political and moral theory. For example, entitlements (a) and (b) are aspects of different models of egalitarianism; (c) is characteristic of classical liberalism, entailing relatively little state intervention; and (d) is related to modified versions of liberalism, such as that of Professor Ronald Dworkin based on the idea of a right to equal concern and respect.[45]

However, none is adequate in itself as a statement of principle, because each leaves open further questions. For example, entitlements (a) and (b) require us to explain what is meant by equal treatment and similar positions respectively, and in what spheres equality is needed (as there may be areas of life where equality is not a requirement, and equality itself might, like justice, signify different values in each field).[46]

---

[45] R. Dworkin, *Taking Rights Seriously* (London: Duckworth, 1976), 272–8.

[46] M. Walzer, *Spheres of Justice: A Defence of Pluralism and Equality* (Oxford: Basil Blackwell, 1983), argues that this is a positive advantage when justifying the criterion of equality as an element in justice.

As Peter Westen has argued,[47] one of the reasons for the enduring appeal of the rhetoric of equality is that it can be accommodated within most moral and political theories, and only on careful analysis does it become clear that it means something different in each of them. Until one has decided in what sense one is seeking to promote equality (in other words, what politico-moral theory one espouses), it is not possible to pursue equality. This leads Westen to regard the idea of equality as empty, in the sense that it does not specify any determinate values of its own independently of the political or moral values on which particular models of equality are founded. In the UK and the EU, legal intervention has aimed less at establishing substantive equality than at combatting inequality of opportunity in education, housing, employment, and obtaining goods and services. The object is not really to produce equality of opportunity (which is accepted as being impossible), but rather to ensure that inequalities could not be imposed on criteria which were impossible to justify on moral grounds. This understandably limits the extent to which the legislation can produce real advances for equality.[48] However, popular commitment to that objective varies with economic conditions. Equal access to employment, and equal treatment when working, are ideals which can be embraced without too much opposition when the economy is booming and well-remunerated work is plentiful, but which come under pressure at times of recession.

3.4 EQUALITY AND DISCRIMINATION

(1) THEORY OF ANTI-DISCRIMINATION LAW[49]

Discrimination, when it consists of an ability to differentiate right from wrong and good from bad, is an essential part of everyday life. Much of education, and arguably the whole of culture, is directed to establishing acceptable criteria for preferring one work of art, objective, technique, or person to another, and encouraging people to develop their critical faculties to enable them to discriminate effectively according to those criteria. Discrimination becomes morally unacceptable only when it takes a particular form, namely treating a person less favourably than others on account of a consideration which is morally irrelevant. The criterion in question may be the person's colour, nationality, religion, ethnic origin, sex, political beliefs, or one of an infinite number of other factors. This unacceptable form of discrimination is often an

---

[47] P. Westen, *Speaking of Equality: an Analysis of the Rhetorical Force of Equality in Moral and Legal Discourse* (Princeton, NJ: Princeton University Press, 1991). For debate over Westen's views, see K. Greenawalt, 'How Empty is the Idea of Equality?', (1983) **83** *Columbia Law Review* 1167–85, a reply to P. Westen, 'The Empty Idea of Equality' (1982) **95** *Harvard Law Review* 537–96.

[48] S. Fredman, 'Less Equal than Others—Equality and Women's Rights', in Gearty and Tomkins (eds.), *Understanding Human Rights*, 197–217.

[49] C. McCrudden (ed.), *Anti-Discrimination Law* (Aldershot: Dartmouth, 1991) is a useful collection of essays; McCrudden's helpful 'Introduction,' xi–xxxi, includes a valuable bibliography. See also J. Gregory, *Sex, Race and the Law: Legislating for Equality* (London: Sage, 1987).

emanation of prejudice (in its pure form of a prejudgment in the absence of evidence) against a person on account of that person's inherent characteristics over which he or she has no control, but (depending on one's moral and political philosophy and the circumstances in which a dispute arises) any criterion may be regarded as either relevant or irrelevant.

The outlawing of certain types of discrimination is justified on the basis of the simple premise that there are certain criteria for treating people differently which should never be regarded as morally relevant, or which are relevant in an admissible way only in a restricted range of situations which can be defined by law. There is usually no objection to discriminating in favour of or against a person on the basis of their voluntary actions, since those are the result of a choice for which it is reasonable to expect the person to accept the consequences (whether good or bad) in accordance with the liberal notions of individual will and individual responsibility. If one has a choice between two acts, either morally reprehensible A or morally admirable B, and one chooses to do the morally reprehensible A, there is no reason why one should not be judged and treated accordingly, although, if the choice is constrained by factors beyond one's control (for example, social and economic circumstances might constrain the range of options available to people in certain social classes or settings), the choice is more apparent than real, and it might reduce the moral force of the action.

If the reason for discriminating is unrelated to one's voluntary acts, and is based instead on matters which are entirely beyond one's control (skin colour, status, family background, nationality, disability, sex,[50] etc.), there is a danger that one will be systematically discriminated against in all situations, losing out all or most of the time on that account. This is socially divisive, because it produces an underclass of systematically disadvantaged people who are unable to improve their position by lawful means. If the differential treatment is based on decisions or actions over which one has some control, but that control is limited by psychological commitments (religion, political beliefs) or the conventions of one's social group (dress, hairstyle), the morality of differential treatment is at best questionable. In such cases, the person seeking to justify differential treatment bears the burden of establishing its moral propriety in the circumstances in question.

The conclusion to which this points is that differentiating between people is not wrong as long as the criteria applied are morally acceptable. What grounds are morally acceptable, and by what principles can one decide whether criteria for differentiating are acceptable? It is usual to start from a presumption in favour of equality. This has two elements. First, people are presumed to be morally equal in the sense of being equally entitled to respect for their moral status by virtue of being human beings. As noted in Chapter 1, this idea forms one of the foundations of the notion of human rights. The principle of moral equality does not always require that all actions be judged in the same way, since standards common to all may require that we distinguish between people with different levels of responsibility for their actions, by reason of mental or physical impairment or exigent circumstances.

---

[50] However, where a person chooses to undergo gender reassignment therapy the position is more complicated.

Equality as an idea is relevant mainly when there is conflict as to the proper distribution of resources of some sort. Treating people as moral equals does not necessarily entail equal treatment, in the sense of distributing identical benefits and burdens to all. It will do so only when the claimants are in morally identical positions. Our voluntary actions, including the way in which we use our rights in the different situations in which we find ourselves, mean that we may cease to be in identical moral positions as soon as we start acting voluntarily. The principle of moral equality merely requires that we judge and treat people as moral equals: we are to be regarded as equally responsible for our actions, which fall to be judged according to common standards (this is one of the principles underpinning the rule of law doctrine). It involves taking account of inequalities in respect of particular characteristics, in order to give effect to the principle of treating people as equals at a higher level of abstraction. Since people who are entitled to be treated as moral equals do not necessarily have equal incomes, wealth, or needs, the principle of moral equality may lead to unequal treatment, with burdens being placed disproportionately on those best able to bear them in order to supply benefits to those in need. This is the basis for the system of 'transfer payments' through progressive taxation and social security payments, and the provision of public services, such as health care and education for all, paid for by means of a system of national insurance contributions and taxes levied on those in remunerated work or with accumulated wealth. Questions of practical equality are related to the resource being distributed and the benefit which it confers: people may be equally wealthy and equally morally good, but when treatment for sickness is being distributed there is no good reason to provide it equally to people who are ill and those who are well: people's different needs, and the extent to which they can be met by the resource under consideration, are morally relevant grounds for differentiating between people in distributing the resource.

This raises problems when it is proposed to legislate against discrimination on particular grounds. To what characteristics is the law to insist that people should be blind, and in which contexts? This problem has a reverse side, in the form of two related issues which any system of social rights and anti-discrimination law must address. First, to what extent does the ideal of equality demand that, as well as being treated on common principles in the distribution of resources and burdens, people should be put in positions where they are equally able to formulate and achieve their goals for life? In other words, does equality imply equality of opportunity, which may be impossible unless people have a right to specially favourable treatment, on the basis of criteria to which we would normally want people to be blind, in order to compensate for the pervasive social effects of past discrimination? Classically, liberal rights theory provides for a limited degree of equality of opportunity. People have equal opportunity in so far as they have equal freedoms. The job of the state is to protect those freedoms, but not to put people into a position where they can make the most of them. But this leads to a problem, noted in Chapter 1: the freedoms turn out to be of unequal value to different people, because some are unable to exploit them, because of physical or mental attributes, or financial, social, or family disadvantages. Secondly, to use freedoms effectively people rely on a reasonable range of choices being available, and those are determined by factors, such as the economic structure of society and the extent to which different activities and products are valued, which are largely outside the control of any individual. The state may have a role, even under some forms of liberal theory, in ensuring that a decent range of choices is practicably open to all.[51]

The connection between these problems makes their solution particularly complex. The provision of choices by state action is a political matter, and the resources and opportunities which are made available are likely to reflect the system of values which is politically dominant. Those values might be incompatible with the principle of moral equality, in that they systematically undervalue the aspirations of certain groups in society and lead to inadequate choice being available. It is a common feature of discrimination on the grounds of sex and race that it produces (or perhaps is produced by) a dominant system of political values in which the opportunities of the subordinated sex or race are restricted. Equivalent results may flow from discrimination on the grounds of religion, disability, and age. In such a system, an underclass is created, so that, even if members are not formally denied the rights and freedoms guaranteed to others, they are normally unable to make much use of them. The inequality of opportunity which results cannot be broken down simply by removing the formal inequalities of rights. Positive steps are likely to be needed in order to improve the lot of entire underprivileged sections of society, to place them in a position from which they can start to take real benefits from exercising rights and freedoms. In such circumstances, treating people as equals, or treating them with equal concern and respect, is likely to entail unequal treatment which discriminates in their favour, through programmes which are aptly described as positive discrimination or affirmative action. Social rights are useful adjuncts of such programmes, but are not essential. The vital factor is the political will, which may be hard to establish, because favourable treatment for some will mean unfavourable treatment for at least some members of the previously favoured group. It is hard to justify affirmative action within traditional liberal, egalitarian, or utilitarian thinking.

Perhaps the most persuasive philosophical justification for affirmative action so far attempted depends on people with conflicting interests being required to consider problems of distribution of benefits and burdens from each other's perspective, and make a decision as to how to resolve the problem taking account of both the views of the other person and the relative importance to each person of the views they hold. This approach is tempered by restricting the range of views which will be admissible, so that people who desire a state of affairs which is fundamentally incompatible with equality (for example, people who wish to preserve a slave class in society) will not be entitled to have those views taken into account in the dialogue.[52] Establishing the conditions for such a dialogue will itself not be an easy or uncontroversial process.

To make the problem still more intractable, the opportunities which the systematically disadvantaged group seek might not be those which are traditionally favoured

[51] J. Raz, *The Morality of Freedom* (Oxford: Clarendon Press, 1986).

[52] M. Rosenfeld, *Affirmative Action and Justice: A Philosophical and Constitutional Inquiry* (New Haven, Conn.: Yale University Press, 1991).

by the dominant set of values. Although there are women who have always wanted to be free from the restrictive paternalism which prevented them from doing the same work and adopting the same working practices as men, it is a recurrent theme of writings on issues of sex and race equality that what at least some members of the underprivileged group (women or ethnic minorities) really desire is not the opportunity to be like the previously dominant group (men, whites, Christians, etc.) but rather the freedom to pursue their own values in their own ways. Treatment of people as moral equals is seen as demanding respect for (even celebration of) difference, rather than its elimination. If this is not recognized, there is a danger of enhancing the status of women, for example, only to subordinate them once again to a new orthodoxy about their proper place in society.[53] It is not surprising that there has been a growing move away from concern to eradicate sex- or race-based differences towards a concern to minimize sex- or race-based disadvantage.[54] Willingness to treat someone as an equal only if he or she adopts one's own system of beliefs and values is a denial of moral equality rather than an expression of it, and is a deeply patronizing attitude. Nevertheless, it is an attitude which has shaped much of the English approach to racial equality, exemplified by the views of those who consider it to be a duty of immigrants to assimilate to, rather than just integrate with, the British way of life.[55]

A useful way of approaching these issues in the field of sex and race discrimination law is through the framework of international law, discussed above.[56] The European Commission on Human Rights decided that discriminating against people on the grounds of race, at least in respect of important matters such as immigration, may offend against the prohibition on degrading treatment in Article 3 of the European Convention on Human Rights.[57] A failure to provide legal remedies also breaches the obligations of the state under the International Convention on the Elimination of All Forms of Racial Discrimination (1966) and the ILO Conventions discussed above. The discussion which follows is concerned with the manner in which domestic law deals with the problems of discrimination.

(2) GROUNDS OF DISCRIMINATION, OBJECTIVES OF ANTI-DISCRIMINATION LAW, AND INTERNATIONAL LAW

Of common grounds for discriminating, colour, age, disability, race, and sex are matters which are virtually always outside the control of the person concerned (save in the rare case where a person has the opportunity to undergo sex reassignment

[53] See S. Fredman, *Women and the Law* (Oxford: Clarendon Press, 1997), chs. 1 (esp. 30–7) and 4.
[54] See, e.g., in the context of sex discrimination, C. MacKinnon, 'Toward Feminist Jurisprudence' 34 *Stanford Law Review* 703–37 (1982); D. L. Rhode, *Justice and Gender: Sex Discrimination and the Law* (Cambridge, Mass.: Harvard University Press, 1989), *passim*; K. O'Donovan and E. Szyszczak, *Equality and Sex Discrimination Law* (Oxford: Basil Blackwell, 1988), ch. 1.
[55] See V. Bevan, *The Development of British Immigration Law* (London: Croom Helm, 1986), 10–12, 27–8.
[56] See J. Greenberg, 'Race, Sex, and Religious Discrimination in International Law', in Meron (ed.), *Human Rights in International Law*, 307–43.
[57] See Ch. 5, below.

therapy, which presents its own problems). Nationality is usually outside the control of the individual, except in somewhat unusual situations where people have an opportunity to adopt a new nationality. Yet these personal characteristics do not normally adversely affect one's ability to discharge one's obligations as a citizen towards the state or one's fellow citizens. Sex, race, disability, age, and nationality therefore have primacy among the characteristics on the basis of which it is thought to be wrong to discriminate.

Religious beliefs and affiliations are usually things which arise involuntarily. Although sometimes people change their religious beliefs, there may be social or political factors which make it difficult or even dangerous to manifest that change. In Northern Ireland, for example, the main social and political divisions around which society is organized are religious in origin, and tension between the main Protestant and Roman Catholic religious-political communities is rife. For this reason, the law in Northern Ireland has long treated religious discrimination as a principal target for its anti-discrimination rules, in order to make possible some sort of economic and social life encompassing the two communities.

There are other grounds for holding political beliefs and religious beliefs to be morally irrelevant grounds for differential treatment of citizens. In countries which espouse some form of democratic political theory, freedom to choose and express a set of political beliefs, and to join other like-minded people in a political party or interest group, is central to the efficient operation of the democratic process. To discriminate against people on the basis of their choice would tend to undermine the democratic nature of the state. A similar, but not identical, argument applies to religious beliefs. In a society which regards religion as a social good, providing a basis (although not necessarily the only one) for social morality, there are good reasons for permitting people the widest possible choice of religious beliefs in the hope that as many people as possible will find a religion with which they can identify. Like the English law of charities, such societies may take the view that any religion is better than none. Having done so, it would be counter-productive to discriminate against people on the basis of their choices.

The values advanced by anti-discrimination legislation of all types, therefore, are the following.[58] First, it attempts to ensure that opportunities are distributed on morally relevant grounds. Secondly, it attempts to uphold the dignity of individuals and groups in their own eyes and in the eyes of others. Thirdly, it seeks to produce a more level playing field than would otherwise be available for competition for resources, by limiting the grounds on which inequalities can lawfully be introduced. Fourthly, it aims to minimize the social friction which may result from an under-privileged underclass being systematically excluded from a fair share of the fruits of social and economic development.

However, there are limits to the restraints which can legitimately be placed on people's or societies' freedom to adopt principles for differential treatment. One limit arises from what might be called a right to self-defence. Societies must be free to

---

[58] R. Townshend-Smith, *Discrimination Law: Text, Cases and Materials* (London: Cavendish, 1998), ch. 3, contains a useful collection of materials and discussion of the role of law in combatting discrimination.

protect themselves against attack on their fundamental values, so they may discriminate against a religious or political belief if its adherents are necessarily committed, by virtue of their adherence, to acts which undermine the state or the moral and political values on which the state is founded.[59] To defend itself in that way, a society might be forced to discriminate against the implementation of the beliefs concerned, but that discrimination is an indirect result of the legitimate exercise of society's right of self-defence, and should be regarded as an exceptional measure. Tolerance should be the norm, although it imposes certain costs on society, including the labour of adjusting institutions and working practices to accommodate unfamiliar needs.[60]

Another type of limit on anti-discrimination legislation arises from the fact that a criterion for differential treatment might be morally irrelevant nine times out of ten, but relevant on the tenth occasion. While there may be a strong presumption against differential treatment on the ground of (for example) a person's religion, the presumption is rebuttable. There might be circumstances in which people's religious beliefs, if sincerely held, may legitimately be held to bar them from certain opportunities or offices. For example, if the authorities of a religion were to bar its adherents on religious grounds from participating in the dissolution of marriages, it would be unreasonable to insist on its adherents being appointed as judges in a state where divorce is socially and morally acceptable, and where any judge may be called on to adjudicate on divorce petitions. Such a situation almost gave rise to a clash between the UK government and the Vatican in the 1950s.[61]

The general principle, however, is that social and cultural differences, as well as race, colour, sex, age, and nationality, should normally be regarded as morally irrelevant, and that the law should strive to enhance tolerance and eliminate disadvantage flowing from discrimination on such grounds. This is the approach adopted in international human rights law. Objectionable forms of discrimination are an assault on the dignity of human beings and of the human species. As well as special international treaties which aim at the elimination of race and sex discrimination,[62] the general human rights treaties typically contain provisions forbidding discrimination. The most straightforward and far-reaching is contained in the ICCPR. Article 2 guarantees the enjoyment of other rights in the Covenant without distinction of any kind, and Article 3 makes special provision for the equal right of men and women to enjoy the other rights. Article 26 contains a free-standing right to be free of discrimination:

'All persons are equal before the law and are entitled without any discrimination to the equal protection of the law. In this respect, the law shall prohibit any discrimination and guarantee

---

[59] For discussion, see S. Poulter, *Ethnicity, Law and Human Rights: The English Experience* (Oxford: Clarendon Press, 1998), 19–30.

[60] See S. Mendus, *Toleration and the Limits of Liberalism* (Basingstoke: Macmillan, 1989), 8–9; F. Schauer, 'The Cost of Communicative Tolerance', in R. Cohen-Almagor (ed.), *Liberal Democracy and the Limits of Tolerance: Essays in Honour and Memory of Yitzhak Rabin* (Ann Arbor, Mich.: University of Michigan Press, 2000), 28–42.

[61] R. B. Stevens, 'The Independence of the Judiciary: the View from the Lord Chancellor's Office' (1988) **8** *Oxford J. of Legal Studies* 222–48 at 227–9.

[62] For example, the UN Conventions on the Elimination of All Forms of Racial Discrimination (1966), and the Elimination of All Forms of Discrimination against Women (1979).

to all persons equal and effective protection against discrimination on any ground such as race, colour, sex, language, religion, political or other opinion, national or social origin, property, birth or other status.'

The UK is bound by Article 26 in international law, although it does not form part of national law.[63]

The ECHR contains a right in Article 14 which is equivalent to that in Article 2 of the ICCPR. Article 14 provides:

'The enjoyment of the rights and freedoms set forth in this Convention shall be secured without discrimination on any ground such as sex, race, colour, language, religion, political or other opinion, national or social origin, association with a national minority, property, birth or other status.'

This right forms part of UK law, because Article 14 is among the Convention rights which were incorporated under section 1 of the Human Rights Act 1998. In the UK, section 2 of the Act provides that Article 14 is to be interpreted taking account of relevant decisions of the European Commission and Court of Human Rights. That caselaw is significant. The non-discrimination right under Article 14 is curiously drafted. The range of impermissible grounds for discrimination is very wide—far wider than in UK law—and is open-ended. On the other hand, the right appears on its face to be limited to freedom from discrimination in the enjoyment of other Convention rights. As such, it seems very limited, because the Convention rights form a floor and not a ceiling, and many fields of activity in which discrimination is suffered are outside the scope of the Convention rights. In November 2000, the Council of Europe opened for signature a treaty which would partially rectify this. Article 1 of Protocol No. 12 provides:

'1.   The enjoyment of any right set forth by law shall be secured without discrimination on any ground such as sex, race, colour, language, religion, political or other opinion, national or social origin, association with a national minority, property, birth or other status.

2.   No one shall be discriminated against by any public authority on any ground such as those mentioned in paragraph 1.'

This is significantly narrower than Article 26 of the ICCPR, in that the general right to be free of discrimination in paragraph 2 applies only as against public authorities, while the right to have freedom from discrimination secured against everyone, in paragraph 1, applies only to the enjoyment of rights set forth by law. While wider than the restriction to enjoyment of other Convention rights, it does not go as far as the right to equality before the law and equal protection of the law[64] contained in ICCPR,

---

[63] See Lord Lester of Herne Hill QC and S. Joseph, 'Obligations of Non-Discrimination', in D. Harris and S. Joseph (eds.), *The International Covenant on Civil and Political Rights and United Kingdom Law* (Oxford: Clarendon Press, 1995), 563–95. Although now somewhat out of date, it provides a good introduction to the structure of ICCPR Articles 2, 3, and 26.

[64] This phrase has symbolic importance, echoing as it does the equal protection clause in the Fourteenth Amendment to the Constitution of the USA on which the US Supreme Court founded its seminal desegregation decision, *Brown v. Board of Education of Topeka* 347 US 483 (1954). See U. Khaliq, 'Protocol 12 to the ECHR: a Step Forward or a Step Too Far?' [2001] *PL* 457–64.

Article 26. Protocol No. 12 to the ECHR represents a very modest development from Article 14 of the ECHR, and is considerably less extensive than the anti-discrimination provision in Article 13 of the EC Treaty (as amended by the Treaty of Amsterdam in 1997) and the Directives since made under it, not to mention the 'soft law' equality and anti-discrimination provisions of Articles 20 and 21 of the EU Charter of Fundamental Rights (December 2000). None the less, the UK government was quick to announce that it had no intention of ratifying the new Protocol, perhaps fearing that the European Court of Human Rights would interpret it as imposing obligations on the UK going beyond those which the UK had accepted under Community law.

Despite the UK's reluctance to ratify Protocol No. 12, the provisions of Article 14 are by no means a dead letter. The Strasbourg institutions have given Article 14 a surprising degree of practical significance. First, they have drawn attention to the fact that Article 14 imposes a positive as well as negative obligation on states as to the way in which the enjoyment of Convention rights is secured.[65] Secondly, there is no need to show that a Convention right has been violated in order to invoke Article 14. It is enough to show that the matter in relation to which discrimination has occurred falls 'within the ambit' of a Convention right, and to that extent Article 14 has an autonomous reach. As the European Court of Human Rights wrote in the *Belgian Linguistic* case:[66]

'While it is true that this guarantee has no independent existence in the sense that under the terms of Article 14 it relates solely to "rights and freedoms set forth in this Convention", a measure which in itself is in conformity with the requirements of the Article enshrining the right or freedom in question may however infringe this Article when read in conjunction with Article 14 for the reason that it is of a discriminatory nature.'

For example, in *Salgueiro da Silva Mouta v. Portugal*[67] the Lisbon Court of Appeal had refused to grant custody of a child to her father, who had left her mother to enter into a homosexual partnership. The father argued that the failure of the Portuguese courts to enforce earlier access orders in his favour against the mother, and the refusal to give him custody of the child on the ground that he was living in a homosexual relationship, violated both Article 8 taken alone (because it failed to respect his private and family life) and Article 14 taken together with Article 8. The Court declined to decide the Article 8 issue, and instead held that there had been a violation of Article 14 taken together with Article 8, because the Lisbon Court of Appeal had overtly discriminated against the father by reason of his homosexuality. These matters are considered further in Chapter 12, below.

Nevertheless, if the Court finds a violation of a substantive right, it is likely to decline to examine Article 14, on the ground that to do so would serve no useful purpose.[68] Although this is doubtful as a practical matter, it saves the Court from a certain amount of hard work.

A number of points should be borne in mind in relation to the nature of

---

[65] See the Report of the Commission in the *Belgian Linguistic* case, 24 June 1965, Series B, No. 3 (1967), 305–306.

[66] Series A, No. 6, Judgment of 23 July 1968, at 33.

[67] App. No. 33290/96. Judgment of 21 December 1999.

[68] See, e.g. *Dudgeon v. United Kingdom*, Series A, No. 45 (1981).

discrimination within the meaning of the Article. Not every difference of treatment amounts to discrimination. Every evaluative process in life involves differentiating between cases, people, or things. Legal rules are themselves attempts to systematize the process of differentiation by identifying criteria by which it will be proper to treat cases or people differently. Nevertheless, there are some grounds for differentiating between cases or people which are unacceptable. The purpose of Article 14 is to outlaw unacceptable differentiation in securing the enjoyment of Convention rights.

The proper approach to an anti-discrimination provision such as Article 14, therefore, is to decide first whether there is a relevant difference in treatment or outcome; secondly, if there is, what is the ground for that difference, and whether the ground is acceptable; and thirdly, whether the resulting difference is justifiable. Although these can be stated as separate questions, we will see that they overlap in practice.

(i) Relevant difference in treatment

There are two elements here: whether there is a difference, and whether the comparators are relevantly in similar positions such that one would expect them to have been treated alike. There is generally little difficulty about the first element. The second element is, however, sometimes difficult, not least because of the need to identify an appropriate comparator. The way the Court approaches it is not to look for identity of position between different cases, but to ask whether the applicant and the people who are treated differently are in 'analogous' situations. This will to some extent depend on whether there is an objective and reasonable justification for the difference in treatment, which overlaps with the questions about the acceptability of the ground and the justifiability of the difference in treatment. This is why, as van Dijk and van Hoof observe,[69] 'In most instances of the Strasbourg caselaw . . . the comparability test is glossed over, and the emphasis is (almost) completely on the justification test'. However, there are occasions on which the Court has rejected applications under Article 14 purely on the ground that the applicant has provided no evidence that the people who were treated differently had been in analogous situations,[70] or because the comparators are not genuinely in analogous positions.[71] This places a particularly

---

[69] P. van Dijk and G. J. H. van Hoof, *Theory and Practice of the European Convention on Human Rights*, 3rd edn. (The Hague: Kluwer Law International, 1998), 722.

[70] *Fredin v. Sweden (No. 1)*, Series A, No. 192 (1991) (legislation providing for closure of pits had effect of closing only the applicant's pit, but no evidence showing that the applicant was in an analogous position to that of other pit owners).

[71] *Van der Mussele v. Belgium*, Series A, No. 70 (1983) (*avocats*, unlike doctors, vets, dentists, and pharmacists, were required to provide free legal assistance to the poor, but the status and other characteristics of the professions were so different that their positions were not analogous, so no Art. 14 claim could be sustained on that basis); *Johnston v. Ireland*, Series A, No. 112 (1986) (Irish law recognized divorces obtained abroad by people domiciled in the place where they were obtained, but not foreign divorces obtained by people domiciled in Ireland, but this was the result of a normal application of the rules of private international law, which meant that the different categories of people were not in relevantly analogous positions); *Sunday Times v. United Kingdom, Guardian and Observer v. United Kingdom*, Series A, Nos. 216 and 217 (1991) (injunctions restraining publication of *Spycatcher* material granted against UK but not foreign publishers the result of the presence of people within or outside the jurisdiction; publishers within and outside jurisdiction not in analogous position for purposes of assessing differential exercise of judicial jurisdiction). See van Dijk and van Hoof, *Theory and Practice*, 720–722; D. J. Harris, M. O'Boyle, and C. Warbrick, *The Law of the European Convention on Human Rights* (London: Butterworths, 1995), 470–475.

heavy burden on applicants who are alleging indirect, rather than direct, discrimination (i.e. improperly differential treatment arising from members of one group having particular difficulty in meeting the requirements of an apparently general and objective rule). Where there is evidence that the applicants are treated differently despite being in a relevantly analogous position to others, the court will proceed to consider Article 14.[72]

(ii) The ground for the difference

The applicants must be able to establish that the ground on which they have been treated differently from others is *prima facie* improper, and in need of justification. The list of grounds which are improper in Article 14 is illustrative, not exhaustive, and is never closed: as social, legal, and moral standards change, a ground which was once regarded as acceptable (such as transsexualism) may become unacceptable. Grounds which have been held to be inappropriate for one purpose may be appropriate for another. Religion is in itself not an acceptable ground for differential treatment of parents in relation to their rights in respect of their children after the marriage has been dissolved;[73] nor is sexuality or the fact that one parent is now living in a homosexual relationship.[74] Sexuality is not an acceptable reason for differential treatment in relation to disciplinary proceedings in the armed forces, or in relation to investigations into alleged offences.[75] The open-ended nature of the list of improper grounds for differentiation enables changing *mores* to be fed into the protection available under Article 14 without the need for further treaties or legislation, unlike the approach taken in UK and EC law.

There is some evidence that the Court treats certain grounds as calling for particularly close scrutiny, which, as Harris, O'Boyle, and Warbrick point out,[76] make them equivalent to the 'suspect categories' in anti-discrimination law in the USA. Race and sex seem to be such categories.[77] Treating children differently on the basis of whether they were born in or outside wedlock, i.e. legitimacy as a ground of different treatment, is in principle unacceptable,[78] as is differentiation on the basis of race, sex, and (in the light of *Salgueiro da Silva Mouta* and the 'gays in the military' cases[79]) sexual orientation. On the other hand, a ground which might be unacceptable as a reason for less favourable treatment could be acceptable as a ground for more favourable treatment, since the Court (unlike, usually, UK law) accepts positive discrimination as a

---

[72] *Pine Valley Developments Ltd. v. Ireland*, Series A, No. 222 (1991) (legislation to block evasion of planning law prevented the applicants, but not other developers, from using planning permissions previously obtained).

[73] *Hoffmann v. Austria*, Series A, No. 255-C (1993).

[74] *Salgueiro da Silva Mouta v. Portugal*, Judgment of 21 December 1999.

[75] *Smith and Grady v. United Kingdom*, Judgment of 4 October 1999; *Lustig-Prean v. United Kingdom*, Judgment of 4 October 1999.

[76] *Law of the European Convention*, 481.

[77] Ibid., referring to *Patel v. United Kingdom*, Eur. Commn. HR, 36 CD 92, 117; *East African Asians Case*, Commn., 3 EHRR 76 (1976); and *Abdulaziz, Cabales and Balkandali v. United Kingdom*, Eur. Commn. HR, Series B, No. 77, para. 113 and Court Series A, No. 94, para. 85 of the judgment.

[78] *Marckx v. Belgium*, Series A, No. 31 (1979); *Inze v. Austria*, Series A, No. 126 (1987).

[79] *Smith and Grady v. United Kingdom*, Judgment of 4 October 1999; *Lustig-Prean v. United Kingdom*, Judgment of 27 September 1999.

justified form of differential treatment, the basis that 'certain legal inequalities tend only to correct factual inequalities'.[80]

(iii) Can the difference be justified?

A difference in treatment does not violate Article 14 if there is what the Court has described as an objective and reasonable reason for it, and that is the real reason for its adoption. The test is, as Harris, O'Boyle, and Warbrick point out, not dissimilar to the test of 'pressing social need' plus 'proportionality' used in relation to the issue under some other Articles of whether or not an interference with a right is 'necessary in a democratic society'. In this context, the Court treats states as having a margin of appreciation, which is wider in relation to some grounds of differentiation than it is in relation to the 'suspect categories', but the state carries the burden of persuading the Court that differentiation on an objectionable ground is reasonable. Its assertion must be supported by objective evidence.

The rational aim requirement is not usually too hard to satisfy: the protection of young people when imposing differential ages of consent for heterosexual and homosexual activity; encouraging traditional family life when disadvantaging illegitimate children in relation to paternity and inheritance rights, and so on, although there may be evidence that the reason advanced by the state is not the real one, in which case the Court will not accept it.[81]

More difficult to meet is the test of proportionality. The relevant rules must, as the Court has said, 'strike a fair balance between the protection of the interests of the community and respect for the rights and freedoms safeguarded by the Convention'.[82] Thus, in *Marckx* the differences between the treatment of legitimate and illegitimate children went beyond anything reasonably required to encourage traditional family life.

Against this background, we can examine the law in England and Wales.

(3) THE LEGAL MEANING OF AND SETTINGS FOR DISCRIMINATION IN ENGLISH LAW

The structure of the law relating to discrimination in England and Wales is now immensely complex, consisting of a large number of inter-woven strands. The main elements are:

- the Equal Pay Act 1970 (pay for employees), Article 141 (formerly 119) of the EC Treaty (equal protection for men and women in occupation and employment), the EC Equal Pay Directive and Equal Treatment Directive (both relating to employment), the Burden of Proof Directive (covering the burden in relation to claims of sex discrimination in occupation and employment), and the (British)

---

[80] *Belgian Linguistic* case, Series A, No. 6 (1968) at para. 10 of the judgment. See Harris, O'Boyle, and Warbrick, *Law of the European Convention*, 485–486.

[81] *Abdulaziz* case, n.77 above: UK claimed that the reason for treating women differently from men for immigration purposes was their different effects on the labour market, but the evidence showed that this was not the real reason.

[82] *Belgian Linguistic* case, n. 80 at 4.

Sex Discrimination Act 1975 (employment, housing, education, and supply of goods and services), in relation to sex discrimination;

- the Race Relations Act 1976 (employment, housing, education, and supply of goods and services) and the EC Race Equality Directive (employment and access to social assistance) in respect of racial discrimination;

- the Disability Discrimination Act 1995 (employment, housing, education, and supply of goods and services) and the EC Framework Discrimination Directive (employment) cover discrimination on the ground of disability;

- the Framework Directive also deals with discrimination on the grounds of age, religion, and sexuality; and

- Article 14 of the ECHR provides a range of protection against discrimination on many different grounds in the enjoyment of Convention rights, which is part of English law as the result of the Human Rights Act 1998. Section 3 of the 1998 Act also provides that legislation (which probably includes Community legislation when examined in the English courts) is to be interpreted, so far as possible, in a manner compatible with Convention rights, including that under Article 14.

- Finally, non-discrimination is one of the general principles of Community law, capable of limiting (but not extending) the competence of the institutions of the Community and of national institutions when giving effect to Community law.

These interlocking regimes share some common features, but there are important differences. This section tries to tease out the common meaning (where there is one) of some key concepts which are central to nearly all the regimes. The Disability Discrimination Act 1995 forms an exception, because there is a recognition that in some circumstances a disability may actually disqualify a person from certain activities or occupations. That Act is therefore dealt with separately, in section (6) below.

(i) The meaning of discrimination

The need to protect people against discrimination on irrelevant grounds, while allowing differential treatment on grounds which are morally justifiable, is one of the factors underlying the entire structure of British race relations law and British and European sex discrimination law. Another fundamental element is the need, in order to tackle discrimination effectively, to attack it not only at the level of individual acts of discrimination directed against individuals on improper grounds (known as 'direct discrimination'), but also where discrimination results from the operation of a practice or application of criteria for selection which are not in themselves obviously related to the morally illegitimate criteria of sex or race, but which can be more easily satisfied by people of some races or one sex than another race or sex (known as 'indirect discrimination'). In the USA, under Title VII of the Civil Rights Act of 1964, both direct and indirect discrimination have been held to be unlawful, and the courts have been engaged in combatting apparently neutral practices which have a discriminatory impact,[83] although recent caselaw suggests that the conservative majority on the Supreme Court, out of sympathy with the ethos of social equality rights, is making it harder for complainants to prove that criteria for establishing disparate treatment are satisfied.[84]

In most of the domestic legislation, both direct and indirect forms of discrimination are unlawful. In section 1 of both the Sex Discrimination Act 1975 ('the 1975 Act') and the Race Relations Act 1976 ('the 1976 Act') discrimination may be committed in either of two ways: (a) by treating a person, on grounds of race or sex, less favourably than one treats or would treat others; or (b) by applying to that person a requirement or condition such that the proportion of that person's racial group or sex which can comply with it is considerably smaller than the proportion of people of another race or sex. In the case of discrimination under (b), a plaintiff must also show that the requirement or condition cannot be justified otherwise than by reference to the person's race or sex, and is to the detriment of that person because he or she cannot comply with it. However, the 'requirement or condition' test for indirect sex discrimination under UK law may now be incompatible with Community law, since Article 2(2) of the Burden of Proof Directive[85] provides that, for the purposes of EC law, there is indirect discrimination:

'where an apparently neutral provision, criterion or practice disadvantages a substantially higher proportion of the members of one sex, unless that provision, criterion or practice is appropriate and necessary and can be justified on objective factors unrelated to sex.'

The phrase 'provision, criterion or practice' is significantly wider than 'requirement or condition', and emphasizes that there is no need to show difference in treatment between male and female employees in order to establish indirect discrimination.[86] However, the Burden of Proof Directive is not applicable to race and disability discrimination, in relation to which (as we shall see) rather different approaches apply.

Thus, direct discrimination cannot be justified, while indirect discrimination is capable of justification by reference to criteria other than race or sex, and is actionable only on proof of detriment. Harassment on a prohibited ground is actionable as direct discrimination without the need to show that someone of the other sex, or another race, would not have been harassed.[87]

Under UK law, indirect discrimination is justified only if, objectively balancing the discriminatory effect of the requirement or condition against the reasonable needs of the employer, the latter outweigh the former.[88] A belief that it is undesirable to allow

---

[83] *Griggs v. Duke Power Co.* 401 US 424 (1971).

[84] *Wards Cove Packing Co. v. Antonio* 490 US 642, 104 L. Ed. 2d 733 (1989), discussed by R. Townshend-Smith, 'American Civil Rights in Retreat' (1992) 12 *Oxford J. of Legal Studies* 129–34.

[85] Directive 97/80 EC, [1988] OJ L14/6, as amended by Directive 98/52/EC, [1998] OJ L205/66.

[86] As C. Barnard and B. Hepple, 'Substantive Equality' [2000] *CLJ* 562–85 at 569 point out, this casts doubt on the correctness of the decision in *Barry v. Midland Bank* [1999] 1 WLR 1465, [1999] 3 All ER 974, HL.

[87] *British Telecommunications plc v. Williams* [1997] IRLR 668, EAT.

[88] *Hampson v. Department of Education and Science* [1990] 2 All ER 25, CA, at 34 *per* Balcombe LJ (reversed on different grounds [1991] 1 AC 171, [1990] 2 All ER 513, HL); *Webb v. EMO Air Cargo (UK) Ltd.* [1993] 1 WLR 49, [1992] 4 All ER 929, HL.

people to display their membership of a racial group, for example by wearing a turban in school, cannot constitute a justification for rules on school uniform which amount to indirect discrimination, since that would allow discriminators to use as a justification the very attitudes which Parliament intended to combat.[89]

The provisions concerning indirect discrimination are particularly significant, because they emphasize the role of anti-discrimination law in protecting group rights rather than purely providing of remedies for individuals. This is reflected in the arrangements for enforcing the legislation, which combine means of individual redress with proactive monitoring and enforcement by public agencies.

There need be no intention to discriminate, either directly or indirectly. If the person doing the act complained of has no intention to discriminate, but is treating someone less favourably than others because of fear of industrial unrest motivated by prejudice on the part of other people, the act is none the less unlawful direct discrimination.[90] Similarly, a condition for the enjoyment of a benefit is directly discriminatory if it relies on a criterion, set by an independent body, which is itself directly discriminatory. The test, as laid down by a three–two majority in the House of Lords in *James v. Eastleigh Borough Council*,[91] is whether the condition or disadvantage would have applied to the person but for his or her sex or (as the case may be) race. The test is objective, not subjective. In *James*, the majority (Lords Bridge, Ackner, and Goff; Lords Griffiths and Lowry dissented) held that there was direct discrimination where a local authority permitted people of pensionable age to swim free in the authority's public swimming baths. Because the age at which pensions could be claimed differentiated between men and women purely on the ground of sex (the age being sixty for women and sixty-five for men), the condition was discriminatory. Similarly, a council was held to have discriminated directly on the ground of sex when it made more places available for boys than for girls at its single-sex grammar schools.[92]

This 'but for' test involves comparing the way in which the victim was treated with the way in which other people of different sex or race from the victim were or would have been treated in that situation. A question immediately arises as to the relevant group with whose treatment that of a victim should be compared. For example, if a woman is dismissed because of inability to do the job through a pregnancy-related disability, should one compare her treatment with that of men generally who are unable to do the job for which they are hired, pregnant men (a physical impossibility), men suffering from a physical disability, or some other group? The effect can be seen in a decision of the House of Lords under the 1975 Act. In *Webb v. EMO Air Cargo (UK) Ltd.*,[93] Ms. Webb had been appointed by the company in July 1987 to cover for another employee who was due to go on maternity leave in February 1988. The

---

[89] *Mandla (Sewa Singh) v. Dowell Lee* [1983] 2 AC 548, [1983] 1 All ER 1062, HL.

[90] *R. v. Commission for Racial Equality, ex parte Westminster City Council* [1984] ICR 770, DC, [1985] ICR 827, CA; *James v. Eastleigh Borough Council* [1990] 2 AC 751, [1990] 2 All ER 607, HL.

[91] [1990] 2 AC 751, [1990] 2 All ER 607, HL.

[92] *R. v. Birmingham City Council, ex parte Equal Opportunities Commission* [1989] AC 1155, [1989] 1 All ER 769, HL. See further *R. v. Birmingham City Council, ex parte Equal Opportunities Commission (No. 2)* (1992) 91 LGR 14, CA.

[93] [1993] 1 WLR 49, [1992] 4 All ER 929, HL.

appointment began almost at once, because six months' training was required for the job. Soon after starting the training, Ms. Webb discovered that she, too, was pregnant, and would be unavailable for work during the period when the other employee was due to be on maternity leave. The company dismissed her, as she would have been unable to do the job at the time for which they had specifically appointed her. Ms. Webb alleged direct and indirect discrimination on the ground of her sex. The House of Lords decided, on the basis of the 1975 Act, that Ms. Webb was not a victim of direct discrimination, because the crucial factor in her dismissal was not her pregnancy but her unavailability for work during the relevant period. Although a male employee could not have been pregnant, a man who was unavailable for work (for whatever reason) at the precise time for which he had been appointed to do the job would have been dismissed. The woman had therefore not been treated less favourably than a man by reason of her sex. In relation to the indirect discrimination claim, the House held that men were more likely than women to be able to satisfy the condition that they be available for work during the specified period, because they could not become pregnant. However, the condition was justified by the reasonable needs of the company's business, which were weightier in the circumstances than the discriminatory effect of the condition.

There were difficulties in reconciling this with the approach of the European Court of Justice to sex discrimination[94] in cases under Council Directive (EEC) 76/207, the Equal Treatment Directive,[95] Article 2(1) of which states that 'there shall be no discrimination whatsoever on grounds of sex either directly or indirectly by reference in particular to marital or family status'. This had been held by the Court in Case C-177/88 *Dekker v. Stichting Vormingscentrum voor Jong Volwassenen (VJV-Centrum) Plus*[96] to mean that it was unlawful to refuse to appoint a woman who was pregnant on the ground of the financial consequences to the employer of doing so. The consequences of appointing a pregnant person, so far as they follow from the fact of pregnancy, are to be regarded as based on the fact of pregnancy, a ground of discrimination which offends against the Directive. This absolutist approach appears at first sight to be inconsistent with the comparison required under the 1975 Act: according to *Dekker*, if unfavourable treatment results from pregnancy it seems to be automatically unlawful. However, this is not necessarily the case. In a decision delivered on the same day as *Dekker*, the Court introduced the possibility of a comparative element in some circumstances. In Case C-179/88 *Handels- og Kontorfunctionoerernes Forbund i Danmark v. Dansk Arbejdsgiverforening*[97] (the *Hertz* case) Mrs. Hertz returned from maternity leave, but thereafter took considerable periods of sick leave because of complications resulting from her pregnancy. Her employer dismissed her. The Court held that it is within the discretion of Member States to fix periods of maternity leave which allow

---

[94] The European Community has no general race relations legislation in place, although there are measures protecting the freedom of nationals of one Member State to move to and establish business interests in other Member States: see Ch. 7. On the principle of equality in EC law, see A. Arnull, *The General Principles of EEC Law and the Individual* (London: Leicester Univ. Press, 1990), esp. Ch. 13.

[95] See E. Ellis, *European Community Sex Equality Law* 2nd edn.(Oxford: Clarendon Press, 1998), ch. 3.

[96] [1990] ECR I-3941, CJEC.

[97] [1990] ECR I-3979, CJEC.

pregnant women to be absent during the period in which disorders which are inherent in pregnancy and childbirth occur. If disorders occur or continue after that period, they are to be treated in the same way as any other illness. It does not constitute unlawful discrimination to dismiss a woman who is persistently ill over a long period following the end of her maternity leave, whatever the cause of the illnesses, unless a man who was ill for a similar period would not have been dismissed.

Domestic courts, as authorities of the state, are required to take all appropriate measures to give effect to obligations on the state arising under directives, and this includes interpreting domestic law so as to be consistent with Community law whenever possible.[98] However, the combined effect of *Dekker* and *Hertz* in circumstances such as those in *Webb* was not clear. Did Community law permit a comparative approach so as to allow an employer to rely on a person's unavailability for work through pregnancy as a ground of dismissal when the person was taken on to cover that very period and a man would have been dismissed for unavailability at that time? Faced by this problem, the House of Lords in *Webb* decided to adjourn the case to await the response of the Court to a question which the House referred under Article 177 (now Article 234) of the Treaty. The Court of Justice held that it had been unlawful to dismiss Mrs. Webb.[99] She had had a contract for an indefinite period. If her unavailability for work during the period of her pregnancy could have been used as a justification for dismissing her, merely because her presence at work during that period was essential to the proper functioning of the employer's business, it would have rendered the provisions of the Equal Treatment Directive ineffective. The Court's view was reinforced by the EC Pregnancy Directive, offering protection for pregnant and breastfeeding workers for whom there is no male comparator and whom it is therefore illogical to try to protect by way of anti-discrimination legislation.[100] If she had only had a temporary contract, the position would have been different. In the light of the Court of Justice's opinion, the House of Lords decided that section 1 of the Sex Discrimination Act 1975 had to be interpreted as meaning that, where a woman has been appointed for an indefinite period and is dismissed because she is temporarily unable to perform her duties because of pregnancy, that is a relevant circumstance which could not be present in the case of a hypothetical man, so there is no need to find a male comparator under section 1(1)(a).[101] This provides a good example of the effect on the interpretation of UK legislation of the dialogue which our courts conduct with the Court of Justice in this area of law.

Section 2 of the 1975 and 1976 Acts make it unlawful to victimize a person by reason of their having alleged that the victimizer has contravened the Acts, or having brought proceedings against the victimizer under the Acts, or having given evidence or information in connection with such proceedings, or having done anything at all under or by reference to the Acts, whether in relation to the victimizer or any other

[98] Case 14/83 *Von Colson and Kamann v. Land Nordrhein-Westfalen* [1984] ECR 1891, CJEC; Case C-106–89 *Marleasing SA v. La Comercial Internacional de Alimentacion SA* [1990] ECR I-4135.
[99] Case C-32/93 *Webb v. EMO Air Cargo (UK) Ltd.* [1994] ECR I-3567, [1994] QB 718, CJEC.
[100] Directive 92/85 [1992] OJ L348/1; Ellis, *European Community Sex Equality Law*, 261–2.
[101] *Webb v. EMO Air Cargo (UK) Ltd. (No. 2)* [1995] 1 WLR 1454, [1995] 4 All ER 577, HL.

person, unless the allegations were made falsely and not in good faith. Discrimination on the ground of suspected past or intended future actions of those types by the person discriminated against are also unlawful under section 2. Establishing this sort of discrimination by victimization does not require proof of subjective intention to treat the person less favourably than others on one of those grounds. In *Nagarajan v. London Regional Transport*[102] the complainant had held various posts with LRT and a subsidiary, and had brought various sets of proceedings alleging racial discrimination and, subsequently, victimization. He applied for the post of travel information assistant, but was rejected. LRT said that he had been rejected purely on the basis of his performance at his interview, where the panel had noted that he was anti-management. The employment tribunal found that this judgment had been based on his previous complaints, and inferred that the panel had been 'consciously or unconsciously' influenced by those complaints. A majority of the House of Lords (Lord Nicholls of Birkenhead, Lord Steyn, Lord Hutton, and Lord Hobhouse of Woodborough; Lord Browne-Wilkinson dissented) held that 'by reason that' in section 2(1) is interchangeable with 'on racial grounds' in section 1(1). Both involve an objective test, the 'but-for' test.[103] Motive is irrelevant to, or at any rate not determinative of, the question.

As noted above, equal treatment will not always provide equal opportunity. Inequality of opportunity is particularly likely to result where one group suffers from the effects of a history of systematic discrimination which has limited the educational and economic opportunities open to them. In such cases, affirmative action, or positive discrimination, is required to redress the balance by favouring members of that group over members of other groups in order to make up for unavoidable disadvantages. Such action involves the use of race- or sex-conscious selection criteria in order to remove or compensate for, rather than to create, inequality of opportunity. In the USA the decision of the Supreme Court in *Brown v. Board of Education of Topeka*[104] that separate schooling for different racial groups could not be 'equal' within the meaning of the Equal Protection Clause of the Fourteenth Amendment to the Constitution led to court-ordered programmes of bussing children between schools and areas in circumstances which gave rise to considerable unhappiness, and incidentally involved courts in taking an active role in controlling school policy. In a follow-up decision, the Supreme Court felt forced to soften its stance somewhat, giving more weight to the opinions of the local school districts as to the speed at which desegregated schooling could be achieved.[105]

Such action to break down segregation is highly contentious, because it will be seen by the disadvantaged members of previously advantaged groups as a straightforward form of discrimination. Suppose that members of group X have in the past systematically discriminated against members of group Y. Xerxes, a member of group X, has

---

[102] [2000] 1 AC 501, [1999] 4 All ER 65, HL.

[103] *R. v. Birmingham City Council, ex parte EOC* [1989] AC 1155, HL; *James v. Eastleigh BC* [1990] 2 AC 751, HL.

[104] (1954) 347 US 483.

[105] *Brown v. Board of Education* 349 US 294 (1955); see also *Swann v. Charlotte-Mecklenburg Board of Education* 402 US 1 (1971) and *Milliken v. Bradley* 418 US 717 (1974).

himself discriminated against members of group Y, and Yolande, a member of group Y, has herself suffered from discrimination at the hands of members of group X (although Xerxes and Yolande have not encountered one another). Yolande and Xerxes now apply for admission to law school. Yolande benefits from a programme of affirmative action which disadvantages Xerxes. One may regard this as a form of just compensation for Yolande's past disadvantage, and as inflicting no injustice on Xerxes as a past discriminator. However, it is less clear that generally preferential treatment can be justified in order to benefit the disadvantaged group as a whole at the expense of people who have never personally discriminated. There are possible justifications. It might be argued that ethnic diversity in education, housing, professions, etc. benefits the whole of society, and also helps to strengthen the institutions concerned. Another argument is that special action is helpful in producing substantial numbers of (for example) black or women doctors in order to give members of that racial group or sex a role model which will encourage them to take up opportunities which are available. But these arguments have not, on the whole, attracted widespread support in the UK or the USA, being inconsistent with the individualist view of rights on which those legal systems are, by and large, based.

In the USA, some affirmative action programmes have been upheld under the Equal Protection clause of the Fourteenth Amendment and Title VII of the Civil Rights Act of 1964. Although crude affirmative action through quotas has been held to be an unlawful form of state action, less rigid, more judgmental favouring of underprivileged groups in educational settings has been upheld (especially if carried on in order to achieve an appropriately broad educational experience for all).[106] Affirmative action programmes have been treated as appropriate in order to correct direct discrimination against the person whom the affirmative action is designed to benefit, and to remedy 'persistent or egregious discrimination'.[107] The philosophical basis for the latter ground is unclear, but it seems to be taken to justify state grants in aid of business enterprises controlled by members of ethnic minorities.[108] Even affirmative action by means of quotas has been upheld where the action is a temporary measure which has been undertaken voluntarily by a private employer or individual, rather than imposed by a state agency.[109] The American courts and Congress are finding it hard to decide whether (and, if so, when) the Constitution permits them to adopt race- and sex-conscious criteria to benefit certain groups in order to correct past negative discrimination, or whether it requires them to be entirely blind to race and sex.[110]

In the British legislation, this dilemma is on the whole resolved in favour of

[106] *Regents of the University of California v. Bakke* 438 US 265 (1978); D. S. Days III, 'Affirmative Action', in L. Gostin (ed.), *Civil Liberties in Conflict* (London: Routledge, 1988), 85–101.

[107] *Local 28 of the Sheet Metal Workers' International Association v. EEOC* 106 S. Ct. 3019 (1986); *United States v. Paradise* 107 S. Ct. 1053 (1987).

[108] *Fullilove v. Klutznick* 448 US 448 (1980).

[109] *United Steelworkers of America v. Weber* 443 US 193 (1979); *Metro Broadcasting v. FCC* 111 L. Ed. 2d 854 (1990).

[110] See H. J. Abraham and B. A. Perry, *Freedom and the Court: Civil Rights and Liberties in the United States* 6th edn. (New York: Oxford University Press, 1994), 421–37.

race- and sex-blindness. Positive discrimination is generally no less unlawful than other forms of discrimination.[111] There are general obligations placed on authorities responsible for public programmes to ensure that education is provided without discrimination.[112] Local authorities also have a duty to have regard, in the performance of their functions, to the need to eliminate unlawful racial discrimination and promote equality of opportunity and good relations between members of different racial groups, although this has been interpreted by the courts as giving only a limited freedom to authorities.[113] However, there are particular settings in which statute provides that specially advantageous treatment for certain purposes is not to be regarded as unlawful discrimination. For example, vocational training can be offered preferentially to members of one racial group or sex where that group or sex is seriously under-represented in the work-force.[114] In deference to the religious significance of turbans to Sikhs, they are exempted from the requirement to wear protective headgear when riding motorcycles and when working on sites where helmets would normally be mandatory, and it is unlawful to discriminate against Sikhs in respect of employment on account of their lawful refusal to wear protective headgear.[115] The influence of European Community law has led to legislation which permits discrimination in favour of women in employment, vocational training, and in respect of discriminatory practices, where the discrimination is carried out for the protection of women as required by statute,[116] and the Secretary of State has power to exempt from the scope of the sex discrimination legislation certain arrangements authorized by statute to make it easier for single parents to take employment.[117] But these provisions do not amount to a general acceptance of affirmative action to remedy the social effects of past discrimination.

A similarly restrictive position was adopted by the Court of Justice under Community law. In *Kalanke v. Freie Hansestadt Bremen*[118] legislation in Bremen, in Germany, provided that, where a man and a woman who applied for the same job were equally well qualified, the job was to be given to the woman if women were less well represented than men in that particular remuneration bracket. The object was to redress historical inequities which led to men having advantages in access to higher paid jobs. Article 2(4) of the Equal Treatment Directive 76/207/EEC allows removal of existing inequalities in order to promote equal opportunities. However, the Court held that the Bremen rule went beyond the legitimate goal of removing existing inequalities, and sought equal representation, not equality of opportunity, between men and women. It therefore constituted unlawful discrimination under Article 2(1).

However, more recently Community law has moved further towards accepting the

---

[111] *Lambeth LBC v. Commission for Racial Equality* [1990] IRLR 231, CA, at 234 *per* Balcombe LJ.

[112] Sex Discrimination Act 1975, s. 25; Race Relations Act 1976, s. 19.

[113] *Wheeler v. Leicester City Council* [1985] AC 1054, [1985] 2 All ER 1106, HL; *R. v. Lewisham LBC, ex parte Shell United Kingdom Ltd.* [1988] 1 All ER 938, DC.

[114] Sex Discrimination Act 1975, ss. 47, 48; Race Relations Act 1976, ss. 37, 38.

[115] Road Traffic Act 1988, s. 16(2); Employment Act 1989, ss. 11, 12.

[116] Sex Discrimination Act 1975, ss. 51 (as substituted by Employment Act 1989, s. 3(1), (3)), 51A and 52A (inserted by Employment Act 1989, s. 3(1), (3), (4)).

[117] Employment Act 1989, s. 8.

[118] Case C-450/93 [1995] ECR I-3051, [1996] ICR 314, CJEC.

legitimacy of some affirmative action. In *Marschall v. Land Nordrhein-Westfalen*[119] the Court of Justice upheld the validity of a law giving preference to women applicants who are as well qualified as males, as long as the men are considered on their individual merits. Only absolute and unconditional rules were outlawed by *Kalanke*. The Court recognized that equal qualifications did not necessarily mean equal opportunities, when women disproportionately suffer from disadvantages following from career breaks, reduced flexibility in working hours, and a higher level of absence. When Article 119 of the EC Treaty became Article 141 TEC, it was amended so that Article 141(4) now reflects the decision in *Marschall*:

'4. With a view to ensuring full equality in practice between men and women in working life, the principle of equal treatment shall not prevent any Member State from maintaining or adopting measures providing for specific advantages in order to make it easier for the under-represented sex to pursue a vocational activity or to prevent or compensate for disadvantages in professional careers.'

This was possible because in 1997 the new Labour government in the UK accepted the obligations of the Social Chapter, which the previous government had rejected, and which had therefore been relegated to a separate agreement between the other fourteen Member States at Maastricht. Article 141(4) is permissive rather than obligatory, but it opens the way for the UK to amend its equality laws to permit a degree of affirmative action without risking incompatibility with Community law. A similar freedom to undertake a degree of affirmative action in relation to racial equality without contravening EC law is provided by the Article 5 of the Race Directive,[120] which is in similar terms to Article 141(4) TEC and which came into force in 2000.

(ii) Contexts in which discrimination is unlawful

The settings in which discrimination is unlawful are broadly similar in relation to sex and race discrimination, although there are detailed rules dealing with sexually discriminatory terms in contracts of employment under the Equal Pay Act 1970, Article 141 (formerly 119) TEC, and the Equal Treatment Directive and the Equal Pay Directive[121] of the Council of Ministers of the European Community. There are also special provisions in the Framework Directive on Discrimination[122] and the Race Directive,[123] and additional provisions added to the Race Relations Act 1976 by the Race Relations (Amendment) Act 2000, which are considered further below.

[119] Case C-409/95 [1997] ECR I-6363, CJEC. See C. Barnard and B. Hepple, 'Substantive Equality' [2000] *CLJ* 562–85 at 576–9.

[120] Directive 2000/43/EC of 29 June 2000 implementing the principle of equal treatment between persons irrespective of racial or ethnic origin, Art. 5: 'With a view to ensuring full equality in practice, the principle of equal treatment shall not prevent any Member State from maintaining or adopting specific measures to prevent or compensate for disadvantages linked to racial or ethnic origin'. In each case it must be possible to assess each candidate's merits objectively: Case C-158/97 *Badeck and others* [2000] ECR 1-0000; Case C-407/98 *Abrahamsson and others* [2000] ECR 1-5539.

[121] See Ellis, *European Community Sex Equality Law*, chs 2 and 3.

[122] Directive 2000/78/EC of 27 November 2000 establishing a general framework for equal treatment in employment and occupation, dealing with discrimination on the grounds of religion and belief, disability, age, and sexual orientation.

[123] Directive 2000/43/EC of 29 June 2000 implementing the principle of equal treatment between persons irrespective of racial or ethnic origin.

Where the special provisions do not apply, the provisions of the 1976 Act parallel those in the 1975 Act. Both Acts apply generally to employment,[124] education,[125] and the provision of goods, facilities, services, and premises to the public or a section of the public.[126] Private clubs do not constitute a section of the public for this purpose,[127] although those with twenty-five or more members are now subject to the race relations legislation,[128] but not the sex discrimination legislation (enabling single-sex clubs, including the gentlemen's clubs in London and elsewhere, to continue to operate). Goods, facilities, and services constitute a broad category which has enabled some governmental acts to be scrutinized. For example, the Court of Appeal held in *Savjani v. IRC*[129] that tax inspectors were forbidden to discriminate when adopting methods of testing taxpayers' entitlements to tax relief, because the provision of the reliefs allowed by statute was a service within the meaning of the legislation. In that case, the Revenue had unlawfully adopted a practice of imposing requirements of proof on immigrants from the Indian sub-continent claiming child relief for the first time which were not demanded of claimants from elsewhere. On the other hand, the House of Lords has held by a majority of three to two, in *R. v. Entry Clearance Officer, Bombay, ex parte Amin*,[130] that the provisions do not cover the work of agencies whose job is to control or police people's activities, rather than to facilitate them. An officer whose job it was to vet potential immigrants was thus not subject to the sex discrimination legislation, and the same would be true of the race relations legislation. This is not a surprising decision on the facts of the case, given that the very nature of immigration law and procedure is inherently discriminatory,[131] but the general way in which Lord Fraser, speaking for the majority in *Amin*'s case, developed his argument suggested that it would be difficult to apply the legislation to such fields as land use planning and policing.

The position was exacerbated when the Police and Magistrates' Courts Act 1994, section 37 and Schedule 9, repealed section 101 of the Police and Criminal Evidence Act 1984, which had made it a disciplinary offence for a constable to act in a racially discriminatory way. In *Farah v. Commissioner of Police of the Metropolis*[132] a Somalian woman alleged that she had been attacked by white teenagers. She sought assistance from the police, who, instead of protecting her, arrested her for assault and detained her. She claimed damages for (*inter alia*) racial discrimination in respect of the provision of a service. After analysing the authorities, the Court of Appeal held that the police provide a service to members of public seeking assistance, and so were within section 20 of the Race Relations Act 1976 when the plaintiff sought their help. How-

[124] Sex Discrimination Act 1975, s. 6; Race Relations Act 1976, s. 4.
[125] Sex Discrimination Act 1975, s. 22; Race Relations Act 1976, s. 17.
[126] Sex Discrimination Act 1975, ss. 29–32; Race Relations Act 1976, ss. 20–4.
[127] *Charter v. Race Relations Board* [1973] AC 868, [1973] 1 All ER 512, HL; *Dockers' Labour Club and Institute Ltd. v. Race Relations Board* [1976] AC 285, [1974] 3 All ER 592, HL.
[128] Race Relations Act 1976, s. 25.
[129] [1981] QB 458, [1981] 1 All ER 1121, CA.
[130] [1983] 2 AC 818, [1983] 2 All ER 864, HL.
[131] I. Martin, 'Racism in Immigration Law and Practice', in P. Wallington (ed.), *Civil Liberties 1984* (Oxford: Martin Robertson, 1984), 245–57.
[132] [1998] QB 65, [1997] 1 All ER 289, CA.

ever, the Commissioner of Police was not vicariously liable for the acts of his constables, as they are not employed by the Commissioner, so an action lay only against an individual police officer.

The weakness of protection against racial discrimination in the public sector increasingly caused concern, particularly after the Report of the Stephen Lawrence Inquiry[133] concluded that there was institutional racism in the Metropolitan Police which had adversely affected the way the police had investigated the killing of Stephen Lawrence in 1993. Ultimately, section 1 of the Race Relations (Amendment) Act 2000 added a new section 19B to the 1976 Act, making it unlawful for a public authority (including the police) to discriminate on racial grounds in carrying out any of their functions, while section 4 of the 2000 Act added a new section 76A to the 1976 Act providing that, for the purposes of the race equality legislation, a constable is to be treated as being employed by the chief officer of police.[134] In relation to planning, a new section 19A of the Race Relations Act 1976 outlaws discrimination on the ground of race. These provisions are considered further below. However, neither the policing provisions nor those relating to planning extend to sex discrimination.

Barristers are the subject of special provisions. Despite evidence of discrimination against female barristers and those from ethnic minorities, the anomalous, non-contractual relationship between barristers and their clients, and the special training and working practices of the Bar in respect of pupillages and seats in chambers, made it difficult to bring the Bar under the equality legislation. Accordingly, special provision was made in the Courts and Legal Services Act 1990 outlawing discrimination against barristers on the grounds of race and sex.[135]

There are some general exceptions from the reach of both sex and race discrimination law. The regime of the legislation does not apply to matters affecting national security,[136] or to charities established before the legislation came into operation.[137] Nor does it apply to certain intimate settings in which small groups of people have to live, work, or play closely together. Partnerships with fewer than six partners are allowed to discriminate when appointing new partners.[138] People providing accommodation in small premises where the lessor or vendor is to continue to live in close proximity to the occupier or purchaser are not covered,[139] although a local authority social services department cannot rely on this provision to protect it against liability

---

[133] Sir William Macpherson of Cluny, *The Stephen Lawrence Inquiry*, Cm. 4262-I (London: The Stationery Office, 1999), ch. 6.

[134] A new s. 76B of the 1976 Act makes equivalent provision for the National Criminal Intelligence Service and the National Crime Squad.

[135] Sex Discrimination Act 1975, s. 35A, and Race Relations Act 1976, s. 26A, as inserted by the Courts and Legal Services Act 1990, s. 64(1).

[136] Sex Discrimination Act 1975, s. 52; Race Relations Act 1976, ss. 19B(3) (inserted by Race Relations (Amendment) Act 2000, s. 1) and 42.

[137] Sex Discrimination Act 1975, s. 43; Race Relations Act 1976, s. 34 (although provisions in charitable trust instruments which discriminate on the basis of colour are to be disregarded).

[138] Sex Discrimination Act 1975, s. 11; Race Relations Act 1976, s. 10.

[139] Sex Discrimination Act 1975, s. 32; Race Relations Act 1976, s. 22; and note ss. 34, 35 of the 1975 Act and ss. 23–6 of the 1976 Act. See further S. H. Bailey, D. J. Harris, and B. L. Jones, *Civil Liberties Cases and Materials*, 4th edn. (London: Butterworths, 1995), 657–60; E. Ellis, *Sex Discrimination Law* (Aldershot: Gower, 1988), 114–26.

for discrimination in its children's homes, or when placing children in its care with fosterers or giving them the opportunity to take holidays with carers.[140] In employment, it is not unlawful to discriminate on the ground of sex or race where the sex or race of the person to be appointed is a genuine occupational qualification.[141]

(4) RACE RELATIONS LEGISLATION

In this section, attention is drawn to some features of the Race Relations Act 1976 and the regime which it establishes which are not shared with the regimes under other anti-discrimination legislation: the groups against which discrimination is unlawful; the new duty on public authorities to foster racial equality; the work of the Commission for Racial Equality (CRE) established under the 1976 Act; and the likely impact of the EC Race Directive.

(i) Racial grounds and racial groups

Direct discrimination is unlawful if carried out on racial grounds, and indirect discrimination against racial groups is unlawful. The meanings of these terms are related. Racial grounds are defined as colour, race, nationality, or ethnic or national origins; a racial group is a group of people defined by reference to colour, race, nationality, or ethnic or national origin. A person's racial group is any racial group into which he or she falls, so a person may be a member of a number of different racial groups simultaneously, and one racial group may comprise a number of different racial groups.[142]

The problems which have arisen in relation to this definition mainly concern the idea of ethnic origins. Whereas racial groups are identified primarily by biological and geographical factors, an ethnic group has been held to be defined primarily by social and cultural factors, such as language, religion, history, or culture, which are commonly associated with racial groups. The 1976 Act does not provide a remedy for discrimination on religious or linguistic grounds, but the availability of a remedy for discrimination on the ground of nationality or ethnic or national origin may have the effect of mitigating the effects of that omission. For example, a social group with a distinct culture (which may include use of a distinctive language or commitment to a particular religion) may constitute an ethnic group even if members of the group come from such diverse racial and geographical backgrounds that they do not constitute a group defined by race or national origins.

For this reason, the House of Lords held in *Mandla (Sewa Singh) v. Dowell Lee*[143] that a head teacher of a school who refused to allow pupils to wear turbans, thus discriminating against Sikhs, was committing an act of unlawful discrimination under the 1976 Act, because the Sikh community was an ethnic group for the purposes of

---

[140]   *Conwell v. Newham London Borough Council* [2000] 1 WLR 1, [2000] ICR 42, EAT.
[141]   Sex Discrimination Act 1975, s. 7, as amended by Sex Discrimination Act 1986; Race Relations Act 1976, s. 5. See R. Townshend-Smith, *Sex Discrimination in Employment* (London: Sweet & Maxwell, 1989), ch. 8.
[142]   See Race Relations Act 1976, s. 3.
[143]   [1983] 2 AC 548, [1983] 1 All ER 1062, HL.

the Act. Lord Fraser identified two essential conditions for the existence of an ethnic group: a long shared history as a separate group; and a cultural tradition of its own, including family and social customs. In addition, Lord Fraser noted five relevant, though not essential, factors: either common geographical origin or descent from a small number of common ancestors; a common language; a common literature special to the group; a common and distinctive religion; and being a separate group within a larger community. Lord Templeman thought that an ethnic group must have some of the characteristics of a race: group descent, common geographical origin, and a common history. These were not regarded as essential by Lord Fraser, and Lord Templeman does not mention several of Lord Fraser's essential or relevant considerations. The fact that Lords Edmund-Davies, Roskill, and Brandon agreed with both speeches means that there can be no definitive test, or set of tests, for the existence of an ethnic group. We can only say that some elements are probably essential (although we cannot say which), and that several are important.

It follows from *Mandla* that, alongside Sikhs, Jews form an ethnic group.[144] Gipsies also form an ethnic group, so that a 'No Travellers' sign outside a public house potentially constituted indirect discrimination in the provision of goods and services (it was not direct discrimination, because it did not treat gipsies less favourably on racial grounds than travellers who were not gipsies).[145]

On the other hand, the outcome of applying *Mandla* to groups defined principally by ethnicity is far from clear. Christians and Muslims form groups which are too diverse from the points of view of race, colour, nationality, and national origin to be protected, unless they form ethnic groups. The same diversity of membership (resulting from their success in attracting people to their ranks) prevents them from demonstrating common histories, languages, or cultures which might make either of them an ethnic group. Even smaller groups may have difficulty. Rastafarians, who share a strong cultural tradition, are not regarded as having a common ethnic origin for the purposes of the Race Relations Act 1976. Their sixty-year history is regarded as insufficient to count as a shared history for the purpose of applying the test in *Mandla*. The Court of Appeal has held that nothing sufficiently distinguishes Rastafarians from the rest of the Jamaican, or indeed Afro-Caribbean, community in the UK to justify treating Rastafarians as a separate ethnic group. Therefore refusing to employ a Rastafarian as a van driver because he refused to cut off his dreadlocks did not constitute racial discrimination: a requirement for short hair did not discriminate on the ground of ethnic origin.[146] But the test for ethnicity is self-evidently never final and conclusive. A religious group may be sufficiently cohesive, culturally distinct, and monocultural to be an ethnic group today, but lose the protection when it attracts a diverse range of converts to its ranks. Similarly, Rastafarians might, over time, become more culturally distinct from Jamaicans or Afro-Caribbeans, and attract the protection of

---

[144] In *Mandla*, Lord Fraser adopted the approach to this matter of Richardson J in the New Zealand Court of Appeal in *King-Ansell v. Police* [1979] 2 NZLR 531.

[145] *Commission for Racial Equality v. Dutton* [1989] 1 All ER 306, CA. See also *Hallam v. Avery* [2000] 1 WLR 966, [2000] ICR 83, CA.

[146] *Crown Suppliers (Property Services Agency) v. Dawkins* [1993] ICR 517; *sub nom. Dawkins v. Department of the Environment* [1993] IRLR 284, CA.

the Race Relations Act 1976 as a group definable by reference to ethnic origin. This emphasizes the difficulties in attempting to distinguish between religious and ethnic groups, where the *Mandla* tests for ethnicity are used. If a distinctive culture and history are to remain as hallmarks of an ethnic group, people should be separately protected against discrimination on the ground of religion or belief. The Human Rights Act 1998 may offer a way forward in seeking to control discrimination on grounds which restrict people's enjoyment of the right to freedom of religion and belief on grounds other than race.[147]

(ii) The new duty on public authorities

Section 2 of the Race Relations (Amendment) Act 2000 inserted a new section 19B into, and replaced section 71 of, the Race Relations Act 1976. As a result of section 19B, it is now unlawful for any public authority to do any act which constitutes racial discrimination when carrying out any of its functions.[148] 'Public authority' includes any person only some of whose functions are of a public nature, but does not encompass such people in respect of their private functions.[149] Neither House of Parliament, nor anyone exercising functions in connection with proceedings in Parliament, is a public authority for this purpose.[150] Thus far, the definition of 'public authority' follows that in the Human Rights Act 1998, section 6. However, there are some additional exceptions. The Security and Intelligence Services, GCHQ and armed forces units assisting GCHQ are exempt.[151] So are judicial acts, acts done on the instructions or on behalf of someone acting in a judicial capacity,[152] decisions not to institute or not to continue criminal proceedings,[153] and the making, confirming or approving of enactments, Orders in Council, statutory instruments, and other instruments, arrangements, requirements or conditions made by Ministers under statutory powers.[154] Ministers and other authorized persons carrying out 'immigration or nationality functions' are excepted from the duty,[155] but the Home Secretary must appoint a person from outside the Home Office to monitor the effect of the exception for immigration and nationality functions, and to report annually to the Home Secretary, who is to lay a copy of the report before each House of Parliament.[156]

The new section 71(1) and (2) of the 1976 Act imposes a duty on bodies specified

---

[147] For discussion, see G. Moon and R. Allen QC, 'Substantive Rights and Equal Treatment in Respect of Religion and Belief: Towards a Better Understanding of the Rights, and their Implications' [2000] *EHRLR* 580–602.

[148] Race Relations Act 1976, s. 19B(1), (2). See C. O'Cinneide, 'The Race Relations (Amendment) Act 2000' [2001] *PL* 220–32.

[149] Ibid., s. 19B(2)(a), (4).

[150] Ibid., s. 19B(2)(b), (3)(a) and (b).

[151] Ibid., s. 19B(3)(c)–(f).

[152] Ibid., s. 19C(1).

[153] Ibid., s. 19F.

[154] Ibid., s. 19C(2), (3). 'Ministers' include the National Assembly for Wales and members of the Scottish Executive: ibid., s. 19C(5).

[155] Ibid., ss. 19C(4), 19D. 'Immigration and nationality functions' are functions under the legislation listed in s. 19D(5).

[156] Ibid., s. 19E.

in the new Schedule 1A,[157] when carrying out their functions, 'to have due regard to the need—(a) to eliminate unlawful racial discrimination, and (b) to promote equality of opportunity and good relations between persons of different racial groups'. The range of public bodies identified in the new Schedule 1A is very wide. It includes the police and armed forces, and all government departments other than the Security and Intelligence Services and GCHQ. It thus encompasses those exercising immigration and nationality functions, but such people are not required to promote equality of opportunity (although they must have due regard to the need to eliminate unlawful racial discrimination and promote good race relations).[158] The provisions apply to Scotland and to the National Assembly for Wales.[159] The CRE is given power to issue codes of practice, with the approval of the Secretary of State and Parliament, offering practical guidance to people in relation to the performance of their duties under section 71(1) and (2). Any such code is admissible in evidence if relevant to any legal proceedings, and shall be taken into account, although it will not in itself give rise to legally binding or directly enforceable obligations or rights.[160] The CRE also has power to enforce compliance with the duties under section 71(1) and (2), issuing, and taking legal action to enforce, compliance notices[161] (on which, see section (iii) below).

These provisions mark a fundamentally important development in equality law in Britain. For the first time, most public authorities are required to make good race relations and the need to combat racial discrimination an integral element in all their decision-making. Failure to do so will be actionable at the suit of someone who suffers discrimination. There are certain limits. Remedies for discrimination in investigative functions must not prejudice criminal investigations or proceedings;[162] and in relation to indirect discrimination in immigration, the remedy will normally lie only in immigration proceedings.[163] None the less, the new legislation generalizes responsibility for good race relations across the public sector, instead of imposing the responsibility for positive action on the CRE and leaving the rest of the public sector merely to refrain from unlawful discrimination. The commitment is necessary, as the discovery of institutional racism in various public authorities, including the police and the prison service, has made clear. The scale and importance of the challenge which this sea-change represents for public authorities is inestimable.

(iii) The Commission for Racial Equality

The CRE was established under Part VII of the 1976 Act, replacing the Race Relations Board which had operated under the Race Relations Act 1965. The CRE was given a general brief to work towards the elimination of discrimination, to promote equality of opportunity and good relations between members of racial groups, and to keep the

---

[157] Inserted by Race Relations (Amendment) Act 2000, s.2(2) and Sch. 1 and amended by SI 2001, No. 3457. See also SI 2001, No. 3458.

[158] Race Relations Act 1976, s.71A(1).

[159] Ibid., s.71B.

[160] Ibid., s.71C.

[161] Ibid., ss.71D, 71E.

[162] Ibid., s.57(4A)–(4D), inserted by Race Relations (Amendment) Act 2000, s.5.

[163] Race Relations Act 1976, s.57A, inserted by Race Relations (Amendment) Act 2000, s.6(2).

working of the Act under review and make recommendations to the Secretary of State for amending it.[164] To further these ends, the CRE is permitted to give assistance (including financial assistance) to organizations, to undertake or assist research and educational activities, and to issue Codes of Practice giving practical guidance for the elimination of discrimination, and promotion of equality of opportunity between racial groups, in the field of employment.[165]

The CRE has a number of powers in relation to the investigation of suspected discrimination and the enforcement of the law. This exemplifies the twin-track approach to the enforcement of anti-discrimination law, which operates equally under the Sex Discrimination Act 1975, whereby individuals have legal remedies for discrimination which they suffer, while a public agency is responsible for safeguarding wider interests. The two may come together: the CRE is empowered to give assistance to an individual complainant in legal proceedings where the case raises a question of principle or it is unreasonable, in view of considerations including the complexity of the case and the position of the complainant, to expect the complainant to deal with the case alone.[166]

When acting in its own right as an investigator and enforcer, the CRE has power to conduct a formal investigation.[167] Launching a formal investigation, as opposed to conducting general research or informal investigations, has two significant consequences. First, for the purposes of a formal investigation the CRE has power to serve notice on any person requiring that specified information be provided, and may require any person to attend to give oral information and produce documents. Non-compliance with the requirements of a notice is a criminal offence.[168] Secondly, if in the course of a formal investigation the CRE becomes satisfied that a person is committing or has committed an unlawful discriminatory act, or a breach of section 28 (discriminatory practice), 29 (discriminatory advertising), 30 (giving instructions to discriminate), or 31 (putting pressure on another person to discriminate) of the 1976 Act, it can issue a 'non-discrimination notice'. This requires the person not to commit such an act, and where necessary to inform the CRE of steps taken to effect changes to practices or other arrangements and to give information to other people if required. The notice may also require the person to provide such other information as may reasonably be required.[169] At first sight, the formal investigation would seem to be a

---

[164] Race Relations Act 1976, s. 43. See M. Coussey, 'The Effectiveness of Strategic Enforcement of the Race Relations Act 1976', in B. Hepple and E. M. Szyszczak (eds.), *Discrimination: The Limits of Law* (London: Mansell, 1992), 35–49; Bailey, Harris, and Jones, *Civil Liberties Cases and Materials*, 668–74; Townshend-Smith, *Discrimination Law*, 524–36; Gregory, *Sex, Race and the Law*, chs 6 and 7; L. Lustgarten, *Legal Control of Racial Discrimination* (London: Macmillan, 1980); L. Lustgarten, 'Racial Inequality and the Limits of Law' (1986) 49 *MLR* 68–85; C. McCrudden, 'The Commission for Racial Equality: Formal Investigations in the Shadow of Judicial Review', in R. Baldwin and C. McCrudden, *Regulation and Public Law* (London: Weidenfeld & Nicolson, 1987), 227–66.

[165] Race Relations Act 1976, ss. 44, 45, 46.

[166] Ibid., s. 66.

[167] Ibid., s. 48. See G. Applebey and E. Ellis, 'Formal Investigations: the Commission for Racial Equality and the Equal Opportunities Commission as Law Enforcement Agencies' [1984] *PL* 236–76.

[168] Race Relations Act 1976, s. 50.

[169] Ibid., s. 58. The person to whom a notice is addressed has a right of appeal on the merits to a court or tribunal: ibid., s. 59; *CRE v. Amari Plastics Ltd.* [1982] QB 1194, [1982] 2 All ER 499, CA.

powerful weapon in the hands of the CRE. However, in practice its potential is limited.

There are two broad types of formal investigation. In the first type of investigation, the terms of reference for the investigation confine it to the activities of named people. They must be informed that the CRE believe that they have committed an act made unlawful by the Act and that the CRE propose to investigate it, and they must be offered an opportunity to make oral or written representations with regard to it.[170] It follows that the decision to embark on a 'named person' investigation must be reactive, responding to a belief that the person has committed an unlawful act. As a public agency, the CRE is subject to the ordinary principles of judicial review. A decision to launch a 'named person' investigation may therefore be quashed if, before taking the decision, the CRE does not have such a belief,[171] or (perhaps) if it has insufficient evidence to make such a belief reasonable. The usefulness of the power to launch a formal 'named person' investigation has been substantially restricted by this tendency on the part of the courts to interpret restrictively the powers of the CRE to initiate formal investigations proactively. It seems that this is the result of a drafting error in the legislation, which was intended to apply to the course of an investigation, not its inception.[172] In 1985, the CRE proposed an amendment to the 1976 Act to allow them to commence 'named person' investigations without a belief that a named person had committed an unlawful act, but this proposal has not been acted on.

The second type of formal investigation, a general investigation, is less restricted. General notice must be given that the investigation is to take place, but the CRE need not have any prior belief that discrimination is occurring, although there will normally be at least a suspicion. These investigations tend, therefore, to be proactive rather than reactive. Such investigations may be undertaken even where there is no suspicion that anyone has committed an unlawful act, in order to enable the CRE to write a report which will highlight factors putting a strain on good relations between racial groups. For example, the CRE investigated suspected racist practices in the implementation of immigration policy, despite such practices not being capable of being unlawful discrimination within the meaning of the Act. This investigation was permitted because it was directed to promoting good relations between people of different racial groups,[173] and led to a report on *Immigration Control and Procedures* in 1985. However, a general investigation is not as effective as a 'named person' investigation, because general reports flowing from general investigations do not have legal consequences (although there is no reason why a non-discrimination notice could not be issued alongside, or before, the report).

The drafting of the Act is a serious drawback to the CRE's effective operation. Its extensive inquisitorial powers operate only in respect of formal investigations, which are hedged about by what Lord Denning has described as 'elaborate and cumbersome'

---

[170] Race Relations Act 1976, s. 49.

[171] *R. v. CRE, ex parte London Borough of Hillingdon* [1982] AC 779, HL; *In re Prestige Group plc, Commission for Racial Equality v. Prestige Group plc* [1984] ICR 473, [1984] 1 WLR 335, HL; M. Monroe, 'The *Prestige* Case: Putting the Lid on the Commission for Racial Equality' (1985) 14 *Anglo-American L. Rev.* 187–203.

[172] Bailey, Harris, and Jones, *Civil Liberties Cases and Materials*, 672.

[173] *Home Office v. Commission for Racial Equality* [1982] QB 385, [1981] 1 All ER 1042, *per* Woolf J.

machinery, catching the CRE in 'a spider's web spun by Parliament, from which there is little hope of their escaping'.[174]

Recent changes in the law, including the Race Relations (Amendment) Act 2000 imposing a general duty on public authorities to have due regard to the need to eliminate racial discrimination and promote equality of opportunity and good relations between members of different racial groups, offer hope that the legal position may improve. In 1999, the government announced that it intended to bring the powers of the CRE (and also the EOC) into line with those of the more powerful Disability Rights Commission. Yet, even if the CRE were given free rein, there might be a still more fundamental problem to be overcome before the drive for equality of opportunity through anti-discrimination law could become truly effective. As Professor Lustgarten has persuasively argued, the structure of the existing law, stressing negative legal sanctions for infringements of individual's legal rights, makes it unlikely to be able to address the more pervasive social causes of racial discrimination. On this view, to make the legislation effective it would require a real governmental commitment to the idea of equality, leading to amendment of the 1976 Act to permit, and indeed encourage, affirmative action programmes. The Race Relations (Amendment) Act 2000 marks a start in this direction. It also represents a move to make public authorities take positive steps to combat deeply-rooted racial discrimination through steps suggested by Lustgarten, which include utilizing the economic power of the public sector to encourage employers and others to seek and use information about the ethnic make-up of their workforces, change recruiting procedures, dismantle racial barriers, and change training policies.[175] Only in these ways will equality of opportunity between racial groups come much closer.[176]

(iv) The EC Race Directive and its likely impact

The EC Council Directive implementing the Principle of Equal Treatment between Persons Irrespective of Racial or Ethnic Origin[177] came into force on 19 July 2000, and must be implemented by Member States by 19 July 2003. It makes direct and indirect discrimination on racial grounds unlawful in employment and areas of social protection, including social security, health care, education, and access to and supply of goods and services (including housing) available to the public. This will require amendment of the Race Relations Act 1976, because the definition of indirect discrimination in the Directive is wider than that in section 2 of the 1976 Act. In particular, under the Directive it is not necessary to show that a person has suffered as a result of a condition or requirement which it is more difficult for him or her to satisfy than for people of other racial groups. Article 2(b) of the Directive provides that there is indirect discrimination where an apparently neutral provision, criterion, *or practice* puts people of one racial or ethnic origin at a particular disadvantage

[174] *CRE v. Amari Plastics Ltd.* [1982] QB 1194 at 1203, [1982] 2 All ER 499 at 502, *per* Lord Denning MR.
[175] See Lustgarten, 'Racial Inequality' at 78–84.
[176] See B. Parekh, *The Future of Multi-Ethnic Britain* (London: Runnymede Trust and Profile Books, 2000), *passim*.
[177] Directive 2000/43, [2000] OJ L180/22.

compared to others. Liability for the indirect discrimination can be avoided where 'that provision, criterion or practice is objectively justified by a legitimate aim and the means of achieving that aim are appropriate and necessary'. The definition avoids the need for victims to provide statistical evidence to establish that they have suffered substantial or disproportionate adverse impact compared to members of other groups. Such evidence is needed in sex discrimination cases where indirect discrimination is alleged, but would often be impossible to provide in cases of racial discrimination, since in several EC Member States it is unlawful to collect information about people's racial or ethnic origins.[178] This will remove a significant cause of criticism of the Race Relations Act 1976.

The scope of the Directive is limited in that it does not deal with differential treatment by reason of nationality, or different rules governing the immigration, residence, and employment or occupation rights of third-party nationals and stateless individuals. These matters will continue to be governed by national law, although one can hope that the national legislation will harmonize the various regimes as far as possible.[179]

(5) SEX DISCRIMINATION LEGISLATION[180]

The legislation on sex discrimination which is in force in the UK comes from two distinct sources. First, Parliament has passed a number of measures to restrict the unequal treatment of men and women. Most prominent among these statutes are the Equal Pay Act 1970, which introduced to English law the principle that men and women doing comparable work should be treated comparably under their contracts, and the Sex Discrimination Act 1975. Secondly, European Community law has significantly affected the rights of employees by means of Article 141 (formerly Article 119) TEC and the Equal Pay, Equal Treatment, Burden of Proof, Pregnancy, and Part-Time Work Directives of the Council of Ministers, which give rise to enforceable Community rights to which our courts are, in appropriate circumstances, bound to give effect regardless of inconsistent domestic legislation.[181]

As in the race relations legislation, the Sex Discrimination Act 1975 prohibits both direct and indirect discrimination. The Equal Pay Act 1970 was at first thought to deal only with direct discrimination, but as a result of Community law its protection has been held to extend to indirect discrimination as well. The types of discrimination to which the legislation applies should therefore be the same.

[178] See the oral evidence of Adam Tyson to the House of Lords Select Committee on the European Union in the Committee's Report, *EU Proposals to Combat Discrimination*, HL Paper 68 of 1999–2000 at 22.

[179] On the need for harmonization between rules governing discrimination on different grounds, see B. Hepple QC, M. Coussey, and T. Choudhury, *Equality: A New Framework. Report of the Independent Review of the Enforcement of UK Anti-Discrimination Legislation* (Oxford: Hart Publishing, 2000), ch. 2.

[180] On European Community law, see Ellis, *European Community Sex Equality Law, passim*. On domestic law, see Ellis, *Sex Discrimination Law*; Gregory, *Sex, Race and the Law*; O'Donovan and Szyszczak, *Equality and Sex Discrimination Law*; and (in relation to employment) Townshend-Smith, *Sex Discrimination in Employment*, and C. Barnard, *EC Employment Law*, 2nd edn. (Oxford: Oxford University Press, 2000), *passim*.

[181] See generally Ellis, *European Community Sex Equality Law*, chs 1–3; Arnull, *General Principles*, 238–50.

(i) The Equal Pay Act 1970

Despite its title, this seeks to give a right to women to be treated equally to men[182] in respect of all terms of the contract of employment.[183] It achieves this by implying an equality clause into contracts of service, apprenticeship, or for the personal execution of any work of labour, under which women are employed at any establishment in Great Britain.[184] This implied clause modifies any other term of the contract which is or becomes less favourable to the woman than is a similar term in contract of a man employed to do comparable work.[185] Because the Act covers more than traditional master-servant employment relationships, it can be relied on by people who are self-employed contractors taken on for limited periods on a commission basis, as long as the dominant purpose of the contract is to secure the performance of the work by the contractor in person.[186] However, in order to take advantage of the equality clause the woman must establish comparability with a male colleague, and there are only three grounds under section 1(2) of the Act on which this can be done.

The first is where she is 'employed on the like work with a man in the same employment'. For this to apply, their work must be of the same or a broadly similar nature, any differences being of no practical importance (as regards the nature of the differences and the frequency with which they arise in practice)[187] in relation to terms and conditions of employment.[188] The second is where the woman's work is 'rated as equivalent with that of a man in the same employment' in the course of a job evaluation based on factors such as the effort, skill, and decision-making responsibility which the jobs entail.[189] The third ground of comparability is where, apart from any job evaluation, the woman's work and the man's work are of equal value, even if dissimilar in nature. This was not originally in the 1970 Act, but was essential because the Act would otherwise have been of no use to women working in traditionally segregated occupations, because of stereotyping of gender roles, where there would be no direct male comparator. Because of this gap in the provision for equal pay for work of equal value, the Act was held by the European Court to fall short of the requirements of Article 1 of the EEC Equal Pay Directive,[190] made under Article 119 of the Treaty of Rome.[191] To comply with the ruling, the government introduced the third ground of comparability to the Act by means of delegated legislation.[192]

---

[182] The legislation applies equally to women and to men, but men cannot complain under the 1970 Act in respect of terms in women's contracts which give special protection or maternity rights to women: Equal Pay Act 1970, s. 6(1), as interpreted in *Coyne v. Export Credits Guarantee Department* [1981] IRLR 51.

[183] See Ellis, *Sex Discrimination Law*, ch. 2.

[184] Equal Pay Act 1970, s. 1(1), (6).

[185] Ibid., s. 1(2).

[186] *Quinnen v. Hovells* [1984] IRLR 227, EAT; *Mirror Group Newspapers Ltd. v. Gunning* [1986] 1 WLR 546, [1986] 1 All ER 385, CA.

[187] *Shields v. Coomes (Holdings) Ltd.* [1978] ICR 1159, CA.

[188] Equal Pay Act 1970, s. 1(4).

[189] Ibid., s. 1(5).

[190] EEC Directive 75/117, OJ No. L 45/19.

[191] On the equal pay for equal work principle in Art. 119, see Case 61/81 *Commission v. United Kingdom* [1982] 3 CMLR 284; Ellis, *European Community Sex Equality Law*, ch. 2.

[192] Equal Pay (Amendment) Regulations 1983, SI 1983/1794, made under the power conferred by the European Communities Act 1972, s. 2(2), (4).

The Act excepts from its reach provisions relating to death and retirement, but these exceptions have been to some extent undermined by decisions of the European Court of Justice applying the EEC Equal Pay Directive 75/117 and the Equal Treatment Directive 76/207. In particular, it has been held that differential retirement ages and ages for entitlement to occupational pensions, fixed by reference to the ages at which people became eligible for state pensions (men at sixty-five, women at sixty) violated the Equal Treatment Directive.[193] Normally, Community rights under directly effective EEC Council Directives are enforceable only against state agencies, and not against citizens or companies, but in Case C-188/89 *Foster v. British Gas plc*[194] the Court held that the rights could also be enforced against any person or body which had been given responsibility by law for providing a public service, which was under the control of the state, and which had been given special powers, beyond those given by the rules governing relationships between ordinary individuals, to facilitate performance of that function. Moreover, in Joined Cases C-6/90 and C-9/90 *Francovich and Bonifaci v. Italy*[195] the Court held that an individual whose grievance lies against a body which does not fall within the scope of the *Foster* doctrine nevertheless has a cause of action against the state for loss caused by the state's failure to implement a directive in domestic law in such a way as to enable the plaintiff to pursue a remedy against the person or body which actually caused the loss.[196] These developments are manifestations of the Court's determination to ensure that people are not left without adequate remedies for injuries suffered through non-compliance with Community law, whether by the state or private undertakings.[197]

It is therefore a potentially important guarantee of the right to be free of discriminatory provisions in respect of retirement and pensions that the Court has held that the Equal Treatment Directive makes it unlawful to adopt discriminatory retirement ages as between men and women.[198] This is particularly significant in view of the weakness, by and large, of the domestic statutory protection against discrimination in relation to retirement arrangements. Excluded from the Equal Pay Act 1970, differential retirement ages for employees doing different kinds of work have been upheld under the Sex Discrimination Act 1975, without the need to show that the difference is justified by objective criteria relating to the nature of the work. In *Bullock v. Alice Ottley School*,[199] the employers adopted retirement ages of sixty-five for maintenance

---

[193] Case 19/81 *Burton v. British Railways Board* [1982] ECR 555, CJEC; Case 152/84 *Marshall v. Southampton and South-West Hampshire Area Health Authority* [1986] ECR 723, CJEC; Case C-262/88 *Barber v. Guardian Royal Exchange Assurance Group* [1991] 1 QB 344, [1990] 2 All ER 660, CJEC.

[194] [1990] ECR I-3133, [1990] 3 All ER 897, CJEC.

[195] [1992] IRLR 84, CJEC.

[196] E. Szyszczak, 'European Community Law: New Remedies, New Directions? Joined Cases C6/90 and C9/90 *Francovich and Bonifaci v. Italy*' (1992) 55 *MLR* 690–7; M. Ross, 'Beyond *Francovich*' (1993) 56 *MLR* 55–73.

[197] See Case C-213/89 *R. v. Secretary of State for Transport, ex parte Factortame Ltd.* [1990] ECR I-2433, [1991] 1 All ER 70, CJEC and HL.

[198] Case 149/77 *Defrenne v. Sabena* [1978] ECR 1365, CJEC; Case 152/84 *Marshall v. South-West Hampshire Area Health Authority (Teaching)* [1986] QB 401, [1986] 2 All ER 584, CJEC; Case C-188/89 *Foster v. British Gas plc* [1990] ECR I-3133, [1990] 3 All ER 897, CJEC.

[199] [1992] IRLR 564, CA.

workers and gardeners (who were men) and sixty for kitchen workers (who were women). The Court of Appeal, reversing the Employment Appeal Tribunal, held that employers are free to impose different retirement ages for different classes of jobs between which there is no comparability, as long as the ages are not based on direct or indirect gender discrimination. This leaves domestic protection in a weak state for those who are in occupations which are predominantly staffed by people of one sex, and makes recourse to rights under Community law increasingly important.

The Equal Pay Act 1970 permits a person who is aggrieved by unequal contractual terms to bring proceedings against the employer in an industrial tribunal. The employee left to take individual action faces a hurdle in the form of the employer's defence where the variation between the woman's contract and the man's contract is proved to be 'genuinely due to a material factor which is not the difference of sex'.[200] The difference in question must be significant and relevant in all the circumstances surrounding the employment in question.[201] The European Court of Justice has ruled that the fact that the woman worker is part-time where the man is full-time does not justify a differential wage rate where the effect is indirectly to discriminate against women because women are more likely than men to be employed part-time.[202]

The onus under the 1970 Act is on individuals to enforce the law (although employees are likely often to be supported and advised by their trade unions). This leaves something of a gap, in that discriminatory contractual terms may be imposed not by individual employers but by larger scale collective agreements (to which the trades unions would usually be parties), pay structures, and legal structures for regulating wages. Originally, these were the subject of an alternative arrangement, under which a Central Arbitration Committee determined the lawfulness of the agreements or other structures. However, the Divisional Court restricted the scope for decision-making by the CAC,[203] which was in due course abolished by the Sex Discrimination Act 1986. In its place, the 1986 Act nullifies sexually discriminatory provisions in collective agreements, employers' and professional organizations and qualifying bodies, and trades unions' and employers' rules,[204] but there is no procedure for adjudicating on the legality of provisions at the instigation of a collective plaintiff or applicant. As Professor Ellis comments, 'The lack of a collective remedy amounts to a serious gap in the legislative framework in relation to this far-reaching form of discrimination'.[205]

(ii) The Sex Discrimination Act 1975

This was drafted to complement the Equal Pay Act 1970, and to extend protection to fields which are not related to the terms of a contract of employment.[206] Most sections of both Acts came into force on the same day, 29 December 1975. The 1975 Act covers

[200] Equal Pay Act 1970, s. 1(3).
[201] *Rainey v. Greater Glasgow Health Board* [1987] 1 All ER 65, HL, especially at 70 *per* Lord Keith of Kinkel.
[202] Case 96/80 *Jenkins v. Kingsgate (Clothing Productions) Ltd.* [1981] ECR 911, [1981] 1 WLR 972, CJEC.
[203] *R. v. Central Arbitration Committee, ex parte Hy-Mac Ltd.* [1979] IRLR 461, DC.
[204] Sex Discrimination Act 1986, s. 6.
[205] Ellis, *Sex Discrimination Law*, 18.
[206] See Ellis, *Sex Discrimination Law*, ch. 3.

discrimination in the provision of housing, education, and goods, facilities, and services, as well as access to employment and non-contractual aspects of employment conditions, including non-contractual benefits. As far as employment is concerned, therefore, the anti-discrimination legislation is a sort of jigsaw puzzle, containing pieces derived from the 1970 Act, the 1975 Act, and Community law. There is also scope for the position to be affected by delegated legislation, since section 2 of the Employment Act 1989 permits the Secretary of State to make statutory instruments repealing any other instrument, or a provision in an Act passed before the 1989 Act, which appears to the Secretary of State to require anyone to do an act which is inconsistent with the Sex Discrimination Act 1975.

The field of operation of the 1975 Act, and the meaning of discrimination which forms the basis of its reach, are both similar to the Race Relations Act 1976, save that, for the 1975 Act to bite, the discrimination must be by reference to sex rather than race. Like the 1976 Act, the 1975 Act excludes acts done on national security grounds, and provides a defence in employment cases where sex is a genuine occupational qualification. Discrimination against homosexuals on the basis of their sexual orientation is not covered by the legislation, or by the EC Equal Treatment Directive.[207] However, it is possible that the 1975 Act will be reinterpreted under section 3 of the Human Rights Act 1998 in the light of the caselaw of the European Court of Human Rights, which has held that discrimination on the ground of sexual orientation violates ECHR Article 14. This is discussed further below.

Discrimination against transsexuals on the ground that they had undergone, or proposed to undergo, gender reassignment was not originally interpreted as falling within the scope of sex discrimination under the 1975 Act. However, in a landmark judgment the Court of Justice decided that the protection against sex discrimination in the EC Equal Treatment Directive encompassed discrimination on the ground of gender reassignment, which, the Court decided, could not sensibly be separated from sex.[208] The law in the UK was subsequently amended to bring it into line with EC law.[209] However, it has been held that dismissal for poor work resulting from depression caused by medication given as part of gender reassignment is not covered by the 1975 Act, because drug-induced depression is not gender-specific.[210]

There was originally a fear that rules which protect women in the workplace might fall foul of the 1975 Act as being unlawful positive discrimination. The Sex Discrimination Act 1986, section 4, clarified the position by expressly stating that such rules do not contravene the anti-discrimination legislation.

Like the Race Relations Act 1976, but unlike the Equal Pay Act 1970 since the abolition of the Central Arbitration Committee, the Sex Discrimination Act 1975 operates on two levels. First, there is the personal level, at which individuals who

[207] Case C-249/96 *Grant v. South-West Trains Ltd.* [1998] ICR 449, CJEC; *Pearce v. Governing Body of Mayfield School*, *The Times*, 9 October 2001, CA.

[208] Case C-13/94 *P. v. S.* [1996] ICR 795, CJEC.

[209] Sex Discrimination (Gender Reassignment) Regulations 1999, SI 1999/1102; Sex Discrimination (Gender Reassignment) Regulations (Northern Ireland) 1999, SR 1999/311, made under European Communities Act 1972, s. 2. See E. Griffiths, 'The Sex Discrimination (Gender Reassignment) Regulations 1999' [1999] 4 *J. of Civil Liberties* 230–6.

[210] *Ashton v. Chief Constable of West Mercia Constabulary* [2001] ICR 67, EAT.

suffer discrimination in a field covered by the Act can bring civil proceedings for damages or other remedies. This is a compensatory and protective procedure. Secondly, there is a public authority, the Equal Opportunities Commission, with the role of monitoring and encouraging the progress of anti-discrimination initiatives on a broader plane. As the government said when announcing the plans for the Commission, 'Although it will be able to represent individuals in suitable and significant cases, its main task will be wider policy: to identify and deal with discriminatory practices by industries, firms or institutions'.[211]

The EOC has had some notable successes. It has taken legal proceedings against the government in order to establish the applicability of principles of Community law where these are more powerfully anti-discriminatory than the domestic law. This is a valuable function, allowing the EOC to perform a function as a representative plaintiff on behalf of women's collective interests, achieving authoritative statements of law earlier than would be possible relying on the uncertainties of litigation by individual plaintiffs. For example, in Case C-9/91, *R. v. Secretary of State for Social Services, ex parte Equal Opportunities Commission*[212] the EOC brought an application for judicial review of the UK's state pension arrangements, under which men had a retirement age of sixty-five as compared with sixty for women. The EOC argued that the differential ages resulted in the Secretary of State being in breach of the obligation under EEC Council Directive 79/7, Article 5, to take measures necessary to abolish discriminatory provisions which fell within the scope of the Directive. By applying for declarations in an application for judicial review, the EOC was able to test the legality of the provisions of the National Insurance Act 1946 and the Social Security Act 1965. The Divisional Court facilitated the process by making a reference to the European Court of Justice, allowing an authoritative interpretation of the directive's requirements to be obtained.

The EOC also established that rules under which part-time workers had to work for five years before being eligible for redundancy pay, as compared with only two years for full-time workers, were inconsistent with Community law on equal pay and equal treatment of men and women. The government argued that the rules were a legitimate attempt to increase the number of part-time jobs by reducing disincentives for employers to create new posts. The House of Lords held that the threshold requirements were incompatible with Article 119 (now Article 141) TEC and the Equal Pay and Equal Treatment Directives, because it had not been shown that they were objectively justified, or that they had actually produced an increase in the availability of part-time work.[213] Whether the differential treatment is justified will depend on the facts which are proved. In *R. v. Secretary of State for Employment, ex parte Seymour-Smith*[214] the complainants argued that a qualifying period of two years' employment

---

[211] *Equality for Women*, Cmnd. 5724 (London: HMSO, 1974), para. 28. For discussion of the role of the Equal Opportunities Commission, see Ellis, *Sex Discrimination Law*, ch. 5.

[212] [1992] 3 All ER 577, CJEC.

[213] *R. v. Secretary of State for Employment, ex parte Equal Opportunities Commission* [1995] 1 AC 1, [1994] 1 All ER 910, HL (Lords Keith of Kinkel, Lowry, Browne-Wilkinson, and Slynn of Hadley; Lord Jauncey dissented).

[214] [1997] 1 WLR 473, [1997] 2 All ER 273, HL.

before an employee could pursue a claim for unfair dismissal was indirectly discriminatory, because it impacted adversely on women, who tended to have been employed for shorter periods than men. The main questions were how a court should decide whether the differential treatment amounted to indirect discrimination, and (if so) how it could be objectively justified. The Court of Justice, on a reference from the House of Lords, decided that differential treatment would amount to indirect discrimination only if a considerably smaller proportion (rather than number) of women than men were able to fulfil the requirement imposed by the relevant rule, although a small difference might be significant if it was long-standing and entrenched. The Court went on to say that indirect discrimination would be justified if the Member State could show that the rule 'reflects a legitimate aim of its social policy, that that aim is unrelated to any discrimination based on sex, and that it could reasonably consider that the means chosen were suitable for attaining that aim'.[215] This was unsatisfactory. The test for indirect discrimination was made to depend on statistics which might be hard to establish and in any case have no significance (for example, if the workforce was too small for differences to be statistically significant), and is sufficiently indeterminate to lack certainty. The judgment also failed to harmonize the rules on justifying indirect discrimination in EC law. Indirectly discriminatory conduct by an employer is justified only if the measures correspond to a real need, are appropriate to that need, and are necessary to that end.[216] Indirectly discriminatory legislation on entitlement to money (e.g. sick pay) would be justifiable if the Member State could show that it pursued a necessary aim of social policy, and that the means adopted were suitable for attaining the aim.[217] The *Seymour-Smith* test would apply to legislative provisions governing entitlement to seek reinstatement.[218] In the light of that, it is not surprising that the House of Lords had difficulty in applying the Court's reply to the facts of the case.[219] By a bare majority (Lord Goff, Lord Jauncey, and Lord Nicholls; Lord Slynn and Lord Steyn dissenting), they held that there had been a small difference but long-standing and entrenched. However, Lords Goff, Jauncey, and Nicholls went on to hold that the government had been able to justify the rule as being designed to encourage employers to take on more employees, as it was not necessary to show that this had actually been achieved. It remains to be seen whether the position is improved by the Burden of Proof Directive,[220] Article 2(2) of which provides that indirect discrimination occurs where 'an apparently neutral provision, criterion or practice disadvantages a substantially higher proportion of the members of one sex unless that provision, criterion or

---

[215] Case C-167/97 *R. v. Secretary of State for Employment, ex parte Seymour-Smith* [1999] 2 AC 554, [1999] 3 WLR 460, CJEC, at para. 77.

[216] Case 170/84 *Bilka-Kaufhaus GmbH v. Weber Von Hartz* [1986] ECR 1607, CJEC.

[217] Case 171/88 *Rinner-Kuhn v. FWW Spezial-Gebaudereinigung GmbH* [1989] ECR 2734, CJEC.

[218] For criticism of the CJEC's ruling, see C. Barnard and B. Hepple, 'Indirect Discrimination: Interpreting *Seymour-Smith*' [1999] *CLJ* 399–412.

[219] *R. v. Secretary of State for Employment, ex parte Seymour-Smith (No. 2)* [2000] 1 WLR 435, [2000] 1 All ER 857, HL. For another example of the difficulty of applying the test, see *Allenby v. Accrington and Rossendale College and others*, *The Times*, 3 April 2001, CA.

[220] Directive 98/52, extending to the UK Directive 97/80 on the Burden of Proof in Cases of Discrimination based on Sex.

practice is appropriate and necessary and can be justified by objective factors unrelated to sex'.

There are special provisions relating to discrimination on the grounds related to pregnancy and childbirth. The Pregnant Workers' Directive 92/85/EC confers rights to protection against dismissal, to maternity leave with pay, and to steps safeguarding the health and safety of pregnant workers. These rights were given effect in UK law by the Employment Rights Act 1996. One advantage of the Directive is to make it clear that there is no need, in pregnancy cases, to seek to find a male comparator for a pregnant woman, a fruitless search at the best of times. Dismissal or unfavourable treatment on the ground of pregnancy is automatically to be treated as direct discrimination.

(6) DISABILITY, SEXUALITY, AGE, AND RELIGION OR BELIEF

The EU Framework Directive on Discrimination[221] was a hurriedly agreed measure[222] which is intended to provide a structure within which to develop protection against discrimination on the grounds of religion or belief, disability, age, or sexual orientation. The Directive suffers from a combination of seeking to impose a common approach on disparate grounds of discrimination, and from occasionally impenetrable drafting which seems calculated to hide rather than elucidate its meaning (Article 4 being a case in point). It includes both direct and indirect discrimination,[223] with the latter occurring where:

'an apparently neutral provision, criterion or practice would put persons having a particular religion or belief, a particular disability, a particular age, or a particular sexual orientation at a particular disadvantage compared with other persons.'

Indirect discrimination is negatived if the provision, criterion, or practice is justified by a legitimate aim and the means adopted to achieve it are both appropriate and necessary; or, in relation to disability, if national legislation obliges an employer to provide reasonable accommodation in order to eliminate the disadvantage.[224] The divergence between these provisions and both the caselaw of the Court of Justice and the provisions of the Burden of Proof Directive adds a further layer of complexity to an increasingly incoherent mass of EC legal provisions.

The relationship between these provisions and English law is as follows. The Framework Directive will lead to protection against discrimination in employment and occupation on the grounds of sexual orientation, so far denied both in the UK and under EC law,[225] and religion or belief, previously covered only in the law of Northern Ireland, and (in respect of enjoyment of Convention rights under the

---

[221] Council Directive 2000/78/EC of 27 November 2000 establishing a General Framework for Equal Treatment in Employment and Occupation.

[222] See House of Lords Select Committee on the European Union, Fourth Report 2000–01, *The EU Framework Directive on Discrimination*, 19 December 2000.

[223] Art. 1(2). Harassment is a form of discrimination: Art. 1(3).   [224] Art. 1(2)(b).

[225] Case C-249/96 *Grant v. South-West Trains Ltd.* [1998] ICR 449, CJEC. See R. Wintemute, 'Lesbian and Gay Inequality 2000: The Potential of the Human Rights Act 1998 and the Need for an Equality Act 2002' [2000] *EHRLR* 603–26.

Human Rights Act 1998) by Article 14 of the ECHR. It will also provide protection against discrimination in employment and occupation on the ground of age, which has in the past not been covered by UK law except under ECHR Article 14, and disability. This last ground is unlikely to provide more protection than is available under the Disability Discrimination Act 1995, which applies well beyond the field of employment and occupation. The remainder of this section examines that Act and the Disability Rights Commission Act 1999.

(i) The meaning of 'disability'

The first problem is to define 'disability', bearing in mind that disabilities can be continuous or intermittent, and sometimes the possibility that a past disability might recur can be no less likely than a current disability to lead to discrimination. The Act defines disability as 'a physical or mental impairment which has a substantial and long-term adverse effect on his ability to carry out normal day-to-day activities'.[226] There are thus four questions: (1) was there a mental or physical impairment? (2) did it have an adverse effect on his ability to carry out day to day activities? (3) was that adverse effect substantial? (4) was it long-term? If the answer to each question is 'yes', the person has a disability for the purpose of the Act. A mental illness is an impairment for this purpose only if it is 'a clinically well-recognised illness'.[227] In *Goodwin v. Patent Office*[228] the claimant was suffering from paranoid schizophrenia, and could not carry on a normal conversation with colleagues because he thought they were plotting against him. His powers of concentration and communication were also adversely affected. The Employment Appeal Tribunal held that his capacity for carrying on normal life was substantially impaired: even if he could continue everyday life, it was made more difficult for him. He certainly suffered from a disability. On the other hand, there must be a causal connection between the disability and the adverse effect on his ability to carry on normal activities. If a person suffers from an illness but his lack of socialising is the result of his choice, rather than an inability caused by his illness, the case falls outside the Act.[229]

Impairment is long-term if it lasts or is likely to last for at least twelve months, or for the remainder of the person's life if less than twelve months.[230] Severe disfigurement is to be treated as having a substantial effect on the ability to carry out normal activities.[231] A past disability may be treated as a disability.[232] For example, in *Greenwood v. British Airways plc*[233] the claimant had suffered from depression, which had led to extended periods off work for treatment. He had overcome it with drugs and counselling. Back at work, he applied for promotion, but was refused, because of concerns about his history of depression and its effect on his ability to do the job. It

---

[226] Disability Discrimination Act 1995, s. 1(1).
[227] Ibid., Sch. 1, para. 1(1).
[228] [1999] ICR 302, EAT.
[229] *Ashton v. Chief Constable of West Mercia Constabulary* [2001] ICR 67, EAT.
[230] Disability Discrimination Act 1995, Sch. 1, para. 2.
[231] Ibid., Sch. 1, para. 3.
[232] Ibid., s. 2 and Sch. 2.
[233] [1999] ICR 969, EAT.

was held that the depression was a disability, because it could have continuing effects, as shown by fact that he had suffered a further bout of depression on hearing the reason for not being promoted. Depression thus remains a disability if prone to produce continuing effects.

(ii) Fields in which discrimination is unlawful

The legislation covers discrimination on the ground of disability in employment (Part II of the Act), the provision of or access to goods, facilities, or services (section 19), sale or letting of premises (section 22), education (Part IV), and public transport, including taxis (Part V).

(iii) The meaning of 'discrimination'

The demands created by disability vary greatly in each of these settings, so (unlike the other equality legislation) the Disability Discrimination Act 1995 provides a different definition of 'discrimination'. In relation to employment, employers with twenty or more employees[234] and trade organizations have both negative duties not to discriminate,[235] and a positive duty to make reasonable adjustments to prevent working arrangements or physical features of the workplace from putting disabled workers at a substantial disadvantage in comparison with people who are not disabled.[236] In these contexts, discrimination means either treating a disabled person less favourably than others for a reason which relates to the disabled person's disability, or failing to comply with the duty to make reasonable adjustments. The first of these is simple direct discrimination, committed if a person does something, like dismissing a person because of disability-related absence, if a person who is not disabled would not have been dismissed for a similar period of absence.[237] The second is as close as the Act gets to outlawing indirect discrimination. The duty to make reasonable adjustments applies in order to prevent someone from having to be dismissed, as well as at earlier points in the employment relationship, and the test is the reasonableness of the necessary adjustment, not the reasonableness of the employer's refusal to make an adjustment in the circumstances.[238] In neither type of case does the duty arise unless the employer is made aware of the disability.[239] However, unlike the position under the other equality legislation, the Act permits both direct and quasi-indirect discrimination if the employer can show that it is objectively justified.[240]

Broadly similar provisions apply to discrimination in other contexts, except for some fine-tuning. For example, they apply in relation to the provision of goods, facilities and services,[241] except that the grounds on which differential treatment may

---

[234] Disability Discrimination Act 1995, s. 7(1).

[235] Ibid., ss. 4, 13.

[236] Ibid., ss. 6, 15.

[237] *Clark v. Novacold Ltd.* [1999] ICR 951, [1999] 2 All ER 977, CA (the first case under the 1995 Act to reach the CA).

[238] *Morse v. Wiltshire CC* [1998] ICR 1023, EAT.

[239] *O'Neill v. Symm & Co. Ltd.* [1998] ICR 481, EAT.

[240] Disability Discrimination Act 1995, ss. 5, 14.

[241] Ibid., ss. 19, 20, 21.

be justified are expressly limited.[242] There is an exception for small dwellings where accommodation is shared and the landlord resides on the premises, but when the Act applies (once again) justification of discrimination can be made on limited grounds.[243]

It is unlawful discrimination to victimize a person as a result of having brought or supported proceedings for discrimination, or to aid unlawful acts.[244]

(iv) The Disability Rights Commission

In 1999, the government responded to concern that the legislation would be ineffective if it was left to individuals to bring proceedings to enforce it. A strong body was needed to educate the public, conduct research, monitor and enforce the Act, and support victims. The Disability Rights Commission Act 1999 accordingly provided for the establishment of a body, the Disability Rights Commission (DRC), which was general duties to work towards the elimination of discrimination against disabled people, to promote equal opportunities for disabled people, to encourage good practice in the treatment of disabled people (a function going well beyond advancing equal opportunities), and to keep the working of the 1995 Act under review. Its powers include undertaking or commissioning or supporting research.[245] Like the CRE and the EOC, the DRC can conduct formal investigations, issue non-discrimination notices, and enter into agreements instead of taking formal enforcement action.[246] The DRC can assist people in bringing complaints of unlawful discrimination, issue codes of practice (after a draft has been approved by the Secretary of State and laid before, and not disapproved by, Parliament), and offer conciliation services in respect of disputes.[247]

Although it is early in the life of the DRC, its powers are sufficiently wide and flexible to enable it to make a significant contribution to combatting discrimination.

(7) CONCLUSION

The last few years have seen an explosion in the amount of anti-discrimination law, with an attendant increase in its complexity. Rules from many sources are laid on top of one another to form a complex, and sometimes confusing, palimpsest of duties, powers, and enforcement procedures. The emphasis remains on eradicating unjustifiable inequalities of treatment in like cases, but there have been moves particularly at EC level, and in the Disability Discrimination Act 1995, which increasingly allow, or in the case of the 1995 Act require, positive action to create a level playing field as far as possible.

The next step is to look at ways of making the body of law and enforcement procedures more coherent. This does not necessarily mean unifying the criteria for and procedures relating to unlawful discrimination, although a powerful case can be

---

[242] Ibid., s. 20(4).
[243] Ibid., ss. 23, 24(3).
[244] Ibid., ss. 55, 57.
[245] Disability Rights Commission Act 1999, s. 2.
[246] Ibid., ss. 3, 4, 5 (and Sch. 3), and 6.
[247] Ibid., ss. 8, 9, and 10.

made out for making them more systematic and harmonizing their effects.[248] What is needed, perhaps more than anything else, is to recognize that the evil which discrimination represents is not eradicated by imposing uniformity. It requires the acceptance of diversity, while establishing structures which will enable members of all groups to participate positively in, and benefit equally from, our society. It may be that the enactment of the Human Rights Act 1998, with its overall provision outlawing discrimination in the enjoyment of other Convention rights, will be a spur in that direction.

[248] See Hepple, Coussey, and Choudhury, *Equality: A New Framework*, chs 2 and 4; Lord Lester of Herne Hill QC, 'Equality and United Kingdom Law: Past, Present and Future' [2001] *PL* 77–96.

PART II

LIFE, LIBERTY, AND PHYSICAL INTEGRITY

4

THE RIGHT TO LIFE

Life is a significant precondition for enjoying freedom. Other preconditions, such as a capacity for autonomy, and social and economic structures which allow people to choose between realistic options, are valuable only while we continue to enjoy life. It is not surprising, then, that people claim a right to life, and regard it as particularly fundamental. None the less, it is a fragile right. It is easy to think of purposes for which one might be considered justified in taking life, such as self-defence, preventing crime, or war. Unlike the right to be free of torture, the right to life is not generally regarded as absolute. Both the range of entities which have the right and the content of the right in different circumstances are controversial. Does it apply to foetuses, patients suffering from life-threatening illness, or those who have permanently lost (or will never achieve) the capacity for self-determination? If these groups have a right to life, what does it mean in their particular circumstances? Moreover, life depends on a range of support mechanisms in society to advance health, combat disease, and protect against violence. Decent nutrition and clean water are at least as important to most people's prospects of life as therapeutic intervention or policing.

This means that the right to life, as a human right asserted against the state and fellow citizens, has two main aspects. First, it is a negative right, a freedom from interference in the classic liberal tradition. People, including public officials, usually have no right to deprive us of our lives. Secondly, it imposes positive duties on the state. To put it at its lowest, we have a right to protect and vindicate our negative right through legal proceedings, and the state has a duty to put in place appropriate legal rules and procedures. The right to life may impose increasingly onerous positive obligations on the state. For example, the police may be obliged to investigate suspicious deaths and take efficient steps to bring killers to justice; the social security, housing, and social services systems may be obliged to ensure that nobody is left without the means of survival; utilities supplying water and energy may be required to ensure that everyone has access to them and that they meet standards of safety; and there may be an obligation to make medical services available. Whether, and to what extent, these obligations are seen as aspects of a right to life, and whether the state is required to discharge the obligations itself or may rely entirely or partly on market mechanisms, will depend on one's view of the proper role of the state generally, and of the scope of an individual's right to life.

This chapter starts by examining the legal bases for these different understandings of the right to life. It then deals with the duties of the state which flow from the right as it has been developed under the European Convention on Human Rights. Lastly, it considers some hard cases revolving round the outer edges of the right to life.

4.1 THE BASIS OF THE RIGHT TO LIFE

International instruments typically treat the right to life as intrinsic to humans, and as needing to be protected rather than conferred. The European Convention on Human Rights, Article 2, recognizes the right by implication, providing:

'1. Everyone's right to life shall be protected by law. No one shall be deprived of his life intentionally save in the execution of a sentence of a court following his conviction of a crime for which this penalty is provided by law.

2. Deprivation of life shall not be regarded as inflicted in contravention of this Article when it results from the use of force which is no more than absolutely necessary:

    (a) in defence of any person from unlawful violence;

    (b) in order to effect a lawful arrest or to prevent the escape of a person lawfully detained;

    (c) in action lawfully taken for the purpose of quelling a riot or insurrection.'

The International Covenant on Civil and Political Rights, Article 6(1), provides, 'Every human being has the inherent right to life. This right shall be protected by law. No one shall be arbitrarily deprived of his life'. Thus, both these instruments require action from national legislatures to provide legal protection for the right to life. In the UK, this is achieved in two ways: by threatening penal sanctions against those who commit, attempt, or incite to acts intended or likely to lead to death, including aiding and abetting suicide; and by giving the estate of deceased persons the right to sue for damages by way of compensation where death is caused intentionally or negligently.

When we think of a right to life, we normally envisage violations as acts which are likely to cause death directly. But a right to life may be endangered by other events. In the USA, there are *dicta* suggesting that the protection offered to 'life' in the Fourteenth Amendment to the Constitution:

'extends to all those limbs and faculties by which life is enjoyed. The prohibition equally prohibits the mutilation of the body by the amputation of an arm or leg, or the putting out of an eye, or the destruction of any other organ of the body through which the soul communicates with the outer world. The deprivation not only of life, but of whatever God has given to every one with life, for its growth and enjoyment, is prohibited by the provision in question, if its efficacy be not frittered away by judicial decision.'[1]

In so far as an occurrence is life-threatening in the victim's own circumstances, this receives support from the decisions of the European Commission of Human Rights in *X. v. Federal Republic of Germany*[2] and *Simon-Herold v. Austria*,[3] discussed below.

A state might provide protection either directly or by imposing duties on others. For example, French law imposes a duty on passers-by to rescue those who are in

---

[1] *Munn v. Illinois* 94 US 113 (1876) at 142 *per* Field J, dissenting, cited by P. Sieghart, *The International Law of Human Rights* (Oxford: Clarendon Press, 1983), 134.

[2] (5207/71) CD 39, 99.

[3] (4340/69) CD 38, 18.

danger of death, while, by contrast, English law normally does not.[4] Again, it might be thought necessary to criminalize only intentional taking of life, since it is on intentional deprivation that the European Convention on Human Rights concentrates, and the existence of a criminal sanction is unlikely to deter unintentional killing. Article 2(1) of the Convention therefore leaves it to the national authorities to define the scope of the right to life, but insists on the minimal requirement that 'No one shall be deprived of his life intentionally . . . '. In other words, a legal system which failed to criminalize intentional killing would be failing in its obligations under the Convention unless some other form of legal protection were offered. On the other hand, it is for the legislatures of each state to decide whether and in what form to criminalize intentional acts such as drunken driving and medical negligence which, though not intended to cause death, may lead to death, as long as the threshold conditions set under the ECHR are satisfied.

These are ways in which the state responds to the negative aspect of the right to life, freedom from being deprived of life. The European Court of Human Rights has recognized that the right also has a positive aspect under the ECHR. At its most basic level, it is held to entail an obligation on the appropriate state bodies (including the police and the armed forces) to take efficient steps to protect people against immediate risks of fatal harm, whether caused by the activities of state agencies or others, and to act to vindicate the right to life after a person has been killed. But the positive obligations of the state may go further, involving a duty to keep people alive (perhaps against their wills), and to afford them living conditions which minimize the risk of morbidity and mortality. This is particularly likely to be seen where the state takes people into its custody without their consent, whether as prisoners or as compulsory patients (for example, under mental health legislation). Such people lack the opportunity to safeguard their own welfare, so the state which detains them assumes a special responsibility for their welfare.

If the right to life is interpreted as being a right not only to conditions which do not endanger life, but also to a certain quality of life, it provokes debate about public services and health care. Where the state provides such care, its proper scope will give rise to problems. Some of these are matters of principle. If the state is required to act in the patient's best interests, quality of life is likely to be an important consideration in determining the scope of the state's positive obligation in respect of the right to life. Is the individual or the state to decide what is in the individual's best interests? If the individual's view is generally to prevail, what is to be done where the patient wants an outcome which is contrary to public policy, for example encompassing his own death? What is to happen if the patient is for some reason unable to make decisions? Is there a duty to use medical resources in order to save the life of a child whose quality of life is likely to be very low on any criterion with which we are familiar? What is the nature of such a person's right to life? Other questions are more pragmatic. It may be necessary to exclude a certain number of people from treatment because resources are

---

[4] See G. Mead, 'Contracting into Crime: A Theory of Criminal Omissions' (1991) 11 *Oxf. J. of Legal Studies* 147–73; A. Ashworth and E. Steiner, 'Criminal Omissions and Public Duties: the French Experience' (1990) *Legal Studies* 153–64.

scarce. How should issues concerning distribution be settled? Is there a role for courts in deciding them? These questions open up deeply rooted fears of eugenics.

We are dealing here with a mixture of values. We saw in Chapter 1 how Professor Joseph Raz uses the notion of autonomy as the basis for his morality of freedom, but includes duties on the state to maintain the social conditions in which autonomy can be real and worthwhile.[5] Raz argues that the notion of autonomy (which is at the centre of his idea of freedom) must be backed up by state action in support of a relatively wide range of individual interests.[6] This justifies an interventionist state within liberal theory. However, it does not justify a paternalistic use of power. In the case of people who are capable of making decisions for themselves, but are temporarily incapable of doing so or lack the skills or resources to give effect to their preferred choice, Raz's state would act to give effect to the actual or presumed preference of the individual, rather than (as in a paternalist state) the state's own view of what a right-thinking person *ought* to prefer. Thus, a state which allows a person to die, regardless of that person's wishes, because death is thought to be in the person's own best interests or those of society as a whole, undermines that individual's autonomy.

If the value of life lies in its contribution to autonomy, and the value of choice depends on making the right choices, it raises the possibility that life is not of equal value to all living creatures. The value of life to any individual might depend on that individual's capacity for autonomy, i.e. to make choices. Individuals who are incapable of making choices, or choices which society regards as rational, will not be treated as autonomous or free except within narrow limits, and their lives may be considered to be less valuable than those of fully rational individuals. Once a choice is made, rights to autonomy may require that the state provides resources to help to give effect to it, but does the value of autonomy in itself justify preserving the lives of those who are not capable of choice? This may depend on the future prospects. Children are not ordinarily considered to be fully autonomous individuals, although as they get older the law and society recognize that their capacity for understanding and rational choice increases. The likelihood that any particular child is on the way to becoming an autonomous member of society justifies investing human and economic resources in maintaining the child's life and health. The same applies to people who, through illness or accident, are temporarily incapable of exercising rational choice. But there are individuals who are likely never to be capable of exercising free choice (depending on the preferred definition of free choice): amoebas, insects, perhaps all non-humans fall into this category. These individuals will, on Raz's approach, be unable to assert a right to life.

What is the position of humans who are so severely mentally handicapped that they are unlikely ever to be able to make rational choices? The autonomy argument does not help to support a right to have their lives maintained. The most powerful argument for maintaining them is that the dignity of all humans requires us to be concerned for the lives of fellow humans. This right to equal concern (and, perhaps, as Dworkin[7] argues, to respect) is not, however, a right to life. In the context of life-and-

---

5 J. Raz, *The Morality of Freedom* (Oxford: Clarendon Press, 1986), discussed in Ch. 1, above.
6 See Ch. 1, above.
7 R. Dworkin, *Taking Rights Seriously* (London: Duckworth, 1977), ch. 7.

death decisions, it requires decision-makers to keep the interests of the subject in the forefront of their minds, and to safeguard those interests so far as possible within available resources and without failing to give equal consideration to the competing interests of others. It does not follow from recognizing the importance of factors which affect the quality of life that the right to life should have any particular shape.[8] Similar considerations apply in respect of the value of dignity. The remainder of this chapter examines how these and related questions are affected by the European Convention on Human Rights and domestic law.

But autonomy is not the only value underpinning rights and freedoms. Other values include dignity, equality, and personal security. These can generate positive obligations to protect life. Similarly, the Rule of Law brings together values which demand legal remedies for threats to life. Such considerations go beyond the state's classic, liberal obligation to refrain from depriving people of life. Yet they do not necessarily point towards a state having a duty to take active steps to preserve life. For instance, where the primary value is thought to be dignity, a severely disabled person might be regarded as having life which is insufficiently dignified to be worth protecting. Such an argument would reduce the value of the right to life, and the weight of the state's duty to preserve and protect it, although it is not clear who should decide what level of dignity is acceptable. On the other hand, the dignity of the human species might require that all human life be treated as sacrosanct, never to be willingly surrendered.

This would justify overriding people's autonomous decisions in order to maintain life. It would permit a high degree of paternalism if the state were to step in and save my life, or legally require a doctor to do so.[9] It maximizes my future autonomy by preserving my opportunity to make choices in the future, on the (possibly mistaken) assumption that I will continue to be capable of autonomous decision-making. In the mean time, it fails to take seriously my decision to exercise that autonomy in such a way as to end my life. If freedom of choice is the essence of autonomy, are we not required to respect people's earlier choices, even when this limits the scope for protecting their future freedom of choice? If we do not respect past choices, autonomy becomes a form of disguised paternalism: people must be free to choose, as long as they choose in such a way as not to restrict (unreasonably) their freedom to choose; and as any choice restricts future freedom by changing the circumstances in which future choices will be made, the state decides whether any particular choice results in an unreasonable restriction of the chooser's future freedom. If life is a necessary precondition for autonomy, the need to protect it might not depend on the individual's choice to continue it. Instead, autonomy remains the fundamental human value, but life (being so central a condition for autonomy) has to be protected against

[8] R. Dworkin, *Life's Dominion: An Argument about Abortion and Euthanasia* (London: HarperCollins, 1993), explains several ways in which people may fail to understand the reasons for disagreements in the welter of complexity surrounding ideas of life. It is significant that the book's index contains no reference to a right to life. Debate means little unless abstract discussion is directed to real, practical problems.

[9] See above, Ch. 1, section 1.3(2) and Ch. 3, section 3.2; Dworkin, *Life's Dominion*, ch. 3; R. Cohen-Almagor, 'Autonomy, Life as an Intrinsic Value, and the Right to Die with Dignity' (1995) 1 *Science and Engineering Ethics* 261–72.

being curtailed even by an exercise of autonomous choice.[10] On this approach, life is not a right but a liberal duty, or (in Hohfeld's terms) a disability, since the individual is unable to alter his or her own legal position in respect of it.

4.2 THE STATE'S OBLIGATIONS IN RESPECT OF THREATS TO LIFE

Under Article 2(1) of the ECHR, which is now part of municipal law in the UK by virtue of section 1 of the Human Rights Act 1998, people are entitled not to be intentionally deprived of life, except in the circumstances set out in the Convention. It has also been held that the state may be responsible under Article 2 for unintentionally caused death, unless it results from the use of absolutely necessary force for one of the law-preserving purposes listed there.[11] This has been held to impose a number of concomitant positive obligations on the state. Article 2(1) requires the state to ensure that people have the protection of the law for the right to life. The European Court of Human Rights has given substance to this provision, interpreting it to ensure that the right to life is real and effective as a matter of domestic law and practice. It has four distinct aspects: (1) the state's duty to protect people against the risk of harm from the activities of public authorities; (2) its duty to undertake an efficient investigation of suspicious deaths; (3) its duty to protect people against threats to their lives; and (4) the duty to provide arrangements for securing legal accountability of those responsible for a death. This section considers those obligations, and the circumstances in which intentional deprivation of life is permitted, comparing the ECHR with English law, and taking account of the Human Rights Act 1998.

(1) THE DUTY TO PROTECT PEOPLE AGAINST THE RISK OF HARM FROM THE ACTIVITIES OF PUBLIC AUTHORITIES

The state has a responsibility when its own activities expose identifiable individuals to a real risk of harm. The responsibility is twofold. First, there is a duty to minimize the risk, within the bounds of current knowledge, in order to respect the right to life under Article 2 of the ECHR. This may include a positive obligation to track and monitor the condition of people who are known to have been affected. For example, if the state knew that a man had been exposed to state-generated radiation, the European Court of Human Rights has written unanimously in *LCB v. United Kingdom*[12] that the state might have been required by Article 2 to provide advice of its own motion to the parents in relation to their daughter, conceived after the man's exposure, 'if it had appeared likely at that time that any such exposure of her father to

[10] For a similar argument, see M. R. Flick, 'The Due Process of Dying' (1991) 79 *Calif. LR* 1121–67. Flick argues that patients' desires not to be treated should be overridden if there is a reasonable chance of successful treatment; doctors should act paternalistically, overriding autonomy to force patients to accept those 'choices' which preserve the capacity to make choices in the future.

[11] See *Stewart v. United Kingdom*, Eur. Commn. HR, App. No. 10044/82, D. & R. 39 (1985) 162.

[12] Eur. Ct. HR, Judgment of 9 June 1998, RJD 1998-III, 27 EHRR 212, at paras. 38, 40.

radiation might have engendered a real risk to her health'. Probably because of the importance of the right to know about one's medical condition, the Court continued: 'It is perhaps arguable that . . . the state authorities would have been under a duty to have made [the risk] known to her parents whether or not they considered that the information would assist the [daughter].' (The better view is that any duty to disclose information which will have no relevance to her treatment would have arisen under Article 8, rather than Article 2, for reasons which will be explained in the next paragraph.) In the light of the conflicting medical evidence about causation, the Court was not satisfied that the information available to the state brought the positive obligation of assistance into existence.

Secondly, there is a duty to make available to individuals information about the risk to which they were exposed which will enable them either to set their minds at rest or assess the danger, in order to satisfy the right to respect for private life arising under Article 8 of the ECHR.[13] The scope of the duties involves a balance between the rights and interests of different people. Where the activity in question confers no therapeutic benefit, the balance may be struck more readily in favour of an extensive responsibility to the victim than where many people benefit from the activity. In *McGinley and Egan v. United Kingdom*,[14] servicemen claimed to have been exposed to radiation during tests of nuclear weapons on Christmas Island, and to have suffered illness as a result. They claimed additional disability pensions, but were refused. They alleged violations of (*inter alia*) Articles 8 and 6, because they said that the state had not made available to them information about their exposure to radiation. The Court treated the obligation to make information available as a positive obligation under Article 8, the incidence of which depended on striking a 'fair balance . . . between the general interest of the community and the competing interests of the individual, or individuals, concerned'.[15] In view of the level of harm which radiation can cause, and the anxiety and distress which uncertainty about the level of their exposure would have caused, the Court considered that the state ought to have made available information about the level of radioactivity on Christmas Island following the tests, particularly as there was no national security reason for withholding it.[16]

'Where a government engages in hazardous activities, such as those in issue in the present case, which might have hidden adverse consequences on the health of those involved in such activities, respect for private and family life under Article 8 requires that an effective and accessible procedure be established which enables such persons to seek all relevant and appropriate information.'[17]

On the facts, a bare majority of the Court found that the procedure for obtaining documents in proceedings before the Pension Appeal Tribunal satisfied this

---

[13] On rights to information derived from the right to respect for private life, see Sir Stephen Sedley, 'Information as a Human Right', in J. Beatson and Y. Cripps (eds.), *Freedom of Expression and Freedom of Information: Essays in Honour of Sir David Williams* (Oxford: Oxford University Press, 2000), ch. 14; D. Feldman, 'Information and Privacy', ibid., ch. 19; and below, Ch. 13.

[14] Eur. Ct. HR, Judgment of 9 June 1998, RJD 1998-III, 27 EHRR 1.

[15] Ibid., para. 98.

[16] Ibid., paras. 100–101.

[17] Ibid., para. 101.

requirement, although Judges De Meyer, Valticos, Morenilla, and Pekkanen, dissenting, favoured a more extensive positive duty on the state to provide information and, in the case of the first three dissenters, to take active steps to monitor the condition of those at risk continuously, although the existence of such a duty would depend on the state of scientific knowledge from time to time (as implied in the Court's judgment in *LCB v. United Kingdom*, above).

Where the state is engaged in therapeutic activities, such as programmes of immunization, providing blood for transfusion, or supplying blood products, the activities may still present a significant incidental risk of harm to recipients of the intended benefits, but the countervailing interests of others may be more powerful. The right to have one's life protected by law imposes an obligation on states to take appropriate precautions when embarking on a course of action which puts people's lives at risk. In a relatively early case concerning a programme of public immunization against measles which was designed to prevent the disease but which created an incidental threat to life, the European Commission of Human Rights decided that the state was required by Article 2 to impose a supervision and control system in order to reduce as far as possible the number of fatalities which would result.[18] On the facts, the Commission decided that an appropriate regime had been put in place. The same principle would seem to apply to infection of patients being treated for haemophilia with blood products made from blood infected with HIV/AIDS.

Consumer law offers some protection to people who are infected by defective blood products. In *A. and others v. National Blood Authority and another*,[18a] Burton J held that the National Blood Authority was liable under the Consumer Protection Act 1987 (enacted to give effect to Article 6 of the Product Liability Directive (85/374/EEC)) for supplying blood carrying the Hepatitis C virus. The product was defective because it did not 'provide the safety which a person is entitled to expect, taking all circumstances into account . . . '. The Authority could not avail itself of the defence under Article 7(e) of the Directive for producers where the state of scientific and technical knowledge at the time was not such as to allow the existence of the defect to be discovered, because it was well known that some blood and products were affected, but it was not possible to say which packets were carrying the virus. In those circumstances, Burton J decided that the Authority supplied the packets at its own risk.

(i) Taking life in the exercise of crime-control functions

The duty not to deprive people of life under Article 2 of the ECHR admits of exceptions. There are circumstances, recognized by Article 2, in which the right must give way to other interests. Sometimes these are private interests, as when a person is attacked and defends himself. If reasonable self-defence were to be criminal, it might be thought to undervalue the victim's life for the sake of that of an aggressor. Sometimes they are or purport to be public interests, as where the state authorizes capital punishment, or where the death results from a necessary use of force to apprehend a suspected offender. The balance between different interests, or between the rights of

---

[18]   *Association X. v. United Kingdom* (7154/75) DR 14, 31, Eur. Comm. HR (measles).
[18a]   *The Times*, 4 April 2001.

different people to live, is likely to depend on cultural values which can differ widely. The ECHR lays down certain minimum standards, accepting that there are circumstances in which it does not violate Article 2 to deprive someone of life, but the European Court of Human Rights understandably construes limitations to the right to life strictly. The Convention specifies two sets of circumstances in which states may abridge the right to life in the interests of preventing crime, without violating Article 2. The first follows a judicial hearing; the second covers situations in which the right to life can be limited without a judicial hearing.

(1) **Intentional deprivation of life in the execution of a sentence of a court following conviction of a crime for which the death penalty is provided by law**. The international trend is towards the progressive abolition of the death penalty.[19] In South Africa, for example, the Constitutional Court held in *State v. Makwanyane*[20] that it was unconstitutional, both as an unjustifiable interference with the right to life and as an assault on human dignity. In Europe, Germany abolished it in 1949 under Article 102 of the *Grundgesetz*. The Sixth Protocol to the ECHR requires the abolition of the death penalty, save in respect of acts committed in time of war or imminent threat of war. When a state ratifies the Sixth Protocol, it renders otiose the capital punishment exception to Article 2. The UK finally ratified the Sixth Protocol in 1999, and amended the municipal law to remove the last vestiges of the death penalty in peacetime. However, many countries (including the USA[21] and states in the Commonwealth Caribbean) retain the death penalty, and keep people for long periods in very bad conditions awaiting execution. A state which has abolished the death penalty may still violate a person's right to life under Article 2 by extraditing or deporting him to a country in which he is shown to be at risk of being killed, if either the public authorities in that country, their agents, or people acting under their control are likely to be the aggressors, or the authorities there will be unable or unwilling to offer adequate legal and practical protection against the threat.[22] Although it would not violate ECHR Article 2 to deport or extradite someone to a jurisdiction where he is liable to be executed (as long as legal proprieties were first observed), the circumstances attendant on the execution (such as delay and conditions on death row) may cause the extradition or deportation to violate Article 3, the right to be free of inhuman or degrading treatment.[23] By virtue of the duty on public authorities

[19] See W. A. Schabas, *The Abolition of the Death Penalty in International Law*, 2nd edn. (Cambridge: Cambridge University Press, 1997).

[20] 1995 (3) SA 391, 1995 (4) BCLR 665, CC.

[21] Compare *Furman v. Georgia* 408 US 238 (1972) with *Gregg v. Georgia* 428 US 513 (1976) and *McCleskey v. Kemp* 478 US 1019 (1986); 481 US 279 (1987).

[22] See, *mutatis mutandis, Chahal v. United Kingdom*, Eur. Ct. HR, Judgment of 15 November 1996, RJD 1996-V, No. 22; 23 EHRR 413.

[23] *Soering v. United Kingdom*, Eur. Ct. HR, Series A, No. 161, Judgment of 7 July 1989, 11 EHRR 439 (extradition to the USA and 'death row syndrome' in murder cases). The Privy Council has developed a substantial caselaw on delay before execution in the Commonwealth Caribbean, imposing a five-year maximum waiting period before execution in *Pratt v. Attorney-General for Jamaica* [1994] 2 AC 1, PC. See also *Lewis v. Attorney General of Jamaica* [2000] 3 WLR 1785, PC (there is an implied constitutional right to await the outcome of an application to the UN Human Rights Committee under the ICCPR where the state has created a legitimate expectation that a convicted person would be permitted to apply to the Committee); D. O'Brien and V. Carter, 'Constitutional Rights, Legitimate Expectations and the Death Penalty' [2000] *PL* 573–81.

(including courts and tribunals) to act in a manner compatible with Convention rights,[24] it is a matter which will affect the legality of any order for deportation or extradition, whether made under national legislation or EU law, to be enforced through judicial review or habeas corpus applications.

(2) **Deprivation of life which results from the use of force which is no more than is absolutely necessary:**

(a) **in defence of any person from unlawful violence;**

(b) **in order to effect a lawful arrest or to prevent the escape of a person lawfully detained;**

(c) **in action lawfully taken for the purpose of quelling a riot or insurrection.**

This group of abridgements of the right to life allows the state to permit anyone to take another's life in the circumstances set out. It assumes that the killer's main purpose is not to kill, but is to achieve one of the specified aims, and the killing is merely a consequence of using an absolutely necessary amount of force in doing so. In the sense in which the word 'intentionally' was interpreted by the Court of Appeal in *Re A., Children,*[25] the conjoined twins case discussed in section 4.3(5), below, such conduct does not intentionally deprive the victim of life. English law would not normally regard such killing as intentional for the purpose of the law of homicide, if the person performing the act has a legal duty to achieve a legitimate purpose. Thus doctors who are faced with dual duties may choose between them, as long as they act reasonably and in good faith, even if they know that their act may cause death. The list of exceptions applies where people are not under duties to anyone, but defend themselves or intervene to protect others as a matter of discretion.

Under (a), the state may take account not only of self-defence but also of the need to rescue others from unlawful violence, although not from lawful violence or natural hazards or accidental disasters.[26] Under (b) and (c), the action (taken usually, but not necessarily, by law enforcement agencies) must be 'lawful'. This requires that the power to act, and to use force of the type and amount actually employed, must be conferred by law. The terms of the relevant law must be accessible to the public and be sufficiently clear to allow people to foresee what sorts of activity will make them liable to be lawfully killed. Nothing in ECHR Article 2 permits a state to legalize the deliberate taking of life as an act of kindness with a view to relieving suffering. The status of laws which allow people to help those who wish to kill themselves, but are incapable of doing so by reason of disability, is uncertain.[27]

[24] Human Rights Act 1998, s. 6(1).

[25] [2000] HRLR 721, CA.

[26] This is why the exception was not applicable to the doctors in *Re A., Children* [2000] HRLR 721, CA, who wanted to separate the conjoined twins, killing one to save the other from the natural consequences of being joined to the former.

[27] See section 4.3(2), below. *Cp.* P. van Dijk and G. J. H. van Hoof, *Theory and Practice of the European Convention on Human Rights,* 3rd edn. (The Hague: Kluwer, 1998), 302–3: 'It would seem . . . that . . . euthanasia does not *per se* conflict with the Convention. In fact, the value of the life to be protected can and must be weighed against other rights of the person in question, particularly his right, laid down in Article 3, to be protected from inhuman or degrading treatment'. But the Administrative Court held in *R. (Pretty) v. DPP, The Times,* 23 October 2001, that the ECHR does not require assisted suicide to be permitted. The applicant has appealed to HL.

The second group of exceptions is apt to cover any death resulting from the use of force for an authorized purpose. If an innocent bystander is killed by accident, that death will not violate Article 2, as long as the level of force used is no more than absolutely necessary for one of the permitted purposes. The question is, what is meant by 'absolutely necessary'? In *McCann and others v. United Kingdom*,[28] the European Court of Human Rights decided that an anti-terrorist operation conducted by UK security forces in Gibraltar, to prevent three IRA suspects from planting a bomb, had violated their right to life when the anti-terrorist personnel had shot and killed them. The Court adopted a balanced approach to the interpretation of the term 'absolutely necessary'. The right to life was fundamental. The phrase 'necessary in a democratic society', when used in connection with justifications for interfering with other rights such as that to freedom of expression, had been held to indicate the existence of a pressing social need to act in pursuit of a legitimate aim, and a proportionate relationship between the aim and the measures adopted. When dealing with the right to life, the test of proportionality had to be strictly applied, subjecting all aspects of the operation to the most careful scrutiny. In a case where agents of the state had deliberately used lethal force, the scrutiny had to be particularly stringent. The Court would allow the state to justify the use of lethal force where agents honestly believed, with good reason, that their lives or other people's lives were imminently at risk, even if it later turned out that the belief, although honest and reasonable, was mistaken. However, the state would still be responsible if the planning of the operation, the checking of information, and the command and control systems which were in place, were not adequate to ensure a proper level of protection for the right to life.

In the *McCann* case, a bare majority of the Court held that the control system had been inadequate. Taking account of the fact that the agents had been trained to shoot to kill, inadequate steps had been taken to supply the anti-terrorist agents with up-to-date intelligence assessments relating to the risk that the suspects had or were about to detonate a bomb, and to ensure that these were properly considered before anyone gave an order to fire. A similarly demanding level of scrutiny was applied in *Gül v. Turkey*,[29] where the Court held unanimously that the Turkish security forces conducting an operation against the Kurdish separatist PKK organization had used disproportionate force when, without any reasonable belief that their own or anyone else's lives were in danger, they fired a long burst of machine-gun bullets through a door behind which Mehmet Gül was standing, killing him.

On the other hand, in *Andronicou and Constantinou v. Cyprus*[30] a majority of the Court decided that police use of lethal force had not been unjustifiable. A man was holding his fiancée at gun-point in their apartment after a row. A team of police marksmen attended. Negotiations with the gunman seemed to have broken down, and the woman was screaming that her life was in danger. The police burst into the

[28] Series A, No. 324, Judgment of 27 September 1995, 21 EHRR 97, esp. at paras. 147–150 and 200 of the judgment.

[29] Eur. Ct. HR, Judgment of 14 December 2000, App. No. 22676/93.

[30] Eur. Ct. HR, Judgment of 9 October 1997, RJD 1997-VI, 2059, 25 EHRR 491.

apartment firing from automatic weapons. Both the man and the woman were fatally injured by police bullets. The evidence suggested that the negotiations had been conducted inefficiently, there was a lack of crowd control, some information about the weapons at the man's disposal had not been checked and was unreliable, the assault on the apartment had been carried out with insufficient lighting, and a great many rounds had been fired. Nevertheless, the police had been told not to fire unless they believed that their lives or the woman's life were in danger, and their belief that she was in danger was reasonable in the circumstances. The majority of the Court considered that 'it has not been shown that the rescue operation was not planned and organised in a way which minimised to the greatest extent possible any risk to the lives of the couple', and that the use of lethal force, 'however regrettable it may have been, did not exceed what was "absolutely necessary" for the purpose of defending the lives of Elsie Constantinou and the officers . . . '.[31]

The negative formulation of the conclusions ('it has not been shown . . . did not exceed') highlights the importance of the burden and standard of proof in these cases. It is a grave step to hold that a state is responsible for someone's death. Accordingly, the Court has held that the facts establishing state responsibility must be proved beyond reasonable doubt. Where evidence does not show beyond reasonable doubt that death was caused by state agents or those acting under their control, the state will be acquitted of directly violating Article 2 rights.[32]

How does English law measure up to these requirements? Before the Human Rights Act 1998 made Article 2 part of municipal law, the degree of force which could lawfully be used was governed by a series of statutory provisions and common law rules, which now fall to be examined in the light of the duties on the state under Article 2.

The Criminal Law Act 1967, section 3 provides:

'(1)　A person may use such force as is reasonable in the circumstances in the prevention of crime, or in effecting or assisting in the lawful arrest of offenders or suspected offenders or of persons unlawfully at large.

(2)　Subsection (1) above shall replace the rules of the common law on the question when force used for a purpose mentioned in the subsection is justified by that purpose.'

This provides a defence against civil or criminal liability when force is used for one of the purposes set out in section 3(1) and the use of force, and the degree of force, are 'reasonable in the circumstances'. Subsection (2) subsumes the common law of self-defence under the reasonableness test, so that the old requirement that a person threatened with violence must take a safe line of retreat if one is available, rather than resorting to violence, no longer applies if it is reasonable in the circumstances not to

---

[31]　Eur. Ct. HR, Judgment of 9 October 1997, RJD 1997-VI, 2059, 25 EHRR 491, at paras. 186, 194.

[32]　See, e.g. *Kiliç v. Turkey*, Eur. Ct. HR, Judgment of 28 March 2000, App. No. 22492/93; *Mahmut Kaya v. Turkey*, Eur. Ct. HR, Judgment of 28 March 2000, App. No. 22535/93. However, as we shall see below, the burden of proof shifts to the state if a person is shown to have died from non-natural causes while in the custody of agents of the state. The state may also be liable under Art. 2 if it has failed to take adequate protective measures, or to take efficient and effective steps to investigate the case and bring the perpetrators to justice.

retreat: a person lawfully in a place is entitled to insist on remaining there, notwith-standing a risk that others may attack him.[33] The cases show that courts have taken an indulgent view of the test of reasonableness, particularly where police or security forces face a reasonably apprehended threat from criminals or terrorists. Courts allow some leeway to the forces on the ground in deciding whether it is reasonable to use force.[34] Thus the law takes account of the reasonable apprehensions of victims or law enforcers in deciding whether to use force to defend themselves or others, or to make an arrest. On the other hand, when a person uses a degree of force which is objectively unreasonable in the circumstances, section 3 does not protect him, even if he made an honest (but defective) assessment of the appropriate response to the perceived threat.[35]

The Police and Criminal Evidence Act 1984, section 117, is slightly less extensive than section 3 of the 1967 Act in giving authority to use force. It allows a constable to use 'reasonable force, if necessary' for the purpose of exercising any power conferred by that Act which does not specifically require the consent of another person, includ-ing powers of stop and search of the person, arrest, detention, entry to premises, and seizure of items as evidence. This subjects the initial decision to use force to a test of necessity. However, where some force is allowed, the degree of force is governed by a reasonableness test similar to that in the 1967 Act.

These reasonableness tests do not sit comfortably with the way in which the Euro-pean Court of Human Rights has interpreted 'absolutely necessary' under Article 2 of the ECHR. Where an ordinary person is threatened and defends himself, it is accept-able to excuse him from criminal liability if he defends himself in a way which he thinks is necessary, and which is not objectively unreasonable. He probably lacks the training and background information needed to assess the risk and weigh up options for his response to it. The state should not be obliged to criminalize behaviour based on an honest and reasonable reaction to a pressing danger, even if someone dies as a result. On the other hand, where trained agents of the state use lethal force to prevent crime, protect the population, or apprehend offenders, a more demanding standard ought to be expected of them than that of reasonableness. For this reason, the Euro-pean Commission of Human Rights held admissible a complaint concerning use of deadly force by the security forces in Northern Ireland after the British courts had dismissed a claim for damages, and the applicant and the government achieved a friendly settlement.[36]

The traditional approach to assessing criminal liability in such cases under section 3 diverges from that required by the European Court of Human Rights in two respects. *First*, reasonableness does not usually import the requirements of pro-portionality and strict scrutiny which the Court applies in Article 2 cases. *Secondly*, a

---

[33] See *R. v. Julien* [1969] 1 WLR 839, CA; *R. v. Field* [1972] Crim. LR 435, CA; A. P. Simester and G. R. Sullivan, *Criminal Law Theory and Doctrine* (Oxford: Hart Publishing, 2000), 618, 621–2.

[34] See, e.g. *Farrell v. Secretary of State for Defence* [1980] 1 All ER 1667, HL.

[35] *R. v. Clegg* [1995] 1 AC 482, [1995] 1 All ER 334, HL (NI).

[36] *Farrell v. United Kingdom* (6861/75) 3 DR 147, 3 EHRR 466; (9013/80) 5 EHRR 466, Eur. Comm. HR. A subsequent application has been held to be inadmissible: *Stewart v. United Kingdom* (10044/82) 7 EHRR 453.

reasonableness test traditionally focuses on what an individual defendant knew or thought, or should have known or thought. However, the state's obligations under Article 2 go beyond a responsibility to ensure that its agents act reasonably according to their lights. It includes a duty to control its agents adequately, making appropriate arrangements for gathering and processing information, keeping agents informed of intelligence assessments, and preventing the use of a greater degree of force than the intelligence assessments objectively justify. A reasonableness test may be acceptable when deciding whether an individual police officer or soldier who pulls a trigger should be subject to criminal penalties for causing a death, but is not appropriate for deciding the civil liability of state institutions to compensate for a death, or even the criminal liability of the commander of the operation. Under Article 2, one must assess the adequacy of the system for managing an operation to protect life. This demands a careful analysis of the operational implications of different sorts of weaponry and tactics.[37] Only in this way can the requirements of Article 2 be met, and security and police forces made accountable to law for interferences with the right to life. Terrorism presents special problems, because it may be necessary to use or threaten a high level of force in order to protect the community against people who are themselves using or threatening extreme and arbitrary violence. Measures become necessary which would not otherwise be considered justifiable, including the use of deadly force.[38] This must be taken into account. Yet such force demands more, not less, care on the part of agents of the state, and proper accountability to law.

Under the Human Rights Act 1998, these inconsistencies between English law and the ECHR can and should be resolved. Section 3 of the 1998 Act requires us to read and give effect to legislation (such as the 1967 and 1984 Acts) in a manner compatible with Convention rights, so far as possible. It would require no great exercise of a judge's skill to treat 'reasonable force' as meaning 'absolutely necessary' force, as the latter term has been interpreted by the European Court of Human Rights for the purpose of Article 2. This would not generally affect the liability (criminal or civil) of an individual who caused another's death, because the Court has accepted that an honest and reasonable belief that it is necessary to use lethal force for a purpose within Article 2(2) can be pleaded by way of defence to a claim under Article 2.[39] On the other hand, where death is caused by the agent of a public authority or by someone under an agent's control, it would mean that the public authority could not use the agent's honest and reasonable belief as a defence to an action against the state for damages, either under the Fatal Accidents Act 1976 or under section 7 of the Human Rights Act 1998 for a violation of the duty to comply with Convention rights

---

[37] For very instructive accounts of tactics involving deadly force and their implementation, particularly in the context of public order, see G. Northam, *Shooting in the Dark: Riot Police in Britain* (London: Faber and Faber, 1988); P. A. J. Waddington, *The Strong Arm of the Law: Armed and Public Order Policing* (Oxford: Clarendon Press, 1991), ch. 4.

[38] For balanced accounts and evaluations of the measures taken in relation to Northern Ireland, see R. J. Spjut, 'The "Official" Use of Deadly Force by the Security Forces Against Suspected Terrorists' [1986] PL 38–66; G. Hogan and C. Walker, *Political Violence and the Law in Ireland* (Manchester: Manchester University Press, 1989), 64–9.

[39] See, e.g. *McCann and others v. United Kingdom*, above n. 28, at para. 200 of the judgment.

under section 6 of the Act, unless the public authority could establish that the force was used for a purpose permitted under Article 2 and that the degree of force used was strictly proportionate to the legitimate purpose in all the circumstances. It would enable the courts to make public authorities legally accountable for acts of their agents which cause death, as required by Article 2, and to give legal remedies to victims of inadequately planned and organized operations which cause death, as required by Article 6 and Article 13 of the ECHR.[40]

In cases which fall outside section 3 of the Criminal Law Act 1967 and section 117 of the Police and Criminal Evidence Act 1984 (for example, because someone uses force for a purpose other than crime control or the exercise of a power under the 1984 Act, or because the act which causes death does not involve the use of force), the law gives very extensive protection to the right to life, and allows lethal force to be justified only in very restricted circumstances. For example, English law does not recognize duress as a defence to murder (either as a principal or as an accessory) or attempted murder.[41] This has particular repercussions where terrorists try to use innocent people as instruments of violence. For example, a person whose car is hijacked by gunmen and filled with explosives, and who is told to drive it to an army checkpoint where it will be detonated, faces a serious problem if the hijackers threaten to kill him or members of his family if he does not comply. Should someone be killed in the explosion, the driver will not be able to use duress as a defence to a murder charge. Prudentially, it makes sense for him to adopt the course which seems least likely to cause death. But in human rights terms, the state has to decide whether it adequately protects a victim's right to life if it allows a defence of duress in such circumstances. Whether the defence is allowed or not, the state would probably be able to justify the result under Article 2(2)(a). It follows that refusal to recognize the defence of duress to a murder charge is not unjustified, even though little is to be gained in terms of deterrence (since a person in that position is unlikely to know the law or to regard it as a major factor influencing his decision).

The Police and Criminal Evidence Act 1984 expressly preserves common-law powers of arrest in connection with breaches of the peace. It also leaves untouched other common-law powers to take any reasonable steps to prevent or defuse a breach of the peace which is in progress or is reasonably apprehended and imminent. These powers are discussed in detail in Chapter 18, below. Here it should be noted that they permit the use of force, and if the force were to lead to someone's death it would be necessary to decide whether it violated Article 2 of the ECHR. It would not fall within the exceptions to Article 2 unless the force were used in order to effect a lawful arrest (Article 2(2)(b)) or to quell a riot or insurrection (Article 2(2)(c)). The degree of force would then need to be assessed in terms of the decisions of the European Court of Human Rights discussed above. The International Covenant on Civil and Political

---

[40] See *Osman v. United Kingdom*, Eur. Ct. HR, RJD 1998-VIII, (1998) 29 EHRR 245; P. Giliker, '*Osman* and Police Immunity in the English Law of Torts' (2000) 20 *LS* 372–92; C. A. Gearty, 'Unravelling *Osman*' (2001) 64 *MLR* 159–90.

[41] *Abbott v. R.* [1977] AC 755, [1976] 3 All ER 140, PC; *R. v. Howe* [1987] AC 417, [1987] 1 All ER 771, HL; *R. v. Gotts* [1992] 2 AC 412, [1992] 1 All ER 832, HL.

Rights Article 6(1), prohibits 'arbitrary' deprivation of life, which has been held by the UN Human Rights Committee to involve a test of necessity and strict proportionality[42] not notably different, in practice, from that which applies under Article 2 of the ECHR.[43]

The law on breach of the peace in England before 2 October 2000 failed to match up to these standards, because it assessed the justification for the amount of force used by reference to reasonableness, rather than necessity, even where death resulted. Unlike statutory powers to use force, the common-law rules are not subject to the requirement in section 3 of the Human Rights Act 1998 that they should be interpreted so far as possible in a manner compatible with the Convention rights. It is therefore possible that the common law might produce a result which violates Article 2. However, a court deciding a case on the common-law rules, in which the use of force to deal with a breach of the peace had led to a death, would be a public authority with a duty under section 6 of the 1998 Act to act compatibly with Article 2. The court ought to discharge this duty by developing the common law so as to secure congruence between it and the meaning of 'absolutely necessary' under Article 2 of the ECHR, at least where the force was used by a public authority such as the police or army.[44]

(ii) Deaths in the custody of the state

The European Court of Human Rights has held that the state is liable if people die in the custody of the police, security forces, or prisons, unless the state can prove that it had no responsibility for the death. In principle, the Court has imposed a high standard of proof on applicants seeking to establish that a state, through its own agents, is responsible for causing a death. Proof is required to reach the criminal standard, beyond reasonable doubt. However, in practice it is extremely difficult for outsiders to establish what went on behind locked doors of prisons or police stations, or in the course of secret operations by state forces. To prevent states from avoiding liability by refusing to explain events which lie within the exclusive cognisance of their agents, the Court has in effect reversed the burden of proof where someone dies while in the custody of the state. The applicant still has to show that the victim died while in the custody of an organization for which the state was responsible. Thereafter, the burden moves onto the state to explain how the death occurred without responsibility on the part of its agents. The explanation must be credible, and must be supported by convincing evidence.[45] The Court has recently been prepared to draw an inference of death

---

[42] *Suárez de Guerrero v. Colombia*, App. No. 45/1979 at para. 13.2; *Burrell v. Jamaica*, App. No. 546/93.

[43] S. Joseph, J. Schultz, and M. Castan, *The International Covenant on Civil and Political Rights: Cases, Materials, and Commentary* (Oxford: Oxford University Press, 2000), 109–14.

[44] On s. 6 of the 1998 Act giving horizontal effect to the Convention rights where all parties to litigation are private people or bodies, see above, Ch. 2, section 2.6(4)(iv).

[45] *Çakici v. Turkey*, Eur Ct. HR, Judgment of 8 July 1999; *Ertak v. Turkey*, Eur Ct. HR, Judgment of 9 May 2000; *Velikova v. Bulgaria*, Eur Ct. HR, App. No. 41488/98, Judgment of 18 May 2000; *Timartas v. Turkey*, Eur Ct. HR, Judgment of 13 June 2000. The same principles apply under Art. 3 to non-fatal harm allegedly caused by torture or inhuman or degrading treatment or punishment, sustained in state custody: *Tomasi v. France*, Eur Ct. HR, Series A, No. 241-A, Judgment of 27 August 1992; *Ribitsch v. Austria*, Eur Ct. HR, Series A, No. 336, Judgment of 4 December 1995; *Tekin v. Turkey*, Eur Ct. HR, RJD 1998-IV, Judgment of 9 June 1998; *Selmouni v. France*, Eur Ct. HR, RJD 1999-V, Judgment of 28 July 1999.

from the disappearance of a detainee where no body had been found, then to transfer to the state the burden of showing that it was not responsible for the presumed death.[46]

This has the effect of transferring attention from the acts or omissions of individuals to the responsibility of the state system to care for those in its custody. Under the Human Rights Act 1998, where a person dies in custody, the caselaw of the Court indicates that there should be a cause of action in tort for breach of a prison governor's or chief constable's statutory duty under section 6(1) of the Act to safeguard the right to life, and that in the action the governor or chief constable should carry the burden of establishing absence of responsibility for the death. Under the previous law, the ordinary principles of negligence or trespass to the person applied, and suicide by a prisoner did not break the chain of causation if those responsible for the prisoner had been negligent, but the burden of proof of negligence remained on the plaintiff unless the evidential doctrine *res ipsa loquitur* operated.[47]

(2) THE DUTY TO CONDUCT AN EFFICIENT INQUIRY INTO SUSPICIOUS DEATHS

After a death, if there are reasonable grounds for suspecting homicide, the agencies of the state must ensure that an efficient and effective official investigation is conducted. There is a violation of Article 2 where the investigators are too ready to accept the account given by state agents, regardless of the credibility of their account in the light of other evidence. If the police behave in a dilatory way, fail to follow up leads, fail to contact obvious sources of information, and do not adequately check apparent inconsistencies in the evidence or contradictory reports, so that no suspect can be identified and charged, it represents a failure of legal protection for the right to life and violates Article 2. This applies particularly forcefully where agents of the state are implicated, for example where someone has died in custody. The state has a special responsibility to investigate such cases to establish the responsibility of systems and individuals, whether or not anyone is criminally liable.[48] But equivalent duties operate in all cases of violent death.

Occasionally investigative shortcomings are highlighted in a murder case which attracts national attention, such as the Macpherson Inquiry into the police investigation of the murder of Stephen Lawrence.[49] Such failures violate the right to life of the murder victim. Surviving relations of the victim are also indirect victims of the violation, within the meaning given to 'victim' by the European Court of Human

---

[46] Eur. Ct. HR, *Tas v. Turkey*, App. No. 24396/94, Judgment of 14 November 2000.

[47] See, e.g. *Reeves v. Commissioner of Police of the Metropolis* [2000] 1 AC 360, [1999] 3 All ER 897, HL.

[48] *McCann and others v. United Kingdom*, Eur. Ct. HR, Series A, No. 324, Judgment of 27 September 1995; *Kaya v. Turkey*, Eur. Ct. HR, Judgment of 19 February 1998, RJD 1998-I; *Hugh Jordan v. United Kingdom*, Eur. Ct. HR, App. No. 24746/94, Judgment of 4 May 2001; *McKerr v. United Kingdom*, Eur. Ct. HR, App. No. 28883/95, Judgment of 4 May 2001; *Kelly and others v. United Kingdom*, Eur. Ct. HR, App. No. 30054/96, Judgment of 4 May 2001; *Shanaghan v. United Kingdom*, Eur. Ct. HR, App. No. 37715/97, Judgment of 4 May 2001; *R. (Imtiaz Ahmed) v. Secretary of State for the Home Dept.* [2001] EWHC Admin 719; *R. (Touche) v. Inner London North Coroner* [2001] 3 WLR 148, CA; *Terry v. East Sussex Coroner* [2001] 3 WLR 605.

[49] *The Stephen Lawrence Inquiry*, Report of an Inquiry by Sir William Macpherson of Cluny, advised by Tom Cook, the Rt Rev Dr. John Santer, and Dr. Richard Stone, Cm. 4262-I (London: Stationery Office, 1999), esp. chs. 11–25.

Rights under Article 34 of the ECHR. But the police are rarely disciplined, much less prosecuted, for failings in the course of investigating violent crimes, and (as we shall see below) the police enjoy an extensive public-policy immunity from liability for negligence in performing their investigative functions, even where they failed to protect the deceased against a well understood threat of serious violence.

(3) THE RIGHT TO STATE PROTECTION AGAINST THREATS TO ONE'S LIFE

Does a law or government programme which permits the existence of a state of affairs which indirectly makes a person's life more vulnerable breach the requirement of Article 2 of the Convention and Article 6 of the Covenant that the right to life be protected by law? There are indications that Article 2 might be interpreted so as to require the law to take account of, and protect against, such indirect threats. The Commission has held in *X. v. Federal Republic of Germany*[50] that to allow a person to be evicted from his home when, because of his state of health, eviction may endanger his life, may infringe Article 2. The Commission also declared admissible a complaint by a prisoner in *Simon-Herold v. Austria*[51] that the conditions and treatment which he suffered in prison had led to serious illness and breached Article 2. This is particularly significant for prisoners, who are unable to control their surroundings, and are entirely reliant on the state for opportunities to maintain health. If the decisions of the Commission are followed, it seems that there might be a duty on national author-ities under Article 2 to frame all law so as to require decision-makers to have regard in all cases (including applications for recovery of property) to the risk to health and life which might result from depriving a person of means of support or housing. The common law already treats public bodies as being under a legal obligation to protect people against a threat to health and dignity through destitution. Only clear words in a statute can authorize the withdrawal of publicly funded support from someone whose life and dignity depend on it.[52] The weight of this obligation is likely to be enhanced by the Human Rights Act 1998.

This derives interesting support from a decision of the Supreme Court of Canada concerning the impact of the Charter of Rights and Freedoms, section 7 ('Everyone has the right to life, liberty and security of the person and the right not to be deprived thereof except in accordance with the principles of fundamental justice') and section 1 (Charter rights guaranteed 'subject only to such reasonable limits prescribed by law as can be demonstrably justified in a free and democratic society') on the testing of nuclear weapons. In *Operation Dismantle v. R.*,[53] a group challenged the Canadian government's policy of allowing American cruise missiles, capable of carrying nuclear warheads, to overfly Canada. The plaintiffs argued that the policy created a threat to life which infringed the right guaranteed under section 7 of the Charter. The Supreme

[50] (5207/71) CD 39, 99.

[51] (4340/69) CD 38, 18; a friendly settlement was later achieved: Eur. Comm. HR, Report of 19 December 1972.

[52] *R. v. Secretary of State for Social Security, ex parte Joint Council for the Welfare of Immigrants* [1997] 1 WLR 275, [1996] 4 All ER 385, CA.

[53] (1985) 18 DLR (4th) 481, SC Canada.

Court accepted that the policy was justiciable under the Charter, even though it concerned international relations. Nevertheless, the challenge was struck out, because it was inevitable that the plaintiffs would fail at trial to prove that the policy represented a sufficiently direct and substantial threat to the plaintiffs' interests to justify granting them a remedy. Despite this, the recognition that rights to life and personal security may be infringed by government programmes suggests that Article 2 of the European Convention on Human Rights might prove to have interesting implications for government policy. The obligation to provide protection against risks arises in several ways, as the caselaw on Article 2 demonstrates.

First, state liability under Article 2 is engaged in respect of a death where 'the authorities knew or ought to have known at the time of the existence of a real and immediate risk to the life of an identified individual or individuals from the criminal acts of a third party', and 'they failed to take measures within the scope of their powers which, judged reasonably, might have been expected to avoid that risk'.[54] In cases against Turkey, the state was held to be liable on this basis when it failed to take action to protect a journalist and a doctor against attacks. It could not be proved that the state's own security forces were responsible, but an official report to the government had warned that attacks were being launched on people suspected of assisting the PKK, the Kurdish separatist guerrilla organization, and the journalist and doctor were widely known to have been threatened. The government took no action to control its forces. The victims were killed, and the state was held to have denied them legal protection for their rights to life.[55] On the other hand, if the police know that a person is harassing someone, but after making appropriate inquiries have good reason to believe that he does not represent an immediate threat to life so that they see no need, or have no power, to take him into custody, there will be no liability under Article 2 if he unexpectedly attacks members of the victim's family.[56]

In England and Wales, this duty is performed through a variety of means, including witness protection schemes for those who put themselves at risk by giving evidence against violent criminals. Bodyguards and a secret dwelling may also have to be supplied, as they were for many years for Salman Rushdie when he came under threat of assassination by fundamentalist Muslims in response to a *fatwah* made against him after the publication of his book, *The Satanic Verses*. The European Commission of Human Rights decided that states have no duty to provide bodyguards indefinitely to protect the lives of people who fear that they are likely to be attacked,[57] but the more recent judgments of the Court in *Osman* and the Turkish cases, mentioned above, suggest that the duty might operate until the state has either removed the threat or made it possible for the victim to avoid it in other ways. It is not clear whether there is a short-term obligation, at least until a person can make alternative arrangements for his or her own protection.

[54] *Osman v. United Kingdom*, Eur. Ct. HR, Judgment of 28 October 1998, RJD 1998-VIII, 3124, at para. 63 of the judgment.

[55] *Kiliç v. Turkey*, Eur. Ct. HR, App. No. 22492/93, Judgment of 28 March 2000; *Mahmut Kaya v. Turkey*, Eur. Ct. HR, App. No. 22535/93, Judgment of 28 March 2000.

[56] *Osman v. United Kingdom*, above n. 54.

[57] *X. v. Ireland* (6040/73) CD 44, 121 Eur. Comm. HR (fear of attack by the IRA).

It may be difficult to establish the practical content and limits of the state's obligations under this head. Sometimes the rights of people who are threatened conflict with the rights of others. For example, if it can be shown that X represents a continuing threat to Y's life, steps to protect Y are likely to interfere with X's rights to liberty, respect for private life, and (so far as it exists in English law) freedom of movement. Protection for Y must be as effective as possible, without interfering with X's rights to a greater extent than is proportionate to the gravity of the threat. It might be legitimate for a court to order X not to go within a mile of Y's home or workplace, and not to attempt to contact him. But if X has not yet committed a serious offence, it would probably not be justifiable to order X's indefinite detention, or to impose restrictions which would make it impossible for him to see his family (unless Y is a member of the family) or to earn a living. Under the Human Rights Act 1998, section 6, courts and police are public authorities with a duty to act compatibly with the Convention rights of all. This requires them to assess the risks carefully and adopt a course of action which has the best chance of protecting Y while minimizing the inevitable interference with X's rights.

The decision of Dame Elizabeth Butler-Sloss P in *Venables and Thompson v. News Group Newspapers Ltd*[58] provides a good example. The applicants had been convicted of the murder of a young child when they were ten years old, and sentenced to indefinite detention. As they approached their eighteenth birthdays, it was decided that they had served the 'tariff' part of their sentences, and that they had made such good progress that they no longer represented a risk to the public. It was therefore likely that they would shortly be released. The Home Office and police were aware of evidence that the teenagers would be at risk of revenge attacks after their release, and that the media would pursue them and publish their whereabouts if they had the opportunity. In order to protect their lives and allow them a reasonable chance of a normal life, it was intended to provide them with new identities on their release. The High Court was asked to order that their new identities should not be published, and to restrain the media from publishing any details which they might obtain about their names or whereabouts after their release. Media organizations objected, claiming that there was a public interest in knowing where convicted murderers were and what they were doing, that they were bound to act responsibly by the Press Complaints Commission's Code of Practice, and that the right to freedom of the press should override the rights of the teenagers. Butler-Sloss P granted the order. While recognizing the importance of press freedom,[59] her Ladyship held that it was outweighed in that particular case, because of the strong evidence that the teenagers' lives would be immediately at risk on release if they were identified, that it would be a continuing threat, that publication of their new identities would substantially increase the risk and would make a normal life impossible for them, and that several media organizations would be likely to reveal their whereabouts and identities, notwithstanding the Code of Practice, if they were allowed to do so. Even convicted murderers have the right to life under Article 2 of the ECHR, the right to be free of inhuman or degrading

---

[58] [2001] 2 WLR 1038.
[59] See Human Rights Act 1998, s. 12(4), discussed below, Ch. 14.

treatment under Article 3, and the right to respect for private life under Article 8. The court's order gave reasonable protection to the teenagers' rights while interfering as little as possible with the rights of others. This shows how the balancing exercise can work to produce fair and sensible results in a framework of human rights law. Had the Human Rights Act 1998 not been in force, it is likely that no court would have had the power to make an order restraining publication of details of the teenagers' identities after they reached the age of eighteen and ceased to be minors (who receive special protection against publicity, backed by the law of contempt of court).[60] The incorporation of the ECHR, particularly Article 2, makes it possible for the teenagers and society to get the benefit of eight years of work dedicated to their reform and rehabilitation.

(4) THE RIGHT TO SECURE THE LEGAL ACCOUNTABILITY OF THOSE RESPONSIBLE FOR A DEATH

The right to life requires the state to provide effective legal means by which Article 2 can be vindicated after an unlawful death. It is not enough to rely entirely on proceedings for compensation. Because of the importance of the right to life, the European Court of Human Rights has held that the official inquiry which follows a suspicious death must be designed to result in criminal proceedings which are likely to lead to the punishment of the person responsible. This is the law both under Article 2 and under Article 13 (the right to an effective remedy before a national authority for violations of Convention rights, which does not form part of English law under the Human Rights Act 1998 but which has influenced the interpretation and application of Article 2).[61] In English law, this is done through inquests, criminal proceedings for homicide, and by civil actions against the person who caused the death. Where the Crown Prosecution Service (CPS) decides not to bring a criminal prosecution after a coroner's inquest has reached a verdict of unlawful killing, the CPS should be prepared to give reasons for not proceeding.[62] Even then, it is usually possible for interested parties to launch a private prosecution. If the high standard of proof required in criminal proceedings makes it unlikely that a conviction could be obtained, a civil action for damages, requiring proof on the balance of probabilities rather than beyond reasonable doubt, may be more likely to succeed.

Some kinds of homicide are crimes in public international law. One of these is genocide. The Convention on the Prevention and Punishment of the Crime of

---

[60] See Ch. 17, below.

[61] See, e.g. *Kaya v. Turkey*, Eur. Ct. HR, RJD 1998-I, Judgment of 19 February 1998 at para. 105; *Cakici v. Turkey*, Eur. Ct. HR, Judgment of 8 July 1999 at paras. 112–13; *Velikova v. Bulgaria*, Eur. Ct. HR, App. No. 41488/98, Judgment of 18 May 2000 at para. 89. See also *Akkoc v. Turkey*, Eur. Ct. H.R., App. Nos. 22947/93 and 22948/93, Judgment of 10 October 2000, at para. 77: the state's obligation under Art. 2(1) 'involves a primary duty on the State to secure the right to life by putting in place effective criminal-law provisions to deter the commission of offences against the person backed up by law-enforcement machinery for the prevention, suppression and punishment of breaches of such provisions'.

[62] *R. v. DPP, ex parte Manning* [2000] 3 WLR 463, DC.

Genocide makes special provision for (among other things) killing 'with intent to destroy, in whole or in part, a national, ethnical, racial or religious group, as such'.[63] States Parties are bound to implement legislation allowing for the prosecution of all persons guilty of these crimes before a competent tribunal of the state where the act was committed, or by an international penal tribunal. States Parties are also to provide for effective remedies, and must ensure that for extradition purposes genocide offences are not treated as political (as normally extradition would not be permitted for political offences). In the UK, these matters are dealt with by the Genocide Act 1969, which incorporates the Genocide Convention in its Schedule. In addition, Part 5 of the International Criminal Court Act 2001 gives courts in the UK jurisdiction to try people for genocide and certain war crimes committed elsewhere, including those which cause death. This would provide additional opportunities to vindicate the right to life through criminal proceedings.

Victims of an alleged violation of Article 2 rights, including indirect victims such as surviving relations or a widow or widower, must be able to test the responsibility of state agencies for a death before an independent and impartial tribunal. This is an aspect of securing accountability for state action which is an essential part of the Rule of Law which is essential to securing respect for human rights in a democratic society. In other words, some aspects of the right to a fair trial under Article 6 and the right to an effective remedy for arguable violations of other Convention rights under Article 13 bolster legal protection for the right to life under Article 2. Where access to a tribunal is blocked, or the available tribunal is insufficiently independent and impartial because one of the judges is a member of the force which is under suspicion,[64] the state breaches one of its duties under Article 2.

In English law, this gives rise to a special problem. A general public-interest immunity from liability for negligence in respect of discretionary and policy decisions made during investigations was established in *Hill v. Chief Constable of West Yorkshire*,[65] when the House of Lords struck out a claim by the relations of a victim of the mass murderer Peter Sutcliffe (known as the 'Yorkshire Ripper') for damages for negligence. The plaintiff claimed that the police had been negligent in their pursuit of Sutcliffe after his first murders, allowing him to kill other people, including the plaintiff's daughter. The House of Lords held that public policy required that the police should be immune from suit in respect of performance of public-interest functions involving highly discretionary elements. In that case, the police could not have identified any particular young woman as likely to be Sutcliffe's next victim, so the case could have been decided on the basis that they owed no duty to any particular young woman in Yorkshire. However, the widely formulated public policy immunity was subsequently applied in cases where a potential victim of crime could have been, or had been, clearly identified. In *Alexandrou v. Oxford*,[66] a case decided in 1990, the *Hill*

---

[63] Art. II. See generally Sieghart, *International Law*, 134–5.

[64] See, e.g. *Incal v. Turkey*, Eur. Ct. HR, Judgment of 9 June 1998, RJD 1998-IV, at paras. 65–73 of the judgment.

[65] [1989] AC 53, [1988] 2 All ER 238, HL.

[66] [1993] 4 All ER 328, CA.

immunity was extended to police who failed to inspect thoroughly shop premises in which a burglar alarm, linked directly to the police station, had been activated, with the result that burglars were later able to steal a considerable amount of property from the shop.

Then in 1992, in *Osman v. Ferguson*,[67] the immunity was applied where the police had failed to stop a man from shooting two members of a family after a long campaign of harassment and violence. A teacher had developed an unhealthy fixation on a pupil, pursuing and harassing him over an extended period, and ramming a car in which he was a passenger. The police knew about this: the teacher had warned them that he might do something criminally insane; but the police failed to stop him. Eventually the teacher followed the boy and his family to their apartment and shot the boy and his father. The father was killed; the boy was severely wounded. The boy and his mother sought to sue the police for negligence. The Court of Appeal struck out the claim, holding that the police were performing functions in the public interest, and public policy required that they should be immune, despite the limited and clearly identifiable class of people to whom the police might have been held to owe a duty of care.

If it was correctly decided, the case demonstrates a failure in English law to provide adequate legal protection for the right to life of identifiable people who were predictably under threat. The police were apparently under no enforceable legal duty to act, took no effective action, and were free of any legal liability for the consequences. The victims applied to Strasbourg under the ECHR, alleging violations of both Article 2, on the basis of the failure of the police to provide adequate protection, and Article 6(1), because the immunity deprived the victims of access to a fair and public hearing of a claim for compensation for the violation of their rights under Article 2. The Court decided by seventeen votes to three that there had been no violation of Article 2, because it was not persuaded that, at the relevant time, the police knew or should have known that the teacher represented a real and immediate threat to the lives of the boy and his father. The school and a psychiatrist had detected no propensity to violence in the teacher, and it had not been unreasonable for the police to take the same view. On the other hand, there had been a violation of Article 6(1). The victims were entitled to have the merits of their claim against the police heard by a court. Their claim in negligence depended on foreseeability of damage, proximity between the parties, and whether it was fair, just, and reasonable to impose a duty of care. There might be reasons for restricting police liability, but the blanket immunity extended to the police by the House of Lords in *Hill* and the Court of Appeal in *Osman* prevented the courts from making a case-by-case assessment of whether it was fair, just, and reasonable to impose a duty of care. The European Court of Human Rights accepted that legitimate public interests favoured restricting police liability in some circumstances, but decided that the rule articulated by the English courts amounted to an automatic immunity for the police, excluding consideration of countervailing interests. This was disproportionate to the legitimate aim, because it effectively deprived the victims of the

---

[67] [1993] 4 All ER 344, CA.

right to have an essential element in their claim determined on its merits by a court.[68]

The decision of the Court might appear to be questionable, on the ground that the police immunity meant that the plaintiffs had never had an arguable cause of action to which a right of access to a court might arise under Article 6. However, this fails to acknowledge two factors. First, the extent of the immunity was open to argument in English law. Indeed, we shall see that subsequent cases have qualified the immunity. It was not clear, therefore, that there was no right to recover. The right to a fair hearing applies to cases where a party is testing the extent of a liability or immunity. It cannot be restricted to cases in which the law is clear. Secondly, in the law of the ECHR the right to a fair hearing to determine one's civil rights and obligations under Article 6 is accompanied by a right to an effective remedy for violation of a Convention right under Article 13. Under the Convention, this ensures that states observe the Rule of Law principle, *ubi ius, ibi remedium* (every right should have a remedy). This would be of little value in hard or innovative cases if it applied only where there had been a clear violation. In order to make the right effective in practice, the Court holds that, 'The effect of Article 13 is thus to require the provision of an "arguable complaint" under the Convention and to grant appropriate relief, although Contracting States are afforded some discretion as to the manner in which they conform to their Convention obligations under this provision'.[69] As the Court made clear in *Osman v. United Kingdom*,[70] 'the requirements of Article 13 are less strict than, and are here absorbed by, those of Article 6 . . . ', so that the Court would have found a violation of Article 13 had it not already found a violation of Article 6.

In *Osman*, the main question was whether the police, as agents of the state, had violated the complainants' rights under Article 2 by failing to offer adequate protection for the right to life. English law did not allow the victims to seek a remedy for that violation from the public authority which was responsible for it. Where there is a real question about the responsibility of a public authority for loss of life, it should be possible for it to be examined on its merits, unless there are very strong countervailing reasons. The decision on Article 6 makes perfect sense when read in the light of this, taking account of the absence of any effective means of litigating in English law the responsibility of the police for the death. The main significance for English law of the finding of a violation of Article 6 is that Article 6, unlike Article 13, is a Convention right under the Human Rights Act 1998, and imposes obligations on courts, as public authorities, in municipal law in the UK.

Subsequent decisions of English courts have established limits on the common-law immunity of the police from liability for negligence in the exercise of their function to protect life. Without at any point suggesting that they were adjusting the law in the light of the decision in *Osman v. United Kingdom*, judges have held that the police may

---

[68] *Osman v. United Kingdom*, at paras. 148–154 of the judgment.

[69] See, e.g. *Mahmut Kaya v. Turkey*, Eur. Ct. HR, App. No. 22535/93, Judgment of 28 March 2000, at para. 124.

[70] At para. 158 of the judgment.

have duties enforceable in negligence towards other officers,[71] and to safeguard people in their custody.[72] In *Waters v. Commission of Police of the Metropolis*,[73] Lord Hutton, *obiter*, questioned the absolutism of the police immunity from liability in investigative matters:

'I consider that in *Swinney v. Chief Constable of Northumbria Police Force*[74] Hirst LJ was right to state that when the police claim immunity against an action for negligence public policy must be assessed in the round, which means assessing the considerations referred to in *Hill's* case[75] together with other considerations bearing on the public interest in order to reach a fair and just decision.'

The implication is that this ought to happen in all cases, not only those in which the person claiming to be a victim was either a colleague of the officers alleged to be responsible or in their custody. If public interest factors for and against allowing immunity are balanced on the facts of each case in this way, English law will meet the requirements of Article 6 of the ECHR.[75a]

Apart from the question of the police immunity in negligence, there is now a statutory cause of action for violating the right to life under the Human Rights Act 1998, which will to some extent mitigate the effect of the immunity of the police from liability in negligence at common law in respect of omissions contributing to death or injury through failure of protection. The victim has a cause of action against the police under the Human Rights Act 1998, sections 6 and 7,[76] relying on the violation of Article 2, which (as interpreted by the Court, in judgments which domestic courts must take into account by virtue of section 2 of the 1998 Act) would focus attention on very similar questions to those which would arise in an action for negligence, although expressed in somewhat different terms.[77]

4.3 CLASHES OF ABSOLUTES

The Convention does not demand that states or private individuals be placed under any positive obligation to save life, or to allocate resources to secure its prolongation. Where English law does impose such an obligation, it is usually on people who are regarded as having special responsibilities, either because of their pre-existing contractual or family relationship to the endangered person, or because (like life-guards

[71] *Waters v. Commissioner of Police of the Metropolis* [2000] 1 WLR 1607, HL, distinguishing *Hill v. Chief Constable of West Yorkshire*, above n. 65.

[72] *Reeves v. Commissioner of Police of the Metropolis* [1999] 3 WLR 363, HL.

[73] [2000] 1 WLR 1607, 1618.

[74] [1997] QB 464, CA, at 484.

[75] [1989] AC 53, HL.

[75a] *Z. v. United Kingdom*, App. No. 29392/95, and *TP and KM v. United Kingdom*, App. No. 28945/95, Judgments of 10 May 2001.

[76] As victims within the meaning given to the word by the Court under Article 34, close relations or a widow or widower would have standing to sue under s. 7 of the 1998 Act.

[77] Where the violation was partly the result of discrimination on racial or other grounds prohibited by Art. 14 (considered in Ch. 3, above), there may also be an actionable violation of the latter Article.

or the police) they have a position which leads society to have higher expectations of them than of the community at large.[78] This may lead to criminal liability, to civil liability, or both. In such cases, liability is imposed in respect of an omission rather than an act.

Particularly difficult problems arise in the context of doctor–patient relationships. The extent of a doctor's duties towards foetuses, to treat severely handicapped neonates, and to keep alive terminally ill patients, are specially sensitive issues. The extent and nature of the regulation which the state exercises over these matters is a significant element in the strength of protection for the right to life. This section considers some aspects of these matters which are particularly relevant to the civil liberties and human rights of the patients concerned.

(1) ABORTION[79]

(i) Do foetuses have a right to life?

While the Convention requires national authorities to protect the right of everyone to life, it does not define 'everyone'. Is there an obligation to protect the life of an unborn foetus? So far, the European Court of Human Rights has not had to decide whether foetuses have a right to life, but there are decisions of the European Commission of Human Rights which suggest that they do not. In *X. v. United Kingdom*[80] the Commission doubted whether 'everyone' in Article 2(1) included a foetus, but thought that even if the right to life began at conception it would be subject to an implied restriction to permit an abortion in order to protect the mother's life or health. The issue arose directly for decision in *Paton v. United Kingdom*,[81] in which the father of an unborn child had unsuccessfully sought to persuade the English courts to prevent the mother from having an abortion. The father argued that the failure to prevent the abortion had infringed the foetus's right to life. The Commission decided that Article 2 applies only to people who have been born, because the life of the foetus is intimately connected with that of the mother. If Article 2 applied to a foetus, the Commission reasoned, abortions would have to be prohibited even where continuation of the pregnancy would present a serious risk to the mother's life, giving the foetus's life a higher value than the mother's, as there is no provision in Article 2 allowing a person to be deliberately killed in order to save the life of another.[82]

In this respect, English law gives more protection to the life of a foetus than is required under the Convention. A number of statutes create criminal offences in

[78] Mead, 'Contracting into Crime'.

[79] See L. L. Tribe, *Abortion: The Clash of Absolutes* (New York: W. W. Norton, 1992), *passim*; Dworkin, *Life's Dominion*, ch. 2.

[80] (8416/78) DR 19, 244.

[81] (1980) 3 EHRR 408.

[82] See the Commission's decision at 413, para. 8, and 415, para. 19. The UN Convention on the Rights of the Child fails to take a position on the applicability of the right to life to foetuses, merely noting in the preamble that children need 'special safeguards and care, including appropriate legal protection, before as well as after birth'. On the approach of the UN Human Rights Committee under the ICCPR, see Joseph, Jenny, and Castan, *The International Covenant on Civil and Political Rights*, 135–7.

order to protect the life of a foetus. A pregnant woman who, with intent to procure her own miscarriage, unlawfully administers to herself any poison or other noxious thing, or uses an instrument or other means to the same end, is guilty of an offence under section 58 of the Offences Against the Person Act 1861. So is anyone who administers drugs or uses an instrument or other means with intent to pro-cure the miscarriage of any woman, whether or not she is in fact pregnant. A person who supplies any poison, noxious thing, instrument, or anything else, knowing that it is intended to be used to procure a miscarriage, commits an offence under section 59. A person who attacks a pregnant woman, injuring her unborn child so that he dies after being born alive, may be guilty of murder or manslaughter of the child.[83]

However, while English law treats foetuses as having *interests* worthy of protection, and as deserving respect,[84] like the European Commission of Human Rights it does not regard them as having *rights* at all. The foetus is not even within the jurisdiction of the English courts until born. Thus, a foetus cannot be made a ward of court until it has been born alive. Indeed, the Commission's decision in *Paton* was influential in persuading the Court of Appeal not to extend the protection of the wardship jurisdic-tion to an unborn child.[85] Similarly, although a child is entitled to sue for prenatal injuries,[86] causes of action do not vest until birth, so a father cannot sue as the unborn child's next friend to seek an injunction restraining a mother or doctor from procur-ing an abortion.[87] The same applies in Scotland.[88] In the USA, where a pregnant woman's right to choose to have an abortion receives some protection from the implied constitutional right to privacy, the Supreme Court (in cases discussed below) has accepted that the state's legitimate interest in the survival of the foetus increases as the foetus matures. The state can therefore justify a higher level of legal regulation of abortion at later stages of pregnancy than in the early stages. In England, the courts at one stage indicated that they would be willing to override a mother's refusal to accept surgical intervention in childbirth in order to safeguard the life of the child.[89] Some US courts have made similar decisions, although the balance of authority now

---

[83] *Attorney General's Reference (No. 3 of 1994)* [1998] AC 245, [1997] 3 All ER 936, HL.

[84] See Dept. of Health and Social Security, *Report of the Committee of Inquiry into Human Fertilisation and Embryology* (Chairman: Dame Mary Warnock), Cmnd. 9314 (London: HMSO, 1984). This is sometimes based on the potential of the foetus to develop into a human being: see the report of the Polkinghorne Committee, *Review of the Guidance on the Research Use of Fetuses and Fetal Material* (Cm. 762). It is a matter of dispute whether foetuses have the potential to become human beings or are already human beings: see, e.g. J. Jarvis Thompson, 'A Defence of Abortion', in R. M. Dworkin (ed.), *Philosophy of Law* (Oxford: Oxford University Press, 1977), 112–28; J. Finnis, 'The Rights and Wrongs of Abortion: A Reply to Judith Thompson', in Dworkin (ed.), *Philosophy of Law*, 129–52.

[85] *Re F. (in utero)* [1988] Fam. 122, [1988] 2 All ER 193, CA. See generally G. Douglas, *Law, Fertility and Reproduction* (London: Sweet & Maxwell, 1991), ch. 6.

[86] Congenital Disabilities (Civil Liability) Act 1976; *Burton v. Islington Health Authority* [1992] 3 All ER 833, CA.

[87] *Paton v. British Pregnancy Advisory Service* [1979] QB 276, [1978] 2 All ER 987. The father lacks standing before the child's birth: *C. v. S.* [1988] QB 135, [1987] 1 All ER 1230, Heilbron J and CA.

[88] *Kelly v. Kelly*, 1997 SC 285; E. J. Russell, 'Abortion Law in Scotland and the *Kelly* Foetus', 1997 SLT 187–93.

[89] *Re S. (Adult: Refusal of Treatment)* [1992] 4 All ER 671.

upholds the mother's autonomy.[90] More recently, the English Court of Appeal has likewise reasserted the more orthodox position that courts and doctors must respect a woman's autonomy and bodily integrity in such cases, accepting her refusal of intervention even if it results in the child's death, as long as the woman has the mental capacity to make the decision.[91] The Supreme Court of Canada has also valued a mother's liberty and autonomy above the interests of a foetus. In *Winnipeg Child and Family Services v. G.*,[92] the court refused to order a pregnant woman to be detained during the pregnancy at the suit of a public authority which wanted to prevent her from damaging the foetus through her addiction to glue sniffing.

(ii) A woman's right to an abortion?

The European Convention, while not mandating protection for the life of a foetus, does not confer on a pregnant woman any right to an abortion on demand either directly or (probably) as an aspect of the right to respect for private life under Article 8. Pregnancy was held not to be a wholly private matter, because the mother's right to respect for privacy was bound up with the life of the developing foetus.[93] It is left to the parties to the Convention to decide whether, and when, to permit abortions. It has been suggested that the Commission, in holding that the foetus has no right to life, must impliedly be recognizing that the pregnant woman has a right to an abortion in at least some circumstances.[94] This does not seem to follow, however. The fact that the Convention might not protect the foetus's interests as rights does not thereby increase the rights of anyone else to be free of the effects of regulation by the state to safeguard the foetus's interests. The relationship between the rights of the woman and those (if any) of the foetus does not affect the relationship between the rights of the woman and the responsibility of the state to protect the interests of those who or which cannot represent themselves. If so, a balance will be needed between the mother's rights under Article 8 and those of the foetus under Article 2. On a matter as sensitive as this states would probably be allowed a wide margin of appreciation,[95] but they might have an obligation to provide some criteria for permissibility of abortions at all stages, and perhaps closer regulation of abortions to avoid social harm than of abortion to protect the mother's health. This is suggested by another case, in which the Commission held that an abortion at 14 weeks did not violate any Article 2 right of the foetus where the law permitted abortion if 'pregnancy, birth or care for the child may place the woman in a difficult position in life', but left open the possibility that there might be circumstances in which a foetus would be entitled to some protection

---

[90] I. Kennedy, *Treat Me Right: Essays in Medical Law and Ethics* (Oxford: Clarendon Press, 1991), ch. 19. On the early US cases, see N. K. Rhoden, 'The Judge in the Delivery Room: The Emergence of Court Ordered Caesarians' (1986) 74 *Calif. LR* 1951–2030.

[91] *St George's Healthcare NHS Trust v. S.* [1999] Fam. 26, [1998] 2 All ER 673, CA. See further Ch. 5, below.

[92] (1997) 1 BHRC 1, SC of Canada.

[93] *Brüggeman and Scheuten v. Federal Republic of Germany* (6959/75) DR 10, 100, Eur. Comm. HR, Report of 12 July 1977; *Paton v. United Kingdom* (8416/78), Eur. Comm. HR, Decision of 13 May 1980, 3 EHRR 408.

[94] M. Rendel, 'Abortion and Human Rights' (1991) 141 *NLJ* 1270–1, at 1271.

[95] See K. D. Ewing and C. A. Gearty, 'Terminating Abortion Rights?' (1992) 142 *NLJ* 1696–8.

under Article 2, which might require some restriction of the right to an abortion.[96] In *Open Door Counselling Ltd. v. Ireland and Dublin Well Woman Centre Ltd. v. Ireland*,[97] the Court left open the possibility that some restrictions on abortion might be required by Article 2 as applied to the foetus. The question is likely to present itself in a concrete form sooner or later.

The development of the law on this subject in Ireland provides a good example of human and constitutional rights providing the setting for a conversation between the European Court of Human Rights, the European Court of Justice, the Irish Supreme Court, the Oireachtas (Irish Parliament), and the Irish people. Under section 58 of the Offences against the Person Act 1861, no abortions were legally available. In 1983, this was reinforced by the guarantee of the unborn child's right to life under Article 40.3.3 of the Constitution, introduced following a referendum instigated by pro-life campaigners. The provision originally provided:

'The state acknowledges the right to life of the unborn and, with due regard to the equal right to life of the mother, guarantees in its laws to respect, and, as far as practicable, by its laws to defend and vindicate that right.'

In *Attorney-General v. X.*[98] the Attorney-General, relying on the right to life of the unborn child under Article 40.3.3, obtained an injunction restraining a pregnant 14-and-a-half-year-old victim of rape from travelling to England for an abortion, arguing that the girl's right to travel (one of the 'unenumerated rights' of the Constitution) was outweighed by her unborn child's right to life. The Supreme Court by a majority discharged the injunction, because there was a real and substantial risk that the girl, if denied an abortion, would commit suicide. In these circumstances, it was held that the girl's right to life outweighed the unborn infant's right to life, and it was not proper to prevent the girl from obtaining an abortion. At around the same time, the European Court of Justice held that abortion clinics offered a service protected by the free movement right in EC law, and this would normally entail a freedom to advertise the service in other Member States.[99] The European Court of Human Rights held that Ireland's censoring of information about abortion services violated the right to freedom of information and ideas under Article 10 of the ECHR.[100] In response, Article 40.3.3 of the Constitution was amended by two Acts following referenda in 1992. After the paragraph set out above, it now provides that the subsection does not limit freedom to travel abroad, or to obtain information about services available in other states (subject to conditions laid down by law).[101] This combination of influences has produced a liberalization of freedom of information about abortions, and

[96] *H. v. Norway*, App. No. 17004/90, Eur. Commn. HR, Decision of 19 May 1992, 73 DR 155. See D. J. Harris, M. O'Boyle, and C. Warbrick, *Law of the European Convention on Human Rights* (London: Butterworths, 1995), 42–3.

[97] Eur. Ct. HR, Series A, No. 246-A, Judgment of 29 October 1992, 15 EHRR 244.

[98] [1992] 1 IR 1, 17, SC of Ireland.

[99] Case C-159/90 *Society for the Protection of Unborn Children v. Grogan* [1991] ECR I-4685.

[100] *Open Door Counselling Ltd. and Dublin Well Woman Centre Ltd. v. Ireland*, Eur. Ct. HR, Series A, No. 246-A, Judgment of 29 October 1992.

[101] See the Regulation of Information (Services Outside the State for Termination of Pregnancies) Act 1995 (Ireland).

freedom to travel abroad to obtain one, which enjoys popular legitimacy in Ireland. The reasoning of the Supreme Court in *Attorney-General v. X.* also implies that there would be no constitutional bar to the legalization of abortion in Ireland itself in situations where there is such a real and substantial risk to the mother's life, even if the risk is of self-inflicted death.

The position in Great Britain was for a long period (and in Northern Ireland still is) much the same as it was in Ireland under sections 58 and 59 of the Offences Against the Person Act 1861. It gave a simple but harsh answer to the problem of balancing the interest in the life of the foetus against the woman's rights to life and to control over her own body. It weighted the interest in the foetus's life above that in the mother's life, health, or happiness. It made a woman or doctor potentially liable to life imprisonment for performing an abortion even when the mother's life and health were threatened by continuing the pregnancy. This liability might be avoided, for example, by invoking the doctrine of double effect: it was possible in some cases to argue that a drug had been administered to save the woman's life, and had only incidentally had the effect of procuring a miscarriage. Alternatively, it was said that performing an abortion to save the woman's life would have been justifiable on ordinary criminal law principles, and so would not have been unlawful within the meaning of section 58 of the 1861 Act.[102] However, even if this is accepted, it arguably left no scope for abortions to preserve mental health or to avoid risks which were not life-threatening. Back-street abortions by unqualified or disqualified practitioners resulted, without the benefit of the appropriate back-up in case of complications, and many women lost their lives as a result.

The balance moved slightly in favour of the woman when the Infant Life (Preservation) Act 1929 was passed. Section 1(1) created a new offence of child destruction, committed by a person who, with intent to destroy the life of a child capable of being born alive, by a wilful act causes the child to die before it has an existence independent of its mother. This section was actually designed to trap people who procured abortions of foetuses at an advanced stage of gestation, when they can be born alive but cannot then survive. It provided that nobody was to be convicted unless it was proved that the act which caused the death had not been done in good faith solely for the purpose of preserving the mother's life. This added nothing substantial to the justification which was available under the 1861 Act, but it placed the burden of proof on the prosecution instead of the defence. This did not, however, help doctors or pregnant women who procured abortions before the child was capable of being born alive; they continued to carry the burden of proof as to the justification under the 1861 Act.

The curious result followed that the criminal law seemed to offer more protection to a less mature foetus than to a more mature one. This is counter-intuitive: as we shall see, in Canada and the USA courts have regarded the state as having a greater interest in protecting more mature than less mature foetuses. The restrictive nature of the proviso, applying only to steps to save the life of the mother, might also seem to

---

[102] In *R. v. Bourne* [1939] 1 KB 687, [1938] 3 All ER 615, the jury was told that, if a doctor was entitled to an acquittal under proviso to s. 1(1) of the Infant Life (Preservation) Act 1929 (below), his action would not have been 'unlawful' within the meaning of ss. 58 and 59 of the 1861 Act.

have put doctors at continuing risk of prosecution in cases where the mother's life was not under immediate threat. However, in *R. v. Bourne*[103] the judge, Macnaghten J, instructed the jury that preserving the mother's life had to be given an extended meaning. As life depends on physical and mental health, an abortion performed to prevent severe harm to the mother's physical or mental health would be regarded as preserving her life.

This was a recognition of the woman's interests, but it did not go as far as women increasingly wanted in allowing them to control their bodies. It did not allow a way of avoiding the stigma attaching to unmarried mothers, nor of saving many families from the social and economic hardship to which having an unwanted child could lead. Often, those who could not face the prospect of a child still relied on illegal abortions. Deaths continued to occur, and back-street abortionists to flourish. As a result, increasing pressure developed during the 1950s and 1960s for an amendment which would permit lawful abortions in a wider range of cases. Governments felt that the moral issues which bore on abortion made it too hot a subject for them to handle, and it was left to the Liberal, Mr. David Steel MP (now Lord Steel), to pilot through Parliament a private member's bill, which received the royal assent as the Abortion Act 1967. This legalized abortions in cases where a pregnancy was terminated by a registered medical practitioner after two registered medical practitioners had formed the opinion, in good faith, either: (a) that continuing the pregnancy would give rise to a risk to the life of the pregnant woman, or of injury to the physical or mental health of the woman or any existing children of her family, greater than the risk if the pregnancy were terminated, taking account of the woman's actual or reasonably foreseeable environment; or (b) that there was a substantial risk that the child, if born, would have suffered from such physical or mental abnormalities as to be seriously handicapped.[104]

The freedom given to doctors to take account of environmental (in this context, social, housing, and economic) matters gave a discretion to allow something close to abortion on demand. Increasingly, interest groups concerned with the life of the foetus (which could not represent itself) claimed that abortions were being performed for the convenience of the mother rather than to prevent a real risk of harm. It was also said that many abortions were performed privately by doctors on women from abroad, who flew in from places where abortion is illegal (such as Ireland) purely to take advantage of the ready availability of the procedure in this country. Finally, although the Act did not affect the Infant Life (Preservation) Act 1929, so it would still be child destruction to perform an abortion where the foetus was 'viable'[105] (i.e. capable of being born alive, albeit only for one or two minutes[106]), it was asserted that viable foetuses were being aborted and, instead of being treated, were left lying around

[103] [1939] 1 KB 687, [1938] 3 All ER 615.
[104] Abortion Act 1967, s.1(1), (2) (now amended by Human Fertilisation and Embryology Act 1990, below).
[105] Abortion Act 1967, s.5(1).
[106] See *Report of the Select Committee on the Infant Life (Preservation) Bill*, HL No. 50 of 1987–88, para. 18; *Rance v. Mid-Downs Health Authority* [1991] 1 All ER 801 at 812 *per* Brooke J.

to die, and then disposed of without the birth being registered.[107] It was not clear when 'viability' began, but it was generally thought to be somewhere between the twenty-fourth and twenty-eighth weeks of pregnancy. Because of delays in obtaining test results under the National Health Service, a doctor could often not offer an abortion to a woman with a seriously abnormal foetus unless the abnormality was detected by the nineteenth week of pregnancy at latest.[108]

After several attempts to introduce amending legislation, the supporters of the life of the unborn foetus finally forced an amendment to the 1967 Act. As amended by section 37 of the Human Fertilisation and Embryology Act 1990, section 1 of the Abortion Act 1967 now provides that an abortion is legal (i.e. does not constitute an offence under section 58 or 59 of the Offences Against the Person Act 1861) if it is performed by a registered medical practitioner[109] and one of the following four conditions is met:

(a) two registered medical practitioners have formed the opinion, in good faith, that continued pregnancy would involve a risk of injury to the physical or mental health of the pregnant woman or any existing child of her family, greater than that involved in termination, and that the pregnancy has not passed the end of the twenty-fourth week; or

(b) a doctor has formed the view, in good faith, that continuing the pregnancy would involve a risk of *grave and permanent* injury to the physical or mental health of the woman (so that in such cases an emergency abortion is now legal without waiting for a second opinion); or

(c) a doctor has formed the view, in good faith, that continuing the pregnancy would involve a risk to the life of the woman (so that in such cases an emergency abortion is now legal without waiting for a second opinion); or

(d) two registered medical practitioners have formed the view, in good faith, that there is a *substantial* risk that the child, if born, would suffer from such physical or mental abnormalities as to be *severely* handicapped (no guidance being given on what is a severe handicap).

In some respects, this represents a tightening of the law, so that the 'environmental' health abortion under (a) is not available after the twenty-fourth week. This should reduce the number of abortions which lead to live births, and the upset and outrage they cause to nursing staff and pro-life groups. However, in other respects, under (b) and (c), the controls are relaxed. It is too early to say how the new regime will affect the availability of abortions, and the protection of the rights of foetuses as

---

[107] See J. K. Mason and R. A. McCall Smith, *Law and Medical Ethics*, 3rd edn. (London: Butterworths, 1991), 117–18.

[108] *Rance v. Mid-Downs Health Authority* [1991] 1 All ER 801 was one such case.

[109] Much of the actual procedure is performed by nurses. However, it has been held (in order to avoid practical resource and staffing problems which could have severely limited the availability of abortions) that 'performed' in s. 1 means 'initiated'. Once a registered medical practitioner has initiated the procedure and instructed nursing staff to continue it, it is treated as performed by (because it is under the authority and control of) the doctor: *Royal College of Nursing of the United Kingdom v. Department of Health and Social Security* [1981] AC 800, [1981] 1 All ER 545, HL.

against their mothers.[110] However, it is continuing evidence of the significance of the state's interest in foetal life in this country, an interest reaffirmed in the provisions, in the Human Fertilisation and Embryology Act 1990, for regulating research on embryos.[111]

It is instructive to compare this approach with those adopted in the USA and Canada. In Canada, where the right to life is constitutionally protected under section 7 of the Charter of Rights and Freedoms, it has been held that the foetus's interest in life does not become a constitutionally protected right until birth.[112] The courts recognize that the state has a legitimate interest in protecting the life of the unborn foetus, partly because of the general social concern to maintain moral standards, which include a proper regard for those potential members of the community who are unable to protect (or even appreciate) their own interests. Accordingly, it is constitutionally proper for the state to regulate abortion by legislation. However, to force a woman to carry a baby to term is an infringement of the mother's right, also under section 7 of the Charter, to security of the person. In assessing the constitutionality of legislation regulating the availability of abortion by reference to the woman's reasons for wanting one, the judges have to weigh the woman's right to security against the state's legitimate interest, according to the criteria set out in section 1 of the Charter: the limits on the woman's right to security of the person must be reasonable, prescribed by law, and demonstrably justified in a free and democratic society. Since the strength of the state's legitimate interest increases as the unborn child matures and comes closer to being a member of the community, the state is entitled to inquire more closely into a woman's reason for wanting an abortion in the later stages of pregnancy than the earlier ones.[113]

In the USA, too, there is a balancing act between the interest of the state in the welfare of the foetus and the rights of the mother, rather than between the rights of the mother and any supposed rights of the unborn child. The rights of women in the USA in this context are privacy rights, rather than rights to personal security, but privacy rights have constitutionally protected status in the USA and are capable of making it unconstitutional for the state to deprive a woman of the opportunity for an abortion.[114] In *Roe v. Wade* the US Supreme Court held, as in Canada, that the state's

---

[110] For discussion of the amendments, see A. Grubb, 'The New Law of Abortion: Clarification or Ambiguity?' [1991] *Crim. LR* 659–70.

[111] Mason and McCall Smith, *Medical Ethics*, 380–4. See further M. Brazier, 'Embryo's "Rights": Abortion and Research', in M. D. A. Freeman (ed.), *Medicine, Ethics and the Law* (London: Stevens & Sons, 1988), 9–22; S. Lee, 'Re-reading Warnock', in P. Byrne (ed.), *Rights and Wrongs in Medicine* (London: King's Fund, 1986), 37–52; J. Montgomery, 'Rights, Restraints and Pragmatism: The Human Fertilisation and Embryology Act 1990' (1991) 54 *MLR* 524–34.

[112] *Borowski v. A.-G. of Canada* (1987) 39 DLR (4th) 731, Saskatchewan CA, *Winnipeg Child and Family Services v. G.* (1997) 1 BHRC 1, SC of Canada.

[113] *Morgentaler, Smoling and Scott v. R.* (1988) 44 DLR (4th) 385, SC of Canada. The account in this paragraph combines the approaches of Dickson CJ and Wilson J. The case is discussed by M. L. McConnell, 'Abortion and Human Rights: an Important Canadian Decision' (1989) 38 *ICLQ* 905–13; G. Marshall, 'Liberty, Abortion and Judicial Review in Canada' [1988] *PL* 199–210; J. Cameron, 'Cross Cultural Reflections: Teaching the Charter to Americans' (1990) 28 *Osgoode Hall LJ* 613–40. The Supreme Court reaffirmed its view in *Tremblay v. Daigle* (1990) 62 DLR (4th) 634.

[114] *Roe v. Wade* 93 S. Ct. 705 (1973).

interest, and so its freedom to interfere, increased as the foetus came closer to full term. The Supreme Court adopted a fairly mechanistic approach to the stages by which the state's interest grows. In the first three months (trimester) of pregnancy, the interest was very weak, and any state interference with a woman's freedom to obtain an abortion was unconstitutional. In the second trimester, the state was entitled to intervene, but only to secure its interest in the health of the *mother*, not the child. In other words, in the second trimester it is permissible to restrict abortion where (for example) the risk to the mother from the abortion exceeds the risk of carrying the child to term.

Only in the third trimester, according to *Roe v. Wade*, was the state entitled to intervene in the interests of the foetus, because by then the foetus is likely to be 'viable', that is, capable of sustaining life independently of its mother if given suitable clinical aid. This is usually thought to happen sometime between the twenty-fourth and twenty-eighth weeks. However, as subsequent cases have made clear, the test for viability depends on the ability of clinicians to save the lives of premature babies. As clinical abilities increase the chances of survival of children born earlier in pregnancy, the moment of viability, and the time when the state is entitled to intervene, will also become earlier. The Supreme Court has therefore subsequently rejected the trimester rule, while maintaining much of the spirit of *Roe v. Wade*.[115] Even then, the limitations imposed by the state will be scrutinized to ensure that they comply with due process requirements. Limiting abortions to cases where there is a risk to the life of the mother was said in *Roe v. Wade* to be unconstitutionally vague (in European Convention terms, too uncertain to meet the 'according to law' criterion), although 'life and health' is acceptable.

This looks, on the face of it, far more liberal than the UK position under the Abortion Act 1967, which specifies the grounds on which abortions may be performed, in a way which would be unconstitutional in the USA (at least in relation to the first trimester). However, it is actually more complicated than that. In the classic liberal individualist tradition of the US Constitution, the American woman's right, to an abortion before the foetus is viable, is in reality a right that the state refrain from stopping her from procuring an abortion. This means that a woman who can afford to pay for an abortion cannot be prevented from having one (before viability). A woman who cannot afford to pay for it has no right that the state shall procure an abortion for her on demand. Where public money is put into a health programme, the state is entitled to specify the way in which the money is to be used.[116] It follows that, while the wealthy can more easily obtain a legal abortion in the USA than in the UK, the poor are likely to be at least as well off in the UK. Here, as elsewhere, we find a

---

[115] *Akron v. Akron Center for Reproductive Health*, 462 US 416 (1983), US Supreme Court, at 455–6 *per* O'Connor J; *Planned Parenthood of South-Eastern Pennsylvania v. Casey* 112 S. Ct. 2791, 120 L.Ed. 2d 674 (1992); *Stenberg v. Carhart* 147 L.Ed 2d 743 (2000). For further discussion, see I. Loveland, 'Affirming *Roe v. Wade? Planned Parenthood v. Casey*' [1993] *PL* 14–24; V. Laird, '*Planned Parenthood v. Casey*: the Role of Stare Decisis' (1994) 57 *MLR* 461–7; L. Heffernan, '*Stenberg v. Carhart*: A Divided US Supreme Court Debates Partial Birth Abortion' (2001) 64 *MLR* 618–27; S. Hannett, 'The Regulation of Abortion in the United States' [2001] *PL* 480–8; below, Ch. 9.

[116] *Harris v. McRae* 448 US 297 (1980); *Webster v. Reproductive Health Services* 492 US 490 (1989) noted by A. I. L. Campbell, 'The Constitution and Abortion' (1990) 53 *MLR* 238–48.

difference between rights which secure negative liberty—the right to be let alone—and discretions which may be exercised to secure positive benefits which make liberty more valuable to the right-holder (see Chapter 1).

In view of the importance which different legal systems attach to the moments when a foetus 'quickens', or becomes 'viable', or is born, in deciding how far the law should protect the interests of that foetus, it is tempting to suppose that foetuses are entitled to protection when they become people, and that there is some easy, mechanical way of identifying when that moment arrives. However, this is a misconception. The process of development is a continuous one. Each watershed is a perceived, rather than real, one: we attach significance to certain developing characteristics for our own purposes, but they have no greater significance in the development of the child than any other. Accordingly, certain methods of non-barrier, post-coital birth control (such as IUD, or the so-called 'morning after pill') raise legal and ethical questions concerning the sanctity of life as profound as does surgical abortion.[117] Like the choice of their birthdays as a time to give people presents, the choice of moments when foetuses should receive additional protection or consideration is conditioned by social or moral considerations. The question, 'When does a person/child/foetus acquire a right to life?' is, in reality, quite different from the question 'When does an ovum/sperm/foetus become a person?' One might want to say that the answer to each should identify the same moment as crucial, but it is not absurd, and it might help to avoid confusion, to consider it possible that the state may have a responsibility to protect entities before they become people (and some, like animals, which will never become people). Conversely, more controversially, and perhaps dangerously, it might be legitimate to suppose that some people towards whom the state has responsibilities may not acquire rights. It is at least as reasonable to say that a person is a being with a right to life as it is to say that the right to life is inherent in every person.

(iii) A right to be aborted?

Is it ever appropriate to hold that a doctor has a duty to a foetus (or the person who the foetus, if born alive, will be) to abort the foetus? Suppose, for example, a foetus is suffering from severe abnormalities which would make an abortion permissible, but the doctor fails to detect this, and the child is born severely disabled. The only circumstances in which loss to the child could be established would be if the child's life could be said to be worse than no life at all. If the child's life, even with its handicaps, is better than non-existence (assuming that such a judgment could ever be made), the child is a net beneficiary of the failure to abort it, and could not establish any loss which would sound in damages. Even if it could be shown that the child's life is worse than non-existence, the Law Commission considered that allowing an action in such circumstances would be contrary to public policy, because it would encourage doctors to perform abortions in marginal cases rather than allowing the pregnancy to proceed and risk liability in damages to the infant.[118] The Law Commission's recommendation

[117] I. Kennedy, *Treat Me Right: Essays in Medical Law and Ethics* (Oxford: Clarendon Press, 1991), ch. 3; Mason and McCall Smith, *Medical Ethics*, 99–100.

[118] Law Com. No. 60, *Report on Injuries to Unborn Children*, Cmnd. 5709 (1974).

may have been enacted in the Congenital Disabilities (Civil Liability) Act 1976, section 4(5), which provides that the Act 'replaces any law in force before its passing, whereby a person could be liable to a child in respect of disabilities with which it might be born'. However, this provision is not unambiguous, as it is not certain that 'any law in force' encompasses an action for wrongful life at common law, and it is possible that the previous common law is at least partly preserved. It has, not surprisingly, been argued that it does not entirely rule out actions for so-called wrongful life.[119]

At common law, independently of the Act, the answer seems to be that it is regarded as contrary to public policy to allow an action by a child for damages for failing to abort that child *in utero*. In *McKay v. Essex Area Health Authority*,[120] an action for negligence brought on behalf of a severely handicapped child, a health authority had failed to detect the fact that a foetus had been infected with the rubella virus. The mother was therefore not offered an abortion. The child was born severely handicapped, and sued for negligence resulting in wrongful life. The Court of Appeal rejected the child's claim, holding that it would be contrary to public policy to impose on doctors a duty to abort, in place of the discretion under the Abortion Act 1967. Such a duty would place a low value on the life of handicapped children, and would come close to giving a right to be born normal (whatever that may be) or not born at all.

It should be noted, however, that the child's lack of any right not to be born does not prevent the mother from recovering damages for her distress, pain, and suffering, and perhaps loss of income, resulting reasonably foreseeably from an unwanted pregnancy and childbirth after a failed sterilization.[121] It has been suggested that it would be reasonable to compensate the child, too, on the basis of a comparison between a handicapped existence and a normal existence.[122] This, however, seems to place responsibility on the doctor for the fact that the child was not born normal. In cases like *McKay*, nothing the doctor could do would result in a normal child being born. The absence of normality cannot, therefore, be laid at the doctor's door, and without doing gross violence to the law of tort the only basis for awarding damages against the doctor would be wrongful life, rather than wrongful deprivation of quality of life. It is therefore submitted that damages should be available only to pay for special medical care needed because of the child's condition, and that ordinary living expenses should be supported through the social security system if necessary. This seems to be the direction in which the law is moving.[122a]

[119] J. E. S. Fortin, 'Is the "Wrongful Life" Action Really Dead?' [1987] *JSWL* 306–13.

[120] [1982] QB 1166, [1982] 2 All ER 771, CA. The events giving rise to the action occurred in 1975 before the Congenital Disabilities (Civil Liability) Act 1976 became law.

[121] In *Emeh v. Kensington and Chelsea and Westminster Area Health Authority* [1985] QB 1012, [1984] 3 All ER 1044, CA, damages were awarded to the parents for the additional cost of bringing up a disabled child. In a Scottish case, *McFarlane v. Tayside Health Board* [1999] 3 WLR 1301, HL, it was held that the cost of bringing up a normal, healthy child was not recoverable, but it is unclear whether the reasoning applies equally to deny recovery of the additional costs of raising a disabled child. In Scotland, such costs have been held to be recoverable in delict: *Anderson v. Forth Valley Health Board*, 1998 SLT 588, Lord Nimmo Smith, Court of Session (Outer House).

[122] See Mason and McCall Smith, *Medical Ethics*, 144–9, and the works cited there.

[122a] See *Parkinson v. St James and Seacroft University Hospital NHS Trust* [2001] 3 WLR 376, CA.

(2) EUTHANASIA AND ASSISTED SUICIDE

If the right to life is to be a genuine right, rather than a duty to remain alive for as long as possible, people must be free to choose to die if they consider it worthwhile to do so.[123] In English law, suicide and attempted suicide are no longer crimes.[124] On the other hand, it is a criminal offence to aid, abet, counsel, or procure someone else's suicide or attempted suicide.[125] This applies to a doctor who helps someone to kill himself ('physician assisted suicide') as it does to other people. A person who commits this offence, for example by participating in a suicide pact and surviving while the other person dies, forfeits any rights to property which he might otherwise have acquired on the other person's death, subject to a court deciding to relieve him of the effects of forfeiture.[126] Active euthanasia (the killing of another person, rather than helping them to kill themselves) is murder in English law. The law thus prevents doctors or others from being put under an obligation to help someone to die, but also outlaws any assistance or encouragement to a person who is considering suicide. One can supply information about means of ending one's life, as long as it does not encourage people to make use of them, and one does not know that the person to whom the information is supplied is considering suicide.[127] As a result, only people who are physically and financially capable of making their own arrangements to end their lives can do so without imposing liability on others.

This represents one compromise between the values of sanctity of life and personal autonomy.[128] It allows people to make decisions about their own lives, but does not permit anyone to assist in the taking of life, even consensually. This is a position which is certainly compatible with, and may be required by, Article 2 of the ECHR. It is clear that no state is permitted to legalize mercy-killing to which the 'victim' does not consent, but does the 'victim's' consent have any force? It might be said that any purported waiver of the right to life should be ignored for legal purposes, because of the right's fundamental nature and on public policy grounds. As already noted, the Convention does not accord the right any more fundamental a status than any other right; indeed, as Sieghart[129] pointed out, the Convention does not grant a right to life but merely recognizes its existence and requires its protection.[130] Nevertheless, it seems clear that euthanasia requires an intentional taking of life, and does not fall within the exceptions in Article 2. The 'victim's' consent is therefore irrelevant, and permitting euthanasia would appear to breach Article 2.[130a]

[123] See D. Giesen, 'Dilemmas at Life's End: A Comparative Legal Perspective', in J. Keown (ed.), *Euthanasia Examined: Ethical, Clinical and Legal Perspectives* (Cambridge: Cambridge University Press, 1997), ch. 14.

[124] Suicide Act 1961, s. 1.

[125] Ibid., s. 2.

[126] *Dunbar v. Plant* [1998] Ch. 412, [1997] 4 All ER 289, CA, on the effects of s. 2 of the Suicide Act 1961 and s. 2 of the Forfeiture Act 1982 on the rights of the survivor of a suicide pact. The majority allowed relief from forfeiture on the facts of the case; Mummery LJ dissented on this point.

[127] *Attorney General v. Able* [1984] 1 All ER 277.

[128] See the essays in Keown (ed.), *Euthanasia Examined*, chs 1, 3, and 5 (by J. Harris) and 2, 4, and 6 (by J. Finnis).

[129] Sieghart, *International Law*, 130–1.

[130] By contrast, it is arguable that Art. 6(1) of the ICCPR, which provides: 'Every human being has the inherent right to life . . .', bestows a right rather than merely recognizing it.

[130a] The need to protect life outweighs rights to dignity and private life: *R. (Pretty) v. DPP*, n. 27 above.

On the other hand, it would not necessarily breach Article 6(1) of the International Covenant on Civil and Political Rights, which provides that the right to life 'shall be protected by law. No one shall be arbitrarily deprived of his life'. As the Covenant speaks of arbitrary rather than intentional deprivation, it is strongly arguable that euthanasia would not breach Article 6(1) if performed with the 'victim's' consent or at his request and after considering the 'victim's' medical circumstances and any other relevant circumstances. The Covenant is therefore less restrictive, and (according to taste) either more or less civilized, than the Convention.

The English approach to euthanasia and assisted suicide is the commonest, but not the only one. In 2000, the Netherlands became the first state in the world to make it legal for doctors to act in a manner intended to kill their patients on request. Previously, euthanasia had been a crime, but the Supreme Court of the Netherlands had held in 1984 that a doctor could in some circumstances invoke the defence of necessity. Thereafter, doctors had not been prosecuted if they could show that they had complied with guidelines issued by the Royal Dutch Medical Association (KNMG), designed to ensure that patients' lives were not ended without their informed request and consent.[131] There was evidence, however, that some doctors were following the guidelines less rigorously than others, leading to concerns that some patients were being killed without their consent.[132] None the less, the Dutch Parliament decided to remove criminal sanctions, allowing euthanasia with consent to become lawful for a wide spectrum of patients, including teenagers. The legalization of consensual euthanasia may well be incompatible with the ECHR. It seems to involve intentional deprivation of life contrary to Article 2(1). Even if the victim's consent were to be held to take the actions of doctors out of the scope of 'intentional deprivation' (and it is by no means clear that it should), the Netherlands would have to show that Dutch law offers sufficient protection to comply with the Convention. In view of the evidence that the medical guidelines were being ignored with impunity in some cases before the new legislation, there is a risk that any protection would be regarded as insufficient if it did not include effective investigation of suspicious deaths and reliable prosecution of doctors who break the rules.

In other parts of the world, there have been attempts to give people a right to the assistance of a physician in ending their lives, or to allow a physician to help (although not obliging him to do so) without incurring criminal liability. It has normally been conditional on the patient being terminally ill, being demonstrably capable of making an autonomous decision, and having voluntarily requested the ending of his life. There may also, as in Oregon's Death with Dignity Act of 1994 (which permitted physician-assisted suicide but not euthanasia), be requirements for counselling, a delay before implementing the decision, and second opinions.[133] However, there is a

---

[131] P. Admiraal, 'Voluntary Euthanasia: the Dutch Way', in S. A. M. McLean (ed.), *Death, Dying and the Law* (Aldershot: Dartmouth, 1996), ch. 7.

[132] J. Keown, 'Euthanasia in the Netherlands: Sliding down the Slippery Slope?', in J. Keown (ed.), *Euthanasia Examined: Ethical, Clinical and Legal Perspectives* (Cambridge: Cambridge University Press, 1997), ch. 16.

[133] C. K. Smith, 'Safeguards for Physician-assisted Suicide: The Oregon Death with Dignity Act', in S. A. M. McLean, *Death, Dying and the Law* (Aldershot: Dartmouth, 1996), ch. 5.

danger that such legislation might in practice offer inadequate safeguards for people who are depressed, or whose lives are undervalued by others because of disability, or whose quality of life could be significantly improved by effective analgesia and pallia-tive care. It has been suggested that euthanasia or physician-assisted suicide could be an alternative to other forms of treatment offering a chance of enhanced experience in the time remaining to a terminally ill patient.[134] As a result, both legislatures and courts have been cautious about permitting active euthanasia or physician-assisted suicide. The US Supreme Court has rejected claims that the Constitution gives a right to die and a concomitant right to the assistance of a physician in committing sui-cide.[135] In Oregon, the Death with Dignity Act was held to be unconstitutional in 1995, violating the equal protection clause of the Fourteenth Amendment to the Constitution of the USA.[136] In Canada, the Supreme Court held by a five–four major-ity that treating assisted suicide as a criminal offence did not violate the right to life of a woman who was too disabled to end her own life without arranging for somebody else to set up the mechanism by which she could kill herself.[137] In Australia, the Federal Parliament overrode legislation passed by the Northern Territory allowing voluntary euthanasia.[138] In the UK, a House of Lords Select Committee on Medical Ethics[139] rejected calls to legalize euthanasia and physician-assisted suicide, but recommended strong development of palliative care. The position in the UK seems unlikely to change in the near future.

(3) TREATMENT TO ALLOW THE PATIENT TO DIE WITH DIGNITY

Sometimes a patient's condition is such that there is no point in striving to prolong his or her life. Judging when that point has been reached will always present problems of two kinds. First, the criteria for pointlessness are not always clear. Secondly, it may not be certain who should make the decision. Both issues depend on the patient's circumstances. This section illustrates how such questions are resolved in English law.

(i) Babies

Once a child is born alive, it has as much right to life as other living people. What implications does this have for the treatment of children born with multiple handi-caps to the point where they are unlikely ever to function as members of the com-munity, and who fall ill? How far is a doctor required to go to preserve life? Are there

---

[134] R. G. Twycross, 'Where there is Hope, there is Life: A View from the Hospice', in J. Keown (ed.), *Euthanasia Examined: Ethical, Clinical and Legal Perspectives* (Cambridge: Cambridge University Press, 1997), ch. 15.

[135] *Washington v. Glucksberg* 117 S. Ct. 2258, US SC (1997); *Vacco, Attorney-General of New York v. Quill* 117 S. Ct. 2293, US SC (1997).

[136] *Lee v. State of Oregon*, cited in Smith, 'Safeguards', at 70.

[137] *Rodriguez v. Attorney General of British Columbia* [1993] 3 SCR 519, SC of Canada.

[138] The Euthanasia Laws Act 1997 (Cth.), Sch. 1 limited the legislative competence of the Legislative Assembly of the Northern Territory to exclude the power to legalize intentional killing, and declared that the Rights of the Terminally Ill Act 1995 (NT) was invalid.

[139] HL 21-I of 1993–94 (London: HMSO, 1994).

cases where a child's life is so miserable that it would, in truth, be better off dead? If so, what are the doctor's duties, and what control does the law exert? The criminal law has so far failed to provide answers to these questions.[140]

These matters have been considered by the Court of Appeal on a number of occasions,[141] usually where the parents have wanted doctors to withhold treatment and the local authority has made the child a ward of court. The decisions make it clear that neither the parents nor the doctors have the final say as to whether a handicapped baby should be allowed to die. The court must decide, and the wishes of parents and doctors must be given some weight, but the court is primarily concerned with the interests of the child. On this view, it will be assumed that continued life is in the child's best interest unless there is compelling evidence to the contrary.

The first case, *Re B. (A Minor) (Wardship: Medical Treatment)*,[142] concerned a child born with Down's syndrome and an intestinal blockage which would have been fatal if not operated on. The question was whether the court, exercising the wardship jurisdiction, should authorize the operation, overriding the wishes of the parents that the child should be permitted to die. On the evidence, it was clear that the baby would be severely mentally and physically handicapped if she survived, but that her faculties would not be completely destroyed. Beyond that, it was too early to offer any prognosis. The court contemplated the possibility that there might possibly be cases in which it was certain that the child's life would be bound to be so demonstrably intolerable and full of pain and suffering that the child ought to be allowed to die. However, in the instant case, if the operation succeeded, baby B 'may live the normal span of a mongoloid child with the handicaps and defects and life of a mongol child, and it is not for this court to say that life of that description ought to be extinguished'.[143] That being so, the court had no alternative but to authorize the local authority to direct that the operation take place. It follows that the doctors would have been neglecting their duty had they failed to operate (otherwise than on medical grounds).

This was, on the principle enunciated, a relatively easy case. The next case, *Re C. (A Minor) (Wardship: Medical Treatment)*,[144] was somewhat more difficult, because baby C was suffering from exceptionally severe hydrocephalus, and, despite anything that could be done for her, was dying. The local authority in whose care she was and the doctors invoked the wardship jurisdiction, asking the judges to decide the extent to which intrusive and unpleasant procedures should be applied to prolong life in the event that the child contracted infections or became impossible to feed through a syringe. The Court of Appeal accepted that the overriding consideration in such

[140] See M. J. Gunn and J. C. Smith, '*Arthur*'s Case and the Right to Life of a Down's Syndrome Child' [1985] Crim LR 705–15, which generated some correspondence in the Criminal LR; Kennedy, *Treat Me Right*, ch. 8.
[141] *Re B. (A Minor) (Wardship: Medical Treatment)* [1981] 1 WLR 1421, [1990] 3 All ER 927, CA; *Re C. (A Minor) (Wardship: Medical Treatment)* [1990] Fam. 26, [1989] 2 All ER 782, CA; *Re J. (A Minor) (Wardship: Medical Treatment)* [1991] Fam. 33, [1990] 3 All ER 930, CA.
[142] [1981] 1 WLR 1421 [1990] 3 All ER 927, CA.
[143] [1990] 3 All ER 927 at 929 *per* Templeman LJ.
[144] [1990] Fam. 26, [1989] 2 All ER 782, CA.

circumstances was that baby C's suffering should be relieved as far as possible, in the judgment of those caring for her, in order to allow her to die, as Ward J expressed it, 'peacefully and with the greatest dignity and the least of pain, suffering and distress'. However, the Court of Appeal made it clear that no court could authorize a doctor to take active steps to terminate a patient's life.

The approach in this case, recognizing the inevitability of the ward's more or less imminent death, was to set broad objectives for the medical staff, but to leave the method of achieving the objectives to their judgment and discretion. The courts have neither the skill nor the foresight to give more detailed instructions to doctors. However, when the child patient is not close to death but is chronically ill and severely handicapped, the judges have to decide when it will cease to be worth trying to save him. This was the situation in *Re J. (A Minor) (Wardship: Medical Treatment)*.[145] Baby J had suffered serious, irreversible brain damage at the time of his premature birth, and was epileptic. He had suffered two periods of collapse requiring ventilation, but if no further collapse occurred he was expected to survive for some years. He was likely to develop severe spastic quadriplegia and to be blind and deaf, and was unlikely ever to be able to speak or develop even limited intellectual abilities. However, he was likely to have a normal sensitivity to pain. Baby J was a ward of court, and the medical team (who in non-wardship cases would have made decisions in consultation with the parents) sought the court's authorization for a treatment plan. The question was whether J should be resuscitated and ventilated if he were to suffer another collapse. Scott Baker J authorized treatment in accordance with a doctor's opinion recommending sucking out his airway to prevent choking, and giving oxygen by face mask, but not to reventilate 'unless to do so seems appropriate to the doctors caring for him given the prevailing clinical situation'. In the event of J contracting a chest infection, the doctor recommended treatment with antibiotics and administering fluids, but no prolonged ventilation. The Official Solicitor, representing the child, appealed, arguing that the court should never withhold consent to treatment which could enable a child to survive a life-threatening condition, regardless of the general quality of the child's life. Alternatively, he argued that treatment should be withheld only in the circumstances outlined in *Re B.*, above, and that these had not been shown to obtain in J's case.

The Court of Appeal did not accept that the *dicta* in *Re B.* laid down a general test to be satisfied before withholding treatment. The judges distinguished between the absolute duty not to kill, and the much more circumscribed duty to keep alive. In deciding how to treat a patient, it was accepted that the interests of the child are the first and paramount consideration, and that there is a strong presumption in favour of taking all steps capable of preserving life, but the court also accepted that in exceptional circumstances it might be in a child's best interests not to have life prolonged. The court has to balance the benefit of prolonging life against the pain and suffering involved in the treatment, taking account of the likely quality and length of the life

---

[145] [1991] Fam. 33, [1990] 3 All ER 930, CA. Subsequently, the Court of Appeal has made it clear that judges cannot order doctors to treat patients in ways inconsistent with the doctors' clinical judgment: *Re J. (A Minor) (Wardship: Medical Treatment)* [1992] 4 All ER 614, CA.

which would follow the treatment. Lord Donaldson MR[146] approved the approach of Asch J in an American case, *Re Weberlist*:[147]

'There is a strident cry in America to terminate the lives of *other* people—deemed physically or mentally defective . . . Assuredly, one test of a civilization is its concern with the survival of the "unfittest", a reversal of Darwin's formulation . . . In this case, the court must decide what its ward would choose, if he were in a position to make a sound judgment.'

This had been applied in a Canadian case, *Re Superintendent of Family and Child Services and Dawson*, where McKenzie J had said:[148]

'The decision can only be made in the context of the disabled person viewing the worth-whileness or otherwise of his life in its own context as a disabled person—and in that context he would not compare his life with that of a person enjoying normal advantages. He would know nothing of a normal person's life having never experienced it.'

In *Re J.*, therefore, Lord Donaldson MR said that the decision-maker must:

'look at it from the assumed point of view of the patient. This gives effect, as it should, to the fact that even very severely handicapped people find a quality of life rewarding which to the unhandicapped may seem manifestly intolerable . . . But in the end there will be cases in which the answer must be that it is not in the interests of the child to subject it to treatment which will cause increased suffering and produce no commensurate benefit, giving the fullest possible weight to the child's, and mankind's, desire to survive.'[149]

Invasive medical procedures cause distress and can be hazardous, and Scott Baker J had been entitled to decide, on the evidence, that the distress was not justified by the unfavourable prognosis and the poor quality of life enjoyed by the patient.

The approach in *Re J. (A Minor) (Wardship: Medical Treatment)* is consistent with a non-paternalistic approach to the problem of the right to life, but is not entirely congruent with autonomy in the sense of maximizing opportunities to make choices, as there might be cases in which a child with some chance of achieving or recovering sufficient intellectual capacity to enable it to choose how it wanted to live might nevertheless be denied treatment on the ground that it would very probably choose to die.

The reasoning respects human life without treating it as an end in itself, worthy of fighting for in all circumstances. It has been developed by judges in cases concerning young babies, in the exercise of the court's wardship jurisdiction, but it is equally applicable to decisions by doctors in consultation with relatives concerning the treatment of adults who for some reason are temporarily or permanently unable to decide whether or not to consent to treatment. The desirability of attempting to resuscitate a heart attack victim, for example, must depend on the distress (if any) which the treatment would be likely to cause to the patient, the likelihood that the treatment would succeed, and the probable quality of life which

---

[146] [1990] 3 All ER 930 at 938.
[147] (1974) 360 NYS 2d 782 at 787.
[148] (1983) 145 DLR (3d) 610 at 620–1.
[149] [1990] 3 All ER 930 at 938.

the patient would enjoy afterwards, judged (so far as possible) from the patient's perspective.

However, one aspect of the reasoning in *Re J. (A Minor) (Wardship: Medical Treatment)* is questionable. It is impossible for a judge or doctor to get inside the mind of a child who, like baby J, is unlikely ever to develop any intellectual capacity. It is instructive to note that, in cases where life is not threatened, judges have adopted a very different approach. In *Re F. (Mental Patient: Sterilization)*[150] the House of Lords held that a court could declare that it would be in the best interests of an adult voluntary in-patient at a mental hospital to undergo a sterilization operation, and that it would not be unlawful for doctors to perform the operation despite the patient's incapacity to consent. The test applied to determine what was in the best interests of the patient was not whether the patient would have chosen to be treated if she had had the necessary capacity, but whether the proposed treatment would be accepted as appropriate by a responsible body of doctors skilled in that form of treatment. Why should this test not apply to decisions about administering potentially life-saving treatment?

The issues in the two cases were essentially similar. The main difference lies in the nature of the wardship jurisdiction which applies to minors only, and takes decision-making responsibilities out of the hands of parents and doctors. In *Re J. (A Minor) (Wardship: Medical Treatment)* treatment was *prima facie* lawful. Indeed, the doctors had a *prima facie* obligation to treat, because it would on the face of it be negligent for a doctor not to try to save a person who is in imminent danger of dying. The patient's presumptive right to life made it necessary to decide whether consent might be given to allowing death to occur. In *Re F.* the doctors favoured treatment, but the treatment would have been a battery in the absence of consent. The patient was incapable of giving consent, and the question was whether in the circumstances treatment could lawfully be administered. Yet the underlying issue was the same: on what basis should the court decide what is in the patient's best interests? In the former case, the Court of Appeal said that the court must decide, balancing the interests as they would be seen by a person in the ward's position. In the latter case, the House of Lords left the decision to a responsible body of medical opinion, with the criminal law and the law of tort providing a review process. (Lord Griffiths would have stipulated that the treatment would always be unlawful unless a court had declared it to be lawful, effectively shifting responsibility back from doctors to courts, but this was rejected by all the other Law Lords.) Perhaps the reason for willingness of the majority of the Law Lords to leave it to the doctors in *Re F.* was that English judges, unlike the European Convention on Human Rights, regard the right to life as more fundamental than, and requiring more extensive judicial oversight than, rights to other aspects of bodily integrity such as the right to procreate.

---

[150] [1990] 2 AC 1, *sub nom. F. v. West Berkshire Health Authority and another (Mental Health Act Commission intervening)* [1989] 2 All ER 545, HL.

(ii) Adults

The problem of a doctor's duties in respect of irretrievably injured patients is not, of course, limited to neonates. Those who suffer traumatic injury may be reduced to a state in which they are not dead (in the sense of brain-stem death now accepted for medical purposes) but are comatose and insensate, have no voluntary bodily functions, and have no hope of recovery. People in what is described as 'persistent vegetative state' (PVS) cannot swallow, and so are dependent on artificial feeding, usually through a nasogastric tube. They may continue to breathe unaided for years after it becomes clear that there is no hope of recovery, but are prone to infections and other secondary conditions which would end their lives unless treated. What are the duties of doctors towards such patients? In *Airedale NHS Trust v. Bland*,[151] in which the courts granted a declaration that it would not be unlawful to stop feeding a PVS patient and to withhold all treatment save that necessary to enable the patient to end his life with dignity and with the least possible suffering, their Lordships accepted that judges could grant declarations to guide doctors where the patient was incapable of giving or withholding consent to further care. The decision is discussed in the next section, but here we can note that it establishes that doctors have no duty to continue invasive care or treatment which confers no therapeutic benefit (in the sense of being likely to lead to an improvement in the patient's condition) and which would not be required by the professional ethics of a responsible body of medical opinion.

(4) WITHHOLDING OR CEASING TREATMENT

While it is criminal to do anything intending to hasten another person's death, there is no absolute legal duty on a doctor to try to save the life of a patient, for four reasons: (i) because treatment without consent is usually a tort and a crime; (ii) because of the doctrine of double effect; (iii) because in some cases the law considers that it is not in the interests of a patient to initiate or continue treatment; and (iv) because the judges recognize there are limits to their proper authority to oversee decisions about the best allocation of resources and treatment in the NHS. These will be considered in turn.

(i) The need for consent to treatment

The first is that any treatment is *prima facie* a trespass to the person, and if the patient is adult and competent to consent it will be unlawful without that consent. A doctor therefore acts lawfully—indeed, could not lawfully act otherwise—when he withholds treatment at the request of a patient who is likely or certain to die without treatment. Thus, a prisoner who is mentally competent to make decisions about his welfare is entitled to refuse food as part of a protest, and the prison authorities have no power to force-feed him against his wishes.[152] This has been called passive, as distinct from active, euthanasia.[153] To ensure that medical staff know of their wishes, some people

---

[151] [1993] AC 789; [1993] 1 All ER 821, HL.
[152] *Secretary of State for the Home Department v. Robb* [1995] Fam. 127, [1995] 1 All ER 677.
[153] See generally Mason and McCall Smith, *Medical Ethics*, ch. 15, especially at 321.

have made advance directives in writing (sometimes called 'living wills'), instructing medical staff to withhold treatment in specified circumstances, and making their wishes known to anyone who might be appointed as their representative in the event that they become incapable for any reason.[154] In such circumstances, the patient voluntarily accepts non-treatment while in a state to do so rationally. The British Medical Association and the General Medical Council regard it as good ethical practice for doctors to comply with advance directives.[155] As a matter of law, the directive will bind doctors as long as the person had the mental capacity to make a decision when he gave it, even if he suffers from severe mental illness at other times.[156] On the other hand, where the patient is suffering from a mental disorder which deprives him of the capacity to make such decisions at the time when he first articulates his refusal of life-preserving treatment, the refusal does not bind doctors.[157] This will be unaffected by the Human Rights Act 1998, since the state normally has a duty under Article 2 to protect the life of those in its care who are unable to make life-or-death decisions for themselves, whatever they think at the time.[158]

Where there is any doubt about the wishes of a patient, that patient should be treated, because the paternalism which decides for someone else when it is best to die is effectively denying them the opportunity to make the most of their lives as autonomous individuals.[159] For this reason, the practice of marking 'DNR', for 'Do Not Resuscitate', on the notes of hospital patients as a way of rationing resources rather than catering for the specific needs of the individual patient, is unethical and quite possibly unlawful. Furthermore, it is wrong in principle to put pressure on a patient to elect to die. In those states where voluntary passive euthanasia has been lawful, the ethical problems for patients, doctors, next of kin, and nursing staff are immense.[160] Where the patient is not mentally competent to confirm the choice to die at the time when the choice is about to be given effect, it will always be impossible to know whether the choice expressed earlier was truly voluntary, whether the consent was informed, and whether or not the patient would want to reconsider were he able to do so. In the Netherlands, as noted above, it seems that the procedural safeguards

[154] A form for an advance directive is printed in Mason and McCall Smith, *Medical Ethics*, at 450–1. See further S. Hornett, 'Advance Directives: a Legal and Ethical Analysis', in Keown (ed.), *Euthanasia Examined*, ch. 17.

[155] British Medical Association, *Advance Statements about Medical Treatment* (London: British Medical Journal Publishing Group, 2000); General Medical Council, *Seeking Patients' Consent: The Ethical Considerations* (London: General Medical Council, 1998), para. 22.

[156] *In re C. (Adult: Refusal of Treatment)* [1994] 1 WLR 290, [1994] 1 All ER 819. See R. Gordon and C. Barlow, 'Competence and the Right to Die' (1993) **143** *NLJ* 1719–20, para. 22.

[157] *B. v. Croydon Health Authority* [1995] Fam. 133, [1995] 1 All ER 683, CA; petition for leave to appeal dismissed [1995] 1 WLR 1640, HL.

[158] See, e.g. *Herczegfalvy v. Austria*, Eur. Ct. HR, Series A, No. 244, Judgment of 24 September 1992, 15 EHRR 432.

[159] See M. R. Flick, 'The Due Process of Dying' (1991) 79 *Calif. LR* 1121–67; Mason and McCall Smith, *Medical Ethics*, 319–25; M. Brazier, *Medicine, Patients and the Law*, 2nd edn. (Harmondsworth: Penguin, 1992), ch. 21.

[160] For a full and interesting discussion, see Kennedy, *Treat Me Right*, chs. 16 (on doctors' duties), 17 (on patients' requests not to receive further treatment), and 18 (on switching off life-support machines).

designed to protect people against involuntary euthanasia have been very hard to enforce and regularly flouted.[161]

(ii) Double effect

The doctrine of double effect allows the doctor to take steps which carry a substantial risk to life in order to treat, in good faith and with the patient's consent, some disease or symptom. This is essential, because virtually any treatment carries some risk to the patient. It is particularly relevant to the euthanasia issue in cases where the primary object (e.g. pain control in terminal cancer treatment) can only be achieved by administering drugs at a level which is likely to shorten life, but enhances the quality of life while it lasts. A trade-off between length of life and quality of life is permissible.[162] However, there is a risk to the doctor if the steps taken turn out not to command the approval of a body of respectable medical opinion, and the consent of the patient has not been obtained. In such circumstances, a charge of murder (or attempted murder if it not clear whether the patient was actually killed by the disease or the treatment) is possible.[163]

(iii) Limitations on the duty to treat

A doctor has no legal or ethical duty to administer treatment which, in the opinion of a responsible body of medical opinion, would not be in the best interests of the patient. This was established as a matter of law in *Airedale NHS Trust v. Bland*.[164] Anthony Bland had suffered catastrophic brain damage as a result of injuries sustained at the Hillsborough football ground tragedy in 1989. His brain cortex showed no sign of activity, and he appeared to have no awareness or capacity to communicate: he was in what is known as 'persistent vegetative state' with no prospect of improvement. He survived because of feeding through a naso-gastric tube. He had given no prior indication of his wishes with regard to continuation or cessation of life in such an event as occurred. In 1992, his doctors decided that continuing to feed him was serving no useful therapeutic purpose. They applied, with the support of his relations, for a declaration that it would not be unlawful to stop feeding a PVS patient and to withhold all treatment save that necessary to enable the patient to end his life with dignity and with the least possible suffering.

---

[161] See J. Keown, 'The Law and Practice of Euthanasia in the Netherlands' (1992) **108** *LQR* 51–78; J. Keown, 'Euthanasia in the Netherlands: Sliding down the Slippery Slope?', in J. Keown (ed.), *Euthanasia Examined*, ch. 16; S. Ost, 'Conceptions of the Euthanasia Phenomenon: A Comparative Discussion of the Law, Individual Rights and Morality within Three Jurisdictions' (2000) 5 *J. of Civil Liberties* 155–92 (on the approaches in the UK, Holland, and the Northern Territory of Australia).

[162] J. Glover, *Causing Death and Saving Lives* (Harmondsworth: Penguin, 1977). The House of Lords Select Committee on Medical Ethics, HL 21-I of 1993–94, recommended that the doctrine of double effect should remain as a defence to a charge of homicide against a doctor arising out of the treatment of a terminally ill patient.

[163] The case of Dr. Leonard Arthur, acquitted on a charge of attempted murder, was one such. Another is *R. v. Cox* (1992) 12 BMLR 38, in which a consultant was convicted on a charge of attempted murder in connection with the death of a patient suffering from a non-terminal disease (chronic arthritis) following an injection of a toxic substance of no therapeutic value.

[164] [1993] 2 WLR 316; [1993] 1 All ER 821, HL.

The House of Lords upheld the decision of Sir Stephen Brown P and the Court of Appeal to grant the declarations.[165] Searching for criteria to apply, their Lordships rejected the American 'substituted judgment' test (which Lord Donaldson had favoured in respect of minors in Re J.) under which the court attempts to decide what the patient would have done if capable of forming a rational view. Instead, where the patient is wholly unconscious, his position is irretrievable, and he has given no advance directive, the court must decide whether further treatment is objectively in the patient's best interests, taking account of the benefit (if any) to the patient, his awareness of it, the effect of treatment on his dignity, and any relevant code of medical ethics.

In the House of Lords, Lord Keith of Kinkel decided that the doctor had no duty to continue care or treatment from which the patient obtained no benefit, at least where the patient was indifferent to it.[166] Lord Goff considered that a doctor owed no duty to treat or care for a person in a way which conferred no therapeutic benefit where the patient was wholly unconscious and there was no prospect of any improvement in his condition, particularly where the care and treatment was invasive and inflicted indignity on the patient. The test was objective, and the former personality of the patient was irrelevant to the determination of his best interests.[167] For this purpose, artificial feeding was an aspect of medical care and treatment. The removal of the nasogastric tube would not constitute murder or manslaughter any more than would turning of a life-support machine when all prospect of recovery had gone. Both were, in reality, omissions to act rather than acts, and homicide liability for omissions arises only where there is a duty to act. As there is no duty to administer treatment or care from which the patient does not, objectively, benefit, withdrawing treatment was lawful. Lord Lowry agreed,[168] and Lord Browne-Wilkinson's speech was to the same effect as Lord Keith's, concentrating on the benefit accruing to the patient from treatment.[169]

Lord Mustill was clearly troubled. Like his brethren, he refused to take account of the wider social benefit of treating or not treating Anthony Bland, although he thought that the nettle of limited resources would ultimately have to be grasped by Parliament.[170] He reluctantly accepted that the criminal law of murder distinguished between acts and omissions, despite considering that 'even if there is any sense in the distinction the current state of the law is unsatisfactory both morally and intellectually',[171] and recognizing 'that this chain of reasoning makes an unpromising start by transferring the morally and intellectually dubious distinction between acts and omissions into a context where the ethical foundations of the law are already open to question'.[172] Both Lord Browne-Wilkinson and Lord Mustill thought that it might appear almost irrational to allow a person to starve slowly to death, but to treat as

---

[165] The moral and ethical problems provoked extensive discussion. See, e.g. J. M. Finnis, 'Bland: Crossing the Rubicon?' (1993) 109 LQR 329–47; J. Keown, 'Restoring Moral and Intellectual Shape to the Law after Bland' (1997) 113 LQR 481–505.

[166] [1993] 1 All ER at 860–1.

[167] Ibid. at 870–2.   [168] Ibid. at 875.

[169] Ibid. at 883–4.   [170] Ibid. at 893.

[171] Ibid. at 891.   [172] Ibid. at 895.

murder a lethal injection producing quick and relatively humane death.[173] But so far, Parliament has not acted to resolve these anomalies, and the intellectually and morally flawed common law approach continues to govern.

The courts regarded *Bland* as a fairly clear case. However, in more marginal cases the prognosis is less certain, and there may be an emergency, such as a dislodged gastrostomy tube, requiring an urgent decision. It may then be difficult to decide what is in the patient's best interests. This is complicated by the promulgation of various different sets of guidelines, from the British Medical Association, the Royal College of Physicians, and a 1996 report by an International Working Party on Persistent Vegetative State, issued by Royal Hospital for Neuro-Disability, Putney. There is a need for these to be harmonized in the light of experience, particularly as subsequent cases have progressively pushed back the boundaries of the jurisdiction.[174] For example, in one case the Court of Appeal granted a declaration in a case where there was no independent medical evidence, and accepted, *obiter*, that there might be emergency situations in which doctors might dispense with an application to the courts before making a decision to cease treatment.[175] In *Bland*, most of their Lordships favoured the *Bolam* test, as applied in *Re F.*: the doctors must reach a view which is supported by a responsible and competent body of relevant medical opinion, preferably with guidance from the British Medical Association. However, Lord Mustill expressed reservations about applying such a test to matters which were ethical rather than medical, and which involved the criminal law of murder and manslaughter rather than civil liability for negligence.[176] Lord Mustill's doubts are compelling. There is little reason to grant a power to the medical professions to authorize the ending of attempts to preserve life on the basis of their own professional standards. Nevertheless, that is what commonly happens, in effect, in accident and emergency rooms at present, and it has largely been sanctioned by courts in the cases discussed in this section. The danger is that decisions will be taken by people who are not publicly accountable for them, while responsibility is passed back and forth between the courts and the medical professions. Their Lordships were surely correct to express the view that the matter should be urgently examined by Parliament: as Lord Mustill said, 'These are problems properly decided by the citizens, through their elected representatives, not by the courts. . . . The whole matter cries out for exploration in depth by Parliament and then for the establishment by legislation not only of a new set of ethically and intellectually consistent rules, distinct from the general criminal law, but also of a sound procedural framework within which the rules can be applied to individual cases'.[177] In the mean time, the right to life appears to operate in these circumstances only if the person concerned is capable of benefiting from it.

---

[173] Ibid. at 884 and 896 respectively. The slow death of a patient by dehydration and starvation takes a heavy emotional toll on families: see B. Jennett, 'Managing Patients in a Persistent Vegetative State since *Airedale NHS Trust v. Bland*', in McLean (ed.), *Death, Dying and the Law*, ch. 2.

[174] *NHS Trust A. v. H., The Times*, 17 May 2001, Dame Elizabeth Butler-Sloss P. See M. Hinchcliffe, 'Vegetative State Patients' (1996) **146** *NLJ* 1579–85; J. Keown, 'Beyond *Bland*: a Critique of the BMA Guidance on Witholding and Withdrawing Treatment' (2000) 20 *LS* 66–84.

[175] *Frenchay Healthcare National Health Service Trust v. S.* [1994] 1 WLR 601, [1994] 2 All ER 403, CA.

[176] [1993] 1 All ER at 895.

[177] [1993] 1 All ER at 889.

Despite the drawbacks of *Bland*, a similar approach has been followed in other jurisdictions. In Scotland, the Court of Session has held that judges must give effect to the best interests of the patient. If he or she derives no benefit from a form of treatment, it does not serve his or her best interests. The court must concentrate on whether a particular treatment confers a benefit, not on whether continued life is a benefit.[178] In New Zealand, the decision to turn off a life support machine has been approached in the same way.[179] In the USA, a somewhat mixed picture emerges. Some states insist on a 'substituted judgment' test, in which a court tries to decide whether the patient would want treatment to be withdrawn, on the basis of what is known about the patient's personality and outlook on life. In other states, courts seek to make an objective assessment as to whether the treatment is in the patient's best interests, as in the UK. As a matter of federal constitutional law, the Supreme Court held in *Cruzan v. Director, Missouri Department of Health*[180] that a state lawfully can require that information about the patient's likely wishes should be made available before permission is given to withdraw life-sustaining treatment, but states are not constitutionally required to do so. The (objective) best interests of the patient can be taken into account, and (unlike the position in the UK) the interests of the family are not necessarily irrelevant to the decision. Thus a substituted judgment test can be applied in New York State[181] and New Jersey,[182] while a New York statute, requiring evidence of the actual wishes of the patient before treatment can be withdrawn, has been upheld.[183] On the other hand, an objective best interests test has been accepted in California[184] and Minnesota.[185]

In Ireland, in *Ward of Court*[186] at first instance Lynch J attempted to merge the best interests test with the substituted judgment test by treating the wishes of the patient as part of the calculation of best interests. As the patient there was a young child, this led to a very complex assessment in which it was assumed that the child would have chosen what a good, loving parent would have wanted for the child. This is obviously highly artificial, and on appeal the Supreme Court took a more straightforward 'best interests' approach. However, this was not easy to reconcile with the constitutional right to life and to legal protection under Article 40.3.1 of the Constitution. Hamilton CJ thought that the right to life was not absolute: it could be waived in exceptional circumstances. By contrast, Denham J decided that the right to life was absolute, but the courts had a duty to protect it only 'as far as practicable', as the Article put it. The court was therefore allowed to authorize cessation of treatment.[187]

---

[178] *Law Hospital NHS Trust v. Lord Advocate*, 1996 SLT 848; *Law Hospital NHS Trust v. Lord Advocate (No. 2)*, 1996 SLT 869.

[179] *Auckland Area Health Board v. Attorney General* [1993] 1 NZLR 235, Thomas J.

[180] (1990) 497 US 261, US SC.

[181] *In re Eichner* 426 NYS 2d 517 (1980).

[182] *In re Quinlan* 355 A 2d 647 (1976).

[183] *In re Storar* 52 NY 2d 263, 531 NE 2d 607 (1988).

[184] *In re Conservatorship of Drabnick* 109 S. Ct. 399, US SC (1988).

[185] *In re Torres* 357 NW 2d 332 (1984).

[186] [1995] 2 ILRM 401.

[187] P. Hanafin, *Death, Dying and the Law in Ireland* (Cork: Cork University Press, 1997) offers a very thorough and persuasive analysis of the decision and the related field of law and ethics.

It might be thought that the incorporation in English law of Article 2 of the European Convention on Human Rights might affect the position. It is arguable that ceasing to administer essential, life-preserving care to a person who is incapable of helping himself amounts to intentional deprivation of life, which is outlawed by Article 2. If it is, the cessation of care cannot be brought within any of the justifications available under the Article. But the European Commission of Human Rights held that states are not compelled to criminalize the withholding of treatment which leads to death.[188] This seems to adopt the distinction between acts and omissions which underpinned the decision in *Bland*, despite the criticisms which Lord Mustill levelled at it: a person is not treated, for the purposes of Article 2, as being intentionally deprived of life by an omission, as long as there are adequate legal safeguards in place. In the first cases of this kind to be brought before an English court after the Human Rights Act 1998 came into force,[189] Dame Elizabeth Butler-Sloss P accordingly held that it did not violate an insensate patient's Article 2 rights to withdraw or withhold life-preserving care where in the circumstances a court was satisfied that the medical team had no legal obligation to provide or continue it, following *Bland*. Her Ladyship further held that the long-drawn-out process of dying would not violate the patient's right to be free of inhuman or degrading treatment under Article 3, because he would not be aware of what was happening to him. The same applied to his right to respect for his family life (although it would seem to be possible that the rights of other members of the family under Article 8 might be relevant, although not decisive).

(iv) Limits to proper judicial oversight of the allocation of resources and treatment in the NHS

The *Bland* case involved a very specific problem, but the courts are more generally reluctant to allow patients to judicialize questions of allocation of resources for treatment, or allocation of particular treatments to individual patients. The UK has a publicly-funded National Health Service. In England and Wales, section 1 of the National Health Service Act 1977 places a duty on the Secretary of State for Health 'to continue the promotion of a comprehensive health service designed to secure improvement—(a) in the physical and mental health of the people of those countries, and (b) in the prevention, diagnosis and treatment of illness'. To this end, the Secretary of State is under a duty to provide such health services as he thinks necessary in order to meet all reasonable requirements.[190] But the NHS is under pressure from a number of directions.[191] Resources for the service have grown less fast than the costs of treatment, and funding arrangements make the provision of services subject to accounting controls. Furthermore, performance indicators for hospitals, with pub-

---

[188] *Widner v. Switzerland*, App. No. 9348/91, 32 D. & R. 190 (1993), Eur. Commn. HR.
[189] *NHS Trust A. v. M.; NHS Trust B. v. H.* [2001] Fam. 348; A. Maclean, 'Crossing the Rubicon on the Human Rights Ferry' (2001) 64 *MLR* 775–94.
[190] National Health Service Act 1977, s. 3.
[191] J. K. Mason and R. A. McCall Smith, *Law and Medical Ethics*, 3rd edn. (London: Butterworths, 1991), 253–61; D. O'Sullivan, 'The Allocation of Scarce Resources and the Right to Life under the European Convention on Human Rights' [1998] *PL* 389–95; E. Haggett, *The Human Rights Act 1998 and Access to NHS Treatments and Services: A Practical Guide* (London: The Constitution Unit, UCL, 2001).

lished league tables, direct attention to the efficiency of a hospital's work rather than to the clinical quality of the service provided. The rights of patients which the government recognizes are related to efficiency, comfort, and speed: the Patient's Charter sets out goals on waiting lists, timeliness of appointments, and so on, because these are more easily measurable and less costly than other standards which might be measured.

Alongside the public sector, there operates a private health care sector: private health insurance schemes, private general practitioners, consultants doing paying client work, hospitals devoted wholly or mainly to private patients, and private services offered in health service hospitals. The gap between the private and public health care systems is being narrowed by the institution of self-governing hospital trusts, funding through public–private partnerships, and the changed role of health authorities from providers of health care to purchasers of health care from increasingly independent providers.

This tends to substitute the market for the political process as the primary mediator of tensions between the desirability of providing treatments of different types and the economics of health care. Where people are unable to obtain necessary treatment for themselves or members of their families, they may resort to litigation in an attempt to force the health authority to provide it by law, or as a means of raising the public profile of their grievance in order to bring pressure to bear on the authority to capitulate. Where this happens, the courts are generally unwilling to force authorities to expend money and other resources in ways different from those indicated by the authorities' professional or political judgment.

The right to receive treatment, or any particular standard of health service provision, is therefore not a legally enforceable right under English or Scottish law. Health service managers have certain duties under the legislation which established the National Health Service, including a duty on health authorities to balance their budgets,[192] but such provisions do not confer legally enforceable rights on patients. As discussed above, in relation to the right to life, the provision of public service health care is at present a matter of considerable political controversy. Although this has not always been the case (until the mid-1980s politicians and managers regarded a commitment to continuously raising the range and standard of provision as being politically non-contentious), spiralling costs have produced serious disagreements as to the ways in which health care should be distributed, administered, and (where necessary) rationed.[193] This has affected the balance between health care in the community—including matters of health education and sanitation—and the treatment of individuals for disease.

Health care resource decisions are of a type which is sometimes called 'polycentric': that is, they involve a number of different interests, which compete and have to be weighed against each other. Because of the adversarial nature of legal procedure, which is based on the assumption that a single plaintiff will normally face a single

---

[192] National Health Service Act 1977, s. 97A, as inserted by Health Services Act 1980, s. 6.

[193] C. Newdick, *Who Should We Treat? Law, Patients and Resources in the NHS* (Oxford: Clarendon Press, 1995), chs 1 and 2.

defendant, it would be difficult to ensure that all these interests were adequately represented before the court. As a result, judges have understandably taken the view that it would be inappropriate to grant remedies for failure to provide particular services or therapies, as this would in effect put the courts in the position of specifying to health providers and managers, health authorities, and indirectly central government, what services should be provided for whom, where they should be based, and how much money should be made available for them.[194] There would be a risk that the courts would have to take over policy making for the health service. Courts in the UK lack developed public interest litigation processes, or even Brandeis brief procedures, which would enable them to hear a wide range of parties on issues of social and medical policy, so the exercise would be doomed to ignominious failure.

It is therefore unsurprising that an attempt to use judicial review to compel the Secretary of State to implement a plan for additional orthopaedic hospital buildings in Birmingham, in order to reduce surgical waiting times and enable people to be treated more quickly, failed in the light of financial constraints. Although the Court of Appeal left open the possibility of judicial review on the ground of irrationality in the *Padfield* sense (that the decision is so unreasonable that no reasonable decision-maker, properly understanding the facts and the law, could have taken it),[195] unreasonableness as a ground of judicial review is notoriously difficult to establish.

Similarly, attempts to compel health authorities to provide treatment denied on the basis of shortage of resources are almost always doomed to failure. In *R. v. Secretary of State for Health, ex parte Walker*,[196] a baby in need of heart surgery had had his operation postponed five times because of a shortage of pediatric intensive care nurses. There was no immediate urgency in the case, and Macpherson J and the Court of Appeal refused to second guess the health authority's allocation of resources. Even where there has been greater urgency for the individual patient, courts have been unwilling to intervene,[197] although the publicity may elicit a change of policy on the part of the health authority or doctors concerned.[198] In *R. v. Cambridge Health Authority, ex parte B.*,[199] the health authority decided that it would not be useful to fund a new and experimental treatment for the applicant, a child suffering from leukaemia who would die without treatment. The authority was influenced by doctors' opinions about the relatively low chance of a successful outcome from the treatment, which was very expensive. At first instance, Laws J quashed the decision, holding that the authority had given insufficient weight to the child's right to life. The Court of Appeal reversed his judgment. The authority had taken account of the right to life, alongside other considerations. They had balanced them in a way

---

[194] See Newdick, *Who Should We Treat?*, 119–37.

[195] *R. v. Secretary of State for Social Services, ex parte Hincks* (1979) 123 Sol Jo 436, Wien J, affirmed (1980) 1 BMLR 93, CA.

[196] (1987) 3 BMLR 32, CA.

[197] *R. v. Central Birmingham Health Authority, ex parte Collier*, 6 January 1988, unreported, CA. The patient in this case was later operated on, but died soon afterwards.

[198] See Mason and McCall Smith, *Law and Medical Ethics*, 260–1.

[199] [1995] 1 WLR 898, [1995] 2 All ER 129, CA.

which could not be said to be wholly unreasonable, so the court had no power to interfere.

These cases all predated the Human Rights Act 1998. It is likely that health authorities and the courts would now have to give greater attention to the right to life in cases where the applicant's life would be immediately threatened by a failure to provide treatment. A health authority, as a public authority within the meaning of section 6 of the 1998 Act, has a duty to act compatibly with Convention rights, including the right to life under Article 2 of the ECHR, when it is exercising a discretion. However, this will probably make little practical difference to the outcome in individual cases. The positive obligations of the state under Article 2 are limited, because one person's right to protection for his life has to be balanced against other people's similar rights. There must be a rational decision-making procedure, which must give appropriate weight to the right to life, but this does not require the authority to give absolute priority to one patient's life in making decisions about allocating resources.

Courts have always been reluctant to review the decisions of health authorities and doctors as to the relative priority to be given to various treatments, and how to allocate places on NHS programmes of (for example) renal dialysis treatment for patients suffering from kidney failure, intensive care cots for premature babies in need of specialized surgery and nursing, or *in vitro* fertilization facilities for couples wanting children. All these engage Convention rights—the right to life under Article 2, the right to respect for private and family life under Article 8, or the right to found a family under Article 12—but the rights are far from absolute. While they must be taken properly into account in the decision-making process, the resulting allocation of resources will rarely be very different. As long as the rights have been duly considered, courts will be unlikely to intervene.

Their approach in the past was markedly non-interventionist. In *R. v. Ethical Committee of St Mary's Hospital (Manchester), ex parte H.*,[200] Schiemann J refused judicial review of a decision by a hospital ethical committee and a consultant of the applicant, who wished to have children but was infertile. She had previous convictions which had led the local Social Services department to refuse her application to become a foster parent or to adopt a child. The Ethical Committee had a policy of excluding from the IVF programme women who were unacceptable as foster or adoptive parents. This was held not to be an unreasonable policy. However, Schiemann J said:

'if the committee had advised, for instance, that the IVF unit should in principle refuse all such treatment to anyone who was a Jew or coloured then I think the courts might well grant a declaration that such a policy was illegal . . . '[201]

Such matters are seen as calling for clinical, managerial, and political judgment in roughly equal measure, and such matters are not seen as being justiciable. This means that NHS patients cannot normally obtain orders that particular treatment

---

[200] [1988] 1 FLR 512, [1987] NLJ Rep 1038, DC.
[201] [1987] NLJ Rep at 1039. For a similar approach under S. Africa's 1996 Constitution, see *Soobramooney v. Minister of Health, Kwa-Zulu Natal*, 1998 (1) SA 765, CC.

or services be provided. On the other hand, a decision not to fund a type of treatment must be capable of being supported by sound reasons. If the reasons which a health authority offers fail to support the decision to refuse funding, the decision is amenable to judicial review.[202] Furthermore, public law has developed to a point at which a patient may be able to challenge a decision not to provide treatment by relying on the doctrine of legitimate expectation, if there has been an unequivocal representation that the treatment would be available, the representation was within the powers of the person making it, and the court considers that it would be unfair to the representee to allow the authority to renege on the undertaking, taking account of competing public interests.[203] An expectation might now be considered to be more legitimate, and more weighty in comparison with competing public-interest considerations, when it serves to protect a Convention right than when it does not.

Where patients are still unable to obtain an order that care be provided, it might be possible to obtain compensation for failure to provide treatment. So far, no case has decided whether a person whose treatment is delayed or denied by the NHS by reason of lack of resources can recover damages for breach of statutory duty. However, for the reasons outlined above, it is likely that courts would regard resource issues as non-justiciable, and would therefore decide that it would be wrong to interpret the statute as conferring rights on patients.

Patients' rights to compensation for non-treatment are limited to those at common law to recover damages for negligence. If resources to treat a patient are available but medical staff fail to treat a patient in circumstances in which no responsible body of medical opinion would regard that failure as medically appropriate, damages will be available. However, where the necessary resources are not available the plaintiff is unlikely to succeed in an action against the health authority for negligence in failing to provide the resources. In the light of recent decisions of the House of Lords on the scope of the duty of care owed by public authorities, it seems likely that the relationship between a health authority (a fortiori a central government department) and a particular patient or potential patient is insufficiently proximate to give rise to a duty to provide resources for that patient. In the field of housing, decisions relating to the allocation of the resources of a public agency between competing claims are regarded as essentially political and non-justiciable in the absence of an express statutory requirement to the contrary.[204] The same is probably true of decisions concerning the funding of different sorts of treatment or care. Any duty owed by planners and decision-makers would seem to lie in the field of public law, and is satisfied if the decision is intra vires, is reached in good faith taking account of relevant considerations, and is not wholly unreasonable. This is consistent with the nature of rights to health care: they are essentially social rather than individual rights, given effect

---

[202] R. v. North West Lancashire Health Authority, ex parte A. [2000] 1 WLR 977, CA.

[203] R. v. North and East Devon Health Authority, ex parte Coughlan [2000] 2 WLR 622, CA; M. Elliott, 'Legitimate Expectation: the Substantive Dimension' [2000] CLJ 421–5; P. Craig and S. Schonberg, 'Substantive Legitimate Expectation after Coughlan' [2000] PL 684–701.

[204] R. v. Hillingdon LBC, ex parte Puhlhofer [1986] AC 484, [1986] 1 All ER 467, HL. The effect of the decision in the housing field was later reversed by the Housing and Planning Act 1986, s. 14.

through governmental action which, domestically as in inter-national law, properly depends on economic and political judgment.

(5) SEPARATING CONJOINED TWINS

In most cases, courts facing a decision about whether or not to allow someone's life to be ended have been able to focus on the rights and interests of a single individual, and the duties of carers towards that individual. There are different formulae for deciding what those rights, interests, and duties are. For example, concentrating on the patient's wishes as revealed at the time or by an advance directive safeguards autonomy. Attempting to deduce what the individual would have decided had he been in a position to express a view about his own treatment (the 'substituted judgment' approach) ensures that the value of autonomy is given weight within a necessarily imperfect decision-making process, on the basis of what is known about the individual's general attitudes, personality, and history. Objectively assessing the individual's best interests tends to put the carers' assessment and obligations at the centre of the picture. But courts have been careful to try not to balance anyone else's rights against the individual's right to life, or *a fortiori* to balance the right to life or individual's best interests against social interests in the efficient use of resources for a socially approved purpose (although the previous section might have suggested to the reader that the pressure for a legitimate way of making decisions about allocation of scarce resources forms an important part of the background to such decisions).

In rare cases, however, a court has to choose to give the life of A priority over the life of B. Some of these cases are relatively straightforward ethically. A self-defence exception to liability for homicide evokes few moral scruples, even if people may differ as to whether or not a particular response to a threat should be regarded as falling within the exception. Other cases are agonisingly difficult. The defence of necessity is difficult, because one's moral and legal obligations when faced with alternative courses of action, each of which is likely to lead to the loss of some lives (perhaps including one's own) will always be controversial. The discussion can be conducted in terms of moral obligations, because the person making the choice will be a moral actor with capacity to choose. Yet one cannot satisfactorily discuss the obligations of the chooser without taking account of the rights of the people who are being placed in the lists of those who are to live or die.

The issue presents itself to courts in its most excruciatingly intractable form when judges are asked to decide, not whether someone in the past has made the right decision (or at any rate an acceptable one), but whether the judges themselves should authorize one of a number of courses of action, any of which will inevitably lead to the premature death of at least one person. The *Bland* case was of this kind, but the judges did not have to decide whether A should die so that B can live. Some abortion decisions are of this type, but judges can relieve their consciences (convincingly or not) by giving lesser moral standing to unborn children than to those who have been born. What is a court to do when asked to choose between the lives of two people, neither of whom has the capacity to express a view, who cannot both survive, but one of whom is slowly but surely causing the death of the other without any fault on the part of either?

This was essentially the position facing the courts in *Re A. (Children)*[205] in England in 2000. Conjoined ('Siamese') twins were born joined from the umbilicus to the sacrum. The lower ends of their spines were fused, and their spinal cords were joined. Each twin had her own vital organs, although they shared a bladder. One twin, Jodie, was alert, healthy, and capable of feeding. The other, Mary, had no functioning lung tissue, and so was unable to breathe for herself. She had a malformed heart, and a very severely abnormal and poorly developed brain. She was surviving only because Jodie's aorta, the major blood vessel carrying oxygenated blood from the heart, fed into Mary's aorta, while the venous return ran from Mary to Jodie. This allowed Jodie's heart and lungs to maintain Mary's life. However, the task was imposing an excessive burden on Jodie's metabolism, particularly as Mary was growing faster than Jodie. If the twins were not separated, there was a very high risk that the pressure of maintaining Mary would cause Jodie's metabolism to collapse, inevitably killing both twins, probably within three to six months, although estimates of life expectancy were admittedly uncertain. In the meantime, Mary would never develop normal mental capacity, would endure developmental delay and learning difficulties, and might well suffer seizures and epileptic fits. Doctors believed that it would be possible to separate them surgically, with a small risk of death to Jodie (estimates varied between 1 per cent and 6 per cent), but Mary would inevitably die at the point when their aortas were divided, cutting off her blood supply. The operation could not realistically be conducted without invading Mary's body space and physical integrity. If the twins were successfully separated, the survivor, Jodie, would have the opportunity of long-term good-quality life, although with a risk of some continuing abnormalities.

The doctors took the view that it would be best to separate the twins, giving Jodie the best chance of survival and a more or less normal life, but leading inevitably to Mary's death. The twins' parents, however, committed Roman Catholics, opposed the operation, believing that God's will should be done without interference. In this view, they had support from the Roman Catholic church. The Roman Catholic Archbishop of Westminster, the Most Rev. Cormac Murphy-O'Connor, made a written submission to the Court of Appeal on relevant aspects of Roman Catholic faith and morality. He stressed five points: human life is sacred and inviolable; a person's bodily integrity should not be violated when it can confer no benefit on that person; it is a grave injustice to preserve one person's life by lethally assaulting another; doctors have no duty to resort to extraordinary means to preserve life; and parents' rights should not be overridden except where they are being used in a way which is clearly contrary to their duties to their children.

In these circumstances, the doctors sought a declaration from the High Court that an operation to separate the twins would not be unlawful. In the High Court, Johnson J, under intense time pressure, granted the declaration. He decided that the court had to act in the best interests of the children, if that course of action was otherwise lawful. He took the view that the quality of Mary's life would be such that it was not in her

---

[205] [2000] HRLR 721, CA.

interests to endure it. Apart from her very limited mental capacity, he thought that being dragged round as an appendage to Jodie would be intolerable. Jodie's interest in life and capacity for a relatively normal existence if separated were thought to out-weigh the danger that she might carry a sense of guilt and psychological problems when she knew that she had survived only at the cost of her twin's life. It was thus in both twins' interests that the operation should proceed. The separation operation could therefore be authorized if it would not otherwise be unlawful. Johnson J found this the most difficult aspect of the case. He took the view that separating the two aortas was not like turning off a life-support machine. It was more closely analogous to withdrawal of food and hydration (as in *Bland*). On that basis, having regard to his decision on the best interests question, the severing of the aortas would not be unlaw-ful. The parents appealed, arguing that Johnson J's decisions as to Mary's best inter-ests, Jodie's best interests, and the legality of the operation were all erroneous.

The Court of Appeal (Ward, Brooke, and Robert Walker LJJ) had the advantage of fuller argument than had been presented to Johnson J, although this made the case seem, if anything, more difficult rather than easier. All three judges accepted that the right to be free of physical interference was fundamental, and that any operation would normally be a crime and a tort if carried out without the patient's consent. Where the patient is a minor who is incapable of giving or refusing consent, the parents' decision (or that of whoever else is empowered at law to make decisions on behalf of the children) must be respected, unless a court decides that a parent is proposing to act in a way which is not in the best interests of the child.[206] The first question, therefore, was whether it had been shown that refusing permission to separ-ate the twins was not in their best interest. The court was clear that separation would be in Jodie's best interests. Unlike Johnson J, however, the judges in the Court of Appeal regarded it as being equally clear that Mary had an interest in survival, although they differed as to what would be in Mary's best interests. For Ward LJ, with whom Brooke LJ agreed without adding to his judgment on the family law issues, it could not be said with confidence that life would be worth nothing to her, and it would be wrong for anyone to hold that somebody else's life is not worth living. Under international human rights law, every life has inherent value, and that is equal, whatever the quality of life might be. It could not be in Mary's best interests to end her life.[207] Robert Walker LJ, on the other hand, thought that the quality of Mary's life was such that it could be said to be in her best interests to be separated, although it would cause her death.[208] But both approaches led to the conclusion that separation satisfied the best interests test. Ward and Brooke LJJ decided that in the extraordinary circum-stances of the case Mary's interests had to be balanced against Jodie's. Although it could not be said that the parents' view of the children's interests was unreasonable, the law required the court to make its own determination. On balance, the best interests of the children would be best served by separation.[209]

---

[206] [2000] HRLR at 748–53 (Ward LJ), 779 (Brooke LJ), 819–22 (Robert Walker LJ).
[207] Ibid. at 758–62 (Ward LJ), 779 (Brooke LJ).
[208] Ibid. at 822.
[209] Ibid. at 764–6 (Ward LJ), 779 (Brooke LJ).

The next question was whether the operation to separate the twins would unlaw-fully kill Mary, who was bound to die as a result. Would it be murder to cut the arteries and veins connecting Mary to Jodie, knowing that it would leave Mary non-viable? Their Lordships analysed this issue in great depth. Brooke LJ delivered a particularly learned judgment on the law of murder and necessity. They rejected the analogy with *Bland* which Johnson J had adopted. Surgical intervention could not be regarded as an omission like withholding hydration and nourishment. It was a posi-tive act, inevitably leading to Mary's death. The House of Lords had held in *R. v. Woollin*[210] that the mental element in murder was made out if the defendant intended to cause death or really serious bodily harm, and that a jury could find that intention when the defendant did not wish for that result, but if and only if he correctly understood that death or really serious bodily harm was a virtually certain result of his act. The court accepted that this principle was of general application. On that basis, it was thought that a jury would be compelled to decide that, in dividing the twins' aortas, the doctors would have intentionally killed Mary, making them guilty of murder.[211] The remaining question was whether the surgeons would have a lawful justification or excuse for dividing the aortas.

In approaching this question, the court inevitably focused principally on the doc-tors' duties. On the face of it, surgeons separating the twins would intentionally[212] cause the death of Mary, in breach of their duty to her. But Ward LJ considered that the doctors had conflicting duties. Not operating to save Jodie could lay the doctors open to a charge of manslaughter by neglect when Jodie died as a result, or a charge of cruelty contrary to section 1 of the Children and Young Persons Act 1933 as inter-preted in *R. v. Sheppard*[213] while she survived.[214] How did the law require doctors to behave in this dilemma?

Their Lordships rejected the doctrine of double effect as a way out of the impasse. It was inapplicable to a case where the therapeutic treatment of one person necessarily involves the death of another person who could not have been expected to enjoy any benefit from it.[215] Turning to varieties of the doctrine of necessity, the authorities established that, save in cases of self-defence, nobody is entitled to kill someone else in order to preserve his own life, although the commission of lesser offences might be excusable.[216] However, the court decided that this should not rule out the taking of human life in situations where neither of the choices open to doctors would secure equal protection for the sanctity of each twin's life. Brooke LJ pointed out that the defence of necessity is not strictly equivalent to duress. In duress, the reason for exculpating a defendant is that his will was irresistibly overborne by the pressure of

---

[210] [1999] 1 AC 82, [1998] 4 All ER 103, HL.

[211] [2000] HRLR at 773 (Ward LJ), 827–8 (Robert Walker LJ). It is arguable, however, that the *Woollin* decision permits, but does not compel, a jury to infer intention from a defendant's appreciation of the inevitability of death or really serious harm.

[212] As that word was defined in *Woollin* for the purposes of the English law of murder.

[213] [1981] AC 394, [1980] 3 All ER 889, HL.

[214] [2000] HRLR at 777–8.

[215] Ibid. at 773–4 (Ward LJ), 791–3 (Brooke LJ), 828 (Robert Walker LJ).

[216] See, e.g. *R. v. Dudley and Stephens* (1884) 14 QBD 273, CCR; *R. v. Howe* [1987] 1 AC 417, HL. See [2000] HRLR at 794–801 (Brooke LJ).

threats or other circumstances. It is possible for a person to make a careful, rational assessment of different options which are genuinely open to him and take advantage of a defence of necessity on choosing the least of the available evils. The reasons usually advanced for denying such a defence would not apply to the case of the twins. There was sufficient diversity of opinion on the morality of the case for there to be no risk of an absolute divorce of law from morality, whichever way the decision went. There was no risk that people would be excessively prepared to take advantage of exceptions to the law to take lives without genuine justification, because conjoined twins are rare, and the choice of saving one twin by killing the other, or losing both, which faced doctors and the court in that case, was even more extraordinary. Brooke LJ wrote:[217]

'According to Sir James Stephen, there are three necessary requirements for the application of the doctrine of necessity:

   (i)   the act is needed to avoid inevitable and irreparable evil;

   (ii) no more should be done than is reasonably necessary for the purpose to be achieved;

   (iii) the evil inflicted must not be disproportionate to the evil avoided.

Given that the principles of modern family law point irresistibly to the conclusion that the interests of Jodie must be preferred to the conflicting interests of Mary, I consider that all three of these requirements are satisfied in this case. Finally, the doctrine of the sanctity of life respects the integrity of the human body. The proposed operation would give these children's bodies the integrity which nature denied them.'

Robert Walker LJ, too, was prepared to extend the doctrine of necessity to cover the case, on similar grounds:

'It is a case of doctors owing conflicting legal (and not merely social or moral) duties. It is a case where the test of proportionality is met, since it is a matter of life and death, and on the evidence Mary is bound to die soon in any event. It is not a case of evaluating the relative worth of two human lives, but of undertaking surgery without which neither life will have the bodily integrity (or wholeness) which is its due. It should not be regarded as a further step down a slippery slope because the case of conjoined twins presents an unique problem.'[218]

Ward LJ agreed with Brooke LJ as to the criminal law aspects, but expressed two distinctive reasons why the operation would not be criminal. First, doctors must not be put in a position where they are liable to be charged with a criminal offence whichever course of action they follow:

'Faced as they are with an apparently irreconcilable conflict, the doctors ... must be given the same freedom of choice as the court has given itself and the doctors must make that choice along the same lines as the court has done. The respect the law must have for the right to life of each must go in the scales and weigh equally but other factors have to go in the

---

[217] Ibid. at 816, referring to Sir James Fitzjames Stephens, *A Digest of the Criminal Law (Crimes and Punishments)* (London: Macmillan, 1887), 9–11. See further Brooke LJ [2000] HRLR at 800–1.

[218] Ibid. at 832 (Robert Walker LJ).

scales as well. For the same reasons that led to my concluding that consent should be given to operate so the conclusion has to be that the carrying out of the operation will be justified as the lesser evil and no unlawful act would be committed.'[219]

Secondly, a defence akin to that of self-defence should be recognized when a doctor helps a person to defend herself against someone who, whether lawfully or unlawfully, is killing her. It would be lawful to kill a six-year-old boy in what Ward LJ called 'self-defence of others' if he was indiscriminately shooting people in a school playground, despite the fact that he was too young to be convicted of a criminal offence:

'I can see no difference in essence between that resort to legitimate self-defence and the doctors coming to Jodie's defence and removing the threat of fatal harm to her presented by Mary's draining her life-blood. The availability of such a plea of quasi self-defence, modified to meet the quite exceptional circumstances nature has inflicted on the twins, makes intervention by the doctors lawful.'[220]

Although the court did not examine separately the doctors' potential liability in respect of other offences, a decision that some variant of the doctrine of necessity protects them against liability for murder means, *a fortiori*, that it must protect them also against lesser offences.

Was the position altered by the coming into force of the Human Rights Act 1998? The decision was made ten days before the Act came into force, but the court accepted that it had to deal with the Act, and particularly Article 2, because the operation was not to be performed until after it had come into force. All three judges rejected an argument that the separation of the twins' aortas would intentionally kill Mary, violating her right to life under Article 2(1). They accepted that the killing of Mary fell to be regarded as intentional for the purposes of the English law of murder, following *Woollin*. They reasoned, however, that under the ECHR 'intention' had an autonomous meaning, equivalent to its more natural and ordinary meaning of 'purpose'. The artificial meaning given to it for the purpose of the English law of murder was inapplicable to its autonomous meaning under the ECHR. This made it unnecessary to imply into Article 2 any special exceptions to the right to life additional to those expressed in the Article itself.[221]

The result was to enable the surgeons to separate the twins lawfully, notwithstanding the objections of the parents. In the event, the operation went ahead as planned. Jodie survived, and has good prospects of a normal life. After the major blood vessels had been separated by the surgeons, two of whom made the fatal incisions simultaneously, it proved impossible to keep Mary alive, and she died as expected. The parents became reconciled to the fates of their children and to the decision of the court, even if they could never agree with it.

The case demonstrates how few absolutes there are in the law of life and death. The reason is that the law has to take account of myriad interests. There would have been no point in deciding the case on the basis of a balancing of the twins' interests if as a

---

[219] [2000] HRLR at 777–8 (Ward LJ).
[220] Ibid. at 778–9 (Ward LJ).
[221] Ibid. at 814–5 (Brooke LJ), 836–7 (Robert Walker LJ). See Maclean, *op. cit.*, n. 189 above.

THE RIGHT TO LIFE

result the doctors had been forced to do something unlawful. Nor would it have been logical for a result to be reached on the foundation of the doctors' duties had it been inconsistent with the fundamental rights of the twins, or of their parents. The case illustrates one of the very limited, but important, roles of human rights law in hotly contested cases. Paying attention to the rights does not always resolve the legal and moral issues. However, it did ensure that the unique claims of each twin could not be obscured behind, or subsumed under, a calculation of social utility, or the best inter-ests of the doctors or the parents. The decision remained an agonising one for all concerned, and depended heavily on medical evidence about the prospects of success-ful surgery and the prognosis for each twin in the event that surgery was denied or delayed. But while the doctors helped to establish where the best interests of each twin lay, the decision about what should be done was not settled by reference to medical evidence or medical ethics, but was determined according to an interpretation of the law. None the less, where the status of the defence of necessity in the law of murder is as unclear as it was shown to be in that case, it seems that the whole of the law, not only the law of human rights, can be seen as serving mainly to ensure that minds are focused on the right questions, rather than reliably offering right answers. This should not surprise us. In matters of life and death, we are dealing with what Professor Laurence Tribe called the 'clash of absolutes'. Under these conditions, rules cannot dictate answers. The best that can be hoped for is to provide answers which are demonstrably not inconsistent with the rules, or (more likely, since the rules conflict) not too inconsistent with too many of them. It is a modest objective, but an important one for anyone interested in rational decision-making and the rule of law.

4.4 CONCLUSION

The right to life, which in a way is incontestably the most fundamental right which we can assert, turns out on close examination to be problematic and surprisingly con-ditional. The law, both domestic and international, provides a substantial measure of protection against arbitrary deprivation of life. However, the point when the right vests in a particular person, the scope of the duties on others which arise from the right, and the scope of people's rights to release other people from those obligations, are all highly controversial. Developments in medical technology and skill, which now make it possible to clone living cells and to preserve some spark of life in people who would previously have been incontestably dead, are likely to ensure that the boundar-ies of this right remain battlegrounds for politicians and human rights advocates for the foreseeable future. Several lessons emerge from the brief survey which we have undertaken.

First, the right to life as it now exists in English law imposes duties on the state which go beyond refraining from depriving people of life. In this field, the caselaw on Article 2 of the ECHR is likely to have an effect on previous rules.

Secondly, while most people subscribe to some version of the doctrine of the sanctity of life, there is a good deal of disagreement about what it actually entails in difficult cases. Traditionally, the courts have shown a good deal of deference to medical opinion when deciding what would be in a person's best interests. The cases of *Bland* and the conjoined twins showed that the law must sometimes take responsibility for deciding itself on the moral and legal implications of ethically controversial medical recommendations, in circumstances where some notions of the sanctity of life come into conflict with some ideas of human dignity and physical integrity. Producing a resolution to the conflict in the form of legal rules or principles is necessary in order to ensure that the right to life can be adequately protected within the framework of the Rule of Law without creating a huge gap between law and morality.

Thirdly, Parliament should ideally grapple with these issues and produce a resolution which will at least have some claim to political and democratic legitimacy, although it will inevitably offend many people's moralities. Generally, however, Parliament has not been willing or able to legislate. This is probably because governments see these highly controversial issues either as net vote-losers, or as calling for the exercise of individual conscience in a way which does not sit comfortably with the normal system of parliamentary government in which the government initiates legislation and whips its supporters into line behind it. The Abortion Act 1967 and the abolition of the death penalty for murder were achieved by private members' bills on free votes. Governments with large legislative programmes of their own are less willing to allow large amounts of parliamentary time for private members' business, and recent governments have always had very large legislative programmes. The courts have therefore had to deal with many delicate issues, by default. They have on the whole done so with great care, and given us the benefit of conclusions backed by fully reasoned judgments (an advantage in terms of legitimacy which Acts of Parliament lack). Those who criticize their judgments should recall that they are of central importance only because of the failure of governments and Parliament to tackle these issues.

Fourthly, human rights cannot always resolve hard cases of this kind. Sometimes they work in a different way. They focus a decision-maker's attention on a set of important values or interests which might otherwise be lost, either because of the complexity of the issues or because the interests belong to people who lack a voice of their own. This is an important function. The Human Rights Act 1998 and the ECHR do not take decisions out of the hands of our politicians or judges, but help to ensure that decisions are taken in the light of proper consideration of the interests of the people who are most closely affected, even if they cannot urge their own cases. The law might not be altered as a result, but its legitimacy can only be enhanced, especially in cases which are morally and legally controversial.

5

OTHER RIGHTS TO BODILY INTEGRITY

Alongside a right to life, people generally enjoy a right to be free of physical interference. This chapter considers the scope and incidents of this right, and the manner of its protection. It covers negative liberties: freedom from physical assaults, torture, medical or other experimentation, immunization and compelled eugenic or social sterilization, and cruel or degrading treatment or punishment. It also encompasses some positive duties on the state to protect people against interference by others.

The right is well established in English law. The primary method of protection is by way of the civil law of tort rather than constitutional, public-law provisions, although criminal law is increasingly important. At common law, any physical interference with a person is *prima facie* tortious. If it interferes with freedom of movement, it may constitute a false imprisonment. If it involves physical touching, it may constitute a battery. If it puts a person in fear of violence, it may amount to an assault. For any of these wrongs, the victim may be able to obtain damages. Where the tort is committed by a person holding a public office, exemplary damages may sometimes be awarded. The same acts may also amount to crimes, making the offender liable to penalties. In order to avoid liability, the defendant has to establish that he had legal authority for the act. This authority may derive from statute (for example, the power to use reasonable force if necessary to make an arrest, under sections 24 and 116 of the Police and Criminal Evidence Act 1984), or from common law powers and duties (such as the power of parents to discipline children, or the duty to prevent breaches of the peace), from the 'victim's' own consent (as where a patient consents to an operation which would otherwise be a battery), from necessity (as where a doctor operates on a patient who is unconscious and unable to consent), or from a court order (as in the case of a court authorizing medical treatment on a ward of court). If the justification is not established, the act is unlawful.

These principles apply equally to interference by private citizens and by state agencies, yet agents of the state have more power than private individuals to interfere lawfully with people's bodily integrity. The duties on state agencies to safeguard the welfare of the weak, to administer the law, to maintain a tolerable level of order, and to regulate many aspects of life, carry with them a wide range of powers to stop, detain, search, hospitalize, imprison, and take into care. Apart from the state, most of the legal powers to interfere with bodily integrity reside with doctors in relation to patients and with parents and teachers in respect of children. Here we will examine some general considerations stemming from international agreements, and those aspects of the powers which raise considerations specifically relevant to the civil liberties and human rights of children, people subject to medical treatment, and convicted offenders. Minimum standards of health care, physical conditions in prisons and hospitals, and freedom from arbitrary arrest and detention are examined in subsequent chapters.

Article 3 of the European Convention on Human Rights (ECHR) provides:

'No one shall be subjected to torture or to inhuman or degrading treatment or punishment.'

Article 7 of the International Covenant on Civil and Political Rights (ICCPR) goes slightly further:

'No one shall be subjected to torture or to cruel, inhuman or degrading treatment or punishment. In particular, no one shall be subjected without his free consent to medical or scientific experimentation.'

It is clear from the instruments, and has been expressly decided by the European Court and Commission of Human Rights, that the obligations of states under these provisions are absolute, non-derogable, and unqualified.[1] As Sieghart observed, 'All that is therefore required to establish a violation of the relevant Article is a finding that the state concerned has failed to comply with its obligation in respect of any one of these modes of conduct: no question of justification can ever arise'.[2] Nevertheless, we will see that a degree of relativism cannot, in practice, be entirely excluded from the application of the notions of inhuman or degrading treatment.

In addition, States Parties have obligations under the European Convention for the Prevention of Torture and Inhuman or Degrading Treatment or Punishment to criminalize torture, provide severe penalties for it, and secure the prosecution of anyone who has committed torture who is present within their jurisdictions. There is a monitoring body, the Committee for the Prevention of Torture (CPT), which will be referred to further below.

Rights to security of the person, which initially look as if they might be relevant, turn out to be unpromising sources of guidance in this context. Article 3 of the Universal Declaration of Human Rights stated: 'Everyone has the right to . . . liberty and security of the person', words echoed in Article 9(1) of the International Covenant on Civil and Political Rights and Article 5(1) of the European Convention. In the European context, 'liberty and security of the person' has been relatively narrowly interpreted: although the Commission has said that liberty and security are two separate rights,[3] it has been held that both refer only to physical liberty and security, and are in effect restricted to freedom from arbitrary arrest and detention.[4]

As interpreted by the European Court of Human Rights, Article 3 of the ECHR

---

[1] *Ireland v. United Kingdom* (5310/71), Report: 25 January 1976; Judgment: 2 EHRR 25; *Tyrer v. United Kingdom*, Eur. Ct. HR, Series A, No. 26 (1978) 2 EHRR 1.

[2] P. Sieghart, *The International Law of Human Rights* (Oxford: Clarendon Press, 1983), 161.

[3] *Kamma v. Netherlands* (4771/71) DR 1, 4; *Engel et al. v. Netherlands* (5100–2/71; 5354/72; 5370/72), Report of 19 July 1974.

[4] *Guzzardi v. Italy* (1981) 3 EHRR 333; *Arrowsmith v. United Kingdom* (7050/72) DR 19, 5; *X. v. United Kingdom* (5877/72) CD 45, 90. See Sieghart, *International Law*, at 142 n.7.

imposes fourfold duties on the state similar to those which arise under Article 2 (the right to life): (1) a duty to refrain from inflicting torture or inhuman or degrading treatment or punishment; (2) a duty to protect people against threats of torture or inhuman or degrading treatment or punishment by state agencies or others; (3) a duty to investigate alleged violations; and (4) a duty to make provision for securing the legal accountability of people who inflict torture or inhuman or degrading treatment or punishment on others. Article 7 of the ICCPR, too, requires prompt state action to investigate alleged abuses, and accessible remedies for victims, as the UN Human Rights Committee's General Comments on Article 7[5] make clear. This chapter follows that structure, but does not neglect the fact that English law in many ways gives greater protection than Article 3 requires.

5.1 THE RIGHT TO BE FREE OF INJURY CAUSED BY AGENTS OF THE STATE

The right to be free of torture and inhuman or degrading treatment or punishment is fundamental to a democratic society, protecting people's dignity as well as their physical integrity. This has been recognized for centuries in England and Wales. In 1688/9, immediately after the accession of King William and Queen Mary, the Bill of Rights provided (among other things): 'That excessive bail ought not to be required nor excessive fines imposed nor cruell and unusuall punishments inflicted'. The prohibition on cruel and unusual punishments was adopted internationally, being incorporated in the Eighth Amendment to the US Constitution in 1789–91, and in many other similar instruments since.

In the series of international human rights instruments agreed since the Second World War, similar provisions appear. Article 5 of the Universal Declaration of Human Rights and Article 7 of the International Covenant on Civil and Political Rights both prohibit torture and cruel, inhuman, or degrading treatment or punishment. This is wider in three respects than the 1689 Bill of Rights: first, in covering torture; secondly, in dealing with treatment generally in addition to punishment; and, thirdly, in covering inhuman or degrading treatment and punishment rather than only cruel and unusual punishment. Article 3 of the ECHR drops the reference to cruelty, contenting itself with forbidding torture or inhuman or degrading treatment or punishment.[6]

---

[5] General Comment 20 (1992), which replaced General Comment 7.

[6] See generally P. J. Duffy, 'Article 3 of the European Convention on Human Rights' (1983) 32 *ICLQ* 316–46. For a brief account of the disagreements which led to the adoption of the present form of Art. 3, see J. E. S. Fawcett, *The Application of the European Convention on Human Rights*, 2nd edn. (Oxford: Clarendon Press, 1987), 41–3.

(1) MEANING OF 'TORTURE'[7]

Torture has been defined in the Convention against Torture and Other Cruel, Inhuman or Degrading Treatment or Punishment, a subsidiary instrument under the aegis of the United Nations.[8] Article 1, paragraph 1, states that for the purposes of the Convention 'torture' means:

'any act by which severe pain or suffering, whether physical or mental, is intentionally inflicted on a person for such purposes as obtaining from him or a third person information or a confession, punishing him for an act he or a third person has committed or is suspected of having committed, or intimidating him or coercing him or a third person, or for any reason based on discrimination of any kind, when such pain or suffering is inflicted by or at the instigation of or with the consent or acquiescence of a public official or other person acting in an official capacity. It does not include pain or suffering arising only from, inherent in or incidental to lawful sanctions.'

This ties the idea of torture to the purpose for which the suffering is inflicted. There are similarities here to the interpretation of torture in the context of the European Convention, Article 3. In two early cases, *Denmark, Norway, Sweden and the Netherlands v. Greece*,[9] and *Ireland v. United Kingdom*,[10] the European Commission of Human Rights took the view that torture was an aggravated form of inhuman treatment which had a purpose such as obtaining information or confessions or inflicting punishment. This approach was adopted by the Court of Appeal of Northern Ireland, for the purpose of deciding whether to exclude confession evidence obtained through torture, in *R. v. McCormick*.[11] However, in *Ireland v. United Kingdom* thirteen judges of the European Court of Human Rights, forming a majority, adopted a more stringent test for torture based on the special intensity of the suffering caused, saying that torture was 'deliberate inhuman treatment causing very serious and cruel suffering'.[12] While accepting that the right under Article 3 is absolute and non-derogable, the majority of the Court said that the treatment must:

'attain a minimum level of severity if it is to fall within the scope of Article 3. The assessment of the minimum is, in the nature of things, relative; it depends on all the circumstances of the case, such as the duration of the treatment, its physical or mental effects and, in some cases, the sex, age and state of health of the victim, etc.'[13]

Thus the so-called 'five techniques' in the *Ireland* case, used by members of the UK security forces against suspected terrorists, were said to constitute torture by the

---

[7] See J. McBride, 'Imperfect Limits to Unacceptable Treatment' (2000) 25 *ELR HR* 29–43.

[8] Adopted by UN General Assembly Resolution 39/46 of 10 December 1984.

[9] (3321–3/67; 3344/67) Report (1969) 12 *Yearbook of the European Convention on Human Rights: The Greek Case.*

[10] (5310/71) Eur. Comm. HR, Report: 25 January 1976 (1976) 19 *Yearbook* 512; Eur. Ct. HR, Series A, No. 25, 2 EHRR 25.

[11] [1977] 4 NIJB 105.

[12] *Ireland v. United Kingdom*, Series A, No. 25, Judgment of 18 January 1978, 2 EHRR 25, at para. 167 of the judgment.

[13] Ibid. at para. 162.

Commission, but not by the majority of the Court: 'wall standing', being spreadeagled for hours against a wall in a physically stressed position; 'hooding', keeping a dark bag over detainees' heads; subjecting the detainees to continuous loud noise; depriving them of sleep before interrogating them; and giving detainees reduced amounts of food and drink. On the other hand, there seems little doubt that the direct application of physical pain by beating on the soles of the feet, electric shocks, kicking people in the genitals, extracting hair, burning with cigarettes, placing a large stick in a person's rectum, and other traditional medieval tortures, would have amounted to torture on anyone's view.[14]

Only four judges in *Ireland v. United Kingdom* thought this definition too restricted, but it was criticized by commentators who suggested that it reflects the idea that there is a common understanding that people should be stigmatized as torturers only if their acts can be characterized as extreme barbarity, thus excluding more subtle psychological and technological methods of overriding the human will which are more readily available to advanced industrial countries than to developing ones.[15] Furthermore, in the same case Judge Fitzmaurice, dissenting, doubted the relevance of the purpose for which the inhuman treatment was meted out, arguing in view of the unconditional wording of Article 3 that torture is constituted by sufficiently inhuman treatment inflicted on a person by compulsion, an objective criterion which did not depend on the subjective purpose of those responsible.

More recently, the European Court of Human Rights has been more willing to find that torture has been established, developing the interpretation of Article 3 dynamically to take a tougher line against oppressive behaviour. While regularly repeating that the minimum level of severity for Article 3 is relative, and reasserting that violations of Article 3 must be proved beyond reasonable doubt, the Court and (previously) the Commission have developed both procedural and substantive law in ways which make it easier to establish torture.[16] On the procedural front, they have been prepared to find torture on the basis of inferences from circumstantial evidence, especially if the respondent state has offered no convincing explanation for a victim's injuries.[17] They have undertaken their own fact-finding missions,[18] and have drawn on relevant findings of other international bodies (such as the European Committee for the Prevention of Torture and Inhuman or Degrading Treatment or Punishment) and authoritative non-governmental organizations.[19] A state cannot avoid being held to have violated Article 3 merely by erecting a wall of silence or non-cooperation.

---

[14] These types of assault were held to amount to torture in *Denmark et al. v. Greece*, above.

[15] See R. J. Spjut, 'Torture under the European Convention on Human Rights' (1979) 73 *AJIL* 267 at 271; N. Rodley, *The Treatment of Prisoners under International Law*, 2nd edn. (Oxford: Oxford University Press, 1999), 93–4.

[16] See McBride, 'Imperfect Limits', n. 7 above.

[17] *Tekin v. Turkey*, Judgment of 9 June 1998, RJD 1998-IV; *Selmouni v. France*, Judgment of 28 July 1999, RJD 1999-V.

[18] E.g. *Aksoy v. Turkey*, Judgment of 18 December 1996, 23 EHRR 553; *Aydin v. Turkey*, Judgment of 25 September 1997, 25 EHRR 251. See K. Altiparmak, 'Turkish Cases relating to Terrorism before the European Court of Human Rights: Procedural Issues' (2000) 5 *Journal of Civil Liberties* 30–48.

[19] E.g *Dougoz v. Greece*, Judgment of 6 March 2001, App. No. 40907/98.

In developing the substantive law, the Court, while remaining of the view that the threshold level of suffering needed for a violation of Article 3 is assessed on a basis which is to some extent relative, has insisted that, once that threshold is crossed, the treatment cannot be justified. Even the need to combat a terrorist campaign such as that being conducted by the PKK in south-eastern Turkey, fighting for a free Kurdistan, cannot justify violation of Article 3 rights.[20] As to the threshold standard, torture is 'deliberate inhuman treatment causing very serious and cruel suffering'.[21] Both physical and mental assaults are capable of amounting to torture. The Court has held that there has been torture where agents of the state have subjected a detainee to 'Palestinian hanging' (having one's arms secured behind one's back and being suspended by the wrists).[22] In *Aydin v. Turkey*,[23] the Court decided that being blindfolded, forcibly stripped and raped causes such a loss of dignity, degradation, and sense of defilement and powerlessness that the combination of physical and mental violence inevitably amounted to torture.[24] The Court accepted evidence that international standards regarded the rape of a female detainee by an agent of the state as torture when done for purposes such as the extraction of information or confessions or the humiliation, punishment, or intimidation of the victim.[25] It therefore seems that torture must be deliberate, cause very severe physical or mental suffering, and be inflicted for one of a number of purposes which include, but are not limited to, obtaining information or confessions. The characteristics and circumstances of the victim are relevant: in *Aydin v. Turkey* the victim's age (17 years), sex, and vulnerability in detention led the Court to hold that other ways in which her captors treated her also amounted to torture. These included being stripped, repeatedly beaten by several people, forced into a tyre, spun round, and sprayed with cold water from high-speed jets over a period of interrogation lasting three days. In *Selmouni v. France*,[26] the Court found that torture had occurred when a suspected drug trafficker in police detention had been made to kneel during interrogations while officers pulled his hair, hit him with a baseball bat or similar implement, kicked him, stood on his feet, threatened him with a syringe and a blowlamp, and urinated on him in front of a woman after telling him to suck the penis of one of the officers. In *Çakici v. Turkey*[27] beatings administered to a suspected Kurdish terrorist in custody, causing a broken rib and laceration to the skull, and the application of electric shocks were held to amount to torture.

Ultimately, however, the definition of torture is of limited importance. Treatment or punishment which causes lesser suffering or which is done for a different purpose

[20] *Aksoy v. Turkey*, Judgment of 18 December 1996, 23 EHRR 553 at para. 81.

[21] Ibid., at para. 82.

[22] Ibid.

[23] Judgment of 25 September 1997, 25 EHRR 251.

[24] Ibid., at paras. 48–51.

[25] The Court noted the decision of the Inter-American Court of Human Rights in *Fernando and Raquel Mejia v. Peru*, 1 March 1996, Report No. 5/96, Case 10,970, and other international legal standards on investigation of allegations of rape made by detainees, in particular UN Convention against Torture, Arts. 11 and 12.

[26] Judgment of 28 July 1999, RJD 1999-V.

[27] Judgment of 8 July 1999.

is not treated as torture, but (as we shall see) may still be inhuman or degrading and so violate Article 3.

The UK legislation on torture, the Criminal Justice Act 1988, section 134, broadly follows the UN Convention against Torture in relation to the quantum of suffering involved, but not on the purposes for which it is inflicted. The Act makes it an offence to inflict severe pain or suffering (thus including psychological torture) on another, where the offender is a public official or person acting in an official capacity, in the performance or purported performance of his official duties, or is acting at the instigation, or with the consent or acquiescence, of such a person performing or purporting to perform his official duties.[28] The definition of torture under the 1988 Act is wider than that adopted by the European Court of Human Rights. On the other hand, unlike Article 3 of the European Convention, the 1988 Act imposes no special liability in respect of inhuman or degrading treatment short of torture, so the extended meaning given to torture is understandable. Section 134 is wide enough to encompass, for example, mistreatment of patients by nurses and medics in the prison medical service, a matter to which we will return in section 5.8 below, as the purpose of the torturer is irrelevant: only the status of the offender as a public official (or someone under his instigation, etc.), acting in purported performance of his official duties, is significant. The maximum penalty is life imprisonment, and the offence is always a serious arrestable offence for the purposes of police investigative powers.[29] The Attorney-General's consent is required for a prosecution in England and Wales.[30]

There is a defence where the defendant had lawful authority, justification, or excuse under the law of the part of the UK where the torture took place, or (if it was inflicted abroad by a UK official) the law of the part of the UK under which the official was purporting to act, or (if it was inflicted abroad by an official of a foreign state) under the law of the country in which it was inflicted.[31] This is rather wider than the relatively narrow exception provided under Article 1, paragraph 1 of the UN Convention relating to lawful sanctions: the defence under the 1988 Act would encompass, for example, duress and mistake of fact as defences. More seriously, it opens the way for national legislation to authorize torture or inhuman or degrading treatment on utilitarian grounds, to cater for some exigent circumstances or pressing military or social need. The European Court of Human Rights has rejected Turkey's claim to justify torture by reference to the need to combat terrorism: under Article 3 of the European Convention on Human Rights the obligation of the state is absolute and non-derogable,[32] and the same applies to the obligations under the UN Convention.[33]

A similar approach has been adopted in Israel, despite the ever-present threat of

---

[28] Criminal Justice Act 1988, s. 134(1), (2).

[29] Ibid., ss. 134(6), 170(2), and Sch. 15, para. 20.

[30] Criminal Justice Act 1988, s. 135.

[31] Ibid., s. 134(5).

[32] *Aksoy v. Turkey*, 18 December 1996, 23 EHRR 553 (para. 81). See also *Ireland v. United Kingdom*, Series A, No. 25, (1978) 2 EHRR 25.

[33] For full discussion, see Rodley, *Treatment of Prisoners*, ch. 3; M. D. Evans and R. Morgan, *Preventing Torture: A Study of the European Convention for the Prevention of Torture and Inhuman or Degrading Treatment or Punishment* (Oxford: Clarendon Press, 1998), ch. 3.

terrorism there. In *Public Committee against Torture in Israel and others v. State of Israel and others*, the Supreme Court of Israel held that the security forces had no lawful authority to use certain techniques to undermine the will of suspects being questioned about terrorist crimes.[34] These techniques included shaking suspects, making them sit in 'the Shabach position' (on a low chair sloping forwards, with arms handcuffed behind the back of the chair), putting them in a 'frog crouch' position (crouching for five minutes at a time on the tips of the toes), hooding them, playing loud music, making them wear tight handcuffs, and depriving them of sleep. The judgment of Barak P (with whom the other judges agreed) recognized that interrogation is a contest between the parties, where the interrogator tries to overcome the interviewee's reluctance to speak, but held that the means adopted had to be consistent with the interviewee's right to be free from violation of his life, body, and dignity under section 2 of Israel's Basic Law: Human Dignity and Liberty (1992). Security forces were entitled to take necessary steps to protect their safety and prevent detainees from escaping, but were not allowed to use force or exert excessive pressure for other purposes.

On the other hand, in some situations it may be ethical to allow a fairly high level of physical pressure in order to avert an imminent threat to life. Israel's Basic Law: Human Dignity and Liberty, section 8 (as amended in 1994), allows for rights to be violated 'by a law befitting the values of the State of Israel, enacted for a proper purpose, and to an extent no greater than is required, or by regulation enacted by virtue of express authorization in such a law'. It would therefore be possible for the Knesset (Parliament) to authorize the use of force for limited purposes. However, in *Public Committee against Torture in Israel and others v. State of Israel and others* the Supreme Court seems to have taken the view that such a law would have to be limited to the 'ticking time bomb' situation, where it was known that people's lives were at risk and there was an urgent need to find out about the danger in order to avert it. In such circumstances, the use of physical pressure might be justified by the doctrine of necessity in order to protect life. There is no such urgency or necessity during the investigation of a criminal act which has already occurred. If a 'ticking time bomb' case were ever to come before the European Court of Human Rights, it would have to decide whether the assessment of levels of suffering for the purposes of Article 3 of the ECHR can be adjusted to take account of the need to protect people's lives from a threat. The answer might depend on matters such as the reliability of information about the existence of a threat, the likely imminence of the threat, and the reasonableness of believing that the person on whom suffering is inflicted has the information which is needed.

Physical torture in the UK is actionable in tort as a battery. The same is probably true of mental torture if it causes psychiatric harm, bearing in mind that psychiatric as well as physical injuries have been held to constitute the criminal offence of assault occasioning actual or grievous bodily harm.[35]

[34] HC 5100/94 and other applications, Judgment of 6 September 1999.
[35] *R. v. Ireland* [1998] AC 147, [1997] 4 All ER 225, HL.

(2) INHUMAN OR DEGRADING TREATMENT OR PUNISHMENT

The international instruments also outlaw inhuman or degrading treatment or punishment. The term 'punishment' imports the idea of a disagreeable experience inflicted as a consequence of conviction for a crime. As such, it is narrower than 'treatment', which is apt to cover anything done to a person in any circumstances. Since any punishment inevitably involves a degree of suffering and humiliation, in order for a punishment to violate Article 3, the humiliation must be different from and greater than the usual and inevitable element of humiliation. 'The assessment is, in the nature of things, relative: it depends on all the circumstances of the case and, in particular, on the nature and context of the punishment itself and the manner and method of its execution'.[36] For example, imprisonment in itself does not violate Article 3, but being imprisoned for a long period in very bad conditions might do so.[37]

While 'treatment' is a very general term, the International Covenant on Civil and Political Rights, Article 7, singles out one form of treatment for special mention: 'In particular, no one shall be subjected without his free consent to medical or scientific experimentation'. This is not particularized in the European Convention, but was held to be a crime against international law by the Nuremberg War Crimes Tribunal.[38] It is very likely that experimentation which presented a serious threat to life or health would be cognizable by the European Court or Commission of Human Rights, as an infringement of the right to life under Article 2 or a special form of torture or inhuman treatment under Article 3. While an experiment which inflicted severe suffering or loss of dignity on a subject would be, respectively, inhuman or degrading treatment, people can be used for experimentation—for example, as part of a sample in a clinical trial of a drug, or in tests for the effects of radioactivity—without knowing it, and without it inflicting any serious injury on them. While it might be argued that experimentation without consent disregards a subject's moral autonomy and dignity, and therefore degrades him the caselaw to date under the ECHR demands that the subject knows at the time that his dignity is threatened in a fairly severe way before treatment will be regarded as degrading. Accordingly, much undisclosed experimentation may fall outside Article 3 of the Convention. The Council of Europe Convention for the Protection of Human Rights and Dignity of the Human Being with regard to the Application of Biology and Medicine (Convention on Human Rights and Biomedicine) entered into force in 1999, but the UK has not signed or ratified either the main Convention or the Additional Protocol on the Prohibition of Cloning Human Beings, which entered into force on 1 March 2001. As a result, the requirements of the Convention for informed consent to medical intervention (Article 5) and for express, informed, and documented consent to being made the subject of research (Article 16) do not apply in the UK. Nor does the prohibition on any intervention seeking to create a human being genetically identical to another human being, whether living or dead, under Article 1 of the Additional Protocol. In England,

---

[36] *Tyrer v. United Kingdom*, Series A, No. 26, Judgment of 25 April 1978, at para. 30 (judicial birching degrading).
[37] See, *mutatis mutandis*, *Dougoz v. Greece*, App. No. 40907/98, Judgment of 6 March 2001.
[38] See further Rodley, *Treatment of Prisoners*, 232–5.

administering a drug without a person's consent would be a battery, but if the patient consents to its administration it ceases to be a battery. English cases have held that consent need not be fully informed in order to provide a defence to an action for battery, although a doctor who had failed to give the patient such information as would be thought reasonable by a reputable body of medical opinion practising in the field might be liable in an action for negligence if harm resulted.[39]

(i) Inhuman or degrading punishment

One of the objects of punishment is to make the offender and others regard the offender's conduct as unacceptable, and this may incidentally lower the offender in his or her own, and other people's, estimation. As noted above, there is no right in national or international law to be free of this inevitable suffering. However, particular problems emerge in relation to corporal punishment and prison conditions for those detained by court order.

Whipping as a judicially imposed penalty was abolished in England and Wales by the Criminal Justice Act 1948, but continued to be used against children and young persons in the Isle of Man. In *Tyrer v. United Kingdom*[40] the European Court of Human Rights held by a majority that a judicially imposed birching, conducted in the Isle of Man on a 15-year-old boy, which caused pain but no serious injury, constituted a degrading punishment. The majority held that the institutionalized infliction of violence on a person by the state, authorized and carried out according to law by state authorities, is intrinsically degrading:

'. . . although the applicant did not suffer any severe or long-lasting physical effects, his punishment—whereby he was treated as an object in the power of the authorities—constituted an assault on precisely that which it is one of the main purposes of Article 3 to protect, namely a person's dignity and physical integrity . . . The institutionalised character of this violence is further compounded by the whole aura of official procedure attending the punishment and by the fact that those inflicting it were total strangers to the offender . . . [I]n addition to the physical pain he experienced, Mr. Tyrer was subjected to the mental anguish of anticipating the violence he was to have inflicted on him.'[41]

This reasoning is not entirely convincing. It was strongly criticized by Judge Fitzmaurice, dissenting. He argued that it is necessary to take account of social standards and expectations when deciding whether something is degrading, because the degrading nature of treatment or punishment had been held in earlier cases to depend on whether it constituted an assault on the victim's personality and lowered the victim in his own eyes and in the estimation of others. Beating is a common, if often controversial, part of child-rearing practice in many cultures, where it does not degrade the victim (although the victim and others may consider it to be cruel). By contrast, beating an adult is an assault on the adult's social and cultural expectations, and is likely to be degrading, although there are circumstances in which violence may legit-

---

[39] *Chatterton v. Gerson* [1981] QB 432, [1981] 1 All ER 257; *Sidaway v. Board of Governors of the Bethlem Royal Hospital and the Maudsley Hospital* [1985] AC 871, [1985] 1 All ER 643, HL.

[40] Eur. Ct. HR, Series A, No. 26 (1978) 2 EHRR 1.

[41] Para. 33 of the judgment.

imately be used against adults (for example, in order to prevent crime) without it being regarded as degrading. The majority decision in *Tyrer* fails to take account of the importance of context.

Furthermore, it seems odd for the majority to concentrate so heavily on the institutional aspects of the punishment. If the fact that it was authorized by law, after a judicial hearing, and inflicted by agents of the state (subject to strict rules about the size of the birch and the manner of infliction), makes the punishment intrinsically degrading, it seems to imply that it would have been preferable had it been administered unofficially and without any safeguards being provided by law. If the intentional infliction by the state of an assault on a person's physical integrity is degrading treatment or punishment, it is hard to see how any punishment which impinges on a person's physical integrity or liberty would not be capable of contravening Article 3. It would have been more convincing had the majority in *Tyrer* concentrated exclusively on the features incidental to the infliction of the punishment as making it degrading.

Despite its argumentational deficiencies, *Tyrer* reflects an international trend towards the abolition of judicial corporal punishment, and the decision was instrumental in encouraging the effective abolition by judicial decision of corporal punishment of adults in Zimbabwe, on the ground that it constitutes inhuman and degrading punishment contrary to the Constitution of Zimbabwe.[42] A similar conclusion was reached, although by a narrow majority, in relation to the corporal punishment of juveniles.[43] However, the culturally determined and relativistic quality of degrading treatment is illustrated by the fact that the Zimbabwe legislature reversed the effect of the latter decision, reinstating the constitutionality of sentences of whipping for juveniles.[44] Other states have outlawed judicial corporal punishment on a different, although no less relativistic, conceptual foundation. In Namibia and South Africa, the courts have held that corporal punishment is incompatible with the constitutional right to respect for human dignity.[45] While respect for dignity underpins the prohibition of inhuman and degrading punishment under ECHR Article 3, more modern bills of rights are more willing to found decisions in this field directly on dignity.

In a 1991 report,[46] the European Committee for the Prevention of Torture and Inhuman or Degrading Treatment or Punishment (CPT) expressed the view that 'the cumulative effect of overcrowding, lack of integral sanitation and inadequate regimes [at Brixton, Leeds, and Wandsworth Prisons] amounts to inhuman and degrading treatment'.[47] Similar concerns have been expressed by Judge Stephen Tumim and

[42] *State v. Ncube* [1988] LRC (Const.) 442, SC Zimb.

[43] *A Juvenile v. State* [1989] LRC (Const.) 774, SC Zimb., noted by A. W. Bradley, 'Inhuman or Degrading Punishment? Judicial Whipping in Zimbabwe' [1991] *PL* 481–4.

[44] Constitution of Zimbabwe Amendment (No. 11) Act 1990.

[45] *Ex parte Attorney-General, Namibia: In re Corporal Punishment by Organs of State* 1991 (3) SA 76 (SC of Namibia); G. J. Naldi. *Constitutional Rights in Namibia* (Kenwyn, SA: Juta & Co, 1995), 48–51; *State v. Williams* 1995 (3) SA 632 (Const. Ct. of South Africa).

[46] *Report to the UK government on the Visit to the UK Carried Out by the European Committee for the Prevention of Torture and Inhuman or Degrading Treatment or Punishment*, adopted by the Committee, 21 March 1991. On the work of the Committee, see M. Evans and R. Morgan, 'The European Convention for the Prevention of Torture: Operational Practice' (1992) **41** *ICLQ* 590–614.

[47] See Evans and Morgan, *Preventing Torture*, 243–7.

General Sir David Ramsbottam, the two most recent former holders of the post of HM's Chief Inspector of Prisons. If this is correct (and the UK government rejected the assertion in its Response to the Report), the UK could be violating the Article 3 rights of a significant number of prisoners. Admittedly, the standards applied by the CPT need not be the same as those applied under Article 3 of the ECHR. Indeed, the Explanatory Report to the European Convention for the Prevention of Torture[48] states (paragraph 27):

'The case-law of the Court and Commission of Human Rights on Article 3 provides a source of guidance for the Committee. However, the Committee's activities are aimed at future prevention rather than the application of legal requirements to existing circumstances. The Committee should not seek to interfere in the interpretation and application of Article 3.'

Before the changes to the ECHR procedures introduced by Protocol No. 11, the European Commission on Human Rights and the Committee of Ministers had decided that overcrowding in mental hospital dormitories, combined with failure to explain medical treatments administered to inmates, did not amount to degrading treatment under Article 3 of the Convention.[49] More recently, however, the Court has held that it is degrading treatment to hold a person awaiting deportation in detention for an inordinate length of time in conditions of overcrowding, without proper sleeping facilities. The Court had regard to the CPT's reports on the sites where the victim was detained, and to the fact that the CPT had decided to revisit the places subsequently.[50] This, together with other indications that the Court is broadening its approach to the interpretation of 'inhuman or degrading treatment', suggests that a heightened level of scrutiny might be applied in future to conditions of detention in penal, as well as other detention, facilities. The matter is discussed further in Chapter 7, below.

(ii) Inhuman or degrading treatment

The European Court of Human Rights has been reluctant to define the term 'inhuman or degrading treatment' too closely. Degrading treatment has sometimes been understood in terms of the high level of humiliation suffered by the victim, while inhuman treatment might be understood in terms of the infliction of a very high level of physical or mental suffering, without reference to humiliation. On the other hand, sometimes treatment has been regarded as degrading without reference to humiliation if a significant level of pain has been inflicted by a public official, especially if the victim was in the custody of the state at the time. No single approach has been followed consistently. The practical effect of the terms can best be understood by examining decisions in their contexts, and trying to assess the Court's objectives by seeing what it does in practice.[51] In general, inhuman treatment is a form of treatment which inflicts severe physical or psychological harm on the victim, while degrading

---

[48] Reproduced in Evans and Morgan, *Preventing Torture*, 394–408.

[49] *B. v. United Kingdom*, Eur. Comm. HR, Report of 7 Oct. 1981, 32 DR 5, 6 EHRR 204.

[50] *Dougoz v. Greece*, App. No. 40907/98, Judgment of 6 March 2001, especially at paras. 46–49.

[51] See M. Addo and N. Grief, 'Is there a Policy behind the Decisions and Judgments relating to Article 3 of the ECHR?' (1995) 20 *ELR* 178–193.

treatment seriously humiliates the victim, lowering him in his own estimation and that of others. In each case, the suffering or humiliation must reach a threshold level of seriousness, which will vary according to the circumstances of the case and the characteristics of the victim. As the Court wrote in *Kudła v. Poland*:[52]

'... ill-treatment must attain a minimum level of severity if it is to fall within the scope of Article 3. The assessment of this minimum is, in the nature of things, relative; it depends on all the circumstances of the case, such as the nature and context of the treatment, the manner and method of its execution, its duration, its physical or mental effects and, in some instances, the sex, age and state of health of the victim ... The Court has considered treatment to be "inhuman" because, *inter alia*, it was premeditated, was applied for hours at a stretch and caused either actual bodily injury or intense physical or mental suffering. It has deemed treatment to be "degrading" because it was such as to arouse in the victim feelings of fear, anguish and inferiority capable of humiliating and debasing them. On the other hand, the Court has consistently stressed that the suffering and humiliation must in any event go beyond that inevitable element of suffering or humiliation connected with a legitimate form of legitimate treatment or punishment ...'

Some examples will illustrate this. In *Dulas v. Turkey*,[53] security forces destroyed a 70-year-old woman's home and property before her eyes, depriving her of shelter and forcing her to leave the village where she had spent her life. This constituted inhuman treatment, although she did not suffer injury to her person. Psychological effects on the relations of people detained and tortured or killed by security forces ('the primary victim') can amount to inhuman or degrading treatment, as in *Kurt v. Turkey*.[54] Factors relevant to assessing the degree of suffering include the closeness of the bond between the complainant and the primary victim (mother and child with continuing family ties in *Kurt*), whether the complainant was present when the primary victim was taken into custody, whether the complainant had tried to obtain an account of the primary victim's whereabouts and welfare, and how the authorities had reacted to such requests.[55] Thus, in *Çiçek v. Turkey*[56] a mother whose two sons had disappeared after allegedly being detained by security forces had met with complacency and lack of assistance from the authorities. This had caused her to suffer severe fear, doubts about the welfare of her sons, and apprehension, and amounted to inhuman and degrading treatment of her.

It is possible that discriminatory treatment might be sufficiently degrading to violate Article 3 rights, as the Commission held in the *East African Asians* case.[57] Although a type of interrogation which victimized homosexuals as such, prying into their private lives and sexual experiences, was not regarded as causing sufficiently severe suffering to constitute inhuman or degrading treatment in *Smith and Grady v.*

[52] App. No. 30210/96, Judgment of 26 October 2000 (Grand Chamber), at paras. 91–2.
[53] App. No. 25801/94, Judgment of 30 January 2001.
[54] Judgment of 25 May 1998, 27 EHRR 373.
[55] *Çakici v. Turkey*, Judgment of 8 July 1999 (where the complainant was a brother of the primary victim and was held not to have had his Art. 3 rights violated).
[56] App. No. 25704/94, Judgment of 27 February 2001.
[57] (1973) 3 EHRR 76.

United Kingdom,[58] the Court left open the possibility that such treatment could in principle violate Article 3 if shown to have been the result of bias based on sexual orientation.

Where people are in the custody of the state, or are being arrested and are under the control of the police or security forces, they are unable to protect their own interests. The Court has therefore been particularly willing to hold that injury amounts to inhuman treatment, because of the oppressive nature of the exercise of state authority over captives and the need for protection in circumstances where violence is especially likely and independent monitoring is difficult. This is coupled with requiring the state to provide a persuasive explanation, supported by credible evidence, to justify any injury which has been shown to have been inflicted on a person while in custody.[59] Indeed, it has been said that any recourse to physical violence against a person deprived of liberty diminishes his dignity and is, in principle, degrading treatment in violation of Article 3, unless the force has been made necessary by his own conduct.[60] For example, where a detainee resists arrest, seeks to escape, or attacks an officer, the use of reasonable force to restrain him or her will not violate Article 3, even if injury results.[61] On the other hand, where the authorities do not use or threaten physical force, a very high level of mental suffering may be required to violate Article 3. The Court has held that highly intrusive questioning about sexual matters does not reach the required level of severity; nor does the imposition of a prison sentence of indeterminate length, at any rate while the prisoner can be regarded as serving the punitive part of the sentence rather than being detained for preventive purposes.[62]

When the state detains someone in custody under legal authority, Article 3 imposes

---

[58] Judgment of 27 September 1999. Mandatory life sentences are not incompatible with Arts. 3 and 5 of ECHR: *R. v. Lichniak, R. v. Pyrah, The Times*, 16 May 2001, CA. Children do not suffer a violation of ECHR Art. 3 from being tried in a public court, but may be unable to guide their defence adequately, so special consideration is needed to secure a fair trial on serious charges: see *Practice Direction (Crown Court: Young Defendants)* [2000] 1 WLR 659. Courts have to balance the right to a fair trial with the need to protect rape complainants against degrading cross-examination regarding previous sexual history between complainant and accused under Youth Justice and Criminal Evidence Act 1999, s. 41, so the section is read down—if evidence is relevant to a defence or an element in the prosecution case, e.g. intention/mistake, the court must allow cross-examination where not doing so would make trial unfair under ECHR Art. 6: *R. v. A. (No. 2)* [2001] 2 WLR 1546, HL, *per* Lord Steyn at 1564, para. 46:

'The effect of the decision today is that under section 41(3)(c) of the 1999 Act, construed where necessary by applying the interpretative obligation under section 3 of the Human Rights Act 1998, and due regard always being paid to the importance of seeking to protect the complainant from indignity and from humiliating questions, the test of admissibility is whether the evidence (and questioning in relation to it) is nevertheless so relevant to the issue of consent that to exclude it would endanger the fairness of the trial under article 6 of the Convention. If this test is satisfied the evidence should not be excluded.'

[59] *Tomasi v. France*, Series A, No. 241-A, Judgment of 27 August 1992, 15 EHRR 1; *Ribitsch v. Austria*, Series A, No. 336, Judgment of 4 December 1995, 21 EHRR 573; *Tekin v. Turkey*, Judgment of 9 June 1998, RJD 1998-IV; *Satik v. Turkey*, App. No. 31866/96, Judgment of 10 October 2000 at para. 54; *Rehbock v. Slovenia*, App. No. 29462/95, Judgment of 28 November 2000.

[60] *Tekin v. Turkey*, Judgment of 9 June 1998, RJD 1998-IV, at paras. 52, 53; *Satik v. Turkey*, App. No. 31866/96, Judgment of 10 October 2000 at para. 54.

[61] *Caloc v. France*, App. No. 33951/96, Judgment of 20 July 2000.

[62] *Hussain and Singh v. United Kingdom*, Judgment of 21 February 1996, 22 EHRR 1; *T. v. United Kingdom and V. v. United Kingdom*, Judgments of 16 December 1999.

positive obligations to ensure that the conditions of detention are decent and that medical attention of an appropriate standard is provided to those who need it. In *Kudła v. Poland*[63] the Court wrote:

'. . . it cannot be said that the execution of detention on remand itself raises an issue under Article 3 of the Convention. Nor can that Article be interpreted as laying down a general obligation to release a detainee on health grounds or to place him in a civil hospital to enable him to obtain a particular kind of medical treatment . . . Nevertheless, under this provision the state must ensure that a person is detained in conditions which are compatible with respect for his human dignity, that the manner and method of the execution of the measure do not subject him to distress or hardship of an intensity exceeding the unavoidable level of suffering inherent in detention and that, given the practical demands of imprisonment, his health and well-being are adequately secured by, among other things, providing him with the requisite medical assistance . . .'

Where children are subjected to physical violence, the position is complicated by their dependent status, but there are clear signs that the Court is increasingly willing to regard them as being specially vulnerable and in particular need of protection through Article 3. In *A. v. United Kingdom*,[64] a nine-year-old boy had been repeatedly caned by his mother's partner; the beating was very painful, and left extensive bruising. The Commission decided that the type and extent of the beating, and the pain which it had caused, had reached a level of severity sufficient to amount to degrading (but not inhuman) treatment, although this did not mean that Article 3 required any physical rebuke of a child, however mild, to be outlawed.[65] The Commission was influenced by the concluding observations of the UN Committee on the Rights of the Child on the UK's initial report under the Convention on the Rights of the Child, where the Committee had commented (in relation to the Children and Young Persons Act 1933) that the 'imprecise nature of the expression of reasonable chastisement as contained in these legal provisions may pave the way for it to be interpreted in a subjective and arbitrary manner'.[66] The Court also decided the case on the basis that the level of suffering fell within the range forbidden by Article 3 because a garden cane had been used, with considerable force, on more than one occasion (although it did not say whether it regarded the case as amounting to inhuman or only degrading treatment).

There was no discussion of whether the treatment humiliated the boy, an essential element in establishing degrading treatment in earlier cases. For example, in *Campbell and Cosans v. United Kingdom*,[67] the Court held that moderate use of the tawse in Scottish schools did not amount to degrading treatment. The judges accepted that widespread public approval in Scotland of the long-standing tradition

---

[63] App. No. 30210/96, Judgment of 26 October 2000 (Grand Chamber), at paras. 93–4.

[64] (1998) 27 EHRR 611.

[65] Commn., Report of 18 September 1997. By contrast, Mr. J. Loucaides would have held that any corporal punishment of a child is inherently degrading, regardless of the level of severity (concurring opinion, (1997) 27 EHRR at 627).

[66] 15 February 1995, CRC/C/15/Add. 34, para. 16.

[67] Eur. Ct. HR, Series A, No. 48 (1982) 2 EHRR 293.

of corporal punishment in schools, while not conclusive, was relevant in deciding that: 'it is not established that pupils at a school, where such a punishment is used, are, solely by reason of the risk of being subjected thereto, humiliated and debased in the eyes of others to the requisite degree at all'. Nor was there any evidence that victims suffered adverse psychological effects which might make them feel humiliated or debased.[68] In *Costello-Roberts v. United Kingdom*,[69] inflicting three strokes with a gym shoe on a seven-year-old boy at his school did not amount to either inhuman or degrading treatment. The Court's new approach in *A. v. United Kingdom* may signal that inflicting a certain level of physical pain on someone who is in one's power will now be treated as inherently humiliating for him. This was already the approach of the Commission: in several cases[70] they had decided that corporal punishment as a disciplinary measure at school constituted degrading treatment.[71] This means that degrading treatment does not necessarily inflict a different kind of suffering from that caused by inhuman treatment; it may simply cause a lower level of the same kind of suffering. Either serious humiliation or a physical assault may suffice.

Sometimes a state has an obligation to protect a person against the risk of being treated in an inhuman or degrading way by another state. In *Soering v. United Kingdom*,[72] it was held that extraditing a murder suspect to Virginia in the USA, where he would be liable to the death penalty, would violate Article 3, because the delays and conditions on death row would expose him to mental suffering ('death row phenomenon') of exceptional severity and duration, having regard to his youth and mental state at the time of the alleged offence.[73] It violates Article 3 to deport a person to a country where he or she is liable to suffer the requisite level of severe harm as a result

---

[68] Judgment at paras. 29–30.

[69] Series A, No. 247-C, Judgment of 25 March 1993.

[70] See Application No. 9303/81, *B. and D. v. United Kingdom*, Eur. Comm. HR, 49 DR 44; *Warwick v. United Kingdom*, Eur. Comm. HR, Report of 18 June 1986 (but the Committee of Ministers was unable to achieve the two-thirds majority necessary to decide whether or not Art. 3 had been violated, so the matter was dropped: Committee of Ministers, Resolution DH(89)5, 2 March 1989); *X. and Y. v. United Kingdom*, App. No. 14229/88, 1 HRCD 228. On 28 September 1988, N. Crequer in *Independent*, 4, reported that the government had paid £51,000 to 16 families who had complained to the Commission about school beatings. Two families, in each of which two children had been victims, received £4,500 each; the others received £3,000 each. In *Y. v. United Kingdom*, Eur. Ct. HR, Judgment of 29 October 1992, the Court ordered a case brought under Arts. 3 and 13 of the Convention to be struck out of the list after noting a friendly settlement under which the UK government agreed to pay £8,000 and costs to the complainant in respect of injuries suffered from four strokes of the cane at an independent school.

[71] By contrast, the Supreme Court of the USA decided by a 5–4 majority that the right to be free of cruel and unusual punishments under the Eighth Amendment to the US Constitution did not make it unconstitutional for state law to permit a school teacher to beat a pupil severely with a wooden paddle. Even if the punishment in that case was cruel and unusual, the constitutional prohibition on cruel and unusual punishments applied only to judicial punishments: *Ingraham v. Wright* 430 US 651 (1977).

[72] Series A, No. 161, Judgment of 7 July 1989.

[73] As a result, the UK government refused to extradite the applicant to the USA on any charge for which the sentence might include the death penalty. The USA, in a diplomatic note, confirmed that in the circumstances US law would prohibit the prosecution of the applicant in Virginia for the offence of capital murder, and the UK was prepared to extradite him on that understanding: Resolution DH(90)8 of the Committee of Ministers, adopted 12 March 1990, appendix.

of state action[74] or because it would be impossible to obtain treatment for a lethal disease.[75]

English law offers extensive protection to people detained by the state, or in its care, against the use of physical force. The law on detention and questioning of suspects, considered in Chapter 6, below, is compatible with Article 3. In prisons, flogging as a disciplinary measure was abolished by the Criminal Justice Act 1967. Corporal punishment of children and young persons as a disciplinary measure in state schools was abolished by the Education (No. 2) Act 1986, section 47, following the decision of the European Court of Human Rights in *Campbell and Cosans v. United Kingdom*[76] that the threat of corporal punishment directed to a pupil, against the wishes of the pupil's parent, violated the right of the parent to have the child educated in accordance with the parent's philosophical convictions, under Article 2 of Protocol No. 1 to the ECHR. The ban was extended to children's homes by the Children Act 1989, section 63, and the Children's Homes Regulations 1991, and to all schools by the School Standards and Framework Act 1998, section 131, substituting new provisions in section 548 of the Education Act 1996. However, physical restraint of a pupil is permitted to avert an immediate danger of personal injury to, or danger to the property of, anyone, including the pupil. Physical restraint of prisoners, and of patients in mental hospitals, also remains possible (discussed in Chapter 7, below). In section 5.5 below we will examine the impact of the various duties under Article 3 of the ECHR on English law governing state-supported medical experimentation and immunization programmes, consent to medical treatment, and rights of children.

5.2 THE DUTY TO PROTECT PEOPLE AGAINST THREATS OF TORTURE OR INHUMAN OR DEGRADING TREATMENT OR PUNISHMENT

Like Article 2 (the right to life), Article 3 of the ECHR gives rise to duties on the state to protect people against foreseeable threats of harm amounting to torture or inhuman or degrading treatment or punishment. This became clear in *A. v. United Kingdom*,[77] in which the Court decided that the law in the UK was inadequate to protect a nine-year-old boy from severe caning by his mother's partner, and that the UK had therefore violated the boy's right to be free of inhuman and degrading treatment.[78] Generally speaking, the law in England and Wales recognizes the state's

[74] *Chahal v. United Kingdom,* Judgment of 15 November 1996, RJD 1996-V, 23 EHRR 413; *Ahmed v. Austria,* Judgment of 17 December 1996, RJD 1996-VI, 24 EHRR 278; *Hilal v. United Kingdom,* App. No. 45276/99, Judgment of 6 March 2001.

[75] *D. v. United Kingdom,* Judgment of 2 May 1997, RJD 1997-III, 24 EHRR 423. *Cp. Bensaid v. United Kingdom,* App. No. 44599/98, Judgment of 6 February 2001, where there was some evidence that treatment for a psychotic illness would be available in Algeria, and it was held that it would not violate Art. 3 to deport the would-be immigrant.

[76] Series A, No. 48 (1982) 2 EHRR 293.

[77] Judgment of 23 September 1998, 27 EHRR 611.

[78] See, *mutatis mutandis,* Ch. 4 above, and J. McBride, 'Protecting Life: A Positive Obligation to Help' (1999) **24** *ELR HR* 43–54.

positive duty to help people to avoid degradation (in relation to the corporal punishment of children, see section 5.5(1) below). At common law, there is a duty (which may only be overridden by clear words in a statute) to provide financial and other assistance to save from starvation those who are unable to support themselves.[79] This is an unusual example of a socio-economic duty in the common law, in harmony with the positive duties flowing from Article 3. In relation to threats of harm by others, the police and the courts provide protection against such treatment in the ordinary run of events by means such as the exercise of powers of arrest and detention, orders against molestation, and the criminal penalties for harassment established by the Protection from Harassment Act 1997. Generally, the duties of the police to protect people operate in public law. In principle, they are enforceable through judicial review proceedings. However, the police have a considerable discretion as to how they deploy their human and other resources in exercising their powers, and the courts will not usually force them to give protection (or a specific level of protection) to particular people.[80]

In private law, the immunity of the police from liability for negligence in failing to protect people against the threats to life and physical injury[81] has been discussed in Chapter 4, above, together with the implications of the Human Rights Act 1998 for that immunity. The reader is referred to that discussion, which applies *mutatis mutandis* to protection against other forms of harm.

It should be noted, however, that the courts have held that the police to owe a duty of care to people in respect of reasonably foreseeable harm where a special relationship can be established between the victim and the police. For example, police officers owe a duty of care in private law to protect fellow officers against sexual harassment or sexual or other assault, whether carried out by another officer[82] or by a suspect in police custody.[83] Such attacks inflict suffering of a kind which would be quite likely to amount to degrading treatment (if not inhuman treatment) under Article 3 of the ECHR. Failing to take reasonable protective steps gives rise to a cause of action, if other conditions (such as proximity) are met. There may also be liability in tort under anti-discrimination legislation if the police offer less protection to a victim against attack because of the victim's race, sex, or disability, since the police are treated as offering services, within the meaning of the term in that legislation, to victims of crime and so have a legal duty not to discriminate in providing those services.[84]

One of the conditions for imposing a duty of care at common law (as distinct from under the equality legislation) is that it be just, fair, and reasonable to impose a duty of care in the circumstances. This has significantly limited the range of private-law

---

[79] *R. v. Eastbourne (Inhabitants)* (1803) 4 East 103, 102 ER 769, especially at 107, 770, *per* Lord Ellenborough CJ; *R. v. Secretary of State for Social Security, ex parte Joint Council for the Welfare of Immigrants* [1997] 1 WLR 275, [1996] 4 All ER 385, CA.

[80] *R. v. Chief Constable of Sussex, ex parte International Trader's Ferry Ltd.* [1999] 2 AC 418, [1999] 1 All ER 129, HL.

[81] *Osman v. Ferguson* [1993] 4 All ER 344, CA.

[82] *Waters v. Commissioner of Police of the Metropolis* [2000] 1 WLR 1607, [2000] 4 All ER 93, HL.

[83] *Costello v. Chief Constable of Northumbria* [1999] ICR 752, CA.

[84] See *Farah v. Commissioner of Police of the Metropolis* [1998] QB 65, [1997] 1 All ER 289, CA.

duties to which public authorities are subject in respect of protecting people from harm. It has been held that it is not just, fair, and reasonable to impose a duty of care on local authorities which negligently fail to protect children against the risk of abuse by their carers.[85] Similarly, a local authority cannot be made liable in damages for negligently failing to protect the owner of a shop and private home against harassment by council tenants and members of their households.[86] However, there is a shift away from giving blanket immunities to public authorities in the performance of their statutory powers and duties. While civil liability may not readily be imposed on them, especially in respect of omissions, the courts are increasingly ready to assess each case on its merits, taking account of the level of control which the authority can in practice exert over the field of activity in issue.[87]

Thus a local authority may be liable if it is instrumental in enabling the abuse to take place, for example by placing a juvenile who is known to be a child abuser with foster-parents who have young, vulnerable children of their own,[88] or where abuse is inflicted on a child in a children's home by someone employed by the authority as a carer in a local authority children's home, or where the police and social services departments disrupt family life with investigations where there is no sufficient reason for interfering.[88a] An authority which is in actual occupation of property (such as a public highway), and which fails to stop people who have based themselves on the land from causing a private nuisance to adjoining landowners, may be liable for the nuisance.[89] This suggests that English law is increasingly adapting itself to the need to protect rights arising under Article 3 and other provisions of the ECHR, in respect of which the earlier decisions have been held to offer inadequate safeguards.[89a] In addition, section 6 of the Human Rights Act 1998 imposes a legally enforceable duty on public authorities to act in a manner compatible with Convention rights, unless they are compelled to violate them by primary legislation which cannot be given effect in a manner compatible with the rights. These developments may prove to have significantly extended the legal duties (in both public and private law) of public authorities to protect people against the sort of harms which constitute inhuman or degrading treatment. This will need to happen because of decisions of the European Court of Human Rights on the right to an effective remedy for breaches of Convention rights under ECHR Article 13, considered further in Chapter 12, below.

---

[85] *X. (Minors) v. Bedfordshire County Council* [1995] 2 AC 633, [1995] 3 All ER 353, HL. See S. H. Bailey and M. J. Bowman, 'Public Authority Negligence Revisited' [2000] *CLJ* 85–132.

[86] *Hussain v. Lancaster City Council* [2000] QB 1, [1999] 4 All ER 125, CA.

[87] See, e.g. *Stovin v. Wise* [1996] AC 923, [1996] 3 All ER 801, HL; *Barrett v. Enfield London Borough Council* [1999] 3 WLR 79, [1999] 3 All ER 193, HL; Bailey and Bowman, 'Public Authority Negligence', 122–32.

[88] *W. v. Essex County Council* [1999] Fam. 90, [1998] 3 All ER 111, CA, affirmed on this point [2000] 2 WLR 601, [2000] 2 All ER 237, HL.

[88a] *L. (A Child) v. Reading Borough Council and another* [2001] 1 WLR 1575, CA; R. Carnwath, 'Welfare Services: Liabilities in Tort after the Human Rights Act' [2001] *PL* 210–19.

[89] *Lippiatt v. South Gloucestershire Council* [2000] QB 51, [1999] 4 All ER 149, CA.

[89a] *Z. v. United Kingdom*, App. No. 29392/95, *T.P. and K.M. v. United Kingdom*, App. No. 28945/95, Judgments of 10 May 2001; R. Carnwath, 'Welfare Services—Liabilities in Tort after the Human Rights Act. Postscript' [2001] *PL* 475–9.

5.3 THE DUTY TO INVESTIGATE ALLEGED ACTS OF TORTURE AND INHUMAN OR DEGRADING TREATMENT

In English law, there is a duty on the police, and sometimes on other agencies, to investigate allegations of behaviour amounting to torture and inhuman or degrading treatment. Before the coming into force of the Human Rights Act 1998, this was subject to three limitations. First, the courts would not ordinarily intervene on public law grounds to require the police to investigate a particular offence, or to oversee the way in which an investigation was carried out, although it would have been regarded as a breach of duty to refuse to investigate a class of offences without regard to the particular circumstances.[90] Secondly, a failure to investigate would not usually give rise to liability in negligence in private law, because the House of Lords held that it was not fair, just, and reasonable to impose a private law duty towards the public at large in respect of the investigation of a crime, or towards a person identified as a likely victim of a known assailant.[91] Thirdly, private law in the UK does not allow people to recover damages for negligently caused mental suffering which falls short of psychiatric illness. It permits a plaintiff to recover for psychiatric illness caused by grave physical injury to a third party, but only if the psychiatric illness was caused by witnessing the injury, the plaintiff had particularly close family ties to the victim of the physical injury, and the risk of psychiatric illness (not only physical injury) was a reasonably foreseeable result of the negligent acts or omissions of the defendant.[92]

It is not clear that this restrictive approach meets the requirements of Articles 3 and 13 of the ECHR. Article 13 provides: 'Everyone whose rights and freedoms as set forth in this Convention are violated shall have an effective remedy before a national authority notwithstanding that the violation has been committed by persons acting in an official capacity'. Because of the fundamental nature of the obligations under Article 3, the European Court of Human Rights held in *Aydin v. Turkey*[93] that Article 13 had been violated where state authorities fail to conduct an adequate investigation of an allegation that someone has been the victim of inhuman or degrading treatment. The adequacy of an investigation was assessed having regard to the speed with which it is instigated, the investigators' independence of the state agencies being investigated (when allegations implicated state officials), the vigour and efficiency

---

[90] *R. v. Commissioner of Police of the Metropolis, ex parte Blackburn* [1968] 2 QB 118, [1968] 1 All ER 763, CA; *R. v. Commissioner of Police of the Metropolis, ex parte Blackburn (No. 3)* [1973] QB 241, [1973] 1 All ER 324, CA.

[91] *Hill v. Chief Constable of West Yorkshire* [1989] AC 53, [1988] 2 All ER 238, HL; *Osman v. Ferguson* [1993] 4 All ER 344, CA.

[92] *Alcock v. Chief Constable of the South Yorkshire Police* [1992] 1 AC 310, [1991] 4 All ER 907, HL; *Page v. Smith* [1996] AC 155, [1995] 2 All ER 736, HL; *Frost v. Chief Constable of the South Yorkshire Police* [1999] 2 AC 455, *sub. nom. White v. Chief Constable of the South Yorkshire Police* [1999] 1 All ER 1, HL. 'Rescuers', i.e. people who go to assist victims of accidents or crimes and suffer psychiatric illness after either being objectively at risk of physical injury or reasonably believing that they are at risk of physical injury as a result, can recover damages from the person whose negligence gave rise to the need for a rescue: *Frost*, above.

[93] Judgment of 25 September 1997, 25 EHRR 251, at paras. 1103–9.

with which it is pursued, and the thoroughness of the report of the findings. If something goes wrong (such as a file being mislaid) which undermines the effectiveness of the investigation and of any possibility of subsequent remedies in respect of the injury, the inadequacy of the investigation will itself amount to a violation of Article 13. Applying this line of reasoning in the law of the UK might seem to pose difficulties, in view of the fact that Article 13 is not one of the Convention rights made part of national law by section 1 of the Human Rights Act 1998. However, in other cases the Court has read the requirements of Article 13 into Article 3 itself.[94] If the authorities adopt an unhelpful, obstructive, and complacent attitude to somebody reporting a suspected death or disappearance, who is emotionally close to the primary victim and was present when he was taken away, the person making the report may also be a victim of a violation of Article 3 if he suffers long-drawn-out fear or apprehension for the primary victim.[95]

Courts in the UK must have regard to the caselaw of the European Court of Human Rights when interpreting Article 3.[96] They are not bound to follow decisions of the Court, although it is likely to lead to a finding of a violation in Strasbourg if our courts give a less extensive interpretation to Article 3 (with obligations which are absolute and non-derogable) than that which the Strasbourg Court applies. In view of the fundamental importance of the right to be free of torture and inhuman or degrading treatment, the significance of a proper investigation to vindicating that right, and the absence from national law of a right to an effective remedy under Article 13 for violations of Article 3, there are particularly strong reasons for national courts to adopt the Strasbourg Court's extended interpretation of Article 3 as including a right to an effective investigation. If national courts do so, it may have one of three effects. The courts may be prepared to expand their public law control over the police, perhaps using judicial review mechanisms to ensure effective investigations of allegations of inhuman or degrading treatment. This would have the disadvantage of involving courts in police decision-making during the conduct of an investigation. Alternatively, the common law duties of investigators may be expanded to make investigators liable to an alleged victim if they fail to take reasonable care when investigating complaints about conduct which amounts to inhuman or degrading treatment. This would require a development of private law obligations in the light of the values of Article 3, perhaps relying on the duty of courts, as public authorities, to act compatibly with Convention rights.[97] Finally, courts could straightforwardly assert that public bodies with investigative functions have a new statutory duty under section 6 of the Human Rights Act 1998 to act compatibly with the rights of victims under Article 3 of the ECHR, and enforce that duty through judicial review, through

---

[94] See, e.g. the approach in *Kaya v. Turkey*, Judgment of 19 February 1998, RJD 1998-I; *Yasa v. Turkey*, Judgment of 2 September 1998, RJD 1998-VI; *Assenov v. Bulgaria*, Judgment of 28 October 1998, RJD 1998-VIII; *Satik v. Turkey*, App. No. 31866/96, Judgment of 10 October 2000, at paras. 58–60 (investigations ineffective: violation of Art. 3); *Caloc v. France*, App. No. 33951/96, Judgment of 20 July 2000 (no violation of Art. 3).

[95] *Çiçek v. Turkey*, App. No. 25704/94, Judgment of 27 February 2001.

[96] Human Rights Act 1998, s. 2.

[97] Ibid., s. 6.

compensatory remedies under sections 7 and 8 of the Act, or through a combination of both types of remedies.

If courts follow the route via section 6 of the Human Rights Act 1998, the caselaw of the European Court of Human Rights under Article 3 may lead them to award damages for mental suffering which falls short of psychiatric illness whether it arises from the infliction of inhuman or degrading treatment or the investigation of allegations of such treatment.

5.4 THE DUTY TO SECURE LEGAL ACCOUNTABILITY AND REMEDIES FOR TORTURE OR INHUMAN OR DEGRADING TREATMENT OR PUNISHMENT

Article 3 of the ECHR (taken together with Article 13), as interpreted by the Court, impose on state authorities a positive duty to secure an effective legal remedy for anyone who suffers assaults on their physical or mental well-being sufficiently serious to amount to inhuman or degrading treatment. This is seen as being essential to provide adequate protection for people against the dangers which Article 3 addresses. Although most of the cases on this have been concerned with treatment meted out by state officials, the state also has a duty to ensure that adequate legal remedies are available against private persons who cause injury of the requisite degree of severity. This positive obligation on the state flows from interpreting Article 3 of the ECHR in the light of Article 1, in which states undertake to 'secure to everyone within their jurisdiction the rights and freedoms defined in Section I of this Convention'. An important part of doing so is providing effective means of imposing legal liability on people who cause others to suffer inhuman or degrading treatment. Part of the purpose is to deter future infringements of Article 3 rights. While civil remedies may be adequate to secure some rights, people's physical and moral integrity and dignity are so fundamentally important that criminal penalties are needed to give adequate protection against serious violations, such as rape or sexual assault.[98]

The type and level of protection which is needed will vary depending on the circumstances and the characteristics of the victim, but, as the Court has said, 'Children and other vulnerable individuals, in particular, are entitled to state protection, in the form of effective deterrence, against such serious breaches of personal integrity'.[99] Generally, protection against abuse is offered by the criminal law. However, section 1(7) of the Children and Young Persons Act 1933 excludes criminal liability where those with responsibilities for the care and control of children employ reasonable

---

[98] See *X. and Y. v. The Netherlands*, Series A, No. 91, Judgment of 26 March 1985, 8 EHRR 235 (decided under Art. 8, but similar principles apply to Art. 3).

[99] *A. v. United Kingdom*, Judgment of 23 September 1998, 27 EHRR 611, at para. 22, citing (*mutatis mutandis*) *X. and Y. v. The Netherlands*, Series A, No. 91, 8 EHRR 235, *Stubbings v. United Kingdom*; Judgment of 22 October 1996, RJD 1996-IV, 23 EHRR 213, and UN Convention on the Rights of the Child, Arts. 19 and 37.

physical punishment. In *A. v. United Kingdom*,[100] a nine-year-old boy's stepfather had apparently hit him regularly with a garden cane, using considerable force, sometimes on his bare legs, and leaving significant bruising. The stepfather was charged with assault occasioning actual bodily harm, but was acquitted after the judge directed the jury that an assault on a child by a person with parental responsibilities could be justified if it had been carried out for the purpose of correcting the child, and was reasonable with regard to the manner of infliction, the instrument used, and quantity of punishment inflicted. The boy complained successfully to Strasbourg that he had not been adequately protected against physical abuse, and had suffered a violation of his Article 3 rights. As the legislation required the prosecution to establish that the treatment meted out to the child had exceeded 'reasonable chastisement', and it had been unable to do so in a case where the suffering amounted to inhuman or degrading treatment, it was held that the law did not offer adequate protection to the boy. The Court also noted that similar rules governed the civil liability of the stepfather for battery, effectively precluding any legal accountability for his actions.

The particular implications of this for the law governing the corporal punishment of children will be considered below, in section 5.5(1). Here it is sufficient to note the general significance for English law of the state's positive obligation to secure legal accountability in order to protect people from inhuman and degrading treatment, bearing in mind that the term encompasses the infliction of severe emotional and psychiatric injury as well as physical assaults. Three matters are relevant: first, the scope of legal liability for such harms; secondly, immunities and defences which might interfere with legal accountability, as in *A. v. United Kingdom*; and, thirdly, the prosecution or extradition of people charged with offences of torture allegedly committed in other countries.

(1) THE SCOPE OF LIABILITY

The law has already developed in recent years to provide additional protection against harm which might constitute inhuman or degrading treatment. A telephone call (even if it is silent, or consists only of heavy breathing) can be a criminal assault occasioning actual or grievous bodily harm if it inflicts psychiatric harm on the recipient by causing fear of immediate and unlawful violence, as long as the caller has the necessary mental element.[101] Psychiatric injury is equated, here, to physical injury: the severity of the harm determines whether it causes grievous bodily harm or actual bodily harm. This sort of indirect assault can be committed in other ways besides telephone calls.[102] The crime is not committed by harassment which does not cause the victim to apprehend immediate unlawful violence, but courts are prepared to infer an apprehension of immediate unlawful violence from the circumstances of the case: they do not adopt a narrow, technical approach to the requirement of immediacy, and

---

[100] Judgment of 23 September 1998, 27 EHRR 611.

[101] *R. v. Ireland* [1998] AC 147, [1997] 4 All ER 225, HL, on the Offences against the Person Act 1861, ss. 18 and 20.

[102] *Cp. R. v. Costanza* [1997] 2 Cr. App. R. 492, CA (threatening letter causing psychiatric harm).

accept that silence may, in context, threaten unlawful violence.[103] Nevertheless, the criminal law gives no protection against degrading treatment which does not threaten immediate unlawful violence, yet causes fear and humiliation but not psychiatric injury. The same applies to civil law, which does not protect against the intentional or negligent infliction of mental anguish or nervous distress falling short of a clinically recognized psychiatric condition.[104]

In this respect, the law may fail to provide adequate protection against some violations of Article 3. It is possible that the obligation to read and give effect to legislation in a manner compatible with Convention rights so far as it is possible to do so, under the Human Rights Act 1998, section 3, might lead to a further expansion of the meaning of 'bodily harm' in the Offences against the Person Act 1861. It will not affect the development of the common law, but a civil court might consider itself, as a public authority, to be obliged by section 6 of the 1998 Act to extend civil liability for negligence or battery to give protection against inhuman or degrading treatment which does not cause clinically recognized physical or psychiatric injury. As the European Court of Human Rights has imposed a positive obligation on states to protect private individuals against inhuman or degrading treatment by other private individuals, this is a situation in which national courts might be prepared to give a measure of horizontal effect to a Convention right, developing private law accordingly.

(2) IMMUNITIES AND DEFENCES

We have already noted that the police have extensive immunities from liability for negligence in conducting inquiries, and are permitted to use reasonable force if necessary to make an arrest and to exercise many other powers. Similarly, the lawful exercise of parental authority over a child may include reasonable corporal punishment. As applied in the past, these immunities and defences may prevent courts from providing adequate protection to victims of inhuman or degrading treatment. Where the defence or immunity is found in a statute and is limited by a conception of reasonableness, courts are likely to approach it in the light of section 3 of the Human Rights Act 1998, holding that an exercise of authority which violates a Convention right, particularly one as fundamental as those under Article 3, can never be reasonable. Where the defence or immunity is found in the common law, it is likely to be developed or limited according to similar considerations, bearing in mind the obligations of courts as public authorities under section 6 of the Act to act compatibly with Convention rights, subject to the operation of the rules of *stare decisis*. If such an approach were to be rejected, it would encourage a multiplicity of applications to Strasbourg under the ECHR.

---

[103] *R. v. Ireland* [1998] AC 147, [1997] 4 All ER 225, HL.
[104] *Alcock v. Chief Constable of South Yorkshire Police* [1992] 1 AC 310, [1991] 1 All ER 353, HL.

(3) PROSECUTION OR EXTRADITION FOR EXTRA-TERRITORIAL OFFENCES OF TORTURE

The UK offers a degree of protection against, and legal accountability for, torture committed abroad by agents of another state. The UN Convention against Torture and Other Cruel, Inhuman or Degrading Treatment or Punishment requires states either to prosecute suspects for such extra-territorial offences or to extradite them to jurisdictions which are prepared to prosecute them. In the UK, section 134 of the Criminal Justice Act 1988 makes torture, wherever it was committed, a criminal offence in the UK from 29 September 1988 when the section came into force. As noted in section 5.1, above, section 134 has a wider definition of torture than the Convention, defining it by reference to the degree of suffering inflicted rather than the purposes of the person inflicting it. This allows the section to take in at least some elements of inhuman and degrading treatment and punishment which fall short of torture, although the threshold level of suffering under the section is higher than that which the European Court of Human Rights now uses in relation to inhuman or degrading treatment under Article 3 of the ECHR.

The doctrine of state immunity, in principle, protects agents of the state, heads of state, and former heads of state against criminal liability in the UK for official acts.[105] However, it does not protect them from criminal liability in this country for torture committed elsewhere after section 134 of the 1988 Act came into force, as torture is an international crime and *jus cogens*, overriding any justifications in national law. Since only a public official (including for this purpose a head of state) can be guilty of torture under the Convention, it would make nonsense of the Convention if the immunity were co-extensive with the offence. Furthermore, torture committed elsewhere is an extradition offence under the Extradition Act 1989 where the torture took place after 29 September 1988 or, at the latest, after the states concerned ratified the UN Convention against Torture, imposing obligations on states either to prosecute or to extradite alleged torturers.[106]

There is a greater problem about obtaining a civil remedy, such as damages, in the UK for torture committed abroad by agents of another state. The English Court of Appeal in *Al-Adsani v. Government of Kuwait*[107] struck out a claim for damages brought by a refugee from Kuwait claiming to have been tortured by agents of the Kuwaiti government. It was held that section 1 of the State Immunity Act 1978 confers immunity on states from civil suit in UK courts, except in relation to matters which are expressly excepted from the immunity (such as death or personal injury caused by an action in the UK, or commercial transactions). There was no room for any implied exception, for example relating to the international crime of torture. This was subsequently approved by three members of the House of Lords in *R. v. Bow Street Metropolitan Stipendiary Magistrate, ex parte Pinochet Ugarte (No. 3)*.[108] Mr. Al-Adsani petitioned the European Court of Human Rights, arguing that the lack of a remedy in

---

[105] State Immunity Act 1978, s. 20, read with Diplomatic Privileges Act 1964, Sch. 1, art. 39(2).

[106] *R. v. Bow Street Metropolitan Stipendiary Magistrate, ex parte Pinochet Ugarte (No. 3)* [2000] 1 AC 147, [1999] 2 WLR 827, [1999] 2 All ER 97, HL.

[107] (1996) 107 ILR 536, CA.

[108] [2000] 1 AC 147, [1999] 2 WLR 827 at 891–2 (Lord Hutton), 914 (Lord Millett), 920–3 (Lord Phillips of Worth Matravers).

the UK for acts of torture committed in Kuwait violated his rights under Article 3 and Article 6 of the ECHR. In 2000, the Court decided that the application was admissible, without prejudging the merits of the case.[109] A judgment on the merits, which at the time of writing is awaited, could have a significant impact on the international law of state immunity.

5.5 APPLYING THE GENERAL PRINCIPLES IN HARD CASES:
PARENTS AND CHILDREN

The rights of children to personal liberty and dignity are necessarily curtailed by reason of the dependent nature of children. As people, children are *prima facie* entitled to enjoy all the rights which attach to people. This is recognized in international law, both in the general human rights treaties and in the special provisions of the UN Convention on the Rights of the Child. On the other hand, as people with special needs they attract special treatment: other (adult) people have responsibilities for their welfare and development, over and above the ordinary responsibilities which we all have for each other's welfare and development; and in order to discharge those developmental responsibilities, and also to protect young people against the worst dangers which threaten as a result of their relative inexperience and incompletely developed understanding, it is necessary to permit interferences with the rights of children which would not be permitted in the case of normal adults. There is therefore a tension, in relation to children's rights, between the desire to protect them against harm and exercise control in order to make possible a more perfect autonomy in their adulthood, and a need to respect them as people in their own right, with their own claims to dignity and self-respect. The way in which these objectives are accommodated in law and child-rearing practices varies between societies and times.

The main constraints on children's civil liberties which do not apply to adults relate to the needs of education and development, and (as an element thereof) socialization and discipline. These are held in the UK to justify a certain amount of restriction of freedom of movement, a subjection to the opinions of parents or guardians and teachers, and a limited liability to treatment which might be regarded as degrading if applied to adults.

(1) PHYSICAL PUNISHMENT IN THE FAMILY

English law allows a certain latitude to parents and others who exercise parental responsibility in bringing up and disciplining the children in their charge. Parental views on upbringing generally are required to be respected by Article 8 of the European Convention (respect for private and family life) and Article 2 of the First Protocol (education in accordance with parents' religious and philosophical convictions).

---

[109] *Sulaiman Al-Adsani v. United Kingdom*, App. No. 35763/97, Decision of 1 March 2000 (Grand Chamber).

As noted above, English law permits parents to apply reasonable force to their children for the purpose of punishing them. As long as the force used is not excessive, and the manner of applying it is reasonable, the parent has a justification which will prevent the infliction making the parent liable for assault or battery.[110] To that extent the child's right to physical integrity is restricted. However, if the manner of infliction is unreasonable or the degree of force threatened or used is excessive, having regard to the age and character of the child, the nature of the offence, and the circumstances of the infliction, the punishment becomes an assault or battery.[111]

The subject of physical punishment of children is a contentious one. The prevailing view among doctors and educational psychologists in this country is that physical punishment has negative results, and is ineffective in the long term in instilling self-discipline or improving the behaviour of a child. It has been argued that the intentional infliction of physical harm on a person degrades both the victim and the inflicter, and perhaps observers as well. In many other European countries, including Sweden, Finland, Denmark, Norway, and Austria, corporal punishment at home has been restricted by law, but an attempt in the House of Lords to introduce criminal sanctions in the Children Act 1989 was unsuccessful. Professor Michael Freeman has suggested that corporal punishment is akin to child abuse.[112] In *A. v. United Kingdom*,[113] as noted above, the European Court of Human Rights held that beatings with a garden cane, administered with considerable force to a nine-year-old boy by his stepfather, violated Article 3 of the ECHR. International pressure to control punishment of children by parents is undoubtedly growing.[114]

The matter has been subject to several official reviews with a view to law reform. The Scottish Law Commission has recommended that in Scotland a parent should be both civilly and criminally liable for striking a child with any implement, whether or not it causes pain or injury, or acting in a way which causes, or risks causing, injury or more than transient pain to a child.[115] In 2000, both the Department of Health in London and the Scottish Executive issued consultation papers on possible changes to

---

[110] Children and Young Persons Act 1933, s.1(7); J. L. Caldwell, 'Parental Physical Punishment and the Law' (1989) 13 *New Zealand Universities LJ* 370–88. A similar freedom previously allowed to teachers in all schools and nursery schools until the Education (No. 2) Act 1986, and in some schools since, has now been entirely abolished: Education Act 1996, s.548, as substituted by School Standards and Framework Act 1998, s.131. However, the section does not apply to teachers employed privately by parents to educate their children at home; it seems that they may continue to employ reasonable physical punishment.

[111] *R. v. Hopley* (1860) 2 F. & F. 202; *Cleary v. Booth* [1893] 1 QB 465, DC; *R. v. Mackie* (1973) 57 Cr. A R. 453, CA; *R. v. Dupperon* [1985] 2 WWR 369, CA of Saskatchewan.

[112] M. D. A. Freeman, *The Rights and Wrongs of Children* (London: Francis Pinter, 1983), 111–14; M. Freeman, 'The Convention: An English Perspective', in M. Freeman (ed.), *Children's Rights: A Comparative Perspective* (Aldershot: Dartmouth, 1996), 93–112 at 100: 'nothing is a clearer statement of the position that children occupy in society, nor a clearer badge of childhood, than the fact that children are the only members of society who can be hit with impunity'.

[113] Judgment of 23 September 1998, 27 EHRR 611.

[114] G. Van Bueren, *The International Law on the Rights of the Child* (The Hague: Martinus Nijhoff, 1998), 88–90; J. Fortin, *Children's Rights and the Developing Law* (London: Butterworths, 1998), 228–34.

[115] Scottish Law Commission, *Report on Family Law* (SLC No. 135, 1992), para. 2.105; C. Barton, 'It's OK to Belt your Kids' (1992) 142 *NLJ* 1262–3.

the law on corporal punishment.[116] They noted that studies have shown that nearly all children have been hit or threatened with physical punishment, often with implements, and that a significant majority of people thought that it should be lawful to smack children, but a very large majority thought that it should be unlawful to use an implement to strike a child. It remains to be seen whether legislation results. So far, no legislation has resulted from the consultation exercises, and it is still regarded as acceptable for children to be physically punished. Indeed, in *Sutton London Borough Council v. Davis*[117] Wilson J upheld the decision of a magistrates' court that the applicant was a fit person to be a childminder, notwithstanding her refusal to undertake not to smack the children in her care and the inflexible policy of the local authority not to permit childminders to smack children.

The right to beat children is apparently confined to parents or guardians, and other people having lawful control or charge of children, such as registered childminders.[118] It has been held that it does not extend to other people who have temporary *de facto*, but not *de iure*, responsibility for the care of the children, such as the child's elder brother.[119] This stems from an understandable desire to limit the range of people who are free to decide whether to inflict violence on the child.

There is more opposition now than formerly to any beating of children, and there are many who would like to see the parent's or guardian's right withdrawn by law. In community homes accommodating children in local authority care, corporal punishment has been abolished. However, there is a grey area surrounding the core meaning of corporal punishment, where it fades into restraint and accepted physical contact with a view to reinforcing an injunction. If all else fails, is it an unjustified assault to strike a child who is intent on sticking his fingers into an electrical socket? Is it an assault, or an unlawful detention, to confine a child to her bedroom after requiring her to surrender her outer garments, as in the 'pin-down' regime operated for a time in children's homes in Staffordshire and elsewhere? The latter is certainly a more extensive assault on the dignity and self-esteem of the 'victim' than is the former. The issues are different in each case. In the former case, the question is whether the beating is punishment or education. In the latter, the issue is whether the manner of the punishment is or is not unjustified. In terms of the Convention, it is fairly clear that the latter is more degrading than the former. But in terms of English domestic law, the question in every case is whether the punishment is of a justifiable type and administered for a justifiable purpose.

For some parents, an attempt to ban corporal punishment in the name of the rights of the child would, apart from being unenforceable, itself amount to an assault on the family and privacy rights of the parents. In Sweden, the Parliament had attempted

---

[116] Department of Health, *Protecting Children, Supporting Parents: A Consultation Document on the Physical Punishment of Children* (London: Department of Health, 2000); The Scottish Executive, *The Physical Punishment of Children in Scotland: A Consultation* (Edinburgh: Scottish Executive, 2000).

[117] [1994] Fam. 241, [1995] 1 All ER 53.

[118] This was recognized by Parliament in the Children and Young Persons Act 1933, s. 1(7). It may now be restricted to people who have parental responsibility for the child under the Children Act 1989, and those to whom the responsibility is delegated.

[119] *R. v. Woods* (1921) 85 JP 272.

to discourage parental beating of children by making the application of corporal punishment contrary to the Code of Parenthood. Members of a Free Protestant sect had petitioned the European Commission, alleging breaches of Article 8 of the Convention. It was said that this infringed their right to respect for family life under Article 8 of the Convention. It interfered with their freedom to organize their families and rear their children in accordance with their religious precepts, they claimed, because, although there were no penal sanctions for breach of the Code, it was taken into account in making decisions about when the state should interfere in child care. It was therefore possible that their children might be more likely to be taken into care by the authorities than the children of parents who had different religious beliefs. The Commission held that the application was inadmissible, but only because the Code had no direct legal effects and the applicants had not shown that they had suffered or were at substantial risk of having their family lives interfered with on this account.[120]

In the domestic law of England and Wales, and other common-law countries where such issues have arisen, it is settled law that, in the nature and extent of corporal punishment, parents must be guided by accepted norms in the society in which they live. Special sets of beliefs, or norms derived from other societies, do not justify punishment which is excessive according the norms of this society. Thus the criminal liability of immigrants and members of religious sects for assaulting their children in the name of discipline will be settled according to standards current in the wider society. In South Africa, the Constitutional Court has held that the state may control the use of corporal punishment in schools without violating the right to religion of the pupils or their parents, because parents with a conscientious commitment to beating their children remain able to do so at home.[120a] In the UK, corporal punishment is banned in schools, as noted in section 5.1 above, but can still be used at home. Following the decision of the European Court of Human Rights in *A. v. United Kingdom*, a consultation process has been under way in which the government has suggested (a) expansion of factors to be taken into consideration when considering defence of reasonable chastisement; (b) restricting defence to common assault only; or (c) clarifying and restricting the class of those who might claim defence to parents and those acting with their express permission. No legislation has been introduced, so the matter has been left to the common law. In *R. v. H. (Reasonable Chastisement)*,[120b] H was charged with assault occasioning actual bodily harm after allegedly hitting his four-year-old son several times with a belt on the back of his legs, leaving bruising, as punishment for not being able or willing to write his name. The Court of Appeal decided in the light of the Convention rights that, of the three options noted above, only (a) was an appropriate exercise of judicial power to develop law, as opposed to a legislative act. Juries should therefore be directed that in relation to reasonableness they must consider (i) the nature and context of the defendant's behaviour, (ii) the duration of the behaviour, (iii) the physical and mental consequences to the child, (iv)

---

[120] *X. and Y. v. Sweden* (8819/79), 29 DR 104 (Commission); see also *G. Hendriks v. Netherlands* (8429/78), 18 DR 225 (Commission); CM Resolution 82/4 of 10 December 1982 (Committee of Ministers).

[120a] *Christian Education South Africa v. Minister of Education*, 2000 (4) SA 757, Const. Ct. of SA.

[120b] *The Times*, 17 May 2001, CA.

the age and personal characteristics of the child, and (v) the reasons given by the defendant for administering punishment. It would not breach Convention rights to make this sort of incremental development in the common law, as hints of such a move could be traced back to early cases on the subject. The reasonableness of a punishment, like the intention of the defendant to use an unlawful degree of force,[121] is therefore always a question of fact for the jury to decide (where there is a jury),[122] although the fact that one is a recent immigrant unfamiliar with local child-rearing practices may be a mitigating factor at the sentencing stage.[123] But this approach does not require a British court or legislature to outlaw all corporal punishment in the home when there is no evidence that the current consensus regards such punishment as unacceptable. As Judge Fitzmaurice observed, dissenting in *Tyrer*, most people in most societies have been subjected to beating or the threat of it as part of growing up, and continue to use it on their own children.

(2) NON-THERAPEUTIC BODILY MUTILATION

Sometimes an insult to the body is inflicted in order to confer a social (rather than clinical or educational) advantage on the subject. When injury is done for such a reason, the question is whether the law will recognize even free consent as sufficient to justify a significant, and often practically irreversible, invasion of a person's bodily integrity. In some circumstances, a subject's consent cannot authorize a procedure (such as homosexual sado-masochistic activity) which inflicts actual bodily harm on him.[124] As to the circumstances in which a person can authorize such an assault, the law is neither clear nor coherent, the Court of Appeal having held in *R. v. Wilson (Alan)*[125] that a woman could lawfully authorize her male partner to carve his initials in her buttocks as a mark of attachment. There is little doubt that at least some pain can lawfully be inflicted on a person, with his or her consent, for religious purposes. The Law Commission has provisionally proposed that the law should be clarified by providing that nobody under the age of 18 should be able to consent to any injury for sexual, religious, or spiritual purposes, but that an adult should be able to consent to any injury which is not severely disabling, regardless of the purpose for which it is inflicted.[126] For the time being, the position remains unclear.

Where the subject of an invasive, painful, potentially irreversible, and non-therapeutic procedure is a child, there must always be a presumption against allowing

[121] This is a part of the *mens rea* of assault: *R. v. Gladstone Williams* (1983) 78 Cr. App. R. 276, CA, although in one case it has been held that, in cases concerning punishment, where the defendant is attempting to justify an application of force which is *prima facie* unlawful, an intention to use any force suffices if the degree of force is objectively unreasonable: *R. v. Smith* [1985] Crim. LR 42, CA, and Commentary by Professor J. C. Smith.
[122] *R. v. Derriviere* (1969) 53 Cr. App. R. 637, CA; in Canada, *R. v. Baptiste* (1981) 66 CCC (2d) 438 (Ontario Provincial Ct.).
[123] *R. v. Geraldes* (1965) 46 CR 365 (CA of Quebec).
[124] *R. v. Brown (Anthony)* [1994] 1 AC 212, [1993] 2 All ER 75, HL.
[125] [1997] QB 47, [1996] 3 WLR 125, CA.
[126] Law Commission, *Criminal Law: Consent in the Criminal Law*, Consultation Paper No. 139 (London: HMSO, 1995), paras. 4.29, 4.49, 10.52–10.55.

the child's consent to justify the act unless it can be shown that the people with parental responsibility for the child also agree to it, or that the procedure is objectively in the child's best interests. This is already the law, for example, in respect of blood tests to establish paternity,[127] examination in relation to child-abuse inquiries,[128] non-therapeutic experimentation,[129] and tattooing.[130]

The same principle would seem, in principle, to apply to various forms of mutilation carried out for religious or social reasons: ear piercing, circumcision, and clitorectomy (sometimes called female circumcision).[131] Arguments that these practices should be permitted in order to give effect to the right to practice religious beliefs founder, because the beliefs in question are those of the parents, and one person's religious freedom should not be used in order to justify an interference with another person's right to bodily integrity.[132] This is a classic example of a case where the parent's freedom ends where the child's nose (or other anatomical protuberance) begins. A stronger argument presents mutilation as necessary in order to protect the child's future as a member of the social or religious group. An uncircumcised Jewish boy is at a social disadvantage in the Jewish community; similar considerations (*mutatis mutandis*) may apply to Muslims and other communities. None the less, in *Re J*.[133] English courts refused to order a five-year-old boy to be circumcised for religious reasons at the request of his Muslim father but against the wishes of his mother. At first instance, Wall J followed the Law Commission[134] in accepting that circumcision for religious purposes could be lawful. To be lawful, both parents would have to consent,[135] or the court would have to be persuaded that circumcision was in the child's best interests. Wall J decided that it was not in the child's best interests to be circumcised, having regard to the division of medical opinion about the long-term effects of circumcision, the child's generally secular upbringing, his age, the fact that

---

[127] *Cf. S. v. McC. (orse S.) and M. (D. S. intervener); W. v. W.* [1972] AC 24, [1970] 3 All ER 107, HL; *In re O. (A Minor) (Blood Tests: Constraint)* [2000] 2 WLR 1284, Wall J, not following *In re R. (A Minor) (Blood Tests: Constraint)* [1998] Fam 66, Hale J.

[128] The Children Act 1989, s. 43(8), provides that the court, when deciding whether to authorize a medical examination of a child, is not to do so if the child does not wish to co-operate and is *Gillick*-competent.

[129] See J. K. Mason and R. A. McCall Smith, *Law and Medical Ethics*, 3rd edn. (London: Butterworths, 1991), 368–74; Law Commission, *Criminal Law: Consent*, paras. 8.38–8.51.

[130] Tattooing of minors, otherwise than by or under the direction of a registered medical practitioner for medical reasons, is an offence: Tattooing of Minors Act 1969, s. 1. See Law Commission, *Criminal Law: Consent*, paras. 9.24–9.26.

[131] Clitorectomy and related practices, but not circumcision of males, are criminal offences unless performed for reasons of medical necessity for the physical or mental health of the patient by a registered medical practitioner or, in certain cases, a registered midwife: Prohibition of Female Circumcision Act 1985, ss. 1, 2.

[132] The Prohibition of Female Circumcision Act 1985, s. 2(2), expressly excludes matters of custom and ritual from consideration when deciding whether an operation is necessary for the mental health of the woman.

[133] [1999] 2 FLR 678, Wall J; [2000] 1 FCR 307, CA. The case is fully discussed by P. W. Edge, 'Male Circumcision after the Human Rights Act 1998' (2000) 5 *Journal of Civil Liberties* 320–37, who provides full citations to the literature on the subject.

[134] Law Commission, *Criminal Law: Consent* at para. 9.2.

[135] Edge, 'Male Circumcision' at 325, points out that the idea that consent by both parents would make circumcision lawful was *obiter* and not supported by detailed consideration of the issues.

circumcision is irreversible, and the risks inherent in the procedure. The social factors were particularly important, but the boy's age played a part in the decision, not least by emphasizing the significance of the social issues: questions of upbringing are less significant when a child is circumcised at only a few days of age (as is usual among Jews), rather than when several years old. The Court of Appeal affirmed the decision, on essentially the same grounds.

Whatever may be the position under English, Islamic, Jewish, or other law, Article 3 of the ECHR, which now forms part of English law and imposes protective obligations on the state, guarantees to children, as to adults, the absolute right to be free from inhuman treatment, which cannot be qualified to give effect to any other right (let alone a social benefit). It is arguable that circumcision and other forms of mutilation, conducted without the victim's 'real' consent and for non-therapeutic purposes, constitute inhuman treatment, particularly if they are irreversible. If so, the UK is failing in its international obligations if its law permits such procedures to be carried out.

Anyone wishing to decide this difficult matter in the context of the Human Rights Act 1998 and the positive obligations of the state under Article 3 of the ECHR must answer the following question. Must treatment humiliate the victim in his or her own eyes or those of ordinary people in that society in order to constitute inhuman or degrading treatment? If it must, circumcising male children may be on a par with ear piercing: a relatively trivial and commonplace form of mutilation; while female circumcision would definitely not be acceptable. On the other hand, if treatment can be inhuman or degrading without unduly humiliating the victim, the legality of the treatment does not depend on local social morality but on internationally accepted standards of objective injury. In principle, this is a preferable approach: it is not objectively acceptable for any society to inflict severe suffering on people, either in the belief that it is for their own good or in order to benefit society. As noted in section 5.1, above, the European Court of Human Rights has gradually tended towards this view. When a certain level of pain is inflicted on children or people under the control of the state, the Court in recent cases has either not looked for humiliation or has assumed it. The question, therefore, is whether male circumcision inflicts sufficient suffering on a child to cross the threshold of degrading treatment under Article 3, taking account of the way in which circumcision is carried out, the long term and short term consequences of the procedure, and the benefits for the child which flow from it. It should be possible to make that assessment in the child's interest without being swayed by social conventions and religious traditions and laws, but it will not be easy. As Carolyn Hamilton observes, 'The acceptability of male circumcision and the unacceptability of female circumcision undoubtedly relies partly on the harm factor, but partly on the fact that male circumcision is a well known practice in the west, and is accepted as a necessary, and wholly religious, practice, for certain religious groups'.[136]

---

[136] C. Hamilton, *Family, Law and Religion* (London: Sweet & Maxwell, 1995), 149.

5.6 APPLYING THE GENERAL PRINCIPLES IN HARD CASES:
ACHIEVING SOCIAL BENEFITS

Sometimes, people are subjected to invasive procedures not solely for their own therapeutic benefit, but at least partly in order to confer an advantage on society. Scientific and medical experiments and immunization programmes confer benefits on society as a whole, as well as often safeguarding particular individuals against disease. But such programmes may sometimes put individuals at risk. This section considers human rights aspects of such interventions.

(1) EXPERIMENTS[137]

Where experiments are performed for the good of the patient, as where the patient's life is threatened by a condition which has resisted treatment by established methods, and it seems that only innovative methods can succeed, there usually is little difficulty in seeking and obtaining the patient's consent. Nor is that consent vitiated by the mere fact that studying the results of the treatment might ultimately prove to be of more benefit to others than to the patient. However, when the experiment is likely to do little or no good to the individual patient, a dilemma arises. The clinical testing of techniques and drugs may be desirable on general utilitarian terms, but harm those who are guinea pigs.[138] In the aftermath of the Second World War, the Nuremberg war crimes tribunal had to decide how to approach the cases of doctors in concentration camps who had performed experiments on inmates. The result was a ten-point code,[139] which was later taken up by the medical profession, refined, and is now encapsulated in the Declaration of Helsinki, drawn up by the World Medical Association in 1964, as revised in 1975.[140] This approach, allowing the medical profession to set its own standards subject to the demands of international humanitarian law and, where the state takes an interest, domestic law, is acceptable only so long as the profession polices the standards rigorously, taking account of public moralities and public interests. Under Article 7 of the International Covenant on Civil and Political Rights, as noted earlier, states have an obligation to guarantee that 'no one shall be subjected without his consent to medical or scientific experimentation', which is treated as a special form of torture or inhuman or degrading treatment. In the UK, this is one of the responsibilities of hospital ethical committees, widely established in accordance with the recommendations of the Warnock Committee report.[141]

---

[137] E. Deutsch, 'Medical Experimentation: International Rules and Practice' (1989) 19 *Victoria University of Wellington LR* 1–10, provides an introduction to this complex field.

[138] See I. Kennedy, *Treat Me Right: Essays in Medical Law and Ethics* (Oxford: Clarendon Press, 1991), ch. 10.

[139] *US v. Rose* 'The Medical Case' (1949), *Trial of War Criminals before the Nuremberg Military Tribunals*, i, ii. See also *Re Brandt and others* (1947) 14 ILR 296 at 298, US Military Tribunal, Nuremberg.

[140] One further subparagraph was added in 1983. The Declaration is printed in Mason and McCall Smith, *Medical Ethics*, 446–9.

[141] Department of Health and Social Security, *Report of the Committee of Inquiry into Human Fertilisation and Embryology* (Chairman: Dame Mary Warnock), Cmnd. 9314 (London: HMSO, 1984).

The distinction between therapeutic treatment and clinical research is blurred in the area of heroic efforts to save life. The category into which a procedure falls would seem to depend both on the balance of risks to the patient and the ethical acceptability of the procedure to the profession. Transplanting a baboon's heart into a young infant who would otherwise have faced certain death from heart disease, and in the event died equally inevitably from the effects of rejection of the heart, was close to the borderline.[142] The patient (or those representing him) must, in principle, have the ultimate right to say yes or no in each case. However, it may be extremely difficult to obtain consent to random sample testing. Seeking consent may not always be possible without undermining the purpose of the experiment. For example, double blind testing (where patients are allocated to groups receiving different types of treatments without either the patients or their physicians knowing which groups are which) presents serious problems, especially where the condition from which people suffer is life-threatening. In such areas, the importance of active monitoring and licensing of experiments is paramount in order to prevent, so far as humanly possible, foreseeable harm (or loss of therapeutic benefit) to a patient. The benefits to society from experiments may be considerable, but it is doubtful whether we should seek those benefits where the cost to innocent members of society, who derive no benefit, is substantial.

(2) IMMUNIZATION

The need to inform people of the effects of immunizations when carrying out a state-sponsored programme designed to eradicate or reduce the incidence of particular diseases presents related difficulties. Epidemiological evidence shows that programmes of mass immunization can enormously benefit the health of the community as a whole. For instance, these programmes virtually eradicated polio, tuberculosis, diphtheria and measles in the UK. Yet, on an individual level, they entail a small but appreciable risk of damage to particular recipients from the immediate effects of vaccines. Usually, there will be no more than a degree of discomfort and perhaps a mild fever, but occasionally there are more serious side effects. The communal benefit of programmes may be put at risk if individual recipients (or their parents) give so much weight to the risk to themselves that substantial numbers refuse the immunization. For example, there was a resurgence of measles after parents refused to accept immunization for their children because of fears about the safety of a triple vaccine (for measles, mumps, and rubella) in the late 1980s and 1990s. The danger of stopping immunization was recently illustrated by the reappearance of tuberculosis in the UK, following suspension of the immunization programme in secondary schools because of a shortage of vaccine in 1998, and increased contact with antibiotic-resistant strains of the bacterium from abroad.

Is it permissible for doctors or the state to encourage people to be immunized by not mentioning or playing down the significance of possible damage? If there is no

---

[142] L. L. Hubbard, 'The Baby Face Case' (1987) 6 *Medical Law* 385; Mason and McCall Smith, *Medical Ethics*, 362–4.

opportunity to obtain real consent in individual cases, does it breach the common-law rights of people who suffer injury? In the UK, this issue has been defused by providing a statutory compensation scheme under the Vaccine Damage Act 1979 for people who suffer damage from vaccine. It is recognized that the people who suffer damage are injured in the interests of the wider community's fight against disease as a social evil, and should be compensated for the special loss which they have sustained in the common cause. A flat-rate payment is made to victims. However, there remains the difficulty (which is hard for most claimants to overcome, particularly in relation to whooping-cough immunization) that claimants must show that the vaccine caused their symptoms.

If parents are deprived of the chance to make informed decisions on behalf of their children, does it breach the right to respect for family life under Article 8 of the Convention? The protection of the community's health is a permitted ground for interfering with the right, under Article 8(2). So long as the state properly weighs the risks, and permits interference only to the extent required for the permitted purpose, it does not breach Article 8 rights; any breach of the right to respect for family life is justifiable, particularly where those who suffer injury have a statutory right to compensation.[143] However, it may also violate the rights of the child to be free of inhuman or degrading treatment under Article 3, where public interest justifications are unavailable once a form of treatment has been held to be inhuman or degrading. So far, it has not been decided whether it is inhuman or degrading to carry out a procedure, which carries a small risk of damaging the subject but offers great benefits both to the individual and to society, without giving full information about the risks when seeking consent.

5.7 APPLYING THE GENERAL PRINCIPLES IN HARD CASES: TREATING INDIVIDUAL PATIENTS

In general, medical treatment constitutes a trespass to the person which must be justified, by reference either to the patient's consent or to the necessity of saving life in circumstances where the patient is unable to decide whether or not to consent.

Rights with regard to medical treatment fall essentially into two categories: first, rights to receive or be free of treatment as needed or desired, and not to be subjected involuntarily to experimentation which, irrespective of any benefit which the subjects may derive, are intended to advance scientific knowledge and benefit people other than the subject in the long term; secondly, rights connected incidentally with the provision of medical services, such as rights to be told the truth by one's doctor (the right to have access to one's medical records is considered in Chapter 9, section 4, below.)

---

[143] *Wain v. United Kingdom* (10787/84) Eur. Comm. HR, 9 EHRR 122, in relation to the administration of the triple vaccine against diphtheria, whooping cough, and tetanus.

As medical treatment is *prima facie* a battery, it is unlawful without the patient's consent. A corollary of this unlawfulness is that the patients normally have a right not to accept treatment, or (to put it slightly differently) a right to choose whether to avail themselves of a form of treatment which is available. However, this right cannot be exercised by people who are incapable, or deemed by law to be incapable, of making the choice. Some categories of patients are therefore liable to have the choice made for them by others. Parents normally make choices on behalf of their children; doctors do so on behalf of patients to whom the Mental Health Act 1983 applies, or who are unconscious; the courts do so on behalf of wards of court and, in certain circumstances, on behalf of others, although in such cases the courts are guided by medical opinion to such an extent that it is the doctors, rather than the courts, who are effectively making the decision.

The position of children is considered in section 5.7(2), and that of prisoners in section 5.7(3), below. This section concentrates on consent by adults. Three particular issues are considered. First, what is meant by consent? Secondly, when (if ever) can a capable adult's decision to refuse treatment be overridden? Thirdly, what steps are available when an adult is incapable of giving a valid consent?

(i) Meaning of consent[144]

English law demands consent in order to protect the doctor, generally assumed to be acting in good faith for the benefit of patients, against actions for battery, and the law is therefore doctor-oriented. If the issue were, 'What must be done in order to safeguard, to the fullest extent possible, the right of the patient as an autonomous person to choose between courses of action affecting him or her?', it would probably produce rules requiring doctors to give to patients full information, in comprehensible language, about their conditions, the treatment options which are available, and the likely effects of each, with (when appropriate) an opinion as to the course of action which is clinically indicated. Consent given in such circumstances would be fully informed, and the right to be free of non-consensual treatment would effectively give the patient an entitlement to participate in the process of making decisions about treatment.

However, the law, being doctor-oriented, has been developed in the context of the question, 'What is a doctor reasonably required to tell and ask a patient in order to protect himself or herself against liability in damages?' The resulting rules have been framed as an aspect of the law of professional negligence rather than patients' rights. Instead of demanding fully informed consent, the law protects doctors against liability where (a) the patient is capable of understanding the implications of the consent, and (b) the doctor has given as much information as a body of respectable medical

---

[144] For a valuable selection of authorities on consent, with commentary, see I. Kennedy and A. Grubb, *Medical Law: Text and Materials*, 2nd edn. (London: Butterworths, 1994), 87–396. The Law Commission has decided against trying to define or explain consent in a draft Bill: see *Criminal Law: Consent*, paras. 4.3–4.38, and *Consent in Sex Offences: A Report to the Home Office Sex Offences Review* (London: Law Commission, 2000), paras. 2.5–2.12.

opinion would consider reasonable, given the scale of the risks, the options available, and the patient's emotional and intellectual state.[145] This is some way short of giving patients a right to be fully informed about their condition and treatment, and so cannot ground a right to give fully informed consent or to participate actively in decision-making (although in practice in many cases medical staff encourage patients to do so). The question is whether there is real consent, rather than whether there is informed consent.

In practice, it is hard to maintain the distinction between the reality of consent and the beliefs on which a patient bases consent. This becomes clear in the rare cases where consent is obtained by way of an express or implied misrepresentation as to the qualifications or purposes of the practitioner carrying out the procedure. In *R. v. Richardson (Diane)*,[146] patients were treated by a dentist who, unbeknown to them, had been suspended from practice by the General Dental Council. It is hard to believe that patients would have consented to treatment of any sort had they known of the suspension, but the Court of Appeal held that she was not guilty of assault on the patients occasioning actual bodily harm. Consent could be vitiated by a mistake as to the identity of the person carrying out the procedure, or as to the nature and quality of the procedure. The patients had known who she was, and had consented to the treatment which she administered. A mistake as to her qualifications did not vitiate that consent. By contrast, in *R. v. Tassbaum*[147] the defendant offered breast examinations to three women. He claimed to have trained as a cancer specialist, and to be conducting a study of breast cancer. In reality, he had no relevant qualification. Two of the women knew him as a lecturer on a computer course which they were studying, and allowed him to examine their breasts. He visited the third at her home, and took her blood pressure and pulse. She would not let him examine her breasts, although she let him put his stethoscope under her bra. Each of them filled in a questionnaire and a consent form. They later said that they would not have let him examine them had they known that he was unqualified. He was charged with indecent assault. His defence was consent. He was convicted, and his appeal was dismissed. The Court of Appeal decided that the women had consented to the nature of his acts, but not to their quality, which was sexual rather than medical. The distinction between the nature and quality of an act is elusive.[148] The women knew who he was, and knew what he proposed to do. In the light of *R. v. Richardson (Diane)*, above, it is hard to see why his lack of qualifications or speculation as to his motives[149] should have negated consent which was objectively real, albeit not fully informed. It is as if the Court of Appeal, recognizing the importance of information to real consent, was keen to

---

[145] *Sidaway v. Board of Governors of the Bethlem Royal Hospital and the Maudsley Hospital* [1985] AC 871, [1985] 1 All ER 643, HL.

[146] [1999] QB 444, [1998] 2 Cr. App. R. 200, CA.

[147] [2000] 2 Cr. App. R. 328, [2000] Crim. LR 686, CA.

[148] See the commentary by Professor Sir John Smith, [2000] Crim. LR 687–9.

[149] The Court of Appeal purported to follow *R. v. Court* [1989] AC 28, HL, but (as Professor Sir John Smith points out in his commentary) the victim in *Court* did not consent to the assault: the only question in the case was whether it was indecent, and it was to that question alone that the perpetrator's sexual motive was held to be relevant.

develop the notion of consent to an act to include information about the actor, but lacked both the authority and the logically coherent arguments which might have enabled it to do so convincingly.

The practice of obtaining a patient's signature on a consent form before (or, especially in the case of dental treatment, after) treatment is of questionable legal effect. A typical clause consenting to surgery is drafted so as to allow a surgeon to do whatever the surgeon considers necessary in the light of circumstances discovered during the operation. As the patient will usually be unconscious at that stage, it might be a useful protection. However, it is not clear that it has any legal effect. If the procedure which is carried out is radically different from that which the patient envisaged, the signing of the consent form could not be said to be real consent to *that* procedure, much less informed consent. If the procedure is urgently needed, although the need was unforeseen, the surgeon would be protected by the doctrine of necessity, regardless of actual consent. If it is not urgent, in England (unlike, perhaps, Scotland) it seems that the consent form will not protect a surgeon who performs a procedure where there is no urgency, so that it would have been reasonable to wait and discuss it with the patient later.[150]

There are further difficulties surrounding the nature of consent to tests. Does the patient have to consent only to a physical intrusion, or must the consent cover the purpose to which the intrusion is directed as well? Take, for example, a patient is suffering from a combination of opportunistic infections. There might be various possible explanations, including the possibility that he is suffering from AIDS. Suppose the doctor decides to take a blood sample, intending to have it tested for (*inter alia*) HIV antibodies. Does the doctor require consent only to the taking of the sample, or must the consent also cover the nature of the intended tests on the sample? It might be difficult to tell the patient that the doctor suspects AIDS, and could cause unnecessary suffering—if the test proves negative, the patient will have been needlessly upset, while, if it proves positive, there is at present no cure for the disease (although treatment may increase life expectancy). But in view of the relevance of purpose to consent in *Tassbaum*, above, it might be regarded as an infringement of the patient's rights to take a sample without telling the patient what it is to be tested for.

The ethical guidance which the British Medical Association offers to doctors advises them to inform patients about the purpose of an investigative procedure for a condition which 'could have serious implications for the patient's employment, social or personal life', and urges doctors whose patients face pressure from employers, insurance companies or others to undergo particular tests or accept treatment to 'do your best to ensure that patients have considered the options and reached their own decision'.[151] This advice is entirely appropriate from the point of view of professional ethics, but the common law has traditionally not made full information a condition for the validity or effectiveness of a patient's consent to tests or treatment.

---

[150] *Devi v. West Midlands Regional Health Authority* [1981] CA Transcript 491. See generally J. K. Mason and R. A. McCall Smith, *Law and Medical Ethics*, 3rd edn. (London: Butterworths, 1991), 228–52.

[151] General Medical Council, *Seeking Patients' Consent: the Ethical Considerations* (London: GMC Publications, 1998), paras. 4, 16.

For legal purposes, one must consider exactly which rights are infringed. If the patient consents to having a needle inserted, knowing that the purpose is to take a blood sample for testing, the right to physical integrity is not infringed merely because the doctor intends to have the sample tested for a condition or conditions which he has not mentioned to the patient. There is no unlawful battery. If any right is infringed, it is either a right to be free of mental suffering (more likely to be infringed if the object of the sampling is disclosed than otherwise) or a right to privacy or confidentiality (which is of uncertain scope in English law, and has never been used to prevent a test but only to prevent disclosure to third parties of the results of the test).[152] A doctor might, perhaps, be liable in negligence for failing to warn the patient of what the test was for, but until it is generally accepted medical practice to tell patients what they are being tested for, it will not be part of the doctor's duty of care as laid down in Sidaway to tell patients the specific tests which it is planned to run on each sample taken.[153] Nor will the failure to disclose the purpose of the test undermine the reality of the consent to it.[154]

A further problem concerns consent to non-treatment. As consent is required to protect the doctor against an action for battery only when treatment is to take place, it seems to follow that no consent is needed where the doctor decides to withhold treatment. The decision may render the doctor liable to an action for negligence, but the consent of the patient is not usually relevant to a negligence claim, which does not normally aim to safeguard the patient's autonomy. The failure of English law to give a *right* to patients to participate in decisions concerning their treatment is a dangerous threat to their autonomy and, sometimes, to their lives, as the freedom of a doctor to write 'DNR' ('do not resuscitate') on a patient's notes illustrates. Even if the patient asked the doctor not to resuscitate him, orally or by way of an advance direction, some steps should be taken, if possible, to ensure that the patient still feels the same way later, when circumstances might have altered. The risk is exacerbated when the doctor has odd ideas. This was made clear by the Cartwright report[155] on the disastrous consequences of a New Zealand doctor's eccentric view that women with cervical cancer did not require any treatment, which has led one commentator to conclude that the Declaration of Helsinki should be incorporated into New Zealand domestic law.[156] If that is right for New Zealand, it would also be good for the UK. The Law Commission was surely right to recommend that consent, in the criminal context, should mean 'a subsisting, free and genuine agreement to the act in

---

[152] X. v. Y. [1988] 2 All ER 648. The European Commission of Human Rights has held that certain mandatory medical tests infringe the right to respect for private life under Art. 8 of the European Convention: X. v. Austria (8278/78), (1979) 18 DR 154 (blood test); Acmanne v. Belgium (10453/83), (1984) 40 DR 251 (chest X-ray and tuberculin test). See P. Sieghart, *AIDS and Human Rights: A UK Perspective* (London: BMA Foundation for Aids, 1989), 30–3.

[153] See J. Keown, 'The Ashes of AIDS and the Phoenix of Informed Consent' (1989) 52 *MLR* 790–800, discussing the conflicting opinions given by leading counsel to various bodies on these points.

[154] However, such a categorical proposition could be over-confident in the light of the unsatisfactory decision in R. v. Tassbaum [2000] 2 Cr. App. R. 328, CA, discussed above.

[155] Judge Cartwright, *Report of the Cervical Cancer Inquiry* (Auckland: NZ Government Printer, 1988).

[156] S. Coney, *The Unfortunate Experiment* (Wellington, NZ: Penguin, 1988), 258.

question'.[157] But even this stops short of requiring that consent should be fully informed.

(ii) Competent adults who refuse to consent

The general rule is that a mentally capable adult who refuses consent to treatment may not lawfully be treated. A person may signify refusal to accept treatment either at the time of the treatment or in advance. As noted in Chapter 4, some patients make advance directives, or 'living wills', directing that they are not to be treated if their condition deteriorates to a point where they are incapable of giving or refusing consent. These directives are effective to bind medical staff subsequently, as long as the person was competent to make a decision at the time of the directive. Even if the patient was suffering from a mental disorder which sometimes made him incompetent, the directive is binding if he was in a lucid period during which they were capable of making a decision.[158] Autonomy is the supreme value in relation to one's own physical integrity.

This was firmly established in *St George's Healthcare NHS Trust v. S.*[159] A pregnant woman suffering from pre-eclampsia rejected medical advice that she should have an induced delivery. She accepted that she could die as a result, but she wanted a natural birth. She had earlier suffered from moderate depression, and was diagnosed as suffering from depression at the time, which led to her being admitted to hospital for assessment under the Mental Health Act 1983. She was subsequently transferred to St George's Hospital. Her capacity to consent to treatment or refuse it was intact or at any rate it was not clear whether it was affected by her medical condition. She fully understood her condition and its implications. The hospital applied for an order allowing labour to be induced, and this was granted in order to safeguard the life of S and the baby, following an earlier first instance decision which called for the interest in autonomy to be balanced against that in preserving life.[160] Thereafter she submitted to intervention, while continuing to withhold her consent to it. The baby was born by Caesarean section. S subsequently appealed against the judge's order and applied for judicial review of both the decision to admit her to hospital under the Mental Health Act 1983 and subsequent decisions about her treatment and transfer to St George's Hospital.

The Court of Appeal reaffirmed the fundamental principle that courts must protect the freedom of people of full age and capacity from any interference with autonomy and bodily integrity. The interests of the foetus could not be ignored, but neither could they justify the removal of the foetus from the mother's body under physical compulsion. The Mental Health Act 1983 could not be used to detain a person merely because her thought processes were bizarre or irrational if she was not suffering from a clinically recognized mental disorder falling within the purview of the Act. People

---

[157] The Law Commission, *Consent in Sex Offences*, paras. 2.10–2.12.

[158] *In re C. (Adult: Refusal of Treatment)* [1994] 1 WLR 290, [1994] 1 All ER 819.

[159] [1999] Fam. 26, [1998] 3 All ER 673, CA. For discussion of these matters and the impact of the ECHR, see E. Wicks, 'The Right to Refuse Medical Treatment under the European Convention on Human Rights' (2001) 9 *Med. L. Rev.* 17–40.

[160] *In re S. (Adult: Refusal of Medical Treatment)* [1993] Fam. 123, [1992] 4 All ER 671.

could not be detained under the Act for a purpose (saving the mother or baby from physical harm) unrelated to treatment for a mental disorder. S had been unlawfully detained. Inflicting a Caesarian section on her against her will was, in addition, a trespass to the person, which was remediable by way of an award of damages. The court provided guidelines to be followed by hospital authorities when the possible need for Caesarian surgery is diagnosed and there is doubt about the capacity of a patient to consent to or to decline treatment. The court stressed that a person may remain competent to make decisions about treatment even while suffering from a mental disorder which justifies detention under the Mental Health Act 1983. When competent, the patient's decision is conclusive. Where there is concern about the patient's competence, an appropriate medical assessment should be made in the light of legal advice. The patient's solicitors should be informed, or (if the patient is unable to instruct solicitors) the Official Solicitor should be notified to protect the patient's interests. Where the hospital applies to a court for a declaration that it would be lawful to treat the patient, the patient should be represented at the hearing or an *amicus curiae* should be appointed. The judge must be provided with all relevant information, which must be accurate. In short, a competent patient's autonomous decision must be respected, and medical staff and courts should not conclude that a patient is incompetent without clear and compelling evidence.

It is not always easy to decide whether a person has capacity to make a decision. Just as mental disorder does not necessarily remove the capacity, other circumstances may overbear the capacity of a person who suffers from no mental disorder but is worn down by a combination of physical and emotional pressures. *In re M.B. (An Adult: Medical Treatment)*[161] concerned a woman in labour who needed and wanted a Caesarian section, but whose panic at the sight of needles prevented her from consenting to the anaesthetic. Butler-Sloss LJ decided that a person need not be suffering from a long-term mental disorder in order to lack capacity. The woman's phobia in that case meant that she was incapable of making a rational decision. She was temporarily deprived of capacity to decide matters for herself. The court could therefore declare that it would be lawful to administer the anaesthetic in her best interests notwithstanding her refusal.

The approach worked to everyone's satisfaction there, but it can have a less satisfactory outcome. *In re T. (Adult: Refusal of Medical Treatment)*[162] concerned a patient, T, whose doctor thought she needed a blood transfusion after a car accident and an emergency Caesarian section. T had been brought up as a Jehovah's Witness. Although she was no longer a member of the sect, after discussing the matter with her mother she had given written instructions to medical staff that she did not want a blood transfusion, as it would be a sin and bar to eternal salvation. On an application by her father and boyfriend, Ward J and the Court of Appeal held that the refusal of consent was vitiated, so doctors could lawfully disregard it and treat T according to their clinical judgment of her best interests.

[161] [1997] 2 FCR 541, [1997] *NLJ* Rep. 600, CA.
[162] [1993] Fam. 95, [1992] 4 All ER 649, CA.

This decision is unsatisfactory. Three factors influenced the judges. First, her doctors had wrongly minimized to T the risks of refusal to her. If correct, this suggests that full and accurate information, while not necessary for consent to be real and effective, may be necessary for a refusal of consent to be binding. If so, the law is both inconsistent and incoherent. Secondly, she had been subjected to undue influence, her will being overborne by the persuasion of her mother when T had been very tired. This comes close to the proposition that refusal of consent to treatment cannot be taken seriously if the patient has been subject to persuasion by a third party, at least if the patient was tired at the time. It is inconsistent with the general principles that the test is one of mental competence, and that a competent patient is free to make decisions on religious or other grounds, whether rational or not. Thirdly, T had later been under the influence of pethidine and in no condition to exercise independent judgment. This depends on the earlier factors being sufficient to undermine the written refusal of consent as a matter of law. If the earlier written direction had stood, it would have bound the doctors when the patient was no longer able to make a decision. Although the decision of the Court of Appeal could not be overruled by the Court of Appeal in *St George's Healthcare NHS Trust v. S.*, it is hard to see how it can stand with it.

(iii) Adults who are unable to consent

Where a patient is incapable of giving consent, the doctrine of necessity or that of implied consent will protect a doctor who embarks on treatment in an emergency.[163] More difficult problems arise where the cause of inability to give a valid consent is the otherwise fit patient's lack of mental capacity. Here, two situations need to be distinguished. Where a patient is detained compulsorily under the Mental Health Act 1983, there is statutory provision for doctors to make decisions on behalf of the patient as to treatment for the mental condition in respect of which the patient has been detained.[164] Such treatment includes taking steps to alleviate the physical effects of the condition. For example, where a patient was suffering from a psychopathic disorder (borderline personality disorder) coupled with post-traumatic stress disorder which caused depression and a compulsion to harm herself, treatment included preventing her from harming herself fatally. Where her drive to harm herself took the form of refusing to eat, it was lawful under section 63 of the Mental Health Act 1983 to feed her through a naso-gastric tube, against her wishes, notwithstanding the first instance judge's decision that she had the capacity to decide whether or not to accept the treatment.[165] The same principle has been held to justify performing a Caesarian section on a pregnant woman suffering from schizophrenia in order to save the baby's

---

[163] See the analysis in *In re A. (Children) (Conjoined Twins: Surgical Separation)* [2001] 2 WLR 480, [2000] HRLR 721, CA. This is subject to any advance directive which the patient has given. These matters are considered in Ch. 4, above.

[164] Mental Health Act 1983, s. 63.

[165] *B. v. Croydon Health Authority* [1995] Fam. 133, [1995] 1 All ER 683, CA (although Hoffmann LJ doubted, *obiter*, whether she should really have been said to have capacity to decide to refuse treatment). See *Herczegfalvy v. Austria*, Eur. Ct. HR, Series A, No. 244, Judgment of 24 September 1992, 15 EHRR 432; and see further Ch. 7, below.

life, when doctors considered that her mental health would suffer if she were to lose the baby.[166]

This is subject to two limitations. First, so-called irreversible treatments cannot be administered without the patient's consent, which must be verified by a specially appointed doctor and two specially appointed non-medical witnesses.[167] These include procedures which result in the destruction of brain tissue or brain function, and the surgical implantation of hormones to control the male sex drive. Such treatment, even if apparently appropriate, can be administered without the patient's properly witnessed consent only if it is necessary to save the patient's life, in which case there is a defence for doctors both under statute and at common law.[168] Secondly, treatment defined as hazardous may be administered only with the patient's consent, verified by the medical officer responsible for treatment or by a specially appointed medical practitioner, unless an appointed medical practitioner certifies that the patient is incapable of giving consent but that the treatment would benefit him.[169] Consent or certification can be bypassed only to save the patient's life or prevent a serious deterioration in his condition, again providing justifications for doctors under either statute or common law.[170]

As noted above, mental disorders do not necessarily deprive a person of the capacity to make decisions about treatment. Treatment for other conditions, unrelated to the mental condition, can be given only with the patient's consent[171] (subject to the limited power of the court under *In re F. (Mental Patient: Sterilisation)*,[172] discussed below, to declare that treatment would not be unlawful). Thus, a patient suffering from schizophrenia, during a lucid period, can refuse consent to be treated for any future recurrence of gangrene in his leg, and that refusal will bind medical staff should there be such a recurrence at a time when the patient's schizophrenia makes him incapable of making decisions about treatment.[173]

Where a patient is not compulsorily detained (or is compulsorily detained and it is thought that treatment unrelated to his mental disorder would be beneficial), there is no provision under the Mental Health Act 1983 for treatment to be given without the consent of the patient. Yet the patient may be incapable of understanding what treatment is proposed, and so be unable to consent. The doctor would be protected by the doctrine of implied consent or necessity when treating the patient for a life-threatening disorder, but has no such protection where the treatment is for a less serious, though perhaps debilitating and unpleasant, condition. The Court of Protection, discharging the responsibility of the Crown as *parens patriae* to care for those

---

[166] *Tameside & Glossop Acute Services Trust v. C.H.* [1996] 1 FCR 753.

[167] Ibid., s. 57.

[168] Ibid., s. 62(1); *In re F. (Mental Patient: Sterilisation)* [1990] 2 AC 1, [1989] 2 All ER 545, HL, below.

[169] Mental Health Act 1983, s. 58.

[170] Ibid., s. 62(1)(b); *In re F.*, above. A patient can withdraw consent at any time: s. 60. For further details, see Mental Health (Hospital, Guardianship and Consent to Treatment) Regulations 1983, SI 1983/893; Mason and McCall Smith, *Medical Ethics*, 402–3.

[171] *St George's Healthcare NHS Trust v. S.* [1999] Fam. 26, [1998] 3 All ER 673, CA.

[172] [1990] 2 AC 1; *sub. nom. F. v. West Berkshire Health Authority (Mental Health Act Commission intervening)* [1989] 2 All ER 545, HL.

[173] *In re C. (Adult: Refusal of Treatment)* [1994] 1 WLR 290, [1994] 1 All ER 819.

who were incapable of looking after their own interests, used to exercise jurisdiction in respect of the affairs of lunatics (as mental patients were then known). It had power to make decisions about medical treatment. Statutes governing the compulsory treatment of mental disorder gradually eroded the common-law jurisdiction of the Court of Protection. Parliament gave wide discretion to doctors. When the Mental Health Act 1983 revised the law in the light of the developing caselaw of the European Commission and Court of Human Rights, the power to take decisions on behalf of voluntary patients was omitted. However, some of these patients were too severely affected by their conditions to be able to understand the nature of the treatment which was recommended for them, or to consent to it. This placed the doctors treating these patients in a dilemma where treatment became, in their view, desirable, but did not relate directly to either the mental condition for which the patient had consented to treatment or to life-threatening disorders for which the principle of necessity (or that of implied consent) might have offered protection.[174]

The House of Lords in *Re F. (Mental Patient: Sterilisation)*[175] decided that the Crown's prerogative powers had been abrogated by statute, and had not sprung up again when the Mental Health Act 1983 omitted to give authority to make decisions on behalf of voluntary patients.[176] However, even without a power to consent on behalf of the patient (which Lord Ackner, alone among the Law Lords, would have been prepared to create under common law), the House decided that the courts had a responsibility to declare prospective treatment to be lawful if in the patient's best interests.[177]

The main difficulty with the decision in *Re F.* is that it replaces autonomy with judicial paternalism, without unambiguous and clear guidelines as to the basis on which the power is to be exercised. It is unfortunate that the main area in which the power is used appears to relate to the sterilization of women who are sexually active but are unable to comprehend the consequences of sexual intercourse, and would be unable to care adequately for any children who might be born as a result. The House of Lords in *Re F.* was inevitably content to be guided by doctors and social workers as to the patient's best interests. The test applied to determine what was in the best interests of the patient was not whether the patient would have chosen to be treated if she had had the necessary capacity, but whether the proposed treatment would be accepted as appropriate by a responsible body of doctors skilled in that form of treatment. This opens the way to major surgery on a patient carried out for any purpose which would be regarded as appropriate by a responsible body of doctors, a

---

[174] See Law Commission Consultation Paper No. 119, *Mentally Incapacitated Adults and Decision-Making: An Overview* (London: HMSO, 1991), 55–60.

[175] [1990] 2 AC 1, [1989] 2 All ER 545, *sub nom. F. v. West Berkshire Health Authority (Mental Health Act Commission intervening)*, HL.

[176] This was similar to the conclusion of B. Hoggett, 'The Royal Prerogative in Relation to the Mentally Disordered: Resurrection, Resuscitation, or Rejection?', in M. D. A. Freeman (ed.), *Medicine, Ethics and the Law* (London: Stevens & Sons, 1988), 85–102 at 96–7.

[177] On the procedure to be followed, see *Practice Note (Sterilisation: Minors and Mental Health Patients)* [1993] 3 All ER 222.

negation of the rights of patients.[178] Furthermore, although Lord Griffiths would have favoured making sterilization unlawful without a court order, the other members of the House in *Re F.* disagreed, so major surgery can be performed with neither consent nor the leave of the court if doctors and health authorities are prepared to take the risk of subsequent court action.

There are two further, though less serious, difficulties with *Re F.* First, it does not remove uncertainty and risk from doctors. While a declaration such as was granted there will protect doctors from subsequent civil action, it could not give guaranteed protection against criminal liability, because neither the doctrine of issue estoppel nor the rules on abuse of process will provide an absolute bar to a prosecution in respect of surgery carried out in accordance with a declaration granted by a civil court.[179] Secondly, the requirement to concentrate on the best interests of the patient may make it difficult for the patient to act altruistically. Suppose, for example, that a mental patient's close relation is suffering from leukaemia and needs a bone marrow transplant. The mental patient would be the most suitable donor, but is not competent to consent to the procedure. Can it be in the mental patient's best interests to undergo it? The answer may depend on whether he would be likely to be gravely upset on discovering, later, that he had been prevented by his mental disorder from making a bone marrow donation with which he would have wished to help his relation. Such matters are not easy to judge.[180]

Legislation is required to resolve the issue of responsibility, and the grounds on which consents are to be given; almost any resolution would be preferable to the present situation. The Law Commission recommended in 1995 that there should be a dual test for the legality of treatment of a person without capacity to consent: first, it should be reasonable; secondly, it should be in the person's best interests. When deciding whether treatment is in a person's best interests, the person's past and present wishes and feelings would be taken into account, if they could be ascertained, but would not be decisive. Other relevant factors would include the desirability of encouraging the person to participate in decisions affecting him; the views of the person's family, carers, attorney (if an enduring power of attorney has been granted), any court-appointed manager, and anyone named by the person as someone to be consulted about such matters. The decision-maker should also consider whether there is a way of achieving the desired purpose in a manner less restrictive of the person's freedom. The consent of a court, or of an attorney or court-appointed manager, should be needed for treatments which lead to permanent infertility if they are

[178] M. D. A. Freeman, 'Sterilising the Mentally Handicapped', in Freeman (ed.), *Medicine, Ethics and the Law*, 55–84; K. McK. Norrie, 'Sterilisation of the Mentally Disabled in English and Canadian Law' (1989) 38 *ICLQ* 387–95; D. Ogbourne and R. Ward, 'Sterilization, the Mentally Incompetent and the Courts' (1989) 18 *Anglo-Amer. LR* 230–40; J. Shaw, 'Sterilisation of Mentally Handicapped People: Judges Rule OK?' (1990) 53 *MLR* 91–106. For a slightly different analysis of *Re F.* and options for reform, see The Law Commission, *Mentally Incapacitated Adults and Decision-Making*, 101–10; The Law Commission, Report No. 231, *Mental Incapacity* (London: The Stationery Office, 1995). On sterilization generally, see G. Douglas, *Law, Fertility and Reproduction* (London: Sweet & Maxwell, 1991), 53–61.

[179] *Imperial Tobacco Ltd. v. A.G.* [1981] AC 718, [1980] 1 All ER 866, HL; D. Feldman, 'Declarations and the Control of Prosecutions' [1981] Crim. LR 25–37.

[180] Cp. *In re Y. (Mental Patient: Bone Marrow Donation)* [1997] Fam. 110, [1997] 2 WLR 556.

employed to relieve the effects of menstruation; for abortion, electro-convulsive therapy, and the use of psychotropic drugs for more than three months; and for withdrawing nutrition and hydration from a person in a persistent vegetative state. The Law Commission made further recommendations about participation in non-therapeutic research. These proposals, if enacted, would do much to clarify the rights of patients and the duties of those caring for them. It is to be hoped that legislation will not be much longer delayed.

(2) CONSENT BY AND ON BEHALF OF CHILDREN

Three special questions arising in relation to the giving of consent to medical procedures for children concern the relationship between the rights of children to give or withhold consent and the rights of adults or the courts to do it for them. The questions are: (i) whether children are capable of giving consent without consulting, or contrary to the wishes of, their parents or guardians; (ii) whether parents, guardians, or courts, can override a child's consent or refusal of consent; and (iii) whether children can veto a consent given on their behalf by a parent or guardian.

(i) Consent by children and young persons

The legal capacity of children to decide for themselves whether or not to obtain medical treatment has only recently been directly addressed in English law. Certain principles are clear.

First, under the Family Law Reform Act 1969, section 8, a person aged 16 but under 18 is entitled to consent to treatment to the same extent as an adult. This recognizes the validity of a consent of a 16-year-old to therapy or experimentation, as long as she is capable of understanding the implications of what is to be done. This does not, however, say anything about whether the young patient's *refusal* of consent is to exclude consent given on her behalf by parent or guardian. This matter falls to be dealt with on general principles applying to minors.

Secondly, parental rights do not extend to vetoing a minor's consent to treatment, whether over or under the age of 16, as long as the minor is of sufficient understanding to comprehend the advice which is given to her and the implications of it. This was established in *Gillick v. West Norfolk and Wisbech Area Health Authority*,[181] where a mother sought to prevent a health authority from allowing doctors under its control to give contraceptive advice to underage children. The rights of parents to control their children's access to contraceptive advice were considered in depth, and it was clear that the same principles applied to obtaining treatment as to obtaining advice. The majority of the House of Lords held that the parent's rights were waning, and children's rights increasing. Parents have responsibilities for their children, and their rights extend only as far as necessary in order to allow them to discharge their responsibilities. As children grow in maturity and understanding, they are to be

---

[181] [1986] AC 112, [1985] 3 All ER 402, HL. See discussion by B. Hoggett, 'Parents, Children and Medical Treatment: The Legal Issues', in P. Byrne (ed.), *Rights and Wrongs in Medicine* (London: King's Fund, 1986), 158–76.

allowed to exercise for themselves those choices of which they are capable of under-standing the implications and consequences. The majority held that the decision whether a child should receive advice on contraception without the parents' consent must be based on the doctor's judgment of the patient's maturity and understanding. Wherever possible, the parents should be consulted, but if the child refuses to agree to the parents being informed the doctor, whose first responsibility is to the patient, must probably accept that, if he considers that the child is mature enough to be given the advice sought.

This is simply another way of saying that, as with adult patients, the doctor is protected by the patient's consent if the consent is 'real', but that the doctor's view of the patient's level of understanding and the significance of the treatment is relevant to the reality of the patient's consent. A 13-year-old might therefore be '*Gillick*-competent' and able to consent to major surgery necessary to treat a life-threatening disorder, or to minor treatment with no long-term implications for an ingrowing toe-nail, but not to major surgery to reconstruct his face for purely cosmetic reasons. A 4-year-old would in all probability not be competent to consent to anything. The child's rights therefore grow with the child's capacity to understand the consequences of exercising them in particular ways, and a child's consent will be more readily acceptable in respect of urgent treatment or advice than other treatment. Such an approach is consistent with the theory that autonomy is the value at the root of the moral justification of freedom: the greater one's capacity to exercise a choice in an informed way, the stronger is one's claim to be free to exercise it.[182]

(ii) When can a parent or court decide to give consent to treatment?

A parent's power to decide whether to allow a child to undergo medical treatment is not unlimited even when the child is an infant. If parents refuse consent to a life-saving procedure, the state can and probably will step in, and appropriate the responsibility for making the decisions. The social services department of the local authority is likely to take the child into care and authorize treatment, or make the child a ward of court and ask the court to do so. Parents' wishes are then relevant, but not decisive: the function of the court is to assess the best interests of the child, having regard to all relevant views and considerations, including the extent to which the parents' commitment and involvement would be essential to a successful outcome of any treatment.[183] For example, in *In re C. (A Child) (HIV Testing)*[184] a baby was born to a mother who was HIV positive. During pregnancy she had rejected advice to deliver the child by Caesarian section in order to reduce the risk of infecting the child, and after birth she breastfed the baby, despite medical advice that this increased the risk of infecting the baby. She did not accept that there was a causative link between HIV and AIDS. She refused to allow the baby to undergo a diagnostic blood test to see whether it was HIV positive. Wilson J ordered that the test should be carried out. It

---

[182] See Ch. 1, above.

[183] See *In re T. (A Minor) (Wardship: Medical Treatment)* [1997] 1 WLR 242, [1997] 1 All ER 906, CA, and the analysis in *In re A. (Children) (Conjoined Twins: Surgical Separation)* [2001] 2 WLR 480, [2000] HRLR 721, CA, discussed in Ch. 4, above.

[184] [2000] Fam. 48, [2000] 2 WLR 270.

was relevant to consider that the proposed test was at least 95 per cent accurate, that drug therapy for HIV positive children was proving to be extremely effective in staving off the onset of AIDS and offering a good quality of life, and that treatment would not impose major burdens on the parents. In those circumstances, it was clearly in the child's best interests to undergo the diagnostic test.

Under the Children Act 1989, a court can make a child assessment order in respect of a child's health, development, or the way he has been treated, and this will normally protect the professional who carries out the assessment. However, the Act expressly states that the child, if of sufficient understanding to make an informed decision (a level of understanding apparently intended to be equivalent to *Gillick*-competence), may refuse to submit to the assessment, and in such circumstances any examination is likely to be an assault or battery, and give rise to criminal liability and liability in damages.[185] Similarly, a court making an interim care order or interim supervision order may give directions concerning a medical or psychiatric examination for the child, and this will normally protect the doctor, but the child, if competent, may refuse to submit to the examination or assessment.[186] The same applies to an order given in an emergency protection order.[187] In relation to a supervision order, the court may include in the order a provision requiring the supervised child to submit to medical or psychiatric examinations, but, where the child has sufficient understanding to make an informed decision, the court is not permitted to include such a requirement unless it is satisfied that he consents to its inclusion.[188] This shows a clear legislative policy of giving the fullest possible rein to a competent child's autonomous decision-making capacity, even to the extent of allowing such a child to override the judgment of a court as to the child's best interests in medical and psychiatric matters.

In extreme cases, a parent who fails to obtain adequate medical treatment for a child may be liable to criminal penalties for offences such as child neglect.[189] If it proves to be too late, and the child dies, the parent may even be guilty of man-slaughter.[190] This state intervention in the parent-child relationship is justifiable because the parent's power to decide on behalf of the child is there to be used in fulfilment of the parent's duty to look after the child, as pointed out in *Gillick*, not to prevent the child receiving care. In addition, if there is any hierarchical ordering of rights, most people would place the child's right to receive appropriate medical treat-ment (in extreme cases, to have its life saved) above the parent's right to decide what is best for the child.

Sometimes, however, the parents are refusing consent to treatment for conscien-tious reasons rather than through mere neglect. For example, they may genuinely believe that it is in the best interests of a severely handicapped child to be allowed to

---

[185] Children Act 1989, s. 43(1), (8).

[186] Ibid., s. 38(6).

[187] Ibid., s. 44(6), (7).

[188] Ibid., Sch. 3, Pt. I, para. 4(4).

[189] Children and Young Persons Act 1933, s. 1, as amended by Children and Young Persons Act 1963 and Children Act 1975, Schs. 3 and 4; *R. v. Sheppard* [1981] AC 394, [1980] 3 All ER 889, HL; *R. v. Young* (1992) 97 Cr. App. R. 280, CA.

[190] However, the statutory offence will usually be more appropriate: *R. v. Lowe* [1973] QB 702, CA.

die, as the parents did in *In re B. (A Minor) (Wardship: Medical Treatment).*[191] The parent's wishes will be only one factor to be considered, and will be relatively insignificant if they conflict with the court's view of the child's best interests on the basis of the medical evidence. On the other hand, the court may decide that it would be wrong to authorize major surgery on a young child against the wishes of the parents, even if the unanimous medical opinion is that the surgery would offer a good chance of a long and normal life while the child would die within two years without the surgery. This was the position in *In re T. (A Minor) (Wardship: Medical Treatment).*[192] A baby had a chance of survival if given a liver transplant. The parents, who were health professionals, felt that the surgery would inflict too much suffering on the child, and refused consent. They had since emigrated, with the child, to a country without liver transplantation facilities. The Court of Appeal, reversing the first instance judge, decided against requiring the mother to bring the child back to the UK to undergo surgery of which the mother disapproved, knowing that she would be the primary carer for a long time, perhaps having to deal with side-effects of the operation and further surgery on her child. The position in which court-ordered surgery on the child would put the parents was relevant to the court's assessment of the welfare of the child, because the child's continued welfare would depend heavily on the willing co-operation of the parents, and particularly the mother.

Certain religious denominations (such as the Jehovah's Witnesses) refuse to permit blood transfusions, so that the intervention of state agencies to allow a blood transfusion to a sick child may violate the parent's right to exercise his or her religion and to bring up children according to his or her philosophical convictions. Nevertheless, the law will treat failure to permit *necessary* treatment as a crime, thereby protecting the autonomy of the child against infringement by adult relations.[193] Where the child is very young, the parent's freedom of religion should not be used to allow a serious detriment to be imposed on a child who is incapable of consent. The parent's religious conviction should no more be allowed to dispose of the issue of the child's treatment if death threatens than should the religious convictions of one whose religion requires child sacrifice.

Where the child is older, and is both *Gillick*-competent and capable of understanding the dictates of the religion and its implications, the position is more difficult. Here, the relevant principles are those which are considered under (iii), below.

(iii) Can the child withhold consent to necessary treatment, or override the consent given by parents or guardians?

If the child wants to refuse treatment which the doctors consider to be necessary, intervention may disregard the child's right to autonomy. Where the child is refusing treatment on religious grounds, intervention disregards the child's right to religious freedom. In such cases, the law has two options open to it. It could require the court to apply the *Gillick* test, and treat the child's wishes as authoritative if the court (or the

---

[191] [1981] 1 WLR 1421, CA.

[192] [1997] 1 WLR 242, [1997] 1 All ER 906, CA.

[193] *R. v. Senior* [1899] 1 QB 283, CCR. For the position if the child, as well as the parent, wants to refuse treatment, see (iii) below.

doctor) is satisfied that the child understands what it is doing and the consequences of its choice.[194] This would respect that child's autonomy and capacity to make decisions, while allowing the court to act to protect children who are, in its opinion, incapable of making such decisions.

Alternatively, the court could say that, while minors sometimes have the right to *seek* advice or treatment without their parents' consent (as in *Gillick*), they have no right to decide to *refuse* treatment where that will threaten their lives. The principle of autonomy, on this view, compels the court to insist that life is maintained, at any rate where a tolerable quality of life will be possible,[195] until the minor comes of age. Only when the law recognizes a person as having full capacity in all matters should it recognize his right to refuse consent to a life-saving treatment. In the meantime, the court would have to balance the wishes of the child against the court's or parent's view of the child's long-term best interests or other relevant objectives. Where there is a risk of death, it will normally outweigh the harm done to a child's autonomy by ignoring the child's wish to be let alone. In relation to treatment for conditions which are not life-threatening, a substantial benefit from the treatment will tend to outweigh the child's short-term objection, but the smaller the benefit is, the more easily it will be outweighed by the child's aversion (always assuming that the child is capable of understanding the issues and their implications). *Gillick*-competence is therefore a relative matter.[196]

The most thorough English judicial examination of these issues was conducted in *Re R. (A Minor) (Wardship: Medical Treatment).*[197] The case arose under the court's wardship jurisdiction. A 15-year-old girl with a history of violent relationships with her parents was received into voluntary care after a fight with her father. While in care she asked not to see her father. Concern about her mental state developed. She had bouts of being flat, expressionless, and resistant to being touched, and sometimes seemed to be experiencing visual and auditory hallucinations and suicidal thoughts. After returning home briefly, she ran off and was found on a bridge threatening suicide. That night she absconded from a children's home, and was found the next day at her parents' home. An interim care order was made, and she was persuaded to return to a children's home, but her behaviour was increasingly disturbed. She was admitted to a psychiatric unit. In her lucid periods, she denied hallucinating, and ultimately refused consent to medication. Doctors sought the local authority's permission to administer anti-psychotic medication. This was at first granted, but, after the patient had telephoned the psychiatric social worker and had a long conversation in which she seemed lucid and rational, the local authority decided that it would not give permission for drugs to be administered against the patient's will. She continued

---

[194] In cases of religious refusal, it would be necessary to consider the stage at which a child can be said to have a religion, and whether the child needs to understand the reasons for the religious injunction, as well as the implications of refusing or accepting treatment.

[195] See *In re C. (A Minor) (Wardship: Medical Treatment)* [1990] Fam. 26, CA, discussed by S. E. Roberts, 'When Not to Prolong Life' (1990) **106** *LQR* 218–22.

[196] See *In re R. (A Minor) (Wardship: Consent to Treatment)* [1992] Fam. 11, [1991] 4 All ER 177 at 187 *per* Lord Donaldson MR.

[197] [1992] Fam. 11, [1991] 4 All ER 177, CA.

to refuse her consent. At this point, the doctors decided that they were not willing to keep the patient in their care unless she consented to treatment. The local authority thereupon commenced wardship proceedings. Waite J, exercising the wardship jurisdiction, gave consent to treatment. The Official Solicitor, representing the child patient, appealed.

The three members of the Court of Appeal (Lord Donaldson MR, Staughton LJ, and Farquharson LJ) agreed that Waite J had acted correctly, on the basis that the girl was not *Gillick*-competent: her decision to refuse treatment had been affected by her immaturity and, perhaps, her medical condition. They held that *Gillick* could have no application to a case where the patient was suffering from mental illness, even with periods of lucidity. In such cases, the court in wardship proceedings had to exercise its discretion in the objective best interests of the child. That would have disposed of the case, but the judges went on to give, *obiter*, two rather different accounts of what the position would have been in relation to a child who could be regarded as *Gillick*-competent. As a result, the principles on which the powers of parents, guardians, and courts to consent to treatment on behalf of children are based remain uncertain.

Staughton LJ, with whom it seems that Farquharson LJ agreed, distinguished between the powers of a parent to override the wishes of a child (exercisable only when the child is not *Gillick*-competent), and the powers of the court in wardship proceedings, where the best interests of the child are paramount and may require the court to override the wishes even of a *Gillick*-competent child. Accordingly, on this view, parents or guardians cannot override the grant or refusal of consent by a *Gillick*-competent child, but a court exercising wardship jurisdiction can.

Lord Donaldson MR took a rather different approach. Starting from the position that the court was protecting not the *interests* of the child but the *rights* (specifically, the right not to be sued for battery) of the doctor treating her, he asked whether only the child was capable of offering the doctor protection. He imagined a door which had to be opened in order to give access to treatment, and suggested that there were several keyholders for the door. One is the child, if *Gillick*-competent; another was the parent or guardian, whether or not the child was *Gillick*-competent; a third was the court, exercising its wardship jurisdiction. Although *Gillick* allowed the competent child to give consent which could not be over-ridden by the parent, *Gillick* did not, he considered, allow the child to refuse treatment where those responsible for her welfare thought it desirable in her interests that treatment should be administered.

On Lord Donaldson's view, then, even a *Gillick*-competent child has no *right* to refuse treatment, but only a right to accept it. It is submitted that this deprives the decision in *Gillick* of much of its force, and runs counter to the approach of the majority in the House of Lords. Lord Scarman, in particular, had spoken of parental rights terminating once the young patient was competent.[198] In addition, it was unnecessary to go that far once it had been decided that, in any case, a mentally ill child could not be regarded as *Gillick*-competent. The effect is to give the medical profession the widest possible discretion, including a discretion in all cases to search round to find someone in authority who can countermand the patient's refusal of

---

[198] *Gillick v. West Norfolk and Wisbech Area Health Authority* [1986] AC 112, [1985] 3 All ER 402, HL.

consent. It is understandable that this might be thought desirable, as in the other English case where the question had arisen the child was a 15-year-old Jehovah's Witness who was endangering his life by refusing a blood transfusion, with his parents' support.[199] In such a case, it is understandable that the court should want to preserve the patient's life until the child is of full age and free from the influence of his parents. However, the best way of dealing with such cases is to invoke the wardship jurisdiction, on the model set out in the judgment of Staughton LJ.

In view of the decision in *Re R.* that the patient was not *Gillick*-competent, it is strongly arguable that the whole of the discussion of the principles governing refusal of consent by *Gillick*-competent children was *obiter*. Nevertheless, when Lord Donaldson reconsidered his approach, in the light of critical commentary on the earlier decision, in *In re W. (A Minor) (Medical Treatment: Court's Jurisdiction)*,[200] he essentially reaffirmed it in a case where the patient was a *Gillick*-competent girl aged 16 who was suffering from anorexia nervosa, and wished to continue to receive treatment of one type when her doctor wanted to change to another type. Lord Donaldson replaced the 'keyholder' analogy with another: consent acts as a 'flak jacket' for doctors, protecting them against criminal or civil liability. The doctor needs only one flak jacket, and it may be provided either by the consent of a *Gillick*-competent minor, or by another person having parental responsibilities, or by the court acting in the best interest of the minor. There is to be what Balcombe LJ called 'a predilection to give effect to the child's wishes on the basis that *prima facie* that will be in his or her best interests', but that predilection can be overborne in appropriate cases. The child's protection against ill-advised consent by a parent lies in the medical ethics of the doctor, or the good sense of the court.

In evaluating these decisions, it should be borne in mind that, as noted above, the statutory scheme for assessment and examination of children under orders made pursuant to the 1989 Act expressly permits a *Gillick*-competent child to override a consent to assessment or examination given by a court. This suggests that the legislative policy lying behind the 1989 Act may be inconsistent with the suggestions in *Re R.* that a *Gillick*-competent child can never effectively veto a consent given by a parent (*per* Lord Donaldson) or a court (*per* Staughton and Farquharson LJJ). Although the statutory provisions are concerned with interim and supervision orders rather than specific issues orders, as Lord Donaldson pointed out in *In re W.*, the House of Lords in *Gillick* treated examinations and advice on the same footing as treatment. It is, therefore, possible that judges will assimilate the principles which apply in wardship to those operating under the Children Act 1989. The balancing approach of Balcombe LJ in *In re W.* points in this direction.

In any case, the question is likely to be academic in most cases. If the child is refusing treatment which doctors regard as desirable to treat a serious condition (*a fortiori* where the condition is life-threatening), courts are very likely in all cases to regard that decision itself as sufficient to indicate that the child is not *Gillick*-competent. This is an area where, even after *Gillick*, children have few rights. However,

---

199 *Re E. (A Minor)*, 21 September 1990, unreported, Ward J.
200 [1993] Fam. 64, [1992] 4 All ER 627, CA. See *In re C. (Detention: Medical Treatment)* [1997] 2 FLR 180; P. de Cruz, 'Adolescent Autonomy, Detention for Medical Treatment and *Re C*' (1999) 62 *MLR* 595–604.

it is at least clear that their views must be taken into account where they are regarded as *Gillick*-competent. Support for this is given by the reasoning of Johnson J in *R. v. M.*[201] A fifteen-year-old girl had suddenly suffered major heart disease. Only a heart transplant could save her. Although her mother had consented to the surgery, M herself refused, expressing a preference for death over surgery and living with a transplant, with all the attendant risks of surgery and rejection and reliance on drugs. M was clearly not suffering from any mental disorder. The doctors were unwilling to proceed without her consent in the absence of authorization from a court, and applied for an order permitting transplantation if a suitable donor should become available. Johnson J quoted at length from the judgments of Lord Donaldson MR and Balcombe LJ in *In re W.* He took account of M's wishes, but decided that they were outweighed, on balance, by the certainty of death if the operation did not take place. It seems that the refusal of a competent teenager is relevant, but courts regard the preservation of a minor's life as being more important than respecting her autonomy, even if she is competent.

5.8 APPLYING THE GENERAL PRINCIPLES IN HARD CASES: MEDICAL TREATMENT IN PRISONS

To what extent do rights in respect of medical treatment—the right to be free from treatment without consent, and the right to a normal quality of medical treatment—form part of the residual rights of prisoners? There is no reason in principle why prisoners, as distinct from people with mental disabilities, should lose any of their medical rights. However, the medical treatment of prisoners is in several respects different from treatment of free people.

First, prisoners are not free to change their medical practitioners. They can normally only make use of those staff employed in the prison service, or practitioners who are prepared to visit the prison, or to whom the prison authorities are prepared to escort the prisoner.

Secondly, the quality of medical facilities in prison is, generally speaking, inferior to that outside. The prison health service has historically been separate from the National Health Service, and is funded from the prisons budget by the Home Office rather than the Department of Health. This has fuelled concerns that prisoners are less well treated than other people. Lord Woolf and Judge Tumim wrote in the report of their inquiry into prison disturbances in 1990, 'Prisoners (and their families) must feel confident that the medical treatment prisoners receive in prison is of comparable standard to that which they would receive in normal life from the National Health Service. The Inquiry has seen a considerable body of evidence which indicates that there is a failure to fulfil this principle'.[202]

---

[201] Unreported, 15 July 1999.

[202] The Rt. Hon. Lord Justice Woolf and His Honour Judge Stephen Tumim, *Prison Disturbances April 1990*, Cm. 1456 (London: HMSO, 1991), paras. 12.131–12.132.

Thirdly, it has been held that the standard of care which the prison health service owes to prisoners is lower than that normally owed by medical staff to patients. Nursing and other staff tend to be less well qualified in prison hospitals than in the NHS, so the courts have so far simply accepted the inevitability that the quality of care will be lower, although there are signs that this may be changing. So it should: there are special security needs in prisons, but the Home Office has refused to allow normal health provision for prisoners even if there is no reason to believe that it would threaten security. As a result, prisoners are treated differently from other people in respect of their health, a context in which neither their need nor their desert justifies such a distinction. This appears to breach the European Social Charter, which the UK ratified in 1961. Part I, paragraph (11) of the Charter provides: 'Everyone has the right to benefit from any measures enabling him to enjoy the highest possible standard of health obtainable'. This provision means that discriminating between citizens in the standard of health care available to them is contrary to the Charter, and breaches the UK's obligations in international law. The UN Standard Minimum Rules for the Treatment of Prisoners suggest that:

'Sick prisoners who require specialist treatment shall be transferred to specialist institutions or civil hospitals. Where hospital facilities are provided in an institution, their equipment, furnishings and pharmaceutical supplies shall be proper for the medical care and treatment of sick prisoners, and there shall be a staff of suitably trained officers.'

Successive reports from the House of Commons Home Affairs and Health Select Committees indicated that these standards were not being reached consistently within the prison medical service, and recommended that the prison health service should be taken over by the NHS.

In 1996, Judge Tumim's successor as HM Chief Inspector of Prisons, General Sir David Ramsbotham, published a thematic review of health care in prisons[203] which led to the establishment of a joint Home Office/NHS task force to examine the provision of health care. The Prisons Board promulgated health care standards for prisons. Every prison was instructed to prepare a health care needs assessment on which service provision could be based. However, 18 months later Sir David reported that no prison had prepared an assessment, nor had the Prisons Board taken any steps to speed up the process. Sir David noted that prison senior medical orderlies, providing primary care, were not qualified as general practitioners, and too many staff (including nursing staff and health care managers) in prison health care centres were unqualified. Prisons were ill equipped to deal with mentally disordered offenders, who comprise up to 70 per cent of the prison population. Many prisoners suffering from severe personality disorders were sent back to prison from hospitals because they were untreatable, but prisons lacked the facilities and special staff to deal adequately with them.[204] More recently, Sir David has reported that the Task Force is taking forward NHS supervision of a process by which the

---

[203] HM Chief Inspector of Prisons, *Patient or Prisoner? A New Strategy for Health Care in Prisons* (London: Home Office, 1996).

[204] HM Chief Inspector of Prisons, *Annual Report 1997–98* (London: HM Inspector of Prisons, 1999), 35–7. On detained children, see *R. (S. R.) v. Nottingham Magistrates' Court* [2001] EWHC Admin. 802.

prison service contracts out primary, secondary, and mental health care to outside providers.[205] It is possible that matters will improve as a result.

Certain specific matters demand more detailed attention.

(1) RIGHT TO CONSENT TO TREATMENT

There is no doubt that prisoners who are not mentally incapable retain the right to consent, or withhold consent, to medical treatment. Any medical procedure carried out without the prisoner's consent is therefore *prima facie* tortious, but treatment to which the prisoner has consented is not.

This presents a particular problem in relation to the treatment of disruptive prisoners. It has been regularly suggested that such people are having drugs administered to them, particularly when put into punishment cells, in order to sedate them and make them easier to manage, even if they have no diagnosed psychiatric condition. This over-administration of drugs for non-therapeutic reasons is a procedure known as the 'chemical cosh', which the Home Office has consistently denied permitting (though it may go on without official sanction).[206] The report by Lord Justice Woolf and Judge Tumim, *Prison Disturbances April 1990*, had this to say in relation to Strangeways Prison in Manchester:

'It was suggested that one prisoner in the punishment cells had been forcibly injected with drugs, but our investigation failed to establish the truth, or otherwise, of what had been alleged. However, . . . [a] full-time medical officer of the prison, . . . when giving evidence, quite inappropriately suggested that drugs could be used for controlling prisoners when they were no more than a nuisance. It is possible therefore that the control of the administration of drugs was not as strict as it could have been . . .'[207]

Later, the report noted:

'. . . there existed among prisoners a suspicion that largactyl was being used too frequently "down the block" for control reasons rather than for medical reasons. We obtained reports from the Director of Prison Medical Services on the allegation. It was categorically denied by those responsible for administering medical treatment at Manchester. However . . . [a]ny rumour or accusation that any particular prisoner is being over-medicated should be taken with the greatest seriousness by prison management. Every effort should be made to communicate to relatives, friends and other prisoners the medical reasons and the necessity for any treatment given, subject only to the need to preserve medical confidentiality. In carrying out these tasks, it may well be necessary to involve medical professionals not connected with the prison service.'[208]

In other words, even if all is being done according to the book, there is sufficient concern to justify putting some treatment, at least, in the hands of independent

---

[205] HM Chief Inspector of Prisons, *Annual Report 1998–99* (London: HM Inspector of Prisons, 2000), ch. 3.

[206] See S. H. Bailey, D. J. Harris, and B. L. Jones, *Civil Liberties Cases and Materials*, 3rd edn. (London: Butterworths, 1991), 686.

[207] Cm. 1456, para. 3.87 (Lord Justice Woolf).

[208] Ibid., paras. 12.132–12.133.

professionals, if only as a public-relations measure to boost confidence in the treatment given.

This would be less of a problem if one could be sure that drugs were administered only where prisoners have consented. But there is some ambiguity over the nature of consent to medical treatment in prison, because the prison hospital officers and prison doctors are prison officers with the same powers under the Prison Rules 1964 as other officers to coerce prisoners. There may be a fine line between advice to a prisoner, perhaps forcefully expressed, and an order, and the prisoner might not be alive to the distinction. The prisoner's freedom of choice may be overborne if the prisoner does not realize that he has that freedom. For this reason, it was argued in *Freeman v. Home Office (No. 2)*[209] that a prisoner had been incapable in law of validly consenting to injections of drugs by prison hospital officers, so that the administration had been a battery. Mr. Freeman was serving a life sentence, and alleged that he had been forcibly injected with drugs for non-therapeutic reasons, in order to control his disruptive behaviour. He argued that valid consent could be given by a prisoner only if the medical staff were not prison officers; only then would the prisoner be able to make a choice without worrying about the effect the choice might have on his treatment in and date of release from prison. Had this been upheld, any treatment by a prison hospital officer or prison doctor would have been a battery. It would have compelled the Home Office to integrate the system of prison medical treatment into the NHS so that prisoners could lawfully receive treatment without their consent only in case of medical necessity or following compulsory admission under section 2 or 3 of the Mental Health Act 1983. However, the trial judge found as a fact that Freeman had consented to treatment, and he and the Court of Appeal held that the consent was valid and effective in law. Prisoners do not lose the capacity to consent to treatment merely because they are in prison. The question is whether their consent is real, not why it was given (although they could sue for negligence if the information on which they were asked to consent did not meet the standards expected by a responsible body of appropriately qualified medical opinion).[210]

The use of drugs to alter a prisoner's state of mind or pattern of behaviour is a particularly sensitive matter, because there will inevitably often be a suspicion on the part of objective observers that the reason for prescribing is in the interests of order and discipline in prison as much as, or more than, the patient's own therapeutic requirements.[211] From this viewpoint, the argument that a prisoner is simply incapable of giving effective consent to medical treatment by a member of the prison medical staff is comprehensible as an attempt to protect prisoners against suffering invasive procedures for the convenience of the prison authorities under the colour of a consent which can only ever be questionable. However, the argument goes too far, because, instead of inviting the court to examine whether a prisoner's consent is real, in view of the pressures under which it is given, it would, if successful, remove the prisoner's right to consent to bona fide medical treatment even where he genuinely

---

[209] [1984] QB 524, [1984] 1 All ER 1036, CA.

[210] *Sidaway v. Board of Governors of the Bethlem Royal Hospital and the Maudsley Hospital* [1984] 1 All ER 1018, CA, affirmed HL [1985] AC 871, [1985] 1 All ER 643.

[211] See M. Brazier, 'Prison Doctors and their Involuntary Patients' [1982] PL 282–300.

wants to do so. This would narrow, rather than widen, the scope of prisoners' residual liberties.

Integrating the prison medical service into the mainstream NHS would have two main benefits in terms of treatment for prisoners with suspected mental disorders. First, it would make it easier for medication to be administered, regardless of lack of consent, to those patients who really needed it. At present, prisoners in a prison service acute psychiatric unit, such as Grendon Underwood, are not compulsorily detained for treatment within the meaning of the Mental Health Act 1983. If they do not take their medication voluntarily, they cannot have it forced on them. Some prisoners become caught up in a cycle of illness, refusing treatment until they become ill enough to be compulsorily detained in an NHS secure mental hospital, such as Broadmoor, and compulsorily treated. When the treatment has returned them to a more rational state, they are transferred back to the prison unit, where they refuse the medication which stabilized their condition and become ill again. An NHS mental hospital regime for all psychiatrically ill prisoners, if such an arrangement could be achieved, would vastly improve the treatment offered to such prisoners.

Secondly, integration into the NHS would offer all prisoners the protection against unjustified compulsory treatment which is provided under the system of reviews and checks instituted by the Mental Health Act 1983 (see Chapter 6, section 5, below), bolstered by independent monitoring of the actions of prison nursing staff. This would be a very desirable development, and would serve to defuse much of the suspicion which prisoners and their families currently express, whether or not it is justified, about the treatment which prisoners receive from prison health officers.

(2) FORCED FEEDING

Hunger striking is one non-violent means of protest by which prisoners can air their grievances lawfully. It is a powerful form of protest. The slow process of wasting, leading eventually in the absence of intervention to death, allows pressure on the authorities to build up gradually over a considerable period. Short of surrendering to prisoners' demands, the only course open to prison authorities is to employ forced feeding. This is an unpleasant and dangerous procedure, which must be performed by a doctor. The prisoner is physically restrained, while a tube is inserted into a nostril and down the throat into the oesophagus. Liquid is then passed through the tube and into the prisoner's stomach. In the UK, the procedure was used against suffragettes who went on hunger strike when imprisoned for offences committed in connection with their campaign to win the right to vote, during the early years of the last century.

The legal and ethical considerations relating to forced feeding are complex. First, it can be said that the state has a responsibility to prevent people from taking their own lives and health, if they can be saved without flouting the law. This was the view of Lord Alverstone CJ in *Leigh v. Gladstone*,[212] an action brought by a suffragette who had been forcibly fed in prison. He held that prison officials had a legal duty, under the Prison Rules and (although this was *obiter*) at common law, to protect the life and

---

[212] (1909) 26 TLR 139. See also *Herczegfalvy v. Austria*, n. 165 above.

health of any prisoner, and that this duty justified what would otherwise have been a serious assault. This paternalistic argument is less convincing now, since suicide has ceased to be a crime by virtue of the Suicide Act 1961, than it was at the time. Today, as noted in section 5(7) above, the right of an adult of sound mind to refuse consent to medical treatment and other forms of battery extends to refusing life-saving treat- ment. This would render unlawful any attempt to force-feed a non-consenting pris- oner who has the capacity to make a decision, as an infringement of his autonomy and physical integrity. For this reason, in *Secretary of State for the Home Department v. Robb*[213] Thorpe J declined to follow *Leigh v. Gladstone*, upholding the prisoner's autonomy. The position would, however, be different if the prisoner were incapable of making a decision.

(3) QUALITY OF TREATMENT

No statute deals with the legal duty on prison authorities to provide any particular standard of medical care for prisoners. In a number of cases the courts have had to deal with the problem of quality of treatment. There has been some indirect support for the view that the standard of care required of health workers in prisons is the same as that which applies to health carers generally, namely that their conduct and advice should be such as would be reasonable in the view of a body of respectable medical opinion.[214] There were *obiter dicta* to this effect in *Freeman v. Home Office (No. 2)*, where Stephen Brown LJ said that prisoners can give valid and effective consent which provides a defence to an action for trespass to the person, and would be entitled to sue for negligence on *Sidaway* principles if the information on which a decision has to be made was inadequate.[215] The existence of the normal private law duty of care was also the basis on which McNeill J, hearing the Crown Office List in *R. v. Secretary of State for the Home Office*,[216] held that an application for judicial review of the failure by the prison medical officer, the governor, and the Secretary of State, to take steps to arrange for a prisoner to have a bone graft as advised by a consultant orthopaedic surgeon (treatment for a bullet wound to the arm sustained while being arrested) was misconceived. It was said to be entirely a private-law matter, governed by normal principles of tort law.

On the other hand, it might seem that a different standard of care for prisoners from that applied to the treatment of other people has been accepted in *Knight v. Home Office*.[217] A court had ordered a man who had pleaded guilty to an offence of violence to be admitted within twenty-eight days to a secure mental hospital. While awaiting admission to hospital he was being held in the hospital wing at Brixton prison. Being known as a suicide risk, he was on 'Special Watch B', being observed every 15 minutes, but he managed to commit suicide by hanging. His administratixes

---

[213] [1995] Fam. 127, [1995] 1 All ER 677.

[214] *Bolam v. Friern Hospital Management Committee* [1957] 1 WLR 582, [1957] 2 All ER 118; *Sidaway*, above.

[215] [1984] 1 All ER at 1043; see also *per* Sir John Donaldson MR at 1044.

[216] [1987] 2 All ER 1049, [1987] 1 WLR 881.

[217] [1990] 3 All ER 237.

and son sued the Home Office for negligence, claiming that in view of his history he should have been held in conditions offering less opportunity for suicide. In particular, it was said that he did not receive appropriate treatment (contact with people on an open ward and opportunity for counselling, therapy, support, and advice). Such treatment would have been given at a psychiatric hospital with between 0.8 and 2 staff per patient, but could not be provided in a prison hospital. Instead, he was held in an ordinary cell or, on some occasions, a special cell stripped of nearly all amenities and furniture (a strip cell). Pill J held that the failure to provide in a prison hospital the facilities which would have been available in a specialist psychiatric hospital did not breach a duty of care to the prisoner. It was not reasonable to expect prison hospitals to provide ideal psychiatric care, given their level of resources. While the standard of reasonable care is that which is reasonably demanded in the circumstances, so that the proper basis for comparison is not the standard currently available in other prisons but the standard applicable to people under a duty to provide health care, the court had to bear in mind the limited resources allocated by Parliament to the prison health service, and the fact that the prison's central function is not to provide health care but to detain people deprived of their liberty. The duty of the prison health service is to provide treatment for mentally ill prisoners, and if necessary to protect them against themselves, but the standard of care to be met in prison was not the same as that in a psychiatric hospital outside prison. In view of the central function of a prison, the level of care provided in the hospital wing at Brixton was held not to breach the duty of care owed to the prisoner.

In resource terms this looks a sensible decision. One can reasonably expect different levels of resource in different situations. As Pill J pointed out, one would not expect a general practitioner's surgery to provide the same level of facilities for treating emergencies as the accident and emergency department at a large hospital. To that extent, the decision is unexceptional. However, when examined in the perspective of civil liberties and human rights it is more than a little worrying that the court was not prepared to consider whether the Home Office was negligent in its provision of resources to the Brixton prison hospital wing, if (and there was no evidence as to this) the prisoner was being denied access to a psychiatric hospital which would have been accorded him earlier had he not been a prisoner. The real ground for serious complaint in terms of the civil liberties and human rights of prisoners is not that different standards of care are expected of different types of medical centre, but rather that (a) prisoners' opportunities for obtaining timely and appropriate treatment are more circumscribed than those of others purely on account of their status as prisoners, (b) the prison medical service, being part of the prison administration, has to treat its patients as prisoners first and patients second,[218] and (c) the European Court of Human Rights has held that it may be degrading treatment which violates Article 3 of the ECHR if the state fails to provide an adequate standard of medical care for people who are compulsorily detained, and so have no opportunity to seek medical assistance on their own account.[219]

---

[218] See R. Smith, 'Prison Doctors: Ethics, Invisibility, and Quality' (1984) **288** *Brit. Med. J.* 781–3.

[219] *Kudła v. Poland*, App. No. 30210/96, Judgment of 26 October 2000.

It is therefore encouraging to note a possibility that the common law is becoming less tolerant of differential standards of medical treatment for prisoners. For example, it has been held that pregnant women in prison are entitled to a proper standard of obstetric care, and that the duties of the prison authorities may be enforced in private law proceedings.[220] It is to be hoped that this will enable the courts to discharge the state's positive obligation to protect the Article 3 rights of prisoners, and will help to stimulate improvements in the medical facilities available to prisoners.

5.9 CONCLUSIONS

The discussion in this chapter has highlighted a number of spheres in which there is a tension between the law in England and Wales and ordinary expectations of human rights. In part, these are the result of a misfit between the terms in which human rights are customarily expressed and the form of English legal rules. For example, English law is not used to thinking about concepts such as torture or inhuman and degrading treatment and punishment (a matter to which we will return, in the context of prison conditions, in Chapter 7), and finds it hard to adapt the legal categories of the common law to such concerns. Much therefore depends on legislation, and the reports and inquiries which may act as a stimulus to legislative reform. For example, there can be no doubt that the Law Commission's recommendations in relation to decision-making for and by mentally incapacitated adults would, if enacted, clarify the law in the area and do so from a rights-based perspective. The problem which may then arise is lack of political commitment to giving effect to worthwhile recommendations, especially where the recommendations would benefit a group which is generally accorded a low priority in political decision-making. For example, prisoners are not, on the whole, seen as a deserving group, and are politically disfranchised, so proposals to improve their lot in line with human rights entitlements are slow to gain ground.

A further problem is that values in these areas are in the process of substantial change and development. The rights of parents over their children are giving way to the rights of children, and the legislature is increasingly recognizing children as having a degree of moral autonomy which deserves respect. At the same time, it is not yet clear how the rights of children as ordinary people can be accommodated to the special responsibilities which adults have towards them. The lines separating adult paternalism (in the strict sense) from juvenile free choice have not yet been drawn firmly, and are still shifting. This is bound to affect perceptions about, for example, the proper extent of parents' disciplinary powers.

Finally, the fields discussed in this chapter and the previous one illustrate another major hurdle which advocates of rights face: the paternalism of professional groups, such as doctors, whose codes of ethics operate largely independently of the state but which may fundamentally affect people's rights, particularly where the law displays

---

[220] *Brooks v. Home Office, The Times,* 17 February 1999. See also *Toumia v. Evans, The Times,* 1 April 1999, CA.

substantial regard for the judgment of the professionals on their own territory. This is less a human rights problem than one of social power, but there are signs that the structures of power are gradually shifting under the influence of human rights.

6

FREEDOM FROM ARBITRARY STOP, SEARCH, ARREST, AND DETENTION

This chapter concerns the extent of powers under English law to interfere with a person's freedom of movement for the purposes of criminal investigations. We start from the proposition that any interference with freedom of movement is *prima facie* a tort. Interferences can, however, be justified under certain circumstances. Historically, the legal justifications included arrest and detention of people in order to bring them before a court, or to restrain a breach of the peace. Arrest powers in respect of breaches of the peace are governed by common law, and are considered in Chapter 18 below. Police powers of arrest in respect of criminal offences are now codified in statute. Arrest and imprisonment in civil proceedings still occur, but are now regarded as anomalous, and will not detain us here.

Three main issues form the background for the legal analysis in this chapter. First, for what purposes and in what circumstances may powers of arrest and detention be exercised? Secondly, what legal safeguards are provided against abuse of arrest powers? Thirdly, how is the law likely to be affected by the Human Rights Act 1998? These questions will not be examined separately, since they overlap at many points, but they provide the themes around which the discussion is organized.

6.1 DEPRIVATION OF LIBERTY, DETENTION, ARREST, AND VOLUNTARY ATTENDANCE DISTINGUISHED

Section 6 of the Human Rights Act 1998 imposes a duty on public authorities to act compatibly with Convention rights unless compelled by primary legislation to act incompatibly. Section 3 of the Act requires that all legislation is to be read and given effect in a manner compatible with Convention rights so far as it is possible to do so. This means that Article 5 of the European Convention on Human Rights (ECHR) provides a framework within which English law on arrest and detention operates. Article 5 provides:

'1.   Everyone has the right to liberty and security of person. No one shall be deprived of his liberty save in the following cases and in accordance with a procedure prescribed by law:

(a) the lawful detention of a person after conviction by a competent court;

(b) the lawful arrest or detention of a person for non-compliance with the lawful order of a court or in order to secure the fulfilment of any obligation prescribed by law;

(c) the lawful arrest or detention of a person effected for the purpose of bringing him before the competent legal authority on reasonable suspicion of having committed an offence or when it is reasonably considered necessary to prevent his committing an offence or fleeing after having done so;

(d) the detention of a minor by lawful order for the purpose of educational super-vision or his lawful detention for the purpose of bringing him before the competent legal authority;

(e) the lawful detention of persons for the prevention of the spreading of infectious diseases, of persons of unsound mind, alcoholics or drug addicts or vagrants;

(f) the lawful arrest or detention of a person to prevent his effecting an unauthorised entry into the country or of a person against whom action is being taken with a view to deportation or extradition.

2. Everyone who is arrested shall be informed promptly, in a language which he under-stands, of the reasons for his arrest and of any charge against him.

3. Everyone arrested or detained in accordance with the provisions of paragraph 1(c) of this Article shall be brought promptly before a judge or other officer authorised by law to exercise judicial power and shall be entitled to trial within a reasonable time or to release pending trial. Release may be conditioned by guarantees to appear for trial.

4. Everyone who is deprived of his liberty by arrest or detention shall be entitled to take proceedings by which the lawfulness of his detention shall be decided speedily by a court and his release ordered if the detention is not lawful.

5. Everyone who has been the victim of arrest or detention in contravention of the provi-sions of this Article shall have an enforceable right to compensation.'

We must first establish the scope of the rights under Article 5. The right to liberty and security of the person is concerned with freedom from arbitrary detention. It does not give rights to a minimum quality of treatment and accommodation when detained, or to freedom of movement; those matters fall under Articles 2 and 3 and Protocol No. 4, Article 2. Furthermore, the European Court of Human Rights has distinguished between a deprivation of liberty, which has the effect of entirely removing a person's freedom, and a restriction of liberty, which does not engage Article 5(1), although the difference is one of degree or intensity, not of substance: one has to assess the detainee's actual circumstances, including the type, duration, effects, and manner of the detention. For example, stopping someone briefly to ask questions, either on the street or at an airport customs control checkpoint, would be unlikely to be regarded as depriving him of his liberty. By contrast, restricting a person to one area of a small island, with restricted social contact, as a form of 'internal exile' for a *mafioso*, was held to deprive him of liberty.[1] Again, Somalian asylum seekers who were detained in the international transit zone at a French airport for twenty days under constant surveillance were held to have been deprived of their liberty, despite being free to

---

[1] *Guzzardi v. Italy*, Eur. Ct. HR, Series A, No. 39, Judgment of 6 November 1980.

leave the country (but not to enter it).[2] Only if there is a deprivation of liberty is it necessary to justify it. The list of permitted justifications in Article 5(1) is exhaustive, and the justifications are to be strictly interpreted.[3]

Where a person is briefly detained on the street or at a customs post in order to check for stolen, prohibited, or dutiable goods, there is a deprivation of liberty, albeit only for a short period: the person is not free to move anywhere without the agreement of the officer until the procedure is complete. Such a detention is probably not within Article 5(1)(c), because it is not for the purpose of bringing the person before a competent legal authority, and under some powers no reasonable suspicion is required. However, it is justifiable under Article 5(1)(b). The person is detained 'in order to secure the fulfilment of [an] obligation prescribed by law', namely the obligation to submit to a search, and will be lawful as long as the conditions precedent to the search are met, the search is carried out in a lawful way, and the period of detention and treatment of the detainee are proportionate to the legitimate purpose of the detention. The same applies to detention for the purpose of obtaining information which a person has a duty to provide, for example under the Terrorism Act 2000.[4]

At common law, too, any deprivation of liberty is *prima facie* unlawful, although it may be justified according to law. A detention may be justified for a number of different reasons. For example, a person may consent, although it can be difficult to distinguish between consent and mere submission. Before the Human Rights Act 1998 came into force, the House of Lords held by a bare majority that a mental patient, who had been taken to hospital without being told whether or not he was being held under a statutory power, and had not tried to leave when placed in an unlocked ward, had not been detained, despite the doctor's statement that he would have been compulsorily detained had he attempted to leave.[5] It is doubtful whether this decision is compatible with Article 5(1) of the ECHR, as the concrete reality of the patient's situation is that he was not free to leave and probably felt constrained to remain.[6] In any case, the decision was concerned with the distinction between voluntary and compulsory hospitalization under the Mental Health Act 1983, and is probably inapplicable outside that field, as the idea of voluntariness carries with it special difficulty where there is doubt about a person's mental capacity to decide whether to stay or to leave.

A detention may be lawful where someone is imprisoned pursuant to a lawful sentence of a properly constituted court; or restrained for his or her own good by a

[2] *Amuur v. France*, Eur. Ct. HR, Judgment of 25 June 1996, 22 EHRR 533.

[3] *Ciulla v. Italy*, Eur. Ct. HR, Series A, No. 148, Judgment of 22 February 1989.

[4] Special latitude may be allowed in assessing the proportionality of detention in relation to terrorism: see, e.g. *McVeigh, O'Neill and Evans v. United Kingdom*, Eur. Commn. HR (1981) 5 EHRR 71.

[5] *R. v. Bournewood Community and Mental Health NHS Trust, ex parte L.* [1999] 1 AC 458, [1998] 3 All ER 289, HL (Lords Goff, Lloyd, and Hope; Lords Nolan and Steyn dissented). The House overruled a unanimous Court of Appeal [1998] 1 All ER 634. See further Ch. 7, below.

[6] See *De Wilde, Ooms and Versyp v. Belgium* (the 'Vagrancy Cases'), Eur. Ct. HR, Series A, No. 12, Judgment of 18 June 1971, 1 EHRR 373 (voluntary surrender to custody does not deprive people of the protection of Art. 5) and the decision of the European Commission of Human Rights in *Walverens v. Belgium*, Report of 5 March 1980.

parent,[7] guardian, or teacher; or detained in hospital according to procedures laid down in the Mental Health Act 1983. Again, legislation may provide for people to be detained for specified purposes in connection with the investigation of crime. Detention need not be preceded by an arrest; it is lawful if it is authorized by law, and is carried out for a lawful purpose and in compliance with required procedures.

An arrest is one of a number of procedures for initiating a lawful detention, and it is distinctive in that it initiates or forms part of a legal process which was traditionally (but is not necessarily today) intended to lead to judicial proceedings. This feature distinguishes arrests and the detentions which follow them from other lawful detentions. It applies both to arrests of people and to arrests of ships in admiralty actions which are said to be conducted *in rem* (that is, a ship is arrested, and proceedings commenced against it, for wrongs notionally committed by it). In criminal matters, the law on arrest underlines the connection between arrests and criminal proceedings in a number of ways. Now part of English law under the Human Rights Act 1998, Article 5(1)(c) of the European Convention on Human Rights provides that an unconvicted person may be arrested in connection with an offence only in accordance with a procedure prescribed by law 'effected for the purpose of bringing him before the competent legal authority on reasonable suspicion of having committed an offence or when it is reasonably considered necessary to prevent his committing an offence or fleeing after having done so'. In other words, arrests must be for the purpose of preventing, or instituting proceedings for, an offence. This reflects the English legal tradition, which usually demands reasonable grounds to suspect that a person has committed one of certain kinds of offences before an arrest is justifiable, and requires that the arrested person be taken to a police station so that a custody officer can decide whether detention should be authorized. (However, in practice the power of arrest is often used for other purposes: see section 6.3(4)(ii), below.)

An arrest, then, is a special way of initiating a lawful detention for particular purposes. An arrest changes the legal rights of the person arrested: he will not be entitled to use reasonable force to resist the arrest or to escape the subsequent detention; he will not be entitled to go on his way unhindered; he will be subject to the lawful application of coercion. Arrest produces a temporary change in the person's status, from free to unfree. Because of this, it has been hedged about with restrictions and formalities. These are designed to ensure that the person arrested is aware of his change of status, and that his liberty is not interfered with for improper purposes or on insufficient grounds. The law places limits on the grounds for arrest, the formalities of arrest, and the procedures which must be observed in relation to detention following an arrest.

---

[7] In a much-criticized decision, *Nielsen v. Denmark*, Eur. Ct. HR, Series A, No. 144, Judgment of 28 November 1988, the Court held that a twelve-year-old child had not been deprived of his liberty when compulsorily detained for over five months in a psychiatric hospital at his mother's request without any independent review of his detention on the basis of his medical condition. Children's liberty was necessarily restricted by properly exercised parental authority, and the Court found no evidence that the mother had acted improperly.

People who voluntarily attend a police station to answer questions or give information are, in theory, neither detained nor under arrest. They are free to go at any time. In the days before the police had power to arrest a person reasonably suspected of an offence in order to question him, the suspect might be induced to go to a police station by a form of words (such as 'I think we had better sort this out down at the station') which did not constitute an arrest, and so left the suspect as a volunteer, but which gave him a clear impression that he had no option but to go with the officers and do as he was told. This produced the fiction of the person helping the police with their inquiries.[8] It was clear that in many cases these volunteers were not acting of their own free will. Several responses are possible. One approach would have been to create a power to detain people for questioning short of arrest, as adopted to a limited extent in Scotland in the Criminal Procedure (Scotland) Act 1995, section 13. Another approach would have been to regulate voluntary co-operation, to try to ensure that it was genuinely voluntary. This was the recommendation of a majority of the Australian Law Reform Commission in 1975, arguing that the unregulated concept of voluntary co-operation, without controls or time constraints, was 'very much stretched in Australian police practice'.[9] In England and Wales, the approach was to leave voluntary co-operation more or less untouched, but to recognize arrest as a legitimate part of an interrogation process, and impose safeguards on detention after arrest for the benefit of suspects.[10]

Volunteers, too, were given extra protection. Even when they are being questioned at a police station and suspected of an offence, they must be allowed to leave unless the police decide to make an arrest, must be given information about the availability of legal advice if they ask about it, and, if it becomes appropriate to caution them, they must be told that they are not under arrest, are free to leave, and are entitled to free legal advice.[11] However, the distinction between detainees and volunteers has been gradually eroded in practice, and is now less significant than the theory would indicate.

After PACE, the necessity principle imposed on detention following arrest (discussed below) meant that there were potential advantages for investigating officers in avoiding an arrest: it helped to evade many of the restrictions and bureaucratic controls imposed by PACE. Although Note for Guidance 1A to Code C stresses that people voluntarily assisting investigations should be treated with no less consideration than detainees, and have absolute rights to communicate with people and to obtain legal advice, some police forces continued to make extensive use of the idea that

---

[8] D. Dixon, *Law in Policing: Legal Regulation and Police Practices* (Oxford: Clarendon Press, 1997), 126–47.

[9] The Law Reform Commission, Report No. 2, *Criminal Investigation* (Commonwealth of Australia: AGPS, 1975), 28–9. For explanation of the position in New South Wales, see Dixon, *Law in Policing*, ch. 5.

[10] A broadly similar solution was adopted in Canada, where, however, the Charter is a powerful constitutional influence on treatment of suspects: Law Reform Commission of Canada, Report No. 29, *Arrest* (1986), ch. 2.

[11] Police and Criminal Evidence Act 1984 (PACE), s. 29; *Code of Practice for the Detention, Treatment and Questioning of Persons by Police Officers* (Code C), paras. 3.15, 3.16. However, failure to comply will not lead to the exclusion from evidence of any statement made by the interviewee if it is clear that the person must have understood the position: *R. v. Rajakuruna* [1991] Crim. LR 458, CA.

people were providing voluntary assistance when, in reality, they had no choice.[12] Some forces have introduced a special form of record-keeping in relation to people who are at police stations voluntarily, to limit the threat to people's rights which flows (paradoxically) from their not having been arrested. However, this emphasizes the blurring of the distinction between suspects being arrested and offering voluntary assistance.

Under ECHR Article 5(1) and the Human Rights Act 1998, a deprivation of liberty does not take place if someone is detained for a very limited time. Searches of the person falling short of arrest entail a detention for only a short period. They probably do not engage Article 5(1), either because the deprivation of liberty falls under a *de minimis* principle or because detaining someone to require them to submit to a search under a legal power is within the exception in Article 5(1)(b), 'the lawful . . . detention of a person . . . in order to secure the fulfilment of any obligation prescribed by law'.[13] However, stops and searches may infringe people's privacy and bodily integrity, so that statutory constraints have been introduced to protect these rights. These are considered in the following section. Thereafter, the chapter examines various aspects of arrest, and the rights which suspects have while in police detention.

6.2 STOP AND SEARCH POWERS

(1) BACKGROUND

Until the passing of the Police and Criminal Evidence Act 1984, there was a patchwork quilt of police powers to stop and search people and vehicles, varying across the country. There were some applicable powers which could be used by constables of any police force in the country, such as the power to stop people and search them on reasonable suspicion of possession of controlled drugs under the Misuse of Drugs Act 1971, section 23(2). Some police forces had local powers to stop people and vehicles and search them for stolen goods, such as that under the Metropolitan Police Act 1839, section 66. Others had no such power. There were no standard conditions for the exercise of the powers.[14] The Royal Commission on Criminal Procedure accepted that the powers were useful and should be retained, and recommended their rationalization.[15] The majority of the Commission recommended that stops and searches for stolen goods and offensive weapons should be available across the country, subject to

---

[12] I. McKenzie, R. Morgan, and R. Reiner, 'Helping the Police with Their Inquiries: The Necessity Principle and Voluntary Attendance at the Police Station' [1990] Crim. LR 22–33; D. Dixon, C. Coleman, and K. Bottomley, 'Consent and the Legal Regulation of Policing' (1990) 17 *J. Law and Soc.* 345–62 at 354–6.

[13] *McVeigh, O'Neill and Evans v. United Kingdom*, Eur. Comm. HR, (1981) 5 EHRR 71 (detention to seek information under anti-terrorism legislation).

[14] The position before PACE was set out by the Royal Commission on Criminal Procedure, *The Investigation and Prosecution of Criminal Offences in England and Wales: The Law and Procedure* Cmnd. 8092–1 (London: HMSO, 1981), hereafter 'RCCP, *Law and Procedure*', 8–10 and App. 1.

[15] Royal Commission on Criminal Procedure, *Report*, Cmnd. 8092 (London: HMSO, 1981), hereafter 'RCCP, *Report*', 25–32.

a requirement of reasonable suspicion and other controls to limit the risk of arbitrary or discriminatory exercise of the search power. The main constraints concerned giving the reasons for the search to the people who were being searched, keeping records of the search, and publishing stop and search statistics for each force showing how often the powers were used and how accurate the constables' suspicions were.

(2) STOP AND SEARCH UNDER THE POLICE AND CRIMINAL EVIDENCE ACT 1984 (PACE)

The Police and Criminal Evidence Act 1984 broadly adopted the Royal Commission's recommendations. It repealed all other stop and search powers, except so far as they were expressly saved by the Act or created subsequently. Some of the more recently established powers allow seizure and retention of material which is visible, but do not authorize a search of the person for concealed items. However, sometimes this masks reality. For example, the Confiscation of Alcohol (Young Persons) Act 1997 was an attempt to control the loutish behaviour often seen when youngsters collect in public or break into empty premises to drink alcohol. Section 1 allows a constable to require a young person to hand over anything in his possession which is, or which the constable reasonably believes to be, intoxicating liquor, and to state his name and address. The power comes into operation if the constable reasonably suspects that a person in a relevant place,[16] who is in possession of intoxicating liquor, is under 18. It also applies where the constable reasonably suspects that an adult in a relevant place is in possession of liquor which he intends should be consumed by someone under the age of 18 in a relevant place; or reasonably suspects that the adult in possession of the liquor is or has recently been with someone under 18 who has recently consumed liquor in a relevant place.[17] It is an offence for anyone to fail to comply with a requirement under the section without a reasonable excuse, once the constable has told him of his suspicion and of the consequences of failing to comply with the request.[18] The Act does not confer a power to search for liquor which might be hidden on a person, but under section 1(5) the constable may arrest without warrant anyone who refuses to comply. The loose concept of reasonable suspicion may make it easy for a constable to justify requiring a person to hand over any liquor which might be hidden, arresting a person who refuses to comply, and conducting a search of the person under powers incidental to arrest (examined below).[19]

PACE changed the scope of existing stop and search powers in three main ways. First, it provided for the first time that all statutory stop and search powers have to be

---

[16] A relevant place for this purpose includes any public place (other than licensed premises), any place to which the public or any section of it has access at the time, on payment or otherwise, as of right or by permission, and any other place to which the person has unlawfully gained access: Confiscation of Alcohol (Young Persons) Act 1997, s. 1(6).

[17] Confiscation of Alcohol (Young Persons) Act 1997, s. 1(1).

[18] Confiscation of Alcohol (Young Persons) Act 1997, s. 1(3), (4).

[19] When the liquor is handed over, the constable may dispose of it 'in such manner as he considers appropriate': Confiscation of Alcohol (Young Persons) Act 1997, s. 1(2). Only an insensitive constable would dispose of it by drinking it in front of the person who has just surrendered it.

exercised in accordance with procedures laid down in the Act and in its associated *Code of Practice for the Exercise by Police Officers of Statutory Powers of Stop and Search* ('Code A'). Secondly, it created a new, uniform stop and search power, applicable on a country-wide basis, for dealing with people reasonably suspected of being in possession of stolen articles, offensive weapons, and certain other items. Some other powers were saved (for example, the power to search for controlled drugs under the Misuse of Drugs Act 1971, section 23). Thirdly, the Act provided a codified statutory scheme for stopping traffic for road checks without the need for reasonable suspicion that the drivers had committed an offence or were in possession of prohibited articles. Some new powers to stop people or vehicles and search them without the need for reasonable suspicion have been introduced since, such as those under section 60 of the Criminal Justice and Public Order Act 1994 and under the Terrorism Act 2000. This section examines powers exercisable on reasonable suspicion. Section (3) below looks at criticisms of the powers. Section (4) below explains the powers to stop, check and search without reasonable suspicion.

(i) Uniform procedures for searches

Before PACE, there were decisions which suggested that many of the formalities which are required on an arrest, such as informing the detainee of the reason for the detention, applied also, by analogy, when people were detained for a search.[20] Under sections 2 and 3 of PACE, the procedures to be followed before, during, and after a search are spelt out.

These provisions apply only to searches, not to stops. Accordingly, a stop which does not lead to a search under a legal power does not entail compliance with the procedures in PACE, sections 2 and 3. Indeed, PACE makes no provision for authorizing a constable to stop a person or vehicle; this power is either to be inferred from section 1(2)(b), which permits a constable to detain a person or vehicle for the purpose of such a search (which would be impossible if the person or vehicle were not stationary), and section 2(9)(b), providing that a power of search does not in itself confer a power on a constable *not in uniform* to stop a vehicle, or alternatively may be derived from another statute. In relation to vehicles on the road, the Road Traffic Act 1988, section 163, makes it an offence for a person driving a vehicle or riding a bicycle to fail to stop when required to do so by a constable in uniform. This allows a stop for any purpose connected with a constable's duties, without the need for reasonable suspicion that the driver has committed an offence. A vehicle may therefore be stopped in order to discover whether there are grounds to suspect a person; this effectively permits random stops which may lead to suspicion which could ground a search of the vehicle or person, or (to some people, more controversially) a suspicion that the person in charge has been drinking, making possible a breath test.[21] This power does not apply to pedestrians, and is not available to constables in plain clothes, so it does not on its own provide all the powers needed to make search powers work.

---

[20] See, e.g. *Pedro v. Diss* [1981] 2 All ER 59, DC; *Lodwick v. Sanders* [1985] 1 WLR 382, [1985] 1 All ER 577, DC.

[21] *Chief Constable of Gwent v. Dash* [1986] RTR 41, DC; *DPP v. Wilson* [1991] Crim. LR 441, DC.

The procedures under sections 2 and 3 of PACE apply to searches of people and vehicles (a term which includes vessels, aircraft, and hovercraft) without making an arrest, under any power which has not been specifically excepted from the need to follow the statutory procedures. The only powers which are excluded are those of constables employed by statutory undertakers, such as the British Transport Police and the British Nuclear Fuels Police (PACE, section 6), and the power to search people at airports under the Aviation Security Act 1982, section 27(2). The procedures are of four kinds: giving information to the person searched; making a record of the search; providing a copy of the record on request; and collating records in each police area so that information about searches can be included, as it must, in the annual reports of the chief officer of police for that area.

Before a search is commenced, the constable must take reasonable steps to bring five matters to the attention of the person to be searched. These are: (a) the constable's name, and the police station to which he is attached;[22] (b) the object of the search, i.e. whether he is searching for stolen goods, weapons, etc., in the light of which the reasonableness of the constable's grounds for suspicion will be judged;[23] (c) the grounds for proposing to make the search,[24] which will facilitate review of the reasonableness of the grounds in the event of a challenge to the legality of the search; (d) the right of the person to request a copy of the record of the search, unless it appears to the constable that it will not be practicable to make a record (for example, where large numbers of people are being searched together: see below);[25] and (e) finally, if the constable is not in uniform, documentary proof that he is a constable, in the form of his warrant card,[26] in order to defuse fears that he might be a mugger or thief pretending to be a policeman, perhaps precipitating a violent reaction from the person in self-defence.[27] Where a constable searches an unattended vehicle, he must leave on or near the car a notice stating that the vehicle has been searched, and giving the name of the police station to which the officer is attached, and to which a request for a copy of the search record and any claim for compensation should be addressed.[28]

The written record of the search mentioned in (d) above is to be made on the national search record form as soon as practicable after every search, unless it is not practicable to do so for operational reasons such as public disorder or the numbers being searched.[29] This must be done on the spot, unless circumstances such as very bad weather or other immediate duties make it impracticable.[30] The record must contain the matters mentioned under (a), (b), and (c) above. In relation to (c), the grounds for making the search, it 'must, briefly but informatively, explain the reason

[22] PACE, s. 2(2)(ii) and (3)(a). Where the constable is making inquiries linked to terrorism, he need only give his warrant number: see Code A, para. 2.4(i).

[23] PACE, s. 2(3)(b).

[24] Ibid., s. 2(3)(c).

[25] Ibid., s. 2(3)(d), (4).

[26] Ibid., s. 2(2)(i); Code A, para. 2.5. Where the investigation is related to terrorism, the constable need not reveal his name.

[27] This occurred, before PACE, in *R. v. Geen* [1982] Crim. LR 604, CA.

[28] PACE, Code A, paras. 4.8, 4.9.

[29] Ibid., s. 3(1); Code A, paras. 4.1, 4.3.

[30] Ibid., s. 3(2); Code A, para. 4.2.

for suspecting the person concerned, whether by reference to his behaviour or other circumstances'.[31] This might be embarrassing, but is essential in making the reasons reviewable. The record must also contain the name (or a description, where the person refuses to give his name) of the person, and a description of any vehicle searched (including the vehicle's registration number); the date and time when the search was made; the place where it was made; the results of the search; and a note of any injury or damage to property which resulted from it.[32] The record must also include a note of the person's ethnic origin,[33] a provision which was initially greeted with suspicion by ethnic minority communities but which is intended to allow records to be monitored for differential treatment by reference to ethnic stereotyping. The records should be monitored by supervising officers to look for evidence that ethnic stereotyping is being used.[34] A study has suggested that managerial intervention, based on such evidence, can be effective in reducing the level of stereotyping in decision-making.[35]

Nevertheless, such stereotyping still seems to be common. In 1996, the British Crime Survey found that African Caribbeans are about 1.5 times more likely to be stopped as white or Asian people, and nearly three times as likely as whites to be stopped more than once in a year. African Caribbeans were 2.5 times more likely than whites, and Asians nearly twice as likely, to be searched after being stopped. In 1997– 98, official figures show that black people were five times more likely to be stopped and searched than white people.[36]

The record has three purposes. The first is to enable the person searched, or the owner or person in charge of a vehicle which was searched, to obtain a copy, either to satisfy himself of the lawfulness of the search or to use it in connection with any complaint or legal proceedings. He must request a copy of the record within a period of twelve months beginning with the date of the search.[37] The second purpose of the record is to enable the behaviour of police officers to be monitored continuously by their senior officers. The recording requirements sometimes perform these functions, but often they are ineffective: most supervising officers do not use the records as a way of supervising the exercise of search powers, and officers seem often not to record the searches which take place.[38] This is a point to which we will return below. The third purpose is to allow for publication of statistical information relating to searches and

---

[31] Code A, para. 4.7. Where the search is conducted under a general authority given under the Criminal Justice and Public Order Act 1994, s. 60, or the terrorism legislation, the record need only state the authority under which the search was conducted: para. 4.7. A written record may be obtained within twelve months of the search: para. 4.7A.

[32] PACE, s. 3(3), (4), (5), (6); Code A, paras. 4.4, 4.5.

[33] Code A, para. 4.5(ii).

[34] Code A, Note for Guidance 4DA.

[35] N. Bland, J. Miller, and P. Quinton, *Managing the Use and Impact of Searches: A Review of Force Interventions*, Police Research Series Paper 132 (London: Home Office, 2000), 9–19.

[36] Home Office, *Statistics on Race and the Criminal Justice System* (London: Home Office, 1998); J. Miller, N. Bland, and P. Quinton, *The Impact of Stops and Searches on Crime and the Community*, Police Research Series Paper 127 (London: Home Office, 2000), 47–50.

[37] PACE, s. 3(7), (8), (9).

[38] D. Dixon, C. Coleman, and K. Bottomley, 'PACE in Practice' (1991) 141 *NLJ* at 1586–7.

road checks, since this must be included in the chief officer's annual report.[39] This allows trends in recorded searches to be tracked, a potentially useful procedure although it must be borne in mind that many searches are not recorded (see below), and changes in the statistics do not make it clear whether they result from changes in search practices or variations in recording practice.

The Act is largely silent on the manner in which searches are to be conducted, but there was clear evidence that insensitivity on the part of constables carrying out searches was damaging the reputation of the police, particularly with young people and members of ethnic minorities who were disproportionately likely to be subjected to searches. Before PACE, the manner in which the powers were used was often objectionable. Officers routinely displayed a lack of sensitivity, used excessive force, and failed to try to obtain people's co-operation or maintain good police–public relations. The anger which built up over racism and so-called 'hard policing' in relation to the use of the powers in London was a major contributing factor leading to the anti-police riots in Brixton in 1981, and also contributed to the riots in the St Pauls area of Bristol.[40] The evidence shows that stops are still carried out in ways which cause ill feeling and damage police–community relations, despite efforts over twenty years.[41]

However, it would be wrong to regard the PACE provisions as aimed solely at improving the quality of policing in areas with substantial ethnic minority populations.[42] A personal search in public is a particularly embarrassing and upsetting experience. It is also a major interference with people's right to privacy, and a relatively minor interference with the right to freedom from physical interference. Five kinds of limits on the extent and manner of the search are accordingly imposed by PACE and Code A.

First, Code A attempts to limit the discretion which might appear to be given to the police by the rather indeterminate standard of 'reasonable grounds for suspicion' which is used in one form or another as the basis for nearly all statutory search powers. The means employed to achieve this limitation are a series of provisions in the Code which give examples of certain types of factors which may or may not give rise to reasonable suspicion. This approach follows the recommendations of the Royal Commission on Criminal Procedure and earlier official bodies, which had concluded that it would not be practicable to give an exhaustive definition of the matters which would be sufficient to provide reasonable suspicion.[43] Noting that there must be some objective basis for the suspicion before it becomes reasonable,

---

[39] PACE, s. 5.

[40] Lord Scarman, *The Brixton Disorders*, Cmnd. 8427 (London: HMSO, 1981), 64–5; D. J. Smith and J. Gray, *Police and People in London: The PSI Report* (Aldershot: Gower, 1985), ch. 15; M. McConville, 'Search of Persons and Premises: New Data from London' [1983] Crim. LR 604–14.

[41] Miller *et al.*, *The Impact of Stops and Searches*, 50–7.

[42] For the suggestion that this is a common view amongst police in some areas, see Dixon, Coleman, and Bottomley, 'PACE in Practice', at 1586–7.

[43] RCCP, *Report*, 9, para. 3.25, expressing agreement with the conclusions of the Advisory Committee on Drug Dependence, *Powers of Arrest and Search in Relation to Drug Offences* (London: HMSO, 1970) and the (Thomson) Committee report, *Criminal Procedure in Scotland (Second Report)*, Cmnd. 6218 (Edinburgh: HMSO, 1975).

taking account of all the surrounding circumstances, the Code points out that officers must consider:

'the nature of the article suspected of being carried in the context of other factors such as the time and the place, and the behaviour of the person concerned or those with him. Reasonable suspicion may exist, for example, where information has been received such as a description of an article being carried or of a suspected offender; a person is seen acting covertly or warily or attempting to hide something; or a person is carrying a certain type of article at an unusual time or in a place where a number of burglaries or thefts are known to have taken place recently.'[44]

Furthermore, in order to foster good community relations and avoid mistrust of the police,[45] personal factors may never be used as the sole basis on which to search a person (although the Code does not prevent a constable from considering them in combination with non-personal factors). The examples which the Code gives of personal factors are: 'a person's colour, age, hairstyle or manner of dress, or the fact that he is known to have a previous conviction for possession of an unlawful article'.[46] This is clearly intended to make it more difficult for constables to indulge their preconceptions or prejudices about particular groups, such as young African Caribbean men, whom previous research has shown to be particularly vulnerable to stops and searches and among whom systemic anti-police feelings have resulted.[47]

The sense that ethnic minorities are disproportionately targeted—whether African Caribbeans, Asians, or (in North London) Irish[48]—is likely to be exacerbated rather than relieved by powers which are aimed (quite legitimately) at street gangs. The Code of Practice allows reasonable suspicion to be based on reliable information indicating that 'members of a particular group or gang, or their associates, habitually carry knives unlawfully or weapons or controlled drugs'.[49] If the members of the gang or group are reliably said to wear distinctive items of clothing or other indications of membership, those items may give reasonable suspicion so as to justify a stop and search.[50] It is not surprising that such groups feel that the standard of reasonable suspicion offers them little protection.

Secondly, people should be treated courteously and considerately.[51] Efforts should be made to secure consent to any search, even if the person initially objects, and the voluntary production of items such as suspected stolen goods, particularly where the person in possession of them may be innocent of the offence.[52] While there is power

---

[44] Code A, para. 1.6.

[45] Code A, Note for Guidance 1AA.

[46] Code A, para. 1.7.

[47] Sir William Macpherson of Cluny, *The Stephen Lawrence Inquiry*, Cm. 4262-I (London: The Stationery Office, 1999), 312, para. 45.10; Miller *et al.*, The Impact of Stops and Searches, 49–57.

[48] J. Mooney and J. Young, *Social Exclusion and Criminal Justice: Ethnic Minorities and Stop and Search in North London* (London: Middlesex University Centre for Criminology, 1999), cited in Miller *et al.*, *The Impact of Stops and Searches*, 48.

[49] Code A, para. 1.6A.

[50] Code A, para. 1.7AA.

[51] Code A, Note for Guidance 1AA.

[52] Code A, paras. 1.7A, 3.2.

to use reasonable force if necessary under most search powers, including that under section 1 of PACE,[53] this should be done only once it has been established that the person is not prepared to co-operate or is actively resisting.[54] These provisions are of questionable value, however. There is judicial authority that passivity should not be assumed to signify consent.[55] None the less, attitudes towards searches may encompass a range of mental states short of active resistance, and the police may treat them as objectively indicating consent. These include acquiescence resulting from ignorance of the right to refuse, fear (sometimes justified) of what the officers might do if the person makes trouble, and reluctant submission to the imbalance of the social power relationship which exists between police officers and ordinary citizens, regardless of the extent of legal powers.[56] This has implications which will be explored further below, section (3)(v).

Thirdly, search powers do not confer any power to detain people against their wills merely to ask them questions[57] or seek grounds for justifying a search, nor can refusal to answer a question give rise to reasonable grounds for suspicion to justify a search.[58] However, some preliminary conversation will inevitably be necessary to see whether suspicions can be set at rest,[59] to try to obtain the person's consent to a search, and to try to impart the information which is demanded by the provisions mentioned above.

Fourthly, no power to search without an arrest is to be construed as conferring a power to authorize a constable to require a person to remove any clothing in public other than an outer coat, jacket, or gloves,[60] or (in terrorism cases) footwear or headgear,[61] although the constable may ask a person to remove other articles of clothing in the hope that he will comply voluntarily.[62] These searches in the street or other public places should usually be limited to a superficial examination of outer clothing and, if necessary, hand baggage. Where a more thorough search, involving removal of other clothing or headgear,[63] is required, it should be conducted nearby but out of the public view, for example in a police station or police van, and if it goes beyond removal of headgear or footwear it must be carried out by an officer of the same sex as the person being searched. Nobody of the opposite sex may be present unless the person being searched requests it (for example, a young boy wanting to be accompanied by his mother or elder sister).[64]

[53] PACE, s. 117.
[54] Code A, para. 3.2.
[55] *Osman v. DPP, The Times,* 29 September 1999, DC, *per* Sedley LJ.
[56] D. Dixon, C. Coleman, and K. Bottomley, 'Consent and the Legal Regulation of Policing' (1990) 17 *J. L. and Soc.* 345–62 at 347*ff*; Dixon, *Law in Policing*, 90–104.
[57] This contrasts with the position in Scotland, where constables have such a power under the Criminal Procedure (Scotland) Act 1995, s. 13.
[58] Code A, paras. 2.1, 2.3.
[59] Code A, para. 2.2.
[60] PACE, s. 2(9)(a).
[61] Terrorism Act 2000, s. 45(3).
[62] Code A, Note for Guidance 3A.
[63] There is an exception for removal of headgear in public under the Terrorism Act 2000, s. 45(3). This is a matter of particular sensitivity to Sikhs and members of other religious groups, such as orthodox Jews, who are required to keep their heads covered. See Code A, paras. 3.5 and 3.5A and Note for Guidance 3c.
[64] Code A, paras. 3.4, 3.5, 3.5A.

Finally, the permissible extent of a search will depend on the type of item which the person is reasonably suspected of possessing. Small and easily concealed items, such as drugs in a search under the Misuse of Drugs Act 1971, section 23(2), may justify a more extensive search than bulkier articles like weapons (where the search is under the Criminal Justice and Public Order Act 1994, section 60, the Firearms Act 1968, sections 47(3) and 49, or section 1 of PACE). If the suspected item was seen to be slipped into a particular pocket the search must not go beyond that pocket unless there are reasonable grounds to suspect that other stolen or prohibited items are concealed in other places, as will usually be the case where (for instance) stolen goods are found in the first pocket searched.[65] A search must be concluded within a reasonable time, and once it is completed the person may no longer be detained, but must be allowed to go or, if there is sufficient cause, arrested.[66]

(ii) The new country-wide search power under PACE, and its relationship with other powers

To tidy up the mess of local search powers, the 1984 Act abolished them, leaving only a few powers extant, including the power to search for controlled drugs under section 23 of the Misuse of Drugs Act 1971.[67] In place of those which were repealed, a new power was enacted, applying to the whole of England and Wales, to search people, vehicles, and anything in or on a vehicle, for stolen articles, prohibited articles, and articles in relation to which a person has committed, is committing, or is going to commit an offence under section 139 of the Criminal Justice Act 1988.[68] The constable must have reasonable grounds for suspecting that he will find the articles in question before embarking on the search.[69] The power may be exercised only in places to which the public have access, on payment or otherwise, as of right (e.g. public footpaths) or by virtue of express or implied permission, and in places other than dwellings to which at the time people have ready access (such as a field adjoining a public highway which are not securely fenced, or with an open gate).[70] People and vehicles may be searched in a garden, yard, or other land occupied with and used for the purposes of a dwelling, but not if the person searched, or the person in charge of the vehicle, resides in the dwelling, nor if the person or vehicle is there with the resident's permission. This preserves the legal privilege of a person's messuage.[71]

If the constable finds any article which he has reasonable cause for suspecting is an article for which search under section 1 is permitted, he may seize it,[72] after which the retention powers and associated duties under section 22(2) of the 1984 Act apply in

---

[65] Code A, para. 3.3.

[66] See Code A, para. 3.3, and (in relation to searches under s. 1 of PACE) PACE, s. 1(2)(b).

[67] PACE, ss. 6, 7; D. Feldman, *The Law Relating to Entry, Search and Seizure* (London: Butterworths, 1986), 284–97; K. Lidstone and C. Palmer, *The Investigation of Crime: a Guide to Police Powers*, 2nd edn. (London: Butterworths, 1996), 41–5. The Annex to Code A provides a list of the main remaining stop and search powers.

[68] PACE, s. 1(2) and (8A), added by Criminal Justice Act 1988, s. 140.

[69] PACE, s. 1(3).

[70] Ibid., s. 1(1).

[71] Ibid., s. 1(4), (5). See Feldman, *Entry, Search and Seizure*, 8–11, 282–3.

[72] Ibid., s. 1(6).

relation to the article. As regards the three categories of articles for which constables may search, stolen goods require no explanation. Prohibited articles fall in two groups. First, there are offensive weapons. These are articles made or adapted for causing injury to persons, and any article intended, by the person having it with him, for use for causing injury to persons, whether he intends to use it for that purpose himself or intends that someone else shall do the injuring. Secondly, there are articles made or adapted for use in the course of, or in connection with, burglary, theft, taking motor vehicles or other vehicles without authority, or obtaining property by deception; together with other articles which are intended, by the person having them with him, to be used for one of those purposes, whether by him or by someone else.[73] The third category of articles, those relating to an offence under section 139 of the Criminal Justice Act 1988, are articles which have a blade or are sharply pointed, whatever use they are intended for, which are in a person's possession in a public place. The only exception is a folding pocket knife which has a blade less than three inches long. If such an article is found on a person, he is guilty of an offence under section 139 of the 1988 Act unless he can establish one of the defences in section 139(5).

(3) CRITICISMS OF THE SEARCH POWERS

The Act was a considerable step forward in terms of the clarity and consistency of the law and of the rights of suspects, who for the first time were entitled by statute to an account of the purposes of the search and the reasons for it. Nevertheless, the provisions relating to stop and search powers were among the most controversial of those proposed in the bills. There was a strong body of opinion favouring the outright repeal of all or most stop and search powers. The main objections to the powers are easily summarized.

(i) The uncertainty of the reasonable suspicion standard

The first objection concerns the difficulty of defining the concept of reasonable suspicion, which was and is used as the threshold requirement for most stops and searches. It has been argued that the test is too flexible to act as any real constraint on an officer. The provisions of Code A, noted above, give too little guidance as to the meaning of 'reasonable'. For example, once the courts have to review the grounds for a constable's suspicion, it is not clear whether the notion implies that there are matters which an officer *must* always consider, or merely requires some reason which is not actually improper for acting in a particular way. Nor is it obvious whether the standard of reasonableness is that of tort, asking whether a reasonable person would reasonably have acted on the the strength of the grounds possessed by the officer, or is that of administrative law, which tends to accept as reasonable any decision which is not so unreasonable that no reasonable person could properly have arrived at it. Before PACE, there were signs in cases on stop and search powers that the standard being applied was closer to that of negligence than to that of administrative law. This gives the best possible protection to people's rights, by judging the police by the

---

[73] PACE, s. 1(7), (8), (9).

standards of a reasonable person rather than asking only whether the constable's view was so unreasonable that no reasonable person could have taken it. However, in relation to reasonable suspicion for arrests there are signs, discussed below, that the courts have abandoned the 'reasonable person' standard, upholding instead any decision which was not wholly unreasonable.[74] This could easily slip across into the field of stop and search powers.

(ii) The reluctance of the police to be bound by the reasonable suspicion standard

There is a risk that the standard of reasonableness cannot or will not be used by the police in practice. There are indications from research into police activities that officers regarded the rules as being, in the typology of David Smith and Jeremy Gray, merely 'presentational' rather than 'inhibitory' or 'working' rules.[75] That is to say, the police had not generally internalized the legal rules, or made them part of the working morality on which they based their decisions about the proper action to take ('working rules'). Often, because the standard of reasonable suspicion is so malleable, and the facts so easily adjusted to make it seem that it was satisfied, the police did not even regard them as significant inhibitory rules (i.e. rules which would discourage them from behaving in certain ways, limiting the range of available action). More recent research has tended to confirm this picture. The idea of reasonable suspicion is out of tune with the way in which the police form suspicions when on the street. The legal rules requiring reasonable suspicion thus form little or no part of police decision-making processes in relation to searches, but officers recognize their presentational importance, i.e. after the event any explanations for stops and searches which might be required in legal proceedings will have to be presented in terms of the reasonableness of their suspicions at the time. The reasons will then tend to be *ex post facto* rationalizations rather than real reasons, and the need for them will not unduly inhibit police searches.[76]

If officers tend to act on the spur of the moment, on hunches, without articulating their grounds of suspicion, the grounds might often be present, so that officers' experience enabled them to identify grounds for suspicion without the need for conscious thought. However, in many cases, researchers before and since PACE have found little sign that this was happening; many stops appear to be conducted without any suspicion. The figures and observational studies suggest that, in the period up to 1999, more stops were being carried out (or more recorded stops, which is a rather different matter),[77] and that they tended to be more productive (at least in terms of

[74] *Mohammed-Holgate v. Duke* [1984] AC 437, [1984] 1 All ER 1054, HL, discussed below, at 6.3(4)(iii) and (v).

[75] Smith and Gray, *Police and People in London*, 440–3.

[76] D. Dixon *et al.*, 'Reality and Rules in the Construction and Regulation of Police Suspicion' (1989) 17 *Int. J. Soc. Law* 185–206.

[77] W. Skogan, *The Police and Public in England and Wales: A British Crime Survey Report*, Home Office Research Study No. 117 (London: HMSO, 1990); compare Dixon, Coleman, and Bottomley, 'PACE in Practice', 1586; N. Bland, J. Miller, and P. Quinton, *Upping the PACE? An Evaluation of the Recommendations of the Stephen Lawrence Inquiry on Stops and Searches*, Police Research Series Paper 128 (London: Home Office, 2000), 29–37, reporting a failure to record about 70 per cent of stop and search encounters.

arrests for burglary). From 1999, when the Macpherson report on the Stephen Lawrence inquiry drew attention to the continuing disproportionate impact of stop and search on ethnic minority communities, additional checks were imposed on stops. The number of recorded stops then fell, but those taking place are more likely to lead to the discovery of stolen or prohibited items.[78]

(iii) Differential use of powers

As already noted, the evidence suggests that decisions to stop and search people tend not to be made even-handedly. Men are more likely to be stopped than women, young people are likelier targets than old people, African Caribbean and Asian people are more vulnerable to searches than Caucasians. There seems to be clear evidence, exploited by opponents of these powers, that police officers regard these factors as important determinants of suspicion. In short, young black males are several times more likely than young white males to be stopped and searched, and young white males are several times more likely to be stopped than middle-aged white females. Little seems to have changed since the early 1980s.[79] In the past, it has been difficult to obtain legal remedies for stops and searches which appear to have been discriminatory. In an action for unlawful imprisonment or trespass to the person, a constable could justify a stop and search by pointing to factors which objectively might give rise to reasonable suspicion that (for example) the detainee had been in possession of controlled drugs. Statistics about the overall impact of the exercise of the power would be irrelevant, unless it could be shown that the individual constable in the particular case had lacked reasonable suspicion or had acted for an improper purpose.

It is possible that the Human Rights Act 1998 will alter this in one of two ways. First, if, as suggested above, a stop for the purpose of a search falls within the ambit of Article 5, differential use of the power engages the right under ECHR Article 14 to equal enjoyment of Convention rights without discrimination.[80] The focus of a claim under Article 14 (like that under most of the Convention rights in the Human Rights Act) is the behaviour of the public authority as a whole, not only the behaviour of individual officers. It is arguable that a police force which can be shown to operate the general rules governing stops and searches in a differential way as between groups, where the effect of the differential treatment is not objectively justifiable, is discriminating within the meaning of Article 14. If an African Caribbean person is stopped several times in a year, the cumulative effect is to suggest that he or she is a victim of a violation of Article 14 (taken in conjunction with Article 5). This might make statistical evidence about the incidence of searches relevant to the claim, placing a heavier than usual burden on the police force to

---

[78] D. Brown, *Investigating Burglary: The Effects of PACE*, Home Office Research Study 123 (London: HMSO, 1991), 76; N. Bland *et al.*, *Upping the PACE?*, 45–6, reporting arrests following about 12–16 per cent of searches and about 2–3 per cent of stops.

[79] See C. F. Willis, 'The Use, Effectiveness and Impact of Police Stop and Search Powers', in K. Heal, R. Tarling, and J. Burrows (eds.), *Policing Today* (London: HMSO, 1985), 94–106; RCCP, *Law and Procedure*, App. 2; Smith and Gray, *Police and People in London*.

[80] See Ch. 3, above.

justify the plaintiff's history of stops and searches, rather than taking each search separately.

Secondly, it has been suggested by the European Commission of Human Rights that the institutionalization of discriminatory treatment may amount to degrading treatment of people who are adversely affected, violating their rights under ECHR Article 3.[81] In view of the mass of evidence of differential use of stop and search powers, and the (admittedly not uncontroversial) finding of Sir William Macpherson's inquiry into the Stephen Lawrence case that institutional racism existed within the Metropolitan Police,[82] this could produce litigation if a person were to suffer sufficiently seriously to be regarded as a victim of degrading treatment. But litigation will not offer a cure. Only leadership from supervising officers, and changes in police training and discipline, will change what one officer described to the Stephen Lawrence inquiry as a 'canteen culture' of racism.[83]

(iv) Effectiveness

There is considerable doubt about the effectiveness of the powers. Huge numbers of stops are recorded; as noted above, these are probably only a small proportion (perhaps 30 per cent) of those which take place. Relatively few stops lead to arrests. Although the Stephen Lawrence Inquiry accepted that stop and search powers are useful and should be retained,[84] it may be argued that they represent a serious interference with people's freedom and dignity in public places, and produce no benefit commensurate with it.

(v) Consensual searches

A final doubt concerns the consensual searches. There is evidence[85] that the consent given to searches is not what one would, in medical contexts, call real or informed consent, but is more in the nature of passive acquiescence. Nevertheless, the police in some forces have used the fact that people do not object to a search to avoid the requirements of section 2 of PACE. In particular, it is certain that there is a substantial under-recording of searches, and the unrecorded searches are likely to be predominantly unsuccessful ones. This makes it very difficult for supervising officers to use the reports as a means of controlling search practices among their subordinates, even when they are inclined to do so. It also deprives many people who are searched of the most important of the protections for their rights which it was the purpose of section 2 to provide, namely that the grounds for and purpose of the search should be recorded and should be made available to the person searched. Some force orders, and a Crown Court decision under the original version of Code A, have insisted that, where a legal power to insist on searching exists, the police must comply with section

---

[81] *East African Asians* case, Eur. Commn. HR (1973) 3 EHRR 76. On Art. 3 generally, see Ch. 5, above.

[82] Macpherson, *The Stephen Lawrence Inquiry*, ch. 6, commenting on the possibility of drawing inferences of racism from evidence of patterns of behaviour.

[83] Police Sergeant Peter Solley, quoted in Macpherson, *The Stephen Lawrence Inquiry*, 263, para. 37.24.

[84] Macpherson, *The Stephen Lawrence Inquiry*, 333, recommendation 60.

[85] e.g. Dixon, Coleman, and Bottomley, 'Consent and Legal Regulation', 345–62; Dixon, *Law in Policing*, 93–104; Bland *et al.*, *Upping the PACE?*, 29–47.

2 procedures.[86] However, the subsequent revised versions of Code A do not unambiguously provide that consensual searches, where there is a power to search, must comply with the recording provisions of PACE and Code A. Many officers are still not recording searches which, to protect suspects' rights and give a proper picture of the frequency with which searches are taking place and their success rates, ought to be recorded.

(4) ROAD CHECKS AND OTHER POWERS TO STOP AND SEARCH WITHOUT REASONABLE SUSPICION

There have long been situations in which a person can be stopped and required to submit to a search or to provide information. Many people are familiar with controls at customs and immigration posts, under the Customs and Excise Management Act 1979 and the Immigration Act 1971. These powers are extended where an examining officer (who may be a member of the police, customs, or immigration services) stops someone at a port of entry in order to combat terrorism, under paragraphs 2 to 6 of Schedule 7 to the Terrorism Act 2000. Such stops are permitted under Article 5(1)(b) of the ECHR to secure the performance of a legal obligation, i.e. the obligation to provide information and submit to a search.[87]

Legislation further provides for a senior police officer to give a blanket authority to stop people or vehicles in a specified area for three purposes. These are: combating terrorism; preventing violence between armed gangs in public; and catching fleeing offenders.

(i) Combating terrorism

The Terrorism Act 2000 allows a police officer of at least the rank of assistant chief constable,[88] who 'considers it expedient for the prevention of acts of terrorism',[89] to give a general authorization for any constable in uniform to stop vehicles[90] or pedestrians[91] in a specified area or at a specified place, and to search the vehicles, pedestrians, drivers of and passengers in vehicles, and anything in or on the vehicle or carried by a driver, passenger, or pedestrian. The authorization may be given orally as long as it is confirmed in writing as soon as is reasonably practicable.[92] It may last for up to twenty-eight days, and is renewable, but it ceases to have effect after forty-eight hours unless it has been earlier confirmed by the Secretary of State (who may cancel the authorization, or change the period for which it is effective).[93] A constable may detain a vehicle or person for as long as is reasonably required to conduct a search at or near the place of the stop,[94] and may search for 'articles of a kind which could be

---

[86] Bland *et al.*, *Upping the PACE?*, at 349–52; *R. v. Fennelley* [1989] Crim. LR 142.
[87] *McVeigh, O'Neill and Evans v. United Kingdom*, Eur. Commn. HR (1981) 5 EHRR 71.
[88] In the case of the metropolitan or City of London police, commander: Terrorism Act 2000, s. 44(4).
[89] Ibid., s. 44(3).
[90] Ibid., s. 44(1).
[91] Ibid., s. 44(2).
[92] Ibid., s. 44(5).
[93] Ibid., s. 46.
[94] Ibid., s. 45(4).

used in connection with terrorism', whether or not he has any grounds for suspecting that articles of that kind will be found on the person or vehicle.[95] Any such article may be seized and retained if found.[96] A search which involves removing clothing other than headgear, footwear, outer coat, jacket, or gloves must not be conducted in public.[97] Because reasonable grounds for suspicion are not needed when stopping a person, there is a risk that ethnic characteristics will play a part in decision-making. The Code of Practice exhorts officers to take particular care not to discriminate, but accepts that ethnic origin may be an appropriate consideration; 'for example, some international groups are associated with particular ethnic identities'.[98]

(ii) Preventing armed violence

A police officer of at least the rank of inspector may authorize the exercise of stop and search powers in a particular locality without reasonable suspicion for a period of up to twenty-four hours, under section 60 of the Criminal Justice and Public Order Act 1994, as amended. An authorization may be given in two situations. The first situation arises where the inspector reasonably believes that incidents or activities involving serious violence may take place in a particular locality, and that it is expedient to use stop and search powers without the need for reasonable suspicion in order to prevent their occurrence. Secondly, an authorization may be given where the inspector reasonably believes that persons are carrying dangerous instruments or offensive weapons in a particular locality without good reason.[99] When an inspector gives an authorization, he must cause a superintendent to be informed as soon as is practicable.[100] A superintendent may extend the authorization for a further twenty-four hours.[101] The authorization and any extension of it must be in writing, signed by the person giving it, and must set out the grounds on which it is given and the locality in which, and period during which, it is to be effective.[102] While an authorization is in force in a locality, any constable in uniform may stop vehicles or pedestrians in the specified locality, and search the vehicles, pedestrians, drivers of and passengers in vehicles, and anything in or on the vehicle or carried by a driver, passenger, or pedestrian, for offensive weapons and dangerous instruments, whether or not the constable has grounds for suspecting that the person or vehicle is carrying such articles.[103] Any such item may be seized if found.[104] The constable may also require any person to remove an item which the constable reasonably believes the person is wearing in order to conceal his identity, and to seize anything which the constable reasonably believes the person intends to wear wholly or mainly for that purpose,[105] although there is no power to search a person for such an item so sections 2 and 3 of PACE do not apply.[106]

---

[95] Ibid., s. 45(1).　　[96] Ibid., s. 45(2).

[97] Ibid., s. 45(3).　　[98] Code A, para. 1.16.

[99] Criminal Justice and Public Order Act 1994, s. 60(1), as amended by Knives Act 1997, s. 8. The Anti-terrorism, Crime and Security Bill 2001 would allow this power to be exercised in respect of any offence.

[100] Criminal Justice and Public Order Act 1994, s. 60(3A), inserted by Knives Act 1997, s. 8(5).

[101] Criminal Justice and Public Order Act 1994, s. 60(3).

[102] Ibid., s. 60(9), as amended by Knives Act 1997, s. 8.

[103] Criminal Justice and Public Order Act 1994, s. 60(4), (5).

[104] Ibid., s. 60(6).

[105] Ibid., s. 60(4A), inserted by Crime and Disorder Act 1998, s. 25.

[106] See Code A, Note for Guidance 1A; DPP v. Avery [2001] EWCA Admin. 748.

(iii) Road checks to catch criminals

Road checks are sometimes useful tools in investigating crime, but interfere (usually only briefly) with the freedom of movement of people who are not suspected of any offence. PACE, section 5, contains a watered-down version of the regime recommended by the Royal Commission on Criminal Procedure[107] for controlling road checks (or road blocks, as they are sometimes called). An officer of at least the rank of superintendent may authorize, in writing, a road check, i.e. an exercise of the power to stop vehicles under section 163 of the Road Traffic Act 1988 (as amended) in such a way as to stop all vehicles, or vehicles selected by any criterion, in a particular locality, continuously or at specified times, for a specified period not exceeding seven days.[108] The permitted purpose of the road check is to ascertain whether any vehicle is carrying a person who has committed or is intending to commit an offence (other than a road traffic or vehicle excise licence offence), or a witness to such an offence, or a person who is unlawfully at large.[109] An officer of lower rank may authorize a road check in case of urgency, but must as soon as practicable report it to a person of the rank of superintendent or above, who may authorize it to continue or order that it be ended.[110]

Before an authorization is given, certain conditions must be met. Where the check is for a person who is unlawfully at large, the officer must have reasonable grounds for suspecting that the person is, or is about to be, in the locality. Where the check is part of a search for witnesses, the officer must have reasonable grounds for believing that the offence was a serious arrestable offence within the meaning of section 116 and Schedule 5 to PACE, explained at 5.6(1)(iii) below. Where the check is for an offender or potential offender, the officer must have reasonable grounds for believing that the offence concerned is a serious arrestable offence, and reasonable grounds for suspecting (the lower standard, which justifies searches of the person and of vehicles, and arrests) that the person is, or is about to be, in the locality of the proposed road check.[111]

The safeguards against improper use of road checks under section 4, apart from the need for a written authorization, are threefold. First, the authorization must specify the name of the authorizing officer, the locality of the check, and (most importantly) the purpose of the check, including any serious arrestable offence in respect of which the authorization is granted.[112] This helps to concentrate the mind of the authorizing officer on the relevant matters. Secondly, any person in charge of a vehicle which is stopped is entitled to a written statement of the purpose of the check if he applies for it within twelve months.[113] This facilitates review of the propriety of the check, in an action for damages, in an application for judicial

---

[107] RCCP, *Report*, 30–2.

[108] PACE, s. 4(1), (3), (11). The authorization is renewable for periods not exceeding seven days: s. 4(12).

[109] PACE, s. 4(2).

[110] Ibid., s. 4(5)–(9).

[111] Ibid., s. 4(4).

[112] Ibid., s. 4(13), (14).

[113] Ibid., s. 4(15).

review, in a defence to a prosecution (for example, for obstructing a constable in the execution of his duty by failing to stop when required to do so), or in disciplinary proceedings following a complaint. Thirdly, the statistics concerning checks in each police area must be collated and included in the chief police officer's annual report.[114] This enables the number of checks and their success rate to be monitored. It is likely to be more effective than the comparable reports of the use of stop and search powers, because the number of checks will be far smaller than the number of searches, and the requirement for authorization by a superintendent is likely to mean that all checks are properly recorded, unlike the position in relation to searches.

Although the restrictions on road checks under section 4 are substantial, there are other powers which permit the police to stop vehicles. These powers are not affected by section 4, which is additional to them, rather than in place of them.[115] Apart from the powers under the Road Traffic Act 1988, already mentioned, there is the important common-law power to control traffic in order to prevent or stop a breach of the peace. This was the legal basis on which the extensive police road blocks were set up around areas containing coalfields during the miners' strike of 1984–85, and (as noted in Chapter 18 below) has the capacity to interfere substantially with people's freedom of movement without the safeguards imposed on road checks set up under section 4 of the 1984 Act.

6.3 GROUNDS FOR ARREST

This section examines the grounds for arresting people in connection with criminal offences. Arrests to prevent or stop a breach of the peace (which in England and Wales, unlike Scotland, is not a substantive offence) are considered in Chapter 18 below. Any arrest deprives a person of liberty, and engages Article 5 of the ECHR. It must be justifiable within Article 5(1), and particularly Article 5(1)(c): the lawful arrest or detention of a person for the purpose of bringing him before the competent legal authority on reasonable suspicion of having committed an offence, or when it is reasonably considered necessary to prevent his committing an offence or fleeing after having done so. Section 6 of the Human Rights Act 1998 makes it unlawful for a public authority to exercise a power in a way which is incompatible with a Convention right unless compelled to do so by primary legislation, while section 3 requires that all legislation is to be read and given effect so far as possible in a manner compatible with Convention rights. The result is that constables must (i) have lawful authority for an arrest, (ii) act in a non-arbitrary way and non-discriminatory way,[116] and (iii) make

---

[114] Ibid., s. 5(1)(b)(ii).

[115] Ibid., s. 4(16).

[116] Arbitrariness is incompatible with lawfulness, as the term is used in the Convention. See *Bozano v. France*, Eur. Ct. HR, Series A, No. 111, Judgment of 18 December 1986; *Lukanov v. Bulgaria*, Eur. Ct. HR, RJD 1997-II, Judgment of 20 March 1997. Discrimination in making arrests may give rise to a claim under Art. 14 in conjunction with Art. 5 similar to that discussed above in relation to stops and searches.

an arrest only where there is reasonable suspicion that the person arrested has committed, is committing, or is about to commit an offence. Any statute must be interpreted, so far as possible, as allowing constables to behave according to those principles.

(1) ARREST UNDER WARRANT

A justice of the peace is empowered to issue a warrant to arrest a person and bring him before a magistrates' court if any information is laid that the person has committed, or is suspected of having committed, an offence.[117] Where the person to be arrested is over 17 years of age, a warrant may issue only where the offence is an indictable offence punishable with imprisonment, or where the person's address is not known with enough precision to allow a summons to be served.[118] Where an arrest is made under warrant for an offence, it is not necessary for the constable who executes it (or a warrant for commitment or distress, unless the warrant concerns non-payment of rates) to have the warrant in his possession at the time he makes the arrest, but the warrant must be shown to the arrestee as soon as practicable.[119] This provision allows a person to be arrested without them being able immediately to check the authority for the arrest, and is a small but significant incursion on rights to be free of arbitrary or unjustified deprivation of liberty. As there is also a power to enter premises, if need be by force, to execute an arrest warrant 'issued in connection with or arising out of criminal proceedings' if the person to be arrested is reasonably believed to be in the premises,[120] this also indirectly allows entry under warrant when the warrant which justifies the entry is not in the constable's possession. This is an infringement of the right to privacy and freedom from interference with property. It is particularly unsatisfactory in view of the fact that, if the entry were under a search warrant, the warrant would have to be in the constable's possession, and shown to the occupier before the search began.[121]

A constable executing a warrant is protected against liability for false imprisonment as long as he arrests the person named in it. If the wrong person is named, for example because the real offender gave a false name and address, the constable who executes the warrant will none the less not be liable in damages for accurately executing the warrant.[121a]

---

[117] Magistrates' Courts Act 1980, s. 1(1). Because the issuing of an arrest warrant affects the liberty of the individual, all procedural requirements must be properly observed: *Brooks v. DPP of Jamaica* [1994] 1 AC 568, [1994] 2 All ER 231, PC.

[118] Magistrates' Courts Act 1980, s. 1(4).

[119] Ibid., s. 125(3), as amended by PACE, s. 33.

[120] Ibid., s. 17(1)(a)(i), (2).

[121] Ibid., s. 16(5).

[121a] *McGrath v. Chief Constable of the Royal Ulster Constabulary* [2001] 3 WLR 312, HL.

(2) CRIMINAL OFFENCES TO WHICH POWERS OF ARREST WITHOUT WARRANT APPLY

The law on arrest without warrant used to depend on the technical and largely illogical distinction between felonies, for which one could be arrested at any time, and misdemeanours. When felonies were abolished by the Criminal Law Act 1967, arrest without warrant was placed on a statutory footing. Section 2 created a class of 'arrestable offences', in respect of which a suspect was liable to be arrested without a warrant. The law was recodified by the Police and Criminal Evidence Act 1984. The main points to note are the following.

The concept of the arrestable offence is retained in section 24(1). The main test for arrestability remains the availability of a sentence fixed by law of five years or more on first conviction for the offence after trial on indictment.[122] This covers most of the types of offence which we would normally consider to be inherently serious. However, a number of other offences, which were thought to be of a kind justifying arrest without warrant but which do not meet those criteria, were added to the list of arrestable offences, making it something of a rag-bag.[123] It is also an arrestable offence to conspire, incite, aid, abet, counsel, or procure the commission of an arrestable offence, and to attempt to commit any such offence other than taking a motor vehicle or other conveyance without authority.[124]

Various offences exist for which a power of arrest without warrant has been granted by other legislation but which do not fall within the definition of an arrestable offence in section 24 of PACE. These offences are, therefore, not 'arrestable offences' despite the fact that a suspect can be arrested for them without a warrant. The only significance of their not being arrestable offences lies in the fact that they can never be 'serious arrestable offences', a sub-group of arrestable offences in respect of which special police powers are sometimes available.

A special power was granted in PACE, section 25, to arrest without warrant for offences in respect of which there would not normally be a power to arrest. This special power arises when (i) an officer has reasonable grounds for suspecting that any offence has been or is being committed or attempted, *and* (ii) the officer has reasonable grounds for suspecting that a particular person has committed or attempted, or is

---

[122] Ibid., s. 24(1)(a), (b).

[123] Ibid., s. 24(1)(c), 24(2) as amended. These arrestable offences are currently offences for which there is a power of arrest under the Customs and Excise Management Acts; offences under the Official Secrets Act 1920 and (with limited exceptions) the Official Secrets Act 1989; causing the prostitution of women or procuring a girl under the age of 21 for the purposes of prostitution, contrary to sections 22 and 23 of the Sexual Offences Act 1956; taking a motor vehicle or other conveyance without authority, or going equipped for stealing, etc., contrary to sections 12(1) and 25(1) respectively of the Theft Act 1968; offences under the Football (Offences) Act 1991; publishing obscene matter contrary to the Obscene Publications Act 1959, s. 2; offences relating to indecent photographs and pseudo-photographs of children (Protection of Children Act 1978, s. 1, as amended); ticket touting (Criminal Justice and Public Order Act 1994, s. 166); publishing material likely to stir up racial hatred (Public Order Act 1986, s. 19); touting for car hire services (Criminal Justice and Public Order Act 1994, s. 167); offences relating to the possession of offensive weapons, blades, and pointed instruments (Prevention of Crime Act 1953, s. 1(1) and Criminal Justice Act 1988, ss. 139, 139A); failure to comply with a requirement to remove an item of face-covering (Criminal Justice Act 1994, s. 60(8)(b) as amended); harassment (Protection from Harassment Act 1997); racially aggravated harassment (Crime and Disorder Act 1998, s. 32(1)(a)); and failing to comply with a football banning order (Football Spectators Act 1989, s. 16(4)).

[124] PACE, s. 24(3), as amended.

committing or attempting, the offence, *and* (iii) it appears to the officer that the service of a summons on that person for that offence is impracticable or inappropriate because any one of what are called the 'general arrest conditions' are satisfied.[125] These conditions are:

(a) that the officer does not know, and cannot readily find out, the person's name (for example, where the suspect is running away);

(b) that the officer has reasonable grounds for doubting whether a name given by the person is his real name (as where the person has no means of identification available);

(c) that the person has failed to give a satisfactory address for serving the summons, or the officer has reasonable grounds for doubting whether an address given by the person is satisfactory for service (for example, where the address is that of a hotel or hostel at which the person has no established roots);

(d) that the officer has reasonable grounds for *believing* (a higher degree of confidence than mere suspicion) that arrest is necessary to prevent the person

   (i)   causing physical harm to himself or another,

   (ii) suffering physical injury,

   (iii) causing loss of or damage to property,

   (iv) committing an offence against public decency, or

   (v)   causing an unlawful obstruction of the highway;

(e) that the constable has reasonable grounds for *believing* that arrest is necessary to protect a child or other vulnerable person from the person arrested.

The object is to allow a person to be arrested where it seems that it would otherwise be impossible to proceed against him by way of summons. The power is open to criticism as extending the wide discretion of the constable to interfere with the liberty of citizens in cases which are, by definition, not terribly serious. It would be less objectionable were the exercise of the constable's discretion to be subject to more closely controlled criteria. As it is, the general arrest conditions give the appearance of a rag-bag without coherent principle.

Conditions (a), (b), and (c) are related to the integrity of the legal process. They treat the arrest as replacing the summons, the commencement of criminal process, in cases where there are reasonable grounds to doubt whether criminal proceedings could be effectively initiated in any other way. This is in line with the justification for making an arrest under Article 5(1)(c) of the European Convention on Human Rights. On the other hand, there are elements of paternalism—protecting the person against himself—in condition (d)(i), while the suspect is to be protected against others in (d)(ii), and other people are protected from the suspect by (d)(i), (d)(iii), and (e). Condition (d)(iv) seems designed to protect general public decency against what Feinberg calls 'harmless wrongdoing', but it is limited to cases where members of the public, going about their ordinary business, cannot reasonably be expected to

---

[125] PACE, s. 25(1), (2).

avoid the person concerned,[126] and so is actually directed more towards Feinberg's category of 'offense to others'. The power to arrest under (d)(v) replaced a similar power in relation to a person causing an unlawful obstruction of the highway under the Highways Act 1980, section 137(2), presumably in order to provide, so far as possible, a comprehensive code of arrest powers in sections 24 and 25 of the 1984 Act.

There is a risk, particularly in relation to the preventive powers of the constable under conditions (d)(iv) and (v), that the power under section 25 might be used to deprive people of the opportunity to protest in public about matters of public concern. If used in this way, the exercise of the powers would be unlawful by virtue of section 6 of the Human Rights Act 1998. It would violate rights under both Article 5(1) (deprivation of liberty for preventive purposes[127]) and Article 10 (freedom of expression) of the ECHR. However, the actual impact of section 25 is minimal in this context, first because (as will be seen in Chapter 18 below) the police have numerous powers, at common law and under statute, to take action to control or stop public protest apart from this section, and secondly because a person must already be reasonably suspected of committing or having committed an offence before the section 25 power may be used (although the offence need not be of a type which itself gives rise to the risk under condition (d) justifying arrest rather than summons).

PACE abolished all other powers for constables to arrest people for an offence without a warrant, or to arrest otherwise than for an offence without a warrant or a court order, except so far as they were expressly saved by Schedule 2 to the Act.[128] This has, however, been construed as applying only to arrest powers conferred on constables *qua* constables. On this view, it leaves in force powers conferred on people generally to arrest someone without a warrant, such as the power to arrest someone who is drunk and disorderly in a public place,[129] or being 'found . . . in any inclosed yard, garden or area, for any unlawful purpose'.[130]

(3) WHO MAY MAKE ARRESTS FOR ARRESTABLE OFFENCES, AND WHEN?

(i) Offences in progress

Anyone may arrest under section 24 of PACE a person who is, or whom he has reasonable grounds for suspecting to be, in the act of committing an arrestable offence. This covers the case where a suspect is caught in the act, in the process of performing the act or omission which the person making the arrest has reasonable grounds for suspecting is an arrestable offence. The person making the arrest is protected against liability if it subsequently turns out that the person arrested was not committing an offence. For example, if somebody sees a person breaking a shop

---

126 Ibid., s. 25(5).

127 See, e.g. *Jecius v. Lithuania*, Eur. Ct. HR, Judgment of 31 July 2000, para. 50.

128 PACE, s. 26(1), (2).

129 Criminal Justice Act 1967, s. 91(1); *DPP v. Kitching* [1990] COD 149, DC.

130 Vagrancy Act 1824, ss. 4, 6; *Gapper v. Chief Constable of the Avon and Somerset Constabulary* [2000] QB 29, [1998] 4 All ER 248, CA.

window, this will normally give reasonable grounds for suspecting that person of criminal damage or burglary, both arrestable offences. If it turns out that the suspect was the owner of the shop who had locked himself out without his keys, and was breaking the window in order to gain access to his own premises, he will not be guilty of any offence, but neither will the arrestor be liable to him in damages for false arrest, false imprisonment, or trespass to the person (so long as no unreasonable force was used to make the arrest).

However, the power of arrest without warrant arises only if the offence which is suspected is, in law, an arrestable offence. If the arrestor wrongly but in good faith believes that an offence is arrestable when it is not, the honesty or reasonableness of his belief will not provide a defence to an action for damages. There is a difference between a reasonable but mistaken exercise of a power which exists in law, and the purported exercise (whether reasonable or not) of a power which does not exist in law. For example, in *Wershof v. Metropolitan Police Commissioner*[131] police officers purported to arrest a solicitor for obstructing them in the execution of their duties, contrary to section 89(2) of the Police Act 1996. There is no power of arrest under that section: the offence is not an arrestable offence, and it was held to be unlawful to arrest for it unless the obstruction gives rise to a breach of the peace or a reasonable apprehension of an imminent breach of the peace, or impedes a lawful arrest.[132] This might seem harsh on a constable following the advice in an authoritative text, and even harder on an ordinary citizen, particularly in the light of the misunderstanding which seems to reign amongst police officers and some judges.[133] However, people are entitled to expect that their liberty will be protected against interference which is not authorized by law. Since ignorance of the law does not excuse a wrongdoer, ordinary citizens (including people such as store detectives and security operatives, who are not constables but who make their livings wholly or partly from combating crime) who make arrests, without knowing whether the offence which they suspect is an arrestable offence in law, do so at their peril.

(ii) Completed and future offences

With regard to arrests for offences for past or apprehended offences, the powers of police officers are in some respects wider than those of ordinary citizens. In respect of completed offences, a constable may make a lawful arrest if he reasonably suspects that an arrestable offence has been committed by the arrestee. The constable will be

---

[131] [1978] 3 All ER 540. See to the same effect *Gelberg v. Miller* [1961] 1 All ER 291, DC, where the court regarded the matter as being of high constitutional significance, and the absence of a power of arrest was ultimately conceded by the Attorney-General; *Riley v. DPP* (1989) 91 Cr. App. R. 14, DC, at 22 *per* Watkins LJ.

[132] It might now also be possible to arrest under PACE, s. 25, if one of the general arrest conditions is fulfilled, but only if the detainee is told that he is being arrested for that reason: *Edwards v. DPP* (1993) 97 Cr. App. R. 301, DC.

[133] The law reports are full of arrests which purport to be for obstructing constables in the execution of their duty: see, e.g. *Stunt v. Bolton* [1972] RTR 435, DC. In some cases where the matter was not central to the case, the judges have not had the law explained by counsel, and so have appeared wrongly to accept, or not to deny, that such arrests are lawful: e.g. *Ledger v. DPP* [1991] Crim. LR 439, DC; *Green v. DPP* [1991] Crim. LR 782. These lapses on the part of counsel are unfortunate: the police must be left in no doubt of the limits to their powers. See the comments of Professor J. C. Smith in his commentary on *Ledger* [1991] Crim. LR at 441.

protected against liability if it turns out that no offence had in fact been committed, so long as he had reasonable grounds to suspect that something which was in law an arrestable offence had been committed.[134] In this regard constables are in a better position than other members of the public who make an arrest (including store detectives), since people who are not constables are permitted to arrest for an arrestable offence only if an arrestable offence has, in fact, been committed.[135] Ordinary members of the public, unlike constables, are not protected against liability to an action for false arrest or false imprisonment if it turns out that no arrestable offence had in fact been committed, however reasonable their suspicions may have been.

In relation to arrests for apprehended offences, constables have a preventive power to arrest someone who is, or whom they have reasonable grounds for suspecting to be, about to commit an arrestable offence.[136] Ordinary citizens have no such anticipatory power, and must usually wait until the offence is in progress before they can lawfully effect an arrest. There is an exception where a citizen reasonably apprehends an imminent breach of the peace, and makes the arrest to prevent it: all citizens, not only constables, have a duty to preserve the peace and are entitled to take reasonably necessary steps to that end.[137]

(4) STRUCTURING THE DISCRETION TO ARREST

There is nothing objectionable on civil liberties grounds about the power to make an arrest in itself. Arrests are permitted under the European Convention on Human Rights, Article 5(1), so long as the deprivation of liberty is 'in accordance with a procedure prescribed by law' and is: '(c) the lawful arrest or detention of a person effected for the purpose of bringing him before the competent legal authority on reasonable suspicion of having committed an offence or when it is reasonably considered necessary to prevent his committing an offence or fleeing after having done so'. The competent legal authority is similar to the 'judge or other officer authorised by law to exercise judicial power' by whom the lawfulness of the detention must be reviewable under Article 5(3): the authority must therefore be independent of the parties and impartial.[138] The extent to which English law complies with these conditions will be considered below.

There are circumstances in which the prosecution process might be frustrated if an arrest were impossible. If there are problems, they concern the width of the discretion which an arresting officer has, and the relative weakness of the principles by which the law structures the discretion and guards against its abuse by police officers.

---

[134] PACE, s. 24(6).

[135] Ibid., s. 24(5); *R. v. Self* [1992] 3 All ER 476, CA; *Davidson v. Chief Constable of North Wales* [1994] 2 All ER 597, CA.

[136] PACE, s. 24(7).

[137] *Albert v. Lavin* [1982] AC 546, [1981] 3 All ER 878, HL.

[138] *Schiesser v. Switzerland*, Eur. Ct. HR, Series A, No. 34, Judgment of 4 December 1979, 2 EHRR 417, at para. 29.

(i) The arresting officer's wide discretion

Normally, when a public official is given a discretionary power by law, limits are placed on it. These include the circumstances in which it can lawfully be exercised (in connection with arrestable offences, as described above); the purposes for which it can be exercised; and the matters which are to be taken into consideration when deciding how it should be exercised. Together, these constraints provide a legal framework within which the official must work if his exercise of power is to be lawful; they are sometimes said to 'structure' discretions. The constraints may be explicitly set out in the statute which grants the power, or they may be implied from the statute by reference to the purposes for which it was supposedly granted.

In relation to arrests without warrant in English law, the principal legal constraints on the exercise of an officer's discretion are the obligation to act in a manner compatible with Convention rights, under section 6 of the Human Rights Act 1998; the requirement, contained in PACE, for reasonable grounds to suspect the person of an arrestable offence; and the further requirement (derived from general principles of administrative law) that the power to arrest should be exercised reasonably and for a proper purpose.

Not all powers of arrest are based on reasonable suspicion of having committed an offence. Sometimes the power arises only in respect of someone who is actually committing an offence. More rarely, there is power to arrest a person without reasonable grounds for suspecting that he or she has committed any particular offence. For example, section 41 of the Terrorism Act 2000 allows a constable to arrest a person whom he reasonably suspects to be a terrorist, defined in section 40 as someone who has committed an offence under the Act or has been *concerned* in the commission, preparation, or instigation of acts of terrorism.[139] In many cases, this power is likely to be used in circumstances which amount to 'reasonable suspicion of *having committed* an offence', as required by Article 5(1)(c). However, if the arrest is made purely in order to facilitate the questioning of a witness whom the arresting officer knows is not suspected of being an offender, and so is not going to be charged with an offence, it would violate Article 5(1), and would be an unlawful exercise of discretion by reason of section 6(1) of the Human Rights Act 1998. The European Court of Human Rights has made it clear that an arrest is justifiable under Article 5(1)(c) only if it is for an offence which was known to the law at the time of the arrest.[140]

It is clearly established that preventive detention of a person to stop him or her from committing future offences is not permitted under Article 5.[141] Even the power to arrest without warrant under section 24 of PACE does not always depend on the

---

[139] For the very wide definition of terrorism, see Terrorism Act 2000, s. 1.

[140] *Wloch v. Poland*, Eur. Ct. HR, Judgment of 19 October 2000, at paras. 109–15: detention on reasonable suspicion of 'trading in children' would have violated Art. 5(1), because such trading was not clearly established as an offence in Polish law. The detention would therefore have been both unlawful, within the meaning of Art. 5(1), and without relevant reasonable suspicion under Art. 5(1)(c). However, W was also detained on reasonable suspicion of incitement to commit offences, which was lawful, so there was no violation of Art. 5(1).

[141] *Lawless v. Ireland*, Eur. Ct. HR, Series A, No. 3, Judgment of 1 July 1961, 1 EHRR 15; *Jecius v. Lithuania*, Eur. Ct. HR, Judgment of 31 July 2000.

constable either holding the suspicion or being in possession of the grounds on which suspicion might reasonably be based.[142] Where an arrestable offence *actually has been or is being* committed, the section provides that anyone may arrest without warrant a person who *is* committing an arrestable offence[143] or who *has* committed one,[144] whether or not there are reasonable grounds to suspect them. Similarly, a constable is permitted to arrest without warrant anyone who *is about to* commit an arrestable offence.[145] In none of these cases are reasonable grounds expressly required, and the arrest (presumably on the strength of a hunch, or of information received which would not be strong enough to ground a reasonable suspicion) is justified by the achievement of the desired end, namely the apprehension of the person who turns out, in fact, to be the offender. Under the Human Rights Act 1998, no statute which confers a discretion to arrest a person for purposes falling within Article 5(1)(c) can make an arrest by a constable, as a public authority, lawful in the absence of reasonable grounds for suspecting the person of an offence which justifies arrest, unless there are clear words forbidding the constable to take account of the absence of reasonable suspicion. For the arrest to be 'lawful' and 'in accordance with a procedure prescribed by law', it must have a proper basis in national law (rather than administrative guidance), and must be in respect of an offence known to law at the time of the arrest.[146] The relevant law must also protect people against arbitrary interference with their liberty.[147]

(ii) Reasonable grounds for suspicion

Under section 24 of PACE, there must be reasonable grounds for suspecting (a) that an arrestable offence has been, is being, or is about to be committed, and (b) that the person being arrested has committed, is committing, or is about to commit it. These are two distinct suspicions, which will be considered separately.

The first matter in relation to which there must, under certain parts of section 24, be reasonable grounds for suspicion is that an arrestable offence has been, is being or is about to be committed. This means that the arresting officer must have reasonable grounds for suspecting that a state of affairs exists which, if it did exist, would constitute an arrestable offence.[148] As noted above, it is not sufficient for him to believe, wrongly, that an offence is arrestable; he must get the legal classification of the offence correct. Were the law otherwise, it would authorize arrests for non-arrestable offences, giving greater arrest powers to ignorant or negligent officers than to those who

---

[142] Unlike the Criminal Law Act 1967, s. 2, which was replaced by s. 24 of PACE.

[143] PACE, s. 24(4)(a).

[144] Ibid., s. 24(5)(a).

[145] Ibid., s. 14(7)(a).

[146] See, e.g. *Grauslys v. Lithuania*, Eur. Ct. HR, Judgment of 10 October 2000; *Wloch v. Poland*, Eur. Ct. HR, Judgment of 19 October 2000.

[147] *Bozano v. France*, Eur. Ct. HR, Series A, No. 111, Judgment of 18 December 1986, 9 EHRR 297; *Lukanov v. Bulgaria*, Eur. Ct. HR, Judgment of 20 March 1997, RJD 1997-II, 24 EHRR 121.

[148] Under ECHR, Art. 5(1)(c), the Commission held that there must be reasonable suspicion that someone has committed an offence where he is arrested because 'it is reasonably considered necessary to prevent his . . . fleeing' as it does where a person is arrested to bring him before a competent legal authority: *Lukanov v. Bulgaria*, 24 EHRR 121, at para. 80 of the Commission's Report.

correctly understand the limits of their lawful authority. The fact that the constable wrongly thought that he had a power of arrest in the circumstances could not confer a power where none existed as a matter of law.

The second necessary suspicion for which there must be reasonable grounds is that a particular person is a guilty party. At this point it is clearly important that the suspicion should be reasonable, as the suspect will suffer an infringement of his liberty. The European Court of Human Rights has pointed out that the reasonableness of a suspicion 'forms an essential part of the safeguard against arbitrary arrest and detention ... [It] presupposes the existence of facts or information which would satisfy an objective observer that the person concerned may have committed the offence. What may be regarded as "reasonable" will however depend on all the circumstances'. In terrorism cases, the need to take effective action against a special threat will make some suspicions reasonable which would not otherwise be so, including suspicions based on intelligence which cannot be disclosed. The state was not required to reveal its sources of information in order to show that reasonable grounds existed, particularly in relation to terrorism. Nevertheless, the Court must even there be furnished with 'at least some facts or information capable of satisfying the Court that the arrested person was reasonably suspected of having committed the alleged offence'.[149]

However, the term 'reasonable grounds to suspect' provides only an indeterminate standard for assessing the adequacy of evidence to justify an arrest. The caselaw on the meaning of the term in the context of arrests (it also appears elsewhere in the law on police powers as a justifying standard, and as we shall see is subject to similar uncertainty whenever it is applied) shows that it does not impose a very rigorous standard on arresting officers, who need only have as much material as a reasonable person would need in the circumstances to hold the relevant suspicion. Since suspicion is a less assured state of mind than belief, less material is needed to produce it in a reasonable person. As Lord Devlin made clear when delivering the advice of the Privy Council in *Shaaban Bin Hussien v. Chong Fook Kam*,[150] reasonable cause does not need to be based on anything which would be admissible in evidence in court; still less need there be what a court would regard as a *prima facie* case:

'"Reasonable cause" is a lower standard than information sufficient to prove a *prima facie* case. Reasonable cause may take into account matters that could not be put into evidence at all or matters which, although admissible, would not on their own prove the case. The circumstances of the case should be such that a reasonable man acting without passion or prejudice would fairly have suspected the person of having committed the offence.'

The malleability of the standard is a recognition of the difficulties facing operational police officers who often have to make difficult judgments in haste. The European Court of Human Rights has even suggested that a suspicion which might be sufficiently reasonably to justify a short detention could be insufficient to justify a

---

[149] *Fox, Campbell and Hartley v. United Kingdom*, Eur. Ct. HR, Series A, No. 182, Judgment of 30 August 1990, 11 EHRR 117, at paras. 32, 34, where insufficient grounds were established and there was a violation of Art. 5(1); *Murray v. United Kingdom*, Eur. Ct. HR, Series A, No. 300-A, Judgment of 28 October 1994, 19 EHRR 193, at paras. 51, 56–63 (reasonable suspicion existed; no violation).

[150] [1970] AC 942, PC, at 948.

longer one.[151] It would be unreasonable to apply too exacting a standard when evaluating their actions with the benefit of hindsight. On the other hand, in the sensitive field of interference with civil liberties, adopting too loose a standard risks removing any realistic chance of obtaining remedies for careless police action. Although the police are called upon to justify their actions after the event by reference to the standard of reasonable suspicion, there is evidence that much investigation proceeds on the basis of hunches.[152] An investigator forms a view of where the truth is likely to lie, and sets out to test (or sometimes simply to confirm) that hypothesis. This is inevitable, and it would probably be impossible to conduct investigations effectively on the basis of the statutory standards. Those standards therefore become *ex post facto* 'presentational' rules rather than inhibitory rules (which are not fully accepted by the police but hold out threats of sanctions which tend to discourage officers from acting in certain ways) or fully internalized working rules,[153] and lose their power to structure police discretion. The power to arrest, like that to stop and search, may then be used in a way which discriminates against certain groups in society according to the experiences (or prejudices) which dictate an officer's hunches.

This is particularly likely to happen when the courts exercise only a very lax scrutiny over the reasonableness of police action. In earlier decades, the courts were quite demanding: for example, it was said that reasonable suspicion arose only if a reasonable constable, not merely an ordinary person in the constable's position, would have thought that the suspect probably committed the offence.[154] However, this can apply in its full rigour only if the arrest is seen as the commencement of criminal proceedings, leading normally to a charge. As we shall see, the House of Lords in *Mohammed-Holgate v. Duke*[155] accepted that in many cases it was reasonable for the police to arrest in order to facilitate the collection of information, and that is now the normal reason for arresting. That being so, it might well be far too early, at the time of arrest, to decide whether the suspect *probably* committed the offence. There ought to be reasonable grounds to suspect that she did, and that seems to demand a lower level of likelihood of guilt than is implied in 'probably'. In practice, however, it is not unusual for the police to arrest people simply to make it easier to obtain information, without any real suspicion that the person being arrested was personally involved in an offence.[156] This breaches Article 5(1)(c) of the European Convention on Human

[151] *Murray v. United Kingdom*, Eur. Ct. HR, Series A, No. 300-A, Judgment of 28 October 1994, 19 EHRR 193, at para. 56.

[152] D. Dixon, K. Bottomley, and C. Coleman, 'Reality and Rules', 185–206, offer an acute and perceptive discussion of the practical effects of the reasonable suspicion requirement, based on an observational study of a North of England police force.

[153] For this classification, see Smith and Gray, *Police and People in London*, 440–3.

[154] See, e.g. *Dallison v. Caffery* [1965] 1 QB 348 at 371, *per* Diplock LJ; *Wiltshire v. Barrett* [1966] 1 QB 312 at 322, *per* Lord Denning MR. See also M. Zander, *The Police and Criminal Evidence Act 1984*, 2nd edn. (London: Sweet & Maxwell, 1990), 61.

[155] [1984] AC 437, [1984] 1 All ER 1054, HL.

[156] Smith and Gray, *Police and People in London*, 462–71, found several examples of this happening in their pre-PACE research on the Metropolitan Police, even where the person arrested was not really suspected of involvement in the offence. This led the authors to express the 'informed opinion' (at 578) that 'people who are known not to have committed an offence but do have information about it would *normally* be arrested in order to bring pressure to bear on them to divulge the information' (italics in original).

Rights: not only must there be reasonable suspicion, but an arrest or detention is lawful under Article 5(1) only if it aims to achieve one of the purposes which are permitted under that paragraph.[157] On the other hand, if there are reasonable grounds for suspecting that the person arrested has committed, is committing, or is about to commit an arrestable offence, the arrest may be legitimate both under the ECHR and in English law, even if no charge is ultimately preferred or there is an ulterior motive (such as the prevention of more serious crime).[158]

It is implicit in the Police and Criminal Evidence Act 1984 that it is permissible to arrest and detain a suspect for a period in order to question him, to seek information about the offence. Arrest cannot properly be regarded as the initiation of a legal process any more; it is part of the investigative process, and must be regulated as such. This may have the effect of extending police powers, but (as the Australian Law Reform Commission noted in 1975) it is not clear whether the appropriate response is to accept the practical reality of police investigative practice, legalize it, and legislate to give the suspect protection against abuse of police powers, or is rather to reassert the old common-law orthodoxy, outlaw police practices, and risk creating a situation in which the police feel forced to bend the law and take liberties (usually other people's) in order to do their jobs, while suspects have no institutional protection.[159]

The courts seem to have become too permissive in dealing with police powers of arrest. In a number of cases, it has come to appear that the courts (and particularly the Court of Appeal and House of Lords) are loath to subject to any searching analysis the basis of police claims that they had reasonable suspicion. In three cases, the Court of Appeal has held that, so long as the police can point to some grounds which might conceivably have led a reasonable person to conclude that a person might have committed an arrestable offence, the courts should be prepared to accept even thin grounds for suspicion as adequate.[160] This approach cannot survive the Human Rights Act 1998, since the caselaw of the European Court of Human Rights, described above, makes it clear that the reasonableness of a constable's suspicion must be carefully assessed in order to provide an adequate safeguard against arbitrary interference with liberty. The job of the courts in actions against anyone, but particularly against public officials, is to ensure that *prima facie* unlawful action can be properly justified, and to award compensation if it cannot be. To adopt a gentler standard in dealing with defendants who are public servants than with others makes inroads on rule-of-law principles, and would suggest that the police have a licence to stretch the law in a manner wholly inconsistent with the duty of public authorities under section

[157] *Bouamar v. Belgium*, Eur. Ct. HR, Series A, No. 129, Judgment of 29 February 1987, 11 EHRR 1 (on detaining a minor for educational purposes).

[158] See *Brogan v. United Kingdom*, Eur. Ct. HR, Series A, No. 145-B, Judgment of 29 November 1988, 11 EHRR 117, at para. 53; *Murray v. United Kingdom*, Series A, No. 300-A, Judgment of 28 October 1994, 19 EHRR 193, at para. 67; *K.-F. v. Germany*, Eur. Ct. HR, Judgment of 27 November 1997, 26 EHRR 390; *R. v. Chalkley* [1998] QB 848, [1998] 2 All ER 155, CA.

[159] The Law Reform Commission, Report No. 2, *Criminal Investigation* (1975), 38–9.

[160] *Ward v. Chief Constable of Avon and Somerset Constabulary*, The Times, 26 June 1986, CA; *Holtham v. Metropolitan Police Commissioner*, The Times, 28 November 1987, CA; *Castorina v. Chief Constable of Surrey* [1988] NLJ Rep. 180, CA.

6 of the 1998 Act.[161] Reasonable suspicion requirements in legislation must now be interpreted accordingly, by virtue of section 3 of the Act.

It has sometimes been suggested that the discretion to arrest should be constrained by statutory rules as to the matters which can and cannot give rise to reasonable cause or grounds, in the hope of excluding sexual and racial prejudices and stereotypes from the decision-making process. However, reasonable cause for suspicion is ultimately a matter of fact and judgment rather than law. The matters which can give rise to it are infinitely various, and successive official reports have rejected as impracticable a catalogue of permissible considerations.[162] A compromise solution has been found in the context of searches of the person, as noted above: Code A specifies certain matters which may *never* be treated as giving rise to reasonable cause for the purpose of conducting a search. A similar approach might be possible in relation to arrests, but there is as yet no code of practice on arrests, and no statutory authority for the Home Secretary to introduce one.

Despite the generally permissive attitude which judges have taken to police actions, there are certain guidelines in the caselaw, especially on the torts of false imprisonment and malicious prosecution, as to what types of considerations constitute reasonable grounds for suspicion. For example, the fact that a suspect has previous convictions for an offence of the same or another type will not on its own normally give reasonable grounds for suspicion, although it may reinforce the strength of other information implicating the suspect.[163] The police are entitled to take account of information from an informant, especially if the informant is professionally involved in crime-fighting, like a store detective.[164] Where the information is hearsay, or the informant is not known to the officers, it may be unreasonable to attach very much importance to it, although this is a matter calling for judgment.[165] The officers should consider whether the informant is known to be reliable, whether witnesses seem sure of their stories, and whether the information appears credible in the light of other known facts.[166] It may be unreasonable to rely on a long delayed complaint, in the absence of other evidence, and where the information concerns the whereabouts of a suspect or of articles which could have been moved, it is particularly important not to rely on it unless it is reasonably up to date.[167] It is not reasonable, when contemplating an arrest under section 25 of PACE, to doubt a suspect's account of his name and address, in the absence of other factors, merely because experience suggests that people who commit offences tend to lie about their names and addresses.[168] Something is needed to suggest that the person in question is lying.

---

[161] For further discussion, see R. Clayton and H. Tomlinson, 'Arrest and Reasonable Grounds for Suspicion', *Law Society Gazette*, 7 September 1988, 22, esp. at 26.

[162] Advisory Committee on Drug Dependence, *Powers of Arrest and Search in Relation to Drugs Offences*; RCCP, *Report*, para. 3.25.

[163] *McArdle v. Egan* (1933) 150 LT 412, CA.

[164] *Davidson v. Chief Constable of North Wales* [1994] 2 All ER 597, CA.

[165] *Lister v. Perryman* (1870) LR 4 HL 521, HL.

[166] Ibid.; *Dallison v. Caffery* [1965] 1 QB 348, [1964] 2 All ER 610, CA.

[167] *Hogg v. Ward* (1858) 3 H. & N. 417, 27 LJ Ex. 443.

[168] *G. v. DPP* [1989] Crim. LR 150, DC.

While the constable need not search round in order to negative any answer which a suspect might possibly give to the allegation,[169] there will be circumstances (such as where there is no great urgency, the information is uncorroborated, etc.) in which it will be unreasonable to act on information which is not itself obviously reliable. The constable must, in short, take reasonable care to inform himself of the facts so far as they can be ascertained, and if he fails to do so the reasonableness of his suspicion should be judged on the basis of the information which he would have had if he had taken reasonable steps, rather than asking merely whether the information which he actually had gave rise to reasonable suspicion.[170]

It would therefore be misleading to accept, without qualification, the assertion made by Purchas LJ in *Castorina v. Chief Constable of Surrey*[171] that the possible need for further inquiries to confirm suspicion was irrelevant to the presence or lack of reasonable grounds for suspicion. The true position is more complicated, particularly in view of the duty on the police under section 6 of the Human Rights Act 1998. An officer may have a suspicion at any time, based on reasonable grounds or otherwise. The power to arrest under section 24 of PACE arises only when there are grounds to support a suspicion, and the grounds are reasonable. The fact that there is a suspicion and that there are grounds for it take the officer only two-thirds of the way towards establishing that he has a power to arrest. The grounds will not be reasonable if a reasonable person would not have regarded them as giving reasonable grounds for an arrest. If a reasonable person, looking at the grounds, would have said that, in the light of all that is known about the suspect, more investigation would be needed to support the indications of guilt before the grounds for suspecting her could be considered reasonable, then more investigation is needed, and failure to check the information will remove the justification for an arrest.

(iii) Whose reasonable suspicion?

Where a constable is doing something (such as making an entry or arrest) which is *prima facie* tortious, there is no room for the application of the maxim *omnia praesumuntur rite esse acta* (everything is presumed to have been done properly). The action is unlawful unless the officer can justify it according the standards laid down by the statutory provisions in question. Generally, the constitutional position of a constable as an independent office-holder, personally responsible for his or her actions, is reflected in statutes which require the person exercising a power of arrest to have the grounds for reasonable suspicion necessary to justify it.[172] For this reason, the decision

---

[169] *Glinski v. McIver* [1962] AC 726 at 745, [1962] 1 All ER 696 at 701 *per* Viscount Simonds.

[170] *Glinski v. McIver* [1962] AC at 768, [1961] 1 All ER at 715 *per* Lord Devlin; *Abrath v. North Eastern Railway Co.* (1883) 11 QBD 440, CA at 450–1 *per* Brett MR, 459–60 *per* Bowen LJ.

[171] [1988] NLJ Rep. 180, CA; see also ambiguous *dicta* in *Ward v. Chief Constable of Avon and Somerset Constabulary*, *The Times*, 26 June 1986, CA.

[172] *O'Hara v. Chief Constable of the Royal Ulster Constabulary* [1997] AC 286, [1997] 1 All ER 129, 134–5 *per* Lord Steyn. See, e.g. PACE, s. 17(2)(a) (entry to premises to make an arrest); *Chapman v. DPP* (1988) 89 Cr. App. R. 190, DC. However, the court in *Chapman* was wrong to suggest that the officer must also have reasonable grounds for believing that it was an arrestable offence. Section 17(1)(b) requires that the entry should be for the purpose of arresting someone for an arrestable offence. If the offence is not, in law, an arrestable offence, the constable's belief that it is, however reasonable, does not justify the arrest.

of the Divisional Court in *Kynaston v. Director of Public Prosecutions*[173] is erroneous so far as it suggests that courts are entitled to assume that a constable was acting lawfully when his acts are *prima facie* unlawful, and that the burden is on the suspect to negative the reasonableness of the grounds for suspicion. However, a question may still arise as to who must be in possession of the grounds for suspicion.

Police officers in many investigations operate in teams. The same officer will not always undertake all parts of an investigation; some officers will be given instructions by more senior officers which they will be expected, on pain of disciplinary sanctions, to carry out, whether or not they are told the reasons for them. Under pressure, the amount of information which can be passed between them, by radio or otherwise, may be limited. In major inquiries, information is collated and analysed centrally from a large number of sources, sometimes with the aid of computers. The officers in charge of the investigation who decide that somebody should be arrested might not pass on all the information on which the decision was based to the officers who are to make the arrest. Where the arresting officer is required to hold a reasonable suspicion, or to be in possession of reasonable grounds for it,[174] is one officer entitled to rely on the judgment of others, and assume that the orders or requests from other officers are based on reasonable grounds, or will the arrest be unlawful unless the arresting officer makes whatever checks, and asks whatever questions, are needed in order to satisfy the required standard?

Where reasonable grounds for suspicion are required in order to justify the arrest of someone who turns out to be innocent, section 24 of PACE requires that the constable personally has reasonable grounds for the suspicion, and it would seem to follow that he is not protected if, knowing nothing of the case, he acts on orders from another officer who, perhaps, does have such grounds. On the other hand, under statutes which require only the objective existence of reasonable grounds for suspicion, it is possible that the officer need neither have the reasonable grounds nor himself suspect anything; he can simply follow orders.[175] One should not interpret differently worded statutes as if they were the same.

In *O'Hara v. Chief Constable of the Royal Ulster Constabulary*,[176] a constable had been told by a senior officer that the plaintiff had been involved in a terrorist murder in Northern Ireland. The senior officer had instructed the constable to arrest the plaintiff. The arrest was made under section 12 of the Prevention of Terrorism (Temporary Provisions) Act 1984, section 12(1), which (like its current equivalent, section 41 of the Terrorism Act 2000), allowed a constable to arrest without warrant 'a person whom he has reasonable grounds for suspecting to be . . . (b) a person who is or has been concerned in the commission, preparation or instigation or acts of terrorism . . .'. The plaintiff was eventually released without being charged, and sued the police for unlawful arrest, arguing that the arresting officer had not had reasonable grounds for suspecting him. The trial judge decided that an official briefing by a senior officer

[173] (1987) 84 Cr. App. R. 200, DC.
[174] As under PACE, s. 24(4)(b), (5)(b), (6), and (7)(b).
[175] Quoted with approval by Lord Steyn, with whom Lords Goff, Mustill, and Hoffmann agreed, in *O'Hara v. Chief Constable of the Royal Ulster Constabulary* [1997] AC 286, [1997] 1 All ER 129, 134.
[176] [1997] AC 286, [1997] 1 All ER 129, HL.

could provide an arresting officer with such grounds. As the plaintiff's counsel had made a tactical decision not to cross-examine the arresting officer about the nature and extent of the information given to him at the briefing, the judge felt able to infer (from admittedly scanty details) that sufficient details had been given to provide the arresting officer with reasonable suspicion, and dismissed the action.[177] The decision was upheld by the Court of Appeal in Northern Ireland.

The House of Lords affirmed the decision. Lords Steyn and Hope (with whose speeches Lords Goff, Mustill, and Hoffmann agreed) stressed that the statute made the lawfulness of the arrest depend on the arresting officer having a suspicion on grounds which are present in that officer's mind and which are objectively sufficient to provide a reasonable basis for that suspicion. Their Lordships were prepared to accept that the evidence had justified the trial judge in inferring that the arresting officer had had reasonable grounds for his suspicion of the plaintiff. This concession does not sit comfortably with the caselaw of the European Court of Human Rights, outlined above, demanding that the state should provide enough evidence to satisfy the court of the reasonableness of any suspicion. None the less, their Lordships were very clear that the arresting officer must himself have the reasonable suspicion. Lord Hope said:

'The statutory power does not require that the constable who exercises the power must be in possession of all the information which has led to a decision, perhaps taken by others, that the time has come for it to be exercised. What it does require is that the constable who exercises the power must first have equipped himself with sufficient information so that he has reasonable cause to suspect before the power is exercised.'[178]

Although police force forces are hierarchically organized and disciplined bodies, this means that, as Lord Steyn said, 'an order to arrest cannot without some further information being given to the constable be sufficient to afford the constable reasonable grounds for the necessary suspicion'.[179]

In relation to arrests based on reasonable suspicion, section 24 of PACE is a provision of this kind. This affects the organization and hierarchical structure of police forces. So far as other cases suggest that constables can unquestioningly accept another officer's suspicion as their own, without any supporting grounds being provided, they no longer represent the law (if they ever did).[180] Decisions based on statutes which permitted an arrest without reasonable grounds for suspicion[181] are irrelevant to arrests under provisions which require reasonable grounds for suspicion, and would in any case probably be decided differently today, as the Human Rights Act 1998, sections 2, 3, and 6 would lead to the implication of a requirement for reasonable grounds by virtue of ECHR Article 5(1)(c).

Even if a statute does not demand that officers who are sent to arrest someone

---

[177] See the speech of Lord Hope [1997] 1 All ER at 136–7.

[178] [1997] 1 All ER at 142.

[179] Ibid. at 135.

[180] See, e.g. *R. v. Francis* (1972) 116 Sol Jo 632, [1972] Crim. LR 549, CA.

[181] See, e.g. *McKee v. Chief Constable of Northern Ireland* [1984] 1 WLR 1358, [1985] 1 All ER 1, HL, on s. 11(1) of the Northern Ireland (Emergency Provisions) Act 1978 (now repealed).

know the grounds giving rise to the suspicion, they will at least need to know the type of offence for which they are making the arrest. If they did not, they would be unable to tell the arrestee of the offence for which he is being arrested, and (as we shall see) this failure would make the arrest unlawful. If a constable sees other constables engaged in a fight, or attempting to detain somebody, but has not been told why, he is not entitled to assume that they are acting lawfully and that there are reasonable grounds to suspect that the person on the receiving end has committed an arrestable offence. If he goes to their assistance, and it turns out that they were acting unlawfully, he will be held not to have acted in the execution of his duty.[182] Professor Sir John Smith has described this as questionable: 'When [the officer] saw his colleagues struggling with a man whom they had arrested, did he not have reasonable grounds for suspecting that an arrestable offence had been committed?'[183] The answer, however, is that, knowing nothing about the offence, his suspicion could only be based on blind faith in his colleagues. This is no ground for depriving somebody of his liberty; the police too often get it wrong (as they did in that case—the purported arrest was for a non-arrestable offence). On the other hand, where an arrest is grounded on an entry in the Police National Computer, the question is whether the officer making the arrest had reasonable grounds for suspicion on the basis of that entry, not whether the person who originally made the entry had reasonable grounds for doing so.[183a]

Lord Steyn pointed out in *O'Hara v. Chief Constable of the Royal Ulster Constabulary*[184] that Article 5(1)(c) of the ECHR is perhaps more in tune with the co-operative and hierarchically organized character of police investigations than most UK statutes, in that Article 5 does not expressly require that the reasonable grounds for suspicion are present in the mind of the arresting officer at the time of the arrest. It also reflects the nature of the ECHR as an international treaty, concerned more with ensuring that state institutions as a whole comply with their obligations than with the state of mind of any particular individual.

(iv) Legality, proper purposes, reasonableness, and natural justice

If there are reasonable grounds for suspicion, or whatever the statute requires, to bring into play the power to arrest a person, on what basis will the officer's exercise of the power be reviewable? Over and above the requirement that there should be reasonable suspicion that a particular person has committed an arrestable offence, the House of Lords made it clear, in *Mohammed-Holgate v. Duke*[185] that, irrespective of the statutory grounds for arrest which apply in particular cases, once the constable is within the four corners of a power to arrest without warrant, the lawfulness of a decision to arrest can be challenged only on general principles of public law governing the exercise of discretions. These principles fall into three main categories.[186]

---

[182] *Riley v. DPP* (1989) 91 Cr. App. R. 14, DC.

[183] Commentary on *Riley v. DPP* [1990] Crim. LR 422.

[183a] *Hough v. Chief Constable of Staffordshire Police, The Times*, 14 February 2001, CA.

[184] [1997] 1 All ER at 133–4.

[185] [1984] AC 437, *sub nom. Holgate-Mohammed v. Duke* [1984] 1 All ER 1054, HL.

[186] *Council of Civil Service Unions v. Minister for the Civil Service* [1985] AC 374, HL at 410–11 *per* Lord Diplock. See generally D. J. Galligan, *Discretionary Powers* (Oxford: Clarendon Press, 1986).

Illegality, or *ultra vires*, requires the official to be acting within the four corners of a power which the official actually has, for a permitted purpose, and not to be acting inconsistently with other legal obligations such as the duty to comply with Convention rights under the Human Rights Act 1998.

Courts have in the past sometimes prepared to take a generous view of the powers granted by a statute. For example, in *Wills v. Bowley*[187] the House of Lords by a majority of three to two (Lords Wilberforce, Bridge, and Russell, with Lords Elwyn-Jones and Lowry dissenting) were prepared to give an expansive reading to a statute which required a constable to 'take into custody, without warrant, and forthwith convey before a justice, any person who within his view commits' one of the offences described in the section.[188] This should not be interpreted literally, the majority said, because it is in the public interest that a constable acting in good faith should be protected as long as he acted on reasonable grounds. The courts had to balance the interest of society in preserving liberty against that in upholding the law and apprehending criminals. The section was therefore to be interpreted as permitting an arrest where the constable honestly believed, on reasonable grounds, that the person to be arrested was committing an offence.[189] The approach of the majority is questionable. Where Parliament has specified the circumstances in which constables are to be protected against liability for interfering with liberty, the protection given by the statute should not be further extended by judicial interpretation.[190] However, the interpretation by the majority does not appear to contravene Article 5(1) of the ECHR. Like much authoritative caselaw of national courts, it is reasonably accessible to the public, and the requirement for reasonable suspicion meets the minimum demands of Article 5(1)(c). It also avoids the risk of arbitrariness in practice and is sufficiently precise to be 'in accordance with a procedure prescribed by law' and 'lawful' as those terms have been interpreted by the European Court of Human Rights.[191]

One way in which a constable exercising a power of arrest may act *ultra vires* is to act in a manner incompatible with Article 5 of the ECHR, which substantively limits the extent of all powers of arrest and detention and all statutory provisions (except so far as the latter cannot be interpreted in a manner compatible with the Article) by virtue of section 6(1) of the Human Rights Act 1998.[192] Another way of acting *ultra vires* is to use a power for an improper purpose. Both in national law before the Human Rights 1998, and under Article 5 of the ECHR, it is proper to arrest someone who is reasonably suspected of an offence in order to question him with a view to obtaining information which will allow the authorities to decide whether to prefer

---

[187] [1983] 1 AC 57, [1982] 2 All ER 654, HL.

[188] Town Police Clauses Act 1847, s. 28. The words conferring the arrest power have now been repealed by PACE, s. 119, and Sch. 7, Part I.

[189] [1982] 2 All ER at 680 *per* Lord Bridge.

[190] St John Robilliard and J. McEwan, *Police Powers and the Individual* (Oxford: Basil Blackwell, 1986), 105.

[191] *Kemmache v. France (No. 3)*, Eur. Ct. HR, Series A, No. 296-C, Judgment of 24 November 1994; *Amuur v. France*, Eur. Ct. HR, Judgment of 25 June 1996, RJD 1996-III, 22 EHRR 533, para. 50.

[192] D. Feldman, 'Convention Rights and Substantive Ultra Vires', in C. Forsyth (ed.), *Judicial Review and the Constitution* (Oxford: Hart Publishing, 2000) 245–68 at 252–6.

criminal charges. An exercise of a statutory power to arrest somebody, where the arrest conditions under the statute are fulfilled, does not become unlawful merely because the arresting officer also had an ulterior purpose such as preventing future criminal acts (at least as long as the ulterior purpose is proper, and does not amount to bad faith on the part of the officer).[193]

Natural justice, or procedural due process, and particularly the idea that a person should be given the chance to respond to allegations which affect his legal position, could play a part in structuring investigative processes. However, English law has generally turned its back on the idea that investigators should comply with the rules of natural justice. The requirement for checking information before using it as the grounds for an arrest is derived from the notion of reasonableness, as noted above, rather than that of fairness to the suspect. If there are other ways of checking suspicions, it will not be necessary to put them to the suspect. Indeed, in criminal investigations it may well be counter-productive to allow a suspect a chance to make representations before arrest. It could alert him allowing him and his associates to escape, destroy or conceal evidence, and salt away the proceeds of crime.

Irrationality as a ground of review of a discretion to arrest goes beyond the idea of reasonable cause for suspicion. The idea that the suspicion which grounds the legality of the arrest should be reasonable is fundamental to the existence of the power in the first place. But in addition, once the power has arisen, the decision to make the arrest (in which the presence of reasonable grounds for suspicion is but one component) should be reasonable. A number of elements are involved here, clustered round what is sometimes called '*Wednesbury* unreasonableness' after the case in which it received its classic formulation.[194] First, the decision should not be so unreasonable that no reasonable officer could properly have made it; secondly, it must be based on relevant considerations; thirdly, it must be made in good faith for a proper purpose.[195]

The notion of unreasonableness is elastic, but, as *Mohammed-Holgate v. Duke* shows, the courts are generally unwilling to question the opinion of experts in the field as to what is reasonable in the light of operational requirements. This deference to perceived expertise is not confined to policing matters,[196] but is particularly marked there. In *Mohammed-Holgate*, a detective constable had reasonable cause to suspect the plaintiff of burglary of jewellery. The detective went to the plaintiff's house, and arrested her without a warrant, because it was likely that a confession would be needed to establish her guilt to the satisfaction of a jury, and the detective believed that the plaintiff would be more likely to confess if taken to a police station and questioned there than if questioned in her own house. At the police station the

---

[193] *Brogan v. United Kingdom*, Eur. Ct. HR, Series A, No. 145-B; *Murray v. United Kingdom*, Eur. Ct. HR, Series A, No. 300-A; *R. v. Chalkley* [1998] QB 848, [1998] 2 All ER 155, CA.

[194] *Associated Provincial Picture Houses Ltd. v. Wednesbury Corporation* [1948] 1 KB 223, CA.

[195] The latter two points are treated here as aspects of irrationality, although for reasons which are not relevant here the House of Lords has suggested that they are, in fact, aspects of illegality rather than irrationality: *R. v. Secretary of State for Trade and Industry, ex parte Lonrho plc* [1989] 1 WLR 525, [1989] 2 All ER 609, HL.

[196] D. Feldman, 'Public Law Values in the House of Lords' (1990) **106** *LQR* 246–76 at 256–7, 263–4.

officers who had originally investigated the burglary, which had occurred four months earlier, would have been available to question the plaintiff; this was regarded as a relevant factor in deciding to arrest her. In the event, no charges were laid against her, and she sued the police for false imprisonment. The county court judge found that the detective's purpose in arresting the plaintiff had been to subject her to the greater stress and pressure involved in an arrest and deprivation of liberty, in the belief that she would then be more likely to confess, but that the police had conducted themselves entirely properly once she was at the police station. The judge held that the arrest had been unreasonable and unlawful, and awarded the plaintiff £1,000 damages.

This decision was reversed by the Court of Appeal, whose decision was upheld by the House of Lords. Lord Diplock, with whom Lords Keith, Bridge, Brandon, and Brightman agreed, noted that the practice of arresting people in order to question them, rather than to initiate charges immediately, was of long standing and had been recognized in the Report of the Royal Commission on Criminal Procedure[197] and in the statutory power given to the police to grant bail to an arrested person where the inquiry cannot be completed forthwith.[198] It was not *Wednesbury* unreasonable to use the period of detention 'to dispel or confirm the reasonable suspicion [which had given rise to the power to arrest] by questioning the suspect or seeking further evidence with his assistance'.[199] In deciding to do so, the detective constable had not taken account of an irrelevant consideration, acted for an improper purpose, or behaved in a way in which no reasonable officer in the circumstances could have behaved. The arrest was therefore within his discretion, and lawful. The reviewability of arrest decisions on *Wednesbury* principles is in accordance with general public-law rules. It supplements the examination of the reasonableness of grounds for suspicion, rather than replacing it. If a decision is *Wednesbury* unreasonable, it will be unlawful in the public-law sense, and will take a constable outside the protection against civil liability offered to him when lawfully exercising a public-law power.

A possible fourth ground for judicial review of official action, *proportionality*, was tentatively advanced by Lord Diplock in the *GCHQ* case, but has so far made little headway in national law;[200] however, it becomes relevant when evaluating an interference with a Convention right under the Human Rights Act 1998.[201]

---

[197] RCCP, *Report*, para. 3.66. Previously, there had been a gap between the rhetoric of the courts, which tended to assume that suspects would be charged and brought before a court immediately on arrest, and the practice of the police, who relied on an informal norm of 24 hours' leeway before bringing an arrested person before a magistrate and had made liberal use of the fiction that people in police stations being questioned had agreed, or been persuaded, to help the police voluntarily with their inquiries. Dixon, 'Detention for Questioning', 7–24.

[198] Magistrates' Courts Act 1980, s. 43(3) as amended. It has now been clearly accepted in the detention and interrogation provisions of PACE and the associated Codes of Practice.

[199] [1984] 1 All ER at 1059 *per* Lord Diplock. However, if it can be proved that the arresting officer knew that there was no possibility of the person being charged, it is open to a jury to decide that the arrest was unreasonable: *Plange v. Chief Constable of South Humberside Police, Independent*, 17 April 1992, CA.

[200] *R. v. Secretary of State for the Home Department, ex parte Brind* [1991] 1 AC 696, [1991] 1 All ER 720, HL.

[201] See J. McBride, 'Proportionality and the European Convention on Human Rights', in E. Ellis (ed.), *The Principle of Proportionality in the Laws of Europe* (Oxford: Hart Publishing, 1999), 23–35.

(v) Conclusion

The flexibility of the 'reasonable grounds' standard leaves police officers a very wide discretion which may be exercised for undisclosed and improper reasons. Regardless of the legal limits on the power, it seems the power to arrest, like that to search people in the street, is used differentially. Police officers use it differently in different areas,[202] and seem to differentiate between racial groups.[203] They also differentiate between people who are polite and submissive and those who are rude, uncooperative, or abusive. The latter are seen as threatening the fragile authority of the police, which must be reasserted by using legal powers so as to put the challengers in their place.[204] There is, in short, far more going on when a constable decides whether or not to arrest a suspect than might be suggested by the need for formal compliance with the legal rules. Because of the nature of police work and the forms of legal control, this is unlikely to be satisfactorily monitored or contained by law. It is too easy for a constable to work out reasonable grounds for suspicion after the event, and judges are (perhaps rightly) wary of substituting their view of reasonable police behaviour for that of the officers on the spot. If the practice of arrest is to match the standards laid down in the ECHR much will depend on the attitudes and training of police officers, and their willingness to take such standards seriously as part of their decision-making and monitoring processes, and the Human Rights Act 1998 is likely to exert pressure on judges to adopt a more questioning approach to justifications which the police offer for arrests in some cases.

6.4 ARREST FORMALITIES

This section examines the formal legal requirements for an arrest. There are certain steps which must be taken to make a lawful arrest out of what would otherwise be a false imprisonment, and further steps which must be taken after the arrest in order to make the subsequent detention lawful.

(1) WHAT CONSTITUTES AN ARREST?

An arrest is not defined in PACE, which merely lays down the conditions for one and steps to be taken when making one. The definition of arrest is therefore a matter for

[202] Royal Commission on Criminal Procedure, Research Study No. 9, *Arrest, Charge and Summons* (London: HMSO, 1980); Home Office, *Statistics on Race and the Criminal Justice System*; Robert Reiner, *The Politics of the Police*, 3rd edn. (Oxford: Oxford University Press, 2000), 128–32.

[203] P. Stevens and C. F. Willis, *Race, Crime and Arrests*, Home Office Research Study No. 58 (London: HMSO, 1979); R. Reiner, 'Police and Race Relations', in J. Baxter and L. Koffman (eds.), *Police: The Constitution and the Community* (Abingdon: Professional Books, 1985), 149–87 at 166–9; Reiner, *Politics of the Police*, 124–36.

[204] See Smith and Gray, *Police and People in London*, 351–4, on the importance in police culture of maintaining control and not losing face; and Reiner, *Politics of the Police*, 93–4, on ways the police classify people with whom they come into contact. For a good example of a case where the desire to avoid losing face seems to have affected events, see *G. v. DPP* [1989] Crim. LR 150, DC (abusive behaviour in a police station).

common law, and may be crucial to the civil and criminal liabilities of police and suspects for two reasons. First, a person is entitled to use reasonable force to resist a battery or a false imprisonment, but not to resist an arrest. Secondly, a constable is entitled to use reasonable force if necessary for certain purposes, one of which is making an arrest, but force will be unlawful (and the constable acting outside the execution of his duty) if directed to an unauthorized purpose, such as holding someone for questioning without arresting him.[205] However, the meaning of arrest, and particularly the distinction between an arrest and a detention, is fraught with problems.

Because of the effect of an arrest on the rights of the person arrested, and particularly the freedom to use reasonable force to resist an unlawful assault or imprisonment, the formalities of arrest stress the need to make it clear to the arrestee that the arrestor requires the arrestee to submit to him and has authority to do so. There must also be a definable moment at which the arrestee's status changes from free to (partially) unfree, and some basis on which the arrestee, and, if necessary, a court or disciplinary tribunal, may decide whether the constable is acting within a legal power. In order to achieve this, there are three essential elements to an arrest.

First, either the arrestee must submit to the arrest, or there must be an act of physical restraint enforcing the arrestee's detention. There may often be a purely formal or symbolic touching of the arrestee, signifying the change in his legal position, followed by submission. At other times, the suspect may submit without any physical touching. Where an arrest takes place in a police station, the suspect having gone there voluntarily, the necessary physical restraint is provided by the surroundings.[206]

Secondly, the arrestor must signify by clear words that he is arresting the arrestee.[207] As this need not happen immediately where it is not reasonably practicable, for instance because the arrestee has escaped before it could be done[208] or is fighting, there is an implication that one may have a lawful arrest when the arrestor attempts physically to take the arrestee into custody, and that this arrest subsequently becomes an unlawful detention only if the arrestee is not made aware of the legal basis for the action as soon as practicable thereafter.[209] The act of physical restraint (such as rugby-tackling a fleeing suspect) must be intended by the arrestor to be in pursuance of a power of arrest. Whether or not it was so intended will be a matter for the trier of fact, to be decided on the basis of the evidence available.[210]

[205] *Rice v. Connolly* [1966] 2 QB 414, [1966] 2 All ER 649, DC; *Kenlin v. Gardiner* [1967] 2 QB 510, [1966] 3 All ER 931, DC.

[206] This is implicit in PACE, s. 29, which provides that: 'Where . . . a person attends voluntarily at a police station or at any other place where a constable is present or accompanies a constable to a police station or any such other place without having been arrested— . . . (b) he shall be informed at once that he is under arrest if a decision is taken by a constable to prevent him from leaving at will'.

[207] PACE, s. 28(1). Where the arrest is made by a constable (but, by implication, not when made by anyone else) this information must be given even if it is obvious.

[208] PACE, s. 28(5).

[209] *R. v. Brosch* [1988] Crim. LR 743, CA. Note, however, that (as Prof. Birch pointed out in her commentary on the case at 744) the Court of Appeal was wrong in supposing (*obiter*) that a constable must inform the arrestee that he is under arrest immediately, whether or not it is practicable to do so.

[210] *R. v. Brosch*, above.

Thirdly, the arrestor must make clear to the arrestee the ground for his arrest on, or as soon as is practicable after, the arrest.[211] If it is longer delayed, the arrest becomes an unlawful detention. If the wrong ground is given, the detention is unlawful.[212] Only limited delay is permitted before the information is given. It is clear that the arrestor is not permitted to delay once it becomes practicable to give a reason for the arrest, even if there might be good reasons for delaying, although the test for practicability may take account of the surrounding circumstances and the effect that giving the information would have on the police operation. In an appeal from Northern Ireland, *Murray v. Ministry of Defence*,[213] the House of Lords decided that giving reasons for arrests and (where a person is *not* resisting restraint) informing a person that she is under arrest might be delayed where necessary in order to prevent a risk that the alarm might be given to others, giving rise to danger. It is clear from the leading speech of Lord Griffiths that this exception was crafted in the light of the exigencies of military policing in Northern Ireland,[214] and it is unlikely that similar delays would be acceptable on the mainland.[215]

Under section 28 of PACE, the danger of an alarm being given will excuse a delay only if it makes it impracticable, rather than merely inconvenient, to give the information. It is, however, significant that the European Court of Human Rights, in *Fox, Campbell and Hartley v. United Kingdom*, accepted that the standard laid down in Article 5(2) of the ECHR that a person who is arrested 'shall be informed promptly, in a language which he understands, of the reason for his arrest and of any charge against him' permitted a person (again in the context of Northern Ireland anti-terrorism policing) to be taken to a police station before being given the information.[216] If this happens before the suspect is questioned, it still allows him to know the suspicion against which he has to defend himself, but it does not allow him or, subsequently, a court to check the grounds for the arrest actually operating in the mind of the arresting officer at the time, so it may restrict the opportunity for review of the lawfulness of detention under Article 5(4).[217]

In the event of delay in giving the information, the arrest will still initially be lawful until such time as it becomes practicable to give the information but the arrestor fails to do so. In the intervening period (if any), the constable will be acting in the

---

[211] PACE, s. 28(3); ECHR, Art. 5(3). Where the arrestor is a constable (and, by implication, not otherwise), this must be done even if the ground is obvious: PACE, s. 28(4).

[212] *Edwards v. DPP* (1993) 97 Cr. App. R. 301, DC.

[213] [1988] 2 All ER 521, HL.

[214] See Lord Griffiths's discussion of 'soldiers . . . employed on the difficult and potentially dangerous task of carrying out a house arrest of a person suspected of an offence in connection with the IRA', circumstances which were held to justify a soldier in following set search and arrest procedures (apparently, whatever they might be): [1988] 2 All ER at 527. This certainly does not reflect the law on the mainland, where the responsibility for adopting appropriate procedures, as laid down by law rather than superior officers, lies on the arresting officer: see above.

[215] The absence of any authority for the exception in *Murray*, and the appearance given by the House of Lords of reasoning back from a desired conclusion rather than forward from principle, laid the decision open to convincing and destructive criticism by Professor Glanville Williams, 'When is an Arrest?' (1991) 54 *MLR* 408–17 and C. Walker, 'Army Special Powers on Parade' (1989) 40 *NILQ* 1–33 at 6–10.

[216] Eur. Ct. HR, Series A, No. 182, Judgment of 30 August 1990, 13 EHRR 157.

[217] For a slightly different view, see Finnie, 'Anti-Terrorism Legislation', 292–3.

execution of his duty, so that an assault on him will be an assault on him in the execution of his duty,[218] despite the fact that it subsequently becomes an unlawful detention. The information may be given in general terms, as long as it makes clear, in the circumstances, the offence (or one of the offences) of which the arrestee is suspected; precision is desirable, but not usually essential.[219] The grounds for the suspicion need not be given. Similarly, when the arrest is made under section 25 (the general arrest conditions), it is sufficient to tell the arrestee the offence for which he is being arrested. It is desirable, but not strictly necessary, to tell the suspect that he will be arrested unless he gives the constable his name and address, and it is probably not necessary, after making the arrest, to tell him that he has been arrested because he has not supplied a name or address, or to tell him that the name and address are required in order to allow a summons to be served.[220] What is important is that the arrestee should know as soon as possible on what grounds his liberty is being restrained.

(2) CAN FAILURES BE RECTIFIED LATER?

If a person is detained unlawfully because the arrestor has failed to inform him of the fact that he has been arrested or of the grounds for arrest, can the detention later be turned into a lawful arrest by giving the arrestee the necessary information? Alternatively, is it necessary for the police to release, then re-arrest, the arrestee? This is a significant issue, as it affects the availability and quantum of damages for false imprisonment. It may also be necessary to decide at what point an unlawful detention becomes an arrest in order to decide whether a detainee who tries to free himself is committing an offence such as assaulting or wilfully obstructing a constable in the execution of his duty. If the detention is unlawful, the constable will not be in the execution of his duty, and any obstruction will have a lawful justification and so will not be wilful.

Before the 1984 Act, the Court of Appeal (Criminal Division) had held in *R. v. Kulynycz*[221] that an unlawful detention may become a lawful arrest when the necessary information is given, and the Court of Appeal (Civil Division) decided in *Lewis v. Chief Constable of the South Wales Constabulary*[222] that the position is the same after the 1984 Act. In that case, the two plaintiffs were sisters who had been travelling in a car when they were stopped, arrested without being told the reason for the arrest, and taken to a police station. There they saw the custody officer, and were separately told, ten and twenty-three minutes respectively after their arrests, that they had been arrested on suspicion of burglary. Five hours later they were both released. They sued

[218] *DPP v. Hawkins* [1988] 1 WLR 1166, [1988] 3 All ER 673, DC.
[219] This was the position under the common-law rules before PACE: *Abbassy v. Metropolitan Police Commissioner* [1990] 1 WLR 385, [1990] 1 All ER 193, CA. As the object of s. 29 of PACE seems to be to codify the common-law rules, deriving from *Christie v. Leachinsky* [1947] AC 573, [1947] 1 All ER 567, HL, there is no reason to suppose that greater particularity is required under the statute.
[220] *Nicholas v. Parsonage* [1987] RTR 199, DC.
[221] [1971] 1 QB 367, [1970] 3 All ER 881, CA.
[222] [1991] 1 All ER 206, CA.

the Chief Constable for false arrest and wrongful imprisonment. The trial judge ruled that the arrest, although initially unlawful, had become lawful when the plaintiffs were told the reason for it, and awarded damages of £200 in respect of periods of unlawful detention of ten and twenty-three minutes respectively. The plaintiffs appealed, but the Court of Appeal upheld the decision. Balcombe LJ, with whom Taylor LJ agreed, started from the position that PACE had not changed the law on the constituents of a valid arrest. He then referred to two *dicta* in earlier House of Lords decisions. The first was from Viscount Dilhorne in *Spicer v. Holt*,[223] a breathalyser case: '"Arrest" is an ordinary English word . . . Whether or not a person has been arrested depends not on the legality of the arrest but on whether he has been deprived of his liberty to go where he pleases'. The other citation was from Lord Diplock in *Mohammed-Holgate v. Duke*:[224]

'arrest is a continuing act: it starts with the arrestor taking a person into his custody (*sc.* by action or words restraining him from moving anywhere beyond the arrester's control), and it continues until the person so restrained is either released from custody or, having been brought before a magistrate, is remanded in custody by the magistrate's judicial act.'

Balcombe LJ held that it followed from treating arrest as a fact rather than a legal concept that a failure to comply with a necessary formality cannot make the act of initiating an arrest a nullity: 'Arrest is a situation . . . Whether a person has been arrested depends not on the legality of his arrest but on whether he has been deprived of his liberty to go where he pleases'.[225] It followed that the arrest, being a *continuing* situation, could be made lawful for the future, though not the past, by complying with the necessary formality and supplying the information.[226]

This end result has common sense to recommend it. There would be little point in requiring a person to be released and then immediately rearrested. However, the means by which the court reached the conclusion is, with respect, unconvincing. If an arrest means no more than factual detention or restraint, why use the word 'arrest' at all? It would make better sense to use the word 'restrain', a nice, factual term without legal overtones. What is required is more careful attention to the legal implications of the terms used, rather than pretending that the terms have no legal significance. It is worth distinguishing between detentions generally, most of which (like those used by schools for disciplinary purposes) have no connection with the legal process, and arrests for the purposes of the criminal process. The word 'arrest' should be used only in relation to detention in reliance on a power conferred for the purpose of upholding the law, as under sections 24 and 25 of PACE. Where a person is detained in purported exercise of a power of arrest which actually exists, but the legal conditions for the exercise of that power are not fulfilled, it makes sense to speak of a purported (but unlawful) arrest, although it would be preferable to limit the use of the word 'arrest' to those detentions which are both objectively capable of being an arrest and are

---

[223] [1977] AC 987 at 1000, [1976] 3 All ER 71 at 79.
[224] [1984] AC 437 at 441, [1984] 1 All ER 1054 at 1056.
[225] [1991] 1 All ER at 210. See also *Murray v. Ministry of Defence* [1988] 2 All ER 521, HL.
[226] Following *R. v. Kulynycz* [1971] 1 QB 367, [1970] 3 All ER 881, CA.

legally justified. On the other hand, if a detention does not purport to be an arrest, or is not made pursuant to a lawful power of arrest, or (having been made lawfully) is not followed by the giving of the required information, it is not an arrest but a detention, and is *prima facie* unlawful and resistable. Where the arrest criteria are objectively not met, it invites analytical confusion to speak of an arrest. Despite the unfortunate tendency to speak of an 'unlawful arrest' in the latter situation, the word 'arrest' should be confined to circumstances where there is something which could objectively be viewed as an arrest, and the question is whether that arrest is justified. Other interferences with people's liberty are detentions, which may or may not be legally justified.[227]

One might go further, and suggest that an arrest is, in truth, a legal term of art, and is used in that sense in PACE. On this view, one either has a lawful arrest or no arrest at all; a purported arrest which fails one of the legal conditions for its validity would be void. This would have the merit of simplicity, but would be impossible to reconcile with the *dicta* from the House of Lords quoted above. But whichever usage one adopts, the police in *Lewis* could have effected a lawful arrest of the plaintiffs at the police station merely by making it clear that the plaintiffs were under arrest and that the reason was that they were suspected of burglary. In effect, it seems that this was what the custody officer did, so it would have been unnecessary to hold that the entire five hours of the plaintiffs' detention had been unlawful. It would certainly not have been necessary for the police to release and then rearrest the plaintiffs, since, if they were not under arrest, they could hardly be required to be released before being arrested.

(3) HOW DETAILED AND ACCURATE NEED THE INFORMATION BE?

The arresting officer need not tell the suspect the precise legal nature of the offence for which the arrest was made. If it is obvious, as where a burglar is caught climbing out of a window of a house with stolen goods in his hands, very little precision in the indication of the offence is needed, although it is desirable to be as precise as possible; all that is required is a clear notification of the fact that the suspect is under arrest. In other cases, however, a general indication of the type of offence is needed, without using technical language which might, in any case, only confuse the arrestee. Of course, the offence for which a person is arrested might be quite different from any charge which is subsequently laid against him. This does not affect the legality of the arrest, which is judged according to the reasonableness of the officer's suspicions on the basis of material available at the time of the arrest.

---

[227] RCCP, *Law and Procedure*, 15. For further discussion, see D. Telling, 'Arrest and Detention: The Conceptual Maze' [1978] Crim. LR 320–31; K. W. Lidstone, 'A Maze in Law!' [1978] Crim. LR 332–42 at p. 332; D. N. Clarke and D. Feldman, 'Arrest by Any Other Name' [1979] Crim. LR 702–7; Williams, 'When is an Arrest?', 408–17. For different views, see M. Zander, 'When is an Arrest not an Arrest?' (1977) 127 *NLJ* 352–4, 379–82; J. C. Smith, [1977] Crim. LR 293, commenting on *Spicer v. Holt* [1977] AC 987.

6.5 TREATMENT FOLLOWING THE ARREST

The ECHR, Article 5(3), provides:

'Everyone arrested or detained in accordance with the provisions of paragraph (1)(c) of this Article shall be brought promptly before a judge or other officer authorised by law to exercise judicial power and shall be entitled to trial within a reasonable time or to release pending trial. Release may be conditioned by guarantees to appear for trial.'

In addition, Articles 2 and 3 of the ECHR impose duties on the police to protect the lives of detainees and to safeguard them against torture and inhuman or degrading treatment while in custody. These obligations have been extensively considered in Chapters 4 and 5, above, and will be referred to in passing in this and subsequent sections of this chapter. How does English law, including the Human Rights Act 1998, satisfy the demands of the ECHR?

Once a lawful arrest has been made, the arresting officer has a number of consequential powers and duties. The object is to provide sufficient protection for the suspect's rights and liberty against abuse of power by the police, while allowing the investigation to continue expeditiously. This calls for a nice sense of balance. The solution adopted in PACE was to place relatively few substantive limits on the powers of the police following arrest, but to introduce administrative and bureaucratic safeguards, requiring records to be kept and copies to be provided to the suspect, with reviews and monitoring of the process being provided by more senior police officers. In the event, the rules, particularly those governing interrogation of suspects, have been given some teeth by the exclusionary rules of evidence contained in sections 76 and 78 of PACE and robustly interpreted by the courts. Section 76 requires the trial court to exclude any confession which has been obtained by oppression or in consequence of anything said or done which was likely in the circumstances to make the confession unreliable. Section 78 as interpreted gives the court an exclusionary discretion where, in the circumstances, it would compromise the proceedings in some way to admit evidence.

The detailed operation of these provisions is a matter for the law of evidence, and is outside the scope of this book. However, we should note that one effect of the ways in which the courts have interpreted them has been to make exclusion of statements a way of protecting the rights given by PACE to suspects in police detention, and arguably to provide a means by which the courts can express their disapproval of police malpractice.[228] It also brings the English position closer to the American exclusionary rule in relation to confessions than was previously the case, partly because the American courts have been moving away from the strict *Miranda* position as the English courts have edged towards it.[229]

---

[228] There is a voluminous literature on this subject. For an excellent treatment, see P. Mirfield, *Silence, Confessions and Improperly Obtained Evidence* (Oxford: Clarendon Press, 1997), *passim*.

[229] M. Berger, 'The Exclusionary Rule and Confession Evidence: Some Perspectives on Evolving Practices and Policies in the United States and England and Wales' (1991) 20 *Anglo-Amer. LR* 63–79.

(1) TAKING THE ARRESTEE TO A POLICE STATION

The main duty, which arises when the suspect is arrested in a place other than a police station, is to take the arrestee to a police station as soon as practicable after the arrest.[230] However, there is power to search the suspect and certain premises before taking the suspect to a police station, and to delay taking the suspect to the police station in order to carry out investigations elsewhere, in specified circumstances. These matters are examined below.

The police station to which an arrestee is taken is normally to be a *designated police station*.[231] Designated police stations are those which are for the time being designated by the chief constable in each police area for use for the purpose of detaining arrestees.[232] In each designated police station there must be at least one custody officer, who is meant to be a sergeant who is independent of the investigation[233] and is generally responsible for ensuring that arrestees are treated in accordance with the requirements of PACE and the Codes of Practice. In particular, Code C provides for regular meals for detainees, drinks with meals and on reasonable request between mealtimes, at least eight hours' rest from questioning and travel in each twenty-four-hour period, the right to an individual cell so far as practicable, and brief outdoor exercise if practicable.[234] The Code also provides that there must be adequate lighting in cells, a reasonable standard of bedding, and access to toilet and washing facilities. Nobody may be interviewed unless adequate clothing has been offered to him and that interview rooms must, as far as practicable, be adequately heated, lit, and ventilated.[235] The custody officer must summon a doctor for a detainee who appears to need one or asks for one. If the detainee complains or shows evidence of improper treatment, the custody officer must call the police surgeon and report the matter to a more senior officer as soon as practicable.[236] These are important safeguards for the right to be free of inhuman or degrading treatment in police custody, under Article 3 of the ECHR and section 6 of the Human Rights Act 1998.[237] The custody officer is also responsible for ensuring that all records are made and kept as required by PACE and the Codes.[238] The role of the custody officer is central to the protection of these

[230] PACE, s. 30(1).

[231] Ibid., s. 30(2).

[232] Ibid., s. 35(1), (4). The chief officer of police in the area has responsibility for designating police stations which seem to provide sufficient accommodation for that purpose: ibid. s. 35(2).

[233] Ibid., s. 36, which also specifies the steps to be taken when this is impracticable. If only one custody officer is appointed for a designated police station, he or she will be off duty for much of the time. On the duties of the chief officer of police in relation to the discharge of the obligations of the custody officer when the custody officer is unavailable, see *Vince v. Chief Constable of the Dorset Police* [1993] 1 WLR 415, [1993] 2 All ER 321, CA; Royal Commission on Criminal Justice, *Report*, Cm. 2263 (London: HMSO, 1993), 31.

[234] Code C, s. 8, especially paras. 8.1, 8.6, 8.7, and 12.2.

[235] Code C, paras. 8.2–8.5, 12.4. However, nothing in the Code gives rise to a private-law cause of action (PACE, s. 67(10)), so it may be difficult to obtain remedies for failure to provide appropriate conditions of detention. This matter is discussed in Ch. 6, below.

[236] Code C, paras. 9.1–9.9.

[237] See *Hurtado v. Switzerland*, Eur. Commn. HR, Series A, No. 280-A, Judgment of 28 January 1994, settled before the Court, and Ch. 5, above.

[238] PACE, s. 39(1).

rights of suspects. Arrestees taken to non-designated police stations would be at a significant disadvantage in relation to the monitoring of their treatment and safe-guarding of their rights.

Nevertheless, sometimes it is permissible to take an arrestee to a non-designated police station. The only circumstances where this is allowed are: (a) where the constable *either* belongs to a body of constables maintained by an authority which is not a police authority, such as the Transport Police, *or* is working in a locality covered by a non-designated police station,[239] *and* it appears to the constable that it will not be necessary to keep the arrestee in detention for more than six hours;[240] (b) where the arrest was made by a single constable, or the arrestee was arrested by someone who was not a constable and handed into the custody of a single constable, and, no other constable being available to assist that constable, it appears to him that he will be unable to take the arrestee to a designated police station without the arrestee injuring himself, the constable, or some other person.[241] If the arrestee is taken to a non-designated police station, he must be transferred to a designated police station within six hours of his arrival, if he has not been released earlier.[242]

The choice of a six-hour period is significant, since the Royal Commission on Criminal Procedure, on whose report much of PACE was based, found that the vast majority of arrestees are released, with or without charge, within six hours. It remains true that it is only in cases which present difficulties that people are usually detained without charge for more than six hours.[243]

As the main independent protection for arrestees' rights is the custody officer, located at the designated police station, it is important that the arrestee should be taken to the police station as quickly as possible. It is too easy for improper pressure to be brought to bear on a suspect if police officers are allowed to drive him round for long periods, carrying on informal discussions, which may or may not be accurately remembered and recorded later. In some cases, where confessions were allegedly made in the backs of cars on the way to police stations, and the evidence of what was said was not reliable, the police having sacrificed reliability by breaking the rules on making records and showing them to the arrestee for comments, it has been held that the evidence should have been excluded as unfair.[244]

Nevertheless, there are circumstances in which the police are entitled to delay taking the arrestee to any police station.[245] These arise in two situations: first, where the police are conducting a search following arrest (considered below); secondly, where the presence of the arrestee is necessary in order to carry out such investigations as it is reasonable to carry out immediately.[246] The latter provision is open to

---

[239] Ibid., s. 30(4).

[240] Ibid., s. 30(3).

[241] Ibid., s. 30(5).

[242] Ibid., s. 30(6).

[243] B. Irving and I. McKenzie, *Regulating Custodial Interviews* (London: Police Foundation, 1988).

[244] *R. v. Hassan Khan, Independent*, 2 March 1990, CA; *R. v. Edwards* [1991] 2 All ER 266, CA.

[245] Whenever there is a delay in taking an arrestee to a police station, the reasons must be recorded when he or she first arrives at a police station: PACE, s. 30(11).

[246] Ibid., s. 30(10).

abuse, and the necessity principle should be strictly applied, with regard (for example) to the urgency of the investigation, and the importance of having the arrestee at the spot (for example, to identify a place or person). It might be necessary and reasonable to take the suspect somewhere else before going to a police station, regardless of any urgency, if the suspect has offered an explanation or alibi and he wishes to be taken to a place or a person to try to supply evidence in support of his account. On the other hand, after a person was arrested at a hotel as part of an investigation into a suspected drugs conspiracy, it was not proper to hold him in his hotel room to prevent him being seen by accomplices leaving the hotel with investigators.[247] Nor is it reasonable to take the suspect to see if a witness to the offence can identify him. All identifications are to be conducted in accordance with the *Code of Practice for the Identification of Persons by Police Officers* (Code D). Again, it is important to restrict the amount of time during which an arrestee is in the hands of investigating officers without any procedural safeguards.

(2) SEARCH OF THE PERSON AND PREMISES FOLLOWING ARREST OTHERWISE THAN AT A POLICE STATION

The operation of the search power varies according to whether the suspect is arrested at a police station, after attending there volutarily, or elsewhere. This section deals with arrests which do not take place in police stations. Those occurring in police stations are dealt with in section (3), below.

(i) Search of the person[248]

If the suspect is arrested anywhere other than in a police station, there is a power for a constable to search him if the constable has reasonable grounds for *believing* that the arrestee may present a danger to him or others.[249] The constable may seize and retain anything he finds which he has reasonable grounds for believing the arrestee might use to cause physical injury to himself or another.[250] This power does not extend to a person who is not a constable, but who makes a citizen's arrest. It is possible that citizens may be able to use their common-law power to take reasonable steps in order to prevent a breach of the peace, if one is reasonably apprehended and appears imminent, as any physical attack on a person would amount to a breach of the peace.[251] In addition, a constable with reasonable grounds to believe that an arrestee may have concealed on him anything which he might use to escape from lawful custody[252] is entitled to search the arrestee,[253] to the extent reasonably required for the purpose of discovering any such item.[254] In each case, when a search is carried out in

---

[247] *R. v. Kerawalla* [1991] Crim. LR 451, CA.
[248] Feldman, *Entry, Search and Seizure*, 227–8, 233–4.
[249] PACE, s. 32(1).
[250] Ibid., s. 32(8).
[251] See Ch. 18 below.
[252] PACE, s. 32(5).
[253] Ibid., s. 32(2)(a)(i).
[254] Ibid., s. 32(3).

public, the arrestee is not to be required to remove clothing other than an outer coat, jacket, or gloves.[255]

All those can be described as non-evidential searches, since they seek to safeguard people and secure the arrestee rather than find evidence. There is an additional power to search an arrestee for evidence relating to any offence (not necessarily the offence for which he has been arrested), if the constable has reasonable grounds for believing that the arrestee may have concealed on him any such evidence.[256] The search must be no more extensive than is necessary for the purpose of discovering any such item,[257] and when it is carried out in public the arrestee is not to be required to remove clothing other than an outer coat, jacket, or gloves.[258] The reasonable grounds for belief may be based on what the constable sees or on other information. In drugs cases, it will usually be reasonable to search for controlled drugs. In other cases, the reasonableness of a belief may be harder to establish.

(ii) Search of premises after arrest other than at a police station

A constable who has reasonable grounds for believing that there is evidence of the offence for which the arrestee was arrested[259] (but not other offences, for which a search would normally require a warrant) is empowered to enter and search any premises[260] in which the arrestee was when arrested, or immediately before he was arrested, for such evidence.[261] Whether the officer has reasonable grounds will depend on the facts of each case. Where the suspect has been arrested on his own premises, there may well be reasonable grounds to believe that there is evidence on the premises, although it will depend to some extent on what crime is suspected and where it is alleged to have taken place. When the suspect is arrested having just left premises, it may still be reasonable to search the premises, even if he was only a visitor there. For example, where officers are watching premises which they believe are being used for drug dealing, and a person is arrested outside the premises and found to be in possession of heroin, it would be reasonable to search the premises for evidence of heroin dealing by him.[262]

The search must be no more extensive than is reasonably required for the purpose of discovering such evidence.[263] In a Crown Court decision, it was held that the power under section 32 is intended to be used immediately following the arrest, and not to give a constable power to return to the scene later—in that case, four hours later—at his convenience and as often as he wants.[264] This has been criticized, as the section

---

[255] Ibid., s. 32(4).
[256] Ibid., s. 32(2)(a)(ii), (5).
[257] Ibid., s. 32(3).
[258] Ibid., s. 32(4).
[259] Ibid., s. 32(6).
[260] For the meaning of 'premises' see below, Ch. 10. When premises are divided into separate dwellings, the power to search is limited to the dwelling in which the arrestee had been immediately before his arrest, together with the common parts of the premises: ibid., s. 32(7).
[261] Ibid., s. 32(2)(b).
[262] Cf. R. v. Beckford (1991) Cr. App. R. 43, CA.
[263] PACE, s. 32(3).
[264] R. v. Badham [1987] Crim. LR 202.

does not provide for any time limit, and the existence of another power to enter premises, under section 18, which is clearly not limited as to time, shows that there was no legislative policy opposed to open-ended entry powers.[265] Nevertheless, the decision seems correct, since (a) section 32 was designed to give statutory effect to a common-law power which was limited to the time and immediate environs of the arrest,[266] and (b) section 18 contains procedural and substantive limitations which are not present in section 32.

Under section 18 of PACE, a constable has power to enter and search any premises occupied or controlled by a person who is under arrest for an arrestable offence, if he has reasonable grounds for suspecting that there is evidence on the premises, other than items subject to legal privilege, which relates to the offence for which the person was arrested or some other arrestable offence which is connected with or similar to that offence.[267] Normally, this power may be exercised only if authorized in writing by an officer of the rank of inspector or above,[268] and the search will take place after the arrestee has been taken to the police station and authority in writing has been applied for and given. However, there is an exception: the constable may conduct the search without authorization, and before taking the arrestee to a police station, if the presence of the arrestee at 'a place other than a police station' is 'necessary for the effective investigation of the offence'.[269] The curious feature of this formulation is that it appears to allow an unauthorized search of the arrestee's premises, even if the place where the arrestee is needed is not his premises. However, it is submitted that the provision must be interpreted purposively as meaning that the power to search without written authorization is to come into operation only where the arrestee's presence is needed, for example, to permit access to the premises.

The relationship between sections 18 and 32 is relatively straightforward. No written authorization is ever required under section 32 to search the place where the person is arrested or was immediately beforehand. If the arrest is not for an arrestable offence, or those premises are not occupied or controlled by the arrestee, they cannot be searched under section 18, but only under section 32. To search other premises, a warrant will normally be needed (if available), unless the premises are occupied or controlled by the arrestee and he has been arrested for an arrestable offence (section

---

[265] Lidstone and Palmer, *Investigation of Crime*, 119.

[266] *Dillon v. O'Brien and Davis* (1887) 20 LR Ir. 300, 16 Cox CC 245; *Chimel v. California* 395 US 752 (1969); *Vale v. Louisiana* 399 US 30 (1970); Feldman, *Entry, Search and Seizure*, 241–8.

[267] PACE, s. 18(1). PACE replaces the common-law power, so there is no power of entry following arrest under a provisional extradition warrant: *R. (Rottman) v. Comr. of Police of the Metropolis, The Times*, 26 October 2001, Admin. Ct.

[268] Ibid., s. 18(4). The authorization must be written on the Notice of Powers and Rights, which under the *Code of Practice for the Searching of Premises by Police Officers and the Seizure of Property found by Police Officers on Persons or Premises* (Code B), para. 5.7, must be given to the occupier of the premises if practicable: see Code B, para. 3.3. In *Cowan v. Condon* [2000] 1 WLR 254, CA, Roch LJ was prepared to infer authorization by speculating on the basis of exiguous evidence. This is unsatisfactory. Provisions designed to protect property rights, required under Article 1 of Protocol No. 1 to the ECHR, ought to be strictly adhered to. The provisions of Code B were apparently not cited to the Court of Appeal, so Roch LJ's judgment on this point can be regarded as *per incuriam*.

[269] PACE, s. 18(5). If the constable searches under this subsection, he must, as soon as practicable, inform an officer of the rank of inspector or above that he has done so: s. 18(6).

18). Even then, some authority is usually required (the inspector's written authorization) unless there is a need to have the arrestee himself present, providing both a reason for acting as quickly as possible and a witness independent of the police. When it comes to the grounds for the entry and search, section 18 is in two respects less demanding than section 32: instead of reasonable grounds to *believe*, section 18 requires only reasonable grounds for *suspecting*; and instead of the search being for evidence of the offence for which the person was arrested, section 18 allows search on the basis of reasonable grounds for suspecting that evidence will be found which relates to that offence or related arrestable offences.

Section 18 is, therefore, a good way of obtaining access to the premises of someone arrested for an arrestable offence, whether or not the person was arrested there. Considering that many arrests are made on or near premises controlled by the arrestee, it is not surprising that the police use section 18 far more often than section 32.[270]

(iii) What may be seized during, and retained after, searches?

A constable searching premises under any of these powers is given certain seizure powers under the sections themselves. After a search of the person under section 32(2)(a), the constable may seize and retain anything he finds, other than items subject to legal privilege, if he has reasonable grounds for *believing* that 'he' (grammatically, meaning the constable, but presumably intended to refer to the arrestee) might use it to escape from lawful custody, or that it is evidence of any offence or has been obtained in consequence of the commission of any offence.[271]

Seizures after searches of premises are more complicated. Nothing in section 32 specifies what may be seized after a search of premises under section 32(2)(b). The powers must therefore be those given by section 19 to a constable who is 'lawfully on premises'. This section gives power to seize anything on the premises, other than items which the officer has reasonable grounds for believing are subject to legal privilege,[272] which the constable has reasonable grounds for *believing* is evidence of, or has been obtained in consequence of the commission of, any offence, whether that which he is investigating or any other. The seizure may, however, be made only if the constable has reasonable grounds for believing that it is necessary to do so in order to prevent it being concealed, lost, tampered with, or destroyed.[273]

Section 18 permits the constable to seize and retain anything, other than items subject to legal privilege, which he has reasonable grounds for suspecting is evidence relating to the arrestable offence for which the arrestee was arrested or to another

---

[270] Lidstone and Palmer, *Investigation of Crime*, 114, 116, report the use of s. 18 to ground 54.2 per cent of searches without warrant, compared to the use of s. 32 in 2.1 per cent of entries. Dixon, Coleman, and Bottomley report s. 18 being used as the basis of 62 per cent of searches in their study: 'PACE in Practice', 1587. For an extensive study of the use of these powers, see K. Lidstone and V. Bevan, *Search and Seizure under the Police and Criminal Evidence Act 1984* (Sheffield: University of Sheffield Faculty of Law, 1992), ch. 3.

[271] PACE, s. 32(9).

[272] Ibid., s. 19(6).

[273] Ibid., s. 19(2), (3). There is also power to require information contained in a computer accessible from the premises to be produced so it can be taken away, on similar grounds: ibid., s. 19(4).

arrestable offence which is connected with or similar to that offence (such as evidence of other burglaries where the person is arrested for burglary).[274] In both section 18(2) and section 19(2) and (3), 'anything' includes vehicles. Although vehicles are within the definition of 'premises' in section 23, and nothing in sections 18 and 19 expressly authorizes seizure of premises, it has been said:

'A constable will not be able to seize and retain premises when they are immovable property because of the physical impossibility of doing so. That practical barrier does not exist where the premises are readily movable such as a vehicle or a tent or a caravan. In my judgment there is no reason why the word "anything" contained in section 18(2) and section 19(2) and (3) should not include "everything" where the nature of the premises makes it physically possible for the totality of the premises to be seized and retained by the police, and where practical considerations make that desirable.'[275]

The necessity condition under section 19 need not be satisfied if the seizure is made under section 18, as the powers in section 19 are additional to, rather than a qualification of, other seizure powers.[276] On the other hand, any seizure which relates to an offence unconnected with that for which the arrest was made will have to be justified by reference to section 19, including the necessity condition.

(3) SEARCH OF THE PERSON AND PREMISES AFTER ARREST AT A POLICE STATION

If a person is arrested at a police station, he must immediately be told that he is under arrest,[277] and he becomes the responsibility of the custody officer or person performing the functions of custody officer, who must decide whether or not a charge or detention should be authorized (the role of the custody officer and the rights of the suspect are described below). If detention is authorized, the custody officer opens a custody record. He must then record everything which the arrestee has with him.[278] This gives rise to powers of search which are the same as those which a custody officer has where the person is brought to the police station having been arrested elsewhere. These are discussed below, in the context of treatment of arrested suspects. All searches are controlled by the custody officer.

Searches of the premises controlled or occupied by a person arrested at the police station are controlled by section 18, above, where the arrest was for an arrestable offence. In other cases, access to premises depends either on the consent of the occupier or on obtaining a warrant to enter (if one is available).

---

[274] PACE, s. 18(2).
[275] *Cowan v. Condon* [2000] 1 WLR 254, CA at 264 *per* Roch LJ (with whom Sir Oliver Popplewell and Butler-Sloss LJ expressed agreement at 265).
[276] PACE, s. 19(5); *Cowan v. Condon* [2000] 1 WLR 254, CA.
[277] PACE, s. 29.
[278] Ibid., s. 54(1).

6.6 RIGHTS OF DETAINED SUSPECTS BEFORE CHARGE

The Royal Commission on Criminal Procedure recommended that the common-law powers in relation to detention without charge, which were uncertain and hard to enforce, should be replaced with a code which would give the powers to the police which were needed in the fight against crime, but would balance them with protections for the rights of suspects. This principle was carried into the Police and Criminal Evidence Act 1984 so successfully that, while civil liberties groups complained that the police were being given sweeping new powers which infringed people's liberties, the police complained that they were being hamstrung by the new rights given to suspects and the complicated procedures put in place to safeguard them. Neither party's assessment was fair, and perhaps the Act's capacity to engender disapproving rhetoric from all sides is the best indication that the right balance was found.

The Act gave suspects a number of enforceable rights for the first time. The suspect's right to inform a person that he had been arrested, first given (but in a more limited form and without any enforcement procedure) by section 62 of the Criminal Law Act 1977, was extended: section 56. A right to legal advice was given for the first time by section 58. The Act extended the period for which people could be held without charge, but only in respect of a new class of 'serious arrestable offences', and a system of reviews was established to authorize detention, including (after a maximum of thirty-six hours) a hearing by a magistrates' court. Elaborate reporting and recording provisions were established to make it as difficult as possible for the police to abuse their powers. The *Code of Practice for the Detention, Treatment and Questioning of Persons by Police Officers* (Code C) laid down standards to be met in the treatment of those in custody. The custody officer was made responsible for ensuring compliance with the Act and Codes, breach of which became a disciplinary offence. This section deals with these matters from the viewpoint of the protection of suspects' rights.[279]

(1) THE RIGHT NOT TO BE HELD UNNECESSARILY

(i) General

The custody officer is responsible for ensuring that suspects are not held at all if there is no necessity for doing so, and are not held for longer than necessary. The necessity principle was recommended by the Royal Commission on Criminal Procedure as the proper basis for police powers of detention, in order to minimize the ambiguity and uncertainty of the detention powers as they operated before PACE.[280] This is an important safeguard for the principle that a person is to be released as soon as the

---

[279] For detailed treatment of the provisions as they affect police powers and procedures generally, see M. Zander, *The Police and Criminal Evidence Act 1984*, 3rd edn. (London: Sweet & Maxwell, 1995); Lidstone and Palmer, *Investigation of Crime*; K. Bottomley *et al.*, *The Impact of Pace: Policing in a Northern Force* (Hull: Centre for Criminology and Criminal Justice, 1991).

[280] RCCP, *Report*, paras. 3.94–3.110.

conditions for detention cease to be satisfied. Detention can no longer be justified under ECHR Article 5(1)(c) once it becomes clear that there are insufficient grounds to bring him before a competent legal authority on reasonable suspicion of having committed an offence. Detaining a person after that time therefore violates a detainee's rights under Article 5(1), unless another legitimate ground for detention under Article 5(1) applies.[281] To give effect to this principle, regular monitoring is needed to ensure that the conditions for detention continue to be fulfilled.

As soon as practicable after a person has been arrested at a police station, has been brought to a station after arrest elsewhere (either without warrant or under a warrant which is not endorsed for bail), or has gone to a police station to surrender to police bail, the Act provides that the custody officer must first decide whether there is sufficient evidence to charge him with the offence for which he was arrested. The custody officer may detain the suspect for such period as is necessary to enable him to make this decision.[282]

If there is enough evidence, the suspect must be either released without charge or charged forthwith,[283] and either released (on bail or without bail) or detained to appear before a magistrates' court. If there is insufficient evidence to charge the suspect, he has a right to be released immediately, on bail or without bail, unless the custody officer has reasonable grounds for believing (not merely suspecting) that detention without charge is 'necessary to secure or preserve evidence relating to the offence for which [the suspect] is under arrest or to obtain such evidence by questioning him'.[284] This gives statutory recognition to the propriety of arresting a person for the purpose of questioning him, making arrest and detention a step in the investigation process rather than the commencement of the prosecution process. Where the custody officer has such grounds, he (and he alone) may authorize detention.[285]

Although the decision to charge or release is the custody officer's, he is not sufficiently independent of his police colleagues to be regarded as a 'judge or other officer authorised by law to exercise judicial powers' within the meaning of Article 5(3) of the European Convention.[286] His review of the grounds for detention therefore does not provide the prompt judicial or quasi-judicial review required by the Article. Nor did review by an executive rather than judicial officer, the Secretary of State, after forty-eight hours, under earlier terrorism legislation. This seems to have been accepted by the government in *Brogan v. United Kingdom*.[287] That this is correct is borne out by the fact that, in practice, the custody officer inevitably relies so heavily

---

[281] *Quinn v. France*, Eur. Ct. HR, Series A, No. 311, Judgment of 2 March 1995, 21 EHRR 529; *K.-F. v. Germany*, Eur. Ct. HR, Judgment of 27 November 1997, RJD 1997-VI, 26 EHRR 390; *Punzelt v. Czech Republic*, Eur. Ct. HR, Judgment of 25 April 2000; *Jecius v. Lithuania*, Eur. Ct. HR, Judgment of 31 July 2000.

[282] PACE, s. 37(1), (10). See E. Cape, 'What Does "Sufficient Evidence to Charge" Mean?' [1999] Crim. LR 874–85.

[283] PACE, s. 37(7).

[284] Ibid., s. 37(2).

[285] Ibid., s. 37(3).

[286] See *Schiesser v. Switzerland*, Eur. Ct. HR, Series A, No. 34, Judgment of 4 December 1979, 2 EHRR 417.

[287] Eur. Ct. HR, Series A, No. 145, Judgment of 29 November 1988. It would, apparently, satisfy the demands of Art. 5(3) for a legal professional to make the decision to detain as long as he was properly independent, in personal and institutional terms, of the prosecution process. The Court will make the

on the account given by the arresting officer (both because of the lack of independent sources of information and because of a desire not to compromise the perceived authority of the arresting officer in the presence of outsiders) that it is almost unknown for him to refuse to authorize detention, at least initially, if the arresting officer requests it.[288] Indeed, the evidence is that the process of authorizing detention quickly became formalized so that the grounds for arrest or detention are rarely checked at all, making the necessity principle entirely ineffective as a protection for suspects' rights.

In practice, it is difficult for the custody officer to attempt very much fact-finding. In order to maintain his independence of the investigation and prevent the booking-in process from turning into an interview without the appropriate safeguards for the suspect, Code C, paragraph 3.4 forbids the custody officer to question the suspect about his involvement in the offence, or about any comments which the suspect may volunteer (although the latter must be recorded). It is therefore unsurprising to find David Dixon *et al.* writing of their observational study of a North of England force:

'in almost all observed cases, custody officers did not inquire into the circumstances of arrest: they simply asked a question such as "What has she been arrested for?", expecting and getting only the briefest of answers (for example, "shop theft" or "breach of the peace") needed to complete the custody record section for "reasons for arrest" . . . We observed no instances of a custody officer refusing to accept a suspect into detention.'[289]

More recent research suggests that the position has not improved.[290]

As soon as detention is authorized, the custody officer must open a custody record for the detainee, and in it must record the reasons for detention.[291] In practice these usually simply parrot the statutory terms (for example, 'detained to obtain evidence by questioning him'). This is partly a protection for the suspect's right to be free of arbitrary detention, by ensuring that a record is kept of his whereabouts (keeping

---

assessment on the basis of the concrete facts of each case. On different facts, a District Attorney was held to be acceptable in *Schiesser v. Switzerland*, Eur. Ct. HR Series A, No. 34, Judgment of 4 December 1979, 2 EHRR 417, but not in *Huber v. Switzerland*, Eur. Ct. HR, Series A, No. 188. Even an investigating judge is insufficiently independent where he would be responsible for referring the case for trial at the end of the investigation: *H. B. v. Switzerland*, Eur. Ct. HR, Judgment of 5 April 2001. *Cp. De Jong, Baljet and Van Den Brink v. Netherlands*, Eur. Ct. HR, Series A, No. 77, (1984) 8 EHRR 20; *Hood v. United Kingdom*, Eur. Ct. HR, Judgment of 18 February 1999; *Findlay v. United Kingdom*, Judgment of 25 February 1999, RJD 1997-I, 24 EHRR 221; *Stephen Jordan v. United Kingdom*, Eur. Ct. HR, Judgment of 14 March 2000 (position of commanding officers deciding on detention following military arrests: insufficiently independent if they have a role in establishing a subsequent court martial or participating in the disposal of the case). It follows that a police officer or member of the Crown Prosecution Service would virtually always be insufficiently independent, but a magistrates' court would satisfy the test under Art. 5(3).

[288] I. McKenzie, R. Morgan, and R. Reiner, 'Helping the Police with Their Inquiries: The Necessity Principle and Voluntary Attendance at the Police Station' [1990] Crim. LR 22–33 at 23–24; D. Dixon, K. Bottomley, C. Coleman, M. Gill, and D. Wall, 'Safeguarding the Rights of Suspects in Police Custody' (1990) 1 *Policing and Society* 115–40 at 129–30.

[289] Dixon *et al.*, 'Safeguarding', 129–30.

[290] D. Brown, *Entry into the Criminal Justice System: A Survey of Police Arrests and their Outcomes*, Home Office Research Study 185 (London: Home Office, 1998), 43. See also Royal Commission on Criminal Justice, *Report*, 28–9.

[291] Code C, para. 2.1; PACE, s. 37(4), s. 39(1)(b).

track of detainees is a basic obligation of public authorities under Article 5 of the ECHR[292] and hence under section 6 of the Human Rights Act 1998), treatment, and decisions affecting him. More significantly, perhaps, it provides a bureaucratic protection for the police officers against disciplinary proceedings for procedural wrongdoing.[293] The suspect must be told the reason for his detention unless he is incapable of understanding what is said, is violent or likely to become violent, or is in urgent need of medical attention.[294]

Once detention has been authorized, the right to be free of unnecessary detention becomes a right to be free of unnecessarily prolonged detention. If the detainee is not promptly released, Article 5(3) of the European Convention guarantees a prompt appearance before a judge or other judicial officer. In *Brogan v. United Kingdom*,[295] the European Court of Human Rights accepted that the length of time which may be allowed to elapse without infringing the 'promptness' requirement had to be judged in the light of the object of the Article, which is to protect an individual's fundamental right to liberty against arbitrary state interference. Under the (now repealed) Prevention of Terrorism (Temporary Provisions) Act 1984, detention without charge for forty-eight hours was permitted, after which time there would be a review by the Secretary of State who could authorize a further period of five days, making a week in all. The majority of the Court held that 'promptly', or '*aussitôt*' as in the French text of the Convention, demands less delay than words like 'speedily'. Even allowing for the special problems of terrorist investigations, only limited flexibility was permitted. Accordingly, the Court held by twelve votes to seven that there had been a breach of Article 5(3) when people were held without judicial control for periods of which the shortest was four days and six hours. Despite this, for security reasons the government felt unable to introduce independent judicial controls on the period of detention without charge in terrorist cases when it replaced the 1984 Act with the Prevention of Terrorism (Temporary Provisions) Act 1989, and entered a derogation from Article 5(3) to cover such cases.[296] The Terrorism Act 2000 introduces a new regime for reviewing the detention of terrorist suspects. An initial review by an officer of at least the rank of inspector, as soon as possible after the arrest, is followed by further reviews at intervals of no more than twelve hours, with a superintendent or still more senior officer conducting the reviews when the suspect has been held for over twenty-four hours.[297] Only a Senior District Judge (Chief Magistrate) or a specially designated District Judge (Magistrates' Court) (previously Chief Stipendiary Magistrate or Stipendiary Magistrate) can authorize detention without charge to continue beyond forty-eight hours, up to a maximum of seven days from the time of arrest in connection with terrorism.[298] These arrangements comply

[292] See, e.g. *Çiçek v. Turkey*, Eur. Ct. HR, Judgment of 27 February 2001, at paras. 166–169.

[293] See McKenzie, Morgan, and Reiner, 'Helping the Police', 24–6.

[294] PACE, s. 37(5), (6).

[295] Eur. Ct. HR, Series A, No. 145 (1988) 11 EHRR 117.

[296] The reservation was held to be valid in *Brannigan and McBride v. United Kingdom*, Eur. Ct. HR, Series A, No. 258-B, Judgment of 26 May 1993.

[297] Terrorism Act 2000, Sch. 8, paras. 21, 24.

[298] Ibid., Sch. 8, para. 29.

with the requirements of ECHR Article 5(3), and allowed the UK to withdraw its reservation in 2001.[299]

In relation to the period for which people can lawfully be detained in non-terrorist cases in England and Wales, PACE imposes an upper limit on detention without charge of twenty-four hours from the time of arrival at the police station following arrest elsewhere, and, where the arrest took place at the station, twenty-four hours from the time of the arrest, in most cases.[300]

The Act specifies that reviews of detention must be carried out within prescribed periods, to ensure that the criteria for detention are still met. Where the suspect has not yet been charged, the criteria for continuing to detain him are the same as those for initial authorization of detention,[301] save that the review must be carried out by a review officer of at least the rank of inspector, rather than the custody officer.[302] Where the suspect has been charged before the review, the review officer is the custody officer, who must order his release (either on bail or without bail) unless: (i) there is reasonable doubt about his name or address; or (ii) the custody officer has reasonable grounds for believing that the person's detention is necessary for his own good or to prevent him causing physical injury to another or loss of or damage to property; or (iii) the custody officer has reasonable grounds for believing that the accused will fail to appear in court, or that detention is necessary to prevent him from interfering with the administration of justice or with the investigation of any offence; or (iv) the person is an arrested juvenile, and the custody officer has reasonable grounds for believing that he ought to be detained in his own interests.[303]

The evidence is that these reviews tend to be as formalized as the initial detention decision. Even the right to make written or oral representations, given by the Act to the detainee (unless he is asleep at the time of the review) and to his solicitor if available at the time of the review,[304] seems to be rarely exercised, largely because solicitors have found that representations rarely make any difference to the outcome of the review.[305] Despite this, the opportunity to make representations, and to do so at a face-to-face meeting with the review officer, has been treated as mandatory in *R. v. Chief Constable of Kent Constabulary, ex parte Kent Police Federation Joint Branch Board*.[306] The Divisional Court there held that a review by video link would be unlawful, and criticized a suggestion in Code C, Note for Guidance 15C, that a review by telephone might be permissible. The government considered that this caused sufficient inconvenience to justify proposing an amendment to the law to permit reviews by either telephone or video link. The Criminal Justice and Police Act 2001, section

---

[299] Human Rights Act 1998, Sch. 2, Part I, which contained the designated reservation, was accordingly repealed by Statutory Instrument on 1 April 2001.

[300] PACE, s. 41(1), (2). See Irving and McKenzie, *Regulating Custodial Interviews*; Dixon *et al.*, 'Safeguarding', 128–9, 132.

[301] PACE, s. 40(8).

[302] Ibid., s. 40(1)(b).

[303] Ibid., ss. 38(1), 40(1)(a).

[304] Ibid., s. 40(12), (13). The review officer need not hear oral representations from the detainee if he considers that the detainee is unfit to make them by reason of his condition or behaviour: s. 40(14).

[305] See Dixon *et al.*, 'Safeguarding', 130–1.

[306] [2000] 2 Cr. App. R. 196, DC.

73(1) inserts section 40A in PACE, allowing the Secretary of State to make regulations to permit reviews by telephone. Until such regulations are made, it follows from the *Kent* decision that a stipendiary magistrate was correct to hold that an authorization of detention after a review where the right to make representations has been improperly denied is invalid. This makes the subsequent detention unlawful, and any magistrates' court to which the police apply for a warrant of further detention after thirty-six hours lacks jurisdiction to grant the warrant.[307]

The time limits within which reviews must be carried out (the first within six hours of the initial authorization of detention, later ones within nine hours of the one before)[308] and the right to make representations on reviews are, therefore, not a strong protection to the rights of suspects to be free of unnecessary detention.

(ii) Detention beyond twenty-four hours

After twenty-four hours from the time when detention was first authorized (not counting time spent being treated in hospital without being questioned by the police),[309] the suspect must be released (either on bail or without bail) if he has not been charged.[310] However, in certain cases there are procedures for continuing detention without charge. This can be authorized by a superintendent or above, at any time after the second review by the review officer but before twenty-four hours have elapsed from the time when detention was first authorized.[311] It can be authorized for a period of up to twelve hours following the time twenty-four hours after detention was first authorized.[312] Before authorizing this continued detention, the superintendent who is responsible for the station must have reasonable grounds for believing: (a) that continued detention without charge is necessary to secure or preserve evidence relating to an offence for which the suspect is under arrest or to obtain such evidence by questioning him, thus maintaining the form of the necessity principle; *and* (b) that the suspect is under arrest for a serious arrestable offence, as distinct from any offence for which an arrest may be made which may justify detention for up to twenty-four hours; *and* (c) that the investigation is being conducted diligently and expeditiously (indicating, again, that the suspect is not being kept waiting in detention for an unnecessarily long time).[313]

The review should be carried out in person, not over the telephone or by video link unless regulations made under section 45A of PACE apply to allow review by video link.[314]

---

[307] *In the matter of an application for a warrant of further detention* [1988] Crim. LR 296.

[308] PACE, s. 40(3). There is provision for postponing a review to the first practicable time if it is not practicable to carry it out before the set time, for example because the suspect is being interviewed and the review officer is satisfied that interrupting the questioning would prejudice the investigation, or if no review officer is available at that time: s. 40(4), (5). In any case, time limits are to be treated as approximate only: s. 45(2).

[309] Ibid., s. 41(6).

[310] Ibid., s. 41(7).

[311] Ibid., s. 42(4).

[312] Ibid., ss. 41(8), 42(1) and (2).

[313] Ibid., s. 42(1).

[314] PACE, s. 45A, inserted by the Criminal Justice and Police Act 2001, s. 73(3), reversing the effect of *R. v. Chief Constable of Kent Constabulary, ex parte Kent Police Federation Joint Branch Board* [2000] 2 Cr. App. R.

The superintendent, besides being more senior than an inspector, is likely to be more remote from the investigating officers, and inspire a good deal of respect. It is not surprising, therefore, that Dixon *et al.* observed in their North of England research force that 'such reviews were more rigorous than inspectors' reviews; investigating officers did not assume that such an extension would be granted (as they did with earlier reviews)'.[315] This offers greater security for the right not to be unnecessarily detained than do the earlier procedures, both because the officers concerned are unlikely to seek a continuation of detention without good reason and because the conditions to be met are likely to form rules which genuinely govern police behaviour at all levels, rather than merely presentational rules which are used to justify behaviour after the event but exercise little real influence over the decision-making process.[316]

(iii) Serious arrestable offences

This is a convenient point at which to explain the nature of serious arrestable offences. A serious arrestable offence, as the name suggests, is an offence which (a) is arrestable within the meaning of section 24 of PACE, discussed earlier, and (b) satisfies one of the statutory criteria for seriousness. These statutory criteria are of two kinds. There are some listed offences which are always serious. It is always a serious arrestable offence to do anything which constitutes offences involving treason, murder, manslaughter, rape, kidnapping, incest with a girl under the age of 13, buggery with a boy under the age of 16 (with or without consent), or indecent assault which constitutes an act of gross indecency.[317] Causing an explosion likely to endanger life,[318] sexual intercourse with a girl under the age of 13,[319] possessing a firearm with intent to injure, using a firearm or imitation firearm to resist arrest, and carrying a firearm with criminal intent,[320] hostage-taking,[321] hijacking,[322] torture,[323] and causing death by reckless driving,[324] are always serious arrestable offences. Endangering safety at aerodromes, hijacking ships, seizing control of fixed drilling platforms,[325] offences relating to indecent photographs and pseudo-photographs of children,[326] and publishing obscene matter,[327] are also always serious arrestable offences,[328] as are those offences

---

196, DC, above. Proposals to permit reviews by telephone and video link are currently before Parliament in the Criminal Justice and Police Bill 2001.

[315] 'Safeguarding', 131.

[316] For the classification of rules, and discussion of presentational rules in particular, see Smith and Gray, *Police and People in London*, 440–3.

[317] PACE, s. 116(2)(a) and Sch. 5, Part I.

[318] Explosive Substances Act 1883, s. 2.

[319] Sexual Offences Act 1956, s. 5.

[320] Firearms Act 1968, ss. 16, 17(1), and 18 respectively.

[321] Taking of Hostages Act 1982, s. 1.

[322] Aviation Security Act 1982, s. 1.

[323] Criminal Justice Act 1988, s. 134.

[324] Road Traffic Act 1988, s. 1.

[325] Aviation and Maritime Security Act 1990, ss. 1, 9, and 10 respectively.

[326] Protection of Children Act 1978, s. 1.

[327] Obscene Publications Act 1959, s. 2.

[328] PACE, s. 116(2)(b) and Sch. 5, Part II.

listed in paragraphs (a) to (e) of the definition of drug-trafficking offences in section 1(3) of the Drug Trafficking Act 1994.[329]

Next, there is a category of offences which, though not intrinsically necessarily serious enough to justify the application of extended police powers to their investigation, may become serious if the facts of particular cases display certain characteristics. These are offences which have led or are intended to lead, or involve a threat which if carried out would be likely to lead, to any of the following consequences:[330]

(a) serious harm to the security of the state or to public order, which brings in, for example, numerous offences under the Official Secrets Act 1911–1989 and the Public Order Act 1986;

(b) serious interference with the administration of justice or with the investigation of offences or of a particular offence, which potentially brings in contempt of court, conspiring to pervert the course of justice, and making a disclosure which prejudices a drug-trafficking investigation;[331]

(c) the death of any person;

(d) serious injury[332] to any person, thus encompassing a threat to infect a person with HIV or to adulterate food with a noxious substance as part of a blackmail plot;

(e) substantial financial gain to any person, so that the amount stolen may make a serious arrestable offence out of a simple theft; and

(f) serious financial loss to any person, judged according to its seriousness for the person who suffers it,[333] so that stealing a small amount from a poor pensioner might be a serious arrestable offence while stealing goods to a larger value from a large store,[334] or from a group of joint owners none of whom has a particularly valuable share,[335] might not be one.

Terrorist offences, and police powers in respect of them, are dealt with separately in the Terrorism Act 2000. We will take note of them where they are relevant.

(iv) Detention beyond thirty-six hours after the first authorization of detention

If the investigating officers feel the need to detain a suspect without charge for more than thirty-six hours in a non-terrorism case, they must apply to the magistrates' court for a warrant of further detention.[336] There must be a full hearing of the

---

[329] PACE, s. 116(2)(c), inserted by Drug Trafficking Act 1994. These offences include laundering the proceeds of drug trafficking.

[330] Ibid., s. 116(3), (4), (6).   [331] See Drug Trafficking Act 1994, s. 53.

[332] 'Injury' includes any disease, and any impairment of a person's physical or mental condition: PACE, s. 116(8).

[333] Ibid., s. 116(7).   [334] *R. v. Smith (Eric)* [1987] Crim. LR 579.

[335] *R. v. McIvor* [1987] Crim. LR 409.

[336] If the application is made after the 36-hour period expires, and the magistrates consider that it would have been reasonable to make it before the time limit expired, the court must dismiss the application: PACE, s. 43(7). The detainee must then be immediately charged or released, on bail or without bail, and cannot be rearrested or subjected to a renewed application for that offence without fresh evidence which has come to light since the application was dismissed: ibid., s. 43(17), (18), (19).

application, at which the suspect will be entitled to be present and represented by a solicitor or barrister.[337] The application for a warrant of further detention must be made on oath by a constable and supported by information, which must state the nature of the offence for which the arrest was made, the general nature of the evidence supporting the arrest, the inquiries which have been made and the further inquiries which the police propose to make, and the reasons for believing that the continued detention of the arrestee is necessary for the purposes of the further inquiries, and must satisfy the magistrates that there are reasonable grounds for believing that the application is justified.[338] Detention is justified only if the offence is a serious arrestable offence, the investigation is being conducted diligently and expeditiously, and detention without charge is necessary to secure or preserve evidence relating to an offence for which the detainee is under arrest or to obtain such evidence by questioning him.[339] If the magistrates are satisfied, they may issue a warrant which authorizes further detention for such a specified period, not exceeding thirty-six hours, as the magistrates think fit having regard to the evidence before them,[340] particularly considering the importance of the necessity principle. If, at the end of the further period, the police still consider it necessary to detain the person without charge, they may make a new application to the magistrates' court for an extension to the warrant of further detention. The criteria and procedures for applying for and granting the extension are the same as those for granting the warrant in the first place,[341] although it is to be expected that magistrates will view the reasons which are said to justify detention without charge with increasing scepticism as time passes. The extension, if granted, will be for a specified period not exceeding thirty-six hours, and the total time spent in detention without charge after the relevant time, within the meaning of section 41(2) of the 1984 Act, must not exceed ninety-six hours.

Strict observance of time limits is not of the essence in relation to the detention provisions: section 45(2) provides, 'Any reference in this Part of this Act to a period or time of day is to be treated as approximate only'. This flexibility makes allowance for problems which may arise in practice. However, the limits are important protections for the fundamental rights of detainees, and going beyond a limit will always require a compelling explanation of the exigencies which made it unavoidable. The onus on the police is very substantial. For example, it has been held that they must contact the magistrates' clerk in good time to allow a bench to be assembled before the time limit expires. If the police fail to do so, bearing in mind such factors as the times of the magistrates' luncheon recess and when the time limits expire, the magistrates will have to reject the application, and the suspect will have to be either charged or released.[342]

---

[337] Ibid., s. 43(2), (3). This means, incidentally, that the power to delay a suspect's exercise of the right to inform a person of his whereabouts and the right to receive legal advice cannot be delayed beyond the 36-hour period.

[338] Ibid., s. 43(1), (14). The detainee must have been provided with a copy of the information: s. 43(2).

[339] Ibid., s. 43(4).

[340] Ibid., s. 43(11), (12).

[341] Ibid., s. 44(1) and s. 43(4).

[342] R. v. Slough Justices, ex parte Stirling [1987] Crim. LR 576, DC.

(v) Detention beyond forty-eight hours in terrorism cases

As noted above, only a Senior District Judge (Chief Magistrate) or designated District Judge (Magistrates' Courts) may grant a warrant of further detention, allowing a terrorist suspect to be detained without charge for more than forty-eight hours from the time of arrest up to a maximum of seven days. An application must be made by an officer of at least the rank of superintendent, and must usually be made before the first forty-eight hours expires. There is some leeway, as an application may be made up to six hours after the end of that period, but the judge must dismiss such an application if he considers that it would have been reasonably practicable for the police to apply within the period.[343] The detainee must be notified of the application, and of the grounds on which it is made and the time when it will be heard. Before this time, the detainee will have been allowed access to legal advice, and he or the advisor will be allowed to make oral or written representations to the judge (although the detainee may be excluded from parts of the hearing if necessary, for example for security reasons).[344] However, the judge may order that specified information on which the police rely in support of their application may be withheld from the suspect or the suspect's legal representative, or both, if there are reasonable grounds for believing that one of the following consequences would follow from disclosing it to them:

- interference with or harm to evidence of a terrorist offence;
- hindering recovery of property obtained as a result of a terrorist offence;
- hindering recovery of property in the possession or under the control of the detainee at the time of the arrest, and intended for use for terrorist purposes, such property being liable to forfeiture under section 23 of the 2000 Act;
- alerting a person suspected of terrorism, making his apprehension, prosecution or conviction more difficult;
- alerting a person so that it would be made more difficult to prevent an act of terrorism;
- interfering with the gathering of information about the commission, preparation, or instigation of an act of terrorism; or
- interference with or physical injury to any person;[345]

or that the detainee has committed and benefited from offences, other than drug trafficking offences, in respect of which a confiscation order might be made, and disclosing the information would hinder the recovery of the value of the benefit.[346] Neither the suspect nor the suspect's legal representative may be admitted to the hearing of an application by the police for an order for non-disclosure.[347] It is arguable that deciding to extend detention on the basis of information which is withheld

---

[343] Terrorism Act 2000, Sch. 8, paras. 29, 30.
[344] Ibid., Sch. 8, paras. 8(2), 31, 33.
[345] Ibid., Sch. 8, para. 34(2).
[346] Ibid., Sch. 8, para. 34(3).
[347] Ibid., Sch. 8, para. 34(4).

from the suspect and his representative would violate the suspect's right to a fair determination of the legality of detention under Article 5(3) of the ECHR.

The judge may grant a warrant of further detention only if satisfied that two conditions are satisfied. Both relate to the necessity for continuing to detain the suspect. The first is concerned with the purpose of the detention: there must be reasonable grounds for believing that further detention is necessary in order to obtain relevant evidence in relation to terrorism, either by questioning the detainee or by detaining him in order to preserve relevant evidence. The second condition is designed to ensure that people are not held for an unnecessarily long time: the police must satisfy the judge that the investigation is being conducted diligently and expeditiously.[348]

A warrant of further detention may be extended at further hearings, up to the maximum period of seven days from the time of arrest, if the judge is satisfied that the conditions for further detention continue to be satisfied. In the meantime, the suspect must be immediately released if the officer having custody of him becomes aware that the conditions for detention are no longer satisfied.[349]

(2) RIGHTS TO HAVE SOMEONE INFORMED OF ARREST AND TO CONSULT SOLICITOR

The evidence so far suggests that, at least until detention is reviewed by a superintendent after twenty-four hours, the necessity principle is of little help in limiting the period of detention. Of more significance to the suspect are the rights which he has while in detention, and the right to be told of his rights at the time of his arrival at the police station after arrest elsewhere, or the time of his arrest at a police station.

The custody officer must tell the suspect clearly about his rights to have someone informed of his arrest, to consult privately with a solicitor, available free of charge, and to consult the Codes of Practice.[350] It must be made clear that these are continuing rights, and, if not exercised at once, may be exercised at any time unless delayed in accordance with the Act. The custody officer is responsible for asking the suspect to sign the appropriate place in the custody record to signify whether or not he wants legal advice at that point, and, if it is requested, the custody officer must act to secure advice without delay.[351] Evidence from the USA, concerning the constitutional requirement, under the Fifth Amendment, that a person be informed of his right of silence and his right to counsel, suggested that the right to be informed can be thwarted by the manner in which the information is given. There is some evidence that the police in England and Wales too were giving the information, deliberately or

---

[348] Ibid., Sch. 8, para. 32.

[349] Ibid., Sch. 8, paras. 36, 37.

[350] Code C, para. 3.1. The right to consult the Codes does not entitle a person arrested on suspicion of drunken driving to delay the taking of any specimen which is authorized under the Road Traffic Act 1988: *DPP v. Billington* [1988] RTR 231, DC; *DPP v. Cornell, The Times*, 13 July 1989, DC; Code C, Note for Guidance 3E. For criticism, see David Tucker, 'Drink-Drivers' PACE Rights: A Cause of Concern' [1990] Crim. LR 177–80.

[351] Code C, para. 3.5.

not, in ways which either discouraged suspects from exercising their rights or inter-fered with their understanding of the rights.[352] To some extent, this should be allevi-ated under the revised Code C, paragraph 3.2 of which provides for suspects to be provided with two written notices, one setting out the above three rights and explain-ing the arrangements for obtaining legal advice, the other setting out his other entitlements while in custody. The suspect can then read the notices at his leisure, if able to do so. Citizens of independent Commonwealth countries, and foreign nation-als, must be informed as soon as practicable of their right to communicate with their countries' High Commissions, Embassies, or Consulates.[353]

There is some difficulty about the idea that a person who declines to exercise his rights does so voluntarily. People in custody are likely to be intimidated by the situ-ation in which they find themselves, and amenable to any suggestion that they should not immediately exercise their rights. For example, suggestions that waiting for a solicitor will slow down the process and delay release might make the suspect feel that it is inappropriate to insist on rights. Consent to delay or waive exercise of rights is therefore questionable, even when it is apparently freely given.[354] For those who regard civil liberties principally as protecting people's autonomy, it goes against the grain to try to protect people against their own weakness. One can, however, justify imposing protection and regulation in situations which are inherently likely to over-whelm people's normal capacity for self-determination and free choice. Being detained in a police station is such a situation.

It is therefore proper to seek to control the extent to which a person who wishes to exercise rights can have his request for a solicitor, or to have someone informed of his arrest, overridden by the police. This is the approach which the Act takes. In particu-lar, there must be a poster prominently displayed in every police station advertising the right to have legal advice.[355] The revised Code of Practice further provides that no attempt should be made to dissuade the suspect from obtaining legal advice, and reminders of the right must be given to the suspect every time an interview begins or recommences after a break, before every review of detention, before identification procedures are initiated, and before an intimate sample is requested.[356]

There is no right to legal advice at common law.[357] Any such right depends on

---

[352] A. Sanders and L. Bridges, 'Access to Legal Advice and Police Malpractice' [1990] Crim. LR 494–509, suggest that the police are using rule-bending 'ploys' when giving information, which result in suspects deciding not to exercise their rights in a significant proportion of cases (498–501). See also M. McConville, A. Sanders, and R. Leng, *The Case for the Prosecution* (London: Routledge, 1991). Other researchers disagree. For example, Dixon *et al.*, 'Safeguarding', 117, write: 'In general, rather than being a deliberate attempt to block access to rights, such practices are the product of a belief that suspects do not benefit from reading the Codes. (Problems increase when such assumptions are taken further, such as assuming that a suspect would not benefit from seeing a legal adviser.)' See also D. Dixon, 'Legal Regulation and Police Malpractice' (1992) 1 *Soc. and Legal Studies* 515–41; Dixon, *Law in Policing*, 152–69; Royal Commission on Criminal Justice, *Report*, 34, paras. 39–40.

[353] Code C, para. 3.3.

[354] Dixon, Coleman, and Bottomley, 'Consent and the Legal Regulation', 356.

[355] Code C, para. 6.3.

[356] Code C, paras. 6.3, 6.4, 6.5, 11.2, 15.3, 16.4 and 16.5; Code D, paras. 2.15(ii) and 5.2.

[357] *R. v. Chief Constable of the Royal Ulster Constabulary, ex parte Begley* [1997] 1 WLR 1475, [1997] 4 All ER 833, HL.

statute. Before PACE, there was a right to make a telephone call to a person under the Criminal Law Act 1977, but there was no sanction for interference with the right. The 1984 Act introduced rights to have someone informed that the suspect has been arrested, and to have legal advice in private, subject to a power to delay, designed to protect the administration of justice. A considerable caselaw has developed round these rights and the power to delay their exercise, but the right to legal advice in particular has been held on a number of occasions to be fundamental to the scheme of the detention provisions under the 1984 Act: this was one of the safeguards which was intended to balance the extension of police detention powers, and any infringement of the right is likely to lead to a challenge to the admission at trial of evidence obtained as a result.[358] Under the Human Rights Act 1998, the right to legal advice may be strengthened by Article 6(3)(c), conferring on anyone charged with a criminal offence the right 'to defend himself . . . through legal assistance of his own choosing'. The European Court of Human Rights has held that denying access to a solicitor even before the suspect is charged may taint a subsequent trial with unfairness, violating Article 6, if the police question the suspect in the absence of a solicitor and induce him to make damaging admissions, or a court later draws adverse inferences from a suspect's failure to answer questions or mention aspects of his defence when questioned without being allowed legal advice.[359] Here, we consider the scope of the rights, and the circumstances which may be held to justify delaying their exercise.

(i) The scope of the right to have someone informed

This right comes into operation whenever a person has been arrested and is being detained in a police station or other premises. Such a person is entitled to have somebody informed, by the police, of the fact that he has been arrested and of where he is being detained. The classes of person whom a detainee is entitled to have contacted are widely drawn. The detainee may request to have a friend or relative contacted, or any other person who is known to him or who is likely to take an interest in his welfare. Once the request has been made, the police must comply with it as soon as practicable, unless delay is authorized.[360] This right applies every time a detainee is moved to new premises or another police station.[361] There may be some difficulty in complying: the person might not be contactable by telephone, and there may be a delay before a constable can be sent to the house to make contact in person. In addition, there may be reasons for an officer to make the call in person rather than by telephone. For example, when the police want to search the detainee's premises and do not want to alert other occupiers beforehand, it is easiest (and avoids the necessity for a formal authorization of delay) simply to deliver the message at the same time as searching the house.[362] In non-terrorism cases, if the first person named by the suspect cannot be contacted, the suspect must be invited to name up to two others; if

---

[358] *R. v. Samuel* [1988] QB 615, [1988] 2 All ER 135, CA.
[359] See, e.g. *Condron v. United Kingdom*, Eur. Ct. HR, Judgment of 2 May 2000, 31 EHRR 1.
[360] PACE, s. 56(1); Terrorism Act 2000, Sch. 8, para. 6(1), (2).
[361] Code C, para. 5.3; Terrorism Act 2000, Sch. 8, para. 6(3).
[362] Dixon *et al.*, 'Safeguarding', 118.

they cannot be contacted either, the custody officer or the officer in charge of the investigation has a discretion to go on trying other people, but need not do so.[363]

Apart from the general right under section 56, the custody officer has special responsibilities under section 57 where the detainee is a child or young person (hereafter 'child') within the meaning of the Children and Young Persons Act 1933. First, such steps as are reasonably practicable must be taken to find out who is responsible for the child's welfare (i.e. his parent or guardian,[364] or other person who has for the time being assumed responsibility for his welfare).[365] That person must then be informed, as soon as practicable, of the arrest and the reason for it, and where the child is being held.[366] These 'rights' are in addition to those in section 56, and are not subject to the provisions authorizing delay, discussed below, which apply in relation to the rights under sections 56 and 58.

Code C, paragraph 5.4, provides that, at the custody officer's discretion, any detainee may receive visits. Under paragraph 5.6 a suspect is entitled to be supplied with writing materials on request, and is to be allowed to speak on the telephone for a reasonable time to one person. These, by contrast with the right under section 56 of PACE, are expressed to be privileges, not rights. They may be at the public expense, at the custody officer's discretion.[367] They do not figure in the 1984 Act itself, and under the Code can be delayed or denied by an officer of at least the rank of inspector who considers that the conditions which would justify delaying the right to have someone informed of the suspect's whereabouts under section 56 apply.[368] Furthermore, the suspect must be told that anything he says or writes (other than a communication to a solicitor, which is likely to attract legal professional privilege) may be read or listened to, and given in evidence, and a telephone call may be terminated if it is being abused (a nicely vague term).[369] Under paragraph 5.8, a record must be made of all letters, messages, telephone calls, or visits made or received.

(ii) The scope of the right to legal advice

Section 58(1) of PACE, and paragraph 7 of Schedule 8 to the Terrorism Act 2000, provide that the detainee is entitled, if he so requests, to consult a solicitor privately at any time. When a request is made, it must be complied with as soon as practicable, and the custody officer must act on it without delay except so far as a delay is authorized in accordance with the section.[370] Where the person detained was a

---

[363] Code C, para. 5.1. Where a friend, relative, or person with an interest in the suspect's welfare contacts the police to inquire about the suspect, the police must give the information if the suspect agrees, unless delay has been authorized: Code C, para. 5.5.

[364] This includes the authority having care of a child who is in the care of a local authority, or a voluntary organization in which parental rights and duties have been vested. On the role of parents as appropriate adults, see (3) below.

[365] Where the child is subject to a supervision order, the person responsible for his supervision must also be informed as soon as practicable.

[366] Children and Young Persons Act 1933, s. 34, as amended by PACE, s. 57.

[367] Code C, para. 5.7.

[368] Code C, para. 5.6.

[369] Code C, para. 5.7.

[370] PACE, s. 58(4); Code C, para. 6.2.

juvenile, or a mentally disordered or mentally handicapped person, either the detainee or the 'appropriate adult' (if one is present) is entitled to request legal advice, and any such request should be acted on immediately.[371]

If a legal adviser arrives uninvited at the police station to see the detainee, the detainee must be told that the adviser is there, and asked whether he wants to see him, even if the detainee has previously declined legal advice.[372] If there is a delay before a solicitor can be contacted or can reach the police station, the suspect must normally not be interviewed (or interviewed further) until he has received the legal advice. There are four exceptions permitted to this rule.

First, delay in exercising the right may in appropriate cases be authorized in accordance with the procedure prescribed in Annex B to Code C. Secondly, an officer of the rank of superintendent or above may authorize an interview to continue or begin if he has reasonable grounds for believing that delay will involve an immediate risk of harm to persons or serious loss of or damage to property, or that awaiting the solicitor's arrival would cause unreasonable delay to the process of investigation. Once sufficient information has been obtained to avert the danger, the interview must cease until the adviser arrives.[373] Thirdly, an officer of the rank of inspector or above may authorize an interview without further delay if the suspect's selected solicitor cannot be contacted, or has indicated that he does not wish to be contacted, or has declined to attend, and the suspect has declined the offer of advice from a duty solicitor or the duty solicitor is unavailable.

The second and third grounds are rather too open-ended for comfort. In such cases there are good public-interest grounds for proceeding as quickly as possible, but it might better balance the rights of the suspect against the public interest in expeditious investigation to advise the suspect of the difficulty and ask if he wants to contact another solicitor who might be able to get to the police station more quickly. Finally, where a suspect who initially asked for advice has changed his mind, and has given agreement in writing or on tape to be interviewed without receiving legal advice, an officer of the rank of inspector or above may permit the interview to start.[374]

Suspects are only statutorily entitled to be advised by solicitors.[375] 'Solicitor' is defined as 'a solicitor who holds a current practising certificate, a trainee solicitor, a duty solicitor representative or an accredited representative included on the register or representatives maintained by the Legal Aid Board' (now the Legal Services Commission).[376] This excludes people who are not subject to the controls enforced by the Law Society, the Legal Services Commission, and the High Court. Nevertheless, the viability of the service depends on some representation and advice at police stations being given by unqualified personnel. In the early years of PACE, the police felt that some wholly inappropriate people were being sent to advise suspects. In Bristol, the police excluded representatives being sent by one particular firm of solicitors. On an

[371] Code C, para. 3.13 and Note for Guidance 3G.
[372] Code C, para. 6.15.
[373] Code C, para. 6.7.
[374] Code C, para. 6.6.
[375] PACE, s. 58(1).
[376] Code C, para. 6.12.

application for judicial review of the exclusion policy, the Divisional Court held that the police had a discretion to exclude people on various grounds, including the suitability of the person on the grounds (*inter alia*) of age, mental capacity, appearance, and supposed criminal orientation.[377] The Code now permits a solicitor to send a 'probationary or non-accredited representative' to give advice on his behalf. It provides that such people shall be admitted to police stations, although an officer of the rank of inspector or above may exclude him or her if the officer 'considers that such a visit will hinder the investigation of crime'.[378] The officer should exercise this discretion in the light of several considerations, including whether the identity and status of the person have been satisfactorily established, and whether he is of suitable character to provide legal advice (this would justify checking whether the person has a criminal record, and excluding him if he has one, unless the conviction was for a minor offence some while ago). In addition, any other matters in a letter of authorization from the solicitor should be considered.[379] If an inspector decides to exclude the clerk or legal executive, he should immediately inform the detainee and the solicitor, who may make alternative arrangements.[380] Note of Guidance 6F suggests that inspectors who consider that a particular solicitor or firm is persistently sending unsuitable people should inform a superintendent, who may wish to complain to the Law Society.

In practice, representatives sent to police stations are sometimes former police officers, who may have close ties with the investigating officers, giving rise to a risk (or at least the appearance of one) that they will be more in sympathy with the police than with their clients. This could reduce the value of the advice and support which they give, and should be borne in mind by courts when considering whether people's rights have been adequately protected by having a clerk in attendance at an interview.[381]

Legal advice is often given on the telephone rather than in person.[382] Where advice is provided by a duty solicitor, the Legal Services Commission requires initial advice to be given by telephone, but the duty solicitor must then attend any subsequent interview or identity parade. The legal aid costs claim will not otherwise be paid.[383] When an adviser does attend at the police station, the detainee is usually entitled to consult the adviser in private.[384]

But in terrorism cases, an officer of at least the rank of Assistant Chief Constable (or, in London, commander) may direct that the consultation is to take place in the

---

[377] *R. v. Chief Constable of Avon and Somerset, ex parte Robinson* [1989] 1 WLR 793, [1989] 2 All ER 15, DC.

[378] Giving proper advice to the suspect is not hindering the investigation of crime, even if the advice is not to answer questions: Code C, para. 6.12. Nor is intervening to stop a suspect incriminating himself, or challenging improper questioning: Code C, Note for Guidance 6D.

[379] Code C, paras. 6.12, 6.13.

[380] A record must be made in the custody record. Code C, para. 6.14.

[381] Dixon *et al.*, 'Safeguarding', 123–5; *cp. R. v. Dunn* [1990] Crim. LR 572, CA.

[382] A. Sanders, L. Bridges, A. Mulvaney, and G. Crozier, *Advice and Assistance at Police Stations and the 24 Hour Duty Solicitor Scheme* (London: Lord Chancellor's Dept., 1990).

[383] Under the franchises for the Criminal Defence Scheme.

[384] Code C, para. 6.1.

sight and hearing of an independent 'qualified officer', i.e. a uniformed officer of at least the rank of inspector who has no connection with the case.[385] The Assistant Chief Constable or Commander may give the direction only if he has reasonable grounds for believing that one of the these consequences will otherwise follow:

- interference with or harm to evidence of any serious arrestable offence;
- interference with or physical injury to any person;
- the alerting of persons who are suspected of having committed a serious arrestable offence but who have not yet been arrested for it;
- hindering the recovery of property obtained as a result of a serious arrestable offence or property subject to forfeiture under section 23 of the 2000 Act (property intended for use for the purposes of terrorism);
- interference with the gathering of information about the commission, preparation, or instigation of acts of terrorism;
- alerting a person and thereby making it more difficult to prevent an act of terrorism;
- alerting a person and thereby making it more difficult to secure a person's apprehension, prosecution, or conviction in connection with the commission, preparation, or instigation of acts of terrorism;
- hindering the recovery of the benefits from a non-drug-trafficking offence of which the detainee is reasonably believed to have committed, and in respect of which he is liable to be subjected to a confiscation order.[386]

The detainee must be permitted to have the adviser present during any interview which takes place while the adviser is available.[387] Once a legal adviser is present in an interview, the police may require him to leave only if his conduct is such that the investigating officer is unable properly to put questions to the suspect. If that occurs, the matter should be referred to an officer not below the rank of superintendent or (if no such officer is readily available) inspector, who will speak to the solicitor and then decide whether the interview should continue in the presence of the solicitor. If he decides that it should not, the suspect will be given an opportunity to consult another solicitor, and the interview will be delayed to allow the replacement to arrive. Removing a solicitor in this way should not occur unless the solicitor's conduct makes it appropriate to consider reporting him to the Law Society and, if he is a duty solicitor, to the Legal Services Commission.[388]

The adviser's role is to advise and support the detainee, not merely to be an independent witness. Not all advisers are conscious of this, and there are good reasons for solicitors or clerks who regularly visit a police station to avoid acting in such a way as to sour their relations with the police. In practice, legal advisers rarely interfere with the conduct of an interview, and tend to assist investigations by encouraging clients to

---

[385] Terrorism Act 2000, Sch. 8, para. 9.

[386] Terrorism Act 2000, Sch. 8, para. 8(1), (4), (5). It would be unlawful to give such a direction without grounds for suspecting the particular solicitor of impropriety, violating ECHR Art. 6(3): *Brennan v. United Kingdom*, Eur. Ct. HR, App. No. 39846/98, Judgment of 16 October 2001.

[387] Code C, paras. 6.8, 6.12.

[388] Code, C, paras. 6.10 and 6.11.

tell their stories more often than they interfere with it by advising silence.[389] The passive adviser is no danger to the police; if anything, there is reason to doubt the usefulness of legal advice to the suspect.[390] In *R. v. Paris, Abdullah and Miller*[391] and *R. v. Heron*,[392] legal advisers had been present at long, hostile, and intimidating interviews of murder suspects. The adviser in each case (a solicitor in *Paris* and an unqualified representative in *Heron*) had failed to intervene. The suspects eventually made damaging statements. In *Paris*, the trial judge admitted them in evidence, but the Court of Appeal later quashed the resulting convictions on the ground that the questioning had been oppressive. In *Heron*, the trial judge refused to admit the statements. It is, perhaps, not surprising that only around thirty-eight per cent of detainees request legal advice,[393] nor particularly worrying that not all of those actually receive it.

(iii) Grounds for delaying exercise of the rights

The criteria for delaying exercise of the right to have someone informed that one has been arrested, and the right to legal advice, are the same, although the application of the criteria varies slightly between the two rights because of the difference between giving information to someone who may be concerned in the crime and obtaining advice from a professional. A further difference lies in the relevant caselaw of the European Court of Human Rights in relation to the right to a fair hearing under Article 6 of the ECHR. So far, it has not been suggested that delaying informing someone of the whereabouts of the suspect violates rights under Article 6, although there is a duty under Article 5 to account to members of the family in due course for people taken into police custody.[394] On the other hand, it may violate the right to a fair trial under Article 6 if a court admits evidence of a confession obtained after long periods of interrogation during which access to legal advice was denied, whatever the reason for the delay.[395] Although this is not possible now under the law of Great Britain and Northern Ireland, it remains possible in the Channel Islands and the Isle of Man. It may also violate Article 6 to draw inferences from a refusal to answer questions or give explanations before the suspect has had access to legal advice, if it has the effect of bolstering the prosecution case or undermining an explanation later given, unless there is very strong prosecution evidence which independently casts doubt on the explanation which the defendant later gives.[396]

---

[389] Dixon *et al.*, 'Safeguarding', 124; D. Dixon, 'Politics, Research and Symbolism in Criminal Justice: The Right of Silence and the Police and Criminal Evidence Act' (1991) 20 *Anglo-Amer. LR* 27–50 at 43–6.

[390] Dixon, *Law in Policing*, 236–58; J. Baldwin, *The Role of Legal Representatives at the Police Station*, RCCJ Research Study No. 3 (London: HMSO, 1992); M. McConville and J. Hodgson, *Custodial Legal Advice and the Right to Silence*, RCCJ Research Study No. 16 (London: HMSO, 1993); Royal Commission on Criminal Justice, *Report*, 38–9.

[391] (1993) 97 Cr. App. R. 99, CA (the 'Cardiff Three case').

[392] Unreported, Leeds Crown Court, discussed by Dixon, *Law in Policing*, 172–3.

[393] C. Phillips and D. Brown, *Entry into the Criminal Justice System: A Survey of Police Arrests and their Outcomes*, Home Office Research Study 185 (London: Home Office, 1997), reporting rates of requests at different police stations ranging between 22 per cent and 50 per cent.

[394] *Çiçek v. Turkey*, Eur. Ct. HR, Judgment of 27 February 2001.

[395] *Magee v. United Kingdom*, Eur. Ct. HR, Judgment of 6 June 2000, at paras. 43–4.

[396] *John Murray v. United Kingdom*, Eur. Ct. HR, Judgment of 8 February 1996, RJD 1996-I; *Averill v. United Kingdom*, Eur. Ct. HR, Judgment of 6 June 2000, at paras. 47–49.

In many respects, however, the two rights are treated alike in national law. In each case, delay may be authorized only by an officer of the rank of superintendent or above, in relation to a person who has been arrested for a serious arrestable offence or under the terrorism provisions.[397] Before the superintendent may authorize delay, he must have reasonable grounds for believing that the exercise of the right in question at the time when the detainee wants to exercise it would have one of three effects in relation to most serious arrestable offences, with other grounds in respect of arrests under the terrorism provisions and offences for which confiscation orders can be made:

(a) it will lead to interference with or harm to evidence connected with a serious arrestable offence[398] (not necessarily that for which the suspect was arrested), or to interference with or physical injury to other people; or

(b) it will lead to the alerting of other people suspected of having committed such an offence but not yet arrested for it; or

(c) it will hinder the recovery of any property obtained as a result of such an offence.[399]

Where the offence is a drug-trafficking offence or one which falls within the provisions of the Criminal Justice Act 1988, Part VI (i.e. offences for which orders can be made to confiscate the proceeds of crime), the exercise of the rights can also be delayed where the superintendent has reasonable grounds to believe that:

(d) the person detained has benefited from the offence, and that the recovery of the benefits in respect of which a confiscation order might be made following conviction will be hindered by the exercise of the right.[400]

Where the person is detained under the Terrorism Act 2000, the exercise of the rights may also be delayed where the superintendent has reasonable grounds to believe that:

(e) it will hinder the recovery of property subject to forfeiture under section 23 of the 2000 Act (property intended for use for the purposes of terrorism);

(f) it will lead to interference with the gathering of information about the commission, preparation, or instigation of acts of terrorism;

(g) by alerting any person, it will make it more difficult to prevent an act of terrorism, or to secure the apprehension, prosecution, or conviction of anyone in connection with the commission, preparation, or instigation of such an act;

(h) by informing someone of the detainee's arrest or allowing access to legal

---

[397] PACE, ss. 56(2), (10), (11); 58(6), (12), (13). The terrorism provisions are those which allow for arrest and detention without warrant in relation to terrorist offences, proscribed organizations and exclusion orders: Prevention of Terrorism (Temporary Provisions) Act 1989, s. 14 and Schs. 2 and 5; PACE, s. 65.

[398] Where a person is detained under the terrorism provisions, 'serious arrestable offence' includes an offence under the Terrorism Act 2000, or an attempt or conspiracy to commit such an offence: para. 8(9) of Sch. 8 to the 2000 Act.

[399] PACE, ss. 56(5), 58(8).

[400] Ibid., ss. 56(5A), 58(8A).

advice, it will hinder the recovery of the value of the benefit of a non-drug-trafficking offence which the detainee is reasonably believed to have committed and benefitted from, and which would make him liable to a confiscation order in respect of property representing the benefits.[401]

It is important to bear in mind the other side of the coin: there are numerous considerations which will *not* justify delaying the exercise of rights. The grounds relied on to justify a delay in the exercise of the rights must be reasonably supportable by reference to the facts as known at the time. For example, in *R. v. Samuel*[402] the police claimed that they had delayed the detained suspect's access to legal advice because they feared that an accomplice still at large might be alerted, yet the suspect's mother had been told of the suspect's arrest hours before the superintendent took the decision to delay access to a solicitor. The Court of Appeal held that an alleged confession made without the benefit of legal advice should have been excluded as a result, and quashed the conviction. In *R. v. Alladice*[403] a suspect had been openly arrested in court, amongst people known to him, and his house had been searched in his mother's presence, so the police claim to have believed that a solicitor might have tipped off other suspects was hard to believe.

Where other suspects remain at large, it may well be reasonable to delay informing a detainee's friends or family that he has been arrested under section 56 of PACE, if they are likely to be in contact with the other suspects. On the other hand, it will not often be reasonable to delay access to legal advice on this ground, unless there are reasonable grounds for believing that the particular legal adviser whom the detainee wants to see is likely to give away to other suspects the fact that the police are on to them. The superintendent must therefore examine separately the grounds for delaying each of the rights.[404] It is not usually argued that the solicitors are likely intentionally to aid or abet a suspect's escape. However, it is sometimes suggested that solicitors are gullible, and can be manipulated by criminals into passing on coded messages without realizing their significance. Some judges are ready to accept that this is a real danger,[405] while others are more sceptical,[406] but all accept two principles: first, that the police are entitled to be suspicious of legal advisers until they know who the adviser is to be (particularly as so many advisers are clerks or 'runners' rather than qualified solicitors); secondly, that they are not entitled to deny access to a reputable and experienced person with no known criminal connections.[407] The second principle is supported by Note for Guidance B4 in Annex B to Code C, advising that the super-intendent may authorize delay 'only if he has reasonable grounds to believe that the specific solicitor will, inadvertently or otherwise, pass on a message from the detained person or act in some other way which will lead' to any of the grounds justifying delay coming about.

---

[401] Terrorism Act 2000, Sch. 8, para. 8(1), (3), (4), (5).
[402] [1988] QB 615, [1988] 2 All ER 135, CA.
[403] (1988) 87 Cr. App. R. 380, CA.
[404] *R. v. Parris* [1989] Crim. LR 214, CA; Code C, Annex B, Note for Guidance B5.
[405] e.g. Lord Lane CJ in *Alladice*, above; *Re Walters* [1987] Crim. LR 577, DC.
[406] e.g. Hodgson J in *Samuel*, above.
[407] *Samuel*, above.

A special problem arises where several suspects are in custody waiting to be interviewed and they ask for the same solicitor. In such cases the risk of accidental contamination of evidence, prejudicing the investigation, is marked, and solicitors, recognizing a risk that they will appear to be helping suspects to co-ordinate their stories, will usually co-operate with police by arranging for the suspects to be advised by different people. Any question of a conflict of interest is for the solicitor to resolve in the light of the relevant code of professional ethics; it is not a matter for the police. On the other hand, where unreasonable delay will be caused to the investigation if the same solicitor has to advise several suspects, the police may be justified in proceeding to interview a suspect before the solicitor has seen him.[408]

As Code C, Annex B, paragraph 3, makes clear, the police are not justified in delaying access to legal advice merely because they fear that a solicitor will advise the suspect to remain silent. Where access has been improperly denied on this ground, a subsequent admission made without the benefit of advice is likely to be excluded from evidence on the ground of unfairness under section 78 of PACE.[409] The right to receive advice must not become a right to receive only such advice as suits the police.

(iv) Ending the delay

Exercise of the rights may only be delayed for as long as the grounds justifying delay continue to obtain,[410] and in any case must end after thirty-six hours (or, in the case of people detained under the terrorism provisions, forty-eight hours) when detained suspects have to be either charged, released, or brought before a magistrates' court.[411] When the authorization of delay no longer applies, the suspect must be told, asked as soon as practicable whether he wants legal advice, and, if he does, it must be obtained in the normal way.[412] If this is not done, and an interview takes place without legal advice for the suspect, the breach of the Code is quite likely to be regarded as making unfair the admission of any statement made as a result.[413]

(3) SPECIAL PROTECTION FOR THE RIGHTS OF VULNERABLE GROUPS

Suspects who are, or who appear to be,[414] juveniles, mentally handicapped, mentally disordered, blind, visually handicapped, or unable to read are in specially vulnerable positions, and the Act and Code C give them special protection in the form of the attendance of an 'appropriate adult'. The appropriate adult's job is not merely to act as a witness, but is to support and advise the suspect in accordance with his best

---

[408] Code C, para. 6.6(b)(ii); Note for Guidance 6G.

[409] R. v. Samuel, above.

[410] PACE, ss. 56(9), 58(11); Terrorism Act 2000, Sch. 8, para. 8(8).

[411] Ibid., ss. 56(3) and 58(5); Terrorism Act 2000, Sch. 8, para. 8(2). In terrorism cases, detainees are entitled to legal advice before the time at which, 48 hours after arrest, an application for a warrant of further detention may be made to a District Judge: Terrorism Act 2000, Sch. 8, para. 29(4)(a).

[412] Code C, Annex B, paras. 4, 9.

[413] See R. v. Walsh [1989] Crim. LR 822, CA.

[414] Code C, paras. 1.5, 1.6.

interests, and to facilitate communication.[415] The custody officer should explain this
to the detainee,[416] and (at least where he is present at an interview) it should also be
explained to the appropriate adult.[417] The appropriate adult may request legal advice
on behalf of the detainee, even if the detainee has declined access to legal advice.[418]

The role of the appropriate adult is a difficult one, and may be harrowing. When
Frederick West was interviewed by Gloucestershire police about the murders of several young women, the police thought he might be mentally disordered. They asked a
female volunteer worker on a young homeless project to act as the appropriate adult.
She was subjected to the traumatic experience of hearing appalling revelations of
sexual and physical abuse of young women, including members of West's family. She
later sued the police for negligence, alleging that they had given her insufficient
support during and after the interviews, and that she had suffered psychological
injury as a result. The Court of Appeal decided by a majority that the police owed no
duty to shield an appropriate adult from the matters revealed during the interviews
which the adult attends, but held unanimously that there might be a duty to offer
appropriate counselling or other psychiatric support afterwards if it is needed.[419]

(i) Juveniles[420]

The Act provides that the custody officer must arrange for an 'appropriate adult' to
attend when a juvenile is detained. The appropriate adult for a juvenile is the parent or
guardian (or, if he is in care, the local authority of voluntary organization in whose
care he is), or a social worker, or, failing either of those, another responsible adult who
is not a police officer or police employee.[421] In exceptional cases where an interview
takes place at the juvenile's educational institution (which is normally forbidden), the
principal or his nominee can act as the appropriate adult, unless the juvenile is
suspected of an offence against the educational institution[422] (which presumably
includes staff and students of the institution), in which case staff would lack the
necessary independence of the investigation. Normally, the preference is to use the
parent or guardian, as being the person most likely to feel responsible for and have a
sympathetic relationship with the juvenile. However, there are circumstances in which
this may not be the case. For example, as the appropriate adult has an advisory role, it
is important that the juvenile should be able to veto the selection of a parent who is
estranged from the juvenile and in whom he puts no trust.[423] The police are therefore
advised not to ask an estranged parent to act as appropriate adult if the juvenile
expressly and specifically objects to his presence.[424]

[415] Code C, para. 11.16.
[416] Code C, para. 3.12.
[417] Code C, para. 11.16.
[418] Code C, para. 3.13.
[419] *Leach v. Chief Constable of Gloucestershire Constabulary* [1999] 1 WLR 1421, [1999] 1 All ER 215, CA.
[420] D. Dixon, 'Juvenile Suspects and the Police and Criminal Evidence Act', in D. Freestone (ed.), *Children and the Law: Essays in Honour of Professor H. K. Bevan* (Hull: Hull University Press, 1990), 107–29.
[421] Code C, para. 1.7(a).
[422] Code C, para. 11.15.
[423] *DPP v. Blake* [1989] 1 WLR 432, DC.
[424] Code C, Note for Guidance 1c.

Even parents who are not estranged might not always be the best people to advise their children in police stations. Some research has shown that parents tend to be anything but sympathetic towards children who have been arrested, reporting one case in which 'a police officer intervened to stop a mother assaulting her 12-year-old daughter with a slipper for having "brought shame on the family". It was evident that some young suspects were afraid of their parents and of being punished when they got home'.[425] Such a parent might be thought to be an inappropriate adult to be giving advice.

Even if the parent is not violent, he may be so unsympathetic as to fail to perform an appropriate adult's functions of advising the suspect and facilitating communication. In *R. v. Jefferson*,[426] a juvenile suspect was being interviewed in connection with public order offences. His father was acting as the appropriate adult. At times, the father behaved properly, intervening to clarify his son's answers or advising him to tell the truth. At other times, he acted as an additional interrogator, asking questions, challenging his son's version of events, and on one occasion flatly contradicting him. The Court of Appeal decided that this behaviour did not disqualify the father from being an appropriate adult.[427] This is an unsatisfactory decision. The capacity of a person to act as an appropriate adult, and his personal qualities, are only part of the picture. It is just as important to consider whether the adult actually conferred on the juvenile the benefits and safeguards envisaged by PACE and the Code of Practice. In assessing the value of the decision as a precedent, it is significant that the description of the appropriate adult's functions was, at the time, not in one of the authoritative paragraphs of the Code, but only in a Note for Guidance. The description is now contained in the authoritative provision of Code C, paragraph 11.16, and should accordingly be given more weight by a court. *Jefferson* can therefore safely be distinguished, and should not be followed on this point.

Another class of parent who would make an inappropriate adult are people of such low intelligence that they are unable to understand the significance of what is happening, let alone advise the juvenile. Where such a person acts as the appropriate adult, it is likely to be regarded as unfair to admit in evidence any statement made by the juvenile during the interview.[428]

All information required to be given to a detainee must be repeated in the presence of the appropriate adult.[429] If the appropriate adult is available at the time of a review of detention, he must be given the opportunity to make representations to the review officer.[430]

A juvenile must not be interviewed in the absence of an appropriate adult, even if

---

[425] P. Softley (with the assistance of D. Brown, B. Forde, G. Mair, and D. Moxon), 'Police Interrogation: An Observational Study in Four Police Stations', in K. Heal, R. Tarling, and J. Burrows (eds.), *Policing Today* (London: HMSO, 1985), 115–30 at 119.

[426] [1994] 1 All ER 270, CA.

[427] Ibid. at 286–7.

[428] *R. v. Morse* [1991] Crim. LR 195, CA.

[429] Code C, para. 3.11.

[430] Code C, paras. 15.1, 15.2.

the juvenile requests it, unless an officer of the rank of superintendent or above considers that delay will lead to interference with or harm to evidence connected with the offence, interference with or physical harm to other people, or the alerting of other suspects not yet arrested; or will hinder the recovery of property obtained in consequence of any offence.[431] If this is ignored, any admission made by the juvenile during the interview is likely to be excluded from evidence at a subsequent trial, either as being unreliable (on the view that juveniles are particularly suggestible or weak-willed) and so inadmissible under section 76(2)(b) of PACE,[432] or on the basis of unfairness under section 78.[433]

Special rules apply where the juvenile is a ward of court. Although leave of the court is not needed before an arrested juvenile can be questioned, leave is needed to interview a ward as a potential witness, whether for the prosecution or the defence, without arresting him.[434] If it is proposed to administer a formal reprimand or warning to the juvenile as an alternative to prosecution, it would first require the court's leave. Reprimands and cautions can be administered only if the juvenile has admitted the offence, which might not be in the ward's best interests.[435]

Whether or not the juvenile is a ward of court, if an interview is desired it should be conducted away from school if at all possible, to protect the child against embarrassment.[436]

(ii) Mentally handicapped or disordered detainees

Where a person arrested for an offence appears to be suffering from a mental handi-cap or a mental disorder, the custody officer must contact the police surgeon (or in urgent cases arrange for the person to be taken to hospital),[437] and contact an appropriate adult, inform him of the person's detention and whereabouts, and ask him to come to the police station. The provisions relating to appropriate adults then apply as they do in respect of juveniles. The appropriate adult for a mentally dis-ordered or handicapped suspect is to be a relative, guardian, or other person respon-sible for his welfare, or someone with experience of dealing with such people who is not a police officer or employed by the police (such as a psychiatric social worker). Failing those, it may be any responsible adult aged 18 or over who is not a police officer or employed by the police.[438] Generally, a person with experience or training in the care of mentally handicapped or disordered people is preferable to an untrained relative, unless the detainee insists on the relative.[439]

---

[431] Code C, para. 11.14, and Annex C, para. 1.

[432] e.g. DPP v. Blake (see n. 316).

[433] R. v. Weekes (1992) 97 Cr. App. R. 222, CA; R. v. Cox (1993) 96 Cr. App. R. 464, CA.

[434] In re K. and others (Minors) (Wardship: Criminal Proceedings) [1988] Fam. 1, [1988] 1 All ER 214; Practice Direction [1988] 1 All ER 223; Practice Direction [1988] 2 All ER 1015; In re R. (A Minor) (Wardship: Criminal Proceedings) [1991] Fam 11, [1991] 2 All ER 193, CA.

[435] Re R., Re G. (Minors) [1990] 2 All ER 633. On reprimands and warnings, see the Crime and Disorder Act 1998, s. 65, as amended by the Criminal Justice and Court Services Act 2000, s. 56.

[436] Code C, para. 11.15.

[437] Code C, para. 9.2.

[438] Code C, para. 1.7(b).

[439] Note for Guidance 1E.

As numerous cases like the Maxwell Confait investigation[440] have shown, people with a mental disorder or a mental handicap may be very suggestible, so no interview is to take place in the absence of an appropriate adult unless an officer of the rank of superintendent or above considers that delay will lead to interference with or harm to evidence connected with the offence, interference with or physical harm to other people, or the alerting of other suspects not yet arrested; or will hinder the recovery of property obtained in consequence of any offence.[441] If an interview is carried out without the appropriate adult, the evidence of any statement made by the detainee is likely to be inadmissible by reason of unreliability under section 76(2)(b) of PACE, or excluded for unfairness under section 78.[442] When deciding whether to exercise the discretion to exclude evidence under section 78, it may be relevant to ask whether there has been a breach of Code C. For example, there is no breach if the police were not told, and had no reason to suspect, that the suspect was suffering from a mental handicap or mental disorder.[443] Nevertheless, if the evidence is admitted, the judge must warn the jury that there is a special need for caution before convicting substantially on the evidence of any admission.[444]

(iii) Blind or visually handicapped detainees

Where a detainee is blind, visually handicapped, or unable to read, the custody officer should ensure that his solicitor, a relative, an appropriate adult, or some other independent person likely to take an interest in him is available to help him to check any documentation and sign anything necessary on his behalf.[445] This is particularly important, as so many of the controls and monitoring systems under PACE rely on records of consents, interviews, and requests being checked and signed by the detainee.

(iv) Deaf and speech-handicapped detainees or appropriate adults, or detainees who do not appear to speak English

Interviews must not be conducted where detainees or appropriate adults appear to be deaf or speech-handicapped, or where detainees appear not to understand English or to be unable to communicate with their solicitors, except in the presence of an interpreter, who must be given an opportunity to check records of interviews and certify their accuracy. The only exception is where a superintendent considers that the usual conditions of urgency obtain under Annex C to Code C.[446] Copies of the various notices which are to be given to detainees are made available, as encouraged by Note

---

[440] Report of the Inquiry by the Hon. Sir Henry Fisher into the Circumstances Leading to the Trial of Three Persons on Charges Arising out of the Death of Maxwell Confait and the Fire at 27 Doggett Road, London SE6, HC 90 of 1977–8.

[441] Code C, para. 11.14 and Annex C, para. 1.

[442] R. v. Everett [1988] Crim. LR 826, CA; R. v. Moss, The Times, 1 March 1989, CA.

[443] R. v. Bailey (Paula) [1995] 2 Cr. App. R. 262, CA.

[444] PACE, s. 77; R. v. Lamont [1989] Crim. LR 813, CA; R. v. Bailey (Paula) [1995] 2 Cr. App. R. 262, CA. On the meaning of 'substantially', see R. v. Campbell (Oliver) [1995] 1 Cr. App. R. 522, CA.

[445] Code C, para. 3.14.

[446] Code C, paras. 3.6, 13.5–13.7, 13.9. Interpreters are provided at public expense, and this should be made clear to the detainee: para. 13.8.

for Guidance 3B to Code C, in Welsh, the main ethnic minority languages, and the principal European languages, when they are likely to be helpful.

(v) Detainees who are ill

The custody officer must immediately call the police surgeon, or arrange for hospital treatment, for a detainee who appears to be ill, mentally disordered, or injured, or who is not responding normally to questions or conversation (unless he is merely drunk), or otherwise appears to need medical attention.[447] Failure in this regard contravenes the Human Rights Act 1998, section 6, and may give rise to a claim for damages if, as a result of the contravention, the detainee's suffering reaches a sufficiently severe level. The right to be free of inhuman or degrading treatment under Article 3 of the ECHR imposes obligations on public authorities to provide appropriate medical services for people in their custody,[448] and if the victim dies it may also give rise to a claim under Article 2 (right to life). The police surgeon must also be called if the detainee requests a medical examination.[449] Generally, the Human Rights Act 1998 and the provisions of section 9 of Code C require the custody officer to be very cautious when dealing with anyone who seems ill.

(4) CONCLUSION

The protective rights given by PACE and the Codes of Practice are dependent on the work, initially, of the custody officer. The primary means of monitoring the performance of the custody officer is by way of entries in the custody record, and monitoring of complaints about treatment, which must be reported immediately to an officer of the rank of inspector or above who is not connected with the investigation. The roles of the custody officer and the review officer are crucial. These roles call for considerable personal authority and independence and the officers may be in a difficult situation. First, they are torn between commitment to the usual police role—a desire to get results by detecting crime—and their statutory responsibilities to remain apart from the investigation and act independently to ensure the detainee is treated properly and given his entitlements. Secondly, they are inevitably subject to pressures imposed by the bureaucratic burden of the recording requirements. Thirdly, there is the pressure from investigating officers, some of whom may be of higher rank than the custody officer.[450]

The Act contemplates that the last point will be catered for by referring any conflict of decisions or directions relating to the treatment or detention of a detainee to an officer of the rank of superintendent or above who is responsible for the police station.[451] This appears to happen rarely in practice. On the other hand, investigating

---

[447] Code C, para. 9.2.

[448] See, *mutatis mutandis, Aerts v. Belgium*, Eur. Ct. HR, Judgment of 30 July 1998, RJD 1998-V; *Kudła v. Poland*, Eur. Ct. HR, Judgment of 26 October 2000; and Chs. 4 and 5, above.

[449] Code C, para. 9.4.

[450] For discussion of some of the main pressures on custody officers, see J. Rodie, 'The Undervalued Custody Officer' (1988) 4 *Policing* 4–27.

[451] PACE, s. 39(6) (custody officer); s. 40(11) (review officer).

officers have expressed concerns about the loss of their control, for example over detention times. They perceive their concerns as being different from those of custody and review officers.[452] Perhaps the most surprising feature of the scheme, therefore, is that it seems, on the whole, to have worked reasonably well so far.

Where the suspect has rights, including access to legal advice, the rights are not easy to enforce by law. The main remedy for breach is the inadmissibility of evidence which fails to satisfy the requirements of section 76(2) of PACE, and the discretion of the court to exclude evidence if it would be unfair to admit it under section 78. The Royal Commission in 1981, in rejecting a proposal for mandatory exclusion of illegally obtained evidence on the US model, relied heavily on studies which did not show any conclusive evidence that the mandatory exclusionary rule actually improved the lot of most suspects.[453] It could only directly affect those suspects who are charged, tried, and plead not guilty, challenging the evidence against them. Others might benefit indirectly, but the preponderance of the research suggested that American police practices were not changed by the rule in a way which safeguarded rights. Instead, the police complied with the letter, but not the spirit, of the rules requiring suspects to be informed of their rights to remain silent and to have counsel: the information would be given in a way which minimized its impact on the suspect.[454] However, there is now some evidence that the exclusionary rule has a real deterrent effect on officers.[455] Even if it had none, it might be a useful, though not a comprehensive, protection for the rights of an accused.[456]

The Royal Commission also rejected a reverse onus exclusionary rule, under which there is a presumption that unlawfully obtained evidence is not to be admitted unless the prosecution is able to justify the unlawfulness by reference to considerations such as the urgency of the situation, the good faith of the officers, and the seriousness of the illegality. The reverse onus rule is broadly the one which operates in Scotland,[457] and was recommended by the Australian Law Reform Commission in 1975.[458] However, the practice in most common law jurisdictions has been to adopt a presumption of admissibility, subject to a discretion to exclude. In Canada, before the enactment of the Charter of Rights and Freedoms gave judges an instrument by which to exclude more unconstitutionally obtained evidence, the exclusionary discretion was very narrow: it arose only where the evidence was of little or no probative value.[459] In England, there was a discretion to exclude evidence where its admittance would be unfair, but this was rarely exercised, and had been narrowed down by the House of Lords to cases

---

[452] Brown, *Investigating Burglary*, 77–8.

[453] RCCP, *Report*, paras. 4.123–4.134.

[454] See, on the exclusionary rule, D. C. Oaks, 'Studying the Exclusionary Rule in Search and Seizure' (1970) 37 *Univ. of Chicago LR* 665. On *Miranda v. Arizona* (1966) 384 US 436, see L. Baker, *Miranda: Crime, Law and Politics* (New York: Atheneum, 1983).

[455] M. W. Oldfield, Jr., 'The Exclusionary Rule and Deterrence: An Empirical Study of Chicago Narcotics Officers' (1987) 54 *Univ. of Chicago LR* 1016–69.

[456] A. J. Ashworth, 'Excluding Evidence as Protecting Rights' [1977] Crim. LR 723–35.

[457] See, e.g. *Lawrie v. Muir*, 1950 JC 19; *McGovern v. HM Advocate*, 1950 JC 33; *Bell v. Hogg*, 1967 JC 49; *Hay v. HM Advocate*, 1968 JC 40.

[458] Report No. 2, *Criminal Investigation*, ch. 11.

[459] *R. v. Wray* (1970) 11 DLR (3d) 673, SC of Canada.

where the prejudicial weight of evidence excluded its probative value.[460] In Australia, a balancing-of-interests test prevailed, with the court deciding whether the illegality was so serious that it would be improper to allow the evidence to be used.[461]

The measured but active use which the English courts have made of sections 76 and 78 of PACE since 1976 has shown a surprising but welcome commitment to the idea of using evidential rules to protect rights. However, other remedies are needed for cases which never reach the stage of a contested trial. Disciplinary proceedings against officers do not give people any right to compensation. Legal proceedings are difficult and often unlikely to succeed. The Human Rights Act 1998 is unlikely to make a significant difference to police practice, because their conduct will usually be compatible with Convention rights as long as they follow the rules in PACE, the Codes of Practice, etc. Refusal of access to legal advice does not make the detention unlawful, so habeas corpus is not an appropriate remedy. The only tort which aggrieved suspects could use to obtain redress is misfeasance in a public office, but this requires proof of knowingly or recklessly acting unlawfully, which is not easily established.

6.7 INTERVIEWS AND THE RIGHT OF SILENCE

(1) THE RIGHT OF SILENCE AND THE PRIVILEGE AGAINST SELF-INCRIMINATION

(i) The privilege against self-incrimination and English law

It used to be possible to assert confidently, as a fundamental principle of the common law, that in a criminal prosecution the Crown must prove the guilt of the accused, and should not be in a position to force the accused to condemn himself. One could also confidently state that the right to refuse to answer questions, and the privilege against self-incrimination at trial, were basic elements in that principle. The European Court of Human Rights has taken a similar view, treating freedom from coerced self-incrimination as an aspect of the right to a fair hearing in the determination of criminal charges under Article 6(1) of the ECHR, and as implied in the right to be presumed innocent until proved guilty under Article 6(2). In a series of cases, it has held that it violates Article 6 to use against a person at trial for an offence statements made or information revealed under the threat of penal sanctions for remaining silent.[462] As the Court wrote in *Heaney and McGuinness v. Ireland*,[462a] although not expressly stated in Article 6,

---

[460] *R. v. Sang* [1980] AC 402, [1979] 2 All ER 1222, HL.

[461] *R. v. Ireland* (1970) 126 CLR 321, HC of Australia; *Bunning v. Cross* (1978) 141 CLR 54, HC of Australia.

[462] See, e.g. *Funke v. France*, Eur. Ct. HR, Series A, No. 256-A, Judgment of 25 February 1993, 16 EHRR 297 at para. 44 (bank statements); *Saunders v. United Kingdom*, Eur. Ct. HR, Judgment of 17 December 1996, RJD 1996-VI, 23 EHRR 313 (replies to DTI inspectors).

[462a] Eur. Ct. HR, App. No. 34720/97, Judgment of 21 December 2000, para. 40.

'the rights invoked by the applicants, the right to silence and the right not to incriminate oneself, are generally recognised international standards which lie at the heart of the notion of a fair procedure under Article 6. Their rationale lies, *inter alia*, in the protection of the accused against improper compulsion by the authorities, thereby contributing to the avoidance of miscarriages of justice and to the fulfilment of the aims of Article 6. The right not to incriminate oneself, in particular, presupposes that the prosecution in a criminal case seek to prove their case against the accused without resort to evidence obtained through methods of coercion or oppression in defiance of the will of the accused. In this sense the right in question is closely linked to the presumption of innocence contained in Article 6.2 of the Convention.

The right not to incriminate oneself is primarily concerned, however, with respecting the will of an accused person to remain silent. The Court would note, in this context, that the present case does not concern a request, through the use of compulsory powers, of material which had an existence independent of the will of the applicants, such as documents or blood samples (also the above-cited *Saunders* case, paragraph 69).'

Like *Funke*, the *Heaney and McGuinness* case 'concerned the threat and imposition of a criminal sanction on the applicants in question because they failed to supply information to the authorities investigating the alleged commission of criminal offences by them'.[462b] Although there were safeguards against *wrongful* confession, 'such protections could only be relevant to the present complaints if they could effectively and sufficiently reduce the degree of compulsion imposed by section 52 of the 1939 Act to the extent that the essence of the rights at issue would not be impaired by that domestic provision'. Not the case: there was a stark choice between giving the information and facing six months in prison.[462c] There was a risk of the information being used in evidence. The degree of compulsion, 'in effect, destroyed the very essence of the privilege against self-incrimination and their right to remain silent'.[462d] As in *Saunders* the requirements of fairness, including the right not to incriminate oneself, apply to all criminal proceedings, and 'the public interest could not be invoked to justify the use of answers compulsorily obtained in a non-judicial investigation to incriminate the accused during the trial proceedings'. The proportionality of an interference with the right could therefore not justify it.[462e] '[S]ecurity and public order concerns of the Government cannot justify a provision which extinguishes the very essence of the applicants' rights to silence and against self-incrimination guaranteed by Article 6.1 of the Convention'.[462f]

It was this principle which underlay the traditional police caution to a suspect in England and Wales until 1994 that he was not obliged to say anything, but that anything said would be recorded and might be used in evidence. However, a person's right to remain silent is now qualified by statute, and applies in full measure only when one is not suspected of an offence.[463] Even here, it is limited by statutes which impose positive obligations on people to disclose information for certain purposes,

---

[462b] Para. 49 of the judgment.
[462c] Ibid., para. 51.
[462d] Ibid., para. 55.
[462e] Ibid., para. 57.
[462f] Ibid., para. 58.
[463]   On the general principle, see *Rice v. Connolly* [1966] 2 QB 414, [1966] 2 All ER 649, DC.

such as regulating corporate and commercial activity or controlling dangerous undertakings.

The privilege originally consisted of a number of different elements:[463a]

(a) a privilege against being compelled to answer questions in legal proceedings, on pain of penalty or committal for contempt, which would tend to expose the witness to (i) an ecclesiastical penalty, particularly for adultery, (ii) a civil penalty, (iii) a civil forfeiture, or (iv) criminal prosecution;

(b) a privilege against being compelled to disclose documents which would tend to expose the person making them to a civil penalty, a civil forfeiture, or criminal liability. Although it has been pointed out in the USA that documents prepared before the compulsion was applied cannot be seen as coerced,[464] the general approach in the UK has been that, 'even if one can see that the reasons which caused the principle to be adopted provide no *logical* justification for such an immunity as the privilege against producing incriminating documents which came into existence before any dispute arose, that immunity holds sway';[465]

(c) a privilege against being compelled, on pain of penalty or committal for contempt, to answer questions posed pursuant to statutory powers which would tend to expose the person to a civil penalty, a civil forfeiture, or criminal liability.

These privileges may interfere with the administration of justice and the performance of statutory responsibilities by officials, because they deny access to sources of information which might be extremely important to a litigant, investigator, or regulator. They have the capacity to thwart significant public interests and the private rights of litigants and third parties.[466] For this reason, the privilege against self-incrimination has been cut down by judicial decision and by statute. As Lord Mustill pointed out in *R. v. Director of the Serious Fraud Office, ex parte Smith*:[467]

'Since the sixteenth century legislation has established an inquisitorial form of investigation into the dealings and assets of bankrupts which is calculated to yield potentially incriminating material, and in more recent times there have been many other examples, in widely separated fields, which are probably more numerous than is generally appreciated.'

[463a] On the history of privilege against self-incrimination, see R. M. Helmolz, Charles M. Gray, J. H. Langbein, E. Moglen, H. E. Smith, and A. W. Alschuler, *The Privilege against Self-Incrimination: Its Origins and Development* (Chicago: University of Chicago Press, 1997, *passim*.

[464] *United States v. Doe* (1984) 465 US 605.

[465] *A T & T Istel Ltd. v. Tully* [1993] AC 45 at 67 *per* Lord Lowry (italics in original).

[466] For penetrating analysis of the balance between these interests, see A. A. S. Zuckerman, 'The Right Against Self-Incrimination: An Obstacle to the Supervision of Interrogations' (1986) 102 LQR 43–70; A. A. S. Zuckerman, *The Principles of Criminal Evidence* (Oxford: Clarendon Press, 1989), ch. 15; A. T. H. Smith, 'The Right to Silence in Cases of Serious Fraud', in P. Birks (ed.), *Pressing Problems in the Law Volume 1: Criminal Justice & Human Rights* (Oxford: Oxford University Press, 1995), 75–88; Mirfield, *Silence, Confessions and Improperly Obtained Evidence*, ch. 2; Australian Law Reform Commission, Report No. 2, *Criminal Investigation*, ch. 5.

[467] [1993] AC 1, HL, at 40. On the privilege against self-incrimination and regulatory public-interest bodies, see also *R. v. Hertfordshire County Council, ex parte Green Environmental Industries Ltd.* [2000] 2 AC 412, HL.

The privilege against self-exposure to a finding of adultery fell into disuse once ecclesiastical courts ceased to be used to enforce morality.[468] When a defendant was made a competent but not compellable witness in criminal proceedings, the Criminal Evidence Act 1898, section 1(e) provided that a defendant who chose to give evidence could be asked questions tending to incriminate him in respect of the offence with which he was charged. Next, in England and Wales section 14(1) of the Civil Evidence Act 1968 removed the privilege against self-exposure to a civil forfeiture, but retained '[t]he right of a person in any legal proceedings other than criminal proceedings to refuse to answer any question or produce any document or thing if to do so would tend to expose that person to proceedings for an offence or for the recovery of a penalty'. This operates in respect of administrative, as well as judicial, decisions imposing penalties which could then be enforced by legal proceedings. So much was made clear in *Rio Tinto Zinc Corporation v. Westinghouse Electric Corporation*,[469] when the Court of Appeal decided, and the House of Lords accepted, that an increased risk[470] of exposure to a penalty for anti-competitive practices could justify a refusal to produce documents or answer questions, where that penalty would be imposed by a decision of the Commission of the European Communities acting in an administrative or regulatory capacity without the need for a prior judicial hearing to determine liability.

The rate of erosion of the privilege against self-incrimination in England and Wales increased as governments sought to enable the regulatory and criminal justice systems to deal more effectively with serious fraud, to combat corporate crime and misbehaviour in the financial markets, and to seize the proceeds of drug-related, terrorist-related, and other major crimes. The tendency to place crime control ahead of freedom from coercion was clear in the controversial recommendation of the Criminal Law Revision Committee in 1972 that courts and juries should be allowed to draw adverse inferences from a suspect's refusal to answer questions put by the police.[471] In 1981, the Royal Commission on Criminal Procedure recommended that suspects should not be compelled to answer questions, and that it should not generally be permissible at trial to draw inferences from silence adverse to an accused. The only exception which the Commission was prepared to contemplate was if the suspect had full information at all times about his rights, and about the evidence against him. Only then would it be proper to draw inferences from a refusal to answer questions. The government was not prepared to give suspects the right to know all the evidence against them, and accordingly PACE retained the suspect's common-law right to refuse to answer questions without suffering any disadvantage.

However, in 1988 the government launched a sustained assault on the right of

---

[468] *Blunt v. Park Lane Hotel Ltd.* [1942] 2 KB 253, CA.

[469] [1978] AC 547 at 606, [1978] 1 All ER 434, HL, affirming CA decisions reported [1978] AC at 558, 572, [1977] 3 All ER 703, 717.

[470] The risk need not originate in the disclosure itself. As the House of Lords held in the *Westinghouse* case, it is sufficient that an existing risk, founded on information already in the hands of an investigative or regulatory agency, would be increased by the disclosure of further information which would tend to confirm or strengthen the case against the person making it.

[471] Criminal Law Revision Committee, 11th Report, *Evidence (General)*, Cmnd. 4991 (London: HMSO, 1972).

silence, based on the view (advanced by the police) that innocent people have nothing to fear from telling the truth, so it should be permissible to draw adverse inferences from a refusal to answer questions. The law in Northern Ireland was changed to allow a trial court to draw such inferences as seem proper from a suspect's failure to mention a fact which he could reasonably have been expected to mention and on which he seeks to rely at trial, and further to treat the failure to mention the facts as being capable of amounting to corroboration of any evidence given against the suspect to which the fact is material.[472] The government announced its intention of introducing comparable legislation for England and Wales, and set up a working group to consider the matter. This group reported in 1989, recommending (unsurprisingly) the course for which the government had already expressed a preference.[473]

The report accepted police assertions that the right to silence, taken together with the statutory rights which suspects were given under PACE, tipped the balance too far in the suspect's favour. The working party was impressed by police evidence that the right of silence is widely invoked, particularly by experienced professional criminals, that those who exercise their right to legal advice are particularly likely to be advised to remain silent, and that this represents a major obstacle to the police in obtaining evidence and securing convictions. The report sparked a storm of protest from critics who attacked its wholesale acceptance of police assertions without adequate research. The critics argued that very few people actually refuse to answer questions,[474] that solicitors do not, in practice, adopt a blanket policy of advising clients not to answer questions, and that there is no evidence that silence often interferes with the ability of the prosecution to secure convictions.[475] Furthermore, the reasons for silence deserve

---

[472] Criminal Evidence (Northern Ireland) Order 1988.

[473] *Report of the Home Office Working Group on the Right of Silence* (London: Home Office, 1989). For a general critique of the report, see A. A. S. Zuckerman, 'Trial by Unfair Means: The Report of the Working Party on the Right to Silence' [1989] Crim. LR 855–65.

[474] For analysis of the figures found in various studies, see R. Leng, *The Right to Silence in Police Interrogation: A Study of Some of the Issues Underlying the Debate*, Royal Commission on Criminal Justice Research Study No. 10 (London: HMSO, 1993); S. Greer, 'Background to the Debate', in S. Greer and R. Morgan (eds.), *The Right to Silence Debate* (Bristol: Bristol Centre for Criminal Justice, 1990), 6–17; S. Greer, 'The Right to Silence: A Review of the Current Debate' (1990) 53 *MLR* 709–30; D. Dixon, 'Politics, Research and Symbolism in Criminal Justice: The Right of Silence and the Police and Criminal Evidence Act' (1991) 20 *Anglo-Amer. LR* 27–50; D. Dixon, 'Common Sense, Legal Advice and the Right of Silence' [1991] *PL* 233–54.

[475] See, in addition to the works cited in the previous note, J. Coldrey, 'The Right to Silence: Should it be Curtailed or Abolished?' (1991) 20 *Anglo-Amer. LR* 51–62. The figures produced by studies conducted by the police tend to suggest that a substantial proportion of people refuse to answer at least some questions for some period. However, the other studies suggest that very few detainees remain silent throughout an interview, and many solicitors and runners are mindful of their need to foster good relations with the police, with whom they come regularly in contact, and may encourage clients to talk: Dixon [1991] *PL* at 235–51. The evidence is that the increase in the proportion of people receiving legal advice is not equalled by the increased use of the right of silence: Brown, *Investigating Burglary*, 80–3. People who have legal advice are charged more often than others, suggesting that the police use other sources of information and do not rely on confessions in most cases: D. Brown, *Detention at the Police Station under the Police and Criminal Evidence Act 1984*, Home Office Research Study No. 104 (London: HMSO, 1989); A. Sanders *et al.*, *Advice and Assistance at Police Stations and the 24 Hour Duty Solicitor Scheme* (London: Lord Chancellor's Dept., 1989). Only where evidence is weak is the right to silence potentially decisive of the results of cases: S. Moston, G. Stephenson, and T. Williamson, 'Police Interrogation Styles and Suspect Behaviour' (unpublished, cited in Brown, *Investigating Burglary*, at 83).

careful analysis, as they are relevant to the circumstances in which it might be appropriate to draw inferences from silence, and the nature of those inferences. In particular, the critics pointed out that people in police stations are under stress, they probably do not know the full details of the case against them, have not had time to give careful thought to what happened, and are likely to be disorientated. Under such circumstances, it is often sensible to say nothing, as there is a real risk that anything which the suspect said in the heat of the moment might turn out to be innocently mistaken, with unjustifiably prejudicial consequences.

In assessing what adverse inferences, if any, it is proper to draw from a suspect's silence, it is important to look at the context in which the refusal to answer questions arose. Did the suspect know what case he was being required to answer? Were there factors, such as lack of access to legal advice or to an appropriate adult, which made it hard for the suspect to understand what was being alleged against him? Were the police exerting unfair pressure? All these matters affect the meaning which can properly be attributed to silence. Yet the Working Party advocated looking only at the explanation offered by the defendant for refusing to answer, rather than at the context as a whole.[476]

The matter was temporarily removed from the political forum when the Royal Commission on Criminal Justice was established to examine that and other aspects of the criminal process. In 1993, the recommendations of the majority of the Royal Commission broadly followed those of the Royal Commission on Criminal Procedure twelve years earlier: the risks of erroneous convictions and of unfair pressure being put on suspects in police custody persuaded them that the privilege against self-incrimination should remain, unless and until the prosecution case has been fully disclosed to the defence.[477] It was possible to write, 'The threat to restrict the right of silence has been repelled, temporarily at least, in mainland Britain'.[478] However, even this qualified degree of confidence proved to be misplaced. Parliament, dismissing the concerns of two Royal Commissions, passed sections 34 to 38 of the Criminal Justice and Public Order Act 1994, significantly restricting the right of silence in criminal proceedings. These provisions are examined in section (ii), below.

Before doing so, it will be useful to set out the limitations on the privilege against self-incrimination as it existed before the 1994 Act and continues to operate where the 1994 Act does not apply. First, it is essentially an evidential privilege. It does not prevent public authorities compelling people to provide information (as long as the method of compulsion is not unlawful under national law or the ECHR). It only prevents any information provided under compulsion from being used in proceedings against the person providing it. Secondly, it follows that it allows people to refuse to answer questions outside criminal proceedings only if proceedings are reasonably likely to be pursued against them. The degree to which a person must be put at risk in order to assert the privilege successfully was established in *R. v. Boyes*:[479]

---

[476] Zuckerman, 'Trial by Unfair Means' [1989] Crim. LR 855–65.

[477] Royal Commission on Criminal Justice, *Report*, 54–5.

[478] See the first edition of this book at 267.

[479] (1861) 1 B. & S. 311 at 330 *per* Cockburn CJ, delivering the judgment of the court on this point. The formulation was approved by the Court of Appeal in *Re Reynolds, ex parte Reynolds* (1882) 20 Ch. D 294

'... the Court must see, from the circumstances of the case and the nature of the evidence which the witness is called to give, that there is reasonable ground to apprehend danger [of penalty] to the witness from being compelled to answer ... [A] judge is in our opinion, bound to insist on a witness answering unless he is satisfied that the answer will tend to place the witness in peril. Further than that, we are of opinion that the danger to be apprehended must be real and appreciable, with reference to the ordinary operation of law in the ordinary course of things—not a danger of an imaginary and unsubstantial character, having reference to some extraordinary and barely possible contingency that no reasonable man would suffer it to influence his conduct.'

The Court went on to decide that a risk that the House of Commons would impeach the witness, after the King had granted a full pardon under the Great Seal for any offence, was in 1861 'simply ridiculous'. Such a 'remote and naked possibility . . . should not be suffered to obstruct the administration of justice'.[480]

Thirdly, the privilege is available to corporations as well as individuals, but an individual acting as an officer of a company can be compelled to reveal information on behalf of the company even if it incriminates him as an individual.[481]

(ii) Adverse inferences from silence under the Criminal Justice and Public Order Act 1994

The 1994 Act and subsequent legislation changed the position of those suspected of or charged with criminal offences in two ways. First, the absolute nature of the right to remain silent in the face of police questioning was restricted by allowing a court or jury at a subsequent trial to draw adverse inferences from silence in certain circumstances. Secondly, defendants at trial were put under pressure to give evidence, with adverse inferences being permitted in some circumstances if a defendant refused to give evidence.

(a) **Silence under police questioning.** Section 34 of the 1994 Act permits a magistrates' court, judge, other court or jury to 'draw such inferences . . . as seem proper' from the failure of a suspect, in certain circumstances, 'to mention any fact relied on in his defence in those proceedings'. The circumstances in which inferences may be drawn are:

- before being charged, the suspect is being questioned having been cautioned as required by Code of Practice C by a constable (or other person charged with the duty of investigating offences or charging offenders) who is trying to discover whether or by whom an offence had been been committed; or

---

Triplex Safety Glass Co. v. Lancegaye Safety Glass (1934) Ltd. [1939] 2 KB 395, and *Blunt v. Park Lane Hotel Ltd.* [1942] 2 KB 253 at 257 *per* Goddard LJ, and by the House of Lords in *Rio Tinto Zinc Corporation v. Westinghouse Electric Corporation* [1978] AC 547.

[480] (1861) 1 B. & S. at 330–331.

[481] *Klein v. Bell* [1955] SCR 309, SC of Canada, at 316–17 *per* Kerwin CJ (delivering the judgment of himself and Taschereau, Estey, and Fauteux JJ), 320–1 *per* Rand J. On the application of the privilege to corporations, see G. McCormack, 'Self-Incrimination in the Corporate Context' [1993] *JBL* 425–43; D. Feldman, 'Corporate Rights and the Privilege against Self-Incrimination', in D. Feldman and F. Meisel (eds.), *Corporate and Commercial Law: Modern Developments* (London: LLP Ltd., 1996), 361–93.

- the suspect is being charged with the offence, or officially informed that he might be prosecuted for it.[482]

Under section 36 of the Act, 'such inferences . . . as appear proper' may also be drawn from a person's refusal or failure on his arrest to account for the presence of any object, or any substance or mark in or on his clothing, footwear, object in his possession or in the place where he is arrested. Such an inference may be drawn only if:

- a constable investigating an offence reasonably believed that the presence of the object, etc. may be attributable to the suspect's participation in the commission of that offence;
- the constable told the suspect of this, specifying the offence, and asked him to account for the presence of the object, etc.; and
- the constable explained to the suspect, in ordinary language, the effect of the provisions in the event of a refusal or failure to account for the presence of the object, etc.[483]

Finally, section 37 of the 1994 Act permits 'such inferences . . . as appear proper' to be drawn from a person's refusal or failure, on his arrest, to account for his presence in a place at or about the time when the offence for which he has been arrested is alleged to have been committed. The circumstances in which such inferences may be drawn are:

- a constable found the suspect at that place at or about the time of the alleged offence (so it does not apply when a witness who is not a constable claims to have found the suspect there);
- a constable investigating the offence reasonably believes that the suspect's presence there may be attributable to the suspect's participation in the commission of that offence; and
- the constable tells the suspect of this, specifying the offence, and asks him to account for his presence there; and
- the constable explains to the suspect, in ordinary language, the effect of the provisions in the event of a refusal or failure to account for his presence there.[484]

Despite the concerns of the Royal Commission on Criminal Justice and other commentators, noted above, that safeguards would be needed to ensure that inferences were drawn only from meaningful refusals to answer, the Act contains few procedural safeguards for suspects. The sections do not require that the police should have told the suspect of the case against him.

Originally, it did not even take account of the suspect's access to legal advice. The legislation was amended after the European Court of Human Rights held by a

---

[482] Criminal Justice and Public Order Act 1994, s. 34(1), (2), (4).
[483] Ibid., s. 36(1), (2), (4).
[484] Ibid., s. 37(1), (2), (3).

majority of fourteen to seven in *John Murray v. United Kingdom*,[485] a case arising out of the equivalent Northern Ireland legislation, that it was unfair to draw adverse inferences at trial from a refusal to answer questions or give explanations during an extended interview at a police station at which the suspect had been denied access to legal advice. Neither the drawing of inferences from silence nor the denial of access to legal advice in themselves violated Article 6(1) taken together with Article 6(3). It was drawing adverse inferences from refusal to answer questions without access to legal advice, at a stage in the inquiry when (because of the legislation) that might irretrievably prejudice the defence, that was unfair. In the light of this, sections 34, 36, and 37 have been amended to provide that, where the investigator requested the explanation at an authorized place of detention (rather than on the street, for example), a refusal to answer cannot give rise to adverse inferences under the Act if the suspect had not been allowed an opportunity to consult a solicitor before the request was made.[486] None the less, the absence of the safeguards recommended by the Royal Commission on Criminal Justice is bound to increase the risk of dangerous convictions.[487] The European Court of Human Rights has decided that the risk is particularly significant when juries, rather than judges, are allowed to draw inferences, because juries are not allowed to explain the weight given to particular items of evidence; it violated the right to a fair hearing under Article 6(1) when the Court of Appeal, having decided that a trial judge had given an incorrect direction to the jury on the drawing of inferences, upheld the conviction on the ground that it was not unsafe.[488]

A refusal to answer cannot be admissible if the answer itself would not have been admissible by reason of any statutory provision or rule of law, and the court in any case can refuse to allow evidence of a refusal to answer to be led if in the circumstances the refusal would be unreliable or relying on it would be unfair.[489] Apart from this, the statute is silent on the inferences which can properly be drawn from a refusal to mention matters later relied on. The courts have fleshed out the notion of a proper inference to some extent. The matter in question must be something the defendant actually relies on in his defence. It must be something which it would have been reasonable to mention, in the circumstances.[490] When assessing the reasonableness of not mentioning something, one should take into account any advice given to the suspect by a legal adviser, if one is present: if a solicitor is present throughout an interview and advises suspects not to answer questions, it can be unfair to draw adverse inferences from a failure to answer, unless the jury is told that if it was satisfied that the applicants' silence at the police interview could not sensibly be attributed to

---

[485] Eur. Ct. HR, Judgment of 8 February 1996, RJD 1996-I, 22 EHRR 29.

[486] Criminal Justice and Public Order Act 1994, ss. 34(2A), 36(4A), 37(3A), inserted by the Youth Justice and Criminal Evidence Act 1999, s. 58.

[487] See H. Fenwick, *Civil Rights: New Labour, Freedom and the Human Rights Act* (London: Longman, 2000), 261–9.

[488] See *R. v. Condron (William)* [1997] 1 WLR 827, CA; *Condron v. United Kingdom*, Eur Ct. HR, Judgment of 2 May 2000 at paras. 63–66.

[489] Criminal Justice and Public Order Act 1994, s. 38(5), (6).

[490] *R. v. Argent* [1997] 2 Cr. App. R. 27, CA, where the Court of Appeal catalogued the considerations relevant when deciding whether any inference (and if so what inference) should be drawn.

their having no answer or none that would stand up to cross-examination it should not draw the adverse inference.[491] If the prosecution suggests that the failure to mention at an interview a line of defence, such as an explanation for possession of an apparently incriminating item, indicates that the defence was subsequently fabricated, the court should be prepared to hear evidence about conversations between the defendant and his solicitor which took place before the interview, if the defendant wishes to offer it.[492]

Where a judge instructs a jury incorrectly that they may draw an inference under section 34, the Court of Appeal has none the less upheld the conviction if not persuaded that the verdict might have been different had the judge given a correct direction.[493] The European Court of Human Rights has held that this denies the defendant a fair trial, as a jury's verdict is not sufficiently transparent to enable a court to speculate fairly about what the jury might have decided in other circumstances. If national courts interpret Article 6 in the same way (and under section 2 of the Human Rights Act 1998 they must take the caselaw of the Strasbourg institutions into account), they would have to modify this aspect of their approach, holding that more verdicts are unsafe than they did before the 1998 Act came into force.

(b) **Adverse inferences from refusal to testify.** Section 35 of the Criminal Justice and Public Order Act 1994 allows a court or jury to draw such inferences as appear proper from the refusal of a defendant to give evidence in his own defence, or from a refusal to answer any question while giving evidence. This applies where the defendant is fit to testify[494] and his guilt remains in issue at the close of the prosecution's case, and the court has satisfied itself (in the presence of the jury if it is a trial on indictment) that the defendant understands that he is now allowed to give evidence, and that a failure to do so, or failure without good cause to answer a question while doing so, will make it permissible for any proper inferences to be drawn. The effect of these provisions is that the court must ask the defendant or his legal representative whether or not the defendant will be giving evidence, and warn him of the possible consequences of not doing so, in front of the jury, unless the representative informs the court that the defendant will give evidence. The process by which the court 'satisfies itself' could be highly prejudicial to the defendant, to the point where it risks making the trial unfair by appearing to bring the judge into the arena.[495] The judges have reduced this risk, in cases where the defendant is represented, by asking the representative (rather than the

---

[491] See *R. v. Condron* [1997] 1 WLR 827, CA; *R. v. Daniel* [1998] 2 Cr. App. R. 373, CA; *Condron v. United Kingdom*, Eur Ct. HR, Judgment of 2 May 2000 at paras. 61, 62.

[492] *R. v. Daniel* [1998] 2 Cr. App. R. 373, CA.

[493] *R. v. Condron* [1997] 1 WLR 827, CA; *R. v. Daniel* [1998] 2 Cr. App. R. 373, CA.

[494] Fitness takes account of mental capability. Where a defendant has a mental age below that of criminal responsibility, or is abnormally suggestible, it may make it undesirable for him to give evidence, but will not necessarily do so. An assessment must be made in each individual case: *R. v. Friend* [1997] 1 WLR 1433, [1997] 2 All ER 1011, CA.

[495] The position does not compromise the judge's appearance of impartiality as much as the equivalent provisions in the Northern Ireland (Evidence) Order 1998, art. 4(2), which requires the judge himself to call the defendant to the witness box. On the potentially farcical implications, see *R. v. Bingham* [1999] 1 WLR 598, HL (on appeal from the Northern Ireland Court of Appeal).

defendant personally) whether the defendant has been advised of the matters set out in section 35.[496]

The courts have accordingly done what they can to restrict the scope of this provision. Magistrates must bear in mind, and judges must tell juries when directing them, that it will often not be proper to draw adverse inferences from a refusal to give evidence. It is proper to draw adverse inferences only the trier of fact decides that the prosecution had established a *prima facie* case, i.e. a case fit to be left to the jury, before the decision of the defendant not to testify. The jury must also be told that the burden to prove guilt lies on the prosecution, and that the defendant was entitled to refuse to testify.[497] Even when inferences are permissible, there are limits to the inferences which would be proper. A finding of guilt cannot be based solely on failure to give evidence: the prosecution case must be fit to leave to the jury, and the jury should draw an adverse inference only if they 'conclude the silence can only sensibly be attributed to the defendant's having no answer or none that would stand up to cross-examination'.[498] But the inference need not be related to the reliability of specific pieces of prosecution evidence. Failing to explain apparently damning evidence forming part of a *prima facie* case may lead to the inference that there is no innocent explanation, and that the defendant is therefore guilty, not merely that specific facts are proved.[499]

(iii) Statutory powers to compel people to provide information or evidence

Statutes have whittled away the privilege against self-incrimination by imposing duties to provide information to investigators in relation to certain complex or particularly serious investigations. For example, under the Official Secrets Act 1920, section 6, an inspector or superintendent, on the authorization of the chief constable and usually with the permission of the Secretary of State, may require a person believed, on reasonable grounds, to have information about an espionage offence, to give any information in his power. Other duties relate to disclosing suspicions or information relating to drug-related or terrorism-related money laundering.

Those provisions do not normally infringe the privilege against self-incrimination. Some provisions aimed at complex frauds go further. The Director of the Serious Fraud Office has power to insist on anyone whom he has reason to believe has relevant information providing it, answering questions, and producing specified documents unless they are subject to legal professional privilege, on pain of imprisonment.[500] The House of Lords has treated the powers of the Serious Fraud Office as defeating the privilege even after the suspect has been charged, and has also limited the scope of the privilege in civil proceedings so that it is not available where the prosecuting authorities state unequivocally that information revealed in the civil

---

[496] *Practice Note* [1995] 1 WLR 657, [1995] 2 All ER 499.

[497] *Murray v. DPP* [1994] 1 WLR 1, HL, at 4 *per* Lord Mustill; *R. v. Cowan* [1996] QB 373, [1995] 4 All ER 939, CA.

[498] Ibid. at 945 *per* Lord Taylor of Gosforth CJ.

[499] *Murray v. DPP* [1994] 1 WLR 1 at 11–12 *per* Lord Slynn, with whom Lords Templeman, Oliver of Aylmerton, and Jauncey of Tulliechettle agreed.

[500] Criminal Justice Act 1987, s. 2.

proceedings will not be used in criminal proceedings against the person providing it.[501] Department of Trade inspectors, and liquidators, also have powers to demand information, and these powers have been held to override the privilege against self-incrimination,[502] and, *a fortiori*, the right to refuse to answer other, non-incriminating, questions.

These powers interact in strange ways. Information provided under coercion to the Serious Fraud Office cannot generally be used as evidence against the person providing it.[503] There was originally no restriction on the power to use information provided to DTI inspectors under the Companies Act 1985, those of the Bank of England under the Banking Act 1987, or those arising under the Insolvency Act 1986. The Serious Fraud Office could use its powers to obtain from the DTI statements made to its inspectors under the Companies Act 1985.[504] When authorities shared information in this way, it evaded the protection of both the common law and statute for the privilege against self-incrimination. The statements could be used in evidence in a prosecution against the person making them. This was held in English courts not to make the trial unfair. However, in *Saunders v. United Kingdom*[505] the European Court of Human Rights held that coercing someone to make a self-incriminating statement and then using it against them made the trial unfair, violating Article 6 of the ECHR. As a result, statutory powers to coerce information have been amended to prevent statements made in the course of a regulatory investigation being used in criminal proceedings against the person who made them.[506]

While the government and Parliament have taken seriously the privilege against self-incrimination as interpreted by the European Court of Human Rights in *Funke* and *Saunders*, British courts have been far less ready to give substance to the right. After the *Saunders* decision but before the Human Rights Act 1998 and the statutory amendments to the law on the use of coerced statements, the Court of Appeal refused to quash

---

[501] *Smith v. Director of Serious Fraud Office* [1992] 3 All ER 456, HL; *AT&T Istel Ltd. v. Tully* [1992] 3 All ER 523, HL. It is not clear how a suspect is to be protected against the use of the information in a private prosecution.

[502] *Ex parte Nadir, The Times*, 5 November 1990, DC (powers of SFO under the Criminal Justice Act 1987, s. 2); *Re London United Investments plc* [1992] 2 All ER 842, CA (powers of DTI inspectors appointed under Companies Act 1985, s. 432); *Bishopsgate Investment Management Ltd. (in provisional liquidation) v. Maxwell* [1992] 2 All ER 856, CA (powers of provisional liquidators under Insolvency Act 1986, ss. 235 and 236).

[503] Criminal Justice Act 1987, s. 2(8).

[504] See *In re Arrows (No. 4)* [1995] 2 AC 75, [1994] 3 All ER 814, HL.

[505] Eur. Ct. HR (1996) 23 EHRR 313.

[506] The Youth Justice and Criminal Evidence Act 1999, s. 59 and Sch. 3 amends Insurance Companies Act 1982, ss. 43A (general investigations into insurance companies) and 44 (obtaining information and documents from companies), Companies Act 1985, ss. 434 (production of documents and evidence to inspectors) and 447 (production of company documents to Secretary of State), Insolvency Act 1986, s. 433 (admissibility in evidence of statements of affairs by debtors), Company Directors Disqualification Act 1986, s. 20 (admissibility in evidence of directors' statements), Building Societies Act 1986, ss. 105 (Secretary of State's powers to investigate affairs of person carrying on building society business) and 177 (investigations into insider dealing), Banking Act 1987, ss. 39 (power of Financial Services Authority to obtain information), 41 (investigations into authorized institutions by FSA), and 42 (investigations by FSA into suspected contraventions), Criminal Justice Act 1987, s. 2 (use of statements made in response to requirements imposed by Director of the Serious Fraud Office), and Friendly Societies Act 1992, s. 67 (inspections carried out on behalf of the Friendly Societies Commission), as well as legislation relating to Northern Ireland and Scotland.

the conviction of a defendant who had been convicted on the basis of self-incriminating statements obtained in a similar way to those in *Saunders*. The Court of Appeal held that the provision used in that case, section 177(6) of the Financial Services Act 1986, amounted to a statutory presumption that admitting the coerced answers would not be unfair, notwithstanding the decisions of the European Court of Human Rights.

Some judges seem equally inhibited now they can deal with Convention rights directly. In a Scottish devolution case, *Brown v. Stott*,[507] the Privy Council, reversing a decision of the High Court of Justiciary, held that a trial of a person for drunken driving using as evidence a self-incriminating statement made by the defendant under a requirement imposed under section 172 of the Road Traffic Act 1988, was not necessarily unfair and so did not violate Article 6. Section 172(2) applies where the police allege that the driver of a vehicle has been guilty of a significantly serious moving traffic offence, including drunken driving, but do not know who the driver was. It allows someone acting on behalf of the chief officer of police to require the keeper of the vehicle to give 'such information as to the identity of the driver as he may be required to give', and any other person 'to give any information which it is in his power to give and may lead to the identification of the driver'. If (as is often the case) the keeper was the driver, this engages the privilege against self-incrimination. Failure to provide the information is an offence punishable by a licence endorsement, with a discretion to impose a fine of up to £1,000 and a period of disqualification. The Privy Council was concerned solely with the question whether the use of self-incriminating information provided by the keeper in response to the requirement at a trial of that person would violate the right to a fair hearing under Article 6(1) and (2) of the ECHR. Nothing in section 172 expressly permits a self-incriminating reply to be admitted in evidence. The case arose under the Scotland Act 1998 at a time when the Human Rights Act 1998 was not in force, so the court could not have used section 3 of the Human Rights Act to interpret section 172 of the 1988 Act in a manner compatible with Convention rights. But the significant feature is the way in which the Privy Council approached the interpretation of the right to a fair trial.

The Privy Council stressed the absolute nature of the right to a fair hearing under Article 6, but noted that the requirements of fairness vary according to circumstances. Individual elements in Article 6 could be restricted, for legitimate purposes in response to a pressing social need, as long as the restriction was proportionate and the trial remains fair overall. Noting that the privilege against self-incrimination was implied into Article 6 rather than being expressly included in it, their Lordships said that implied rights were more open to restriction than elements expressed in Article 6. A number of grounds were given for allowing a restriction of the privilege against self-incrimination in relation to section 172. There was a legitimate and pressing need to regulate driving, which was a privilege, not a right, and is a dangerous activity causing large numbers of deaths and injuries every year. The restriction of the privilege against self-incrimination was not disproportionate, because it does not authorize long-drawn-out or intrusive questioning, improper compulsion, or physically inva-

---

[507] [2001] 2 WLR 817, PC. See R. Pillay, 'Self-incrimination and Article 6: the Decision of the Privy Council in *Procurator Fiscal v. Brown*' [2001] *EHRLR* 75–84.

sive procedures, and is narrowly circumscribed, while the penalty for someone who refuses to provide the information or who provides false information is moderate and non-custodial. Admitting the statement obtained under compulsion would therefore not violate Article 6.

This decision is understandable on pragmatic grounds. Section 172 is undoubtedly a useful weapon in the important fight against criminally dangerous or careless driving. A decision that it was incompatible with Article 6 would have triggered a public reaction which could have undermined respect for the whole idea of human rights in domestic law, as the press response to the decision of the High Court of Justiciary had demonstrated. The Privy Council's approach even had the support of a written argument submitted by JUSTICE, the respected human rights organization. However, aspects of it give rise to concern.

First, the European Court of Human Rights held that it is unfair to convict someone on the basis of a statement which they were compelled to make on pain of a penalty. The Privy Council held that it is not unfair to convict someone on the basis of a statement which they were compelled to make on pain of a penalty, if the penalty for not making the statement would not be too heavy, and the offence is serious, and the requirement to provide information did not authorize improper coercion, and the activity needs to be regulated, and so on. There is no basis for such an approach to the privilege against self-incrimination in the Court's caselaw. The examples which the Privy Council gave relate to evidential presumptions, which can be legitimate and are open to being disproved. Section 172 does not impose extra burdens, perhaps reasonably, on a defendant: it effectively closes off all lines of defence, and relieves the prosecution of the responsibility to prove its case. The privilege is abrogated, not limited. It is a basic principle of Convention law that an interference which takes away the very substance of the right cannot be justified. The Privy Council gave this factor no consideration.

Secondly, the Strasbourg authorities for a relativistic approach all relate to the extent to which a restriction of a right, for example to disclosure of prosecution evidence or the right to see one's accusers, can be compensated by other measures taken by the trial court to secure a fair trial. Once it is accepted that the privilege against self-incrimination is an essential part of a fair trial, it should be abridged, if at all, only if the trial court takes steps to ensure that the trial is fair notwithstanding the violation of the privilege. For example, one might decide to take account of the statement only if there is already at least a *prima facie* case against the defendant from other sources: the strength of other evidence is an important factor in deciding whether the trial could be fair notwithstanding the admission of evidence which is presumptively unfair. However, in the balancing exercise which the Privy Council undertook there is no hint of any attention being paid to that side of the balance.

Thirdly, their Lordships made use of the idea of deference to the judgment of a democratic and representative legislature in deciding what was needed in the Road Traffic Act 1988. There was no evidence that the government or the legislature had considered the implications of the privilege against self-incrimination in relation to section 172. In the absence of such evidence, it is hard to see why courts should defer to government or Parliament in relation to the striking of a balance of the need for

which neither the government nor Parliament appeared to have been conscious. As Lord Steyn said, 'national courts may accord to the decisions of national legislatures some deference *where the context justifies it*'.[508] The context cannot justify deferring to a judgment where there is no evidence that the legislature ever addressed its collective mind to the issue before the court.

Now that the government and Parliament have shown that they take the privilege against self-incrimination seriously as an aspect of Article 6 in response to decisions of the European Court of Human Rights, it is time for the judges to do the same. It is to be hoped that subsequent decisions on the subject will be governed by a stronger concern for principle. If they are not, we could see an interesting exchange developing between national courts and the Strasbourg court.

(2) THE REGULATION OF POLICE INTERVIEWS

PACE and the Code of Practice give certain rights to suspects being held at police stations in relation to the circumstances in which interviews may take place. The Code applies to constables, and to those charged with the duty of investigating crime. It does not apply to the officers of regulatory bodies such as the Bank of England in relation to banking and inspectors appointed by the Department for Trade and Industry in relation to the regulation of companies. Their main role is regulatory, ensuring that the rules protecting the interests of depositors and investors are complied with. It follows that they need not caution people before exercising powers, for example to require them to provide information, even if the suspected breach of regulatory rules is also a serious criminal offence, such as false accounting or fraudulent trading.[509] The same applies, *a fortiori*, to a psychiatrist's therapeutic or diagnostic conversation with a patient. If the patient is so unwise (or unbalanced) as to reveal a carefully formulated plan to kill his stepfather with an airgun, neither PACE nor the Code of Practice prevents the psychiatrist from giving evidence against the patient on a charge of making a threat to kill.[510]

The rights of suspects, where they operate, are as follows.

(i) The caution before being interviewed

If an officer has reasonable grounds for suspecting that a person has committed any offence, he must caution him before any questions[511] are put to him for the purpose of obtaining evidence for possible court proceedings. No caution is needed where merely routine questions are being asked to establish such matters as someone's ownership of a vehicle, or in searching him under stop and search powers,[512] or when a customs officer is asking standard questions of travellers without any particular ground to

---

[508] [2001] 2 WLR at 842 (italics in original).
[509] *R. v. Smith (Wallace)* [1994] 1 WLR 1396, CA (further proceedings, [1996] 2 Cr. App. R. 1, CA) (Bank of England officials); *R. v. Seelig* (1990) 92 Cr. App. R. 106, CA (DTI inspectors).
[510] *R. v. Kennedy* [1999] 1 Cr. App. R. 54, CA. The psychiatrist's obligations of confidentiality under the common law, Art. 8 of the ECHR or any applicable code of medical ethics, were not considered.
[511] A single question may bring the right into play: *R. v. Ward* (1993) 98 Cr. App. R. 337, CA.
[512] Code C, para. 10.1.

suspect them of an offence.[513] If the suspect is not under arrest at the time, he must be so informed and told that he is not obliged to remain with the officer.[514] If the arrest takes place at a police station, the suspect must also be told of his right to legal advice.[515] A caution must be given on arrest, unless the suspect's condition or behaviour makes this impracticable or he has been cautioned immediately before, when reasonable grounds for suspicion first came to light.[516] A caution must also be given each time questioning resumes after a break, unless there is no doubt that the suspect is aware that the caution still applies.[517] The caution should be in the form:

'You do not have to say anything. But it may harm your defence if you do not mention when questioned something which you later rely on in court. Anything you do say may be given in evidence.'

The complexity of this caution is dictated by the qualification of the right of silence, already discussed. Minor deviations are permitted, but the sense must be preserved. The officer may go on to explain the meaning of the caution and its implications if required.[518] Where a juvenile or mentally disordered or mentally handicapped person is cautioned in the absence of an appropriate adult, the caution must be repeated in the presence of the appropriate adult.

Nevertheless, a suspect in a police station is under severe stress. The balance of power is always in favour of the police, on whose territory the suspect and his legal adviser or appropriate adult are.[519] What safeguards are provided to ensure that the interview process itself is fair to him, and is likely to produce reliable results?

(ii) What counts as an interview?

Before the revision to the Codes of Practice, there was some disagreement on this point between different judges. The latest edition of Code C, paragraph 11.1A describes an interview in a somewhat circular way as:

'the questioning[520] of a person regarding his involvement or suspected involvement in a criminal offence or offences which, by virtue of paragraph 10.1 of Code C, is required to be carried out under caution. Procedures under section 7 of the Road Traffic Act 1988 do not constitute interviewing for the purpose of this code.'

In other words, a person must be cautioned before an interview, and an interview is an exchange before which a person must be cautioned. Paragraph 10.1 helps somewhat. It requires a caution to be given before a person who is suspected of an offence is questioned about it:

---

[513] *R. v. Shah* [1994] Crim. LR 125, CA; *R. v. Nelson* [1998] 2 Cr. App. R. 399, CA. A caution is required once suspicions are aroused and the questions are geared to obtaining evidence about an offence: *R. v. Weedersteyn* (1993) 96 Cr. App. R. 464, CA.

[514] Code C, para. 10.2.

[515] Code C, para. 3.15.

[516] Code C, para. 10.3.

[517] Code C, para. 10.5. See *R. v. Manji* [1990] Crim. LR 512, CA; *R. v. Sparks* [1991] Crim. LR 128, CA.

[518] Code C, para. 10.4 and Notes for Guidance 10C, 10D.

[519] Dixon [1991] *PL* at 239.

[520] A single question can amount to an interview: *R. v. Ward* (1993) 98 Cr. App. R. 337, CA.

'If his answers or silence ... may be given in evidence to a court in a prosecution. He therefore need not be cautioned if questions are put for other purposes, for example, solely to establish his identity or his ownership of any vehicle or to obtain information in accordance with any relevant statutory requirement ... or in furtherance of the proper and effective conduct of a search ... or to seek verification of a written record ...'

The early part of this definition is unexceptionable, but the final sentence may underestimate the extent to which the police ask questions in the course of searches which are designed to confirm suspicions, rather than merely seek information. There is also a risk of encouraging the police to play down their suspicion in order to evade the safeguards for the suspect. If a court decides that the police have behaved in a dishonourable way, it is likely to exclude the evidence of any admission which the suspect makes as a result.[521]

It was held in *R. v. Christou*[522] that the protections for interviewees outside police stations come into play only if the suspect knows that the interviewer is a police officer, and is therefore likely to feel the psychological effects of being subject to the legal power of the officer. If the officer is working under cover, masquerading as a criminal, there is no such perceived inequality of power. The result is sensible: to require the interview procedures to be followed in such circumstances would defeat the purpose of much undercover work; but the reasoning offers a potentially easy way for the police to evade the requirements of the Code of Practice. This was noted in *R. v. Bryce*,[523] where the Court of Appeal discouraged it pragmatically by excluding the statements so obtained. This produces satisfying effects which are, however, hard to reconcile on principled grounds. On the other hand, merely setting up an opportunity for criminals to reveal themselves is not unfair. It may put temptation in people's way, for example to fill a van with apparently valuable cartons of cigarettes and park it, unattended and insecure, on a busy street. Someone who tries to steal the cigarettes does it of his own volition, without being incited, induced, or provoked into committing the offence.[524] It is no more unfair than putting attractive goods on display in a department store and deploying store detectives and CCTV cameras to keep watch for shoplifters.

None the less, the approach of the court in *Christou* may facilitate entrapment of suspects by the police. Take, for example, a case in which officers, having received information that a person intended to kill someone, posed as contract killers. In *R. v. Smurthwate*[525] the Court of Appeal accepted that it was not unfair to admit evidence of the conversation which then took place. Although the method of investigation had allowed the police to extract what amounted to an admission from the suspect without the safeguards of the Code of Practice, it was justified because the offence was serious, and they had not instigated it, but had acted on information that the offence was already being planned. The European Court of Human Rights adopted a rather

---

[521] *R. v. Neil* [1994] Crim. LR 441, CA. See also *R. v. Weedersteyn* (1993) 96 Cr. App. R. 464, CA.
[522] [1992] 4 All ER 559, CA.
[523] [1992] 4 All ER 567, CA.
[524] *Williams (Gary) v. DPP* [1993] 3 All ER 365, DC.
[525] [1994] 1 All ER 898, CA.

similar approach in *Schenk v. Switzerland*,[526] where covert police methods had been used against a suspected drug dealer. There had been good information that the suspect had a propensity to indulge in drug dealing, a serious offence, so it had not been unfair to admit the evidence against him.[527] A later case, *Teixeira de Castro v. Portugal*,[528] went the other way. Undercover police officers had approached someone who had no known propensity for drug dealing, and asked him to supply them with heroin. He agreed, and was duly convicted. The European Court of Human Rights held that he had not had a fair trial. The Court set out two tests for the fairness of a trial using evidence from entrapment. First, if officers instigate an offence, and there is no evidence that it would have been committed without their instigation, the evidence will have been unfairly obtained. Secondly, the use of the evidence of the *agent provocateur* in those circumstances makes the trial unfair.

The Court of Appeal attempted to reconcile these cases in *R. v. Shannon*.[529] A *News of the World* journalist had posed as an Arab sheikh wanting to buy drugs. He had approached the defendant, who (it was alleged) had agreed to obtain drugs and supply them without (it was said) the journalist having actively persuaded him to do so. The evidence was passed to the police and the defendant was convicted. On appeal, the Court of Appeal decided that admitting evidence of *agents provocateurs* would make a trial unfair, violating Article 6.1, only if (a) the *agents provocateurs* in that case were police officers, and (b) the officers had actively instigated or incited the offence. The evidence had therefore been rightly admitted.[530] But the line is not easy to draw. In *Nottingham City Council v. Amin*,[531] two people hailed a taxi driver outside the area in which he was licensed to ply for hire. He stopped to pick them up. They turned out to be special constables. He was charged with unlicensed plying for hire. The magistrate dismissed the charge, on the ground that he had been entrapped by the police. The Divisional Court accepted that *Teixeira de Castro* appeared to indicate that it would always be unfair to admit evidence of an offence committed as a result of active steps taken by officers, but was not persuaded that it could represent a general rule. The police had not persuaded or pressurized the driver. Finally, in *R. v. Loosely*[531a] the House of Lords applied *Teixeira de Castro* where officers instigated an offence by someone who was not suspected of having committed similar offences or of having a predisposition to commit such offences, without it being part of a properly authorized investigation. Such cases could now be stayed as an abuse of process, or evidence could be excluded under section 78 of PACE. This may not go beyond earlier decisions, but it shows that the ECHR can help to identify the elements which are central to principled, consistent decision making.

---

[526] Eur. Ct. HR (1988) 13 EHRR 242.

[527] The Court emphasized that questions relating to the admissibility of evidence were primarily a matter for the national courts. In *Khan v. United Kingdom*, Eur. Ct. HR, Judgment of 12 May 2000, the Court made it clear that this depended on national courts taking proper account of the impact of admitting the evidence on the fairness of the proceedings as a whole.

[528] Eur. Ct. HR (1998) 28 EHRR 101.

[529] [2001] 1 WLR 51 at 69–70.

[530] See also *R. v. Chalkley* [1998] QB 848, CA.

[531] [2000] 1 WLR 1071, DC.

[531a] [2001] UKHL 53, 25 October 2001, HL.

(iii) The duties of the investigating officer

The first point to note is that, once an interview begins, the custody officer drops out of the picture. When the custody officer allows an investigating officer to take the suspect into an interview room for questioning, or out of the police station (for example, to conduct a search of the suspect's premises),[532] the investigating officer becomes responsible for ensuring that the provisions of PACE and the Codes are complied with. The investigating officer must account for the treatment of the suspect when he delivers him back to the custody officer at the end of the interview, but during it the custody officer has no power to protect the suspect's rights. The review officer can intervene, but only if a review becomes due.[533] Where no appropriate adult or legal adviser is present, there is ample room for different accounts of what happened to be given by the officer and the detainee, particularly as the detainee's perception of events is likely to be affected by the pressures of his position. Tape recording of interviews is not normally possible outside police station interview rooms.[534]

Protecting the integrity and reliability of the interview therefore depends heavily on the good sense and honesty of the interviewer. To minimize the opportunities for the record of an interview to be intentionally or unintentionally corrupted, there are extensive provisions in the Codes concerning methods of recording of interviews. If the interview is tape-recorded, there should be no problem (unless it is later alleged that some impropriety occurred before the tape was turned on or after it was turned off). Tape recording has worked well, and the police have on the whole become supporters of it. It has several benefits for them. It frees them from the need to make laborious, manual, verbatim records, which slowed down the pace of questioning and could destroy the effect of a line of questions.[535] It tends to improve rapport with interviewees, and tends to discourage challenges to confessions. It also restricts allegations of 'verballing' (crediting suspects with statements which were never made), as verballing can now only take place outside formal interviews, and such statements are unlikely to be considered fairly admissible unless the suspect voluntarily repeats them on tape.

(iv) The recording requirements

In order to control the practice of conducting interviews outside police stations, evading the tape-recording requirements, Code C provides that, after arrest for an offence, a suspect must not be interviewed about that offence except at a police station or other authorized place of detention, unless the delay would be likely to lead to one of the consequences which would justify a superintendent in authorizing delay in exercising the rights to have someone notified of the arrest and to have access to legal advice: interference with or harm to evidence, interference with or physical harm to

---

[532] This must be authorized by the custody officer: Code C, para. 12.1.

[533] PACE, s. 39(2), (3).

[534] See Code E, and the Code of Practice on recording interviews in terrorism cases to be made by the Home Secretary under the Terrorism Act 2000, Sch. 8, para. 3.

[535] C. F. Willis, J. Macleod, and P. Naish, *The Tape-Recording of Police Interviews with Suspects: A Second Interim Report*, Home Office Research Study No. 97 (London: HMSO 1988), ch. 3.

other people, alerting suspects not yet under arrest, or hindering recovery of the proceeds of an offence.[536]

One possible source of corruption to the record remains, however. The tape is rarely fully transcribed unless there is a dispute about the record. In other cases, a summary of the interview is made, which often becomes more important than the tape for practical purposes. A survey of these summaries found that they are of uneven quality, being misleading, distorted, of poor quality, or omitting much relevant detail in nearly half of the summaries examined, although the police are said to be paying more attention now to training officers in techniques of accurate summarizing.[537]

Where tape recording is not available, the officer must make an accurate record of the interview, wherever it occurs. The record must be made during the course of the interview, unless in the officer's view this would not be practicable or would interfere with the conduct of the interview, and must be either a verbatim record or an adequate and accurate summary.[538] Where the record is not made during the interview, it must be made as soon as practicable afterwards, and the reason for the delay recorded in the officer's pocket book (where the order of pages can be checked, and ESDA tests most easily applied to establish whether there have been later insertions or deletions).[539] Unless it is impracticable, the interviewee and, if present, an appropriate adult or solicitor, must be given the opportunity to read the record (or, if he cannot read, have it read to him), and to sign it as correct, or to indicate the respects in which he considers it to be inaccurate.[540] The police have sometimes taken liberties with these requirements. In *R. v. Canale*[541] the officers failed to make a contemporaneous record. They recorded their reasons with the cryptic note 'BW', which (they later explained) stood for 'best way'. Lord Lane CJ commented, 'In the officers' view the reason for failing to record the interview contemporaneously was that the best way was not to record the interview contemporaneously, which of course is not a reason at all'.[542] The judicial criticism which followed led the Metropolitan Police to tighten the controls exercised over interrogation techniques. It is to be hoped that the police will treat these provisions with the respect which they deserve, as they are important protections for suspects, and the courts have shown an increasing willingness to exclude evidence which is obtained in breach of these provisions.[543]

(v) Styles of interviewing

The Codes give no guidance on the conduct of interviews. Under PACE, section 76(2), a confession, if challenged by the defence, is inadmissible unless the prosecution can

---

[536] Code C, para. 11.1.

[537] J. Baldwin and J. Bedward, 'Summarising Tape Recordings of Police Interviews' [1991] Crim. LR 671–9.

[538] Code C, para. 11.5.

[539] Code C, paras. 11.7, 11.9.

[540] Code C, paras. 11.10, 11.11.

[541] [1990] 2 All ER 187, CA.

[542] [1990] 2 All ER 187, at 190.

[543] *R. v. Doolan* [1988] Crim. LR 747, CA; *R. v. Delaney* (1988) 88 Cr. App. R. 339, CA; *R. v. Canale*, [1990] 2 All ER 187, CA.

prove beyond reasonable doubt that it was not obtained (a) by oppression, or (b) in consequence of anything said or done which was likely, in the circumstances, to render unrealiable any confession which might be made in consequence thereof. Furthermore, if the circumstances surrounding the confession (or alleged confession) are such that it would taint the proceedings with unfairness to admit the evidence, it may be excluded (and usually should be excluded) under section 78. A considerable body of caselaw has built up round these provisions, but their value in protecting the rights of suspects is limited, because the admissibility or exclusion of evidence is a valuable sanction against police malpractice only if the case comes to court (i.e. is not dropped beforehand) and is contested (i.e. the accused does not plead guilty). However, the caselaw has had the effect of establishing some ground rules for police interviews, breach of which may make confessions inadmissible or liable to exclusion.

(a) **The meaning of oppression.** '"Oppression" includes torture, inhuman or degrading treatment, and the use or threat of violence'.[544] This statutory exegesis of the term is not exhaustive, and the Court of Appeal has treated oppressive conduct as extending beyond those types of treatment to take in potentially any burdensome, harsh, or wrongful exercise of authority, or unjust or cruel treatment of subjects and inferiors. There are conditions, however: oppression will probably not be found in the absence of improper behaviour by the investigator.[545]

This has two implications. First, it means that the conduct must produce a situation which oppresses the suspect more severely than is inevitable when in detention. Secondly, it imports a subjective element to the evaluation of police conduct: the investigators must probably be aware that what they are doing is improper, and intend it to produce an effect on the suspect, before conduct falling short of inhuman or degrading treatment will be held to amount to oppression. In *R. v. Fulling*,[546] the defence argued that a confession had been or may have been obtained by oppression. The defendant, a woman, had been arrested on suspicion of having been one of a number of people who had allegedly made fraudulent claims from insurance companies in respect of bogus burglaries. She refused to say anything under repeated questioning over a period of more than twenty-four hours. Eventually, one of the investigators told her that her cohabitant had been having an affair for three years with one of the other suspects, a woman who had been arrested and was in a cell next to the defendant's. At this stage, it was said, she could no longer face being in the cell, and confessed. On these facts, the trial judge not surprisingly rejected the suggestion of oppression, and the Court of Appeal dismissed the defendant's appeal.

However, where conscious and serious impropriety by the police is alleged and is not disproved beyond reasonable doubt by the prosecution, the evidence of any confession resulting from it is to be excluded on the ground of oppression. For example, in *R. v. Ismail*[547] the prosecution conceded, and the Court of Appeal accepted, that the trial judge had rightly excluded evidence of a confession on the

---

[544] PACE, s. 76(8). On the meaning of torture and inhuman and degrading treatment under international law, see Chs 5 and 7.

[545] [1987] QB 426, [1987] 2 All ER 65, CA.

[546] Ibid.   [547] [1990] Crim. LR 109, CA.

ground of oppression. The defendant had been arrested in relation to an indecent assault, and was detained at a police station. The investigating officer had misled the custody officer as to the purpose of an interview, making it impossible for the custody officer to perform his duty when deciding whether or not to permit the interview. The defendant was not offered the chance to obtain legal advice, and the recording requirements were breached during the interview. Although the suspect continued to deny the allegations at that interview, there were three later interviews, culminating in a signed confession. The Court of Appeal held that the effects of the oppression at the earlier interview, together with other breaches of PACE and Code C, might well have lingered on, affecting the suspect's will to a point where it was unfair to admit the evidence.[548]

Heavy-handed or bullying interview techniques may amount to oppression. In *R. v. Beales*[549] the suspect had been arrested for assaulting a two-year-old boy. The interviewing officer had misrepresented the evidence against the suspect, inventing some evidence which did not in fact exist, had misrepresented the effect of the suspect's own answers, and had adopted a hectoring and bullying demeanour throughout the interview to the point where, after thirty-five minutes, the suspect had accepted that he must have assaulted the child although he claimed to have no recollection of having done so. The trial judge accepted that this strayed into the realms of oppression, and held that the admission was inadmissible. The Court of Appeal reached the same conclusion in *R. v. Paris, Abdullah and Miller*,[550] where (despite the presence of a solicitor) investigating officers had subjected the suspects to long-drawn-out, repetitive, aggressive, hectoring interrogation which eventually produced a confession. The confession evidence ought not to have been admitted, because it had been obtained by oppression. The convictions were quashed.[551]

(b) **Hectoring, bullying, and strategems.** Generally, it will not be necessary to stigmatize hectoring and bullying behaviour as oppressive in order to have resulting confessions excluded. It will often be possible to rule the evidence inadmissible on the ground that the manner of the interview made the confession unreliable, under section 76(2)(b), or to exclude the evidence on the basis that it would be unfair to admit it, under section 78, even if there is no breach of PACE or the Codes of Practice. Much will depend on the age and competence of the suspect, and, if there was police impropriety, whether it had the effect of depriving the suspect of his protective rights under PACE. It has been held, for example, that evidence of confessions should be excluded where suspects or their solicitors have been misled about the strength of the evidence against their clients,[552] and where bullying or hectoring

---

[548] It is not clear whether the evidence of the final interview was excluded under s. 76(2)(a) or s. 78. See the commentary by D. J. Birch [1990] Crim. LR at 110–11. On the potentially lingering effects of oppression on the mind of the suspect and (a different matter) the fairness of proceedings for the purposes of s. 78, see also *R. v. Davison* [1988] Crim. LR 442, a first instance decision.

[549] [1991] Crim. LR 118, a Crown Court decision.

[550] (1993) 97 Cr. App. R. 99, CA (the 'Cardiff Three case').

[551] See also *R. v. Heron*, unreported, Leeds Crown Court, discussed by Dixon, *Law in Policing*, 172–3.

[552] *R. v. Mason* [1987] 3 All ER 481, CA; *R. v. Blake* [1991] Crim. LR 119; *R. v. McGovern* [1991] Crim. LR 124, CA.

approaches have been adopted at interviews, particularly with a young or vulnerable suspect.[553]

Nevertheless, in one respect oppression may have a longer lasting effect than other forms of unfairness or impropriety. Oppression in an earlier interview is likely to be accepted as tainting the quality or fairness of evidence obtained at later interviews with the same person. Where police misbehaviour does not amount to oppression, courts will look for clearer evidence that it continued to put the suspect at a disadvantage or under pressure in later interviews before excluding evidence of those later interviews,[554] although it will sometimes be clear that it has done so.[555] It is particularly likely to have had a continuing effect when it reduces the effectiveness of the protective provisions of PACE, such as the protective role of the custody officer or (most powerfully) the usefulness of the right to legal advice.[556] This reflects the increasingly protective attitude of the courts towards interviewees, which is developing in the light of growing realization of the pressures (sometimes subtle, at other times less so) which can lead a person, especially if young, mentally handicapped or disordered, or confused, to confess to crimes which they could not possibly have committed.

Where the police use a stratagem rather than oppression to overcome a suspect's resistance, it may lead to breaches of the Code of Practice by allowing the police to evade requirements which apply to formal interviews. We have seen how stratagems have been permitted in cases where the suspect is put in a position where he volunteers information without being pressurized by an exercise of police power or authority, as long as the police do not initiate the exchange and deceive the suspect with a view to evading the Code's requirements.[557] The same applies where the police put two suspected offenders together in a bugged cell in the hope that they will be able to record them making damaging admissions in conversation with each other. In these cases, courts tend to admit the evidence none the less, because the admission is voluntary. Neither PACE nor the Code of Practice protects a suspect from taking the opportunity to speak voluntarily and incriminatingly to another, even if the police have engineered the opportunity and wired the cell, or one of the suspects, with recording equipment.[558] Even if there is a breach of the Code, there is usually no causal link between the breach (normally a failure to comply with the requirements for a contemporaneous record) and the damaging admission. The suspect will have volunteered information without being asked questions by people in authority. In such circumstances, there is no unfairness or injustice in admitting the evidence[559] (although the position is probably different if an undercover police officer insinuates himself into a suspect's home and family life, in an attempt to reduce her inhibitions

---

[553] R. v. Everett [1988] Crim. LR 826, CA; R. v. Beales [1991] Crim. LR 118.

[554] Y. v. DPP [1991] Crim. LR 917, DC.

[555] R. v. Canale [1990] 2 All ER 187, CA; R. v. Gillard and Barrett [1991] Crim. LR 280; R. v. Ismail, above.

[556] R. v. McGovern [1991] Crim. LR 124, CA; see also Matto v. Wolverhampton Crown Court [1987] RTR 337, DC.

[557] R. v. Christou [1992] QB 979, [1992] 4 All ER 559, CA, and R. v. Bryce [1992] 4 All ER 567, CA.

[558] R. v. Bailey [1993] 3 All ER 513, CA.

[559] Ibid.; R. v. Roberts (Stephen) [1997] 1 Cr. App. R. 217, CA.

and induce admissions). The discretion allowed under section 78 of PACE is very wide. The trial judge's assessment of fairness is unlikely to be upset on appeal unless it is clearly based on wrong principles or is wholly unreasonable.[560]

6.8 INTERFERENCE WITH BODILY SECURITY:
FINGERPRINTS, SEARCHES, AND SAMPLES

(1) SEARCH BY CUSTODY OFFICER

The Police and Criminal Evidence Act 1984 makes provision for a number of different types of invasion of people's personal security and integrity. The first is a power for the custody officer to search the detainee on arrest at the police station or arrival at the police station after arrest or committal elsewhere, in order to make a record of the items which the person has on him.[561] This power is not a duty: it is to be exercised only when it seems possible that the custody officer will have continuing duties in respect of the person over an extended period.[562] The custody officer is entitled to seize and retain anything the detainee has on him, except for clothes and personal effects,[563] which are defined in Code C, paragraph 4.3 as 'those items which a person may lawfully need or use or refer to while in detention but do not include cash or other items of value'. They ought, therefore, to include a watch (essential in order to check the time limits around which the detention provisions revolve), spectacles, and the notices given out by the custody officer. Clothes and personal effects may be retained by the custody officer only if:

(a) he believes (not necessarily on reasonable grounds) that the detainee may use them to cause physical injury to himself or anyone else, to damage property, interfere with evidence, or to assist an escape; or

(b) he has reasonable grounds for believing that they may be evidence in relation to any offence (not necessarily the one for which the detainee was arrested).[564]

Any constable may search a detainee anywhere and at any time for anything in (a) above, and may seize anything he finds, other than clothes and personal effects, which are liable to seizure only if they fall under either (a) or (b) above.[565]

The power to search does not extend to an intimate search, which must be separately authorized (see below). It may, however, extend to a strip search in the police

---

[560] *R. v. Jelen and Katz* (1989) 90 Cr. App. R. 456, CA; *R. v. Ali (Shaukat)*, *The Times*, 19 February 1991, CA; *R. v. Bailey* [1993] 3 All ER 513, CA; *R. v. Quinn* [1995] 1 Cr. App. R. 480, CA; *R. v. Dures* [1997] 2 Cr. App. R. 247, CA.

[561] PACE, s. 54(1), (2).

[562] Code C, Note for Guidance 4A.

[563] PACE, s. 54(3), (4).

[564] Ibid., s. 54(4). The person must be told the reason for the seizure unless he is violent or likely to become so, or is incapable of understanding what is said: s. 54(5).

[565] Ibid., s. 54(6A), (6B), (6C), added by the Criminal Justice Act 1988, s. 147(b).

station (i.e. one which involves removing more than outer clothing), so long as the custody officer considers it to be necessary in order to remove an article which the detainee would not be entitled to keep while in custody.[566] A strip search is an embarrassing and upsetting procedure, representing a major invasion of privacy. It engages the right to respect for private life under Article 8(1) of the ECHR, and is justifiable only if conducted in accordance with the law, and is necessary in a democratic society for one of the legitimate aims listed in Article 8(2). The Code of Practice would probably constitute a sufficient grounding in positive law for the search to be 'in accordance with the law'. As there must be a pressing social need, normally either to protect safety or for the detection of crime, such searches ought not to be routine. To protect against a subsequent Human Rights Act claim, as well as in the interests of good administration, the purpose of and grounds for the search should be recorded.[567] Any search must be carried out by a constable of the same sex as the detainee.[568]

(2) FINGERPRINTING

(i) During the investigation

Normally, an 'appropriate consent' is needed before a person's fingerprints can be taken.[569] The appropriate consent for a person of seventeen years of age or over is that of the person himself. If the person is under seventeen years old but over fourteen, the person and his parent or guardian must both consent; if he is under fourteen, the parent or guardian's consent alone is sufficient,[570] and reasonable force can then be used against the child if necessary in order to take the fingerprints.[571] Because of concern over the reality of consent when a person is in custody, the consent of the person to be fingerprinted must be in writing if he gives it at a police station.[572] However, where a person is charged with, or told that he will be charged with, a recordable offence and has not had his fingerprints taken in the course of the investigation, the appropriate consent may be dispensed with. In its place, the Act provides for an authorization (normally in writing, but confirmed in writing if given orally) by an officer of at least the rank of superintendent, who must have reasonable grounds (a) for suspecting that the person has been involved in a criminal offence, and (b) for believing that fingerprints will tend to confirm or disprove his involvement[573] (for

---

[566] PACE, s. 54(7); Code C, para. 4.1 and Annex A, Part B.

[567] Code A, Annex A, paras. 10–12.

[568] Ibid., s. 54(8), (9).

[569] Ibid., s. 61(1). The Anti-terrorism, Crime and Security Bill 2001 would allow more extensive examinations to take place to establish identity.

[570] Ibid., s. 65, on the meaning of 'appropriate consent'.

[571] Ibid., s. 117; Code D, para. 3.2.

[572] Ibid., s. 61(2).

[573] Ibid., s. 61(3), (4), (5). Under the Terrorism Act 2000, Sch. 8, para. 10, an authorization may also be given if the superintendent is satisfied that it is necessary to do so in order to assist in determining whether a person has been concerned in the commission, preparation, or instigation of acts of terrorism, or has been involved in a terrorism offence. There are also powers to take fingerprints of suspected illegal immigrants under the Immigration Act 1971, Sch. 2, para. 18(2).

example, where fingerprints were found at the scene of the crime which cannot otherwise be accounted for).

Where fingerprints and samples (on which see below, subsection (3)) are retained by the police, the information derived from them and computerized data-management and imaging technology have made possible a computerized fingerprint database covering many people, giving rise to fears of a threat to privacy and to people's freedom from police interference. The police are allowed to make speculative searches of the database, electronically cross-matching prints taken in the course of an investigation with those taken previously anywhere in the country.[574] Normally, the Data Protection Act 1998 would restrict such processing of electronic data, but the Act allows extensive exemptions for criminal investigation purposes.[575] There is one specific restriction: fingerprints and samples taken for the purpose of a terrorism investigation under the Terrorism Act 2000 may not be cross-matched against fingerprints and samples taken under PACE for the purpose of investigating a non-terrorism offence.[576] This is because the rules which restrict the period for which fingerprints and samples may be retained (see below) do not apply when the prints and samples were taken for the purpose of a terrorism investigation.[577] Apart from this, the main statutory safeguards against abuse of this power, as so often under PACE, are based on the giving of reasons and keeping records when the prints are first taken.

If a person's fingerprints are taken without the appropriate consent, he must be told the reason beforehand, and the reasons must be recorded (in the custody record if he is in police detention at the time) as soon as practicable after taking the fingerprints.[578] In addition, if given by a suspect who is later cleared of the offence, the police are required to destroy the fingerprints as soon as possible, except in terrorism cases; and if given by someone else for the purposes of an investigation, they must be destroyed as soon as they have fulfilled the purpose for which they were taken. Copies and computer records must also be destroyed. People may, if they wish, witness the destruction of their own fingerprints, and in the case of computerized records, are entitled to a certificate stating that access to the data has been made impossible.[579] They must be told of this right.[580] Nevertheless, suspicions that the provisions were being breached, depending as they do on the police complying with rules which do not work in their interests, have been confirmed in a recent case. The judiciary failed to provide the police with any incentive to keep the rules, holding that evidence derived from unlawfully retained samples could be admitted as evidence against a person in relation to a subsequent offence. The discretion to exclude evidence under section 78 of PACE will not be used to control breaches of the rules, at any rate when the offence involves serious violence.[581] A person whose fingerprints or samples have

---

[574] PACE, s. 61(7A), 63A(1).

[575] See Ch. 9, below.

[576] Terrorism Act 2000, Sch. 8, para. 14(2), (3).

[577] See Terrorism Act 2000, Sch. 8, para. 10.

[578] PACE, s. 61(7), (8).

[579] Ibid., s. 64, as amended by Criminal Justice Act 1988, s. 148; Code D, para. 3.4.

[580] Code D, para. 3.1.

[581] *Attorney-General's Reference (No. 3 of 1999)* [2001] 2 WLR 56, HL.

been unlawfully detained suffers an interference with his right to respect for private life under Article 8(1) of the ECHR, and it cannot be justified under Article 8(2) because the retention was not in accordance with the law. The subject ought therefore to have a cause of action under the Human Rights Act 1998. The Criminal Justice and Police Act 2001 allows fingerprints and samples, and records derived from them, to be retained indefinitely in certain cases for data matching purposes. It operates retrospectively as well as prospectively. This removes the right of action in national courts under the Human Rights Act, but, by depriving the subject of an effective remedy for the violation of his right under Article 8, is likely to violate the right to such a remedy under Article 13. The Anti-terrorism, Crime and Security Bill, if enacted, would extend the retention regime to immigrants' fingerprints.

(ii) After conviction

There is special provision under section 27 of PACE for fingerprinting people who have been convicted of a recordable offence, have not been in police detention at any time in relation to the offence (because they were proceeded against by way of summons rather than arrest), and have not had their fingerprints taken at any time in relation to the offence. Within a month of the conviction, a constable may require the person to attend a police station within seven days to be fingerprinted. After conviction for a recordable offence, the appropriate consent to fingerprinting is not required.[582] If the person fails to attend, a constable may arrest him without warrant. Detention in such a case will be limited to the time necessary to take the fingerprints.

(3) INTIMATE AND NON-INTIMATE SAMPLES

Modern science, particularly in relation to DNA analysis, has made samples of body tissue and body products important to the investigation of many crimes, particularly serious offences of violence such as rape. The rules on taking, retaining, and using samples are in many ways similar to those relating to fingerprints. Intimate samples (defined in section 65 of PACE, as amended, as a sample of blood, semen or other tissue fluid, urine, or pubic hair, a dental impression, or a swab taken from a person's body orifice other than the mouth[583]) may be taken only with the appropriate consent (which has the same meaning as in relation to fingerprinting) and then only if an officer of the rank of superintendent or above authorizes it in writing (or, if authorized orally, with confirmation in writing as soon as practicable). The sample may be authorized only if the superintendent has reasonable grounds (a) for suspecting that

---

[582] PACE, s. 61(6). A recordable offence is one which is potentially punishable with imprisonment, and certain other specified non-imprisonable crimes such as loitering or soliciting for the purposes of prostitution, possessing a weapon with a blade or point in a public place, tampering with a motor vehicle, and improper use of a public telephone communications system: National Police Records (Recordable Offences) Regulations 1985, SI 1985/1941, as amended.

[583] Like the definition of intimate searches, this shows the validity of the 'thin end of the wedge' critique of new police powers. Originally, saliva was an intimate sample, but was down-graded to a non-intimate sample when it proved inconvenient for the police to wait for a medical practitioner to take the sample, or to be required to obtain the suspect's consent.

the person concerned has been involved in a recordable[584] offence, and (b) for believing that the sample will tend to prove or disprove his involvement.[585] The person must be informed of the grounds for the authorization, which must also be recorded (in the custody record if the person is in custody at the time). A sample (other than a sample of urine) must be taken by a registered medical practitioner, except that a dental impression must be taken by a registered dental practitioner.[586]

This power raises fewer problems than the power to conduct intimate searches. The appropriate consent cannot be dispensed with, although there are serious doubts as to the propriety of allowing a parent or guardian to give consent on behalf of a child who is *Gillick*-competent and is refusing his consent: the Act seems to be premised on the same assumptions as those which informed the *obiter* discussion of Lord Donaldson MR in *Re R. (A Minor) (Wardship: Medical Treatment)*,[587] and which, as noted in Chapter 5 above, are incompatible with the approach taken to consent to medical examinations in the Children Act 1989. In most cases, therefore, the interests of doctors and detainees are protected. The interests of justice are also protected, by section 62(10) of PACE and paragraph 13(1) of Schedule 8 to the Terrorism Act 2000, which permit a court or jury to draw such conclusions from refusal of consent as appear proper. In particular, the refusal may be treated as capable of corroborating any evidence against the defendant to which his refusal is relevant.

A non-intimate sample is a sample of hair (other than pubic hair), a sample taken from a nail or under a nail, a swab taken from part of a person's body, including the mouth not any other body orifice, and a footprint or similar impression of part of a person's body, other than a hand (which would constitute a fingerprint).[588] Non-intimate samples normally require the person's written consent, but this may be dispensed with if an officer of the rank of at least superintendent authorizes the taking of the sample. This may be done on the same grounds as justify giving authority for taking an intimate sample.[589] A non-intimate sample may also be taken without the appropriate consent from a person who has been charged with, or informed that he will be prosecuted for, a recordable offence,[590] or someone who has been convicted of such an offence, acquitted of it on the ground insanity, or found to be unfit to plead to it.[591] After a non-intimate sample has been authorized, reasonable force may be used

---

[584] Down-graded from 'serious arrestable'.

[585] PACE, s. 62(1), (1A), (2), (3), (4). In terrorism cases, under the Terrorism Act 2000, Sch. 8, para. 10, an authorization may also be given if the superintendent is satisfied that it is necessary to do so in order to assist in determining whether a person has been concerned in the commission, preparation or instigation of acts of terrorism, or has been involved in a terrorism offence.

[586] Ibid., s. 62; Terrorism Act 2000, Sch. 8, para. 13(3).

[587] [1991] 4 All ER 177, CA.

[588] PACE, s. 65 as amended.

[589] Ibid., s. 63; Terrorism Act 2000, Sch. 8, para. 10.

[590] This applies only if no sample was taken during the course of the investigation, or up to two were taken, neither of which was adequate: PACE, s. 63(3A)(b).

[591] Ibid., s. 63(3A), (3B), (3C). The substitution of recordable for serious arrestable offence as the threshold for taking samples without consent by the Criminal Justice and Public Order Act 1994, and the extension of the powers in the Criminal Evidence (Amendment) Act 1997, provide examples of the way a fairly limited power granted after careful consideration of the balancing of competing interests in the Police and Criminal Evidence Act 1984 can be incrementally applied in ways which would have been unacceptable at the time the power was originally created only a decade or so earlier.

if necessary to take it.[592] This may be traumatic for the person from whom it is taken, but it is far less degrading and dangerous, and so less objectionable, than the power to conduct intimate searches.

On the retention of samples and information derived from them, see (2) above.

(4) INTIMATE SEARCHES

A physical examination of a person's body orifices other than the mouth ('an intimate search')[593] is highly intrusive, and is *prima facie* a serious battery, invasion of privacy, and interference with bodily integrity. It has the capacity to cause serious injury to the person being searched, besides being degrading and humiliating. If carried out insensitively (for example, there have been anecdotal reports of women being required to stand naked on a table with their legs apart, and to jump up and down, in the presence of male officers) it comes close to the kind of degrading treatment which would fall foul of Article 3 of the European Convention on Human Rights. In *McFeeley v. United Kingdom*,[594] the European Commission of Human Rights held that such searches were not degrading treatment within the meaning of ECHR Article 3 when conducted in terrorism cases. However, the threshold of degrading treatment has changed since 1980,[595] and in any case respected authors have suggested that the European Court of Human Rights might apply more demanding standards in a case not involving terrorism than the Commission did in a case of suspected terrorism.[596]

One would normally expect that no such search would be permitted without the consent of the person searched. However, Parliament decided that there are circumstances in which these fundamental individual rights may properly be overridden to advance some other interest. These interests lie in the safety of the person concerned or other people, preventing escape, and detecting drugs offences (drugs are often hidden in body orifices, sometimes even being swallowed in bags to avoid detection).

An intimate search must be specially authorized by an officer of at least the rank of inspector.[597] He must have reasonable grounds for believeing (not merely for suspecting) that a person who has been arrested, and is in police detention at the time,[598] may have concealed on him either: (a) something which he could use to cause physical injury to himself or others (the usual example is a razorblade), and which he might use for that purpose while in the custody of the police or a court; or (b) a Class

---

[592] PACE, s. 117.

[593] Ibid., s. 65. Originally, an examination of the mouth was an intimate search. However, when this was found to be inconvenient for the police, it was downgraded to a non-intimate search. This provides another good example of the incremental nature of police powers generally, and supports arguments against new powers which suggest that they will be merely the thin end of the wedge.

[594] (1980) 20 DR 44.

[595] See Ch. 5, above.

[596] D. J. Harris, M. O'Boyle, and C. Warbrick, *The Law of the European Convention on Human Rights* (London: Butterworths, 1985), 83.

[597] The Criminal Justice and Police Act 2001, s. 79, allows an inspector to authorize such searches, rather than a superintendent as previously. This reduction in the level of protection against potential violations of ECHR Art. 3 should be deprecated.

[598] There is no power to arrest someone purely in order to carry out an intimate search.

A drug (within the meaning of section 2(1) of the Misuse of Drugs Act 1971), which he had in his possession, with intent to supply it or to smuggle it, before his arrest (thus excluding possession for his own use, or drugs received from a fellow prisoner after his arrest), and that the article cannot be found without an intimate search.[599] There is no power to authorize a search for evidence of offences, however serious, unless that evidence is reasonably believed to consist of a Class A drug. However, once the search has been carried out, anything found can be seized if the custody officer (a) believes (reasonable grounds being unnecessary) that the person may use it to cause physical injury to himself or another, to damage property, to interfere with evidence, or to assist him to escape, or (b) has reasonable grounds for believing that the article may be evidence of any offence.[600]

The grounds which would be needed for such a search would therefore be substantial. There would need to be evidence (and more evidence than is needed to justify the arrest) that the person is in possession of the article, and that (in the case of a search for an injurious article) the person is liable to use it, or (in the case of a drugs search) the person is a dealer in or courier of drugs, and Class A drugs in particular. But no independent authority reviews the evidence on which the authorization is given before the search is made.[601]

The safeguards for the detainee are therefore somewhat limited. The Code of Practice requires that the reasons for the search be explained to the person concerned before the search takes place,[602] so the person presumably has a chance to persuade the officers that no search is justified or himself to remove the articles in question, making a search unnecessary. Once it is decided that the search should go ahead, there are safeguards of two sorts.

First, there are safeguards against arbitrary behaviour and abuse of power. Like other such safeguards under the PACE detention provisions, these consist of requirements as to the giving of information (for example, about the reasons for the search and the reasons for seizing anything found)[603] and record-keeping.[604] These records are to be collated for each police area, and the chief constable's annual report must give information about the number and purpose of searches, the manner in which they were conducted, and the results, allowing for some monitoring of the global use of the powers.[605]

Secondly, there are some safeguards for the dignity and physical safety of the detainee. A Class A drugs search may be conducted only at a hospital, a doctor's surgery, or other place used for medical purposes, and must be conducted by a suitably qualified person: a registered medical practitioner or registered nurse.[606]

---

[599] PACE, s. 55(1), (2).

[600] Ibid., s. 55(12).

[601] In this respect, a person detained under PACE is in a worse position than one being searched by a customs officer at the port of entry, who can insist on the grounds for a search being reviewed by a justice of the peace: Customs and Excise Management Act 1979, s. 164(2).

[602] Code C, Annex A, para. 1.

[603] PACE, s. 55(3), (13); Code C, Annex A, para. 1.

[604] Ibid., s. 55(10), (11).

[605] Ibid., s. 55(14), (15), (16).

[606] Ibid., s. 55(4).

Other intimate searches are normally to be carried out by a suitably qualified person, but may be conducted at a police station as well as the other places in which a drugs search would be permitted. A non-drug search may be carried out by a police officer of the same sex as the person searched, if an officer of at least the rank of inspector considers that it would be impracticable for the search to be conducted by a medically qualified person. This power is rarely exercised, and comes into play typically where the case is urgent and no medically qualified person is readily available.[607] Juveniles may be searched only in the presence of an appropriate adult (which has the same meaning as under the detention provisions), unless the juvenile signifies, in the presence of the adult, that he does not wish the adult to be present and the adult agrees. When an appropriate adult is in attendance on a juvenile or a mentally disordered or mentally handicapped person, the adult may be present for the search, but must be of the same sex as the person searched, unless the detainee specifically requests the presence of a particular adult of the opposite sex.[608]

Intimate searches raise problems of two sorts, apart from the inevitable degradation and risk of physical injury from an intrusive procedure, which may sometimes be conducted by an unqualified person. The first problem is a general one, concerning the relationship between the power to conduct an intimate search and the general purposes and values of a legal system. The idea of a person being held down while her vagina or anus is physically searched against her will is repulsive to civilized feelings. If a film or video were to portray such a scene, it would be generally regarded as worthy of condemnation and, perhaps, prosecution. It is hard to imagine how a legal system could be justified in authorizing police officers to commit such acts, without even the check of a prior review by an independent person of the grounds for a search. This is a case where the law has conferred a power which contravenes the civilized values which it is the main job of law to foster.

The other problem is more specific, and relates to the position of doctors and nurses who are asked by the police to conduct an intimate search against the will of the person to be searched. The doctor is not protected by any statutory authority against an action for trespass to the person. As there is no medical necessity for the procedure, the doctor or nurse is, on normal principles (for which see Chapter 5 above), not entitled to ignore or override the absence of consent from the detainee unless there is statutory authority or a court order. There is no judicial determination of the best interests of the detainee. The only statutory authority justifying the use of force against a non-consenting person to exercise a power under PACE is in section 117 of PACE, and that protects only a police officer, not a doctor or nurse. The doctor is therefore apparently not protected against an action for trespass. Furthermore, if the detainee suffers injury as a result of the procedure, the doctor or nurse may be liable in damages for negligence. If the injury results from the detainee's struggles, it is hard to see how a doctor could defend a negligence action: there could hardly be a more clear-cut case of medical negligence than that of a doctor performing a non-therapeutic, intrusive procedure on a person who is actively resisting, in

---

[607] PACE, s.55(5) (as amended by the Criminal Justice and Police Act 2001, s. 79, allowing an inspector rather than a superintendent to give the authorization), (6), (7).

[608] Code C, Annex A, para. 5.

circumstances where that is obviously likely to make the procedure particularly risky. Unless the courts produce some previously unknown public-policy defence for doctors carrying out searches at the request of the police, the only case in which the doctor is likely to succeed is if it can be shown that, on the balance of probabilities, the risk to the detainee from the concealed article is greater than the risk from performing the procedure, so that the doctor was acting in the detainee's best interests.

Even in cases where the doctor or nurse acts lawfully, it is far from clear that he or she would be acting ethically. The British Medical Association has recommended to its members that they should not conduct intimate body searches for evidence of drugs offences without the free and informed consent of the detainee, and stigmatized the power to conduct intimate body searches as oppressive and objectionable.[609] This is surely correct. Article 1 of the Declaration of Tokyo (1975) provides:

'The doctor shall not countenance, condone or participate in the practice of torture or other forms of cruel, inhuman or degrading procedures, whatever the offence of which the victim of such procedures is suspected, accused or guilty, and whatever the victim's beliefs or motives, and in all situations, including armed conflict and civil strife.'

The power to conduct intimate searches may be very useful to the police, but its benefits are achieved at too high a price in human dignity and standards of civilized behaviour to be compatible with the responsibilities of the medical profession and the principles of a civilized legal system.

6.9 TREATMENT AFTER CHARGE

Once a detainee has been charged, he must be either released (on bail or without bail) or brought before a magistrates' court, where he will either be released on bail, remanded in custody to await committal proceedings or trial, or remanded into police custody to enable the police to investigate other offences.

Once charged, and if they are not being investigated in relation to other offences, defendants generally have a right to be released on bail, which may be withheld only in accordance with the conditions specified in the Bail Act 1976. If a juvenile is to be detained, the custody officer has a duty to ensure that he is held in secure local authority accommodation if possible, but if the custody officer is not satisfied that there is appropriately secure local authority accommodation available he may detain him at the police station.[610]

The court has power to impose conditions on the grant of bail, such as curfews, or requirements that the defendant should live at a specified address, surrender his passport, or report regularly to the police station. These conditions must be for the purpose of ensuring that the defendant appears for trial and does not commit

---

[609] See W. Russell, 'Intimate Body Searches: For Stilettos, Explosive Devices, et al.' (1983) **286** Brit. Med. J. 733.

[610] PACE, s. 38(6); R. v. Chief Constable of Cambridgeshire, ex parte M. [1991] 2 QB 499, [1991] 2 All ER 777, DC.

offences in the mean time. As part of a drive to combat drug abuse, drug use is a relevant condition when considering whether to grant bail,[611] and urine samples can be required to check on compliance with any drug-related condition which is attached to a grant of bail.[612] The conditions may affect other rights, such as the right to freedom of movement. Furthermore, as noted in Chapter 18 below, a court can (but ought not to) use bail conditions to limit the freedom of a defendant to exercise rights to protest and express political views pending trial. Such potential abuses of bail procedures need careful monitoring.

If remanded in custody, the accused is entitled to have a summary trial or committal hearing within a set time (in most places now seventy days, although there are some regional variations), and there is a limit to the time which may elapse between committal and trial on indictment (now 112 days). The period may be extended by the court, but if the procedures are not complied with the defendant must be given bail.[613] When a person with special needs (such as a child with psychological problems, or a physically disabled adult) is remanded in custody, the conditions of detention must be suitable for their needs. Detention in conditions which, because of their special circumstances, are demeaning, cause undue hardship, or are therapeutically inappropriate may violate ECHR Articles 3, 5, and 8.[614]

6.10 CONCLUSION

At the end of this huge chapter, it is worth taking a paragraph to identify some of the threads which run through it. First, it would be wrong to claim that PACE and the Codes of Practice represented major infringements of people's rights in this area. The principal new powers are the country-wide power to search the person for stolen or prohibited articles, and the power to hold people without charge for over twenty-four hours in respect of serious arrestable offences. The search power is open to criticism, but no more than other search powers which existed before and, like that under the Misuse of Drugs Act 1971, section 23(2), remain in force. The power to detain without charge is an extension of the previous law.

Secondly, counterbalancing the new powers are new (or newly stated in statutory form) rights for detainees. The right to legal advice, the right of members of vulner-

---

[611] Bail Act 1976, s. 4(9), added by the Criminal Justice and Court Services Act 2000, s. 58.

[612] PACE, ss. 63B, 63C, added by the Criminal Justice and Court Services Act 2000, s. 57. Under the Bail Act 1976, ss. 3(6ZAA) and 3AA, and the Children and Young Persons Act 1969, ss. 23(7) and 23AA (as amended and inserted by the Criminal Justice and Police Act 2001, ss. 131 and 132), courts can impose a requirement that the defendant should submit to electronic tagging as a condition of bail, to check that conditions of bail are being complied with.

[613] Prosecution of Offences Act 1975, s. 22(3); Prosecution of Offences (Custody Time Limits) Regulations 1987, SI 1987/299, as amended; *R. v. Sheffield Justices, ex parte Turner* [1991] 2 WLR 987, [1991] 1 All ER 858, DC. On the effect of a new charge being laid, see *R. (Wardle) v. Crown Court at Leeds* [2001] 2 WLR 865, HL.

[614] *Price v. United Kingdom.* Eur. Ct. HR, App. No. 33394/96, Judgment of 10 July 2001; *R. (S.R.) v. Nottingham Magistrates' Court* [2001] EWHC Admin 802; *Napier v. The Scottish Ministers, The Times,* 15 November 2001.

able groups to have an appropriate adult present, and the right to communicate with people outside the police station are all important. The efficacy of the first of these rights depends crucially on the operation of an effective twenty-four-hour duty solicitor scheme. This is a case, therefore, where civil liberties depend crucially on the expenditure of public money to make the detainee's freedom to obtain legal advice a real one. This illustrates the point made by Raz (Chapter 1 above) about the way in which many individual freedoms depend on social and governmental action to make them realizable.

Thirdly, there are questions about the adequacy of the safeguards. Many of these depend on the requirement for reasonable grounds for belief or suspicion. There is some scepticism, supported by the observational studies, about the ability of such statutory standards to control police behaviour. Others turn on record-keeping, an exercise of questionable value unless senior officers and defence solicitors are routinely prepared to spend time checking the records. In these areas, police attitudes are more important than legal rules. As an aid to changing those attitudes, the approach of the courts to the detention and questioning provisions, excluding substantial numbers of alleged confessions under section 78 of PACE for breaches of the rules, or holding them to be inadmissible under section 76, is potentially powerful, as well as being, in my view (although some others disagree), a welcome and belated reassertion of the values of the rule of law in relation to the law governing policing.

Finally, there are a few (mainly fairly limited) areas in which the implementation of the European Convention on Human Rights in English law by way of the Human Rights Act 1998 may make a difference to the way in which ordinary people are treated.

7

RIGHTS UNDER RESTRAINT: DETENTION
OF PRISONERS AND PATIENTS

This chapter considers the detention of people for reasons which have nothing to do with criminal investigation: the conditions in which people are imprisoned after conviction, and the detention of people for medical reasons. We will consider both the justification for detention and the rights of those who are detained.

The provisions of English law governing the punishment and treatment of convicted offenders are highly complex. While some forms of punishment have been abolished (such as flogging and hanging),[1] other types of punishment available to sentencers have proliferated.[2] The main form of sentence which has implications for the right to liberty is imprisonment. Sections 7.1 to 7.4 deal with the conditions under which imprisonment is lawful. Section 7.5 examines the compulsory treatment of patients under the Mental Health Act 1983.

7.1 CONDITIONS OF IMPRISONMENT IN INTERNATIONAL HUMAN RIGHTS LAW AND UK LAW

(1) INTERNATIONAL STANDARDS

Deprivation of liberty as a punishment is within the contemplation of the European Convention on Human Rights, Article 5(1)(a), so long as it follows conviction by a competent court and is 'in accordance with a procedure prescribed by law'. Where these conditions are not complied with, Article 5(5) requires that victims 'shall have an enforceable right to compensation'. As noted in Chapter 5, Article 10(3) of the International Covenant on Civil and Political Rights insists that the essential aim of the treatment of prisoners is to be 'their reformation and social rehabilitation'. Article 10(1) further requires that people deprived of their liberty are to be treated with humanity and with 'respect for the inherent dignity of the human person'. Article 7 of the International Covenant on Civil and Political Rights (ICCPR), and Article 3 of the European Convention on Human Rights, each outlaws torture and inhuman or

---

[1] The last vestiges of capital punishment—for treason and piracy—were abolished by the Crime and Disorder Act 1998, s.36, following Parliament's decision to include ECHR Protocol No. 6 among the Convention rights in the Human Rights Act 1998. See Ch. 4, above.

[2] See Powers of Criminal Courts (Sentencing) Act 2000.

degrading treatment or punishment. The implications of these provisions for conditions of imprisonment and medical detention form one of the themes of this chapter.[3]

Under the ICCPR, the Human Rights Committee has held that conditions of detention amount to inhumanity and fail to respect the dignity of the person where people were held in isolation, yet subjected to continuous surveillance, were malnourished, kept without natural light or exercise, and denied family visits, over a long period.[4] Other examples include cases where a prisoner was kept for a long period in isolation in a dirty cell which was excessively hot in summer and cold in winter, without light,[5] or in a grossly overcrowded cell with men, women, and children in filthy, vermin-infested conditions, without proper sleeping arrangements or windows.[6] These are very serious conditions, which could easily threaten physical or mental health. The Human Rights Committee has also treated solitary confinement in a small cell as amounting to inhuman treatment under Article 7 when it continued for ten years.[7]

Under Article 3 of the European Convention, the Commission found a breach of the prohibition on inhuman or degrading treatment in *Denmark et al. v. Greece*,[8] where prisoners were subjected to severe overcrowding in cells and corridors used as sleeping and living accommodation with little natural light, were given no beds or mattresses, and experienced refusal to provide, or delays in providing, medical treatment for significant illnesses, and these conditions continued for long periods. On the other hand, the Commission was prepared to treat some fairly awful conditions of imprisonment as compatible with the minimum guarantees of Article 3. For example, in *Kröcher and Möller v. Switzerland*[9] it decided that being kept for two months in solitary confinement, under constant artificial light, subject to surveillance, did not violate Article 3. Applications relating solely to solitary confinement have accordingly had no success.[10]

More recently, however, the European Court of Human Rights, while reiterating that the duration of the treatment and the degree of suffering which it causes must reach a certain level of severity in order to violate Article 3, has shown itself readier to find that the conditions of imprisonment have amounted to inhuman or degrading treatment. As Phillippa Kaufmann observes,[11]

---

[3] See generally N. Rodley, *The Treatment of Prisoners under International Law*, 2nd edn. (Oxford: Clarendon Press, 1999), ch. 9.

[4] *Estrella v. Uruguay*, Application No. 79/1980, and *Cámpora v. Uruguay*, Application No. 66/1980.

[5] *Manera v. Uruguay*, Application No. 123/1982.

[6] *Griffin v. Spain*, Application No. 493/1992, UN doc. CCPR/C/57/WP.1 (1996).

[7] *Edwards v. Jamaica*, App. No. 529/1993, UN doc. CCPR/C/60/D/529/1993 (1997).

[8] (3321–3/67, 3344/67) (1969) 12 *Yearbook of the European Convention on Human Rights The Greek Case*; (1968) 11 *Yearbook* 690, 730.

[9] (8463/78) Eur. Comm. HR (1983).

[10] See, e.g. *Brady v. United Kingdom* (8575/79) 3 EHRR 297, Eur. Comm. HR; P. J. Duffy, 'Article 3 of the European Convention on Human Rights' (1983) *ICLQ* 316 at 329–35; G. Zellick, 'Human Rights and the Treatment of Offenders', in J. A. Andrews (ed.), *Human Rights in Criminal Procedure* (The Hague: Martinus Nijhoff, 1981), 375–416.

[11] P. Kaufmann, 'Prisoners', in K. Starmer, *European Human Rights Law: The Human Rights Act 1998 and the European Convention on Human Rights* (London: Legal Action Group, 1999), ch. 16 at 457.

'the question whether the conditions of confinement violate article 3 is one which is particu-larly dependent on the evolving standards which flow from the Convention's status as a living instrument. What were considered to be "normal conditions of confinement" in the mid-1970s may well be unacceptable now.'

The Court has held that seriously defective medical care, including failing to provide psychiatrically qualified medical staff to treat a prisoner known to suffer from severe mental disorder, inadequately monitoring his condition, and failing to maintain proper medical notes, violated Article 3, because of the positive obligations on state authorities for the health of those in their care.[12] Keeping prisoners in dirty, over-crowded, insanitary conditions, without proper sleeping facilities for over sixteen months while awaiting deportation, with few opportunities for outdoor exercise or recreation, has been held to violate Article 3.[13] The Court has also left open the possibility that imposing a life sentence without hope of release on a juvenile, or refusing for an unreasonable time to specify a date at which a juvenile might hope to be released, would violate Article 3 of the ECHR, taking account of the prohibition on life imprisonment of a child without possibility of release in Article 37 of the UN Convention on the Rights of the Child.[14] There are signs of a growing convergence between the standards of the various international adjudicative and monitoring bodies on unacceptable treatment of prisoners.

Some international instruments go further in laying down detailed standards for prison authorities to observe. The United Nations Standard Minimum Rules for the Treatment of Prisoners set out principles of good practice in the treatment of prisoners and the management of prisons, to be applied in the light of local condi-tions. These are aspirational principles. They include a requirement for prisoners normally to be accommodated at night in single cells (rule 9(1)), and to be allowed natural light, fresh air, and artificial light when desired (rule 11). Sanitation should be such as to permit prisoners to comply with the needs of nature when necessary, and in a clean and decent manner (rule 12). There are provisions relating to medical services (rules 22–6), and requiring communication with family and reputable friends, including visits, at regular intervals (rule 37).

The European Prison Rules, adopted in 1987,[15] attempt to outline the proper objectives of prison authorities in setting standards for treatment and accommoda-tion of prisoners. European Prison Rule 71(3), for example, requires authorities to

---

[12] *Keenan v. United Kingdom*, Eur. Ct. HR, App. No. 27229/95, Judgment of 3 April 2001, at paras. 113–15. *Cp. Kudła v. Poland*, Eur. Ct. HR, App. No. 30210/96, Judgment of 26 October 2000, at paras. 94–100.

[13] *Dougoz v. Greece*, Eur. Ct. HR, App. No. 40907/98, Judgment of 6 March 2001, where the Court took account of the views of the European Committee for the Prevention of Torture on its visits to Greece.

[14] *T. and V. v. United Kingdom*, Eur. Ct. HR, App. Nos. 24724/94 and 24888/94, Judgments of 16 December 1999, at paras. 96–9 of the judgments. The Court also took account of Rule 17.1(b) of the UN Standard Minimum Rules for the Administration of Juvenile Justice, adopted by the UN General Assembly in 1985 (the 'Beijing Rules'), which are not binding in international law but were treated as representing a certain level of international consensus: 'Restrictions on the personal liberty of the juvenile shall be imposed only after careful consideration and shall be limited to the possible minimum'.

[15] Recommendation No. R(87)3 of the Committee of Ministers of the Council of Europe, adopted 12 February 1987.

provide useful work or other purposeful activities to keep prisoners actively employed for a normal working day; rule 14(1) provides that prisoners shall normally be lodged at night in individual cells unless it is considered that there are advantages in sharing with other prisoners; rule 17 requires that sanitary arrangements 'enable every prisoner to comply with the needs of nature when necessary and in clean and decent conditions'. However, neither the UN Standard Minimum Rules nor the European Prison Rules are binding in international law or in the domestic law of the UK. They are intended as guidelines for national authorities, and also for the Human Rights Committee and the European Court of Human Rights when relevant to human rights complaints which they are considering.

(2) STANDARDS IN THE UK[15a]

The UK's current legal regime for prisons is governed by statute—the Prison Act 1952—and subordinate legislation (the Prison Rules 1999). The Rules are contained in a Statutory Instrument, and are justiciable to the extent that the court, on an application for judicial review of disciplinary penalties, can determine whether the governor or Board of Visitors which decided the case interpreted the rule correctly, and whether it is *intra vires* in the sense of being consistent with the Prison Act and other primary legislation.

On the other hand, it has also been decided that a breach of the rules by the governor or prison officers will not in itself give rise to an action for breach of statutory duty at the suit of an aggrieved prisoner.[16] Instead, they typically impose obligations on prisoners. As Stephen Shaw pointed out,[17] what is now rule 31(1) of the Prison Rules 1999, dealing with work, provides that prisoners 'shall be required to do useful work', making it in effect one of the pains of imprisonment rather than a dignity-enhancing right, and placing no obligation on the authorities to provide useful work for the prisoners to do. The Woolf/Tumim report suggested instituting contracts between prison authorities and inmates,[18] setting out the kind of regime which each establishment would undertake to provide for its inmates, while each inmate would agree to comply with the responsibilities placed on him by the contract, giving progressively more preparation for release as the end of the sentence approached.[19] In reality, such arrangements can impose no legal obligation on prison authorities to provide opportunities for work of that kind, which depend on resources and often on winning contracts to supply outside companies, so they are always likely to be used more to discipline or control prisoners than to help them to prepare for release.

By the early 1990s it was clear that many British prisons fell below the standard

[15a] See generally S. Livingstone and T. Owen QC, *Prison Law*, 2nd edn. (Oxford: Clarendon Press, 1999).

[16] *R. v. Deputy Governor of Parkhurst Prison, ex parte Hague; Weldon v. Home Office* [1991] 3 All ER 733, HL.

[17] S. Shaw, 'Prisoners' Rights', in P. Sieghart (ed.), *Human Rights in the UK* (London: Human Rights Network, 1988), 40–9 at 42.

[18] Cm. 1456, paras. 12.120–12.129.

[19] Ibid., paras. 14.57–14.83.

envisaged in the UN Standard Minimum Rules and the European Prison Rules. Successive reports had made recommendations for improving minimum standards of prison conditions. The May Committee of Inquiry into the UK Prison Service in 1979 recommended that conditions should be improved to remove the need for prisoners to share cells (something which Jeremy Bentham's panopticon prison designs in the early years of the nineteenth century were intended to eliminate) and slop out their excreta from buckets. In 1983, both HM Chief Inspector of Prisons and the House of Commons Select Committee on Education, Science, and the Arts, called for a code of standards to be introduced legislatively. As Stephen Shaw commented,[20] 'Establishing a code of more specific, enforceable standards—a role neither the Convention on Human Rights nor the European Prison Rules were designed to fulfil—has become a unifying demand of all the parties to the penal debate, with the critical exception of the British government'. Little was done in response: there has never been much political capital to be made from helping prisoners.

The European Committee for the Prevention of Torture and Inhuman or Degrading Treatment (CPT),[21] the monitoring agency under the European Convention for the Prevention of Torture and Inhuman or Degrading Treatment or Punishment,[22] visited a number of prisons and police stations in the UK in 1990. Its Report[23] found some things to praise, but made a number of damning criticisms. These included:[24]

(a) overcrowding, with several people to a cell designed for one;

(b) the need to defecate in buckets in the presence of other people in a confined space used as a living area is degrading;

(c) slopping out the buckets when cells are unlocked in the morning is debasing for the prisoners and supervising officers;

(d) lack of decency even where toilet facilities are available, especially within shared cells;

(e) inadequate exercise and work facilities, leading to many prisoners being locked in cells for twenty-two or more hours a day, while work which was available tended to be dull and repetitive and did not involve skills which might be useful to the prisoner on release.

The CPT's conclusion was that 'the cumulative effect of overcrowding, lack of integral sanitation and inadequate regimes amounts to inhuman and degrading treatment'.[25] This is in line with criticisms levelled at prison conditions by Judge Stephen Tumim, HM Chief Inspector of Prisons, in a series of reports both before and after the CPT's report. In looking at the cumulative effect of conditions and treatment, the CPT's approach is in line with that of the Human Rights Committee to

[20] Shaw, 'Prisoners' Rights', 42.
[21] On the work of the CPT, see M. D. Evans and R. Morgan, *Preventing Torture: A Study of the European Convention for the Prevention of Torture and Inhuman or Degrading Treatment or Punishment* (Oxford: Clarendon Press, 1998), chs 5–8.
[22] Discussed by Evans and Morgan, *Preventing Torture*, ch. 4; A. Cassese, 'A New Approach to Human Rights: the European Convention for the Prevention of Torture' (1989) 83 *Amer. J. Int. L.* 128–53.
[23] Adopted by the CPT on 21 March 1991 and published as CPT/Inf (91) 15 on 26 November 1991.
[24] Report, paras. 40, 45, 47, 50, 53–6.   [25] Report, para. 57.

establishing breaches of Articles 7 and 10 of the International Covenant on Civil and Political Rights. The conditions were perhaps not as bad as those which had at the time led the European Commission of Human Rights and the European Court of Human Rights to uphold complaints of inhuman or degrading treatment. But since then the Strasbourg Court has embraced the idea that prison conditions can amount to inhuman or degrading treatment,[26] making it possible that the standard to be applied under the Human Rights Act 1998 is moving closer to that used by the CPT.

Although the government rejected most of the findings of the CPT in 1990, the Woolf/Tumim report in 1991 found that prisoners had legitimate grievances and, often, no satisfactory way of ventilating them which would offer a reasonable likelihood that they would be dealt with. In response, the government established a Prisons Ombudsman, to examine complaints. However, the position of the Prisons Ombudsman as an administrative institution without statutory authority has undermined any real chance that the position could be used to improve conditions substantially.[27] Unsatisfactory standards in prisons remain.

The Woolf/Tumim report in 1991 found that there was still a high level of overcrowding, coupled with inadequate sanitation for prisoners in their cells, in a number of prisons. The report noted, 'Successive Chief Inspectors [of Prisons] have made it clear that they regard the practice of slopping out as uncivilised, unhygienic and degrading'.[28] The report identified overcrowded and insanitary conditions in prisons as factors in creating the conditions for the prison riots of 1990.[29] The government initiated a major building and renovation programme, and greatly reduced both the number of prisoners who were forced to slop out and the proportion of inmates in multi-occupancy cells. However, the prison population increased during the decade,[30] and the building programme has not kept pace with it.

It is therefore not surprising that conditions in many penal establishments continue to provoke censure from HM Chief Inspector of Prisons. For example, in 2000 an inspection of Birmingham Prison found appalling conditions and a deep malaise affecting virtually all aspects of prison life, in an institution which already spent less per prisoner than comparable establishments and had been told to cut its budget by a further £860,000.[31] Under the Human Rights Act 1998, it will become increasingly

[26] See, e.g. *Dougoz v. Greece*, Eur. Ct. HR, App. No. 40907/98, Judgment of 6 March 2001.

[27] For a thorough evaluation of the scheme, see P. E. Morris and R. J. Henham, 'The Prisons Ombudsman: A Critical Review' (1998) 4 *European Public Law* 345–78.

[28] Ibid., para. 11.101.

[29] Ibid., paras. 11.81–11.112.

[30] Admissions to prison fell in the early 1990s, but rose again so that by 1999 they were higher than in 1989. The daily average prison population also rose over the decade as a whole. In 1999 the average male population was about a third higher than in 1989 (64,771, compared with 48,610), and the average female population was approaching double the 1989 level (3,247 compared with 1,761): Home Office, *Prison Statistics, England and Wales 1999*, Cm. 4805 (London: The Stationery Office, 2000), Table 1.4. Lack of toilet facilities in cells has been held to breach ECHR Art. 3: *Napier v. The Scottish Ministers*, *The Times*, 15 November 2001.

[31] HM Chief Inspector of Prisons for England and Wales, *HM Prison Birmingham: Report of an Announced Inquiry 10–18 July 2000* (London: Home Office, 2001). Similar problems were found to afflict other establishments to varying degrees. See, e.g. HM Chief Inspector of Prisons for England and Wales, *Stoke Heath Young Offender Institution: Report of an Announced Inquiry, 2–6 October 2000* (London: Home Office, 2001); ibid., *HM Prison Brixton: Report of an Unannounced Inspection 26–29 June 2000* (London: Home Office, 2001).

hard for prison authorities to avoid being held to have violated the right of prisoners to be free of inhuman or degrading treatment, particularly as financial constraints cannot be prayed in aid to justify such treatment.

It is difficult for prisoners to keep in touch with the outside world. Although a series of decisions of the European Court of Human Rights and English courts led to some relaxation of the restrictions on correspondence, rule 35(2)(a) of the Prison Rules 1999 allows convicted prisoners to send and receive only one letter per week. Personal contact is even more limited. The Woolf/Tumim report pointed out that the normal allowance of visits (now one or two thirty-minute visits every four weeks for convicted prisoners: Prison Rules 1999, rule 35(2)(b)) is woefully inadequate for maintaining family contact.[32] This gives rise to questions about compliance with the right to respect for family life under Article 8 of the ECHR. While it is permissible to restrict contact in order to maintain security, the state may have an obligation to a child of a prisoner to interfere as little as possible with family relationships, and (as where a child is taken into the care of a public authority) to arrange matters so that there is a reasonable chance of an existing parent-child relationship being maintained and resumed successfully on an inmate's release. The relationship between imprisoned women and their babies and young children is particularly difficult. Apart from the degrading experience of some women who have been shackled during labour in hospital, there is a shortage of mother and baby units in prison. Even those mothers and babies who are allowed to remain together are separated once the toddlers reach the age of eighteen months. The Home Office is concerned about the welfare of the children, and rightly regards a prison upbringing as less than ideal. It may, however, be better than being separated from a mother with whom one has bonded, and put into the care of a local authority until the mother has completed what may be a long sentence: see page 443, below.

Home leave can be offered to prisoners as a matter of discretion, but it is a privilege, not a right. The purpose is to start the process of reintegration into life outside the prison, and to allow prisoners to re-establish the relationships with family and society which are important to avoiding re-offending after release. Because it has not been regarded as a right, legal protection for it has been very limited. The practice of allowing prisoners to apply for home leave after completing one third of their sentence was held not to give rise to a legitimate expectation, so the Home Secretary could lawfully change the system, making prisoners eligible only after serving half their sentence, in his unfettered discretion.[33] This is unlikely to be significantly affected by Article 8 of the ECHR becoming part of national law under the Human Rights Act 1998, except perhaps to require the Home Secretary to leave more room for family circumstances to be taken into account more flexibly and at an early date.

---

[32] Rt. Hon. Lord Justice Woolf and His Honour Judge Stephen Tumim, *Prison Disturbances April 1990*, Cm. 1456 (London: HMSO, 1991), paras. 14.225 *et seq.*

[33] *R. v. Secretary of State for the Home Department, ex parte Hargreaves* [1997] 1 WLR 906, [1997] 1 All ER 397, CA.

7.2 THE INITIATION OF IMPRISONMENT IN THE UK

In general, the requirements of Article 5(1)(a) of the European Convention on Human Rights—that imprisonment must only follow conviction by a competent court, and must be in accordance with a procedure prescribed by law—are met by English law, which lays down in detail the circumstances in which detention or imprisonment can be imposed as a punishment for offences, and the maximum terms which can be imposed. In Northern Ireland, the power to impose detention without charge by administrative order (internment), utilized from 1971 to 1975 in Northern Ireland to contain suspected terrorists, finally fell out of the legislation when the Northern Ireland (Emergency Provisions) Act 1996 was passed, reflecting the belief that armed conflict would cease and security would improve.[34] Although such preventive detention violated ECHR Article 5,[35] the UK could lawfully reintroduce it and derogate from its obligations under Article 5 if there were to be a renewed 'public emergency threatening the life of the nation' within the meaning of Article 15, under which states are allowed a 'margin of appreciation' in deciding what steps are strictly required to deal with the emergency.[36] The Anti-terrorism, Crime and Security Bill 2001 would introduce a form of detention without trial for certain suspected international terrorists, accompanied by a derogation from ECHR Article 5.

There was formerly a lacuna in relation to the enforceable right to compensation for unlawful detention, required by Article 5(5). At common law, a judge of a superior court of record enjoys an immunity from suit in relation to acts done judicially. The immunity is designed to allow judges to act fearlessly as they think right, so long as they are acting in good faith in purported performance of their duties.[37] Magistrates, by contrast, had no common law immunity, but have long been protected by statute. Until 1997, they were immune from liability when acting within their jurisdiction, but when acting outside jurisdiction they might be liable (although if acting in the execution of his office as a justice, damages would be limited to one penny unless the plaintiff proved bad faith and lack of reasonable and probable cause).[38] If a person was imprisoned for an offence for which he was not liable to imprisonment as a matter of law, or was imprisoned for longer than the law allowed, he would have suffered a punishment greater than that assigned by law, and so would have been able to recover damages at large for the imprisonment.[39] However, if the person could lawfully have been committed to the term of imprisonment but the order was vitiated by a procedural error, his damages were limited to one penny.[40] This difference

---

[34] e.g. Lord Colville, *Review of the Northern Ireland (Emergency Provisions) Act*, Cm. 1115, ch. 11.

[35] See Ch. 6, above.

[36] *Ireland v. United Kingdom*, Eur. Ct. HR, Series A, No. 25, Judgment of 18 January 1978, 2 EHRR 25.

[37] See *Sirros v. Moore* [1975] QB 118, [1974] 3 All ER 776, CA. For analysis and critique of judicial immunity, see A. Olowofoyeku, *Suing Judges: A Study of Judicial Immunity* (Oxford: Clarendon Press, 1993).

[38] Justices of the Peace Act 1979, ss. 44, 45, 52; *In re McC. (A Minor)* [1985] AC 528, [1984] 3 All ER 908, HL; *R. v. Waltham Forest Justices, ex parte Solanke* [1986] QB 983, [1986] 2 All ER 981, CA.

[39] *R. v. Manchester City Magistrates' Court, ex parte Davies* [1989] QB 631, [1989] 1 All ER 90, CA.

[40] *R. v. Waltham Forest Justices, ex parte Solanke* [1986] QB 983, [1986] 2 All ER 981, CA.

according to the nature of the judge was criticized by Lord Denning MR, but was reaffirmed by the House of Lords.[41]

The difference has since been largely removed. Section 51 of the Justices of the Peace Act 1997[42] now gives an immunity to magistrates (and to their clerk when exercising the functions of a justice) in respect of acts or omissions either in the execution of their duty or with respect to any matter within their jurisdiction. Where a magistrate or clerk does something purportedly in the execution of his duty, but in law outside his jurisdiction (for example, by imposing a sentence for which there was no lawful authority, or by committing a serious procedural irregularity),[43] section 52 provides that an action lies only if it is proved that he acted in bad faith. This removes the anomaly which Lord Denning tried unsuccessfully to remove by judicial decision.

But there is a less satisfactory result: it leaves many people without remedies for the injurious effects of unlawful orders. In general, judicial officers have immunity even if they violate a Convention right under Schedule 1 to the Human Rights Act 1998. Although courts are public authorities, bound by section 6 of the Act to behave in a manner compatible with Convention rights unless compelled by primary legislation to do otherwise, section 9(1) provides that proceedings in respect of an alleged violation of a Convention right by a judicial act may be brought only by exercising a right of appeal or by applying for judicial review. By section 9(3), damages may usually not be awarded for such an act done in good faith. However, there is a limited exception which allows damages to be awarded 'to compensate a person to the extent required by Article 5(5) of the Convention', that is, damages for an arrest or detention in contravention of the provisions of Article 5. It is not enough to show that the order for arrest or detention was unlawful. For damages to be awarded, the claimant must have been a victim of a violation of Article 5 (either in respect of the original arrest or detention, or through over-long detention or failure to provide a proper review of the lawfulness of detention) as a result. Such damages are to be awarded against the Crown, for which purpose the Minister responsible for the court which committed the violation must be either a party to, or joined in, the proceedings.

When a person who was convicted and sentenced has his conviction quashed, there is a limited statutory right to compensation under the Criminal Justice Act 1988. The person must show beyond reasonable doubt that there has been a miscarriage of justice, either by proving that the conviction resulted from non-disclosure of evidence which was not wholly or partly due to him, or by producing new evidence. It is for the Home Secretary to decide whether or not a person is entitled to compensation, subject to judicial review on the usual public-law grounds. If he decides that compensation is due, he appoints an assessor, who must be legally qualified, to determine the amount which is to be paid.[44]

---

[41] *In re McC. (A Minor)* [1985] AC 528, [1984] 3 All ER 908, HL.

[42] The Justices of the Peace Act 1997 consolidates the Justices of the Peace Act 1979 with amendments made by the Police and Magistrates' Courts Act 1994, Part IV.

[43] See *In re McC. (A Minor)* [1985] AC 528, [1984] 3 All ER 908, HL.

[44] Criminal Justice Act 1988, s. 133 and Sch. 12.

7.3 RIGHTS AND REMEDIES IN DETENTION IN NATIONAL LAW

Generally, three questions arise in relation to prisoners. First, what rights do prisoners retain when they enter captivity? Secondly, what special rights (if any) accrue to them? Thirdly, how are their rights enforceable?

(1) RETAINED RIGHTS

At common law, it used to be the case that prisoners, at any rate if convicted of felonies, lost all their civil rights and liberties. They even lost the right to bring legal proceedings, so that they became, in legal terms, non-people. In Australia, this view, derived from early nineteenth-century English law, prevailed for longer than in the UK.[45]

However, this view is inconsistent with modern attitudes to rights. In the USA it has long been held that a prisoner's right to apply to federal courts for a writ of habeas corpus cannot be inhibited by states,[46] and habeas corpus has therefore become an important weapon in the armoury of convicted murderers seeking to delay or avoid execution of the death penalty. The right of access to courts also demands a right to legal advice from advisers with legal training, and adequate library facilities.[47] In England and Wales, too, a convicted prisoner does not now become a non-person. Rule 3 of the Prison Rules 1999 provides that the purpose the training and treatment of convicted prisoners is to encourage and assist them to lead a good and useful life. Rule 32 requires prison authorities to provide educational classes at every prison, to encourage prisoners to profit from them, and to pay special attention to prisoners with special educational needs. Rule 33 requires the authorities to provide a library in every prison, and allows every prisoner to have and exchange books from the library (subject to directions of the Home Secretary). This reflects the insistence in Article 10(3) of the International Covenant on Civil and Political Rights that the essential aim of the treatment of prisoners is their reformation and social rehabilitation, as noted in section 7.1, above.

Consistently with the UK's obligations under international law, courts have held that prisoners retain all their rights except so far as they are taken away expressly by legislation or by necessary implication, having regard to the nature of imprisonment.[48] Indeed, there is a presumption that any civil right is retained unless it is taken away expressly, or its loss is an inevitable consequence of imprisonment.[49] Where a

---

[45] *Dugan v. Mirror Newspapers Ltd.* (1978) 142 CLR 583, HC of Australia. The law was changed in New South Wales by Felons (Civil Proceedings) Act 1981 (NSW).

[46] *Ex parte Hull* 312 US 546 (1941); *Johnson v. Avery* 393 US 483 (1969).

[47] *Procunier v. Martinez* 416 US 421 (1974): ban on interviews with law students or paralegals unconstitutional; *Bounds v. Smith* 430 US 817 (1977).

[48] *R. v. Hull Prison Board of Visitors, ex parte St Germain* [1979] 1 QB 425; *Raymond* v. *Honey* [1983] 1 AC 1, [1982] 1 All ER 756; *R. v. Secretary of State for the Home Department, ex parte Leech* [1994] QB 198, [1993] 4 All ER 539, CA. The same is true in Canada: *Solosky v. R.* (1979) 105 DLR (3rd) 745 at 760 *per* Dickson J in the Supreme Court of Canada.

[49] *R. v. Secretary of State for the Home Department, ex parte Simms* [2000] 2 AC 15, [1999] 3 WLR 328, 331 *per* Lord Steyn (with whom Lords Browne-Wilkinson, Hoffmann, and Millett expressed agreement), approving the *dictum* of Judge LJ in the Court of Appeal, [1999] QB 349 at 367.

right is retained, it may be permissible to restrict it in the interests of security or good discipline, but where it is a fundamental right, such as freedom of expression, and is being exercised for a legitimate purpose, such as to engage the investigative power of the press to correct what is alleged to be a miscarriage of justice, the prison authorities must show that the interference is justified by a pressing social need. The more substantial the interference with a fundamental right, the stronger will be the justification required if it is not to be regarded as unreasonable, and hence unlawful, in the public law sense.[50] Furthermore, as an aspect of the constitutional principle of legality, legislation (both primary and subordinate, and including the Prison Rules) is normally presumed to be made subject to fundamental rights. It will be regarded as restricting fundamental rights only if, and so far as, it does so clearly and unambiguously. It will not be interpreted as conferring a delegated power to make orders or give directions which take away a right unless it confers that power clearly, by unambiguous express words or necessary implication.[51]

The right which is most obviously lost on incarceration is that to liberty, and there are other rights which are inevitably restricted, either in order to maintain security and order in prison or because a person's freedom of choice is automatically attenuated under conditions of imprisonment. Restrictions here, as in the USA, include limitations on privacy rights and freedom of communications.[52] The nature of the rights which are lost and those which are retained has been the subject of attention both in the English courts and, under various Articles of the European Convention on Human Rights, in the European Commission and Court of Human Rights.[53]

A less obvious right for prisoners to lose is the right to vote in local and national elections. The Representation of the People Act 2000 deprives convicted persons who are serving a sentence of detention in a penal institution of the right to vote. Excluding prisoners from the ranks of those entitled to a say in democratic decision-making reinforces the sense that they are outcasts from civil society, and might be thought to be inconsistent with the idea of retained rights, since there is no security reason or other objectively rational necessity to deprive them of a basic right of citizens. However, Parliament is free to legislate inconsistently with fundamental, constitution rights as long as it does so clearly and unambiguously. The free expression of the people, guaranteed under Article 3 of Protocol No. 1 to the ECHR, has been held to be compatible with prisoners not being able to express their individual views, and the

---

[50] *R. v. Secretary of State for the Home Department, ex parte Simms* [1999] 3 WLR 328 at 340 *per* Lord Steyn, with whom Lord Browne-Wilkinson and Lord Hoffmann agreed.

[51] *R. v. Secretary of State for the Home Department, ex parte Pierson* [1998] AC 539 at 573–5 *per* Lord Browne-Wilkinson, 587–90 *per* Lord Steyn; *R. v. Secretary of State for the Home Department, ex parte Simms* [1999] 3 WLR 328 at 340 *per* Lord Steyn, 341–2 *per* Lord Hoffmann.

[52] *Turner v. Safley* 482 US 78 (1981).

[53] See G. Douglas and S. Jones, 'Prisoners and the European Convention on Human Rights', in M. P. Furmston, R. Kerridge, and B. E. Sufrin (eds.), *The Effect on English Domestic Law of Membership of the European Communities and of Ratification of the European Convention on Human Rights* (The Hague: Martinus Nijhoff, 1983); G. Richardson, 'Time to Take Prisoners' Rights Seriously' (1984) **11** *J. L. and Soc.* 1–23. For a comparative survey of prisoners' rights in the UK, Australia, the US, and Canada, see G. Hawkins, *Prisoners' Rights: A Study of Human Rights and Commonwealth Prisoners*, Human Rights Commission Occasional Paper No. 12 (Canberra: AGPS, 1986).

Court of Appeal has held that discriminating against prisoners in the enjoyment of rights under that Article does not violate their non-discrimination rights under Article 14 of the ECHR, because prisoners are inevitably treated less favourably than others in many ways.[54] The decision on the discrimination point is slightly surprising, since discrimination is required to be justified by reference to objective and rational criteria under Article 14, and it is not clear what they are in the case of prisoners' voting rights.

(2) COMMUNICATION AND LITIGATION

Prisoners retain the right at common law and under Article 6 of the European Convention on Human Rights to have access to the courts to have their civil rights and obligations determined, and it is a contempt of court for anyone, including the prison authorities, to attempt to interfere with the exercise of the right (for example, by intercepting or censoring letters which are attempting to initiate court proceedings).[55] However, this does not necessarily encompass a right to be transported to court at public expense for a hearing, unless it is necessary for the prisoner to appear in order to present his or her own case or give evidence. Where the prisoner is given legal aid, and the proceedings are conducted without witnesses (like a normal judicial review hearing), the Home Secretary retains a discretion to require a prisoner to pay for transport and escort services, subject to judicial review on ordinary public-law principles.[56]

Prisoners also retain the right to respect for their correspondence under Article 8 of the Convention. The Prison Rules and Standing Orders, which previously made provision for routine examination, reading, and stopping of correspondence, have been substantially liberalized following decisions of the European Court of Human Rights holding that the restrictions violated the right to respect for correspondence under Article 8(1) were not in accordance with a procedure prescribed by law, and went further than was justified by reference to any of the permissible justifying purposes for interference under Article 8(2).[57] The Home Office adapted the Prison Rules, but English courts responded relatively slowly. Revisions to the Prison Rules allowing mail to be sent unread to a legal adviser and any court (previously Rule 37A(1) of the Prison Rules 1964) were held not to apply to letters in connection with an application to the European Commission of Human Rights, because the Commission was regarded (probably wrongly) as not exercising any judicial functions.[58] The European

---

[54] R. (Pearson) v. Secretary of State for the Home Department, Hirst v. Attorney-General, The Times, 17 April 2001, CA.

[55] Raymond v. Honey [1983] 1 AC 1, [1982] 1 All ER 756, HL.

[56] R. v. Secretary of State for the Home Department, ex parte Wynne [1993] 1 WLR 115, [1993] 1 All ER 574, HL.

[57] See Golder v. United Kingdom, Eur. Ct. HR, Series A, No. 18, Judgment of 21 February 1975; Silver v. United Kingdom, Eur. Ct. HR, Series A, No. 61, Judgment of 25 March 1983; Boyle and Rice v. United Kingdom, Eur. Ct. HR, Series A, No. 131, Judgment of 27 April 1988; and McCallum v. United Kingdom, Eur. Ct. HR, Series A, No. 183, Judgment of 30 August 1990, where the government conceded that there had been a breach of Art. 8; Campbell v. United Kingdom, Eur. Ct. HR, Series A, No. 233, Judgment of 25 March 1992, 15 EHRR 137.

[58] Guilfoyle v. Home Office [1981] QB 309, [1981] 1 All ER 943, CA.

Court of Human Rights, however, held the opening of such mail to be an unjustifiable interference with the inmate's right to respect for privacy of correspondence under Article 8 of the Convention,[59] and the Home Office altered the Rules.[60] Only then did the courts begin to treat the right to communicate in connection with legal proceedings as an aspect of a fundamental right of access to a court. In *R. v. Secretary of State, ex parte Leech*,[61] Steyn LJ said of the right of unimpeded access to a court, 'Even in our unwritten constitution it must rank as a constitutional right'. The Court of Appeal held that the Prison Act 1952, interpreted on the presumption that it was not intended to restrict constitutional rights, conferred no power to interfere with it. The House of Lords reiterated the importance of legal professional privilege as a fundamental right relating to access to courts in *R. (Daly) v. Secretary of State for the Home Department*.[61a] A Home Office Security Manual purported to instruct prison governors to search cells, examining all papers to ensure that nothing had been written by a prisoner or stored between leaves which might endanger prison security. Searches were to be conducted in the absence of inmates, to prevent intimidation and prevent prisoners from learning about search techniques. The material to be examined included communications with lawyers. The House of Lords held that this violated the retained right to communicate confidentially with a lawyer under the seal of legal professional privilege. Such a practice could be authorized only with express statutory authority, and section 47(1) of the Prison Act 1952, empowering the Secretary of State to make rules of the regulation and control of prisoners, was not a sufficiently clear and unequivocal authorization to make the order excluding prisoners from cells during searches lawful, except where in an individual case the prisoner tried or had tried in the past to intimidate the searchers or to endanger security. The order interfered with the right to a greater extent than was justified by section 47(1), and was unlawful. Furthermore, it interfered with the prisoner's right under ECHR Article 8(1), and was disproportionate to the legitimate aim of preventing disorder or crime, bearing in mind that the court must make its own assessment of proportionality under the Human Rights Act 1998.[61b]

In *R. v. Secretary of State for the Home Department, ex parte Simms*,[62] the House of Lords extended the principle to allow a prisoner to be interviewed by journalists as part of a campaign against an alleged miscarriage of justice. Lord Steyn regarded the press as one of the means by which prisoners gain access to justice, bearing in mind the limitations of other parts of the criminal justice system revealed by high-profile miscarriages of justice. Interviews could be restricted in order to prevent disruption in prison or threats to security. But the Home Office would have to demonstrate a real

---

[59] *Campbell v. United Kingdom*, Eur. Ct. HR, Series A, No. 233, Judgment of 25 March 1992.

[60] See now Prison Rules 1999, r. 39.

[61] [1994] QB 198, [1993] 4 All ER 539, 548, CA.

[61a] [2001] 2 WLR 1622, HL.

[61b] On the proper approach to issues of proportionality, the House of Lords disapproved the approach adopted by the Court of Appeal in *R. (Mahmood) v. Secretary of State for the Home Department* [2001] 1 WLR 840, CA, which would have allowed courts to interfere with an official assessment of proportionality only if the assessment was irrational.

[62] [2000] 2 AC 15, [1999] 3 WLR 328, HL.

risk of serious disruption, or threat to security, bearing in mind the identity of the journalist concerned, in order to establish the pressing social need for, and proportionality of, the interference.[63]

But these cases are all concerned with communication about legal matters. The English courts have not yet recognized prisoners' freedom of expression and communication on other matters as fundamental. While many petty restrictions on correspondence have been removed, in accordance with the recommendations of the Woolf/Tumim report, contact with the outside world remains limited, making it hard for prisoners to maintain or establish the contacts which are important to successful reintegration into the community after release.[64]

(3) INHUMAN AND DEGRADING TREATMENT AND REGIMES AND CONDITIONS OF IMPRISONMENT

Another retained right, not surprisingly, is freedom from torture and inhuman or degrading treatment or punishment. The prison regime must respect these rights, both because it is a requirement of common law, the ECHR and the Human Rights Act 1998, and because it helps to maintain order.

As noted above, neither the Prison Act 1952 nor the Prison Rules 1999 lay down standards of accommodation for prisoners or standards of treatment. The rules require the provision of 'clothing adequate for warmth and health in accordance with a scale approved by the Secretary of State' (rule 23(3)), food which is 'wholesome, nutritious, well prepared and served, reasonably varied and sufficient in quantity' (rule 24(2)), bedding 'adequate for warmth and health' (rule 27), and 'toilet articles necessary for [the prisoner's] health and cleanliness' (rule 28(1)). But most facilities are subject to the Home Secretary's discretion, including the number of prisoners sharing sleeping accommodation (rule 26), or to institutional requirements ('if circumstances reasonably permit' or similar expressions), including physical education, time in the open air, and work (rules 29–31). Certain rules provide for detailed matters: for example, rule 45 provides that a prisoner may be segregated from other prisoners 'for the maintenance of good order and discipline or in his own interests', a provision much used to keep sex offenders apart from other prisoners who might be likely to attack them. There is also provision in rules 46 and 48 for a violent or refractory prisoner to be confined in a 'close supervision centre' for the maintenance of good order and discipline or to protect officers, other prisoners or other persons, and to be placed in a special cell until he has ceased to be refractory or violent. Such forms of confinement would usually be justified under Article 3 of the ECHR as being for the protection of the life and well-being of the offender or others, as long as the conditions of detention do not inflict an unacceptable level of suffering taking account of the facilities available and the period for

---

[63] [1999] 3 WLR 328 at 337–9.

[64] Cm. 1456 (1991), 407–9. The need for prison authorities to check letters where there is a reasonable suspicion that this is required in the interests of security was recognized by the Supreme Court of Canada in *Solosky v. R.* (1979) 105 DLR (3rd) 745.

which the offender is segregated. But there is no comprehensive set of standards for prison authorities to meet.

Meanwhile, prisoners have attempted to press their claims to improved conditions through the courts, by bringing applications for judicial review and actions for damages for false imprisonment or trespass to the person, claiming that the conditions in which they have been confined breach the Prison Rules, the Bill of Rights 1689, or common-law standards. While judicial review applications have had some impact on prison disciplinary and other procedures, they have so far failed to make any impact on the substance of prison conditions and regimes. For example, it has been held that fairness requires disclosure to a prisoner of at least the gist of the reasons for a decision not to reclassify a Category A prisoner as Category B. This security categorization is based on an assessment of, among other things, the risk posed by a prisoner and the progress made towards being suitable for release. Category A is the highest security category. The prison regime of Category A prisoners is particularly restrictive, and a decision not to downgrade a categorization affects the prisoner's prospects of being released on licence. Only the gist of the reasons need be disclosed, as long as that allows the prisoner to make meaningful and useful representations when seeking a review of the decision; if more information is needed for that purpose, it must be disclosed.[65] A reasonable time must be allowed to prisoners to make representations, and procedures should be operated flexibly to ensure fairness.[66] However, a court would only review the substance of the decision if it was wholly unreasonable in the public law sense, unless conditions amounted to degrading treatment, violating ECHR Article 3.[66a]

In this, our courts are doing no better, but probably no less well, than the US federal courts, which generally defer to the expertise of prison administrators on the conditions which prison authorities can reasonably be expected to provide and the rules by which they are governed, which, unlike many other types of administrative rules, are not subjected to strict scrutiny analysis.[67] However, the US Supreme Court has used the prohibition on cruel and unusual punishment, under the Eighth Amendment to the US Constitution, to impose a thirty-day limit on the period for which prisoners may be held in isolation cells in Arkansas prisons. The court acknowledged, and was influenced by, the fact that prisoners in Arkansas suffered bad nutrition, violence, and overcrowding, and described conditions as 'a dark and evil world completely alien to the free world'.[68] This, however, is a small step on a long road.

All the means so far used in England and Wales to seek damages to compensate for bad conditions have been unsuccessful, but there is a possibility that a new approach, based on a common-law duty of care (i.e. a simple negligence action), coupled with the applications of ECHR Article 3 via the Human Rights Act 1998, might enjoy more success. In the text which follows, the possible heads of recovery will be examined.

[65] R. v. Secretary of State for the Home Department, ex parte Duggan [1994] 3 All ER 277, DC; R. v. Secretary of State for the Home Department, ex parte McAvoy [1998] 1 WLR 790, CA.

[66] R. (Hirst) v. Secretary of State for the Home Department, The Times, 22 March 2001, CA.

[66a] See Price v. United Kingdom, Eur. Ct. HR, App. No. 33394/96, Judgment of 10 July 2001; Napier v. The Scottish Ministers, The Times, 15 November 2001, OH (Lord Macfadyen).

[67] Turner v. Safley 482 US 78 (1981), especially at 84–5; L. Fisher, American Constitutional Law (New York: McGraw-Hill, 1990), 1065; G. P. Alpert (ed.), Legal Rights of Prisoners (Beverly Hills, Calif.: Sage, 1980).

[68] Hutto v. Finney 437 US 678 (1978) at 680.

(4) FALSE IMPRISONMENT

False imprisonment is a tort of strict liability, consisting of depriving someone entirely of their liberty without legal authority. Where the authority for a prisoner's detention is a court order, it provides the prison governor with a defence to an action for false imprisonment or an application for habeas corpus. However, 'The defence of justification must be based upon a rigorous application of the principle that the liberty of the subject can be interfered with only upon grounds which a court will uphold as lawful'.[69] Thus where statute requires a person to be released after a particular time, it has been established for nearly 400 years that a public officer who imprisons him for a longer period than is authorized by statute, or in an unauthorized place, is liable for false imprisonment.[70] If a prison governor, with the statutory duty to calculate the release date, gets it wrong, the governor is not protected from liability by having acted in good faith in reliance on judicial decisions interpreting the relevant legislation which were subsequently overruled, nor by reliance on Home Office guidance (although those factors would make it inappropriate to award exemplary or punitive damages). This orthodoxy was firmly re-asserted in *R. v. Governor of Brockhill Prison, ex parte Evans (No. 2).*[71] The governor had calculated the prisoner's statutory release date on the basis of decisions which were subsequently overruled. The prisoner obtained her release by applying for habeas corpus and judicial review,[72] and claimed damages for false imprisonment. The House of Lords upheld the claim, and the award of £5,000 damages for fifty-nine days of unlawful imprisonment. There was no reason to create a new defence for the state which would deprive prisoners of protection for, and compensation for loss of, their right to liberty. 'In the present case, the state (through the legislature) has defined the power of detention; the state (through the executive) has detained the plaintiff in excess of that power; it creates no injustice that the state should compensate the plaintiff'.[73]

Similarly, it is well established that a prisoner whose liberty within the prison is restricted in an allegedly unauthorized way can maintain an action for false imprisonment, as where an imprisoned debtor (normally permitted a good deal of freedom within the prison walls) was confined to a secure part of the prison known as the 'strongroom'.[74]

Section 12(1) of the Prison Act 1952 now provides that a prisoner may be lawfully confined in any prison, and there is provision for remand prisoners to be held in police cells under the Imprisonment (Temporary Provisions) Act 1980. In a number of first-instance decisions, it was held that these provisions provide a defence for the Secretary of State or prison authorities against an action for false imprisonment

---

[69] *R. v. Governor of Brockhill Prison, ex parte Evans (No. 2)* [2000] 3 WLR 843 at 855 *per* Lord Steyn.

[70] *Scavage v. Tateham* (1601) Cro. Eliz. 829, 78 ER 1056 (justice of the peace detaining suspected robber at justice's house for eighteen days; statute authorized detention for only three days at a gaol).

[71] [2000] 3 WLR 843, HL.

[72] *R. v. Governor of Brockhill Prison, ex parte Evans* [1997] QB 443, [1997] 1 All ER 439, DC.

[73] *R. v. Governor of Brockhill Prison, ex parte Evans (No. 2)* [2000] 3 WLR at 867 *per* Lord Hobhouse of Woodborough.

[74] *Yorke v. Chapman* (1839) 10 Ad. & El. 207, 113 ER 80.

where the imprisonment has been authorized according to law and occurs in a place prescribed by law: the prisoner was said to have a cause of action for false imprisonment in respect of the *nature* of the imprisonment, as Goddard LJ said in *Arbon v. Anderson*,[75] but he could sue in relation to the *conditions* of imprisonment only if his treatment or other attendant circumstances amounted to a breach of statutory duty or some other tort.[76] This attitude was based on a policy of protecting prison discipline: as Goddard LJ said in *Arbon v. Anderson*:[77] 'It would be fatal to all discipline in prisons if governors and warders had to perform their duty always with the fear of an action before their eyes if they in any way deviated from the rules'. Lord Denning MR echoed that in *Becker v. Home Office*:[78] 'If the courts were to entertain actions by disgruntled prisoners, the governor's life would be made intolerable. The discipline of the prison would be undermined'.

The importance of this consideration has tended to be downgraded in legal argument in more recent times. Prison governors' disciplinary decisions have been opened up to judicial review,[79] the right of prisoners to have access to the courts has been upheld,[80] and it has been made clear that officials of the state will be required to demonstrate that a pressing social need justifies interfering with prisoners' fundamental rights, and that any interference is proportionate.[81] However, the tort of false imprisonment is not a promising vehicle for controlling prison conditions. It is concerned with the authority for detention rather than the conditions of detention. Admittedly there were cases in which judges were prepared to say that sufficiently bad conditions might take gaolers outside the scope of the authority to detain a prisoner given either by statute or by a court order, if the conditions were either intolerable[82] or seriously prejudicial to a prisoner's health.[83] But in *R. v. Deputy Governor of Parkhill Prison, ex parte Hague*[84] the House of Lords unanimously held that, when people are in prison pursuant to a court order, the order justifies the imprisonment (subject to any statutory limit on detention), and the prison governor and those officers who act in accordance with his directions are protected against liability for false imprisonment by section 12 of the Prison Act 1952. This means that the tort of false imprisonment offers no protection to prisoners against being detained in intolerable conditions. As Lord Bridge said:[85]

---

[75] [1943] KB 252 at 254–5, [1943] 1 All ER 154 at p. 156.

[76] *Arbon v. Anderson* [1943] KB 252, [1943] 1 All ER 154; *Williams v. Home Office (No. 2)* [1981] 1 All ER 1211, affirmed on procedural grounds [1982] 2 All ER 564, CA; *R. v. Gartree Prison Board of Visitors, ex parte Sears, The Times*, 20 March 1985.

[77] [1943] KB 252 at 255, [1943] 1 All ER 154 at 156–7.

[78] [1972] 2 QB 407 at 418, [1972] 2 All ER 676 at 682.

[79] *Leech v. Deputy Governor of Parkhurst Prison* [1988] AC 533, [1988] 1 All ER 485, HL.

[80] See, e.g. *Raymond v. Honey* [1983] 1 AC 1, [1982] 1 All ER 756, HL.

[81] See, e.g. *R. v. Secretary of State of the Home Department, ex parte Simms* [2000] 2 AC 15, [1999] 3 WLR 328, HL.

[82] *R. v. Commissioner of Police of the Metropolis, ex parte Nahar, The Times*, 28 May 1983, *per* Stephen Brown J.

[83] *Middleweek v. Chief Constable of the Merseyside Police* (1985) [1990] 3 All ER 662 at 668 *per* Ackner LJ.

[84] [1992] 1 AC 58, [1991] 3 All ER 733, HL.

[85] [1991] 3 All ER at 746.

'the proposition that the conditions of detention may render the detention itself unlawful raises formidable difficulties. If the proposition be sound, the corollary must be that when the conditions of detention deteriorate to the point of intolerability, the detainee is entitled immediately to go free. It is impossible, I think, to define with any precision what would amount to intolerable conditions for this purpose ... The law is certainly left in a very unsatisfactory state if the legality or otherwise of detaining a person who in law is and remains liable to detention depends on such an imprecise criterion and may vary from time to time as the conditions of his detention change.'

Lord Jauncey delivered a judgment to the same effect, and Lords Ackner, Goff, and Lowry agreed with both Lord Bridge and Lord Jauncey. A prisoner suffering such conditions would be entitled to a public-law remedy by way of judicial review, but the private law of false imprisonment is not to be pressed into service to combat defective conditions.

(5) BREACH OF STATUTORY DUTY

The tort of breach of statutory duty has been explored as an alternative way to provide remedies for poor conditions or special regimes in prison. A breach of the Prison Act 1952 may give rise to an action for damages if the provision breached is one which is capable of giving rise to a right in an individual prisoner. For instance, section 14(2) of the Act provides: 'No cell shall be used for the confinement of a prisoner unless it is certified by an inspector that its size, lighting, heating, ventilation and fittings are adequate for health . . .'. As this is clearly intended to benefit the prisoner, a breach of the provision should ground an action for breach of statutory duty. If this is so, those in prison are better off than people detained in police stations. The conditions of the latter are governed by the Code of Practice (Code C), section 8 of which lays down standards for the conditions which should be provided for detainees in police stations. However, section 67(10) of PACE provides that failure to comply with the Code does not in itself give rise to civil or criminal liability, although the Code is admissible in evidence and may be relevant to the scope of any duty of care in a negligence action,[86] and breach of the Code may also make an officer liable to disciplinary proceedings.[87]

A breach of merely regulatory or administrative provisions of the Prison Act 1952, or of the Prison Rules 1999, for example by denying a prisoner association under rule 45 in circumstances where segregation is not justified under the rule, would not be actionable as a breach of statutory duty. The Prison Rules are said to be regulatory only, intended to provide a framework for the running of the prison system rather than to confer rights on individual prisoners. As noted above, this is consistent with the language in which the rules are framed, and is one of the main differences between the Prison Rules 1999 and the European Prison Rules promulgated by the Council of Europe.

As the Prison Rules 1999 are merely regulatory, breach of the Rules does not give rise to an action for breach of statutory duty, as they are generally not intended to

---

[86] PACE, s. 67(11).
[87] Ibid., s. 67(8).

give rights to prisoners or to operate for their benefit. This was established in *R. v. Deputy Governor of Parkhurst Prison, ex parte Hague.*[88] Not only can a breach of the rules not ground an action in itself, but the House of Lords accepted that it cannot deprive the prison authorities of the benefit of any defence to an action for false imprisonment based on section 12(1) of the Prison Act 1952. This makes it impossible to use a breach of statutory duty action as a means of obtaining compensation for intolerable prison conditions at present, although the tort might become useful if the nature of the Prison Rules were to change in the future. In the meantime, a breach of the Prison Rules 1999, or the Prison Act 1952, is likely to provide no more than a basis for an application for judicial review of the act, omission, or decision in question. This may be a useful remedy, but will be more effective in relation to disciplinary matters, where the court's discretion is likely to be exercised in favour of the prisoner once illegality, irrationality, or procedural impropriety is shown, than in respect of general prison conditions, where the discretion is likely to be used to avoid dictating to the Home Office on matters of policy and resource allocation and management.

(4) THE BILL OF RIGHTS 1689

It was accepted in *Williams v. Home Office (No. 2)*[89] that the prohibition on cruel and unusual punishment in the Bill of Rights 1689 is capable of giving rise to an action in damages, since breach of the prohibition makes the punishment unlawful unless the particular punishment is authorized by the Prison Act 1952. (The Prison Rules, being merely secondary legislation, cannot override the prohibition in the Bill of Rights.) It may also be possible to apply for judicial review of a decision to place a prisoner in a particular type of accommodation on the ground that the conditions amount to cruel or unusual punishment.[90] It is not clear whether breach of the Bill of Rights 1689 is a special tort, or whether it is a type of breach of statutory duty.

This resulted, in *Ex parte Herbage (No. 2)*, in the majority of the Court of Appeal holding that leave to apply for judicial review had been properly granted where the applicant, who was seriously overweight and as a result was immobile and could not climb stairs, had on that account been accommodated on the ground floor of the hospital wing at Pentonville Prison, which was the prison psychiatric hospital. There he was surrounded by schizophrenics, psychopaths, and others in conditions which made it impossible for him to sleep. This, he argued, amounted to cruel and unusual punishment. In the same way it was argued in *Williams* that the plaintiff's detention in the special control unit at Wakefield Prison was actionable as a cruel and unusual punishment. He had been denied association and, for a time, exercise, kept without visual or auditory relief, had insufficient light, had dull and repetitive work sewing mailbags, was subject to constant surveillance and searches, denied the opportunity to

---

[88] [1992] 1 AC 58, [1991] 3 All ER 733, HL, approving *dicta* of Tudor Evans J in *Williams v. Home Office (No. 2)* [1981] 1 All ER at 1240–2.

[89] [1981] 1 All ER 1211.

[90] *R. v. Secretary of State for the Home Dept., ex parte Herbage (No. 2)* [1987] QB 1077, [1987] 1 All ER 324 (CA majority decision, May LJ dissenting).

gain remission for good behaviour, and was subject to indefinite prolongation of his term in the unit. This raises a number of issues.

First, the Bill of Rights speaks only of punishments, and not (unlike the ECHR) of treatment generally. What is a punishment? In *Williams*, Tudor Evans J accepted that confinement in the unit, being part of the sentence which the plaintiff was serving, was a punishment.[91] However, in *Ex parte Herbage* the applicant had not been convicted of any offence, but was remanded in prison awaiting extradition to the USA for trial on fraud offences. It is hard to see how a person who is awaiting trial or extradition can be said to be undergoing punishment. If, as seems likely, remand prisoners are not protected by the Bill of Rights prohibition on cruel and unusual punishments, their rights are paradoxically protected less well than those of convicted prisoners.

Next, when is punishment cruel and unusual? The judge in *Williams* decided that the Bill of Rights prohibits punishments only if they are both cruel and unusual: the words are to be read conjunctively, not disjunctively. In reaching this decision he followed a decision of the Supreme Court of Canada in *R. v. Miller and Cockriell*[92] that the words were to be read conjunctively in the context of the Canadian Bill of Rights 1960, in preference to a contrary opinion of Heald J in *McCann v. R.*[93] There had been no previous suggestion, particularly in the judicial and academic literature on the Eighth Amendment to the US Constitution, that it was proper to read the words conjunctively. Nevertheless, Tudor Evans J adopted the conjunctive interpretation. A regime might therefore be cruel, judged according to prevailing standards of morality, yet not be unusual (and hence not be actionable) if prison practice here and abroad lags behind public morality. He went on to hold that the special control unit had not been unusual, because the conditions in it were not notably different from those under certain other regimes in English prisons—notably those applied to prisoners segregated at their own request under what is now rule 45 of the Prison Rules 1999—or from control units abroad, notably in the USA and British Columbia.

Tudor Evans J then turned to the question whether the regime was cruel. He adopted a two-standard test for cruelty. First, there are minimal standards accepted by public standards of morality, and any regime which falls below those standards will automatically be cruel. Secondly, a regime may be at or above that standard, but still be cruel if the suffering it imposes is disproportionate to any legitimate penological objective. These matters are to be judged objectively, by reference to the standards current in the society in question at the present time.[94] This approach is consistent with some of the caselaw of the US Supreme Court in relation to the death penalty, which was held to be cruel in *Furman v. Georgia*[95] because it was not shown to serve any penological objective which could not be achieved otherwise.[96] Tudor Evans J decided that the standards did not fall below the irreducible minimum required of

[91] [1981] 1 All ER 1211 at 1242.
[92] (1975) 70 DLR (3d) 324.
[93] (1975) 68 DLR (3d) 661.
[94] [1981] 1 All ER 1211 at 1245.
[95] 408 US 238 (1972).
[96] However, the US Supreme Court has subsequently resiled from that view. See, e.g. *Gregg v. Georgia* 428 US 513 (1976); *McCleskey v. Kemp* 478 US 1019 (1986); 481 US 279 (1987).

prisons by public morality. He then decided that the need to maintain order and contain inveterate trouble-makers in prison justified the use of segregation and control units, having regard to the fact that the long-term segregation of prisoners in poor conditions for the purpose of maintaining order had been accepted as necessary in 1968 by a subcommittee of the Advisory Council on the Penal System, chaired by Professor Radzinowicz[97] and in 1973 by the Home Office working party established to consider ways of controlling disruptive maximum security prisoners in the light of widespread prison disturbances in 1972.

This approach to the issue of cruelty is unsatisfactory, and is in reality inconsistent with the professed aim of judging these matters objectively according to prevailing standards of public morality. The judge, instead of assessing whether the regime was necessary in the light of a publicly accepted penal objective, was content to be guided by the opinion of a Home Office working party, having no claim to be independent of the executive, and which had not been required by its terms of reference or otherwise to direct its attention to the demands of public morality. Like so many other Home Office working parties, this one had been given a limited and functional brief, with no scope to review penal policy. This made the judge's approach a mere rubber stamp for the executive decision to implement the regime of its working party: hardly a satisfactory way of protecting prisoners against cruel and unusual punishments. Special control units were abolished in 1975, and the main reason for their abolition was the public outcry generated by publicity about the treatment of prisoners in the units.

(5) MISFEASANCE IN A PUBLIC OFFICE

Any prison officer who, in the performance of his duties as a prison officer, intentionally commits an unlawful act or omission, realizing that it is likely to cause loss or injury to a prisoner, is liable in damages for misfeasance in a public office to the prisoner if loss or injury results.[98] However, this tort is unlikely to come often into play; even when the elements of the tort are present, it will usually also constitute a battery or some other tort which will be easier to establish, depending on a less demanding mental element on the part of the tortfeasor.

(6) NEGLIGENCE

As has already been observed, in *Ex parte Hague* the House of Lords rejected attempts to build a remedy for intolerable prison conditions on the twin bases of false imprisonment and breach of statutory duty. However, their Lordships accepted that there ought to be a remedy, and expressed the view (*obiter*) that it lay in the field of negligence rather than intentional torts. As Lord Bridge put it:[99]

---

[97] *The Regime for Long Term Prisoners in Conditions of Maximum Security* (London: Home Office, 1968).

[98] *Bourgoin SA v. Ministry of Agriculture, Fisheries and Food* [1986] QB 716, [1985] 3 All ER 585, CA; *R. v. Deputy Governor of Parkhurst Prison, ex parte Hague* [1990] 3 All ER 733 at 707, CA, *per* Taylor LJ; [1991] 3 All ER 733, HL, at 745 *per* Lord Bridge.

[99] [1991] 3 All ER 733 at 746.

'Whenever one person is lawfully in the custody of another, the custodian owes a duty of care to the detainee. If the custodian negligently allows, or, a fortiori, if he deliberately causes, the detainee to suffer in any way in his health he will be in breach of that duty. But short of anything that could properly be descibed as a physical injury or an impairment of health, if a person lawfully detained is kept in conditions which cause him for the time being physical pain or a degree of discomfort which can properly be described as intolerable, I believe that could and should be treated as a breach of the custodian's duty of care for which the law should award damages.'

This has the advantage of allowing compensation to be obtained without making the detention itself unlawful, but immediately raises the difficult issue of the extent of the duty of the prison authorities. In any such action, the court would have to consider whether a prison governor has discharged the duty of care which he owes to a prisoner. It would not be necessary to decide what the threshold of tolerability is; the questions would be: (a) was it reasonably foreseeable that the conditions would cause physical injury, impairment of health, or intolerable pain or discomfort? and, if the answer to that is yes, (b) would it have been reasonable for the governor to alleviate the conditions? The difficulty for plaintiffs is likely to come under part (b), since the governor's ability to improve conditions is likely to be heavily dependent on matters outside his control. Much may depend on the level of resources provided by the prison department of the Home Office, on the state of and amount of space in the buildings, and on the number of prisoners whom the governor is required to accommodate. If an action is brought against the governor, these contingencies are likely to restrict the scope of his duty of care. If an action is brought against the Home Office, the court is unlikely to be prepared to hold that government has a common-law duty to provide a particular level of resource for prisons, as so to hold would impose on the judges the task of setting public expenditure targets, a job for which they are ill suited under the doctrine of the separation of powers.

It seems to follow that liability in negligence is likely to be most readily incurred where prisoners are subjected to special regimes which are dictated by disciplinary or other special considerations rather than by staff shortages or inadequacy of resources. It might have offered a way in which Messrs. Williams, Weldon, and Hague could have improved their lot, but does not offer a way of securing compensation for the general run of poor conditions in British prisons. However, the scope of negligence liability is limited. In *H. v. Home Office*,[100] where through the negligence of the prison authorities a prisoner's conviction for sexual offences was discovered by fellow inmates, making it necessary to keep the prisoner in protective solitary confinement under what is now rule 45(1) of the Prison Rules 1999, the Court of Appeal held that the severe restriction of educational and recreational facilities and loss of quality of life could not give rise to damages for negligence. In the light of the Court of Appeal's decision in *Hague* (later affirmed by the House of Lords), the court decided that negligence damages were available for intolerable conditions, but that a regime of solitary confinement authorized under the Prison Rules could not, as a matter of law,

---

[100] *Independent*, 6 May 1992, CA.

be regarded as so intolerable as to give rise to an action for breach of a duty owed to a prisoner.

This is important. Although Lord Bridge suggested in *Hague* that, in practice, the problem will not often arise, we have already seen the mounting evidence that conditions in Britain's prisons are sometimes inhuman or degrading. It is hard to imagine how one could live in such conditions without suffering impaired mental health or intolerable mental discomfort. At the same time, the remedies depend so heavily on the supply of resources from government that it is hard to imagine that a duty of care in tort would ever be adequate to provide a remedy for those who are condemned to live in those conditions.

At common law and under the Fatal Accidents Act 1976, gaolers owes a duty of care to those in their custody to take reasonable steps to prevent them from committing suicide if that is reasonably foreseeable. If the gaolers fail to put in place an appropriate monitoring regime, they may be liable in damages. The quantum of damages is likely to be reduced (probably by half) by reason of contributory negligence under the Law Reform (Contributory Negligence) Act 1945 if the person in custody was of sound mind and made a choice to kill himself.[101]

(7) THE HUMAN RIGHTS ACT 1998

The Convention rights which are part of English law by virtue of the Human Rights Act 1998 have considerable humanizing potential. The following could, over time, prove to be important implications of the Act.

(i) Medical treatment and psychiatric supervision in prison

In *Keenan v. United Kingdom*[102] the European Court of Human Rights held that a prison regime in which a mentally disordered person was segregated from other prisoners as a disciplinary measure, in addition to an award of additional days in prison, causing him to suffer paranoid episodes and suicidal thoughts, and where he received inadequate medical treatment and monitoring, constituted inhuman and degrading treatment and punishment. The violation of ECHR Article 3 stemmed from a number of events: segregating someone who was known to be ill and a possible suicide risk; treatment by a prison medical officer who had no psychiatric qualifications and treated the prisoner without reference to a qualified psychiatrist; and failing to take proper steps to ensure proper treatment and monitoring when the prisoner was awarded additional punishment, despite the known mental illness. Similarly, committing a severely disabled Thalidomide victim to prison for seven days violated Article 3.[102a]

We noted in Chapter 5 the poverty of the arrangements for providing prisoners with medical, and particularly psychiatric, treatment in many prisons. Although prison medical officers can and do call in outside medical practitioners, rule 20(3) of the Prison Rules 1999 makes it clear that the outside practitioner works within the

[101] *Reeves v. Commissioner of Police of the Metropolis* [2000] 1 AC 360, HL.
[102] Eur. Ct. HR, App. No. 27229/95, Judgment of 3 April 2001.
[102a] *Price v. United Kingdom*, above, n. 66a.

prison 'under the general supervision of the medical officer', which does nothing to quell fears that administrative convenience and discipline are major determinants of the type and quality of care which is delivered to prisoners. Some prison governors, as well as HM Chief Inspector of Prisons, are worried about the standard of health care. At Brixton Prison in 2000, the governor expressed his concern. Inspectors observed falsification (in the form of advance completion) of records of the timing of observations of people on 'suicide watch', which might lead to liability in negligence if a prisoner were to be able to commit suicide as a result.[103] The inspectors also found 'conditions on wards that were an affront to human decency, poor professional practice and in one case illegal practice'.[104] If English courts can build on the standards being set by the European Court of Human Rights under Article 3,[105] using the legal duty under section 6 of the Human Rights Act 1998 to create legally enforceable minimum standards of health care for prisoners, it will be a major contribution to the protection of human rights in prisons, bearing in mind that (as noted in Chapter 5, above) the common law has so far tolerated a lower standard of care in prisons than in the wider community for the purpose of the law of negligence.

(ii) Overcrowding and segregation, and related conditions

As noted earlier, the European Court of Human Rights has recently held that over-crowding, coupled with poor sleeping arrangements, and lack of access to the open air and exercise, over a substantial period constitute degrading treatment contrary to ECHR Article 3.[106] The conditions considered there were extreme, and are unlikely to be replicated in a penal institution in the UK. This may limit the extent to which the Human Rights Act can influence day-to-day prison conditions for ordinary prisoners. In the same way, the Strasbourg organs have not held that solitary confinement, on its own, constitutes degrading treatment, although the Commission has implied that the position might be different if measures were imposed in order to punish someone in a deliberately humiliating or debasing way, so as to be disproportionate to the legitimate aim of maintaining order, discipline, and security in prison.[107] This is unsatisfactory. It introduces a subjective element of intention or motive into the objective standard of inhuman or degrading treatment in a manner which is inconsistent with decisions of the Court, for example in *Tyrer v. United Kingdom.*[108] It is to be hoped that the reasoning would not be followed, bearing in mind the dynamic nature of ECHR interpretation.

It is noteworthy that the Court in *Keenan v. United Kingdom* held both that punishing a young, mentally ill man for breaches of prison discipline with a period of

---

[103] *Reeves v. Commissioner of Police of the Metropolis* [2000] 1 AC 360, HL. See also *R. (Imtiaz Amin) v. Secretary of State for the Home Department* [2001] EWHC Admin 719.

[104] HM Chief Inspector of Prisons for England and Wales, *HM Prison Brixton: Report of an Unannounced Short Inspection 26–29 June 2000* (London: Home Office, 2001), 71. See also H. Arnott, 'HIV/AIDS, Prisons and Human Rights' [2001] *EHRLR* 71–7.

[105] In addition to *Keenan*, above, see, e.g. *Kudła v. Poland*, Eur. Ct. HR, App. No. 30210/96, Judgment of 26 October 2000.

[106] *Dougoz v. Greece*, Eur. Ct. HR, App. No. 40907/98, Judgment of 6 March 2001.

[107] *Ensslin, Baader and Raspe v. Germany*, App. Nos. 7572/76, 7586/76 and 7587/76, 15 D. & R. 35.

[108] (1978) 2 EHRR 1. See Ch. 5, above.

segregation and an additional period of imprisonment gave rise to an arguable case of inhuman or degrading treatment, and that the UK was liable under Article 13 because the legal and administrative systems failed to provide him with an effective remedy for the potential violation of Article 3. In response to the government's argument that a person in Mr. Keenan's position could not have made use of a legal remedy even if one had been provided, the Court said that this made it all the more important for such disciplinary awards to be subject to automatic and speedy review of the order for segregation.[109] The Court of Appeal has held that a prison disciplinary charge is not a 'criminal charge', and so does not bring into play the right to an independent and impartial tribunal under ECHR Article 6(1) or the rights of defence under Article 6(3).[110] This sits a little uncomfortably with the view of the Court in *Keenan* that segregation constitute a 'punishment' for the purposes of Article 3. But if the Court of Appeal was correct, it exposes the weakness in the system of domestic remedies which results from the failure to include the right to an effective remedy for violations of Convention rights, under ECHR Article 13, in the list of Convention rights made part of domestic law by section 1 of, and Schedule 1 to, the Human Rights Act 1998. Whenever a disciplinary punishment gives rise to an arguable violation of another Convention right, *Keenan* shows that the UK has an obligation in international law, under Article 13 of the ECHR, to provide a remedy before a national authority which will be effective in the circumstances of the case. The omission of Article 13 from the 1998 Act means that national courts cannot do anything to provide such a remedy. The responsibility passes to the government and Parliament.

   Certain control and disciplinary measures are simply unacceptable under the Convention, as they are under national law. Depriving a prisoner of food in order to force him to wear clothes, or failing to adopt measures to prevent insanitary behaviour by prisoners as part of a protest from threatening health, or adopting an inflexible approach to discipline which failed to achieve compliance with Article 3 standards, might violate Convention rights and be unlawful as a matter of ordinary public law.[111] Before the Human Rights Act 1998, English law allowed a mentally competent prisoner to choose to refuse food, even to the point at which he died.[112] Under the Human Rights Act 1998, the responsibility of prison authorities for the safety of people in their custody under Articles 2 and 3 cannot compel them to force-feed such prisoners, in disregard of an autonomous and competent decision and in contravention of national law. On the other hand, both national law and the Articles 2 and 3 permit the authorities to force-feed people whose refusal of food is putting life or health seriously at risk if they are mentally disordered in ways which make them legally incompetent to make that decision.[113]

---

[109] Eur. Ct. HR, App. No. 27229/95, Judgment of 3 April 2001, at paras. 123–6.

[110] *Greenfield v. Secretary of State for the Home Department, The Times,* 6 March 2001, CA. See also *Mathewson v. The Scottish Ministers, The Times,* 24 October 2001, OH (Lord Reed).

[111] See Prison Rules 1999, r. 24; *R. v. Governor of Frankland Prison, ex parte Russell* [2000] 1 WLR 2027; and *cp. McFeeley v. United Kingdom,* Eur. Commn. HR, (1980) 3 EHRR 161, and Kaufmann, in Starmer, *European Human Rights Law,* 457–63.

[112] *Secretary of State for the Home Department v. Robb* [1995] Fam. 127, [1995] 1 All ER 677.

[113] *B. v. Croydon Health Authority* [1995] Fam. 133, [1995] 1 All ER 683, CA; and see *X. v. Germany* (1985) 7 EHRR 152, Eur. Commn. HR.

(iii) Maintaining family relationships

The difficulty of maintaining contact with one's family while in prison is exacerbated by the sometimes very long distances between the family home and the prison, and by the fact that Category A women prisoners have no access to mother-and-baby units. The Court of Appeal has since held that the young children of imprisoned mothers have a right under ECHR Article 8 to have individual consideration given to their need for maternal contact. The prison authorities are entitled to have a policy on such matters, and may restrict or exclude mother-child cohabitation as a general rule for security and related operational reasons which fall within the legitimate aims under Article 8(2). However, if there is evidence that the child would suffer serious harm as a result of separation, it may outweigh the security considerations, with the result that a refusal to allow a child to remain with his or her mother in such circumstances could be a disproportionate interference with the child's right to respect for family life. This may mean that a woman has to be accommodated in an open prison where a mother-and-baby unit is available, even if security considerations would normally militate against it.[114] In *Togher v. United Kingdom*,[114a] the Commission declared admissible a complaint that forced separation from her ten-day-old baby violated both Article 3 and Article 8 of the ECHR, and in a friendly settlement the UK paid the applicant £10,000, preventing the Commission or the Court from exploring the wider implications of separating mothers from their babies. On the other hand, the distance between home and prison has been held not to violate Article 8 rights in itself.[115] This is a particular problem for women prisoners: the relatively small (although growing) number of them in the prison system means that there are fewer establishments for them, increasing the chance that their families will have long journeys, particularly if a prisoner has particular needs which require access to a special unit or type of regime. The Human Rights Act 1998 will not make a significant contribution to resolving these problems unless Article 8 is applied dynamically.

Nor is the Act likely in the short term to improve opportunities for contact between prisoners and their spouses. Conjugal visits are not allowed in the UK, unlike some other European countries, so intimacy is impossible, as is starting a family before the prisoner becomes eligible for temporary release on licence (home leave). Requests for access to facilities for artificial insemination are considered on their individual merits in the light of a range of considerations relating to the age and fertility of the parties (particularly the woman) and the welfare of the potential offspring, but the Home Office starts from the position that loss of an opportunity to procreate is inherent in a sentence of imprisonment, and artificial insemination should be allowed only in exceptional circumstances. The Court of Appeal has held[116] that this is not an irrational position to adopt, and that the considerations to which the Home Office has regard are permissible grounds for restricting the right to respect for family life and the right to

---

[114] *R. (P.) v. Secretary of State for the Home Department*, [2001] 1 WLR 2002 CA.
[114a] Eur. Commn. HR, App. No. 28555/95, Admissibility decision 16 April 1998; Report on friendly settlement 25 October 1999.
[115] *Wakefield v. United Kingdom*, Eur. Commn. HR, 66 D. & R. 251.
[116] *R. v. Secretary of State for the Home Department, ex parte Mellor*, [2001] 3 WLR 533, CA.

found a family under ECHR Article 8 and 12. More interesting, perhaps, will be the response of the English courts to complaints about the impact of limited contact opportunities on the rights of existing children to maintain relationships with members of their families. So far, the Strasbourg bodies have been willing to regard very extensive restrictions on Article 8 rights as justifiable,[117] but it is arguable that the test of proportionality should be applied flexibly, in the light of developing European standards, taking particular account of the rights and interests of children. There is a danger that a parent's imprisonment will effectively negate the right of children to contact with the parent, undermining the reality of the right in a way which it would be hard to regard as proportionate. In this area, as in others, norms and expectations are evolving constantly. In *Messina v. Italy (No. 2)*,[117a] the Court, while accepting that imprisonment inevitably interferes with familial rights under ECHR Article 8, stressed the need for prison authorities to help prisoners maintain contact with their close families.

7.4 DETERMINACY OF SENTENCE AND THE RIGHT TO RELEASE

The normal rule is that a prisoner is entitled to know the term, or the maximum term, which he will have to serve, although supervision may continue after release and may be enforced by electronic monitoring and drug testing to ensure that the offender is complying with conditions of release.[118] Normally, statute sets the maximum penalty, and leaves the sentencing court to impose a penalty within that maximum taking account of the circumstances of the offence, the level of culpability of the defendant, fairness between people convicted of similar offences, the needs of deterrence, and the interest in protecting the public against serious offenders. There have always been some offences carrying a mandatory sentence. At present, the only serious offence in this category is murder, for which the penalty is life imprisonment or, for people under eighteen, detention during Her Majesty's pleasure.[119] In provisions of the Crime (Sentences) Act 1997 now consolidated in the Powers of Criminal Courts (Sentencing) Act 2000, Parliament provided for a strong presumption in favour of a life sentence for anyone convicted of certain serious crimes[120] for a second time.[121] The court need not impose a life sentence where it is of the opinion that there are exceptional circumstances, relating to one of the qualifying offences or to the offender, which justify not doing so, and states in open court what the circumstances are.[122] The object is to allow the Home Secretary and the Parole Board to control the person's release date in order to protect the public against the risk that the offender will commit

---

[117] *Boyle and Rice v. United Kingdom*, Eur. Ct. HR, Series A, No. 131, Judgment of 27 April 1988, 10 EHRR 425.

[117a] App. No. 25498/94, Judgment of 28 September 2000, at para. 61.

[118] See, e.g. Criminal Justice and Court Services Act 2000, ss. 62, 63, 65.

[119] Powers of Criminal Courts (Sentencing) Act 2000, s. 90.

[120] The offences are: attempt, conspiracy, or incitement to murder; soliciting murder; manslaughter; wounding or causing grievous bodily harm with intent; rape or attempted rape; intercourse with a girl under the age of thirteen; possession of a firearm with intent to injure; use of a firearm to resist arrest; carrying a firearm with criminal intent; robbery when in possession of a firearm or imitation firearm (Powers of Criminal Courts (Sentencing) Act 2000, s. 109(5)).

[121] Ibid., s. 109(1).   [122] Ibid., s. 109(2), (3).

further serious violent or sexual crimes.[123] Having regard to that purpose, exceptional circumstances exist, relieving the court of the duty to impose a life sentence, when a qualifying serious offence is committed by someone against whom there would be no need to protect the public in the future. The characteristics of the offender and the offence are central to the need for future protection.[124] Furthermore, the imposition of a life sentence under section 2 would be liable to amount to inhuman or degrading treatment (violating ECHR Article 3) and the right to liberty (violating ECHR Article 5(1)) if it were applied in a disproportionate way or otherwise arbitrarily.[125] The Court of Appeal accordingly held that section 2 must be applied 'so that it does not result in offenders being sentenced to life imprisonment when they do not constitute a significant risk to the public', judged according to the evidence before the court.[126]

The Crime (Sentences) Act 1997 also introduced a presumption that a person convicted on a third occasion of certain types of crime would receive a minimum term of imprisonment: seven years in the case of trafficking in a Class A drug, and three years in the case of domestic burglary.[127] In these cases, the statute itself provides that the court may decide that it is inappropriate to impose that sentence having regard to specific circumstances relating to the offences or the offender which would make the sentence unjust.

In other cases, there is a wider discretion as to sentence, but (except in relation to discretionary life sentences) the maximum term to be served will be specified at the start. Even in these cases, however, the period actually served is to some degree uncertain. First, a prisoner serving from two months to three years in prison, whose conduct in prison is of a prescribed standard, may be awarded up to twelve 'early release days' in the first two months of the term, and up to six early release days for each subsequent two-month period. These days bring forward the date at which the prisoner is eligible for release on licence.[128] Prisoners serving over three years do not benefit from early release days, but must be released after serving five-sixths of their terms if the Parole Board so recommends.[129] If the prisoner is guilty of disciplinary offences in prison, additional days of detention may be imposed, postponing the date when the prisoner would be eligible or entitled to be released by reference to the early release days or the five-sixths rule.[130]

---

[123] Home Office, *Protecting the Public: The Government's Strategy on Crime in England and Wales*, Cm. 3190 (London: HMSO, 1996), para. 10.11; *R. v. Buckland* [2000] 1 WLR 1262, CA, at 1268 *per* Lord Bingham of Cornhill CJ.

[124] *R. v. Offen* [2001] 1 WLR 253, CA, at 271–2 *per* Lord Woolf CJ applying the approach laid down in the Human Rights Act 1998, s. 3.

[125] In *R. v. Secretary of State for the Home Department, ex parte Evans (No. 2)* [2000] 3 WLR 843, HL, at 858, Lord Hope of Craighead accepted that an *intra vires* sentence might be challengeable under the Human Rights Act 1998 if 'it is arbitrary because, for example, it was resorted to in bad faith or was not proportionate'.

[126] *R. v. Offen* [2001] 1 WLR 253, 277, CA.

[127] See now Powers of Criminal Courts (Sentencing) Act 2000, ss. 110, 111.

[128] Crime (Sentences) Act 1997, s. 11.

[129] Ibid., s. 12. Because the effect of ss. 11 and 12 is that prisoners do not become eligible for parole until they have served a significantly larger proportion of their sentences than previously, s. 26 requires courts to impose a sentence of two-thirds the term which would have been considered appropriate before those provisions came into force.

[130] Ibid., s. 14.

The Home Secretary always has power to release prisoners in exceptional circumstances on compassionate grounds, usually after consulting the Parole Board.[131]

Detention in accordance with a determinate sentence imposed by a court is justified under ECHR Article 5(1)(a), without the need for further reviews of detention under Article 5(4). However, an effective remedy is needed to review (if necessary, automatically) an award of additional days of detention for a disciplinary offence in circumstances where the award may give rise to an arguable case of a violation of Article 3 in the prisoner's individual circumstances, for example if it subjects the prisoner to a period during which he will be denied proper treatment for a serious illness.[132] At present, no such remedy is available in the UK.

The position with regard to life imprisonment is more complicated. For life prisoners, release on licence is their one hope of release, but they have no right to release. There are established procedures for deciding whether or not to release prisoners on licence. If released, the prisoner remains permanently liable to be recalled to prison.[133] The power to release on licence used to lie entirely in the Home Secretary's discretion. The process of decision-making was secretive, and no due-process guarantees were provided. After the trial, the judge would recommend to the Home Secretary the minimum period which, in his view, the offender should serve in prison in order to meet the retributive and deterrent objectives of the sentence, taking account of the circumstances of the offence and the offender. The Lord Chief Justice might recommend an increase or limitation of this so-called 'tariff period'. The Home Secretary then had an unfettered discretion to decide when to release the prisoner, increasing or limiting the tariff period taking account of the need to protect the public at the end of the recommended period, in the light of any advice from the Parole Board.

This was altered in the light of decisions of the European Court of Human Rights that this violated discretionary life prisoners' rights under Article 5 of the ECHR,[134] and decisions of English courts giving discretionary life prisoners the right, arising out of the rules of natural justice, to know the 'tariff' period of imprisonment recommended by the trial judge and any facts which might affect the Home Secretary's or Parole Board's decision, and to make representations in writing.[135] As regards mandatory life prisoners, if there was a considerable discrepancy between the judge's recommendation and the Home Secretary's decision, and no reasons were given for departing from the recommendation, the decision might be open to review on the ground of irrationality.[136] The procedures were put on a statutory footing by the Criminal Justice Act 1991, and are now contained in the Crime (Sentences) Act 1997 and the Powers of Criminal Courts (Sentencing) Act 2000, as amended.

---

[131] Crime (Sentences) Act 1997, s. 10.

[132] *Keenan v. United Kingdom*, Eur. Ct HR, App. No. 27229/95, Judgment of 3 April 2001.

[133] Crime (Sentences) Act 1997, s. 31(1).

[134] *Weeks v. United Kingdom*, Eur. Ct. HR, Series A, No. 145, Judgment of 5 October 1988, 10 EHRR 293; *Thynne, Wilson and Gunnell v. United Kingdom*, Eur. Ct. HR, Series A, No. 190, Judgment of 25 October 1990, 13 EHRR 666.

[135] *R. v. Parole Board, ex parte Wilson* [1992] QB 740, [1992] 2 All ER 576, CA; *R. v. Secretary of State for the Home Dept., ex parte Doody* [1994] 1 AC 531, [1993] 3 All ER 92, HL.

[136] *R. v. Secretary of State for the Home Dept., ex parte Doody* [1994] 1 AC 531, [1993] 3 All ER 92, HL.

(1) SETTING THE TARIFF FOR, AND RELEASING PRISONERS FROM, DISCRETIONARY LIFE SENTENCES

Prisoners serving discretionary life sentences (including those sentenced for a third serious qualifying offence under the Crime (Sentences) Act 1997, section 2) now have the 'tariff' period fixed openly by the court as part of the sentence.[137] As soon as the tariff period set by trial court expires (or after the end of any determinate sentence imposed at the same time as the life sentence, if the determinate sentence is longer than the tariff period), the prisoner must be released on licence if the Parole Board so directs. The Parole Board must decide whether 'it is no longer necessary for the protection of the public that the prisoner should be confined'.[138] Review by the Parole Board, as an independent body with final decision-making power, satisfies the requirements of ECHR Article 5(4) for a speedy decision by a 'court' as to the lawfulness of detention. Its position is bolstered by the need to comply with public law principles. Discretionary life prisoners are entitled as a matter of natural justice to see, or at least to be informed of the gist of, reports about the appropriateness of releasing them, to make representations to the Parole Board, and to be told the reasons for decisions affecting them.[139]

The Parole Board can only act when a case has been referred to it by the Home Secretary, but the prisoner can require the Home Secretary to refer the case after the end of the tariff period if there has been no previous reference. Because release depends in part on an assessment of dangerousness, the prisoner may make progress, after an initial decision to refuse parole, which would make it inappropriate to continue to detain him. To satisfy ECHR Article 5(4), cases must therefore be regularly reviewed. The prisoner is not entitled under the Crime (Sentences) Act 1997 to a further review until two years after the most recent one,[140] but the Parole Board must be prepared to review the case earlier if there are circumstances in a prisoner's case which make it possible that sufficient progress to justify release will have been made in less than two years (for example, where a prisoner's violent behaviour is the result of alcohol abuse, and he is taking active steps to tackle the problem).[141]

(2) SETTING THE TARIFF FOR, AND RELEASING PRISONERS FROM, MANDATORY LIFE SENTENCES

Unlike a discretionary life sentence, in theory a mandatory life sentence for murder has no 'tariff' period. The Home Secretary may release a mandatory life sentence prisoner at any time if recommended to do so by the Parole Board, and after consult-

---

[137] Crime (Sentences) Act 1997, ss. 2(4), 28(3).

[138] Ibid., s. 28(6).

[139] *R. v. Parole Board, ex parte Bradley* [1991] 1 WLR 134, [1990] 3 All ER 828, DC; *R. v. Parole Board, ex parte Wilson* [1992] QB 740, [1992] 2 All ER 576, CA.

[140] Crime (Sentences) Act 1997, s. 28(7).

[141] *Oldham v. United Kingdom*, Eur. Ct. HR, App. No. 36273/97, Judgment of 26 September 2000, *The Times*, 24 October 2000. The period within which review is needed under Art. 5(4) will depend on the particular facts of each case, so sometimes the two-year review period will be lawful: *R. v. Parole Board, ex parte MacNeil*, *The Times*, 18 April 2001, CA.

ing the Lord Chief Justice and (if available) the trial judge. The Parole Board may made a recommendation for release only if the case has been referred to it by the Home Secretary, who is thus entirely in control of the process.[142] The Home Secretary may also release a prisoner if satisfied (usually after consulting the Parole Board) that there are exceptional circumstances justifying it on compassionate grounds.[143]

In practice, the courts and the Home Secretary recognize that there are degrees of seriousness of murders. As Lord Mustill said:

'. . . as every law student knows, although many who speak in public on the subject appear to overlook, it is possible to commit murder without intending to kill . . . In truth, the mandatory life sentence for murder is symbolic.'[144]

Accordingly the then Home Secretary, Mr. Leon Brittan, decided in 1983 to import the idea of a 'tariff' into decisions about parole for murderers. As developed by his successor Mr. Douglas Hurd and subsequent Home Secretaries, it works as follows. As soon as possible after the trial, the judge, through the Lord Chief Justice, advises the Home Secretary of the period of incarceration which, in the judges' view, is required for retribution and deterrence. In the light of that, the Home Secretary sets a first review date (in effect, the end of the informal 'tariff period'), taking account of the need to uphold public confidence in the system and to reflect concern about violent crime. A whole life tariff (i.e. a decision that retribution and deterrence require the prisoner's incarceration for the whole of his or her natural life) is in principle not incompatible with the discretion of the Home Secretary, but it is appropriate in only the most heinous crimes, such as active participation in the kidnapping, torture, and killing of children.[145] However, the European Court of Human Rights has left open the possibility that persistently refusing to set a tariff for a prisoner, leaving him in a state of uncertainty as to whether or when he might become eligible for release, might constitute inhuman punishment, violating ECHR Article 3, particularly if the prisoner is a child.[146] Once the tariff period has expired, decisions are guided principally, but not exclusively, by the need to protect the public.[147]

The European Court of Human Rights has so far contributed nothing to the protection of adult mandatory life prisoners in this context, because in *Wynne v. United Kingdom*[148] it accepted uncritically the formal, or theoretical, proposition that the

---

[142] Crime (Sentences) Act 1997, s. 29.

[143] Ibid., s. 30. A mandatory life sentence is not inhuman, degrading, or arbitrary, because the indeterminate period of imprisonment in practice takes account of the circumstances of the crime and the offender: *R. (Lichniak) v. Secretary of State for the Home Department* [2001] 3 WLR 933, CA.

[144] *R. v. Secretary of State for the Home Department, ex parte Doody* [1994] 1 AC 531, [1993] 3 All ER 92, 96, HL.

[145] *R. v. Secretary of State for the Home Department, ex parte Hindley* [2000] 2 WLR 730, [2000] 2 All ER 385, HL.

[146] *T. and V. v. United Kingdom*, Eur. Ct. HR, App. Nos. 24724/94 and 24888/94, Judgments of 16 December 1999, at para. 100. In those cases, failing to set a new tariff for over a year after the previous tariff had been quashed in judicial review proceedings, when the prisoners would not in any case have been eligible for release for some years to come, did not inflict suffering of the level necessary to violate Art. 3.

[147] *Official Report, House of Commons*, 6th Series, vol. 49, col. WA 505–508 (Mr. Brittan); *Official Report, House of Commons*, 6th Series, vol. 120, col. WA 347–349 (Mr. Hurd).

[148] Eur. Ct. HR, Series A, No. 294-A, Judgment of 18 July 1994, 19 EHRR 333.

'tariff' for a whole life sentence is always the whole of the prisoner's natural life. It followed that there was never a need, under Article 5(4), for the legality of the detention to be reviewed by a court after sentence. In reality, the administrative 'tariff' ascertained by reference to the first review date is the punitive and deterrent element, thereafter detention is primarily to protect society against danger. It is to be hoped that the Court will take a more realistic approach in the future.

The Court has already done so in relation to juveniles sentenced to be detained during Her Majesty's pleasure for murder, accepting that a punitive element existed in such a sentence. Setting the tariff is properly to be regarded as part of the sentencing process. This used to be done by the Home Secretary, but the Court held that this denies the defendant a determination by a tribunal independent of the executive, required by Article 6(1) of the ECHR. The Court also drew attention to the open-ended nature of a sentence of detention during Her Majesty's pleasure, unlike that of a mandatory life sentence, to hold that the refusal of regular reviews of the tariff period, for juveniles who were developing in maturity, violated Article 5(4).[149] Furthermore, under the ECHR proper steps have to be taken to justify continued detention after the tariff period. There was a violation of Article 5(4) in that context because the Parole Board did not conduct an adversarial process, and could not order the release of the prisoner.[150] As a result, the Home Secretary, Mr. Jack Straw, announced[151] that he would legislate to require courts to determine the tariff period in open court when sentencing a child to be detained during Her Majesty's pleasure, and would in the meantime accept the advice of the Lord Chief Justice on the appropriate tariff in individual cases. The legislation is now in place.[152] But the discretion of the Home Secretary with regard to mandatory life sentences on adults remains (except in Northern Ireland), with the apparent support of the European Court of Human Rights.

Fortunately, English courts have hedged the discretion about with due process safeguards for prisoners by applying public law principles. The practice of successive Home Secretaries of setting what is in effect a tariff gives prisoners the legal right to regard a mandatory life sentence as a set period for punishment and deterrence, after which due process rights apply to fixing any further period of detention. Furthermore, before setting the first review date, the Home Secretary is obliged to give a prisoner the opportunity to make representations, and to that end must tell the prisoner what factors will be taken into account when setting the penal element. The prisoner must be told the substance of the advice from the trial judge and the Lord Chief Justice. The Home Secretary is not bound by the advice of the judges, but, if departing from it, must tell the prisoner the reasons for doing so, facilitating an application for judicial review.[153]

---

[149] *T. and V. v. United Kingdom*, Eur. Ct. HR, App. Nos. 24724/94 and 24888/94, Judgments of 16 December 1999, at paras. 111–121.

[150] *Hussain and Singh v. United Kingdom*, Eur. Ct. HR, Judgment of 21 February 1996, RJD 1996-I, 22 EHRR 1.

[151] See *Official Report, House of Commons*, 13 March 2000, cols. 21–24.

[152] Powers of Criminal Courts (Sentencing) Act 2000, s. 82A, inserted by Criminal Justice and Court Services Act 2000, s. 60. *Cp.* Life Sentences (Northern Ireland) Order 2001.

[153] *R. v. Secretary of State for the Home Department, ex parte Doody* [1994] 1 AC 531, [1993] 3 All ER 92, HL.

Rule of Law principles have been further injected into the decision-making process. The Home Secretary is required to act in a judicial manner when setting the penal element, and must not be swayed by irrelevant matters such as a populist press campaign harnessing public hatred for the offender without proper regard for the offender's age and other circumstances.[154]

Once set, the length of the penal element is not immutable. The Home Secretary must be ready to reduce it if subsequent representations establish that he had wrongly supposed that there were aggravating features of the offence. It would irrational (in the public law sense) not to reduce the tariff element in those circumstances.[155] Mr. Jack Straw, when Home Secretary, accepted that the tariff element could also be reduced if the prisoner made exceptional progress, and in any case should be reviewed at regular intervals (including after twenty-five years' imprisonment).[156]

It is not clear whether a tariff, once set, can be increased by the same Home Secretary or a successor. In *R. v. Secretary of State for the Home Department, ex parte Pierson*,[157] there was difference of opinion on this point. Lord Steyn and Lord Hope of Craighead thought it would be contrary to principle for one Home Secretary to increase a tariff already set by another. Lord Browne-Wilkinson and Lord Lloyd of Berwick disagreed, and Lord Goff expressed no conclusion. It is at least clear that in making any decision about the tariff, the Home Secretary is required to act judicially, and must not be swayed by orchestrated outpourings of public antagonism towards the offender.[158] If the Home Secretary sets a tariff in excess of that recommended by the Lord Chief Justice, reasons and an opportunity to make representations must be given.[159]

After a mandatory life prisoner has served the punishment and deterrence element of the sentence, the Home Secretary may release him on licence, after consulting the Parole Board.[160] As noted above, the European Court of Human Rights has declined to apply the right to an independent review under ECHR Article 5(4) to mandatory life prisoners, even after the end of their tariff periods, although the decision is probably based on a misconception about the purpose of incarceration after that time. Although the legislation offers no guidance as to relevant criteria for release on licence, the main relevant factor at that stage is preventing danger to the public. It has been held to be legitimate for the Home Secretary to take account of non-violent offences committed during an earlier period of release on licence, because the public can properly be protected against a wide range of serious offences.[161] Conditions imposed to protect the victim's family must respect the right of the licensee to take employment and keep in touch with his family after release.[161a]

[154] *R. v. Secretary of State for the Home Dept., ex parte Venables and Thompson* [1998] AC 407, [1997] 3 All ER 97, HL.
[155] *R. v. Secretary of State for the Home Dept., ex parte Pierson* [1998] AC 539, [1997] 3 All ER 577, HL.
[156] Official Report, House of Commons, 10 November, 1997, cols. 419–420.
[157] [1998] AC 539, [1997] 3 All ER 577, HL.
[158] *R. v. Secretary of State for the Home Dept., ex parte Venables* [1998] AC 407, [1997] 3 All ER 97, HL.
[159] *R. v. Secretary of State for the Home Dept., ex parte Doody* [1994] 1 AC 531, [1993] 3 All ER 92, HL.
[160] Crime (Sentences) Act 1997, s. 29.
[161] *R. v. Secretary of State for the Home Dept., ex parte Stafford* [1999] 2 AC 38, [1998] 4 All ER 7, HL.
[161a] *Craven v. Secretary of State for the Home Dept.*, unreported, 5 October 2001, Admin. Ct.

(3) RECALLING PRISONERS AFTER RELEASE ON LICENCE

In relation to the recall of life sentence prisoners who have been released on licence, section 32 of the 1997 Act provides for the Home Secretary to revoke a licence and recall a person to prison on the recommendation of the Parole Board. The Home Secretary is permitted to act without a recommendation from the Board only if it appears to him that it is expedient in the public interest to recall the person to prison before it would be practicable to seek a recommendation from the Board, but this is an emergency measure to be used only if there is an urgent need for action to protect the public.[162]

The person has a right to make representations with respect to his recall, and to be informed on his return to prison of the reasons for recall and of the right to make representations. If he makes representations, the Home Secretary must then refer the case to the Parole Board, and must immediately release the person again on licence if the Parole Board so directs or recommends.[163] In practice, the Home Secretary as a matter of course refers the cases of recalled prisoners to the Parole Board for their advice. The Board has power under the Criminal Justice Act 1991, section 32(2) to give advice in such cases. The advice on an informal reference is provisional and tentative only, given without the benefit of hearing the prisoner's representations. It is a speedy process which can only benefit the prisoner, and does not fetter the Board's decision-making on a later, formal, reference. The advice does not bind the Home Secretary.[164] Where the Home Secretary rejects the informal advice of the Board that recall is unnecessary, a formal reference should be expedited.[165] This is particularly important where the recall disrupts employment prospects or arrangements for child care.

(4) CONCLUSIONS

In the field of determinacy of sentences, one can see how developments in public law principles in England and Wales, and the growing willingness on the part of the judges to apply them to protect prisoners against arbitrary use of executive discretion. Alongside the use of public law principles by domestic courts, the European Court of Human Rights has impelled Parliament and successive governments to impose a degree of order and regularity on the operation of discretionary life sentences and the detention of juvenile murderers. The result has been to assert the Rule of Law in an area previously devoid of legal regulation. Little remains to be done by the Human Rights Act 1998. Perhaps the main area for further development by domestic courts will be to encourage Parliament to extend the tariff regime introduced for children to

---

[162] Crime (Sentences) Act 1997, s. 32(1), (2), as interpreted in *R. v. Parole Board, ex parte Watson* [1996] 1 WLR 906, [1996] 2 All ER 641, CA. There are separate provisions allowing renewal of detention where a person commits a further offence while on licence or breaches a condition of the licence: see Powers of Criminal Courts (Sentencing) Act 2000, s. 116.

[163] Crime (Sentences) Act 1997, s. 32(3)–(5).

[164] *R. v. Parole Board, ex parte Watson* [1996] 1 WLR 906, [1996] 2 All ER 641, CA; *In re Cummings* [2001] 1 WLR 822, CA.

[165] *In re Cummings* [2001] 1 WLR 822, CA, at 829–30 *per* Lord Phillips of Worth Matravers MR.

adults serving mandatory life sentences. There is no principled reason to continue to rely on the misunderstanding of the tariff system for adults in order to avoid legal accountability for treating them arbitrarily.

7.5 DETENTION UNDER HEALTH LEGISLATION

(1) MEDICAL DETENTION IN EUROPEAN HUMAN RIGHTS LAW AND ENGLISH LAW

(i) The European Convention on Human Rights

Article 5(1) of the Convention provides: 'No one shall be deprived of his liberty save in the following cases and in accordance with a procedure prescribed by law: ... (e) the lawful detention of persons for the prevention of the spread of infectious diseases, of persons of unsound mind, alcoholics or drug addicts, or vagrants ... '. In an important judgment in *Witold Litwa v. Poland*,[166] the European Court of Human Rights has observed of these categories:

'There is a link between all these persons in that they may be deprived of their liberty either in order to be given medical treatment or because of considerations dictated by social policy, or on both medical and social grounds. It is therefore legitimate to conclude from this context that a predominant reason why the Convention allows the persons mentioned in paragraph 1(e) of Article 5 to be deprived of their liberty is not only that they are dangerous for public safety but also that their own interests may necessitate their detention ... '

This dual focus on the welfare of the individual and of the public led the Court in that case, after considering the *travaux préparatoires*, to give a wide interpretation to the word 'alcoholics' as including anyone abusing alcohol in a way which endangers himself or others. But it also led the Court to interpret 'lawful detention' as meaning that the detention must be necessary to protect either the individual concerned or the public. As there was no real evidence that the applicant, when taken to be detained in a sobering-up centre, had 'posed a threat to the public or himself, or that his own health, well-being or personal safety were endangered', and considering that he was almost blind and that other less restrictive measures could have been taken, the Court concluded that it had not been shown to be necessary to confine him, leading to a finding of a violation of Article 5(1).[167] This approach allows states to deprive people of liberty for the public benefit, but imposes a necessity condition which can have implications for the procedures used to authorize detention. For example, in *Verbanov v. Bulgaria*[168] it was held that detaining a person as being of unsound mind could be justified only if the assessment of his state of mind was based on certification by a qualified doctor with appropriate psychiatric expertise.

---

[166] Eur. Ct. HR, App. No. 26629/95, Judgment of 4 April 2000, para. 60.
[167] Ibid., paras. 62, 77, 80.
[168] Eur. Ct. HR, App. No. 31365/96, Judgment of 5 October 2000, paras. 46–7.

The purpose of detention is usually to treat the person so that they will no longer represent a threat to themselves or others, particularly in relation to those detained for reasons of mental or physical health. The Court has insisted that the accommodation and treatment regime provided for detainees under sub-paragraph (e) must be appropriate to that aim. If a person is detained under a court order for psychiatric treatment after an offence, it will not be lawful to accommodate them in a prison psychiatric wing unless it offers a proper therapeutic environment with an appropriate level of specialist psychiatric expertise. The Court assesses this in the light of evidence, including reports from the European Committee for the Prevention of Torture and Inhuman or Degrading Treatment or Punishment.[169]

When the detainee no longer requires treatment, he should in principle be released. It may be appropriate to impose conditions, in order to ensure that he adapts properly to life in the community, and to defer release until facilities (such as specialized hostel accommodation) can be arranged. States have an obligation to provide, or arrange for the provision, of necessary facilities with reasonable expedition. The Court will not permit a continuing failure to arrange appropriate facilities in the community to justify continued detention of someone who is not in need of in-patient treatment, as it would amount to indefinite detention which cannot be justified by reference to the purposes of Article 5.[170]

Thus Article 5(1) lays down obligations of six types in cases under sub-paragraph (e):

- to ensure that the detention powers are applied only to the kinds of people and purposes specified in the Article;
- to ensure that the detention is in accordance with a procedure prescribed by law;
- to ensure that it is necessary;
- under Article 5(4), to provide access to proceedings in which the lawfulness of the detention can be speedily determined and in which release can be ordered if the detention is unlawful;
- to ensure that the detainee is placed in an appropriate environment and given appropriate treatment for the condition which justified detention;
- to release the detainee when the justification for detention no longer exists, providing the appropriate facilities to meet any conditions for release which appear to be appropriate to protect the individual or the community.

In addition, detained patients retain the right to be free of inhuman and degrading treatment under ECHR Article 3, although some kinds of non-consensual treatment, such as the forcible administration of drugs or nutrition, may be justified in the patient's interests if he is unable, by reason of the illness, to make a legally effective decision in respect of treatment. The state has an obligation to protect the lives of people in its care under these circumstances, and treating a patient without his or her consent for that purpose, in a manner approved by experts in the light of current

---

[169] *Aerts v. Belgium*, Eur. Ct. HR, Judgment of 30 July 1998, para. 49.

[170] *Johnson v. United Kingdom*, Eur. Ct. HR, RJD 1997-VII, Judgment of 24 October 1997, 27 EHRR 196. Cp. *R. (K.) v. Camden and Islington Health Authority* [2001] 3 WLR 553, CA.

medical knowledge and understanding, would not be regarded as inhuman or degrading.[170a]

(ii) Preventing the spread of infectious diseases

The Secretary of State has power to order the hospitalization and, if considered necessary, exceptionally, to prevent or control an epidemic, detention in quarantine of people who have infectious diseases, in order to prevent the spread of the disease.[171] This could, if necessary, be invoked in relation to a disease such as AIDS. However, the evidence is that, as it is relatively difficult to transmit the HIV virus under normal circumstances, the compulsory detention of sufferers would be unreasonable and unnecessary. It would therefore breach the necessity principle, which the European Commission and Court of Human Rights have imposed in respect of the other grounds for depriving people of their liberty under Article 5 of the European Convention.[172] As Sieghart argued,[173] there is no reason for failing to impose the same standard of necessity in relation to medical detention under Article 5(1)(e). Indeed, there are signs that the necessity principle does apply: in relation to detention of people of unsound mind, the Court has held (as noted above) that the continued detention of a patient after the condition has been relieved is usually a breach of Article 5, suggesting that the necessity principle applies at least to that limb of Article 5(1)(e). In addition, detention of HIV-positive or AIDS patients in an emergency would have to be reviewed by a 'court', i.e. a body independent of the executive which conducts a full inquiry on the basis of evidence, to which a detainee can make representations, and which has the power finally to determine the lawfulness of the detention. The absence of such a procedural protection would breach Article 5(4).

At the moment, AIDS is not a notifiable disease in the UK (i.e. a disease all cases of which must be reported to the Department of Health), although health authorities are required by the AIDS (Control) Act 1987 to provide regular reports on the number of cases in their areas (but without identifying the sufferers) to the Minister, so that the progress of the disease may be monitored. The identification and control of people who are HIV-positive or suffering from pre-AIDS or AIDS raises serious civil rights and civil liberties issues, some of which are examined in the section on privacy, below. The matter has attracted considerable controversy abroad. Sweden has a programme of compulsorily detaining and isolating sufferers in hostels away from centres of population, and in Sydney, New South Wales, in 1989 a prostitute who was found to be HIV-positive was imprisoned for some days before being released when it was found that there was no legal power to detain her. Compulsory detention of all sufferers, on the Swedish model, seems to go further than necessary to protect other

---

[170a] See *Herczegfalvy v. Austria*, Eur. Ct. HR, Series A, No. 244, Judgment of 24 September 1992, 15 EHRR 432, and Chs 4 and 5, above.

[171] Public Health (Infectious Diseases) Regulations 1985, SI 1985/434. See in particular reg. 3.

[172] *Lawless v. Ireland*, Eur. Ct. HR, Series A, No. 3, (1961) 1 EHRR 15, *Bouamar v. Belgium* Eur. Ct. HR, Series A, No. 129, Judgment of 29 February 1987, 11 EHRR 1; *Caprino v. United Kingdom*, Eur. Comm. HR, Report: (1980) DR 12, 14 at 20.

[173] P. Sieghart, *AIDS and Human Rights: A UK Perspective* (London: BMA Foundation for AIDS, 1989), 41–6.

people, and would almost certainly be held to breach Article 5 of the European Convention.

On the other hand, it is arguable that some action may be necessary if the sufferers are in jobs which raise particular risks of passing on the disease. Those who deal regularly with bleeding patients, such as ambulance officers, surgeons, and dentists, or who have sexual intercourse with others, such as prostitutes, may well put their patients or clients at risk. Nevertheless, it does not seem necessary to detain such people. Counselling on methods of controlling the risks, and if need be regular monitoring of procedures, is often all that is required. Detention may be required where, for example, a sufferer is found bleeding heavily in public, but arguably only for as long as it takes to control the bleeding and ensure that it is unlikely to begin again. At the moment, there is no legal procedure for securing such a detention lawfully in the UK.

(iii) People suffering from mental disorders[174]

Article 5(1)(e) of the ECHR permits detention of people of unsound mind. The notion of 'unsound mind' is potentially very wide and indeterminate. However, it has been somewhat tied down by the Commission and the Court, which have imposed three limitations.[175] First, there must be objective criteria on the basis of which an appropriate medical expert forms the opinion that the patient is suffering from a recognized psychiatric disorder, in accordance with contemporary understanding of mental disorders. Secondly, the disorder must be such as to necessitate confinement either to treat the patient or to protect himself or others, or both. Thirdly, the lawfulness of continuing to detain a person must depend on a reliable medical assessment that the patient is still suffering from the condition which initially justified detention. Once the patient's condition has been stabilized, so that he no longer represents a serious threat to himself or others, he ought to be released.[176]

In England and Wales, the Crown had ultimate responsibility for the care of people of unsound mind. The royal prerogative included powers in respect of their welfare and the management of their affairs. These powers were exercised by the Court of Protection. The legal framework for the treatment and detention of mental patients was progressively put on a statutory footing, and the prerogative powers were finally

---

[174] For a critical appraisal of the current law, see G. Richardson, *Law, Process and Custody: Prisoners and Patients* (London: Weidenfeld and Nicolson, 1993), chs 9 and 10; and the very full review by an expert committee, chaired by Professor Genevra Richardson, appointed to advise the Department of Health on the operation of the Mental Health Act 1983: *Review of the Expert Committee: Review of the Mental Health Act 1983* (London: Department of Health, 1999). The government's proposals for change were published in a White Paper, *Reforming the Mental Health Act, Part I: The New Legal Framework; Part II: High Risk Patients*, Cm. 5016-I and 5016-II (London: The Stationery Office, December 2000).

[175] *Winterwerp v. Netherlands*, Eur. Ct. HR, Series A, No. 33, Judgment of 24 October 1979, 2 EHRR 387; *Luberti v. Italy*, Eur. Ct. HR, Series A, No. 75, Judgment of 23 February 1984, 6 EHRR 440; *Ashingdane v. United Kingdom*, Eur. Ct. HR, Series A, No. 93, Judgment of 28 May 1985, 7 EHRR 528; *Johnson v. United Kingdom*, Eur. Ct. HR, RJD 1997-VII, Judgment of 24 October 1997, 27 EHRR 196; *Verbanov v. Bulgaria*, Eur. Ct. HR, App. No. 31365/96, Judgment of 5 October 2000.

[176] *Luberti v. Italy*, Eur. Ct. HR, Series A, No. 75, Judgment of 23 February 1984, 6 EHRR 440; *Johnson v. United Kingdom*, Eur. Ct. HR, RJD 1997-VII, Judgment of 24 October 1997, 27 EHRR 196.

superseded in 1960 when the Mental Health Act 1959 entered into force.[177] Following various challenges to the regime under the Mental Health Act 1959, before the European Commission and Court of Human Rights, a series of statutes revised the law, which was consolidated in the Mental Health Act 1983.

The definition of mental disorder remains somewhat unclear, containing elements deriving from different periods in the development of psychological and psychiatric study. Section 1(2) of the Mental Health Act 1983 defines it as 'mental illness, arrested or incomplete development of mind, psychopathic disorder and any other disorder or disability of mind'. The government propose to introduce a new definition of the conditions which can trigger intervention in forthcoming legislation. It will be intended to be broad enough to cover all possible cases of concern, with patients' rights and interests being protected by rigorous procedural safeguards.[178]

Under the 1983 Act, there are two classes of patients: those admitted voluntarily, or informally, to hospital, and those admitted compulsorily, or using the formal statutory procedures. These will be considered in sections (2) and (3) below.

(2) INFORMAL OR VOLUNTARY ADMISSIONS

These may be treated in the usual way by their general practitioner or others. If it becomes desirable for them to enter hospital for psychiatric treatment, and they do so voluntarily, they can be admitted, but are free to leave at will.[179] The Law Commission noted in 1991 that:

'well over 90 per cent of admissions to mental hospitals are now on an informal basis. This is probably because, in practice, compulsion is only needed when a patient actively refuses to cooperate with the treatment or care which his doctors or other professionals consider that he needs for his own sake or for the protection of others.'[180]

Such patients fall outside the statutory regime which protects those admitted compulsorily (on which see section (3), below). Yet their condition may be such as to prevent them from exerting any control over, or consenting to, their admission or treatment, or of understanding the nature and implications of treatment or care. They are left in a legal limbo. The problem was graphically illustrated in *R. v. Bournewood Community and Mental Health NHS Trust, ex parte L. (Secretary of State for Health and others intervening).*[181] The applicant was an autistic and profoundly mentally retarded forty-eight-year-old man, unable to speak and of very limited understanding. He had spent over thirty years residing at the hospital before being released into the community as a trial measure in 1994. He lived with people who regarded him as one of the family, and attended a day centre. One day he became agitated there, and after being sedated by a doctor was taken by ambulance to the hospital, where a doctor

---

[177] For a good, brief account of the history, see Law Commission Consultation Paper No. 119, *Mentally Incapacitated Adults and Decision-Making: An Overview* (London: HMSO, 1991), 55–60.

[178] *Reforming the Mental Health Act, Part I: The New Legal Framework*, paras. 3.3–3.7, 3.14–3.18.

[179] Mental Health Act 1983, s. 131.

[180] Law Commission, *Mentally Incapacitated*, 73 (footnote omitted), citing DHSS figures for 1982–86.

[181] [1999] 1 AC 458, [1998] 3 All ER 289, HL.

assessed him as needing in-patient treatment. He was put in an unlocked ward. The doctor would have compulsorily admitted him had he tried to leave, but he seemed compliant. The doctor could have authorized detention for up to seventy-two hours, in order for an application to be made to the court.[182] However, the formal procedures would then have had to be observed, including a right to have the legality of the detention reviewed.

In due course L was returned to the family caring for him, but meanwhile proceedings had been launched to determine the lawfulness of the detention. The Court of Appeal decided that he had been detained without statutory authority. The hospital appealed to the House of Lords. Lord Goff, with whom Lord Lloyd of Berwick and Lord Hope of Craighead agreed, accepted that he had been detained in the ambulance, but held that he had not been detained at the hospital, because the ward door had been unlocked. Lord Nolan and Lord Steyn disagreed. The reality of the position was that he would have been compulsorily detained had he tried to leave, his behaviour was closely monitored, he was sedated to keep him compliant, and his outside carers were denied access for some time in case he tried to leave with them. He was in fact subject to the control of medical staff to such an extent that he was wholly deprived of his liberty. On this point, the view of Lord Nolan and Lord Steyn is respectfully to be preferred, as being more in tune with the need for the law to protect people from being deprived of their liberty by an arbitrary exercise of authority.

On either view, the question then arose whether the detention (either in the ambulance or also at the hospital) could be justified in law. All of their Lordships held that it could. Section 131 of the Mental Health Act 1983 authorized the admission, and the common law doctrine of necessity justified treatment which was reasonably considered to be in L's best interests as someone who could not make or communicate decisions about his welfare.[183] This made L's future liberty depend entirely on the good judgment and good faith of the hospital staff.

The admission of such patients is therefore not necessarily truly voluntary. There must be concern about treating patients while they are apparently co-operating but perhaps not genuinely consenting.[184] The understandable desire on the part of relatives and professionals to avoid having to stigmatize people leads to the compulsory procedures being rather rarely used, but as a result:

'For what may be very good, practical and humane reasons, important decisions may be taken on behalf of mentally incapable people with none of the safeguards which would be available if they or their families were actively opposed.'[185]

---

[182] Mental Health Act 1983, s.5(1), (2). If the doctor in charge or his delegate is not available when the patient tries to discharge himself, and it is immediately necessary to restrain the patient, a nurse can restrain the patient from leaving the hospital for up to six hours or (if sooner) until it is practicable to secure the doctor's attendance: ibid., s.5(4).

[183] In re F. (Mental Patient: Sterilisation) [1990] 2 AC 1, sub nom. F. v. West Berkshire Health Authority (Mental Health Act Commission intervening) [1989] 2 All ER 545, HL, on which see above, Ch. 3.

[184] Concerns have been expressed by the Mental Health Act Commission: First Biennial Report 1983–85, 11; Second Biennial Report 1985–87, 50; Third Biennial Report 1987–89, 35, cited in Law Commission, Mentally Incapacitated, 74.

[185] Law Commission, Mentally Incapacitated, 95.

There was concern when *Ex parte L.* was being litigated that the Mental Health Review Tribunals would have been swamped, and excessive demands and difficulties have been made of the medical and bureaucratic procedures for protecting patients, had it been held always to be necessary to admit patients in L's position formally. However, this is not a sufficient reason for denying to a whole class of patients the protections which are accorded to others in clinically and therapeutically indistinguishable positions. Lord Steyn pinpointed the anomaly in his speech in *Ex parte L.* when he said:

' . . . neither habeas corpus nor judicial review are sufficient safeguards against misjudgments and professional lapses in the case of compliant incapacitated patients. Given that such patients are diagnostically indistinguishable from compulsory patients, there is no reason to withhold the specific and effective protections of the 1983 Act from a large class of vulnerable mentally incapacitated individuals. Their moral right to be treated with dignity requires nothing less. The only comfort is that counsel for the Secretary of State has assured the House that reform of the law is under active consideration.'[186]

So far, however, no legislative change has been forthcoming, although in its White Paper on *Reforming the Mental Health Act* the government have expressed a willingness to change the law to protect 'not uncompliant' patients without resorting to compulsory admission.[187]

Children who are detained for treatment present special cause for concern. Normally they will have been admitted with their parents' consent, so that they are formally voluntarily rather than involuntarily detained patients. However, they will not themselves necessarily have consented either to detention or to treatment. The safeguards which apply to adults who are detained compulsorily do not apply to these 'voluntary' child patients. Where a local authority social services department is responsible for the care of the child, some external and interdisciplinary monitoring of the child's treatment can take place. In cases where there is a difference of opinion between the parents and the local authority, the authority can apply to have the child made a ward of court, whereupon the Family Division of the High Court takes responsibility for all decisions relating to the welfare of the child, and must give its consent before 'voluntary' detention or treatment is allowed. Yet there remain cases in which children are detained without their consent, though with the agreement of their parents on their behalf, and where no external monitoring is available.

This would, on the face of it, seem to be contrary to the European Convention's guarantees under Article 5. In *Nielsen v. Denmark*,[188] the European Court of Human Rights took a different view. The applicant was a twelve-year-old illegitimate child who had been admitted to a mental hospital at his mother's request. There was no procedure under Danish law for an independent judicial body to determine the lawfulness of his detention, and he claimed that this breached Article 5(1). For the Danish government, it was first argued that for the state to intervene in a matter of this sort,

---

[186] [1998] 3 All ER at 309. Habeas corpus and judicial review are inadequate in these cases because the Administrative Court cannot authoritatively assess the medical condition and therapeutic needs of the patients: see *X. v. United Kingdom*, Eur. Ct. HR, Series A, No. 46, Judgment of 5 November 1981, 4 EHRR 188.

[187] *Reforming the Mental Health Act, Part I: The New Legal Framework*, 20–1, paras. 2.39–2.40 and ch. 6.

[188] Eur. Ct. HR, Series A, No. 144, Judgment of 28 November 1988, 11 EHRR 175.

overriding the parent's wishes, would be incompatible with respect for family life under Article 8. This argument was unanimously rejected. The Court accepted that the state had obligations under Article 5 to protect children against infringements of their right to liberty, and that this justified some degree of interference with parental decisions. However, by a narrow nine to seven majority the Court held that there had been no breach of Article 5. According to the majority, the parent's decision to have her son committed was within the constraints on children's rights necessarily connected with their upbringing. At that age, it was normal for some decisions to be taken for children by parents. The responsibility of the state to safeguard the child's liberty did not go beyond ensuring that expert medical advice was provided for the child.

This narrows the responsibilities of the state, and protection for the rights of children, almost to vanishing point. Allowing the state to evade its responsibility to protect children, or to provide procedures whereby children can protect themselves, against ill-conceived and potentially harmful parental action makes children liable to be committed to mental institutions by their parents without any right to have the rationality or legality of the committal tested by anyone except medical professionals, who have neither training nor legitimacy as protectors of rights. It makes the child liable to arbitrary interference with his liberty, dignity, privacy, and family life without any legal remedy. It is hard to reconcile with the view which the Court has taken in more recent cases of the positive obligation of states to protect the welfare of children.[189] Where the state fails to take appropriate action to provide special protection for the child who is temporarily or permanently deprived of his family environment, it will also contravene Articles 16 and 20 of the UN Convention on the Rights of the Child. The decision in *Nielsen* is therefore an unsafe basis on which to seek to justify or develop the current state of English law. It is reassuring to note that the government propose to bring children within the protection of mental health legislation.[190]

(3) FORMAL OR COMPULSORY ADMISSIONS

Compulsory admissions to hospital, as noted above, are the exception rather than the rule. Patients are admitted to hospital by hospital managers, and thereafter detained, on the authority of sections 2, 3, or 4 of the 1983 Act. The purpose must be to offer appropriate treatment. There is no power in England and Wales to detain (or to continue to detain) for preventive purposes a person who is not suffering from a treatable condition,[191] although such a power now exists in Scotland in relation to untreatable restricted patients following a conviction,[192] and the government plans

[189] See Ch. 5, above.

[190] *Reforming the Mental Health Act, Part I: The New Legal Framework*, 20, paras. 2.35–2.38.

[191] See *Reid v. Secretary of State for Scotland* [1999] 2 AC 512, [1999] 1 All ER 481, HL, where it was held that treatment to alleviate or prevent the deterioration of symptoms of a condition, without affecting the underlying condition itself, could be regarded as treatment.

[192] Mental Health (Public Safety and Appeals) (Scotland) Act 1999, s. 1, an Act of the Scottish Parliament upheld against a Convention rights challenge under the Scotland Act 1998 in *Anderson v. The Scottish Ministers, The Times*, 29 October 2001, PC (no requirement in Art. 5 or implied from *Winterwerp* that detention must be for treatment; not arbitrary to take account of public safety).

to introduce legislation for England and Wales to permit preventive detention of people suffering from certain severe personality disorders which make them a threat to the public.[193] Any such legislation would raise serious issues under ECHR Article 5.

There are currently three types of admission.

(i) Admission for assessment

Under section 2 of the Mental Health Act 1983, two requirements for admission to hospital must be satisfied. They are: (a) that the patient is suffering from a mental disorder of a nature or degree which warrants detention in hospital, at least for a limited period; and (b) that it is necessary that the patient be detained, in the interests of his own health or safety or with a view to the protection of other persons. The effect of an admission is that the patient, once admitted, may be detained for up to twenty-eight days for assessment, after which he must be released unless an admission is justified under section 3.

The process is subject to various safeguards. First, the application must be made by the patient's nearest relative, or someone authorized to act on the patient's behalf, or by an approved social worker. The applicant must have seen the patient within the previous fourteen days. Secondly, the application must be supported by two registered medical practitioners, one of whom must be a psychiatrist. Thirdly, the patient must be informed of the legal effects of admission, and his rights must be explained to him. Fourthly, the patient is immediately entitled to have the admission reviewed by the hospital manager, and, at any time during the first fourteen days following admission, is entitled to apply to a Mental Health Review Tribunal to have his case reviewed. The manager or the tribunal can order his release if they disagree with the doctors' assessment.

(ii) Admission for treatment

Under section 3 of the 1983 Act, the patient can be admitted for treatment. The conditions for admission under section 3(2), all of which must be satisfied, are that (a) the patient is suffering from a mental illness, psychopathic disorder, or mental impairment, of a nature or degree which makes it appropriate for him to receive in-patient treatment; (b) where the patient is suffering from psychopathic disorder or mental impairment, the treatment is likely to alleviate or prevent deterioration of his condition; (c) it is necessary for the health or safety of the patient, or the protection of other persons, that he should receive such treatment; and (d) the treatment cannot be provided unless the patient is detained under section 3. The section therefore cannot be used in order to protect other people; it must enable treatment to be given which will benefit the patient. Nor can section 3 be used initially purely for providing care and nursing, or treatment which is not likely to benefit the patient, unless the patient is suffering from mental illness. However, if the period of detention is being extended, there is an alternative ground to (b) if the patient is suffering from mental illness or *severe* mental impairment and is unlikely, if discharged, to be able to care

---

[193] *Reforming the Mental Health Act, Part II: High Risk Patients*, ch. 3.

for himself, to obtain the necessary care, or to guard himself against serious exploitation.[194]

Patients have three safeguards under section 3:

- The application for admission must be made by the closest relative or person authorized to act on the patient's behalf or an approved social worker (who must normally have consulted the relative). If the nearest relative is not consulted, the detention is unlawful, and the patient can obtain his release by way of a writ of habeas corpus.[195] If the nearest relative objects, the application should not be made (section 11(4)), although a court may replace the nearest relative if he appears not to be acting in the best interests of the patient.[196]

- The application must be founded on the written recommendations of two registered medical practitioners, each stating that the conditions for admission under section 3 are complied with, and including particulars of the grounds for their opinions in relation to conditions (a) and (b) above, and the reasons for thinking that (c) and (d) are met, specifying whether other methods of dealing with the patient are available and, if they are, why they are inappropriate.[197]

- The patient has the right to apply to have his case reviewed by a Mental Health Review Tribunal.

After being admitted under section 3, the patient can be detained for up to six months, and detention can be renewed (initially for a further six months, and thereafter for periods of up to a year at a time) if the conditions for detention are still satisfied.[198] During the period of detention, the medical officer responsible for treating the patient may give the patient leave of absence, subject to any conditions which the medical officer considers necessary in the interests of the patient or for the protection of others.[199] If, while the patient is on leave but before the end of the authorized period of detention, it appears to the responsible medical officer that it is necessary to recall the patient to hospital in the interests of his health or safety or for the protection of others, he may be recalled.[200] This is likely to be the case, for example, if the patient stops taking prescribed drugs so that his condition, which had been stabilized, deteriorates. It has the effect of making possible a period of compulsory treatment in the community. Furthermore, a Mental Health Review Tribunal may make an order for discharge conditional on the patient making use of supervision or accommodation facilities in the community, in which case the responsible local authority or health authority has a duty under section 117 to take steps to provide those services with all reasonable expedition and diligence, in order to avoid a violation of the

---

[194] Mental Health Act 1983, s. 20(4).

[195] *In re S.-C. (Mental Patient: Habeas Corpus)* [1996] QB 599, [1996] 1 All ER 532, CA.

[196] Mental Health Act 1983, s. 29; *R. v. Central London County Court, ex parte London* [1999] QB 1260, [1999] 3 All ER 991, CA.

[197] Ibid., s. 3(3).

[198] Mental Health Act 1983, s. 20(1), (2).

[199] Ibid., s. 17(1).

[200] Ibid., s. 17(4). Where the patient has been on leave for over six months, he may be recalled only if he has either returned to hospital or been transferred to another hospital, or he is absent without leave at the end of the period of leave: s. 17(5).

necessity condition for detention under ECHR Article 5(1)(e) and the 1983 Act.[201] If agreement can be reached between the responsible medical officer, the relevant local authority and the relevant health authority on a supervision application, a plan can be put in place to ensure that a patient still suffering from mental disorder in some circumstances will receive after-care following and as a condition of discharge.[202] But the obligation under section 117 depends on resources being available.[202a]

However, neither an initial admission under section 3 nor a recall under section 17 can be used to force a patient to attend for short-term treatment as an out-patient: admission and recall must lead to him becoming a detained patient again. This leads to some inconvenience where all that is needed is to administer drugs regularly to a patient who can then be left to his own devices, but McCullough J held, in *R. v. Hallstrom, ex parte W. (No. 2), R. v. Gardner, ex parte L.*,[203] that the power to recall for compulsory out-patient treatment is not available, and that attempts by two doctors to use the power in that way was not justified by the Act. McCullough J also expressed the view that it would be an abuse of power to recall a patient from leave for one night purely in order to prevent the period of six months' leave, after which he would not be liable to recall under section 17, from expiring.

(iii) Emergency admission

This procedure, under section 4 of the 1983 Act, is available where the applicant has seen the patient within the previous twenty-four hours, and requires a recommendation from just one doctor, who need not be a psychiatrist but should, if practicable, have previous acquaintance with the patient.[204] The admission is for a period of seventy-two hours, after which time the patient must be released unless it is converted into an admission for twenty-eight days for treatment, obtaining an additional supporting opinion from a psychiatrist. If this is done, the patient must be told of the legal position and has the right, within fourteen days, to apply for review by a Mental Health Review Tribunal, as under section 2.

(4) RATIONALES FOR DETENTION, AND PATIENTS' LIBERTIES

The compulsory detention of mental health patients is justified either on the basis of a paternalistic test, acting in the patient's own best interests, or a protective test, safeguarding other people against the patient. This raises problems for a civil liberties theory based on personal autonomy. Is paternalism compatible with idea of autonomy? As we have seen above, in relation to consent to medical treatment in Chapters 4 and 5, enforced treatment of someone who is incapable of consenting or unwilling to consent is not necessarily incompatible with the patient's autonomy. Treatment may

---

[201] *Johnson v. United Kingdom*, Eur. Ct. HR, RJD 1997-VII, Judgment of 24 October 1997, 27 EHRR 196; *R. v. Ealing District Health Authority, ex parte Fox* [1993] 1 WLR 373, [1993] 3 All ER 170, Otton J; *R. v. Mental Health Review Tribunal, ex parte Hall* [2000] 1 WLR 1323, [1999] 4 All ER 883, CA.

[202] Mental Health Act 1983, ss. 25A–25J, inserted by Mental Health (Patients in the Community) Act 1995, s. 1.

[202a] *R. (K.) v. Camden and Islington Health Authority* [2001] 3 WLR 553, CA.

[203] [1986] QB 1090, [1986] 2 All ER 306, DC.

[204] Mental Health Act 1983, s. 4(3).

be necessary in order to restore the patient's rationality to a point where he is capable of evaluating options and making rational choices. In other words, it may restore a sick person's capacity for autonomy; he might even be said to have a right to be compulsorily treated (at any rate on an interest, or benefit, theory of rights).

This, however, depends on adopting a model of autonomy which makes it inseparable from rationality, and so denies people the option of choosing to be systematically irrational. This has the capacity to empower professionals to impose their ideas of right bases for choice on the patient. That is acceptable if the patient has been convicted of an offence: there is no *prima facie* compelling reason to respect the freedom of a person to choose criminality. On the other hand, most compulsory patients have not been convicted of any offence. The risk is that the line which separates personal or political eccentricity from illness will become obscured, as it did, notoriously, in the Soviet Union. This risk is particularly acute under section 3 of the 1983 Act, as mental illness is not defined in the Act and depends on professional judgment. The Act does limit the extent to which a doctor can use the category of mental illness to enforce his own view of right behaviour on an unwilling person. It specifies in section 1(3) that 'promiscuity or other immoral conduct, sexual deviancy or dependence on alcohol or drugs' are not on their own to be regarded as constituting a mental disorder. Mann J accordingly decided that, despite the contrary opinion of the doctors in the case, a person's sexual attraction to young girls cannot on its own justify a diagnosis of psychopathic disorder.[205]

Although in that case there was an avenue for correcting the error of the doctors and the mental health review tribunal, the case shows fears that doctors will make the test of mental disorder over-inclusive, labelling a wide range of conduct as psychopathic merely because it is antisocial and perhaps leading to what has been called 'an undue medicalization of deviant behaviour'.[206] All the tests essentially rely on the medical expertise of the examining doctors, in consultation with social workers and the patient's family. We depend heavily on the objectivity and professional judgment of doctors, with the independent Mental Health Review Tribunals as an important safeguard against medical misjudgment. Perhaps the extensive powers under the 1983 Act mean that we have to trust them more than is ideal.

Even if one is satisfied that paternalism is justifiable on civil liberties grounds, there is at first sight a curious anomaly in that mental patients appear to be subjected to this sort of paternalism in cases where patients with purely physical disorders are not. This is explicable only on the basis that the disorder suffered by a mentally disordered patient interferes with the capacity to make decisions in a way which purely physical disorders do not; this explains and, perhaps, justifies a more interventionist line in relation to decision-making for mental patients than would be thought admissible in relation to other patients. As Professor Tom Campbell has pointed out in an acute discussion of the problem, it may reflect an assumption that humanity is, in some way, linked to rationality, and that the capacity to exercise rights is a feature of humanity

---

[205] *R. v. Mental Health Review Tribunal, ex parte Clatworthy* [1985] 3 All ER 699, DC.

[206] J. K. Mason and R. A. McCall Smith, *Law and Medical Ethics*, 3rd edn. (London: Butterworths, 1991), 401. See also J. Jacob, 'The Right of a Mental Patient to his Psychosis' (1976) 39 *MLR* 17–42.

which is, in turn, diminished if mental disorder reduces one's capacity for rationality.[207]

There is a further threat to civil liberties in the power to detain mentally ill patients on the basis that they pose a threat to others, without the need for any criminal offence to have been proved against them. This protective detention is not available in respect of people who suffer no mental disorder (although the latter may be required to be bound over to keep the peace or be of good behaviour). It is justifiable only if the prediction of dangerousness is reliable. In many cases, it will be based on assaults which the patient has already carried out, whether or not he has been charged with them. In other cases, it will be based purely on informed guess-work. There is no general correlation between mental illness and criminality, and predictions of future dangerousness are unreliable. Very great care is therefore needed when admitting a patient compulsorily on protective grounds. At present, admission under section 3 is permitted only in order to receive treatment, not simply to keep the patient out of circulation for a period. However, if the treatment is unsuccessful and the patient is thought to be dangerous, a renewed admission under section 17 can be permitted, even if there is unlikely to be any improvement in the patient's condition from further treatment, merely as a measure of containment. Furthermore, the government propose to introduce a new power to detain people with severe personality disorders who cannot be treated but who are likely to represent a danger to the public.[208] In view of the necessity test under ECHR Article 5(1)(e), a high standard of proof should be required of anyone applying for an order for detention in these circumstances. Detention should be allowed only if there is clear evidence that the patient is violent, and the matter should be decided by a court, rather than being left to doctors and managers subject to review by a Mental Health Review Tribunal.

(5) REVIEW OF DETENTION[209]

After detention has been authorized, the patient has the right to apply for release first to the hospital manager, and secondly (within fourteen days, in the case of admissions under section 2) to a Mental Health Review Tribunal.[210] Sections 72 and 73 of the Mental Health Act 1983 require a tribunal to order the discharge of a patient if it is satisfied that the conditions for detention are no longer satisfied. This appears to place the onus of satisfying the tribunal on the patient, whereas the presumption in favour of liberty at common law and under the ECHR should lead to the tribunal being required to order discharge unless satisfied that the conditions for detention continue to be satisfied. On the latter formulation, the onus would lie on those seeking to justify further detention. The Court of Appeal has therefore held that the formulation in the

[207] T. Campbell, 'The Rights of the Mentally Ill', in T. Campbell, D. Goldberg, S. McLean, and T. Mullen (eds.), *Human Rights: From Rhetoric to Reality* (Oxford: Basil Blackwell, 1986), 123–47 at 125–32.
[208] *Reforming the Mental Health Act, Part II*, above.
[209] See Richardson, *Law, Process and Custody*, ch. 11.
[210] See Richardson, *Law, Process and Custody*, ch. 12; G. Richardson and D. Machin, 'Judicial Review and Tribunal Decision Making: A Study of the Mental Health Review Tribunal' [2000] *PL* 494–514.

Act is incompatible with the rights of patients under the Human Rights Act 1998, and has made a declaration of incompatibility under section 10 of that Act.[211] A remedial order to amend sections 72 and 73 to remove the incompatibility was made in November 2001. Until the order came into force, at least a few people may have been detained in violation of their rights under ECHR Article 5, and will be entitled to compensation under Article 5(5). However, the remedial order (which was made by the urgent procedure because individual liberty was at stake) makes no provision for compensation.

The European Convention on Human Rights, Article 5(4), gives those who lose their liberty a right to have the legality of their detention reviewed regularly by a 'court', and the European Court of Human Rights has held that this right applies to those compulsorily detained for treatment for mental disorders following convictions for criminal offences as it does to other patients. Patients who are detained for treatment for mental disorders may recover or have their conditions stabilized, and once that has happened there may be no further medical (as opposed to retributive, deterrent, or political) reason for detaining them in mental hospitals. It was therefore an infringement of a patient's right under Article 5 for the decision to release him, recommended on medical grounds by doctors or a Mental Health Review Tribunal, to be subject to the approval on non-medical grounds by the Secretary of State. This was the position in English law, in relation to those detained after conviction or being found unfit to plead, under the regime of the Mental Health Act 1959. Decision-making processes of this sort were disapproved by the European Court in several cases, including *X. v. United Kingdom*.[212] The law was accordingly changed, and under the Mental Health Act 1983 the Mental Health Review Tribunal has authority to order the discharge of any patient without the Secretary of State being able to override the order.[213] As the patient is entitled to make representations to the tribunal, and the tribunal is independent of the executive, it satisfies the requirements for a 'court' under Article 5(4). None the less, where a sentencing court makes a hospital order under section 37 of the Act coupled with a restriction order under section 41 in order to protect the public, the Secretary of State retains considerable power to influence the decision of the Tribunal, and to recall the patient after release in order to protect the public, with or without evidence of mental disorder.[214] The Secretary of State is not bound to accept the Tribunal's view of the patient's medical condition, and is entitled to take advice from an Advisory Board on Restricted Patients in coming to his decision. The normal principles of public law still require the Secretary of State to inform the patient of at least the gist of the advice given by the Board, and to give him an opportunity to make worthwhile representations in respect of it before the

---

[211] *R. (H.) v. Mental Health Review Tribunal, North and East London Region, and Secretary of State for Health* [2001] 3 WLR 512, CA.

[212] Eur. Ct. HR, Series A, No. 46, Judgment of 5 November 1981. See also *van Droogenbroeck v. Belgium*, Eur. Ct. HR, Series A, No. 50, Judgment of 24 April 1982, 4 EHRR 443; *Winterwerp v. The Netherlands*, Eur. Ct. HR, Series A, No. 33 (1979) 2 EHRR 387, and *Van der Leer v. Netherlands*, Eur. Ct. HR, Series A, No. 170 (1989) 12 EHRR 567.

[213] Mental Health Act 1983, ss. 72, 73.

[214] *R. v. Secretary of State for the Home Dept., ex parte K.* [1990] 1 All ER 694, CA; further proceedings [1991] 1 QB 270, [1990] 3 All ER 562, CA.

Secretary of State makes a decision.[215] The European Commission of Human Rights declared admissible a complaint that this violated Article 5(4).[216]

To protect applicants for release who are notorious criminals against media campaigns designed to prejudice the tribunal against them, and to satisfy the requirement of the European Convention that the review of detention should be carried out by a court, it has been held that the Mental Health Review Tribunal is a court of law for the purposes of the law of contempt of court, and attempts to prejudice its proceedings are punishable as such.[217]

The tribunal must give reasons for its decisions.[218] The reasons must be sufficiently clear to show that the conditions for detention remain satisfied, and must be based on an adequate evaluation of the evidence.[219] It is subject to the supervisory jurisdiction of the courts, either by way of case stated or by way of the application for judicial-review procedure. The supervisory jurisdiction has been used both by aggrieved patients and by the Department of Health to ensure that the tribunal observes the rules and to clarify the principles on which the tribunal acts.[220] When it was first invoked by a patient against a doctor who had admitted her, the judicial review application was met with the argument that it constituted 'civil proceedings', which are not available in respect of anything purporting to be done in pursuance of the 1983 Act unless the act was done in bad faith or without reasonable care.[221] This would have excluded judicial review on the basis of most of the classic heads of review (*ultra vires*, natural justice, and irrationality). This argument succeeded at first instance, but was rejected by the Court of Appeal. As it appeared that the 1983 Act was intended to protect doctors against actions for damages or criminal liability rather than to take away a patient's access to a forum for testing the legality of the detention, the Court of Appeal applied the principle that judicial review cannot be excluded except by the most clear and explicit statutory language, and restricted the scope of the term 'civil proceedings' to the type of damages action for false imprisonment or trespass to the person at which it was aimed.[222]

If the tribunal discharges a patient, a social worker cannot apply for compulsory re-admission to prevent the patient's release unless the patient's condition has changed materially between the date of the decision and the date of release.[222a]

[215] *R. v. Secretary of State for the Home Department, ex parte Harry* [1998] 1 WLR 1737, [1998] 3 All ER 360, Lightman J.

[216] *Benjamin and Wilson v. United Kingdom*, Eur. Commn. HR, App. No. 28212/96, Decision of 23 October 1997.

[217] *Pickering v. Liverpool Daily Post and Echo Newspapers plc* [1991] 2 WLR 513, [1991] 1 All ER 622, HL.

[218] Mental Health Review Tribunal Rules 1983, SI 1983/942, 23(2).

[219] *Bone v. Mental Health Review Tribunal* [1985] 3 All ER 330; *R. v. Mental Health Review Tribunal, ex parte Clatworthy* [1985] 3 All ER 699, DC; *R. v. Mental Health Review Tribunal, ex parte Pickering* [1986] 1 All ER 99, DC.

[220] *R. v. Oxford Regional Mental Health Review Tribunal, ex parte Secretary of State for the Home Dept.* [1988] AC 120, [1987] 3 All ER 8, HL; *Secretary of State for the Home Dept. v. Mental Health Review Tribunal for Mersey Regional Health Authority* [1986] 1 WLR 1170.

[221] Mental Health Act 1983, s. 139(1).

[222] *Ex parte Waldron* [1986] QB 824, *sub nom. R. v. Hallstrom, ex parte W.* [1985] 3 All ER 775, CA.

[222a] *R. (Von Brandenburg) v. East London and The City NHS Mental Health Trust* [2001] 3 WLR 588, CA.

(6) ARRESTING MENTAL PATIENTS

In certain cases, there are powers to arrest or forcibly remove mentally disordered people from wherever they happen to be. The first of these powers, rarely used, is exercisable only for the benefit of the person to be detained. Under section 135 of the Mental Health Act 1983, an approved social worker can lay an information on oath before a justice of the peace showing that there is reasonable cause to suspect that a person, who is believed to be suffering from a mental disorder, has been or is being ill-treated, neglected, or not kept under proper control, or is living alone but is unable to care for himself. The social worker need not name the patient.[223] If it appears to the justice that the facts are as described by the social worker, and that the person is within his geographical jurisdiction, he may issue a warrant authorizing any constable, who must be accompanied by an approved social worker and a medical practitioner, to enter, if need be by force, the premises specified in the warrant where the person in believed to be, and, if they think fit, to remove him to a place of safety, which may be a police station (although this is not encouraged).[224]

The second power requires no warrant and is given only to constables in public places. Under section 136(1) of the 1983 Act, a constable may remove to a place of safety anyone whom he finds in a place to which the public have access and who appears to be suffering from a mental disorder. This power may be exercised either in the person's own interests or for the protection of other persons. This power is, unfortunately, being used increasingly frequently as people are returned to the community after the closure of long-stay mental hospitals without adequate housing and hostel provision being made. It presents constables with a problem: it requires them first to decide whether the person is suffering from a mental disorder or from a mental handicap (to which the section does not apply), and then to make an assessment of the person's dangerousness to others and to himself. These matters are not easy for someone who lacks experience in the care or treatment of people with mental disorders or mental handicaps. It will be much simpler for the constable if the person is reasonably suspected of having committed an offence, which will give rise to a power of arrest either under section 24 of PACE (if it is arrestable) or under section 25(d)(i) or (ii) (in order to protect that person or another from causing or suffering physical injury). If an arrest is made under one of those provisions, the person is a suspect who must be taken to a police station and there dealt with in accordance with the regime outlined in Chapter 6, above.

Where a person is at a police station after being detained under section 136 of the Mental Health Act 1983, the Code of Practice under PACE stresses the importance of having him assessed as soon as possible by an approved social worker and a doctor.[225] The person can be detained for up to seventy-two hours under section 135 or section 136, but must not be held in a police station for longer than necessary to interview and examine him and make suitable arrangements for his treatment or care.[226] A

---

[223] Mental Health Act 1983, s. 135(1), (5).

[224] Ibid., s. 135(1), (4).   [225] Code C, para. 3.10.

[226] Mental Health Act 1983, ss. 135(3) and 136(2); Code C, para. 3.10. See further K. Lidstone and C. Palmer, *The Investigation of Crime: A Guide to Police Powers*, 2nd edn. (London: Butterworths, 1995), 493–5.

police cell is self-evidently inappropriate as a place of safety for a mentally disordered person.

A final, somewhat draconian, power arises where a person who has been admitted to a hospital as a compulsory patient under the Mental Health Act 1983 absents himself without leave, or overstays a leave of absence given under section 17 of the 1983 Act. Such a person is unlawfully at large, within the meaning of PACE, section 17(1)(d), which permits a constable to enter and search any premises, without a warrant, for the purpose of recapturing a person who is unlawfully at large and whom he is pursuing. In *R. v. D'Souza*,[227] the Divisional Court held that 'pursuit' might be delayed, allowing for those handling the situation to proceed with 'patience, sensitivity, calmness and tact'. In that case, however, constables and nurses broke into the house of the patient's parents to recapture her, and were attacked by her and her father. Both were convicted of assaulting constables in the execution of their duty. The Divisional Court upheld the conviction, and the patient appealed to the House of Lords. Their Lordships unanimously allowed the appeal, holding that the word 'pursuing' could not be widened to encompass mere seeking. A pursuit necessarily involved chasing the patient, and an entry to premises under section 17(1)(d) of PACE must follow more or less immediately on arrival at the premises.

The interpretation of 'pursuing', which will apply to all cases where the police seek to enter premises under section 17(1)(d) of PACE, may indicate a shift away from the view that the police should unquestioningly be given the powers which they claim to need, although it remains to be seen whether this will be extended from cases in which criminal procedure overlaps with mental health law to straightforward criminal investigations. In any case, the decision is a welcome reassertion of the principle that the courts should respect statutory limitations on officials' powers to interfere with the rights and liberties of citizens, preventing the police from evading the minimal safeguards demanded where a warrant is issued under section 135 of the 1983 Act.

(7) LEGAL REDRESS FOR AGGRIEVED PATIENTS

Apart from review by a Mental Health Review Tribunal, the primary legal means by which compulsorily admitted patients have been able to test the lawfulness of their detention are the writ of habeas corpus,[228] which is given priority in the business of the High Court, and an application for judicial review. Although neither habeas corpus nor judicial review offers an apt procedure for challenging medical judgments, they are capable of testing the formal legality of a detention. For example, in *In re S.-C. (Mental Patient: Habeas Corpus)*[229] a patient had been compulsorily admitted under an application for admission wrongly stating that all the preconditions for compulsory admission had been satisfied. In fact, the nearest relative had not been consulted as required by section 11 of the Mental Health Act 1983. The detention was

---

[227] [1992] Crim. LR 119, DC; [1992] 1 WLR 1073, [1992] 4 All ER 434, HL.

[228] D. Clark and G. McCoy, *The Most Fundamental Legal Rights: Habeas Corpus in the Commonwealth* (Oxford: Clarendon Press, 2000), contains an illuminating comparative analysis of developments in the use of the writ.

[229] [1996] QB 599, [1996] 1 All ER 532, CA.

unlawful and habeas corpus issued. Section 6 of the Act provides that an application for admission 'duly completed in accordance with the provisions of this Part of this Act' provides sufficient authority for admission, but the error as to an essential pre-condition for admission meant that the application was not 'duly completed'. Habeas corpus also provides an effective remedy where a person who is entitled to be unconditionally discharged continues to be detained.[230] However, it cannot be used to compel a tribunal to order the unconditional discharge of a patient if the tribunal considers that conditional release would be more appropriate to protect the public, and other authorities are dilatory in putting in place the necessary arrangements.[231] This could lead to a violation of Article 5(1) of the ECHR.

Under Article 5(5) of the ECHR, a person who has been arrested or detained in contravention of Article 5 shall have an enforceable right to compensation. This is provided in English law by civil actions for damages. In the context of the detention of patients in mental hospitals, the scope for such proceedings is somewhat restricted, in that section 139 of the Mental Health Act 1983 provides, so far as material:

'(1)   No person shall be liable, whether on the ground of want of jurisdiction or any other ground, to any civil or criminal proceedings to which he would have been liable apart from this section in respect of any act purporting to be done in pursuance of this Act or any regulations or rules made under this Act, or in, or in pursuance of anything done in, the discharge of functions conferred by any other enactment on the authority having jurisdiction under Part VII of this Act, unless the act was done in bad faith or without reasonable care.

(2)   No civil proceedings shall be brought against any person in any court in respect of any such act without the leave of the High Court; . . .'

As noted above, it was held in *Ex parte Waldron*[232] that subsection (1) did not exclude applications for judicial review. It does, however, exclude actions for damages for false imprisonment or trespass to the person against anyone in respect of acts purporting to be done in pursuance of the legislation. It will always be necessary to prove negligence or bad faith leading to a potential violation of ECHR, Article 5(5), for reasons explained below. This leaves open the possibility of an ordinary action for negligence on the basis of the duty of care which all doctors owe to their patients and which, it was held in the context of prisons, everyone who detains anyone owes to the detainee.[233] It also leaves open the possibilities of actions for misfeasance in a public office, or malicious abuse of legal process.

It has also been said that admitting a compulsory patient in reliance on an apparently proper application for admission under section 6 of the 1983 Act will protect the hospital authorities against liability in damages, even if the detention turns out to be unlawful because of non-compliance with a precondition for making the application.[234]

---

[230] See, *mutatis mutandis, R. v. Governor of Brockhill Prison, ex parte Evans* [1997] QB 443, [1997 1 All ER 439, DC; Clark and McCoy, *The Most Fundamental Right*, ch. 5.

[231] *R. v. Mental Health Review Tribunal, ex parte Hall* [2000] 1 WLR 1323, [1999] 4 All ER 883, CA.

[232] [1986] QB 824, *sub nom. R. v. Hallstrom, ex parte W.* [1985] 3 All ER 775, CA.

[233] *Hague v. Deputy Governor of Parkhurst Prison* [1991] 3 All ER 733, HL; above, section 7, 3(2) and (3).

[234] *In re S.-C. (Mental Patient: Habeas Corpus)* [1996] QB 599, [1996] 1 All ER 532, CA.

The statutory limitation of liability is worrying in civil liberties terms. It is probably a recognition of the particular risks which those caring for mental patients run, especially when treating patients compulsorily, of being subjected to unfounded allegations of abuse and to vexatious litigation. However, small-scale and large-scale abuses do sometimes occur in mental hospitals. The requirement in section 139(2) that plaintiffs should not begin an action without obtaining leave from the High Court, akin to the restriction imposed on habitually vexatious litigants, is a powerful protection. Although the plaintiff need not convince the court that he has a *prima facie* case or even that there is a serious issue to be tried, he must show that the case is not clearly hopeless, and that it deserves the fuller consideration which it will receive if the action is allowed to proceed. This balances the rights of patients to access to the courts against the need to protect doctors against harassment by clearly hopeless litigation.[235] Together with the inherent credibility problem facing a mental patient who sets his word against that of a doctor or nurse, this ought to be sufficient protection for carers against harassment. The further protection offered in subsection (1) is a sign of the special tenderness of the law for professionals, and, perhaps, for doctors most of all, and seems arguably to be excessive. It is curious that this shield is given in the mental health legislation when no such protection is given by statute to prison governors and their staff, who are at least as likely to be subjected to problems and harassment as mental health carers. The protection given to carers under the Mental Health Act 1983 is more extensive than that which is available to doctors in Scotland under the Mental Health (Scotland) Act 1984 or Scots common law.[236] The Scottish approach should, in principle, also apply in England and Wales.

The availability of a negligence remedy still keeps the door open to some legal scrutiny of hospital regimes. It is consistent with the position in relation to negligence liability for prison conditions, established in *Hague v. Deputy Governor of Parkhurst Prison*, above, page 434, that Henry J in *Furber v. Kratter*[237] was prepared to give leave under section 139(2) of the Mental Health Act 1983 for a mental patient to bring an action for damages for negligence in respect of an allegedly unnecessarily harsh hospital regime. It was alleged that the patient, after an attack on a ward sister, had been put naked and alone in a cell, containing only a mattress, and left there for sixteen days without care, clothing, or reading and writing materials, for punitive rather than therapeutic reasons. Henry J held that there might be a cause of action in negligence in respect of the discomfort, suffering, and loss of amenity which the patient allegedly suffered. In this respect, at least, English law provides a remedy in relation to a matter which does not fall within Article 5 of the ECHR, which was held in *Ashingdane v. United Kingdom*[238] not to be concerned with conditions of detention for mental patients.

The effect of the Human Rights Act 1998 is to make it possible for a patient to

---

[235] *Winch v. Jones; Winch v. Hayward* [1986] QB 296, [1985] 3 All ER 97, CA. This case was part of a long-drawn-out attempt by Miss Winch to obtain redress for her treatment by doctors, the courts, and the Public Trustee following a dispute over her mother's estate: it began in 1977, and continued into the 1990s.

[236] See *Black v. Forsey*, 1988 SC (HL) 28.

[237] *The Times*, 21 July 1988; *Independent*, 9 August 1988; full text available on Lexis.

[238] Eur. Ct. HR, Series A, No. 93 (1985) 7 EHRR 528.

DETENTION OF PRISONERS AND PATIENTS

obtain damages for a detention which violates Article 5 of the ECHR, as well as for violations of other Convention rights which are not concerned simply with the justification for detention. In relation to Article 5, the requirement that people detained for treatment must be afforded an appropriate therapeutic environment and properly qualified staff to treat their condition, developed in cases such as *Aerts v. Belgium* (explained in section 7.5(1) above page 453), has the potential to extend an absolute right to compensation for inappropriate or sub-standard treatment regimes to mental patients (including those serving terms of imprisonment) for the first time. Because of section 9 of the Human Rights Act 1998, even members of judicial bodies (such as Mental Health Review Tribunals) may be liable to pay damages where the effect of a decision is to cause a violation of Article 5.

This is in addition to, and separate from, any compensation which might be payable under the 1998 Act in respect of inhuman or degrading treatment under Article 3. It seems that the European Court of Human Rights, having been alerted to a real threat to the dignity and liberty of patients and prisoners in relation to medical treatment, is filling a legal vacuum both by extending the reach of Article 3 and by insisting that powers to interfere with liberty under Article 5 must be exercised for a demonstrably proper purpose. We can expect this to enrich the legal remedies for interference with human rights and civil liberties under English law.

8

FREEDOM OF MOVEMENT INTO AND OUT OF BRITAIN

8.1 BACKGROUND

From the earliest times, commercial necessity has combined with diplomatic propriety to dictate that in normal circumstances people should be free to enter and leave the country with a minimum of restriction and formality. In Magna Carta of 1215, subsequently confirmed repeatedly without material alteration in this regard, Chapter 41 recognized the right of merchants to be safe and secure in leaving, entering, staying, and travelling in England to buy and sell, unless they came from enemy countries in time of war. In that event, they were to be held safely until it was known how English merchants were treated in their country; if our merchants were safe there, theirs were to be safe here. By Chapter 42, there was a more general provision, covering people who were not merchants, that (apart from short periods in time of war for the common good of the realm) anyone was to be permitted to leave and re-enter the realm safely and securely, subject to his allegiance to the King, excepting only those who had been imprisoned or outlawed according to law, and enemy aliens. In the USA, the Supreme Court has recognized the right to travel abroad as an aspect of personal liberty, and thus constitutionally protected under the Fifth and Fourteenth Amendments to the Constitution, with their due process requirements.[1] These rights are necessarily restricted by any form of immigration or emigration law, and it is one of the purposes of sections 1 to 3 of this chapter to examine the extent of the restriction in England and Wales, and its relationship with principles enshrined in human rights treaties.

There is also, under some constitutions, a right for citizens and others to move freely within the country. As already noted, Chapter 41 of Magna Carta recognized that merchants had this right in England. The right of citizens to move freely without penalty is guaranteed under the Indian Constitution of 1949, and by the US Constitution.[2] It is also guaranteed under certain international human rights instruments. There used to be a statutory power to curtail the movement of particular individuals

---

[1] *Kent v. Dulles* 357 US 116 (1958).

[2] *Aptheker v. Secretary of State* 378 US 500 (1964); *US v. Guest* 383 US 745 (1966); *Shapiro v. Thompson* 394 US 618 (1969); *Griffin v. Breckenridge* 403 US 88 (1971); *Dunn v. Blumstein* 405 US 1 (1972), 23. Cp. *Marston v. Lewis* (1973) 410 US 679; *Burns v. Fortson* 410 US 686 (1973), on residency requirements as a precondition to voting rights in a state.

between Northern Ireland and mainland Britain by making 'exclusion orders' under the terrorism legislation. This power no longer exists under the Terrorism Act 2000. On the other hand, new powers have been created by other statutes to prevent individuals or classes of people from going to specified areas, in order to limit opportunities for anti-social behaviour. These are considered in Chapter 18, below.

The principal provisions in international law are: Article 13 of the UN Declaration on Human Rights (1948); the Fourth Protocol (1968) to the European Convention on Human Rights, to which the UK is not a party; and Article 12 of the International Covenant on Civil and Political Rights (1976), to which the UK entered a significant reservation on ratification allowing it to continue to apply such immigration and emigration legislation as the government may deem necessary from time to time in respect of persons not at the time having the right to enter and remain in the UK.[3]

(1) EMIGRATION

Article 12(2) of the ICCPR provides: 'Everyone shall be free to leave any country, including his own'.[4] The UK has made no reservation to this paragraph. Indeed, the UK, and, earlier, England, can be said to have shown a high level of respect for the right to leave the country. Unlike the regime under the now defunct Soviet Union, which severely restricted emigration of people wanting to go to the West by allowing people to leave only if they had an exit visa and making it very difficult to obtain one (giving the word 'refusenik' to the English language, via Yiddish), governments in this country have not tried to stop those who wanted to leave from doing so, unless they were trying to evade the process of law. Indeed, English governments from medieval times gave moral, and sometimes material, support to those going abroad on commercial ventures, knowing that success as a trading nation, and the acquisition and development of the colonies, largely depended on the freedom given to British explorers, traders, and adventurers to go where they wanted.

There has been a presumption that Britons would be free to travel abroad. Far from needing a passport or visa to permit egress, a special writ (ne exeat regno) was required in order to prevent a person leaving the country. When the British passport was developed, it was a guarantee of protection from the Crown for British travellers abroad, and a demand for protection from the authorities in the countries through which the traveller would pass. Although issuing a passport was and is a discretionary exercise of a prerogative power, it started as an expression of official support for freedom of movement, an express extension of royal protection and the King's peace to the person of the holder, not as a condition for its exercise.

Today, the British passport is a condition for entry to most other countries. It has

---

[3] See P. Sieghart, *The International Law of Human Rights* (Oxford: Clarendon Press, 1983), 174–5, 464–5; N. Mole, 'Immigration and Freedom of Movement', in D. Harris and S. Joseph (eds.), *The International Covenant on Civil and Political Rights and United Kingdom Law* (Oxford: Clarendon Press, 1995), ch. 9, 299–300.

[4] This provision reflects Art. 13(2) of the Universal Declaration, and is identical to Art. 2(2) of the Fourth Protocol to the ECHR.

therefore become both a necessity for international travel, and a mechanism for official surveillance and control of cross-border movement. The control element is enhanced by the need for special visas to enter certain countries.[5] Because it has become a practical necessity for anyone travelling abroad to have a passport, refusing a person's passport application substantially limits his freedom of movement.[6] The courts have therefore extended judicial review to the decisions by which passports are denied: they are no longer seen as privileges, but as *prima facie* rights attracting judicial protection against arbitrary executive infringement.[7] This is in some ways a more rights-conscious approach than that which operates in the USA. In *Kent v. Dulles*[8] the US Supreme Court held that the Secretary of State had exceeded his statutory authority in withholding passports, during the McCarthy anti-communist witch hunts, from people who had associations with the Communist Party. Perhaps wary of becoming too embroiled in political controversy, the court did not rule on the further question of the constitutionality of withholding passports from US citizens, and so restricting their ability to travel abroad. When the constitutional issue was squarely raised later in *Haig v. Agee*[9] the court decided that there was no constitutional protection for the right to travel abroad. Accordingly, it upheld the power of the executive to revoke the passport of Philip Agee, a former CIA agent, who was planning to make revelations which would identify American agents still operating abroad.[10] This almost certainly violates Article 12 (which did not then bind the USA). Although Article 12(3) permits states to restrict freedom of movement, the power is limited:

'The above-mentioned rights shall not be subject to any restriction except those which are provided by law, are necessary to protect national security, public order (*ordre public*), public health or morals or the rights and freedoms of others, and are consistent with the other rights recognized in the present Covenant.'

The UN Human Rights Committee (the monitoring body for the ICCPR) in its General Comment on Article 12 wrote that the word 'necessary' imports considerations of proportionality, as under the ECHR. The conditions of necessity and proportionality 'would not be met, for example, if an individual were prevented from leaving a country merely on the ground that he or she is the holder of "State secrets"'.[11]

Our law has historically been, to say the least, no less liberal, and may be more liberal, than that of the USA in this regard. However, this may be changing. Two kinds of restriction have appeared. First, in an effort to stop violent behaviour by supporters

---

[5] See J. Torpey, *The Invention of the Passport: Surveillance, Citizenship and the State* (Cambridge: Cambridge University Press, 2000), *passim*.

[6] On the principles on which passports are granted or refused, see S. de Smith and R. Brazier, *Constitutional and Administrative Law*, 6th edn. (Harmondsworth: Penguin, 1989), 454–5.

[7] *R. v. Secretary of State for Foreign and Commonwealth Affairs, ex parte Everett* [1989] QB 811, [1989] 1 All ER 655, CA.

[8] (1958) 357 US 116.

[9] (1981) 453 US 280.

[10] The court also held that the ban on travel abroad did not infringe Mr. Agee's First Amendment rights to freedom of speech.

[11] Human Rights Committee, General Comment No. 27, 18 October 1999, 7 IHRR 1, paras. 14, 16.

of UK soccer teams abroad, a court can make an 'international football banning order' to stop a person people leaving the country to attend football matches abroad. An order may be made as part of the sentence imposed on a person who has been convicted of, or subject to a complaint about, an offence involving violence against people or property, or public disorder or drunkenness at or on the way to or from a match, including during overnight stops in transit. A court must make the order if satisfied that there are reasonable grounds to believe that making the order would help to prevent violence or disorder at or in connection with football matches of a kind designated under the Football Spectators Act 1989. If the court does not make an order, it must state in open court its reasons for not being satisfied that the conditions for making an order are met.[12] A court may also make an international football banning order, subject to similar conditions, against a person who has been convicted of equivalent offences abroad.[13] Such an order would be a disproportionate interference with the right to leave the country under ICCPR Article 12(2), unless there is in a particular case sufficient evidence that the person subject to it would be responsible for offences abroad if permitted to attend a particular match or matches, and the order could be limited to those matches. It has been held that the legislation is compatible with the right to freedom of movement in Community law, because it is justifiable on the ground of public policy to restrict the freedom of movement of those responsible for football violence for preventative purposes (subject to a test of proportionality in individual cases). Nor does the legislation impose a retrospective penalty for football-related offences contrary to ECHR Article 7, because the purpose is preventative and protective rather than punitive.[13a]

Secondly, the Criminal Justice and Police Act 2001, section 33 provides a power for courts to impose a 'travel restriction order' on someone sentenced to four years' imprisonment or more for a drug trafficking offence. The offender who is subject to an order to surrender his passport will not be permitted to travel abroad for at least two years, and potentially for life, after release from custody. The object is to disrupt trafficking by preventing traffickers from travelling abroad, but there is nothing in the Bill which expressly limits the orders to purposes which are legitimate under ICCPR Article 12(3) or to periods for which, or circumstances in which, they would be proportionate to the aim. Nor could an order be suspended or set aside during its currency, save in exceptional circumstances on compassionate grounds. This gives rise to a risk of a disproportionate interference with the right to respect for family life under ECHR Article 8, as well as rights to freedom of movement, of establishment, and of provision of services under European Community law.[14] It is important to guard against creeping incursions on freedom of movement, as on other rights,

---

[12] Football Spectators Act 1989, s. 15(1), (2), (2A), (3), as substituted by Football (Offences and Disorder) Act 1999, s. 1, and Football (Disorder) Act 2000, s. 1 and Sch. 1. For these purposes, an absolute or conditional discharge counts as a conviction: see s. 15(4) of the 1989 Act, as substituted. See also Football (Disorder) (Amendment) Bill 2001.

[13] Football Spectators Act 1989, s. 22, as amended by Football (Offences and Disorder) Act 1999, s. 5.

[13a] *Gough v. Chief Constable of Derbyshire; R. (Miller) v. Leeds Magistrates' Court; Lilley v. DPP, The Times*, 19 July 2001, DC (Laws LJ and Poole J).

[14] See the critique by the Joint Committee on Human Rights, First Report 2000–01, *Criminal Justice and Police Bill*, HL Paper 69, HC 427 (London: The Stationery Office, 2001), paras. 34–43.

limiting it little by little for reasons which seem good at the time but which cumulatively undermine the very essence of the right.

(2) IMMIGRATION[15]

International law recognizes the right of sovereign states to control entry to their territories by nationals of other states. It does, however, impose responsibilities on states in respect of their own nationals, and also imposes duties in respect of those foreign nationals who have been lawfully admitted to a state's territories. Under Article 12(4) of ICCPR, 'No one shall be arbitrarily deprived of the right to enter his own country'. This is a relatively narrow formulation of the right. It assumes that the right exists, rather than requiring that such a right be created where it does not exist. Article 12(4) also implies that a non-arbitrary deprivation of this right is permissible. Accordingly, the UK government, on ratifying the ICCPR on 20 May 1976, entered a reservation in the following terms:

'The government of the UK reserve the right to continue to apply such immigration legislation governing entry into, stay in and departure from the UK as they may deem necessary from time to time and, accordingly, their acceptance of article 12(4) and of the other provisions of the Covenant is subject to the provisions of any such legislation as regards persons not at the time having the right under the law of the UK to enter and remain in the UK. The UK also reserves a similar right in regard to each of its dependent territories.'

Article 12(4) therefore offers less protection to individuals than is envisaged under Article 13(2) of the Universal Declaration ('Everyone has the right to leave any country, including his own, and to return to his country'), or Article 3(2) of the Fourth Protocol to the ECHR ('No one shall be deprived of the right to enter the territory of the state of which he is a national').

The UK's reservation set out above represents successive governments' attitudes to immigration control since the mid-1960s. This is somewhat different from the approach taken to immigration until the twentieth century. On the whole, it is fair to say that British officials have over the centuries displayed a respectable level of tolerance towards those who came to settle here, and discharged their responsibilities towards refugees fleeing from oppression elsewhere. For a long time, until well into the twentieth century, it was officially accepted that racially discriminatory entry requirements were undesirable, although, under our constitution, there was nothing to stop Parliament from introducing such requirements.[16] So long as people from foreign parts have been self-supporting, contributed positively to a thriving economy, amused the British public, and supported the English cricket team, they have generally been tolerated and even encouraged, making up for shortages of labour, skills, or capital in the domestic economy.

[15] See generally I. A. MacDonald and N. Blake, *Immigration Law and Practice*, 4th edn. (London: Butterworths, 1997). On the historical and political background, see V. Bevan, *The Development of British Immigration Law* (London: Croom Helm, 1986), ch. 2; A. Dummett and A. Nicol, *Subjects, Citizens, Aliens and Others: Nationality and Immigration Law* (London: Weidenfeld & Nicolson, 1990).

[16] See Dummett and Nicol, *Subjects, Citizens, Aliens*, 136–41, for discussion of the parliamentary debates on the British Nationality Act 1948.

Yet British attitudes to foreigners have never been unconditionally friendly. The massacre of the Jews in 1189, following the accession of King Richard I, in all major English cities except Winchester, remains perhaps the most notorious of the outpourings of popular hatred on an alien community over the succeeding centuries. Politicians making immigration policy, and the officials operating it, have generally been severely utilitarian,[17] and even official approval has not always protected settlers from a certain level of discrimination, abuse, and occasional outbursts of violence. Groups which have been assimilated into the wider community have tended to be better received than those which have wanted to retain their cultural or religious practices and lifestyles.[18] Jews and Muslims, Afro-Caribbeans, Gypsies and East African Asians are only some of those who, accepted into the country as refugees or economic migrants, or actively encouraged to come in times of labour or skill shortage, have become the butt of those who lose most heavily when economies turn down in their eternal cycles. When times are hard, there are regular calls to exclude people from the country, sometimes on blatantly racial criteria.[19]

The first systematic attempt to forge an immigration policy and to give it statutory form[20] was the Aliens Act 1905, which required immigration officers to refuse entry to people who were deemed undesirable. These included people who, if admitted, would be liable to extradition; those who could not show that they would be able to support themselves and their dependants; and those who, because of their physical condition, were likely to become a charge on the rates or a detriment to the public. The general principle was that all who were not undesirable would continue to be allowed to enter. Large numbers of immigrants, initially those from Central and Eastern Europe (particularly Jews) and later, after the Second World War, increasingly from the New Commonwealth, entered under these provisions. However, more recently there has been increasing anti-immigration feeling, often mixed with racism based largely on colour, to which the politicians have been sensitive. Since the enactment of the Commonwealth Immigrants Act 1962, as Professor J. M. Evans has written, immigration policy has aimed primarily at limiting immigration from the (predominantly black) New Commonwealth, while allowing descendants of the (mainly white) emigrants who had settled the lands of the Old Commonwealth to return to the mother country. To be respectable, it was necessary to find 'appropriate legal means for implementing this objective without resorting to laws that expressly discriminate on grounds of race or ethnic origin'.[21]

The form which immigration law takes has tended, therefore, to swing between two approaches. When times are good and immigrant labour or skills are needed to boost the economy, the law imposes only those controls which are needed to ensure that undesirable individuals are excluded. When times are harder, immigration is

[17] See, e.g. Z. Layton-Henry, *The Politics of Immigration* (Oxford: Blackwell, 1992), chs 1, 2, 7, 8, 9; L. London, *Whitehall and the Jews 1933–1948* (Cambridge: Cambridge University Press, 2000), *passim.*
[18] See S. Poulter, *Ethnicity, Law and Human Rights: The English Experience* (Oxford: Clarendon Press, 1998), esp. ch. 1.
[19] Layton-Henry, *Politics of Immigration*, chs. 4, 6, 8.
[20] For a concise introduction to the history of the development, see S. S. Juss, *Immigration, Nationality and Citizenship* (London: Mansell, 1993), ch. 2.
[21] J. M. Evans, *Immigration Law*, 2nd edn. (London: Sweet & Maxwell, 1983), 3.

restricted to those who are strictly within groups which have been given rights to enter by reason of their pre-existing connection with the UK. At present, the dominant approach is restrictive of immigration.

Any sort of immigration control is bound to make entry from abroad more difficult for foreigners than for Britons (however defined). Under the ECHR, the Commission and the Court have accepted that international law recognizes the right of states to control entry to their territories.[22] However, it has been held that the controls, in their effects, must either treat alike all those who are not British nationals, or at any rate not differentiate between people on the basis of arbitrary racial categories. In the *East African Asians*[23] case, the European Commission of Human Rights decided that immigration-control legislation which discriminated against people by singling them out for differential treatment purely on the ground of their race might constitute a special form of affront which would amount to degrading treatment, violating Article 3 of the ECHR by lowering them in rank, position, reputation, or character in their own and other people's eyes. Legislation imposing tighter controls on entry by people from the New Commonwealth (in that case, Asians expelled from African states, particularly Uganda) than from the predominantly white Old Commonwealth was of that kind. The Asians were then admitted in accordance with the decision of the Commission, and the law was reviewed to apply the same standards without reference to race, so the Committee of Ministers took no further action on the violation.[24] To the extent that the substance of immigration controls in any country is likely to reflect social and cultural prejudices, compliance with the Commission's standards may be hard to achieve.[25] In view of the political history of immigration in the last forty years, it is noteworthy, but not surprising, that the immigration service is excluded from most duties under the race relations legislation (examined in Chapter 3, above).[26]

Furthermore, the operation of any controls on entry may be more or less in tune with the requirements of the Convention. In the case of the UK, the steps taken to determine whether people are entitled to enter—whether they are indeed who they say they are, and are related to those who claim to be their parents or other relatives—can be demeaning and unreliable. X-ray tests for determining age were used until 1981, when the experts changed their minds about their reliability; vaginal tests, to determine whether women, claiming to be the fiancées of men settled here, were virgins, were discontinued in 1979 after an outcry over the discriminatory nature of such tests on Asian women. But extensive powers to arrest and search people and fingerprint them apply, and the Home Secretary has power to make provision by

[22] *Patel and others (The East African Asians) v. United Kingdom*, Applications Nos. 4403–19/70, CD 36, 92; Report: (1981) 3 EHRR 76, Eur. Comm. HR; *Vilvarajah and others v. United Kingdom*, Eur. Ct. HR, Judgment of 30 October 1991. Series A, No. 215, 14 EHRR 248.

[23] *Patel and others v. United Kingdom*, Applications Nos. 4403–19/70, CD 36, 92; Report: (1973) 3 EHRR 76, Eur. Comm. HR.

[24] Resolution DH(77)2, Committee of Ministers.

[25] See Dummett and Nicol, *Subjects, Citizens, Aliens*, ch. 14.

[26] See Race Relations Act 1976, ss. 19D, 71A (inserted by Race Relations (Amendment) Act 2000, ss. 1 and 2).

regulations for collection of further information about people's 'physical characteristics'.[27] Widespread executive discretion within the system to relax the rules, or to apply them in a racially discriminatory way, results in a system which appears to be rule-based but which, because of the strange status of the Immigration Rules, can operate in an unpredictable and unprincipled way.[28] Rights, and remedies for unfairness, are worthy of examination in this field.

The next three sections of this chapter are therefore concerned with people from abroad: their entry by right, as having a right of abode or EU citizenship, as refugees, or by executive discretion; their removal (by way of deportation); and their remedies.

8.2 RIGHTS OF ENTRY[28a]

The Immigration Act 1971, as amended, provides the structure governing immigration to the UK. Its provisions are fleshed out by the Immigration Rules 1994, as amended by the various Statements of Changes to the Immigration Rules presented to Parliament annually by successive Home Secretaries. The Rules have an uncertain status: they have a foundation in section 3 of the Immigration Act 1971, but are not statutory instruments. They govern official action and decision-making and so have legal effects. They are subject to judicial review for illegality, procedural impropriety, and irrationality. In particular, they are subject to common law fundamental rights, so that a Rule which interferes with such a right and is not expressly and unequivocally authorized by statute is unlawful.[29] Likewise, a Rule which is incompatible with a Convention right is unlawful unless required by primary legislation to be made in that way. The Rules are also subject to the overriding discretion of the Secretary of State.

(1) CITIZENSHIP, NATIONALITY, AND RIGHTS OF ENTRY

The right to enter and leave the UK without any let or hindrance, except such as is required or permitted under statute or Community law, is given to people by section 1(1) of the Immigration Act 1971, on the basis of their citizenship status under the British Nationality Act 1981, and by Article 18 (formerly Article 8a) of the EC Treaty given effect by the Immigration (European Economic Area) Order 1994.[30] Irish citizens, under section 50(1) of the British Nationality Act 1981, are not aliens. A Common Travel Area free of most immigration restrictions operates between the UK and

---

[27] Immigration Act 1971, ss. 28G, 28H, Sch. 2, paras. 25B, 25C, inserted by Immigration and Asylum Act 1999; Immigration and Asylum Act 1999, ss. 141, 144. See also Anti-terrorism, Crime and Security Bill 2001.

[28] C. Harlow and R. Rawlings, *Law and Administration*, 1st edn. (London: Weidenfeld & Nicolson, 1984), chs 16 and 17.

[28a] See generally I. Macdonald QC and F. Webber, Macdonald's *Immigration Law and Practice*, 5th edn. (London: Butterworths, 2001).

[29] *R. v. Secretary of State for the Home Department, ex parte Saleem* [2001] 1 WLR 443, CA.

[30] SI 1994, No. 1895.

Ireland, although the Home Secretary's power to deport Irish citizens, if this is conducive to the public good, may be invoked. This section provides a very brief outline of the main substantive rules.[31]

(i) Those with rights of abode before the British Nationality Act 1981 came into force (1 January 1983)[32]

This category includes:

- all who had citizenship of the UK and Colonies by virtue of having been born, adopted, naturalized, or (save in the case of women married to a citizen before the passing of the 1971 Act) registered, in some part of the UK or Islands;

- those whose parent was a citizen of the UK and Colonies with a right of abode at the time when the child was born or adopted, or whose grandparent had citizenship of the UK and Colonies at the time when the parent was born or adopted; citizens of the UK and Colonies who have at any time been settled in the UK, and had at that time been ordinarily resident there as a citizen for the previous five years or more;

- Commonwealth citizens born to or legally adopted by a parent who at the time of birth or adoption had citizenship of the UK and Colonies by reason of having been born in the UK; and

- women who are Commonwealth citizens and either are or have been married to a citizen of the UK and Colonies or a Commonwealth citizen who, during the marriage, had a right of abode under the above rules, or would have had but for dying before the British Nationality Act 1948 commenced.

All these people were 'patrials' who became British citizens under the 1981 Act. They had a close connection with the UK, and were predominantly white.

Other Commonwealth citizens, who might have no other citizenship apart from that of a former British colony, were left with no place in which they had an unquestionable right to settle: they were left 'stranded on the beach by the ebbing tide of British imperialism'.[33] They might hold British Dependent Territories Citizenship, British Overseas Citizenship, or have the status of British subjects or British protected persons, but they are not British citizens and have no right of abode, unless they fall within one of the other categories below.

A person who claims to be entitled to a right of abode as a British citizen must prove it either by producing a current UK passport describing the person as having a right of abode, or by a certificate of entitlement issued by the UK government.[34] If

---

[31] On the substantive law, see MacDonald and Webber, *Immigration Law and Practice*. A concise account is provided in A. W. Bradley and K. D. Ewing, *Constitutional and Administrative Law*, 12th edn. (London: Longman, 1997), 487–96.

[32] Immigration Act 1971, s. 2, as saved by the British Nationality Act 1981, s. 11, in respect of people with a right of abode before the commencement of the 1981 Act. See Evans, *Immigration Law*, 2nd edn., 70–2.

[33] Evans, *Immigration Law*, 68. See I. Martin, 'Racism in Immigration Law and Practice', in P. Wallington (ed.), *Civil Liberties 1984* (Oxford: Martin Robertson, 1984), 245–57.

[34] Immigration Act 1971, ss. 3(9) (as substituted by Immigration Act 1988, s. 3), 33.

immigration officers claim that apparently valid documents are forgeries, or that the person in possession of them is not the person named in them, the burden lies on the officers to prove it on the balance of probabilities.[35]

(ii) People who acquired a right of abode on or after 1 January 1983

This group includes:

- people who have been born to or adopted by, or are descended from, British citizens, and

- people who have become naturalized or have registered as British citizens,

on or after 1 January 1983.[36] These complex classes of people also have a right to enter without let or hindrance, and to settle.

The first group of people includes the children of people settled in the Falkland Islands, who were given British citizenship after the Falklands War by the British Nationality (Falkland Islands) Act 1983. The familial connection which is essential to establishing the right of abode can now be tested fairly accurately by using DNA-profiling methods, which have shown that most people are honest when claiming to be related to people who have a right to enter. The stringent tests for familial connection which are employed by entry clearance officers and immigration officers do not breach the right to respect for family life under Article 8 of the ECHR; indeed, by stressing the significance of the family relationship, they are, in a sense, expressions of this respect.[37]

Naturalization as a British citizen is in the discretion of the Home Secretary, subject to certain conditions. Generally, an applicant must have resided in the UK for five years, must be of good character, must have a sufficient knowledge of English, Welsh, or Scottish Gaelic, and must intend to maintain his principal home in the UK.[38] When assessing an application, the Home Secretary is required to observe the normal rules of fairness. Although not required to give reasons for decisions,[39] the Home Secretary must give the applicant an opportunity to make representations so as to satisfy him that the conditions are met. In order to make effective representations possible, the Home Secretary must inform the applicant of any areas of concern, at least where they would not be immediately obvious to the applicant.[40]

Certain people who would not otherwise be entitled to a right of abode may acquire one if the Home Secretary registers them as British citizens.[41] There is one special category of people who are entitled to registration on application, because the

---

[35] R. v. Secretary of State for the Home Department, ex parte Obi [1997] 1 WLR 1498, Sedley J, and see *dicta* in *Akewushola v. Secretary of State for the Home Department* [2000] 1 WLR 2295, CA.

[36] British Nationality Act 1981, ss. 1–11. See Evans, *Immigration Law*, 72–90; S. H. Bailey, D. J. Harris, and B. L. Jones, *Civil Liberties Cases and Materials*, 4th edn. (London: Butterworths, 1995), 687–93.

[37] *Kamal v. United Kingdom*, Application No. 8378/78, 20 DR 168; (1982) 4 EHRR. 244, Eur. Commn. HR.

[38] British Nationality Act 1981, s. 6 and Sch. 1.

[39] British Nationality Act 1981, s. 44(2).

[40] R. v. Secretary of State for the Home Department, ex parte Fayed [1998] 1 WLR 763; [1997] 1 All ER 228, CA.

[41] British Nationality Act 1981, ss. 1(3) and (4), 3(1) and 4.

UK was considered as having continuing obligations to them. When Hong Kong was being handed back to China in 1997, there was concern about the fate of Hong Kong residents with a type of British status which did not confer a right of abode in the UK,[42] but who had no other nationality or citizenship. The British Nationality (Hong Kong) Act 1997 requires the Home Secretary to register such people as British citizens if they are ordinarily resident in Hong Kong at the time of their application and were ordinarily resident there either (a) immediately before 4 February 1997 or (b) immediately before they acquired their British status if that happens on or after 4 February 1997.

(iii) EU citizens[43]

Nationals of all Member States of the EU are EU citizens.[44] Article 18 (formerly Article 8a) of the EC Treaty provides:

'Every citizen of the Union shall have the right to move and reside freely within the territory of the Members States, subject to the limitations and conditions laid down in the Treaty and by the measures adopted to give it effect.'

This goes considerably beyond the original position in Community law, under which the right to freedom of movement and establishment was limited to people moving between Member States for economic purposes. The new rules were given effect in the UK by the Immigration (European Economic Area) Order 1994.[45] The older, economic rights to free movement remain. There are specific rights for workers to accept offers of employment in other Member States, and to move with their families for that purpose.[46] There is a right of establishment for self-employed people and undertakings, for the purposes of business.[47] Finally, there is a right to supply services in other Member States.[48] These rights may be restricted on the grounds of public policy, public security, or public health.[49] The explanation of these rights lies outside the scope of this book.

Before the Treaty of Amsterdam, control of movement between Member States was governed by the 'Schengen *acquis*', by which Member States were to enforce controls on entry to their territory from third countries (i.e. non-Member States), but there would be no internal border controls between Member States. The UK, always keen to maintain its border controls, was not a party to Schengen. At the Treaty of Amsterdam, a framework was provided for bringing freedom of movement and residence within EC law. Article 14 (formerly Article 7a) of the EC Treaty requires the Council of the EC to adopt measures on the free movement of persons by 2002 to remove

[42] The categories are: (a) British Dependent Territory citizens by virtue only of having a family connection with Hong Kong; (b) British Overseas citizens; (c) British subjects; (d) British protected persons.

[43] See S. Peers, *EU Justice and Home Affairs Law* (London: Longman, 2000), chs 4 and 5.

[44] Art. 17 (formerly Art. 8) EC.

[45] SI 1994, No. 1895.

[46] EC Treaty, Arts. 43–8.

[47] Ibid., Arts. 49–55.

[48] Ibid., Arts. 56–60.

[49] Ibid., Arts. 39(3), 46, and 55.

barriers to migration within the EU, but the UK has derogated from this provision in order to allow her to continue border controls. In addition, the Amsterdam Treaty committed the EC to harmonizing the law on a range of immigration-related issues. The UK is participating in this enthusiastically, seeing it as a way of limiting the burden which it carries in relation to asylum seekers. Article 62 of the EC Treaty now requires the Council to adopt, by 2002, measures on the removal of controls at borders, including uniform treatment of third country nationals, and Article 63 imposes a similar requirement in respect of measures on refugees, asylum, illegal immigration, visas, conditions for entry, etc. The process of drafting and consulting on these measures in now under way.

(2) REFUGEES

The Universal Declaration on Human Rights, Article 14, specifies everyone's right to seek and enjoy in other countries asylum from persecution, but neither the International Covenant on Civil and Political Rights nor the European Convention on Human Rights includes this right. Instead, the right is protected by the Convention Relating to the Status of Refugees ('the Refugee Convention'), adopted by the UN Conference on the Status of Refugees and Stateless Persons at Geneva in 1951. It entered into force in 1954. While the original Convention applied only to those who became refugees as a result of events occurring before 1 January 1951, that restriction was removed by the Protocol Relating to the Status of Refugees which was adopted by the UN General Assembly in 1966 and entered into force in 1967. In 1951, the UN established the Office of High Commissioner for Refugees. The High Commissioner has on occasion intervened in litigation concerning the treatment of refugees.[50] The Executive Committee to the Office, and the High Commissioner, have the task of providing advice and guidance respectively as to the interpretation and implementation of the Convention and Protocol.[51]

The UK is a party to the Refugee Convention, and national immigration law is applied so as to be compatible with it. People who are seeking asylum in the UK as political refugees from another country form a relatively small but growing and, from a human rights standpoint, very important group of entrants. Applications for asylum have risen as people displaced by, or fleeing from, ethnic violence, especially in the Former Republic of Yugoslavia (Kosovo, Serbia, and Montenegro), Sri Lanka, and Somalia. In the twelve months to 30 June 2000, there were 77,690 applications in all (a rise of 19,850 over the previous twelve months), of which 21,515 came from nationals of those countries. Of the total, 14 per cent were recognized as refugees and granted asylum, 15 per cent were not recognized as refugees but were given exceptional leave

---

[50] See, e.g. *R. v. Secretary of State for the Home Department, ex parte Sivukamaran (UN High Commissioner for Refugees intervening)* [1988] AC 958, [1988] 1 All ER 193, HL.

[51] The High Commissioner publishes (*inter alia*) the *Handbook on Procedures and Criteria for Determining Refugee Status*, which, however, is not binding on any domestic court or decision-maker: *R. v. Secretary of State for the Home Department, ex parte Sivakumaran (UN High Commissioner for Refugees intervening)* [1988] AC 958, [1988] 1 All ER 193, HL.

to remain, and the remainder were refused leave.[52] The administrative burden imposed by these applications is considerable, and the humanitarian implications of wrong decisions are deeply troubling. The diplomatic sensitivity of cases where people claim to be refugees, and the gravity of the threat to life and liberty which refugee status implies, has resulted in all asylum decisions in England being taken by the Home Office, in the light of the Convention and Protocol.[53]

The Home Secretary's discretion in national law to admit or refuse those seeking asylum is governed by the Immigration Rules 1994, Part 11. The Asylum and Immigration Appeals Act 1993, section 2 provides that the Rules must not 'lay down any practice which would be contrary to the Convention'. This gives rise to a difficulty. The Convention is an international treaty which is interpreted and given effect in different ways in different countries. For example, the English courts appear to give a wider meaning to 'persecuted' and 'membership of a particular social group' than courts in France and Germany. This has implications for such matters as the identification of other countries as 'safe third countries' to which asylum seekers may be removed, and for the harmonization of national rules on asylum between Member States of the EU. The House of Lords has made it more difficult for the executive to 'level down' protection for asylum seekers to that offered by the least receptive state, holding that the Home Secretary must treat the Refugee Convention as having a single correct meaning and adopting the interpretation given by the highest national court in the UK for all purposes connected with applications to the UK.[54] The English courts can therefore strike down a decision to reject a claim for asylum on the basis that the Secretary of State has misconstrued the Convention or Protocol when interpreting the rules, in the same way that they can treat any misinterpretation of the rules as an error of law.[55] While the advice or guidance offered by the Executive Committee and UN High Commissioner for Refugees are not part of the rules, it is open to the courts to review the Secretary of State's decision for unreasonableness or failure to take account of relevant considerations, for example if he does not give adequate consideration to a matter which, under the Convention and Protocol, he is required to consider.[56]

On the other hand, the courts will not review factual decisions made by the immigration authorities under the legislation and Immigration Rules unless they are said to be *ultra vires* or procedurally flawed,[57] although they will subject to particularly close scrutiny decisions which, if flawed, may imperil life or liberty.[58] The proper remedy for people affected by factual decisions which are merely wrong is to appeal, rather

[52] K. Jackson and R. McGregor, *Control of Immigration: Statistics United Kingdom, First Half 2000* (London: Home Office, 2000), para. 16 and Table 3.1.

[53] Immigration Rules 1994, r. 328.

[54] *R. v. Secretary of State for the Home Department, ex parte Adan* [2001] 2 WLR 143, HL.

[55] *R. v. Chief Immigration Officer, Gatwick Airport, ex parte Kharrazi* [1980] 1 WLR 1396, [1980] 3 All ER 373, CA.

[56] *Bugdaycay v. Secretary of State for the Home Department* [1987] AC 514, [1987] 1 All ER 940, HL.

[57] *R. v. Secretary of State for the Home Department, ex parte Sivakumaran (UN High Commissioner for Refugees intervening)* [1988] AC 958, [1988] 1 All ER 193, HL.

[58] *Bugdaycay v. Secretary of State for the Home Department* [1987] AC 514 at 535–7, [1987] 1 All ER 940 at 955–6 *per* Lord Templeman.

than to apply for judicial review.[59] The Immigration and Asylum Act 1999, sections 11, 12, 65, and 72, together with Immigration Rule 386, now provide that a person who has been refused asylum is not to be deported until the time for making an appeal has expired, or any appeal has been disposed of, save in limited circumstances.

(i) The basis of refugee status

Under the Refugee Convention, a person is a refugee if he:

(a) is outside the country of his nationality;

(b) has a well-founded fear of being persecuted for reasons of race, religion, nationality, membership of a particular social group, or political opinion; and

(c) is unable or, because of that fear, unwilling to avail himself of the protection of that country.[60]

A considerable caselaw has developed in the UK on the meaning of these requirements. The main elements in the UK's interpretation of the Convention are as follows.

- The definition in the Convention of a refugee is exhaustive. Other people are not protected by it. Stateless people, who have been deprived of a nationality and so have no right of abode anywhere, are not refugees for this purpose unless they satisfy the other tests in the Convention.[61]

- A person has a well founded fear of persecution only if he subjectively fears persecution, and that fear is objectively justified. In *R. v. Secretary of State for the Home Department, ex parte Sivakumaran (UN High Commissioner for Refugees intervening)*[62] the applicants, Tamils from Sri Lanka, were fleeing from brutal treatment meted out by the Sinhalese and Indian armies in quelling the Tamil insurrection in Sri Lanka, and claimed that they feared persecution if they were returned to Sri Lanka. The House of Lords held that it was for the Secretary of State to decide whether a subjective fear of persecution was objectively well-founded, in the light of all the available evidence.[63] Agreeing with the US Supreme Court, the House accepted that the asylum-seeker did not need to show that he was more likely than not to be persecuted.[64] The test was whether there was, objectively, a 'reasonable chance', a 'serious possibility', or 'substantial grounds for thinking', that the fugitive will be persecuted if returned. As it

---

[59] Judicial review is a remedy of last resort, normally to be used only when other avenues have been tried, unless there is no other equally convenient procedure for challenging the decision: *R. v. Secretary of State for the Home Department, ex parte Swati* [1986] 1 WLR 477, [1986] 1 All ER 717, CA.

[60] Art. 1A(2) of the Convention.

[61] *Revenko v. Secretary of State for the Home Department* [2000] 3 WLR 1519, CA.

[62] [1988] AC 958, [1988] 1 All ER 193, HL.

[63] Their Lordships rejected the test advanced on behalf of the UN High Commissioner for Refugees, who had argued for a basically subjective test of well-foundedness, as well as of fear.

[64] *Immigration and Naturalization Service v. Cardoza-Fonseca* (1987) 94 L. Ed. 2d 434 US Supreme Court. For comparison of the US and UK positions, see Sajid Qureshi, 'Opening the Floodgates? Eligibility for Asylum in the USA and the UK' (1988) 17 *Anglo-Amer. LR* 83–107.

seemed to the Home Office that military efforts to root out Tamil extremists did not amount to persecution of Tamils as such, the Home Secretary was entitled to conclude that the Tamils' fear of persecution was not well-founded (although a subsequent appeal by the Tamils on the facts was upheld, and the Secretary of State's decision reversed, by the immigration adjudicator). It follows that a person may have a well-founded fear of persecution as a result of having made a bogus asylum claim in the UK falsely claiming to have been the victim of past persecution in his country of nationality (although in such a case the decision-maker could justifiably be very sceptical about the existence of a subjective fear of persecution or its well-foundedness).[65]

- The reason for the persecution must be race, religion, nationality, membership of a particular social group, or political opinion. It is not enough to show that those who are persecuted are predominantly of one race, etc., if their membership of that race, etc. is not the reason for the persecution.

- The state or its agents need not be responsible directly for the persecution. The Convention protects people who are persecuted by non-state factions within the country, if the state is either unwilling or unable to protect victims. This situation may arise, for example, if the victims are socially excluded, or treated by law as entitled to less protection than others,[66] or are people who flout or live outside prevailing social *mores*. It may also arise if state authority has broken down because of a civil war.[67] The decision-maker must therefore decide on the basis of available facts whether or not the state in question offers adequate protection.[68]

- People do not form a 'particular social group' merely by reason of being persecuted for the same reason. 'Social group' and the other terms are interpreted *eiusdem generis*. Members of a social group must therefore share some common characteristic which is either immutable or such that it would be unreasonable to expect people to choose to change it. The group need not have any pre-existing cohesiveness; there need be no social link between its members. Thus in *R. v. Immigration Appeal Tribunal, ex parte Shah*[69] Lord Steyn, Lord Hoffmann, and Lord Hope of Craighead held that women in Pakistan form a social group, because Islamic law, recognized by the state, treats them as entitled to lesser human rights than men. This gives weight to the way in which the law of status in the country in question defines groups for different treatment. If members of the group suffer persecution by reason of being women, they are entitled to the protection of the Convention. A narrower view, supported by Lord Steyn and

---

[65] *M. v. Secretary of State for the Home Department* [1996] 1 WLR 507, [1996] 1 All ER 870, CA.

[66] *R. v. Immigration Appeal Tribunal, ex parte Shah* [1999] 2 AC 629, [1999] 2 All ER 545, HL (women in Pakistan treated as entitled to lesser human rights than men).

[67] *Adan v. Secretary of State for the Home Department* [1999] 1 AC 293, [1998] 2 All ER 453, HL (civil war in Somalia).

[68] *Horvath v. Secretary of State for the Home Department* [2000] 3 WLR 379, HL (Immigration Appeal Tribunal entitled to conclude, on the evidence, that state authorities in Slovakia were able to provide adequate protection to Romanies against attacks by skinheads).

[69] [1999] 2 AC 629, [1999] 2 All ER 545, HL.

Lord Hutton, would treat women suspected of adultery, who were liable to legal penalties including public flogging and stoning to death as well as violent retribution by the husband's family, as a social group. However, this approach is more open than the former to the criticism levelled at it by Lord Mustill, dissenting. Lord Mustill argued that both approaches allow the mere fact of persecution to create a social group, thus bringing the Convention into play whenever there is systematic, as opposed to random, persecution, without regard to the reason for it. Such a criticism is harder to justify in relation to an approach which uses the pre-existing law of the place in question to identify social groups for this purpose.

- Fleeing one's country of nationality should be a last resort. A person should normally avail himself of any safe haven within that country, if it would be reasonable for him to relocate and live there. It would not be reasonable if it was unduly harsh to expect him to move to a safe area before seeking refuge abroad, having regard to the accessibility of the safe area, the practicalities of moving and living there, and the dangers or hardships which would be encountered. However, the evidence must show that moving to another part of the country would in reality enable the refugee to obtain proper protection against the risk of persecution, torture, etc.[70]

The grounds which justify a person in seeking asylum clearly exclude people who are emigrating in order to escape famine or to seek improved economic or social conditions. States may provide sanctuary for such people as an humanitarian gesture, but have no obligation to do so under the Convention. Thus the Hong Kong authorities have felt justified in returning to Vietnam large numbers of illegal Vietnamese immigrants who are considered to be economic migrants, without a well-founded fear of persecution from the Vietnamese authorities on their return. The same applies to people who are at risk of discrimination which does not amount to persecution.[71]

(ii) The rights of refugees

A person claiming to be a refugee seeking asylum is not to be removed from the UK without having the application decided, and must generally not be removed while there is a right of appeal against an unfavourable decision. However, there are exceptions. Under section 11 of the Immigration and Asylum Act 1999, the Home Secretary may be able to certify that another EU state is the responsible state for deciding an applicant's claim under a standing arrangement (such as the Dublin Convention), for example because that state is the first place the applicant entered within the EU. The asylum seeker may then be removed to that state, which is to be regarded as one where the person will be safe for the purposes of the Refugee Convention, as long as he is not a national or citizen of the state. Section 65 gives the applicant a right to appeal against the Home Secretary's certificate on the ground that any of his ECHR rights

---

[70] *Hilal v. United Kingdom*, Eur. Ct. HR, App. No. 45276/99, Judgment of 6 March 2001; *R. v. Secretary of State for the Home Department, ex parte Robinson* [1998] QB 929, [1997] 4 All ER 210, CA. See also *Karanakaram v. Secretary of State for the Home Department* [2000] 3 All ER 449, CA.

[71] *Velmira Blanusa v. Secretary of State for the Home Department*, unreported, 18 May 1999, CA.

has been violated. However, the legislation, giving effect to the standing arrangement, displaces the previous requirement for the Home Secretary to satisfy himself (subject to review by UK courts) that the third country will comply with the Refugee Convention as interpreted by UK courts, and will not send the claimant on to another country where there is a danger of a violation of the Refugee Convention so interpreted.[72] Under section 11, the claimant is not usually to be removed from the UK until time to appeal has expired, or any appeal has been decided.

But the Home Secretary is empowered to certify under section 72(2)(a) of the 1999 Act that the allegation that someone has violated the claimant's Convention right is 'manifestly ill founded'. If such a certificate is issued, the claimant loses the right of appeal under section 65. The term 'manifestly ill founded' is familiar: it is a ground on which the European Court of Human Rights is to reject applications alleging that a person's rights have been violated. The Court, and the Commission in earlier days, has sometimes used the 'manifestly ill founded' ground to reject a complaint after a cursory inspection of the merits. It would be clearly contrary to the Rule of Law to allow the Home Secretary to determine the merits of an appeal against his own decision or that of a member of his staff. It would be likely to violate the fundamental common law right of access to an independent court or tribunal to protect one's other legal rights.[73] Such a right can be taken away only by unequivocal, express words in primary legislation.[74] In relation to an analogous certificate to the effect that a person's claim to have suffered persecution for the purposes of the Refugee Convention is manifestly ill-founded, it has been held that the Home Secretary can issue the certificate only if the claim does not disclose any facts capable of amounting to persecution under the Convention. There is no power to issue a certificate, depriving the claimant of a right of appeal, merely because the Home Secretary disbelieves the claimant's statement of facts. That is a matter for the appellate body.[75] This is correct as a matter of constitutional principle. Section 72(2)(a) of the 1999 Act should be interpreted in the same way. So should powers to exclude asylum claims by suspected international terrorists under the Anti-terrorism, Crime and Security Bill 2001.

The Home Secretary also has power, under section 12 of the 1999 Act, to remove an asylum seeker to another country of which he is not a national or a citizen if the third country is a Member State of the EU not covered by a standing arrangement such as the Dublin Convention, or a country designated as a safe country for asylum purposes by the Home Secretary which will not return the claimant to his country of origin in breach of the Refugee Convention (as interpreted by the English courts).[76]

---

[72] Asylum and Immigration Act 1996, s. 2(2)(c), as interpreted in *R. v. Secretary of State for the Home Department, ex parte Adan* [2001] 2 WLR 143, HL.

[73] See, e.g. *Raymond v. Honey* [1983] 1 AC 1, [1982] 1 All ER 756, HL; *R. v. Secretary of State for the Home Department, ex parte Leech* [1994] QB 198, [1993] 4 All ER 539, CA.

[74] *R. v. Secretary of State for the Home Department, ex parte Pierson* [1998] AC 539, HL, at 573–5 *per* Lord Browne-Wilkinson, 587–90 *per* Lord Steyn; *R. v. Secretary of State for the Home Department, ex parte Simms* [1999] 3 WLR 328, HL, at 340 *per* Lord Steyn, 341–2 *per* Lord Hoffmann.

[75] *R. (Gavira) v. Secretary of State for the Home Department, The Times*, 15 May 2001, Admin. Ct., dealing with a certificate under the Asylum Appeals Act 1993, Sch. 2, para. 5, as substituted by the Asylum and Immigration Act 1996, s. 1.

[76] Immigration and Asylum Act 1999, s. 12(7)(c); *R. v. Secretary of State for the Home Department, ex parte Adan* [2001] 2 WLR 143, HL.

Moves have been made to introduce blanket designations of countries as 'safe' to facilitate removal of asylum seekers. These are always questionable, as a country which may be safe for one person, or people of a particular race or political or religious creed, may be unsafe for others. The power to designate countries as safe is exercised by the Home Secretary statutory instrument, subject to the affirmative resolution procedure. The fact that a statutory instrument designating a country as safe has been approved by Parliament after a debate does not prevent the courts from conducting judicial review of the validity of the order. Because the designation, if mistaken, puts people at risk of death, torture or inhuman or degrading treatment, as well as persecution, the Court of Appeal has held that it is open to a court to review such instruments not only for illegality and procedural impropriety, but also for irrationality if the known facts and previous decisions of the courts on the basis of them are simply incompatible with the Home Secretary's conclusion that the country in question is generally safe. Thus in R. (Asif Javed) v. Secretary of State for the Home Department[76a] the Court of Appeal struck down a statutory instrument designating Pakistan as a generally safe country, in the light of clear evidence that women and Ahmadis are likely to suffer persecution there. The fact that the order had been approved by Parliament after debate did not make it improper for the courts to conduct their own review of the material facts or to conclude that the judgment of the Secretary of State had been irrational. The courts, not Parliament, retain responsibility for deciding whether the subordinate legislation approved by Parliament is valid by reference to the tests of *ultra vires*, including irrationality. The deference to the judgment of the Secretary of State and Parliament did not permit either of them to make legally binding a factual conclusion which was clearly wrong. A party seeking to establish the irrationality of such an order bears a heavy evidential burden, but where the burden is discharged, the court has jurisdiction to review, particularly where human rights as fundamental as that under ECHR Article 3 are in issue.

When reviewing a decision by the Home Secretary that a country is 'safe' for the purposes of the Refugee Convention, two kinds of issues arise. First, the Home Secretary must satisfy the courts that the claimant will not be persecuted or at risk of death, torture, etc. in the third country itself. Courts (including the European Court of Human Rights) will have regard to reports of international non-governmental organizations such as Amnesty International as well as institutions such as the UN and European Committees for the Prevention of Torture.[77] Secondly, the Home Secretary must satisfy the court that the third country will not interpret or apply the Refugee Convention so as to return the applicant to a country where he would be at risk of persecution, death, etc. in circumstances where the applicant would not have been liable to direct return from the UK. The third country must adopt what the UK courts would regard as a 'correct' interpretation of the Convention.[78] Thus where a person fleeing Uganda, because of a well-founded fear of persecution there, came to this country via Kenya, where there was no risk of persecution, the Home Secretary

---

[76a] [2001] 3 WLR 323, CA.

[77] *R. v. Secretary of State for the Home Department, ex parte Canbolat* [1997] 1 WLR 1569, [1998] 1 All ER 161, CA.

[78] *R. v. Secretary of State for the Home Department, ex parte Adan* [2001] 2 WLR 143, HL.

was not entitled to return him to Kenya without giving serious consideration to the risk that the Kenyans would return him to the Ugandan authorities.[79] There is a right of appeal on human rights grounds under section 65 of the 1999 Act, subject to the Home Secretary's power to issue a certificate under section 72(2)(a), noted above.

When a claim for asylum has been made, the refugee is entitled not to be expelled or returned to the frontiers of any territory where his life or freedom would be threatened on account of his race, religion, nationality, member of a particular social group, or political opinion, until the claim has been assessed and found to be ill-founded.[80] While in the UK awaiting a decision, asylum seekers enjoy a right at common law not to be left destitute. This right can be taken away by primary legislation, or by subordinate legislation authorized by statute, but only if (in each case) the primary legislation does so expressly and using clear and unambiguous language. Such legislation has been passed, together with provisions giving power to disperse asylum seekers to 'reception zones' in different parts of the country.[81]

Many refugees have to enter the country in ways which would normally be illegal. For example, they might have been compelled to travel on false passports, without obtaining a valid entry clearance before leaving. They might have lied (or been economical with the truth) on first confronting an immigration officer at the port of entry, because of trauma, language difficulties, or suspicion of officials. They are also likely to have been stowaways on the ship or aircraft on which they arrived, having bribed an employee to let them board. Since 1987, carriers have been discouraged from taking people on board officially without valid travel documents by a charge of £2,000 (which can be increased by the Home Secretary by order, and is recoverable as a civil debt) for each passenger who arrives on board a carrier's aircraft, ship, or vehicle without appropriate documentation. Carriers are also subject to a penalty in respect of stowaways.[82]

There may be good reasons for refugees to leave their countries without proper papers, or to be fearful about presenting themselves to the authorities in the UK. In the first half of 2000, some 70 per cent of asylum applicants applied from within the country,[83] often having misled the immigration officer as to the purpose of their visit on arrival. Rules 340 and 341 of the Immigration Rules 1994 make it clear that a failure to apply for asylum immediately on arrival in the UK, or the use of false papers, will

---

[79] *R. v. Secretary of State for the Home Dept., ex parte Bugdaycay* [1987] AC 514, [1987] 1 All ER 940, HL.

[80] Art. 33(1) of the Convention (the so-called 'non-refoulement' provision), 33(2). Where the person is a suspected international terrorist and threat to national security, the application need not be considered: Anti-terrorism, Crime and Security Bill 2001, Part 4.

[81] See *R. v. Secretary of State for Social Security, ex parte Joint Council for the Welfare of Immigrants* [1997] 1 WLR 275, [1996] 4 All ER 385, CA, holding regulations depriving asylum seekers of benefits to be *ultra vires*; Asylum and Immigration Act 1996, ss. 9, 10, and 11 (excluding asylum seekers expressly from eligibility for housing under the homelessness legislation, from child benefit, and from various other social security benefits); Immigration and Asylum Act 1999, ss. 95 and 96 (under which regulations have been made allowing asylum seekers to receive services and vouchers but not cash benefits), 101 (reception zones). This policy was under review in November 2001.

[82] See now Immigration and Asylum Act 1999, ss. 32, 40. There are defences to the penalty, the burden of proving that they apply being on the carrier: s. 34. There is also power to detain the ship, aircraft, or vehicle on which a clandestine entrant arrived: ibid., ss. 36, 37.

[83] Jackson and McGregor, *Control of Immigration: Statistics United Kingdom, First Half 2000*, para. 17.

not automatically lead to the rejection of a claim for asylum. On the other hand, significant delay in claiming refugee status, the use of false documents, failure to co-operate with the investigation of a claim, or (as Rule 342 shows) the behaviour of a claimant's agent, may cast doubt on a claimant's credibility, and lead the Home Secretary to reject the claim as being without foundation. Under Rule 329, the claimant will be allowed to remain in the UK pending a determination of his claim to asylum.

It is an offence to attempt to enter the country by deception. However, Article 31(1) of the Refugee Convention provides:

'The contracting states shall not impose penalties, on account of their illegal entry or presence, on refugees who, coming directly from a territory where their life or freedom was threatened in the sense of article 1, enter or are present in their territory without authorisation, provided they present themselves without delay to the authorities and show good cause for their illegal entry or presence.'

The state thus has an obligation in international law to mitigate any criminal liability for illegal entry in the case of people fleeing directly to the UK to protect their lives and freedom, with a bona fide desire to seek asylum in the UK or elsewhere, whose quest reasonably involved them in breaching the law.[84] Although the Refugee Convention has not been legally incorporated into UK law (although it has been said that its provisions 'have for all practical purposes being incorporated'[85]), the courts have to some extent been able to ensure that asylum seekers are not left at the mercy of prosecuting authorities. Thus merely disembarking without proper papers does not make the refugee an illegal entrant for the purpose of the Immigration Act 1971, as this would have the effect of making virtually all refugees illegal entrants. Only an entrant who evades immigration control, or tries to use false papers in order to deceive the immigration officer and gain entry, is an illegal immigrant.[86] Furthermore, a person who presents himself to the immigration authorities and claims asylum within a short time of gaining entry is, on the face of it, entitled to assume that the state will comply with its obligations under Article 31 of the Refugee Convention. It is not settled whether primary responsibility for securing compliance lies with the judiciary, through judicial review of a decision to prosecute on the ground that it violates legitimate expectations or, possibly, amounts to an abuse of process, or with the executive by way of a pardon.[87] Either way, it is clear that courts now expect the executive, through its various agencies, to protect asylum seekers against criminal liability where Article 31 of the Refugee Convention applies, although a short period of detention to enable a speedy decision to be made will not necessarily violate the Refugee Convention or ECHR Article 5.[87a]

---

[84] See R. v. Uxbridge Magistrates' Court, ex parte Adimi [2000] 3 WLR 434, DC, at 443 per Simon Brown LJ.

[85] R. v. Secretary of State for the Home Department, ex parte Sivakumaran [1988] AC 958, HL, at 990 per Lord Keith of Kinkel.

[86] See R. v. Naillie [1993] AC 674, [1993] 2 All ER 782, HL.

[87] R. v. Uxbridge Magistrates' Court, ex parte Adimi [2000] 3 WLR 434, DC. Simon Brown LJ favoured judicial control through the doctrine of legitimate expectations, following a dictum of Lord Woolf MR in R. v. Secretary of State for the Home Department, ex parte Ahmed [1998] INLR 570, CA, at 583. Newman J favoured executive responsibility through a pardon.

[87a] R. (Saadi and others) v. Secretary of State for the Home Dept. [2001] EWCA Civ. 1512, CA.

Once it has been accepted that a person is a refugee and has not come from a safe third country, he is entitled to settle in the UK. He has certain obligations, particularly to conform to laws and regulations and measures taken to maintain public order.[88] He may, therefore, be removed from the country if, but only if, this is necessary on grounds of national security and public order, following a decision reached in accordance with due process of law. The refugee must be given time to find a third country prepared to accept him.[89] He should not be removed if the only country to which he could go is one to which he is unwilling to go because of a well-founded fear of persecution, or where he would be at risk of a violation of the rights to be free of deprivation of life, torture, or inhuman or degrading treatment or punishment. If he is a suspected international terrorist and threat to national security, there will be power to detain him until a safe country can be found.[90]

(3) OTHER GROUPS: DISCRETIONARY ADMITTANCE

Those people who wish to enter but do not have a right of abode under the above rules are admitted under the Immigration Rules 1994, which permit the imposition of limits on the circumstances in which people may be admitted, and the period and purposes for which they are allowed to stay. Those who may be admitted as temporary entrants include visitors for short periods as tourists or for private medical treatment, and students (other than Iraqis, whose entry was severely curtailed during the run-up to the Gulf War in 1990–91) who have been accepted for full-time courses at educational institutions. Other categories may be admitted for limited periods in the first instance, but with the possibility of being allowed to remain for longer, or indefinite, periods subsequently. These include people with work permits, including permits for training and work experience who have jobs which have been made open to them before arrival; people seeking to establish themselves in business or in self-employment, with the means to do so and to support themselves; people with the means to support themselves without taking employment; dependents of such people; and fiancés and fiancées, with an entry clearance, entering for the primary purpose of marrying people settled in the UK and intending to live with them permanently as man and wife. This, and particularly the independent-means head of admittance, has been characterized as replacing a test based on colour of skin with one based on the colour of money.[91] This impression was strengthened by arrangements for Hong Kong residents after the colony was returned to China in 1997. The status of British Nationals (Overseas)[92] did not confer a right of abode in the UK on Hong Kong residents. The British Nationality (Hong Kong) Act 1990, the British Nationality (Hong Kong) (Selection Scheme) Order 1990[93] established a scheme whereby the Home Secretary could confer British citizenship, with a right of abode, on up to 50,000 Hong Kong residents nominated by the Governor of Hong Kong. It became

---

[88] Refugee Convention, Art. 2.   [89] Ibid., Arts. 32, 33(2).

[90] Immigration Rules 1994, rr. 369, 385; Anti-terrorism, Crime and Security Bill 2001, Part 4. See (4) below.

[91] G. Robertson, *Freedom, the Individual and the Law*, 6th edn. (Harmondsworth: Penguin, 1989), 318–19.

[92] See Hong Kong Act 1985.   [93] SI 1990, No. 14.

clear that people were to be selected from the wealthiest members of Hong Kong society.

In addition, the Home Secretary has a discretion to admit people who would not be entitled to enter on normal criteria.[94] This may be done on compassionate grounds. In 1998, 4,270 people were recognised as refugees, while 2,410 were given exceptional leave to remain after being refused refugee status, and a further 3,700 people were accepted on other discretionary grounds outside the legislation and the Rules.[95]

(4) MIGRANTS AND HUMAN RIGHTS

Apart from the Refugee Convention, UK immigration law is subject to the human rights of migrants in two ways. First, the UK has an obligation in international law to respect the rights of everyone under international human rights instruments to which the UK is party. The European Court of Human Rights has held that states violate certain rights if they send people back to countries where they are at risk of suffering acts such as torture or inhuman or degrading treatment. Secondly, those principles now form part of municipal law in the UK under the Human Rights Act 1998, so a person threatened with removal can challenge an order for deportation on the ground that it would violate his Convention rights under the Act. The effect of the rights is considered in section 8.3 below.

8.3 DEPORTATION

The power of the Secretary of State for the Home Department to deport people who are not British citizens is given by section 3 of the Immigration Act 1971. There is no power to deport British citizens; Commonwealth and Irish citizens who were settled here on 1 January 1973 become exempt from deportation after five years' residence.[96]

The power to deport applies in four groups of cases.[97] The first is where people who have entered with limited leave to remain overstay their leave, or break one of the conditions attached to their leave to enter (as where a person who enters as a visitor is found to have taken employment). The second is where the Secretary of State deems a person's deportation to be conducive to the public good. The third is where another person to whose family the deportee belongs has been, or has been ordered to be, deported. The fourth is where a person over the age of 17 years has been convicted of an offence for which he is punishable with imprisonment, and the court on his conviction made a recommendation for his deportation. In all these cases, the Home

---

[94] See C. Vincenzi, 'Extra-Statutory Ministerial Discretion in Immigration Law' [1992] PL 300–21.

[95] See Jackson and McGregor, *Control of Immigration: Statistics United Kingdom, First Half 2000*, Table 4.1 (*Cp.* Table 3.1).

[96] Immigration Act 1971, s. 7. On the meaning of these categories see section 8.2(1), above.

[97] Immigration Act 1971, s. 3(5), (6), as amended by the British Nationality Act 1981.

Secretary has a discretion which is exercised in accordance with the Immigration Rules 1994. The first and fourth cases present no special civil liberties problems in principle (although there is an issue, discussed below, about the human rights implications of deporting people ordered by criminal courts to be detained for treatment for mental disorders). This section examines (1) deportation for the public good, (2) deportation of members of the primary deportee's family, and (3) human rights restrictions on deportation.

(1) PERSON'S DEPORTATION DEEMED CONDUCIVE TO THE PUBLIC GOOD

There are no rules laid down for deciding when this is the case. In deciding the matter, the Home Secretary considers personal factors relating to the deportee, and in particular his age, length of residence, strength of local connections, personal history, including character, conduct and employment record, domestic circumstances, previous criminal record, compassionate circumstances, and any representations made on the person's behalf (by friends, relatives, MPs, etc.).[98] Deportation orders are made on this ground in about 100 cases annually,[99] most often to remove people who have been convicted of offences without the court making any recommendation for deportation.[100] However, there are a few cases where it seems that deporting (or refusing entry to) people has infringed civil liberties or human rights.

For example, the power to deport has several times been invoked to remove foreign nationals with political views which the government finds uncongenial. Rudi Dutschke, a student activist, was removed in 1971; successive Home Secretaries have apparently considered it appropriate to remove or exclude foreign nationals whose public utterances would be likely to offend sections of the community, or whose very presence might be offensive.[101] In some cases, the power has been used to remove people who are thought to be threatening particular harm to national security. This is always a matter for concern, as the government asserts, and the courts have traditionally conceded, exclusive authority to determine what national security requires.[102] Because judges are reluctant to insist that the Home Secretary provides convincing evidence for a claim about national security, the European Court of Human Rights held in *Chahal v. United Kingdom*[103] that judicial review of a deportation order did not provide an effective remedy (as required by ECHR Article 13) for a deportee who claimed that removing him to India would put him at risk of torture or inhuman or degrading treatment (a violation of ECHR Article 3). Furthermore, the lack of procedural safeguards during the decision-making process left the deportee without a way of judicially testing the legality of his detention and deportation, in violation of ECHR Article 5(4). As a result, a special appeal procedure had to be established by the

---

[98] Immigration Rules 1994, r. 364.

[99] Jackson and McGregor, *Control of Immigration: Statistics United Kingdom, First Half 2000*, Table 5.3.

[100] Evans, *Immigration Law*, 272.

[101] Ibid., 272–3.

[102] For full discussion, see L. Lustgarten and I. Leigh, *In from the Cold: National Security and Parliamentary Democracy* (Oxford: Clarendon Press, 1994), 183–91.

[103] Eur. Ct. HR, Judgment of 15 November 1996, 23 EHRR 413.

Special Immigration Appeals Commission Act 1997, noted further in section 8.4 below.

There are several examples of the difficulty of holding the Home Secretary to account for deportation orders made on national security grounds. Mark Hosenball and Philip Agee, Americans who had published information which was said to have prejudiced national security and put the lives of British agents in the field at risk in the course of an account of the activities of the CIA, were removed in 1977, despite the facts that the damage was no less likely to be caused with them abroad than with them here, and that it was unclear what further damage could be done to make their presence here unconducive to the public good in the future.[104] Large numbers of Iraqi or Kuwaiti residents were deported during the Gulf crisis in 1990–91, on information (often highly dubious) from the security services that those people represented a security threat.[105]

The protean nature of the concept of national security makes the power to deport on this ground very wide. Courts have accepted that it is not necessary for the deportee's activities to threaten security in the UK directly. The Home Secretary is said to be entitled to treat a threat of terrorism against a foreign state as indirectly threatening the UK's national security. Thus courts have upheld deportation orders against a Sikh who was said to be threatening national security by fomenting violence in India,[106] and an Islamic clergyman who was said to be involved in fund-raising and recruiting among British Muslims in support of a terrorist organization.[107] However, opinions about the reality of the threat may differ. In *Chahal v. United Kingdom*[108] the European Court of Human Rights held that deportation of a militant Sikh to India would breach the UK's responsibilities under the ECHR by exposing him to a risk of torture or inhuman or degrading treatment at the hands of the Indian police and security forces. The English courts had said that the Home Secretary was entitled to accept a statement from the Indian High Commission that Mr. Chahal would be protected like any Indian citizen. The European Court of Human Rights made its own assessment, having regard to reports by the UN Special Rapporteur on Torture and the Indian Human Rights Commission, and decided that there was a risk of unauthorized misbehaviour by the Indian police against which other state agencies might be unable to protect Mr. Chahal. Similarly, in *Secretary of State for the Home Department v. Rehman*[109] (the case of the Islamic clergyman) the Special Immigration Appeals Tribunal heard in closed session evidence from the Home Office and submissions on it from the Special Advocate appointed to represent the interests of the deportee in relation to matters which could not be disclosed to him for security reasons. The

---

[104] *R. v. Secretary of State for the Home Dept., ex parte Hosenball* [1977] 1 WLR 766, [1977] 3 All ER 452, CA.

[105] *R. v. Secretary of State for the Home Department, ex parte Cheblak* [1991] 1 WLR 890, [1991] 2 All ER 319, CA.

[106] *R. v. Secretary of State for the Home Department, ex parte Chahal* [1995] 1 WLR 526, [1995] 1 All ER 658, CA.

[107] *Secretary of State for the Home Department v. Rehman* [2000] 3 WLR 1240, CA.

[108] Eur. Ct. HR, Judgment of 15 November 1996, 23 EHRR 413.

[109] [2001] 3 WLR 877, HL.

Tribunal, described by the Court of Appeal as 'singularly well qualified',[110] rejected the Home Secretary's submission that national security was threatened. On appeal by the Home Secretary, the Court of Appeal reversed the decision without having heard the sensitive Home Office evidence or submissions from the Special Advocate. The House of Lords upheld the decision of the Court of Appeal, holding that an overseas threat could be a threat to national security and that the Home Secretary was best placed to decide whether proven facts made deportation conducive to the public good. This threatens to undermine the procedural protection for the deportee introduced to meet the requirements of the ECHR as disclosed in the *Chahal* case.

In another group of cases, members of the Church of Scientology have been excluded on the basis that the teachings and practices of that church are damaging to its adherents. Even where the people concerned have been EC nationals exercising their *prima facie* right to free movement of workers and freedom of establishment, their exclusion has been held to be justified as coming within the exception for public policy.[111] This interferes with freedom of expression and, in the latter case, freedom of religion (if, unlike the English courts, one regards scientology as a religion). The courts are not entirely powerless to impose minimal procedural standards on the process of making decisions about what is conducive to the public good. In 1995, the founder of the Moonies, Rev. Moon, was refused entry to the UK on the ground that his presence would not be conducive to the public good, although he had been given clearance to enter in 1992. The Home Secretary refused to explain why his presence would have been compatible with the public good in 1992 but not in 1995, so Rev. Moon was unable to make worthwhile representations. This was held to be a breach of the duty to act fairly in administrative law, and the refusal of leave was quashed on an application for judicial review.[111a] None the less, the protection at common law has historically been very limited.

Finally, and squarely within the group of cases which concern political freedom, it has sometimes been suggested that the deportation power has been used to get round restrictions on extradition. There are various formalities which must be complied with before a person can be extradited to face trial in another country, including the conclusion of an extradition treaty between the two countries concerned, and a judicial hearing to establish cause for extradition. There are also substantive limitations, of which the most important is that the offence for which the person is to be extradited must not be one regarded by the courts as a political offence. It is often easier, and more conducive to good international relations, to deport a person as someone whose presence is not conducive to the public good rather than to go through the tortuous and often unsuccessful process of extradition. However, to use deportation in this way evades a person's due-process protections against being returned to face political charges in another jurisdiction. The use of extradition in this

[110] [2000] 3 WLR 1240, CA at 1246, para. 17 of the judgment.

[111] *Schmidt v. Secretary of State for Home Affairs* [1969] 2 Ch. 149 (a case of refusal to renew leave to remain, rather than a deportation during the term of a right to remain); *Van Duyn v. Home Office* [1974] 1 WLR 1107, Ch. D; *Van Duyn v. Home Office* [1974] ECR 1337, ECJ.

[111a] *R. v. Secretary of State for the Home Department, ex parte Moon*, Sedley J, 1 November 1995, unreported, noted in (1996) 1 *J. of Civil Liberties* 98–9.

way is an abuse of power. The argument was first raised in *R. v. Governor of Brixton Prison, ex parte Soblen*,[112] where Soblen was wanted for trial in the USA, and the US government had asked the British government to return him to them. The offence for which Soblen was wanted in the USA was espionage, an offence for which extradition is not available. Soblen wanted to go instead to Czechoslovakia, which was prepared to accept him, but the Home Secretary ordered his deportation to the USA. This order was upheld by the Court of Appeal in habeas corpus proceedings, as it had not been shown that the Home Secretary would not have removed Soblen to the USA even had the request for his delivery not been made. It is therefore open to the court to review a deportation decision for an abuse of power if it is an attempt at disguised extradition, although it seems that the deportation order will be regarded as an abuse of power in such cases only if the desire to achieve extradition by the back door was the sole reason for making the order.[113] 'Where disguised extradition from another country has resulted in a person being brought improperly to the UK in order to face criminal charges, a prosecution is capable of amounting to an abuse of process and may be stayed by the court'.[113a] In *R. v. Mullen*[113b] a person was improperly deported from Zimbabwe to the UK without access to a lawyer, in violation of Zimbabwean law and international human rights. The deportation took place as a result of collusion between the security services of Zimbabwe and the UK in order that he should be arrested in the UK for terrorist offences. After the deportee had been arrested and convicted, he appealed, arguing that there had been an abuse of process (the degradation of the lawful administration of justice) which could be said to make the conviction unsafe for appeal purposes, even though the trial itself had been fair, as the trial should never have taken place.[113c]

(2) FAMILY OF PERSON DEPORTED

One of the difficulties which may flow from a deportation is that the deportee's family will be split up, breaching the right to respect for family life under Article 8 of the European Convention on Human Rights. This is, to some extent, taken into account by the Secretary of State when exercising his discretion under the Immigration Rules 1994. As regards the deportee, the family connection may be a factor (in relation to domestic or compassionate circumstances) influencing the Home Secretary to allow him to remain. Following one case, *Uppal v. United Kingdom (No. 2)*,[114] the Home Secretary revoked a deportation order after the European Commission of Human Rights held that it might breach the applicant's Article 8 rights by dividing the family. If it has been decided to deport him, or not to revoke a deportation order, on the other

---

[112] [1963] 2 QB 243, CA.

[113] *R. v. Bow Street Magistrates, ex parte Mackeson* (1982) 75 Cr. App. R. 24, CA; *R. v. Guildford Magistrates' Court, ex parte Healy* [1983] 1 WLR 108, DC.

[113a] *R. v. Horseferry Road Magistrates' Court, ex parte Bennett* [1994] 1 AC 42, [1993] 3 All ER 138, HL; *R. v. Latif* [1996] 1 WLR 104, [1996] 1 All ER 353, HL.

[113b] [1999] 3 WLR 777, CA.

[113c] For discussion of the theoretical issues involved, see A. Ashworth, 'Testing Fidelity to Legal Values: Official Involvement and Criminal Justice' (2000) 63 *MLR* 633–59.

[114] (1981) 3 EHRR 399.

hand, the family ties will militate in favour of deporting the rest of the family as well. At this stage, therefore, if the family wants to remain, it will do well to stress its independence of the deportee, its connection with other relatives in the UK, other ties with the UK, the spouse's independent employment record, the family's ability to support itself here, and the disruptive effect on the children and their education if they were to be forcibly removed.[115] The human rights implications are considered next.

(3) DEPORTATION AND HUMAN RIGHTS

As noted above, removing a person from the UK may breach his rights in international law under the ECHR, and rights in municipal law under the Human Rights Act 1998. At the basic level of due process, detaining a person claiming refugee status pending return to his country of origin without a proper hearing may breach the right to have the legality of detention tested judicially under Article 5(4). In relation to more substantive rights, the European Court of Human Rights has held that states have a positive duty to protect people against violation of certain rights by other states. These rights include the right not to be intentionally deprived of life, the right to be free of torture and inhuman or degrading treatment, and the right to respect for private and family life. Where there is a positive obligation to take appropriate steps to protect people against such violations, or a negative duty to avoid putting people at risk of them, it may preclude deportation, either generally or to particular countries in which the deportee would be at special risk. However, not all Convention rights impose such duties. Under the Human Rights Act 1998, it has been held that the right to education under Article 2 of Protocol No. 1 to the ECHR does not prevent the deportation of a child of parents who were being removed to Poland, although it would admittedly disrupt the child's education.[116]

The European Court of Human Rights has gradually increased the rigour of the protection offered to deportees by ECHR Article 3. As noted in Chapters 5 and 7, above, there has been a gradual relaxation in the degree of harm necessary to constitute a violation of Article 3, and an extension of the positive duties of states. For instance, in *D. v. United Kingdom*[117] the Court held that returning a person suffering from AIDS to a country where no treatment would be available would constitute inhuman or degrading treatment under Article 3. In *Bensaid v. United Kingdom*[118] the Court carefully examined the type, quality, and accessibility of mental health care available to a deportee in Algeria before deciding that it would not violate Article 3 to deport to Algeria a person suffering from a long-term schizophrenic condition. In *R. (X.) v. Secretary of State for the Home Department*[119] the Court of Appeal accepted that removing a person with a mental illness could engage Article 3, but decided that the worsening of a patient's condition from being removed to Malta, where appropriate treatment would be available, was not sufficiently serious to amount to a violation of

---

[115] Immigration Rules 1994, rr. 36–368.
[116] *R. v. Secretary of State for the Home Department, ex parte Holub, The Times*, 13 February 2001, CA.
[117] Eur. Ct. HR, Judgment of 2 May 1997, RJD 1997-III, 24 EHRR 423.
[118] Eur. Ct. HR, Judgment of 6 February 2001, 33 EHRR 205.
[119] [2001] 1 WLR 740, CA.

Article 3. It is therefore clear that English law can now offer a proper opportunity to obtain a judicial assessment of the effect of deportation on the patient's medical condition in the light of Article 3 standards, taking account of the accessibility of appropriate medical care in the country to which the patient is to be removed, as long as our courts do not defer to the view of the executive or introduce the idea of proportionality into the assessment: a violation of an Article 3 right cannot be justified by reference to countervailing considerations or interests.

The Court has also become more willing to make its own assessment of the risk, perhaps in response to growing awareness that states are too ready to accept a third country's assessment of its own situation at face value. At first, the Court was inclined to examine claims in the light of the information available to the respondent state at the time when it took the decision to remove the applicant. On that basis, the Court decided in *Vilvarajah v. United Kingdom*,[120] by a majority of eight to one, that there were no substantial grounds for believing that the Tamils who had failed to establish refugee status in *R. v. Secretary of State for the Home Department, ex parte Sivakuma-ran (UN High Commissioner for Refugees intervening)*[121] would, if expelled, be sub-jected to a real risk (rather than a mere possibility) of treatment of a severity sufficient to give rise to a breach of Article 3. More recently, however, the Court has taken account of reports by international institutions such as the UN Special Rapporteur on Torture, national bodies such as the Indian Human Rights Commission, and national or international non-governmental organizations such as Amnesty International when assessing the risk to a deportee, and has directed its attention much more clearly to the position at the time the particular applicant would arrive in the country in question. This more rigorous review led to a finding in *Chahal v. United Kingdom*[122] that India was not a safe country to which to return a Sikh militant. The decision cast doubt on the compatibility with Article 3 of any blanket designations of a country as safe for deportation purposes.

A further issue which arises under Article 13 of the European Convention concerns the adequacy of the administrative-law remedies available in England and Wales to protect the Article 3 rights of people who have claimed and been refused refugee status. In *Vilvarajah*'s case, above, in addition to alleging a breach of Article 3, the Tamil refugees alleged a breach of Article 13, on the ground that proceedings before the English courts had failed to provide an adequate remedy to enforce the rights of the refugees under the Convention. The Commission took the view, by thirteen votes to one, that the domestic remedies available to the applicants were not effective, breaching Article 13. The Court, emphatically differing from the clear opinion of the Commission, decided by seven votes to two that judicial review proceedings were an effective remedy in cases of this sort. In an earlier decision, *Soering v. United King-dom*,[123] the Court had held that judicial review could be adequate protection for a person's Article 3 rights, because the English courts could review the reasonableness of a decision (in that case, an extradition decision) on *Wednesbury* principles, and

---

[120] Eur. Ct. HR, Judgment of 30 October 1991.
[121] [1988] AC 958, [1988] 1 All ER 193, HL.
[122] Eur. Ct. HR, Judgment of 15 November 1996, 23 EHRR 413.
[123] Eur. Ct. HR, Series A, No. 161, Judgment of 7 July 1989.

would have jurisdiction to quash a decision where a serious risk of inhuman or degrading treatment was established. These decisions are more persuasive now that under the Human Rights Act 1998 many decisions incompatible with Convention rights are automatically illegal, rather than merely potential irrationality. Nevertheless, in some cases the courts are unable or very reluctant to review decisions by reference to substantive standards, particularly where national security is said to be in issue. For this reason, the European Court of Human Rights held in *Chahal v. United Kingdom*[124] that judicial review did not offer an effective remedy for violations of Convention rights in cases relating to national security, leading to new appeal procedures in such cases.

The right to respect for family life under ECHR Article 8 may affect deportation decisions and immigration rules. The European Court of Human Rights accepts that states have a legitimate interest in maintaining immigration controls, so it is open to states to justify separating members of a family by reference to the criteria set out in Article 8(2).[125] To be justifiable, an order which seriously interferes with the relationship between family members must satisfy tests of legal certainty, necessity, and proportionality. The Immigration Act 1971 provides a basis in law for removing foreign nationals sufficient to meet the requirement for legal certainty. The necessity, or pressing social need, condition will usually be met if the state is acting in good faith to protect the integrity of its system of immigration law. The most usual point at issue relates to proportionality. A decision to divide a family must carefully strike a balance between the interests of members of the family and the interest in maintaining immigration control.[126] It will be relevant to consider the strength of the ties between family members, whether it would inflict unreasonable hardship on other members of the family to move abroad and continue their lives with the deportee, as well as the impact of any offences which the deportee has committed and the risk of allowing him to remain in the UK.[127] For example, even before the Human Rights Act 1998 came into force, rights under the ECHR had to be taken into account when considering a person's right not to be deported under EC law. In *B. v. Secretary of State for the Home Department*[127a] the Court of Appeal held that it would be disproportionate to deport a sex offender to Sicily. He had settled in the UK with his parents when he was seven years old, and had lived in this country for about thirty-five years without acquiring British nationality. He had been to Sicily only twice in the previous twenty years. His ties with the UK were so much stronger than those with Sicily that a

---

[124] Eur. Ct. HR, Judgment of 15 November 1996, 23 EHRR 413.

[125] For full discussion of Article 8, see Chapter 9, below.

[126] See, e.g. *Ahmut v. Netherlands*, Judgment of 28 November 1996, 24 EHRR 62.

[127] See, e.g. three cases where removal was disproportionate: *Berrehab v. The Netherlands*, Eur. Ct. HR, Series A, No. 138, Judgment of 21 June 1988, 11 EHRR 322 (removal of ex-husband and father of child after divorce from Dutch wife not proportionate to protection of the Netherlands' economic interests); *Moustaquim v. Belgium*, Eur. Ct. HR, Series A, No. 193-A, Judgment of 18 February 1991, 13 EHRR 802 (disproportionate to remove Moroccan national living in Belgium from age of one after committing many serious offences, but without significant family or means of support in Morocco); *Beldjoudi v. France*, Eur. Ct. HR, Series A, No. 234-A, Judgment of 26 March 1992, 14 EHRR 801 (deporting Algerian criminal to Algeria disproportionate when his wife might well not be able to enter Algeria with him).

[127a] [2000] HRLR 439, CA.

decision to deport him was quashed as a disproportionate interference with his right as a worker to remain in the UK under Community law, of which rights under the ECHR were said to be a part. If there are other ways, besides remaining in the UK, by which the family tie could be maintained, it will often not be disproportionate to deport a member of the family (always assuming that there are good reasons for doing so), or to refuse to allow a member of the family to enter or remain in the UK.[128] However, the courts must make their own assessment of the relative weights of competing considerations when deciding whether deportation is a disproportionate interference with a right. It is not sufficient merely to defer to the view of the original decision-maker so long as that view is not obviously irrational.[129]

8.4 RIGHTS OF APPEAL AND DUE PROCESS

International-law obligations accepted by the UK impose two kinds of procedural constraints on the expulsion of aliens. First, under the ICCPR, Article 13, an alien lawfully within the territory of a state may be expelled:

'only in pursuance of a decision reached in accordance with law and shall, except where compelling reasons of national security otherwise require, be allowed to submit the reasons against his expulsion and to have his case reviewed by, and be represented for the purpose before, the competent authority or a person or persons especially designated by the competent authority.'

While the UK government, on ratification, made reservations in respect of the application of this provision to Hong Kong, no reservation was entered in respect of its application in the UK itself. As we shall see, the executive review and appeal system is now broadly in accord with this provision.

Secondly, people who are detained in order to be removed as illegal immigrants, or deported for any reason, have their liberty interfered with. Article 5(4) of the European Convention on Human Rights, providing for an entitlement to take proceedings speedily to test the lawfulness of detention, and Article 6(1), providing (*inter alia*) that in the determination of civil rights and obligations everyone is entitled to a fair and public hearing within a reasonable time by an independent and impartial tribunal established by law, between them lay down a framework against which to assess the procedures for challenging the legality of detentions pending removal.

The review and appeal processes in these cases are of three types: review by an official, appeals to an adjudicator or tribunal, and review by a court. There used to be a special procedure where a person was refused entry, or served with a notice of deportation, on the ground that it was conducive to the public good. No appeal was

---

[128] See *R. (Mahmood) v. Secretary of State for the Home Department* [2001] 1 WLR 840, CA, esp. *per* Lord Phillips of Worth Matravers MR at paras. 38–67.

[129] *R. (Daly) v. Secretary of State for the Home Department* [2001] 2 WLR 1622, HL, disapproving statements to the contrary in *R. (Mahmood) v. Secretary of State for the Home Department* [2001] 1 WLR 840, CA.

provided in such a case. The Home Secretary was advised by a three-person advisory committee. The deportee could make representations to the committee, but would often be denied any detailed information about the reason for thinking that it would be conducive to the public good to remove him, in order to protect security interests. Judicial review and habeas corpus were attenuated in such cases by the courts' deference to executive judgments about the public interest generally and national security in particular.

All this changed after the European Court of Human Rights decided in *Chahal v. United Kingdom*, above, that the UK's arrangements for making deportation decisions in national security cases violated the right to a judicial assessment of the legality of detention under ECHR Article 5(4), and neither the administrative procedures nor judicial review constituted the effective remedy required by Article 13 for violations of Convention rights.

At the same time, a wave of public fear about increasing numbers of immigrants, and asylum seekers in particular, led Home Secretaries in the 1990s to discourage immigrants and to restrict the time taken by appeals in order to speed up the removal of illegal immigrants or what were often referred to as 'bogus' asylum seekers. As well as removing asylum-seekers' eligibility for state benefits, time limits for appeals were cut, and the Home Secretary was given power to short-circuit appeals by certifying that claims were manifestly ill-founded. However, the Human Rights Act 1998 and the influence of Strasbourg are showing signs of re-establishing concern for human rights and due process in immigration procedures.

(1) OFFICIAL REVIEW OF THE DECISION

There is a procedure for administrative review of a deportation order. The deportee can apply to have the deportation order revoked.[130] This matter is normally decided by officials of the Home Office, acting in the name of the Home Secretary,[131] but may be decided by the Home Secretary in person (with advice from his officials) if the deportation involves particularly sensitive political, legal, or diplomatic issues.

(2) APPEALS TO AN ADJUDICATOR, THE IMMIGRATION APPEAL TRIBUNAL, OR THE SPECIAL IMMIGRATION APPEALS COMMISSION[131a]

Following, or instead of, the administrative review, there is an appeal process. A person aggrieved by refusal of entry or of entry clearance, conditions attached to clearance or leave to enter, variation of leave, a deportation order, a violation of a

---

[130] See Immigration Rules 1994, rr. 390–5.

[131] It is normal for the decision on deportation to be taken by immigration inspectors authorized by the Home Secretary to act on his behalf, and this practice was upheld by the House of Lords in *Oladehinde v. Secretary of State for the Home Department* [1991] 1 AC 254, [1990] 3 All ER 393, as falling within the principle that duties placed on a Minister might lawfully be discharged by any member of the Home Office: *Carltona Ltd. v. Commissioners of Works* [1943] 2 All ER 560, CA.

[131a] See Judge David Pearl, 'Immigration and Asylum Appeals and Administrative Justice', in M. Harris and M. Partington (eds.), *Administrative Justice in the 21st Century* (Oxford: Hart Publishing, 1999), 55–65.

Convention right, directions for removal, the country proposed for removal, refusal of asylum, or removal after rejection of an asylum claim, normally has a right of appeal to an Immigration Adjudicator, with a further appeal to the Immigration Appeals Tribunal.[132] However, neither the adjudicator nor the Tribunal has jurisdiction over decisions based on what is conducive to the public good, or over refusal of asylum or authorization of detention pending removal on national security and international terrorism grounds. In such cases, an appeal now lies to the Special Immigration Appeals Commission, a tribunal which acts judicially and has power to determine the case (although the Commission cannot require asylum to be granted to a suspected international terrorist believed to threaten national security), subject to an appeal on questions of law to the Court of Appeal.[133]

The appellant before the Commission faces a difficulty and potential unfairness caused by the refusal of the Home Secretary to reveal material which might affect national security. This limits the appellant's ability to respond to, or even know of, the case against him or her. For understandable reasons, the 1997 Act allows the Commission to receive in closed session evidence and submissions which cannot be disclosed to the appellant or his or her legal representatives. To mitigate the unfairness, which can lead to a violation of the right to a fair hearing under ECHR Article 6,[134] the Act provides for the appointment of a Special Advocate to represent the appellant's interests in relation to such matters, receiving relevant information, asking questions and making submissions in closed session without either disclosing the information to the appellant or the appellant's representatives or taking instructions from them. This is a sensitive task. It is unfortunate that no similar arrangement applies under the statute on a further appeal to the Court of Appeal. Although that court has used its inherent jurisdiction to seek ways round the problem, the only reported case in which it has done so leaves the impression that the Court of Appeal as ultimate decision-maker feels more constrained than the Commission about hearing or testing sensitive security-related evidence.[135] This could have the effect of undermining, in cases going to the Court of Appeal, the protection which the procedure of the Commission offers to the UK against liability under Articles 5(4), 6(1) and 13 of the ECHR, by leaving the deportee's right to liberty without adequate judicial protection.

The Home Secretary has power in some circumstances to remove the right of appeal to the Immigration Appeal Tribunal by certifying that an asylum-seeker's claim to asylum does not disclose a valid ground for asylum under the Refugee Convention.[136] This does not allow the Home Secretary to assess the truthfulness of any assertions of fact, but only to certify his opinion of the applicability of the Refugee Convention to the facts set out in the application.[137]

---

[132] Immigration and Asylum Act 1999, ss. 59, 61, 63, 65, 66, 67, 69, 71.

[133] Special Immigration Appeal Commission Act 1997, ss. 2, 4; Anti-terrorism, Crime and Security Bill 2001, Part 4.

[134] See *Chahal v. United Kingdom*, Eur. Ct. HR, Judgment of 15 November 1996, 23 EHRR 413.

[135] *Secretary of State for the Home Department v. Rehman* [2000] 3 WLR 1240, CA, currently under appeal to the House of Lords.

[136] Asylum Appeals Act 1993, Sch. 2, para. 5, as substituted by Asylum and Immigration Act 1996, s. 1. See also s. 2 of the 1996 Act (safe third country certificates).

[137] *R. (Gavira) v. Secretary of State for the Home Department*, The Times, 15 May 2001.

(3) REVIEW BY A COURT

Finally, there are two processes whereby the legality of detention may be tested in the courts. These are, first, an application for habeas corpus, and, secondly, an application for judicial review. They can be used in tandem.

(i) Habeas corpus[138]

Habeas corpus is a writ which requires a person to justify the detention of another. The initial evidential burden lies on the applicant to show some reason to think that the validity of the order authorizing detention might be doubtful. This is a substantial burden, particularly where the power to detain is expressed in a way which makes it dependent on the Home Secretary's subjective state of mind or belief.[139] Only if that burden is discharged is there a legal obligation on the detainer to justify the detention, rather than on the detainee to show that it is unlawful.[140]

There are limits to the usefulness of habeas corpus. The power of the court in habeas corpus proceedings is limited to considering whether the detention is within the legal powers of the person authorizing it. It does not extend to reviewing the procedure adopted in the course of making a decision which the decision-maker had power to make.[141] It will therefore be possible to challenge factual determinations made by the immigration authorities only if they are jurisdictional facts, which must be correctly decided in order to ground the power to make the order for detention, deportation, or removal. A finding that a person is an illegal entrant is of this sort, and so is reviewable by a court on a habeas corpus application.[142] On the other hand, an allegation of breach of natural justice or fairness, or an argument that the decision was unreasonable or the decision-maker was influenced by improper motives or irrelevant considerations, will not be entertained in a habeas corpus application; the only course in such cases is to apply for judicial review.[143]

If the order for detention is quashed on one of these other grounds, the detention will be without valid authorization, and habeas corpus will then be available to secure the detainee's release. The use of *certiorari* in aid of habeas corpus in this way is well established in Canada, and it would seem to be equally possible and convenient to bring a habeas corpus application alongside an application for judicial review in England and Wales.[144]

---

[138] See R. J. Sharpe, *The Law of Habeas Corpus*, 2nd edn. (Oxford: Clarendon Press, 1989); D. Clark and G. McCoy, *The Most Fundamental Legal Rights: Habeas Corpus in the Commonwealth* (Oxford: Clarendon Press, 2000), ch. 1.

[139] *R. v. Governor of Brixton Prison, ex parte Ahsan* [1969] 2 QB 222, DC; Sharpe, *Habeas Corpus*, 86–7.

[140] *Khawaja v. Secretary of State for the Home Department* [1983] AC 74, [1983] 1 All ER 765, HL.

[141] *R. v. Secretary of State for the Home Department, ex parte Muboyayi* [1992] QB 244, [1991] 4 All ER 72, CA.

[142] *Khawaja v. Secretary of State for the Home Department* [1983] AC 74, [1983] 1 All ER 765, HL.

[143] *R. v. Secretary of State for the Home Department, ex parte Cheblak* [1991] 1 WLR 890, [1991] 2 All ER 319, CA; *R. v. Secretary of State for the Home Department, ex parte Muboyayi* [1992] QB 244, [1991] 4 All ER 72, CA.

[144] Sharpe, *Habeas Corpus*, 51–3; *Khawaja v. Secretary of State for the Home Department* [1984] AC 74 at 99, [1983] 1 All ER 765 at 774 *per* Lord Wilberforce.

The immigration authorities must normally show that the jurisdictional requirements are satisfied on the balance of probabilities, that being the civil rather than criminal standard of proof. This standard is flexible, however, and a higher standard of probability is needed to tip the balance where the issue affects individual liberty.[145] Nevertheless, where the Home Secretary claims that deportation is conducive to the public good by reason of national security, the court will not test the accuracy of the statement, which is based on an evaluation which lies within the exclusive competence of the Home Secretary.[146] There is therefore little room to test a deportation order made on these grounds: the leading commentator on habeas corpus refers[147] to 'the contrast between a stated willingness to intervene on the one hand, and a queasiness about actually giving relief on the other' in cases where 'the terms of the statute are broad, and the element of public interest to be considered influences the court to shy away from intervention'. Habeas corpus is not available to a suspected international terrorist reasonably believed to be a threat to national security under the Anti-terrorism, Crime and Security Bill 2001, Part 4.

(ii) Application for judicial review

This is a procedure which permits the adequacy of the procedure leading up to the making or confirmation of an order for removal or deportation to be tested by the court on the usual administrative-law principles: illegality, irrationality, and procedural impropriety. It therefore has a wider reach than habeas corpus. Nevertheless, there is one general limitation: an applicant will not be given leave to apply for judicial review if there are other, more appropriate, channels open to him in seeking a remedy. Thus applicants will normally be expected to have made use of the appeal procedures, if they are available, before resorting to the courts.[148] The courts are a second line of defence.[149]

When judicial review is sought in relation to a decision to deport for the public good on national-security grounds, there is a special problem: the courts regard national-security judgments as the exclusive preserve of the executive, and will not quash an executive decision on such matters unless it is manifestly unsupported by proper reasons or evidence.[150] When an applicant is someone who would be an illegal entrant but is claiming asylum as a refugee, the judgment of the Secretary of State as to the reasonableness of the applicant's fear of persecution, and as to whether the applicant could be returned safely to a third country without well-founded fear of being

---

[145] *Khawaja*, above; *R. v. Secretary of State for the Home Dept., ex parte Momin Ali* [1984] 1 WLR 663, [1984] 1 All ER 1009, CA.

[146] *R. v. Secretary of State for the Home Dept., ex parte Cheblak* [1991] 1 WLR 890.

[147] Sharpe, *Habeas Corpus*, 122–3.

[148] *R. v. Secretary of State for the Home Dept., ex parte Swati* [1986] 1 WLR 477, [1986] 1 All ER 717, CA.

[149] *R. v. Secretary of State for the Home Dept., ex parte Cheblak* [1991] 1 WLR 890.

[150] *Council of Civil Service Unions v. Minister for the Civil Service* [1985] AC 374, [1984] 3 All ER 935, HL; *R. v. Secretary of State for Home Affairs, ex parte Hosenball* [1977] 1 WLR 766, [1977] 3 All ER 452, CA; *R. v. Secretary of State for the Home Dept., ex parte Cheblak* [1991] 1 WLR 890. Facts on which the decision is based must be proved on a balance of probabilities, while the policy decisions based on the facts are largely unreviewable: *Farakhan v. Secretary of State for the Home Dept.*, unreported, 1 October 2001, Admin. Ct.; *Secretary of State for the Home Dept. v. Rehman* [2001] 3 WLR 877, HL.

returned from there to the country where the risk of persecution exists, are political judgments given by Parliament exclusively to the Secretary of State, and these judgments likewise will not be questioned by the courts unless manifestly without foundation,[151] although the burgeoning understanding of the state's obligations under human rights law (both national and international) may call forth a more rigorous standard of review from the courts than has previously been seen. The Antiterrorism, Crime and Security Bill 2001 would entirely exclude judicial review from cases falling under the provisions of Part 4 (people certified as suspected international terrorists believed to threaten national security).

8.5 CONCLUSION

The risks to civil liberties which arise in the field of freedom of movement are not, on the whole, the result of a failure of English law to recognize a *prima facie* right to move freely. Generally speaking, people enjoy freedom of movement within the UK, and freedom to leave the UK. So far as immigration law is concerned, the right of states to control entry to their territories is well established in international law as an incident of sovereignty, and the terms on which entry is granted are part of the internal affairs of the state with which other states are not generally regarded as having a legitimate concern.

If this suggests that the law of migration and asylum in the UK is stable and principled, it gives a misleading impression. Immigration law is highly politicized, and shows signs of becoming more so. It is riven by tensions and contradictions. In this, it displays in microcosm the stresses afflicting the English law of civil liberties and human rights. The account given in this chapter reveals an interaction of systems of law and systems of administration. Immigration law has a politically-driven statutory framework, adjusted to the way public opinion seems to be blowing. At international level, there is a different legal framework under the ICCPR, the ECHR and the Refugee Convention. This is far less subject than domestic law to the roller-coaster of public opinion within any one state. It limits the freedom of governments to remove various classes of potential immigrants, and requires increasingly sophisticated judicial safeguards for the interests of people who have little or no voice in national political processes. Governments seek to ameliorate the effect of international requirements, for example by designating certain countries as safe for the purpose of deporting asylum seekers, or using Community law to establish standing arrangements with countries within the European Community for allocating responsibility to deal with asylum applications. Within the state, much of the normative structure

---

[151] *R. v. Secretary of State for the Home Department, ex parte Bugdaycay* [1987] AC 514, [1987] 1 All ER 940, HL, distinguishing *Khawaja* on the ground that the power of review in the latter case related to objective factual judgments as to the legality of entry, not to impressionistic judgments about conditions in other countries; *R. v. Secretary of State for the Home Department, ex parte Muboyayi* [1992] QB 244, [1991] 4 All ER 72, CA: Home Secretary's decision to return to France a Zairean claiming asylum not reviewable.

within which administrative discretion is exercised is provided by non-statutory rules. The Refugee Convention itself has a strangely amorphous presence in UK law; the ICCPR is rarely deployed; only the ECHR (or more accurately, most of the rights under it) now form part of municipal law directly.

The adjudicators, Tribunal, Commission, and courts are left to handle these bodies of rules, and to explain their inter-relationships. Judges have added a further level of norms through fundamental common law rights, including procedural rights which cannot be taken away except by clear words in primary legislation.[152] This produces strains between institutions and their respective responsibilities. For example, while the courts (international and national) have recently injected a measure of respect for due process into immigration matters, it remains to be seen whether the Special Immigration Appeals Commission can successfully provide the independent judicial scrutiny of decisions about what is conducive to the public good, as required by the European Court of Human Rights, or whether its work turns out to be hamstrung by the Court of Appeal's more conservative approach (particularly on national security matters) so that it becomes an institution which merely gives an appearance of legitimacy to uncontrolled administrative discretion. A complex dialogue is developing between the Home Secretary, Parliament, the adjudicators, the Tribunal, the Commission, the national courts, and the European Court of Human Rights. Maintaining checks and balances between them is a matter of high constitutional importance in a politically charged field. Their management of the task will be one of the measures of the success of the Human Rights Act 1998, particularly in the wake of the anti-terrorism legislation of late 2001.

---

[152] See, e.g. *R. v. Secretary of State for the Home Department, ex parte Saleem* [2001] 1 WLR 443, CA (statutory power to make Immigration Rules insufficiently precise to permit making of rules deeming notice of decisions to have been received, denying opportunity to make use of appeal procedures).

PART III

PRIVACY

9

THE SCOPE OF LEGAL PRIVACY

Part III as a whole examines aspects of privacy-related rights. This chapter surveys the geography of the subject. Starting with an introduction to the idea of privacy, it then looks at the way in which aspects of privacy developed, and the difficulties which flow from them. This will be illustrated, first, by reference to the development of privacy law in the USA, then by examining its substantial impact on international human rights law, and thirdly by sketching its more limited effect on English law. The chapter concludes with a brief reflection on the importance of privacy in legal analysis.

The three chapters which follow examine certain aspects of privacy law in England and Wales in more detail. Chapter 10 explains the legal protections against unreasonable entries, searches, seizures, and surveillance. Chapter 11 looks at the special position of confidential information, in relation to both the civil and the criminal justice systems. Chapter 12 deals with sexuality and the family, which are particularly sensitive aspects of personality and autonomy protected by privacy interests.

9.1 WHAT IS PRIVACY?[1]

(1) PRIVACY, INDIVIDUALISM, AND COMMUNITY

The desire for a private area in life is deeply rooted, and derives its justification from three sources. The first is the notion of personal autonomy, which (as we saw in Chapter 1) is a powerful element in the ideology of freedom. Although not strictly necessary to freedom of choice, privacy, in the sense of a protected field of decision-making within which an individual or a group of individuals is free from the meddling of outsiders, helps to produce the conditions in which freedom of choice can be exercised without interference. This is linked to the desire for defensible space, a physical area marked off in some way from other areas, to which a person, family, or group may withdraw and wherein they may protect themselves against all comers, unless entry is clearly justified by some supervening public interest.[2] The second

---

[1] For the philosophical background, see A. F. Westin, *Privacy and Freedom* (London: Bodley Head, 1967), and the excellent essays in J. R. Pennock and J. W. Chapman (eds), *Privacy: Nomos XIII* (New York: Atherton Press, 1971).

[2] The link between privacy, urban planning, domestic architecture, and design through western history is instructively explored in P. Ariès and G. Duby (General eds.), *A History of Private Life*, trans. A. Goldhammer, 5 vols. (Cambridge, Mass.: Harvard University Press, 1987–91).

element is the idea of utility: it is arguable that people operate most effectively and happily when they are allowed to make their own arrangements about domestic and business matters without interference from the state. This utilitarian argument also justifies extending privacy rights beyond the home and family, as many business relationships depend on maintaining privacy in the forms of confidentiality and freedom of contract. Thirdly, surveillance of individuals and the collection and use of personal information about them without their consent fails, in some degree, to respect their dignity and separateness, and what Professors Lustgarten and Leigh have called 'mental and emotional security':[3]

'Imagine being unable to draw the curtain in your bedroom, so that others can see you naked at any time of their choosing. The fear and revulsion this image evokes has little to do with the beauty or otherwise of one's body, but everything to do with one's sense of *self*. If I have no control over what is known about me, I am seriously diminished as a person both in my own eyes and in those which are capable of intruding upon me.'

It is no answer to a person suffering from 'existential insecurity'[4] to assert that they have nothing to fear if they have nothing to hide. We all have things we would rather not make accessible to others, from a sense of decency, dignity, or respect for intimacy. In short, some level of privacy is a necessary condition for human flourishing.

Such privacy rights are often said to be predominantly individualistic,[5] but they are better conceptualized as part of a balance between the interests of individuals, groups, and the state. They protect a sphere of action and decision-making for individuals against the power of the state, wielded in the public interest. Indeed, the notion of privacy arose, historically, before the emergence of the modern nation state, and so may constrain people's conception of the legitimate sphere of the state in social life.[6] Because they tend to restrict the activity of the state, privacy rights are politically controversial. Socialist, Marxist, and communitarian critics have characterized the public–private distinction as an ideology of classical liberalism, and have argued that the notion of the private sphere tends to place the individual outside society, minimizing the scope for the notion of social responsibility.[7] Claims to privacy can be used to prevent the state from taking action to force people to take responsibility for others, or organizing society for the benefit of the weakest groups. More recently, feminist legal theorists have suggested that, by regarding the family as pre-eminently a part of the private rather than the public sphere of social life, the state is discouraged from interfering to change the power structures within the family which systematically disadvantage women. They also argue that similar considerations are relevant to relations within the workplace, and in other social settings which are traditionally

---

[3] L. Lustgarten and I. Leigh, *In from the Cold: National Security and Parliamentary Democracy* (Oxford: Clarendon Press, 1994), 39–40 (emphasis in original).

[4] Ibid., 41.

[5] S. Lukes, *Individualism* (Oxford: Basil Blackwell, 1973).

[6] M. J. Horwitz, 'The History of the Public/Private Distinction' (1982) **130** *Univ. of Pennsylvania LR* 1423–8; G. Duby, 'Foreword to *A History of Private Life*', in P. Veyne (ed.), *A History of Private Life: I. From Pagan Rome to Byzantium* (trans. A. Goldhammer) (Cambridge, Mass.: Harvard University Press, 1987), viii.

[7] E. Kamenka, 'Public/Private in Marxist Theory and Marxist Practice', in S. I. Benn and G. Gaus (eds.), *Public and Private in Social Life* (London: Croom Helm and St. Martin's Press, 1983), 267 at 273–4.

regarded as governed by the private arrangements of participants rather than public interests.[8] It has been rightly observed that the idea of private family life effectively eradicated the rights of children, so that the effects of the UN Convention on the Rights of the Child are 'firstly to question the public/private dichotomy; secondly, and even more fundamentally, to disaggregate the rights of children from the rights of "families", to constitute children as independent actors with rights *vis-à-vis* their parents and *vis-à-vis* the state'.[9]

However, we must not underestimate the importance of privacy to maintaining a functioning community. Communitarians rightly emphasize the nature of society as a community of communities, of different sizes and with different purposes, but with overlapping memberships. Families, friends, and lovers; streets, estates and regions; schools, workplaces, and religious associations; political parties, tennis clubs, Rotary groups and masonic lodges, are just a few of the social structures and relationships through which people pursue their interests and provide social solidarity. Privacy allows these groups to form and function without undue interference. Without it, people would be inhibited in forming intimate relationships on which friendship and family life are based; indeed, it has been suggested that facilitating intimate relationships is the core of privacy.[10] There is no need to limit the core of privacy in this way: identifying with causes, indulging in play, and so on, are socially as well as individually worthwhile activities which privacy helps to make possible. Privacy is socially valuable.[11] There is thus a persuasive argument that privacy encapsulates values which should form a basic part of a liberal constitution, alongside others such as equality and freedom of expression.[12]

On the other hand, spheres of privacy may allow inequality and abuse to become entrenched. The notion of privacy must therefore not allow individuals or groups to displace entirely the interests of other individuals or groups (whether insiders or outsiders) or of society. Nothing in the idea of privacy dictates the extent of the private and the public spheres relative to each other, or the balance of power between members of a private group. That is a matter for social decision-making according to political principles. A willingness to argue about it is an essential part of the practical politics of liberalism.[13] The argument is reflected in economics in debates about the proper extent (if any) of state ownership or state regulation in the management of an economy. In morality, it is reflected in debates about the extent to which people should be free to pursue their sexual preferences, considered in Chapter 12 below, or to control their bodies, a matter examined in the context of abortion and medical procedures in Chapters 4 and 5 above. In law, it shows up in debates within private

[8] See, e.g. K. O'Donovan, *Sexual Divisions in Law* (London: Weidenfeld and Nicolson, 1985), esp. at 12–19; S. Fredman, *Women and the Law* (Oxford: Clarendon Press, 1997), esp. at 44–58, 413–6.
[9] B. Cass, 'The Limits of the Public/Private Dichotomy: A Comment on Coady and Coady', in P. Alston, S. Palmer, and J. Seymour (eds.), *Children, Rights and the Law* (Oxford: Clarendon Press, 1992), 140–7 at 142.
[10] J. C. Inness, *Privacy, Intimacy, and Isolation* (Oxford: Oxford University Press, 1992), ch. 6.
[11] See D. Feldman, 'Privacy-related Rights and their Social Value', in P. Birks (ed.), *Privacy and Loyalty* (Oxford: Clarendon Press, 1997), ch. 2, at 16–28.
[12] See E. Barendt, 'Privacy as a Constitutional Right and Value', in Birks (ed.), *Privacy and Loyalty*, ch. 1.
[13] Lukes, *Individualism*, 62.

law, for example on the scope of freedom of contract[14] or the law of private nuisance, and in public law in disagreements over whether or not a separate and exclusive procedure is needed for public-law matters.

The public and private spheres necessarily interact. They are not mutually exclusive: an area of activity or piece of information may be in the public domain for some purposes yet remain subject to protection for privacy interests for other purposes.[14a] Understanding the separateness of individuals and the cohesiveness of social groups, to which the idea of privacy is central, is an important reason for choosing a method for making social decisions which gives weight to the preferences or interests of each person, whether on the basis of a democratic system giving equal weight to the vote of each adult citizen or through the mediation of some form of utilitarian calculation.[15]

Individual or group privacy and social action are, therefore, constantly interacting, and the tension between them is a dynamic one which each society in each period resolves by producing a balance, albeit one which is temporary and unstable. Three factors tend to limit the extent of the protected sphere of privacy. The first is the responsibility which the state adopts for the welfare of its citizens. This has both a public-interest aspect and an individual-rights aspect. Public service provision is an example of the public interest aspect. The people responsible for planning public services, such as health, housing, and education, require information, often personal and sensitive information, about everyone in the community, to enable them to forecast how many people will be needing their services over a period, and what kind of services are likely to be most in demand. This information has to be obtained by means which, to a greater or lesser extent, interfere with people's privacy: censuses, access to records held by other parts of the government machine, questionnaires, health records, and other means. The other side of the state's responsibilities is the role which it has in upholding individual rights, and protecting the welfare of those who are in too weak a position to look after their own interests. In the privacy field, child-care law provides a good example of this: it may be necessary to interfere with a parent's privacy rights in order to protect the rights of children to be free from abuse.

The second factor is the need (if such is accepted) for regulation. Bodies such as Oftel (regulating the telecommunications industry), the Financial Services Authority (with responsibility for the financial services industry), and the governing bodies of professions, such as the Law Society, need information in order to be able to regulate the members of their professions and protect the interests of consumers of services. Investigative and regulatory agencies, set up for the welfare of the public, need to obtain information about the people and business undertakings which are being

[14] For a stimulating discussion, see H. Collins, 'The Decline of Privacy in Private Law' (1987) 14 *J. of Law and Soc.* 91–103.

[14a] For an argument that private and public are not mutually exclusive categories, so that there can be good privacy-related arguments for prohibiting the re-publication of facts which are or have in the past been in the public domain, see E. Paton-Simpson, 'Private Circles and Public Squares: Invasion of Privacy by the Publication of Private Facts' (1998) 61 *MLR* 318–40.

[15] Westin, *Privacy and Freedom*, 33; Lukes, *Individualism*, ch. 9.

investigated and regulated, and this can sometimes justify considerable inroads into the principle of privacy. Invoking the legal process, to remedy an injury or contest a claim, itself involves a loss of privacy.

Thirdly, the public interest in freedom of information may impose limits on the right to privacy. For example, people who wish to carry out construction work on their private land may well need consent for the development from their planning authority. For this, they will need to submit a proposal and plans which will be available for inspection by anyone interested enough to visit the local town hall to see what is being proposed. This entails a restriction of the right to privacy, which is justified by the public interest in making planning decisions on an informed basis in the light of consultation with concerned members of the community. Again, we will see in Chapter 11 below that the legal remedies available to restrain a breach of confidence will not be granted if the defendant can show that publication of the information would be in the public interest, for example by disclosing a possible miscarriage of justice. In these areas, the privacy interest falls to be balanced against the achievement of social objectives in the wider public interest.

This might seem to leave privacy rights in a relatively weak position. They are protected only so far as they are compatible with public interests. This is reflected in the structure of ECHR Article 8, discussed in section 9.3 below: a public authority may interfere with the right to respect for private and family life, home and cor- respondence for a number of legitimate social purposes, as long as the interference satisfies conditions of legal certainty, necessity, and proportionality. The feature of privacy which gives it special status as a human right, rather than merely one among many competing public interests, is its close connection with the ideas of dignity and autonomy. This is why the state may interfere with privacy-related rights, but must rigorously justify doing so.

(2) POSITIVE AND NEGATIVE ASPECTS OF PRIVACY RIGHTS

Autonomy-related rights have both a negative and a positive aspect, as described in Chapter 1. The negative aspect is freedom from intrusion, the right to be let alone, which Dean William Prosser identified as the core sense of privacy.[16] The positive aspects are more elusive and controversial. First, there is a duty on the state and other individuals to foster the conditions in which privacy can be enjoyed. There are, for example, limits to the extent to which a person can realistically expect to enjoy privacy if the only accommodation available to her is a box in a shop doorway on the streets of London or Bristol. Secondly, alongside a right to protect oneself against intrusion in one's private affairs, there may be a right to have access to information held about one, by government or private bodies, which is sensitive and may affect one's ability to give effect to an autonomous decision, or to protect oneself against a medical or environmental threat. For instance, my privacy interests may be infringed if my doc- tor decides not to reveal the nature of my medical condition, as this may prevent me from exercising my freedom of choice as regards career, treatment, or marriage, in a

---

[16] W. L. Prosser, 'Privacy' (1960) **48** *Calif. LR* 383–423, and the discussion in section 9.2, below.

properly informed way. Where a choice is fully informed, a person's ability to give effect to it may be affected without their knowledge if somebody else makes available to potential employers, banks, or insurers, personal information which is misleading or wrong, without giving them an opportunity to correct the record. Thirdly, where there are circumstances in which it is justifiable to interfere with a person's privacy, the strength of the interest in privacy may demand the imposition of special procedures before an interference can take place in any individual case, or require specific considerations to be taken into account in decision-making, such as the desirability of working to reunite families as quickly as possible if it has been necessary to take a child into care.

The way in which these aspects of privacy develop, and the difficulties which flow from them, can be illustrated by an examination, first, of the development of privacy law in the USA, and then of its substantial impact on international law.

9.2 THE DEVELOPMENT OF PRIVACY AS A LEGAL VALUE:

US CASE STUDY

The process by which privacy came to articulated as a central legal value in common law systems took its first great leap forward in the USA. In 1888, the great judge and legal writer Thomas Cooley argued that there was a 'right to be let alone' which might be the essence of privacy.[17] He derived the right largely from English decisions on consent to medical treatment and related matters, but he argued that they could provide a basis for legal remedies for interference with a range of non-physical interests, including reputation and dignity. Three years later, the idea of a 'right to be let alone' was taken up by Gray J in the US Supreme Court.[18] In the meantime, there had appeared an article by Warren and Brandeis[19] which has a better claim than most to be described as 'seminal'. Like Cooley, the authors argued inductively from a number of English cases, but concentrated on confidentiality and property rights rather than cases on physical integrity. Warren and Brandeis argued that underpinning property protections and the equitable rules on confidentiality was a deeper unifying principle, namely the protection of privacy against modern technological and commercial developments.[20] After a slow start, the privacy principle, which, Warren and Brandeis

---

[17] T. Cooley, *A Treatise on the Law of Torts*, 2nd edn. (Chicago: Callaghan and Co., 1888), 29.

[18] *Union Pacific Railway Co. v. Botsford* 141 US 250 at 251 (1891).

[19] S. D. Warren and L. D. Brandeis, 'The Right to Privacy' 4 *Harv. LR* 193–220 (1890).

[20] Warren and Brandeis relied heavily on *Prince Albert v. Strange* (1848) 2 De G. & Sm. 652, where Knight Bruce V-C had granted an injunction restraining the defendant from publishing etchings made by Queen Victoria and the Prince Consort of their family life. The Vice-Chancellor regarded the proposed publication, without consent, as an invasion of the plaintiff's rights of property and his privacy and home life. For evaluation and criticism of the reasoning of Warren and Brandeis, on which there is a huge literature, see e.g. Prosser, 'Privacy' 48 *Calif. LR* 383–423 (1960), a hugely influential article in its own right; L. Brittan, 'The Right of Privacy in England and the United States' 37 *Tulane LR* 235–68 (1963), which examines the patchy response of English law to the challenge of privacy, and discusses Lord Mancroft's Right of Privacy Bill, introduced to the House of Lords in March 1961 but later dropped in the face of government opposition;

argued, was immanent in the common law, came to exercise a powerful influence in the USA.

Much of the early development was directed to protecting privacy interests against unauthorized commercial exploitation. After the New York Court of Appeals, by a majority, had rejected a claim by a woman whose picture had been used, without her consent, in a flour advertisement, a public outcry led to a New York statute which gave protection against having one's name or image appropriated without written consent for the purposes of advertising or trade.[21] Subsequently, courts outside New York recognized a tort of interference with privacy at common law. In fact, American tort lawyers regarded privacy as a group of four torts, protecting different sorts of interests: (i) intrusion on seclusion, solitude, or private affairs, the classical 'right to be left alone', particularly by the press, which had particularly exercised Warren and Brandeis and which violates interests in property, reputation and feelings; (ii) publication of embarrassing private facts about the plaintiff, violating reputation and feelings; (iii) publicity which places the plaintiff in a false light in the public eye, which is a form of injury to feelings, reputation, honour, and dignity, and may also cause economic loss, combining elements of defamation and injurious falsehood but going further than either; (iv) appropriating the plaintiff's name or likeness for the defendant's advantage, which covers the commercial exploitation cases in which the tort was first applied.[22] This four part categorization was adopted in the *Restatement of the Law of Torts*, paragraph 867.

Subsequently, privacy came to be regarded as a constitutional right. The process by which this came about is somewhat complex. Privacy is nowhere mentioned in the text of the US Constitution. Nevertheless, the courts have been able to find an implied right of privacy. The Fourth Amendment provides: 'The right of the people to be secure in their persons, houses, papers, and effects, against unreasonable searches and seizures, shall not be violated . . . '. The First Amendment, preventing Congress from making any law respecting an establishment of religion, or prohibiting the free exercise thereof, or abridging the right of the people peaceably to assemble, has been interpreted as protecting autonomy rights (including, by implication, freedom of association) which are central to individual autonomy aspects of privacy. Privacy has been treated as one of the liberties protected by due process requirements, despite not being enumerated in the Constitution. The Ninth Amendment provides: 'The enumeration in the Constitution, of certain rights, shall not be construed to deny or disparage others retained by the people'. These retained rights are held to include privacy rights, which are then within Fifth and Fourteenth Amendment due process

---

E. J. Bloustein, 'Privacy as an Aspect of Human Dignity: An Answer to Dean Prosser' (1964) **39** *New York Univ. LR* 962–1007; H. Kalven, 'Privacy in Tort Law: Were Warren and Brandeis Wrong?' (1966) **31** *Law and Contemp. Problems* 326; W. F. Pratt, 'The Warren and Brandeis Argument for a Right to Privacy' [1975] *PL* 161–79; R. Wacks, *Personal Information: Privacy and the Law* (Oxford: Clarendon Press, 1989), 31–9.

[21] *Robertson v. Rochester Folding Box Co.* 171 NY 538, 64 NE 442 (1902); New York Sess. Laws, 1903, c. 132, ss. 1–2.

[22] This is based on Prosser, 'Privacy' 48 *Calif. LR* at 389. See further, T. Gibbons, Personality Rights: The Limits of Personal Accountability, (1997/8) **3** *Yearbook of Media and Entertainment Law* 53–74.

guarantees. The Fifth Amendment provides that no person shall 'be deprived of life, liberty, or property, without due-process of law', and Section 1 of the Fourteenth Amendment extends the due-process protection so that it operates against the states as well as the Federal authorities.

Out of all this, judges constructed a constitutional right to privacy. In *Griswold v. Connecticut*[23] Douglas J, writing for the US Supreme Court, argued that the core cases of privacy under the First, Third, Fourth, Fifth, and Ninth Amendments were surrounded by 'penumbras' and 'emanations', fading gradually away from the core cases, in which privacy rights could be shown to be consistent with the core values. The potential scope of the emanations of privacy are uncertain, and the reasoning is controversial. In particular, judges and scholars who hold that judges should not create new rights by embellishing the constitutional text disapprove of reasoning which leaves judges free to give the due process clause in the Fourteenth Amendment a controversial substantive content in line with their personal opinions; while those who believe that the proper way of interpreting the Constitution is to ask what its framers thought they meant by particular provisions, rather than to develop its concepts in line with changing social conditions, argue that the framers would not have recognized many of the interests which fall within the modern reach of privacy. In *Griswold*, therefore, Goldberg J, joined by Warren CJ and Brennan J, relied squarely on the Ninth Amendment, but this reasoning is little more helpful, as it is hard to identify with any certainty the content of the unenumerated, retained rights which it protects.[24]

Despite these doubts, the constitutional right to privacy has been remarkably durable, albeit of uncertain extent. Unlike the right to privacy in tort, the constitutional right is soundly based in the right to make decisions about the conduct of one's own life, within the sphere of personal autonomy. The right of parents to decide what their children should study and where they should be educated was vindicated in two early cases.[25] The Supreme Court called up echoes of the assertion in the Declaration of Independence of the rights to life, liberty, and the pursuit of happiness, arguing that the Constitution protected the rights:

'to contract, to engage in any of the common occupations of life, to acquire useful knowledge, to marry, to establish a home and bring up children, to worship God according to the dictates of his own conscience, and generally to enjoy those privileges long recognized at common law as essential to the orderly pursuit of happiness to free men.'[26]

The interest at the root of the constitutional protection for privacy, therefore, is personal autonomy. In the constitutional sphere, the issue is the extent to which the individual should be protected against interference from public authorities, and the

---

[23] 381 US 479 (1965).

[24] For discussion of such reasoning, see extracts from 'Nomination of Robert H. Bork to be Associate Justice of the Supreme Court of the United States', hearings before the Senate Committee of the Judiciary, 100th Cong., 1st sess. 114–21, 149–51, 240–2 (1st of 5 parts), 1987, as reproduced in L. Fisher, *American Constitutional Law* (New York: McGraw-Hill, 1990), 1226–32.

[25] *Meyer v. Nebraska* 262 US 390 (1923); *Pierce v. Society of Sisters* 268 US 510 (1925).

[26] *Meyer v. Nebraska* 262 US 390 (1923) at 399.

core meaning of privacy is 'the right to be let alone—the most comprehensive of rights and the right most valued by civilized men'.[27] The focus is different from, and in some ways narrower than, that of the private right which developed in tort, yet it has proved to be remarkably extensive in its own sphere.

Privacy rights have been held to underlie the Fourth Amendment,[28] so that one of the tests for an unreasonable search and seizure is whether the public authority has violated the victim's legitimate interest in privacy. This has been used to justify more restricted Fourth Amendment rights in respect of automobiles and mobile homes than in respect of homes and offices.[29] Privacy in one's associations with others was the basis for holding that the First Amendment right of peaceable assembly has a penumbra which extends constitutional protection to the freedom of political, social, and economic association more generally. This freedom was unconstitutionally interfered with when the state attempted to compel organizations to disclose their membership lists.[30] The right to privacy, this time in respect of marital relationships, justified holding unconstitutional a state statute which made it an offence for a married couple to employ contraceptives.[31]

Most famously, and most controversially, in *Roe v. Wade*[32] the right to privacy was recognized as creating a realm of protection for the autonomy of women in respect of their bodies. This restricted the grounds on which the state was entitled to intervene in the progress or termination of pregnancy. Yet if *Roe v. Wade* and its progeny made a powerful demonstration of the power of privacy, they also illustrated its limitations. The majority in the Supreme Court accepted that the woman's privacy rights were not absolute. They had to be set against the state's legitimate interest in preserving the life and health of both the woman and the child. To that end, the state might legitimately legislate to regulate abortions, but the interests served would change as the pregnancy progressed. Regulation to protect the interests of the unborn child was legitimate from the time of viability, i.e. the moment when the child became capable of an existence independent of the mother, around the beginning of the third trimester of pregnancy. Before that, the state may intervene only to protect the life and health of the mother. Statistical evidence suggested that the risks to the mother of termination in the first trimester were no greater than the risks of childbirth, so the decision on abortion there was to be left to the mother and her medical advisers. In the intervening period (i.e. roughly in the second trimester) the state could regulate abortions only to minimize the risk to the mother, in effect acting paternalistically to

[27] *Olmstead v. US*, 277 US 438 (1928) at 478, *per* Brandeis J, one of the authors of the seminal article, and by this time a Justice of the Supreme Court. In this case, he was dissenting from a majority decision that telephone tapping did not violate the Fourth Amendment to the Constitution, because the tap involved no trespass. *Olmstead* was later overruled in *Katz v. US* (1967) 389 US 347.

[28] *Boyd v. US* 116 US 616 (1886) at 630; *Mapp v. Ohio* 367 US 643 (1961) at 656.

[29] *California v. Carney* 471 US 386 (1985); *New York v. Class* 475 US 106 (1986). This has replaced an earlier rationale for allowing warrantless searches of automobiles, based on the risk that they might be driven away and be out of the state before a warrant could be obtained: *Carroll v. US* 267 US 132 (1925). But *cp.* *Minnesota v. Carter*, 525 US 83 (1998).

[30] *NAACP v. Alabama* 357 US 449 (1958); *NAACP v. Button* 371 US 415 (1963).

[31] *Griswold v. Connecticut* 381 US 479 (1965).

[32] 410 US 113 (1973).

avoid her privacy rights being exercised in a way which unnecessarily endangered her.

The dissenters in *Roe v. Wade* noted that the Fourteenth Amendment protected privacy rights not absolutely, but only against infringement without due process of law. This would point towards a rationality test for constitutionality: does the impugned law have a rational relationship to a legitimate state objective? They argued that allowing a legislature to weigh the respective interests of women and unborn children was within such a relationship. It was, they argued, improper for the court, under the colour of the due-process clause, to impose its own weighting of the competing priorities on the people and legislatures of the states without any clear constitutional foundation.

These arguments gained ground as the Supreme Court became more conservative under the influence of appointments to the Bench by Presidents Ronald Reagan and George Bush. The court held that the positive obligations on the state, arising from the privacy-based abortion rights of the mother, are restricted. In particular, states are under no obligation to make public funds or services available to people for non-therapeutic abortions. The court has also moved away from the trimester-by-trimester growth in the state's legitimate interest in protecting first the mother, and later the fetus. States are now regarded as having an interest in life at all stages of pregnancy, and are in principle entitled to make a value judgment that favours child-birth over abortion, so long as they do not interfere with the mother's liberty without due process of law.[33] The majority of the court in *Webster v. Reproductive Health Services* refused to review *Roe v. Wade*, but relegated the mother's right from a fundamental constitutional right to an abortion (at least in the first trimester) to a liberty protected by due-process requirements. Accordingly, they did not find it necessary to provide any criteria for determining the extent of this state interest at different times, so it is up to the states to provide legislative frameworks which take adequate account of the various interests involved.

It was widely expected that conservative forces would triumph and the decision in *Roe v. Wade* would be overruled when the Supreme Court was forced to address the central issue of the woman's constitutional right to an abortion. The moment of truth came in *Planned Parenthood of South-Eastern Pennsylvania and others v. Casey and others*.[34] The court had to rule on the constitutionality of the Pennsylvania Abortion Control Act of 1982. The petitioners challenged requirements that the woman should give informed consent, and be provided with information at least twenty-four hours before the procedure, that she should give notice to her husband if she is married, and if a minor should normally have parental consent. There were exceptions for medical emergencies. In a decision with which few people on either side were entirely happy, the central holding in *Roe* survived, but not unscathed. Remarkably, three Republican appointees, O'Connor, Kennedy, and Souter JJ, decided that they could not reconcile the overruling of *Roe* with their respect for the doctrine of precedent. They decided that the constitutional guarantee of liberty defined in *Roe* had not proved unworkable,

---

[33] *Webster v. Reproductive Health Services* 109 S. Ct. 3040 (1989).
[34] 112 S. Ct. 2791, 120 L.Ed. 2d 674 (1992).

and that neither social facts, legal principles, nor scientific knowledge had altered since 1973 in ways which compelled them to reverse the earlier decision.[35] The undue burden test, as developed by Justice O'Connor in *Webster*, was to provide the criterion of due process against which restrictions on pre-viability terminations would be judged.

The three central Justices were supported by Stevens J, in holding that the only requirement of the Pennsylvania statute which constituted an undue burden was the requirement of spousal notice, and by Stevens and Blackmun JJ in refusing to overrule *Roe v. Wade*. However, Justice Blackmun, while praising the three for 'an act of personal courage and constitutional principle', criticized them for qualifying the right of women to decide on an abortion without state interference by permitting burdens on the exercise of the right as long as they are not undue burdens. He clearly feared that this left the door open to further restrictions on privacy rights by the court. Rehnquist CJ, and White, Scalia, and Thomas JJ, dissented, arguing that neither the right to an abortion nor the undue burden test had any foundation in the language of the Constitution. In any case, they argued, the right to an abortion could not be described as fundamental, since its regulation had long been acceptable to society. State legislation restricting abortion should be regarded as unconstitutional only if not rationally related to a legitimate state objective.

This represented a draw in the fight over abortion rights. The provisions of the Pennsylvania statute were upheld, except the requirement for notice to be given to the husband. It would now be difficult for the court to depart from the view that there is a constitutional right to privacy which protects against undue interference a woman's decision to terminate her pregnancy. Nevertheless, for the moment it seems that constitutional privacy protection, if not actually on the retreat, is unlikely to be extended dynamically into new fields, and its basis and implications remain highly controversial.

This concern about the derivation and scope of constitutional privacy rights has grown into a major political, as well as legal, dispute in the USA. A gradual restriction of the privacy right, and extension of the powers of legislatures, in recent Supreme Court decisions, has moved alongside changes in support for political factions. During the 1980s, American conservatives gained the ascendancy over liberals; pro-life groups made headway at the expense of pro-choice groups; evangelical religious fundamentalism advanced against 1960s humanism; and judicial activism retreated in the face of the changes.[36] One aspect of the growth of religious and constitutional fundamentalism—both characterized by a largely uncritical commitment to a sacred text—was that the focus of constitutional inquiries changed. Instead of asking questions about the legitimate range of underlying rights, such as privacy, in a Constitution committed to individual freedom, the new conservative judges asked questions about surface rights, such as whether the Constitution entrenches a

[35] As Barendt, 'Privacy as a Constitutional Right and Value' at 9, points out, O'Connor J's opinion is couched entirely in terms of liberty, and does not mention privacy at all.

[36] See the essays in M. L. Goggin (ed.), *Understanding the New Politics of Abortion* (Newbury Park, Cal.: SAGE Publications, 1993).

fundamental right to carry on the particular activity under consideration. Any right which is not apparent in the Constitution became, at best, a liberty to be protected only by the partial shield of due process.

This change of emphasis can be observed in *Bowers v. Hardwick*.[37] Hardwick, a practising homosexual adult, challenged the constitutionality of a Georgia statute under which he had been charged with sodomy with another adult male in the bedroom of his house. The majority of the Supreme Court held that the statute did not infringe his constitutional rights. They declined to extend the right to privacy so as to give constitutional due-process protection to a right to commit sodomy. Freedom to commit sodomy was not of the same character as other freedoms traditionally protected by the constitutional right to privacy (marriage, contraception, abortion, procreation, family relationships, child-rearing, and education). Nor was it within the range of those fundamental liberties which had been implied into the Constitution because they were deeply rooted in the nation's history and traditions, or necessary for ordered liberty and justice.[38] The liberty fell within the protection of the rationality requirement, under the due-process clause, but the rationality test was satisfied, as there is nothing irrational about making laws which are based on moral judgments. The court would be slow to give too substantial a content to the due-process clause, in the absence of clear constitutional justification.

In other words, the majority saw the case as raising the spectre of a fundamental right to engage in homosexual activity, and retreated from it, taking refuge behind the legislative authority of the state and its people. Dissenting, Blackmun J, joined by Brennan, Marshall, and Stevens JJ, argued that the case was in reality about a deeper issue, the right to be let alone. The level of generality at which an issue is conceptualized fundamentally affects the nature and scope of the resulting right, particularly where the rights in question are not expressly stated in the Constitution.

Between 1993 and 2001, President Clinton's administration presided over a partial resurgence of liberalism, but that seems likely to be swiftly reversed by the Southern conservatism of President George W. Bush from 2001. In US constitutional law, the scope and derivation of the right to privacy remain a fragile product of controversial judicial glosses on the constitutional text.

This introduction to privacy theory, and its emanation in US constitutional law, suggests three questions with which the remainder of this chapter, and Chapters 10 to 12 below, are concerned. First, how is the right to privacy to be formulated, and what is its scope in international human rights law and in English law? Secondly, what is the scope of protection for the negative aspects of rights? Thirdly, what is the scope of the positive rights implied by a right to privacy?

---

[37] 478 US 186 (1986).
[38] See *Moore v. East Cleveland* 431 US 494 (1977) at 503 (Powell J).

9.3 PRIVACY IN INTERNATIONAL LAW AND UNDER THE HUMAN RIGHTS ACT 1998[39]

(1) THE FORMULATION OF THE RIGHT: POSITIVE AND NEGATIVE OBLIGATIONS

Most international human rights instruments today recognize a right to privacy in one form or another. There is, however, an interesting contrast between the formulation of this right under the various instruments to which the UK is a party. The International Covenant on Civil and Political Rights (ICCPR) provides in Article 17:

'(1)   No one shall be subjected to arbitrary or unlawful interference with his privacy, family, home or correspondence, nor to unlawful attacks on his honour and reputation.

(2)   Everyone has the right to the protection of the law against such interference or attacks.'

This is identical to Article 12 of the Universal Declaration of Human Rights, save that the latter does not divide the Article into two paragraphs. Children are given rights in similar terms under Article 16 of the UN Convention on the Rights of the Child, which the UK ratified in 1991.

Several points about the formulation merit attention. It starts with a negative right: freedom from *arbitrary or unlawful* interference with the interests enumerated. Interference with privacy, family, home, and correspondence can be justified if not arbitrary or unlawful. This limited negative right is coupled with a positive right: the state must ensure that the law protects people against arbitrary and unlawful interference with those interests. The interests themselves are not defined, and privacy in particular is a difficult interest to delimit, particularly as a non-arbitrary interference is justifiable. Does a right to privacy encompass a right to perform in private acts which outrage prevailing ideas of decency? Would criminalizing such acts in order to reinforce popular views on morality or decency be regarded as arbitrary, or would it be justifiable? There is no answer to these questions within the ICCPR. It is clear, however, from the inclusion of the right to be free of unlawful attacks on honour and reputation in Article 17 of ICCPR that the Article is intended to protect human dignity, and that this is the foundation for the rights under the Article rather than serving democracy or any of the other basic values which have been postulated as grounding privacy rights.

The position under Article 8 of the European Convention on Human Rights (ECHR), which now forms part of national law in the UK under section 1 of, and Schedule 1 to, the Human Rights Act 1998, is somewhat different. Article 8 provides:

'(1)   Everyone has the right to respect for his private and family life, his home and his correspondence.

(2)   There shall be no interference by a public authority with the exercise of this right except such as is in accordance with the law and is necessary in a democratic society in the

---

[39] See J. Michael, *Privacy and Human Rights* (Paris: Dartmouth and UNESCO, 1994), *passim*.

interests of national security, public safety or the economic well-being of the country, for the prevention of disorder or crime, for the protection of health or morals, or for the protection of the rights and freedoms of others.'

The rights conferred by this provision are both more extensive and more clearly drawn than those under Article 17 of ICCPR. The formulation of Article 8(1) does not speak of privacy, but of private and family life, although this difference may be insubstantial. More significantly, it does not link the rights which it confers to honour or reputation. Article 8 is about doing and living, not about maintaining dignity for its own sake. The rights conferred by Article 8(1) are subject only to the tightly drawn exceptions authorized by Article 8(2) which specify the grounds on which public authorities may justify interference in pursuance of a defined set of public-interest objectives.

Most important of all, the ECHR is unique among international human rights instruments in the way in which rights are conceived in relation to private life. Instead of giving a right to be free of arbitrary or unlawful interference[40] with privacy, Article 8 provides for a right to respect for everyone's private and family life, home, and correspondence. This movement from a right to freedom from interference with privacy to a right to respect for it might seem to weaken the right, as there may be circumstances in which it could be argued that interfering with a person's privacy would not indicate any lack of respect. Examples would be interfering with privacy paternalistically, to protect the individual against further loss of autonomy resulting from untreated illness, deficient family management, or poor child-rearing practices. Sir James Fawcett, speaking of the *travaux préparatoires*, noted that:

'What began in the Teitgen proposals as "inviolability", and became "immunity from arbitrary interference", then protection from governmental interference (*immixtions gouvernementales*), ended tamely as "respect". These changes may in part reflect various opinions, expressed in the Consultative Assembly but overruled, that "in these cases [under Article 8] no rights regarded as essential for the function of the democratic institutions were at stake".'[41]

This potential limitation on the negative (freedom from interference) aspects of the right to privacy should not blind us to the considerable extension of the right which the notion of respect may entail, and which has been influential in the caselaw of the Court on Article 8. As observed in Chapter 8, respect for correspondence was held to

---

[40] Thus the Universal Declaration, Art. 12, the ICCPR, Art. 17, and the UN Convention on the Rights of the Child, Art. 16. The American Convention on Human Rights, Art. 11(2), forbids 'arbitrary or abusive interference' with anyone's 'private life, hisfamily, his home, or his correspondence . . . '. The American Declaration of the Rights and Duties of Man confers on every person the rights (*inter alia*) to protection of the law against abusive attacks upon his private and family life (Art. V), to the inviolability of his home (Art. IX), and to the inviolability and transmission of his correspondence (Art. X). The African Charter on Human and Peoples' Rights does not confer a right to private or family life, although Art. 29 imposes duties on every individual to 'preserve the harmonious development of the family and to work for the cohesion and respect of the family; to respect his parents at all times, to maintain them in case of need'.

[41] J. E. S. Fawcett, *The Application of the European Convention on Human Rights*, 2nd edn. (Oxford: Clarendon Press, 1987), 211 (footnotes omitted). The significance of a protected sphere of privacy for democracy was mentioned in section 8.1 above.

limit significantly the power of prison authorities to interfere with prisoners' letters. Respect for private life has also generated protection against telephone interception, and forced the UK to prevent a telephone undertaker from releasing information to the police about numbers dialled by a subscriber, without legal authority or the subscriber's knowledge or consent.[42] Furthermore, a right to respect is capable of imposing positive duties on public authorities, because it can be interpreted as requiring them to take active measures to enable people to have a private and family life, going beyond providing remedies for interference.[43]

The European Court of Human Rights has regularly affirmed that positive obligations on the state arise from Article 8. These include framing the law in such a way that people are not inhibited in choosing a mode of private life; ensuring that appropriate *de facto*, as well as *de iure*, family relationships are possible and protected; making available suitable remedies for people whose private or family life is interfered with; and allowing people access to information[44] about their early lives, threats to their health, and decisions taken concerning them. The nature of these positive obligations has been worked out from case to case in a way which is sensitive to the contexts in which cases arise and which many common lawyers will find attractive. The guiding principle was first expounded in *Marckx v. Belgium*,[45] concerning the treatment of children born out of wedlock under Belgian law, where the Court stated that Article 8 does not merely compel the state to abstain from arbitrary interference with family life:

'... in addition to this primarily negative undertaking, there may be positive obligations inherent in an effective "respect" for family life. This means amongst other things, that when the state determines in its domestic legal system the regime applicable to certain family ties such as those between an unmarried mother and her child, it must act in a manner calculated to allow those concerned to lead a normal family life. As envisaged by Article 8, respect for family life implies in particular, in the Court's view, the existence in domestic law of legal safeguards that render possible as from the moment of birth the child's integration into his family.'

The Court there unanimously accepted that Article 8 imposed positive as well as negative obligations, although some judges dissented as to the nature and scope of those obligations in the context of the legal regime affecting family relationships and their concomitant rights, powers, obligations, and responsibilities. In subsequent cases, the positive obligations have been developed in the context of child-care decisions which affect the family. In a series of cases concerning the procedures for removing children from their parents under the English law which existed before the Children Act 1989 came into force, the Court held that the state has a positive

---

[42] *Malone v. United Kingdom*, Eur. Ct. HR, Series A, No. 82, Judgment of 2 August 1984, 7 EHRR 14.

[43] See D. Feldman, 'The Developing Scope of Article 8 of the European Convention on Human Rights' [1997] *EHRLR* 265–74.

[44] See D. Feldman, 'Information and Privacy', in J. Beatson and Y. Cripps (eds.), *Freedom of Expression and Freedom of Information: Essays in Honour of Sir David Williams* (Oxford: Oxford University Press, 2000), 299–324.

[45] Eur. Ct. HR, Series A, No. 31, Judgment of 13 June 1979, 2 EHRR 330, at para. 31.

obligation to ensure that parents are involved in the process of decision-making at least to the extent necessary to provide the requisite protection for their interests under Article 8(1). English law failed to provide for such involvement.[46] This was one of the factors which led to the enactment of a revised set of child-care procedures in the 1989 Act, discussed in Chapter 12 below.

There may also be an obligation on the state to provide legal protection for people by imposing criminal liability on those who gravely interfere with their private lives. In *X. and Y. v. Netherlands*[47] the Court held that the Netherlands had failed to respect the private life of a mentally handicapped teenager who had been forced to have sexual intercourse by the son-in-law of the governor of the home in which she was a resident. The man's behaviour did not constitute rape under Dutch law, and the offence of abusing a dominant position so as to cause a minor to commit an indecent act could be prosecuted only on a complaint laid by the victim. Because of her mental condition, the girl was not competent to lay a complaint. This lacuna in the criminal law was held to be a failure to respect the girl's private life, because in such situations only the criminal law could provide deterrent effect adequate to protect her.

Finally, the right to respect for private and family life has been held to impose an obligation in some circumstances to make available to a person information relating to himself, his private affairs, or environmental matters which affect him, held by a public authority.[48]

The idea that rights under the Convention may carry with them positive obligations on the state beyond anything expressly stated in the text of the Convention has also been applied to other Articles of the ECHR, where the obligations are necessarily incidental to the rights in question and are required in order to permit effective access to procedures for giving effect to the right. For example, the right to have civil rights and obligations determined by an independent and impartial tribunal after a fair and public hearing, under Article 6, has been held to impose on the state an obligation to make available effective access to a court or tribunal, and provide legal aid to the person who alleges an infringement of civil rights. In *Golder v. United Kingdom*,[49] the Court held by a majority that Article 6(1) implied a right of access to a tribunal, and that interfering with correspondence between a prisoner and his solicitor in connection with contemplated legal proceedings breached that right. In *Airey v. Ireland*,[50] a majority of the Court held that the right to have access to a hearing when applying for a judicial separation could be made effective only if appropriate legal assistance was provided by the state, and that refusal of legal aid therefore breached a positive obligation arising out of Article 6(1).

---

[46] *W. v. United Kingdom*, Eur. Ct. HR, Series A, No. 121, Judgment of 8 July 1987, 10 EHRR 29.

[47] Eur. Ct. HR, Series A, No. 91, Judgment of 26 March 1985, 8 EHRR 235.

[48] *Gaskin v. United Kingdom*, Eur. Ct. HR, Series A, No. 160, Judgment of 7 July 1989, 12 EHRR 36. This does not apply where the material is held for the purposes of national security, e.g. for vetting the person for a sensitive post, provided that there are adequate means (such as review by an independent ombudsman and a board) by which the decision not to release the information can be reviewed: *Leander v. Sweden*, Eur. Ct. HR, Series A, No. 116, Judgment of 26 March 1987, 9 EHRR 443. See further *Guerra v. Italy* (1998) 26 EHRR 357, Eur. Ct. HR; *McGinley and Egan v. United Kingdom* (1999) 27 EHRR 1, Eur. Ct. HR.

[49] Eur. Ct. HR, Series A, No. 18, Judgment of 21 February 1975.

[50] Eur. Ct. HR, Series A, No. 32, Judgment of 9 October 1979, 2 EHRR 305.

(2) THE SCOPE OF THE PROTECTED INTERESTS UNDER ARTICLE 8 ECHR[51]

What, then, are the interests protected, expressly or by implication, under Article 8(1)? In his dissenting opinion in *Marckx v. Belgium*[52] Judge Sir Gerald Fitzmaurice identified the core evil at which the Article was aimed as being subjection to 'the whole gamut of fascist and communist inquisitorial practices such as had scarcely been known, at least in Western Europe, since the eras of religious intolerance and oppression, until (ideology replacing religion) they became prevalent again in many countries between the two world wars and subsequently'. But Sir James Fawcett pointed out that, although Article 8(1) was 'designed, primarily at least, to protect the physical framework of personal life: the family from separation, the home from intrusion, and correspondence from being searched or stopped . . . it goes to inner life as well'.[53]

Accordingly, 'private and family life',[54] 'home', and 'correspondence' have been interpreted widely. Article 8 has a core purpose: as the Court observed in *Hokkanen v. Finland*,[55] 'the essential object of Article 8 is to protect the individual against arbitrary interference by the public authorities'. There are also core cases. The right to respect for one's home is clearly violated by a programme of burning down the houses of people who are regarded by the state as associated with militant opposition or terrorist groups.[56] But more peripheral interests may also be protected, sometimes by imposing positive duties on the state. Respect for private and family life is seen as encompassing various forms of space, activity, information and communication, physical and moral integrity, personal relations, and personal identity. This expansive interpretation is supported by reference to notions of dignity and personal autonomy which are central to liberal theory and are held to underpin privacy-related rights. The interpretation of Article 8 is dynamic and continuous, so any account is only a snapshot of a developing process caught at a single moment. At present, the main interests protected are as follows.

(i) Protection of the home in its environment

The home, private life, and family life to some extent go together, since the home is the setting for much private and family life. 'Home' is a wide term, including any place which is in fact currently used (rather than intended for use) as a private home, even if the use as a home is unlawful,[57] as long as the public do not have access to the place otherwise than for private business.[58]

---

[51] See S. Grosz, J. Beatson QC, and P. Duffy QC, *Human Rights: The 1998 Act and the European Convention* (London: Sweet & Maxwell, 2000), 265–91; Feldman, 'Developing Scope of Article 8' [1997] *EHRLR* 265–74.

[52] Eur. Ct. HR, Series A, No. 31, Judgment of 13 June 1979, 2 EHRR 330.

[53] Fawcett, *Application*, 211.

[54] 'These words are doubtless to be read disjunctively, but they are closely linked.' Fawcett, *Application*, 211.

[55] Eur. Ct. HR, Series A, No. 299-A, Judgment of 23 September 1994, at para. 55.

[56] *Akdivar v. Turkey*, Eur. Ct. HR, Judgment of 16 September 1996, 23 EHRR 143.

[57] *Buckley v. United Kingdom*, Eur. Ct. HR, (1997) 23 EHRR 101, at para. 54 of the judgment.

[58] See *Loizidou v. Turkey*, Eur. Ct. HR (1997) 23 EHRR 513; *Pentidis v. Greece*, Eur. Commn. HR, Report of 27 February 1996, 24 EHRR CD 1; struck out of list by Court, Judgment of 9 June 1997, RJD 1997-III, No. 39 (refusal of permission to use building as place of worship for Jehovah's Witnesses does not engage Art. 8, although it violated Art. 9).

As noted above, Article 8 protects against a state-supported programme of burning down the homes of members of disfavoured groups.[59] It also imposes a positive obligation on state agencies to take reasonable steps, using their legal powers of regulation and enforcement, to protect people's homes against pollution and similar hazards, created by private enterprises, which make it unsafe or excessively unpleasant to live in a particular area. While a failure to use a power may be justified, it will fall to be assessed by reference to the criteria in Article 8(2), including that of proportionality.[60]

The right to respect for the home extends to ensuring that a scheme requiring that people who want to live in a particular area, but lack residence qualifications, obtain licences to do so is administered with proper attention to the particular circumstances of an individual's situation. In particular, it breached Article 8 when the Guernsey Housing Authority refused a licence to a couple who had built a residence for themselves and their family at a time when they possessed residence qualifications but who had since lost them by absence. During their absence, the couple had let the property to people approved by the Housing Authority, contributing to the housing stock in the island. On their return, they had no other home in the UK or elsewhere. The property was vacant. The licensing scheme was an interference with Article 8(1), and, while in principle justifiable under Article 8(2), its application on the facts of the case was disproportionate.[61] On the other hand, it is permissible to restrict the use of land in order to advance public interests in orderly development and conservation. This has been held to justify refusing to allow a person to live in a caravan on her own land, placed there without planning consent.[62] However, the decision depended significantly on the margin of appreciation which the Strasbourg Court allows to states in developing land-use planning controls. Municipal courts will not be so hampered in applying rigorous standards of review. If planning controls are taken to the point where Romanies and other travellers are unable to find a place for their homes, it may come to be regarded as depriving them of the very essence of the right to respect for their homes under Article 8(1) and as violating the right to be free of discrimination under Article 14.

Article 8 has also been held to carry with it positive obligations on the state which go much further. For example, the appropriate state bodies have an obligation to use their powers under public health and land-use planning law to control polluters whose activities make it difficult or unhealthy for people to live in their homes in affected areas: even if the level of harm caused to inhabitants of the area is insufficient to amount to inhuman or degrading treatment under ECHR Article 3, the failure of agencies of the state to control the pollution can nevertheless violate Article 8. The state may also violate the right to respect for the home by failing to warn inhabitants

---

[59] *Akdivar v. Turkey*, Eur. Ct. HR, Judgment of 16 September 1996, 23 EHRR 143.

[60] *López Ostra v. Spain*, Eur. Ct. HR, Series A, No. 303-C, Judgment of 9 December 1994, 20 EHRR 277.

[61] *Gillow v. United Kingdom*, Eur. Ct. HR, Series A, No. 109, Judgment of 24 Nov. 1984, 11 EHRR 335. See also *Wiggins v. United Kingdom*, Application No. 7456/76, Report: 13 DR 40, Eur. Comm. HR

[62] See, e.g. *Chapman v. United Kingdom*, Eur. Ct. HR, App. No. 27238/95, Judgment of 18 January 2001.

of an area about a threat to their health from environmental factors known to a state agency.[63]

(ii) Privacy in public and private space

Almost everyone must carry on life partly in public, and private interests need protection in public places as well as on private property. Article 8 goes some way towards achieving this. For example, although being sent to prison or school necessarily limits one's autonomy and control over space, the right to respect for correspondence applies in prisons.[64] Children have a right to respect for private life when at school, which may manifest itself in relation to disciplinary matters among others.[65] The formulation of Article 8 in terms of respect for private life, rather than property, means that it is capable of extending to any place where people live their lives. This includes business premises, where people are protected against arbitrary invasion by state agencies, and where employees have a legitimate expectation that their private discussions and telephone conversations will be respected.[66] In principle, protection should also be available to people who have to live all their lives on the street through homelessness. There is an urgent need to regulate the use of closed-circuit television cameras, and the dissemination of material recorded by them, in order to ensure that people who lose their homes do not also lose all their dignity. English courts have shown themselves unwilling to offer protection through administrative law.[67] But the state has positive duties in respect of personal information and pictures which it holds, and the duty could and should lead to a requirement for a regulatory regime for the use of surveillance over private activities by cameras in public places.[68]

On the other hand, there is an understandable desire to ensure that people are not given protection for what most people would regard as inappropriate exploitations of privacy. The question is whether the person has, in all the circumstances, a reasonable or legitimate expectation of privacy. On private premises, even drug dealers are

---

[63] *Guerra v. Italy*, Eur. Ct. HR (1998) 26 EHRR 357.

[64] See, e.g. *Golder v. United Kingdom*, Eur. Ct. HR, Series A, No. 18, Judgment of 21 February 1975; *Silver v. United Kingdom*, Eur. Ct. HR, Series A, No. 61, Judgment of 25 March 1983; *Boyle and Rice v. United Kingdom*, Eur. Ct. HR, Series A, No. 131, Judgment of 27 April 1988; *McCallum v. United Kingdom*, Eur. Ct. HR, Series A, No. 183 (1990); *Campbell v. United Kingdom*, Eur. Ct. HR, Series A, No. 233, Judgment of 25 March 1992.

[65] *Costello-Roberts v. United Kingdom*, Eur. Ct. HR, Series A, No. 247-C, Judgment of 25 March 1993.

[66] *Niemietz v. Germany*, Eur. Ct. HR, Series A, No. 251-B, Judgment of 16 December 1992; *Halford v. United Kingdom*, Eur. Ct. HR, Judgment of 25 June 1997, RJD 1997-III, No. 39, 24 EHRR 523.

[67] See *R. v. Brentwood Borough Council, ex parte Peck, The Times*, 18 December 1997, DC, where Harrison J extended the incidental powers of local authorities to a point where neither the deployment of cameras nor the commercial exploitation and dissemination by a council of upsetting and embarrassing pictures of a person attempting suicide was subject to any legal control.

[68] See Feldman, 'Privacy-related Rights and their Social Value', 44–9; *Rotaru v. Romania*, Eur. Ct. HR, App. No. 28341/95, Judgment of 4 May 2000; K. S. Williams, C. Johnstone, and M. Goodwin, 'Closed Circuit Television (CCTV) Surveillance in Urban Britain: Beyond the Rhetoric of Crime Prevention', in J. Gold and G. Revill (eds.), *Landscapes of Defence* (London: Longman, 2000); A. von Hirsch, 'The Ethics of Public Television Surveillance', in A. von Hirsch, D. Garland, and A. Wakefield (eds.), *Ethical and Social Perspectives on Situational Crime Prevention* (Oxford: Hart Publishing, 2000), 59–76.

entitled to the protection of Article 8,[69] but drug dealers in public places have no legitimate expectation that public officials will respect the privacy of their business.[70]

(iii) Personal and business communications

Under Article 8(1) of the ECHR, correspondence is specifically protected. The Court is concerned to treat the various elements in Article 8(1) on an equal footing, contributing cumulatively to the protection of privacy interests. This has prompted the Court to extend the ideas of private life and the home so as to cover the same range of fields and activities that are protected as correspondence, including business premises.[71] This was taken to its furthest extreme so far in *Halford v. United Kingdom*,[72] holding that Article 8 had been violated by an unregulated interception of calls made by a serving police officer from work. The range of correspondence which is protected includes correspondence from those, such as prisoners, who might be regarded as necessarily enjoying only a restricted range of privacy interests. The importance of confidentiality to market operations and to some aspects of legal procedure has caused some people (particularly in capitalist and mixed economies) to use the idea of privacy to protect what are in reality business interests.

(iv) Personal information: data protection and access[73]

States have several kinds of obligations in respect of personal information. The right to respect for private life is continuously engaged when a public authority seeks, collects, stores, processes, compares, or disseminates personal information or opinions about, or images of, a data subject, even if the information is concerned with the data subject's alleged acts in the public (or political) domain.[74] The state must justify any such treatment by reference to the principles of ECHR Article 8(2). Certain types of information are regarded as particularly important or intimate, and so impose specially heavy obligations on the state to ensure that it is collected in ways which respect private life, stored in ways which safeguard its security, checked for accuracy, made available to the data subject, and not disclosed without strong reasons.

---

[69] *Khan v. United Kingdom*, Eur. Ct. HR, App. No. 35394/97, Judgment of 12 May 2000, where a violation was found of Art. 8 because there was no legal authority for, or judicial regulation of, the placing of a microphone on the outside wall of a suspect's dwelling.

[70] *Lüdi v. Switzerland*, Eur. Ct. HR, Series A, No. 238 (1992) 15 EHRR 173. *Cp. Kruslin v. France*, Series A, No. 176-A, Judgment of 24 April 1990. For discussion, see JUSTICE, *Under Surveillance: Covert Policing and Human Rights Standards* (London: JUSTICE, 1998).

[71] See, e.g. *Malone v. United Kingdom*, Series A, No. 82, Judgment of 2 August 1984; *Huvig v. France*, Eur. Ct. HR (1990) 12 EHRR 547; *Niemietz v. Germany*, Eur. Ct. HR, Series A, No. 251-B, Judgment of 16 December 1992.

[72] Eur. Ct. HR (1997) 24 EHRR 523. See also *Kopp v. Switzerland*, Eur. Ct. HR, (1999) 27 EHRR 91; *Valenzuela Contreras v. Spain*, Eur. Ct. HR (1999) 28 EHRR 483; *Amann v. Switzerland*, Eur. Ct. HR, Judgment of 16 February 2000.

[73] For accounts of the international arrangements in relation to this, see J. Michael, *Privacy and Human Rights* (Paris: Dartmouth/UNESCO Publishing, 1994); Feldman, 'Information and Privacy', 304–16.

[74] *Rotaru v. Romania*, Eur. Ct. HR, App. No. 28341/95, Judgment of 4 May 2000.

The intimate fields which demand special protection include information about health,[75] social security,[76] and sexuality.[77]

The state's positive obligations under Article 8 include giving people access to information about their own backgrounds and histories when they have been in the care of a public authority. Refusal to give access must be justifiable under the principles of Article 8(2), and the decision-making procedures must enable those principles to be reliably applied.[78] There is also a duty to make available information about threats to people's health.[79] States must also take appropriate steps to ensure that information stored about people is capable of being checked for accuracy, is held for no longer than necessary, and is not used for an illegitimate purpose.[80]

This means that the Human Rights Act 1998 will have implications for the sharing of information about people's past criminal activities, for example by circulating information about the predilections of convicted shoplifters or paedophiles. It also affects the type of information which could be included (whether legibly or in machine-readable form) in an identity card, if one were ever to be introduced compulsorily in the UK: the obligations of the state to protect people's privacy would require each piece of information to be properly justified, and would demand powerful technological and legal protections for the confidentiality of any personal information. The field is becoming considerably more complex because of developments in information technology and the explosion in the range of legal rules which seek to regulate the use of information. The impact on data protection law, confidentiality, and investigative powers will be considered as they become relevant in this and subsequent chapters.

(v) Personal status and identity

Article 8 ECHR has been applied to the legitimacy of children in *Marckx v. Belgium*.[81] The choice of a name has, however, been treated rather differently. One's name is an aspect of one's private and family life, but the choice of a name is not immune from state interference. The state can justify preventing a person from choosing a new name if, in the opinion of the competent state authority, he suffers little inconvenience from having the existing name and the proposed new name does not identify him particularly directly with his family. However, if restrictions on taking new names discriminate between people without an objective, rational justification or in a manner disproportionate to any legitimate state objective, there will be a violation of Article 14 taken together with Article 8.[82] This aspect of identity has implications for

---

[75] *Guerra v. Italy*, Eur. Ct. HR (1998) 26 EHRR 357; *McGinley and Egan v. United Kingdom*, Eur. Ct. HR (1999) 27 EHRR 1; *Z. v. Finland*, Eur. Ct. HR, Judgment of 25 February 1997, RJD 1997-I.

[76] *M.S. v. Sweden* (1997) 3 BHRC 248.

[77] *Lustig-Prean v. United Kingdom*, Eur. Ct. HR, Judgment of 27 September 1999.

[78] *Gaskin v. United Kingdom*, Series A, No. 160, Judgment of 7 July 1989.

[79] *Guerra v. Italy*, Eur. Ct. HR (1998) 26 EHRR 357.

[80] See, e.g. *Leander v. Sweden*, Series A, No. 116, Judgment of 26 March 1987.

[81] Eur. Ct. HR, Series A, No. 31, Judgment of 13 June 1979.

[82] *Burghartz v. Switzerland*, Eur. Ct. HR, Series A, No. 280-B, Judgment of 22 February 1994; *Stjerna v. Finland*, Eur. Ct. HR, Judgment of 25 November 1994, Series A, No. 299-B; *Guillot v. France*, Eur. Commn. HR, Judgment of 24 October 1996, RJD 1996–V.

identity cards, which must not identify a person in ways which cause unnecessary embarrassment.[83]

(vi) Sexual identity and gender

There are signs of a growing consensus about the desirability of respecting people's decisions about their genders.[84]

(vii) Sexuality

Linking privacy with philosophical notions of autonomy, self-fulfilment, and self-expression has made privacy interests relevant to freedom of action and life-style, not merely to freedom from interference. This expansion has been fostered, in the context of the ECHR, by the fact that Article 8(1) is drafted in terms of respect for private life, rather than privacy. This made it possible to treat the criminalization of homosexuality as a violation of homosexuals' right to respect for private life.[85] However, not all sexual activity automatically attracts the protection of Article 8. It would not protect non-consensual sex. It is not clear whether the Strasbourg Court would extend the idea of private life to sado-masochism: in *Jaggard, Laskey and Brown v. United Kingdom*[86] the majority of the Court only reluctantly accepted the government's concession that a rule of law treating adult sado-masochists as incapable of consenting to batteries against themselves engaged Article 8(1). It is extremely unlikely, in the current state of European attitudes, that sexual activity between adults and children would engage Article 8(1). Even if it did, the state would have little difficulty in justifying legally restricting it under Article 8(2). While the state is entitled to impose restrictions on sexual freedom to protect vulnerable people, a discriminatory restriction which is not justified by reference to an objective and rational criterion, or is disproportionate to any legitimate, justifying objective, will violate Article 8. Thus there was a violation where English law made it an offence for male homosexual acts to take place when more than two men were present, but no such restriction was imposed on other types of sexual activity.[87] As well as engaging Article 8, sexuality is a 'suspect category' for the purpose of the anti-discrimination provision under Article 14, and discrimination on the grounds of sexuality (for example, in relation to child custody matters) will be hard to justify.[88]

---

[83] See *B. v. France*, Eur. Ct. HR, Series A, No. 232-C, Judgment of 25 March 1992.

[84] See *Rees v. United Kingdom*, Series A, No. 106, Judgment of 17 October 1986, 9 EHRR 56; *Cossey v. United Kingdom*, Series A, No. 184, Judgment of 27 September 1990; *X., Y. and Z. v. United Kingdom* (1997) 24 EHRR 143; *Sheffield and Horsham v. United Kingdom*, Judgment of 30 July 1998, 27 EHRR 163. Refusal to recognize a reassigned gender in circumstances which cause people particular embarrassment, such as on an identity card which must be produced on demand to officials, will violate Art. 8: *B. v. France*, Series A, No. 232-C, Judgment of 25 March 1992. See further Ch. 12, below.

[85] See *Dudgeon v. United Kingdom*, Series A, No. 45, Judgment of 22 October 1981; *Norris v. Ireland*, Series A, No. 142, Judgment of 26 October 1988; *Modinos v. Cyprus*, Series A, No. 259, Judgment of 22 April 1993; *Lustig-Prean v. United Kingdom*, Eur. Ct. HR, Judgment of 27 September 1999.

[86] Eur. Ct. HR (1997) 24 EHPR 39.

[87] *A. D. T. v. United Kingdom*, Eur. Ct. HR, App. No. 35765/97, Judgment of 31 July 2000.

[88] *Salgueiro da Silva Mouta v. Portugal*, Eur. Ct. HR, App. No. 33290/96, Judgment of 21 December 1999.

(viii) Family life: respecting the family unit when taking children into care, and facilitating continued contact

The idea of family life has been given an extended meaning under Article 8. It requires the state to respect the value of mutual enjoyment of a wide range of *de facto* relationships of personal intimacy and genetic closeness. The question is not whether a relationship is recognized by law or is socially approved, but whether a genuine, familial inter-relationship subsists between the parties.[89] The categories of such relationships is not closed, but by way of example the idea of family life includes:

- the mutual enjoyment by parent and child of each other's company;[90]

- relationships between members of the extended family, such as uncle and nephew, where there has been a real tie between them;[91]

- the relationship between a man and his child, conceived when the man and the mother were unmarried but living together, following the break-up of the relationship;[92]

- the relationship between a man and his child conceived during an extra-marital affair between the mother and the man.[93]

A decision to take a child into the care of a public authority is draconian and has far-reaching consequences. The Strasbourg Court allows a significant area of discretion in relation to the initial decision to take a child into care where there is any element of urgency, because the initial decision to take a child into care is often necessarily taken under pressure of circumstances suggestive of urgency with less opportunity for careful reflection, while there is far less reason for refusing to take account of other people's rights in making subsequent decisions. None the less, where there is time the right to respect for family life has been held to require fair procedural protections provided by law for parents when their children are in danger of being taken into care.[94]

Once the child is in care, there will be time for considered decision-making, and the standard of review will be more demanding. The duty of a public authority is to re-establish family relationships as quickly as can safely be achieved. Public authorities must not normally place the children and manage their contacts so as to make a restoration of family relationships unlikely.[95] However, the rights and interests of all

---

[89] *Marckx v. Belgium*, Eur. Ct. HR, Series A, No. 31, Judgment of 13 June 1979; *Berrehab v. The Netherlands*, Eur. Ct. HR, Series A, No. 138, Judgment of 21 June 1988.

[90] *Andersson v. Sweden*, Eur. Ct. HR, Series A, No. 226, Judgment of 25 February 1992.

[91] *Boyle v. United Kingdom*, Eur. Ct. HR, Series A, No. 282-B, Judgment of 28 February 1994 (uncle denied contact with child in care following abuse allegations, without legal process to determine issue—friendly settlement following determination on merits by Commission).

[92] *Keegan v. Ireland*, Eur. Ct. HR, Series A, No. 290, Judgment of 26 May 1994 (adoption of child without father's consent violated father's Art. 8 rights).

[93] *Kroon v. The Netherlands*, Eur. Ct. HR, Series A, No. 297-C, Judgment of 27 October 1994 (legal presumption of the child's legitimacy, preventing real father from legally recognizing the child as his own, violated rights under Art. 8; law of state must enable family ties to be developed, and legally recognized and safeguarded).

[94] *W. v. United Kingdom*, Eur. Ct. HR, Series A, No. 121-A, Judgment of 8 July 1987.

[95] *Olsson v. Sweden (No. 1)*, Eur. Ct. HR, Series A, No. 130, Judgment of 24 March 1988; *Hokkanen v. Finland*, Eur. Ct HR, Series A, No. 299-A, Judgment of 23 September 1994.

parties must be taken into account, not just the person complaining to the Court.[96] Even in Strasbourg, it has been accepted that there must be strong judicial scrutiny of decisions about child care. As the Court has frequently said, its review 'is not limited to ascertaining whether a respondent state exercised its discretion reasonably, carefully and in good faith . . . [T]he Court . . . must look at [the decisions] in the light of the case as a whole; it must determine whether the reasons adduced to justify the interferences at issue are "relevant and sufficient" . . . '[97] A similar approach is likely to apply in the UK under the Human Rights Act 1998.

The Court's insistence that an interference with family life, in order to be justifiable, must be regulated by procedures adequate to ensure that the various interests are taken fairly into account[98] introduces due-process values to a range of decision-making functions which might not fall naturally within Article 6(1). This may require the courts to exercise their powers in such a way as to oversee the implementation of a local authority's care plan for a child, extending the supervision of courts over the statutory functions of social services departments beyond that which has previously been customary under the Children Act 1989, in order to provide adequate safeguards for the rights of members of the family. This would be closely analogous to the approach of the Court of Appeal to another power under the Children Act 1989, the making of a secure accommodation order in respect of a child under section 25 of the Act. Examining the compatibility of such orders with the child's right to liberty under ECHR Article 5, the Court of Appeal has held that such an order can be said to be for the purpose of educational supervision (in a broad sense) under Article 5(1)(d). Although section 25 does not expressly mention the educational needs of the child as a criterion for making an order, judges must consider any application in the light of the educational implications in order to comply with Article 5,[99] and must allow a child full rights of defence in order to satisfy Article 6.[100]

(ix) Family life and immigration and deportation decisions

As noted in Chapter 8, the right to respect for family life may affect deportation decisions and immigration rules, as it includes a right not to have the family broken up by a deportation decision unless the state has carefully struck a balance between the interests of members of the family and the interest in maintaining immigration control.[101] This is already having an effect on the approach of English courts to reviewing deportation orders.[102]

---

[96] *Glaser v. United Kingdom*, Eur. Ct. HR, App. No. 32346/96, Judgment of 19 September 2000.

[97] *Olsson v. Sweden (No. 1)*, Eur. Ct. HR, Series A, No. 130, Judgment of 24 March 1988, at para. 68. See to same effect *Scozzari and Giunta v. Italy*, Eur. Ct. HR, Apps. Nos. 39221/98 and 41963/98, Judgment of 13 July 2000, at para. 148.

[98] *W. v. United Kingdom*, Eur. Ct. HR, Series A, No. 121-A, Judgment of 8 July 1987.

[99] *In re K. (A Child) (Secure Accommodation Order: Right to Liberty)*, *The Times*, 29 November 2000 [2001] FCR 249, CA.

[100] *In re M. (A Child) (Secure Accommodation Order)*, *The Times*, 5 April 2001, CA.

[101] See, e.g. *Ahmut v. Netherlands*, Eur. Ct. HR, Judgment of 28 November 1996, 24 EHRR 62.

[102] See, e.g. *R. v. Secretary of State for the Home Department, ex parte R.*, *The Times*, 29 November 2000, Gage J.

(x) Personal integrity

This is a collective description of a rather diffuse set of interests concerned with the people's abilities to carry on their lives in an autonomous and dignified way. Respect for private life has been treated as requiring states to avoid causing or allowing seriously adverse effects on a person's physical and moral or psychological integrity. Physical integrity is straightforward, and overlaps with rights considered in Chapters 4 and 5 above. In *Costello-Roberts v. United Kingdom*,[103] involving corporal punishment of a child at a private school, it was held that the standard of harm needed to violate Article 8 in respect of a person's physical integrity would generally be similar to the standards applied in respect of inhuman or degrading treatment under Article 3, which (as noted in Chapter 5, above) has since been extended to cover excessive punishment of children. None the less, the Court in *Costello-Roberts* left open the possibility that Article 8 might in some situations have a reach wider than Article 3. The Court did not indicate where this might happen, but an example might be non-consensual medical treatment which did not inflict suffering of sufficient seriousness to violate Article 3.

Moral or psychological integrity is a more difficult concept, but might be engaged by a serious interference with a person's ability to pursue a chosen life-style or plan for life which was not protected by any of the other Convention rights, such as freedom of religion or the right to marry and found a family. In *Botta v. Italy*,[104] the Court wrote:

'Private life, in the Court's view, includes a person's physical and psychological integrity; the guarantee afforded by Article 8 of the Convention is primarily intended to ensure the development, without outside interference, of the personality of each individual in his relations with other human beings . . . '

However, it would have to be possible to define the obligations of the state with sufficient clarity to allow it to take whatever action is required to secure the appropriate level of respect for the choice.

In *Botta v. Italy*, the applicant and a friend, who were both physically disabled, went on holiday to the seaside. They found that the bathing establishments were not equipped with facilities enabling disabled people to reach the beach and the sea. The Court rejected the applicant's claim that this violated his right to respect for private life under Article 8. The Court noted that Recommendation No. R(92)6 of 9 April 1992 of the Committee of Ministers of the Council of Europe urged states to 'guarantee the right of people with disabilities to an independent life and full integration in society, and recognize society's duty to make this possible', making all leisure, cultural, and holiday activities accessible to them without discrimination. The Court also took account of Recommendation 1185 (1992) of the Parliamentary Assembly of the Council of Europe on rehabilitation policies for disabled people, and Article 15 of the Revised Social Charter on the right of people with disabilities to independence, social integration, and participation in the life of the community. The Italian state had enacted laws to give effect to these rights and recommendations.

---

[103] Eur. Ct. HR, Series A, No. 247-C, Judgment of 25 March 1993, 19 EHRR 112.
[104] Eur. Ct. HR, Judgment of 24 February 1998, 26 EHRR 241, at para. 32 of the Judgment.

The Court apparently did not accept the argument advanced by the Italian state and the Commission that positive obligations could not arise under Article 8 in respect of economic or social rights, which required a more flexible and discretionary approach than could be provided under Article 8. Indeed, in earlier cases states had been held to have positive obligations with regard to such matters as the impact of industrial pollution on people's homes, and environmental risks to health. Instead, the Court considered that the notion of 'respect' for private life gave rise to positive obligations under ECHR Article 8 where there is:

'a direct and immediate link between the measures sought by an applicant and the latter's private and/or family life . . . In the instant case, however, the right asserted by Mr. Botta, namely the right to gain access to the beach and the sea at a place distant from his normal place of residence during his holidays, concerns interpersonal relations of such broad and indeterminate scope that there can be no conceivable direct link between the measures the state was urged to take in order to make good the omissions of the private bathing establishments and the applicant's private life. Accordingly, Article 8 is not applicable.'[105]

This implies that a state or public authority which accepts an obligation in respect of social or economic rights which directly and immediately affect a person's ability to lead their lives independently to the full may have to discharge that obligation in ways which take account of positive obligations under Article 8. The boundaries of these positive obligations in respect of what may best be regarded as physical and moral integrity will no doubt be established incrementally as the Court and national courts develop their approaches to Article 8 dynamically.

(3) GROUNDS ON WHICH INTERFERENCES MAY BE JUSTIFIED UNDER ARTICLE 8(2) ECHR

In order to justify an interference with the right to respect for private and family life, home, and correspondence, the state must show that the interference, of which the applicant is a victim, complies with the criteria laid down in Article 8(2). This paragraph lays down three separate tests which must be satisfied. These can be loosely described as the tests according to rule-of-law criteria, purpose, and necessity/proportionality.

(i) Rule-of-law criteria

Any interference must be 'in accordance with the law'. This term, on the face of it, appears to require only that the interference be compatible with domestic law.[106] However, that would make it difficult for any pan-European standards to be applied to the legislation and procedures of states in Convention litigation. Accordingly, the Court has given, through its caselaw, a more extensive content to the term. Both here and in Article 10, it is represented in the French text by the term 'prévue par la loi',

---

[105] 26 EHRR 241, at paras. 34–35.
[106] *Cp. De Wilde, Ooms and Versyp v. Belgium (No. 1),* Eur. Ct. HR, Series A, No. 12, Judgment of 18 June 1971, 1 EHRR 373, at 412, para. 93.

suggesting that the public authority's interference must be grounded in some positive provision of the domestic law, rather than merely being not inconsistent with any such provision. The Court has treated the requirement similarly, applying to Article 8(2) the interpretation developed for the purposes of Article 10(2), in the context of the law of contempt of court, in the *Sunday Times* case.[107] In each place, it has treated 'in accordance with law' as importing general principles based on the ideal of the rule of law, providing a critical standard, external to the vagaries of any particular domestic legal system, by which to evaluate the provisions of the legal systems of all the parties to the Convention. As the Court held in *Malone v. United Kingdom*:[108] 'the phrase "in accordance with the law" does not merely refer back to domestic law but also relates to the quality of the law, requiring it to be compatible with the rule of law, which is expressly mentioned in the preamble to the Convention'.

There are two rule of law principles which have been developed in the caselaw of the Court. First, the law must be accessible enough for the citizen to be able to have an adequate indication of the legal rules which will be applicable to any case. This means that the interference must be governed by law, not by administrative practice. Secondly, the law must be formulated with sufficient precision to enable a person to regulate his conduct, foreseeing the consequences of his actions.

These two tests are not absolute, for a number of reasons. It may be permissible to have regard to administrative rules, even if they lack legal status, when deciding whether the way in which the law would be applied is sufficiently clear to enable people to anticipate their rights and liabilities. All laws are to some extent uncertain, and their interpretation and application will often rely on developing practices in connection with them. For this reason, in *Silver*'s case[109] the Court accepted that the published Standing Orders issued by the Prison Department of the Home Office in relation to monitoring and intercepting prisoners' correspondence could be taken into account in deciding whether the application of the law to particular prisoners' situations was sufficiently certain. By contrast, it would not have been permissible to have regard to unpublished guidelines to officers, such as Circular Instructions, as these would not have assisted the person subject to interference to anticipate the way in which the application of the law would affect him. In the same way, in *Malone*'s case in 1984 it was not clear that statements of executive practice on interception of communications, contained in a report in 1957 by Birkett LJ,[110] a discussion paper and a White Paper on interception of communications,[111] and various statements in Parliament by Home Office Ministers, were either a full or an up-to-date account of

[107] Eur. Ct. HR, Series A, No. 30, Judgment of 26 April 1979, 2 EHRR 245. See further Ch. 16, below.

[108] Eur. Ct. HR, Series A, No. 82, Judgment of 2 August 1984, 7 EHRR 14, at para. 67. See also, in the context of interception of prisoners' letters, *Silver v. United Kingdom*, Eur. Ct. HR, Series A, No. 61, Judgment of 25 March 1983, 5 EHRR 347.

[109] Eur. Ct. HR, Series A, No. 61, Judgment of 25 March 1983, 5 EHRR 347.

[110] *Report of the Committee of Privy Councillors Appointed to Inquire into the Interception of Communications* (Chairman: Birkett LJ), Cmnd. 283 (London: HMSO, 1957).

[111] Home Office, *The Interception of Communications in Great Britain*, Cmnd. 7873 (London: HMSO, 1980); Home Office, *The Interception of Communications in Great Britain*, Cmnd. 9438 (London: HMSO, 1985).

the relevant practices. They were therefore insufficient to satisfy the second limb of the 'according to law' test.

In relation to laws regulating citizens' behaviour, there is no justification for failing to make clear the circumstances in which rights or liabilities are to arise. There are special problems, however, in relation to laws conferring discretionary powers on public authorities, especially when the powers relate to the investigation of crime or the maintenance of national security. In these cases, the purpose of granting the power might be frustrated were it possible for the subjects of investigation to antici-pate where and when they were likely to be the objects of surveillance or interception of communications. Nevertheless, even here the law should lay down the conditions under which, and purposes for which, the power may lawfully be exercised, with at least sufficient clarity to provide some control over the behaviour of the authorities. If this is not done, there is inadequate legal protection in domestic law against arbitrary interferences with the rights under Article 8(1), particularly where the interferences necessarily take place in secret.

In *Malone*, where an English judge had decided that telephone tapping was lawful because nothing in the law made it unlawful, and its use by public authorities was regulated by administrative rules of practice, the Court held that the UK system for authorizing interceptions failed the 'according to law' test, because at the time it could not be said with certainty what elements in the arrangements were incorporated in legal rules and which ones depended entirely on the discretion of the executive. The same applied to 'metering' of calls, whereby the telephone undertaker, having col-lected the telephone numbers called from a particular instrument for the purposes of its business, released this information to the investigating authorities without the caller's knowledge or permission. Metering was held to raise an issue under Article 8 because the numbers dialled formed an integral element in the communication by telephone, and so concerned the private life of the caller.

It is not necessary for the legal grounding for the practice to be provided by statute. As the Court recognized in the *Sunday Times* case, a common-law system may give rise to legal norms which are sufficiently certain to satisfy the 'in accordance with the law' requirement. Nevertheless, where principles are developed by judicial decision, those decisions must have the effect of creating legal norms. In common-law systems, such as those operating in the UK, the authority of judges to make law in this way is recognized and institutionalized by the doctrine of *stare decisis*. In systems which do not recognize judicial decisions as creating binding—or sufficiently binding—legal norms, some other form of legislation will be required. For example, under French law, judges are considered to have authority to interpret legislation but not normally to make binding law; there is no formal doctrine of judicial precedent. Perhaps because of this, the Court held in *Huvig v. France* and *Kruslin v. France*[112] that prin-ciples regulating telephone tapping, developed in France by way of administrative guidance and judicial decisions, were evidence of a practice with regard to tapping, but did not provide sufficient foundation in law to satisfy the requirement that inter-ferences with private life should be 'in accordance with the law'.

---

[112] Eur. Ct. HR, Series A, No. 176-B, Judgment of 24 April 1990, 12 EHRR 528, 547.

(ii) The purpose test

If the interference has sufficient grounding in law, and is sufficiently certain, to satisfy the rule-of-law part of the test, it must next be shown that the interference was adopted for one of the purposes specified in Article 8(2). Interferences are permitted only if 'in the interests of national security, public safety or the economic well-being of the country, for the prevention of disorder or crime, for the protection of health or morals, or for the protection of the rights and freedoms of others'. Besides the obvious matters which this list covers, it has been held by the Commission to deny prisoners their conjugal rights while in prison,[113] and to justify surveillance of visits to prisoners by members of their families,[114] and requirements that the prisoners wear prison uniforms and be subjected to searches by staff and restrictions on association with other prisoners.[115]

Interferences with Article 8(1) rights in the investigation of crime may be difficult to justify under the criteria in Article 8(2). Sir James Fawcett suggested that on a literal interpretation Article 8(2) would allow the state to justify interferences which are intended to prevent crimes, but not interferences designed to contribute purely to the investigation of past crimes.[116] However, there will often be an appreciable risk that crimes will be repeated if the offender is not caught, so the detection of crime often makes a worthwhile contribution to public safety, the prevention of disorder, and the protection of the rights of others. It is important to note that, in relation to all the legitimate interests which may justify interference under Article 8(2), the Court recognizes that the state has a certain amount of leeway: if a state decides that a measure serves one of the legitimate purposes, the Court will be fairly slow to override its judgment. This is considered further in relation to the next requirement.

(iii) Necessity and the proportionality requirement

If an interference is securely grounded on rule of law principles, and serves a legitimate purpose under Article 8(2), it still must be shown to be 'necessary in a democratic society' in the interests of that purpose. On the face of it, this is a difficult phrase to which to give substantive content. There are many notions of democracy, and it is not obviously appropriate for the Court to lay down standards for states as to the type of democracy which is to be preferred. 'Necessary' is also susceptible of different interpretations. It might be taken to mean that an interference will be justified only if the Court is satisfied that the legitimate objective could not have been achieved without it, carrying the meaning 'indispensable'. This would give the Court immense power over a state's domestic policy-making, and might be thought to be unacceptable. Alternatively, at the other extreme, it might mean that any measure is acceptable which is not obviously unnecessary.

In practice, the Court has found an elegant way of avoiding many of the pitfalls. It has accepted that states must be allowed a substantial discretion (the 'margin of

---

[113] *X. and Y. v. Switzerland*, Application No. 8166/78, 13 DR 241, Eur. Comm. HR.
[114] *X. v. United Kingdom*, Application No. 8065/77, 14 DR 246.
[115] *McFeeley and others v. United Kingdom*, Application No. 8317/78, 3 EHRR 161, Eur. Comm. HR.
[116] Fawcett, *Application*, 235.

appreciation') in making policy choices. On the other hand, the freedom is not unconstrained.[117] States must recognize that securing social interests may involve costs both to society and to individuals. The measures adopted must be shown to satisfy two principles. First, they must be a response to a 'pressing social need'. Secondly, they must not exact a higher price than is necessary and acceptable in a democratic society, 'two hallmarks of which are tolerance and broadmindedness';[118] in the terms used by the Court, the interference must be proportionate to the legitimate objective pursued.

When deciding whether these two principles are met, the Court has regard to the margin of appreciation allowed to state legislatures, judiciaries, and executives in identifying situations as problems and framing measures which are appropriate to the local conditions. However, the scope of the margin of appreciation has been held to vary according to the type of interest which the interference is designed to further. Where a right is interfered with in order to protect morals, the margin of appreciation is wide, because moral standards vary greatly from time to time and from place to place, and national authorities must have the freedom to respond to local views on morality. For this reason, the Court in the *Handyside* case was prepared to accept, in the context of Article 10 (freedom of expression), that it could be considered necessary to impose criminal sanctions on the publishers of *The Little Red Schoolbook*, a publication which was aimed at children and contained accurate, but explicit, advice on matters such as masturbation, homosexuality, and abortion. Where the Court considers that the purpose is less subject to local or national variations, it allows a narrower margin. Accordingly, the majority of the Court in the *Sunday Times* case decided that the prejudgment rule in English contempt of court law could not be justified on the basis of being necessary to maintain the authority and impartiality of the judiciary under Article 10(2).

Under Article 8(2), the margin of appreciation in relation to the protection of morals appears to be more limited than under Article 10, perhaps because the rights protected under Article 8 are essentially private while freedom of expression under Article 10 implies a right to publicize one's moral view, imposing it on others rather than merely indulging it in private. In *Dudgeon v. United Kingdom*, a majority of the Court accepted that the prevailing moral view in Northern Ireland was opposed to homosexuality, but considered that this could not be decisive as to the necessity for imposing restrictions on the private manifestation of an aspect of human personality. The judgment of the majority noted that the law had not in recent years been enforced, and that there was no evidence that this had harmed moral standards or vulnerable social groups in the province. It concluded that there was no pressing social need to criminalize homosexuality. In any case, the Court decided that criminalizing private consensual homosexual acts between adults was disproportionate to any social need:

---

[117] The *Handyside* case, Eur. Ct. HR, Series A, No. 24, Judgment of 7 December 1976, 1 EHRR 737; *Sunday Times* case, Eur. Ct. HR, Series A, No. 30, Judgment of 26 April 1979, 2 EHRR 245; applied to Art. 8(2) in the *Klass* case, Eur. Ct. HR, Series A, No. 28, Judgment of 6 September 1978, 2 EHRR 214.

[118] *Dudgeon v. United Kingdom*, Eur. Ct. HR, Series A, No. 45, Judgment of 22 October 1981, 4 EHRR 149, at para. 53.

'On the issue of proportionality, the Court considers that such justifications as there are for retaining the law in force unamended are outweighed by the detrimental effects which the very existence of the legislative provisions in question can have on the life of a person of homosexual orientation like the applicant. Although members of the public who regard homosexuality as immoral may be shocked, offended or disturbed by the commission by others of private homosexual acts, this cannot on its own warrant the application of penal sanctions when it is consenting adults alone who are involved.'[119]

The Court felt unable to overlook the changes which had occurred in the moral attitudes of other Member States of the Council of Europe, which no longer regarded homosexual behaviour in itself as deserving criminal punishment. This shows that the margin of appreciation, even in relation to a matter as variable as morality, is restricted both by general European thought and by the need for tolerance in a democratic society. This approach will be welcome to some people who live in countries which are less tolerant than others in Europe. However, the juxtaposition of tolerance and democracy in the Court's jurisprudence is not entirely unproblematic. Toleration of opinion and expression is necessary in order to maintain the democratic order. In relation to such toleration, the rights guaranteed, particularly under Articles 9 and 10 of the Convention, buttress democracy, and interference is hard to justify within a democratic society, particularly where it aims merely to avoid offence to other people.[120] When one considers the right to respect for private life, this too has an important democratic role, as noted above. Yet, we said in section 9.1 that the proper sphere of private as distinct from public life is always a subject for debate within a liberal democracy, and Article 8(2) acknowledges that respect for private life may be restricted to preserve health and morals. That being so, it gives an appearance of inconsistency to accept, on the one hand, that morality and the scope of private life fall within the sphere of state sovereignty, as mediated through democratic decision-making processes, and yet to assert, on the other hand, that the scope of private life may be restricted by a democratic state only so far as is consistent with the Court's view of the proper balance between competing interests.

This, however, is inevitable when democratic states agree to subscribe to international standards for protecting individual rights within the states. There is a tension between (a) the demands of sovereignty and democratic self-determination within states, and (b) the standard of protection for individual rights which is demanded by the Convention. Having once agreed to an international process for adjudicating on breaches of rights under the Convention, it does not lie in the mouths of states to claim the freedom to restrict those rights in pursuance of democracy and self-determination without any limitation according to the principles of the Convention. Private life, being pre-eminently necessary for self-fulfilment and the enjoyment of other rights guaranteed under the Convention, is particularly in need of protection from the Court against too wide a margin of appreciation being allowed to states.

For this reason, it is proper for the Court to impose procedural requirements on

---

[119] Eur. Ct. HR, Series A, No. 45, Judgment of 22 October 1981, 4 EHRR 149, at para. 60.
[120] *Lingens v. Austria*, Eur. Ct. HR, Series A, No. 103, Judgment of 8 July 1986, 8 EHRR 103, at para. 41.

states which interfere with the right to respect for Article 8(1) interests. A state will be unable to show that the risk to society which the interference is designed to avert outweighs the harm to individuals from the measures adopted, unless there are procedures which ensure that those interests are taken into account and that, so far as is compatible with the object of the interference, abuses of power may be remedied. For example, where the interference is necessarily not known to the individual concerned (as where his telephone is secretly tapped), there must be an independent authority to authorize the interference. In *Klass v. Federal Republic of Germany*[121] the Court decided that the provisions of Germany's Law G10 on telephone tapping to protect national security complied with the requirements of Article 8 of the ECHR. Under Law G10, authority to intercept communications was granted by a Minister of the government, applying criteria laid down in the statute. The decision was reviewable and reversible by a Commission, headed by a person qualified for judicial office and independent of government. The Commission must also decide whether the person subject to surveillance should be notified. At the end of the surveillance, the Minister must decide whether the person should be notified, so that he can enforce his legal rights, or whether this would be incompatible with national security. If he decides not to notify, the decision must be ratified by the Commission, and reconsidered at regular intervals to see whether the conditions for withholding notification are still satisfied. During the surveillance, the Commission acting *ex proprio motu*, or at the instance of the person under surveillance if he suspects what is happening, may consider the legality of the surveillance and, if appropriate, order its termination. Finally, the person believing himself to be under surveillance may challenge the order before the *Bundesverfassungsgericht* (constitutional court). Responsibility to Parliament for the overall use of the power is also maintained: the Minister has to report half-yearly to a board consisting of five members of the Parliament, which had a monitoring role.

The Court in *Klass* accepted that this set of measures was adequate, at least in the context of national-security investigations. It is not clear whether it would provide sufficient protection against interference with private life in the course of investigations which concerned ordinary crime rather than national security. The Court was prepared to accept, where national security was concerned, that it was not essential to have the surveillance authorized by a judicial officer independent of the executive, but it regarded judicial authorization as desirable. It may be that allowing non-judicial authorization by a member of the executive would be regarded as disproportionate to the legitimate object pursued in ordinary criminal cases.

If so, it will cause problems for the UK, as the Regulation of Investigatory Powers Act 2000 allows the Home Secretary (or, sometimes, a civil servant) to issue warrants authorizing interceptions of communications in a range of cases going beyond those involving national security. The 2000 Act replaces the Interception of Communications Act 1985, which was a response to *Malone*'s case. The 1985 Act put the rules on a statutory basis, although it failed to make the law fully compatible with the Convention. This is considered further in Chapter 10, below.

---

[121] Eur. Ct. HR, Series A, No. 28, Judgment of 6 September 1978, 2 EHRR 214.

9.4 THE LEGAL SCOPE OF PRIVACY IN ENGLAND AND WALES: DOMESTIC LAW APART FROM, AND UNDER THE INFLUENCE OF, THE HUMAN RIGHTS ACT 1998

The form in which privacy rights are recognized in any legal system is a matter for that system, and will be affected by cultural and political factors which are peculiar to particular societies. As noted above, some societies, like the USA and Canada, offer constitutional protection to certain privacy interests. Other societies, such as the UK, do not give legal protection to privacy as such, but protect some of the interests which are normally classified as privacy interests by way of rights of property or confidentiality. The extent, as well as the form, of the rights will also be a matter for political decision and will vary between societies.

(1) THE SLOW MOVEMENT TOWARDS NEGATIVE PRIVACY RIGHTS IN ENGLISH LAW

Until recently, English law left little scope for the protection of privacy as such. Compared with the interests in property and personal integrity, privacy has had only limited importance in English culture. It need not have been so. Early in English legal history, the idea of the 'peace' acquired an importance which affected a number of subsequent developments.[122] The idea that a person's home and family life were to be free from violent intrusions was powerful. The King's peace eventually developed to cover the whole country, but its roots were in the idea of personal, rather than national, security. The peace of the King was, originally, the peace of the householder writ large. It entitled the monarch to levy compensation for violent acts in the vicinity of the court, which followed the monarch's person travelling round the country. This peace offered the protection of the royal courts and of the King's military force to those in the vicinity of the court. It could be extended in two ways: by granting the protection of the King's peace to individuals who were travelling on royal business or who were performing tasks which benefited the realm; and, more artificially, by announcing that the whole country would come within the King's peace on certain days when there were special reasons (usually religious) for preserving peace, or by asserting that particular parts of the country, usually those of special economic significance such as the main roads, were within the King's peace. The extension of the King's peace from a personal and localized form of protection to a general one took place by stages over several centuries.

The peace of the commoner's homestead mirrored the original, localized, peace of the King. It gave a right of compensation for those brawling within the homestead. It was not simply related to property rights, and could have developed into a legally protected sphere of personal freedom from interference and oversight, which is the

---

[122] On the early history, see Sir Frederick Pollock, *Oxford Lectures and Other Discourses* (London: Macmillan, 1890), 65–90; Sir Carleton Kemp Allen, *The Queen's Peace* (London: Stevens & Son, 1953), 23–66; J. K. Weber, 'The King's Peace: A Comparative Study' (1989) **10** *J. of Legal Hist.* 135–60.

essence of a right to privacy. However, it took another turn, no doubt influenced by prevailing economic forms and structures. It became associated at common law with the idea of real property. It spawned the law of nuisance—interference with quiet enjoyment of property rights—rather than a law of privacy. The common law proved resistant to the introduction of new protected interests, so that when other interests acquired economic importance it fell to equity rather than the common law to protect them. For example, equitable relief—particularly in the form of injunctions—was employed to restrain breaches of confidence unrelated to property interests. A famous example was the action brought successfully by the Prince Consort to restrain unauthorized publication of certain etchings made by Queen Victoria and himself, which, apart from considerations of copyright, would have opened to the public eye the home life of the royal family. It was on cases like this that the Warren and Brandeis argument, that the common law protected (*inter alia*) the interest in the privacy of the family in the form of a right to be let alone, was based.

Despite the procedural fusion of law and equity late in the nineteenth century, neither Parliament nor the judges took the opportunity to develop a coherent law of privacy. There was a good deal of law which had the effect of protecting particular privacy-related interests. In public law, there was legislation for protecting computerized data and controlling harassment, powers of entry, and surveillance. In private law, there were remedies for breach of confidence, trespass to land or personal property, copyright and nuisance. But until relatively recently, neither judges nor legislators thought in terms of a right of privacy as such. The main reason for this was the difficulty of defining privacy with any clarity.[123] Concern about intrusions by journalists led the Calcutt Committee to suggest that there might be a need for legislation to give rights of privacy against the press, if the press was unable to ensure that its agents observed an appropriately high standard of responsibility in pursuing news stories. The National Heritage Select Committee in the House of Commons and other official reports reached a similar conclusion, and calls for such legislation have been echoed by judges both judicially and extra-judicially, but so far Parliament has not acted.[124]

The lack of a right to privacy as against the state became evident in *Malone v. Metropolitan Police Commissioner (No. 2)*,[125] which concerned telephone tapping by the police. In the course of a criminal trial, the defendant, Mr. Malone, alleged that the police had been intercepting some of his telephone calls, and metering (i.e. obtaining a print-out of the numbers called) all of them. After being acquitted of the criminal charges, Mr. Malone brought a civil action against the police, claiming a declaration

---

[123] *Report of the Committee on Privacy* (Chairman: Kenneth Younger), Cmnd. 5012 (London: HMSO, 1972), 17.

[124] *Report of the Committee on Privacy and Related Matters* (Chairman: David Calcutt), Cmnd. 1102 (London: HMSO, 1990); *Kaye v. Robertson* [1991] FSR 62, CA; National Heritage Committee, Fourth Report, *Privacy and Media Intrusion,* HC 294-I of 1992–93, paras. 30–7; Department of National Heritage, *Review of Press Self-Regulation* (Sir David Calcutt QC), Cm. 2135 (1993); *Infringement of Privacy* (The Lord Chancellor's Department and The Scottish Office, 1993); Sir Thomas Bingham, 'Should there be a Law to Protect Rights of Personal Privacy?' [1996] *EHRLR* 450–62, suggesting that the courts might create rights through the common law if Parliament failed to act. See further below.

[125] [1979] Ch. 344, [1979] 2 All ER 620.

that the interception had been unlawful on the grounds that it constituted a breach of confidence, a trespass, and an unlawful interference with his privacy. In accordance with standing policy, the police refused to confirm or deny that they had intercepted the telephone calls, and the litigation was conducted on the assumption that they had done so.

Sir Robert Megarry V-C dismissed the claims. Any interception had been carried out electronically from outside the plaintiff's premises, so there was no trespass against the plaintiff's property. The law of trespass could not be adapted to deal with the sophistication of modern technologies of communication and interception. The claim in breach of confidence failed, because, although the subject-matters of tele-phone conversations were capable of being confidential in nature, there was no express or implied undertaking of confidentiality imposed on those who were party to the conversations, by reason either of the circumstances in which the communication took place or of the relationship between the parties. Indeed, Megarry V-C appears to have taken the view that communicating by telephone, notorious for its crossed lines and lack of security, indicated a willingness that the conversation should not be regarded as confidential (this is even more true of mobile telephones, which can easily be intercepted by radio, than of the old-fashioned line-based telephones). Finally, Sir Robert held that English law did not entertain actions for interference with privacy unless the interference amounted to one of the established causes of action in tort or equity. He accepted that this appeared to be inconsistent with the demands of Article 8 of the European Convention on Human Rights, but took note of the fact that the Convention was not then capable of creating directly enforceable rights in English law. He felt unable to develop the common law along the lines of American law. As English common law was devoted to maintaining an undifferentiated mass of liberty (subject to any legal inroads made on it), rather than identifying and protecting a range of specific liberties,[126] he took the view that anyone is entitled to do anything which is not prohibited by law, and argued that on ordinary rule of law principles this applied equally to agents of the state and to citizens.

This was unsatisfactory, as it ignored an important aspect of the rule of law. In treating like cases alike, and unlike cases differently, the law should take account of differences between the status and interests of the state and its agents, on the one hand, and private citizens on the other. Individuals have liberties. State agencies have only powers, which are conferred for the good of the public. When a state agency interferes with an individual, it must be required to identify a specific power or authorization, and to justify every exercise of the power. If the courts fail to insist on this, they cannot perform one of their essential functions under the rule of law: namely, to make public bodies legally accountable for their actions in such a way as to restrict the scope for abuse of power. This was reaffirmed when the European Court of Human Rights held, as noted in section 9.3(3) above, that the English practice of interception was insufficiently grounded in law to allow it to be justified under ECHR Article 8(2).

We will see in the chapters which follow how legislation has gradually supplied the

---

[126] See Ch. 2, above.

deficiency which the Strasbourg Court identified in *Malone*'s case. However, until the Human Rights Act 1998 there was no statute which specifically and expressly recognized, much less conferred, a right of privacy. However, there were a number of developments at common law, influenced to some extent by the jurisprudence of the Strasbourg Court and, later, the Human Rights Act 1998, which eventually led to a point where it is possible to say, with only a small degree of tentativeness, that a right of privacy exists in both public and private law.

This happened very gradually, and only the main steps can be noted here. First, the law of breach of confidence was extended to cover cases where there was no pre-existing relationship of confidence, based on a familial, commercial, or employment connection, or a contract for confidentiality, between the parties. This extension allowed the law of breach of confidence to form the basis for injunctions restraining a newspaper from publishing photographs of Diana, Princess of Wales taken surreptitiously by Mr. Bryce Taylor, the owner of a gymnasium in which she had been working out.[127] Mr. Taylor was reported as suggesting that the Princess had secretly wanted to be photographed,[128] but there can never be a defence of implied consent when the photography or other surveillance is conducted clandestinely, and so unknown to the victim.

Concern about harassment, whether by the press or by stalkers of other kinds, has led to judicial and legislative innovations. In *Khorasandjian v. Bush*,[129] the Court of Appeal, by a majority, held that the daughter of lessees of domestic premises, living with her parents but without a proprietary interest in the property, could claim an injunction in the tort of private nuisance to restrain a former boyfriend who persistently made nuisance telephone calls to her at the premises. This was overruled by the House of Lords in *Hunter v. Canary Wharf Ltd.*[130] The case concerned interference with television signals caused to local residents by the building of the Canary Wharf tower-block in London. A majority of their Lordships (Lord Cooke of Thorndon dissenting) held that the tort of private nuisance protected only property interests, leaving people in the position of the daughter in *Khorasandjian v. Bush* without a remedy in nuisance. The House left untouched another development on which the decision in *Khorasandjian* could have been based, namely an emergent tort of harassment. This tort, coupled with the law of assault, was used by the Princess of Wales to obtain injunctions against two people in 1996. A German doctor who had stalked her for a long time, waving placards and distributing leaflets about her relationship with Dodi Fayed, the son of the owner of Harrods, Mohammed Fayed, was banned from going within five miles of her.[131] A freelance photographer, Martin Stenning, who had frequently pursued her on a motorcycle, was later restrained from approaching within

---

[127] *HRH The Princess of Wales v. MGN Newspapers Ltd.*, unreported, 8 November 1993 (transcript: Association of Official Shorthand Writers Ltd.), discussed by H. Fenwick and G. Phillipson, 'Confidence and Privacy: A Re-examination' [1996] *CLJ* 447–55.

[128] See the *Independent*, 17 November 1993, 11, reporting an interview first published in London's *Evening Standard*.

[129] [1993] QB 727, [1993] 3 All ER 669, CA.

[130] [1997] AC 655, [1997] 2 All ER 426, HL.

[131] *The Times*, 28 June 1996, 11. See also *The Times*, 13 January 1996, 1; 8 March 1996, 2; 25 April 1996, 2.

300 metres of her, harassing her or interfering with her safety, security or well-being, or molesting or assaulting her.[132]

Judicial decisions also extended the criminal law of assault to cover telephone calls which put a person in fear of violence or caused psychiatric injury.[133] However, there was a risk that the law failed to protect people adequately against interference with their enjoyment of their homes (as distinct from their property or persons), leaving the UK in violation of its positive obligations under Article 8 of the ECHR.

Subsequently, Parliament has enacted the Protection from Harassment Act 1997. Section 1 makes it an offence to pursue a course of conduct which amounts to harassment of another person and which the perpetrator knows or ought to know amounts to such harassment. Section 4 creates a separate offence which is committed by someone whose course of conduct puts another person in fear of violence on at least two occasions, if the perpetrator knows or ought to know that the conduct will cause such fear on each occasion. To protect a victim or potential victim of either offence, a court dealing with a person under the Act can make a restraining order under section 5, prohibiting the defendant from doing anything described in the order. This has implications for peaceful picketing and freedom of assembly and protest. In such contexts, the power to make an order must now be read and given effect in the light of those rights, as a result of the Human Rights Act 1998, sections 1, 3, and 6. The same applies to the power to make an anti-social behaviour order under section 1 of the Crime and Disorder Act 1998, and (if it is enacted) the power to stop protests outside people's homes, proposed in the Criminal Justice and Police Bill 2001 in order (principally) to protect from harassment the families of staff at laboratories conducting experiments on live animals, such as Huntingdon Life Sciences Laboratories, which were the site of major protests by animal rights campaigners in 2000 and 2001.

These developments illustrate the growing concern about, and willingness to respond to, the weakness of protection against interference with privacy (including privacy interests in public places) and the home. Much of the concern concentrated on intrusions by the press. In *Kaye v. Robertson*[134] the Court of Appeal accepted that there was no power to restrain an interference with privacy as such in English law. Journalists had photographed and interviewed an actor from a well-known television series, who was seriously ill in hospital following an accident. The newspaper claimed an 'exclusive' for the story. No permission had been given by or on behalf of the hospital. The actor, who was recovering from brain surgery, was in no position to give or withhold real consent when the journalists burst into his hospital room. The actor sought an injunction restraining publication of the interview and photographs. He succeeded at first instance on the ground of defamation, as the implication that the actor had consented to be interviewed by the *Sunday Sport* would inevitably have

---

[132] *The Times*, 16 August 1996, 1. The affidavit sworn in support of the application is reproduced in *The Times*, 17 August 1996, 2. For coverage of an unrelated incident involving Stenning, see *The Times*, 23 August 1996, 4.

[133] *R. v. Ireland* [1998] AC 147, [1997] 4 All ER 225, HL. See Ch. 5, above.

[134] [1991] FSR 62, CA.

lowered him in the opinion of right-thinking people.[135] On appeal, the Court of Appeal reversed the decision as regards defamation, as it was not inevitable (although it was thought to be likely) that a jury would have held that the material was defamatory. English courts are wary of interfering with press freedom by granting prior restraint of alleged libels, save in very clear cases.[136] The court also rejected claims based on passing off and trespass to the person. Nevertheless, a narrower injunction was granted to restrain malicious falsehood, as the court thought it clear that the journalists knew that the actor had not given informed consent to the interview as the 'exclusive' label on the story implied, and publication of the story in the *Sunday Sport* would greatly reduce the value of the actor's potentially valuable commercial right to sell the story of his accident to other newspapers later.

All three judges in the Court of Appeal expressed concern that privacy rights needed to be protected against the press, and were more in need of protection than is press freedom. It is felt that the press, or elements in it, abuse their freedom, and that the balance between the press and individuals needs to be redressed by law. Glidewell LJ regarded the case as 'a graphic illustration of the desirability of Parliament considering whether and in what circumstances statutory provision can be made to protect the privacy of individuals'. Leggatt LJ went further, hoping 'that the making good of this signal shortcoming in our law will not be long delayed'. Sir David Calcutt, in his *Review of Press Self-Regulation*,[137] recommended that new criminal offences and a new tort of invasion of privacy should be introduced to deal with people who invade privacy to obtain personal information with a view to its publication. Such privacy laws, aimed exclusively at those who publish information, and leaving untouched those who invade privacy for other purposes (whether private or public), would provide protection which would be too narrow to satisfy those who are concerned at the powers of the security service and investigative agencies, and too wide to be acceptable to those who regard the press as a principal guardian against corruption in public life. Sir David, moving away from the relatively non-interventionist view he had expressed two years earlier, did not feel that the Press Complaints Commission Code of Practice was being enforced sufficiently rigorously to provide reliable protection for people. The House of Commons National Heritage Select Committee took a similar view, but so far, no legislation has materialized.[138]

However, the courts have not let the matter rest. Individual judges have increasingly regarded privacy as fundamental, and as an interest which the law should protect.[139]

---

[135] Cf. *Tolley v. J. S. Fry & Sons Ltd.* [1931] AC 333, HL, where an amateur golfer whose image was used without permission in an advertisement for chocolate was held to have been defamed by the implication that he had compromised his amateur status by selling the right to use his image.

[136] See Ch. 14, below.

[137] Cm. 2135 (London: HMSO, 1992), ch. 7.

[138] See National Heritage Committee, Fourth Report, *Privacy and Media Intrusion*, HC 294-I of 1992–93, paras. 30–7; Department of National Heritage, *Review of Press Self-Regulation* (Sir David Calcutt QC), Cm. 2135 (1993). The government issued a consultation paper: The Lord Chancellor's Department and the Scottish Office, *Infringement of Privacy* (London: The Lord Chancellor's Department and The Scottish Office, 1993).

[139] See, e.g. *Morris v. Beardmore* [1981] AC 446 at 464, [1979] 2 All ER 753 at 763 *per* Lord Scarman; *Attorney General v. Guardian Newspapers Ltd. (No. 2)* [1990] 1 AC 109 at 255, [1988] 3 All ER 545 at 639 *per* Lord Keith of Kinkel.

In *R. v. Khan (Sultan)*[140] a majority of the House of Lords refused to lend their authority to the proposition that there was no right to privacy in English law. Lords Browne-Wilkinson, Slynn of Hadley, and Nicholls of Birkenhead considered that a matter of such importance should not be decided until it was raised squarely on the facts of a case before the House.[141] In *Earl Spencer v. United Kingdom*,[142] the European Commission of Human Rights rejected a claim by the family of Lady Spencer, step-mother of the Princess of Wales, that UK law had failed to protect the Princess against publication of photographs of her undergoing treatment at a private clinic, taken without consent by a photographer with a telephoto lens. The Commission decided that the family should have pursued an action for breach of confidence, which, in the light of developments in the law since *Kaye v. Robertson*, offered a reasonable prospect of an effective remedy for that sort of interference with privacy. They had not exhausted their domestic remedies, so their application to Strasbourg was inadmissible.

Since the Human Rights Act 1998 came into force, the issue has come closest to arising directly in *Douglas v. Hello! Ltd.*[143] in the context of a dispute over the publication of photographs of a wedding of a pair of film actors. Michael Douglas and Catherine Zeta-Jones had entered into an exclusive agreement with the publishers of *OK!*, a weekly magazine, to publish photographs of their California wedding in exchange for a very large sum of money and a profit-sharing arrangement. A few days before the issue of *OK!* carrying the photographs was to appear, its publishers learned that *Hello!*, another weekly magazine, was about to publish unauthorized photographs (albeit blurred and ill-defined) of the wedding taken by a photographer with a hidden camera. An interim order was made to restrain the distribution of that week's issues of *Hello!* in the UK, pending trial of an action for breach of confidence, malicious falsehood, and interference with contractual relations. The publishers of *Hello!* appealed successfully. The Court of Appeal decided that, under section 12(3) of the Human Rights Act 1998, it had to look in interim proceedings at the merits of the case, granting an injunction against publication only if the court is satisfied that the applicant is likely to establish at trial that publication should not be allowed. This did not clash with the requirements of the ECHR: it simply supplemented, in cases involving publications, the usual 'balance of convenience' principle for granting pre-trial relief. The claimants' chance of establishing a claim to an injunction at trial were too weak to justify an interim order.

In the course of their judgments, the three judges made instructive comments about privacy rights in English law. Brooke LJ identified as a difficult issue the question whether there is a positive duty on courts, as public authorities, under ECHR Article 8 and the Human Rights Act 1998, to provide a remedy for invasion of privacy by private persons or bodies where Parliament had failed to do so, and left the matter

---

[140] [1997] AC 558, [1996] 3 All ER 289, HL.

[141] [1997] AC at 571, 572 and 582–3, [1996] 3 All ER at 291, 292 and 302, *per* Lords Browne-Wilkinson, Slynn, and Nicholls respectively.

[142] [1998] EHRR CD 105, Eur. Commn. HR.

[143] [2001] 2 WLR 992, CA. See N. Moreham, '*Douglas and others v. Hello! Ltd*—the Protection of Privacy in English Law' (2001) 64 *MLR* 767–74.

for a case where it was necessary to decide it.[144] Sedley LJ went further, holding that the common law (irrespective of any duty arising under the 1998 Act) had developed to a point at which there was at least a 'powerfully arguable case' that the claimants had a right of privacy which English law 'will today recognize and, where appropriate, protect'. This right, grounded in breach of confidence, extends not only to those whose trust has been abused but also to 'those who simply find themselves subjected to an unwanted intrusion into their private lives. The law no longer needs to construct an artificial relationship of confidentiality between intruder and victim: it can recognize privacy itself as a legal principle drawn from the fundamental value of personal autonomy'.[145] Keene LJ likewise considered it 'unlikely that *Kaye v. Robertson*,[146] which held that there was no actionable right of privacy in English law, would be decided in the same way on that aspect today . . . Consequently if the present case concerned a truly private occasion, where the persons involved made it clear that they intended it to remain private and undisclosed to the world, then I might have concluded that in the current state of English law the claimants were likely to succeed at any eventual trial'.[147]

Here was the rub. All three judges decided that the happy couple, by entering into the publication agreement with *OK!*, had deprived their wedding of the necessary quality of privacy. They agreed that section 12(4) of the 1998 Act, which requires courts to 'have particular regard to the importance of freedom of expression', and in relation to journalistic, literary, or artistic material to, *inter alia*, 'any relevant privacy code', could not elevate rights under ECHR Article 10 above other rights. The right to freedom of expression included the limitations contained in Article 10(2), which permitted interference to protect other rights if appropriate. It is on this basis that Dame Elizabeth Butler-Sloss P granted an injunction restraining publication of details of the post-release identities and whereabouts of the two boys imprisoned for the murder of James Bulger: releasing the details would compromise their right to life, as well as their right to a private life.[148] In the *Douglas* case, Brooke LJ considered, in relation to the claim in breach of confidence, that a claimant who put himself outside the rules on privacy in the Press Complaints Commission Code of Practice would be unlikely to be able to benefit from the Convention right to respect for private life in relation to that occasion.[149] As Sedley LJ put it, 'by far the greater part of that privacy has already been traded and falls to be protected, if at all, as a commodity in the hands of the [publishers of *OK!*]'.[150]

This is encouraging, as it distinguishes the emerging privacy right from commercial rights. One of the criticisms of non-constitutional privacy law in the USA has been

---

[144] [2001] 2 WLR at 1017, para. 91. See R. Singh, 'Privacy and the Media after the Human Rights Act' [1998] *EHRLR* 712–29; G. Phillipson and H. Fenwick, 'Breach of Confidence as a Privacy Remedy in the Human Rights Era' (2000) 63 *MLR* 660–93.

[145] Ibid. at 1025, paras. 125–6.

[146] [1991] FSR 62, CA.

[147] [2001] 2 WLR at 1036, para. 167.

[148] *Venables and Thompson v. News Group Newspapers Ltd.* [2001] 2 WLR 1038.

[149] Ibid. at 1018–19, paras. 93–5.

[150] Ibid. at 1031, para. 144. Brooke LJ agreed: see at 1020, para. 101.

the way it confuses a right to privacy with a right to exploit publicity about oneself. The Court of Appeal in *Douglas* made it clear that this confusion is unlikely to afflict English privacy law. A right to exploit publicity is in principle remediable by compensation for loss of profits, either by way of damages or through the equitable remedy of account of profits. It is only privacy in the pure sense of a right to be free of intrusion or wholly unwanted publicity which will usually be protected by restraining publication.

(2) POSITIVE RIGHTS PROTECTING PRIVATE AND FAMILY LIFE

On the basis of the notion that the most fundamental interests in privacy relate to personal information, the law has increasingly acted to provide protection for it. This protection is of two kinds. First, there are provisions restricting the use to which people can put personal information about others which they hold. Secondly, there are statutes which permit people to claim access to information banks, in order to discover what information is held about them, and to correct mistaken records.

(i) Restrictions on the use of personal information

Protecting privacy is partly a matter of preventing unauthorized access to, or use of, personal information. This is achieved partly through the principle of breach of confidence, and partly through criminal law. In relation to computerized information, the Computer Misuse Act 1990 makes it a criminal offence to secure unauthorized access to computerized data. The object was to deal with 'hackers' who gain unauthorized access to computer systems to obtain or corrupt records or programs, thus protecting commercial interests as well as personal privacy. It protects against unauthorized use by people within organizations as well as those hacking in from outside. When a person has authority to access some information, but goes further and accesses other information not covered by the authority, he commits an offence under the Act.[151]

Officials who hold information, obtained in the course of their official business, may (subject to limited exceptions) use it only for the purpose for which it was obtained. There is a general principle of equity which imposes such a restriction as an element in the obligation of confidentiality.[152] But the use of breach of confidence in this context involves a balancing exercise between public interests and the core right. At common law, the protection offered by the doctrine of breach of confidence is fairly weak when information or images are in the hands of a public authority using them for the purpose of carrying out its proper functions.[153] Matters may improve somewhat under the Human Rights Act 1998. As explained above, ECHR Article 8

---

[151] *R. v. Bow Street Metropolitan Stipendiary Magistrate, ex parte government of the United States of America* [2000] 2 AC 216, [1999] 4 All ER 1, HL.

[152] See *Marcel v. Metropolitan Police Commissioner* [1992] 1 All ER 72, CA, and Sir Nicolas Browne-Wilkinson's first-instance judgment at [1991] 2 WLR 1118, [1991] 1 All ER 845.

[153] See, e.g. *R. v. Chief Constable of North Wales, ex parte A.B. and C.D.* [1999] QB 396, DC and CA; *Woolgar v. Chief Constable of Sussex Police* [2000] 1 WLR 25, CA; *R. (A.) v. Chief Constable of C.* [2001] 1 WLR 461.

requires that any storage, use, or disclosure of information about a person be justified by reference to Convention standards. It must be in accordance with the law, pursue a legitimate aim, and be a proportionate response to a pressing social need. The impact of this will be considered further in subsequent chapters.

The requirements of common law and the Human Rights Act 1998 are reinforced by some statutes, which authorize the collection of information but prohibit disclosure. Examples include information gathered in connection with assessing people's tax liabilities,[154] information gathered by the Parliamentary Commissioner for Administration (ombudsman),[155] and material and information collected from authorized telephone taps.[156] There are also more general prohibitions on disclosure under the Official Secrets Act 1989, considered further in Chapter 15 below.

Many of these provisions do not admit a public-interest justification for disclosure.[157] In such cases, as under the Health and Safety at Work Act 1974, section 28, it meant that it might be impossible legally to warn the public about a danger being created by a commercial polluter. The interests which are protected by non-disclosure requirements, therefore, may concern individuals' privacy, but the requirements are often designed to protect commercial interests. To some extent, it may be possible to imply a public-interest exception into the legislation to protect the right of a whistle-blower to freedom of expression under ECHR Article 10 and section 3 of the Human Rights Act 1998.[158] To protect public-interest whistle-blowers against being dismissed or otherwise victimized by their employers, the Public Interest Disclosure Act 1998 inserted provisions into the Employment Rights Act 1996, particularly sections 43A to 43K. Dismissal or victimization may give rise to unlimited compensation where a worker (including many employees of the Crown) reasonably makes a disclosure in the reasonable belief that it is in the public interest to do so. However, the Act does not protect the self-employed, volunteers, or members of the police and security services.[159]

(ii) Access to, and correction of, stored information

Vast amounts of personal information about people are held by an increasing range of bodies. Employers, bankers, doctors, solicitors, and others, hold records on their employees, customers, clients, and patients. Educational establishments hold records on their students, and sometimes on students' families. Government departments which administer programmes such as social security hold detailed personal information about many people. The police have always relied heavily on collecting and

---

[154] E.g. Taxes Management Act 1970, s. 6 and Sch. 1.

[155] Parliamentary Commissioner Act 1967, s. 11.

[156] Interception of Communications Act 1985, Sch. 2.

[157] For full discussion of this and related issues, see Y. Cripps, *The Legal Implications of Disclosure in the Public Interest*, 2nd edn. (London: Sweet & Maxwell, 1994), *passim*; Y. Cripps, 'The Consequences of Disclosure in the Public Interest', in C. Forsyth and I. Hare (eds.), *The Golden Metwand and the Crooked Cord: Essays in Honour of Sir William Wade QC* (Oxford: Clarendon Press, 1998), 297–317.

[158] See L. Vickers, 'Whistleblowing in the Public Sector and the ECHR' [1997] PL 594–6.

[159] For discussion of the Act, see Y. Cripps, 'The Public Interest Disclosure Act 1998', in J. Beatson and Y. Cripps, *Freedom of Expression and Freedom of Information: Essays in Honour of Sir David Williams* (Oxford: Oxford University Press, 2000), 275–87.

collating reports about people, not all of whom are suspected of offences. Until relatively recently, these gobbets of information were routinely held on paper, and their mass and the lack of centralization made it hard, and in normal circumstances too much trouble, to link them. As a result, no one person or body could put together a complete view of the activities of individuals based on records. This was traditionally regarded as an important safeguard for individuals: if the state could not find out all about its citizens, it could not easily control them; liberty and autonomy could be preserved.[160] Full information is a tool of repression, particularly when coupled with the ability (now provided by computer networks) rapidly to combine, process, and match large amounts of information from diverse sources.

The early history of income tax provides a good example of this principle. On the introduction of income tax[161] during the Napoleonic Wars, the need for the first time to assess people's income raised a threat to the confidentiality of people's private and business affairs. This was eased by having income from different sources assessed under different schedules to the Act by different surveyors, and so began the schedular system of income tax which survives to the present, although the various schedules are no longer assessed by different people. The advent of computers, the phenomenal growth in their storage capacities and processing and transmission speeds, and the development of networking systems such as the internet, have revolutionized the position. A portable computer is now far more powerful than the batteries of machines which helped to plan and implement lunar landing expeditions only thirty years ago. This has facilitated a vast explosion in the amount of information which can be stored, and the ability to retrieve, collate and cross-match information speedily. Combined with improved telecommunications, it has also made it far easier to transfer information from one user to another over large distances, even internationally, virtually instantaneously.[162] Despite attempts by government to play down the implications,[163] this poses two risks to civil liberties.[164]

First, information which is held can do far more damage than previously if passed on to other people, even if it is correct, but particularly if it is wrong, while technology such as DNA profiling has increased the amount of sensitive information which can be stored. Security vetting procedures in relation to job applications may sometimes be needed, but can lead to people being denied jobs without ever knowing the grounds on which they have been rejected, or being able to challenge incorrect information.[165] Security vetting at the BBC no longer takes place except for those

---

[160] See the observations of Sir Nicolas Browne-Wilkinson in *Anchor Brewhouse Developments Ltd. v. Berkeley House (Docklands Developments) Ltd.* (1987) 284 EG 625.

[161] Property and Income Tax Act 1798; see B. E. V. Sabine, *A History of Income Tax* (London: Allen & Unwin, 1966).

[162] See, generally, *Report of the Committee on Data Protection* (Chairman: Sir Norman Lindop), Cmnd. 7341 (London: HMSO, 1978); D. Campbell and S. Connor, *On the Record: Surveillance, Computers and Privacy —The Inside Story* (London: Michael Joseph, 1986); Wacks, *The Protection of Privacy*, ch. 4; Wacks, *Personal Information*, ch. 6.

[163] See, e.g. White Paper on Data Protection, Cmnd. 8539 (1982).

[164] Campbell and Connor, *On the Record*, ch. 3; S. Davies, *Big Brother: Britain's Web of Surveillance and the New Technological Order* (London: Pan Books, 1996), ch. 2.

[165] For discussion, see S. Fredman and G. S. Morris, *The State as Employer* (London: Mansell, 1989), 232–6.

concerned in war reporting. Previously, all applicants for jobs were vetted. For example, in 1977 MI5 advised the BBC not to appoint a Ms. Hilton, because as a student she had been secretary of the Scotland–China Association, which MI5 regarded as subversive, despite the fact that its members included eminent churchmen and a former governor of Stirling Castle.[166] There is a serious risk that capacity to cross-match information will be used in ways which are not compatible with the right to respect for private life under Article 8. For example, in 1995 the Conservative government produced a consultation paper on an identity card.[167] It supported the idea of a compulsory card on the basis of questionable claims about the benefits a card would have for individuals and the crime-control potential of cards, without addressing the serious risks to privacy if more than very minimal information about the bearer was contained in, or accessible through the use of, the card.[168] The idea was dropped after responses made clear the complexity of the issues. Proposals to extend the accessibility and use of personal information would now have to be properly assessed by reference to data protection and human-rights standards before being put into the public domain. But the privacy of one's life is seriously compromised by the need to use other electronically processed cards to obtain money or credit or to make payments or obtain access to buildings, and by the use of telephone and e-mail communications which are all too readily monitored by public authorities and private enterprises.[169]

Secondly, it has proved to be at least as easy for people to break into computer databanks and abstract information as it ever was to break into a file registry and acquire information from paper files. Amateur computer hackers do it for fun, but professionals can exploit the security problems which face databank managers.[170] These difficulties can be exaggerated, but there is some cause for concern. At present, information is too diffuse to be easily collated on any very large scale. However, it would be very much easier if people had a single reference number which they were required to use for all purposes, such as an identity card number or a national insurance number. The Lindop Committee noted that linkages between databases were technically possible; they are now commonplace. The adoption of a 'universal personal identifier' would remove some of the existing obstacles.[171] National Insurance numbers are already close to providing such an identifier. Information collected by commercial enterprises such as credit-rating agencies for the purpose of assessing people's creditworthiness may be passed on, or even sold, for commercial purposes. The ability to pool information from medical records, which are increasingly being computerized, insurance applications, credit applications, etc., could pose a major threat to privacy, even without linking these databanks with those held by government.

---

[166] *Independent*, 21 October 1988, 3. On proceedings in Strasbourg, see *Hilton v. United Kingdom*, Eur. Commn. HR (1988) 57 D. & R. 108.

[167] Home Office, *Identity Cards*, Cm. 2879 (London: HMSO, 1995).

[168] See Davies, *Big Brother*, ch. 7.

[169] Davies, *Big Brother*, chs 8, 9, and 10.

[170] See, e.g., B. Hugill, 'Pay Up and Snoop on thy Neighbour', *Observer*, 6 March 1994, 10; Davies, *Big Brother*, ch. 8.

[171] Cmnd. 7341, para. 6.08.

Problems concerning the accuracy and security of records are common to paper and computerized records, but are raised in an acute form by computer databanks. Wherever they arise, a number of interests have to be balanced. The state has a legitimate interest in collecting information for its manifold purposes, and these include the vetting of people who hold or apply for jobs which are sensitive in terms of national security, or more recently involve dealing with children. As the late Harry Street pointed out, this is inevitable and essential, but the great task is to ensure that the information on which the process depends is reliable.[172] This interest in securing reliability would seem to indicate that there is a public, as well as a private or individual, interest in allowing the subjects of records to have access to them to check and if necessary correct them, at least where this can be done without threatening security.

However, here another interest enters the balance. Third parties may be concerned, either as informants, or as advisers or referees who have expressed opinions about the subject of the record, or as subjects whose affairs are bound up with those of the main subject of the record. They might have spoken or written in confidence, and have a privacy interest of their own in preventing the subject from finding out who they are. It may therefore be necessary to restrict access to records which would allow the subject to identify others, if an overriding privacy or national-security interest would be endangered by allowing full access; but any restriction should go no further than necessary to achieve the purpose. These matters have, to some extent, now been covered by legislation, although the secrecy and lack of accountability which currently characterizes in policing and national-security activities, and very wide exemptions from the legislation, make it impossible to be confident that the safeguards are adequate or that human-rights and data-protection principles are being considered properly in relation to each dealing with personal information.

Awareness of the danger of uncontrolled access to and use of personal information posed by computer power, even in its relatively primitive days, was promoted by organizations such as the Campaign for Freedom of Information and led to the passing of the Data Protection Act 1984, which provided a legal framework for controlling the use of computerized personal data.[173] It was already seen as an international problem. The Act was drafted in the light of the OECD *Guidelines on the Protection of Privacy and Transborder Flows of Personal Information* (1980), and the Council of Europe *Convention for the Protection of Individuals with Regard to Automatic Processing of Personal Data* (1981). The growth of the world wide web and global markets, the resulting expansion of cross-border data flows and their huge economic importance, made it increasingly important to approach controls on an international level during the 1980s and 1990s. There was an explosion of international standards, both 'hard law' in the form of treaties between states and 'soft law' in the form of recommendations and guidelines issued by international bodies. These mainly reflect similar standards, which have influenced the interpretation of judicially enforceable provisions such as Article 8 of the ECHR and so have acquired a degree of legal force.[174]

---

[172] H. Street, *Freedom, the Individual and the Law*, 5th edn. (Harmondsworth: Penguin, 1982), 245.
[173] For full discussion, see C. Tapper, *Computer Law*, 4th edn. (London: Longman, 1989).
[174] See Feldman, Information and Privacy, 304–7.

Ultimately, Member States of the European Community accepted that control over data affected the operation of inter-state trade. The EC Council adopted the Data Protection Directive 95/46,[175] providing the foundation for harmonizing standards of data protection across the Community. The Directive states expressly that its purpose is to give effect to the right to privacy. The UK enacted the Data Protection Act 1998 to implement the Directive. Although the Act does not mention privacy, it is central to the purposes of the Act and to the functions of the regulatory machinery which it established.

Both the Data Protection Act 1984 and the Data Protection Act 1998 put in place a protective regime for personal data. The most significant change between the 1984 Act and the 1998 Act is the extension in the range of data which are covered. The 1984 Act protected only computerized data. It left an obvious lacuna in relation to trad-itional paper files. People had no right of access to such files, and there was no legal regime regulating the circumstances in which other people's rights of confidentiality, or other interests, could justify denying people access to their records.[176] This was later held to violate the right to respect for private life under ECHR Article 8.[177] The gap was partly filled by three pieces of legislation. The first was the Access to Personal Files Act 1987, which originated as a Private Member's Bill introduced by Mr. Archy Kirk-wood MP. It had a limited impact, giving a right of access in respect of files containing personal information, if held by a Housing Act local authority or a local social services authority. The authorities' obligations in respect of access were set out in regulations made by the relevant Secretary of State under section 3, but they applied in relatively few fields of administration. The Act is now repealed and replaced by the Data Protection Act 1998, from the time when its provisions covering personal files on paper come into force.

Information supplied to a local authority by a health professional was exempted from disclosure under the 1987 Act. Doctors have very intimate information about people, and wield substantial power. Furthermore, the doctor's normal obligation of confidentiality in relation to the patient has been watered down. First, disclosure of information about patients in an anonymized form has been held to raise no issue of confidentiality.[178] Secondly, there is what Professor Gerald Dworkin has called 'extended confidence', in which medical records are routinely open to a whole 'health care team', including nurses, secretaries, administrators, and social workers, as well as doctors, although the General Medical Council requires doctors to ensure that patients understand how information will be shared within the team.[179] Secondly, the scope of the duty of confidence may be restricted by the public-interest exception.[180] Thirdly, the General Medical Council recognizes that, in addition to the above

---

[175] [1995] OJ L281/31.

[176] *Gaskin v. Liverpool City Council* [1980] 1 WLR 1459, CA.

[177] *Gaskin v. United Kingdom*, Eur. Ct. HR, Series A, No. 160, Judgment of 7 July 1989, 12 EHRR 36.

[178] *R. v. Department of Health, ex parte Source Informatics Ltd.* [2000] 2 WLR 940, CA.

[179] G. Dworkin, 'Access to Medical Records: Discovery, Confidentiality and Privacy' (1979) 42 *MLR* 88 at 90; General Medical Council, *Confidentiality: Protecting and Providing Information* (London: General Medical Council, 2000), paras. 7–10.

[180] *W. v. Egdell* [1990] Ch. 359, [1990] 1 All ER 835, CA.

relaxations, the obligation does not prevent disclosure where the patient has consented expressly, where patient is unable to consent, and where disclosure is required by law. Where information is required for the purposes of audit or research, doctors should either obtain consent or arrange for information to be supplied in an anonymized form unless it is essential to make disclosure under other conditions.[181] Nevertheless, where the interests of patients may be affected by a disclosure, it is important that the patient should be able to make sure that the information recorded is accurate, and to know what is being said about him, unless there are compelling reasons for keeping the record closed.

For this reason, the Access to Medical Reports Act 1988 and the Access to Health Records Act 1990 extended to patients a right to know what is being recorded or disclosed about them. The 1988 Act deals with reports written by doctors for insurance companies and employers. The 1990 Act applies to information relating to the physical or mental health of an individual who can be identified from that information, or from other information in the possession of the holder of the record, where the record has been made by or on behalf of a registered medical practitioner, dentist, optician, pharmacist, nurse, midwife, health visitor, chiropodist, dietician, occupational therapist, orthoptist, physiotherapist, clinical psychologist, child psychotherapist, speech therapist, art or music therapist employed by a health-service body, or a scientist employed by a health-service body as a head of a department.[182] Access is to be allowed to children only if they are *Gillick*-competent (section 4(1)), and may be excluded where the information, in the opinion of the holder, would be likely to cause serious harm to the physical or mental health of the patient or anyone else, or was provided by or relates to another individual who could be identified from the information, unless the latter has consented to disclosure.[183] Incorrect information is to be rectified.[184]

The 1988 and 1990 Acts continue to operate alongside the Data Protection Act 1998, as the Secretary of State is empowered to exempt information about health from the access right of data subjects under the 1998 Act.[185] The remainder of this section explains the main features of the 1998 Act.

The Data Protection Act 1998 imposes duties on data controllers who are established in the UK and are processing data in the context of that establishment, and those who are established outside the European Economic Area but are using equipment in the UK to process data otherwise than for the purpose of transit through the UK.[186] The first duty is to notify the official regulator, the Information Commissioner,[187] of 'registrable particulars' of controllers and their activities, together with a general

---

[181] See General Medical Council, *Confidentiality*, paras. 15–39.

[182] Access to Health Records Act 1990, ss. 1, 2.

[183] Ibid., s. 5.   [184] Ibid., s. 6.

[185] Data Protection Act 1998, s. 30(1).

[186] Data Protection Act 1998, s. 5(1). The Act envisages that activities of data controllers established in other EEA states will be governed by equivalent legislation in those states giving effect to the EC Data Protection Directive.

[187] The Data Protection Registrar under the Data Protection Act 1984 was renamed the Data Protection Commissioner by s. 6(1) of the Data Protection Act 1998, and became the Information Commissioner when she took responsibility for freedom of information by virtue of the Freedom of Information Act 2000, s. 18.

description of the organizational and technical measures which they are taking against unauthorized or unlawful processing of personal data, and against accidental loss or destruction of, or damage to, personal data.[188] It is a criminal offence to process personal data without being registered, or to fail to notify the Commissioner of changes to the registered details.[189] The 'registrable particulars' which must be notified are:

- the data controller's name and address, and the name and address of any nominated representative;
- a description of the personal data being or to be processed by or on behalf of the data controller;
- a description of the category or categories of data subjects to whom they relate (e.g. customers, patients, experimental research subjects, people coming to the notice of investigators, informants, etc.);
- a description of the purpose or purposes for which the data are being or are to be processed;[190]
- a description of any recipient or recipients to whom the data controller intends or may wish to disclose the data;
- the names, or a description, of any countries or territories outside the European Economic Area to which the data controller directly or indirectly transfers, or intends or may wish to transfer, the data;
- a statement (where applicable) of the fact that personal data are being, or are intended to be, processed in circumstances where the prohibition on unregistered processing is excluded either by reason of not consisting of computerized information being automatically processed, or by a regulation made by the Home Secretary on the ground that the processing appears to the Home Secretary to be unlikely to prejudice the rights and freedoms of data subjects.[191]

The notified details are held on a register which the Commissioner maintains.[192]

Next, data controllers must comply with eight data protection principles when processing (although some data controllers are exempt from certain principles). The Commissioner has powers to enforce the principles. The Act also gives rights to data subjects, which they can enforce through ordinary courts. We will now consider (a) the data which are covered by the Act, (b) the activities in relation to the data which are covered, (c) the data protection principles, (d) the enforcement powers of the Commissioner, (e) the rights of data subjects, and (f) the exceptions and exemptions which the Act grants.

(a) *The data which are protected.* The Act protects 'personal data',[193] i.e. data which relate to a living individual (the 'data subject') who can be identified either from the

---

[188] Data Protection Act 1998, s. 18(2).
[189] Ibid., ss. 17(1), 20 and 21(1), subject to the exceptions in s. 17(2)–(4) and the defence in s. 21(3).
[190] 'Processed' has a very wide meaning, explained below.
[191] Data Protection Act 1998, s. 16(1).
[192] Ibid., ss. 18, 19.
[193] Ibid., s. 1(1).

data themselves or from the data together with other information which is, or is likely to come into, the possession of the data controller. They include any expression of opinion about the individual and any indication of the intentions of the data controller or any other person in respect of that individual. It follows that individuals, but not organizations, are protected; the object is to bolster individual liberty and privacy, not commercial or group rights. There are four kinds of 'data' within the meaning of the Act. The first two are categories of computerized information, the third is information held in non-electronic form, and the last may be of either type:

- information which is being processed by means of equipment operating automatically in response to instructions given for that purpose;
- information recorded with the intention that it should be processed by means of such equipment;
- information which is recorded as part of a 'relevant filing system' or with the intention that it should form part of such a filing system; and
- an accessible record not falling within one of the other categories (i.e. a record made by or on behalf of a health professional, relating to the physical or mental health or condition of an individual, and relating to the care of that individual; a record relating to a present or past pupil at a state school or special school, maintained by or on behalf of the school's governors or a teacher at the school; or a record maintained by a social services department or a housing authority).[194]

A 'relevant filing system' for the purpose of the third category of data is:

'a set of information relating to individuals to the extent that, although the information is not processed by means of equipment operating automatically in response to instructions given for that purpose, the set is structured, either by reference to individuals or by reference to criteria relating to individuals, in such a way that specific information relating to a particular individual is readily available.'[195]

For example, a set of files held by a university would be a relevant filing system if:

- it contained a file for each of a number of students or staff, organized in alphabetical order of name, or by each individual's identification number (assuming that there is an index of reference numbers), or by year of matriculation, graduation or appointment (assuming that there are annual lists of students or staff); or
- it contained a file for each year's set of examination results, in which individual students were identifiable, assuming that there is an index of students taking examinations in each year.

On the other hand, a filing system would not be a relevant filing system if it contained notes of decisions of committees organized by topic (e.g. computer facilities, module

---

[194] Ibid., ss. 1(1), 68 and 69, and Schs. 11 and 12.
[195] Ibid., s. 1(1).

descriptions, programme admission criteria) in such a way that specific information relating to particular individuals was not readily accessible. Applying the same principles in a different context, the paper files of the Security Service (MI5) holding information about particular individuals and arranged person by person (or, perhaps, organization by organization) would be relevant filing systems, but files on operations undertaken by the Service, or on topics such as Communist subversion since 1920, would not.

Special safeguards for the rights and freedoms of data subjects apply in relation to 'sensitive personal information', defined as personal data consisting of information as to:

- the data subject's racial or ethnic origin;
- his political opinions;
- his religious beliefs or other beliefs of a similar nature;
- whether he is a member of a trade union;
- his physical or mental health or condition;
- his sexual life;
- the commission or alleged commission by him of any offence;
- any proceedings for any offence committed or alleged to have been committed by him, the disposal of such proceedings, or the sentence of any court in such proceedings.[196]

(b) *The activities which are covered in relation to the data.* The Act governs the processing of personal data. 'Processing' has a wide meaning, making it possible for the Act to contribute to discharging most, if not all, of the UK's obligations in relation to personal information under ECHR Article 8. The word 'processing' is defined as:

'obtaining, recording or holding the information or data or carrying out any operation or set of operations on the information or data, including—

   (a) organization, adaptation or alteration of the information or data,

   (b) retrieval, consultation or use of the information or data,

   (c) disclosure of the information or data by transmission, dissemination or otherwise making available, or

   (d) alignment, combination, blocking, erasure or destruction of the information or data . . .'

This avoids some problems which arose under the Data Protection Act 1994, section 5, which made it an offence (*inter alia*) to use personal data for an unregistered purpose. In *R. v. Brown (Gregory)*[197] the defendant was a police officer who had improperly made use of the Police National Computer to check registration numbers

---

[196] Data Protection Act 1998, s. 2.
[197] [1996] AC 543, [1996] 1 All ER 545, HL.

of vehicles to assist a friend who ran a debt collection company. The question was whether merely calling up information on screen amounted to 'using' the data. In the House of Lords, the majority (Lords Goff of Chievely, Browne-Wilkinson, and Hoffmann) decided that 'use' was an ordinary word which, in its ordinary sense, involved doing something with the computerized information. Merely retrieving it and looking at it did not constitute 'use'. Lords Griffiths and Jauncey of Tulliechettle, dissenting, interpreted the section in the light of the 1981 Council of Europe Convention for the Protection of Individuals with regard to Automatic Processing of Personal Data, which the 1984 Act was enacted to implement. The object of the Convention was to protect the right to privacy (Article 1). The majority's approach did not achieve this. The dissenters thought that a person used information stored in a computer if he informed himself of its contents, so that he could decide whether or not to go on to apply the information for any particular purpose. The very broad meaning of 'process' in the 1998 Act avoids such disputes.

(c) *The data protection principles.* The eight principles[198] are as follows:

1. Personal data shall be processed fairly[199] and lawfully. In particular, personal data shall not be processed unless one of the following conditions is met:[200] (i) the data subject has consented; (ii) the processing is necessary for the performance of a contract to which the data subject is a party, or for taking steps at the data subject's request with a view to entering into a contract; (iii) the processing is necessary for compliance with any non-contractual legal obligation to which the data controller is subject; (iv) the processing is necessary in order to protect the vital interests of the data subject; (iv) the processing is necessary for the administration of justice, or for the exercise of statutory functions conferred on any person, of functions of the Crown, a Minister or a government department, or other functions of a public nature exercised by any person in the public interest; or (vi) the processing is necessary for the purposes of legitimate interests pursued by the data controller or by the third party or parties to whom the data are disclosed, except where the processing is unwarranted in any particular case by reason of prejudice to the rights and freedoms or legitimate interests of the data subject.

Where sensitive personal data are involved, they are not to be processed unless one of the following conditions is satisfied:[201] (i) the data subject has explicitly consented; (ii) the processing is necessary for the purposes of exercising or performing any right or obligation which is conferred by law on the data controller in connection with employment; (iii) the processing is necessary in order to protect the vital interests of the data subject in circumstances where consent cannot be given by or on behalf of him or her, or the data controller cannot reasonably be expected to obtain consent, or in order to protect the vital interests of another person where consent by or on behalf of the data subject is being unreasonably withheld; (iv) the processing is carried out as part of the legitimate activities of a non-profit-making body existing for political, philosophical, religious or trade-union purposes, with appropriate safeguards for the rights and freedoms of data subjects, if the information

---

[198] Data Protection Act 1998, s. 4 and Sch. 1, Part I. The principles are to be interpreted in accordance with Part II of Sch. 1.

[199] On the meaning of 'fairly', see Data Protection Act 1998, Sch. 1, Part II, paras. 1–4.

[200] Ibid., Sch. 2.

[201] Ibid., Sch. 3.

relates to members of the organization or people who have regular contact with it, and the information is not disclosed to a third party without the data subject's consent; (v) the information has been made public as a result of steps taken deliberately by the data subject; (vi) the processing is necessary for the purpose of, or in connection with, any legal proceedings, for the purpose of obtaining legal advice, or otherwise for the purposes of establishing, exercising or defending legal rights; (vii) the processing is necessary for the administration of justice, or for the exercise of statutory functions conferred on any person, or of functions of the Crown, a Minister or a government department; (viii) the processing is necessary for medical purposes and is undertaken by a health professional or someone who owes an equivalent duty of confidentiality; (ix) the processing of information as to racial or ethnic origin is necessary for the purpose of monitoring, promoting or maintaining equality of opportunity, and is carried out with appropriate safeguards for the rights and freedoms of data subjects; or (x) the data are processed in circumstances specified by an order made by the Secretary of State.

2. Personal data shall be obtained only for specified and lawful purposes, and shall not be further processed in any manner incompatible with those purposes.[202]

3. Personal data shall be adequate, relevant, and not excessive in relation to those purposes.

4. Personal data shall be accurate and kept up to date.[203]

5. Personal data shall not be kept for longer than necessary for the specified purposes.

6. Personal data shall be processed in accordance with the rights of data subjects under the Act.[204]

7. Appropriate technical and organizational measures shall be taken against unauthorized processing, accidental loss or destruction of, or damage to, personal data.[205]

8. Personal data shall not be transferred to a country or territory outside the European Economic Area unless that country or territory ensures an adequate level of protection for the rights and freedoms of data subjects in relation to the processing of personal data.[206]

(d) *The regulation and enforcement powers of the Commissioner.* The Commissioner combines her registration function with advisory, educational, monitoring, and enforcement roles. A data controller can ask the Commissioner for an assessment of his compliance with the data protection principles,[207] and the Commissioner must make a preliminary assessment of processing which is of a kind specified in an order made by the Secretary of State as appearing to him to be particularly likely to cause substantial damage or distress to data subejcts or otherwise significantly to prejudice their rights and freedoms.[208] Because the sixth data protection principle requires respect for the rights of data subjects, the Commissioner has a role in protecting those rights alongside proceedings which data subjects can take in the courts. The

---

[202] See further Data Protection Act 1998, Sch. 1, Part II, paras. 5 and 6.
[203] See further ibid., Sch. 1, Part II, para. 7.
[204] On the rights of data subjects, see below. See further ibid., Sch. 1, Part II, para. 8.
[205] See further ibid., Sch. 1, Part II, paras. 9–12.
[206] See further ibid., Sch. 1, Part II, paras. 13–15.
[207] Ibid., s. 42.
[208] Ibid., s. 22.

Commissioner can require information from a data controller, subject to the rules on legal professional privilege and to a limited privilege against self-incrimination,[209] and has available powers to enter and inspect premises.[210] If the Commissioner is satisfied that a data controller has contravened or is contravening a data protection principle, she has power to serve an enforcement notice specifying in some detail the steps to be taken, the time within which they must be taken, and what processing (if any) will be permitted meanwhile.[211] Data controllers have rights to appeal to the Information Tribunal against notices.[212] This creates a potentially powerful regulatory, monitoring, and reporting body[213] for data collection and processing, covering all public and private computerizable personal records, including those collected for research purposes.

(e) *The rights of data subjects.* The Act gives a data subject the following rights over data controllers:

- the right to be informed whether the data controller is processing personal data relating to that data subject;
- the right to be given a description of the personal data, the purposes for which they are being or are to be processed, and the recipients or classes of recipients to whom they are or may be disclosed;
- the right to have the information, and any available information about the source of the information, communicated in an intelligible form;
- the right to be informed of the logic involved in making any personal evaluations (for example, of credit-worthiness or employability) automatically on the basis of the personal data;[214]
- a right to give notice requiring the data controller to cease, or not to begin, processing any personal data of which he is the data subject, on the ground that, for specified reasons, the processing is causing or is likely to cause substantial and unwarranted damage or distress to any person;[215]
- a right to give notice requiring the data controller to cease, or not to begin, processing data relating to the data subject for the purpose of direct marketing;[216]
- a right to give notice requiring a data controller to ensure that no decision which significantly affects the data subject is taken solely on the basis of processing of personal data by automatic means for the purpose of evaluating such matters as the data subject's performance at work, credit-worthiness, reliability, or conduct.[217]

---

[209] Ibid., ss. 43, 44.
[210] Ibid., s. 50 and Sch. 9.
[211] Ibid., s. 40.
[212] Ibid., s. 48. The Tribunal was renamed by the Freedom of Information Act 2000, s. 18.
[213] The registrar's annual reports are published as House of Commons Papers.
[214] Data Protection Act 1998, s. 7(1). There are some restrictions in s. 7(2)–(6). If the data controller wrongfully fails to comply, a court can order compliance: s. 7(8).
[215] Ibid., s. 10. A court can order compliance: s. 10(4).
[216] Ibid., s. 11. A court can order compliance: s. 11(2).
[217] Ibid., s. 12. A court can order compliance: s. 12(8).

Besides being able to take proceedings in court to enforce compliance with these rights, data subjects can claim compensation for damage, and for distress linked to the damage, caused as the result of a contravention by a data controller of the requirements of the Act. Data subjects can also claim compensation for distress without any damage if the contravention relates to the processing of data for certain 'special purposes', namely journalism and artistic or literary purposes.[218] This gives a remedy against the press (among others) for a range of failures, including holding or using inaccurate personal data. Data controllers have a defence if they can prove that they had taken such care as in all the circumstances was reasonably required to comply with the requirement concerned.[219] A court can order a data controller to rectify, block, erase, or destroy data which are inaccurate, together with any other personal data which contain an expression of opinion which appears to be based on the inaccurate data.

The court can also order rectification, blocking, erasure, or destruction of personal data if the data subject has suffered damage through the data controller's breach of requirements of the Act in relation to the data, if satisfied that there is a substantial risk of further contraventions in relation to those data.[220]

(f) *The exceptions and exemptions which the Act grants.* The Act grants certain exemptions from its regime, or parts of it.

- **National security:** The data protection principles, the rights of data subjects, requirements for notification by data controllers, the enforcement powers of the Commissioner, and the offence of knowingly or recklessly obtaining, disclosing, or procuring the disclosure of personal data without the consent of the data controller, do not apply if the exemption from the provision in question is required for the purpose of safeguarding national security. A Minister's certificate to that effect is conclusive, subject to an appeal against the certificate to the Information Tribunal.[221] In terms of ECHR Article 8 this may be justified by the national-security exception in Article 8(2), but it would probably need to be shown that there was appropriate machinery for the necessity and proportionality of the exemption to be assessed in relation to each case.

- **Crime and taxation:** Personal data processed for the prevention or detection of crime, the apprehension or prosecution of offenders, or the assessment or collection of any tax or duty or of any imposition of similar nature, enjoy a limited exemption to the extent to which the application of requirements to the data would be likely to prejudice those purposes. When that applies, the data are exempt from the first data protection principle (fair and lawful processing) except in respect of the particular conditions for processing data noted above. They are also exempt from the data subject's rights under section 7 of the Act to obtain information about the data held in relation to them, noted in the first four bullet points under (e), above.[222] The first data protection principle and the rights in section 7 are together referred to as the 'subject information provisions'.

---

[218] Data Protection Act 1998, s. 13(1), (2). The special purposes are defined in s. 3.
[219] Ibid., s. 13(3).　　　　[220] Ibid., s. 14(1), (4).
[221] Ibid., s. 28.　　　　[222] Ibid., s. 29.

Although the other rights and principles apply, as do the Commissioner's enforcement powers in respect of them, it emphasises the relative weakness of privacy controls over data sharing activities under arrangements for inter-agency co-operation such as Youth Offending Teams, under section 115 of the Crime and Disorder Act 1998. Despite Home Office guidance on the use of the powers, there is little consistency of approach between police forces. The same applies to the sharing of information between tax and social security bodies under the Social Security Administration (Fraud) Act 1997, sections 1 and 2, and sharing of information about a person's record of sex offences under sections 17 and 47 of the Children Act 1989.[223] It is somewhat reassuring that all these provisions must now be given effect as far as possible in a manner compatible with ECHR Article 8, by virtue of the Human Rights Act 1998.

- **Health, education, and social work:** The Secretary of State has power under section 30 of the Data Protection Act 1998 to make orders excluding or modifying the effect of the subject information provisions. This may be done in respect of information about a person's physical or mental health or condition, information about school pupils, and information held for social work purposes. While this could be restrictive of rights, the Human Rights Act 1998 means that the power to make and apply orders can lawfully be exercised only in a manner compatible with Convention rights, including that established under Article 8 by the *Gaskin* case, above.

- **Regulatory activities:** Regulatory bodies need not comply with the subject information provisions where to do so would be likely to prejudice the proper discharge of their functions.[224]

- **Journalism, literature, and art:** Personal data being processed only for these purposes have certain exemptions if the processing is undertaken with a view to publication by any person of journalistic, literary, or artistic material, subject to certain conditions, as provided by section 32. This exemption is designed to protect the Convention right to, and public interest in, freedom of expression. The conditions are that the data controller must reasonably believe (i) that, having regard to the special importance of the public interest in freedom of expression, publication would be in the public interest, and (ii) that, in all the circumstances, compliance with the provision in question is incompatible with the purposes of journalism, literature, or art. This assessment must be made on a case-by-case basis. If the conditions are satisfied, the personal data may be unprotected by any or all of the rights under section 7 in respect of obtaining information about personal data processed by the data controller, the right to prevent damaging or distressing processing, the right to forbid wholly automated evaluations, and the power of courts to order rectification, blocking, erasure, or destruction of data. In order to protect the rights of others, particularly their privacy rights, there is a further exception for payroll and accounting data, while

---

[223] See *Re L. (Sexual Abuse: Disclosure)* [1999] 1 WLR 299, CA.
[224] Data Protection Act 1998, s. 31.

people who maintain membership and mailing lists, and other data, on behalf of clubs and for purely domestic purposes, are exempted by section 33.

• **Research, history, and statistics:** Section 33 permits further processing of personal data for research purposes, including historical and statistical research, and excludes the rights under section 7 in respect of obtaining information about personal data processed by the data controller, as long as the data are not processed to support measures or decisions with respect to particular individuals, and are not processed in a way that is likely to cause substantial damage or distress to any data subject.

• **Information available to the public under any enactment:** Section 34 exempts such information from the subject information provisions, the fourth data protection principle (ensuring that data are accurate and up to date), the power of courts to order rectification, blocking, erasure, or destruction of data, and provisions forbidding disclosure.

• **Legal disclosures:** Section 35 exempts from the non-disclosure provisions any personal data which are required to be disclosed under an enactment, rule of law, or court order. It also exempts personal data from non-disclosure provisions if disclosure is necessary for the purpose of, or in connection with, any current or prospective legal proceedings, or for the purpose of obtaining legal advice, or is otherwise necessary for the purposes of establishing, exercising, or defending legal rights.

• **Domestic purposes:** Section 36 exempts from data protection principles, the rights of data subjects, and the notification and registration requirements, any personal data processed by an individual (not a corporation) only for the purposes of that individual's personal family or household affairs. Thus there is no need for individuals to register in respect of their social address and telephone lists, as long as they are kept separately from business lists.

• **Other exemptions:** Section 37 of, and Schedule 7 to, the Act give miscellaneous limited exemptions. Confidential reference given in connection with the current or prospective education, training, or employment of the data subject, of the provision or prospective provision of any service by the data subject. Personal data are exempt from the subject information provisions on a case-by-case basis to the extent to which the application of any of the provisions would be likely to prejudice the combat effectiveness of the armed forces. Personal data processed in connection with the appointment of QCs and judges and the conferral of honours are exempt from all the subject information provisions, and the Secretary of State may by order exempt from those provisions personal data processed for the purpose of assessing a person's suitability for employment by or under the Crown or for any office to which appointments are made by Her Majesty, a Minister, or a Northern Ireland department. Personal data used for management planning or management forecasting are exempt from the subject information provisions to the extent to which their application would be likely to prejudice the conduct of an enterprise's business or other activity. There are

exemptions for those providing corporate financial services, for records of negotiations, for examination scripts and similar papers, for data to which a claim to
legal professional privilege can be maintained, and for data which, if disclosed,
would expose the person to proceedings for an offence other than an offence
under the Act. Finally, the Secretary of State has power under section 38 to
exempt other data by order. Personal data may be exempted from the subject
information provisions or the non-disclosure provisions, if and to the extent that
he considers it necessary in order to safeguard the interests of the data subject or
the rights or freedoms of any other person.

All these statutory provisions serve to protect the interests of individuals in their
dignity and their private lives. They should also help to encourage record holders to
ensure that the information which they record is accurate and fair. The 1998 Act
marks a significant step forward. Some difficulties remain. Medical researchers, for
example, are finding that the requirement for initial consent to data processing from
the data subject is making it difficult to establish large-scale studies using statistical
data, and puts important studies at risk. Conversely, there is concern about the width
of the exemptions, particularly in respect of national security and the investigation
and prosecution of crimes. However, the provisions represent an important effort to
strike a balance between private rights and public interests in accordance with internationally approved data protection principles and the right to respect for private life
under ECHR Article 8. The legislation, which must be interpreted in the light of all
the Convention rights, not only Article 8, shows that Parliament is beginning to take
seriously the positive obligations on the state which flow from the right to private and
family life under Article 8 of the ECHR.

9.5 PRIVACY: THE FOUNDATION

In this chapter we have explored the reaction to privacy-based rights in international,
US, and English law. We have noted distinctions between positive and negative aspects
of privacy rights, and have observed different conceptions about the foundational
values which are said to mandate the protection of privacy, and respect for private and
family life. There is the view, advanced by Westin and Wacks, that privacy is fundamentally concerned with the control of information. Against this is the view of many
judges, both in the US Supreme Court and in the European Court of Human Rights,
that the value of privacy or private life is more far-reaching, and protects personal and
political autonomy, self-determination, family relationships, and similar interests
which have nothing directly to do with information. So far as the ECHR is concerned,
it is plausible to argue that the extensive interpretation given to Article 8 is the result
of the rights being framed in terms of respect for private and family life, rather than
merely a right to privacy. This cannot, however, explain either American developments or the evolutionary way in which the European Court of Human Rights has felt
able to develop the notion of private and family life.

It is important to work out where one stands on the question of the fundamental justification for privacy rights, because it is likely to dictate the use to which one can put them. Treating them as essentially about information has the attraction that it makes them relatively easy to handle, and gives them a clear and easily delimited scope. However, it seems artificial to choose a foundational theory for a right merely because that makes the right easier to handle. It allows the practical tail to wag the theoretical dog. If there are good reasons to extend the notion of privacy beyond information, or even to treat the core meaning of privacy as something unrelated to information, we should brace ourselves to grapple with the conceptual problems in order to make our conception of the private sphere of life generate usable principles. Underlying this chapter has been an assumption that this task is worth attempting.

Historically and theoretically, the notion of privacy has emerged from a political ideal of the individual, the family, and small groups of people working together consensually for a common object, as the basic elements in society. The rights to respect for private and family life, home, and correspondence, as under ECHR Article 8, or the core constitutional privacy rights under the US Constitution (as interpreted by the judges), are founded on the fundamental importance of these units to people's psychology and self-fulfilment, to their opportunity to participate in democratic political processes, and to the welfare of society. Rights to respect for personal information, far from being core elements in the definition of privacy, are usually parasitic on these foundational privacy rights: respect for individual dignity, self-determination, family relationships, etc. Other rights, such as the commercial right to exploit the potential public (rather than private) value of one's information or personality, are derived from a source entirely unrelated to privacy. All the tort and constitutional rights which are grouped together in American privacy law are valuable aids to autonomy. But it is autonomy itself, the freedom to pursue one's own objectives and life-style and to enjoy personal space, which is the fundamental justification for privacy-related (as so many other) rights.

If one accepts that privacy rights have an importance which is logically and historically prior to the interest in personal information, it means that a legal right to respect for privacy need not be reduced to a mere manifestation of the legal categories and remedies from which Warren and Brandeis derived its existence. Once the significance of privacy has been acknowledged, its centrality to the development of legal protection for personal autonomy can be exploited. It can take off in new directions, and have effects which are unrelated to personal information. For example, the use of privacy to extend the rights of women in *Roe v. Wade*, or the restriction of rights to be free of unreasonable searches and seizures (under the Fourth Amendment to the US Constitution, or section 8 of the Canadian Charter of Rights and Freedoms) to situations in which the litigant has a legitimate privacy interest of his own to protect, are expressions of the basis of privacy jurisprudence in human dignity and personal autonomy.

Such developments as these will not be random or unprincipled, so long as the judges base developments securely in the fundamental values of autonomy. This avoids reducing privacy to a redundant or empty concept. It has life and purpose, without becoming unmanageably vague. Adopting a model of privacy based on liberal values does not exempt privacy from political processes, as the scope of the private sphere of life is ultimately a political matter. It does, however, demand that people (including legislators, judges, and other public officers) respect those expectations of privacy which have been accepted as appropriate for all by means of the democratic process. The three chapters which follow examine the extent to which this ideal is realized in various areas of English law.

10

FREEDOM FROM UNREASONABLE
ENTRIES, SEARCHES, SEIZURES,
AND SURVEILLANCE

10.1 BACKGROUND

In England and Wales before the Human Rights Act 1998 we relied mainly on the common law to protect us against arbitrary exercises of public power. As noted in Chapter 9, English law was very late in developing a right to privacy. In the field of search and seizure, this meant that the common-law rights concerning property and confidentiality bore the main burden of protecting privacy-related rights. Much of the law of entry, search, seizure, and surveillance therefore concerns the circumstances in which the law will recognize exceptions to rights to property and confidentiality in the public interest. Exceptions have been introduced both by statute and by common law. Some of these rely on a degree of control being exercised by an independent judicial officer, who has to decide whether to grant a search warrant authorizing the interference. However, an increasing number rely on the competence and good sense of the officers concerned.

Other countries have based their controls on entries, searches, and seizures squarely on a right to privacy, and have been much less willing to permit searches and seizures without independent judicial safeguards. In the USA, the Fourth Amendment to the federal Constitution guarantees the right to be free of unreasonable search and seizure, and provides that no warrant shall issue save on probable cause. As regards other invasions of privacy interests, they constitute a deprivation of liberty under the Fifth and Fourteenth Amendments, and must observe due process requirements, including (normally) independent authorization. Any interference with privacy, or search and seizure, without a warrant is *prima facie* unreasonable, and so unconstitutional, although there are exigent circumstances in which it will not be regarded as unreasonable.[1] In Canada, section 8 of the Canadian Charter of Rights and Freedoms, forming

---

[1] *Katz v. United States* 389 US 347 (1967). Exigent circumstances justifying warrantless search or seizure include cases where the police are in hot pursuit of a suspect (*Warden v. Hayden* 387 US 294 (1967)); situations where evidence is in plain view of officers acting with justification, and might be destroyed if not seized immediately (*Coolidge v. New Hampshire* 403 US 443 (1971)); and searches for weapons on arrest (*Chimel v. California* 395 US 752 (1969)). See also *Minnesota v. Carter*, 525 US 83 (1998), and generally W. C. LaFave, *Search and Seizure: A Treatise on the Fourth Amendment*, 3 vols. (St Paul: West, 1978).

Part I of the Constitution Act 1982, guarantees the right to be free of unreasonable searches and seizures. It has been held that this provision too is grounded in a privacy right, and the courts have decided that a system of independent authorization prior to a search and seizure is normally required where there is a reasonable expectation of privacy.[2] Each situation must be examined to determine whether there was such an expectation, and whether an interference with it was reasonable. For example, students attending school have a reasonable expectation of privacy at school, but it is lower than it would be at home because school authorities have responsibilities to maintain a safe environment and an atmosphere which encourages learning. They must take action against students with illicit drugs, and to that end will find it easier to justify a warrantless search than would police officers. While a warrantless search is *prima facie* unreasonable, school authorities must be able to act quickly and maintain discipline, and for those purposes they need a power to search without a warrant. Such searches are accordingly not unreasonable if they are carried out on reasonable grounds, with statutory authority, for a proper purpose, and in a manner which minimizes the intrusion on privacy.[3]

In the UK, the Human Rights Act 1998, incorporating the right to respect for private life and the home under ECHR Article 8 into domestic law, makes it likely that English law will move in the same direction. Any official entry to, or surveillance or search of, a person's private premises engages Article 8(1), as explained in Chapter 9, above. The interference can be justified under Article 8(2), but the European Court of Human Rights has exercised particularly strict scrutiny of searches, etc., which are permitted without prior judicial authorization. The Court requires states to demonstrate that national law provides adequate safeguards for the rights of people who are affected. In particular, the national law must prescribe the grounds on which interference may be permitted, the officers who can authorize it, the manner in which it is to be carried out, and the procedures for obtaining remedies for improper searches, in such a way to ensure that the interference is necessary for one of the legitimate purposes under Article 8(2), intrudes on the right as little as possible to give effect to that aim, and guarantees an effective remedy for an aggrieved individual.[4] Warrants for searches which cannot be justified under ECHR Article 8(2) are now unlawful by virtue of section 6(1) of the Human Rights Act 1998, unless primary legislation requires the warrant to be issued, or the search to be conducted, in those circumstances or in that way, notwithstanding the incompatibility.

The new right under the 1998 Act provides an important underpinning of principle to the law in this area. The common law provided only weak protection against abuse of power by officials searching premises. Judges could have provided some protection for privacy by refusing to accept any new common-law exceptions to property and confidentiality rights, and by restrictively interpreting legislation which infringed

---

[2] *Hunter v. Southam Inc.* (1984) 11 DLR (4th) 641; *Kokesch v. R.* (1990) 1 CR (4th) 62.

[3] *R. v. M. (M.R.)*, Supreme Court of Canada, 26 November 1998.

[4] See, e.g. *Niemietz v. Germany*, Eur. Ct. HR, Series A, No. 251-B, Judgment of 16 December 1992, 16 EHRR 97; *Funke v. France*, Eur. Ct. HR, Series A, No. 256-A, Judgment of 25 February 1993, 16 EHRR 297; *Mialhe v. France*, Eur. Ct. HR, Series A, No. 256-C, Judgment of 25 February 1997, 16 EHRR 332; *Cammenzind v. Switzerland*, Eur. Ct. HR (1999) 28 EHRR 458.

such rights. However, English courts showed too great a deference towards police officers' estimations of the powers which they require. Well before Parliament set some boundaries to police powers in the Police and Criminal Evidence Act 1984, the Court of Appeal had twice extended powers of seizure under warrant, without any statutory justification,[5] and failed notably to protect items subject to legal professional privilege from seizure under warrant.[6] Parliament attempted to reassert sensible limits on police powers (including the protection of privileged material) in the Police and Criminal Evidence Act 1984, but judges nearly always refused to exclude evidence obtained or retained unlawfully, and so failed to discourage, and may even have actively encouraged, investigators to disregard the limits of their powers. More recently, Parliament itself has been willing to allow extraordinary discretion to the police and the security and intelligence services to authorize their own bugging, burgling, and surveillance activities, subject to limited external control.

In many other common law countries, by contrast, the judges seek to protect citizens' rights, regarding it as the legislature's role to provide additional police powers in the public interest if that is thought appropriate (subject to any overriding constitutional limitations on legislative power). New Zealand courts refused to follow the English judicial extensions to police powers in the 1970s.[7] New Zealand judges followed their Canadian brethren, and were in turn ultimately followed by the High Court of Australia, in recognizing that the common-law doctrine of legal professional privilege conferred a right which could be asserted even against a search warrant, unless a statute expressly provided that the warrant was to override claims to privilege.[8] The New Zealand Court of Appeal also fashioned a constitutional remedy in damages for unreasonable searches which violated the New Zealand Bill of Rights Act 1990.[9] This shows a considerable commitment to rights-based, liberal values. It is to be hoped that the Human Rights Act 1998 will stimulate a move in the same direction among judges in the UK.

Even before the 1998 Act, there were signs of a change of attitude among the English judiciary. In *Marcel v. Commissioner of Police of the Metropolis*[10] Sir Nicolas Browne-Wilkinson V-C said: 'Search and seizure under statutory powers constitute fundamental infringements of the individual's immunity from interference by the state with his property and privacy—fundamental human rights'. Sir Nicolas (now Lord) Browne-Wilkinson is well known for his concern to protect individual rights against the state, of which his judgment in the first *Spycatcher* case, although later reversed by the Court of Appeal and House of Lords, was a notable example.[11] His was not a lone voice: when *Marcel*'s case went to the Court of Appeal, the judges, while

---

[5] *Chic Fashions (West Wales) Ltd. v. Jones* [1968] 2 QB 299, [1968] 1 All ER 229, CA; *Ghani v. Jones* [1970] 1 QB 693, [1969] 3 All ER 1700, CA.

[6] *Frank Truman Export Ltd. v. Metropolitan Police Commissioner* [1977] QB 952, [1977] 3 All ER 431; *R. v. Justice of the Peace for Peterborough, ex parte Hicks* [1977] 1 WLR 1371, [1978] 1 All ER 225, DC.

[7] *McFarlane v. Sharpe* [1972] NZLR 838, CA of NZ.

[8] *Solosky v. R.* (1979) 105 DLR (3d) 745, SC Canada; *Rosenburg v. Jaine* [1983] NZLR 1, CA of NZ; *Baker v. Campbell* (1983) 153 CLR 52, HC of Australia.

[9] *Attorney-General v. Simpson (Baigent's Case)* [1994] 3 NZLR 667.

[10] [1991] 2 WLR 1118 at 851, [1991] 1 All ER 845 at 851.

[11] *Attorney-General v. Guardian Newspapers Ltd.* [1987] 1 WLR 1248, [1987] 3 All ER 316.

reversing the decision on the duties owed by the police to people from whom items are seized, agreed with most of Sir Nicolas's judgment, and the passage quoted above was specifically approved by Sir Christopher Slade.[12] The movement towards privacy rights at common law has accelerated, as noted in Chapter 9, above.

The following sections of this chapter therefore address the current scope of entry, search, seizure, and surveillance powers in England and Wales, in the light of people's human rights. Search and seizure powers exercisable in public places, and those related to arrests and detention in police custody, have been examined in Chapter 6, above. Here, we look at other types of search and surveillance.

10.2 THE BASIC PRINCIPLE AND RELATED SAFEGUARDS

The fundamental principle is summed up in two well-known statements: that 'Everyone has the right to respect for his private and family life, his home and his correspondence',[13] and 'That the house of every one is to him as his castle and fortress, as well for his defence against injury and violence, as for his repose'.[14] These are not unqualified rights. The right to respect for privacy under ECHR Article 8 is subject to qualifications permitted by that Article. The common-law 'home as castle' doctrine was already, by 1604, subject to numerous limitations: it applied only to dwellings, not to outbuildings or business premises; it gave way to legal process in the name of the King, whether civil proceedings in the King's name or felonies in which the King was always deemed to have an interest; it prevented breaking in, but entry through an unbolted door was permitted in order to serve legal process or distrain for rent; and it applied only to outer doors, so that once on the premises lawfully an officer could force inner doors, cupboards, etc., if necessary.[15] In the seventeenth century, justices of the peace developed the practice of granting warrants to enter premises to search for stolen goods, and this received grudging judicial acceptance. At the same time, statutes began to provide powers of entry for public officials, with or without warrant, notably in respect of regulatory schemes for press licensing. This practice snowballed over the following 300 years, until now there are many entry and search powers for public officials of all kinds, in relation to health and safety, licensing, child care, smuggling, the provision of public utilities, and for many other purposes.

Lord Hoffmann summed up the position when delivering the judgment of the Judicial Committee of the Privy Council in *Attorney-General of Jamaica v. Williams*,[16] the right to be free of non-consensual entries to or searches of one's premises:

'is not absolute. As Lord Camden CJ said,[17] the search must be "justified by law". There are

---

[12] [1992] 1 All ER 72 at 86.
[13] European Convention on Human Rights, Art. 8(1).
[14] *Semayne's case* (1604) 5 Co. Rep. 91a at 91b.
[15] See D. Feldman, *The Law Relating to Entry, Search and Seizure* (London: Butterworths, 1986), 7–11, 47–53.
[16] [1997] 3 WLR 389, PC, at 391–2 (footnote added).
[17] *Entick v. Carrington* (1765) 2 Wils. 275, 291.

cases in which the power to enter and search without the consent of the occupier is necessary for the proper functioning of a democratic society. Such powers have long existed at
common law and under various statutes.'

These powers have chipped away at the general principle of security for the home to a
point where it is fair to say that protection for security and privacy depends on
safeguards provided by law against *abuse* of the entry and search powers, rather than
on any blanket prohibition on entry and search. This chapter examines these safeguards, and particularly those which operate in the field of criminal investigation,
which have been substantially overhauled by the Police and Criminal Evidence Act
1984 (hereafter 'PACE') and the ponderously named *Code of Practice for the Searching
of Premises by Police Officers and the Seizure of Property found by Police Officers on
Persons or Premises* (hereafter 'Code B'), issued under section 66 of PACE.

The safeguards are of three sorts. First, compliance with certain conditions justifies
an entry or search, making it lawful. These include consent given by or on behalf of
the occupier, the possession of a valid search warrant, or reasonable grounds for
suspecting that a person who is to be arrested for an arrestable offence is in the
premises. Secondly, there are legal principles governing the way in which entry to
premises may be obtained. Thirdly, there are rules governing the way in which
searches are to be conducted and the range of articles which may be seized.

These statutory safeguards relate to entries to and searches of premises. 'Premises'
is a term of art, defined for the purposes of PACE (rather unhelpfully) by sections
23 and 118(1). It is said to include any place (which the Act does not define), and
the safeguards seem therefore to cover entry to gardens, farmyards, and the like,
rather than merely (as one might have expected) to buildings. The wide meaning of
'place' is a way of extending the protection against abuse of power by the police: the
effect of an area being a 'place' is that the police must comply with the rules under
PACE and Code B when entering and searching it. In order to avoid any risk that
the notion of 'any place' could be narrowed down by judicial interpretation, section
23 specifies that it includes any vehicle, vessel (which in turn includes any ship, boat,
raft, or other apparatus constructed or adapted for floating on water),[18] aircraft,
hovercraft, and offshore installation[19] (such as an oil-drilling platform). Perhaps
most significantly, it also includes any tent or movable structure. This means that
the police must observe the safeguards of the Act, including the need to obtain
consent or a warrant or have other statutory authority, before entering caravans.
The Act thus protects the privacy interests of travellers, a group who are often on
the receiving end of popular and police prejudice. The practical significance of this
in ordinary cases is somewhat reduced, however, since we will see that in most cases
where a constable enters through a gate he will be taking advantage of an implied
permission from the occupier, and will not be relying on any power under PACE or
other legislation to which the safeguards of PACE and the Code of Practice are
attached.

Alongside powers of entry and search, investigators have increasingly resorted to

---

[18] PACE, s. 118(1).
[19] As defined in the Mineral Workings (Offshore Installations) Act 1971, s. 1.

covert entry, burglary, in order to obtain information or plant surveillance devices, and have used increasingly sophisticated techniques of surveillance (either techno- logical or using human agents), and interception of communications. The law of interception of communications was put on a statutory footing in 1985 in order to make it justifiable under ECHR Article 8(2).[20] Covert entry to premises and interfer- ence with property by the Security Service (MI5) were put on a statutory footing in 1989, extended to the Secret Intelligence Service (MI6) in 1994. The police were given similar powers in 1997. Surveillance by technological devices and human sources was given a legal basis only in 2000, when the Regulation of Investigatory Powers Act 2000 sought to provide a foundation which would be compatible with ECHR Article 8 in time for the coming into force of the Human Rights Act 1998 on 2 October 2000. These developments are explained in the sections which follow.

10.3 CONDITIONS JUSTIFYING ENTRY AND SEARCH

(1) CONSENT[21]

Many entries to premises and searches are carried out by consent. Even since 1 Janu- ary 1986, when the statutory police powers to enter and search premises after arrest- ing someone came into effect,[22] it seems that around one-third of all post-arrest searches are still carried out with the consent of the occupier.[23] In an attempt to make it clear to householders that they are entitled to refuse, as well as to consent to, a search, Code B provides that, before seeking consent, the officer in charge must tell the occupier the purpose of the proposed search and inform him that he is not obliged to consent and that anything seized may be produced in evidence. If the person con- cerned is not at the time suspected of an offence, he must be told of that fact as well.[24] Where a search is conducted with the occupier's consent, that consent must be given in writing, if possible on the Notice of Powers and Rights which officers carry with them, before the search commences.[25] Finally, if the consent is given under duress, or is withdrawn during a search, the officer is not permitted to continue to search.[26]

That, at least, is the theoretical position. However, the reality may well be somewhat different. The elasticity of the notion of consent, and its unreality where people do not know that they have the right to refuse, was noted in Chapter 6 in relation to stop and

---

[20] See the discussion of the *Malone* cases in Ch. 9, above, and the examination of interception of communi- cations in Ch. 11, below.

[21] Feldman, *Entry, Search and Seizure*, ch. 2; K. Lidstone and V. Bevan, *Search and Seizure Under the Police and Criminal Evidence Act 1984* (Sheffield: University of Sheffield Faculty of Law, 1992), 44–8; D. Dixon, *Law in Policing: Legal Regulation and Police Practices* (Oxford: Clarendon Press, 1997), 104–9.

[22] PACE, ss. 18, 32. See Ch. 5, above.

[23] K. Lidstone and C. Palmer, *The Investigation of Crime: A Guide to Police Powers*, 2nd edn. (London: Butterworths, 1995), 98, 114; Lidstone and Bevan, *Search and Seizure*, tables 3.2, 3.3, pp. 45–6.

[24] Code B, para. 4.2.

[25] Code B, para. 4.1.

[26] Code B, para. 4.3.

search powers. The same applies with respect to consent to entry to premises and to searches of premises. Officers often obtain what passes for consent by bluff, relying on the occupiers' ignorance of their rights, unquestioning belief that the police have power to search if they want to, and an implication of guilt if access is refused. Alternatively, they may try to gain entry by a stratagem, for example by pretending not to be police officers, or misleading the occupier as to their reason for wanting to enter. It has been held that this does not automatically make any subsequent search unlawful,[27] but if the occupier refuses entry it may be unlawful to use force to enter: a forcible entry is lawful only if it is necessary and the level of force used is reasonable, and it is often not necessary to use force until the occupier has had a proper opportunity to admit the officers, knowing what they have come for (unless, for example, there is good reason to think that giving notice would defeat the purpose of the entry, or there is an urgent necessity to enter to save someone's life).[28]

If access is refused, less experienced officers may regard it as causing a loss of face, and may try to get round it by means of an unlawful search. Instead of seeking informed consent to a search, the officers might try to obtain permission civilly but informally, creating an atmosphere which is as friendly as possible and gives an 'air of consent'[29] without letting occupiers know that they have a right to refuse.[30] This militates against compliance with the provisions of Code B on giving information and recording consents, and probably leads to a substantial under-recording of searches which do not rely on legal authority. Where the occupier is in custody, the consent, recorded on the custody record, is likely to be particularly artificial. The information need not be given, nor consent recorded, before entry to the premises. It is the search, not the entry, which requires written consent. Any demand for written consent, or provision of information, before entry would be highly unrealistic.

Moreover, the need for express consent to entry applies only in respect of houses and flats. Anyone normally has an implied licence from the occupier to go through a garden gate and up a path to the door of a house, or into a block of flats and up to the floor on which the flat in question is situated, in order to conduct legitimate business with the occupier. There is also implied consent to carrying on the officer's lawful business on the driveway of a house (for example, by inspecting a car which is suspected of having been involved in an accident).[31] This licence can be negated by clear words (for example, a notice on the gate expressly denying entry to hawkers or police officers), but otherwise takes effect. On the other hand, at the outer door there is no implied consent to entry to the house or flat, even if the door is open; nor is

---

[27] R. v. Longman [1988] 1 WLR 619, CA.

[28] O'Loughlin v. Chief Constable of Essex [1998] 1 WLR 374, CA: occupier refused entry to officers who said they had come to ask some questions about damage to a car; in fact they intended to arrest his wife for criminal damage to the car. The use of force to enter was unlawful (Roch and Buxton LJ, Thorpe LJ dissenting on the facts).

[29] Dison, Law in Policing, 107.

[30] D. Dixon, C. Coleman, and K. Bottomley, 'Consent and the Legal Regulation of Policing' (1990) 17 J. Law and Soc. 345–62 at 352–3.

[31] Robson v. Hallett [1967] 2 QB 939, [1967] 2 All ER 407, DC; Lambert v. Roberts [1981] 2 All ER 15, CA; Pamplin v. Fraser [1981] RTR 494, DC; Brunner v. Williams [1975] Crim. LR 250, DC; Morris v. Beardmore [1981] AC 446, [1980] 2 All ER 753, HL.

there any implied consent to entering any place to commit a crime.[32] In business premises during business hours, the implied licence normally goes further, permitting a visitor with lawful business to enter the building, as one expects that business visitors will be actively encouraged by the occupiers (it would be a poor shop propri-etor who insisted on every potential shopper obtaining individual consent to entry). This implied licence carries over to police officers and other authorized officials who have lawful business on business premises, even if their business is not related to the occupier's. However, outside business hours there is no implied consent to people entering business premises, even if they have a legitimate reason for wanting to get in (as, for example, where a police officer sees a door open at night, and enters in case a burglary is taking place).[33]

Where express consent to entry is needed, it may take a number of forms. An invitation from the householder will, of course, be adequate, but it seems that anyone with a right of occupation, including children if of sufficient age and understanding, can invite people on to the premises, although in the case of a consent by a child it would appear that the responsible adult is entitled to withdraw or override the invita-tion.[34] It seems, too, that any invitee may have authority to invite a visitor on to the premises, although the invitation will normally be subject to revocation by the occu-pier unless the visitor has an independent right to remain (for example, in order to stop a breach of the peace).[35]

In the case of hotels, hostels, student halls of residence, and lodging houses, where people occupy rooms as licensees but do not have rights to exclude the landlord from them, the guests or lodgers can normally invite people to their rooms, but so can the landlord. People living in such accommodation are therefore peculiarly vulnerable to invasion of their limited privacy, for instance by having their rooms searched by the police by virtue of a consent given by the landlord or the landlord's agent (for example, the warden of a hostel). This is recognized by Code B, which includes Note for Guidance 4A, advising that in lodging houses or similar accommodation a search should not be made solely on the basis of the landlord's consent unless the tenant is unavailable and the matter is urgent. Naturally, where the landlord refuses consent and the occupier is not present the police can enter only if they have some other authority, such as a search warrant.

Consent may also be given by conduct. Moving backwards from the door when a constable explains who he is and why he is there is likely to be interpreted as acqui-escence by the police and the court.[36] However, one should be cautious about accept-ing that acquiescence implies consent. In many cases, the police avoid asking for

---

[32] *R. v. Lundry* (1981) 128 DLR (3rd) 726, Ontario CA; *R. v. Jones and Smith* [1976] 1 WLR 672, [1976] 3 All ER 54, CA. *Cp.* the position when executing legal process: *Southam v. Smout* [1964] 1 QB 308, [1963] 3 All ER 104, CA, and Feldman, *Entry, Search and Seizure*, 49–51.

[33] *Great Central Railway v. Bates* [1921] 3 KB 578, DC.

[34] *R. v. Thornley* (1980) 72 Cr. App. R. 302; *Riley v. DPP* (1989) 91 Cr. App. R. 14, DC. Other examples include *R. v. Collins* [1973] QB 100, [1972] 2 All ER 1105, CA; *Robson v. Hallett* [1967] 2 QB 939, [1967] 2 All ER 407, DC; *Morris v. Beardmore* [1981] AC 446, [1980] 2 All ER 753, HL.

[35] *McGowan v. Chief Constable of Kingston upon Hull* [1968] Crim. LR 34, DC; *Jones and Jones v. Lloyd* [1981] Crim. LR 340, DC.

[36] *Faulkner v. Willetts* [1982] RTR 159, DC.

consent, merely implying that they have a power to enter: asking for consent implies that people have a right to say no, and that would put the police at risk of a loss of face as well as some inconvenience.[37]

Consent to entry may be withdrawn by the person who gave it, unless the visitors have some independent authority for remaining, such as the need to prevent or stop a breach of the peace. Consent may also be withdrawn by anyone with express or implied authority from the occupier to do so, such as an office or shop manager, or (as in *McArdle v. Wallace (No. 2)*)[38] the adult son of a café owner, who asked a constable to leave when the latter was making inquiries about some goods which he thought might have been stolen. Where one cohabitant has issued an invitation, the other is not empowered to revoke it unilaterally while the visitors are engaged on the business for which they were invited in.[39] Clear words are needed in order to revoke a licence, particularly when the person on the premises is there on legitimate public business. It is a question of fact whether the revocation has been made suffiently unequivocally. Accordingly, it was held in *Snook v. Mannion*[40] to be legitimate for magistrates to decide that the words 'Fuck off!', which might signify mere abuse, were not a revocation of the licence.

Once the licence to enter or remain on premises has been withdrawn, the visitor must start to leave. He must be allowed a reasonable time in which to do so, but if he attempts to remain on the premises, or fails to leave after a reasonable period, he becomes a trespasser, and may be removed by the occupier, using reasonable force if necessary.[41] Use of force against a constable is always dangerous, however. If the force is used too early, it will constitute a breach of the peace, justifying the constable and others in remaining or re-entering in order to quell it. Even if the constable has become a trespasser, developments which produce a reasonable apprehension of a breach of the peace will justify the constable in being there, so that he will once again be in the execution of his duty and will no longer be a trespasser,[42] although the officer will be acting unlawfully under section 6 of the Human Rights Act 1998 if remaining on the premises is an unnecessary or disproportionate interference with the occupier's right to respect for private life or home under ECHR Article 8.[43] Despite a suggestion to the contrary in an *obiter dictum* in *Kay v. Hibbert*,[44] the better view is that the police have no authority to remain on premises in order to complete inquiries once their licence has been withdrawn,[45] unless they are acting under some specific power independent of the original licence, for example in order to make an arrest for an arrestable offence, or to conduct a search under warrant.

---

[37] Dixon *et al.*, 'Consent', 352–3.

[38] (1964) 108 Sol. Jo. 483, DC; see also *McArdle v. Wallace* [1964] Crim. LR 467, DC.

[39] *R. v. Thornley* (1980) 72 Cr. App. R. 302, CA.

[40] [1982] RTR 321, DC; see also *Gilham v. Breidenbach (Note)* [1982] RTR 328, DC.

[41] *Davis v. Lisle* [1936] 2 KB 434, [1936] 2 All ER 213, DC.

[42] *Robson v. Hallett* [1967] 2 QB 939, [1967] 2 All ER 407, DC; *R. v. Lamb* [1990] Crim. LR 58, DC; *McLeod v. Commissioner of Police of the Metropolis* [1994] 4 All ER 553, CA, criticised by D. Feldman, 'Interference in the Home and Anticipated Breach of the Peace' (1995) 111 *LQR* 562–5.

[43] *McLeod v. United Kingdom*, Eur. Ct. HR (1999) 27 EHRR 493.

[44] [1977] Crim. LR 226, DC.

[45] *Davis v. Lisle* [1936] 2 KB 434, [1936] 2 All ER 213, DC.

(2) WARRANTS

Before the 1984 Act came into force, the availability of search warrants was haphazard. Search-warrant provisions, usually stipulating that an information for a warrant was to be laid before a justice of the peace, were often included in statutes creating or codifying criminal offences. Those under section 26 of the Theft Act 1968 and section 23(1) of the Misuse of Drugs Act 1971 were particularly widely used. However, no warrants were available for offences which were unregulated by statute. (The common-law warrant to search for stolen goods had long been superseded by statutory provisions.) It followed that warrants were available to search for evidence of illegal betting,[46] but not for evidence of murder.[47] This could be very frustrating for investigators, tempting them to commit unlawful acts in order to obtain evidence of grave offences.

This was remedied by PACE. Operating alongside the statutory provisions authorizing the grant of search warrants in relation to specific statutory offences are retained, section 8 created a new power for a justice of the peace to grant a warrant to search for evidence of serious arrestable offences in certain circumstances, whether or not there is another specific statutory power to grant a search warrant for that particular offence.[48] The power is rarely used, because the police can generally seek a search warrant under a statute directly related to their investigation, but it is sometimes valuable. A warrant under section 8 may be granted where the justice of the peace is satisfied that there are reasonable grounds for believing (not merely for suspecting) that each of five conditions is satisfied.[49] They are:

(a) that a serious arrestable offence has been committed;[50]

(b) that there is material, on specified premises, which is likely to be of substantial value (either alone or together with other material) to the investigation of the offence;

(c) that the material is likely to be relevant evidence;[51]

(d) that it does not consist of items subject to legal privilege, or excluded or special procedure material;[52] and

(e) that any one of four further conditions applies.

These four further conditions are:[53]

(i) that it is not practicable to communicate with anyone entitled to grant access to the premises; or

(ii) that it is not practicable to communicate with anyone entitled to grant access to the material; or

[46] Betting, Gaming and Lotteries Act 1963, s. 51.

[47] *Ghani v. Jones* [1970] 1 QB 693, [1969] 3 All ER 1700, CA.

[48] PACE, s. 8(5).

[49] PACE, s. 8(1).

[50] On the meaning of 'serious arrestable offence' see PACE, s. 116 and Sch. 6; Ch. 6, above.

[51] This means anything which might be admissible at trial: s. 8(4).

[52] On these categories, for which special provision is made, see below.

[53] PACE, s. 8(3).

    (iii) that entry to the premises will not be granted unless a warrant is pro-
          duced; or

    (iv) that the purpose of the search may be frustrated or seriously prejudiced if
          a constable cannot obtain immediate entry on arrival (for instance,
          because it is thought that the occupier might destroy the evidence unless
          taken by surprise).

There was, before PACE, no codified set of requirements to be satisfied before warrants could be granted. The matter was governed by a combination of common-law
rules, mainly based on little-known cases of considerable antiquity, and statutory
preconditions. It was, perhaps, not surprising that most justices of the peace (and,
indeed, circuit judges) displayed little understanding of the responsibilities which they
bore by law. One pre-PACE study found that magistrates normally issued warrants
more or less automatically on request, without any real attempt to test the strength of
the grounds for issuing them.[54]

Yet the role of the issuing justices was, and remains, central to the safeguards
against the abuse of search-warrant procedures. They are administering an *ex parte*
procedure in which the occupier of premises has no opportunity to be heard, and
they bear a heavy responsibility for ensuring that warrants, which authorize a grave
interference in people's private and family lives, are not issued without due cause.
They have important legal duties in that regard, which include ensuring that the
statutory preconditions to the grant of a warrant are satisfied, and that there are no
reasons to exercise their discretion against granting one.[55] If this obligation is
ducked in any case, the procedure will have failed to give that respect to the private
life of the person whose premises are to be entered and searched which is required
under Article 8(1) ECHR. The interference with private life will not be justifiable
under Article 8(2), because the search, without any independent check on the
grounds for it, is liable to be regarded as disproportionate to the legitimate purposes
of the search in a democratic society (except, perhaps, where national security is at
stake).[56]

This is not a sign of the over-sensitivity of the ECHR to the rights of suspects. It is
an indication of the significance of the issuing authority (magistrate or judge) as one
of the crucial safeguards justifying a serious interference with people's rights. In non-
Convention common-law countries, the courts understand this, and have been reso-
lute in quashing warrants whenever there are indications that the issuing justice has
had his independence undermined, misunderstood his role, or misconstrued the relevant legislation. In the USA, a magistrate may not be paid only when he issues
warrants, as this gives a financial incentive to authorize searches.[57] A warrant issued
without probable cause appearing from the applicant's affidavit, including the reasons
for the applicant's belief in information given by others, is invalid.[58] Where the

---

[54] K. W. Lidstone, 'Magistrates, the Police and Search Warrants' [1984] Crim. LR 449.

[55] For detailed discussion of these responsibilities, see Feldman, *Entry, Search and Seizure*, 72–91.

[56] See the discussion in Ch. 9, above.

[57] *Connally v. Georgia* 429 US 245 (1977).

[58] *Grau v. United States* 287 US 124 (1932).

affidavit is verified by an inappropriate officer, it cannot be used as the foundation for an application, and a warrant granted on the strength of it is invalid.[59] The common-law position in Canada, New Zealand, Australia, and England and Wales, is similar.[60]

It follows that any failure to observe the due process requirements for dealing with applications for a warrant is not the fault of the law. It is, instead, the result of lack of familiarity with the legal requirements, or failure to comprehend or apply them, on the part of the issuing magistrate or judge. This is exacerbated by a paucity of training for judges and magistrates in their responsibilities with regard to warrants, and the difficulty of obtaining reliable evidence of what passed between the applicant and the magistrate or judge when the application was made. Only rarely will a reviewing court have available to it evidence that the issuing magistrate did not bother to look at the written information, calling it 'a load of garbage' which she 'didn't have to read', as in the Australian case of *R. v. Sing, ex parte Harrison.*[61] Unfortunately, as we shall see, judges in England and Wales have been reluctant to use the words on the face of the warrant as indicating the state of mind of the issuing authority. This makes it hard to exercise an appropriate level of supervision in cases where extraneous evidence is lacking.

Issuing authorities, therefore, need to be educated. There are provisions in PACE which seek to alert justices to their responsibilities, and to impress on police officers their duty of candour when applying for warrants. A warrant obtained otherwise than in accordance with the provisions of section 15 of PACE will not justify a subsequent entry and search, since courts regard entry, search and seizure as a composite process governed by a statutory code under PACE, breach of which at any point undermines the lawfulness of the process.[62] Section 15(2) requires the constable who applies for a warrant to state the grounds for the application and the enactment under which the warrant is sought, and to specify the premises which it is desired to enter and search and (so far as practicable) the articles or people to be sought. Section 15(3) requires the application to be supported by a written information, which, under Code B, paragraph 2.6, must state the enactment under which the application is made, the premises to be searched and the object of the search, and the grounds on which the application is made. Where the object of the search is to find evidence of an offence, the written statement of grounds must include an indication of how the evidence relates to the investigation. Section 15(4) requires a constable applying for a warrant

[59] *Albrecht v. United States* (1927) 273 US 1.

[60] For Canada, see *Imperial Tobacco Sales Co. v. A-G for Alberta* [1941] 2 DLR 673; *R. v. Colvin, ex parte Merrick* [1970] 3 OR 612 (where, however, there was a statutory requirements for the grounds to be stated in the information); *Royal American Shows Inc. v. R., ex parte Hahn* [1975] 6 WWR 571; *Re Alder and R.* (1977) 37 CCC (2nd) 234. For New Zealand: *Mitchell v. New Plymouth Club (Inc.)* [1958] NZLR 1070. For Australia: *R. v. Tillett, ex parte Newton* (1969) 14 FLR 101; *George v. Rockett* (1990) 93 ALR 483, HC of Aust. For England and Wales: *Jones v. German* [1897] 1 QB 374, CA; *IRC v. Rossminster Ltd.* [1980] AC 952, HL (where, however, the majority did not regard failure on the part of the issuing judge to state in the warrant that he was satisfied as being sufficient evidence that he had misunderstood his role); *R. v. Guildhall Magistrates' Court, ex parte Primlaks* [1989] 1 WLR 841, DC.

[61] (1979) 36 FLR 322.

[62] *R. v. Chief Constable of Lancashire, ex parte Parker* [1993] QB 577, [1993] 3 All ER 56, DC; *R. v. Chief Constable of the Warwickshire Constabulary, ex parte Fitzpatrick* [1999] 1 WLR 564, [1998] 1 All ER 65, DC.

to answer on oath any questions which the justice of the peace or judge asks. The object of all this is to ensure that the issuing authority, as protector of the privacy and property of the occupier of premises, can thoroughly test the strength of the grounds for issuing a warrant. Note for Guidance 2A to Code B suggests that, where the application is based on information from an informant, the name of the informant need not be disclosed, but the constable should be ready to answer questions about the reliability of the source.

However, the observance of these requirements seems to remain patchy, and depends as much on the administrative arrangements made by the clerk to the justices, or by senior police officers themselves, for checking on applications as on the performance of the justices themselves. Too often, justices are asked to grant warrants at night, at home, and without the opportunity for them to take advice. Most justices receive no training in recognizing and discharging their responsibilities in relation to search warrants. Evidence suggests that warrants are still too readily granted without appropriate questioning of officers. The police often have a free choice as to the magistrate whom they approach, subject to any direction issued by the clerk to the justices. This perhaps makes it unsurprising that researchers from the University of Hull found that no officer whom they interviewed had had a warrant application refused.[63] This might mean that the police always prepare their warrant applications in an unexceptionable way. In a research study by Bevan and Lidstone of applications for warrants to search for stolen goods under the Theft Act 1968, following up a pre-PACE study, it was noted that in 61 per cent of the cases studied the only information given to the magistrate was that the application was made 'as a result of information received from a previously reliable source', or some variant on that formula. Magistrates rarely asked about this, because they believed (without asking) that the informants would have been at risk if their identities were revealed, which was sometimes but by no means always the case.[64] The requirement for consent applies to routine scene-of-crime searches of premises where the occupier is thought to be the victim of crime just as it does to searches of premises where the occupier is suspected of having committed an offence.[64a]

Of course, it is very hard to test reliability objectively. As Bevan and Lidstone point out, the success of the search is only a crude indication. If nothing is seized, goods which were on the premises could have been removed; if articles are seized, they might not be the items which were originally sought. Dixon *et al.* found that of the searches under warrant for drugs which they examined, only 10 per cent resulted in drugs being seized, but searches very often resulted in the seizure of suspected stolen goods;

---

[63] Dixon *et al.*, 'PACE in Practice' (1991) 141 *NLJ* 1586 at 1587. I know from anecdotal reports of two cases in which a magistrate has refused to issue warrants; the magistrate concerned has never again been approached for one.

[64] Lidstone and Palmer, *Investigation of Crime*, 102.

[64a] *R. v. Sanghera*, The Times, 26 October 2000, CA, where a search of the premises in which an armed robbery was alleged to have taken place, two days after the alleged robbery, revealed the allegedly stolen money concealed on the premises, implicating the occupier. However, despite the breach of Code C, it was held that the evidence could be admitted following a balancing exercise conducted under section 78 of PACE, because there was no question of the reliability of the evidence and the court had to be fair to the prosecution as well as the defence.

overall, goods not covered by the warrant were seized in 47 per cent of searches under warrant.[65] There should be concern at the continued unwillingness of magistrates to press constables about the reliability of their information. Contrary to the intention of the legislation, it seems likely that the requirement in Code B, paragraph 2.4, that a senior officer must authorize the application for a warrant, is a more substantial protection for the privacy of an occupier of premises than is the application itself. The officer (usually an inspector) is likely to satisfy himself that the investigating officer complied with the other requirements of Code B: that he has taken reasonable steps to check that his information is accurate, recent, and has not been provided maliciously, that anonymous information is corroborated, and that reasonable inquiries have been made to find out about the nature and location of the articles sought, the nature of the premises, whether they have been searched recently, and what is known about the likely occupier.[66]

When the justice of the peace or judge has decided to issue the warrant, it is essential to draw the warrant accurately, so that the officers and occupiers know what they are entitled to do. It must specify the name of the applicant, the date on which it is issued, the enactment under which it is issued, the premises to be searched, and (so far as practicable) the articles or people to be sought.[67] It is the responsibility of the magistrate or judge to ensure that the warrant specifies the names of any people who are authorized to accompany the constable executing it.[68] If the form of the warrant is defective, the warrant may not protect the officers who execute it. If the procedure by which a warrant is obtained or the form of the warrant is defective, it will be liable to be quashed on an application for judicial review.

It is hard to monitor the grounds on which warrants are sought and granted. The written information ought to contain a reasonable amount of information, although not the details concerning reliability of sources, but the informations are not required to be kept or analysed. A search record is made, and the warrants are endorsed with the results of the search and returned to the issuing court,[69] but the warrant will not show the grounds on which it was issued. This makes it difficult to assess the effectiveness of review by the issuing magistrates, and we are heavily reliant on research of the type conducted by Bevan and Lidstone, referred to above. A provision requiring the informations for warrants and the records of searches to be collated, and statistical information included in the annual report of the chief officer of police for each area (such as is required in respect of searches of the person and road checks under Part I of PACE), would go some way towards monitoring the quality of the work of magistrates in this field.

---

[65] Dixon *et al.*, 'PACE in Practice', 1587.

[66] Code B, paras. 2.1–2.3.

[67] PACE, s. 15(6). On the permissible scope of a warrant, and the limits of possible particularity in their formulation, see *R. v. Central Criminal Court, ex parte AJD Holdings Ltd.*, *The Times*, 24 February 1992, DC; *R. v. South Western Magistrates' Court, ex parte Cofie* [1997] 1 WLR 885, DC; *R. v. Chief Constable of Warwickshire Constabulary, ex parte Fitzpatrick* [1999] 1 WLR 564, [1998] 1 All ER 65, DC.

[68] See PACE, s. 16(2); *R. v. Reading Justices and others, ex parte South West Meats Ltd.* [1992] Crim. LR 672, DC. This is good practice, but may not be obligatory where warrants are issued to people other than constables: see *R. v. Hunt* (1994) 68 TC 132, CA.

[69] PACE, s. 16(9), (10), (11); Code B, paras. 7.1–7.3.

In the mean time, one is left with an impression that justices of the peace do not provide the independent judicial scrutiny of proposed entries and searches under warrant which is needed to ensure that interferences with the right to respect for a person's private life and home are justified, as demanded by Article 8(2) of the European Convention on Human Rights. The formal trappings of scrutiny are there, but the substance is sadly lacking in most cases. The English courts have in the past sometimes been unwilling to exert an appropriate degree of control by way of judicial-review proceedings. For example, in *IRC v. Rossminster Ltd.*[70] the House of Lords by a majority rejected an application for review of a warrant, issued by a circuit judge, which failed to state that the judge had satisfied himself of the matters which were conditions precedent to the lawful grant of a warrant, making it seem that the judge had relied unquestioningly on the opinion of the person applying for the warrant. The majority held that this did not make the warrant invalid on its face, or provide convincing evidence that the judge had misunderstood or failed to fulfil his responsibilities. A similar attitude prevailed in *R. v. Billericay Justices and Dobbyn, ex parte Frank Harris (Coaches) Ltd.*,[71] where the court refused to assume that the magistrate had failed to consider relevant matters merely because the affidavits did not affirm that he had considered them. The judges felt that it was permissible to assume that the magistrate had considered the matters in question, because he was very experienced.

Again, in *Attorney-General of Jamaica v. Williams*,[72] a customs officer, investigating suspected fraudulent importation of motor vehicles to evade duty, obtained a search warrant from a justice of the peace under a statutory provision which authorized warrants to enter premises and search for and seize 'uncustomed or prohibited goods, or any books or documents relating to' such goods. The warrant did not refer to the statutory provision under which it was issued, and purported to authorize search of persons as well as premises, and seizure of (*inter alia*) articles other than those mentioned in the statute. The Court of Appeal of Jamaica held that the warrant was invalid on its face. The Judicial Committee of the Privy Council reversed the decision. Lord Hoffmann, delivering the judgment of the Committee, reasserted the duty of magistrates to make an independent assessment of the existence of reasonable cause to issue the warrant, and not merely to rubber-stamp the application of an officer. However, the Committee did not feel able to infer from the errors in the warrant that the justice had not been satisfied that the conditions for issuing the warrant had been met. 'The fact that the justice may have held erroneous beliefs about the source or extent of the power, or may have been satisfied on other matters irrelevant to the exercise of the power, is not inconsistent with the recital' that there was reasonable cause for issuing the warrant.[73] The mention of articles in the warrant which were not permitted by the statute to be seized could not make a seizure of them lawful, so the Committee thought that nothing would be gained by treating it as invalidating the warrant. Although section 19(1) of the Constitution of Jamaica restricted the power

---

[70] [1980] AC 952, [1980] 1 All ER 80, HL.
[71] [1991] Crim. LR 472, DC.
[72] [1997] 3 WLR 389, PC.
[73] Ibid. at 399.

to create authority to search, it 'was intended to serve a higher purpose than to promote accuracy in drafting in the revenue protection division'.[74]

With respect, this makes a nonsense of the protective role of magistrates and the supervisory rule of the courts in relation to invasions of privacy and property rights under warrant. The Committee accepted that one purpose of a search warrant is to enable the occupier of premises to satisfy himself that officers are acting lawfully,[75] but did not accept that this justified the implication of formal requirements as to the contents of a warrant. What the Committee characterized as 'infelicities' in the warrant[76] could, in fact, have misled the occupier of premises as to the powers of the officers, particularly if the occupier did not have ready access to the text of the relevant legislation (which, in any case, was not mentioned in the warrant). The Committee apparently regarded a fundamentally important protection for the rights of occupiers and the principles of the rule of law as a mere aid to drafting.

If this attitude prevails, it leaves magistrates or judges effectively unchecked when issuing warrants, because courts will not take seriously a failure to show that the conditions for issuing the warrant have been complied with. This undermines the protective scheme put in place by Parliament when powers to grant search warrants are issued, and does nothing to force the magistrates or judges to comply with the rules laid down. Lord Salmon, dissenting in *Rossminster*, argued that the warrant showed evidence of invalidity on its face, which was not contradicted by other evidence. It is submitted that his view is preferable, in that it upholds rule of law values, and is more in tune with common sense and with common-law developments elsewhere in the world where the draconian nature of the search warrant is recognized and the importance of safeguards is respected.[77] It is likely that the presumption in favour of Convention rights which the Human Rights Act 1998 puts in place, and the resulting need to satisfy the requirements of ECHR Article 8(2) in order to establish that warrants and searches are lawful, will lead to a new attitude of increased vigilance by the courts in their supervisory role over warrants and searches.

Even before the 1998 Act there were already a few signs that England's defective judicial attitude to warrants may indeed be changing. For example, in *R. v. Reading Justices and others, ex parte South West Meats Ltd.*[78] the Divisional Court granted *certiorari* to quash a search warrant which failed to specify the number of people who might enter premises with the constable who was to execute it, as well as awarding exemplary damages against the police and the Intervention Board for Agricultural Produce in respect of the manner of the search and seizure conducted under it. In another case, *Darbo v. Director of Public Prosecutions,*[79] the Divisional Court quashed

---

[74] Ibid. at 401–2.

[75] Ibid. at 400, citing Feldman, *Entry, Search and Seizure,* 129.

[76] [1997] 3 WLR 389 at 401.

[77] See Feldman, *Entry, Search and Seizure,* 132–6; *R. v. Tillett, ex parte Newton* (1969) 14 FLR 101; *George v. Rockett* (1990) 93 ALR 483, HC of Australia.

[78] [1992] Crim. LR 672, DC.

[79] [1992] Crim. LR 56, DC; full text on Lexis *sub nom. Darbo v. Crown Prosecution Service.* See also *Ex parte Bradlaugh* (1878) 3 QBD 509.

the defendant's conviction on a charge of wilfully obstructing a constable in the execution of her duty. The constable was searching premises with a warrant issued under the Obscene Publications Act 1959. Section 3 of the Act permits a search for obscene articles, meaning things tending to deprave and corrupt people who are likely to come in contact with them. The magistrate had drawn the warrant as permitting search for 'books, magazines, films and video cassettes and photographs, and any other material of a sexually explicit nature'. The final six words were wider than the obscene articles for which search could lawfully be authorized under section 3. The Divisional Court held that this made the warrant *ultra vires*, despite the fact that it had been executed by experienced officers who knew what they were looking for. The presence of the police on the premises was therefore unlawful, and they were not in the execution of their duty when obstructed.

These cases provide a welcome reminder to justices of the peace, and those who seek and execute warrants, of their responsibilities to ensure that the statutory preconditions to the grant of a warrant are met, and that the warrant authorizes no more extensive an interference with rights of privacy and property than is necessary and permitted under the statute. It is to be hoped that the message is getting through.

(3) PROTECTING CONFIDENCES: EXCEPTIONS FROM THE SEARCH-WARRANT PROCEDURE

A group of further statutory provisions in PACE are designed to give additional protection to privacy interests and the interest in the free exercise of journalistic activity against unjustified infringement. For the first time in England and Wales, it is provided by section 9 that no warrant may issue to permit search for items subject to legal privilege, a special class of confidential material defined in section 10, arising out of the relationship between lawyer and client. Much other confidential material, and material held for the purposes of journalism, is protected against warrants issued by magistrates, except in respect of certain material relevant to drug-trafficking offences. Access to the protected types of material may be obtained only by way of an application to a circuit judge, which will normally be *inter partes*. These provisions are examined elsewhere.[80] They protect specific privacy interests by insisting on a special procedure with particular access conditions, without making it impossible for investigators to get access to evidence.[81]

---

[80] On confidential material generally, see Ch. 11, below. On journalistic material, see Ch. 14, below.

[81] However, in Scotland the law has lacked equivalent protection for journalistic and confidential material, and a search warrant issued in Scotland for execution in England can be given effect even if no such warrant could have been issued in England: *R. v. Manchester Stipendiary Magistrate, ex parte Granada Television Ltd.* [2000] 2 WLR 1, [2000] 1 All ER 135, HL. This threatens the balance of proportionality, and will need to be reconsidered under the Human Rights Act 1998. The decision of the Divisional Court, [1999] QB 1202, which the House of Lords reversed, is in principle to be preferred, and is likely to be influential if the issue arises again under the 1998 Act.

(4) ARRESTS AND SIMILAR APPREHENSIONS[82]

The police have power to enter premises to make an arrest under section 17 of PACE. The power applies where a constable has reasonable grounds for believing that the person whom he is seeking is in the premises. Where premises consist of a number of separate dwellings (such as a block of flats) the constable may enter any one dwelling only if there are reasonable grounds for believing that the person is in that dwelling unit.[83] The purposes for which entry may be made are restricted by section 17(1) to: (a) executing a warrant of arrest or commitment issued by a magistrates' court; (b) arresting a person for an arrestable offence; (c) arresting a person for one of a number of offences which are not arrestable offences under section 24 of PACE but are thought to be sufficiently serious to justify a power of entry;[84] (d) arresting a child or young person remanded or committed to local authority accommodation;[85] (e) recapturing a person who is, or is deemed to be, unlawfully at large while liable to be detained in a prison, remand centre, young offender institution, secure training centre, or any other place by virtue of a sentence of a court;[86] (f) recapturing a person who is unlawfully at large and whom the constable is pursuing;[87] and (g) saving life or limb,[88] or preventing serious damage to property. The search must be limited to the extent reasonably required for the purpose for which the entry was effected.[89]

(5) WRITTEN AUTHORITIES TO ENTER PREMISES, ISSUED BY NON-JUDICIAL OFFICERS

A number of statutes permit entry to premises under written authorizations which are not issued by a judicial authority on the basis of an evaluation of reasonable cause to enter on the facts of the particular case. Many statutes allow regulatory bodies to authorize their officers to enter and inspect premises in the performance of their statutory functions, such as enforcing health and safety requirements, building regulations, food safety, and so forth. An unusual example of an authorization issued by a judicial officer but without reference to the facts of any individual case is the Customs and Excise writ of assistance, a general authority for officers of Customs and Excise to enter any premises where there is reasonable cause to suspect that anything liable to

---

[82] Feldman, *Entry, Search and Seizure*, ch. 8; see also Ch. 6, above.

[83] PACE, s. 17(2).

[84] Political Uniforms (Public Order) Act 1936, s. 1; entering and remaining on premises (Criminal Law Act 1977, ss. 6, 7, 8, or 10), restricted by PACE, s. 17(3) to constables in uniform only; engendering fear of, or provoking, violence (Public Order Act 1986, s. 4).

[85] Children and Young Persons Act 1969, ss. 23(1) and 32(1A).

[86] For example, a prisoner released on licence who has been recalled, or who has breached a condition of the licence.

[87] See *D'Souza v. DPP* [1992] 1 WLR 1073, [1992] 4 All ER 545, HL.

[88] For a common-law power for any person to do this, see *Handcock v. Baker* (1800) 2 Bos. & P. 260. Defendants heard the screams of a woman being murdered by her husband, entered the house, and saved her. The husband sued for trespass. He argued (*inter alia*) that the defendants should have left the woman to her legal remedies. Lord Eldon CJ at 262–3 commented: 'a wife is only bound to apply to those remedies, where it is probable that the injury to be apprehended will be prevented by such application'. The common-law power has been abolished as it applies to constables: PACE, s. 17(5); but it survives for other people.

[89] PACE, s. 17(4).

forfeiture under the Customs and Excise Acts is kept or concealed, and to search the place and seize any such goods which may be found. Writs of Assistance are issued at the start of each monarch's reign out of the Office of the Queen's Remembrancer in the Queen's Bench Division of the High Court, and remains in force until six months after the end of the monarch's reign.[90] All of these are, in effect, general warrants for entry, allowing officials a wide-ranging freedom, subject to the general principles of public law and the Human Rights Act 1998 governing the way in which official discretion may be exercised.

Some authorizations are based on an evaluation of the available information relating to the case, but are not issued by a judicial officer. The most commonly used is the power of a police officer of at least the rank of inspector to authorize a constable to enter the premises of a person who is under arrest and in police custody has already been noted.[91] Other, less common but very important, powers include that of the Secretary of State to issue warrants for interception of communications (considered in Chapter 11, below), and warrants for the Security and Intelligence Services and the police to enter premises and do other acts in relation to property.

(i) Covert entry and seizure: the Security and Intelligence Services[92]

In 1989, in an uncharacteristic burst of unsolicited openness, the government decided to put the Security Service, MI5, on a statutory footing. Peter Wright, in his book *Spycatcher*, had recounted stories of bugging and burglary by the Service in England, actions for which there was no legal authority or public accountability. One of the objects of the Security Service Act 1989 was, in the words of the long title, 'to enable certain actions to be taken on the authority of warrants issued by the Secretary of state, with provision for the issue of such warrants to be kept under review by a Commissioner . . .'. Section 1 of the Act defined the functions of the Security Service as being 'the protection of national security and, in particular, its protection against threats from espionage, terrorism and sabotage, from the activities of agents of foreign powers and from actions intended to overthrow or undermine parliamentary democracy by political, industrial or violent means', and 'to safeguard the economic well-being of the United Kingdom against threats posed by the actions or intentions of persons outside the British Islands'.[93]

These functions gave the Service a very wide brief.[94] They were further broadened in 1994, by which time the collapse of the USSR and its eastern European allies, which had been the target of much activity by the Security Service and the Secret Intelligence Service (MI6) during the Cold War, seemed to have removed part of those services' *raison d'être*. In response to growing concern about major criminal networks, the

---

[90] Customs and Excise Management Act 1979, s. 161; Feldman, *Entry, Search and Seizure*, 293–5.

[91] PACE, s. 18. See Ch. 6, above.

[92] See H. Fenwick, *Civil Rights: New Labour, Freedom and the Human Rights Act* (Harlow, Essex: Longman, 2000), ch. 8.

[93] Security Act 1989, s. 1(2), (3).

[94] For commentaries on the Security Service Act 1989, see I. Leigh and L. Lustgarten, 'The Security Service Act 1989' (1989) **52** *MLR* 801–36; K. D. Ewing and C. A. Gearty, *Freedom under Thatcher: Civil Liberties in Modern Britain* (Oxford: Clarendon Press, 1990), 175–88; L. Lustgarten and I. Leigh, *In from the Cold: National Security and Parliamentary Democracy* (Oxford: Clarendon Press, 1994), ch. 14.

Intelligence Services Act 1994 amended section 1 of the 1989 Act so that (as further amended subsequently) the functions of the Security Service now include acting in support of police forces, the National Criminal Intelligence Service, the National Crime Squad and other law enforcement agencies in the prevention and detection of serious crime. The powers of entry to or interference with property which were conferred on the Service are framed in terms of those wide functions. The Director-General of the Security Service is responsible (*inter alia*) for ensuring that arrangements are in place to secure that no information is obtained by the Service except so far as necessary for the proper discharge of its functions, or is disclosed except for that purpose or for preventing or detecting serious crime or for the purpose of any criminal proceedings. The Director-General is also responsible for ensuring that the Service does not take action to further the interests of any political party.[95]

The 1994 Act also allowed the law to intrude further into the secret world, providing for the first time a legal foundation for the existence and work of the Secret Intelligence Service, MI6, and the Government Communication Headquarters (GCHQ), which serves as a listening post monitoring radio and telecommunications traffic across the world. This was remarkable: until forced into the open by the determination of Mrs. Thatcher, then the Prime Minister, to ban trade unions at GCHQ in 1984, no government had even acknowledged the existence of GCHQ (although its huge site on the outskirts of Cheltenham can hardly have gone unnoticed by even the least observant locals).

The Act authorizes the continued existence of the Secret Intelligence Service, under the authority of the Secretary of State. The functions of the Service are to obtain and provide information relating to the actions or intentions of people outside the British Islands, and to perform other tasks relating to their actions or intentions, in the interests of national security (with particular reference to the UK's defence and foreign policy), of the economic well-being of the UK, or in support of the prevention or detection of serious crime.[96] The Service is under the control of its Chief, who is responsible for ensuring that no information is obtained unless it is necessary for the proper discharge of the Service's functions, and that none is disclosed unless necessary for the proper discharge of those functions, or in the interests of national security, for the purpose of the prevention or detection of serious crime, or for the purpose of criminal proceedings. The Chief is also required to ensure that the Service 'does not take any action to further the interests of any UK political party'.[97]

In relation to GCHQ, the 1994 Act provides for its continued existence, to monitor and interfere with electromagnetic, acoustic, and other emissions and the equipment producing them, and to advise and assist the UK's armed forces, government and other bodies about languages and cryptography and similar matters. These functions are exercised in the interests of national security, particularly the UK government's defence and foreign policies, or in the interests of the economic well-being of the UK in relation to actions or intentions of people outside the UK, or in

---

[95] Security Service Act 1989, s. 2(1), (2).
[96] Intelligence Services Act 1994, s. 1.
[97] Ibid., s. 2(1), (2).

support of the prevention or detection of serious crime. The Director of GCHQ is to ensure that there are arrangements for securing that GCHQ obtains no information except such as is necessary for the proper discharge of its functions, that GCHQ discloses no information except for those purposes or for the purpose of any criminal proceedings, and that it takes no action to further the interests of any UK political party.[98]

In respect of all three services, the 1994 Act then provides that no entry on or interference with property or with wireless telegraphy is to be unlawful if it is authorized by a warrant issued, not by a judge, but by the Secretary of State. A Secretary of State's warrant may be granted, specifying the action which is authorized, if the Secretary of State:

(a) thinks that the action is necessary in order to obtain information which is likely to be of substantial value in assisting the Service to perform any of its functions;[99] and

(b) is satisfied that the information cannot be obtained by other means; and

(c) is satisfied that satisfactory arrangements are in force to ensure that no information obtained will be disclosed by the Service except for a purpose permitted under the 1989 and 1994 Acts.[100]

Warrants remain in force for six months, but may be renewed.[101]

The extension of security and intelligence service functions into criminal investigations was highly contentious. It threatened the normal system of accountability for policing, which was already under strain as a result of the growing tendency towards police squads operating at regional or national level, of which the establishment of the National Crime Squad and the National Criminal Intelligence Service was an inevitable part. There was concern that the security and intelligence services would obtain warrants from the Secretary of State in criminal investigations in relation to property in the UK in ways which would circumvent the protection for individual rights and rule-of-law values embodied in the normal regime for regulating search warrants in criminal cases. The issue is partially addressed by amendments to section 5 of the 1994 Act. As amended, it restricts the availability of warrants under the Act for investigating serious crime. No warrant may be issued to the Secret Intelligence Service for that purpose in relation to property in the British Islands. A warrant may be issued to the Security Service for that purpose in relation to property in the British Islands, but only if the proposed action relates to conduct which constitutes (or would, if it took place in the UK, constitute) an offence or offences, and either is an offence for which a person aged 21 or over without a previous conviction could

[98] Intelligence Services Act 1994, ss. 3 (as amended by the Anti-terrorism, Crime and Security Bill 2001), 4.

[99] In the case of GCHQ, a warrant must relate to its monitoring or interference function, not its advisory and assistance functions: ibid., s. 5(2) (a)(iii).

[100] Ibid., s. 5(1), (2).

[101] Ibid., s. 6(2), (3). Where a warrant is issued by an official in the absence of the Secretary of State, it expires after two working days unless extended. The Secretary of State must cancel a warrant if satisfied that the action which it authorizes is no longer necessary: ibid., s. 6(4).

reasonably be expected to be sentenced to a term of imprisonment of three years or more,[102] or:

- involves the use of violence;
- results in substantial financial gain; or
- is conduct by a large number of persons in pursuit of a common purpose,[103] a category which would include even minor public-order offences committed by environmental groups, campaigners for human rights in the UK or abroad, or opponents of mistreatment of animals.

To increase openness and allay concerns about the inadequacy of political or legal controls over the exercise of these powers by the security and intelligence services, the Security Service Act 1989 established a Security Service Commissioner, who had to hold or have held high judicial office. The Commissioner had particular responsibility for keeping under review the way in which the Secretary of State exercised the power to issue warrants, and reported annually to the Prime Minister, who was to lay a copy of the report before each House of Parliament. A Tribunal was established to examined complaints from members of the public about the behaviour of the Security Service, but, where the complaint concerned anything done in relation to property, the Tribunal referred the complaint to the Commissioner, who first ascertained whether a warrant had been issued, and, if one had been, determined whether it had been properly issued or renewed in accordance with judicial review principles. However, the merits of the decision to issue a warrant were not reviewable.[104] A similar arrangement, with a Commissioner and a Tribunal, was put in place in 1994 to scrutinize warrants issued to the Secret Intelligence Service and GCHQ.[105]

The separate arrangements for the different services have now been replaced with a single Intelligence Services Commissioner and a Tribunal under sections 59 and 67 to 70 of the Regulation of Investigatory Powers Act 2000. The new Commissioner has responsibilities for monitoring the exercise of the power to issue warrants to the services to interfere with property or wireless telegraphy under the 1994 Act, and authorizations to carry out surveillance and investigation of encrypted information under Parts II and III of the 2000 Act (explained below), but has no power to review individual warrants. Instead, the new Tribunal is given exclusive jurisdiction to hear and decide complaints of unlawful conduct in connection with, or improper grant of warrants or authorizations for, interference with property or wireless telegraphy, interception of communications, surveillance, or investigation of encrypted material under the 1994 and 2000 Acts.[106] The members of the Tribunal must be lawyers of at least ten years' standing who are not Members of Parliament, and the President must be a person who holds or has held a high judicial office.[107] It is the only tribunal before

---

[102] This does not set the standard very high, bearing in mind, for example, that most drug couriers can expect a sentence of seven years or so on first conviction.

[103] Intelligence Services Act 1994, s. 5(3), (3A) and (3B).

[104] Security Service Act 1989, s. 4 and Sch. 2.

[105] Intelligence Services Act 1994, ss. 8 and 9 and Schs. 1 and 2.

[106] Regulation of Investigatory Powers Act 2000, s. 65.

[107] Ibid., Sch. 3.

which a person can argue that the security or intelligence services have violated their Convention rights under the Human Rights Act 1998.

(ii) Bringing covert entry by the police within the law

It was not long before police forces began to ask why the security and intelligence services could obtain ministerial warrants to legalize bugging and burgling activities for purposes which included combatting serious crime, when the police, for whom the pursuit of serious criminals was a core activity, had no legal authority for such activities, relying instead on Home Office guidance which would not provide a defence in court. Parliament gave way to police pressure, creating a power in Part III of the Police Act 1997 for very senior police officers to authorize their officers to take such action in their area[108] as the authorization might specify in relation to property or wireless telegraphy. No action is to be authorized unless the authorizing officer believes (without any requirement for reasonable grounds) that the action is necessary because it is likely to be of substantial value in the prevention or detention of serious crime, and the objective cannot reasonably be achieved by other means. No entry on or interference with property or wireless telegraphy is unlawful if authorized in this way.[109] A serious crime is defined as one which *either* is an offence for which a person aged 21 or over without a previous conviction could reasonably be expected to be sentenced to a term of imprisonment of three years or more, *or*:

- involves the use of violence;
- results in substantial financial gain; or
- is conduct by a large number of persons in pursuit of a common purpose.

The authorizing officers are the Chief Constable of a police force, the Commissioner of Police (or, in the Metropolitan Police, an Assistant Commissioner), the Director General of the National Crime Squad or a person holding the rank of assistant chief constable in the squad who is designated by the Director General, the Director General of the National Criminal Intelligence Service, and chief officers of certain other investigative bodies.[110]

This appears very permissive and lacking in independent control, but, after strong lobbying by civil liberties groups who warned of the risks of abuse of power and incompatibility with rights under ECHR Article 8, the legislation included certain safeguards. If the authorizing officer believes that the authorization relates to property which is used wholly or mainly as a dwelling or hotel bedroom, or constitutes office premises, or is likely to result in anyone acquiring knowledge of matters subject to legal privilege, confidential personal information or confidential journalistic material, the authorization does not take effect unless it has been notified to and approved by a

---

[108] See also Police Act 1997, s.93(1)(ab) and (1A), inserted by Regulation of Investigatory Powers Act 2000, s.75: power to authorize actions outside the area in order to maintain or retrieve surveillance equipment.

[109] Police Act 1997, ss. 92, 93(1).

[110] Ibid., s.93(5), as amended by Regulation of Investigatory Powers Act 2000, s.75.

Commissioner appointed for this purpose.[111] The Commissioner must not approve the authorization unless he is satisfied that there are reasonable grounds for believing that the action is necessary because it is likely to be of substantial value in the prevention or detention of serious crime, and the objective cannot reasonably be achieved by other means. In other words, the Commissioner must make an independent assessment of the grounds for the application, not merely satisfy himself that the authorizing officer acted within his powers. A Code of Practice issued under section 103 of the Police Act 1997 provides further protection for privacy interests, for example by reminding officers of an undertaking that the powers would not be used to breach the Seal of Confession between priest and penitent in the Roman Catholic tradition.[112]

(iii) Extending regulation to surveillance and the use of human sources by Security and Intelligence Services, police and others: the Regulation of Investigatory Powers Act 2000[113]

The institutions overseeing these powers have been consolidated, and further legal powers conferred, by the Regulation of Investigative Powers Act 2000, passed to bring the procedures into line with the requirements of the Human Rights Act 1998, and particularly ECHR Article 8. There are now three Commissioners in England and Wales: one dealing with interception of communications, one with surveillance, and one with the functions of MI5, MI6 and GCHQ. There is a single Tribunal to deal with all complaints arising in connection with the powers under discussion here. In relation to the substance of the powers, Part I of the Act, which replaces the Interception of Communications Act 1985, and Part III, which gives powers to investigate encrypted electronic data, will be examined in Chapter 11, below. The remainder of this section looks at Part II of the Act, which regulates by law, for the first time (and decades after many other countries), surveillance by means of technological devices and human sources. (The earlier legislation was able to authorize steps taken to placing surveillance devices on private property, but did not regulate the use of surveillance devices placed elsewhere, the collection of information from devices wherever placed, or the use of human sources.) These provisions operate alongside the powers given by the Intelligence Services Act 1994 and Part III of the Police Act 1997.

Part II of the 2000 Act provides that conduct to which it applies is lawful if an authorization has been given in accordance with the Act, and the conduct is in accordance with the authorization.[114] The conduct to which Part II applies is of three kinds: 'directed surveillance'; 'intrusive surveillance'; and 'the conduct and use of

---

[111] Police Act 1997, s. 97. The Chief Commissioner and a number of other Commissioners are appointed for this purpose by the Prime Minister. They hold or have held high judicial office, and have security of tenure equivalent to that of a High Court judge. See Police Act 1997, s. 91.

[112] *Intrusive Surveillance Code of Practice* (Home Office, 1999).

[113] Fenwick, *Civil Rights*, ch. 10; Y. Akdeniz, N. Taylor, and C. Walker, 'Regulation of Investigatory Powers Act 2000 (1): Bigbrother.gov.uk: State Surveillance in the Age of Information and Rights' [2001] Crim. LR 73–90.

[114] Regulation of Investigatory Powers Act 2000, s. 27(1).

covert human intelligence sources'.[115] As will become clear, these types of conduct do not necessarily involve any trespass, but there was a clear risk that they would be unlawful. They often interfere with privacy and had no legal basis, and so constituted an unjustifiable interference with rights under ECHR Article 8 which would be unlawful by virtue of section 6 of the Human Rights Act 1998. In addition, there was (and remains) a clear risk that surveillance would violate the emerging right to privacy at common law, discussed in Chapter 9, above.[116] There was thus probably no need for the Act to make unauthorized surveillance a criminal offence or a tort, although this may need to be reconsidered, depending on the future direction of the courts' caselaw on privacy at common law and under Article 8.

The Act does not define 'surveillance' exhaustively, but provides that it includes:

- monitoring, observing or listening to persons, their movements, their conversations, or their other activities or communications;[117]

- recording anything monitored, observed, or listened to in the course of surveillance; and

- surveillance by or with the assistance of a surveillance device.[118]

However, it does not include:

- the use of, or conduct of, a covert human intelligence source for obtaining or recording (with or without a surveillance device) any information disclosed in the presence of the source, as the position of human intelligence sources is dealt with separately; or

- an entry on or interference with property or wireless telegraphy which would be unlawful unless authorized under the Intelligence Services Act 1994 or Part III of the Police Act 1997, as such entry or interference falls to be assessed under those provisions.[119]

(a) **Intrusive surveillance** is surveillance that is covert (i.e. carried out in a manner calculated to ensure that the subjects of the surveillance are unaware of it[120]) and targets anything taking place on any residential premises or in any private vehicle. This conduct clearly engages the right to respect for private life and the home under ECHR Article 8(1), and was previously uncontrolled by law unless it involved a trespass, making it impossible for such surveillance to be justified under ECHR Article 8(2) and also violating the right of the subject of surveillance to an effective remedy for the

---

[115] Regulation of Investigatory Powers Act 2000, s. 26(1).

[116] See further H. Fenwick and G. Phillipson, 'Breach of Confidence as a Privacy Remedy in the Human Rights Act Era' (2000) 63 *MLR* 660–93.

[117] Interception of communications fall within the surveillance regulation regime only if it falls outside the regulation of interceptions under Part I of the Act because one of the parties to the communication has consented to the interception so that no warrant has been issued in respect of it: Regulation of Investigatory Powers Act 2000, s. 48(4).

[118] Ibid., s. 48(2). A 'surveillance device' is any apparatus designed or adapted for use in surveillance: s. 48(1); and 'apparatus' includes any equipment, machinery or device, and any wire or cable: s. 81(1).

[119] Ibid., s. 48(3).

[120] Ibid., s. 26(9)(a).

violation of Article 8.[121] The Regulation of Investigatory Powers Act 2000, by putting this on a statutory footing and giving the Tribunal jurisdiction to entertain complaints, including allegations of violations of Convention rights, seeks to remedy the position.

Intrusive surveillance may be conducted by means of a technological device or a person who is present on or in the premises or vehicle.[122] There is an overlap between intrusive surveillance and the use of a human covert intelligence source. If an agent-in-place infiltrates a target's residential premises or vehicles by becoming his lover or obtaining employment as his gardener, driver, or housekeeper, or a person already occupying such a position is recruited by the police or intelligence services to provide information, the source is conducting intrusive surveillance while in the house or car, but is merely a covert human intelligence source when they are out shopping or going for a picnic. The fairly tight controls which the Act puts in place in relation to intrusive surveillance, whether by technological device or human agency, are a response to cases in which the police used highly intrusive means to try to obtain damaging admissions from suspects.[123] This attracted some judicial disapproval, and, being unregulated by law, would have been unlawful both in European human rights law and, when the Human Rights Act 1998 came into force, in national law as an unjustifiable violation of rights under ECHR Article 8.

If the surveillance is carried out by means of a device which is not situated on or in the premises or vehicle, the surveillance is still intrusive if the device 'consistently provides information of the same quality and detail as might be expected to be obtained from a device actually on the premises or in the vehicle'.[124] Investigators cannot evade the statutory controls by employing high-quality apparatus from a distance. Using a tracking device on a vehicle is not intrusive surveillance. Nor is an interception of communications which falls within the surveillance regulation regime only because one of the parties to the communication has consented to the interception so that no interception warrant has been issued in respect of it.[125]

Intrusive surveillance can be authorized by the Secretary of State if the application is made by a member of any of the intelligence services or of the armed forces, or by an official of the Ministry of Defence or someone holding designated rank or office with another public authority with power to apply for authorizations.[126] If the application is made by a member of a police force, the National Crime Squad, NCIS, or a customs officer, the authorization can be given by a 'senior authorizing officer'.[127] In

---

[121] *R. v. Khan (Sultan)* [1997] AC 558, [1996] 3 All ER 289, HL; *Khan v. United Kingdom*, Eur. Ct. HR, Judgment of 12 May 2000; *P. G. and J. H. v. United Kingdom*, Eur. Ct. HR, App. No. 44787/98, Judgment of 25 September 2001.

[122] Regulation of Investigatory Powers Act 2000, s. 26(3).

[123] See, e.g. a policewoman striking up a relationship with a suspect in the Rachel Nickell murder case to try to obtain a confession (*The Times*, 15 September 1994), and a confession taped by a policewoman planted with a view to becoming the suspect's lover to gather evidence in the Hall murder case (*Independent*, 12 March 1994).

[124] Regulation of Investigatory Powers Act 2000, s. 26(5).

[125] Ibid., s. 26(4).   [126] Ibid., ss. 32(1), 41(1).

[127] Ibid., ss. 32(1), 33. Senior authorizing officers are chief constables of police forces outside London, the Commissioner and Assistant Commissioners of the Metropolitan Police, the Commissioner of the City of London Police, and the most senior officers of other bodies entitled to seek authorizations: see s. 32(6). In urgent cases, where it is not reasonably practicable for the decision to be made by the senior authorizing officer, an authorization may be given by someone acting on his behalf: s. 34.

each case, the relevant person must believe that a necessity condition and a proportionality condition are satisfied. The former condition is that an authorization is necessary in the interests of national security, in the interests of the economic well-being of the UK, or (in the case of a police or customs authorization only—this does not apply to the intelligence services[128]) for the purpose of preventing or detecting serious crime. The authorizing person must consider whether the information which is needed could reasonably be obtained by other means.[129] The proportionality requirement imports into decision-making the principle which is familiar from the caselaw of the European Court of Human Rights on ECHR Article 8(2).[130]

Where a senior authorizing officer grants an authorization to police or customs officers, it does not take effect until it has been considered, and approved in writing, by a Surveillance Commissioner[131] (there is an exception in cases where the person who grants the authorization gives notice that the case is one of urgency, and notifies a Surveillance Commissioner[132] of the reasons for coming to this conclusion). The Surveillance Commissioner is to give approval only if he is satisfied that there are reasonable grounds for believing that the necessity and proportionality conditions are met on the facts of the case.[133] If satisfied at any time that there were no reasonable grounds for granting the authorization, a Surveillance Commissioner may quash it retrospectively, and order the destruction of any records relating wholly or mainly to information obtained by the authorized conduct after the time when the decision takes effect,[134] i.e. the date on which there ceased to be reasonable grounds for it. If satisfied that there are no longer reasonable grounds to continue an authorization which was originally properly granted, he may cancel it prospectively.[135] The senior authorizing officer may appeal against a decision of a Surveillance Commissioner to the Chief Surveillance Commissioner, who may alter or reverse the decision.[136] If not quashed, cancelled, or renewed, an authorization normally has effect for three months.[137]

The drafting of these provisions is slightly odd, in that there is a logical gap between being satisfied that conditions are met and being satisfied that conditions are not met. There is a similar logical gap between being satisfied that there are reasonable grounds, and being satisfied that there are no reasonable grounds. One might not be sure, and the Act seems to contemplate a situation where one is no longer satisfied

[128] Regulation of Investigatory Powers Act 2000, s. 42(3).

[129] Ibid., s. 32(1)–(4).

[130] See J. McBride, 'Proportionality and the European Convention on Human Rights', in E. Ellis (ed.), *The Principle of Proportionality in the Laws of Europe* (Oxford: Hart Publishing, 1999), 23–35; D. Feldman, 'Proportionality and the Human Rights Act 1998', in Ellis (ed.), *Principle of Proportionality*, 117–44.

[131] Ibid., s. 36(1), (2), (3).

[132] The Chief Surveillance Commissioner and ordinary Surveillance Commissioners are lawyers who hold or have held high judicial office, appointed for a term of three years by the Prime Minister under the Police Act 1997, s. 91: Regulation of Investigatory Powers Act 2000, s. 81(1). There is also power to appoint Assistant Surveillance Commissioners: Regulation of Investigatory Powers Act 2000, s. 63.

[133] Ibid., s. 36(4).

[134] Ibid., s. 37(2), (4), (5).

[135] Ibid., s. 37(3).

[136] Ibid., ss. 38, 39.

[137] Ibid., s. 43(3).

that the conditions are met, but cannot quash or cancel the authorization because one is not satisfied that they are not met either. In a different context, the Court of Appeal has held that it violates the right to liberty under ECHR Article 5 to allow a tribunal to free a mental health patient only if satisfied that the conditions for detaining him are no longer met, rather than requiring them to free him when no longer satisfied that the conditions are met.[138] As cases arising under these provisions will never reach a court, the legality of action being capable of being determined only by the Tribunal, there is a very good reason for persons granting and reviewing authorizations, and the Tribunal itself, to read and give effect to the Act in such a way as to protect Article 8 rights adequately. In this context, where access to a court has been denied so that the declaration of incompatibility is not available as a quasi-remedy, the interpretative requirement in section 3 of the Human Rights Act 1998 should lead public authorities to cancel an authorization whenever they are no longer satisfied that the conditions for its continuance are met.

Where the Secretary of State grants an authorization to the intelligence services, it is in the form of a warrant which remains in effect for up to six months, unless cancelled on the ground that the Secretary of State is satisfied that the necessity or proportionality condition is no longer met.[139] The warrant takes effect immediately. There is no requirement for approval by a judicial officer. The only control which is independent of the executive is a complaint to the Tribunal, after the event, by an aggrieved party; but people will often not know that they have been subjected to intrusive surveillance, so this may prove to be an ineffective remedy for the purposes of ECHR Article 13, and to violate the right of access to a court to protect the common-law right to privacy as a civil right under ECHR Article 6 and section 6 of the Human Rights Act 1998.

The person who grants or renews an authorization must cancel it if satisfied that the requirements for making it are no longer satisfied.[140]

(b) **Directed surveillance** is surveillance which is covert but not intrusive, and is undertaken for the purposes of a specific investigation or operation, in such a manner as is likely to result in the obtaining of private information about any person (whether or not that person is the target of the surveillance). Surveillance is not directed surveillance if undertaken as an immediate response to events or circumstances which are such that it would not be reasonably practicable to seek an authorization under the Act.[141] Monitoring premises using equipment exclusively for the purpose of detecting the installation or use of a television receiver (television detector vans seeking to catch people who are using televisions without having bought a licence) is neither intrusive nor directed surveillance.[142]

Directed surveillance may be authorized by a police officer of the rank of superintendent or above (or, in cases of urgency, inspector or above), and people of equivalent seniority in the security and intelligence services, armed forces, and civilian

[138] See Ch. 7, above.
[139] Regulation of Investigatory Powers Act 2000, ss. 42(1), 44(4), 45.
[140] Ibid., s. 45.
[141] Ibid., s. 26(2).
[142] Ibid., s. 26(6).

public authorities with power to undertake such surveillance.[143] As in relation to intrusive surveillance, a person may authorize directed surveillance only if he believes that necessity and proportionality conditions are fulfilled. The necessity condition here is that the authorization is necessary for one of a number of purposes, more extensive than the purposes for which intrusive surveillance may be permitted:

- in the interests of national security;
- for the purpose of preventing or detecting any crime or preventing any disorder;
- in the interests of the economic well-being of the UK;
- in the interests of public safety;
- for the purpose of protecting public health;
- for the purpose of assessing or collecting any tax, duty, levy or other imposition, contribution or charge payable to a government department; or
- for any other purpose specified in an order made by the Secretary of State.[144]

This seems at first sight to set a low threshold for authorizing directed surveillance. The crime and disorder function seems particularly wide. However, these are all legitimate aims capable of justifying an interference with privacy-related rights under ECHR Article 8(2): the European Court of Human Rights has accepted that protecting tax revenues is an aspect of advancing the economic well-being of a country,[145] and it would be unlawful and *ultra vires* (because of sections 3 and 6 of the Human Rights Act 1998) for the Secretary of State to use the order-making power to authorize an interference for a purpose which did not fall within the legitimate aims listed in ECHR Article 8(2). Furthermore, the test of necessity in the Act, and that of necessity in a democratic society (pressing social need and pro-portionality) under the ECHR and the Human Rights Act 1998, will, if properly applied, significantly supplement the relatively weak purposive constraints in the Act. The lawfulness of the grant of an authorization, and of conduct under it, will therefore depend crucially on the facts of individual cases and the way in which powers under the Act are exercised.

Unlike an authorization of intrusive surveillance, that for directed surveillance takes effect when granted, and remains in force for up to three months (renewable for three months, or six months in the case of an authorization granted to a member of the intelligence services).[146] There is no independent check on individual warrants by a Surveillance Commissioner. The only checks come from the Chief Surveillance Commissioner's general monitoring of and reporting to the Prime Minister on sur-veillance functions under Part III of the Police Act 1997 and section 62 of the Regula-tion of Investigatory Powers Act 2000, and from the entitlement of a person who

---

[143] The Regulation of Investigatory Powers (Prescription of Offices, Ranks and Positions) Order 2000, SI 2000 No. 2417, made by the Secretary of State in exercise of powers to designate authorizing officers conferred by Regulation of Investigatory Powers Act 2000, s. 30(1) and (3) and s. 78(5).

[144] Regulation of Investigatory Powers Act 2000, s. 28(1)–(3).

[145] See, e.g. *Funke v. France*, Eur. Ct. HR, Series A, No. 256-A, Judgment of 25 February 1993, 16 EHRR 297, at para. 52 of the judgment.

[146] Regulation of Investigatory Powers Act 2000, s. 43(3)(c), (4); s. 44(5).

thinks he is the victim of improper surveillance to complain to the Tribunal if he manages to discover that the surveillance has taken place.

(c) **Use of a covert human intelligence source.** The use of informers and specially tasked agents appears to have been increasing in the investigation of serious crime, particularly terrorism, for some time.[147] They sometimes represented threats to privacy which clearly engaged ECHR Article 8. Before the Regulation of Investigatory Powers Act 2000, they were regulated only by guidance from the Association of Chief Police Officers and by protocols within each police force, and equivalent administrative rules within the security and intelligence services. These arrangements were insufficient to make the use of human sources 'in accordance with the law' within the meaning of ECHR Article 8(2). The 2000 Act therefore provides a legal framework for the use of such sources.

Section 29 of the 2000 Act allows the designated persons within public authorities to authorize the conduct or use of a covert human intelligence source. This is a person who establishes or maintains a relationship with someone else (whether of a personal, business or other nature) for the purpose, of obtaining information, providing access to information for a third party, or disclosing information obtained by the use of the relationship or as a consequence of the existence of the relationship. To qualify, the relationship must be conducted in a manner calculated to ensure that the other party to it is not aware of the source's purposes or disclosures. As noted above, this class of activity overlaps with intrusive surveillance, but it may be kept on a strictly business or, at any rate, non-intimate level.[148]

The grounds for granting an authorization and the accompanying legal regime are the same as for directed surveillance, above, except that the person authorizing use of a covert human intelligence source must be satisfied that any necessary arrangements are in place for managing the source, overseeing the use made of him, maintaining records, and ensuring that the records which disclose the identity of the source will not be disclosed to anyone except on a need-to-know basis.[149]

(iv) Conclusion

The developments show both the positive and negative aspects, in terms of the protection of civil liberties generally, of developments in relation to covert policing and the deployment of the security and intelligence services over the past decade or so. On the positive side, a number of activities which were previously unregulated by law have

---

[147] See S. Greer, *Supergrasses: A Study in Anti-Terrorist Law Enforcement in Northern Ireland* (Oxford: Clarendon Press, 1995); JUSTICE, *Under Surveillance: Covert Policing and Human Rights Standards* (London: JUSTICE, 1998), ch. 2. Examples include reported attempts to infiltrate New Age convoys (*The Times*, 15 April 1993), Yardies (*Sunday Times*, 1 August 1993), and gangs of football hooligans (G. Armstrong and D. Hobbs, 'Tackled from Behind', in R. Giulianotti, N. Bonney, and M. Hepworth (eds.), *Football, Violence and Social Identity* (London: Routledge, 1994); capture of children dealing in drugs by a teacher working under cover with the drug squad in Sunderland (*The Times*, 18 February 1995, 2); and any number of people jailed after the hit-men commissioned to kill or injure turned out to be undercover police officers (e.g. the Stanfield case, *The Times*, 23 April 1992; the Morgan case, *Independent*, 21 March 1995; and the Redwood case, *Independent*, 14 July 1995). See also *The Times*, 11 July 1995, 8.

[148] See above, text at n. 123.

[149] Regulation of Investigatory Powers Act 2000, s. 29.

now been brought under the law. Practices which seriously interfered with people's reasonable expectation of privacy, sometimes in the most intimate parts of their lives, are regulated for the first time. The formal arrangements now in place satisfy the requirement in ECHR Article 8(2) that any interference with privacy-related rights must be in accordance with the law, and it is strongly arguable that they also make it possible to be less fearful than before that unregulated interference was being used for illegitimate aims and in circumstances where the interference was disproportionate to those aims. Injecting an element of external review into the process through the work of the various Commissioners and the Tribunal has the potential to improve safeguards for rights. Codes of Practice provide, in a quasi-legislative form, rules of a kind which are likely to command the respect of bureaucrats within the police and security and intelligence services. The need to show that each warrant authorization to be demonstrably justifiable under ECHR Article 8(2) in the circumstances of the case, resulting from the Human Rights Act 1998, section 6, and the power of the Tribunal to quash warrants or authorizations, and to order the destruction of records of information obtained in consequence of them, could considerably extend the protection of the rule of law.

This is bolstered by new institutional arrangements for monitoring them. In 1994, a new Intelligence and Security Committee was established to examine the expenditure, administration, and policy of the three services. It was a response to unfavourable comparisons between the virtual exclusion of external accountability for the work of the security and intelligence services in the UK and the element of scrutiny combined with security provided by a committee of Privy Councillors in Canada.[150] The UK Intelligence and Security Committee consists of members of both Houses of Parliament, none of whom must be a Minister. They are appointed by the Prime Minister after consultation with the Leader of the Opposition. They report annually to the Prime Minister, and the report (edited if necessary to maintain security) is laid before Parliament.

On the other hand, the developments have a negative side. One effect of the legislation has been to legitimate, incrementally, a number of activities which many people would previously have regarded as quite improper and unacceptable. Conduct originally carried on outside the law on a plea of state necessity and national security was first legitimized by Home Secretary's warrants under statute for the Security Service, then extended to investigation of so-called 'serious' crimes when investigated by the security and intelligence services, then authorized for the police in similar cases. Extraordinary techniques have become legally, if not morally, acceptable, although they may still give rise to argument about whether a civilised legal system should make use of their fruits as evidence.[151] If they have not become standard, it is partly because of the high cost (in terms of financial, technical, and human resources) of intensive surveillance operations, and partly because of the sense of balance and proportion which probably predominates in most parts of police forces and, perhaps, the security and intelligence services.

---

[150] Lustgarten and Leigh, *In from the Cold*, 548–66.
[151] P. Mirfield, 'Regulation of Investigatory Powers Act 2000 (2): Evidential Aspects' [2001] Crim. LR 91–107.

The provisions give further cause for concern. The notion of 'national security', which provides one of the planks on which an exercise of the powers can be grounded, is so vague that it can be invoked in a very wide variety of circumstances, and seems to be unconnected with any clear, controlling conception of what is necessary in a democratic society.[152] It will be interesting to see whether the Surveillance Commissioners and the Tribunal take a more robust approach to it than the courts, which have traditionally deferred to a Minister's view of the demands of national security. The Commissioners and the Tribunal will have access to a wider range of information than has been made available to courts. This could justify them in making their own assessments of necessity in relation to national security. Time will tell. But there are other weaknesses in the safeguards for rights and liberties. There is no statutory control on the types of conduct which can be authorized, or the places which may be entered or placed under surveillance, or the material which may be seized or copied, or the means adopted for doing it. The work of the various Commissioners and the Tribunal under the 1994, 1997, and 2000 Acts is of the greatest importance, and calls for the most careful scrutiny in the coming years.

10.4 ENTRY TO AND SEARCH OF PREMISES[153]

(1) GENERAL CONSIDERATIONS

Under PACE, there is a uniform set of procedures to be followed by constables who enter premises under statutory powers. These were drafted with a view to complying with the requirements of ECHR Article 8(2), and (subject to a few matters noted below) ensure that entries and seizures are in accordance with the law, and are a proportionate response to pressing social needs in the fight against crime. It has been said that police action in relation to an entry to and search of premises is a 'composite process' which must be in accordance with the statutory rules on entry and search under section 16 of PACE and, where the entry is under warrant, the statutory rules on applying for and granting the warrant under section 15 of PACE.[154] As Jowitt J said in *R. v. Chief Constable of Warwickshire, ex parte Fitzpatrick*:[155] 'It is clear that sections 15 and 16 are intended to provide a statutory code by which the applications for, issue and execution of search warrants are to be governed'. To be lawful, the obtaining of the warrant (if there is one) and the search, together with any seizure, must comply with the statutory code and with any special statutory provisions governing the particular search. There should therefore be few special problems under the Human

---

[152] For a full analysis, and an attempt to develop a 'democratic conception of national security', see Lustgarten and Leigh, *In from the Cold*, ch. 1.

[153] This section concentrates on the police. It does not consider covert entry and surveillance, or the activities of the security and intelligence services, which were discussed in the preceding section.

[154] *R. v. Chief Constable of Lancashire, ex parte Parker* [1993] QB 577, DC, at 584 *per* Nolan LJ, giving the judgment of the court.

[155] [1999] 1 WLR 564, DC, at 575.

Rights Act 1998. Where there is a doubt, section 6 of the Act reminds us that the police must exercise their discretion in a manner compatible with those Convention principles if their conduct is to be lawful.

Entries to and searches of premises, especially dwellings, are serious infringements of privacy and property rights, and place occupiers under considerable stress. Searches are therefore to be conducted with due consideration for property and privacy, causing no more disturbance than necessary, and using force only when this is necessitated by the occupier's lack of co-operation.[156] Searches are to be conducted at a reasonable hour from the occupier's point of view, unless this might frustrate the object of the search.[157] The occupier's consent to entry is to be sought, after explaining the authority under which the officer seeks entry, unless the premises are known to be unoccupied, or everyone entitled to grant access is known to be absent, or there are reasonable grounds for believing that alerting people in the premises would frustrate the objects of the search or endanger people.[158]

Once on the premises, a Notice of Powers and Rights must be given to the occupier, specifying the power under which the search is to be carried out and summarizing the extent of the statutory search power, explaining the rights of occupiers (including the right to compensation in appropriate cases), and stating that a copy of Code B may be consulted at any police station.[159] This notice should be given before the search begins, if practicable, unless the officer in charge believes that doing so would frustrate the objects of the search or endanger people. If the occupier is not present, a copy of the notice is to be left on the premises, endorsed with the name of the officer in charge, the name of his police station, and the date and time of the search.[160] Where the occupier is present, he must be allowed to ask a friend, neighbour, or other person (it might, for example, be a solicitor) to witness the search, unless the officer in charge has reasonable grounds for believing that this would seriously hinder the investigation.[161] It might do so, for example, if the third person is a suspect, or if it would frustrate the investigation to have to wait for the person to arrive. In any case, the search need not be delayed for an unreasonable period (judged in the light of the purposes and difficulties facing the searcher, as well as the position of the occupier) in order to give time for the person to arrive, so it will often not be practicable for a solicitor to reach the premises in time to witness the search. It is significant that there is no obligation on the officer to tell the occupier of the right to have a third person present.

No more than reasonable force may be used.[162] Searches may be carried no further than necessary to achieve the object of the search, and once the things specified in the warrant have been found, or the officer is satisfied that they are not on the premises,

---

[156] Code B, para. 5.10. For a study of police practice generally in relation to searches, see Lidstone and Bevan, *Search and Seizure*, chs 4 and 6.

[157] PACE, s. 16(4); Code B, para. 5.2 and Note for Guidance 5A.

[158] Code B, para. 5.4.

[159] Code B, para. 5.7.

[160] Code B, para. 5.8. In terrorism investigations, the officer should be identified by warrant number rather than by name.

[161] Code B, para. 5.11.

[162] PACE, s. 117.

the search must end.[163] When the officer in charge leaves the premises, he must satisfy himself that they are secure,[164] a very important provision when force has been used against an outer door or window in order to gain entry.

(2) ENTRY UNDER WARRANT[165]

There are some special rules governing the execution of warrants, designed to ensure that an authorization to enter premises, invading property and privacy, is not abused by the searchers. Warrants must be executed within one month of issue, and may be used only once.[166] This sensible provision takes account of the fact that the factors which justified issuing the warrant may cease to apply later. A warrant may be executed by any constable,[167] and may authorize people who are not constables to accompany the constable.[168] This reflects the view in relation to warrants issued to officials other than police constables that (unless a statute expressly requires it) the names of those people who are permitted to enter need not be recorded in the warrant.[169] Furthermore, not everybody who enters will necessarily be subject to police discipline procedures, and may not know the scope of the powers under statute or even the purpose of the search. It makes a clear briefing by the officer in charge, to all who will be involved, in advance of the entry, particularly important. Allowing other people to enter may be useful: it permits the police to take experts, social workers, or customs officers, as appropriate. However, there is a risk of abuse. In particular, it became a common practice in some cases of suspected fraud to combine execution of search warrants by the police with execution of a search order in civil proceedings (formerly known as an *Anton Piller* order). This is an interim injunction whereby a court orders a defendant in civil proceedings to permit the claimant's solicitor to have access to premises and to seize evidence: see section 10.6, below. If constables attend, it allows them and the claimant's solicitor to pool their powers. This has been disapproved by the courts,[170] even though it has been held by the European Court of Human Rights that it is not incompatible with Article 8 of the European Convention on Human Rights.[171] One of the purposes of requiring the police when executing a search warrant to provide the occupier with a Notice of Powers and Rights and a copy of the warrant is so that the occupier knows what is within the powers of the searching officers. If the search becomes entangled with the execution of an *Anton Piller* order, which confers different powers on searchers and

---

[163] Ibid., ss. 16(8), 17(4); Code B, para. 5.9. The question must be approached from the standpoint of the officer in charge of the search, and knowledge in his possession at the time. See *R. v. Chief Constable of Warwickshire, ex parte Fitzpatrick* [1999] 1 WLR 564, DC, at 575 *per* Jowitt J.

[164] Code B, para. 5.12.

[165] Feldman, *Entry, Search and Seizure*, ch. 6.

[166] PACE, ss. 15(5), 16(3); Code B, paras. 5.1, 5.3.

[167] Ibid., s. 16(1).

[168] Ibid., s. 16(2).

[169] *R. v. Hunt* (1994) 68 TC 132, CA.

[170] *ITC Film Distributors Ltd. v. Video Exchange Ltd.* [1982] Ch. 431, [1982] 2 All ER 241; affirmed CA, *The Times*, 17 June 1982.

[171] *Chappell v. United Kingdom*, Eur. Ct. HR, Series A, No. 152 (1989) 12 EHRR 1.

different safeguards for the occupiers, there is likely to be confusion as to the powers of the various people on the premises, who has seized what, and what remedies the occupier has against whom.

Similarly, there are dangers in the police executing warrants in company with other public officials acting in pursuit of their own objects. In *R. v. Reading Justices, ex parte South West Meats Ltd.*,[172] the police executing a warrant were accompanied by officials of the Intervention Board for Agricultural Produce. The warrant should have been executed by a constable, assisted by the officials of the Board, but instead the officials of the Board conducted the search, decided what should be seized, and retained it, despite the fact that the seizure powers belonged to the police and any items seized should have been retained by the police. This was held to be a trespass involving an abuse of power sufficiently serious to merit the award of exemplary damages of £22,000 on top of the compensatory damages of £3,000. It illustrates the risks of confusion and illegality which can arise where different groups of people, or officials, enter simultaneously without being clear about who is entitled to do what. It also shows the substantial damages which can result. In each case, the magistrate issuing the warrant must specify, in the warrant, the number of extra people who are permitted to enter. It is oppressive to leave the occupiers open to having their premises invaded by a group of people of unspecified number and identity, at the discretion of the police officer concerned.[173]

Where the occupier is present, the officer seeking to execute the warrant must identify himself, producing documentary evidence of identity if he is not in uniform. He must also produce the warrant, which must therefore be in his possession at the time of entry.[174] On the natural reading of section 16(5) of PACE, which speaks of 'the time at which a constable seeks to execute a warrant to enter and search', it might appear that this ought to be done before entry, but such a requirement would often frustrate the purpose of the search. It might give time for drugs to be flushed down a toilet, or for violent suspects to prepare and arm themselves. Accordingly, the Court of Appeal held in *R. v. Longman*[175] that if necessary the officer may obtain entry by a trick, complying with the statutory requirements once in the premises.

This might give rise to some concern on two counts. First, it could appear to do violence to the words of the statute. This may be overstated. The subsection is providing for obligations on officers when the occupier is present at the time when the warrant is executed. It does not actually say when the obligations have to be discharged, although there is an implication that the subsection must be complied with sooner rather than later. On this reading, the Court of Appeal's interpretation was correct. Even if one disagrees about the literal interpretation, the court was doing its best to adopt a construction of the subsection which is workable, and the fault—if there is any—would properly lie with Parliament for approving language which would seem to impose an obligation on officers which tends to undermine the

---

[172] (1991) 4 Admin. LR 401, [1992] Crim. LR 672, DC.

[173] *R. v. Reading Justices and others, ex parte South West Meats Ltd.* (1991) 4 Admin. LR 401, [1992] Crim. LR 672, DC.

[174] PACE, s. 16(5).

[175] [1988] 1 WLR 619.

purpose of the warrant. Secondly, it might seem to be inappropriate in principle for a court to be seen to encourage officers to gain entry to premises by a trick. People should know, when asked to consent to entry, whether they are letting in a constable, a gas official, or a burglar. However, as a matter of law, once the door is open there is authority for the proposition that a constable may enter to execute a warrant without further formalities.[176] At least part of the rationale for the formalities laid down in the statute is to prevent the unnecessary breaking of outer doors and other violence. Where the occupier is thought to be violent or likely to destroy evidence, it would seem to be good police practice to gain access with as little force as possible. While tricks should not be encouraged too widely, neither should they be too readily condemned.

Once officers are on the premises under the authority of a warrant, they have the obligations mentioned above with regard to the Notice of Powers and Rights. In addition, they must give a copy of the warrant to the occupier (if practicable, before the search begins, unless this would frustrate the object of the search or endanger people), or leave a copy on the premises if they are unoccupied. The copy of the warrant should be endorsed in the same way as the Notice of Powers and Rights.[177] The idea is that the occupier should be able to satisfy himself that the people on the premises are acting lawfully, and take advantage of the rights which the Act and Code B offer to ensure that the subsequent search is conducted properly and that the occupiers know what remedies are available to them afterwards.

It was noted above that warrants may never be issued authorizing searches for items subject to legal privilege, and that certain items which are held in confidence or for the purposes of journalism ('special procedure material' or 'excluded material') are also excepted from the normal search-warrant jurisdiction. The treatment of items subject to legal privilege and items held in confidence is considered in Chapter 11, and journalistic material in Chapter 14, below. There are some circumstances in which a circuit judge may issue a search warrant in respect of material which falls into the categories of special procedure material or excluded material, and there are special rules about the execution of those warrants, which are considered in Chapter 11.

10.5 SEIZURE

(1) GENERAL PRINCIPLES

One of the curious features of the elaborate structure of protection for rights of property and privacy is the laxity of the controls over seizures by the police. This is unlike the basic principle in the USA and Canada, where the starting-point is that searches and seizures are infringements of rights to privacy. As such, they must be

---

[176] *Southam v. Smout* [1964] 1 QB 308, [1963] 3 All ER 104, a case concerning entry on civil process; *Re Agnes Securities and R.* (1976) 70 DLR (3d) 504.
[177] Code B, para. 5.8.

properly authorized, and any search without prior authorization in the form of a warrant, from a magistrate or other officer or judge independent of the investigation, is regarded as *prima facie* unreasonable and unconstitutional.[178] This is subject to exceptions, established by the courts; an American commentator has described these as growing so rapidly that they threaten to become the rule,[179] but one still starts from the position that it is for the police or legislature to justify carrying out or authorizing a warrantless search. In England and Wales, by contrast, there is nothing in law to stop the legislature from launching unchecked incursions on the right to privacy. However, legislation must now be read and given effect (so far as possible) in a manner compatible with Convention rights under the ECHR, and conduct which is incompatible with a Convention right and is not required by primary legislation will be unlawful by virtue of section 6 of the Human Rights Act 1998.

In the course of searching premises, the police may seize anything for which they were authorized to search, and certain other items as well.[180] As noted in Chapter 6, when searching premises following an arrest under section 18 or 32 of PACE, the police can seize evidence of certain offences besides that for which the arrest was made. When the police are searching under warrant, they are entitled to seize anything authorized by the statute under which the warrant was issued. In addition, under section 19 any constable lawfully on premises (whether by the consent of an occupier, or under warrant or other statutory authority) may seize anything which he innocently comes across (other than items which the constable has reasonable grounds to believe are subject to legal privilege), in relation to which two conditions, referred to below as the *evidential* condition and the *necessity* condition, are satisfied. Premises are widely defined, including such mobile items as vehicles and caravans. If a constable searching a vehicle, for example, concludes that the evidential and necessity conditions are satisfied in respect of it, sections 18 and 19 have been interpreted as permitting the police to seize and retain the vehicle itself, as well as items found in or on it.[181]

The *evidential* and *necessity* conditions, discussed below, must be applied in such a way as to satisfy the tests for seizure under the Human Rights Act 1998. In relation to the right to respect for private life under ECHR Article 8, a seizure must be in accordance with the law, for a legitimate aim (criminal investigation is such an aim), and a proportionate response to a pressing social need. Justifying an interference with the right to property under Article 1 of Protocol No. 1 also depends on the seizure being lawful, in pursuit of a legitimate state aim, proportionate. If powers of seizure are exercised in a disproportionate way, they therefore become unlawful by virtue of section 6 of the 1998 Act.

While this probably does not substantially alter the scope of the statutory powers of

---

[178] *Coolidge v. New Hampshire* (1971) 403 US 443; *Katz v. United States* (1967) 389 US 347 at 357, US Supreme Court; *Hunter v. Southam Inc.* (1984) 11 DLR (4th) 641, SC of Canada; *Kokesch v. R.* (1990) 1 CR (4th) 62, SC of Canada.

[179] L. Fisher, *American Constitutional Law* (New York: McGraw-Hill, 1990), 866.

[180] Feldman, *Entry, Search and Seizure*, 192–7; Bevan and Lidstone, *Investigation of Crime*, 130–4; Zander, *The Police and Criminal Evidence Act 1984*, 44–6.

[181] *Cowan v. Condon* [2000] 1 WLR 254, CA.

seizure under PACE, it may have two incidental effects. First, it may make it necessary to disapply a common-law power for trespassing officers to seize evidence, if that power has survived PACE. This matter is discussed below. Secondly, it should extend the supervisory powers of the courts to review the legality of warrants and seizures. In the past, it has been said that a seizure of particular items which might or might not be within the warrant or statutory power will be held to be unlawful only if the seizure was so unreasonable that no reasonable constable could have thought that it was justified.[182] Under the Human Rights Act 1998, a disproportionate seizure violates ECHR Article 8 and is *ultra vires*. The courts must make their own assessment of the proportionality of such a seizure, rather than allowing the view of the officer to stand unless it can be stigmatized as irrational: it goes to legality, not rationality.[183] This will increase the intensity of review of police seizures.

(i) The evidential condition

There should be reasonable grounds to believe that the item either is evidence in relation to some offence (not necessarily that which the constable entered to investigate), or has been obtained in consequence of the commission of an offence, whether or not the person in possession of it is suspected of the offence.[184] The only real limitation which structures the officer's discretion under the evidential requirement is the criterion of reasonable grounds for the belief. It is potentially a significant restraint on abuse of power, as it allows the law of tort to step in: an indiscriminate seizure will be tortious, both at common law and under the Human Rights Act 1998. To satisfy the reasonable-grounds standard, every item must be examined in order to decide whether it is evidence and whether it is necessary and proportionate to seize it.

Where large quantities of material are being looked at, this may be inconvenient for all concerned, but it is clear that seizing any item without checking first to see whether it is subject to seizure, or seizing an item which cannot reasonably be regarded as being evidence or otherwise covered by a warrant, will be an unlawful interference with goods, and substantial damages (including, if appropriate, exemplary damages for abuse of power by a public authority) will be recoverable.[185] In *Reynolds v. Metropolitan Police Commissioner*,[186] police officers investigating a suspected insurance fraud had taken large quantities of documents and had sorted them later, returning some and retaining others. In an action for trespass to goods, the jury found for the defendant police officers. The Court of Appeal allowed an appeal by the plaintiff, because the jury had not been asked to decide whether, in relation to each file, book, bundle, or separate document, the officer had reasonable cause to believe that it, or part of it, was of evidential value. If he had not, the seizure was unjustified and tortious. This important principle remains unaltered by PACE.

---

[182] See, e.g. *R. v. Chief Constable of Warwickshire Constabulary, ex parte Fitzpatrick* [1999] 1 WLR 564, [1999] 1 All ER 65, DC.

[183] See Feldman, 'Proportionality and the Human Rights Act'; *R. (Daly) v. Secretary of State for the Home Department, The Times*, 25 May 2001, HL, *per* Lord Steyn.

[184] PACE, s. 19(2)(a), (3)(a).

[185] See, e.g. *R. v. Chief Constable of Warwickshire Constabulary, ex parte Fitzpatrick* [1999] 1 WLR 564, [1999] 1 All ER 65, DC.

[186] [1985] QB 881, [1984] 3 All ER 649, CA.

Generally, however, the evidential requirement is a relatively weak condition, which serves only to ensure that the seizure serves a public interest in the administration of criminal justice. Where that public interest can be invoked, the evidential requirement does not provide any limit on interference with property and privacy rights. For example, under section 19 the police constable may seize any evidential item which he does not have reasonable grounds for believing to be subject to legal privilege.[187] This means that confidential or journalistic material, falling within the categories of special procedure or journalistic material and thus outside the normal search-warrant juris- diction, may be seized during a search under warrant, despite the fact that no warrant could have issued to search for it. For any substantial limitation, we rely on the necessity condition.

There is no power under section 19 to seize material which there are reasonable grounds to believe to be items subject to legal privilege. Material cannot lawfully be taken away for inspection to see whether it is or is not subject to legal privilege. Where such material is inextricably mixed with other material which is of evidential value and is not subject to legal privilege, it has been held that there is no power to seize any of the material.[188] However, the Criminal Justice and Police Act 2001, sections 50 to 70, for the first time allows seizures of material intermixed with items which could not normally be seized, subject to appropriate safeguards for the confidentiality of the material in question and the rights of parties with interests in it.

(ii) The necessity condition

There should be reasonable grounds to believe that it is necessary to seize the item in order to prevent its concealment, loss, or destruction.[189] This is meant to limit the power to seize items without a warrant, or outside the scope of a warrant, where seizure is not actually necessary. In practice, it means that seizure is likely to be lawful only where the person in possession is suspected of being implicated in the offence, or is connected to a suspect, or where the police need to copy or carry out tests on the item. The limitation is particularly important in view of the fact that special- procedure material and excluded material, for which it might well have been impos- sible to obtain a search warrant, is not privileged from seizure under section 19. The concern shown to prevent searches for confidential items being authorized by a magistrate, who is, in theory at least, independent of the police investigation, does not extend to preventing their seizure by the police on the spur of the moment without any independent authorization or check. The privacy interest in such material is required to be respected under ECHR Article 8 and the Human Rights Act 1998. Interference is justified only if it complies with the conditions in Article 8(2), one of which is that interference is necessary (in a democratic society) for the purpose of the prevention of crime (including the detection of crime). Strict compliance with the necessity condition is therefore essential if privacy interests are to be adequately protected in accordance with the Convention.

---

[187] See s. 19(2), (3), (6).
[188] *R. v. Chesterfield Justices, ex parte Bramley* [2000] QB 576, [2000] 1 All ER 411, DC.
[189] PACE, s. 19(2)(b), (3)(b).

The constable may photograph or copy anything which he is empowered to seize.[190] This should make it possible to leave most business records in place, minimizing the risk that a search and seizure will bring a business crashing down. That this can happen when massive seizures take place is shown by the aftermath of the *Rossminster* case: vast amounts of client and business information were seized, with the effect that the company was unable to continue trading. After the House of Lords had refused to quash the warrant or order the Inland Revenue officers to return the material, the company which was being investigated was unable to continue in business, despite the fact that no criminal proceedings were ever brought for the alleged tax fraud in relation to which the warrants had been granted. A seizure of business documents may be a quick and relatively easy way of driving a person or company out of business without the need to establish that he or it is guilty of any criminal offence. Copying of evidence will almost always be preferable.

The police may also demand access to information, including confidential information, which is held in or is accessible from a computer on the premises, if the material is covered by the warrant or other statutory authority or the conditions under section 19 are satisfied.[191] The constable can require the information to be produced in a form in which it is visible and legible and in which it can be taken away, so a print-out may be necessary.

Where the police are searching following an arrest or under a search warrant, the statutory powers to seize evidential material under PACE have been held to co-exist with a common law power to seize goods which show the person arrested or the occupier of premises to be implicated in any crime, so long as they act reasonably and detain the goods for no longer than necessary.[192]

(2) TRESPASSING CONSTABLES

The above powers apply where the constable is lawfully on premises. (Constables who have had consent to their presence withdrawn and are in the process of leaving when they see the evidence are still lawfully on the premises, unless they have taken an unreasonable time to depart: see section 10.3(1), above.) It might be thought that the statutory provision of seizure powers in section 19 for a constable who is lawfully on premises impliedly precludes any seizure powers for a constable who is trespassing. Such a view might draw strength from the maxim *expressio unius, exclusio alterius*: if a power is expressed to be applicable in one situation, it can be implied that it is unavailable in others. Such a conclusion would draw support from other considerations, such as the natural desire not to encourage the police to enter premises without authority.

However, this is not necessarily correct. If an officer is trespassing, but on property in which the complainant has no property or privacy interest, the officer may still be

---

[190] PACE, s. 20(5).

[191] Ibid., ss. 19(4), 20(1).

[192] *Dillon v. O'Brien and Davis* (1887) 16 Cox CC 245; *Chic Fashions (West Wales) Ltd. v. Jones* 1968] 2 QB 299, CA; *Ghani v. Jones* [1970] 1 QB 693, CA, at 706 *per* Lord Denning MR; *Cowan v. Condon* [2000] 1 WLR 254, CA.

in the execution of his duty. For example, it is arguable that a suspect who hops over a hedge into somebody else's premises in order to evade detection or arrest should not be allowed to protest that the constable who follows is acting outside his duty *vis-à-vis* him, even though an action for trespass might lie at the suit of the owner or occupier of the premises. This view has been adopted by the High Court of Australia,[193] and in the USA it has been held that a person other than the occupier has no standing to assert privacy interests under the Fourth or Fourteenth Amendments against a trespassing constable.[194] ECHR Article 8 protects all who have a reasonable expectation of privacy, even on other people's property with their consent,[195] although they are unlikely to be entitled to rely on Article 8 if they, like the constable, are trespassing.

The position is more doubtful where the constable is trespassing on premises occupied by an owner of the items seized. At common law in England and Wales before PACE, there was power to seize evidence of grave offences, and it did not depend on the officer being lawfully on the premises at the time.[196] As explained by Lord Denning MR in *Ghani v. Jones*,[197] the power was limited to cases where the police have reasonable grounds for believing: (i) that a serious crime has been committed; (ii) that the item to be seized is either the fruits of the crime, or the instrument with which it was committed, or is material evidence; (iii) that the person in possession has committed or is implicated in the crime, or his refusal to surrender the item is quite unreasonable.[198] There had been a profoundly unsatisfactory suggestion in a previous decision that a search without reasonable grounds might be justified after the event by the finding of evidence of sedition, because of the public interest in obtaining such evidence.[199] This was rightly disapproved in *Ghani v. Jones*. Making the legality of police behaviour depend on events occurring after the search would have prevented occupiers from establishing their legal rights with reasonable certainty, breaching the requirement in the ECHR Article 8(2) that any interference with the right to respect for privacy, the home, and family life should be in accordance with law.[200] None the less, the court accepted that a constable liable in trespass could none the less lawfully exercise the limited common law power to seize property.

It is at least possible that, where the constable is not lawfully on premises, the common-law power of seizure survives, by virtue of section 19(5) of PACE: 'The powers conferred by this section are in addition to any power otherwise conferred'. In *Cowan v. Condon*[201] the Court of Appeal held that this preserved common law powers of seizure under search warrants or following arrests. However, it is far from clear section 19 should be interpreted as preserving the seizure power which *Ghani v. Jones* conferred on trespassing constables. To treat that power as preserved would

---

[193] *Halliday v. Nevill* (1984) 155 CLR 1, by a majority, Brennan J dissenting.

[194] *Brown v. US* (1973) 411 US 223.

[195] *Khan v. United Kingdom*, Eur. Ct. HR, Judgment of 12 May 2000.

[196] *Ghani v. Jones* [1970] 1 QB 693, [1969] 3 All ER 1700, CA; Feldman, *Entry, Search and Seizure*, 260–8.

[197] [1970] 1 QB 693, [1969] 3 All ER 1700, CA.

[198] This was an afterthought, and is of questionable authority. See R. M. Jackson, [1970] *CLJ* 1; *McLorie v. Oxford* [1982] QB 1290, [1982] 3 All ER 480, DC.

[199] *Elias v. Pasmore* [1934] 2 KB 164.

[200] For explanation of the implications of this term, see Ch. 8 above.

[201] [2000] 1 WLR 254, CA.

complicate the law considerably. For example, it would make it very difficult to decide whether a person who interferes with a trespassing constable, who is attempting to secure evidence of a grave crime, is assaulting or wilfully obstructing the constable in the execution of his duty, committing an offence under section 89 of the Police Act 1996, as normally a trespassing constable is not in the execution of his duty.[202] It would also be difficult to argue that the conduct of a constable making a seizure is lawful, or in accordance with the law, for the purposes of justifying incursions on rights under the Human Rights Act 1998, where the constable is trespassing at the time. One aspect of the principle of legality which underpins the ECHR is to enforce the principles of the Rule of Law, keeping state officials within powers conferred by law. There may be public-interest grounds for allowing the police to seize evidence of grave crimes even when trespassing, even if the police presence on the premises is unlawful, but if such a power is to be conferred it should be done consciously and explicitly by Parliament, not by way of the turning of a judicial blind eye to unlawful action.

The common law power conferred by *Ghani v. Jones* has been roundly rejected by the New Zealand Court of Appeal, which accepted that the previous, more restricted, common-law powers might need to be reformed, but decided that it was the job of the legislature, not the courts, to restrict individual rights and codify police powers if necessary.[203] In Canada, the courts, assisted by the enactment of the Charter of Rights and Freedoms, have developed an exclusionary rule for unreasonable (including most trespassory) searches.[204] This is a more rights-based approach, treating rights as entitled to protection by the courts. In the same way, the US Supreme Court, interpreting the Fourth Amendment to the Constitution, has developed a mandatory exclusionary rule to prevent the police from using as evidence anything seized in the course of an unconstitutional search,[205] although since the 1970s the court, dominated increasingly by conservatives, has developed exceptions to the exclusionary rule. Even in England, where in *Ghani v. Jones* the extended powers was applied in a number of cases before PACE,[206] the Royal Commission on Criminal Procedure recommended in 1981 that items seized during a search under warrant, but in excess of the authority conferred by the warrant, should not be admissible in evidence, although they rejected any more extensive exclusionary rule for illegally obtained evidence.[207]

There is, therefore, much to be said for the view expressed by Jowitt J, with whom Rose J agreed, in *R. v. Chief Constable of Warwickshire Constabulary, ex parte Fitzpatrick* in relation to goods seized during the execution of a search warrant which are outside the scope of the warrant:[208]

---

[202] For full discussion, see Feldman, *Entry, Search and Seizure*, 409–16.

[203] *McFarlane v. Sharpe* [1972] NZLR 838, CA of NZ.

[204] E.g. *Kokesch v. R.* (1990) 1 CR (4th) 62, SC of Canada.

[205] *Weeks v. United States* (1914) 232 US 383; *Mapp v. Ohio* (1961) 367 US 643.

[206] *R. v. Hinde* (1977) 64 Cr. App. R. 213, CA; *Frank Truman Export Ltd. v. Metropolitan Police Commissioner* [1977] QB 952, [1977] 3 All ER 431; *Malone v. Metropolitan Police Commissioner* [1980] QB 49, [1979] 1 All ER 256, CA. *Ghani v. Jones* was also applied in New South Wales: *GH Photography v. McGarrigle* [1974] 2 NSWLR 635.

[207] RCCP, *Report*, para. 3.49.

[208] [1999] 1 WLR 564, 575.

'. . . sections 15 and 16 are intended to provide a statutory code by which the applications for, issue and execution of search warrants are to be governed. I do not accept that by an oversight Parliament has omitted to provide for the case in which articles have been seized for which the search warrant has provided no authority, leaving such a case to be dealt with by the common law . . . [A] search has exceeded the purpose for which the warrant was issued—namely the search for and seizure of material covered by the warrant in respect of which the criteria [in sections 15 and 16] have been satisfied—when material which does not satisfy those criteria has been seized.'

If that is true of cases where the police have entered premises lawfully in reliance on a warrant, it should apply *a fortiori* where there is no warrant and the police are trespassers. The power formulated in *Ghani v. Jones* was intended to provide for a situation in which Parliament had not addressed, as a matter of general principle, the proper scope of police powers of seizure, and no warrant was available for evidence in murder investigations. Parliament subsequently addressed both issues in PACE, and limited the power in section 19 to constables who are lawfully on premises. In the light of the interpretative principle in section 3 of the Human Rights Act 1998, courts should not be too quick to interpret section 19(5) of PACE, which is far from clear and unequivocal, as leaving in existence a common-law power designed to deal with a problem which no longer exists, and of questionable compatibility with basic Rule of Law principles.

(3) RETENTION OF ITEMS SEIZED

At common law, after an item had been lawfully seized the police were not to keep it, or prevent its removal by the person in possession, for longer than necessary, using a copy if practicable. The lawfulness of the conduct was to be judged by the circumstances at the time, not by what happens afterwards.[209] This power continues,[210] but as it is significantly narrower than that under sections 19 and 20 of PACE, below (except where the constable was trespassing or otherwise acting unlawfully when the items were seized, as to which see the discussion above) it is rarely, if ever, of any practical importance.

Under PACE, the principles are somewhat refined. When items have been lawfully seized for the purposes of a criminal investigation, the police may retain them for use as evidence at trial, for forensic examination, for investigation in connection with an offence, or (where there are reasonable grounds for believing that it has been obtained in consequence of an offence) to establish the lawful owner.[211] If seized by an officer

---

[209] *Ghani v. Jones* [1970] 1 QB 693 at 708–9, [1969] 3 All ER 1700 at 1704–5 *per* Lord Denning MR.

[210] See *Cowan v. Condon* [2000] 1 WLR 254, CA. For example, in *Flynn v. Commissioner of Police*, 6 December 1993, CA, unreported (available on Lexis), the police seized a car which was alleged to have been obtained by deception. It was seized from travellers with no fixed address, and the police refused to release it to them pending criminal proceedings. The Court of Appeal upheld the police action, applying *Ghani*: as the people claiming the car might be difficult or impossible to track down if the car were later to be needed as evidence, the police were not in breach of their duty in holding the car pending trial in case it was needed, even if it was not clear beforehand how the car itself could be of evidential value.

[211] PACE, s. 22(2).

lawfully on premises, under section 19 or (in relation to computerized records) section 20 of PACE, the retention powers are wider: such material may be retained for as long as is necessary in all the circumstances.[212] This has serious implications for the people from whom the material is seized. If they are not implicated in the offence, their control over the items is restricted in the public interest; the seizure may interfere with their lawful business activities and cost them a great deal of money. If the items are seized from a suspect who is subsequently charged, police control of the items may make it difficult to prepare the defence adequately. In either case, there is a risk that the police may make the items available to other people who derive an illegitimate advantage from seeing them, whether business competitors, litigants in civil proceedings against the person from whom the items were seized, or investigators in other jurisdictions who could not otherwise have obtained access to the material.[213] For all these reasons, it is important that there should be safeguards on the use which may be made of the material while in police custody.

The first safeguard for people from whom material is seized is that the police must, on request within a reasonable time, provide a list or description of the material to the person from whom it was seized.[214] This does not go as far as the Royal Commission on Criminal Procedure, which recommended that there should be a duty to give a receipt for all items on seizure.[215] Secondly, the person, or his representative, must be allowed supervised access to it, to examine it or have it photographed or copied, unless the officer in charge of an investigation has reasonable grounds for believing that this would prejudice the investigation of an offence or any criminal proceedings.[216] Refusal to allow access may be challenged by an application for judicial review.[217] Thirdly, the police hold property under section 22 of PACE only for the purposes authorized. There is no power to apply it to any other purpose without either the consent of the owner or person from whom it was seized, whose property it remains, or some other legal authority. They owe a duty to maintain the confidentiality of materials which they have seized, subject only to their power to use them for police purposes; however, this duty may be overridden by a countervailing public interest. The clearest example is where a court orders the police to produce material, which is admissible in evidence in other proceedings, under a *subpoena duces tecum*, but there are other possible exceptions. For example, it is permissible to pass information about suspected child abuse between the police and social services without the

---

[212] Ibid., s. 20(1).

[213] The last category is now largely covered by statute, since the Criminal Justice (International Co-operation) Act 1990, s. 7, provides for warrants to be issued to search for and seize evidence of offences committed in other jurisdictions following a direction of the Secretary of State at the request of foreign authorities, and for any evidence found to be transmitted to the foreign authorities. On the role of the Secretary of State, see *R. v. Central Criminal Court, ex parte Propend Finance Property Ltd.* [1996] 2 Cr. App. R. 26, DC.

[214] Code B, para. 6.8.

[215] RCCP, *Report*, para. 3.47.

[216] Code B, para. 6.9; the position is the same as at common law, on which see *Arias v. Metropolitan Police Commissioner, The Times*, 1 August 1984, CA.

[217] *Allen v. Chief Constable of Cheshire, The Times*, 16 July 1988, CA.

prior approval of the court.[218] The police as bailees of items seized have a duty to take reasonable steps to keep them safely and in good condition.[218a]

The power to seize and retain property is granted to the police for specific and limited purposes. Once those purposes have been fulfilled (for example, criminal proceedings in relation to which an item has been retained as evidence are at an end, or a decision has been taken not to pursue them), the police no longer have any right to continue to retain the property. They must then return it to the person who appears to have the best claim to it. If the items have been stolen, the person with the best title to the goods will usually be the victim of the theft. If that person cannot be traced, the person from whom they were seized is entitled to their return (unless the goods have been forfeited by a court order). Even if the person from whom the goods were seized was implicated in the offence, they will have acquired possessory title which is good against all the world, except for someone who can establish better title. Sections 19 and 22 of PACE do not confer such title on the police. Accordingly, if the police refuse to return the goods, they would have no defence to an action for wrongful detention of them. The equitable doctrine *ex turpi causa non oritur actio* (no action will lie to protect a right or interest acquired wrongfully) no longer operates to prevent a wrong-doer from relying on possessory title acquired wrongfully, unless he or she has been divested of that title under a statutory power or by someone with a stronger claim to possession in the ordinary law of personal property.[218b]

10.6 SEARCH ORDERS IN CIVIL PROCEEDINGS

Besides entry and search in criminal matters, there is a special type of order which requires a party to civil proceedings to give access to his premises to another party, in order that the latter can seek evidence. This is called a 'search order', previously known as an *Anton Piller* order after the first case of its type to reach the Court of Appeal.[219] The order is a form of coerced discovery, originally used only in exceptional and emergency cases where there was a serious risk that a conventional order for discovery would be ineffective, because the party subject to it would destroy or hide evidence and thwart the other party's chances of success in the litigation.[220] The making of an order therefore reflects on the honesty of the party against whom it is

---

[218] *Marcel v. Commissioner of Police of the Metropolis* [1992] 1 All ER 72, CA, especially *per* Nolan LJ and Sir Christopher Slade at 85, 89; *In re G. (A Minor) (Social Worker: Disclosure)* [1996] 1 WLR 1407, [1996] 2 All ER 65, CA (Butler-Sloss LJ and Sir Roger Parker; Auld LJ dissented).

[218a] On the duties of the police as bailees, see *Sutcliffe v. Chief Constable of West Yorkshire* [1996] RTR 86, CA, an action by the wife of the so-called 'Yorkshire Ripper' for the return of the vehicle in which he had been arrested.

[218b] *Costello v. Chief Constable of Derbyshire Constabulary* [2001] 1 WLR 1437, CA, applying *Tinsley v. Milligan* [1994] 1 AC 340, [1993] 3 All ER 65, HL, and *Webb v. Chief Constable of Merseyside Police* [2000] QB 427, [2000] 2 WLR 546, [2000] 1 All ER 209, CA, in preference to Feldman, *Entry, Search and Seizure*, 313, para. 11.41.

[219] *Anton Piller KG v. Manufacturing Processes Ltd.* [1976] Ch. 55, [1976] 1 All ER 779, CA.

[220] *EMI v. Pandit* [1975] 1 WLR 302, [1975] 1 All ER 418.

made. It is a draconian step, equivalent in many ways to a civil search warrant,[221] to be employed only where absolutely necessary and clearly justified. Moreover, as the essence of such an order is surprise, it is crucial that the person on whom the order is served should have no warning, and so the application is *ex parte*, imposing a heavy responsibility on the party applying to put all relevant information before the court. At the same time, it is important that all rights should be adequately protected in the execution of the order: it is *prima facie* a contempt of court to refuse access to premises or material when access is demanded in reliance on an *Anton Piller* order, so the consequences for the person subject to the order are potentially very serious.

In *Anton Piller KG v. Manufacturing Processes Ltd.*[222] Ormrod LJ specified three conditions for the grant of an order, and Lord Denning MR added a fourth. The conditions were: (i) that the applicant must show an extremely strong *prima facie* case, making it very likely that he will succeed at trial; (ii) that the actual or potential damage to the applicant must be very serious; (iii) that there is clear evidence that the defendants have in their possession incriminating documents or things, and that there is a real possibility that they may destroy that material before an *inter partes* application could be made; and (iv) that the inspection under the order will do no real harm to the defendant or his case.

However, as time went on it became clear that orders were being granted more or less as a matter of course, without adequate supporting information or consideration of the issues, and that orders were being executed by solicitors for the plaintiff without proper regard for the need to safeguard the rights of the defendant. After one case, in which the plaintiffs obtained an order in respect of pirated films, knowing that the police intended to execute a warrant to search for obscene material at the same time but without telling the judge that this was so, the defendant applied to the Strasbourg organs, arguing that the grant of the order and the manner of its execution infringed ECHR Article 8. The Commission declared the application to be admissible, but in due course the Court decided that the infringement of the defendant's privacy rights had been justifiable under Article 8(2).[223] This did nothing to allay the deep concern which developments were causing both to some judges[224] and to practitioners and academics.[225]

This concern led to a wide-ranging review of the procedures for executing *Anton Piller* orders in the course of a judgment by Sir Donald Nicholls V-C in *Universal Thermosensors Ltd. v. Hibben.*[226] First, orders are to be executed during office hours on

---

[221] M. Dockray, 'Liberty to Rummage: A Search Warrant in Civil Proceedings?' [1977] *PL* 369–88; A. Staines, 'Protection of Intellectual Property Rights: *Anton Piller* Orders' (1983) 46 *MLR* 274–88.

[222] [1976] Ch. 55, [1976] 1 All ER 779, CA.

[223] *ITC Film Distributors v. Video Exchange Ltd.* [1982] Ch. 431, [1982] 2 All ER 241, affirmed CA, *The Times*, 17 June 1982; *Chappell v. United Kingdom* (10461/83), Eur. Ct. HR, Series A, No. 152, 12 EHRR 1.

[224] *Columbia Pictures Ltd. v. Robinson* [1987] Ch. 38, [1986] 3 All ER 338 at 365–71, 375–80 *per* Scott J; *Lock International plc v. Beswick* [1989] 1 WLR 1268, [1989] 3 All ER 373 (Hoffmann J).

[225] M. Dockray and H. Laddie, 'Piller Problems' (1990) 106 *LQR* 601–20. Hugh Laddie QC was counsel who, in effect, invented the orders, representing the plaintiffs in the first cases; Professor Dockray has been one of the foremost academic commentators on them.

[226] [1992] 1 WLR 840, [1992] 3 All ER 257.

working days, so that the defendant can quickly obtain legal advice before the plaintiff's representatives begin to search. Secondly, where the order is to be executed at a private house and it is at all likely that a woman will be there alone, the solicitor serving the order must be a woman, or be accompanied by one. Thirdly, unless it is seriously impracticable, a detailed list of items to be seized must be prepared at the premises before any items are removed, and the defendant must be given an opportunity to check it. Fourthly, injunctions restraining people from informing anyone other than a lawyer about the order must not last too long. A week, as in that case, was far too long. Fifthly, orders must provide that they are not to be executed at business premises save in the presence of a representative of the company or trader in question, unless there is good reason for doing otherwise. Sixthly, it must not be possible for directors or employees of a plaintiff company to search the files of the defendant company if the two companies are business competitors. Finally, the court must consider ordering the plaintiff to instruct, and pay for, an independent solicitor with experience of *Anton Piller* orders to supervise the execution of the order, and to prepare a written report on what takes place.[227] This is to be served on the defendant. The plaintiff should in any case be required to return to court within a few days for an inter partes hearing. As Sir Donald Nicholls said:

' . . . in suitable and strictly limited cases, Anton Piller orders furnish courts with a valuable aid in their efforts to do justice between two parties. Especially is this so in blatant cases of fraud. It is important therefore that these orders should not be allowed to fall into disrepute. If further steps are necessary to prevent this happening, they should be taken. If plaintiffs wish to take advantage of this truly Draconian type of order, they must be prepared to pay for the safeguards which experience has shown to be necessary if the interests of defendants are fairly to be protected.'

Furthermore, the order must contain a proviso safeguarding the respondent's privilege against self-incrimination, although he is free to choose not to rely on the privilege if he so wishes.[228] If the respondent is likely to suffer violent reprisals for making disclosures about third parties in obedience to the order, that is a matter to be taken into account, but the public interest in the administration of justice is not normally to be subordinated to threats of violence.[229] The orders are now governed by Practice Direction annexed to Part 25 of the Civil Procedure Rules.

---

[227] For an account of the work of the independent solicitor in one case, see *IBM United Kingdom Ltd. v. Prima Data International Ltd.* [1994] 1 WLR 719, [1994] 4 All ER 748.

[228] *Rank Film Distributors Ltd. v. Video Information Centre* [1982] AC 380, [1981] 2 All ER 76, HL; Supreme Court Act 1981, s. 72; *IBM United Kingdom Ltd. v. Prima Data International Ltd.* [1994] 1 WLR 719, [1994] 4 All ER 748; *Coca-Cola Co. v. Gilbey* [1995] 4 All ER 711.

[229] *Coca-Cola Co. v. Gilbey* [1995] 4 All ER 711.

10.7 SOME CONCLUDING REFLECTIONS

There is a developing and welcome recognition among judges that the public interest in the detection of crime and the administration of the civil justice process does not justify wholesale and uncontrolled interference with individual rights. This has been most obvious in decisions of judges in relation to civil proceedings, but is gradually permeating criminal matters as the influence of the Human Rights Act 1998 exerts itself. Parliament provided some safeguards for rights in PACE, but has shown itself too ready to extend intrusive powers of investigation with only limited protection for those whose lives are affected by official actions. This is particularly evident in legislation extending legal authority to conduct bugging, burgling, and surveillance activities on premises, often without prior judicial approval. In these cases, aggrieved parties have their access to courts abridged. Even access to the Tribunal is restricted by the fact that there is no obligation to inform people that they have been the subject of surveillance, so as to allow them to pursue a remedy. In this, the UK lags behind Germany's legal rules in providing safeguards for people's rights in relation to surveillance by the security and intelligence services.[230]

Again, Parliament permits officers to enter premises under sections 18 and 32 of PACE without judicial authorization. The police can also use the occupier's consent to avoid legal limits on their powers of entry.[231] We have no requirement for a judicial hearing *inter partes* after the execution of every search warrant, to check the legality of what took place; instead, the aggrieved party is left to pursue remedies by way of judicial review. We make no provision for a person to take legal advice before a warrant is executed.

It will be interesting to see whether the Human Rights Act 1998 affects all these areas for the better, both in Parliament and the courts, in coming years.

[230] See *Klass v. Germany*, Eur. Ct. HR, Series A, No. 28, Judgment of 6 September 1978, 2 EHRR 214.
[231] See Lidstone and Bevan, *Search and Seizure*, 44–7, 157–60.

11

PROTECTING CONFIDENCES

Although it may be misleading to regard the protection of personal information as central to the idea of privacy (see section 9.5 above), protecting such information undoubtedly has an important role to play in maintaining the conditions necessary for private life. This chapter examines the treatment of confidential information in English law, principally in the context of protection for personal information, as an aspect of rights to respect for privacy. 'Personal information' has been defined by Professor Wacks as consisting of 'those facts, communications, or opinions which relate to the individual and which it would be reasonable to expect him to regard as intimate or sensitive and therefore to want to withhold or at least to restrict their collection, use, or circulation'.[1] The advantage of speaking of personal information rather than privacy, according to Wacks, is that it enables one to avoid dependence on the problematic notion of privacy, which, he suggests, is largely parasitic on other legal categories such as property and confidentiality. However, ECHR Article 8, forming part of English law by virtue of section 1 of, and Schedule 1 to, the Human Rights Act 1998, while not expressly mentioning personal information, guarantees respect for much of it as an aspect of a person's private and family life, home, and correspondence. Community law also respects these rights at all stages of inquiries conducted by the EC Commission, although the Court of Justice has given a narrower reach to the rights in Community law than the European Court of Human Rights has given them under the Convention machinery: the Strasbourg court, unlike the Luxembourg court, extends Article 8 rights to commercial, rather than only domestic, premises.[2] English law incorporates the wider, Strasbourg, version of these privacy-related standards for normal purposes. The relationship between the Human Rights Act 1998, the Strasbourg court's jurisprudence and Community law in national courts is complex and the effects of the relationship are at present uncertain, but UK courts would be likely to interpret the rights under Community law in the light of the Strasbourg jurisprudence when dealing with Community law proceedings concerning the powers of UK bodies taking action as competent authorities on behalf of the Commission or implementing Community law.

The present chapter looks at the limits imposed on the confidentiality element in privacy rights in English law by the need to further public interests, and particularly

---

[1] R. Wacks, *Personal Information: Privacy and the Law* (Oxford: Clarendon Press, 1989), 26.

[2] Compare Cases 46/87 and 227/88, *Hoechst AG v. Commission* [1989] ECR 2859, CJEC, with *Niemietz v. Germany*, Eur. Ct. HR, Series A, No. 251-B, Judgment of 16 December 1992.

the interest in the prevention and detection of crime. The Human Rights Act 1998, section 6 requires any discretion which may interfere with respect for private and family life, home or correspondence to be exercised in a manner compatible with Convention rights. Article 8 now provides a basis for striking the balance between competing interests in national law. Article 8(2) of the European Convention on Human Rights provides that the exercise of the right to respect for a person's private and family life, home, and correspondence, may be subjected only to such interference 'as is in accordance with the law and is necessary in a democratic society in the interests of national security, public safety or the economic well-being of the country, for the prevention of disorder or crime, for the protection of health or morals, or for the protection of the rights and freedoms of others'. In the context of protecting confidential information against publication, the right to respect guaranteed under ECHR Article 8 comes into conflict with the right to free expression and communication of information and ideas guaranteed under Article 10 of the same Convention. Neither right is unqualified. The circumstances under which it is legitimate to interfere with the right to freedom of expression are examined generally in Chapter 13 and with particular reference to the media in Chapter 14.

The scheme of this chapter is as follows. In section 11.1, the scope of the protection for confidential material is considered. In what circumstances do professional or business relationships give rise to duties of confidentiality, in the sense of duties to keep secrets? When can these be overridden? The two sections which follow examine aspects of the relationship between the interest in maintaining confidences and the public interest in the administration of criminal justice. Where these interests come into conflict, what protections against forced disclosure are offered to holders of confidential material? Section 11.2 opens the examination of procedures for confidential material in criminal investigations, concentrating on items subject to legal privilege. Section 11.3 examines the treatment of other confidential material in criminal investigations, and section 11.4 looks at the control of interception of communications. Some conclusions about the importance of confidentiality interests in the criminal justice system are suggested in section 11.5.

11.1 THE SCOPE OF DUTIES OF CONFIDENCE

The duty of confidence operates in equity and in contract. It protects information of certain limited classes. The protection primarily takes the form of equitable remedies, such as injunctions restraining disclosure. If the disclosure has already been made other remedies may be granted, such as damages, or an account of profits made through improper disclosure, so that the person entitled to the information rather than the wrongdoer may benefit. In order to enjoy protection, the subject matter of the information must be such as to justify treating it as confidential. It must usually not be in the public domain. If there has been an authorized disclosure to anyone, the information may lose its confidential quality unless a duty was imposed on the confidant in turn to hold the information in confidence. Finally, even if the information in question passes these tests for confidentiality, the protection may be lost if the court takes the view that the disclosure in question serves a public interest of such importance that it overrides the interest in maintaining confidentiality. Each of these elements will be examined separately.

(1) THE CONFIDENTIAL QUALITY OF THE INFORMATION

Treating information or material as worthy of legal protection on the ground of confidentiality presupposes a judgment about the value of maintaining the confidentiality of information of that type. The information must arise from or be significant to a relationship or activity which the law recognizes as particularly worthy of support, and must engage some legitimate interest which would be adversely affected by disclosure. If disclosure would not adversely affect anyone's interests, it will not engage a duty of confidentiality. For example, in *R. v. Department of Health, ex parte Source Informatics Ltd.*[3] the Court of Appeal held that pharmacists could pass data concerning the prescribing habits of doctors to commercial organizations to guide marketing by drug companies. Patient data was anonymized, so disclosure did not affect patients' right to privacy or confidentiality.

Initially, the judges regarded the confidentiality of information as worthy of protection if it related to either of two fields of human activity. Information about commercial or manufacturing processes carried on for profit was protected,[4] because of the market value of business information in a free or mixed economy. Information about family relationships, particularly the secrets of the marriage bed, were protected,[5] because of the keen personal interest in preserving an area of life in which intimate relationships could be developed and nurtured without the risk of publicity, and because of the importance of the family to the organization and stability of society. Generally, disclosing commercial information can be remedied by an award of damages or an account of profits, whereas disclosing personal details is more likely to be capable of protection only by preventing disclosure. The classification of material as private or commercial will therefore be relevant to the type and level of protection available. In *Douglas v. Hello! Ltd.*,[6] the Court of Appeal refused to restrain a magazine from publishing unauthorized photographs of the wedding of two film actors because they had entered into an exclusive publication deal with a rival magazine. For the purpose of the law of confidence and privacy, this had converted photographs of their wedding from essentially private material into essentially commercial material, not meriting an order restraining publication.

---

[3] [2000] 2 WLR 940, [2000] 1 All ER 786, CA. The common law position is now capable of being restricted by statutory instrument in relation to patient information. The Secretary of State has power to make regulations imposing additional restrictions on disclosure of patient information for such purposes as he considers necessary or expedient, or in the public interest: see Health and Social Care Act 2001, s. 60.

[4] *Coco v. A. N. Clark (Engineers) Ltd.* [1969] RPC 41.

[5] *Prince Albert v. Strange* (1849) 2 De Gex & Sm. 652, (on appeal) 1 Mac. & G. 25; *Margaret, Duchess of Argyll v. Duke of Argyll* [1967] 1 Ch. 302, [1965] 1 All ER 611.

[6] [2001] 1 WLR 992, CA. For general discussion of the scope for such developments, see G. Phillipson and H. Fenwick, 'Breach of Confidence as a Privacy Remedy in the Human Rights Act Era' (2000) 63 *MLR* 660–93.

The doctrine of confidentiality has been significantly expanded in recent years. A person who has a job involving secret work, such as officers of the security and intelligence services, is under a duty not to disclose information about the work, as well as being bound not to disclose any information coming into his possession in the course of the work.[7] It covers any relationship within which there is a recognized public interest in fostering frank discourse. For example, a duty to hold information in confidence *prima facie* operates in the relationships between patient and medical adviser, penitent and priest, client and lawyer, and pupil and teacher. It also operates in the absence of a pre-existing relationship between the parties, if the information is such that disclosing it would seriously damage the subject's interest in maintaining respect for his private life. Thus breach of confidence, alongside an emerging tort of harassment, was used by the late Diana, Princess of Wales to restrain the publication of certain photographs taken of her in secluded situations, as noted in Chapter 9, above. In the same way, it is capable of providing remedies for unauthorized publication of photographs of a bride and groom taken by a press photographer covertly, against their wishes, as *Douglas v. Hello! Ltd.*, above, demonstrates.

More generally, the doctrine operates wherever a public authority (as distinct from a private person or body) holds personal information about anyone. Even if the information is not strictly private—for example, it may relate to a person's previous convictions, which are a matter of public record—the authority is not permitted to disclose the information in ways which would injure the subject's ability to conduct private and family life, unless justified in doing so by a compelling public interest. This relatively recent development of common-law confidentiality allows English law to address the state's obligations under ECHR Article 8. It was pointed out in Chapter 9 that Article 8, as interpreted by the European Court of Human Rights (for example, in *Rotaru v. Romania*[8]) requires the state to ensure that the way in which it acquires, stores, and processes information, the period and purposes for which it is kept and processed, arrangements for maintaining the accuracy of the information and informing the data subject about it, and the circumstances in which, purposes for which, and people to whom it is disclosed, all comply with the provisions of Article 8(2), even if the information relates to the data subject's alleged public political activities in the past.

Under section 6 of the Human Rights Act 1998, the legality of disclosures by public authorities depends partly on the existence of a pressing social need to make the disclosure in order to prevent (or detect) crime, and the proportionality of any disclosure to the object which is to be achieved. English courts have been making such assessments through the machinery of the law of breach of confidence. The relevant principles have been applied to cases involving disclosure of information about a person's conduct or convictions in response to a subpoena addressed to the police in civil proceedings, between public authorities, between the police and shopkeepers in respect of the activities of a convicted shoplifter, between the police and caravan site

---

[7] *Attorney-General v. Guardian Newspapers (No. 2)* [1990] 1 AC 109, [1988] 3 All ER 545, HL. This obligation has been put on a statutory footing by the Official Secrets Act 1989.

[8] Eur. Ct. HR, App. No. 28341/95, Judgment of 4 May 2000.

owners and education authorities in relation to people who are said to represent a danger to children, and between the police and a professional disciplinary body in respect of the professional conduct of a nurse.[9] The Human Rights Act 1998 is likely to result in the relevant principles being applied more systematically, rather than to a sea change in the approach. The main change is likely to be a growing awareness that private life, protected by Article 8, goes far beyond anything previously regarded as confidential information. This may continue the expansion in the range of information protected by the duty. For instance, so far as certain decisions have suggested that information about a person's previous employment is not covered by Article 8,[10] they are inconsistent with *Rotaru v. Romania* and will have to be reconsidered in the light of the obligations on courts and other public authorities under the Human Rights Act 1998, sections 2 and 6. If the law of breach of confidence cannot continue to be developed to respond to the requirements of ECHR Article 8, data subjects will have to resort to the cause of action founded directly on an allegation of unlawfulness under sections 6 and 7 of the Act.

(2) CONFIDANT'S OBLIGATION TO HOLD INFORMATION IN CONFIDENCE

Normally, a person who receives information is free to transmit it to others. The assumption is that if A is prepared for B to know something, there is no harm in C and D knowing it as well, so B commits no wrong in repeating it. However, when the information is of a confidential nature and is not in the public domain, B is not free to disclose it if he is subject to an obligation of confidence. Such an obligation may be expressly imposed contractually by A at the time of transmission to B, if A provides some consideration for B's undertaking. Alternatively it may be implied from the circumstances of the transmission.[11] Express imposition of a duty is straightforward, but the implication of a duty is more difficult to predict. Once again, the public interest which the courts see as being served by the activity in question, or the harm to the public interest which might flow from disclosure of information of the type in question, is likely to determine both the existence and the scope of any duty of confidence. Generally, the judges have accepted that a public interest is served by confidentiality in particular relationships, such as those between lawyer and client, doctor and patient, and more recently journalist and source, although that interest will not always override competing public interests favouring disclosure.[12] The more personal or commercially sensitive information is, the more likely it is that it will be subjected to an implied duty of confidence. When disclosure of sensitive material is

---

[9] *Marcel v. Commissioner of Police of the Metropolis* [1992] Ch. 225, [1992] 1 All ER 72, CA; *Hellewell v. Chief Constable of Derbyshire* [1995] 1 WLR 804, [1995] 4 All ER 473; *R. v. Chief Constable of the North Wales Police, ex parte A.B.* [1999] QB 396, [1998] 3 All ER 310, CA; *R. v. Local Authority and Police Authority in the Midlands, ex parte L.M.* [2000] 1 FLR 612; *Woolgar v. Chief Constable of Sussex Police* [2000] 1 WLR 25, [1999] 3 All ER 604, CA. This is in addition to statutory powers of disclosure.

[10] See, e.g. *R. v. Worcester County Council, ex parte S.W.* [2000] 3 FCR 174 at 189–90, paras. 26–9, *per* Newman J.

[11] See generally F. Gurry, *Breach of Confidence* (Oxford: Clarendon Press, 1984).

[12] *Parry-Jones v. The Law Society* [1969] 1 Ch. 1, [1968] 1 All ER 177, CA; *British Steel Corporation v. Granada Television Ltd.* [1981] AC 1096, [1981] 1 All ER 417, HL; *X. v. Y.* [1988] 2 All ER 648.

permitted, because there is a public interest in the object in view, the information must be used only for that purpose. For example, in civil litigation documents disclosed to the other side on discovery may be used only for the purposes of the litigation, and unless read in open court must not be published or used for any other purpose,[13] unless the court gives leave for such use on the ground that it serves an overriding public interest.[14] In the same way, confidential information about a drug which the manufacturer passes to an advertising company for use in connection with a promotion may not be passed on to a television company for use in making a programme critical of the effects of the drug.[15]

(3) INFORMATION NOT IN THE PUBLIC DOMAIN

Normally, information loses its confidential quality when it enters the public domain. This is because equity does not act in vain, and the courts will not grant injunctions to prevent disclosure by one person of information which is already readily available and may easily be obtained or communicated by others. It was partly for this reason that the government failed to obtain permanent injunctions restraining publication of allegations about the activities of MI5 after they had been widely distributed following the publication of the book *Spycatcher*.[16] It also explains why a party to legal proceedings to whom material disclosed for the purposes of the proceedings is free to use for other purposes those parts of the material which are used or read in open court,[17] and why a statement made to the police under caution, which is covered by confidentiality, can be reproduced after it has been read in open court.[18]

However, this principle is neither universally applicable nor straightforward to use in those areas where it does apply, for two reasons. First, it is not always clear when information comes into the public domain. If it were necessary only that the information should have been disclosed to one unauthorized person, a wrongdoer could evade the protection of the law by the very act of wrongdoing which the law is intended to prevent or discourage. Generally speaking, if X passes confidential information to Y, in breach of a duty owed by X to Z to keep the information secret, the recipient Y will be subject to a duty to Z to keep the information from further disclosure, similar in scope to the duty owed by X to Z. This will, at any rate, be the position if Y knows that X is acting improperly in disclosing the information.[19] There

---

[13] *Home Office v. Harman* [1983] 1 AC 280, [1982] 1 All ER 532, HL.

[14] *Customs and Excise Commissioners v. A. E. Hamlin & Co.* [1984] 1 WLR 509, [1983] 3 All ER 654; *Marcel v. Commissioner of Police of the Metropolis* [1992] Ch. 225, [1992] 1 All ER 72, CA.

[15] *Schering Chemicals Ltd. v. Falkman Ltd.* [1982] QB 1, [1981] 2 All ER 321, CA, concerning the anti-arthritis drug Primodos.

[16] See Ch. 15, below.

[17] *Mahon v. Rann* [1998] QB 424, [1997] 3 All ER 687, CA; Criminal Procedure and Investigations Act 1996, s. 17.

[18] *Bunn v. British Broadcasting Corporation* [1998] 3 All ER 552.

[19] *Fraser v. Evans* [1969] 1 QB 349, [1969] 1 All ER 8, CA. In relation to the newspaper serialization of Peter Wright's book *Spycatcher*, this was the position of the *Sunday Times*, against whom an order for an account of profits was made, in *Attorney-General v. Guardian Newspapers Ltd. (No. 2)* [1990] 1 AC 109, HL. See further Ch. 15, below.

are *dicta* suggesting that a certain number of people must acquire access to the information before it will be regarded as having come into the public domain: a disclosure to a few people, for example by printing a few hundred copies of a book and distributing them privately as presents, will not suffice, because the people who have immediate access do not constitute the public, or a section of the public.[20] Perhaps the moment when material passes into the public domain is the moment when it passes beyond individuals selected by the person making the disclosure.[21] There may also be arguments for restraining re-publication of material which was once in the public domain, where it would undermine a person's privacy and time has passed since the original publication.[21a]

Secondly, remedies for breach of confidence operate *in personam*, not *in rem*. The question is, strictly, whether or not the defendant is subject to a duty not to disclose information, so it is theoretically possible that particular people may be subject to duties not to speak out even after the information has been made public by others. This is because public interests may affect a defendant in a different way from other people. For example, it may be that if Mr. Wright, the author of *Spycatcher*, were to come within the jurisdiction of the English courts, he could be restrained from making further disclosures about matters which came within his knowledge during his service with MI5, because of a public interest in maintaining the mutual confidence of members of MI5, past and present, by enforcing a principle that they should never speak on such matters, even if they have already been disclosed by other sources. In *Attorney-General v. Guardian Newspapers Ltd. (No. 2)*,[22] the House of Lords acknowledged that a lifelong duty of confidence was owed by members of the security service, and this duty has since been backed by criminal sanctions in section 1 of the Official Secrets Act 1989.[23] Despite interfering with Mr. Wright's freedom to impart information under ECHR Article 10(1), this duty might be justifiable under Article 10(2) as serving the legitimate aim of protecting national security and, arguably, information received in confidence, if it can be shown that the extent of the restriction is necessary and proportionate to that aim. Proportionality will depend on the content of the information, the purpose of the disclosure, and the damage which the disclosure would do, among other considerations.

In *Attorney-General v. Blake*[24] a former spy had acted as a double agent for the USSR while holding office in the UK's Secret Intelligence Service (MI6). After his conviction on espionage charges in England, he escaped from prison to the USSR, from where he had his autobiography, *No Other Choice*, published in the UK. A majority in the House of Lords treated his contractual obligation of confidentiality to

---

[20] See, e.g. Lord Jauncey in *Lord Advocate v. The Scotsman Publications Ltd.* [1990] 1 AC 812 at 827, [1989] 2 All ER 852 at 862.

[21] See for general discussion Gareth Jones, 'Breach of Confidence—after *Spycatcher*' [1989] *CLP* 49–69.

[21a] See E. Paton-Simpson, 'Private Circles and Public Squares: Invasion of Privacy by the Publication of A Private Facts' (1998) 61 *MLR* 318–40.

[22] [1990] 1 AC 109, [1988] 3 All ER 545, HL.

[23] See Ch. 15, below.

[24] [2000] 3 WLR 625, HL.

MI6 as being sufficiently analogous to a fiduciary duty to justify ordering Mr. Blake to account to the state for the profits which he had derived from the book in the interests of justice. The ordinary remedies for breach of confidence were said to be inadequate to vindicate the interest of MI6 which the publication had violated. Lord Hobhouse of Woodborough dissented, arguing that the interests of justice could not justify using private law for a non-compensatory purpose. With respect to the majority, Lord Hobhouse's comments are compelling. The House was unanimous in rejecting the suggestion that a public law injunction could be granted to deprive an offender of the proceeds of crime (indirectly derived from it, in that case) in circumstances lying outside those in which Parliament had provided a statutory means of confiscating proceeds. The majority speeches give the appearance of having then strained every sinew to achieve by means of private law what they had held to be beyond their powers in public law. This skews the nature and purpose of private law remedies unacceptably. In that case, the state had no private interest to protect, and was seeking to use private law to punish Mr. Blake, rather than to protect private interests.

A newspaper or publisher to whom Mr. Wright or Mr. Blake disclosed information would be in a different position from Mr. Wright or Mr. Blake, because the newspapers or publishers are under no prior obligation of secrecy, and indeed have a responsibility to keep the activities of the state under public scrutiny in the public interest. The balance of rights and public interests, which the tests of necessity and proportionality embody, falls in different places according to the position and obligations of the particular defendant.

It follows that the public domain principle is sufficiently flexible to take account of the need to discourage a person who has lawful access to confidential information[25] from misusing it, while not committing the law to a position where it appears to be attempting to hold back the inevitable rise of the tide of publicity, or to prevent the press from performing public interest functions. This connects with the following issue.

(4) OVERRIDING PUBLIC INTERESTS JUSTIFYING DISCLOSURE

Even if the person holding information is otherwise subject to a duty to hold it in confidence, there may be countervailing public interests which are sufficiently weighty to justify, or even compel, disclosure. This was at one time expressed in the maxim that there is no confidence in an iniquity: people who commit acts or omissions which are contrary to law or morals have no legitimate claim to keep them secret. However, the iniquity defence to a claim for breach of confidence is merely an example, albeit a central one, of a wider principle which allows for disclosure in the public interest.[26] It is usually in the public interest to reveal information about

---

[25] Such a person is sometimes called a confidant, but this wrongly implies that he will always have had the information confided in him by another. Sometimes, as in many of the *Spycatcher* allegations, the person making the disclosure has the information from personal, first hand knowledge, but is under a legal obligation not to disclose it.

[26] *Lion Laboratories Ltd. v. Evans* [1985] QB 526, [1984] 2 All ER 417, CA.

wrongdoing,[27] but the public interest may also favour disclosure of other information which is of importance to the public or to certain people, even if it does not show that anyone has done anything legally or morally wrong. For example, it may be in the public interest to disclose confidential information which tends to show that a person who has been accused of a crime is innocent, or to reveal a risk to public health or safety.[28] The importance of these interests is reflected in the weight which they carry as possible justifications under Article 8(2) of the European Convention on Human Rights for interfering with privacy rights.

An example of factors which might make it desirable to disclose confidential information is *W. v. Egdell*.[29] The plaintiff, W, while suffering from a condition subsequently diagnosed as paranoid schizophrenia, had shot a number of people. He had been detained under a restriction order made under the Mental Health Act 1959. The psychiatrist treating him formed the view that W's condition was being controlled by medication, that W understood the need to continue with the medication, and that he could in due course be released. W applied to have his case reviewed by a Mental Health Review Tribunal with a view to conditional discharge. His solicitors instructed Dr. Egdell, another psychiatrist, to examine W and to provide a report to the solicitors for use at the tribunal hearing. Dr. Egdell considered that W's condition might have been misdiagnosed, and that W could have been suffering from a paranoid psychosis, which is more difficult to control through medication than paranoid schizophrenia. Dr. Egdell also thought that W had an abnormal personality, and might still have an unhealthy interest in guns and explosives. He strongly recommended that no steps towards releasing W should be taken until these and other matters had been fully investigated. On receiving the report, W's solicitors withdrew the application to the tribunal. However, Dr. Egdell communicated the report to the doctors treating W, and caused it to be sent to the Home Office. W brought proceedings for breach of confidence, arguing that Dr. Egdell had an obligation of confidence towards his patient, W. Scott J rejected the claim. Besides owing a duty to W, Dr. Egdell owed a duty to the public. In relation to a patient who was held in a secure hospital under an indefinite restriction order following serious crimes the duty to the public would require the doctor to place his report before the appropriate authorities where it was in the public interest to do so,[30] regardless of the patient's wishes.[31]

This shows that the public interest restriction on duties of confidence is not

---

[27] See, e.g. *S. v. S. (Judgment in Chambers: Disclosure)* [1997] 1 WLR 1621, where the tax authorities sought disclosure of material from a private hearing relating to ancillary relief in matrimonial proceedings wherein the judge had made a finding of tax evasion against the husband.

[28] *R. v. Ataou* [1988] 2 All ER 321, CA. In the context of AIDS treatment, see *X. v. Y.* [1988] 2 All ER 648, discussed below.

[29] [1990] Ch. 359, [1990] 1 All ER 835.

[30] Scott J said ([1989] 1 All ER 1089 at 1104) that the duty to inform the authorities arose if, in the doctor's opinion, it was in the public interest to do so. Since the scope of the legal duty of confidence is a matter of law, not medical ethics, it should be made clear that the court, not the doctor, has the last word on the assessment of the public interest, although the doctor must make a personal assessment when deciding how to behave, and that assessment will carry considerable weight in subsequent proceedings, particularly if it is consistent with official standards of medical conduct and ethics and was reached in good faith.

[31] See to the same effect *R. v. Kennedy* [1999] 1 Cr. App. R. 54, CA; *cp.* General Medical Council., *Confidentiality: Protecting and Providing Information* (London: General Medical Council, 2000).

dependent on iniquity: W's medical condition could not be said to be equivalent to legal or moral wrongdoing. A wide variety of public interests may come into play, which may have unfortunate consequences for the individuals concerned. For example, it means that patients like W, who are detained following criminal offences, do not enjoy the benefit of as extensive an assurance of confidentiality in their dealings with doctors as do other people. Nevertheless, where people are detained for the protection of society it is essential that the law of confidence should not make it possible to undermine that protection, although perhaps the courts, rather than individual doctors, ought to be responsible for making the final decision as to where the balance of public interests lies, as they are in other fields.[32] On the other hand, where the public interest in dissemination of the information is outweighed by the interests of the patient in confidentiality and his right to respect for private life under ECHR Article 8(1), the court will restrain disclosure, even if that involves restricting the freedom of the press to publish, as *X. v. Y.*,[33] considered below, makes clear. Section 12 of the Human Rights Act 1998, which enjoins courts to have particular regard to the importance of freedom of expression in cases involving the press, is unlikely to affect this, in the light of the approach to that section adopted in *Douglas v. Hello! Ltd.*[34]

In order to decide whether a person who holds confidential information is justified in disclosing it, the interests favouring disclosure must be weighed against the interests (both public and private) which support maintaining the confidence. Only if the former outweigh the latter will disclosure be justified. Although the public interest in free, informed debate on matters of social importance may tend to support disclosure of information, sometimes disclosing confidential information would tend to inhibit or prejudice other worthwhile activities which are themselves in the public interest. In *X. v. Y.*[35] Rose J granted a permanent injunction restraining a newspaper from publishing information from confidential hospital records on two practising doctors who were suffering from AIDS. Freedom to publish the medical details was supported by the public interest in freedom of the press, and by the marginal assistance to informed public debate concerning AIDS which would flow from it. But it would also have been very likely to discourage patients from going to hospital to receive monitoring and counselling. There is a powerful public interest in ensuring that patients are monitored and counselled, so that they can organize their lives as positively as possible while avoiding the risk of infecting other people. On careful consideration, Rose J decided that the balance of public interests decisively favoured upholding the confidentiality of the information by granting the injunction.

Even if it is legitimate to disclose the information, the public interest might not support a generalized, public disclosure. It might be suitable only to permit disclosure to particular people, or for specific purposes. For instance, it might be proper to disclose evidence that somebody has committed a crime only to the police, and

[32] *Cp.* the remarks of Lord Bridge in *X. Ltd. v. Morgan Grampian (Publishers) Ltd.* [1991] 1 AC 1 at 48, [1990] 2 All ER 1 at 13.
[33] [1988] 2 All ER 648.
[34] [2001] 2 WLR 992, CA, discussed in Ch. 9, above.
[35] [1988] 2 All ER 648.

information about a suspected breach of the rules of a regulatory organization to the regulator, not to splash it across the pages of a newspaper.[36] There are two questions. First, is it legitimate to disclose the confidential material at all? Secondly, how and to whom is it in the public interest to disclose it? In *W. v. Egdell*, although it was proper in the circumstances for the psychiatrist to arrange for the report to be transmitted to the doctors who were responsible for the day to day management of W (for W's own medical benefit), and to the Home Office and the review tribunal (for the benefit of the public), it would not have been appropriate to communicate the report to the press.

The scope of the duty of confidence thus depends on the circumstances of the case. Of the public interests which restrict duties of confidence, one of the most compelling is that in the due administration of justice. It is because of this interest that the courts have held that a duty of confidence does not shield a person, as of right, from having confidential information or communications divulged for the purpose of providing evidence in legal proceedings. Only one type of documents and communications enjoys such protection as of right: the category covered by legal professional privilege. This includes many communications between lawyer and client for the purpose of seeking or giving legal advice, and material brought into existence predominantly for the purpose of contemplated litigation, and is considered in section 11(2), below. In relation to other classes of confidential material and information, although a judge has a discretion to relieve a witness from the obligation to produce documents or answer questions when the answer will entail a breach of an undertaking of confidentiality, the judge will have to weigh the competing interests—the importance of the material to the proceedings, and the harm which would flow from disclosure— and decide where the balance falls.

Although journalists, doctors, and others have no privilege at common law which protects confidences and sources of information, there are several special statutory provisions which give some limited protection to journalists and their sources.[37] The European Court of Human Rights established in *Goodwin v. United Kingdom*[38] that freedom of the press under ECHR Article 10 entails the right of journalists to refuse to disclose the identities of their sources, in order to prevent compelled disclosure having a chilling effect on people's willingness to give information to the press in the public interest. Under the Human Rights Act 1998, this is likely to enhance the protection for journalists' sources in national law.[39] In addition, in relation to criminal investigations, Parliament has legislated to clarify the balance which is to be struck between the competing public interests when evaluating claims by investigators to have access to confidential material, defining the scope of the duty of confidence in the light of the public interest in the prevention and detection of crime, and offering procedural safeguards against unjustified seizure. The overall effect should be to secure compliance with ECHR Article 8, by specifying the circumstances in which the privacy

---

[36] *Francome v. Mirror Group Newspapers Ltd.* [1984] 1 WLR 892, [1984] 2 All ER 408, CA.
[37] See Ch. 14 below.
[38] Eur. Ct. HR (1996) 22 EHRR 123.
[39] But see *Ashworth Hospital Authority v. MGN Ltd.* [2001] 1 WLR 515, CA, where disclosure was ordered. The House of Lords has given leave to appeal.

interests covered by the law of confidence can be interfered with for the prevention of disorder or crime, and by ensuring that any interference is in accordance with the law and goes no further than is necessitated by a pressing social need. However, the legislation may not always achieve these purposes.

11.2 CONFIDENTIALITY AND CRIMINAL INVESTIGATIONS

(1) BACKGROUND TO THE PACE PROVISIONS

A number of relationships of trust involve the parties in giving and receiving personal information in circumstances which import an obligation of confidence. Such information may sometimes be very useful to an investigator seeking information about criminal offences or suspects. Although it would often offend the conscience of most people to allow the police to invade the offices of a lawyer, doctor, or priest in search of information, the public interest in preventing or detecting crime or maintaining public order might sometimes be held to outweigh the interest in maintaining the integrity of those relationships. For example, where the information is likely to make it possible to prevent serious harm to innocent victims of a threatened crime, an interference would be for a legitimate objective in terms of Article 8 of the European Convention on Human Rights, and would be justifiable if in accordance with the law and necessary in a democratic society for the achievement of the legitimate objective. The European Court of Human Rights has amplified these terms in a number of judgments. To comply with the requirements for justifying an apparent infringement of Article 8(1), the criteria for interference must be laid down by law, they must be reasonably clear and accessible, there must be adequate legal safeguards against abuse, and the extent of any interference must be proportionate to the object pursued.[40] Under the Human Rights Act 1998, section 6, it is unlawful to exercise a power in a manner incompatible with Convention rights unless primary legislation demands it. The requirements of the Act form a structure for balancing privacy-related rights against public interests in the context of confidentiality and investigative powers.

Many statutes give powers to officials to demand the production of documents which are relevant to their investigations, regardless of duties of confidence which may subsist in relation to the material. For example, the Director of the Serious Fraud Office has power to require a person, by a written notice, to 'produce at a specified time and place any specified documents which appear to the Director to relate to any matter relevant to the investigation or any documents of a specified class which appear to him so to relate'.[41] Failure to comply with the requirement, without reasonable excuse, is a criminal offence,[42] even if the person who is required to provide

---

[40] *Malone v. United Kingdom,* Eur. Ct. HR, Series A, No. 82, Judgment of 2 August 1984, 7 EHRR 14.
[41] Criminal Justice Act 1987, s. 2(3).
[42] Ibid., s. 2(13).

information has already been charged with an offence.[43] A search warrant may be issued by a justice of the peace if the person fails to comply with the requirement, or it is not practicable to serve a written notice, or serving a notice might seriously prejudice the investigation.[44] Documents in respect of which a person could claim legal professional privilege at common law are not subject to this power,[45] but there is no exception for other categories of confidential material. Parliament has here decided that the importance of combating serious or complex fraud takes absolute priority over the interests which were given some protection under PACE in respect of crimes which pose a less immediate or extensive social problem.

The powers of the Director of the Serious Fraud Office were introduced at a time when revelations of improper trading and fraud in the city were threatening to undermine public trust in the markets on which the Conservative government relied to extend share ownership to a wider range of individual members of the public than had previously held shares. Comparable powers have long been available to Inland Revenue and Customs and Excise investigators, in order to protect the public purse,[46] and to regulatory bodies such as the Department of Trade and Industry and the Bank of England. Generally, the statutes contain no express protection for confidential material (although the Criminal Justice and Police Act 2001, section 85 empowers the Secretary of State to extend such safeguards to investigations by Department of Trade and Industry inspectors). These provisions rely mainly on the investigators themselves to balance the public interest in the investigation of crime against the interests of suspects and their advisers. The principal judicial safeguard arises under section 6 of the Human Rights Act 1998: public authorities act unlawfully if they exercise their powers to require people to provide information in circumstances which amount to a violation of the right to respect for private life and correspondence. This requires investigators to apply principles of necessity and proportionality when deciding whether to demand information, and what information to require, for particular purposes. It gives legal force to what was previously good practice, and allows courts to review the place where investigators strike the balance.

By contrast, the provisions of the Police and Criminal Evidence Act 1984 authorizing police access to confidential material provide for an independent check, and set out detailed tests for access to confidential material which encapsulate the results of Parliament's painstaking assessment, during the long drawn out passage of several versions of the Bill between 1982 and 1984, of the needs of the police and the factors affecting the proportionality of intrusions on privacy. Under the pre-existing law, when under statute a search warrant could be issued (often by a magistrate) to enter premises to search for and seize prohibited items (such as controlled drugs or forgeries), confidential material could be seized, including documents subject to legal

---

[43] R. v. Director of Serious Fraud Office, ex parte Smith [1993] AC 1, sub. nom. Smith v. Director of Serious Fraud Office [1992] 3 All ER 456, HL. On the current law concerning the privilege against self-incrimination, see Ch. 6, above.

[44] Criminal Justice Act 1987, s. 2(4).

[45] Ibid., s. 2(9).

[46] E.g. Taxes Management Act 1970, ss. 20, 20A; Customs and Excise Management Act 1979, s. 167.

professional privilege. The statute was regarded as having overridden the protection offered by the duty of confidence or privilege.[47] Under the Police and Criminal Evidence Act 1984 (PACE), there are several different categories of confidential material, which are regarded as having different weights in the balance of interests, and so have different levels of protection against coerced disclosure. The PACE provisions apply to powers of search and seizure enacted in legislation passed before PACE,[48] but have been incorporated into most later search powers, including that given in section 8 of PACE itself. The main exceptions are search powers to make it easier to track down proceeds of drug trafficking and property intended to support terrorism. The protections for confidential information are somewhat truncated in such cases, which are examined below.

(2) ITEMS SUBJECT TO LEGAL PRIVILEGE

The material which is most securely protected is that falling within the category of 'items subject to legal privilege'. Section 9 of PACE provides that no warrant may be issued to search for such items. Legal professional privilege[49] is well established in civil litigation, where it operates as a shield against compulsory disclosure[50] which might otherwise require a party to litigation to reveal the advice received from lawyers or the information on the basis of which that advice was given, together with communications between lawyers and third parties in connection with litigation or contemplated litigation. There is an equivalent, if slightly narrower, privilege in European Community law against coerced disclosure of communications between lawyer and client as part of the 'rights of the defence' in EC Commission investigations and enforcement procedures.[51] The privilege bolsters the adversarial nature of civil litigation, where the core assumption has historically been that each party must establish its own case, and must not be forced to establish the other side's case for it. The adversarial nature of the civil process has been somewhat watered down—disclosure itself makes inroads on it—but the privilege remains important in civil litigation.

So far as the privilege prevents the courts from receiving valuable evidence, it could perhaps be regarded as irrational. The privilege in respect of lawyer-client communications is absolute,[52] demonstrating judges' view of its fundamental importance. Indeed, after many years of being treated as a mere rule of procedure and evidence, the privilege has now been re-conceptualized as an aspect of a substantive legal right

[47] *Parry-Jones v. The Law Society* [1969] 1 Ch. 1, [1968] 1 All ER 177, CA; *Frank Truman Export Ltd. v. Metropolitan Police Commissioner* [1977] QB 952, [1977] 3 All ER 431; *R. v. Justice of the Peace for Peterborough, ex parte Hicks* [1977] 1 WLR 1371, [1978] 1 All ER 225, DC.

[48] PACE s. 9(2).

[49] For a concise account, see N. Andrews, 'Civil Procedure', in P. Birks (ed.), *English Private Law*, vol. II (Oxford: Oxford University Press, 2000), 958–63.

[50] Disclosure was formerly known as discovery. It was renamed by Civil Procedure Rules (CPR) 31, which now governs it. For a concise account, see Andrews, 'Civil Procedure', in Birks (ed.), above, 950–8.

[51] Case 136/79, *National Panasonic v. Commission* [1980] ECR 2033, CJEC; Case 155/79, *A. M. & S. Europe Ltd. v. Commission* [1982] ECR 1575, CJEC; Cases 46/87 and 227/88, *Hoechst AG v. Commission* [1989] ECR 2859, CJEC.

[52] *R. v. Derby Magistrates' Court, ex parte B.* [1996] AC 487, [1995] 4 All ER 526, HL.

incorporating a general duty of confidentiality,[53] bringing England and Wales into line with the long-standing position in Australia, Canada, New Zealand, and the USA.[54] On the other hand, a bare majority of the House of Lords has held in *In re L. (Police Investigation: Privilege)*[55] that the privilege for communications between lawyers and third parties in connection with litigation is not absolute, and is weaker when the litigation to which they related was less adversarial, for example in relation to child care under the Children Act 1989. Reports prepared for the Children Act litigation could therefore be disclosed to the police for the purpose of investigating allegations that the mother had unlawfully administered a drug to the child. In terms of human rights, one can see how restricting the privilege in this way helps the state to perform its positive obligation under the ECHR to protect the rights of children, but there is a danger that *ad hoc* restrictions of the privilege will eventually undermine its central core.

Despite its significance in civil litigation, before 1984 the privilege had never become properly established in English pre-trial criminal procedure. This was partly because there is no general system of advance disclosure of evidence by the defence in criminal proceedings, so there was little room for importing from civil procedure a shield against pre-trial disclosure. Another possible reason was that the privilege is grounded in public policy, particularly the public interest in encouraging candour between client and lawyer. In criminal cases, the importance of encouraging candour might be outweighed, more easily than in civil actions between private individuals, by the public interest in deciding cases on the basis of the best available evidence. On the other hand, warrants to search for evidence of crimes are somewhat akin to coerced discovery in pre-trial criminal proceedings, and it seemed anomalous to have a privilege which protected parties to civil litigation but not defendants in criminal trials. Section 10 of PACE addressed this issue.

(i) What are 'items subject to legal privilege'?

The drafters of PACE defined 'items subject to legal privilege' so as to extend protection to broadly the same types of material as had until then attracted legal professional privilege in civil litigation. The material is defined in section 10. Subject to a single, but very important, exception, an item is subject to legal privilege if it is in the possession of a person who is entitled to possession of it, and it falls within one of the following categories, as set out in section 10(1):

> (a) communications between a professional legal adviser and his client or any person representing his client made in connection with the giving of legal advice to the client;

---

[53] *R. v. Derby Magistrates' Court, ex parte B.* [1996] AC 487, [1995] 4 All ER 526, HL.

[54] *Baker v. Campbell* (1983) 153 CLR 52, HC of Australia; *Carter v. Northmore Hale Davy & Leake* (1995) 183 CLR 121, HC of Australia; *Solosky v. R.* (1979) 105 DLR (3d) 745, SC Canada; *Re Gowling & Henderson and R.* (1982) 136 DLR (3d) 292; *Rosenburg v. Jaine* [1983] NZLR 1, CA of NZ; *Clark v. United States* 289 US 1, 77 L Ed. 993 (1933); *United States v. Upjohn* 449 US 383, 66 L Ed 2d 584 (1981), US Supreme Court; Annotation, 81 Am Jur 2d, 242–3.

[55] [1997] AC 16, [1996] 2 All ER 78, HL (Lord Jauncey of Tulliechettle, with whom Lord Lloyd of Berwick and Lord Steyn agreed; Lord Mustill and Lord Nicholls of Birkenhead dissented).

(b) communications between a professional legal adviser and his client or any person representing his client or between such an adviser or his client or any such representative of his client and any other person made in connection with or in contemplation of legal proceedings and for the purposes of such proceedings; and

(c) items enclosed with or referred to in such communications and made—

　　(i)　in connection with the giving of legal advice; or

　　(ii)　in connection with or in contemplation of legal proceedings and for the purposes of such proceedings[.]

The categories are not identical with those which apply under common law in civil litigation, although there are substantial similarities. The common law privilege protects only material prepared for or communicated to or from solicitors and barristers, and protects it only from disclosure in civil litigation. The privilege does not protect documents from disclosure in other kinds of proceedings, such as tax investigations, and does not cover material in the hands of accountants and other tax advisers. There are express statutory privileges protecting advisers against enforced production of communications between them and their clients for the purposes of the Taxes Acts,[56] and some other specialist advisers whose work has a legal content.[57] There is also a special statutory extension of legal professional privilege in civil matters to certain people licensed to do legal work under the Courts and Legal Services Act 1990, section 63. PACE contains no equivalent express extension, but the term 'professional legal adviser', which is not defined in the Act, may include people such as accountants and licensed conveyancers who give legal advice as part of their professional duties.

Apart from this, paragraph (a) broadly reflects the common law position under which a solicitor's records of transactions, most draft and final contracts, and other papers accumulated in connection with conveyancing and commercial transactions, are not privileged, because they are not made in connection with the giving of advice.[58] Similarly, a solicitor's diary note (or equivalent) of the time when a client called for a consultation is not privileged, so the solicitor can be ordered to produce it if it is relevant to a police investigation and other conditions for making an access or production order are met.[59] In civil litigation, however, the scope of protected legal advice has been somewhat extended by recent decisions which aim to take account of the variety of advice which modern solicitors are called on to give. For example, lawyers may advise on all aspects of the purchase of a house or business, including how to negotiate the contract and how to finance the purchase. Where the lawyer gives advice on how it is prudent to proceed in the light of the legal situation, that advice (and material communicated in order to obtain it) is covered by common law legal

---

[56] Taxes Management Act 1970, s. 20B(8), (9).

[57] Andrews, op. cit. at 959, n. 471, calls these 'quasi-lawyers', who include patent and trade mark agents (Copyright, Designs and Patents Act 1988, ss. 280, 284).

[58] For the common law position, see *Balabel v. Air India* [1988] Ch. 317, [1988] 2 All ER 246, CA. Under PACE, see *R. v. Inner London Sessions Crown Court, ex parte Baines & Baines (A Firm)* [1988] 1 QB 579, [1987] 3 All ER 1025, DC.

[59] *R. v. Manchester Crown Court, ex parte Rogers* [1999] 1 WLR 832, DC.

professional privilege.[60] Lawyers frequently give advice on the commercial as well as legal viability of complex business operations, often as part of a multi-disciplinary team including accountants, investment bankers, and others. In order to avoid over-complicating the task of deciding what communications or materials are, or are not, privileged, and to reflect the reality of modern legal practice, it has been held that all communications in respect of professional advice given to a client in a solicitor's professional capacity in relation to a proposed transaction is privileged, including communications between members of the multi-disciplinary team for the purpose of preparing the advice.[61] It is not yet clear whether the privilege under section 10(1)(a) of PACE covers as wide a range of material, but it would be inconvenient if section 10 of PACE were to be so restrictively interpreted as to allow the privilege a wider scope in some proceedings than others.

Paragraph (b) covers communications between legal advisers and experts for the purpose of litigation, and paragraph (c) extends the protection to items enclosed with those communications for the purpose of litigation. For example, in *R. v. R.*[62] the solicitors for a man charged with sexual offences sent a blood sample from their client to a forensic scientist for DNA testing. The defence team decided not to use the report at trial. The prosecution subpoenaed the expert and the judge allowed them to question him about the sample and his report to the defence solicitors. The defendant was convicted and appealed, arguing that the sample and the report were privileged and the judge had been wrong to allow the prosecution to call the expert. The Court of Appeal agreed that the sample, and information and reports derived from it and sent to the defendants' solicitors, had been privileged. The prosecution should not have been permitted to put them before the jury (although the court upheld the conviction, because other evidence against the defendant was so strong that the conviction was not unsafe or unsatisfactory).

Paragraphs (b) and (c) have parallels in, but may be different in scope from, the common law rules. For example, the privilege at common law applies only to material and communications *made for* the *predominant* purpose of obtaining or giving legal advice or of pending or contemplated litigation.[63] This test has two significant features. The first is also a feature of paragraph (c) of section 10 of PACE: an item is not privileged if it existed before the need for advice arose.[64] This prevents a criminal client from depriving the police and courts of relevant evidence by the simple expedient of lodging them with his solicitor with a request for advice. The second feature of the common law rule is not expressly present in the PACE provisions: the predominant purpose for which the item was made must have been to obtain legal advice or for the purpose of litigation. The absence of such a requirement seems to enable the PACE provisions to avoid the complication, only partially resolved by the common

---

[60] *Balabel v. Air India* [1988] Ch. 317, [1988] 2 All ER 246, CA.

[61] *Nederlandse Reassurantie Groep Holding NV v. Bacon & Woodrow* [1995] 1 All ER 976, where Colman J applied the observations of Taylor LJ in *Balabel v. Air India*, above.

[62] [1994] 1 WLR 758, CA.

[63] *Waugh v. British Railways Board* [1980] AC 521, [1979] 2 All ER 1169, HL.

[64] *R. v. Guildhall Magistrates' Court, ex parte Primlaks Holdings Co. (Panama) Inc.* [1990] 1 QB 261, DC.

law,[65] which arises where a report or plan is originally prepared because the party's insurer insists on it, or in obedience to a company's standing instructions, rather than because litigation is contemplated at the time, but is later passed to lawyers for the purpose of preparing for litigation.

In other respects the common law privilege appears to be wider than the PACE protection. Unlike paragraph (c) of section 10, the common law rules cover items which have not been enclosed with or referred to in communications, as long as the items in question were created for the predominant purpose of contemplated legal proceedings.[66] It is also possible that there are other circumstances in which items which attract privilege at common law might fall outside paragraph (c) for the purposes of criminal investigations. For instance, at common law, if a solicitor makes a selection of documents which are not themselves privileged for the purpose of contemplated legal proceedings, the collection is privileged at common law.[67] Under paragraph (c) the selection is privileged, if at all, only once the material has been communicated to somebody (for instance to counsel in order to obtain an opinion).

Since the effect of PACE was to create a new privilege in criminal proceedings, rather than to reproduce or restrict an existing one, there is no reason to presume that section 10 was drafted or should be interpreted so as to produce results identical with the common law rules operating in civil litigation. The government, originally committed to only a very narrow privilege in criminal matters, conceded wider protection during the debates on the first and second Police and Criminal Evidence Bills; the privilege moved closer to that operating in civil litigation, until the drafters seem to have tried to adopt at least some of the private-law rules. It would have been simpler to have said in section 10 no more than, 'Any item in respect of which legal professional privilege would apply in connection with civil litigation is an item subject to legal privilege for the purposes of this Act'. However, there may be good policy grounds for having narrower privileges in criminal investigations than in civil litigation, because of the strong public interest in the discovery of offenders.

Balanced against this, the privilege serves several interests in relation to criminal investigations. There is a public interest in people being able to obtain the best legal advice in relation to their cases, on the basis of full information, an interest related to the public interest in the fairness of the adversarial system of criminal justice. There is also a private interest in maintaining the confidentiality of lawyer-client and related communications, including those relating to clients other than the suspect, although the privilege is usually thought to be founded on public rather than private interests. The privilege prevents police searches, under warrant, of solicitors' files which contain material relating to the affairs of many clients. While an order for production of documents in the hands of a solicitor permits the solicitor to deliver only those documents which are covered by the order, a police officer executing a search warrant may rummage in any files, including those of other clients of the solicitor, which are reasonably thought likely to contain evidence. The police try to be as sensitive as

---

[65] *Guinness Peat Properties Ltd. v. Fitzroy Robinson Partnership (A Firm)* [1987] 1 WLR 1027, [1987] 2 All ER 716; *Ventouris v. Mountain* [1991] 1 WLR 607, [1991] 3 All ER 472, CA.

[66] *Waugh v. British Railways Board* [1980] AC 521, [1979] 2 All ER 1169, HL.

[67] *Lyell v. Kennedy (No. 3)* (1884) 27 Ch. D 1, CA; *Dubai Bank Ltd. v. Galadari (No. 7)* [1992] 1 All ER 658.

possible to problems of confidentiality, but warrants present a potential threat to the confidentiality interests of all the solicitor's clients. PACE protects the privacy interests of all of them, not just those of the suspect.

There is an important limitation on the scope of legal privilege under PACE. Section 10(2) reads: 'Items held with the intention of furthering a criminal purpose are not items subject to legal privilege'. There is a similar, but not identical, exception at common law in relation to material which is communicated between lawyer and client in order to further (rather than merely obtain legal advice about) a crime or fraud.[68] On its face, the phraseology of section 10(2) seems to mean that an item loses its privileged status if the person holding it intends, by doing so, to further a criminal purpose. The relevant intention appears to be that of the person holding the item. Where a solicitor holds items which fall within section 10(1), the items ought, on a literal reading, to remain privileged as long as the solicitor does not intend by holding them to further a criminal purpose. The fact that the solicitor may, by holding them, unknowingly further the criminal purpose of his client or a third party would not deprive the item of its privilege. That interpretation was accepted in *R. v. Crown Court at Snaresbrook, ex parte Director of Public Prosecutions,*[69] an early case on section 10. The Court of Appeal applied the same test in relation to civil matters in 1986 in an interlocutory appeal concerning discovery of documents.[70] This view is fortified by practical considerations affecting the position of the solicitor, who may be unable to obtain the information necessary to contest a warrant or an order for production if the relevant alleged intention to further a criminal purpose is that of somebody who may not be known to him or the client.[71] A test for privilege which depends on the intention or purpose of someone who does not hold the material in question and whose evidence cannot be obtained imposes grave hardship on the practitioner and the client.

The approach has the merit of simplicity, but it creates practical difficulties for the police, and may not reflect the intention of the drafters of section 10(2). There are cases in which the police are seeking material which is thought to implicate not the person holding it (the solicitor), but the client, or an associate of the client. If a

[68] *R. v. Cox and Railton* (1884) 14 QBD 153; *Barclays Bank v. Eustice* [1995] 1 WLR 1238.

[69] [1988] QB 532, [1988] 1 All ER 315, DC. A petition for leave to appeal was dismissed: [1987] 1 WLR 1502, HL.

[70] *Banque Keyser Ullmann SA v. Skandia (UK) Insurance Co. Ltd.* [1986] 1 Lloyd's Rep. 336, CA.

[71] It is an offence to tip off a person about investigators' knowledge or action in connection with a drug trafficking or terrorist investigation: Drug Trafficking Act 1994, s. 53(1)–(3); Terrorism Act 2000, s. 39(1)–(4). This replaces offences which used to apply to lawyer-client communications, making it potentially a criminal offence for a solicitor to inform the client that an order for production has been sought, let alone seek instructions from the client about the intentions of the client or of people who might be the target of the investigation: Prevention of Terrorism Act 1989, s. 17; Drug Trafficking Offences Act 1986, s. 31, although it was suggested that a solicitor taking instructions would have a reasonable excuse giving a defence under those sections: *R. v. Central Criminal Court, ex parte Francis & Francis (A Firm)* [1989] AC 364 at 386, [1988] 3 All ER 775 at 792, *per* Lord Griffiths; *cp.* D. Feldman, 'Conveyancers and the Proceeds of Crime' [1989] *Conv.* 389–402 at 398. The new legislation restricts the offences do not apply to communications between professional legal adviser and client (or client's representative) in connection with giving legal advice, or to communications between professional legal adviser and any person for the purpose of current or contemplated legal proceedings. The privilege does not apply where matters are disclosed 'with a view to furthering any criminal purpose'. See Drug Trafficking Act 1994, s. 53(4), (5); Terrorism Act 2000, s. 39(6).

criminal intention on the part of the client or the client's associate were irrelevant, much useful material might be lost to the police. At common law, both in England and Wales and in the USA, the privilege belongs to the client, not to the solicitor, so the intention of the client should, in principle, be at least as relevant as that of the solicitor.[72] There is no reason for a more extensive privilege to be permitted in pre-trial criminal than in pre-trial civil matters.

In *R. v. Central Criminal Court, ex parte Francis & Francis (A Firm)*[73] the House of Lords by a majority interpreted the 'criminal intention' exception to privilege in section 10(2) of PACE as relating to the intention of the client or even a third party, not just the solicitor's state of mind. A circuit judge had granted an order requiring a firm of solicitors to produce to investigators material which, it was thought, would enable them to trace the whereabouts of assets thought to be the proceeds of drug trafficking. The order was obtained *ex parte* under the Drug Trafficking Offences Act 1986, which contains an exception for items subject to legal privilege as defined by section 10 of PACE. The material in question concerned advice about the purchase of a business by the solicitors' client, using funds allegedly given to the client by a third party who was a suspected drug trafficker. The advice was *prima facie* privileged, but the police argued that the holding of the material by the solicitors was part of a plan by the suspect to launder the ill-gotten gains, and that this criminal purpose of a third party excluded the privilege by virtue of section 10(2) of PACE. The solicitors applied for judicial review of the order, relying the decision of the Divisional Court in *R. v. Crown Court at Snaresbrook, ex parte Director of Public Prosecutions*,[74] interpreting section 10(2) literally. The Divisional Court decided that, since the privilege was that of the client, not the solicitor, the relevant intention was that of the client or a third party, not the solicitor.[75] The decision was upheld on appeal by a bare majority of the House of Lords.[76]

As a piece of statutory interpretation, this flies in the face of the literal meaning of the words of the statute, as Lord Bridge and Lord Oliver pointed out in dissent. It also over-extends the exception. The legal background to the statute might justify taking account of the intention of the client, but does not automatically justify allowing the intention of a third party to defeat the privileged relationship between lawyer and client. The majority of the House of Lords read extra words into section 10(2), and justified this by referring to the difficulties which the police face in tracing the proceeds of drug trafficking. However, if a statute is to make inroads into the common law rights of citizens, the intention to do so must be clear from the statute, either expressly or by necessary implication. The decision in *ex parte Francis and Francis* sits uncomfortably with later developments recognizing legal professional privilege as a

---

[72] *R. v. Cox and Railton* (1884) 14 QBD 153; *O'Rourke v. Darbishire* [1920] AC 581 at 604, PC; *Clark v. United States* 289 US 1, 77 L. Ed. 993 (1933), US Supreme Court; *United States v. Zolin* 491 US 554, 105 L. Ed. 2d 469 (1989), US Supreme Court.

[73] [1989] AC 346, [1988] 3 All ER 775, HL.

[74] [1988] QB 532, [1988] 1 All ER 315, DC.

[75] [1989] AC 346, [1988] 1 All ER 677, DC.

[76] [1989] AC 346, [1988] 3 All ER 375, HL (Lords Brandon, Griffiths, and Goff, Lords Bridge and Oliver dissenting).

substantive right, as in Australia, Canada, New Zealand, and the USA.[77] It requires reconsideration, either by Parliament or by the House of Lords.

(ii) Protection given to items subject to legal privilege

Such items are, in principle, intended to receive virtually absolute protection from seizure and enforced production. Section 9(2) removes from earlier statutes any power to grant a search warrant for such material, and the exemption has been incorporated in all search powers passed subsequently. The person applying for a warrant or an order for production or access carries the burden of satisfying the issuing authority that the items sought are not subject to legal privilege, and the issuing authority must take seriously the obligation to scrutinize applications and to protect the privilege. Where the people in possession of items are solicitors or barristers, it should normally be difficult to persuade a judge that it is proper to grant a warrant or order under PACE.[78] There is no alternative means of seeking production of items subject to legal privilege. Furthermore, when conducting a search on premises, a constable may not use powers of seizure to seize any item which the constable has reasonable grounds for believing to be subject to legal privilege.[79] In the past, when ordinary items were inextricably mixed with items subject to legal privilege, neither could be taken away.[80] This caused great difficulties for investigators. The Criminal Justice and Police Act 2001 now provides, in sections 50 and 51, that an official investigator with a power of seizure is lawfully on premises or lawfully conducting a search of a person, and finds such mixed items part of which would be liable to seizure if not mixed with items subject to legal privilege, the investigator may seize the whole of the items. Notice must be given under section 52 when the power has been exercised. Once there has been an opportunity to examine the material, which must take place as soon as reasonably practicable (section 53), items subject to legal privilege which can be severed must be returned as soon as reasonably practicable, together with excluded or special procedure material which could not lawfully be retained under section 22 of PACE (see sections 54 to 56 of the 2001 Act). There is a procedure under section 59 of the 2001 Act whereby a person with an interest in the seized property can apply to a circuit judge for the return of the property. If an application is made, sections 61 and 62 provide that the investigators must secure the property so that it cannot be examined, copied, or used by the investigators except with the consent of the applicant or in accordance with a direction of the circuit judge, pending a hearing of the application. In addition, it will usually be a disproportionate interference with the rights of privacy and property of the people interested in the material, under ECHR Article 8 and Protocol No. 1, Article 1, to deny them the opportunity to inspect and take copies of the material for their own legitimate purposes, if there is no pressing, public-interest reason for refusing to allow them such access. The material may be needed in order to allow professional people to

---

[77] *R. v. Derby Magistrates' Court, ex parte B.* [1996] AC 487, [1995] 4 All ER 526, HL; *General Mediterranean Holdings SA v. Patel* [2000] 1 WLR 272, [1999] 3 All ER 673.
[78] *R. v. Guildhall Magistrates' Court, ex parte Primlaks Holdings Co. (Panama) Inc.* [1990] 1 QB 261, DC.
[79] PACE s. 19(6).
[80] *R. v. Chesterfield Justices, ex parte Bramley* [2000] QB 576, DC.

conduct their business and to protect the interests of third parties. If the investigators act disproportionately in refusing access in such circumstances, their behaviour will violate the Convention rights of those affected, and will be unlawful by virtue of section 6 of the Human Rights Act 1998.

The privilege applies in all investigations, regardless of the seriousness of the offence under investigation. This extensive protection is explicable by reference to the particularly tough pressure which the Law Society and the lawyers in Parliament exerted during the passage of the Police and Criminal Evidence Bill in its various versions between 1982 and 1984. It reflects the lawyer's perception of the importance of the legal process to civilized society, and of the centrality of uninhibited communication between lawyer and client in order to make an adversarial legal process work. By contrast, protection for the secrets of the doctor-patient or priest-penitent relationships is less thorough.

(3) OTHER CONFIDENTIAL MATERIAL

Confidential items, even if they are not subject to legal privilege, may have some protection, whether they are in the hands of solicitors or others. Instead of the absolute protection against coerced disclosure accorded to items subject to legal privilege, there are restrictions on coerced disclosure, and procedural safeguards additional to those which apply to other types of material. Section 9 of PACE provides for special treatment of two types of material: excluded material, which is particularly sensitive and arises in the course of a confidential professional relationship; and special procedure material, which with one exception[81] is imparted in confidence but does not arise out of such a sensitive professional relationship, and is not of such a sensitive nature, as excluded material. These two kinds of material are to be accessible to investigators only in the limited circumstances and subject to the restrictive procedures laid down under Schedule 1 of the Act. The procedure, an application— usually *inter partes*—to a circuit judge for an order for the production of or access to the material, with a search warrant issued only if an order has failed or seems bound to fail, is common to both types of material. However, the substantive grounds on which the material is to be accessible differentiate between the two types of material. The Act makes it in some respects easier to obtain an order in respect the less sensitive category, special procedure material, than in respect of the more confidential category of excluded material. Yet, as we shall see in section 11.3 this generalization hides a number of curiosities.

---

[81] Journalistic material, defined in s. 13, is special procedure material even if it is not held in confidence. If held in confidence, it is excluded material. The provisions relating to journalistic material are explained in Ch. 14, below.

11.3 EXCLUDED MATERIAL AND SPECIAL PROCEDURE MATERIAL

Three matters require consideration. First, the nature of excluded and special procedure material must be explained. Secondly, the conditions under which an order
may be made in respect of each category must be examined. Next, the procedure for
obtaining access must be considered. At each stage, we will try to assess the impact of
the legislation and its implementation on the privacy and confidentiality interests of
the people who are most closely affected.

(1) THE NATURE OF EXCLUDED MATERIAL AND SPECIAL PROCEDURE MATERIAL

(i) Excluded material

Excluded material is defined in section 11 of PACE. Apart from journalistic material
held in confidence, which is one of the subjects of Chapter 14 below, there are only
two kinds of excluded material.[82]

(a) **Personal records** which a person has acquired or created in the course of any
trade, business, profession, or other occupation or for the purposes of any paid or
unpaid office, and which he holds in confidence.

Personal records need not be in documentary form—for instance, computerized
records and X-ray photographs are included—but must concern an identifiable
individual. The material must relate either: (i) to that individual's physical or mental
health; or (ii) to spiritual counselling or assistance given or to be given to him; or (iii)
to counselling or assistance, for the purposes of his personal welfare, given or to be
given to him by a voluntary organization or individual who has responsibilities for his
personal welfare by reason of the adviser's office or occupation, or who has responsibilities for his supervision by reason of a court order.[83] Thus medical records are
included under (i), and material relating to advice from one's Minister of religion
under (ii). Social workers' and teachers' records would be included under (iii) so far
as they relate to counselling and assistance for individual clients and pupils, but not
where they concern the social workers' or teachers' other duties in respect of the
clients or pupils. Citizens' Advice Bureaux, the Samaritans, and similar voluntary
organizations, would be covered under (iii), since their advisers have responsibilities
for the welfare of those who seek their advice.

Those bodies also satisfy the further requirement that the person or organization
should hold the material in confidence. The Act provides that a person holds material
(other than journalistic material) in confidence if he holds it subject either to an
express or implied undertaking to hold it in confidence, of the sort described in
section 11(1) above, or to a statutory restriction on disclosure or obligation of
secrecy.[84] The legislation thus protects both privacy interests in personal information

---

[82] PACE, s. 11(1).
[83] PACE, s. 12.
[84] Ibid., s. 11(2).

and public interests in secrecy where they concern personal records, as under the Data Protection Act 1998 and the Regulation of Investigatory Powers Act 2000.

(b) **Human tissue or tissue fluid** taken for the purposes of diagnosis or medical treatment and which the person holds in confidence.[85]

This provision has important limitations. Blood samples taken to establish the blood type of an injured person following a road accident in order to match it for a blood transfusion are excluded material, and cannot be subjected to a search warrant; but blood or urine samples taken from the same injured person for testing under statutory powers to establish whether he has been driving illegally are not excluded material, since they are not taken for the purpose of diagnosis or treatment. Section 62 of PACE imposes statutory restrictions on the period during which, and purposes for which, samples and information derived from them can be retained and used. However, as noted in Chapter 6, above, these safeguards for the privacy rights of individuals have been progressively reduced by statute in the interests of the investigation of crime, and the courts have been reluctant to exclude evidence derived from material or information which the police have retained illegally.[86]

This means that there is some protection for privacy, but it is far from absolute: it can be overridden when Parliament has decided that there are adequate countervailing public interest grounds for doing so. Parliament attaches great weight to the integrity and security of the person. Thus, although a search of a person's body orifices can be made in certain circumstances for specific types of material (as described in Chapter 6 above), and surgery may be authorized by a court if the patient is incapable of consenting and the surgery is for the best interests of the patient (as described in Chapter 5), there is no legal procedure for authorizing a surgical procedure to be performed on a non-consenting person for a purpose which is not in that person's interests. For example, bullets removed from a person shot during a criminal enterprise are not excluded material, as they are neither tissue nor tissue fluid, but the Act does not authorize the making of an order for the surgical removal of the bullets against the victim's will in order to use them as evidence.[87]

This protection for privacy interests is limited in two ways. First, there are circumstances in which samples which are taken may be accessible to the police. Secondly, although the police may not be able to obtain an order giving them access to the material, they will be able to seize such material if they come on it while lawfully on premises, if they have reasonable grounds for believing that it is relevant evidence in relation to any offence, and that it is necessary to seize it in order to prevent it being concealed, lost, altered, or destroyed.[88] To illustrate these points, take the following scenarios.

---

[85] Ibid., s. 11(1).

[86] *R. v. Kelt* [1994] 1 WLR 765, CA; *Attorney-General's Reference (No. 3 of 1999)* [2001] 2 WLR 56, [2000] 1 All ER 577, HL.

[87] On the Canadian position, see *Re Laporte and R.* (1972) 29 DLR (3d) 651.

[88] PACE, s. 19(3).

Case 1. A driver, D, has been seriously injured in a road accident in which a pedestrian was killed. D is taken unconscious to hospital with a head wound which is bleeding profusely. While he is still unconscious, a doctor suturing D's wound collects some of the blood flowing it, and has it stored in case it later becomes necessary to establish whether it contained alcohol. The police learn of the existence of the sample, and ask for it to be handed over. The doctor refuses to hand it over unless the police obtain a court order.

The blood was not taken for the purposes of diagnosis or treatment, and so is not excluded material. It may be special procedure material (see below), but it is likely that an order for production will be granted on an application under Schedule 1 of PACE. This is, however, without prejudice to the discretion of a trial court to exclude evidence derived from the sample under section 78 of PACE, on the ground that the circumstances surrounding the taking of the sample (the blood having been taken without D's consent, and without any procedural safeguards to ensure, for example, that D can have part of the sample independently tested) would make the proceedings unfair were the evidence to be admitted.

Case 2. A driver, D, is in hospital being treated for injuries following a road accident. Nobody else was injured. A police officer, who has reasonable grounds for believing that D was drunk at the time of the accident, is waiting to interview D when he sees the doctor taking a sample of blood from D in order to match its type to enable D to be given a transfusion. The officer insists on taking away the part of the sample which is left over when the Medical Laboratory Scientific Officer has completed the blood group test.

In this case, the doctor took the blood sample in order to treat D, and there is no doubt that in a search warrant or Schedule 1 application the doctor and other hospital staff should be treated as having an obligation of confidence in respect of the sample. It would, therefore, be excluded material. Nevertheless, the seizure powers of the police officer under section 19 of PACE can be lawfully exercised in respect of excluded or special procedure material which the officer finds while lawfully on the premises, without the need to obtain an order for access or production under the restrictive rules in Schedule 1.[89]

This makes it clear that, whatever may have been the original intention, the effect of the legislation is to protect the professional or voluntary adviser against invasion of privacy by the police, and to prevent the police, when seeking evidence against a suspect, from ransacking the records or premises of third parties with a duty of confidence. It does not always protect the privacy of the suspect as such.[90] Nor does it protect against confidential material being seized from an adviser when officers come on it without infringing the adviser's privacy or property interests.

Compare the position in a system where the decision has to be based on consti-

---

[89] *Cp. R. v. Apicella* (1985) 82 Cr. App. R. 295, CA, on the position under the pre-PACE law.

[90] See A. A. S. Zuckerman, 'The Weakness of the PACE Special Procedure for Protecting Confidential Material' [1990] Crim. LR 472–8.

tutional rights. The Canadian Supreme Court, in *R. v. Dyment*,[91] held that taking a blood sample from an unconscious patient for investigative purposes constitutes a seizure within the meaning of section 8 of the Canadian Charter of Rights and Freedoms, and if made without a warrant the seizure requires to be justified by reference to urgency or some other pressing need if it not to be regarded as unreasonable and so unconstitutional. According to La Forest J, with whom Dickson CJC concurred, the case invol1ved seizure rather than mere finding, and so fell to be reviewed under section 8 of the Charter, because the taking infringed a privacy interest of the patient. Even before the Charter, Canadian judges had allowed an action for replevin to reclaim a sample taken for non-therapeutic purposes from an unconscious patient and passed to the police, holding that the blood was the patient's property and there was no lawful ground for refusing to deliver it to the patient on demand.[92] Although replevin is not an entirely satisfactory remedy in these circumstances, because it raises difficult and unresolved questions about the extent to which people can have proprietary interests in parts of their bodies, these decisions, unlike PACE, genuinely offer protection to the subject of the confidential information or the person from whom samples are taken, rather than merely protecting that person's advisers. This shows how different political judgments about the proper balance between the interests in effective criminal investigation and those in protecting the various parties to confidential relationships may influence the development of legal rules and their effects, particularly in relation to the protection of rights.

(ii) Special procedure material

Special procedure material is defined in section 14 of PACE. One type of special procedure material is journalistic material, which is subject to special rules considered in Chapter 14 below. Material other than journalistic material is special procedure material if it does not consist of items subject to legal privilege or excluded material, and is in the possession of a person who—

(a) acquired or created it in the course of any trade, business, profession, or other occupation, or for the purpose of any paid or unpaid office; *and*

(b) holds it subject to either an express or implied undertaking to hold it in confidence, or a restriction or obligation of secrecy contained in any enactment.

It follows from this definition that much of the material held by professional advisers for their business purposes, relating to their clients' affairs, will be special procedure material, even if it does not meet the stringent conditions needed to qualify as excluded material.

The emphasis is once again on protecting the adviser rather than the beneficiary of the duty of confidence. The status of the material depends on the person in whose possession it is. Even if an adviser created or acquired the information as set out in paragraph (a), the material is not special procedure material when it is in the

---

[91] (1988) 55 DLR (4th) 503, SC of Canada.
[92] *Capostinsky v. Olsen* (1981) 27 BCLR 97.

possession of the client, but only when in the possession of the adviser. If an accountant acquires material in confidence from a client for the purpose of giving business advice, and creates a document setting out that advice confidentially, the material and the document are special procedure material in the hands of the accountant, but cease to be special procedure material when dispatched to the client. The object is to protect confidential advisers and their other clients against invasions of privacy, not to protect suspects in ways which might thwart the process of criminal investigation even if nobody else's interests are affected. This reflects the origin of these provisions in pressure from professional and voluntary organizations.

(2) CONDITIONS FOR MAKING ORDERS FOR ACCESS OR PRODUCTION

Circumstances in which courts may grant orders requiring people to give investigators access to excluded and special procedure material are as follows. Schedule 1 to PACE provides for two sets of 'access conditions' under which courts may order a person to produce or give access to the protected types of material.

(i) The first set of access conditions

This applies only to special procedure material. An order may be granted for production of or access to special procedure material if three requirements are met. These are that:

1   there are reasonable grounds for believing that a serious arrestable offence (as explained in Chapter 6 above) has been committed, and that there is, on specified premises, special procedure material which is likely to be relevant evidence, and which does not contain excluded material;

2   other methods of obtaining the material have been tried unsuccessfully, or have not been tried because they appeared at the time to be bound to fail; and

3   access to or production of the material is in the public interest, having regard to both the likely benefit to the investigation, and the capacity in which the person in possession of the material holds it.[93]

The general requirement that the judge must be satisfied of the matters does not mean that a criminal, or even a civil, standard of proof need be met. In *R. v. Norwich Crown Court, ex parte Chethams*[94] the Divisional Court decided that the question is whether the judge is satisfied, not whether the matter has been proved to a criminal, or even a civil, standard. Similarly, in relation to condition (a), Mann LJ doubted, in *Ex parte Chethams,* that the word 'likely' meant 'more probable than not', preferring the meaning 'such as might well happen'. This is a sensible approach, given that the application is a stage in an investigative procedure, and is not well suited to making final determinations of questions of fact of a kind to which notions of the standard of proof in legal proceedings are usually directed.

---

[93] PACE, Sch. 1, para. 2.
[94] Unreported, 13 February 1991, DC; text available from Lexis.

At the same time, it has been pointed out that circuit judges, as the people responsible for ensuring that the statutory scheme operates properly, must be scrupulous in ensuring that the relevant criteria are met.[95] Accordingly, requirement (b) is fairly strict. An applicant under Schedule 1 to PACE need not show that every remotely possible means of obtaining material has been tried or seriously considered, but those which are readily available, including alternative legal means, should be tried or seriously considered, and the judge should be told why they failed or seem to be impracticable. In *R. v. Lewes Crown Court, ex parte Hill*,[96] the police wanted material relating to four bank accounts, which they thought were likely to provide evidence in respect of seventeen charges of theft then pending against the applicant. They obtained an order under section 7 of the Bankers' Books Evidence Act 1879, but this was later quashed on the ground that the application had been seriously defective. The applicant then granted access to some material by consent, but refused to produce other material without a court order. Instead of applying for another order under the 1879 Act, the police successfully sought an order for production under Schedule 1 to PACE. However, when applying for the Schedule 1 order, the police did not tell the circuit judge of the circumstances surrounding the quashing of the order under the 1879 Act. Because of this inadequacy in the disclosure to the judge, it was later held on an application for judicial review of the order that there had been no material on which the judge could properly have been satisfied that it appeared that a proper application under the 1879 Act would have been bound to fail, and the order was quashed.

One curious result of the drafting of requirement (b) is that the all-important factor was the view of the officers when they applied for the Schedule 1 order as to the likely effectiveness of other means of obtaining the material. The real likelihood of obtaining the material by other means is irrelevant. In *Ex parte Hill* the police argued at the judicial review hearing that an application under the 1879 Act had, in reality, been bound to be at most partially successful, because the police wanted access not only to records of the suspect's bank accounts, which would have been covered by the 1879 Act, but also to correspondence, which is not within the meaning of 'bankers' books' under the Act. However, because this problem with the 1879 Act had not been in the minds of the applicants at the time when it was decided to apply for a production order under PACE, it could not be said that other means of obtaining the material had appeared to be bound to fail. Accordingly, condition (b) had not been met.

The requirement protects advisers against coerced disclosure. No similar requirement applies to search warrants in respect of material which is not excluded or special procedure material, despite the greater threat which the execution of a warrant poses to privacy and property interests.[97] This is because such warrants are likely to affect only the interests of the suspect, not those of the professional advisers and their other, unimplicated, clients.

---

[95] See *R. v. Leeds Crown Court, ex parte Switalski* [1991] Crim. LR 559, DC, *per* Neill LJ (transcript from Lexis).

[96] (1990) 93 Cr. App. R. 60, [1991] Crim. LR 376, DC.

[97] *R. v. Billericay JJ and Dobbyn, ex parte Frank Harris (Coaches) Ltd.* [1991] Crim. LR 472, DC.

Requirement (c), as it has been interpreted so far by the courts, is more easily satisfied than (b). Once a circuit judge decides under (a) that there is material, in specified premises, which is likely to be both relevant evidence and of substantial value to the investigation of a serious arrestable offence, it is always likely to be open to the judge to decide, under (c), that it is in the public interest that access or production should be ordered. However, it does not follow automatically that it will be in the public interest to make an order in all cases where requirement (a) is satisfied. On the wording of Schedule 1 to PACE, this is a matter of judgment for the circuit judge, and may demand detailed consideration of the countervailing public interests in order to arrive at a balance of interests under (c). A judge might in appropriate cases, without committing a reviewable error of law, decide that (a) is satisfied, yet refuse an order on the ground that it would not be in the public interest to grant one.

Nevertheless, one decision suggests that the judge has no such freedom. In *R. v. Northampton Crown Court, ex parte Director of Public Prosecutions*,[98] Taylor LJ, delivering the judgment of the Divisional Court, held that it would be *Wednesbury* unreasonable—so unreasonable that no reasonable judge could properly do it—to accept that relevant evidence is on premises, and that it would be of substantial value to an investigation into a serious arrestable offence, but then to hold that it would not be in the public interest to order production or access. A broadly similar approach has been adopted in respect of applications for production of journalistic material, although in these cases the competing public interest factors were at least examined.[99] Any such examination seems to be made otiose by the *Northampton* decision, in which Taylor LJ did not explain what scope, if any, was left for considering the public interest under requirement (c). An interpretation which narrows a statutory judicial discretion to weigh competing interests to a point where the statutory provision loses all possible effect is highly questionable. It is inconsistent with the usual approach where Parliament gives a power to an administrative official to be exercised in the light of a judgment about the balance of public interests. In such cases, judges normally hold that it is the job of the designated decision maker to strike that balance, and a considered judgment as to the public interest would be interfered with only if it is exercised perversely or on wrong principles. It is not clear why different considerations should be thought to apply where the discretion is exercised against granting an order. The tendency, here and in cases involving journalistic material, to dismantle the protection given to confidential material by the Act suggests a determination to ensure that the police are not inconvenienced by the new legislation, even to the point of flouting the clear meaning of a statute. This may indicate a view, which would be hard to sustain on constitutional grounds, that the protection for confidential information under the Act where people are suspected of serious arrestable offences is incompatible with the public interest, despite having been enacted by Parliament.

When a court restricts confidentiality rights by refusing to permit the circuit judge

---

[98] (1991) 93 Cr. App. R. 376, DC.

[99] *Chief Constable of Avon and Somerset v. Bristol United Press, Independent,* 4 November 1986; *R. v. Bristol Crown Court, ex parte Bristol Press & Picture Agency Ltd.* (1986) 85 Cr. App. R. 190, DC. See further section 14.4(3), below.

to exercise the discretion granted by Parliament, to make a judgment about the balance of public interests, it threatens the justification, which might otherwise be available under ECHR Article 8(2), for any consequent interference with respect for private life and correspondence. Under the Human Rights Act 1998, courts, as public authorities, must exercise powers in a manner compatible with rights under ECHR Article 8. If a court makes an order which is incompatible with a Convention right, section 9 provides that it is not to be actionable (unless it involves a deprivation of liberty), but can ground an appeal or application for judicial review. Orders in relation to confidential material are always likely to interfere with rights under Article 8(1), especially if they are concerned with excluded material made up of personal records and bodily tissues, etc. The interference must be justified under Article 8(2). In section 9 of, and Schedule 1 to, PACE, Parliament has decided when an interference with these rights is necessary in a democratic society and proportionate to a pressing social need. In the light of that, judges and other officials would appear to breach the Convention if they dispense with a protection for the right, based on a public interest, which the legislature thought necessary. Orders made in disregard of any element in the safeguards under Schedule 1 are not 'in accordance with the law', and are also presumptively disproportionate to any legitimate aim. They will therefore be unlawful by virtue of section 6 of the Human Rights Act 1998, and so invalid.

(ii) The second set of access conditions

These, under paragraph 3 of Schedule 1 to PACE, is applicable to excluded material as well as special procedure material. The conditions are that:

1   there are reasonable grounds for believing that there is material which consists of or includes excluded material or special material (but does not include items subject to legal privilege) on specified premises;

2   but for the prohibition in section 9 of PACE on issuing search warrants for such material, a search of the premises for that material could have been authorized by a warrant issued to a constable under an enactment other than Schedule 1 itself; and

3   the issue of a warrant would have been appropriate.

A general point about the relationship between the two sets of access conditions emerges from paragraph 3. Whereas the first set of access conditions extends the powers of the police to obtain access to material which would often not previously have been accessible, the second set imposes limitations on access to material for which they could otherwise have obtained a search warrant. This narrower basis for access is the only one on which the police may obtain access to the particularly sensitive category of excluded material. If, even apart from section 9(2) of PACE, no search warrant would be available in respect of particular material or a particular suspected crime, the police will be unable to obtain access to excluded material. It is in this sense that the material is 'excluded' from investigations. On the other hand, if a power to issue a search warrant would otherwise be available, the police may utilize the second set of access conditions to seek access to excluded material, even if the offence in question is not a serious arrestable offence.

Taking the specific requirements of the second set of access conditions in turn, the first presents few problems, as long as the applicant is able to satisfy the circuit judge of reasonable grounds for believing that the material is on the premises, and is not subject to legal privilege. The latter point requires special attention when the premises in question are those of a solicitor. The fact that other material, which does not consist of either items subject to legal privilege or excluded or special material, is present does not prevent material falling within the definition from being special procedure material.[100]

Condition (b) is less straightforward. Statutory powers to issue warrants which were enacted before PACE are within the scope of the condition. However, powers enacted in or after PACE will not be within the condition if the legislation in question provides that they may not be used to seek excluded material. For example, the general power in section 8 of PACE to grant search warrants for evidence of serious arrestable offences does not apply to excluded material or special procedure material.[101] It could therefore not be said that a warrant to search for such evidence which consists of excluded or special procedure material would be available but for section 9(2). It follows that the police cannot seek an order under Schedule 1 paragraph 3 for access to excluded material by reference to such a provision. For example, before section 8 of PACE was enacted, there was no procedure whereby a search warrant could be obtained to search for evidence of murder. Murder investigations therefore fall outside the second set of access conditions. It follows that murder investigators cannot seek access to a person's medical records by way of a production or access order under Schedule 1, because such records are excluded material which are available only under the second set of access conditions, which do not apply in murder cases.[102] In such cases only special procedure material may be sought, and that must be sought under the first, rather than the second, set of access conditions.

Condition (c) of the second set of access conditions clearly envisages that wider questions than those which relate to mere jurisdiction to issue a warrant will arise, but the nature of these considerations is not expressed. The provision is calculated to allow for consideration of factors affecting the proportionality of making an order for access or production, which is necessary to ensure that the order is not invalid as a violation of a Convention right under ECHR Article 8. The grant of a search warrant is a discretionary act, and any judge or magistrate who is considering an application for a warrant should endeavour to strike an appropriate balance between the rights of those affected under ECHR Article 8 and the public interest in preventing and detecting crime. The issuing authority should take account of the nature of the offence, the capacity in which the person holding the material does so, whether it would be feasible to obtain access to the material in a less dramatic way, and whether an order for access or the less intrusive order for production of the material is more

---

[100] R. v. Preston Crown Court, ex parte McGrath, unreported, 13 October 1992, DC.
[101] PACE, s. 8(1)(d).
[102] R. v. Central Criminal Court, ex parte Brown, unreported, DC, 30 July 1992 (text available from Lexis).

appropriate. Even before the Human Rights Act 1998 it was incumbent on every issuing authority to take account of these matters on general public law principles,[103] and the 1998 Act reinforces the obligation. Judges considering applications under the second set of access conditions should consider whether it would have been appropriate to grant a warrant in respect of excluded material in the light of the balance of public interests, having regard to such considerations as ought to be considered by justices issuing warrants. It should be borne in mind that orders to produce or allow access to material, directed to people such as solicitors, bankers, building societies, and investment advisers, impose a considerable administrative and financial burden on them, which they are not in a position to pass on to the customers or clients concerned. Customers will often not even be informed of the order, let alone asked to authorize expenditure in complying with it: there is no contractual obligation on a banker, for instance, to pass information about receipt of an order for production to a customer whose affairs are affected by it. Access should therefore be by consent whenever possible, allowing the person holding the material to arrange matters so as to cause a minimum of disruption to business.

(3) PROCEDURAL PROTECTIONS FOR CONFIDENCES UNDER SCHEDULE 1 TO PACE

If consensual access cannot be achieved, the procedures laid down for applying for orders are calculated, like much of the law considered in this chapter, to protect the interests of the adviser who holds material rather than the interests of the client, whose interests are principally affected by breaches of confidence. It seems to be assumed, usually correctly, that the client is a suspect, and necessarily suffers some detriment in the public interest. The procedures are straightforward.

The officer applying for an order must obtain the consent of an officer of at least the rank of superintendent. This is normally given as a matter of course, the investigating officers being in the best position to decide whether and when it is appropriate to apply.[104] Notice is served on the people who appear to hold the material,[105] informing them of the application for an order directed to them and of their right to appear to contest the application. The notice need not be served on a suspect on whose behalf the material is being held.[106] The police have a discretion as to whether to supply, in advance of the hearing, the evidence on which they base their application for the order. If supplying the evidence poses no risk to the success of the investigation, they may supply it, but if there is a risk that it would be used to prejudice the investigation they may withhold it until the hearing.[107]

The police will have to describe the material sought to the person in possession of it

---

[103] D. Feldman, *The Law Relating to Entry, Search and Seizure* (London: Butterworths, 1986), 117–20.

[104] Code B, para. 2.4; Lidstone and Bevan, *Search and Seizure under the Police and Criminal Evidence Act 1984*, 145–6.

[105] PACE, Sch. 1, para. 4.

[106] *R. v. Leicester Crown Court, ex parte DPP* [1987] 1 WLR 1371, [1987] 3 All ER 654, DC.

[107] *R. v. Central Criminal Court, ex parte Adegbesan* [1986] 1 WLR 1292, [1986] 3 All ER 113, DC; *R. v. Crown Court at Inner London Sessions, ex parte Baines & Baines (A Firm)* [1988] 1 QB 579, [1987] 3 All ER 1025, DC.

when the notice is served, because, once the notice has been served on a person holding the material, that person must not conceal, destroy, alter, or dispose of the material to which the application relates without the leave of a judge or the written permission of a constable, until the application has been dismissed or abandoned or any order made has been complied with.[108] Breach of this rule makes the person liable to be dealt with as if for contempt of court. The notice must therefore make the material to which the application relates as clear as possible, to prevent a situation in which a person is liable to be penalized for destroying material which he had not way of knowing that he ought not to have destroyed. In particular, the notice should contain a description of everything which the police hope to obtain, even if that gives rise to some risk that the suspect will be forewarned and the material tampered with.[109] The requirement has the incidental benefit of making it harder for the police to embark on fishing expeditions. Normally, the information should be in documentary form, and will usually be included in the written notice, but it will suffice to give the information orally, so long as the police can prove that it was in fact given.[110]

At the hearing before a circuit judge, the applicant will give evidence, and may be cross-examined. The applicant must take care not to make misleading or unsupported allegations concerning the person holding the material sought. Any evidence placed before the judge to support the application must, if not previously supplied to the respondent with the notice, be made available to the respondent, and, if it would be difficult for the respondent to deal with it on the spur of the moment, the judge should allow an adjournment.[111] The officer need not give the name of any informant, but should be prepared to give sufficient details to the judge to satisfy him that the information supporting the application is likely to be reliable.[112] At the end of the hearing, the circuit judge will decide whether to grant the order, and in what terms.

Either party may challenge the decision by way of an application for judicial review to the Administrative Court under Part 54 of the Civil Procedure Rules.[113] Under the Human Rights Act 1998, section 6, a judge (as a public authority) would act unlawfully if he makes an order on insufficient grounds or in circumstances where the order is a disproportionate interference with the rights of the professional person or anyone else whose rights to privacy under ECHR Article 8 are adversely affected by it. The judge to whom an application for an order is made must make a proper assessment of the necessity for and proportionality of the order sought in the circumstances of the case. On an application for judicial review, the Administrative Court must make its own assessment of the merits of the application so far as they relate to the issues of

---

[108] PACE, Sch. 1, para. 11.

[109] R. v. Central Criminal Court, ex parte Adegbesan [1986] 1 WLR 1292, [1986] 3 All ER 113, DC.

[110] R. v. Crown Court at Manchester, ex parte Taylor [1988] 2 All ER 769, DC.

[111] R. v. Crown Court at Inner London Sessions, ex parte Baines & Baines (A Firm) [1988] 1 QB 579, [1987] 3 All ER 1025, DC.

[112] R. v. Crown Court at Middlesex Guildhall, ex parte Salinger [1993] QB 564, DC, at 575 per Stuart-Smith LJ. The application was made under the terrorism legislation, but the considered the same principles to be applicable as in applications under Sch. 1 to PACE.

[113] These applications are regarded as being in a criminal cause or matter, so any appeal from the decision of the Divisional Court lies, with leave, directly to the House of Lords: Carr v. Atkins [1987] QB 963, [1987] 3 All ER 684, CA.

necessity and proportionality under ECHR Article 8, since an order which constitutes an unjustifiable interference with the Convention rights would be *ultra vires*. This introduces a stronger element of supervision by the Administrative Court than was previously available under general public law principles (including *Wednesbury* irrationality) at common law.[114] The general public-law principles continue to operate alongside the Human Rights Act 1998, so (irrespective of interference with Convention rights) an order will be quashed if the judge acted without authority or on the wrong principles, or somebody failed to observe the proper procedures, or the decision was one which no reasonable judge could have reached.

Once an order has been made and is not being challenged by way of review or appeal, the person to whom it is addressed must comply with it within seven days, unless the judge is persuaded to allow a longer period,[115] perhaps because of the administrative difficulties which are involved in finding and making available the material. The material must be produced for a constable to take away, or made available for inspection. Where material is contained in a computer, it must be provided in a form in which it is visible and legible, and, if the order is for production rather than merely for access, it must be in a form in which it can be taken away. All material produced pursuant to an order is to be treated as if it were material seized by a constable, so sections 21 and 22 of PACE (allowing material to be copied or retained by the police for certain purposes: see Chapter 10 above) apply to it.[116]

Two features of the procedure for obtaining an order make it clear that the object in the past has been to protect people such as advisers who innocently hold material about a suspect, rather than protecting the privacy or confidentiality interests of the client. First, the notice of an application for an order is to be served on the person who appears to be in possession of the material sought, not on the person who is the subject of the records or samples. The reason is simple: the investigation might be hampered if the subject found out about it; he might decamp, or destroy or hide evidence.[117] It has even been regarded as an open question whether the subject has standing to apply for judicial review of an order which has been addressed to the subject's advisers.[118]

Secondly, although there is normally nothing to stop the person holding the material from telling the client of the notice, the police will often strongly discourage such a course. This makes it more difficult for the person holding the material to contest the application. Indeed, applications for orders are rarely contested. While solicitors have sometimes, with the support of the Law Society, contested applications or challenged orders which have been made, other professionals, such as bankers, rarely have any incentive to risk incurring substantial and unrecoverable costs in protecting the interests of a client who is suspected of a crime. Even were an adviser

---

[114] D. Feldman, 'Proportionality and the Human Rights Act 1998', in E. Ellis (ed.), *The Principle of Proportionality in the Laws of Europe* (Oxford: Hart Publishing, 1999), 117–44 at 127–9; *R. (Daly) v. Secretary of State for the Home Department, The Times*, 25 May 2001, HL, *per* Lord Steyn.

[115] PACE, Sch. 1, para. 4.

[116] Ibid., Sch. 1, paras. 5, 6.

[117] *R. v. Crown Court at Leicester, ex parte DPP* [1987] 1 WLR 1371, [1987] 3 All ER 654, DC.

[118] *R. v. Central Criminal Court, ex parte Carr, Independent*, 5 March 1987, DC.

minded to contest the application, it would usually be difficult to do so without contacting the client to obtain information relevant to the case.[119] Moreover, there are certain statutes which make it an offence for a person to advise another that an order has been applied for or obtained, specifically where the case concerns the proceeds of drug trafficking or money for use in terrorism. Although it has been suggested (*obiter*) that a solicitor's duty to the client would justify giving the information in order to obtain instructions,[120] it is not clear either that this is correct, or that it would apply to other professions (as there is no duty on a banker, for example, to take instructions from customers in these circumstances[121]) or to people who voluntarily hold material about subjects under investigation.

However, the Human Rights Act 1998 may have affected this, since courts, as public authorities, now have an obligation to act compatibly with the Convention rights of all who may be affected, not only those who happen to be parties to the proceedings. This may sometimes make it necessary for procedures to be adapted to ensure that the rights of those to whom information is thought to relate can be properly considered in the course of an application for an order.

(4) SEARCH WARRANTS FOR CONFIDENTIAL MATERIAL

There is a further, more draconian procedure available to the police in respect of material normally accessible under Schedule 1: the grant of a search warrant. This power is to cater for three types of case. The first class comprises cases in which it would be ineffective to go through the production order procedure, either because it would be impossible to find anyone with authority to comply with the order or because the purpose is to prevent an unlawful disclosure of material which is likely to be disclosed before any order could be made or executed. The second class comprises cases where the process of applying for an order for production, with notice being given, would be seriously counter-productive, allowing for the disappearance of evidence, proceeds of crime, or suspects. The third class comprises cases where a production order has been granted but has not been complied with.

There are two separate sets of grounds on which a warrant may be issued.

First, if an order for production has been made on the basis of the second set of access conditions (in other words, on the ground that it would have been possible and proper to issue a search warrant but for section 9(2) of PACE) and has not been complied with, a circuit judge may grant a warrant authorizing a constable to enter and search the premises where the material is reasonably believed to be.[122]

---

[119] See C. Graham and C. Walker, 'The Continued Assault on the Vaults—Bank Accounts and Criminal Investigations' [1989] Crim. LR 185–97; D. Feldman, 'Conveyancers and the Proceeds of Crime' [1989] *Conv.* 389–402; A. A. S. Zuckerman, 'The Weakness of PACE Special Procedure for Protecting Confidential Material' [1990] Crim. LR 472–8; K. Lidstone and V. Bevan, *Search and Seizure under the Police and Criminal Evidence Act 1984* (Sheffield: University of Sheffield Faculty of Law, 1992), 144–8.
[120] *R. v. Central Criminal Court, ex parte Francis & Francis (A Firm)* [1989] AC 346, [1988] 3 All ER 775, HL, *per* Lord Griffiths.
[121] *Barclays Bank plc (trading as Barclaycard) v. Taylor* [1989] 1 WLR 1066, [1989] 3 All ER 563, CA.
[122] PACE, Sch. 1, para. 12(b).

Secondly, a circuit judge may issue a warrant without first making an order for production under paragraph 4 of Schedule 1 to PACE, if satisfied that either set of access conditions is fulfilled and also satisfied that one of the following preconditions applies:[123]

(a) that it is not practicable to communicate with any person entitled to grant entry to the premises in question;

(b) that it is not practicable to communicate with anyone entitled to grant access to the material sought;

(c) that the material in question is the subject of a statutory restriction on disclosure or obligation of secrecy, and is likely to be improperly disclosed if a warrant is not issued; or

(d) that service of notice of an application for an order, as would normally be required, may seriously prejudice the investigation.

There is some overlap between heads (a) to (d). In particular, 'not practicable' has been regarded as having a wider meaning than 'not feasible' or 'physically impossible', so, when deciding whether it would be practicable to communicate with a person for the purposes of (a) and (b), it is permissible to consider whether communicating with them would lead to the destruction of evidence, or similar consequences, which would be equally relevant to (d).[124]

Granting a warrant to search for excluded and special procedure material is a serious matter. The judges have made it clear that warrants under Schedule 1 to PACE are not to be applied for or granted routinely,[125] as routine applications would distort the statutory scheme of protection provided under section 9 and the remainder of Schedule 1 to PACE. The courts have also been prepared to examine warrant applications rather more critically than applications for production orders. Four principles have been established in the caselaw.

First, where a warrant is sought on the basis that it would be impracticable to communicate with a person entitled to grant access to the premises or the material, the police have a heavy duty to discharge if they are seeking material on business premises, particularly if it is in a solicitor's office. Where there are receptionists, partners, assistants, and so forth, readily available on the premises, it will not usually be impracticable to contact them, at least during office hours.[126] There is an exception to this, however, where the occupants of the premises to be searched, who hold the material sought, are themselves under suspicion in the investigation of the offence. In these circumstances, it might not be practicable (giving that word a broad meaning) to communicate with a person with authority, as that person might be implicated in the offence.[127]

Secondly, when granting a warrant, the circuit judge must take care to ensure that it

123 Ibid., Sch. 1, paras. 12(a), 14.
124 *R. v. Leeds Crown Court, ex parte Switalski* [1991] Crim. LR 559, DC.
125 *R. v. Crown Court at Maidstone, ex parte Waitt* [1988] Crim. LR 384, DC.
126 *R. v. Maidstone Crown Court, ex parte Waitt* [1988] Crim. LR 384, DC.
127 *R. v. Leeds Crown Court, ex parte Switalski* [1991] Crim. LR 559, DC.

is no wider than is justified by the information supporting the application. In *R. v. Central Criminal Court and British Railways Board, ex parte A.J.D. Holdings Ltd., Royle & Stanley Ltd.*,[128] a fraud investigation, where the information supporting the application for a warrant referred to grounds for seizing 'all records of business details relating to the finances of [Royle & Stanley Ltd.] namely: letters, notes . . . ', the judge granted a warrant authorizing a search for and seizure of 'material likely to be relevant evidence of that offence, namely: letters, notes [etc.]', without limiting the seizeable items by reference to business records concerning the finances of the company. On an application for judicial review of the warrant,[129] it was therefore held that the warrant as drawn was wider than could be supported by reference to the information, and was invalid.

Thirdly, the police and the circuit judge must comply strictly with the formal requirements for warrants and searches. The warrant, which must be produced to the occupier of premises, a copy of which must be provided, under section 16(5) of PACE, must provide all the information required by section 15. If any part of that information is unavailable, for example because it is on separate pages inadequately attached to the cover sheet of the warrant, or contained in a schedule which comes adrift from the main body of the warrant, the search will be unlawful.[130] The warrant must also identify so far as practicable the items to be sought, so as to constrain a general rummage through confidential papers.[131]

Fourthly, if a search is conducted in reliance on a warrant which turns out to be invalid, (a) reliance on the warrant will not make the search lawful, and (b) the police will not be permitted to retain any material seized as against the lawful owner.[132] Furthermore, even if the warrant is valid, it will not be held to authorize the seizure or retention of items which do not fall within the description in the warrant of the materials for which search is authorized.[133]

In addition to these principles, entry to search for excluded and special procedure material is hedged about with procedural safeguards. Like applications for production orders, applications for Schedule 1 warrants must be authorized by an officer of at least the rank of superintendent.[134] Empirical evidence suggests that this requirement does not result in many applications being rejected by the superintendent. The main value of the requirement seems to be it underlines in the minds of investigating officers the seriousness of invoking the search warrant jurisdiction in these circum-

---

[128] [1992] Crim. LR 669, DC.

[129] This is the proper procedure for challenging a warrant. Having once granted a warrant, the circuit judge is *functus officio*, and has no power to hold an *inter partes* hearing to consider revoking the warrant: *R. v. Liverpool Crown Court, ex parte Wimpey plc* [1991] Crim. LR 635, DC.

[130] *R. v. Chief Constable of Lancashire, ex parte Parker* [1993] QB 577, [1993] 2 All ER 56, DC.

[131] PACE, s. 15(6)(b). See *R. v. Central Criminal Court and British Railways Board, ex parte A.J.D. Holdings Ltd., Royle and Stanley Ltd.* [1992] Crim. LR 669, DC. On the degree of specificity required in warrants, see Ch. 10, above.

[132] *R. v. Central Criminal Court and British Railways Board, ex parte A.J.D. Holding Ltd., Royle & Stanley Ltd.* [1992] Crim. LR 669, DC; *R. v. Chief Constable of Lancashire, ex parte Parker* [1993] QB 577, [1993] 2 All ER 56, DC.

[133] *R. v. Central Criminal Court and British Railways Board, ex parte A.J.D. Holding Ltd., Royle & Stanley Ltd.* [1992] Crim. LR 669, DC.

[134] Code B, para. 2.4.

stances.[135] Once the superintendent has authorized the application, it goes to a circuit judge, supported by a written information in a similar way to other warrant applications. If it is made on the ground that applying for a production order may seriously prejudice the investigation, the application (or, more correctly, the information in writing supporting the application) must indicate the basis for believing that to be so.[136] This ought to apply also where the application is made on the basis that it is impracticable to communicate with anyone entitled to grant access to the premises or material because communicating with them would let the cat out of the bag and interfere with the investigation. Issuing a warrant without giving a hearing to the profession advisers who will be affected is an extraordinary and draconian measure. Judges have a special responsibility to prevent abuse of the procedure. Accordingly, it has been held that a judge who issues a warrant under Schedule 1 to PACE must give reasons for doing so.[137]

(5) PROCEEDS OF CRIME LEGISLATION: DRUG TRAFFICKING, MONEY LAUNDERING, AND TERRORISM

In certain fields which are regarded as being of special importance, the law allows investigators more extensive access to private information, and reduces to some degree the safeguards against abuse of the powers. Sometimes, people who have information, or even suspicions, about crime-related conduct have a positive obligation to inform the police without waiting to be asked for it. As part of a European Community initiative to combat money-laundering, banks, credit unions, and investment institutions are required to have in place procedures to prevent their services being used to launder money derived from drug trafficking or other serious crime, or to handle the proceeds of terrorist-related crime, or to make financial assistance available for the purposes of terrorism, in the course of their business. In particular, they must ensure that they can identify their customers and any principal on whose behalf the immediate customer is acting. They and their supervisory bodies must keep appropriate records, and ensure that any suspicion of money laundering by a customer is reported to the police.[138] There is also a general duty, imposed on anyone who in the course of a trade, profession, business, or employment acquires knowledge of or suspects drug money laundering, to disclose it to a constable as soon as is reasonably practicable, unless it is protected by legal professional privilege.[139] There is an equivalent duty in respect of people who, in the course of their business, etc. come to believe or suspect that a person has raised, held, used, helped to conceal, or laundered funds for terrorism purposes.[140] It is a criminal offence to fail to comply with any of these duties.

---

[135] Lidstone and Bevan, *Search and Seizure under the Police and Criminal Evidence Act 1984*, 145–6.

[136] Code B, para. 2.7.

[137] *R. v. Southampton Crown Court, ex parte J. and P.* [1993] Crim. LR 962, DC.

[138] Money Laundering Regulations 1993 and 2001, made under s. 2(2) of the European Communities Act 1972 to implement EC Council Directive 91/308/EEC on the prevention of the use of the financial system for the purpose of money laundering (OJ L166, 28 June 1991, 77).

[139] Drug Trafficking Act 1994, s. 52.

[140] Terrorism Act 2000, s. 19. The non-terrorism legislation is about to be consolidated and extended by the Proceeds of Crime Bill 2001. The terrorism provisions are being extended by the Anti-terrorism, Crime and Security Bill 2001.

These duties force disclosures which may interfere with the rights of business people or their customers under ECHR Article 8. There are circumstances in which the disclosure may not be justifiable in terms of the criteria in Article 8(2): the suspicion or belief which must be disclosed does not depend on the existence of reasonable grounds for the belief or suspicion, and disclosing an unreasonable belief or suspicion to the police may be disproportionate to the legitimate aim of preventing crime. Although banks, etc. are not usually public authorities for the purposes of the Human Rights Act 1998, section 6, they would seem to be performing public functions when making disclosures to the police pursuant to a duty imposed by statute. In order to avoid a violation of Article 8, a failure to disclose information to the police should attract the defence which the legislation offers for people who have a 'reasonable excuse' for not making the disclosure.

Sometimes, people are not under a duty to disclose information or suspicions about money laundering in connection with drug trafficking or other serious crime, or about offences in connection with terrorist funds. For example, they may have acquired information outside the course of their business, or it might be covered by legal professional privilege. In such cases, they are permitted to disclose the information to the police, and do not act unlawfully in doing so, notwithstanding any legal restriction on disclosure which would normally apply.[141]

To supplement these duties and powers of disclosure, Parliament has enacted variants on the PACE procedure allowing investigators to obtain access and production orders in cases concerning drug trafficking, terrorism, and the tracing of proceeds of crime. Under section 55 of the Drug Trafficking Act 1994, the police can apply *ex parte* (without giving notice to the person holding material) to a circuit judge for an order for access to or production of special procedure material in connection with an investigation into drug trafficking. A circuit judge may make an order if satisfied:

1   that there are reasonable grounds for suspecting that a specified person has carried on or benefited from drug trafficking; and
2   that there are reasonable grounds for suspecting that specified material is likely to be of substantial value to the investigation, and does not consist of items subject to legal privilege or excluded material; and
3   that there are reasonable grounds for believing that it is in the public interest that the material should be produced or that access to it should be given, having regard to the benefit likely to accrue to the investigation from the material and the capacity in which the person holding the material does so.[142]

There is a similar power under the Terrorism Act 2000, Schedule 5, paragraph 5 to apply *ex parte* to a circuit judge for an order for access to or production of material for the purposes of a terrorist investigation. The power in respect of terrorism is wider than that relating to drug trafficking investigations: the 2000 Act, unlike the

[141] Criminal Justice Act 1988, ss. 93A(7), 93B(5), inserted by Criminal Justice Act 1993, ss. 29 and 30; Drug Trafficking Act 1994, s. 50(3); Terrorism Act 2000, s. 20. These provisions help to implement the EC Money Laundering Directive 91/308/EEC.
[142] Drug Trafficking Act 1994, s. 55(4).

1994 Act, applies to excluded material as well as special procedure and ordinary material.[143]

Broadly equivalent provisions apply (*mutatis mutandis*) under the Criminal Justice Act 1988, section 93H in relation to material of substantial value to an investigation into whether anyone has benefited from criminal conduct in respect of which a confiscation order could be made under the Proceeds of Crime Act 1995, or into the whereabouts of the proceeds of such crimes.[144] Unlike the access and production provisions under the Drug Trafficking Act 1994 and the Terrorism Act 2000, the *ex parte* procedure under section 93H applies only in respect of proceeds of crime investigations, not to investigations into substantive offences. If the police want access to special procedure material for the purposes of an investigation into a substantive non-terrorist, non-drug-trafficking offence, they must make an *inter partes* application in the standard way under Schedule 1 to PACE. An order under section 93H of the 1988 Act is invalid if the dominant purpose of the police in seeking it was to further an investigation into a substantive offence rather than to pursue the proceeds of crime for the purpose of seeking a confiscation order.[145] The power to make an order under section 93H is narrower than that relating to terrorism in a further respect: it allows the police to apply for an order *ex parte* only in respect of special procedure material, not (like the Terrorism Act 2000) the more sensitive category of excluded material.

Once an order is served, it is a contempt of court to refuse to comply with it or to conceal, destroy, or otherwise deal with the material covered by it without the leave of the court. In addition, it is an offence for a person without a lawful authority or reasonable excuse to make any disclosure which is likely to prejudice the investigation, unless the disclosure is made by a professional legal adviser in circumstances which attract legal professional privilege as defined by relevant legislation.[146] Where the subject of the investigation is a client or customer of the person who holds the material which is sought, it would therefore appear, on the face of it, to be unlawful for the person to whom the order is addressed to tell the client that the order has been made, or to seek instructions as to whether to release the material or challenge the order. If the people holding the material are unable or unwilling to test the validity of the order, this may force them to choose either to release it in circumstances where the release may be unjustified, or to inform the client and risk criminal liability. In *R. v. Central Criminal Court, ex parte Francis & Francis*, Lord Griffiths, *obiter*, suggested

---

[143] There are limited defences under both Acts: see Feldman, 'Conveyancers and the Proceeds of Crime' [1989] *Conv.* 389 at 396–401.

[144] Criminal Justice Act 1988, s. 93H, inserted by Proceeds of Crime Act 1995, s. 11. A confiscation order can be made in respect of any indictable offence other than a drug trafficking offence, and specific non-indictable but potentially highly profitable offences relating to the use of places for public dancing, music or other entertainment, use of licensed premises for an unlicensed activity, offences relating to sex establishments, and offences relating to supplying obscene videos: Criminal Justice Act 1988, Sch. 4.

[145] *R. v. Southwark Crown Court, ex parte Bowles* [1998] AC 641, [1998] 2 All ER 193, HL, affirming the decision of the Divisional Court *sub nom. R. v. Crown Court at Guildford, ex parte DPP; R. v. Crown Court at Southwark, ex parte Bowles* [1998] QB 243, [1996] 4 All ER 961.

[146] Criminal Justice Act 1988, s. 93D, inserted by Criminal Justice Act 1993, s. 32; Drug Trafficking Act 1994, s. 53; Terrorism Act 2000, s. 39.

that a professional's duty to look after the affairs of a client might provide a lawful authority or reasonable excuse for informing the client that the investigation is in progress, where this is necessary in order to take instructions from the client.[147] However, if this justification relies on a contractual obligation owed by professionals to their clients, it is severely limited in scope. It has been held that bankers have no contractual obligation to inform their customers about production orders made or sought in respect of material concerning the client.[148] A *fortiori* social workers and voluntary agencies, with no contractual obligations to their 'clients', would find it hard to base a reasonable excuse or lawful justification on the fiduciary relationship which links them to the 'client'. In any case, Lord Griffiths made his suggestion before Parliament provided legislative protection for communications subject to legal professional privilege. It would now be arguable that Parliament has consciously decided not to extend protection to communications which do not attract that privilege. Informing clients that orders under the 1988, 1994, or 2000 Acts have been made in respect of material which relates to them is at best a risky business.[149]

It follows, therefore, that it will often be the responsibility of the person holding the material to decide whether to challenge the order by way of an application for judicial review, or apply for its variation or discharge, and what material should be produced in complying with the order. It is important that sufficient information should be served with the order to make it possible for these decisions to be taken. The information which formed the basis for the making of the order may be highly sensitive in drug trafficking and terrorism cases, and there may be good reasons for not disclosing it, either to the circuit judge to whom the application for the order is made, or to the people holding the material sought. Everyone may have to work on less extensive information in cases where the source of the information is secret than in ordinary cases arising under Schedule 1 to PACE.

In *R. v. Middlesex Guildhall Crown Court, ex parte Salinger*,[150] a journalist applied for judicial review to require a judge to order the police to serve him with the grounds on which a production order had been made under the terrorism legislation. The case concerned video recordings and other records of interviews conducted by Mr. Salinger in Libya with two Libyans suspected of having planted the bomb which blew up a Pan American World aircraft over Lockerbie in December 1988. The court held that the overall objective should be to provide as much information, preferably in writing, as early in the proceedings, as is consistent with the security of the operation. The court laid down four guidelines: the judge should be given a written statement of the evidence relied on to support the application for an order, although this need not disclose the nature or source of the information if it is too sensitive to allow disclosure; a judge who makes an order should give directions as to the information

---

[147] [1989] AC 346 at 386, [1988] 3 All ER 775 at 792.

[148] *Barclays Bank plc (trading as Barclaycard) v. Taylor* [1989] 1 WLR 1066, [1989] 3 All ER 563, CA.

[149] The dilemma is discussed by C. Graham and C. Walker, 'The Continued Assault on the Bank Vaults— Bank Accounts and Criminal Investigations' [1989] Crim. LR 185–97; D. Wheatley, 'Guilty . . . said the Red Queen?' (1989) 139 *NLJ* 499–500; and D. Feldman, 'Conveyancers and the Proceeds of Crime' [1989] *Conv.* 389–402.

[150] [1993] QB 564, [1993] 2 All ER 310, DC.

which should be served on the recipient, and that information should normally be served in the form of a written statement from the constable, which should be as full as possible without compromising security; if it is inappropriate to serve any information at that stage, the judge should consider whether it would be appropriate to serve any in the event of the recipient of the order applying for its variation or discharge; and application for variation or discharge of an order should be heard by the judge who originally made the order. The judge has the job, at every stage, of being as fair as possible to the recipient of the order without defeating the purpose of making it or putting at risk the security of the operation. This is no easy task.

Where confiscation of proceeds of crime or forfeiture of assets intended for use for terrorist purposes is envisaged, an order for disclosure of information or documents is available in High Court proceedings, including an application for a restraint or charging order under the legislation, freezing the assets of those who are thought to have benefited from crime. In order to discover the extent and whereabouts of a person's assets, an investigator applying for a restraint order can seek discovery and administer interrogatories, as if applications for restraint orders were ordinary High Court litigation in which all the usual interlocutory orders were available.[151]

Useful as these powers are to those who have to track down the proceeds of crime with a view to having them confiscated, they raise issues of principle which were not properly debated when the 1988, 1994, and 2000 Acts were passed. Compelling disclosure of material is a major incursion on the right of silence, although this might be of diminishing significance in view of the recent sustained assault on the right of silence by the judges and politicians. Perhaps more significant is the manner in which the rights of suspects in the criminal justice process have been steadily undermined by employing civil procedures, such as discovery and restraint orders, in criminal investigations, moving from a principle that the prosecution must prove all elements of its case on a playing field which, if not level, is tilted in favour of the subject, to a belief that there are certain matters which are so serious that the protections which the legal process normally offers to subjects can justifiably be relaxed. This is an unattractive feature of the legislation, but it is one shared with proceeds of crime legislation in many parts of the world, including some (notably the USA) in which the existence of constitutional guarantees of due process would have led one to expect a higher regard for principle.[152] It remains to be seen whether the provisions of the Human Rights Act 1998 can inject some much-needed respect for rights into the system.

---

[151] *In re O. (Restraint Order: Disclosure of Assets)* [1991] 2 QB 520, [1991] 1 All ER 330, CA; M. S. Dockray, 'Restraint Orders' (1991) **107** *LQR* 376–80; *In re Thomas (Disclosure Order)* [1992] 4 All ER 814, CA.
[152] D. Feldman, 'Individual Rights and Legal Values' (1989) **18** *Anglo-American L. Rev.* 261–88.

11.4 INTERCEPTING COMMUNICATIONS

(1) THE PRE-1985 POSITION

Until 1985, there was no clear legal regime for regulating the interception of communications in the UK. There was no legal procedure which was required to be invoked for authorizing an interception, either of mail or of telephone calls, and (as noted in Chapter 9) at common law it seemed that none was needed. Megarry V-C held in *Malone v. Commissioner of Police of the Metropolis*[153] that interception of telephone calls did not constitute a civil wrong, because no protected interest was affected, and it was not a crime. Therefore no special authorization was needed to justify them. The method of interception involved no trespass to the plaintiff's property, and confidentiality did not attach to telephone conversations. This applied whether the people intercepting them were public officials acting in the performance of their functions, private investigators, industrial spies, or mere trouble makers. Nor did metering of calls—the monitoring of telephone numbers dialled from the plaintiff's line—breach any confidentiality right, as metering is an essential part of the process of charging for calls made, and disclosing the results to an official authorized by a warrant from the Secretary of State was neither criminal nor tortious, because section 80 of the Post Office Act 1969 provided that information from interceptions might lawfully be passed to a person holding office under the Crown.

Intercepting mail, by contrast, was a criminal offence,[154] and might also constitute a civil wrong in that it constituted an interference with the proprietary interests of the sender or recipient of the package. It therefore needed special authority, but the authorization was administrative. It was given by senior officials of the Post Office, rather than a judicial officer. The Post Office Act 1953 provided that an interference with a postal packet was not to be criminal if authorized by a warrant issued under the hand of the Secretary of State, but did not lay down criteria for giving an authorization.[155] Warrants issued by the Secretary of State both for mail interceptions and for telecommunication interceptions shielded the officials by virtue of the Post Office Act 1969, section 80.

The conditions for issuing warrants for interceptions, whether of mail or telephone conversations, were laid down by the Secretary of State in rules of practice, which had no legal force, and were publicized only in the Report of a Committee of Privy Councillors established under the chairmanship of Lord Justice Birkett in 1957 to examine the matter.[156] Different sets of conditions applied, depending on whether the interception was designed to assist a criminal investigation or to protect state security.

---

[153] [1979] Ch. 344, [1979] 2 All ER 620; V. Bevan, 'Is Anybody There?' [1980] *PL* 431–53; Ewing and Gearty, *Freedom Under Thatcher*, 56–61.

[154] Post Office Act 1953, s. 58.

[155] Ibid., s. 58(1), proviso.

[156] *Report of the Committee of Privy Councillors Appointed to Inquire into the Interception of Communications*, Cmd. 283 (London: HMSO, 1957). For discussion, see V. Bevan, 'Is Anybody There?' [1980] *PL* 431–53.

In relation to crime, the conditions were stated by the Home Secretary to be: (a) the crime had to be really serious; (b) normal methods had to have been tried unsuccessfully; (c) there had to be good reason for believing that a conviction would result from the evidence obtained by the interception. In relation to security matters, two conditions were applied: an interception could be authorized only in respect of major subversion, terrorism, or espionage, which was likely to injure the national interest, and the material to be obtained had to be of direct use in compiling the information necessary for the security service (MI5) to carry out its functions in protecting state security. There was no external review of the working of the system: the Birkett Committee in 1957 took the view that the best safeguard against abuse lay in the final responsibility of the Secretary of State.[157]

Following the *Malone* case, when reform was under consideration, a White Paper was produced detailing the procedures,[158] and Lord Diplock was appointed to review the operation of the procedures for issuing and implementing warrants. Lord Diplock's annual reports had some effect in widening, rather than narrowing, the range of cases in which warrants might be granted, for example by loosening the definition of serious crime. Neither he nor Lord Bridge, who succeeded him in 1982, found irregularities in the issue of warrants in respect of the 500 or more authorized telephone taps conducted each year between 1980 and 1985. Generally speaking, the government seemed satisfied that administrative controls were working adequately, although others were concerned at evidence from former officers of the Security Service, such as Cathy Massiter, that either the guidelines were not being adhered to or unauthorized telephone tapping was being carried on by officers of the Service.[159]

Two factors combined to persuade the government to change its position, and put interception on a statutory footing. First, the plaintiff in *Malone v. Commissioner of Police of the Metropolis* lodged a petition under the European Convention on Human Rights, arguing that both the uncontrolled interception of telephone conversations and metering (i.e. recording the numbers called and the duration of the calls, but not the content) contravened his right to respect for private and family life, home, and correspondence under Article 8. The European Court of Human Rights held that the threat of legally unregulated interception and metering was an interference with private life and correspondence, and could not be justified under Article 8(2) because it was not 'in accordance with the law' as that term was interpreted by the Court. The approach of the Court is explained further in section (3), below. Secondly, the privatization of telecommunications services in the Telecommunications Act 1984, which put control over lines into the hands of British Telecom, a private corporation, made it important to regulate interceptions by law, and to criminalize unauthorized interceptions.

---

[157] *Report of the Committee of Privy Councillors*, Cmd. 283, para. 139.
[158] *The Interception of Communications in Great Britain*, Cmnd. 7873 (London: HMSO, 1980), paras. 7–14.
[159] See Ewing and Gearty, *Freedom Under Thatcher*, 51–65.

(2) THE INTERCEPTION OF COMMUNICATIONS ACT 1985[160]

The Interceptions of Communications Act 1985:

- made it a criminal offence to carry out unauthorized interception of communications via a 'public telecommunication system' (section 1(1));

- provided for interception warrants to be granted to the police or the security and intelligence services by the Home Secretary in the interests of national security, for the purpose of preventing or detecting serious crime,[161] or for the purpose of safeguarding the economic well-being of the UK (section 2);

- exempted from the warrant requirement any communication if the public authority had reasonable grounds for believing that either of the parties to it had consented to the interception (section 1(2)(b));

- required arrangements to be made to secure that disclosures of material flowing from an interception under warrant are kept to a minimum, and that material is destroyed as soon as retention is no longer necessary for one of the purposes for which a warrant could be issued (section 6);

- prohibited the use of intercepts in evidence (section 9);

- prohibited any evidence being adduced or questions being asked in legal proceedings tending to show that any official or person engaged in running a telecommunications system has carried out an interception of communications,[162] or that a warrant had been issued, subject to limited exceptions (section 9);

- established an Interception of Communications Tribunal to which a person who suspected that his communications were being intercepted could complain, although the Tribunal's powers were limited to examining interceptions under warrant, and it could offer only very limited remedies;

- established an Interception of Communications Commissioner, to keep under review the granting of interceptions warrants and to report to the Prime Minister annually.

The Act had several shortcomings. First, being limited to public telecommunication systems, it was held not to regulate interception of communications before they reached the public system, or interception of pager messages transmitted by private operators.[163] This confirmed legal advice given to the police and Customs and Excise in 1992. After that, Customs and Excise officers, as servants of the Crown, intercepted pager messages under section 5 of the Wireless Telegraphy Act 1949. The police, not

---

[160] I. Leigh, 'A Tapper's Charter?' [1986] *PL* 8–18; I. J. Lloyd, 'The Interception of Communications Act 1985' (1986) **49** *MLR* 86–95; Ewing and Gearty, *Freedom Under Thatcher*, 65–83.

[161] But not for the purpose of prosecuting suspects: *R. v. Preston* [1994] 2 AC 130, [1994] 3 All ER 638, HL.

[162] 'Communication' for the purpose of section 9 included any electrical impulse or signal to be transmitted from the telephone number from which the impulse or signal was sent to the telephone number with which it was connected, and so included a printout of numbers dialled by a person whose telephone use was being logged by a device attached to the line, even if the content of the call was not being monitored: *Morgans v. DPP* [2000] 2 WLR 386, [2000] 2 All ER 522, HL. See now Regulation of Investigatory Powers Act 2000, Part I, discussed below.

[163] See *R. v. Taylor-Sabori* [1999] 1 WLR 858, CA.

being servants of the Crown, were unable to use that authority, so they applied to circuit judges for production orders under Schedule 1 to PACE until a judge at Worcester Crown Court held in 1998 that there was no power to grant an order in respect of material not yet in existence, and that in any case it could not authorize the police to act in a manner unlawful under the 1949 Act. Thereafter an informal arrangement was made for the Home Office to authorize police interceptions of pager messages by warrants under the 1949 Act, without formal independent oversight.[164] Similarly, intercepting a telephone conversation by monitoring the radio signals passing between the base unit and handset of a cordless telephone did not require a warrant, although a tap on the line to intercept the message after it was transmitted from the base unit down the telephone line would have done.[165] Nor did the Act regulate interception of communications outside the UK.[166] Such interceptions, and those on an employer's internal telephone network, were still not 'in accordance with the law', and so were unjustifiable under Article 8(2).[167] The same applied to interceptions.

Secondly, unilateral consent to interception given by one party to a communication left the other party at risk of serious invasion of privacy for which no remedy could be obtained. This was a particularly serious problem when the consent was given by a police informer,[168] at a time when there was no statutory regulation of the use of such informers to obtain private information about people.[169] The dangers were exacerbated by a judicial decision interpreting the legislation as preventing questions being asked to establish whether or not a public authority had reasonable grounds for believing that a party had consented, on the ground that this would tend to permit a challenge to the legality of official interceptions, the confidentiality which it was the policy of the Act (particularly section 9) to protect.[170]

Thirdly, certain oddities and difficulties arose from the prohibition in section 9 on the use in court of evidence from interceptions. In particular, it was only in 2000 that the House of Lords finally settled the difficulties, holding that section of the 1985 Act prevented evidence being adduced if it had been obtained as a result of an interception by an officer of the Crown or other person who could be authorized to carry out interceptions, whether carried out under warrant, with the consent of a party, or unlawfully, except in a prosecution for unlawful interception or in proceedings before the Tribunal.[171] However, it seemed that evidence obtained by a private person through an unlawful interception could still be admitted as evidence, and questions could be asked to establish its unlawfulness, as such a case would fall outside the

[164] See Lord Nolan, *Annual Report of the Interception of Communications Commissioner for 1998*, paras. 18–27.
[165] *R. v. Effik* [1995] 1 AC 309, [1994] 3 All ER 458, HL.
[166] *See R. v. Governor of Belmarsh Prison, ex parte Martin* [1995] 1 WLR 412, [1995] 2 All ER 548, DC; *R. v. Aujla (Ajit Singh)* [1998] 2 Cr. App. R. 16, CA; *R. v. Taylor-Sabori* [1999] 1 WLR 858, CA.
[167] *Halford v. United Kingdom*, Eur. Ct. HR, Judgment of 25 June 1997, RJD 1997-III, No. 39, 24 EHRR 523.
[168] As in *R. v. Rasool* [1997] 1 WLR 1092, [1997] 4 All ER 439, CA.
[169] See now Regulation of Investigatory Powers Act 2000, Part II, considered in Ch. 10, above.
[170] *R. v. Owen* [1999] 1 WLR 949, CA.
[171] *Morgans v. DPP* [2000] 2 WLR 386, [2000] 2 All ER 522, HL overruling *R. v. Rasool* [1997] 1 WLR 1092, [1997] 4 All ER 439, CA, and *R. v. Owen* [1999] 1 WLR 949, CA, and disapproving *dicta* of Steyn LJ (as he then was) in the CA in *R. v. Effik* (1992) 95 Cr. App. R. 355, 365, on this point.

policy of the 1985, which was to maintain the confidentiality of interceptions by officials.

Fourthly, section 9 of the Act conflicted with the prosecutor's duty to make full disclosure of unused material to the defence, in order to ensure that any material which might assist the defence was available.[172] It was finally held that investigators had a duty to make information about interceptions available to counsel for the prosecution, who had no duty to disclose them to the defence, but was responsible for ensuring that anything possible was done to secure fairness at trial, including (for example) making statements conceding certain facts which favoured the defence if that could be done without disclosing the source of the information.[173]

Fifthly, there were doubts about the effectiveness of the oversight exercised by the Tribunal in individual cases and the Commissioner in respect of the general operation of the warrant system. The Tribunal's effectiveness was undermined by the absence of a requirement for people to be told when their communications had been intercepted as soon as that could be done without prejudicing the object of the interception. The result is that the remedies for unlawful interception in violation of ECHR Article 8 can hardly have been said to be adequate. The Commissioner's effectiveness in reviewing the overall compliance of investigative agencies with the Act was doubtful, because the part-time nature of the office militated against day-to-day involvement and comprehensive oversight of the system. Despite a doubling in the number of warrants issued to over 1,800 annually between 1992 and 1998, the Tribunal never found a complaint to have been substantiated, and the Commissioner identified few occasions for strictures.[174]

(3) THE PRINCIPLES OF ECHR ARTICLE 8 AS INTERPRETED BY THE EUROPEAN COURT OF HUMAN RIGHTS IN RELATION TO INTERCEPTION AND METERING OF COMMUNICATIONS

The European Court of Human Rights has now decided a significant number of cases about interception and monitoring of communications, including telephone calls, by the police and security forces. It has progressively developed a clear set of principles governing both the types of official conduct constituting an interference with the right under ECHR Article 8(1), and the requirements to be satisfied before a state can justify an interference by reference to the criteria in Article 8(2).

(i) When is Article 8(1) engaged?

Telephone conversations fall within the scope of 'private life' and 'correspondence',[175]

---

[172] *R. v. Ward (Judith)* [1993] 1 WLR 619, [1993] 2 All ER 577, CA; Criminal Procedure and Investigations Act 1996, ss. 3, 5, 7, and 9, and the Code of Practice issued by the Home Secretary under s. 23.

[173] *R. v. Preston* [1994] 2 AC 130, [1994] 3 All ER 638, HL.

[174] L. Lustgarten and I. Leigh, *In from the Cold: National Security and Parliamentary Democracy* (Oxford: Clarendon Press, 1994), 51–72; N. Taylor and C. Walker, 'Bugs in the System' (1996) 1 *Journal of Civil Liberties* 105–124; JUSTICE, *Under Surveillance: Covert Policing and Human Rights Standards* (London: JUSTICE, 1998), ch. 2; Lord Nolan, *Annual Report of the Interception of Communications Commissioner for 1998*, Cm. 4364 (London: HMSO, 1999).

[175] *Klass v. Germany*, Eur. Ct. HR, Series A, No. 28, Judgment of 6 September 1978.

and (together with letters) are protected whether they originate in or are sent to a person's home or business premises.[176] An interception interferes with the right to respect for private life and correspondence even if no use is subsequently made of the material.[177] The knowledge that someone might be intercepting the conversation would inhibit free communication and constitute a lack of respect for the privacy of the participants.[178]

(ii) Justifying an interference 1: is it 'in accordance with the law'?

This requirement of Article 8(2) has two elements. First, the interference must be lawful according to national law, as interpreted in national courts. Secondly, it must also meet international standards arising from the notion of the rule of law: any interference with the right must have a sound foundation in positive national law, and the law in question must meet certain tests of quality. If there is no positive law authorizing and regulating the interference, it cannot be in accordance with the law under Article 8(2). The rule of law requires that safeguards be put in place against abuse of power. Arbitrariness is incompatible with the rule of law, and the law which governs interceptions must sufficiently restrict the capacity for arbitrary interference.[179] The law in question must therefore be sufficiently accessible to those likely to be affected by the interference to allow them to foresee reasonably clearly what its impact might be, and plan their behaviour accordingly.[180] It need not be entirely contained in statute: reliance on caselaw and on the opinions of academic writers may together establish an adequate basis,[181] but only if the matter is reasonably settled. Thus French provisions for regulating telephone tapping were not adequately clear or accessible, and so were not in accordance with the law, when essential safeguards had to be deduced from scattered judicial decisions in which the trend of authority was not yet settled.[182] Furthermore, where the person whose communications are intercepted is unaware of the interception, and so is unable to take steps to test its lawfulness, it is particularly important to put in place procedural safeguards, independent of the state, to ensure that interception is not authorized improperly. Authorization by a member of the executive, without supervision by an independent judge, is always likely to fall foul of Article 8(2), especially if the communications are likely to affect the privacy interests of third parties (for example, where the person whose telephone is being tapped is a lawyer).[183]

The issue of third-party interests regularly arises where communications are

---

[176] *Niemietz v. Germany*, Eur. Ct. HR, Series A, No. 251-B, Judgment of 16 December 1992, 16 EHRR 97; *Halford v. United Kingdom*, Eur. Ct. HR, Judgment of 25 June 1997, RJD 1997-III, 24 EHRR 523; *Kopp v. Switzerland*, Eur. Ct. HR, Judgment of 25 March 1998, RJD 1998-II, 27 EHRR 91.

[177] *Kopp v. Switzerland*, Eur. Ct. HR, Judgment of 25 March 1998, RJD 1998-II, 27 EHRR 91.

[178] *Malone v. United Kingdom*, Eur. Ct. HR, Series A, No. 82, Judgment of 2 August 1984, 7 EHRR 14.

[179] *Klass v. Germany*, Eur. Ct. HR, Series A, No. 28, Judgment of 6 September 1978.

[180] *Malone v. United Kingdom*, Eur. Ct. HR, Series A, No. 82, Judgment of 2 August 1984, 7 EHRR 14.

[181] *Kopp v. Switzerland*, Eur. Ct. HR, Judgment of 25 March 1998, RJD 1998-II, 27 EHRR 91.

[182] *Kruslin v. France*, Eur. Ct. HR, Series A, No. 176-A, Judgment of 24 April 1990, 12 EHRR 547; *Huvig v. France*, Eur. Ct. HR, Series A, No. 176-B, Judgment of 24 April 1990, 12 EHRR 528.

[183] *Kopp v. Switzerland*, Eur. Ct. HR, Judgment of 25 March 1998, RJD 1998-II, 27 EHRR 91. In a concurring opinion, Judge Pettiti suggested that the time had come to recognize legal professional privilege as an aspect of the rule of law under Art. 8, but the Court did not go quite so far.

intercepted, since many people are likely to contact, or be contacted by, the person whose communications are targeted. Many of these will be purely fortuitous contacts, but may end up on official records without knowing it. In *Amann v. Switzerland*,[184] the applicant was an importer of depilatory devices, including the battery-operated 'Perma Tweez', which he advertised in magazines. A woman from the Soviet embassy telephoned him to order one. Her calls were being intercepted. It led to Mr. Amann being investigated, and a card being opened on him in the card index of the Federal Public Prosecutor's Office. Mr. Amann complained of a violation of Article 8 in his case. The European Court of Human Rights decided that the interception of the telephone call to him interfered with his right under Article 8(1). Although there was legislation dealing with interceptions in Switzerland, and some safeguards against arbitrariness were in place, the Court held that the legislation did not regulate in detail the treatment of people whose communications were fortuitously and necessarily recorded in the course of surveillance of criminal suspects or security targets. Special precautions are needed to protect the rights and interests of such people. Because the legislation did not provide such precautions, the interference was not in accordance with the law, and could not be justified under Article 8(2). Furthermore, there was no sufficient basis in law for the creation of the index card on the applicant, or for its storage, leading to further violations of Article 8.

(iii) Justifying an interference 2: is it in pursuit of a legitimate aim?

Where an interference is shown to be in accordance with the law, it must next be shown to have been in pursuit of one of the legitimate aims listed in Article 8(2): in the interests of national security, public safety, or the economic well-being of the country; for the prevention of disorder or crime; for the protection of health or morals; or for the protection of the rights and freedoms of others. The aims most often prayed in aid in relation to interception of communications are the interests of national security and the economic well-being of the country, neither of which has been defined by the Court, or the prevention of crime, which has been treated as including detection of criminals. A wide margin of appreciation has been allowed to states in deciding what is in the interests of national security, because of the special sensitivity of information on that subject,[185] but less discretion would be likely to be permitted in relation to the other legitimate aims.

(iv) Justifying an interference 3: is it 'necessary in a democratic society' for the legitimate purpose?

As noted earlier, the Court has interpreted 'necessary in a democratic society' as meaning that there must be a pressing social need to be addressed, and the means adopted must be proportionate to it. Proportionality means that the measure must not interfere with the right further than necessary, and must in any case not deprive a person of the very essence of the right. The sufficiency of safeguards against abuse of power and remedies for aggrieved parties are relevant to proportionality. In *Klass v.*

---

[184] Eur. Ct. HR, App. No. 27798/95, Judgment of 16 February 2000.
[185] *Klass v. Germany*, Eur. Ct. HR, Series A, No. 28, Judgment of 6 September 1978.

Federal Republic of Germany,[186] the Court approved the safeguards in force in West Germany on telephone tapping for security purposes: Law G10 provided for warrants to be issued by a designated Minister only in relation to suspected criminal activity affecting state security; it imposed reviews of individual warrants by a Commission presided over by a person qualified for judicial office, capable of acting of its own motion. It provided that a person whose communications have been intercepted should normally be informed of the fact at the conclusion of the period of interception, unless there are national security grounds for continuing to keep the matter secret. Proceedings for compensation could then be brought in ordinary courts if appropriate. Law G10 also subjected the entire process of granting warrants to the general oversight of a special Parliamentary Board. These safeguards were regarded as meeting the 'in accordance with the law' and 'necessary in a democratic society' criteria in security cases, although the Court did not lay down any minimum standards which such legislation must meet in order to satisfy the justifying conditions of Article 8(2), or say whether more demanding criteria would be applied to interceptions in ordinary criminal investigations than in national security cases.

(v) The Human Rights Act 1998

The above principles are applicable as part of the law on interception of communications in the UK by virtue of section 1 of, and Schedule 1 to, the Human Rights Act 1998. By section 2, the legislation authorizing interception of communications must be read and given effect so far as possible in a manner compatible with the right under ECHR Article 8, including the justifications under Article 8(2) for interfering with the right. For this purpose, section 2 provides that Article 8 must be interpreted taking account of the caselaw of the European Court of Human Rights. In the light of this, the next section examines Part I of the Regulation of Investigatory Powers Act 2000, which now provides the legislative basis for interception of communications in the UK.

(4) THE REGULATION OF INVESTIGATORY POWERS ACT 2000, PART I[187]

The Regulation of Investigative Powers Act 2000, Part I, was an attempt by the Labour government to provide a statutory framework for the legitimate interception of communications which would address the problems of the Interception of Communications Act 1985, meet the requirements of the ECHR in preparation for the coming into force of the Human Rights Act 1998, and respond to the growing demands of employers for legal authority to monitor employees' use of telephone and, more particularly, e-mail systems, not least to discourage unlawful or inappropriate messages. In many respects, the new provisions followed the 1985 Act, but with some significant adaptations.

---

[186] European Court of Human Rights, Series A, No. 28, Judgment of 6 September 1978, 2 EHRR 214.

[187] See H. Fenwick, *Civil Rights: New Labour, Freedom and the Human Rights Act* (Harlow, Essex: Longman, 2000), ch. 9.

(i) Offence of unauthorized interception of communications

Under section 1(1) of the 2000 Act, it continues to be a criminal offence intentionally
and without lawful authority to intercept in the UK a communication in the course of
its transmission through public postal services or public telecommunication systems.
A telecommunication system is widely defined as 'any system which exists . . . for the
purpose of facilitating the transmission of communications by any means involving
the use of electrical or electro-magnetic energy',[188] thus including radio transmissions
not intended for general reception.[189] On the other hand, the Act reverses *Morgans v.
Director of Public Prosecutions*[190] by providing that 'traffic data', i.e. data merely identifying the origin or the destination of the message, the apparatus used or the pieces of
the message, or activating the equipment, do not constitute communications.[191] Thus
monitoring or metering the data will not be capable of being authorized by an
interception warrant. However, to avoid leaving such activities, which interfere with
privacy rights under ECHR Article 8, without a legal basis, a separate system is
provided for authorizing them, as explained below.

The Act adopts a fairly wide definition of 'public telecommunications system' and
'public postal service', including those offered to the public or a substantial section of
the public.[192] It also brings other communications systems within the statutory
regime of regulation, filling one of the big gaps in the 1985 Act. Section 1(2) makes it
an offence to intercept in the UK, intentionally and without authority, any communication in course of transmission by means of a private system, unless under section
1(6)(a) the person carrying out the interception is entitled to control the operation or
use of the system. This exception has caused concern, as it allows employers to meter
and intercept their employees' communications over or originating from the employers' private networks. For these purposes, a private telecommunication system is one
which is directly or indirectly attached to a public system for any purpose, and which
includes apparatus in the UK for making that attachment.[193]

(ii) Grounds for authorizing interceptions of communications

The Act provides blanket permission to intercept communications in certain circumstances, and allows the Secretary of State to authorize certain other interceptions by
warrant. The blanket permissions apply where:

- both the sender and the intended recipient of the communication have
  consented;[194]

- either the sender or the intended recipient of a communication has consented,
  and surveillance by means of the interception has been authorized by a surveillance authorization under Part II of the 2000 Act (explained in Chapter 10,
  above);[195]

---

[188] Definitions of terms are contained in Regulation of Investigatory Powers Act 2000, s. 2.
[189] Ibid., s. 2(3).
[190] [2000] 2 WLR 386, [2000] 2 All ER 522, HL.
[191] Regulation of Investigatory Powers Act 2000, s. 2(5), (9).
[192] Ibid., s. 2(1).   [193] Ibid.
[194] Ibid., s. 3(1).   [195] Ibid., s. 3(2).

- the interception consists of conduct by or on behalf of a postal or telecommunication service provider for a purpose connected with the provision or operation of the service (such as keeping records for charging purposes, or testing the system), or with the enforcement of any enactment relating to the use of such services;[196]

- the communication is intercepted in the course of its transmission by wireless telegraphy by a person designated under an order made by the Secretary of State to intercept wireless telegraphy transmissions for purposes connected with the issue of licences under the Wireless Telegraphy Act 1949, to prevent or detect interference with wireless telegraphy, or to enforce enactments contained in that Act or otherwise relating to an interference with wireless telegraphy;[197]

- the interception takes place in the course of transmission by a telecommunication system for the purpose of obtaining information about a person who is, or is reasonably believed to be, abroad, and the interception relates to the use of a foreign public telecommunication system (subject to certain conditions);[198]

- the conduct is authorized by regulations made by the Secretary of State on the ground that it appears to him to constitute a legitimate practice for the purpose of record keeping or monitoring for business purposes, including the work of government departments (fostering fears about eavesdropping on employees and customers);[199]

- interceptions by the authorities in prisons, high security psychiatric hospitals, and state-run hospitals under certain conditions,[200] removing the need to assume that prisoners with notice of the existence of telephone surveillance had consented to the interception;[201]

- the conduct in the exercise, in relation to any stored information, of any other statutory power that is exercised for the purpose of obtaining information (such as a surveillance authorization) or of taking possession of any document or property (such as a search warrant).[202]

The first two of these permissions removes a danger under the previous legislation that a person's right to privacy might be abrogated, without his knowledge and without external control, by unilateral consent given by someone else. For example, if a person (X), having an extra-marital sexual liaison with a prominent public figure (Y), saw an opportunity to make money by selling the story to a newspaper, X might have initiated a call to Y and recorded (or allowed an accomplice to record) their intimate conversation. The recording might then have been sold to a newspaper, and a transcript published. No offence would have been committed, because of the consent

---

[196] Ibid., s. 3(3).
[197] Ibid., s. 3(4), (5).
[198] Ibid., s. 4(1).
[199] Ibid., s. 4(2), (3), (7).
[200] Ibid., s. 4(4), (5), (6).
[201] See *R. v. Owen* [1999] 1 WLR 949, CA (overruled on other grounds in *Morgans v. DPP* [2000] 2 WLR 386, HL).
[202] Regulation of Investigatory Powers Act 2000, s. 1(5)(c).

of X. This left Y without a remedy, because breach of privacy was not tortious in itself, and a defamation action would be met with a defence of truth. It would now be criminal. In addition, the aggrieved party may have a private law remedy under the emergent tort of invasion of privacy, examined in Chapter 9 above.

The other circumstances in which there is lawful authority for intercepting a communication is when the interception is in accordance with a warrant issued by the Secretary of State under section 5 of the 2000 Act. The decision to leave the power to grant all interceptions warrants in the hands of the Secretary of State, contrary to the recommendation (in respect of criminal investigations) by the Royal Commission on Criminal Procedure,[203] is controversial. It fails to provide for the independent, prior scrutiny by a person or body with judicial experience which is offered in a number of other countries, notably Canada and Australia.[204] The European Court of Human Rights in the *Klass* case thought it desirable that, in principle, interceptions should be under judicial supervision.[205] Although it was not held to be a requirement of Article 8 of the Convention, subsequent decisions have made it clear that the absence of such safeguards will be taken into consideration when deciding whether the independent safeguards against arbitrariness are sufficient to meet the rule of law requirements which arise from the term 'in accordance with the law' in ECHR Article 8(2). This consideration may be decisive, particularly where the target of the interception is likely to be a party to highly sensitive, private communication by virtue of his position, for example as a lawyer or doctor.[206] Even in Australia, where issuing a warrant is regarded as a ministerial, rather than a judicial, function, the officer executing it is required to act judicially.[207]

Section 5 of the Act lays down the conditions for the grant of a warrant. The Secretary of State must not issue a warrant unless he considers both that it is necessary for one of four specified purposes, and that the interference which the interception would represent is proportionate to what is sought to be achieved by carrying it out.[208] The necessity and proportionality conditions are lifted from ECHR Article 8(2) and the caselaw of the European Court of Human Rights, and will be given effect accordingly, as required by section 3 of the Human Rights Act 1998. The necessity for a warrant (but not its proportionality) must be kept under review, as the Secretary of State must cancel it if he consider that it is no longer necessary for one of the purposes

---

[203] Royal Commission on Criminal Procedure, *Report*, Cmnd. 8092 (London: HMSO, 1981), para. 3.57, recommending that in criminal matters an application for a warrant should be made to a magistrate.

[204] Lustgarten and Leigh, *In from the Cold*, 78–86.

[205] *Klass v. Federal Republic of Germany*, Eur. Ct. HR, Series A, No. 28, Judgment of 6 September 1978, 2 EHRR 214.

[206] See, e.g. *Kopp v. Switzerland*, Eur. Ct. HR, Judgment of 25 March 1998, RJD 1998-II, 27 EHRR 91, at para. 74.

[207] *Hilton v. Wells* (1985) 157 CLR57, HC of Australia, dealing with warrants under the Telecommunications (Interception) Act 1979 (Cth); *Love v. Attorney-General (NSW); Peters v. Attorney-General (NSW)* (1990) 169 CLR307, HC of Australia, dealing with warrants under the Listening Devices Act 1984 (NSW). A judicial officer may exercise the jurisdiction only as *persona designata*. If acting by virtue of a judicial office, the issue of a warrant violates the constitutional doctrine of the separation of powers, and is unconstitutional.

[208] Regulation of Investigatory Powers Act 2000, s. 5(1), (2).

permitted by the 2000 Act.[209] When deciding whether it is necessary, the Secretary of State must consider whether the information which is needed could reasonably be obtained by other means.[210]

The purposes for which a warrant may be issued are:[211] (a) in the interests of national security; (b) for the purpose of preventing or detecting serious crime; (c) for the purpose of safeguarding the economic well-being of the UK (but only in respect of information relating to the acts or intentions of persons outside the British Islands[212]); and (d) for the purpose of giving effect to an international mutual assistance agreement (i.e. an agreement with a foreign state under which each takes action on behalf of the other in connection with the investigation of serious crime) in circumstances which appear to the Secretary of State to be equivalent to those in which a warrant could be issued under (b). The first three deserve attention.

(a) *National security.* This is a legitimate purpose for interfering with rights under ECHR Article 8, but neither the ECHR nor the Act defines national security. Indeed, it would probably be impossible, and might counter-productive, to do so exhaustively. The first Commissioner to be appointed under the Interception of Communications Act 1985, Lloyd LJ, pointed out in his first annual report that national security is not confined to the 'major subversion, terrorism, or espionage' test which was applied under the pre-1985 interception guidelines, and regarded certain warrants issued on national security grounds unrelated to subversion, terrorism, or espionage, as having been properly granted.[213] More recently, Lord Nolan, presenting a very broad understanding of the term, wrote:

'It is generally understood to refer to the survival and well-being of the state and community and includes such matters as threats to the security of the Nation by terrorism, espionage and major subversive activity but is not confined to these matters. The normal object of a national security warrant is to assist in the build up of an intelligence picture, for example about a suspected terrorist or terrorist group. This process is often long drawn out. There have, however, been many occasions in the field of counter-terrorism where interception has played a vital part in cases of great urgency.'[214]

This passage, and particularly the reference to the well-being of the community alongside the survival of the state, indicates a far wider meaning than the core (but not exhaustive) remit of the Security Service as identified in the Security Service Act 1989, section 1: 'threats from espionage, terrorism and sabotage, from the activities of agents of foreign powers and from actions intended to overthrow or undermine parliamentary democracy by political, industrial or violent means'. It is also very much wider than the minimal 'democratic conception of national security' proposed by Professors Lustgarten and Leigh:

---

[209] Ibid., s. 9(3).

[210] Ibid., s. 5(4).

[211] Ibid., s. 5(3).

[212] Ibid., s. 5(5).

[213] *Interception of Communications Act 1985, chapter 56: Report of the Commissioner for 1986,* Cm. 108 (London: HMSO, 1987).

[214] Lord Nolan, *Annual Report of the Interception of Communications Commissioner 1998,* para. 14. The Secretary of State is entitled to conclude that terrorism committed abroad can threaten the UK's national security: *Secretary of State for the Home Dept. v. Rehman* [2001] 3 WLR 877, HL.

'... certain activities—notably political violence and covert attempts to influence a nation's political processes—*are* incompatible with both the institutions and ideals of a democratic state and cannot be tolerated. All states are entitled to protect their territory from invasion or attempts to detach portions of it by insurrection. In addition, efforts to gain access to certain narrow and specific categories of information ought to be prevented to protect any nation's immediate or longer term defence needs. Therefore these matters deserve to be regarded as ones whose "security", in the sense of safeguarding, requires protection.'[215]

The relative breadth of Lord Nolan's conception of national security leaves a considerable margin of discretion in the hands of the Secretary of State. While some degree of indeterminacy is inevitable, it would be desirable that the boundaries of a power such as this, which allows interference with the confidentiality of communications in ways which make it difficult if not impossible for the parties to the communication even to discover whether the interference has occurred, with rather more certitude than has so far been accomplished. This is particularly important in view of the substantial evidence that, before the 1985 Act, the Security Service and successive Secretaries of State interpreted their national security function as justifying surveillance on, and interception of the communications of, some people who were concerned in wholly legitimate, democratic, political activity, but who espoused causes with which the establishment was out of sympathy. For example, it seems that members of the Campaign for Nuclear Disarmament were targets of telephone interceptions.[216] There is at least some credible basis for suggesting that CND posed a threat to national security, if one accepts that security benefited from, or even depended on, maintaining a nuclear capability. However, that claim is politically contentious, and it seems that the Security Service was advancing the government's (or its own) political perception of the national interest by checking those who manifested support for opposing views. Concerns on this front are only partially alleviated by the instruction given by Mr. Harold Wilson, when Prime Minister in 1966, and reaffirmed by every subsequent Prime Minister, that the telephones of MPs are not to be tapped.

Perhaps this is inevitable, in a politically charged field such as national security. However, it seemed that all active opposition to government might attract surveillance. In 1986, Harriet Harman (now a Member of Parliament) and Patricia Hewitt (now a Minister, and previously the author of an incisive critique of the English law of civil liberties[217]), both of whom had been officers of the National Council for Civil Liberties, complained to the European Commission of Human Rights that they had been placed under surveillance by MI5 after being labelled as subversives, relying on evidence from the former MI5 officer, Miss Cathy Massiter. They alleged violations of their right to respect for private life under Article 8 of the Convention, and of the lack of an effective domestic remedy contrary to Article 13. The Commission held in 1989 that their rights had been breached, because keeping information about somebody's

---

[215] Lustgarten and Leigh, *In from the Cold*, 35 (italics in original; footnote omitted).

[216] For discussion of the evidence, see Ewing and Gearty, *Freedom Under Thatcher*, 51–5, 61–5; *R. v. Secretary of State for the Home Department, ex parte Ruddock* [1987] 1 WLR 1482, [1987] 2 All ER 518; Leigh, 'The Security Service, the Press and the Courts' [1987] *PL* 12 at 13–17.

[217] P. Hewitt, *The Abuse of Power* (Oxford: Martin Robertson, 1981).

private life is an interference with the right to respect for private life,[218] and the Commission decided that it followed that collecting such information must equally constitute an interference. It could not be justified, because it was not in accordance with the law, there being no rules in English law conferring or regulating the power of the Security Service to collect such information. Furthermore, because there was no legal procedure allowing subjects of information gathering to obtain appropriate remedies, there had been a breach of Article 13 as well. The British government later concluded a friendly settlement with the applicants, and enacted the Security Service Act 1989. As a result, the Committee of Ministers decided that no further action was required.[219] This indicates the weakness of a safeguard for privacy which depends on so elastic a notion as national security.

(b) *Preventing or detecting serious crime.* This is within the 'prevention of crime' purpose for which interceptions are permitted under ECHR Article 8(2), as interpreted by the European Court of Human Rights. 'Serious crime' is defined by section 81(2)(b) and (3) of the 2000 Act. A crime is serious for this purpose if, and only if either:

(a) it is an offence for which a first offender aged twenty-one or over could reasonably expect to receive a sentence of at least three years' imprisonment; or

(b) it involves the use of violence, results in substantial financial gain, or is conduct by a large number of people in pursuit of a common purpose.

This is wider than the non-statutory guidelines in operation before the 1985 Act came into force,[220] in that it includes offences resulting in substantial financial gain, facilitating the use of interception against white-collar criminals.

(c) *Safeguarding the economic well-being of the UK.* Like national security, this is a legitimate aim under ECHR Article 8(2), but is not defined in either the Act or the Convention. Since an interception for this purpose is to be considered necessary only if the information which it is considered necessary to acquire relates to the acts or intentions of people outside the British Islands,[221] it is clear that the object is to protect access to markets abroad on which our economy depends, and to prevent the acts of foreign powers or commercial organizations abroad from destabilizing the economy. It is wide enough to cover the activities of foreign dealers in buying and selling strategic shares and currencies in the markets. The damage which such transactions can do to the national economy was demonstrated in the attack on sterling on the international currency exchanges which led to its withdrawal from the European Exchange Rate Mechanism in September 1992. Lord Nolan has noted that the power to obtain a warrant to safeguard the economic well-being of the nation is a protective power. By contrast, the remits of the Security Service, the Secret Intelligence Service and GCHQ extend to acting in the interests of the economic well-being of the UK,

---

[218] *Leander v. Sweden,* Eur. Ct. HR, Series A, No. 116, Judgment of 26 March 1987.

[219] *Harman and Hewitt v. United Kingdom,* Eur. Comm. HR, Application No. 12175/86; Report of 9 May 1989, and Resolution of the Committee of Ministers, 14 EHRR 657.

[220] *Cp. The Interception of Communications in Great Britain,* Cmnd. 7873, para. 4.

[221] Regulation of Investigatory Powers Act 2000, s. 5(5).

allowing them to exercise their general functions to promote it positively as opposed to merely protecting it; but they can only obtain interception warrants for the narrower, protective purpose.[222]

(iii) Procedural and formal matters in relation to interception warrants

A warrant may be issued only on an application by the head of a police force or a person of equivalent seniority in one of the other law enforcement, security, and intelligence organizations which can be authorized to undertake an interception.[223] A warrant must be issued under the hand of the Secretary of State, except in urgent cases where the Secretary of State has expressly authorized its issue, when it may be signed by a senior official of the department. In the latter case, the warrant must be endorsed with a statement that the Secretary of State expressly authorized its issue.[224] Once issued, a normal warrant stays in force for three months, and is renewable for a further period of six months in the case of a warrant issued in the interests of national security or to safeguard economic well-being, or for a further three months in the case of a serious crime warrant. A warrant issued under the hand of an official stays in force for five working days, and is renewable by the Secretary of State for three months. At the end of the first renewal period, the warrant may be renewed for further periods of one month at a time, unless the Secretary of State endorses it with a statement that the renewal is considered necessary for the purposes of national security or for safeguarding the economic well-being of the UK, in which case the renewal takes effect for six months.[225] These periods are longer than those previously permitted under the Interception of Communications Act 1985. During the currency of a warrant, the Secretary of State may modify it at any time,[226] and must cancel it if satisfied that it is no longer necessary for a permitted purpose or, in the case of a warrant in respect of a person outside the UK, that the person is in the UK.[227]

The warrant must be addressed to the person who applied for it.[228] It must name or describe a single person as the subject of the interception, or a single set of premises as those in relation to which the interception is to take place.[229] Unless the Secretary of State issues a certificate in respect of an external interception warrant,[230] a warrant must also contain a schedule which describes the communications subject to interception, specifying the addresses, numbers, apparatus, or other factors or combination of factors to be used for identifying the communications which are to be intercepted. The factors must be likely to include communications from or intended for the person or premises named as the interception subject.[231] This helps to avoid general warrants for interceptions. However, the restrictions do not apply to warrants for the interception of external communications (i.e. those sent or received outside the British Islands) if the Secretary of State signs a certificate at the time of issuing the warrant, certifying the descriptions of intercepted material which he considers it

[222] Lord Nolan, *Annual Report of the Interception of Communications Commissioner 1998*, para. 16.
[223] Regulation of Investigatory Powers Act 2000, s. 6.
[224] Ibid., s. 7.   [225] Ibid., s. 9(6).   [226] Ibid., s. 10.
[227] Ibid., s. 9(3), (4).   [228] Ibid., s. 7(3)(a).   [229] Ibid., s. 8(1).
[230] Ibid., s. 8(4), (5).   [231] Ibid., s. 8(2), (3).

necessary to have examined for one of the purposes permitted under section 5 of the Act.[232]

(iv) Conduct authorized by the warrant

The warrant may authorize or require its addressee to secure, by such conduct as may be described in the warrant, one or more of the following:

- the interception of such communications as are described in the warrant, in the course of their transmission by a postal service or telecommunication system described in the warrant;

- the making of a request to a foreign country under a mutual assistance agreement, for the provision of assistance in the form of an interception;

- the provision of described assistance to a foreign country under a mutual recognition agreement, by way of an interception;

- the disclosure of material intercepted and related communications data in such manner as is described in the warrant.[233]

A warrant also authorizes such other conduct (including the interception of communications not identified by the warrant) as is necessary in order to do what is expressly required or authorized by the warrant, together with anything done to obtain related communications data and conduct by people required by the addressee of the warrant to assist in giving effect to it.[234] When the addressee of the warrant requires others, such as service providers, to assist in conducting the interception, they have a legal obligation to comply, enforceable by the Secretary of State in civil proceedings.[235] The Secretary of State may make orders requiring service providers to maintain a capability to assist with interceptions,[236] and must make a contribution to the cost of interceptions out of public funds.[237]

(v) Authorizing interception of communications data

The Regulation of Investigatory Powers Act 2000 provides a somewhat watered down system for authorizing the obtaining and disclosure of communications data. This category of material consists of traffic data comprised in or attached to a communication, information about a person's use of a postal service or the whole or part of a telecommunication service, and other information held or obtained by a postal or telecommunication service provider.[238] Obtaining and disclosing that material is lawful for all purposes if it is authorized or required by an officer within the police force or other organization concerned, who is designated for the purpose under regulations made by the Secretary of State, and the conduct is in accordance with or in pursuance of the authorization or requirement.[239] People are also immune from civil liability (but not judicial review or any criminal liability) in respect of conduct which is incidental to the authorization and which could not reasonably have been authorized under another statutory provision.[240]

---

[232] Ibid., s. 8(4)–(6).   [233] Ibid., s. 5(1).   [234] Ibid., s. 5(6).
[235] Ibid., s. 11.   [236] Ibid., s. 12.   [237] Ibid., s. 14.
[238] Ibid., s. 21(4).   [239] Ibid., s. 21(2).   [240] Ibid., s. 21(3).

An authorization may be given only if it is necessary for one of a number of purposes, all of which fall within legitimate aims which may justify an interference with privacy under ECHR Article 8(2):

* in the interests of national security;
* for the purpose of preventing or detecting crime (not only serious crime) or preventing disorder;
* in the interests of the economic well-being of the UK (not only to safeguard those interests: this allows for positive action to advance them);
* in the interests of public safety;
* for the purpose of protecting public health;
* for the purpose of assessing or collecting any tax, duty, levy or other imposition, contribution or charge payable to a government department (which probably falls within the 'economic well-being' ground in any case);
* for the purpose, in an emergency, of preventing death or injury or any damage to a person's physical or mental health, or of mitigating any injury or damage to a person's physical or mental health; or
* for any other purpose which is specified for these purposes by order made by the Secretary of State.[241]

Any such authorization will also need to meet a proportionality test,[242] to avoid being unlawful by virtue of ECHR Article 8(2) as given effect in national law by the Human Rights Act 1998, sections 1 and 6. In the same way, although not expressly stated in the 2000 Act, any additional purpose specified by the Secretary of State under his order-making power will be invalid to the extent that it is outside the legitimate aims of an interference with privacy rights under ECHR Article 8(2) and the 1998 Act.

An authorization must be in writing, and must describe the conduct it authorizes and the communications to be obtained, and specify (*inter alia*) the position held by the authorizing officer and the manner in which any required disclosure of the data is to be made.[243] The authorizing officer may issue a notice to a postal or telecommunication operator who, it appears to the officer, is or may be in possession of or capable of obtaining communications data. The notice requires the operator to disclose all data in his possession or subsequently obtained, and if not in possession of the data to obtain it.[244] The authorization and any notice remains in force for one month, except that a notice and is renewable for the same period.[245] The Secretary of State must arrange for appropriate contributions to be made towards the costs of postal and telecommunication operators incurred in complying with obligations imposed on them pursuant to authorizations.[246] Any notice to an operator must be cancelled if the authorizing officer is satisfied that it is no longer necessary for a permitted purpose or is no longer proportionate to what is sought to be achieved by obtaining the

---

[241] Regulation of Investigatory Powers Act 2000, s. 22(1), (2).   [242] Ibid., s. 22(5).   [243] Ibid., s. 23(1), (2).
[244] Ibid., s. 22(4). Such a notice must meet a proportionality test: s. 22(5).
[245] Ibid., s. 23(4)–(7).   [246] Ibid., s. 24.

communications data,[247] so both authorizations and notices must be kept under review during their currency.

A Code of Practice, issued under section 71 of the Act, and given effects by section 72 equivalent to those of the PACE Codes of Practice, deals with the implementation of the powers. However, unlike the Code of Practice on Surveillance, it does not address the delicate problems posed for Article 8 rights by interceptions which violate the Seal of Confession between priest and penitent in the Roman Catholic tradition or legal professional privilege. These are major gaps in the legislative scheme at present.

(vi) Electronic data protected by encryption

Encryption is a method of concealing the content of messages sent electronically (for example by e-mail). Where investigators have obtained encrypted material, the Act permits them to apply to a judge, or in the case of material obtained under a Secretary of State's warrant, to the Secretary of State, for permission to issue a notice directed to a person who is believed on reasonable grounds to be in possession of a key to the encryption, requiring him to put the material into intelligible form. For a notice to be issued, the person with the appropriate permission must believe on reasonable grounds that it is necessary for, and proportionate to the objects sought to be achieved by, ordering the disclosure in the interests of national security, for the purpose of preventing or detecting crime, or in the interests of the economic well-being of the UK.[248] If the person is not in possession of the key, he or she must disclose every key which is in his possession at the time.[249] This is a massive power, and the main safeguard is administrative. Those using it must ensure that arrangements are in force to ensure that the keys are not used to obtain access to information other than that in respect of which a notice could be given, that the necessity and proportionality conditions are fulfilled in relation to all information, that any key or information is stored securely, and that all records of the key are destroyed as soon as they are no longer needed for the purpose of putting the encrypted information into intelligible form.[250] The task of tracking down the person who is likely to have a key is simplified by the Electronic Communications Act 2000, section 1 of which requires providers of cryptography support services to register with the Secretary of State. Complaints about the operation of powers under the Regulation of Investigatory Powers Act 2000 can be made to the Tribunal established under section 65 of the Act.

(vii) Restrictions on the use of material

As the Birkett report noted in 1957, it would be wrong for material obtained in an authorized interception to be disclosed to private people or private bodies. It should be used only for the public purposes for which the interception was authorized.[251] This is also demanded by Article 8(2) of the European Convention on Human Rights,

---

[247] Ibid., s. 23(8).

[248] Ibid., ss. 49 and 50 and Sch. 2. In certain cases where the information is obtained under a statutory power, no further authorization to issue a notice is required: ibid., Sch. 2, para. 4.

[249] Ibid., s. 50(3), (7).

[250] Ibid., s. 55.

[251] *Report of the Committee of Privy Councillors*, Cmnd. 283, para. 152.

as interpreted by the European Court of Human Rights: an interference with respect for correspondence cannot be justified as necessary in a democratic society unless the law gives adequate protection against the disclosure of private communications for an improper purpose by providing for the destruction of recordings and records when they have fulfilled their legitimate purpose.[252] Section 15 of the Regulation of Investigatory Powers Act 2000 caters for this by requiring the Secretary of State to make arrangements in respect of all interception warrants to secure that the material or data are stored in a secure manner,[253] and that the extent of any disclosure of material or data, the number of people to whom material or data are disclosed, the extent to which material or data are copied,[254] and the number of copies made, are limited to the minimum necessary to the purpose for which the warrant is granted.[255] Each copy made must be destroyed as soon as its retention is no longer necessary for that purpose.[256] These requirements do not apply to material or data which have been passed to the authorities of another country pursuant to the warrant.[257] They apply to communications data only if the data are related to intercepted communications.[258]

The 2000 Act continues the policy of the Interception of Communications Act 1985 by keeping intercepted material out of the public domain. An unauthorized disclosure by an officer of any information about or derived from an interception is a criminal offence. To the same end, the 2000 Act allows the yield of interceptions to be used for investigations but not to be adduced as evidence in court.[259] However, the regime is more balanced and easier to apply than the provisions of the 1985 Act which led to the serious difficulties described in section (2) above. Section 17(1) of the 2000 Act sets out the general rule in broad terms:

' . . . no evidence shall be adduced, question asked, assertion or disclosure made or other thing done in, for the purposes of or in connection with any legal proceedings which (in any manner)—

(a) discloses, in circumstances from which its origin in anything falling within subsection (2) may be inferred, any of the contents of an intercepted communication or any related communications data; or

(b) tends (apart from such disclosure) to suggest that anything falling within subsection (2) has or may have occurred or be going to occur.'

The matters falling within subsection (2) are:

• conduct by the addressee of an interception warrant, a person holding office under the Crown, a member of National Criminal Intelligence Service or the

---

[252] *Kruslin v. France*, Eur. Ct. HR, Series A, No. 176-A, at para. 34 of the judgment.

[253] Regulation of Investigatory Powers Act 2000, s. 15(5).

[254] 'Copy' includes any extract from or summary of the material or data which identifies itself as the product of an interception, and any record of the identities of the interception subjects or the people to whom communications data relate which refers to an interception: ibid., s. 15(8).

[255] Ibid., s. 15(1), (2).   [256] Ibid., s. 15(3). For the meaning of 'necessary', see s. 15(4).

[257] Ibid., s. 15(6), (7). For additional safeguards in respect of warrants for the interception of external communications, see s. 16.   [258] Ibid., s. 15(2).

[259] Ibid., s. 19. This applies both to interceptions by unauthorized people, and to unauthorized interceptions by people engaged in running the system who are sometimes authorized to conduct interceptions: Morgans v. DPP [2001] AC 315, HL; *R. v. Sargent* [2001] 3 WLR 992, HL.

National Crime Squad, a person employed by or for the purposes of a police force, or a person providing, or employed for the purposes of any business providing, a postal or public telecommunication service, which constituted or would constitute the offence of unauthorized interception contrary to section 1 of the Act;

- the making of a request to foreign authorities under a mutual assistance agreement, without the Secretary of State's warrant, for them to carry out an interception;

- the issue of an interception warrant;

- the making of an application for an interception warrant; or

- the imposition of any requirement on any person to provide assistance with giving effect to an interception warrant.

However, this comprehensive concealment of all interception-related activity from courts is subject to certain exceptions, contained in section 18. Some are designed to allow statutory procedures to operate. Thus it does not apply to criminal proceedings for an offence contrary to section 1 of the Act, or to civil proceedings to compel an operator to offer assistance in giving effect to a warrant, or to proceedings before the Tribunal to test the legality of an interception warrant or further proceedings so far as they may be possible, or proceedings before, or arising out of proceedings before, the Special Immigration Appeals Commission or the Proscribed Organisations Appeal Commission.[260] Nor does the prohibition apply to anything done in relation to proceedings for unfair dismissal where the grounds for dismissal were conduct which constitutes an offence of unauthorized interception or failure to comply with an obligation to assist in an interception or making an unauthorized disclosure of intercepted material or data.[261] The prohibition does not extend to disclosures relating to interceptions which were lawful by virtue of one of the blanket authorizations in sections 1(5)(c), 3, or 4.[262] Nor does it extend to communications data acquired under section 22 of the Act.

The Act also provides a clear statutory balance between the right of an accused person to a fair trial on a criminal charge, both at common law and under ECHR Article 6(1), and the public interest in keeping interceptions secret. Disclosure can be made to the prosecutor in any criminal proceedings, so that he can decide how to perform his duty, established in relation to intercepted material under the 1985 Act in *R. v. Preston*,[263] of securing the fairness of the prosecution. There is also power for a judge to order disclosure to him alone (but not to any member of the defence team) if satisfied in exceptional circumstances that such disclosure is essential in the interests of justice. After inspecting disclosed material, the judge may direct the prosecutor to make any admission of fact which the judge thinks

---

[260] Ibid., s. 18(1). Information disclosed in proceedings before the two Commissions, or in further proceedings arising therefrom, must not be passed to the applicant or his representatives: s. 18(2).

[261] Ibid., s. 18(3), (6).

[262] Ibid., s. 18(4), (5). On the blanket statutory authorizations, see above, pp. 668–74.

[263] [1994] 2 AC 130, [1993] 4 All ER 638, HL.

essential in the interests of justice, as long as the admission does not contravene the requirements of section 17(1), above.[264] This compromise requires the utmost care and good faith on the part of counsel for the prosecution and investigators to ensure that facts which could assist the defence are made available, and that no assertion is made on the basis of interception material or communications data which could not be adduced as evidence. A person who considers that he has suffered a detriment as a result of the operation of these rules may apply to the Tribunal under section 65 of the Act. The tribunal has power, under section 67(7), to award compensation or make 'any such . . . other order as they think fit', which is wide enough, in theory at least, to permit the tribunal to quash a criminal conviction. The power might, for example, be used in that way if it turns out that there was an unfairness at trial which violated the right to a fair trial under ECHR Article 6(1).

(viii) Remedies

The Regulation of Investigatory Powers Act 2000 introduces a raft of new remedies for people who suffer under the interception of communications regime. A person whose communications are intercepted by a controller or user of a private telecommunication system without lawful authority has an action in private law.[265] This is useful so far as it relates to users of the system, but its value as against controllers of systems is limited by the very extensive authority which the Act gives them to intercept communications on their systems.[266]

The Act revamps the system of public law remedies for unauthorized or improperly authorized interception of communications, acquisition, or disclosure of communications data, or notices requiring production of encryption keys. A Tribunal is established under section 65 of the Act, to serve as the only appropriate forum for litigating complaints in relation to these activities, including complaints of violations of Convention rights in the course of them. The Tribunal exercises a judicial review jurisdiction in relation to alleged violations of Convention rights, has an investigative role in relation to complaints about interceptions of communications, surveillance and related matters, and acts as a normal tribunal in other cases.[267] Its members seem to have sufficient guarantees of independence of the executive[268] to satisfy the requirements of ECHR Article 6(1). There is a one-year time limit for complaints, unless the Tribunal decide that it is equitable to consider a complaint outside that time period.[269] The Tribunal can call on the Interception of Communications Commissioner, the Intelligence Services Commissioner, the Investigatory Powers Commissioner for Northern Ireland, and the Surveillance Commissioners or Assistant Commissioners for assistance, and call for all such documents and information as they require from people holding office under the Crown and others who are involved in the process of

---

[264] Regulation of Investigatory Powers Act 2000, s. 18(7)–(10).
[265] Ibid., s. 1(3).
[266] Ibid., s. 4.
[267] Ibid., s. 67(1), (2), (3).
[268] Ibid., Sch. 3.
[269] Ibid., s. 67(5); Human Rights Act 1998, s. 7(5).

intercepting communications, conducting surveillance, etc.[270] If the Tribunal decide that a complaint has been substantiated, they can make an award of compensation and such other order as they think fit, including quashing or cancelling any warrant or authorization, or ordering the destruction of any records of information obtained under a warrant or authorization or held by any public authority in relation to any person.[271]

Operating alongside the Tribunal is a Commissioner, who must hold or have held high judicial office, and who is responsible for keeping under review:

- the performance of the Secretary of State's functions in relation to interception of communications, and of his duties in relation to information obtained under interception of communications, acquisition of communications data, and investigation of encrypted information provisions of the Act;

- the exercise and performance of powers and duties conferred or imposed on other people by the interception of communications, acquisition of communications data, and investigation of encrypted information provisions of the Act; and

- the adequacy of arrangements to ensure that intercepted material, etc. is securely stored and is not improperly disclosed.[272]

The Commissioner must also assist the Tribunal to carry out its functions.[273] Everyone holding office under the Crown, or working in one of the bodies which can obtain authorization carry out interceptions, etc., or is required to assist in them, must give to the Commissioner any documents or information which he or she may require for the purpose of carrying out his functions.[274] The Commissioner must report to the Prime Minister on any contravention of the Act, may make other reports at any time, and must make an annual report to the Prime Minister. The Annual Report is laid before Parliament, with a note stating if any material has been edited out of the report on the grounds that its inclusion would be prejudicial to national security, the prevention or detection of serious crime, the economic well-being of the UK, or the continued discharge of the functions of a public authority whose activities fall within the Commissioner's purview.[275]

The system of remedies, particularly in relation to the operation of the Tribunal, may prove to be a distinct improvement on very weak remedial provisions previously available. The limited appeal to a court against a decision of a Tribunal in respect of the detrimental effect of denying someone the right to use information about interceptions in civil proceedings is welcome.[276] However, it is less than satisfactory that the ordinary courts are entirely excluded from other aspects of the process, unless the Secretary of State provides by order for an appeal to or review by courts. Nor is there any appeal from a decision of the Tribunal, unless the Secretary of State provides for one, either to the courts or to a specially constituted appeal tribunal, by order.[277] This effectively outflanks the blow struck for the rule of law by the House of Lords in

---

[270] Regulation of Investigatory Powers Act 2000, s. 68(2), (6), (7), (8).
[271] Ibid., s. 67(7).   [272] Ibid., s. 57(2).   [273] Ibid., s. 57(3).
[274] Ibid., s. 58(1).   [275] Ibid., s. 58(2)–(7).   [276] Ibid., s. 67(9).
[277] Ibid., s. 67(8), (10).

Anisminic Ltd. v. Foreign Compensation Commission[278] in holding that, in the absence of the clearest words, a clause ousting the jurisdiction of the courts could not be interpreted as giving an inferior tribunal an uncontrolled discretion to determine the scope of its own jurisdiction. In a case arising before the Interception of Communications Act 1985 came into force, Taylor J held that the courts could review an exercise of the Secretary of State's power to issue warrants, and seek evidence that the exercise was consistent with the published guidelines, since people have a legitimate expectation that their communications will not be officially intercepted save in accordance with those guidelines.[279] The 1985 Act compared unfavourably with the direction which the common law seemed to be taking, and the 2000 Act takes only a small step back in the direction of openness in the process of review of governmental interference with privacy rights.

(5) EVALUATION OF PARTS I AND III OF THE REGULATION OF INVESTIGATORY POWERS ACT 2000

The Act represents a step towards full implementation of the principle of legality—the idea that all official action should be justifiable according to law and subject to an accountability mechanism which is governed by law—and the provision of remedies for breach of privacy in English law. The work of the Tribunal has the capacity to be a significant influence working towards accountability for the secret work of the police and the security service. The Act also marks an important recognition, by Parliament and the government, of the legitimacy of claims under the Human Rights Act 1998 and of the developing caselaw of the European Court of Human Rights under ECHR Article 8. The 2000 Act is certainly a huge step forward in most respects from the position adopted in the Interception of Communications Act 1985. The remedial provisions may need further strengthening in order to meet Article 8 standards, and the safeguards for privacy rights arguably rely too much on administrative safeguards to command confidence. Much will depend on the thoroughness and transparency with which the Tribunal and the Interception of Communications Commissioner set about their tasks under the Act in the coming years, and on the ability of people who think that they may have a claim to bring it.

There are perhaps two particularly important changes now required to further the process of making interception of communications Convention compliant in the UK. First, it should be easier for people to obtain information about interceptions of their communications, and so to test their propriety. The restriction on questions in legal proceedings means that one way of finding out about an interception—the one employed in *Malone*'s case—is blocked. Once a warrant has been issued, there is no provision for the subject of an interception authorization to be informed of the interception after it has taken place. Such a provision, unless in an individual case the

---

[278] [1969] 2 AC 147, [1969] 1 All ER 208, HL.

[279] *R. v. Secretary of State for the Home Department, ex parte Ruddock* [1987] 1 WLR 1482, [1987] 2 All ER 518. The applicants failed, on the evidence, to establish that it would have been improper to issue a warrant. See I. Leigh, 'The Security Service, the Press and the Courts' [1987] *PL* 12–21 at 13–17.

disclosure would threaten national security, would make it realistically possible for people to protect their rights under Article 8. Just such a disclosure principle is found in Germany's G10 law covering national security surveillance, and was approved by the Court in the *Klass* case.[280] In the absence of such a general principle, there is a risk that the Tribunal will be held in Strasbourg not to be an effective remedy for the violation of Convention rights under Article 8, leading to a violation of Article 13.

Secondly, the legislation and the Code of Practice on Interception do not offer adequate—or, indeed, any—systematic protection for sensitive communications which, for the purposes of PACE, would fall into the categories of items subject to legal privilege, excluded material, and special material. Recent decisions of the European Court of Human Rights[281] indicate a requirement for a sliding scale of safeguards for privacy rights under ECHR Article 8: the more intimate or confidential information is, the stronger will be the required safeguards if an interference with privacy is to be regarded as being in accordance with the law and proportionate to a legitimate aim. The safeguards in the 2000 Act need to be adjusted to ensure that they take account of this principle.

11.5 CONCLUSIONS

The conclusions which can be drawn from this chapter's survey of confidentiality and its protection are rather more encouraging than were those in the equivalent chapter of the first edition of this book. There are signs that privacy is being taken more seriously by courts and by Parliament. Although the individual privacy interests which are protected by the doctrine of confidentiality are too easily defeated by public interests (which are often relatively slight) in advancing criminal investigations, the operation of the Human Rights Act 1998, and the express inclusion of necessity and proportionality tests in the Regulation of Investigatory Powers Act 2000 are hopeful signs of a promising development. This may be particularly valuable as a check on a tendency to legislate and adjudicate in the field of criminal procedure in ways which run counter to the values of fairness and respect for individual freedom. The ECHR has had some beneficial impact on English law already, and may have more in the future as the impact of the Human Rights Act 1998 accrues.

At present, however, every new piece of legislation and judicial decision such as those relating to the confiscation of the proceeds of crime, extending the powers of the police and the courts to extract information from people against their wills for the purposes of imposing penalties on them or others, threatens both human rights and values, such as the right of silence, the right to legal advice and assistance, the placing of the burden of proof on the prosecution, and the right not to incriminate oneself, which are usually regarded as appropriate to a civilized legal system. We owe it to

---

[280] *Klass v. Federal Republic of Germany*, Eur. Ct. HR, Series A, No. 28, Judgment of 6 September 1978, 2 EHRR 214.

[281] See, e.g. *Kopp v. Switzerland*, Eur. Ct. HR, Judgment of 25 March 1998, 27 EHRR 91.

ourselves to examine such legislation carefully, in the light of human rights principles, to ensure that we are not restricting confidentiality rights more severely than absolutely necessary, and that the safeguards are adequate. Judges, politicians, and commentators must vigilantly scrutinize all proposals for new or extended powers, for example those to combat money laundering or drug trafficking, confiscate proceeds of crime, or facilitate the dissemination of personal information between investigative bodies. We can too easily become desensitized to the serious civil liberties implications of such creeping extensions of state power. If we do, we may wake one day to find that, by a series of small steps, each of which seemed justifiable at the time, we have fundamentally undermined the ethos of our legal system, and produced one in which legal protections for the individual are insignificant, and the legal power of the investigative arms of the state is overwhelming. It will be interesting to see whether the Human Rights Act 1998 can contribute to arresting this trend.

12

SEX, SEXUAL ACTIVITY, AND FAMILY LIFE

This chapter deals with a range of privacy interests which are particularly closely related to people's freedom to organize the most intimate details of their lives according to their own preferences. The first matter to be considered is the allocation of individuals to a particular sex, particularly important when a person's legal status, rights, and obligations are affected (section 12.1). Secondly, the chapter addresses people's sexual orientations, and their freedom (or lack of it) to give expression to their sexual predilections privately or publicly (section 12.2). The third topic relates to family life, particularly as it affects rights in respect of children (section 12.3). The interests considered in this chapter are related to each another. At one level, they advance people's freedom to choose a lifestyle and to give effect to it, so long as it does not interfere unduly with the rights of others. This seems to demand relatively limited state intervention, setting the boundaries between competing claims to freedom, and policing them, but not otherwise intervening in the conduct of citizens. But people's freedom is constrained by their physical attributes and by the social and legal norms which are built on those attributes. It is the duty of the state to ensure that the legal norms are fair. It must both avoid discriminating against people, and protect people against discrimination, on the basis of factors over which they have no control, as discussed in Chapter 3 above. The right to protection against discrimination justifies relatively extensive state intervention, although the state will still not be making choices for people, or taking responsibility for their choices.

The role of the state, and the level of interference with individual choice which is justifiable, is more extensive when protecting children within families. Children's interests need special protection, because children are not often parties to the decision to found a family, which will usually have been taken by adults before the birth or adoption of the child (although children of one union may sometimes have a say in the formation of subsequent unions by their parents). Once born or adopted into the family, children will normally be unable, for a considerable time, to protect their own interests against those of parents or guardians. In this period, the state may take responsibility for monitoring and, if necessary, assuming the care of the children. Nevertheless, in a society which is built on the notion that the family is (in the words of Article 10(1) of the International Covenant on Economic, Social and Cultural Rights) 'the natural and fundamental group unit of society',[1] to be accorded '[t]he

---

[1] The European Social Charter (1961), Art. 16, describes the family as 'a fundamental unit of society'.

widest possible protection and assistance . . . particularly for its establishment and while it is responsible for the care and education of dependent children', some room must be left to parents to implement their opinions about the best way of bringing up children. Principles must be developed to control the way in which the state intervenes in family life, to try to ensure, as far as possible, that the parents' freedoms and ways of life are not unnecessarily prejudiced by the state's imposition of its notions of proper child rearing practice. As Lord Mackay of Clashfern said when he was Lord Chancellor, 'The threat to the poor and to minority groups, whose views of what is good for a child may not coincide closely with that of the majority, is all too apparent'.[2]

Each of the interests on which this chapter touches therefore makes substantial demands on society to adjust its legal system so as to recognize different forms of relationship and to protect those who embark on them. English law has only recently begun to grapple with these problems, and its approach is shaped by principles developed by the European Court of Human Rights under the European Convention on Human Rights (ECHR), which now forms part of national law. Under the Human Rights Act 1998, section 3, all legislation must be read and given effect, so far as possible, in a manner compatible with the Convention rights incorporated into national law by section 1 and interpreted taking account of the Strasbourg jurisprudence as required by section 2. A public authority which acts incompatibly with a Convention right acts unlawfully, by virtue of section 6, unless primary legislation, interpreted in accordance with section 3, compels the incompatible act. For the purposes of this chapter, the main relevant provisions of the ECHR are:

- Article 3, providing that no one is to be subjected to inhuman or degrading treatment (on which see Chapter 5 above);

- Article 8, guaranteeing respect for private and family life, subject to such limitations as are in accordance with the law and necessary in a democratic society for one of a number of purposes, including the protection of health and morals (on which see generally Chapter 9 above);

- Article 12, which guarantees the right of men and women of marriageable age to marry and found a family, according to the national laws governing the exercise of this right (considered further below); and

- Article 14, which requires the states to secure the enjoyment of these and the other rights and freedoms guaranteed in the Convention without discrimination on grounds such as sex, birth, or other status, including (as interpreted by the Court) sexuality (see further Chapter 3 above).

In addition, the United Nations Convention on the Rights of the Child, which was concluded in 1989, includes a number of provisions which require States Parties to the Convention to protect families as a whole. The Preamble declares that the States Parties are 'convinced that the family, as the fundamental group of society and the

---

[2] Lord Mackay, 'Perceptions of the Children Bill and Beyond' (1989) 139 *NLJ* 505–8 at 508, quoted in S. M. Cretney, *Elements of Family Law*, 2nd ed. (London: Sweet & Maxwell, 1992), 301.

natural environment for the growth and welfare of all its members and particularly children, should be afforded the necessary protection and assistance so that it can fully assume its responsibilities within the community'. Accordingly, the Convention imposes certain duties on States Parties in respect of children, including a duty to treat their interests as a primary consideration in all actions concerning them (Article 3), and the duty to undertake measures to implement children's economic, social, and cultural rights to the maximum extent of their available resources (Article 4). The UK is a State Party, having acceded to the Convention in 1991.

12.1 A RIGHT TO A SEXUAL IDENTITY

Sex is one of any person's most significant characteristics. A considerable body of theory has developed exploring the unfortunate consequences of this. In particular, it has been convincingly argued that the distinction between men and women has formed the basis for discriminatory social structures in nearly all societies, in which '[f]or the most part men occupied the "public" sphere of political and commercial activity, women occupied the "private" sphere of domestic life, and the law respected those boundaries'.[3] However regrettable it may be, a person's sex has both legal and social consequences.[4] Socially, sex is one of the factors which defines one's self-image and the expectations of others. It also affects one's legal status and capacity to enter into legal relationships with others (although its legal significance has diminished where statute has eroded the common law disabilities affecting women, and particularly married women).[5] For example, possibilities for marriage, with its attendant privileges and responsibilities, are limited by the requirement that the parties must be of different sexes. Criminal liability may attach to homosexual acts which do not attach to similar acts between people of different sexes. Since the ability to enter into close, legally protected personal relationships, and the freedom to express one's sexual desires, are important and (within certain limits) legitimate aspects of personal autonomy, the assignment of a sex is fundamental to legal personality.

However, sex is not clear-cut, and may conflict with gender (the psychological and social experience of being considered a man or woman). People's biological sex may be uncertain or ambiguous. Where an individual's body is partially or totally unable to respond to the signals which normally stimulate the development of the physical characteristics of one sex rather than the other, the body's physical characteristics can be insufficiently differentiated to allow a sex to be clearly attributed to the individual. Sometimes neither male nor female physical features are fully developed, or occasionally an individual combines the gonads of both sexes. The social importance of being either male or female is such that, in such cases, an early decision will usually be made

---

[3] D. L. Rhode, *Justice and Gender: Sex Discrimination and the Law* (Cambridge, Mass.: Harvard University Press, 1989), 9.

[4] K. O'Donovan, *Sexual Divisions in Law* (London: Weidenfeld and Nicolson, 1985), ch. 3.

[5] E.g. Married Women's Property Act 1882.

by doctors and parents to bring up the child as either a boy or a girl, with appropriate surgical adjustment of the child's physical attributes.[6]

More commonly, an individual may feel like a woman but appear to display the physical characteristics of a man (or vice versa). Such a person suffers a disjunction between self-image and the expectations of others. This condition, known medically as gender identity dysphoria, will always be profoundly uncomfortable and can lead to serious psychological disturbances. Growing understanding on the part of the medical professions has led to increased availability of therapy. Drugs and surgical procedures can bring a person's physiognomy more closely into line with his or her psychology, and counselling can help people to cope with the social, psychological, and sexual difficulties which such treatments (or a decision not to undergo them) may engender. Nevertheless, medical reassignment of sex can lead to legal difficulties.

(1) THE GENERAL APPROACH IN ENGLISH LAW

In view of the personal, legal, and social implications of this type of treatment, which will include surgical removal of external genitalia and may also include reconstructive surgery (for example, in the case of male-to-female transsexuals, surgically fashioning an artificial vagina), one might expect it to be legally regulated. In some countries, laws set an age below which consent to such treatment may not lawfully be given, or limit the circumstances in which the treatment may lawfully be carried out.[7] English law, by contrast, does not regulate the treatment differently from any other medical treatment. There is no such special regime as there is in respect of reproductive medicine under the Human Fertilisation and Emryology Act 1990. As in the context of other types of medical treatment, legal rules safeguard people against having therapy imposed on them without their consent. Although there is a category of harm, or physical invasion of one's body, to which people are incapable of consenting as a matter of law and which would constitute the crime of maim at common law, it seems to be accepted that one can lawfully make a decision to accept castration and related surgery, with proper medical safeguards, if responsible medical opinion would regard it as appropriate therapy for gender identity dysphoria.[8] To put it at its lowest, it should be no less possible to consent to such surgery than to consent to extensive cosmetic surgery.

The fact that treatment is not against the law does not mean, of course, that it is necessarily readily available to all who want or need it. Like other treatments offered by the National Health Service, the needs of those who seek it must compete with the needs of people seeking other treatments in the battle for resources, and must pass through the filter of medical ethics which denies this radical treatment to those for whom it is not regarded as medically necessary. In the UK, a very small proportion—

---

[6] In *W. v. W. (Physical Inter-sex)* [2001] 2 WLR 674, Charles J explains this in the light of an expert medical opinion.

[7] According to A. Cremona-Barbaro, 'Medicolegal Aspects of Transsexualism in Western Europe' (1986) 5 *Med. Law* 89, cited by J. K. Mason and R. A. McCall Smith, *Law and Medical Ethics*, 3rd edn. (London: Butterworths, 1991), 41, the minimum age is eighteen in Sweden and twenty-five in Germany.

[8] *Corbett v. Corbett* [1971] P. 83, [1970] 2 All ER 33.

said to be around one per cent—of those who seek treatment are regarded as suitable to receive it.[9] Like other rights related to health care, the right to sex reassignment therapy is thus an example of a qualified legal liberty, or limited freedom from interference with a decision to undergo it, rather than a right to have it giving rise to a claim against the state or medical practitioners. The practical worth of the liberty allowed by law is restricted by fiscal, moral, and professional controls. Health authorities have no positive duty, at common law or under ECHR Article 3 or 8, to make available particular treatments for particular diseases, even if they are life-threatening: medical judgment has a role in deciding how best to use public resources to benefit individuals.[10]

However, health authorities have some obligations in respect of people who suffer from gender identity dysphoria. Their needs in respect of this clinically recognized, treatable medical condition must be balanced against those of others who call on the National Health Service for assistance. It is permissible to give a relatively low priority to the treatment of gender identity dysphoria in comparison with other conditions, but (on ordinary principles of administrative law) it is unlawful to apply the general rule without regard to medical judgment about the needs of particular patients. Gender identity dysphoria has a devastating effect on some people, causing severe psychiatric illness and sometimes leading to suicide attempts. A health authority's resource allocation decisions must take account of these factors in individual cases, in the light of evidence about the severity of a person's suffering and the effectiveness of different forms of treatment.[11] It is also possible that a representation that treatment would be provided might give rise to a legally enforceable expectation.[12]

Although English law does not impose any special impediments to obtaining gender reassignment therapy, neither has it so far been prepared to recognize therapy as changing a patient's legal status. A person who was registered as male at birth is not permitted to have that allocation of sex altered after treatment to replace the physical stigmata of manhood with those of womanhood, and vice versa. This can interfere with the right to marry. Marriage in English common law was defined as the union of one woman and one man, for life, to the exclusion of all others. Although the provision for divorce by statute, and recognition of certain polygamous marriages celebrated abroad, has watered down the absolute nature of this commitment, the law still assumes that people are capable of having only one sex, which they retain throughout life, and which is identified exclusively by reference to the biological characteristics of genitalia, chromosomes, and hormones, at the time of birth. There is a duty to register a birth within forty-two days, and the child's sex must be declared.[13] Thereafter, there is no power to have the register of births altered to reflect the result of sex reassignment therapy, save in the case of a genuine mistake in the original registration. Nor is there any means of authorizing the issue of a sex reassignment certificate, recognizing

---

[9] Mason and McCall Smith, *Law and Medical Ethics*, 41.

[10] *R. v. Cambridge Health Authority, ex parte B.* [1995] 1 WLR 898, [1995] 2 All ER 129, CA; *R. v. North West Lancashire Health Authority, ex parte A.* [2000] 1 WLR 977, CA.

[11] *R. v. North West Lancashire Health Authority, ex parte A* [2001] 1 WLR 977, CA.

[12] *Cp. R. v. North and East Devon Health Authority, ex parte Coughlan* [2000] 2 WLR 622, CA.

[13] Births and Deaths Registration Act 1953, s. 2; SI 1968, No. 2049, reg. 16.

the changed position following therapy, as there is in South Australia.[14] As a result, a small group of people who are psychologically of one sex, and have had the genitalia of the opposite sex surgically removed, are condemned to go through life officially recorded as having been born with the opposite sex. This can be ameliorated to some extent by administrative measures. A passport and driving licence can be issued showing the new gender and name, and state agencies discourage the use of a birth certificate for the purposes of identification. However, personal details cannot be altered for the purposes of national insurance, social security, or pensions.

The once and for all assessment of sex on the register of births reflects the position at common law. In *Corbett v. Corbett*,[15] a biological man had undergone sex reassignment therapy, including surgery, to become a woman, April Ashley. She had gone through a marriage ceremony in Gibraltar with a man, who subsequently petitioned in England for nullity. After an extensive review of the authorities and medical opinions, Ormrod J held that under English law it is of the essence of a marriage that it should be between a person of the male sex and one of the female sex. He distinguished between sex, which he regarded as determined by physical characteristics, and gender, the psychological and social attributes relating to a person's sex. Surgery might change external genitalia, but could not alter a person's chromosomal structure. A man remained a man, and a woman a woman, regardless of surgery, from their births to their deaths. He was prepared to accept that Miss Ashley might have been female by gender, but, testing sex by reference to genital, chromosomal, and gonadal features at birth, he held that she remained of the male sex. Sex, rather than gender, was held to be essential to capacity to marry because marriage is the basis for the family, and a capacity for heterosexual intercourse is essential to marriage. Adopting the physical sex at birth as a determinant of capacity to marry, the judge held that the 'marriage' had been between two men, and was void.

The law as to nullity of marriage is now laid down by statute. Section 11 of the Matrimonial Causes Act 1973 provides that a marriage is void if the parties to it are not respectively 'male and female'. In *S.-T. (formerly J.) v. J.*[16] in the Court of Appeal Sir Brian Neill said, *obiter*, 'the words used in section 11 of the 1973 Act are "male and female" which, I suppose it might be argued, indicate a test of gender rather than sex'.[17] However, no English court has accepted that argument as a basis for distinguishing *Corbett v. Corbett* as a pre-Act decision. In *Franklin v. Franklin (otherwise Jones)*,[18] Ian Franklin went through a ceremony of marriage in England with someone who had been registered as a male (Robert Duxbury) at birth, but had later undergone gender reassignment therapy and taken the name Harley Jones. On an unopposed application for a declaration of nullity, Judge Dobry QC decided that Harley Jones remained biologically male despite reassignment surgery, and that the

---

[14] Sexual Reassignment Act 1988 (South Australia), s. 7(8)(b).

[15] [1971] P. 83, [1970] 2 All ER 33.

[16] [1998] Fam. 103, [1998] 1 All ER 431, CA.

[17] [1998] 1 All ER at 476.

[18] News reports are carried in the *Daily Telegraph*, 9 November 1990, 3, and the *Guardian*, 9 November 1990, 8. See generally S. M. Cretney, *Elements of Family Law*, 2nd edn. (London: Sweet & Maxwell, 1992), 15–16.

marriage was void, having been solemnized between two males. In *S.-T. (formerly J.) v. J.*,[19] Ward LJ, *obiter*, reviewed the reception in other common law jurisdictions of the physical test for sex laid down in *Corbett v. Corbett*.[20] Broadly, a post-operative transsexual may have the capacity to marry according to his or her reassigned gender in some states of the USA, in Australia, and in New Zealand: as long as by the surgery 'the anatomical or genital features of a genuine transsexual are made to conform to the person's gender, psyche or psychological sex, then identity by sex must be governed by the conference of those standards'.[21] In *S.-T.*, both Ward LJ and Potter LJ accepted that the *Corbett* test might need to be reconsidered in the light of growing scientific understanding of transsexualism, although they thought that it would be inappropriate to allow a person born as a woman to marry as a man without external male genitalia, whether produced by surgery or otherwise.[22] However, in *Bellinger v. Bellinger*[23] Johnson J followed *Corbett*, accepting that the issues needed to be comprehensively addressed but taking the view that it was for Parliament, rather than the courts, to make any changes which might be thought desirable.

This is unfortunate. The decisions treat the physical distinction between men and women as absolute, whereas in fact individuals are now scientifically regarded as lying on a continuum, with female physical characteristics at one extreme and male ones at the other. The law is thus out of touch with scientific understandings. Furthermore, it is hard to sustain the logic of Ormrod J's reasoning in *Corbett*. A marriage which does not produce children is not void, or even voidable, on that account, so the function of founding a family, while it might form a social justification for the institution of marriage, does not form the basis for the legitimacy of any individual marriage. Non-consummation makes a marriage voidable but not void, so inability to perform heterosexual intercourse should not in principle make it impossible for two people to contract a valid marriage. The essential basis for the relationship, it might be thought, is love and support, rather than intercourse or child-rearing. To speak as if sexual intercourse is 'the essential role of a woman in marriage'[24] seems to relegate the matrimonial home to a form of legitimized brothel.

This leaves English law in an incoherent state. A male-to-female transsexual can marry a female-to-male transsexual in England, but the apparently male party will be treated by law as the bride and the female party as the groom. A male-to-female transsexual can marry a woman, and a female-to-male transsexual can marry a man. English law will recognize the marriage of a male-to-female transsexual and a man, or a female-to-male transsexual and a woman, as long as the marriage is formally valid according to the *lex loci celebrationis* and at the time of the ceremony both parties are

---

[19] [1998] Fam. 103, [1998] 1 All ER 431, CA.

[20] [1998] 1 All ER at 445–7.

[21] [1998] 1 All ER at 446, discussing *M.T. v. J.T.* (1976) 355 A 2d 204, Superior Ct. of NJ, App. Div. Ward LJ also considered *M. v. M.* [1991] NZFLR 337, NZ Fam. Ct., and *M. v. M.*, unreported, 30 May 1991, Ellis J in NZ SC.

[22] [1998] 1 All ER at 447 *per* Ward LJ, 470 *per* Potter LJ.

[23] *The Times*, 22 November 2000.

[24] *Corbett v. Corbett* [1971] P. 83 at 106 *per* Ormrod J. See O'Donovan, *Sexual Divisions in Law*, 65–7.

domiciled[25] in countries under whose laws they have capacity to contract that marriage (since capacity to marry is governed by the law of the parties' domiciles). Thus a male-to-female transsexual domiciled in the Netherlands and a man domiciled in the Netherlands could marry in Amsterdam; the marriage would be valid under Dutch law and would be recognized under English law, even if both parties were British nationals. It is at least arguable that a legal system which treats its own domiciliaries less favourably (in respect of recognition of marriage) than people domiciled elsewhere is improperly discriminating against them in the enjoyment of their right to marry, contrary to ECHR Article 14 taken together with Article 12. Even if it is not unlawfully discriminatory, the law in this area is an unprincipled mess and needs to be reconsidered.

(2) THE EFFECT OF THE ECHR AND THE HUMAN RIGHTS ACT 1998 ON ENGLISH LAW

Neither the ECHR itself nor the incorporation of ECHR Articles 3, 8, and 12 in national law by the Human Rights Act 1998 is likely to have a direct or immediate impact on the legal recognition of a transsexual's reassigned gender. Since one's sex is a significant feature of one's private life, it might have been expected that a state's refusal to recognize a change of sex constitutes a failure of the respect for private life guaranteed under Article 8 of the Convention. As it also makes it hard for transsexuals to marry, one might have thought that such a refusal would violate a person's right to marry under Article 12. It might even demean the person concerned in his or her own eyes and in the eyes of other members of society sufficiently to constitute degrading treatment contrary to Article 3. However, the caselaw does not support these expectations, although the European Court of Human Rights appears to be edging towards accepting that states have a duty to recognize reassigned gender for at least some purposes.

The Commission, before its abolition, was more activist than the Court. In an early decision, the Commission held admissible a petition alleging that a West German administrative decision to refuse to rectify the petitioner's birth certificate after sex reassignment therapy gave rise indirectly to a breach of Article 5(1) (liberty and security of the person) and Article 6(1) (right to a fair and public hearing by an independent and impartial tribunal established by law to determine civil rights and obligations). Following this, the government reached a friendly settlement in which it agreed to rectify the birth certificate.[26] This appears to be the only case in which those Articles have been invoked by a transsexual petitioner. In another decision, this time concerning the refusal of Belgian law to reassign a person's status on their change of sex, the Commission held that Article 8 and Article 12 had been breached, and Belgian law was amended in consequence.[27] The case was referred to the Court, which how-

---

[25] 'Domicile' for this purpose has a technical meaning in private international law: a person acquires a new domicile if he or she takes up residence in a new country with the intention of residing there indefinitely.

[26] *X. v. Federal Republic of Germany*, Application No. 6699/74, Report of 11 October 1979, 17 CD 21.

[27] *Van Oosterwijck v. Belgium*, Application No. 7654/76, Report of 1 March 1979 upholding the complaint on the merits.

ever did not examine the merits, holding instead that, contrary to the Commission's initial decision, the petitioner had not exhausted domestic remedies, so the complaint had been inadmissible.[28]

The Court has been more cautious than the Commission, particularly in relation to the right to marry and found a family.

(i) The right to marry and found a family (ECHR Article 12)

Decisions about transsexuals' rights to marry takes place against the background of the Court's very restrictive approach to Article 12 generally. Article 12 gives the right to marry only 'according to the national laws governing the exercise of this right'. This imposes on states a positive obligation to provide by law for marriage, and to regulate its inception and its incidents, but leaves a wide discretion to the state as to the kind of law which it puts in place to govern marriage, as long as the law does not deny people the very essence of the right.

Thus a state is free to make rules preventing marriage on the basis of the current marital status of the parties, and to make its own decision about whether or not to make available a procedure to dissolve a marriage. The right to marry does not imply a right to escape from marriage. In *Johnston v. Ireland*,[29] a man whose marriage had broken down wanted to remarry, but was prevented from doing so by the constitutional prohibition on divorce and on the recognition of foreign divorces which Article 41.3.2 of the Irish Constitution then contained. (It was amended in 1995 following a referendum.) Mr. Johnston argued that he was denied the right to marry and found a family. The Court, following the Commission, held that the *travaux préparatoires* showed that the right to a divorce had been deliberately omitted from both Article 12 and Article 5 of Protocol No. 7. It would therefore have been improper for the Court to employ a dynamic interpretation to provide for such a right. A state can therefore limit potential husbands or wives to one bite of the cherry. On the other hand, where a divorce has been granted the state is not permitted to impose on one of the parties a period of time during which he or she is not permitted to remarry. That would threaten the substance of the right to marry in countries where the state, by allowing a dissolution, has demonstrated that it does not intend to limit the parties to marriage on one occasion only. This was established in *F. v. Switzerland*,[30] in which the Court was impressed by the importance of preventing so far as possible the disadvantages to children of being born out of wedlock. The state may also regulate the rights and obligations of the parties to marriage, both during it and on any dissolution, so long as the provisions are not discriminatory; the circumstances in which a dissolution or annulment may be granted (as long as a non-consensual marriage is always treated as null); and the obligations of the parties after the divorce or annulment, providing always that the rights of any children under Article 8 are taken properly into account and that the interests of any children are paramount.

In relation to transsexuals, the Court (unlike the Commission) has for most

---

[28] *Van Oosterwijck v. Belgium*, Eur. Ct. HR, Series A, No. 40, Judgment of 6 November 1980, 3 EHRR 557.
[29] Eur. Ct. HR, Series A, No. 112, Judgment of 18 December 1986, 9 EHRR 203.
[30] Eur. Ct. HR, Series A, No. 128, Judgment of 18 December 1987, 10 EHRR 411.

practical purposes consistently denied to transsexuals the right to marry. In *Rees v. United Kingdom*,[31] a female-to-male transsexual complained of alleged breaches by the UK of Articles 8 and 12. As regards the right to marry, the Court in *Rees* unanimously rejected the complaint. It noted that Article 12 protects the right to marry 'according to the national laws governing the exercise of this right'. The exercise of the right is therefore subject to national law. A state is free to prefer a traditional view of marriage, as a relationship between people of opposite sex, to a more flexible view, and to embody that preference in its national law governing marriage. While any restriction must not deny to anyone the very essence of the right, the law in the UK did not do so.[32] The Court did not explain this, but it can only refer to the fact that a male-to-female transsexual remains free to marry a woman.

The Court reaffirmed this view in two later cases. In *Cossey v. United Kingdom*,[33] the petitioner was a male-to-female transsexual who had changed her name to Caroline in 1972, and had dressed as a woman and adopted a female role since then. She had undergone hormone therapy and breast augmentation implant surgery between 1972 and 1974, and had then undergone gender reassignment surgery. She enjoyed a full life as a woman, psychologically and physically, and was capable of sexual intercourse with a man. She held a passport as a woman, and worked as a successful fashion model. In 1983 she wished to marry a Mr. L, but was told by the Registrar General that such a marriage would be void in English law because she would be classified as a man. The Registrar General also stated that she could not be given a birth certificate showing her sex as female, because the birth certificate merely records details as at the date of birth. Miss Cossey lodged an application to the European Commission of Human Rights, alleging breaches of Articles 8 and 12. Her engagement was broken off. A subsequent marriage to a Mr. X was later declared to be void by the High Court. The Commission decided by ten votes to six, following the *Rees* case, that there had been no violation of Article 8, but found a violation of Article 12 by the same margin.[34] The UK government referred the case to the Court. All the judges accepted that the case was indistinguishable from *Rees*. By fourteen votes to four the Court held that there was no breach of Article 12, reaffirming the decision in *Rees*. The majority observed that Miss Cossey's inability to marry a woman was not the result of any legal impediment, and argued that Article 12, speaking of men and women having the right to marry, gives support to the traditional view of marriage as a union of two people biologically of different sexes. The number of Contracting States which treated marriage between a male/female transsexual and a man as valid was insufficient to suggest that there had been a general abandonment of the traditional concept of marriage. Attachment to that concept was held to provide sufficient reason for allowing national law to maintain exclusively biological criteria for determining sex for the purpose of capacity to marry.[35]

---

[31] Eur. Ct. HR, Series A, No. 106, Judgment of 17 October 1986, 9 EHRR 56.
[32] *Rees* at paras. 49 and 50 of the judgment.
[33] Eur. Ct. HR, Series A, No. 184, Judgment of 27 September 1990, 13 EHRR 622.
[34] *Cossey v. United Kingdom*, Application No. 10843/84, Eur. Commn. HR, Report of 9 May 1989.
[35] Judgment at paras. 45–6.

A similar decision was reached subsequently in *Sheffield and Horsham v. United Kingdom*[36] by eighteen votes to two. Miss Kristina Sheffield, born as a male and always resident in the UK, had undergone gender reassignment after a marriage (subsequently dissolved) during which she had fathered a daughter. Miss Rachel Horsham had been born a male in the UK, but had lived in the Netherlands since 1974 and had obtained Dutch citizenship in 1993. She underwent gender reassignment surgery in Amsterdam in 1992. She obtained a court order under which the Dutch Registrar of Births issued her with a birth certificate showing her to be female. The British Consulate issued her with a passport showing her new name and sex, but the British authorities refused to amend her British birth certificate. She wanted to marry a man, but could not do so in the UK. In its judgment, the Court said that it:

'recalls that the right to marry . . . refers to the traditional marriage between persons of opposite biological sex . . . [T]he wording . . . makes it clear that Article 12 is mainly concerned to protect marriage as the basis of the family. Furthermore, Article 12 lays down that the exercise of this right shall be subject to the national laws of the Contracting States. The limitations thereby introduced must not restrict or reduce the right in such a way or to such an extent that the very essence of the right is impaired. However, the legal impediment in the UK . . . cannot be said to have an effect of this kind (see the . . . *Rees* judgment . . .).'

This is, with respect, a weak argument. It cannot mean that there no limits to a state's freedom to make national law concerning the capacity to marry, as that would make Article 12 entirely vacuous. The Court could only have thought that the legal impediment to marriage did not impair the very essence of the right of transsexuals to marry on the basis that they remain free to marry as long as they marry someone of the opposite sex to their own original sex. This is odd. A female-to-male transsexual, who regards himself as a man, would normally want to marry a woman, but is regarded by the law as a woman, and so is unable to marry any person whom he might realistically want to marry (unless she happens to be a male-to-female transsexual). For practical purposes, the Court's approach makes the right to marry illusory for transsexuals, depriving them of its very essence, in a manner inconsistent with the ethos which (as noted in Chapter 2 above) is said to inform the Court's interpretation of the Convention as a whole.[37]

Furthermore, to say that the state is free to prefer a traditional view of marriage as a union of people of opposite sexes fails to justify excluding from the rights and obligations of marriage those people whose psychological and social gender develops differently from their biological sex as understood at birth. It may once have been correct to say that Article 12 protects marriage because it is the basis of the family, but family arrangements are far more varied now than they were fifty years ago. Many marriages are childless by choice, many children are born out of wedlock, and the stigma which used to attach to such children has been eroded (in part because of decisions of the Court under ECHR Article 8). Marriage is only one of the bases of the family, and founding a family is only one of the possible reasons for getting married. The Court

---

[36] Eur. Ct. HR, Judgment of 30 July 1998, 27 EHRR 163.

[37] This point is made in the dissenting opinion of Judge van Dijk, with whom Judge Wildhaber agreed, in *Sheffield and Horsham v. United Kingdom*, above.

underestimated the objects of marriage in the same way as Ormrod J in *Corbett v. Corbett*.

The Court also assumed (unlike Ormrod J) that sex is always unambiguous. Biological sex, at birth and later, is sometimes not easy to establish by reference to the appearance of genitalia. Doctors in such circumstances assign to a baby the sex which they think he or she is most likely to be able to support socially in later life. Chromosomal sex is not evident to the child/adult or to social contacts at any time, and medical and scientific developments in the field have been so rapid that the medical view of a person's sex may change within a small part of the person's lifetime.[38] For example, it seems that the practice in western countries in the 1940s with regard to physical inter-sex babies was to be guided by the choice of the parents, while today 'in cases of real difficulty and uncertainty there is probably a bias towards assigning an inter-sex child to the female gender and lifestyle with appropriate surgical intervention'.[39] It is hard to see why the state should be free to place such reliance on a doctor's decision, made without foreknowledge of the later development of the child or science, in making law to govern capacity to marry. Indeed, in relation to physical inter-sex people it has been held that the best approach for legal purposes is to assess the person's sex (for the purpose of capacity to marry) in the light of the person's entire physical and psychological history up to the time of the intended marriage.[40]

None the less, the decision in *Sheffield and Horsham v. United Kingdom*, flawed as it is, shows that ECHR Article 12 has little potential for helping to resolve the deficiencies of English law relating to transsexuals, unless the English courts take a view of the right to marry under Article 12 considerably closer to that of the old European Commission of Human Rights than to that of the Strasbourg Court.

(ii) The right to respect for private life (ECHR Article 8)

In a number of cases involving the UK, the European Court of Human Rights has held (albeit by an ever-narrowing majority) that the right to respect for private life does not yet require the state to recognize a transsexual's reassigned gender for legal purposes, either by way of issuing a new birth certificate or by allowing the person to be recorded as the mother (or, as the case may be, father) of a child born to the person's partner or adopted by them.[41] In *Rees v. United Kingdom*,[42] *Cossey v. United Kingdom*,[43] *X. Y. and Z. v. United Kingdom*[44] and *Sheffield and Horsham v. United Kingdom*,[45] the Court noted that Article 8's guarantee of respect for private life is not always clear cut. While the notion of respect sometimes carries with it a duty on the

---

[38] Mason and McCall Smith, *Law and Medical Ethics*, 3rd edn., 42–3.

[39] *W. v. W. (Physical Inter-sex)* [2001] 2 WLR at 683 *per* Charles J, referring to the expert evidence of a consultant endocrinologist, Dr. Conway.

[40] *W. v. W. (Physical Inter-sex)* [2001] 2 WLR 674.

[41] On the latter point, see further section 12(3) below on family life.

[42] Eur. Ct. HR, Series A, No. 106, Judgment of 17 October 1986, 9 EHRR 56, at para. 37.

[43] Eur. Ct. HR, Series A, No. 184, Judgment of 27 September 1990, 13 EHRR 622, at paras. 37–8.

[44] Eur. Ct. HR, Judgment of 22 April 1997, RJD 1997-II, 24 EHRR 143, at para. 41.

[45] Eur. Ct. HR, Judgment of 30 July 1998, 27 EHRR 163, at paras. 51–2.

state to take positive action to advance the right, deciding what positive steps are demanded by the respect which is properly due involves balancing the general interests of the community against the interests of the individual concerned. In striking that balance, the state necessarily enjoys a margin of appreciation. The Court held that the diversity of practices between states in relation to recognition of sexual reassignment showed that there was no settled view amongst the parties to the Convention as to the appropriate response. In such a case the state had a substantial 'margin of appreciation' (although some judges have increasingly criticized the use of this concept[46]). To decide whether the state has overstepped its discretion, one must assess whether the actions of the state interfere with a transsexual's private life more than is justified by any countervailing general public interest.

The Court has not regarded the inability to secure rectification of the register of births as a serious matter in itself. The register was considered to record only historical information (the view taken at the time of birth), and in the absence of special provision for secrecy (such as operates in respect of adoption and legitimation) any change would be visible in the register and might be a cause of continuing embarrassment.[47] Although biological sex is determinative for the purposes of marriage, pensions,[48] and some (but not all) employment law matters,[49] for most legal purposes sex makes no difference in English law. People are free to use any name of their choice, and are not required to carry an identity card or any other document displaying their given names or sex. Passports and driving licences can be issued in a person's new names, although there is an administrative discretion as to the prefix or title (if any) which is included. A male-to-female transsexual has been treated as a woman by agreement with the authorities for National Insurance purposes. Because of this, the majority of the Court has not generally regarded refusal of official recognition of the change of sex as interfering sufficiently with transsexuals' private lives to amount to a failure of the respect due under Article 8. Kristina Sheffield, one of the applicants in *Sheffield and Horsham v. United Kingdom*, pointed out that she often suffered great embarrassment on being required to disclose her previous name. For example, when she applied for a visa to enter the USA, when she acted as surety to a friend in court, and when required to state her sex in order to obtain motor insurance. She had even been dissuaded from acting as an alibi witness for a friend because of the fear of introducing an element of sensationalism into the court proceedings. Yet the majority of the Court regarded these as legitimate occasions of inquiry about previous identity,

---

[46] E.g. Judge de Meyer in s. III of his separate opinion in *Z. v. Finland*, Eur. Ct. HR, Judgment of 25 February 1997, RJD 1997-I, and in s. II of his separate opinion in *X., Y. and Z. v. United Kingdom*, Eur. Ct. HR, Judgment of 22 April 1997, RJD 1997-II, 24 EHRR 143.

[47] *Rees* at paras. 40 and 43 of the judgment, reiterated by the majority in subsequent cases.

[48] The National Insurance Commissioner has applied the test of biological sex at birth when sex was contested in respect of retirement ages: Decision CP6/76.

[49] The Sex Discrimination Act 1975 demands that people be classified as either men or women for its purposes, and the *Corbett* test was originally applied: *White v. British Sugar Corporation* [1977] IRLR 121. However, the position has changed following the decision of the European Court of Justice in Case C–13/94, *P. v. S. and Cornwall County Council* [1996] ICR 795, CJEC: Sex Discrimination (Gender Reassignment) Regulations 1999, SI 1999, No. 1102. See E. Griffiths, 'The Sex Discrimination (Gender Reassignment) Regulations 1999' (1999) 4 *J. of Civil Liberties* 230–6.

and concluded that the detriment was not sufficiently serious to outweigh the public interest in requiring people to reveal their previous identities.[50]

In only one case has the Court decided that the detriment was serious enough to outweigh the public interest. In *B. v. France*,[51] the applicant was a male-to-female transsexual. She alleged a breach of Article 8 in that the French authorities had refused to alter her birth certificate to show her new sex and forename. The authorities had taken the view that she had intentionally brought about the change of sex by artificial processes, and considered that recognizing the change would allow a person voluntarily to alter his or her civil status. The French *Cour d'appel* accepted that there are cases where irreversible necessity compels an amendment to a person's status, but held that such necessity was not established in B's case. She had undergone cosmetic surgery to change her external appearance, but had not undertaken hormone therapy, counselling, and reconstructive surgery. In particular, she had not gone through the procedures approved by the National Council of France's Medical Association, namely treatment by a qualified medical team in the course of which they reach the conclusion that the transsexual's position is genuine and irreversible and that no form of psychological or psychiatric treatment will help. In short, there was only very weak evidence for regarding Miss B's surgery as treatment for gender identity dysphoria, bringing her physiognomy into line with her psychological and social gender. This should have made her position under Article 8 less promising than that of the applicants in *Rees, Cossey, X., Y. and Z.,* or *Sheffield and Horsham.*

None the less, the European Court of Human Rights held, by fifteen votes to six, that the French decision infringed Article 8. The Court distinguished *Rees* and *Cossey* because of differences between French and English law concerning the effects of refusal to recognize a change of sex. On the balance between the interests of the community and those of the individual, the Court took account of Miss B's determination to change her sex, and of the ease with which an annotation could be inserted on Miss B's birth certificate to reflect her current status, as had been allowed in other cases in France. The refusal of some courts in France to allow a change of forenames was also a factor which distinguished the French position from that in England, and was relevant to respect for private life. In view of the legal requirement in France (but not England) for people to carry identity cards identifying their sex, and to show them on demand, the Court held that the discrepancy between B's apparent sex and that recorded in official documents had reached a sufficient degree of seriousness to be considered incompatible with her right to respect for her private life, and not to be justified by the state's margin or appreciation. It was for the state to decide how to remedy the breach as a matter of national law.[52] The Court awarded one hundred thousand French francs for non-pecuniary damage as just satisfaction under old Article 50 (now Article 41).

[50] Eur. Ct. HR, Judgment of 30 July 1998, 27 EHRR 163, at paras. 15–20, 59.
[51] Eur. Ct. HR, Judgment of 25 March 1992, noted by S. Millns, 'Transsexuality and the European Convention on Human Rights' [1992] *PL* 559–66.
[52] A further complaint that France's treatment of Miss B had been inhuman and degrading and had violated her rights under Art. 3 was not proceeded with.

In the light of this, the Court's continued attachment in other cases to the reasoning in *Rees* is little short of bizarre. In section V of his dissenting opinion in *Sheffield and Horsham*, Judge van Dijk pointed out that the specific incidents of detriment on which Katrina Sheffield relied were only symptoms of 'a continuous risk of being forced to reveal her pre-operative gender which she deliberately and at great cost has abandoned'. As the state is able to make administrative concessions for some purposes, it cannot plausibly be argued that it would be impossible to find a less distressing way to safeguard the interests of third parties and protect the historical nature of the register of births. A person's gender is central to his or her personality and aspirations, and to society's expectations. A consistent refusal by law to accept a person's commitment to a reassigned sex, involving major surgery and drug therapy over an extended period, and confirmed by doctors, constitutes a serious violation of respect for that person's private life. Such a violation can be justified under Article 8(2) only if it is in accordance with the law, and is necessary in a democratic society for one of the legitimate purposes[53] listed in that Article. It is hard to see how an interference of this magnitude can be said to be necessary for any of those purposes, or justified by any other compelling public interest which can stand against the fundamental violation of the subject's private life and self-esteem. Only if the interference is shown to be for a legitimate purpose does the margin of appreciation become relevant.[54] As Judge Martens pointed out, dissenting in *Cossey v. United Kingdom*,[55] the margin of appreciation is a doctrine of judicial self-restraint, which comes into play to prevent judges from substituting their ideas of the correct response to an interference with Article 8 rights for those of the government of the state, so long as the state is taking some steps to remedy the interference. The margin cannot be invoked to deflect the Court's criticism from a state which has refused to take any action to remedy a serious and apparently unjustifiable violation of rights.[56]

In *Rees*, the Court stated that the matter should be kept under review in the light of social and scientific developments. Subsequently, the medical professions internationally have increasingly reached a consensus that gender identity dysphoria is to be recognized as a clinical condition which can be best treated (at least in some cases) by a combination of counselling, drug therapy, and surgery to bring the sufferer's bodily appearance into line with his or her psychological and social gender identity. Some evidence has also emerged that gender may have a physical foundation, being determined by a sexual differentiation to the brain occurring after birth. Post-mortem studies of the brains of a small number of people have been said to reveal certain morphological differences between the brains of transsexuals and those of non-transsexual controls. If it is correct that these changes occur after birth, it would make

---

[53] They are: the interests of national security, public safety, or the economic well being of the country; the prevention of disorder or crime; the protection of health or morals; or the protection of the rights and freedoms of others.

[54] This point is well made by Judge Martens in his dissenting opinion in *Cossey*, by the joint partly dissenting opinion of Judges Bernhardt, Thór Vilhjámsson, Spielmann, Palm, Wildhaber, Makarczyk, and Voicu in *Sheffield and Horsham*, and by the dissenting opinion of Judge van Dijk in the latter case.

[55] Eur. Ct. HR, Series A, No. 184, Judgment of 27 September 1990, 13 EHRR 622.

[56] See T. Walton, 'A Measure of Appreciation' (1992) 142 *NLJ* 1202–4.

attribution of sex by reference exclusively to external genitalia at birth unreliable. Societal developments include a 1989 resolution of the European Parliament[57] calling on Member States of the European Community 'to enact provisions on transsexuals' right to change sex by endocrinological, plastic surgery, and cosmetic treatment, on the procedure, and banning discrimination against them', and Recommendation 1117 of the Parliamentary Assembly of the Council of Europe, also adopted in 1989, encouraging harmonization of the laws and practices of the various Member States in the field of recognizing reassignments of sex. A study of 37 Member States of the Council of Europe, undertaken by Liberty and submitted to the Court during the *Sheffield and Horsham* litigation in 1998, found that twenty-three states permit birth certificate entries to be changed in respect of post-operative transsexuals, the position was unclear in ten states, and only four (Albania, Andorra, Ireland, and the UK) expressly forbade such alterations. Finally, European Community law has recognized sex or gender reassignment as falling within the meaning of sex for the purpose of EC anti-discrimination law.[58] Nevertheless, the Court has refused to depart from the decision, by narrow majorities of ten–eight in *Cossey* and eleven–nine in *Sheffield and Horsham*, indicating that there had been no relevant scientific developments, and that the growing convergence of legal systems on this issue has not yet reached a sufficient consensus to justify departing from the earlier decisions.

At the same time, the majority in *Rees* and in *Cossey* emphasized their consciousness of the seriousness of the problems and distress which transsexuals face, and stressed the need to keep the appropriate legal measures under review in the future in the light of current circumstances.[59] In *Sheffield and Horsham* the Court was concerned to note that the UK appeared to have taken no steps to review the law.[60] The majority appeared to be giving a signal that it was on the point of reconsidering its approach to these cases. The appearance is reinforced by the strength of the dissenting opinions in the case, concluding that the balance of fairness now tipped clearly in favour of recognizing reassigned gender as an aspect of respect for private life. Perhaps most significant is the separate opinion of the UK's judge, Sir John Freeland, concurring with the majority but admitting that his vote was cast 'after much hesitation and even with some reluctance . . . I acknowledge that continued inaction on the part of the respondent state, taken together with further developments elsewhere, could well tilt the balance in the other direction'.

In *Cossey*, Judge Martens in his dissenting opinion castigated the majority for their caution in the face of moral attitudes which, while changing everywhere in Europe, were changing more slowly in some countries than in others. For the Court to adapt its interpretation of the Convention to relevant societal change only if almost all Member States had adopted the new ideas was, said the Judge:

'inconsistent with the Court's mission to protect the individual against the collectivity and to do so by elaborating common standards. Caution is indeed called for, but in another

---

57 [1989] OJ C256/33.
58 Case C-13/94, *P. v. S. and Cornwall County Council* [1996] ICR 795, CJEC.
59 *Rees* at para. 47; *Cossey* at paras. 41–2.
60 *Sheffield and Horsham* at para. 60.

direction: if a collectivity oppresses an individual because it does not want to recognize societal changes, the Court should take great care not to yield too readily to arguments based on a country's cultural and historical peculiarities.'[61]

This is a compelling argument, up to a point. A human rights court should be slow to allow the views of groups in some of the countries within its jurisdiction to deprive individuals of redress for humiliation resulting from lack of respect for a central element in their private lives. At the same time, there are difficulties which the dissenting judges did not directly address. As in all situations where a judicial body confronts an executive body, important but unstated considerations of institutional politics were in play in *Cossey*. Any international human rights agency ultimately depends for its success on maintaining its moral authority over the states within its jurisdiction. There is always a tension between the agency and the state which is subject to it. By giving too little weight to deeply held cultural or moral beliefs in particular states, an agency can weaken its own authority in respect of those states for all purposes, without benefiting the oppressed individuals in the case immediately before it. It is proper for a court to weigh the seriousness of the alleged violation of the particular rights in issue against the deleterious effects which might follow from going too far, exacerbating the tension to a point where the court's moral authority over the state concerned is overborne by that state's commitment to the moral standards which the court is overriding.

Ultimately, therefore, the question is sociological: how deeply committed are the states or the peoples of Europe to the values which support the oppression of which the petitioner complains? If, like Judge Martens in *Cossey* and the dissenting judges in *Sheffield and Horsham*, one considers that there is a growing public tolerance for unconventional modes of existence, and acceptance of the importance of privacy, it is important to take account of these social developments in interpreting the Convention. Nevertheless, as Judge Martens himself accepted, this is not capable of proof.[62] By using the recommendations of supra-national and international parliamentary institutions as evidence for these social changes, the dissenting judges adopted a mode of sociological interpretation which gives great weight to the views of members of a cosmopolitan elite (which, incidentally, lacks legislative or executive authority in Member States, although the members of the European Parliament are at least directly accountable to their electorates back home), but may not reflect the views of ordinary citizens in European states. The question in the end is whether, in interpreting difficult Convention provisions in a context in which moral views appear to be changing, the Court should have given more weight to the established hardships which transsexuals face than to speculation about the moral views of a range of European societies.

The deep divisions within the Court, and between the Commission and the Court,[63] together with the promise—or threat—in *Rees*, *Cossey*, and *Sheffield and*

---

[61] Dissenting opinion in *Cossey* at para. 5.6, 13 EHRR at 663. See also 644, 664.

[62] 13 EHRR at 660–1.

[63] The Commission's delegate at the hearing in *Cossey* told the Court that the Commission had referred the *Cossey* case to the Court in the hope that the Court would depart from the judgment in *Rees*. The Commission's delegate in *Sheffield and Horsham* took the same line.

Horsham that the matter would continue to be kept under review in the light of social and scientific developments, make it probable that the Court is preparing to change tack. The decision of the Court in *B. v. France*[64] makes it clear that there are circumstances in which even the margin of appreciation will not protect a state which fails to recognize a change of sex for domestic legal purposes. The decision shows that an important factor, in deciding whether a refusal to recognize a change of sex amounts to a violation of the right to respect for private life under Article 8, is the impact which the refusal has on the individual in the light of the effects of civil rights and obligations related to legal status. As matters stand, this results in an apparently curious position. Article 8 effectively gives rights to transsexuals in some, but not all, states to recognition of their changed sex. People in countries where few disabilities, obligations, or embarrassments are imposed on transsexuals by operation of law have no right to official recognition of their reassigned sex. However, this misses the point of Article 8. Respect for private life is not simply a matter of protecting people from the embarrassment of external scrutiny of their personal situations. It involves respect for the individual's own dignity, and sense of being valued. This has been recognized independently by the German *Bundesverfassungsgericht* and by the Appellate Division of the Superior Court of New Jersey, in decisions cited in the dissenting opinion of Judge Martens in *Cossey*.[65] In the New Jersey case, the court ruled that recognition would 'promote the individual's quest for inner peace and personal happiness, while in no way disserving any societal interest, precept of public order or precept of morality'.[66] It is an important aspect of the right to respect for, rather than merely avoidance of discrimination resulting from, private life. The Strasbourg Court, and the courts, government and Parliament of the UK, should now discharge their responsibilities in this area.

(iii) Implications under the Human Rights Act 1998

As noted above, some English judges have said that the *Corbett* test might need to be reconsidered in relation to post-operative transsexuals in the light of growing scientific understanding of transsexualism.[67] In *Bellinger v. Bellinger*[68] Johnson J accepted the Attorney-General's view that it must be left to Parliament, rather than the courts, to make any changes which might be thought desirable. That case concerned an application for a declaration that a male-to-female transsexual was validly married to a man within the terms of section 11 of the Matrimonial Causes Act 1973. The marriage had been contracted before the Human Rights Act 1998 came into force. It is arguable that the Human Rights Act could open the way to a judicial reconsideration of the issues. The argument would run as follows.

Under section 6 of the Act, public authorities (including registrars of births and

---

[64] Eur. Ct. HR, Judgment of 25 March 1992, noted by S. Millns, 'Transsexuality and the European Convention on Human Rights' [1992] *PL* 559–66.

[65] 49 BVerfGE 286; *M.T. v. J.T.* (1976) 2 FLR 2247, respectively. See 13 EHRR at 647–8.

[66] *M.T. v. J.T.*, above.

[67] *S.-T. (formerly J.) v. J.* [1998] 1 All ER 431, CA, at 447 *per* Ward LJ, 470 *per* Potter LJ; *Bellinger v. Bellinger*, *The Times*, 22 November 2000, *per* Johnson J.

[68] *The Times*, 22 November 2000.

marriages and courts) act unlawfully if they behave in a manner incompatible with Convention rights, including the right to respect for private life under ECHR Article 8. Section 2 makes it clear that English courts must take into account the interpretation given to Convention rights by the Strasbourg organs. In the context of the private life of transsexuals, the knife-edge majorities and strong dissents in the Strasbourg Court, and the consistent view of the Commission (before its abolition) that the decision in *Rees* should be reconsidered, deserve to be given considerable weight by national courts and other public authorities. It would be open to them to decide that it now violates Article 8 in national law to refuse to recognize a person's reassigned gender post-operatively. Public authorities would then be required by section 3 of the 1998 Act to read and give effect to other legislation, including section 11 of the Matrimonial Causes Act 1973, in a manner compatible with the interpretation which the national courts (rather than the Strasbourg Court) would have given to the right to respect for private life. Nothing in the Act compels courts to refuse to recognize reassigned gender. Courts have previously treated 'male' and 'female' in section 11 as meaning the same as 'man' and 'woman' did at common law, importing the *Corbett* test, but that interpretation of section 11, like the *Corbett* test itself, are products of judicial action, not of primary legislation. A judicial reading of legislation must change if it proves to be incompatible with a court's interpretation of a Convention right.

If a court accepted each stage in that argument, there would be no need to await the tortuous processes of parliamentary legislation to effect a change to the status of transsexuals in English law. Courts might be cautious about allowing their dynamic interpretation of Convention rights to run too far ahead of Strasbourg where their decisions could be seen as affecting the character of an institution as sensitive as marriage. They might also be influenced, in the context of capacity for marriage, by the Strasbourg Court's decisive (although, as has been argued above, misguided) rejection of the use of ECHR Article 12 to create a right for transsexuals to marry according to their reassigned genders. Furthermore, it would be difficult for a court to introduce a significant change if it had major financial or legal ramifications calling for legislation to authorize additional public expenditure or amendments to other legislation. But these are questions of judicial policy and practicality rather than jurisdiction or legal doctrine. The question will be whether there is a judicial will to use the Human Rights Act 1998 to remedy what is increasingly seen as a substantial injustice to people suffering from a recognized and treatable medical disability. As seven judges put it in a joint partial dissent in *Sheffield and Horsham v. United Kingdom*:[69]

'The present applicants have undergone, following appropriate medical advice and counselling, painful and gruelling gender re-assignment surgery. This has undoubtedly involved substantial hardship and, as in the case of Ms. Sheffield, the dislocation of personal relationships. When required to prove their identity in certain situations they are placed in a situation where they are obliged to choose between hiding their new sex—which may not

---

[69] Eur. Ct. HR, Judgment of 30 July 1998, 27 EHRR 163, *per* Judges Bernhardt, Thór Vilhjámsson, Spielmann, Palm, Wildhaber, Makarczyk, and Voicu.

be either possible or lawful—or revealing the truth about themselves and facing humiliating and possibly hostile reactions. It is no longer possible, from the standpoint of Article 8 of the Convention and in a Europe where considerable evolution in the direction of legal recognition is constantly taking place, to justify a system such as that pertaining in the respondent state, which treats gender dysphoria as a medical condition, subsidises gender re-assignment surgery but then withholds recognition of the consequences of that surgery thereby exposing post-operative transsexuals to the likelihood of recurring distress and humiliation.'

(3) SOME IMPLICATIONS OF *CORBETT* FOR THE CRIMINAL LAW

The rule in *Corbett* refusing to recognize the reassigned gender of post-operative transsexuals has implications for criminal liability. Certain offences can be committed only by or against people of a particular sex. Rape is penile penetration of the vagina or anus of a man or woman who does not consent.[70] A post-operative male-to-female transsexual cannot commit rape (except by aiding and abetting it), since surgery on a male/female transsexual removes the male genitalia without which rape is impossible. It is not clear whether a female-to-male transsexual could commit rape as a principal. It would be physically possible for a surgically constructed penis to be inserted into a vagina or anus. Although surgical techniques have not yet succeeded in constructing a sexually functional penis for female-to-male transsexuals, the *actus reus* of rape does not require ejaculation, but only penile penetration. The question would be whether a surgically constructed penis would be regarded as a penis for the purposes of rape. It would be incoherent for the law to convict a transsexual of rape on the basis that he had a penis while not recognizing him as a man for other purposes. Yet that has been recommended by a review of sex offences following a public consultation process.[71]

The current law may also leave a transsexual victim of non-consensual penile penetration less well protected than other people. The position in relation to anal penetration has improved since it was included in the definition of rape in 1994. However, it is not clear whether penile penetration of a surgically constructed artificial vagina without consent would constitute rape. If the law refuses to treat such an organ as a vagina within the meaning of the legislation, the defendant would be guilty only of indecency between men[72] or an indecent assault on a man.[73] Such a result might be considered absurd. There are good reasons for ignoring the victim's chromosomal sex when deciding whether a man is guilty of raping her. In particular, the offender is not in any position to know what anyone's chromosomal sex is, and has to go entirely by external appearances.

The law need not ignore an artificial vagina. In *S.Y. v. S.Y.*,[74] a husband applied for a

---

[70] Sexual Offences Act 1956, ss. 1(1) (as amended by the Sexual Offences (Amendment) 1976 and the Criminal Justice and Public Order Act 1994) and 44.

[71] Home Office, *Setting the Boundaries: Reforming the Law on Sex Offences* (London: Home Office, 2000), vol. 1, 15, para. 2.8.4.

[72] Sexual Offences Act 1956, s. 13.

[73] Ibid., s. 15.

[74] [1963] P. 37, [1962] 3 All ER 55, CA.

decree of nullity of marriage on the ground that the wife (who had been registered as female at birth) had only a vestigial vagina, which made consummation impossible. The court found that a vagina could have been corrected surgically by forming an artificial passage, and held that the law would then recognize sexual intercourse as constituting consummation. The decree was therefore refused. Willmer LJ, *obiter*, said that if true sexual intercourse were impossible for a woman with an artificial vagina, she could not be raped, and he regarded such a result as 'bordering on the fantastic'.[75] This might be thought to support the claim that a male/female transsexual with an artificial vagina could be raped. The decision in *S.Y.* was distinguished in *Corbett v. Corbett*,[76] on the ground that a woman with a vestigial vagina was nevertheless a woman, while a male-to-female transsexual remained chromosomally a man. However, this merely goes to show that we are on slippery ground when assigning a sex to people in the grey area between the two sexes. The wife in *S.Y.* was regarded in 1962 as a woman, albeit imperfectly formed, while today it has been suggested that she would probably be classified as a chromosomal male with testicular feminization.[77]

There is therefore much to be said for the recommendation of the Home Office Sex Offences Review: 'The law must give protection from all sexual violence. Whether or not sexual organs are surgically created, the law should apply. Accordingly we thought to put it beyond doubt that the law should apply to surgically constructed organs— whether vaginal or penile'.[78]

Certain other offences are defined in ways which depend on the offender or victim being a man or a woman, and so create difficulties when either is a transsexual. The offence of loitering or soliciting in a public place for the purposes of prostitution can be committed only by a 'common prostitute',[79] and it has been held that a man cannot be a common prostitute.[80] There is a separate offence of soliciting by men for an immoral purpose.[81] It is also an offence for a man to live on the earnings of prostitution.[82] In *R. v. Tan*,[83] charges arose out of acts of prostitution performed by a woman, Moira Tan, and a male-to-female transsexual, Gloria Greaves, the proceeds being shared with a man, Brian Greaves. Gloria Greaves was convicted of being a man living on the earnings of Tan's prostitution, contrary to section 30 of the Sexual Offences Act 1956; and Brian Greaves was convicted of living on the earnings of prostitution of a man, Gloria Greaves, contrary to section 5 of the Sexual Offences Act 1967. On appeal, although it would have been open to the Court of Appeal to overrule *Corbett*, the defendants did not launch a frontal assault on the earlier decision, attempting instead to distinguish it. It was argued on their behalf that the *Corbett* doctrine should

---

[75] [1963] P. at 60, [1962] 3 All ER at 62–3.
[76] [1971] P. 83, [1970] 2 All ER 33.
[77] Mason and McCall Smith, *Law and Medical Ethics* 3rd edn., 43.
[78] Home Office, *Setting the Boundaries*, vol. 1, 15, para. 2.8.4.
[79] Street Offences Act 1959, s. 1(1).
[80] *DPP v. Bull* [1995] QB 88, [1994] 4 All ER 411, DC.
[81] Sexual Offences Act 1956, s. 32.
[82] Ibid., s. 30.
[83] [1983] QB 1053, [1983] 2 All ER 12, CA.

be restricted to the law of marriage, and Gloria should be regarded (as she regarded herself) as a woman, so that neither conviction could stand. The Court of Appeal rejected this, holding that it would be unacceptable to adopt different approaches to assigning sex for different purposes. *Corbett* was followed, so that people were treated as having the biological sex assigned at birth. Gloria should not be treated as a man for the purpose of capacity to marry but as a woman for the purpose of repelling a charge under section 30 of the Sexual Offences Act. The same reasoning would apply to other offences which can be committed by members of only one sex.

Nevertheless, the use of purely biological criteria for assigning sex remains questionable in principle. The defendants in *Tan* had argued that, for the purposes of section 30 of the 1956 Act and section 5 of the 1967 Act, a person should be considered a woman if she had become philosophically or psychologically or socially female. This approach would not have required any steps to be taken by hormone therapy or surgery to change the physical state of the person. It would have allowed people to redefine their sexes at will, and that would have made it too easy to evade liability for offences which have a person's sex as an essential part of their definition. Yet if it would be unacceptable that a person should be able to define his or her own sex at will, it might still be justifiable to base assignment of sex on a combination of physical, psychological, philosophical, and social factors, rather than on physical characteristics alone. The need for consistency does not dictate that the law should adopt a one-dimensional criterion. At present, however, the only proposal for reform in this area is to bring the law of soliciting by men into line with that governing soliciting by women for the purpose of prostitution.[84]

12.2 SEXUAL FREEDOM

If there are circumstances in which the right to be treated by law as being of the sex which best reflects one's psychological make-up is protected by the right to respect for private life under Article 8(1) of the Convention, the same is true of respect for the means whereby a person gives expression to the sexuality which is part of his or her sexual constitution. But there have traditionally been legal limits on sexual freedom. In England and Wales, the law interferes with sexual freedom in two ways. First, it imposes criminal liability in respect of disapproved acts. Secondly, it discriminates, or permits people to discriminate, against people of particular sexual orientations.

Criminal liability is imposed partly to protect vulnerable people (such as children, those suffering from mental disorder or disability, and people subject to the authority of others) against having sexual activity forced on them when they are not in a position to choose rationally for themselves or to refuse to co-operate. In

---

[84] Home Office, *Setting the Boundaries* vol. 1, 103–4, paras. 6.6.12–17. The Home Office review also suggests new provisions on recruiting and exploiting men and women for sexual purposes for reward (ibid., 116, paras. 7.7.1–4), but it is not clear whether such legislation would apply to recruitment and exploitation by men and women equally.

addition, the law is used to protect sexual morality. The latter aim is somewhat controversial. In the second half of this century, the principle expounded by John Stuart Mill in his essay *On Liberty*, that the sole ground for restricting a person's freedom should be that it causes harm to others,[85] has grown in popularity. Mill argued that people who are specially likely to have a distorted view of their own interests or who are likely to be at a disadvantage in protecting them—young or mentally handicapped people, or those subject to the orders of others—must be specially protected against harm, but otherwise people should be free to decide for themselves what constitutes a harm for them and what would be a good. Mill's principle has formed the foundation for two important official reports: the *Report of the Committee on Homosexual Offences and Prostitution*[86] (the Wolfenden Report), which recommended a relaxation of the punishment of homosexual acts; and the *Report of the Committee on Obscenity and Film Censorship*[87] (the Williams Committee Report), which used it as a basis for recommendations for reform of the law of obscenity.

However, Mill's rationalist view that identifiable harm to identifiable people constitutes the sole justification for imposing criminal liability was contentious. It was opposed by moralists of many persuasions. Lord Devlin attacked it in a famous Maccabean Lecture, asserting the proper role of law as protector of established moral standards, rather than an instrument for changing moral views. He argued that there is a core of social morality which binds societies, and which must be maintained, using the criminal law in support if needed, lest civil society collapse. The Law Lords, in 1961, followed the Devlin line, asserting a power to create new criminal offences in order to protect public morality as understood by the judges.[88]

Chief among offences which consist of sexual behaviour considered immoral or socially harmful was buggery.[89] This is constituted at common law by sexual intercourse involving penetration *per anum* by a man with another man or a woman, or *per vaginam* by a man or woman with an animal. Not only is consent not a defence, but the consenting party is guilty of the offence as a principal. Section 12 of the Sexual Offences Act 1956, providing that: 'It is an offence for a person to commit buggery with another person or with an animal', merely incorporates the common law definition. The moral passions engendered by the issue of homosexual buggery in particular made the issue too hot for government to handle, and it was not until 1967 that the law in England and Wales was liberalized, as a result of a private member's Bill which became the Sexual Offences Act 1967.[90]

In many states of the USA, too, buggery is illegal. Although the federal courts have developed a constitutional right to privacy which includes a right to contraception and some consensual sexual activity, the Supreme Court has retreated from giving

---

[85] See Ch. 1, above.

[86] Cmd. 247 (London: HMSO, 1957).

[87] Cmnd. 7772 (London: HMSO, 1979), examined further in Ch. 16, below.

[88] *Shaw v. DPP* [1962] AC 220, [1961] 2 All E R 446, HL.

[89] See J. C. Smith and B. Hogan, *Criminal Law*, 7th edn. (London: Butterworths, 1992), 476–9.

[90] In Scotland, the change was introduced later by the Criminal Justice (Scotland) Act 1980, s. 80. The law in Northern Ireland changed in 1982: see below.

constitutional protection to buggery, at any rate between men. In *Bowers v. Hard-wick*,[91] the Court upheld by a five–four majority a Georgia statute which criminalized sodomy between consenting adults in private. The majority held that there is no fundamental right to homosexual buggery such as might benefit from due process protection under the Fourteenth Amendment. The minority argued that the case was about the fundamental right to privacy, not about buggery *per se*, but they were outvoted.

The European Court of Human Rights has a rather better record on protecting sexual freedom. In 1981 the Court held in *Dudgeon v. United Kingdom*[92] that the blanket criminalization of homosexual acts violated the rights of homosexual men to respect for their private lives. That case concerned the law in Northern Ireland, which was altered as a result to bring it more closely into line with that in mainland Britain.[93] Similarly, in *Norris v. Ireland*[94] the Court held that Ireland's total ban on homosexual acts violated the right to respect for private life. The Court reiterated this in *Modinos v. Cyprus*.[95]

Article 8(2) permits states to restrict practical expressions of that respect in order to protect health and morality (allowing governments to take account of prevailing moral standards in its territory) or the rights and well-being of others, so long as any interference with the right is in accordance with the law and necessary in a democratic society. This gives scope for argument about the demands of morality, health, and the rights or well-being of others, and the extent to which it necessitates interferences with people's sexual freedom. In *Dudgeon* the Court decided that the state's legitimate interest in protecting the health and morals of its citizens, and particularly of its youth, must be respected by allowing the UK government a wide margin of appreciation in setting the age at which men could lawfully consent to homosexual activity. A minimum age of twenty-one was within the margin of appreciation. But the margin of appreciation has its limits. In *Norris*, the Court held by a majority of eight votes to six that the total ban on homosexual activity in Ireland went further than could be considered necessary for the protection of the morals of youth, and, being disproportionate to any aim which could legitimately be pursued under Article 8(2), fell outside the margin of appreciation and violated Article 8. However, even a minimum age to protect youth may fall victim to the ban on discrimination under Article 14 if the age set for homosexuals is higher than that set for heterosexuals. For this reason, the Commission decided by fourteen votes to four that English law violated Article 14, taken together with Article 8, in *Sutherland v. United Kingdom*,[96] leading to a friendly settlement when the ages of consent were equalized at 16 by the Sexual Offences (Amendment) Act 2000.[97]

[91] (1986) 478 US 186, discussed by Anon., 'The Supreme Court, 1985 Term: Leading Cases: Right to Privacy' (1986) 100 *Harv. LR* 200–20 at 210–20; A. Lester, 'The Overseas Trade in the American Bill of Rights' (1988) 88 *Columbia LR* 537–61 at 558–61; J. Michael, 'Homosexuals and Privacy' (1988) 138 *NLJ* 831.

[92] Eur. Ct. HR, Series A. No. 45, Judgment of 22 October 1981, 4 EHRR 149.

[93] Homosexual Offences (Northern Ireland) Order 1982.

[94] Eur. Ct. HR, Series A, No. 142, Judgment of 26 October 1988, 13 EHRR 186.

[95] Eur. Ct. HR, Series A, No. 259, Judgment of 22 April 1993, 16 EHRR 485.

[96] Eur. Commn. HR, App. No. 25186/94, Report of 1 July 1997.

[97] Eur. Ct. HR, Judgment of 27 March 2001 striking the case out of the Court's list.

In what follows, it should be borne in mind that these principles now form part of English law by virtue of the Human Rights Act 1998.

(1) HOMOSEXUAL ACTS[98]

It would be wrong to imagine that the criminal law was aimed exclusively at homosexual acts. Buggery may be either a heterosexual or a homosexual act, as will be clear from the definition of the offence given above. Furthermore, homosexual acts between women have never been criminal, although indecent assault on a woman (whether by a man or another woman) is an offence under the Sexual Offences Act 1956, section 14. Most female homosexual acts, such as cunnilingus, masturbation, and tribadism, are capable of amounting to indecent assaults, but normally partners in a female homosexual act would be able to give consent, which would prevent the act from being an assault, if it did not produce bodily harm. However, under section 14(2) a girl under the age of sixteen cannot give a consent which would prevent an act being an assault for the purposes of the section. This effectively means that the age of consent for homosexual activity by women is sixteen, the same as for heterosexual activity.[99]

On the other hand, there was for many years a total ban on male homosexual acts, which would all constitute either buggery or acts of gross indecency between men regardless of age or consent. It was left to a private member's Bill to translate into law the more liberal sexual atmosphere of the 1960s. The Sexual Offences Act 1967, section 1(1) provided that 'a homosexual act in private shall not be an offence provided that the parties consent thereto and have attained the age of twenty-one years'. As noted above, the age of consent was reduced, first to eighteen in 1994,[100] then (against strong opposition from the House of Lords which led to the invocation of the Parliament Act 1911) to sixteen with effect from 8 January 2001.[101] Homosexual acts are defined as buggery and acts of gross indecency.[102] Gross indecency has not been defined either by statute or by the courts, despite being the subject of a separate statutory offence, but acts of gross indecency include fellatio, masturbation, genital apposition, and other forms of contact with other people's genitals.[103] The reform left untouched situations in which homosexual practices were deemed to be prejudicial to good discipline. The 1967 Act preserved criminal liability for buggery by members of the armed forces or by members of the crew on board a merchant ship.[104] This

[98] T. Honoré, *Sex Law* (London: Duckworth, 1978), ch. 4.

[99] See Sexual Offences Act 1956, s. 6.

[100] Sexual Offences Act 1956, s. 12(1A), inserted by Criminal Justice and Public Order Act 1994, s. 143; Sexual Offences Act 1967, s. 1, as amended by Criminal Justice and Public Order Act 1994, s. 145 (now repealed).

[101] Sexual Offences Act 1956, s. 12(1A) and (1C) and Sexual Offences Act 1967, s. 1, as amended by Sexual Offences (Amendment) Act 2000, s. 1.

[102] Sexual Offences Act 1967, s. 1(7).

[103] For discussion, see Honoré, *Sex Law*, 90.

[104] Army Act 1955, s. 66; Sexual Offences Act 1967, ss. 1(5), 2. This was held not to give rise to an admissible petition under the European Convention on Human Rights, because of the special need to prevent disorder in the army: Eur. Comm. HR, Application No. 9237/81, *B. v. United Kingdom*, 34 DR 68 (1983), 6 EHRR 354.

criminal liability has now been abolished.[105] In order to protect particularly vulnerable groups, people suffering from a severe mental handicap are deemed to be incapable of giving the necessary consent at any age, and staff are criminally liable for homosexual acts committed against patients in mental hospitals.[106] When the age of consent was reduced to sixteen, it was made a criminal offence for a person in a position of trust in relation to a person under eighteen to engage in sexual activity with the person to whom he or she is in a position of trust.[107] These provisions, while removing some unfairness and improving the lot of homosexual men, leave some curiosities.

(i) The limited meaning of privacy

Without attempting a definition of the phrase 'in private', section 1(2) of the 1967 Act specifies two situations which are not to be treated as being in private. One is a public lavatory. This is unexceptionable, if one accepts that part of the purpose of the prohibition is to protect the sensibilities of members of the public who would be shocked or upset by seeing homosexual acts, and would have no warning of what was going on before entering the lavatory. However, unlike some other legislation,[108] there is nothing in the language of the Act to limit it in this way.[109] Using criminal law to safeguard sensibilities is hard to justify within the strict definition of Mill's harm principle, but may be acceptable if (with Feinberg[110]) one regards a serious assault on one's deeply held moral beliefs as so offensive as to amount to a form of personal harm. More controversially, the subsection provides that a homosexual act is not in private when more than two people take part or are present. This is an extraordinary provision. It has no parallel in the law relating to heterosexual acts, and is quite unjustifiable if the acts are taking place on private premises, all the participants and observers are consenting adults, and other people are excluded. Once it is accepted that homosexual acts in private between consenting adults ought not in principle to give rise to criminal sanctions, it is hard to see any justification for imposing the wholly arbitrary limitation that only two people may be present, making it impossible for male homosexual voyeurs to satisfy themselves lawfully unless they are content to watch one other man masturbating alone. It flies in the face of the principle of equal treatment for men and women, and has been held to discriminate in such a way as to violate ECHR Article 8 taken together with Article 14 (the non-discrimination provi-

---

[105] Criminal Justice and Public Order Act 1994, ss. 146 (England and Wales), 147, and 148 (Northern Ireland and Scotland). See G. R. Rubin, 'Section 146 of the Criminal Justice and Public Order Act 1994 and the "Decriminalisation" of Homosexual Acts in the Armed Forces' [1996] Crim. LR 393–405.

[106] Sexual Offences Act 1967, s. 1(3), (4).

[107] Sexual Offences (Amendment) Act 2000, ss. 3, 4.

[108] E.g. Town Police Clauses Act 1847, s. 28, as interpreted in *Cheeseman v. DPP* [1992] QB 83, [1991] 3 All ER 54, DC.

[109] For a reform proposal to remedy this by treating men and women alike and respecting the privacy of those who do not invite public attention or behave in a way that causes distress, see Home Office, *Setting the Boundaries*, vol. 1, 100–2, 123–6.

[110] J. Feinberg, *Offense to Others* (New York: Oxford University Press, 1985), chs 7 and 9.

sion).[111] The Home Office review of sex offences has rightly recommended that the limitation to a maximum of two people, and other restrictions on homosexual activity which do not also apply to heterosexuals, should be abolished.[112]

(ii) Heterosexual buggery

Until fairly recently, heterosexual anal intercourse was a criminal offence. It is now lawful if both parties consent and are at least sixteen years old, and the activity takes place in private.[113] To some extent this is more permissive than the legalization of homosexual acts, because the restrictive meaning given to 'private' in relation to homosexual acts[114] does not apply to heterosexual acts. The Home Office review of sex offences, following in the footsteps of the Criminal Law Revision Committee,[115] has rightly recommended the abolition of the whole offence of buggery, placing the law of anal intercourse on the same footing as that governing other forms of sexual behaviour.[116]

Other legal provisions discriminate in a number of ways against people's wishes to take part in sexual practices which others would regard as unconventional or immoral. This discrimination generally takes the form of criminal offences specifically aimed at certain types of sexual activity, or used to penalize expressions of some selected types of sexual behaviour. However, there are also circumstances in which certain sexual predilections may justify discrimination against a person in the field of employment: see Chapter 3 above and subsection (8), page 725, below.

(2) ACTS BETWEEN MALES IN PRIVATE OR IN PUBLIC

There are offences which are committed by acts between males, but not to acts between males and females or between females. Under the Sexual Offences Act 1956, section 13, it is an offence for a man (but not a woman) to commit an act of gross indecency with another man whether in public or in private, or to be a party to or procure the commission of such an act.[117] It is now not an offence, however, for a man to procure the commission of an act of gross indecency between himself and another man, if that act would be lawful by virtue of section 1 of the Sexual Offences Act 1967 as amended, being a homosexual act in private between two men who have attained the age of sixteen years.[118] The Home Office review of sex offences has recommended

---

[111] *A. D. T. v. United Kingdom*, Eur. Ct. HR, App. No. 35765/97, Judgment of 31 July 2000. In a subsequent case where a group of people (the 'Bolton Seven') were convicted of offences arising out of consensual homosexual activities taking place in a group of seven people, the UK government has offered those convicted £15,000 each in an attempt to stave off a further challenge in Strasbourg before the law can be changed: *Guardian*, 27 July 2001, 5. It remains to be seen whether the offer will be accepted.

[112] Home Office, *Setting the Boundaries*, vol. 1, 102, paras. 6.6.3–6.

[113] Sexual Offences Act 1956, s. 12(1A), inserted by Criminal Justice and Public Order Act 1994, s. 143 and amended by Sexual Offences (Amendment) Act 2000, s. 1.

[114] Sexual Offences Act 1956, s. 12(1B), inserted by Criminal Justice and Public Order Act 1994, s. 143.

[115] CLRC Fifteenth Report, *Sexual Offences*, Cmnd. 9213 (London: HMSO, 1984), para. 6.7.

[116] Ibid., 102, para. 6.6.10.

[117] 'Man' includes 'boy': Sexual Offences Act 1956, s. 46.

[118] Sexual Offences Act 1967, s. 4(2).

the abolition of the offence of gross indecency. The review noted that the offence deals with same-sex behaviour between consenting people in private, and recommended that it should be repealed as being uncertain in meaning, discriminatory and unnecessarily intrusive on private life.[119]

(3) OTHER ACTS IN PRIVATE: ASSAULT, INDECENT ASSAULT, AND SADO-MASOCHISM

A man or woman who indecently assaults any woman or man in public or in private is guilty of an offence.[120] This effectively outlaws certain types of violent sexual activity even between consenting adults in private, whether homosexual or heterosexual. In particular, sado-masochism, which is said to form an element in the sexual techniques of many people,[121] is probably always illegal in England and Wales under current caselaw, but the law in this respect is not easy to reconcile with principle.

It is a battery intentionally to inflict on a person violence, or to put someone in fear of immediate violence, which causes or is intended or likely to cause actual bodily harm. The subject's consent will justify bodily harm in some circumstances: for example, if the victim is of an age and mental condition which permits the law to recognize that consent, at least so long as the harm is no more than trifling (on which see below) or is inflicted for a therapeutic purpose (see Chapter 5, above). Sir James Fitzjames Stephen, in his *Digest of Criminal Law*,[122] suggested that one was entitled to consent to bodily harm so long as it does not amount to a maim (which, as noted above in connection with sex reassignment therapy, is an offence at common law). But in *Attorney-General's Reference (No. 6 of 1980)*[123] the Court of Appeal held that nobody may give an effective consent to any degree of bodily harm unless some public interest is served thereby. On that ground, it was held that young men who agreed to settle an argument by a fist fight were guilty of assault, and could not use each other's consent to the fight to justify the bodily harm which resulted. The court accepted (*obiter*) that a public interest was served by properly conducted games and sports, lawful punishment of children, reasonable surgical procedures, and dangerous exhibitions. In a later case it was held that boys could consent to rough and undisciplined play.[124]

However, the judges acknowledge no public interest in sado-masochism between consenting adults. In two cases it has been held that the law will refuse to recognize consent where the purpose of inflicting the violence is to secure sexual gratification. In *R. v. Donovan*[125] the defendant had beaten a girl, aged seventeen, with a cane, with her consent. His purpose was to obtain sexual pleasure. He was convicted on charges

---

[119] Home Office, *Setting the Boundaries*, vol. 1, 101–2.

[120] Sexual Offences Act 1956, s. 14 (indecent assault on a woman) or 15 (indecent assault on a man).

[121] Law Commission, Consultation Paper No. 139, *Consent in the Criminal Law* (London: HMSO, 1995), 134, paras. 10.18–19.

[122] 4th edn., 148–9.

[123] [1981] QB 715, [1981] 2 All ER 1057, CA.

[124] *R. v. Jones* [1987] Crim. LR 123, CA.

[125] [1934] 2 KB 498, CCA.

of indecent assault and common assault. The Court of Criminal Appeal decided that the girl's consent was irrelevant, because it would be contrary to public policy to take account of consent where the sole purpose was sexual gratification. The conviction was quashed on the technical ground that the jury had not been asked to consider whether the degree of violence used was intended or likely to cause bodily harm. In *R. v. Brown (Anthony)*[126] the House of Lords by a bare majority (Lords Templeman, Jauncey, and Lowry; Lords Slynn, and Mustill dissented) upheld convictions under sections 20 and 47 of the Offences against the Person Act 1861 arising out of a sado-masochistic encounter, notwithstanding the participants' consent. It is not clear what the *ratio decidendi* of *Brown* is. It is at least possible, and may be probable, that the decision goes well beyond the facts of the case, and has the effect of outlawing mere love bites or scratches as it does more extreme forms of sado-masochistic activity. There is some support in the majority speeches for all the following propositions:

(a) that consent is no defence in respect of an act that is intended or likely to do actual bodily harm, or injury; or

(b) that consent is no defence in respect of an act that is intended or likely to do actual bodily harm or injury and which forms part of a cult of violence; or

(c) that consent is no defence in respect of an act that is intended or likely to do actual bodily harm or injury and which is not directed to a socially worthwhile purpose;[127] or

(d) that consent is no defence in respect of an act that is intended or likely to do actual bodily harm or injury and which is not regulated by pre-set rules and a system of independent and impartial refereeing; or

(e) some other combination of the factors in (a) to (d).

Which of these is the *ratio* depends on the objectives of the criminal law in this area. A decision of the Court of Appeal subsequent to *Brown*, it was clear that the court was uncomfortable with the breadth of possibilities (a), (c), and (d). In *R. v. Wilson (Alan)*[128] a woman persuaded her husband to brand his initials on her buttocks with a knife as a mark of her attachment to him. When the scars were noticed at a medical examination, the police were informed and the boyfriend was prosecuted and convicted. The Court of Appeal allowed his appeal, holding that the girlfriend's consent sufficed to provide a defence where there was no element of immorality and no public interest interfering with her autonomy. The branding was considered to be closer to tattooing than to the facts of *Brown*, so the rationale of *Brown* (whatever it might be) did not apply.

It is difficult to reconcile *Wilson* with *Brown*. If the infliction of bodily harm is to be criminal, regardless of consent, unless there is a public interest in allowing it, the

---

[126] [1994] 1 AC 212, [1993] 2 All ER 75, HL.

[127] See D. Kell, 'Social Disutility and the Law of Consent' (1994) 14 *Oxford J. Legal Studies* 121–55 for a full discussion of this issue and possible alternative formulations.

[128] [1997] QB 47, CA.

decision in *Wilson* would be well-nigh unjustifiable. *Wilson* gives proper weight to individual privacy and autonomy. If *Wilson* is correct, *Brown* can only be justified if one can identify on the facts of the case a legitimate state interest in denying or restricting respect for a person's autonomy in relation to the integrity of his or her own body which distinguishes sado-masochism from other reasons for submitting to serious bodily harm. In *Brown*, a number of interests were suggested. There was some discussion of the health risks stemming from sado-masochism. This is unconvincing, however. As the Law Commission was told, sado-masochism grew in popularity when people realised that it carried less risk of infection with HIV and other sexually transmitted diseases. Certain practices, such as breath restriction, are very unsafe if carried on in solitude and regularly lead to deaths, but are fairly safe if carried out under the supervision of other people. Making communal sado-masochistic activity unlawful, forcing people into solitary masochistic acts, greatly increases the dangers to health and life. It also makes it dangerous for sado-masochistic groups to undertake health and safety education.[129]

Another concern expressed by the majority in *Brown* was that a young person's ability to resist the lure of sado-masochistic acts might be overridden by older people. But similar risks and concerns arise in the mind of sensible observers from other kinds of sexual activity, rugby or association football, professional boxing, or rock-climbing. Something extra must have been present to justify giving these considerations such weight that they could override the interest in respecting the autonomy of sane adults.

This extra element might perhaps be found in the difference between sex and violence. Violence is not in itself usually seen as a good thing. Although there are situations where physical violence is part of an activity which is regarded as socially acceptable (rugby football, rough play amongst children, perhaps boxing matches, and beating children), most people in this country instinctively share the views most economically expressed by Lord Templeman at the end of his speech in *Brown*:[130] 'Society is entitled and bound to protect itself against a cult of violence. Pleasure derived from the infliction of pain is an evil thing. Cruelty is uncivilised'. If the activity is classified as violent, pleasure derived from it is 'evil', and the act of inflicting it is to be regarded as 'cruelty' which is 'uncivilised'. For moral reasons, in order to protect standards of public decency, the courts will not permit people to legalize such acts of cruelty, unless no significant bodily harm results to the subject.

On the other hand, if an activity is classified as private and sexual, pleasure derived from it is not an 'evil thing', and is often good, even if accompanied by pain. Accordingly, it is permissible to allow a person to consent to it, although public policy demands that consent cannot effectively be given to acts which inflict particularly serious forms of bodily harm. The interests which are at stake are the satisfaction of natural cravings, the expression of one's sexual identity, and the right not to be exploited as an unwilling means to someone else's end. The need for consent allows

---

[129] Law Commission, Consultation Paper No. 139, *Consent in the Criminal Law*, 135–6, 140–2, paras. 10.25, 10.37–38.
[130] [1993] 2 All ER 75 at 84.

people who do not want to partake in sexual activity to assert their own desires and needs. The general freedom to consent permits people to enjoy sexual encounters to which they feel drawn, but is restricted in certain situations to prevent people's real desires from being overborne by superior authority.

Whether or not a person is permitted to consent to the actions of another directed towards him or her seems likely, then, to depend on a matter of classification: is the activity of which the actions form part properly to be regarded as violence or sex? The majority in *Brown* decided to classify the case as being about violence rather than sex, and this affected the relative weight they attributed to competing considerations of public policy and individual rights. Lord Templeman made this clear:

'The assertion was made on behalf of the appellants that the sexual appetites of sadists and masochists can only be satisfied by the infliction of bodily harm and that the law should not punish the consensual achievement of sexual satisfaction. . . . [T]he argument would be acceptable if sado-masochism were *only* concerned with sex, as the appellants contend. In my opinion sado-masochism is not *only* concerned with sex. Sado-masochism is *also* concerned with violence.'[131]

Lord Templeman assumes, first, that an activity can be neatly pigeon-holed as either violent or sexual; and, secondly, that violent behaviour is without redeeming value. Both assumptions are false, or, at least, over-simplifications. First, sado-masochism occupies an area in which the field of apparently violent conduct overlaps with the field of privacy and sex.[132] As the testimony of willing participants in consensual sado-masochistic encounters shows,[133] behaviour which appears violent to outsiders has a different social meaning to participants,[134] who regard it as a means of giving pleasure or fulfilment or an expression of love by causing emotional and physical sensations which produce those feelings in the other participants. Far from being unregulated, the violence is ritualistic, carefully administered, and controlled by the person who is subject to it rather than the person administering it.[135] If this is violence, it is far from anti-social. As Lord Mustill said at the start of his dissenting speech, 'My Lords, this *is* a case about the criminal law of violence. In my opinion, it *should be* a case about the criminal law of private sexual relations, if about anything at all'.[136]

Secondly, to imply (as Lord Templeman does) that carefully controlled, planned, and consensual violence as part of a sexual encounter has no redeeming social value, but to accept that boxing or rough and undisciplined play have social value which justifies the infliction of bodily harm, turns reality on its head. The object of respecting consent to the rough and tumble of sport (like consent to medical treatment) is

---

[131] [1993] 2 All ER at 82 (italics added).

[132] Law Commission, Consultation Paper No. 139, *Consent in the Criminal Law* (London: HMSO, 1995), 146, paras. 10.50–51.

[133] Law Commission, Consultation Paper No. 139, *Consent in the Criminal Law*, 131–40.

[134] N. Bamforth, 'Sado-Masochism and Consent' [1994] Crim. LR 661–4; Law Commission, Consultation Paper No. 139 *Consent in the Criminal Law*, 145, para. 10.48.

[135] Law Commission, Consultation Paper No. 139, *Consent in the Criminal Law*, 137–40, paras. 10.31–36.

[136] [1993] 2 All ER at 101 (italics added).

primarily to protect the individual interests of the participants as they perceive them, rather than to advance any public interest. It is a recognition of individual autonomy, the right of individuals of sufficient understanding to make their own decisions about what is good for them. In principle, this should apply equally to people's sexual preferences. Indeed, it is hard to see how the interest (whether public or private) in allowing people to express their sexuality, which forms a fundamental part of people's personality, could be less important than the interest in allowing people to pursue sports. Sport is fun, but sex, for many people, is more than fun: it is a form of self-expression.

To sum up, the decision in *Brown* is unsatisfactory whether viewed from the perspective of legal coherence or that of public policy. It is explicable only on the basis of an attachment to legal moralism, the Devlinesque view that law must enforce a core of morality in order to maintain the bonds holding society together.[137] However, even this hardly provides a justification in the light of evidence about the prevalence of sado-masochistic practices in mainstream heterosexual relationships in the UK.[138] It appears to infringe the privacy rights of both homosexuals and heterosexuals, can hardly be a genuine response to a pressing social need such as to make it necessary in a democratic society for the purposes of ECHR Article 8(2), and in any case seems disproportionate to any legitimate object which the law might be pursuing. Surprisingly, however, when three of the defendants in *Brown* complained to the European Court of Human Rights about their convictions, arguing that they violated their right to respect for private life under ECHR Article 8, they were unsuccessful.[139] The Court was seduced by the superficial appearance of violence and injury to the participants, even casting doubt on the UK government's concession that the convictions engaged the right to respect for private life: at least some judges were apparently of the view that the presence of violence might take at least some sado-masochistic encounters in private outside the scope of private life under ECHR Article 8(1), perhaps because in the *Brown* case participants had videotaped encounters and distributed the tapes among members of the group. At any rate, it cannot be assumed safely that the Court will regard all sexual activity in private as being protected by the right to respect for private life. When the Court turned its attention to the justification for interfering with the right to respect for private life, it accepted uncritically that refusing to accept the legal effectiveness of consent to actual bodily harm pursued the legitimate aim of protecting health and morals. When it came to applying the tests of pressing social need and proportionality, the Court allowed a wide margin of appreciation to the state, and concluded that the rule adopted in *Brown* was within the margin.

The Court often allows a wide margin of appreciation in cases involving immorality, but the decision is disappointingly out of line with the Court's decisions on criminalizing homosexual acts. In national law under the Human Rights Act 1998 the

---

[137] This is essentially the argument advanced by W. Wilson, 'Consenting to personal injury: how far can you go?' (1995) 1 *Contemporary Issues in Law* 45–60.

[138] Law Commission, Consultation Paper No. 139, *Consent in the Criminal Law*, 133–4, paras. 10.17–20.

[139] *Jaggard, Laskey and Brown v. United Kingdom*, Eur. Ct. HR, Judgment of 19 February 1997, RJD 1997-I, 24 EHRR 39.

margin of appreciation is not applicable, so in domestic proceedings the 1998 Act might provide a stronger argument for departing from *Brown* than there would be in Strasbourg for finding a violation of ECHR Article 8: the institutional politics of relationships between international tribunals and national authorities do not affect national judges. But even apart from the Human Rights Act 1998, the decision of the House of Lords in *Brown* is both unprincipled and incoherent.[140] The Law Commission has provisionally recommended a change in the law to allow people aged eighteen or over to consent to injuries intentionally caused for sexual (and also for religious and spiritual) purposes.[141] In the light of the more recent reduction of the age of consent for other sexual activity to sixteen, there is an argument for putting the age at which a person could give valid consent to injury inflicted in the course of a sado-masochistic encounter to sixteen. However, so far there has been no sign that any government is prepared to grasp this nettle. Sado-masochism was notably excluded from the Home Office review of sex offences. The courts created the problem by their decisions in *Donovan* and *Brown*, and it could well be left to the courts to resolve it.

The offence of indecent assault[142] presents a further difficulty. Any offence which contains as part of its definition a requirement of indecency is subject, even more than offences founded on immorality, to the whims and fashions of social acceptability. An indecent assault is an assault or battery (i.e. an intentional, non-consensual act putting the victim in fear of immediate violence, or actually inflicting violence) which is indecent. But what is needed to establish indecency? If the objective nature of the act is incapable of being regarded as indecent, the assault or battery is not indecent, regardless of the intention of the perpetrator. Thus removing a girl's shoe, or touching the bottom of her skirt, are not indecent assaults (although they may amount to common assaults), even if the perpetrator derives sexual gratification from the act.[143] It seems that there are only two ways in which an assault or battery may be indecent.[144]

First, if the nature of the act is unquestionably indecent in the circumstances, the assault is indecent whatever the defendant intended. As Lord Griffiths has said, 'A man might strip a woman with the motive of obtaining sexual gratification or, alternatively, with the motive of revenge to humiliate her; but whichever his motive he would undoubtedly be guilty of indecent assault because his intentional stripping of her clothing is an indecent affront to her sexual modesty'.[145] This use of criminal law to protect people against forcible affronts to their sexual modesty is a legitimate attempt to prevent harm and safeguard privacy.

Secondly, if the objective nature of the act in its context is equivocal, the assault will

---

[140] For detailed discussion, see L. H. Leigh, 'Sado-masochism, Consent, and the Reform of the Criminal Law' (1976) 39 *MLR* 130–46.

[141] Law Commission, Consultation Paper No. 139, *Consent in the Criminal Law*, 147–8, paras. 10.54–5.

[142] Sexual Offences Act 1956, ss. 14 (indecent assault on a female) and 15 (indecent assault on a male).

[143] *R. v. George* [1956] Crim. LR 52 (Streatfield J, Lincoln Assizes); *R. v. Thomas* (1985) 81 Cr. App. R. 331, CA.

[144] Smith and Hogan, *Criminal Law*, 7th edn., 468–71.

[145] *R. v. Court* [1989] AC 28 at 35, [1988] 2 All ER 221 at 224 *per* Lord Griffiths.

be indecent if the perpetrator had an indecent purpose, and evidence of purpose is admissible to establish the offence. This was decided by a majority of the House of Lords in *R. v. Court*,[146] where the defendant, a shop assistant, had placed a twelve-year-old girl customer across his knees and spanked her over her shorts. There was nothing in the nature of the spanking to show that this was anything other than a misguided and unjustified disciplinary chastisement. However, when the police asked the perpetrator why he had done it, he was unwise enough to admit that he was indulging a buttock fetish. This admission was held to be admissible in order to establish the indecency. The reasoning of the majority was that the offence includes as part of its mental element the intention to behave in a way that ordinary people would regard as indecent. Evidence of motive was admissible to prove this element. However, it is inconsistent to assert that the *mens rea* includes this element of subjective indecency when the objective nature of the act is equivocal, but not when the act is objectively indecent. It is an odd offence in which the *mens rea* alters from subjective to objective depending on the exterior manifestations of the behaviour which is to be penalized. The indecency should properly be regarded as part of the *actus reus* of the offence, not the *mens rea*. It might be desirable to treat the perpetrator's indecent motive as potentially an element of the *actus reus* of an indecent assault, and evidence of the admission might properly have been admitted for that purpose, but not as an element of the *mens rea*.

Furthermore, it is far from clear that it achieved a desirable result. To include the motive of the defendant as an element in the *actus reus* of the offence comes close to using the criminal law to penalize immoral thoughts. The effect of *Court* is that more severe penalties may be imposed on a defendant for an assault which affords him sexual satisfaction than for an exactly similar assault which affords him some other sort of satisfaction. For example, a shopkeeper who suspects a child of shoplifting might derive considerable moral satisfaction from giving the child a spanking to teach him a lesson. This would probably amount to a common assault and battery, with a maximum penalty of one year's imprisonment on conviction on indictment.[147] It seems a little unfair that another shopkeeper whose satisfaction is sexual as well as moral would be liable to up to ten years' imprisonment for indecent assault.[148] The objective quality of the two acts, and their impact on the victim, are the same, so the increased liability is entirely attributable to moral disapproval of certain motives or sources of satisfaction. A harm-based, utilitarian justification for imposing criminal liability provides no justification for distinguishing between the two cases.

(4) PAEDOPHILIA

An act of indecency on a child which amounts to an assault is always criminal. Children under the age of sixteen are unable to consent validly to any act which

---

[146] [1989] AC 28, [1988] 2 All ER 221 (Lord Keith of Kinkel, Lord Fraser of Tullybelton, Lord Griffiths, and Lord Ackner; Lord Goff of Chieveley dissented).

[147] Offences Against the Person Act 1861, s. 47.

[148] Sexual Offences Act 1956, Sch. 2, as amended by the Sexual Offences Act 1985, s. 3.

amounts to an indecent assault, even if it does not cause any bodily harm.[149] This is because of the perceived need to protect children from exploitation, and safeguard them against potentially serious errors of judgment due to lack of experience and understanding. For the same reasons, committing any act of gross indecency, not amounting to an assault, with or towards a child under the age of fourteen, or inciting a child under that age to commit such an act with oneself or another, is an offence.[150] In addition, it is an offence, without legitimate reason, to take, distribute, show, or advertise indecent photographs or pseudo-photographs of a child,[151] or knowingly to possess one for one of those purposes[152] or for one's personal use.[153] The effect is to make virtually any sexual activity involving children illegal. The restriction of the right to respect for paedophiles' private lives, which this entails, is justifiable under Article 8(2) of the European Convention on Human Rights by reference to the protection of the rights of the children concerned, even without reference to the object of protecting health and morality.

The Secretary of State for Health has a duty to keep a list of people who are considered unsuitable to work with children, going beyond those who have been convicted of offences against children to include people removed or suspended from positions involving contact with children as a result of misconduct which harmed or placed at risk a child. This statutory scheme, put in place by the Protection of Children Act 1999, includes provision for a Tribunal to deal with complaints about unjustified inclusion on the list or disclosure of information, and inaccuracy of records. It replaces a government-run Consultancy Service Index which prospective employers could consult, and should prevent a possible incompatibility between the Index and the rights to a fair hearing and to respect for the private lives of people included on the list. In particular, there was a risk that the Index lacked an appropriate foundation in positive law and failed to provide adequate safeguards for the private lives of people included on it, potentially violating ECHR Articles 6 and 8.[154] The Act supplements the provisions for obtaining criminal records certificates under the Police Act 1997, Part V. However, there is some doubt as to the accuracy of information maintained under both arrangements, so there could be significant problems arising under the Data Protection Act 1998 and ECHR Article 8 as incorporated into national law by the Human Rights Act 1998 (on which see Chapter 9 above).

(5) ACTS BETWEEN MALES IN PUBLIC

It is an offence under section 32 of the Sexual Offences Act 1956 for a man (or boy) 'persistently to solicit or importune in a public place for immoral purposes'. Although 'originally introduced to regulate the activity of men seeking the services of female

---

[149] Sexual Offences Act 1956, ss. 14(2) (girls), 15(2) (boys).

[150] Indecency with Children Act 1960, s. 1.

[151] Protection of Children Act 1978, s. 1(1), as amended by Criminal Justice and Public Order Act 1994, s. 84.

[152] Protection of Children Act 1978, s. 1(1)(c), as amended.

[153] Criminal Justice Act 1988, s. 160, as amended by Criminal Justice and Public Order Act 1994, s. 84.

[154] *R. v. Secretary of State for Health, ex parte C.* [2001] HRLR 400, CA, at 407–8 *per* Hale LJ.

prostitutes ... [i]n practice the charge is one laid almost exclusively against men soliciting other men'.[155] The classic setting for this is a public toilet. The offence presents two problems. First, it discriminates against men, since women cannot be convicted of it. Secondly, people's conceptions of an immoral purpose may differ, so there is a risk that a defendant might be convicted in one part of the country, or by one jury, in relation to a purpose which would have led to an acquittal elsewhere or by a differently constituted jury, not because different views are taken as to the evidence but because different moral standards prevail. This risk is only partly relieved by the decision in *Crook v. Edmondson*[156] that the immorality must relate to sexual conduct to fall within the section. Sexual mores have changed markedly over the last forty-five years, although at different rates and in different directions depending on geographical location, social class, and ethnic or cultural background. In a number of cases since the Sexual Offences Act 1967 legalized certain homosexual acts in private between consenting adults, defendants have argued that homosexual purposes should no longer be regarded as immoral within the meaning of the Act. The changes in standards of sexual morality have been acknowledged by the Court of Appeal to the extent that it is now for the jury to decide whether a particular purpose is immoral, although the trial judge must not leave a case to the jury unless satisfied that the purpose is at least capable of being properly regarded as immoral.[157] At the same time, the Court of Appeal has accepted that there are serious problems involved in dealing with crimes which rely on immorality as part of their definition. There may be a tendency for jurors to be overly influenced by the offensiveness of a defendant's conduct when accosting somebody, allowing their attention to be distracted from the immorality or otherwise of the defendant's purpose in soliciting. Judges must carefully direct juries as to what is required of them. When a defective direction leads to a conviction, the Court of Appeal will still uphold the conviction the court concludes that it is not 'unsafe', for example because, even had the jury been properly directed, they would have been bound to convict.[158] In *R. v. Gray*[159] the Court of Appeal asserted that any jury would inevitably have decided that homosexual activity was immoral, albeit not illegal. Although in *R. v. Kirkup*[160] the Court of Appeal made it clear that this was a decision on a question of fact, not law, the court still felt compelled to accept that it remained legally open to a jury to conclude that homosexuality could be regarded as immoral, and that a jury was so likely to have concluded that it was immoral that the conviction could not be quashed.[161]

With respect, however, this approach seems defective in law and questionable in morality. If the morality or otherwise of a purpose is a question for the jury, it must be

---

[155] Home Office, *Setting the Boundaries*, vol. 1, 103, para. 6.6.12.
[156] [1966] 1 All ER 833, DC.
[157] *R. v. Ford* [1978] 1 All ER 1129, CA; *R. v. Gray* (1981) 74 Cr. App. R. 324, CA; *R. v. Goddard* (1991) 92 Cr. App. R. 185, CA; *R. v. Kirkup* [1993] 1 WLR 774, [1993] 2 All ER 802, CA.
[158] Criminal Appeal Act 1968, s. 2 as amended.
[159] (1981) 74 Cr. App. R. 324, CA.
[160] [1993] 1 WLR 774, [1993] 2 All ER 802, CA.
[161] [1993] 2 All ER at 807, 809; see also *R. v. Ford* [1977] 1 WLR 1082, [1978] 1 All ER 1129, CA; *R. v. Gray* (1981) 74 Cr. App. R. 324, CA.

a question of fact from a legal point of view. If so, it is hard to see how the Court of Appeal in 1992 could be required as a matter of law to follow the factual conclusion of a differently constituted court, eleven turbulent years earlier, that a jury could not have regarded homosexual activity as other than immoral. In *R. v. Kirkup*,[162] Staughton LJ said that there was no evidence before the court to convince it that moral judgments had altered significantly since 1981. This, however, misstates the issue. When considering whether a conviction is safe under section 2 of the Criminal Appeal Act 1968, as amended, the Court of Appeal ought to look to the prosecution to convince them that standards of morality are so clear as a matter of fact that no jury could have taken the view that homosexuality is not immoral. The burden of proof is on the prosecution. By shifting it to the defence, the Court of Appeal erred in law.

This exacerbates a problem which the Court of Appeal in *Kirkup* acknowledged, and which would exist in any case. It is not satisfactory for judges to have to decide questions of morality as a basis for criminal liability. The only way to avoid this is for Parliament and the courts to refrain from creating offences which are premised on unspecified moral postulates. Merely to refer to popular morality leaves the standards of criminal liability to be determined by jurors, which is scarcely less objectionable than having them decided by judges. One may question whether it is appropriate for anyone to be entitled to decide that somebody else's purposes deserve punishment by reason of immorality. In the spirit of Mill, Wolfenden, and Hart, some identifiable harm should be required in order to justify criminalizing conduct. Mere immorality of purpose is not enough. The offence under section 32 of the Sexual Offences Act 1956 is objectionable as an attempt to criminalize conduct which may be harmless, merely by reason of the immorality of the ulterior object of the actor.

In the light of the developments in the caselaw of the European Court of Human Rights, section 32 of the Sexual Offences Act 1956 calls for urgent reconsideration by Parliament and, failing that, by the courts. It is now clear that discrimination on the ground of a person's homosexuality to amount (at least *prima facie*) to a violation of the right to respect for private life taken together with the right to be free of discrimination (ECHR Articles 8 and 14).[163] If Article 8 is engaged, the inherent uncertainty of the term 'immoral purposes' makes it probable that any failure of respect is not 'in accordance with the law', and so cannot be justified under the Convention.[164] Happily, the Home Office sex offences review has recommended the abolition of the offence under section 32, and its possible replacement with regulation of soliciting by men for the purposes of prostitution equivalent to the offence committed by women under section 1 of the Street Offences Act 1959.[165] It is to be hoped that Parliament acts speedily on this recommendation.

Other parts of the law regulating sexual activity display a similarly prurient concern

---

[162] [1993] 2 All ER at 808.

[163] *Salgueiro da Silva Mouta v. Portugal*, Eur. Ct. HR, App. No. 33290/96, Judgment of 21 December 1999.

[164] *Cp. Hashman and Harrup v. United Kingdom*, Eur. Ct. HR, Judgment of 25 November 1999, 30 EHRR 241, at paras. 38–41 (binding over to be of good behaviour violated Art. 10 because the *contra bonos mores* standard, defined as 'wrong rather than right in the judgment of the majority of contemporary fellow citizens', was too imprecise and lacking in objectivity to satisfy the test of being 'prescribed by law').

[165] Home Office, *Setting the Boundaries*, vol. 1, 103–4, paras. 6.6.12–17.

to discover and punish immoral purposes or thoughts, apart from any harm which may be done by their manifestation. Some examples follow.

(6) OTHER SEXUAL ACTIVITY IN PUBLIC

Behaviour which is acceptable in private is not necessarily acceptable in public. The sight of sexual activity (whether heterosexual or homosexual) is deeply offensive to many people. The injury to feelings which this sort of offence engenders may be severe enough to constitute a harm against which it is justifiable to seek protection from the criminal law.[166] At the same time, people's susceptibilities to this sort of outrage, and the kinds of behaviour which precipitate it, vary greatly. If the code of public conduct sanctioned by the criminal law were designed to avoid outraging the most susceptible citizens, the range of behaviour and expression to which we could give vent in public might be absurdly restricted. The framers of criminal law have tended to balance the interest in free expression against that in freedom from outrage by treating the problem essentially as one of public order: conduct has been treated as criminal, both formerly under the Public Order Act 1936, section 5, and now under the Public Order Act 1986, section 4, if the outrage which it is intended or likely to occasion makes it likely to precipitate public violence.[167]

However, there are signs that Parliament and the courts are inclined to press criminal liability rather further than this might suggest. Section 5 of the Public Order Act 1986 makes it an offence to use threatening, abusive, or insulting words or behaviour, or disorderly behaviour, within the hearing or sight of a person likely to cause harassment, alarm, or distress thereby. This has the capacity to allow public displays of physical affection, particularly between homosexuals, to be penalized. Although showing affection for another person could not normally be regarded as insulting (unless that person did not consent to the display, and regarded it as implying a sexual orientation which he or she found insulting[168]), the Divisional Court held in *Masterson v. Holden*[169] that magistrates were entitled to decide that heterosexuals might feel insulted at seeing two homosexuals cuddling and kissing each other on the lips in Oxford Street, London at 1.55 a.m. If this is correct, and the same approach is applied to prosecutions under section 5 of the Public Order Act 1986, the freedom of homosexuals (particularly, perhaps, men) to express their feelings in public will be severely curtailed, since it would seem to follow from the decision that magistrates would often be justified in deciding that the behaviour would be likely to cause harassment or distress to a heterosexual observer.

However, the decision in *Masterson v. Holden* is of questionable authority. It gives a more expansive interpretation to 'insulting' than is justified by the decision of the House of Lords in *Brutus v. Cozens*[170] that 'insulting' should be given its natural

---

[166] Feinberg, *Offense*, ch. 9.

[167] See further Ch. 18, below.

[168] *Parkin v. Norman* [1983] QB 92 at 100–1, [1982] 2 All ER 583 at 588–9, *per* McCullough J.

[169] [1986] 1 WLR 1017, [1986] 3 All ER 39, DC. The defendants were charged under the Metropolitan Police Act 1839, s. 54(13).

[170] [1973] AC 854, [1972] 2 All ER 1297, HL, a case on s. 5 of the Public Order Act 1936.

meaning. The approach in *Masterson* is therefore hard to support as a matter of law. It is also objectionable in principle. It extends criminal liability more widely than is authorized by Parliament, and it does so in a manner which is likely, in practice, to discriminate against homosexuals, since it is unlikely that any prosecutor or magistrate would consider a heterosexual couple publicly kissing to be insulting. Even leaving aside the possibility of improper discrimination on the basis of sexual orientation, the use of the criminal law to penalize normal behaviour expressive of affection, whether between heterosexuals or homosexuals, where there is no risk of public disorder or violence being caused, seems insensitive and inappropriate.

The interpretation and application of the law in this area may be affected by the Human Rights Act 1998, and particularly the right to respect for private life under ECHR Article 8. It is inevitable that people carry aspects of their private lives into public spaces, and expressions of affection deserve respect in public as they do not intrude on others so as to cause annoyance. An interference with people's freedom to give expression to their feelings would violate ECHR Article 8 unless it could be justified. The justification depends partly on a test of proportionality. Only in the most extreme circumstances will it be proportionate to criminalize someone for expressing affection in public. The facts of *Masterson* provide a classic example of a disproportionate application of legislation. By virtue of section 3 of the 1998 Act, legislation which might have that affect must be read and given effect in the light of ECHR Article 8 so far as it is possible to do so. This should be enough to consign *Masterson* to oblivion. However, ideally Parliament should make the law clear. The Home Office sex offences review has recommended that the law on sexual activity in public 'should apply to all sexual behaviour in public and not in particular to same sex behaviour . . . Like the CLRC we thought the discreet couple should not be penalised, the nuisance was not the sexual activity itself but the fact that it is seen by others and that it occurs in situations where it is likely to cause distress or offence'.[171] The review proposed that the matter should be dealt with by a new offence, consisting of sexual behaviour which a person knows or should know is likely to cause distress, alarm, or offence to others in a public place, and would enable a warning to be given before the criminal law is invoked.[172] With regard to the application of the proposed law, the review notes:

'It will be important that any new or amended offence should operate in a gender and sexuality neutral way. A man and a man—or a woman and a woman—kissing and holding hands in public should no more be criminalised than a man and a woman behaving in the same way. It will be equally important, not least to satisfy the clarity required by the ECHR, that as far as possible the test and standards applied to any new offences should be national and not merely local.'[173]

This offers a sensible and principled way forward.

---

[171] Home Office, *Setting the Boundaries*, vol. 1, 124–6, paras. 8.4.4, 8.4.6, referring to Criminal Law Revision Committee, Fifteenth Report, *Sexual Offences* (London: HMSO, 1984).

[172] Ibid., 126, paras. 8.4.9, 8.4.11, and Recommendation 56.

[173] Ibid., para. 8.4.10.

(7) PROSTITUTION, KEEPING A DISORDERLY HOUSE, AND RELATED OFFENCES[174]

The law takes a dim view of prostitution, sometimes said to be the world's oldest profession. While prostitution is not actually unlawful in itself, a range of criminal offences penalize those who manage prostitutes, permit their premises to be used for prostitution, or keep, manage, or let premises which are used as a brothel.[175] A brothel requires the presence of at least two prostitutes. A person who provides sexual services for money to one customer at a time, or provides no sexual services at all, on his or her premises can be charged with keeping a disorderly house at common law if the services are available to the public and are such as outrage public decency (provision for flagellation, humiliation, bondage, and torture apparently falls into this category) or are otherwise calculated to harm the public interest to such an extent as to call for punishment.[176] This threatened to disrupt the smooth commercial development of social fashions when the police decided to target fetishist theme clubs. In London, police officers dressed in leather and rubber to infiltrate a club on sado-masichistic nights as part of a surveillance operation which led to the manager being charged with keeping a disorderly house. When the case was tried at Southwark Crown Court, the jury acquitted the manager, showing that at least some people in England have a stronger sense of humour, proportion, and tolerance than the police had given us credit for.[177]

Women who loiter or solicit in a public place for the purpose of prostitution commit an offence.[178] Men who persistently solicit women for the purpose of prostitution commit an offence,[179] and it is a special offence (because of the harassment to women caused by kerb-crawlers) to use a car to solicit a woman for the purpose of prostitution in a manner or in circumstances likely to cause annoyance to the woman or nuisance to other people in the neighbourhood.[180] This form of annoyance constitutes a harm which may justify criminal sanctions, but it is hard to see how prostitutes who merely loiter waiting to be picked up by punters do any harm. Parliament will not attempt the impossible task of driving prostitution out of society, but seeks instead to make it a marginal, hole-in-the-corner activity which it is difficult to pursue without falling foul of the law in one way or another. For people who for some reason depend on prostitutes to satisfy their sexual appetites, this battery of legal obstacles makes the fulfilment of that part of their private lives constituted by their sexual appetites into a difficult and uncomfortable affair.

---

[174] Honoré, *Sex Law*, ch. 5.

[175] Sexual Offences Act 1956, ss. 31, 33, 34, 35, 36; Sexual Offences Act 1967, s. 6. For reform proposals, see Home Office, *Setting the Boundaries*, vol. 1, 116–7, paras. 7.7.1–7.8.3, also recommending a full review of the law of prostitution.

[176] *R. v. Tan* [1983] 2 All ER 12, CA.

[177] For an account of the case, see J. Cusick, 'Club Manager Cleared over "Disorderly House"', *Independent*, 30 March 1996, 3.

[178] Street Offences Act 1959, s. 1.

[179] Street Offences Act 1985, s. 2.

[180] Ibid., s. 1.

(8) SEXUAL ORIENTATION AS A GROUND FOR DISCRIMINATION[181]

As explained in Chapter 3 above, a person's sex is generally not a legitimate ground for discriminating against him or her, but neither English law nor Community law has in the past directly protected people against discrimination on the ground of their sexual orientation. There was hope that this might be changing when the European Court of Justice in *P. v. S. and Cornwall County Council*[182] decided that the Community rules on sex discrimination protected transsexuals.[183] These hopes were dashed in *Grant v. South-West Trains Ltd.*,[184] but may be rekindled by the EC Framework Directive on Discrimination. By contrast, the European Court of Human Rights has held that taking legal or administrative action against a person on account of his or her sexual orientation infringes the right to respect for their private lives under ECHR Article 8(1), and is a violation unless it can be justified under Article 8(2). Because of the importance of sexual orientation to a person's identity and sense of worth, the Court has regarded an infringement as being particularly hard to justify. This is markedly different from the approach of English courts to the issue. The long-standing deference of the courts to the executive's judgments about national security has had a strange effect in relation to the national security implications of homosexuality. The risk to security from blackmail is small when the person concerned is open about his or her homosexuality. Yet in *Hodges v. Director, GCHQ*,[185] a man employed at GCHQ in a security-related capacity 'came out', publicly acknowledging his homosexuality. He was told that he was to be moved to other, less sensitive duties. Internal appeal processes having failed, he applied for judicial review of the decision. The Divisional Court accepted that in all likelihood Mr. Hodges posed less of a security risk after coming out than he had previously, and that the decision to move him therefore seemed hard to justify rationally, but nevertheless refused to quash the decision, concluding that it would be inappropriate to conclude that the decision was one which no reasonable Director of GCHQ could have reached.[186] Similarly, in *R. v. Ministry of Defence, ex parte Smith*[187] the Court of Appeal decided that the administrative discharge of homosexuals from the armed forces after highly intrusive interrogations, despite engaging fundamental rights, was not so unreasonable as to be unlawful on ordinary principles of administrative law.

[181] R. Wintemute, 'Sexual Orientation Discrimination', in C. McCrudden and G. Chambers (eds.), *Individual Rights and the Law in Britain* (Oxford: Clarendon Press, 1994), 491–533; R. Wintemute, *Sexual Orientation and Human Rights: The United States Constitution, the European Convention, and the Canadian Charter* (Oxford: Clarendon Press, 1995), *passim*; R. Wintemute, 'Lesbian and Gay Inequality 2000: the Potential of the Human Rights Act 1998 and the Need for an Equality Act 2002' [2000] *EHRL Rev.* 603–26.

[182] Case C–13/94, [1996] ICR 795, CJEC.

[183] R. Wintemute, 'Recognizing New Kinds of Direct Sex Discrimination: Transsexualism, Sexual Orientation and Dress Codes' (1997) 60 *MLR* 334–359.

[184] Case C–249/96, [1998] ICR 449, CJEC. See N. Bamforth, 'Sexual Orientation Discrimination after *Grant v. South-West Trains*' (2000) 63 *MLR* 694–720.

[185] [1988] COD 123.

[186] See S. Fredman and G. S. Morris, *The State as Employer: Labour Law in the Public Services* (London: Mansell, 1989), 372–3.

[187] [1996] QB 517, [1996] 1 All ER 257, CA.

By contrast, in *Smith and Grady v. United Kingdom*[188] and *Lustig-Prean and Beckett v. United Kingdom*,[189] the European Court of Human Rights held that the state had failed to show that the interference with Article 8 rights was proportionate to a legitimate aim under Article 8(2). This difference in approach shows that the onus lies on the state or a public authority to offer convincing proof of proportionality, rather than the onus lying on the applicant to establish unreasonableness. The burden on the state is particularly heavy in view of the importance of the right to the individuals concerned. Furthermore, treatment which discriminates against a person by reason of sexual orientation in relation to other Convention rights is likely to violate Article 14.[190]

These rights under the ECHR are now part of English law by virtue of the Human Rights Act 1998. However, the protection is limited. Article 8 protects private life only against public authorities (unless the courts develop the horizontal effect of Article 8 more aggressively than currently appears likely), while Article 14 does not offer a free-standing right to be free of discrimination, but only a right not to be discriminated against in the enjoyment of other Convention rights. There may, therefore, still be cases in which it is permissible to dismiss a person by reason of their sexuality, although the right to freedom of expression under ECHR Article 10 may bolster Article 8 rights in a case such as *Boychuk v. Symons Holdings Ltd.*,[191] where a lesbian employee was held to have been fairly dismissed for refusing to remove a Gay Liberation badge. But if the expression adversely affects the employee's ability to do the job (for example because of the reaction of customers, as in *Boychuk*), or if the employer is providing a public service such as education or residential child care, in respect of which there is considerable public disquiet at the risk of child abuse, it may still not be unfair to dismiss a teacher or carer who has been convicted of an act of sexual impropriety, even if it was not connected with the job.[192]

In principle, it is unacceptable to discriminate against homosexuals. The reasons go beyond the objection to discrimination in itself. People's homosexuality is not necessarily patent. If a person chooses to dress or behave in ways which make clear their homosexual orientation, they are making a statement about their own personality. Such statements are an emanation of the person's private life, commitments, and beliefs, and as such are entitled to respect. In terms of human rights, to subject people to disadvantage on the ground of their self-expression violates the right to respect for their private lives, contrary to Article 8(1) of the European Convention on Human Rights, because it undermines their self-esteem. But the matter does not end there. By openly associating themselves with a group which is increasingly playing a political role, agitating for respect and fair treatment, the homosexual who declares his or her sexual orientation may be making a political, as well as a personal, statement. The right to freedom of expression is protected by Article 10 of the Convention, considered further in Chapters 13 to 18 below. Article 10 protects people against

---

[188] Eur. Ct. HR, Apps. Nos. 33985/96 and 33986/96, Judgment of 27 September 1999.

[189] Eur. Ct. HR, Apps. Nos. 31417/96 and 32377/96, Judgment of 27 September 1999.

[190] See generally Ch. 3, above; *A. D. T. v. United Kingdom*, Eur. Ct. HR, App. No. 35765/97, Judgment of 31 July 2000.

[191] [1977] IRLR 395, EAT.

[192] *Nottinghamshire County Council v. Bowley* [1978] IRLR 252, EAT.

discrimination on the ground of their expressed views if the discrimination amounts to an interference with their freedom to express the views, although it is a potential weakness of Article 10 that it permits states to justify an interference if it is prescribed by law and necessary in a democratic society for (*inter alia*) the protection of health or morals.[193]

Many, if not all, of these complexities would be resolved if the UK's government were to change its present stand of opposition to ratifying the free-standing anti-discrimination right under Protocol No. 12 to the ECHR, and include it among the Convention rights in the Human Rights Act 1998, at the same time implementing the EU Framework Directive on Discrimination. As it is, the law in England and Wales remains a mass of potentially conflicting principles and rules. The UK may be in breach of the free-standing non-discrimination right under Article 26 of the International Covenant on Civil and Political Rights, but at present there is no judicial or quasi-judicial remedy for that breach in national law or (unless and until the UK ratifies the first Optional Protocol to the ICCPR to allow people to complain of alleged violations to the UN Human Rights Committee) in international law.

12.3 SOME OTHER ASPECTS OF FAMILY LIFE

This section notes the impact of certain other aspects of the right to respect for private and family life under Article 8 of the European Convention on Human Rights, and some associated rights, on people's rights in English law. Whereas the earlier parts of the chapter have been concerned mainly with questions of legal status and criminal liability, this section illustrates the interaction of principles of civil liberties and human rights with the technicalities of law.

(1) THE RIGHT TO MARRY

ECHR Article 12 confers a right to marry only on people of marriageable age, which is not defined, and 'according to the national laws governing the exercise of this right'. English law provides for a minimum age of sixteen. (If a party is under eighteen, each parent with parental responsibility for the party, or the guardian, or a court should have consented to the marriage, but a marriage without that consent is not invalid on that ground.)[194] As noted in section 12.1 above, the parties must be respectively male and female,[194a] must not be related to each other within prohibited degrees of

---

[193] On the possibility that freedom of expression might protect physical manifestations of same-sex love, see Wintemute, *Sexual Orientation and Human Rights*, 49–50 and 52 (on the position in the USA), 114–7 (on the position under the ECHR).

[194] Marriage Acts 1949 to 1986, ss. 2, 3 as amended.

[194a] The Court of Appeal of New Zealand has held by a majority that there is no unlawful discrimination in issuing marriage licences only to opposite-sex couples: *Quilter v. Attorney-General* [1998] 1 NZLR 523, (1997) 2 BHRC 461, discussed by A. Butler, 'Same-Sex Marriage and Freedom from Discrimination in New Zealand' [1998] *PL* 396–406. See generally I. Karsten QC, 'Atypical Families and the Human Rights Act: The Rights of Unmarried Fathers, Same Sex Couples and Transsexuals' [1999] *EHRL Rev.* 195–207.

consanguinity or affinity, and must be unmarried. A person domiciled in England and Wales cannot lawfully contract a marriage which is in fact (rather than potentially) polygamous anywhere in the world, even if it would be permitted according to the *lex loci celebrationis*.[195] Although polygamy is prohibited, serial monogamy is permitted: there are procedures for dissolving marriages which have irretrievably broken down, and the parties to a dissolved marriage are then free to remarry as often as they wish. Indeed, in *F. v. Switzerland*[196] the state had sought to impose a period during which the guilty party to a divorce could not remarry (in the case of the guilty party in a divorce granted for adultery, up to three years). The Court held that this threatened the essence of the right to marry where the state, by allowing a dissolution, had demonstrated that it did not intend to limit the party's right to marry to one occasion only.

But this is not the case in all jurisdictions. In Ireland, for example, the influence of Roman Catholic canon law, with its insistence on the lifelong nature of the marriage vows, has resulted in civil law offering no procedure for divorce to Irish citizens. The European Court of Human Rights has held that neither the right to marry nor the right to respect for private and family life demands that people should have a legal channel for ending marriages into which they have entered. In *Johnston v. Ireland*[197] the Court held that the total absence in the Republic of Ireland of a procedure for dissolving a marriage once it has been validly entered into did not violate either Article 8 or Article 12 of the Convention. The *travaux préparatoires* showed that the right to a divorce had been deliberately omitted from both Article 12 and Article 5 of Protocol No. 7. It would therefore have been improper for the Court to to create such a right by interpretation.

(2) THE RIGHT TO FOUND A FAMILY

The right to marry and the right to found a family in ECHR Article 12 are linked in that marriage is seen as a precursor to the founding of a family, and Article 12 prevents a state from denying to married people the right to found a family unless there are Convention-compliant justifications for doing so. The paradigm of an interference with the right to found a family would be non-consensual sterilization or abortion. The right to marry does not depend on an intention to found a family, and a family may exist without or in spite of a marriage (as we will see below). However, the European Court of Human Rights, like the English common law exemplified in *Corbett v. Corbett*, has consistently held that people who lack the anatomical paraphernalia required for procreation cannot assert a right to be allowed to marry,[198] although a state may permit them to do so in its discretion. There is an alternative view that the rights to marry and found a family are entirely distinct, so that it would be possible for people who cannot procreate to assert a right to marry. This view was taken by Mr.

[195] Matrimonial Causes Act 1973, s. 11(d); Private International Law (Miscellaneous Provisions) Act 1995, Sch., para. 2(2).
[196] Eur. Ct. HR, Series A, No. 128, Judgment of 18 December 1987.
[197] Eur. Ct. HR, Series A, No. 112, Judgment of 18 December 1986, 9 EHRR 203.
[198] See the *Rees, Cossey,* and *Sheffield and Horsham* cases, discussed in section 12(1) above.

Schermers in his dissenting opinion in the Commission in *W. v. United Kingdom.*[199] This has not so far achieved widespread institutional support, but if it were to do so it might have significant implications for the nature of marriage, for example by making it possible to argue for a right to same-sex marriage.

If the right to found a family were to be treated as giving rise to positive obligations on the state, it could impose significant economic, medical, and social responsibilities on society. For example, if founding a family is taken to include child-rearing, the right might in appropriate circumstances include pre-natal, obstetric, neo-natal, and post-natal care and support, from medical services, social services, and through the social security system. For infertile couples, there might be a right to assisted reproduction, unless there were Convention-compliant reasons for denying the service to them. If the right to found a family then came to be regarded as entirely independent of the right to marry, the services and support for reproduction would need to be supplied as a matter of right to all intending parents, including single parents and same-sex couples, unless a Convention-compliant justification could be found for limiting the obligations of the state or setting off other people's rights against those of the intending parent or parents. Support for such an interpretation of Article 12 might be found in the right to be free of discrimination in the enjoyment of other Convention rights, under Article 14. Treating intending parents differently on the ground of their marital status discriminates on the ground of status. However, Article 14 has so far not been interpreted in that way, and the right to found a family under Article 12 has until now been limited to married couples.

Adoption provides one means of founding a family. At the same time, adoption brings to an end the parental responsibilities of the natural parents, bringing into play their right to respect for family life under Article 8 where a child in the care of a local authority is placed for adoption without the agreement of the natural parents. The law must resolve potential conflicts between prospective adoptive parents and natural parents. Article 12 does not seem to require any particular system of adoption, nor recognition of foreign adoption orders.[200] The Adoption Act 1976 as amended regulates adoption in England and Wales in ways which are designed to protect the interests of the child as well as those of the natural and the adoptive parents. In relation to the Article 8 rights of natural parents, the Act usually requires the consent of the parent before an adoption can take place, but to protect the best interests of the child it provides that the court can dispense with the parents' consent if it is unreasonably withheld.[201] Under ECHR Article 8, now forming part of English law by virtue of the Human Rights Act 1998, the courts should usually give an opportunity to a father who is no longer cohabiting, but who has maintained contact with or support for the child, to make representations before authorizing adoption, as such fathers have rights under ECHR Article 8 which may be overridden only when justified by reference to the criteria in Article 8(2). ECHR Article 6(1) also provides them with a

---

[199] App. No. 11095/84, 63 DR 34 (1989).

[200] *X. and Y. v. United Kingdom*, App. No. 7229/75, 12 DR 32 (1977); *X. v. Netherlands*, App. No. 8896/80, 24 DR 176 (1981). However, the position might be different if the matter were re-litigated now.

[201] Adoption Act 1976, s. 6.

right to a fair hearing before their parental rights and responsibilities are terminated by adoption, although all these requirements may have to give way to an established need to protect the physical or emotional welfare of the child.[202]

In the past, a conservative attitude was taken to the kinds of people who should be permitted to adopt children. Adopters were overwhelmingly financially independent, securely married couples under the age of forty. The growing number of children in the long-term care of local authorities, coupled with the falling number of secure marriages and a shortage of potential adopters of older and disabled children, led to a rethink. It came to be accepted that the best interests of a child were better served by giving the opportunity to enjoy a secure family life than by keeping the child in care. The criteria for judging the acceptability of potential adoptive parents came to focus on their capacity to offer a secure home life rather than on stereotypes of happy families. Adoption by single parents and same-sex couples has become relatively commonplace. It is not now regarded as contrary to public policy to allow an unmarried person in a same-sex relationship to adopt a child, and it is not reasonable for a natural mother to withhold consent to an adoption on that ground if the adoption is judged to safeguard and promote the welfare of the child throughout childhood.[203] This gives an opportunity to found a family to people who would not fall within the scope of the orthodox interpretation of the right to do so under ECHR Article 12. The government is conducting a full review of the principles which should guide adoption law in modern conditions. A White Paper was published late in 2000.[203a] The Adoption and Children Bill 2001 will, if passed, improve the adoption regime. In particular, it will make the welfare of the child the paramount consideration in adoptions as in other areas of family law.[204]

There was concern among some practitioners that the Human Rights Act 1998 might force judges and local authorities to prefer the rights of parents under the Act to the best interests of the child, where they came into conflict. This was based on a misconception. A parent's right to respect for private and family life can legitimately be restricted under ECHR Article 8 in order to protect health, morals, and the rights and freedoms of others, as long as the restriction is proportionate to a pressing social need to protect the child. The European Court of Human Rights has consistently interpreted and applied Article 8(2) in a manner which gives primacy to the interests of the child in health and development in cases where they conflict with the rights of adults even allowing the right to a public hearing and the public delivery of judgment

---

[202] *Keegan v. Ireland*, Eur. Ct. HR, Series A, No. 290, Judgment of 26 May 1994, 18 EHRR 342; *Kroon v. The Netherlands*, Eur. Ct. HR, Series A, No. 297-C, Judgment of 27 October 1994, 19 EHRR 263; *In re H. (A Child) (Adoption: Disclosure), In re G. (A Child) (Adoption: Disclosure), The Times*, 5 January 2001, Dame Elizabeth Butler-Sloss P.

[203] Adoption Act 1976, s. 6; *In re W. (A Minor) (Adoption: Homosexual Adopter)* [1998] Fam. 58, [1997] 3 All ER 620.

[203a] Department of Health White Paper, *Adoption: A New Approach*, Cm. 5017 (London: The Stationery Office, 2000) with annexed Draft National Adoption Standards for England, Scotland, and Wales.

[204] In adoption proceedings, the court must currently have regard to all the circumstances, but the welfare of the child is the first consideration: Adoption Act 1976, s. 6. This is similar but not identical to the principle governing decisions relating to a child's upbringing under the Children Act 1989, s. 1 that the best interests of the child are paramount.

under ECHR Article 6 to be compromised where it is necessary in the children's interests in proceedings concerned with the custody and residence of children.[205] The Court of Appeal has adopted this approach when refusing applications by parents who have been responsible for domestic violence for contact with their children. Where the parents have not changed their behaviour or for any other reason contact would give rise to a real risk of physical or emotional harm to the child, the court has a positive duty under Article 8 to protect the child against that risk, if necessary by restricting or even annihilating any chance of re-establishing a family relationship between the parents and children concerned.[206]

Social, technological, and scientific developments have provided additional ways of founding a family. One is surrogacy, in which a person or couple commission another woman to bear a child for them, usually using either an implanted foetus developed by in vitro fertilization (IVF) or using the woman's own ovum fertilized by artificial insemination using the sperm of the male commissioning partner or a donor. Before the passage of the Human Fertilisation and Embryology Act 1990, a woman who bore a child was treated as the mother of the child. If she was married her husband was presumed to be the child's father, although this presumption might be rebutted by evidence that the woman had been inseminated (artificially or otherwise) with sperm from another man, who would then be treated as the father. It made no difference that the mother had carried the baby under an agreement with another woman to act as surrogate for the other. The position remains the same under section 27 of the 1990 Act. However, there are two ways in which the parental responsibilities and rights of the surrogate may be terminated. First, the party or parties who commissioned the arrangement may adopt the child. Secondly, section 30 of the 1990 Act, drafted hurriedly during the passage of the Bill and subject to a number of serious criticisms, introduced the notion of a 'parental order', which requires the child to be treated in law as the child of the commissioning parties.[207] Such an order requires the free and fully informed consent of the surrogate and the legal father of the child to the making of the order, unless the person in question cannot be found or is incapable of agreeing. An unreasonable refusal to consent cannot be overridden.

In the absence of adoption or a parental order, it is possible that treating a child born to a surrogate mother as her child (and, if she is married, that of her husband) might violate two sets of Convention rights. First, the commissioning parties will often be the biological parents. Refusing to recognize them in law as the child's parents may violate their right to respect for family life under ECHR Article 8(1), unless the refusal could be justified on the grounds set out in Article 8(2). Secondly,

---

[205] See, e.g. *Johansen v. Norway*, Eur. Ct. HR, Judgment of 7 August 1996, 23 EHRR 33 at para. 78: '. . . the parents cannot be entitled under Article 8 of the Convention to have such measures taken as would harm the child's health and development'. On private hearings and restrictions on releasing judgments in residence cases, see *B. v. United Kingdom* and *P. v. United Kingdom*, Eur. Ct. HR, Apps. Nos. 36337/97 and 35974/97, Judgment of 24 April 2001; *The Times*, 15 May 2001.

[206] *In re L. (A Child) (Contact: Domestic Violence)* [2001] 2 WLR 339, CA, especially at 352 *per* Dame Elizabeth Butler-Sloss P.

[207] For discussion, see G. Douglas, *Law, Fertility and Reproduction* (London: Sweet & Maxwell, 1991), 158–61.

the child's right to respect for his or her biological relationship with the commission-ing parties might be infringed. On the other hand, there may be powerful arguments of public order and morality for refusing recognition in some or all such cases.

Another method of founding a family is by IVF. Where the conception is brought about by artificial insemination, the legal father is the person whose sperm were used. If the sperm are those of the woman's partner, there is no legal problem. However, if the process involves use of sperm provided by a donor, the Human Fertilisation and Embryology Act 1990, section 8, amends the usual legal rules on parenthood. When a married woman is artificially inseminated with the sperm of a third party, her hus-band is to be treated as the father unless he can prove that the sperm was not his and that he did not consent to the insemination.[208] If the insemination took place in the course of a treatment provided for the mother and a man, regulated under the licens-ing regime laid down for such treatment by the 1990 Act, the man is to be treated as the father.[209] However, this only applies where the partner is, in law, a man. The European Court of Human Rights has held that the state is under no obligation to allow a female-to-male transsexual to be registered as the father of a child, even if he is filling the role of the child's father, despite the disadvantages which the child may suffer as a result.[210]

The 1990 Act also regulates the circumstances in which gametes or embryos may be stored or used for the purpose of allowing a woman to give birth to a child. The Act was passed to resolve legal and ethical difficulties discussed in the *Report of the Committee of Inquiry into Human Fertilisation and Embryology*.[211] The Act is designed to protect the interests of all those involved in the process, including the mother, the child, other members of the family, and the sperm donor. In order to protect the interests of the sperm donor in controlling the use to be made of his genetic material, licences for storing and using gametes and embryos under the Act require the user to ensure that gametes are used only if their donor has consented in writing to their use after proper counselling, and has not withdrawn that consent.[212] The Human Fertil-isation and Embryology Authority in its discretion under the Act imposes further requirements (which it is free to vary or waive in particular cases) as conditions of a licence. For example, it restricts the export of stored sperm. This may frustrate the desire of a person to found a family, but generally the restrictions will be justifiable under the Human Rights Act 1998 and ECHR Article 12, because they will be a legitimate way of protecting compelling social interests or the rights and interests of other parties.

However, in rare cases it may work real unfairness. *R. v. Human Fertilisation and Embryology Authority, ex parte Blood*[213] was such a case. Mr. and Mrs. Blood were trying to conceive a child when Mr. Blood contracted meningitis. While he was in a

---

[208] Human Fertilisation and Embryology Act 1990, s. 28(5), (2).

[209] Ibid., s. 28(3).

[210] *X., Y. and Z. v. United Kingdom*, Eur. Ct. HR, Judgment of 22 April 1997, RJD 1997-II, 24 EHRR 143.

[211] Cmnd. 9314 (London: HMSO, 1984).

[212] Human Fertilisation and Embryology Act 1990, Sch. 3.

[213] [1999] Fam. 151, [1997] 2 All ER 687, CA. See D. Morgan and R. G. Lee, 'In the Name of the Father? *Ex parte Blood*: Dealing with Novelty and Anomaly' (1997) 60 *MLR* 840–56.

coma, two samples of sperm were taken from him and stored. Despite having wanted his wife to conceive his child, he was unable to consent in writing to the use of his sperm: he died without regaining consciousness. Mrs. Blood wanted to use them to conceive her late husband's child. The Authority took the view under the Act that it would be unlawful to use the sperm for that purpose in the UK, because of the lack of written consent. On an application for judicial review of the decision, this was upheld by Sir Stephen Brown P and the Court of Appeal. Mrs. Blood also sought to have the sperm delivered to her so that she could take it to Belgium, a European Community Member State, where the requirement for consent did not apply. On this point, the Authority decided against exercising its discretion in her favour. Parliament had carefully considered the requirement for consent, and it would allow the intention of Parliament to be evaded if the sperm were to be delivered to Mrs. Blood for treatment abroad without the donor's consent. The Court of Appeal quashed this decision, holding that it conflicted with Community law. Articles 59 and 60 (now 49 and 50) of the EC Treaty prohibit restrictions on the freedom of a person established in one Member State of the Community to provide services within the Community to nationals of other Member States. The court adopted the opinion of Advocate-General Van Gerven in *Society for the Protection of Unborn Children Ireland Ltd. v. Grogan*[214] that medical treatment for profit is a service, and that restrictions on access to the service in another Member State may impede intra-Community trade in services and so in principle infringe the right to provide such services. The Authority should have considered whether the refusal to allow the export of the sperm was a proportionate response to a recognized public interest for the purposes of EC law. After further consideration, the Authority gave permission for Mrs. Blood to take the sperm to Belgium, and in due course Mrs. Blood was delivered of her late husband's child.

This is a happy ending, of sorts, but it is hardly satisfactory that a decision of such ethical sensitivity should have been decided ultimately by reference to the law of international trade. It is essentially an aspect of the right to found a family and the right to respect for private and family life. The case should have been determined accordingly. If the case had arisen now, the main basis for reviewing the decision of the Authority would be, and ought properly to be, Mrs. Blood's rights under ECHR Articles 8 and 12 by virtue of the Human Rights Act 1998.

(3) THE RIGHT TO RESPECT FOR FAMILY LIFE

As noted at the outset of this chapter, international law regards the family as the fundamental unit in society, and requires states to protect it. The European Court of Human Rights has made it clear that children as well as adults have the right to respect for family life under ECHR Article 8. The idea of the family is not defined solely by national law: it is a factual, rather than a legal, construct, and is so regarded in the caselaw of the Court. The idea of family life has accordingly been extended to protect the value of mutual enjoyment of a wide range of *de facto* relationships of personal

---

[214] Case C–159/90, [1991] ECR I–4685, CJEC, at 4708–15.

intimacy and biological closeness. The question is not whether national law regards people as related to each other, but whether they have close, continuing, and practical ties. At the core of the notion is the mutual enjoyment by parent and child of each other's company.[215] A family relationship may subsist between a child borne out of wedlock and his or her father,[216] and between an estranged father and his child to whom he has rights of access and for whom he provides financial support.[217]

Other examples of family life protected under Article 8 include the following situations, as long as there is a real and practical bond to be preserved:

- relationships between members of the extended family, such as uncle and nephew;[218]

- the relationship between a man and his child, conceived when the man and the mother were unmarried but living together, following the break-up of the relationship,[219] consistent with Article 9 of the UN Convention on the Rights of the Child: 'States Parties shall respect the right of the child who is separated from one or both parents to maintain personal relations and direct contact with both parents on a regular basis, except if it is contrary to the child's best interests';

- the relationship between a man and the child conceived during an extra-marital affair between the mother and the man.[220]

Among the relationships which attract the protection of Article 8 are those between siblings, half-siblings, and step-siblings. Contact is not easily maintained after adoption if the children are placed with different families.[221] In this area, it is not clear that English law yet gives sufficient weight to the right of the children in maintaining contact if they wish to do so.

In respect of the more general sense of 'family', there were clear signs that the broader, fact-based sense of the word, largely divorced from both legal technicality and moral censoriousness, was taking hold in England and Wales even before the Human Rights Act 1998 came into force. In *Fitzpatrick v. Sterling Housing Association Ltd.*,[222] the plaintiff had lived for eighteen years in a stable homosexual relationship with a Mr. Thompson in a flat of which Mr. Thompson had been a protected tenant under the Rent Act 1977. After Mr. Thompson's death, the plaintiff applied to take

[215] *Andersson v. Sweden*, Series A, No. 226, Judgment of 25 February 1992, 14 EHRR 615.

[216] *Marckx v. Belgium*, Eur. Ct. HR, Series A, No. 31, Judgment of 13 June 1979, 2 EHRR 330.

[217] *Berrehab v. The Netherlands*, Eur. Ct. HR, Series A, No. 138, Judgment of 21 June 1988, 11 EHRR 322.

[218] *Boyle v. United Kingdom*, Eur. Ct. HR, Series A, No. 282-B, Judgment of 28 February 1994, 19 EHRR 179 (uncle denied contact with child in care following abuse allegations, without legal process to determine issue—friendly settlement following determination on merits by Commission).

[219] *Keegan v. Ireland*, Eur. Ct. HR, Series A, No. 290, Judgment of 26 May 1994, 18 EHRR 342 (adoption of child without father's consent violated father's Art. 8 rights).

[220] *Kroon v. The Netherlands*, Eur. Ct. HR, Series A, No. 297-C, Judgment of 27 October 1994, 19 EHRR 263 (legal assumption of the child's legitimacy, preventing real father from legally recognizing the child as his own, violated rights under Art. 8; law of state must enable family ties to be developed, and legally recognized and safeguarded).

[221] See, e.g. *In re T. (Minors) (Adopted Children: Contact)* [1996] Fam. 34, [1996] 1 All ER 215, CA; *In re S. (A Minor) (Adopted Child: Contact)* [1999] Fam. 283, [1999] 3 WLR 504, [1999] 1 All ER 648, Charles J.

[222] [1999] 3 WLR 1113, [1999] 4 All ER 705, HL.

over the tenancy of the flat. Under the Act, he was eligible to do so if either he had
been living with the tenant as husband or wife, or he had been a member of the
original tenant's family. The House of Lords unanimously held that a same-sex couple
could not be said to live as husband and wife, those words being gender-specific. But
the House held by a majority (Lords Slynn of Hadley, Nicholls of Birkenhead, and
Clyde; Lords Hutton and Hobhouse of Woodborough dissented) that they could be
said to have been living as members of a family, because they had been in a secure
and loving relationship which went well beyond the superficial and transient. While
the word 'family' might mean different things in different contexts, it had to be
applied in the light of modern, unprejudiced opinions. In a similar spirit, the
Supreme Court of Canada has held that a statute which allowed unmarried mixed-
sex couples to apply for support at the end of the relationship, but purported to deny
that right to same-sex couples, violated the guarantee of equality under section 15 of
the Canadian Constitution's Charter of Rights and Freedoms, and was not 'demonstrably justified in a free and democratic society' so as to be saved by section 1 of the
Charter.[222a]

This non-technical meaning of 'family' prevents the right to respect for family life
from generating a right to remarry following divorce (discussed above). In *Johnston v.
Ireland*,[223] a man who was separated from his wife claimed that the prohibition on
divorce in Ireland prevented him from forming a family with another woman. The
Court rejected this argument. The absence of any means of obtaining a divorce did
not prevent the parties to the marriage from entering into lasting unions with other
people, and so did not infringe the right to respect for family life. The law merely
prevented the parties to the extra-marital union from solemnizing their union in legal
form. On the other hand, the state must ensure that its law does not disadvantage
children of an unsolemnized union. Where the law of illegitimacy subjects the child of
an extra-marital union to legal disadvantages as compared with children of a valid
marriage, it constitutes a lack of respect for the family life of the child and an unjustifiable discrimination in respect of Convention rights which violates Article 8 and
Article 14 taken together with it.[224]

Alongside the non-technical meaning of 'family', the state's obligations under Article 8 are extensive. First, there are duties to avoid interfering arbitrarily with family
life. The right to respect for private life has an impact on immigration and deportation decisions, as noted in Chapter 8 above, and on prisoners, as noted in Chapter 7
above. One issue arising in relation to immigrants concerns people who are entitled to
remain in the country because he has married a person who is entitled to reside there,
but from whom he is then divorced. No family relationship will then subsist between
the parties to the dissolved marriage, so Article 8 will not prevent the deportation of
the person who has no entitlement to reside there in his or her own right. However, if
there are children of the union, each child has a family relationship with each parent,

[222a] *M. v. H.* (1999) 171 DLR (4th) 577, SC Canada, on s.29 of the Family Law Act 1990 (Canada);
E. Hitchings, '*M. v. H.* and Same-Sex Spousal Benefits' (2000) 63 *MLR* 595–607.

[223] Eur. Ct. HR, Series A, No. 112, Judgment of 18 December 1986, 9 EHRR 203.

[224] *Marckx v. Belgium*, Eur. Ct. HR, Series A, No. 31, Judgment of 13 June 1979, 2 EHRR 330; *Johnston v.
Ireland*, Eur. Ct. HR, Series A, No. 112, Judgment of 18 December 1986, 9 EHRR 203.

whether or not the children reside with them, which continues after the parents have divorced or separated. The natural parent-child relationship is entitled to respect, and is protected under Article 8(1). It will be an improper interference with the right to respect for family life if a state deports a parent whose children will remain behind, unless the deportation can be justified under Article 8(2).[225]

For example, it has been held to be disproportionate to remove an unsuccessful asylum seeker from the UK without his wife and three children, from whom he was separated but still kept in close touch.[226] Even where a person has committed serious offences while settled in the country, it may be disproportionate to deport him if he has been residing here for a long time, has family ties here, and has no real connection with the country to which he would be deported. In *B. v. Secretary of State for the Home Department*,[227] the Court of Appeal quashed an order for the deportation to Sicily of an EU citizen who had lived here since 1955, and had family here, despite the fact that he had been sentenced to five years' imprisonment for serious sex offences against his daughter. That decision applied Article 8 of the ECHR as an element of judicial review under EC law, and the same result would be reached under the Human Rights Act 1998.[228] On the other hand, where a person has committed serious offences and has subsisting links with the country to which he is to be deported and weaker family ties in this country, the deportation is less likely to be regarded as disproportionate.[229]

In relation to prisoners, we saw in Chapter 7 that the Human Rights Act 1998 has not given rise to a right to donate sperm to inseminate a prisoner's wife, either under Article 8 or under Article 12. A further aspect of respect for family life concerns prisoners with young children, and those who give birth while in prison. The operation of Article 8 means that prison authorities must take account of the need for mothers to be close to their babies early in life as far as possible. This is relevant, for example, to decisions about the classification of prisoners, to enable them to be allocated to a prison at which the mother-baby bond can be disrupted as little as possible.[230]

Although the primary role of Article 8 is to combat arbitrary interference by the state, the notion of respect imposes some positive obligations on the state to safeguard the family life of parents and children. First, the right to respect for family life requires the state to provide fair procedural protections by law for parents and children when there is a risk of the children being taken into care.[231] The approach should be to provide all relevant evidence to all parties, unless there are compelling reasons for

---

[225] *Berrehab v. Netherlands*, Eur. Ct. HR, Series A, No. 138, Judgment of 21 June 1988, 11 EHRR 322.

[226] *R. v. Secretary of State for the Home Department, ex parte R.*, The Times, 29 November 2000, Gage J.

[227] [2000] HRLR 439, CA.

[228] See *Ezzouhdi v. France*, Eur. Ct. HR, App. No. 47160/99, Judgment of 13 February 2001.

[229] *Cp. C. v. Belgium*, Eur. Ct. HR, App. No. 21794/93, Judgment of 7 August 1996.

[230] A complaint to Strasbourg on this basis was held to be admissible by the European Commission of Human Rights, leading to a friendly settlement, in *Madeleine Taylor v. United Kingdom*, App. No. 28555/95, Report of 25 October 1999.

[231] *W. v. United Kingdom*, Eur. Ct. HR, Series A, No. 121-A, Judgment of 8 July 1987, 10 EHRR 29. On the high standard of proof required in cases involving suspected sexual abuse, see C. Keenan, 'Finding that a Child is at Risk from Sexual Abuse: *Re H. (Minors) (Sexual Abuse: Standard of Proof)*' (1997) 60 *MLR* 857–65.

withholding certain information or evidence in order to protect the children. A party wanting to withhold evidence should apply to the court for a judge to decide whether non-disclosure would be justified. If decisions are taken without allowing the parties to deal with allegations affecting them on the basis of all the relevant evidence, it will fail to respect their family lives and (in the absence of justification sufficiently compelling to satisfy a judge that it meets the tests of pursuing a legitimate aim and proportionality) it will violate both Article 8 and, in relation to a court hearing and similar proceedings, also the right to a fair hearing under Article 6.[232] There is thus an overlap between this aspect of Article 8 and the right to a fair hearing under Article 6(1).

English law already largely incorporates a strong presumption in favour of disclosure of evidence unless that would be likely to result in harm to the child. In *In re D. (Minors) (Adoption Reports: Confidentiality)*,[233] the guardian ad litem of children in adoption proceedings promised the children that anything they told him would be confidential. The House of Lords held that this undertaking could confer no general right on the children to have the guardian's report kept from the other parties. Because of the importance of fairness in legal proceedings, there was a strong presumption in favour of disclosure of all evidence to the parties. Material could be withheld to protect the children against the risk of harm, but that risk had to be assessed in the light of the likelihood of harm resulting and the seriousness of the harm. A high degree of risk was needed to justify limiting the fairness of legal proceedings; the case for non-disclosure must be compelling if it is to prevail. A similar approach has been held to apply under the Human Rights Act 1998 to deciding whether to inform a father that his child may be freed for adoption, the criteria to be fulfilled for withholding information at the request of the mother in the latter case being explicitly based on Article 8(2).[234]

The state also has positive obligations towards children when deciding whether to take them into care and in formulating and giving effect to a care plan when they are in care. The history of the law in this area in England and Wales is instructive. The decision to remove a child from his family, and decisions about subsequent care of the child, are always difficult. In a number of cases, children who were not taken into care have been killed or seriously injured in their families, and the social services departments of the local authorities concerned, which are primarily responsible for deciding whether or not to intervene, have been severely criticized. As public concern grew during the 1970s and 1980s about the prevalence of physical and later sexual abuse of children by those close to them, pressure grew on social workers and doctors to act to remove children from risk in cases of suspected abuse. However, taking children into care is always a shattering event for the children, parents, and their wider families and friends. If the state interferes in families without adequate cause, suspicion is cast on the innocent, and there is a risk that families will be broken up

---

[232] *T. P. and K. M. v. United Kingdom*, Eur. Ct. HR, App. No 28945/95, Judgment of 10 May 2001.

[233] [1996] AC 593, [1995] 4 All ER 385, HL.

[234] *In re H. (A Child) (Adoption: Disclosure); In re G. (A Child) (Adoption: Disclosure), The Times*, 5 January 2001, Butler-Sloss P.

because of child-rearing practices which do no real harm to the children but are not regarded as ideal by the social workers concerned. When large numbers of children were diagnosed as having suffered sexual abuse in Cleveland, and were unceremoniously whisked away from their families, a backlash started, as parents mobilized public opinion in a challenge to the decisions.

As media attention turned towards the parents' and children's plight, concern focused on four issues. First, doubts were expressed about the methods of diagnosis used, about the types of questioning which led children to make (or appear to make) allegations of abuse, and about the tendency to interpret the children's responses to questions uncritically in the light of the interviewers' preconceived idea that abuse had taken place. Secondly, it became clear that decisions were taken at case conferences attended only by the police, doctors, and social workers, at which the parents were often given no opportunity to challenge the evidence or to answer the allegations before the children were taken into care. Thirdly, the process of seizing children, usually without warning and often in dawn raids on their homes by police and social workers, was insensitive and unnecessarily cruel to all concerned. Fourthly, the families often had no adequate legal procedure for challenging the decision to remove their children.

The matter was examined, in the light of the Cleveland cases, by a judicial inquiry, conducted by Dame Elizabeth Butler-Sloss. In a full and thorough report,[235] which criticized many aspects of local authority decision-making and implementation, Dame Elizabeth made numerous recommendations concerning safeguards on the conduct of interviews with children, and proper decision-making procedures. At about the same time, the Divisional Court, in a series of cases in which parents applied for judicial review of case conference decisions, held that parents whose conduct is impugned and whose children are liable to be taken into care as a result are usually entitled to be informed of the fact and to be allowed to make representations, in person or in writing, to the case conference which would make decisions about the children. This was held to be required by the principles of procedural fairness in most cases, although there might be situations in which the urgency of the case, or the risk of serious harm to the child, might justify a different course.

Simultaneously, in a string of judgments the European Court of Human Rights upheld complaints from parents that their children had been taken into care without adequate legal or administrative safeguards. First, the Court established that respect for family life entailed the institution of fair procedures when decisions are made by social service officers affecting the integrity of the family unit. In *W., B., and R. v. United Kingdom*,[236] the Court held that the right to respect requires that the parents be involved in the decision-making process to a degree sufficient to enable them to protect their interests. The arrangements then in place for involving the parents in decisions to place the children of the applicants in long-term fostering with a view to adoption were found to be insufficient for that purpose. Similarly, it was held that a local authority, when making decisions about access to children in care, must take

---

[235] *Report of the Inquiry into Child Abuse in Cleveland*, Cm. 412 (London: HMSO, 1988).
[236] Eur. Ct. HR, Series A, No. 121, Judgments of 8 July 1987, 10 EHRR at 29, 87, and 74 respectively.

account of relevant considerations, including the views of the parents. It followed that parents should normally be informed of the course which the authority was contemplating and be given an opportunity to make representations. Failure to give that opportunity evinced a lack of respect for family life which would violate Article 8 in the absence of good reasons, based on the legitimate objectives in Article 8(2), for not informing the parents and giving them an opportunity to put their point of view. Furthermore, the right to remain together as a family is a civil right which is protected under Article 6(1), with the effect that adequate opportunities for independent review of the decision must be available to the children and their parents in order to satisfy the right to a fair and impartial hearing by an independent tribunal in determining civil rights and obligations.[237]

Under the Convention, therefore, the obligation on the state to respect family life goes beyond taking steps to prevent harm to children. The risk of harm to children has to be weighed against the interests of the parents and the value of maintaining the family unit, which would be threatened by intervention. Parents or guardians are regarded as having substantive rights, as well as procedural rights, because of the right to respect for their private and family life and their cultural and ethical traditions. As it is put in the UN Convention on the Rights of the Child, Article 3, paragraphs 1 and 2, the best interests of the child are to be a primary consideration, but (because the family is regarded as the fundamental social unit for ensuring the well-being of children) protection and care offered to children is to take into account the rights of duties of parents, legal guardians, or other individuals who are legally responsible for the child, and to this end the state is to 'take all appropriate legislative and administrative measures'.

It is therefore not necessarily sufficient for the authorities simply to conclude that the child would be better off in care. The initial decision to take a child into care is often necessarily taken under pressure of circumstances suggestive of urgency with limited opportunity for careful reflection. But even at the initial stage, making a care order without sufficient reasons to justify it will violate Article 8, and may lead to liability to pay damages under the Human Rights Act 1998.[238] The European Court of Human Rights applies a more rigorous standard of scrutiny to decisions about care plans and access to children in care than to an initial decision to take a child into care.[239] There is far less reason for refusing to take account of everyone's interests, particularly in relation to the reunification of the family, in making subsequent decisions.

When a child is in care, public authorities must develop a care plan which so far as possible advances the goal of reuniting and reintegrating the family. If the authorities fail to consider actively how best to do this, or fail to take appropriate steps towards that end or to give active consideration to whether and when to terminate the care

[237] O. v. United Kingdom, Eur. Ct. HR, Series A, No. 120, Judgment of 8 July 1987, 10 EHRR 82.

[238] K. and T. v. Finland, Eur. Ct. HR, Judgment of 27 April 2000, 31 EHRR 484. On potential liability for negligence and misfeasance in a public office, see L. (A Child) v. Reading Borough Council [2001] 1 WLR 1575, CA, and Sir Robert Carnwath, 'Welfare Services: Liabilities in Tort after the Human Rights Act' [2001] PL 210–19.

[239] See, e.g. Johansen v. Norway, Eur., Ct. HR, Judgment of 7 August 1996, RJD 1996-III, 23 EHRR 33.

order, Article 8 will be engaged. It is not enough that the authorities act in good faith. They must actively pursue the reintegration of the family unless, and save to the extent that, the goal is shown to be impossible or is incompatible with a compelling aim under Article 8(2).[240]

When deciding whether to take a child into care, public authorities must ensure that they act with reasonable speed when there is evidence of a real threat to the health and welfare of a child in its home environment. In *Z. and others v. United Kingdom*,[241] those responsible for child care had failed to respond over a number of years to evidence that four children were being inadequately cared for and were suffering physical and emotional harm as a result. It was accepted that the level of suffering amounted to inhuman and degrading treatment. The state was liable under Article 3. It was not necessary to consider the position under Article 8: in this context the two Articles work closely together. The House of Lords had denied the children a remedy in negligence against the local authority.[242] This gave rise to a violation of the right under ECHR Article 13 to an effective remedy for the violation of their Article 3 right.[243] Now the Human Rights Act 1998 is in force, a remedy would be available in the form of an action under section 7 of the Act for a breach of the duty under section 6(1) to comply with Convention rights.

When children are taken into care, the local authority has duties both to the children and to the people who foster them. At common law, they must take reasonable care to avoid putting the children in a situation where they are in danger of abuse, and must act on suspicions that carers are causing them harm.[244] Under the Human Rights Act 1998, allowing children in care to be subjected to abuse gives rise to strict liability under ECHR Article 3 if (as is very likely) the harm reaches the level of inhuman or degrading treatment.[245] The local authority probably owes a duty of care at common law to members of a family which fosters a child in care. If the child is known to have a propensity for harming or abusing other children, the foster family should be warned so that they can protect their own children. The House of Lords has held that there is an arguable claim against the local authority in negligence if insufficient information is given and harm results.[246] There is a need for all concerned

[240] *Olsson v. Sweden (No. 1)*, Eur. Ct. HR, Series A, No. 130, Judgment of 24 March 1988, 11 EHRR 259 (failure to consider whether to reunite family, and adoption of care plan—including fostering the children far apart—which made reunification unlikely; *cp. Olsson v. Sweden (No. 2)*, Eur. Ct. HR, Series A, No. 250, Judgment of 27 November 1992); *Hokkanen v. Finland*, Eur. Ct. HR, Series A, No. 299-A, Judgment of 23 September 1994, 19 EHRR 139; *E. P. v. Italy*, Eur. Ct. HR, App. No. 31127/96, Judgment of 16 November 1999, 31 EHRR 463; *K. and T. v. Finland*, Eur. Ct. HR, App. No. 25702/94, Judgment of 27 April 2000, 31 EHRR 484.

[241] Eur. Ct. HR, App. No. 29392/95, Judgment of 10 May 2001.

[242] *X. (Minors) v. Bedfordshire County Council* [1995] 2 AC 633, [1995] 3 ALL ER 353, HL.

[243] The European Court of Human Rights in *Z. v. United Kingdom* found a violation of Art. 13 rather than Art. 6, because the House of Lords' decision had been based on a balance of interests in the light of the facts of each case, rather than a blanket immunity irrespective of the merits which would have denied the plaintiffs a hearing. In reality, the rules of *stare decisis* will mean that in future cases this will be a distinction without a difference, unless (as is possible) courts take seriously their obligations under Arts. 3 and 8 and evaluate the competing interests afresh in each case on its merits.

[244] *Barrett v. Enfield London Borough Council* [1999] 3 WLR 79, HL.

[245] *Scozzari and Giunta v. Italy*, Eur. Ct. HR, App. Nos. 39221/98 and 41963/98, Judgment of 13 July 2000.

[246] *W. v. Essex County Council* [2000] 2 WLR 601, HL.

(courts as well as local authorities) to act with celerity when dealing with child-care issues. A delay of a few months may have devastating effects on children and other members of their families. The right under Article 6 to a fair hearing within a reasonable time requires much faster determination of legal issues in such cases than in the general run of litigation.[247]

The courts, as public authorities, have considerably enhanced positive duties in child-care cases by virtue of the Human Rights Act 1998. English law has moved steadily from the idea of parental rights over their children towards the notion of parental responsibility. This trend was exemplified by the decision of the House of Lord in *Gillick v. West Norfolk and Wisbech Area Health Authority*[248] that parental rights derive from the primary responsibilities of parents to care for and maintain their children. The Children Act 1989, sections 2 and 3, reinforced the emphasis on parental responsibility, making it the foundation of the legal relationship between parents and their children;[249] and the emphasis on responsibilities (particularly paternal responsibilities) for maintaining children is fundamental to the scheme of the Child Support Act 1991, which requires fathers to support their children financially, and imposes penalties, in the form of withheld social security benefits, on a parent who refuses to disclose information about the other parent, unless the Secretary of State considers that there are reasonable grounds for believing that it would lead to a risk of harm or undue distress being caused to prevent the parent or any child living with him.[250]

Whether or not influenced by the European Convention, judges in judicial review proceedings in the late 1980s began to insist on parents being given an opportunity to participate in case conferences where decisions were being made which intimately and adversely affected the parents' lives, despite any inconvenience which this might cause to the health and social workers. Failure to offer an opportunity for parents to put their cases was characterized as a breach of principles of natural justice or fairness, vitiating the decisions reached. This included not only decisions about access, but also a decision to place a child's name on a child abuse register as a suspected victim of abuse.[251]

Although administrative law was introducing procedural rights for the parents, the availability of review of decisions on their merits was cut down. Wardship had been used as a means of testing whether or not a local authority's decision was, in substance, in the best interests of the child. However, in *A. v. Liverpool City Council*[252] the House of Lords had held that it would be inappropriate for the English High Court to allow the wardship jurisdiction to be used to review the merits of child-care decisions taken by local authorities under their statutory powers. Henceforth, the exercise of a

---

[247] *E.P. v. Italy* (1999) 31 EHRR 463.

[248] [1986] AC 112, [19851 3 All ER 402, HL.

[249] See R. White, P. Carr, and N. Lowe, *A Guide to the Children Act 1989* (London: Butterworths, 1990), ch. 2.

[250] See Cretney, *Elements*, ch. 10.

[251] *R. v. Norfolk County Council, ex parte M.* [1989] QB 619, [1989] 2 All ER 359; *R. v. Harrow LBC, ex parte D.* [1990] 3 All ER 12, CA.

[252] [1982] AC 363, [1981] 2 All ER 385, HL.

local authority's statutory powers was to be reviewable only on ordinary judicial review principles, for illegality, procedural impropriety, or irrationality. In *In re W. (A Minor) (Wardship: Jurisdiction)*[253] the House of Lords, while recognizing the hardship which this caused to parents who were apparently the victims of injustice, reluctantly refused to overrule its earlier ruling.

This did not meet the requirements of the European Convention on Human Rights. The absence of a legal procedure for testing the merits of a decision to terminate access by a parent to a child in care was held to breach Article 6(1) of the Convention in *O. v. United Kingdom*,[254] while undue delay in deciding proceedings relating to access was held to violate the right to respect for family life in *H. v. United Kingdom*.[255] Despite this, in *In re M. and H. (Minors) (Local Authority: Parental Rights)*[256] the House of Lords refused to depart from its earlier decisions.[257]

The Children Act 1989, section 1(1), reasserts the primacy of the child's interests. It provides that the child's welfare is to be the paramount consideration when a court is deciding any question relating to the upbringing of the child (the welfare principle). However, despite recommendations by Dame Elizabeth Butler-Sloss in the Cleveland Report that the House of Lords' decisions should be reconsidered,[258] the Act did nothing to alter the approach of the House of Lords, preferring instead to restrict the freedom of the local authorities to invoke the wardship jurisdiction.[259] Nevertheless, under the Act a child may enter care only by an order of the court, acting on a report from the local authority and in accordance with the welfare principle. Voluntary entry into care, with the consent or at the request of a parent without review by a court, is ended. Before making a care order or a supervision order in respect of a child,[260] the court must be satisfied:

(a) that the child is suffering or is likely to suffer significant harm; and

(b) that the harm or likelihood of harm is attributable to the care given to the child, or likely to be given if an order is not made, not being what a parent could reasonably be expected to give, or the fact that the child is beyond parental control;[261] and

(c) that it is in the best interests of the child to make the order, and making the order would be better for the child than making no order.[262]

The court must also take account of the arrangements which the authority has made, or proposes to make, for permitting people to have access to the child, in accordance

---

[253] [1985] AC 791, [1985] 2 All ER 301, HL.

[254] Eur. Ct. HR, Series A, No. 120, Judgment of 8 July 1987, 10 EHRR 82.

[255] Eur. Ct. HR, Series A, No. 120, Judgment of 8 July 1987, 10 EHRR 95.

[256] [1990] 1 AC 686, [1988] 3 All ER 5, HL.

[257] Child Care Act 1980, Part IA, added by Health and Social Services and Social Security Adjudications Act 1983, s. 6 and Sch. 1.

[258] *Child Abuse in Cleveland*, Cm. 412 (1988).

[259] Children Act 1989, s. 100.

[260] These provisions apply to children under the age of seventeen years, or (if married) sixteen years.

[261] Children Act 1989, s. 31(2).

[262] Ibid., s. 1(1), (5).

with the presumption that the child in care has a right to parents and certain other people.[263]

This last point is important in the light of the decision of the European Court of Human Rights in *Andersson v. Sweden*[264] that restriction of parental access to children in care violates Article 8(1) of the European Convention on Human Rights, and is justifiable under Article 8(2) as being for the protection of health and morals, or the rights of the child, only if the restriction is proportionate to the threat. In that case, the authorities had stopped all letters and telephone contact. This was held to be unnecessary and disproportionate, and deprived the authorities of the benefit of the justification under Article 8(2). Similarly, it has been held in *Eriksson v. Sweden*[265] that an indefinite prohibition on a mother removing her daughter from a foster home, when there was no longer any ground for considering that the mother was unable to care for the child, breached the rights of the mother and the child under Article 8.

The Human Rights Act 1998 has had the significant effect of encouraging courts to extend their supervision over the work of local authorities in child care matters after a care plan has been agreed for the children. In order to offer adequate safeguards against violations of the right to respect for family life, the Court of Appeal has held that the Act puts a positive obligation on the courts to exercise continuing control to ensure that a care plan is actually put into effect, for example by making a supervision order or an interim care order, and imposing a duty on the local authority to return to court if the care plan becomes impossible to operate for any reason, including financial and resource reasons.[266]

(4) CHILD'S KNOWLEDGE OF FAMILY BACKGROUND

Knowing about one's family background, and having an opportunity to identify with it, has been recognized as an important psychological need. For children and adults, knowing where we come from is a significant element in our sense of identity. The freedom to adopt a name which reflects one's family background, without undue interference by the state, has been recognized as an aspect of private and family life falling within ECHR Article 8(1). The state can, within its discretion under Article 8(2), prevent one from choosing a new name if in the opinion of the competent state authority the inconvenience arising from having one's present name is not very great and one's connection with the family represented by the new name is not very direct. But any interference must be necessary and proportionate to meet the requirements of Article 8(2), and it may violate the right to equal enjoyment of the right (under Article 14 taken together with Article 8) if the restriction on choosing a name discriminates between people without objective and rational justification.[267] English law

---

[263] Ibid., s. 34.

[264] Eur. Ct. HR, Series A, No. 226, Judgment of 25 February 1992, 14 EHRR 615.

[265] Eur. Ct. HR, Series A, No. 156, Judgment of 22 June 1989, 12 EHRR 183.

[266] *In re W. and B. (Children); In re W. (Children),* unreported, 23 May 2001, CA, currently under appeal to HL.

[267] *Burghartz v. Switzerland,* Eur. Ct. HR, Series A, No. 280-B, Judgment of 22 February 1994, 18 EHRR 101; *Stjerna v. Finland,* Eur. Ct. HR, Series A, No. 299-B, Judgment of 25 November 1994; *Guillot v. France,* Eur. Ct. HR, Judgment of 24 October 1996, RJD 1996–V.

does not seriously threaten to violate Article 8 on this ground: in relation to personal nomenclature, the law is very permissive (unlike that in some other states). This aspect of respect for private life would, however, have implications for any plans to introduce a compulsory identity card scheme in the UK.

The significance of knowledge about our history has been acknowledged by the European Court of Human Rights, which decided in *Gaskin v. United Kingdom*[268] that people who have been in care have 'a vital interest, protected by the Convention, in receiving the information necessary to know and understand their childhood and early development'. This confers a *prima facie* right of access to their files, subject however to the need for confidentiality of public records, important for receiving objective and reliable information and for protecting third parties.

Mr. Gaskin alleged that he had been ill-treated while in care, and wished to see his file to find out about his past and come to terms with it. He applied to the High Court for an order of discovery under section 31 of the Administration of Justice Act 1970, permitting the court to order disclosure to a person who is likely to be a party to legal proceedings in respect of personal injury, but this was refused. The Court of Appeal agreed with the judge that the public interest in maintaining confidentiality in such documents clearly outweighed the applicant's interest in obtaining the information.[269] Thereafter the DHSS issued Circular LAC(83)14, setting out the principles which were to govern disclosure of information: access to documents was to be permitted if the contributor of each confidential document consented to its disclosure. On this basis, the council released some documents to Mr. Gaskin, but withheld others, and there was no procedure available for challenging the refusal of contributors to the file to permit access.

The European Court of Human Rights held unanimously that the applicant had had no right to receive the information under Article 10, but held by sixteen votes to one that the withholding of personal files gave rise to an issue under Article 8, and by eleven votes to six that the refusal of access constituted an unjustified interference with the right to respect for private and family life. The majority accepted that the confidentiality of the file served a legitimate aim under Article 8(2), and that, in achieving that aim, the state enjoyed a margin of appreciation which permitted it in principle to make access dependent on the consent of the contributor. However, in such a system the interests of the individual seeking access had to be protected against lack of consent by a contributor who was unavailable or who improperly refused consent. An independent authority should have been able to decide whether to override the absence of consent in such circumstances. The English system at the relevant date had no independent review body, and so the restriction on access was disproportionate to the aim pursued. However, by the time the decision in *Gaskin* was delivered, the Access to Personal Files Act 1987 had been passed,[270] and regulations had been made under it which gave rights of access to personal files equivalent to those envisaged in the judgment.

---

[268] Eur. Ct. HR, Series A, No. 160, Judgment of 7 July 1989, 12 EHRR 36, at para. 49 of the judgment.
[269] *Gaskin v. Liverpool City Council* [1980] 1 WLR 1459, CA.
[270] See now Data Protection Act 1998, above, Ch. 9.

In *Gaskin,* the applicant at least knew who had been his genetic parents and who had been responsible for his upbringing. However, in some cases this knowledge may be unavailable, and the individual's sense of identity may be confused. A child might be adopted early in life, or be born to a surrogate mother, or be conceived by means of artificial insemination using sperm, ovum, or both, from a person or people other than those who are to bring up the child.[271] The Warnock Committee considered how easy it should be for children to find out who their genetic or carrying parents are, if they have been brought up as their own children by others.[272] Socially, genetic parenthood is usually not particularly important, and both the social parents and the donors of sperm or ova and surrogate mothers might wish the contributions of outsiders to be confidential, allowing the children to regard themselves exclusively as offspring of the social parents. Yet, psychologically, a child might feel incomplete, forced to make do with only a partial self-image and understanding, if genetic information is withheld.

This is a field in which the English law has so far come only a limited way towards keeping up with the implications of fast-moving social and scientific developments. Different considerations apply to adopted children, to those conceived by artificial means but carried by the woman who later brings up the child as its mother, and to those who are conceived artificially and carried by a surrogate, with a view to being brought up by others.

(i) Adopted children

Adoption is a legal procedure for changing the legal parentage of the child.[273] It used to be considered inappropriate to tell children or adoptive parents anything about the children's biological parents. When most children were adopted as very young babies, this was comprehensible: babies could be brought up in the security of their new family without threatening intimations that another identity and background might be lurking. Now that more than half of all adoptions are of children aged five or over, and a very large proportion of adoptive parents are already related to the child concerned,[274] this is less sensible. It is now thought to be good practice to bring children up in the knowledge of their backgrounds as far as possible. This has been reinforced by two statutory provisions which facilitate the discovery of background information and the establishment of links with a child's natural parents, once the adopted person has reached the age of eighteen, and will be further enhanced if the Adoption and Children Bill 2001 is passed.

Section 51 of the Adoption Act 1976 (as amended by the Children Act 1989, Schedule 10, paragraph 20) provides that a person who has been adopted is entitled to be provided by the Registrar General of Births, after reaching the age of eighteen, with a copy of the record of the person's birth from the births register. The person must first be informed that counselling is available, but the right appears to be absolute if

---

[271] G. Douglas, *Law, Fertility and Reproduction* (London: Sweet & Maxwell, 1991), chs 6, 7; G. Douglas and N. V. Lowe, 'Becoming a Parent in English Law' (1992) 108 *LQR* 414–32.

[272] *Report of the Committee into Human Fertilisation and Embryology* (Chairman: Dame Mary Warnock), Cmnd. 9314 (London: HMSO, 1984), paras. 4.21–4.22, 6.6, 7.7.

[273] See Cretney, *Elements,* ch. 12.

[274] Ibid., 230.

the person decides to exercise it. However, there is a public policy exception implied in the Act, allowing the Registrar General to refuse to provide counselling or to release the information in certain exceptional circumstances. This was decided in *R. v. Registrar General, ex parte Smith*.[275] The applicant, who had been adopted at the age of nine weeks, had been imprisoned for life for the unprovoked murder of a stranger in a park. While in prison, he killed a cell-mate, apparently in the belief that the man was his adopted mother. He was convicted of manslaughter by reason of diminished responsibility, and sent to Broadmoor. While there, he applied for a copy of the record of his birth from the register of births. The Registrar General obtained medical reports which suggested that the applicant might react emotionally by redirecting some of his hostility from his adopted mother towards his natural mother, and that he might put his natural mother's life in danger if he were ever to escape or be released. The Registrar General refused to release the information sought, and the applicant applied for judicial review of the decision.

The Divisional Court and the Court of Appeal held that public policy exceptions to apparently unqualified statutory rights might be implied in an Act where they appeared to reflect the likely intention of Parliament. In the circumstances of the case, concerning a double killer with an abnormal personality, Sir Stephen Brown P considered that there was 'a very real and present apprehension for the safety of the . . . natural mother'; identifying her 'might even be tantamount to signing her death warrant'.[276] Staughton LJ agreed, holding that the exception could not depend on showing that the person had the present intention of attacking his natural mother. He thought that a statutory duty might not be enforced 'if there is a significant risk that to do so would facilitate crime resulting in danger to life'.[277]

McCowan LJ thought that a person would not be permitted to enforce his right under section 51 'if there is a current and justified apprehension of a significant risk that he might in the future use the information obtained to commit a serious crime'.[278] With respect, the 'serious crime' formulation might be considered rather too flexible for comfort. A right given by Parliament without express qualification is not lightly to be limited. It is submitted that the formulation by Staughton LJ is to be preferred, as imposing the restriction on the exercise of the right which is most clearly justified by considerations relating to the welfare of third parties.

Section 51A of the Adoption Act 1976 (added by the Children Act 1989, Schedule 10, paragraph 21) provides for the Registrar General to keep an Adoption Contact Register. The register is in two parts. In one part, the name and address is kept of any adopted person over the age of eighteen who has exercised, or is in a position to exercise, the right under section 51, and who notifies the Registrar General of a wish to contact a relative. In the other part of the register is kept the name and address of any person who has attained the age of eighteen, has satisfied the Registrar General that he is a relative of the adopted person and has the information necessary to obtain

275 [1991] 2 WLR 782, [1991] 2 All ER 88, CA.
276 [1991] 2 All ER at 93.
277 Ibid. at 95.
278 Ibid. at 96.

a copy of the adopted person's birth certificate, and has notified the Registrar General of a wish to contact the adopted person. The Registrar General shall then transmit to the adopted person the name and address of any relative listed in the register. The register is not open for public inspection by the general public: only the adopted person can initiate the contact.

The adoption register cannot be edited to remove details in order to protect an adopted child against harm. Where a birth mother was violently opposed to the idea of adoption, and it was feared that she would seek to track down the child in circumstances where that would be likely to harm the child seriously, the court held that it could make an order that information on the register was not to be disclosed to any person during the minority of the child without the leave of court. Although the decision in *R. v. Registrar General, ex parte Smith* was not entirely on all fours with the case, similar principles were applied to protect the safety of the child.[279] The balancing process required under ECHR Article 8(2) would be very likely to produce the same result if a similar case were to arise under the Human Rights Act 1998.

(ii) Children born to surrogate mothers

If the parties who commissioned the surrogacy arrangement adopt the child, the child will in due course be able to obtain information about his or her birth and may be able to contact relatives in the usual way under sections 51 and 51A of the Adoption Act 1976, after reaching the age of eighteen. Alternatively, if a parental order is made under section 30 of the 1990 Act, it does not affect the entry in the register of births, so a person will normally be able to discover the identity of his or her birth mother by consulting the register.

(iii) Children born by other artificial insemination techniques

Where a child has been conceived by a procedure governed by the rules in the Human Fertilisation and Embryology Act 1990, there may be good reasons to permit the child to find out about his or her genetic parents. For instance, people may need to discover whether they or their offspring may be prone to suffer a hereditary disorder. The Warnock Committee recommended that children should be able, on reaching the age of eighteen, to find out basic details of the ethnic origin and genetic health of the donors of the sperm, egg, or embryo, but considered that the identity of the donors should never be disclosed, in order to protect confidentiality and minimize the extent to which the donors' existence could intrude into the child's family relationships.[280] The statutory scheme follows these general principles. Section 31 of the 1990 Act requires the Human Fertilisation and Embryology Authority to maintain a register, and permits a person aged eighteen or over to demand information from the authority showing whether a person other than his legal parents was a biological parent of the applicant. While regulations may specify the amount of information to be given, section 31(5) provides that the regulations are not to require the authority to identify

---

[279] *In re X. (A Minor) (Adoption Details: Disclosure)* [1994] Fam. 174, [1994] 3 All ER 372, CA.
[280] *Report of the Committee of Inquiry into Human Fertilisation and Embryology*, Cmnd. 9314, paras. 4.21–4.22, 6.6, 7.7.

the biological parent.[281] This is the worst of all possible worlds. Applicants are to be told that they are, or might be, the biological offspring of people other than those who have been regarded as their parents up to that time, thus whetting their curiosity, but are disabled from obtaining information which might assuage the curiosity. This problem would be significantly mitigated if the Adoption and Children Bill 2001 is passed.

12.4 CONCLUSIONS

English law has a mixed record in relation to rights concerned with sex, sexuality, and family life. In relation to child-care law, parental rights and responsibilities, and the role of social service agencies in maintaining or intervening in the family unit, the UK has done reasonably well in responding to concerns expressed by both the European Court of Human Rights and the various reports on child-care matters which have appeared in the last decade. Legislation has also been generally effective in providing a right for people to find information about their histories, while balancing the right against the needs of good administration and other people's right to confidentiality. On the other hand, the law has failed to respond as effectively where morality, particularly sexual morality, is implicated; but in these areas the European Court of Human Rights has proved as disappointing as Parliament, and less dynamic than the Commission.

It is, perhaps, fair to conclude that the rights of individuals are protected in proportion to the political significance of the groups from which they come. Members of groups which lack wide political support, such as the mental patient in *R. v. Registrar General, ex parte Smith*, homosexuals, or transsexuals, find their rights-claims are not taken as seriously, either by Parliament or courts, as members of populous, popular, and increasingly vocal groups, such as parents. The rights of the underprivileged are liable to be too easily overridden by arguments which, on analysis, appear unconvincing. It is in this area, perhaps, that the Human Rights Act 1998 may make its most significant impact, improving both the quality and the equality of treatment of those whose private and family lives collide with public authorities.

---

[281] Douglas, *Law, Fertility and Reproduction*, 132–6.

PART IV

EXPRESSION

13

FREEDOM OF EXPRESSION

Part IV of the book is concerned with expression and its protection. The present chapter examines the nature of freedom of expression, the reasons why it is important, and the general extent to which it is guaranteed under international and English law. Chapter 14 looks at a special aspect of freedom of expression, the freedom of the media. The chapters which follow examine the balance between freedom of expression and other interests, as translated into law in the context of the protection of state interests (Chapter 15), individuals' sensibilities and moral welfare (Chapter 16), the administration of justice (Chapter 17), and public order (Chapter 18).

This chapter begins with an explanation of the nature and content of the right to free expression, taking account of the formulation of the right in international human rights instruments and under the Human Rights Act 1998. There follows a brief account of some of the leading justifications advanced for protecting freedom of expression, noting the problem of setting limits to the freedom, particularly where the people exercising it do not respect the freedom of others. The Chapter ends with two sections examining the extent of freedom of expression in English law, and the way in which it is specially protected or particularly restricted in certain situations.

13.1 THE NATURE OF FREEDOM OF EXPRESSION IN INTERNATIONAL AND NATIONAL LAW

The right to freedom of expression is protected by all the major international human rights instruments.[1] In Article 19 of the UN Universal Declaration of Human Rights and Article 10 of the European Convention on Human Rights (ECHR), it is stated to include rights to hold opinions and to receive and impart information and ideas. The International Covenant on Civil and Political Rights (ICCPR), Article 19, separates the right to hold opinions in Article 19(1) from freedom of expression in Article 19(2), but includes in the latter the right to seek, as well as receive and impart, information and ideas. The ICCPR and the ECHR recognize that the exercise of these freedoms carries with it special responsibilities, and so may be subject to restriction

---

[1] See P. Sieghart, *The International Law of Human Rights*, 327–36; J. P. Humphrey, 'Political and Related Rights', in T. Meron (ed.), *Human Rights in International Law: Legal and Policy Issues* (Oxford: Clarendon Press, 1984), 171–88.

for specified purposes. The ECHR contains the most extensive grounds for restricting the freedom, which apply to the right to hold opinions as well as to the other elements in freedom of expression. ECHR Article 10, which now forms part of national law by virtue of the Human Rights Act 1998, provides:

'(1)   Everyone has the right to freedom of expression. This right shall include freedom to hold opinions and to receive and impart information and ideas without interference by public authority and regardless of frontiers. This Article shall not prevent States from requiring the licensing of broadcasting, television or cinema enterprises.

(2)   The exercise of these freedoms, since it carries with it duties and responsibilities, may be subject to such formalities, conditions, restrictions or penalties as are prescribed by law and are necessary in a democratic society, in the interests of national security, territorial integrity or public safety, for the prevention of disorder or crime, for the protection of health or morals, for the protection of the reputation or rights of others, for preventing the disclosure of information received in confidence, or for maintaining the authority and impartiality of the judiciary.'

The blanket authority to license broadcasting, television, and cinema enterprises under ECHR Article 10(1) does not depend on there being a justification for restricting the freedom under Article 10(2). By contrast, ICCPR Article 19 requires any licensing regime has to be justified by reference to the permitted grounds for restrictions set out in Article 19(3).[2] Neither the ECHR nor the ICCPR permits licensing regimes to be imposed on the dissemination of printed material, which may be restricted only in accordance with ECHR Article 10(2). The ICCPR allows fewer restrictions of expression than does the ECHR. Article 19 of the ICCPR does not permit any restriction of the freedom to hold opinions without interference, guaranteed by Article 19(1). Article 19(2) and (3) provides:

'(2)   Everyone shall have the right to freedom of expression; this right shall include freedom to seek, receive and impart information and ideas of all kinds, regardless of frontiers, either orally, in writing or in print, in the form of art, or through any other media of his choice.

(3)   The exercise of the rights provided for in paragraph 2 of this article carries with it special duties and responsibilities. It may therefore be subject to certain restrictions, but these shall only be such as are provided by law and are necessary:

(a) for respect of the rights and reputations of others;

(b) for the protection of national security or public order (*ordre public*), or of public health or morals.'

The ICCPR binds the UK in international law but does not yet form part of national law, although on ordinary principles of interpretation courts may have regard to it in order to resolve uncertainties in legislation,[3] including the Human Rights Act 1998.

In the past, English law avoided the need to define the limits of freedom of expression, concentrating instead on exceptions to the principle. The doctrines of Parliamentary sovereignty and the dualism of national and international law made it

---

[2] Licensing of broadcasting media is considered in Ch. 14 below, and that of the cinema in Ch. 16 below.
[3] See Ch. 2, above.

difficult to impose a normative legal framework on issues of expression, so there was little point in worrying about the precise scope of the freedom. The Human Rights Act 1998 has changed that. English law now contains a right to free expression in the terms of ECHR Article 10. Restrictions of the right fall to be assessed by reference to Article 10(2), so the scope of the right is of primary importance. The caselaw of the European Court of Human Rights provides helpful guidance.

The Court has always stressed the importance of freedom of expression as a mainstay of the liberal-democratic form of society which the ECHR is intended to safeguard. Such a society does not aim to achieve consensus, and does not confer a privilege on received wisdom or views which are favoured by a majority or by those in authority. Liberal-democratic society embraces the difficult task of maintaining cohesion through diversity, establishing a framework of respect and tolerance within which conflict can be accommodated. The underlying assumption is that disagreement, even about fundamental values, is healthy and needs protection.[4] For this reason, the freedom normally covers expression of unpopular as well as popular ideas. As the Court said, on the first of many occasions, in *Handyside v. United Kingdom*:[5]

'Subject to paragraph 2 of Article 10, it [Article 10(1)] is applicable not only to "information" or "ideas" that are favourably received or regarded as inoffensive but also to those that offend, shock or disturb the state or any sector of the population. Such are the demands of pluralism, tolerance and broadmindedness without which there is no "democratic society".'

In this spirit, the Court has treated Article 10(1) as encompassing any action or inaction intended to have expressive content. Communicative acts and publications clearly fall within Article 10(1) (although it has not yet been decided whether this includes music). Although the European Commission of Human Rights decided in *X. v. United Kingdom*[6] that the expression of an opinion through the performance of the act of sexual intercourse was not a protected form of expression, it is questionable whether the distinction between the form and the content of expression can be maintained. Homosexual intercourse in public, if intended to make a point about the propriety of legal or political restrictions on gay men and lesbians, would on its face be expressive. Context is important. In the USA, the Supreme Court accepts that the manner of expression may be an integral part of the communication of ideas itself, giving expression to the strength of feeling as well as the intellectual content of the ideas expressed. Accordingly, the court has held that the First Amendment to the Constitution, in precluding Congress from making any law which abridges freedom of speech, protects 'symbolic speech', such as burning a flag to protest against US government policy,[7] or burning a cross outside a house occupied by a black family, to symbolize a racist political programme,[8] as well as verbal expression. It also protects an expression of opinion expressed in offensive terms, for example 'Fuck the Draft' emblazoned on a jacket worn in a courthouse, to assert opposition to conscription

---

[4] See the discussion in section 13.2, below.
[5] Eur. Ct. HR, Series A, No. 24, Judgment of 7 December 1976, 1 EHRR 737, at para. 49 of the judgment.
[6] App. No. 7215/75, 19 DR 66.
[7] *Texas v. Johnson* 109 S. Ct. 2533 (1989).
[8] *R. A. V. v. City of St Paul, Minnesota* 112 S. Ct. 2538, 120 L. Ed. 2d 305 (1992).

into the US army to fight in Vietnam.[9] It would be strange if, under the European Convention on Human Rights, which is drafted in terms of expression rather than speech, the range of types of expression protected were to be narrower than under the speech-based US First Amendment. If it were so, under the Convention a mime might not be protected despite carrying the same message as a speech. Of course, this does not mean that all speech is accorded an equal value. Even under the First Amendment to the Constitution of the USA, it is easier to justify interfering with some kinds of speech than others. Loud, amplified music at a political gathering could be controlled to protect local residents against the undesirable impact of the noise on their lives, as long as it was regulated without regard to the content of the ideas being advanced by the music.[9a] Nude dancing, although a form of expression, can be controlled on the basis of its secondary effects (said to include damage to public health, safety and welfare, being associated with violence, sexual harassment, public intoxication, prostitution, and the spread of sexually transmitted diseases) rather than because of the content of the expression.[9b] But judgments about what speech is of a sufficiently low value to justify restricting First Amendment rights on the basis of secondary effects are not always easy or uncontroversial, and there is a danger of certain types of speech being suppressed as much because of their content as because of their inseparable secondary effects.

Artistic works, including films, are covered, although licensing of cinema is permitted under Article 10(1).[10] Membership of a political party and participating in a demonstration (even if merely takes the form of obstructing people acting lawfully) are expressive acts, allowing people to identify themselves with a set of opinions and values, and so fall within the idea of expression.[11] The right to communicate coupled with the right to receive information and ideas protects the publication of material which governments consider to be prejudicial to national security,[12] although (unlike ICCPR Article 19) ECHR Article 10 does not give a right to seek information (which may, however, arise under Article 8, as noted in Chapter 9, above).

As one would expect, in view of the importance of free expression in a democracy, political expression is particularly strongly protected. The freedom of people participating in the political process attracts strong safeguards, especially if they wish to be

---

[9] *Cohen v. California* 403 US 15 (1971).

[9a] *Ward v. Rock Against Racism*, 419 US 781 (1989).

[9b] *City of Erie v. Pap's A.M., tdba 'Kandyland'*, 2000 US LEXIS 2347, discussed by P. N. S. Rumney, '*City of Erie et al. v. Pap's A.M., tdba "Kandyland"*: Low-Value Speech and the First Amendment' [2001] *PL* 158–67.

[10] *Müller v. Switzerland*, Eur. Ct. HR, Series A, No. 133, Judgment of 24 May 1988, 13 EHRR 212; *Chorherr v. Austria*, Eur. Ct. HR, Series A, No. 266-B, Judgment of 25 August 1993, 17 EHRR 358; *Otto-Preminger-Institut v. Austria*, Series A, No. 295-A, Judgment of 20 September 1994, 19 EHRR 34.

[11] *Vogt v. Germany*, Eur. Ct. HR, Series A, No. 323, Judgment of 26 September 1995, 21 EHRR 205 (membership of, and acting as prospective candidate for, German Communist Party); *Steel and others v. United Kingdom*, Eur. Ct. HR, Judgment of 23 September 1998, RJD 1998-VII (anti-road-building protesters); *Hashman and Harrup v. United Kingdom*, Eur. Ct. HR, Judgment of 25 November 1999 (hunt saboteurs).

[12] *Vereinigung Demokratische Soldaten Österreich and Gubi v. Austria*, Eur. Ct. HR, Series A, No. 302, Judgment of 19 December 1994; *Vereiniging Weekblad Bluf! v. The Netherlands*, Eur. Ct. HR, Series A, No. 306-A, Judgment of 9 February 1995, 20 EHRR 189.

candidates for elective office[13] or are already members of a legislative body.[14] Criticism of government, even if expressed in insulting terms, is likely to be even more extensively protected than other contributions to debate, because it is essential to a democracy. Accordingly, while there is no absolute freedom of political expression, the Court has held that 'interferences with the freedom of expression of an opposition member of parliament, like the applicant, call for the closest scrutiny on the part of the Court'.[15] Political opposition to government in general deserves special protection, because in a liberal democracy 'a person opposed to official ideas and positions must be able to find a place in the political arena'.[16]

At the same time, freedom of expression under the ECHR is never unlimited. Words and other forms of expression can damage people and undermine, as well as promote, the bonds of tolerance and respect which hold liberal societies together. Racist speech does little to aid race relations. Political speech can undermine politics. In Israel in 1995, speeches and publications by members of extreme religious parties condemning the policy of the then Israeli government in developing a rapprochement with the Palestinians contributed to, and perhaps directly caused, the assassination of Prime Minister Yitzhak Rabin, precipitating the reactionary swing in Israeli politics which has done so much to disrupt the peace process in the Middle East.[17] This is an extreme example of a general truth: free speech has costs.[18] In the words of ECHR Article 10(2), the exercise of the freedom 'carries with it duties and responsibilities'. As ECHR Article 17 reminds us:

'Nothing in this Convention may be interpreted as implying for any state, group or person any right to engage in any activity or perform any act aimed at the destruction of any of the rights and freedom set forth herein or at their limitation to a greater extent than is provided for in the Convention.'

Article 10(2) furthers this principle by allowing states to restrict freedom of expression under certain conditions. The exception must by 'prescribed by law', pursue one of the legitimate aims for a restriction exhaustively listed in Article 10(2), and be 'necessary in a democratic society' for that purpose.[19] In *Sunday Times v. United Kingdom*,[20] the question arose whether the English common-law offence of contempt of court by prejudging the result of pending legal proceedings was 'prescribed by law' within the meaning of Article 10(2). The *Sunday Times* argued that the law was so vague and uncertain, and the principles on which the House of Lords had upheld the conviction for contempt were so novel, that they could not be said to have been

---

[13] *Vogt v. Germany*, Eur. Ct. HR, Series A, No. 323, Judgment of 26 September 1995, 21 EHRR 205.

[14] *Castells v. Spain*, Eur. Ct. HR, Series A, No. 236, Judgment of 23 April 1992, 14 EHRR 445.

[15] *Castells*, above, at para. 42 of the judgment.

[16] *Piermont v. France*, Eur. Ct. HR, Series A, No. 314, Judgment of 27 April 1995, 20 EHRR 301, at para. 76.

[17] See R. Cohen-Almagor, 'Boundaries of Freedom of Expression before and after Prime Minister Rabin's Assassination', in R. Cohen-Almagor (ed.), *Liberal Democracy and the Limits of Tolerance: Essays in Honor and Memory of Yitzhak Rabin* (Ann Arbor, Mich.: University of Michigan Press, 2000), 79–98.

[18] F. Schauer, 'The Cost of Communicative Tolerance', in Cohen-Almagor (ed.), *Liberal Democracy*, 28–42.

[19] For a general account of the meaning of these terms, see Ch. 2 above.

[20] Eur. Ct. HR, Series A, No. 30, Judgment of 26 April 1979, 2 EHRR 245.

prescribed by law. The Court held that two of the requirements which flow from the expression were:

(1) the law must be adequately accessible: the citizen must be able to have an indication that is adequate in the circumstances of the legal rules applicable to a given case;

(2) a norm cannot be regarded as law unless it is formulated with sufficient precision to enable the citizen to regulate his conduct: he must be able—if need be with appropriate advice—to foresee, to a degree that is reasonable in the circumstances, the consequences which a given action may entail.[21]

The Court recognized that any law is to a greater or lesser extent vague, and any type of law is subject to interpretation, and so their practical effects may be to some degree uncertain. The need for law to be reasonably flexible was also recognized. Like the ECHR, national law is a living organism. National courts had to be responsible for interpreting the law in such a way as to minimize any unavoidable uncertainty, but as long as they did so the practical effect of the rules could be said to be prescribed by law.[22] The Court therefore accepted that the common law could be regarded as 'law' for the purpose of authorizing a restriction under Article 10(2) (any other conclusion would in any case have been contrary to the intention of the drafters of the Convention: see paragraph 47 of the judgment), and after looking at the leading decisions and the formulation of the principles in *Halsbury's Laws of England*[23] the Court concluded that the applicants had not been without an adequate indication of the existence of the 'prejudgment principle': 'Even if the court does have certain doubts concerning the precision with which that principle was formulated at the relevant time, it considers that the applicants were able to foresee, to a degree that was reasonable in the circumstances, a risk that publication of the draft article might fall foul of the principle'.[24]

The question whether or not a restriction is necessary in a democratic society for one of the purposes specified in Article 10(2) is by its very nature open to controversy. As this has been interpreted by the Court, the main requirements are that the restriction should be directed to meeting a 'pressing social need', and that it should be proportionate to that need.[25] The Court has felt that, as long as the restriction is prescribed by law and a plausible case can be made for the need for the restriction for an authorized purpose, a democratic government must be allowed a measure of

---

[21] Para. 49 of the majority judgment.

[22] *Otto-Preminger-Institut v. Austria*, Eur. Ct. HR, Series A, No. 295-A, Judgment of 20 September 1994, 19 EHRR 34. For example, when the House of Lords in *R. v. R.* [1992] 1 AC 599, [1991] 4 All ER 481 departed from the previously understood rule that a wife was always presumed to consent to sexual intercourse with her husband, the European Court of Human Rights held that there had been sufficient indications of a movement in that direction in the caselaw to allow a husband to foresee possible criminal liability for rape, so the conviction did not violate ECHR Article 7: *S. W. v. United Kingdom*, Eur. Ct. HR, Series A, No. 335-B, Judgment of 22 November 1995, 21 EHRR 363. See also *Rekvényi v. Hungary*, Eur. Ct. HR, App. No. 25390/94, RJD 1999-III, at para. 34; *Tammer v. Estonia*, Eur. Ct. HR, App. No. 41205/98, Judgment of 6 February 2001, at para. 37 (criminal liability for using 'insulting' language prescribed by law, because of the way the national courts had applied the term 'insulting').

[23] 3rd edn. (current at the time of the events which gave rise to the application), vol. viii, paras. 11–13.

[24] At para. 52 of the judgment.

[25] This is explained in Ch. 2, above.

discretion ('margin of appreciation') as to the form of restriction which it imposes. None the less, this discretion is circumscribed. The Court is the ultimate arbiter of the existence of a pressing social need and of the proportionality of the restriction. The state must convincingly establish the need for the restriction, providing any relevant evidence to support the claim.[26] In relation to proportionality to a legitimate aim, national authorities must show that they applied standards which conformed to Article 10, and had relevant and sufficient reasons for deciding that their actions were proportionate, based on an acceptable assessment of the relevant facts.[27]

This means that the circumstances in which a restriction on freedom of expression can be justified, and the types and level of safeguards which are demanded, are very sensitive to the nature of an exercise of free expression (including to some extent the content of the expression) and the context in which it takes place. Political expression, including robust criticism of politicians, is strongly protected. There is no absolute right to legal protection when criticizing politicians, who do not lose the right to protect their reputations or to enjoy a protected area of private life when they enter politics. Nevertheless, the importance of political debate means that '[t]he limits of acceptable criticism are accordingly wider as regards a politician as such than as regards a private individual. Unlike the latter, the former inevitably and necessarily lays himself open to close scrutiny of his every word and deed by both journalists and the public at large, and he must consequently display a greater degree of tolerance'.[28] It will be hard to justify interfering with free expression in relation to politicians. By contrast, public servants are generally expected to be politically neutral in their work. The Court therefore held in *Janowski v. Poland*[29] that it was easier to justify criminalizing insulting abuse of public servants than similar abuse of politicians. For public servants, that generosity has a down side: the desirability of maintaining their political neutrality makes it possible to justify restricting their own participation in political activities, at least where the country's history gives rise to legitimate fears about the risk of totalitarianism through a political party's domination of the public service, as in former Soviet Bloc countries.[30]

When assessing the justification for interfering with freedom of expression, the Court draws a distinction between assertions of fact and value judgments. Where a person makes a factual assertion which is demonstrably false and damages someone, it is reasonably easy to justify imposing a penalty or a duty to compensate the victim and refrain from repeating the falsehood, particularly if the speaker failed to take

[26] *Lingens v. Austria*, Eur. Ct. HR, Series A, No. 103, Judgment of 8 July 1986, at para. 41; *Nilsen and Johnsen v. Norway*, Eur. Ct. HR, App. No. 23118/93, RJD 1999-III at para. 43; *Tammer v. Estonia*, Eur. Ct. HR, App. No. 41205/98, Judgment of 6 February 2001, at paras. 59–60.

[27] *Sunday Times v. United Kingdom*, Eur. Ct. HR, Series A, No. 30, Judgment of 26 April 1979, at para. 62; *Lingens v. Austria*, Eur. Ct. HR, Series A, No. 103, Judgment of 8 July 1986, at para. 40; *Barfod v. Denmark*, Eur. Ct. HR, Series A, No. 149, Judgment of 22 February 1989 at para. 28; *Janowski v. Poland*, Eur. Ct. HR, App. No. 25716/94, RJD 1999-I at para. 30; *News Verlag GmbH & Co. KG v. Austria*, App. No. 31457/96, RJD 2000-I at para. 52; *Tammer v. Estonia*, Eur. Ct. HR, App. No. 41205/98, Judgment of 6 February 2001, at para. 61.

[28] *Lingens v. Austria*, above, at para. 42. See to the same effect *Oberschlick v. Austria*, Eur. Ct. HR, Series A, No. 204, Judgment of 23 May 1991, at paras. 57–9.

[29] Eur. Ct. HR, App. No. 25716/94, RJD 1999-I, Judgment of 21 January 1999.

[30] *Rekvényi v. Hungary*, Eur. Ct. HR, App. No. 25390/94, RJD 1999-III.

reasonable care to check his or her information. Legal liability may attach to factual
assertions without violating Article 10 rights if the assertions are not supported by a
reasonable basis of investigation and information, particularly if the defendant is a
journalist, since abiding by proper standards of journalistic ethics (for example, by
taking reasonable care to check facts before publishing) is one of the duties and
responsibilities of journalists to which Article 10(2) refers.[31] However, much debate,
especially about matters of public or political interest, is about values and their application to particular situations. Value judgments are not demonstrably true or false,
but they are at the core of political dialogue. The Court therefore scrutinizes particularly rigorously any attempt to restrict people's freedom to form, express, or give effect
to value judgments.[32] For example, it has been held in that it violates the Article 10
right of a secondary-school teacher (a public servant) to freedom of expression to
dismiss her on the ground of her membership of, and prospective parliamentary
candidature on behalf of, the German Communist Party (DKP).[33]

Even expressions of value judgments may be restricted or penalized to give effect to
the responsibilities and duties which accompany the freedom. The responsibilities
which attach to freedom of expression include a duty to avoid making damaging,
value-based criticisms without any appropriate foundation of fact. If a value judgment is based on a factual premise, the state is entitled to insist on there being a
sufficient factual basis for the value judgment. However, if a person is restrained,
penalized, or made liable in respect of a value judgment, the law must allow him to
justify the statement by leading evidence to establish a factual basis for the value
judgment in question. If rules of evidence or of law effectively prevent a person from
establishing the truth of an allegation (for example by not allowing truth as a defence
to a charge of criminal libel), the Court has held that the interference with freedom
of expression cannot be justified, because a person who is entitled as a matter of
human-rights law to make a claim if it is supported by a reasonable basis of fact must
be permitted by national law to advance relevant evidence by way of justification.[34]
Furthermore, the person making the statement need not necessarily personally
undertake research, even if he or she is a journalist, if there are official reports or
statistics on which it is reasonable to rely in support of the factual assertion or
judgment.[35]

Many of the controversial issues in any society are not party-political. There is none

---

[31] *Barfod v. Denmark*, Eur. Ct. HR, Series A, No. 149, Judgment of 22 February 1989, 13 EHRR 493;
Thorgeirson v. Iceland, Eur. Ct. HR, Series A, No. 239, Judgment of 25 June 1992, 14 EHRR 843; *De Haes and
Gijsels v. Belgium*, Eur. Ct. HR, Judgment of 24 February 1997 RJD 1997-I, 25 EHRR 1; *Fressoz and Roire v.
France*, Eur. Ct. HR, App. No. 29183/95, Judgment of 21 January 1999, RJD 1999-I, at para. 54; *Bladet Tromsø
and Stensaas v. Norway*, Eur. Ct. HR, App. No. 21980/93, Judgment of 20 May 1999, RJD 1999-III.

[32] This has been a consistent thread in the caselaw since *Lingens v. Austria*, Eur. Ct. HR, Series A, No. 103,
Judgment of 8 July 1986.

[33] *Vogt v. Germany*, Series A, No. 323, Judgment of 26 September 1995, 21 EHRR 205.

[34] *Castells v. Spain*, Eur. Ct. HR, Series A, No. 236, Judgment of 23 April 1992, 14 EHRR 445; *Jerusalem v.
Austria*, Eur. Ct. HR, App. No. 26958/95, Judgment of 27 February 2001.

[35] *Bladet Tromsø and Stensaas v. Norway*, Eur. Ct. HR, App. No. 21980/93, Judgment of 20 May 1999, RJD
1999-III (disproportionate to convict newspaper and journalist of defamation when they based their attack
on seal-hunters on an official report on the subject).

the less a strong public interest in openly debating them, and Article 10 protects contributions to the debate as extensively as purely political debate.[36] This approach has been applied to restrict actions for defamation in respect of allegations that the police had mistreated people,[37] injunctions restraining the publication of scientific opinions about the potential dangers of food cooked in microwave ovens,[38] and prosecutions for defamation in respect of newspaper allegations, using an official report, of inhumane methods used when culling seals.[39]

Article 10 protects the provision of information about services available to people in other countries, even if they would be illegal if provided in the country where the information is provided. For example, an injunction preventing the dissemination in Ireland of information about abortion services abroad was held to violate Article 10.[40] That information closely touched the lives and health of women, but commercial advertising and information more generally is protected, not least because of consumers' right under Article 10(1) to receive information of interest to them as long as the advertising is truthful,[41] although it may be easier to justify restricting such advertising than it would be to justify restricting public-interest publications. For example, the Court has been ready to countenance significant restrictions on advertising by lawyers, in order to maintain the standing of the profession,[42] and other grounds for regulating advertising, such as to protect consumers' safety and health in respect of tobacco or liquor advertising, are likely to provide an even stronger justification. This would be in line with the majority decision of the Supreme Court of Canada that a ban on tobacco advertising was an illegitimate interference with the right to freedom of expression under the constitutional Charter of Rights and Freedoms.[42a] It is possible that any attempt by the Secretary of State in England and Wales to use his new power under section 60 of the Health and Social Care Act 2001 to make regulations restricting the freedom of pharmacists to sell to drug companies information about the prescribing habits of particular doctors, using material in which the patients concerned are anonymized, would be challenged as a disproportionate interference with the pharmacists' freedom to impart commercially useful information under ECHR Article 10 (the object of any restriction would be to make it difficult for companies to target their advertising for drugs in ways which might inflate the cost to the National Health Service of providing medication).

[36] *Thorgeirson v. Iceland*, Eur. Ct. HR, Series A, No. 239, Judgment of 25 June 1992, 14 EHRR 843, at para. 64.

[37] *Thorgeirson v. Iceland*, above.

[38] *Hertel v. Switzerland*, Eur. Ct. HR, Judgment of 25 August 1998, RJD 1998-VI, 28 EHRR 534.

[39] *Bladet Tromsø and Stensaas v. Norway*, Eur. Ct. HR, App. No. 21980/93, Judgment of 20 May 1999, RJD 1999-III.

[40] *Open Door Counselling Ltd. and Dublin Well Woman Centre Ltd. v. Ireland*, Eur. Ct. HR, Series A, No. 246-A, Judgment of 29 October 1992, 15 EHRR 244.

[41] *Markt intern Verlag v. Germany*, Eur. Ct. HR, Series A, No. 165, Judgment of 20 November 1989, 12 EHRR 161; *Casado Coca v. Spain*, Eur. Ct. HR, Series A, No. 285-A, Judgment of 24 February 1994, 18 EHRR 1.

[42] *Casado Coca v. Spain*, above.

[42a] *R.J.R.-MacDonald Inc. v. Attorney General of Canada* [1995] 3 LRD 653, SC of Canada (a five-to-four majority decision).

Some other forms of expression, while within Article 10(1), are less fully protected. The Court has been ready—perhaps too ready—to accept governments' justifications for restricting pornographic or blasphemous material, because of the damage it may be thought to do to the moral standards of a society and to the sensibilities of believers (on which see Chapter 16, below). The weakest protection of all is accorded to racist expression and the promulgation of racial hatred. The Court interprets Article 10 in the light of Article 20 of the ICCPR, which requires the prohibition of propaganda for war and advocacy of national, racial, or religious hatred that constitutes incitement to discrimination, hostility, or violence. This permits states to control, under ECHR Article 10(2), publicity given to racist views and hate speech, as long as the controls satisfy the tests of legality, necessity, and proportionality.[43] The approach, which is markedly different from that adopted by the US Supreme Court under the First Amendment to the US Constitution, is further supported by reference to the outlawing of abuse of rights under ECHR Article 17, and Article 4 of the International Convention on the Elimination of All Forms of Racial Discrimination, which provides:

'States Parties condemn all propaganda and all organizations which are based on ideas or theories of superiority of one race or group of persons of one colour or ethnic origin or which attempt to justify or promote racial hatred and discrimination in any form, and undertake to adopt immediate and positive measures designed to eradicate all incitement to, or acts of, such discrimination and, to this end, with due regard to the principles embodied in the Universal Declaration of Human Rights and the rights expressly set forth in article 5 of this Convention, *inter alia*:

> (a) shall declare an offence punishable by law all dissemination of ideas based on racial superiority or hatred, incitement to racial discrimination, as well as acts of violence or incitement to such acts against any race or group of persons of another colour or ethnic origin, and also the provision of any assistance to racist activities, including the financing thereof;
>
> (b) shall declare illegal and prohibit organizations, and also organized and all other propaganda activities, which promote and incite racial discrimination, and shall recognize participation in such organizations or activities as an offence punishable by law;
>
> (c) shall not permit public authorities or public institutions, national or local, to promote or incite racial discrimination.

Against this background of international law, the reluctance of the European Court of Human Rights to accord significant protection to racist speech under ECHR Article 10 is understandable. The emphasis on the duties and responsibilities of those exercising freedom of expression, the refusal to countenance any element of absolutism in the right, and a keen sensitivity to the political and social context of expression, are key features of the jurisprudence of the Court under ECHR Article 10. This makes collective interests weightier in Europe than in the USA in the definition of rights to

---

[43] *Jersild v. Denmark*, Eur. Ct. HR, Series A, No. 298, Judgment of 23 September 1994, 19 EHRR 1.

free expression. Some people have argued that American First Amendment jurisprudence should guide the interpretation of ECHR Article 10 under the Human Rights Act 1998.[44] However, this underestimates the deep differences between the legal, social, and political cultures of the USA and Europe which make social welfare, even in post-Thatcher Britain, a far more powerful consideration than in the more individualistic ethos of post-Clinton America.[45]

That this runs through the ECHR is clear from the approach of the Court to assessing proportionality. In *Tammer v. Estonia*,[46] a journalist was convicted of publishing an insulting report on the private and family life of a former politician, Ms. Laanaru. The journalist argued that his conviction violated ECHR Article 10. The Court decided that it was justifiable as a proportionate response to a pressing social need to protect the reputation and rights of Ms. Laanaru, noting that the offensive words expressed a value judgment about parts of Ms. Laanaru's private life which related to no matter of real public concern or general importance, was not a contribution to political discussion, and could in any case have been expressed without resorting to insulting expressions. Furthermore, the penalty imposed was relatively a minor fine.[47] What is said, the way in which it is said, the public importance of what is said, the context in which it is said, and the impact of the restriction or penalty on the speaker, are all relevant to making decisions about proportionality under Article 10. It does not make the right to freedom of expression entirely transparent, but it allows courts to take account of matters which reasonable people might properly think were relevant to decisions of that kind.

Freedom of expression under ECHR Article 10 does not stand alone. It operates alongside, and is complemented by, other rights, including freedom to manifest a belief under ECHR Article 9, freedom of peaceful assembly and association under ECHR Article 11, and the right to be free of discrimination in the enjoyment of all these Convention rights under ECHR Article 14. Freedom of assembly is considered in Chapter 18, below. The effect of ECHR Articles 9 and 14 in providing protection for forms of expressive behaviour can be illustrated by reference to *Thlimmenos v. Greece*.[47a] The applicant, a Jehovah's Witness, was sentenced to a term of imprisonment for refusing on religious grounds to enlist in the army for religious reasons (he objected to wearing a military uniform). After his release, he wanted to become a chartered accountant, but was refused entry to the profession because his conviction for a felony was said to make him an unfit person, in accordance with a general rule that people convicted of felonies were not fit to enter the profession. In the circumstances of the case, this was held to discriminate against Jehovah's Witnesses on

---

[44] See, e.g. I. Loveland, 'A Free Trade in Ideas—and Outcomes' in I. Loveland (ed.), *Importing the First Amendment: Freedom of Speech and Expression in Britain, Europe and the USA* (Oxford: Hart Publishing, 1998), 1–21.

[45] *Cp.* E. Barendt, 'Importing United States Free Speech Jurisprudence?', in T. Campbell and W. Sadurski (eds.), *Freedom of Communication* (Aldershot: Dartmouth, 1994), 57–75; Sir Stephen Sedley, 'The First Amendment: A Case for Import Controls?', in Loveland (ed.), *Importing the First Amendment*, 23–7; D. Feldman, 'Content Neutrality', ibid., 139–71.

[46] Eur. Ct. HR, App. No. 41205/98, Judgment of 6 February 2001.

[47] Ibid. at paras. 65–70.

[47a] Eur. Ct. HR, App. No. 34369/97, Judgment of 6 April 2000, 31 EHRR 411.

grounds which violated ECHR Article 14 taken in conjunction with ECHR Article 9. Excluding the applicant from the accountancy profession was held to pursue no legitimate aim, as an objection to wearing a military uniform did not call in question his honesty or morality, and was not likely to interfere with his ability to perform the duties of an accountant. There was therefore no reasonable and objective justification for the state's refusal to treat the applicant differently from other felons. This shows that people need not be treated differently from others in order to suffer unlawful discrimination under Article 14. While like cases should be treated alike, Article 14 also requires that people in relevantly different situations should be treated in accordance with those differences. In any case, it was held to be disproportionate to impose a further penalty for refusing to enlist when he had already served his prison sentence. The effect is to provide a network of rights protecting many types of expressive behaviour.

13.2 THE JUSTIFICATIONS FOR, AND LIMITS OF, FREEDOM OF EXPRESSION

(1) THE IMPORTANCE OF FREEDOM OF EXPRESSION

The liberty to express one's self freely is important for a number of reasons, which help to shape the development and application of the law on freedom of expression.[48] First, self-expression is a significant instrument of freedom of conscience, personal identity, and self-fulfilment.[49] From the point of view of civil liberties, this is probably the most important of the justifications which can be offered for free speech. In Chapter 1, the commitment to liberty was grounded mainly in the idea of individual autonomy, an ability to live a life according to choices consciously made between a reasonable range of options. The freedom to choose between values, to have fun through communication, to identify and be identified with particular values or ideas, and to live one's life according to one's choice, is the essence of liberty. Freedom of expression has an important role to play here. If one takes seriously one's choice of values, it will be important to be able to express them through words and action alike. Such expression does not only serve the instrumental goal of persuading others or advancing understanding. It is also the means by which people acknowledge and start to put into effect their commitments to selected values and choices, thereby defining

---

[48] See F. Schauer, *Free Speech: A Philosophical Enquiry* (Cambridge: CUP, 1982); D. F. B. Tucker, *Law, Liberalism and Free Speech* (Totowa, NJ: Rowman & Allanheld, 1985); E. Barendt, *Freedom of Speech* (Oxford: Clarendon Press, 1987), ch. 1; T. Campbell, 'Rationales for Freedom of Communication', in Campbell and Sadurski (eds.), *Freedom of Communication*, 17–44; R. Moon, *The Constitutional Protection of Freedom of Expression* (Toronto: University of Toronto Press, 2000), 8–31. For examples of the theory of free speech influencing judicial reasoning, see *Irwin Toy Ltd. v. Attorney-General of Quebec* [1989] 1 SCR 927, SC Canada; *Secretary, Ministry of Information and Broadcasting, Government of India v. Cricket Association of Bengal* [1995] AIR SC 1236, SC of India, at 1255–6 *per* Sawant and Mohan JJ.

[49] For discussion, see Schauer, *Free Speech*, chs 5 and 6; Tucker, *Law, Liberalism and Free Speech*, 11–56.

an important aspect of their personal identities.[50] The choice of language can be as important as the ideas being expressed, if (for example) the use of a particular language (Breton in France, French in Quebec, Welsh in Wales, Gaelic in Scotland, etc.) is part of one's identification with and support of a minority community or a threatened culture.[51] Language rights are generally respected in England and Wales. There is a right to equal treatment of the Welsh and English languages in legal proceedings in Wales, so that jurors and witnesses can take oath or affirm in Welsh.[51a] But this does not give an absolute right to have one's child taught in the language of one's choice at public expense. When English parents living in Wales wanted their child to be taught mainly in English, while their local school taught mainly in Welsh, the local education authority was not compelled to provide free transport to another school where the child could be taught mainly in English.[51b] This does not seem to be a disproportionate or illegitimate interference with language rights.

This has important implications for the types of expressive action which merit protection by law. It becomes impossible to restrict the freedom to verbal forms of expression, much less to the content of ideas expressed. Any act may have expressive content, if it amounts to an expression of one's chosen values. Conversely, there may be verbal or written textual outpourings which do not merit protection, because they do not express any such choice between values. For this reason, Edwin Baker has argued that, while the First Amendment to the US Constitution 'bars certain governmental restrictions on non-coercive, nonviolent, substantively valued conduct, including nonverbal conduct',[52] it does not bar controls on commercial speech, including advertising. The latter are not substantively valuable: they are not expressions of life choices, but are (at best) instrumentally useful ways of exercising commercial freedom, or informing potential purchasers about products.[53] This would be a more powerful argument if the liberty model were the only theoretical framework for justifying protection for freedom of expression, but it is not. There are others, which overlap with it in core areas, but also extend beyond it to justify free speech on other grounds at the peripheries.

The second justification concerns the contribution of communication to the growth of knowledge and understanding. Freedom of expression enables people to contribute to debates about social and moral values. It is arguable that the best way to find the best or truest theory or model of anything is to permit the widest possible

[50] J. Raz, 'Free Expression and Personal Identification', in J. Raz, *Ethics in the Public Domain: Essays in the Morality of Law and Politics* (Oxford: Clarendon Press, 1994), 131–54.

[51] On language rights under ICCPR Article 19, see *Guesdon v. France*, UN HR Cttee., Comm. No. 219/1986; *Ballantyne, Davidson and McIntyre v. Canada*, UN HR Cttee., Comms. Nos. 359/1989 and 385/1989; *R. L. M. v. France*, UN HR Cttee., Comm. No. 363/1989. For Canadian approaches, see *Ford v. Attorney General of Quebec* [1988] 2 SCR 712, SC Canada; L. Green, 'Freedom of Expression and Choice of Language', in W. J. Waluchow (ed.), *Freedom of Expression: Essays in Law and Philosophy* (Oxford: Clarendon Press, 1994), 135–52; Moon, *Freedom of Expression*, 65–8.

[51a] See *Practice Direction (Crown Court: Welsh Language)* [1998] 1 WLR 1677.

[51b] *R. v. Dyfed County Council, ex parte S. (Minors)*, The Times, 25 July 1994, CA.

[52] C. E. Baker, *Human Liberty and Freedom of Speech* (New York and Oxford: Oxford University Press, 1989), 5. The main argument is developed in ch. 3.

[53] Baker, *Human Liberty*, ch. 9.

range of ideas to circulate. The interplay of these ideas, challenging each other and allowing the strengths and weaknesses of each to be exposed, is more likely than any alternative strategy to lead to the best possible conclusion. This treats freedom of expression as an instrumental value, advancing other goods (the development of true or good ideas) with a consequential benefit for the individual and society. This is the basis on which freedom of expression appealed to John Milton, in *Areopagitica*, and to the utilitarian mind of John Stuart Mill, who gave the most famous, and most convincing, justification for freedom of speech in *On Liberty*.

Mill argued on utilitarian grounds that there was a distinction in principle between facts and opinion. When dealing with opinions, all should be freely expressed, subject to any restrictions necessary to protect against identifiable harm. This wide freedom would benefit individuals by allowing them to choose between the widest possible range of opinions, where none could be definitively shown to be right or wrong, maximizing personal autonomy. It would also extend freedom of political choice, and bolster democratic processes by encouraging rational debate which, it was confidently expected, would render it more likely that the best solution would be found for any problem. Assertions of fact, on the other hand, could by definition be either true or false. There would be good reason to allow free expression of the truth, as this would lead to advances in knowledge and material improvements in society, but this does not justify permitting free expression of falsehoods. However, it is not always possible to say whether an assertion is true or false, and many benefits may flow from allowing statements of fact to be asserted so that they may be tested, even if they are ultimately found to be false (this is particularly important in the physical sciences if one accepts Karl Popper's portrayal of scientific advance as occurring through the testing and falsification of factual hypotheses).[54] This cannot in itself justify the publication of factual claims which are known to be false, but on a rule-utilitarian analysis the benefits of a general principle permitting freedom of expression are held to outweigh the disbenefits resulting from particular applications of the rule. It is therefore preferable to permit freedom to express opinions and facts, even if untrue, rather than to adopt a general rule which permits censorship and coercion in relation to expression.

This approach is sometimes linked with the notion of a market-place of ideas, in which the best ideas win through the operation of market forces. The market-place theory was influential in the USA, where it was developed by the Supreme Court to justify First Amendment protection for unpopular speech, such as advocacy of racist theories by the Ku Klux Klan,[55] but also to deny protection to those forms of expression—such as obscenity—which were regarded as offering nothing worthwhile to the market-place of ideas, and so having no redeeming social merit.[56] Obscenity was considered to be useful, if at all, only as a sex aid.[57] However, the fact that it adds

[54] K. Popper, *The Logic of Scientific Discovery* (London: Hutchinson, 1959); K. Popper, 'Science: Conjectures and Refutations', in his *Conjectures and Refutations*, 4th edn. (London: Routledge & Kegan Paul, 1972), 33–65.

[55] *Brandenburg v. Ohio* 395 US 444 (1969).

[56] *Roth v. United States* 354 US 476 (1957). See the discussion by Baker, *Human Liberty*, 8–11.

[57] Schauer, *Free Speech*, 182.

nothing valuable to the market-place of ideas does not necessarily mean that obscenity, or any other form of expression, ought not to be protected. A privacy issue then arises: even if material is of purely prurient interest, and is resorted to as an aid to (let us say) masturbation, it is hard to see how the state can have a sufficient interest in its effects to justify making it unavailable for use by consenting adults.[58]

The market-place-of-ideas model has implications for commercial speech. In a market economy, commercial speech, including advertising, may be useful in order to permit information about products and the relative merits of commercial competitors to be promulgated, facilitating informed choices by customers. Thus in a liberal society with a market economy, freedom of expression could be thought to support an important aspect of collective economic life. This depends on the assumption that the information will be presented to the market, through advertising, in a way which enables potential customers to choose between products. That is, of course, highly questionable. Much very successful advertising gives remarkably little information about the product. Magazine and poster advertisements for cigarettes rely almost wholly on image, and purposely give no information (save the health warning required by law) about the qualities of the product. The same applies to most liquor advertisements. The argument does not justify protection for all commercial speech, unless one takes the view that, on a utilitarian analysis, the social costs involved in vetting commercial speech would outweigh the benefits.

A third justification for free expression is that it allows the political discourse which is necessary in any country which aspires to democracy.[59] It reinforces the personal-autonomy justification by mandating protection for the political expression of those who regard participating in politics as an aspect of their self-fulfilment as people and citizens. The power of this justification depends on the view which one adopts about the structural arrangements which democracy entails. A democratic rationale for freedom of expression makes perfect sense if applied to a society in which the operative model of democracy is one in which the people have the right to participate directly in day-to-day governmental decision making, or to have their views considered in the choice of policies by government. It works less well if the prevailing model is one in which the people merely choose a government, which is then free to get on with the job of governing until the time comes for it to account to the people for the way in which it has used power. The representative system, such as we have in the UK, would offer less support to free-expression rights than a participatory system.

Nevertheless, a measure of free speech (and more especially freedom of information) remains necessary to any sort of democracy. As the Privy Council observed in *Hector v. Attorney-General of Antigua and Barbuda*:[60]

---

[58] H. Kalven, Jun. (ed. by J. Kalven), *A Worthy Tradition: Freedom of Speech in America* (New York: Harper & Row, 1988), 34.

[59] The leading exponent of this democratic justification is A. Meiklejohn, *Political Freedom: The Constitutional Powers of the People* (New York: OUP, 1965). For discussion, see Schauer, *Free Speech*, ch. 3.

[60] [1990] 2 AC 312, [1990] 2 All ER 103, PC.

'In a free democratic society it is almost too obvious to need stating that those who hold office in government and who are responsible for public administration must always be open to criticism. Any attempt to stifle or fetter such criticism amounts to political censorship of the most insidious and objectionable kind . . . [I]t is no less obvious that the very purpose of criticism levelled at those who have the conduct of public affairs by their political opponents is to undermine public confidence in their stewardship and to persuade the electorate that the opponents would make a better job of it than those presently holding office . . . [T]heir Lordships cannot help viewing a statutory provision which criminalises statements likely to undermine public confidence in the conduct of public affairs with the utmost suspicion.'[61]

Fourthly, it has been suggested that it is good for people to be forced to respect each other's right to self-expression, especially if they disapprove of the way it is being exercised, because it helps to develop a capacity for tolerance. This, it is said, can be done most easily in the relatively harmless sphere of speech acts, making it more likely that people will extend the same attitude to other fields which are not as obviously harmless.[62] This controversially assumes both that speech is relatively harmless—often, but not always, the case—and that tolerance in one field can and should be translated into tolerance of other activities. Alternatively, accepting that speech is sometimes dangerously harmful, it can be argued that allowing harmful speech stimulates opponents of racist or sexist speech to campaign in ways which ultimately overcome the harm and revolutionize the law and society.[63]

Fifthly, freedom of expression facilitates artistic and scholarly endeavour of all sorts. This is not, perhaps, a separate head of justification. It is a specialized form of the first and second heads, and depends on accepting that art and scholarship are valuable in their own right.

These justifications draw mainly on three values: personal autonomy, which is served by maximizing the range of information and choice of opinions to which people have access; truth, which may be advanced by full information and open debate (at any rate if conducted under conditions of fairness in which no one ideology is permitted to dominate or dictate the terms of the discussion);[64] and democracy, which depends on some choice at least being available in the market-place of ideas, as well as drawing strength from the combination of personal autonomy of electors and legislators in the political sphere and the hope that it will lead to the selection of the 'best', or 'most true', policies. For example, where a government proposes to introduce a law regulating commercial advertising, the autonomy of consumer choice favours free advertising, subject to any controls needed to ensure that people are not misled by false claims which advertisers might make for products. Were there no constraints on freedom of expression, the difficulty would arise that one of the objects of upholding free expression—truth—could be defeated if it were in a person's commercial interests to do so. There is an element, as the Williams Committee noted, of

[61] [1990] 2 All ER at 106.

[62] L. C. Bollinger, *The Tolerant Society: Freedom of Speech and Extremist Speech in America* (New York: Oxford University Press, 1986), especially ch. 8.

[63] D. A. J. Richards, 'Free Speech as Toleration', in Waluchow (ed.), *Free Expression*, 31–57.

[64] See J. Habermas, *Communication and the Evolution of Society*, trans. T. McCarthy (London: Heinemann, 1979).

bad expressive coinage driving out the good,[65] and it is important to regulate expression to limit the extent to which this can happen.

There will inevitably be situations in which these values come into conflict with each other or with other values, but this does not mean that the liberal harm principle is incoherent. It merely means that the principle itself cannot determine the area within which the principle is to operate. For instance, does the interest in democracy require respect for the right of political activists to make demonstrably untrue statements in an attempt to curry favour with the electorate? Is there a trade-off between the demands of truth and the demands of democracy? What happens if there is an expression of opinion which is so offensive to right-thinking people that it is likely to provoke public disorder and violence?

(2) CONFLICTS OF VALUES: TOLERANCE AND THE NEED TO MAINTAIN RESPECT FOR RIGHTS

There is a dilemma for liberals. Classical liberalism has seen the threat to freedom as coming from over-powerful governments and legislatures. On this model, expression needs to be protected against governmental interference. Any attempt by the state to regulate speech is suspect. Adopting this model, American First Amendment constitutional jurisprudence aims almost exclusively to protect all speakers against regulation by government. The harms which certain types of speech inflict on audiences and society as a whole, in terms of emotional or psychological harm and a diminution of respect or self-respect, are largely ignored. Opportunities to protect against the harm caused by particular views, such as racist opinions and Holocaust denial, are further restricted by the requirement that any limitation of free speech must be neutral as between competing viewpoints. The capacity of government to advance collective goods or prevent social harms by restricting individuals' freedom of speech is heavily circumscribed, if not eliminated, by a test such as the 'clear and present danger' test for the acceptability of any abridgment of speech.[66] One can be too liberal; free expression may operate in a way which undermines respect for people and damages society as a whole. It can harm people's dignity and self-respect, threaten other freedoms, including the freedom to participate in society on an equal footing, and weaken the argument in favour of free expression itself.

This is an abuse of the right, and must be restrained. It fails to respect the fundamental justifications for free expression. If people are allowed to get away with behaviour which inflicts harm in ways which do not advance the objectives which make free expression valuable, it may undermine the rationales for the freedom, and erode the public tolerance which makes freedom of expression possible. This may lead to the conclusion that people who abuse the right to free expression sacrifice to the extent of the abuse. The practical problem relates to the kind and extent of restrictions

---

[65] *Report of the Committee on Obscenity and Film Censorship* (Chairman: Professor Bernard Williams), Cmnd. 7772 (London: HMSO, 1979).

[66] C. McCrudden, 'Freedom of Speech and Racial Equality', in P. Birks (ed.), *Pressing Problems in the Law 1: Criminal Justice and Human Rights* (Oxford: Oxford University Press, 1995), 125–48; D. Feldman, 'Content Neutrality', in Loveland (ed.), *Importing the First Amendment*, at 141–56.

on freedom which are appropriate and justifiable.[67] As noted above, ECHR Article 10(2) accepts that the right carries with it responsibilities, and restrictions on the right are necessary in order to give effect to the responsibilities, and Article 17 prohibits the use of rights in ways which destroy the rights of others. This is expressed in the International Covenant on Civil and Political Rights, Article 5, paragraph 1 as follows: 'Nothing in the present Covenant may be interpreted as implying for any state, group or person any right to engage in any activity or perform any act aimed at the destruction of any of the rights and freedoms recognized herein or at their limitation to a greater extent than is provided for in the present Covenant'. The concept of an act which aims at destroying or limiting a right may seem fairly narrow, but an act may be part of a larger programme which has that aim. All such acts may justifiably be restrained by law, or states would awake one morning to find that a series of acts, none of them individually capable of destroying the right, have effectively taken it away incrementally.

ECHR Article 17 and ICCPR Article 5(1) refer to acts which are *aimed at* the destruction of rights. This may sometimes unduly restrict a state's duty to control expression. Sometimes it is clear that a person's, or party's, political objectives, if implemented, would infringe rights, but it is not clear that the person or party aims to produce those effects. 'Aim' appears to have a subjective meaning: it is not enough merely that the person or party is intentionally doing something which has, or is objectively likely to have, a destructive effect; the person or party must subjectively intend to produce that effect, or (perhaps) recognize the risk and be prepared to live with it. But it may be highly desirable to restrain expression which can objectively be seen to threaten rights, even if that is not the intended consequence. Subjective tests are appropriate when apportioning blame for harms caused to others. They are not so relevant when considering whether restrictions are required to safeguard the rights of others. The latter is not a matter of blame, but concerns the proper steps to respond to a pressing social need and an assault (albeit possibly inadvertent) on the rights of others.

If one accepts that the objective test is appropriate, and that it will sometimes be necessary to restrict the freedom of expression of people who are not morally blameworthy in order to protect the rights of others, it may be hard to decide at what point, or to what extent, it is proper to intervene. The American Nazis who planned to hold a meeting in an area of Skokie, Illinois, which had a very substantial Jewish population, raised this problem. The US Federal Court of Appeals held that the right of free speech under the First Amendment of the Constitution overrode other competing values,[68] but it is questionable whether this is a liberal resolution of the problem or merely a legalistic one.[69] Had there been no constitutional provision giving priority to

[67] For discussion, see R. Abel, *Speech and Respect* (London: Stevens & Sons, 1994); Schauer, 'The Cost of Communicative Tolerance', above; O. Fiss, 'Freedom of Speech and Political Violence', in Cohen-Almagor (ed.), *Liberal Democracy*, 70–8.

[68] *Collin v. Smith* (1978) 578 F.2d 1197 (7th Circuit), affirming 447 F. Supp. 676 (ND Ill.). The US Supreme Court denied certiorari, over a dissent by Blackmun J; *Smith v. Collin* (1978) 439 US 916. In the event, the Nazis did not march through Skokie, but held a meeting in another nearby area.

[69] See J. Feinberg, *Offense to Others* (New York: OUP, 1985), 86–96; L. H. Tribe, *Constitutional Choices*

free speech interests over others, the conundrum could not have been resolved within the resources of free speech theory alone. To be helpful in these situations, a free speech principle should, as Dr. Geoffrey Marshall has pointed out, either be multi-tiered, arranging interests in hierarchical order, or incorporate a distinction between the core and periphery of free speech protection 'so as to permit suppression of those [forms of speech] that fall outside the topmost level or privileged core of the area protected by the principle'.[70] Before the Human Rights Act 1998, the constitution in the UK did not compel one type of interest to be given priority over others. Now the Convention rights form part of national law. Even the standards contained in the ECHR do not entirely settle the relative weight of different rights: although there is an implicit ordering of rights in the ECHR,[71] the Court has never been willing to arrange the rights protected by the Convention in hierarchical order. Nevertheless, the Convention at least provides criteria for judging when social and individual interests not amounting to human rights justify restricting the exercise of a human right. As will be seen in Chapter 18 below, the implicit ordering of interests in the UK's constitutional order was not wholly favourable to free expression: the common law and statute actually exhibited a preference for public peacefulness and the avoidance of incitement over freedom of expression, without considering whether the substance of the views expressed threatened liberal democratic values. Under the Human Rights Act 1998, the use of discretion to limit freedom of expression will at last have to be judged by reference to rights-based criteria.

There is a further problem. Sometimes, it seems to the state that it is necessary to abridge people's rights to free speech in order to safeguard or advance some pressing national interest. Liberals may accept that this can be necessary—the state is responsible for fostering and maintaining the conditions which make liberty possible and, perhaps, valuable[72]—but will want to impose fairly stringent tests to be satisfied before such a restriction, which benefits no individual's rights directly and limits the rights of all, is acceptable. Very often, this requires legislatures or courts to conduct a balancing exercise. Where a particular exercise of the right to freedom of expression violates another person's rights, for example the right to reputation or privacy, the legislature or court must decide which takes priority in the circumstances. This can be seen in the way that the US law on defamation accords less protection to the reputations of public figures, who put their reputations on the line by the nature of the life-

---

(Cambridge, Mass.: Harvard University Press, 1985), 219–20; D. Galligan, 'Preserving Public Protest: The Legal Approach', in L. Gostin (ed.), Civil Liberties in Conflict (London: Routledge, 1988), 39–64; N. Dorsen, 'Is There a Right to Stop Offensive Speech? The Case of the Nazis at Skokie', and S. Sedley, 'The Spider and the Fly: A Question of Principle', in Gostin (ed.), Civil Liberties, 122–35 and 136–44, respectively; L. W. Sumner, 'Hate Propaganda and Charter Rights', J. Weinstein, 'An American's View of the Canadian Hate Speech Decisions', and J. Magnet, 'Hate Propaganda in Canada', in Waluchow (ed.), Free Expression, at 153–74, 175–221, and 223–50 respectively; L. W. Sumner, 'Should Hate Speech be Free Speech? John Stuart Mill and the Limits of Tolerance', and I. Cotler, 'Holocaust Denial, Equality, and Harm: Boundaries of Liberty and Tolerance in a Liberal Democracy', in Cohen-Almagor (ed.), Liberal Democracy, 133–50 and 151–81 respectively; Moon, Freedom of Expression, 126–47.

[70] G. Marshall, 'Press Freedom and Free Speech Theory' [1992] PL 40–60, at 60.
[71] See Ch. 2, above.
[72] See Ch. 1.

styles which they have chosen, than to other citizens. English defamation law makes no such distinction.[73]

In context of criminal liability for speech, under the First Amendment to the US Constitution the Supreme Court has developed a number of tests to aid in the balancing exercise. One, the 'bad tendency' test, which asked whether the speech in question had a tendency to undermine society or created a palpable risk of harm, gave relatively weak protection to free speech.[74] It was rapidly supplanted by another, the 'clear and present danger' test. This is simple to state but hard to apply. It asks whether there is a clear and present danger that the speech in question will bring about substantive evils that Congress is constitutionally entitled to outlaw.[75] If there is, the liberty of speech is protected only by the due-process reasonableness and certainty requirements of the Fifth and Fourteenth Amendments. Impressive as the clear-and-present-danger test sounds, one authority on the US Constitution has noted that the test has sometimes been rather easily satisfied: 'The clear-and-present-danger test supposedly favours free speech more than the bad-tendency test, but these standards are applied unevenly'.[76] As Peter Macmillan suggested, in its day-to-day operation this test 'amounts to little more than a restatement of the bad tendency test: the court will overrule the legislature only when legislative judgement is unreasonable. This in turn may well amount to no more than the protection offered by the due process clause'.[77] The protection for free speech has been to some extent improved by a requirement that advocacy consisting of pure speech (unmixed with non-verbal action) is not to be proscribed unless it is directed to incite unlawful action,[78] but the lesser protection accorded to categories of expression designated as 'speech-plus' (i.e. combined speech and action), and 'fighting words', still leaves the right to free speech somewhat exposed.

This emphasizes the gap between employing the rhetoric of strong protection for civil liberties or human rights and producing results which consistently respect freedoms in practice, even under a constitution which protects free speech as a fundamental right. Ultimately, freedom depends on the good sense and balance of legislatures, governments, and courts. When one of them loses its sense of balance, as arguably happened in the British Government's desperate efforts to stop publication of a book which had already been published round the world—*Spycatcher*, by Peter Wright—in the mid-1980s, it is hard to protect freedoms or to avoid making the law look an ass.[79]

---

[73] This is considered in Ch. 14.

[74] *Frohwerk v. United States* 249 US 204 (1919); *Debs v. United States*, 249 US 211 (1919).

[75] *Schenk v. United States* 249 US 47 (1918) at 52, *per* Holmes J. See further *Whitney v. California* 274 US 357 (1927) at 366 *per* Brandeis J; *Dennis v. United States* 341 US 494 (1951).

[76] L. Fisher, *American Constitutional Law* (New York: McGraw Hill, 1990), 535.

[77] P. R. Macmillan, *Censorship and Public Morality* (Aldershot: Gower, 1983), 478.

[78] *Brandenburg v. Ohio* 395 US 444 (1969).

[79] This is considered further in Chs 15 and 16.

(3) STIFLING PUBLICATION: PRIOR AND SUBSEQUENT RESTRAINT[80]

Because of the high value usually placed on freedom of expression, it is thought to require particularly strong grounds to justify using the law to attempt to prevent a person from speaking, as opposed to penalizing them afterwards if their expression justifies it. Grounds which might suffice for penalizing expression after the event, such as the harm or offence which it causes, will not always suffice to justify prior restraint. Indeed, in the USA it used to be thought that the First Amendment to the Constitution protected the press only against prior restraint. In the market-place of ideas, there is something to be said for allowing people to speak, because what they say might be socially valuable, even if it is punishable. The social utility of the utterance may mitigate the penalty, if indeed there is any prosecution. Even if an utterance is damnable, liberal society usually considers that there is a right to publish first and be damned afterwards, rather than being restrained from publishing at all. Not only does prior restraint interfere with freedom of expression, it takes away society's opportunity to judge for itself whether a publication is worthy of condemnation. The decision is instead left to a judge or censor, who is likely to be unaccountable for his decision, if only because people will be unable to judge whether the censor was right. Even the judge may not have the best evidence available, as prior restraint often occurs at an interim stage in proceedings without full examination of the facts on the merits. Nevertheless, this approach is open to certain counter-arguments.

First, in some ways a person's awareness that he may later be subject to subsequent restraint inhibits publication, and is a disguised form of prior restraint. It is undeniable that a person may be influenced in deciding whether to publish by the knowledge that he may make himself liable to criminal penalties or damages by doing so. Even subsequent condemnation, therefore, has some effect on the freedom of expression of a rational person. However, this can be exaggerated. At least the decision whether or not to publish is left to the publisher, respecting his autonomy. He may decide to run the risk only for matters which he feels to be particularly important, but if there is a serious threat of offence or harm flowing from the publication it is right that the threat should be avoided except where justified by important matters.

Secondly, it might be thought illogical to be prepared to punish somebody for doing something, but not to be prepared to ban it beforehand. On the other hand, this again is a reflection of a liberal attitude in society, which allows people to make decisions about their action beforehand (treating knowledge of likely legal consequences as merely one reason for acting in a particular way, which may be outweighed by other reasons)[81] so long as they are prepared to take responsibility for their actions subsequently when called to account by the community.

Thirdly, prior restraint may be more objectionable when it bars publication permanently than when it defers it for a short time, for example pending trial of an action. Fourthly, it may be more objectionable to restrain merely offensive or embarrassing ones than those which cause actual damage. Fifthly, the degree of the restriction is significant. At its most extreme, prior restraint may be more objectionable if

---

[80] Barendt, *Freedom of Speech*, 114–25.
[81] J. Raz, *Practical Reason and Norms* (London: Hutchinson, 1975).

designed to silence any public expression by a person than if it is designed simply to restrain publication of a particular item of information or opinion. This point was ignored by the Privy Council, in considering the impact on freedom of expression of requirements for publishers to pay large licensing fees and lodge sums by way of indemnity against legal liabilities, in *Attorney-General for Antigua v. Antigua Times*.[82] However, the US Supreme Court was alive to the threat in *Grosjean v. American Press*[83] and *Minneapolis Star and Tribune Co. v. Minnesota Commissioner for Revenue*.[84] It is important to be conscious of the fact that prior restraint, like subsequent restraint, has gradations of seriousness, and may be justified in order to deal with a particularly pressing need.

The mechanisms of prior restraint in English law are now restricted both by the general terms of ECHR Article 10 and by the specific provisions of section 12 of the Human Rights Act 1998. This applies whenever a court is considering whether to grant interim relief before trial which might affect the exercise of the Convention right to freedom of expression. In all such cases, the court 'must have particular regard to the importance of the Convention right to freedom of expression'.[85] No such relief is to be granted to the applicant *ex parte* (where the respondent is neither present nor represented) unless the court is satisfied either that the applicant has taken all practicable steps to notify the respondent, or that there are compelling reasons why the respondent should not be notified.[86] Furthermore, no publication is to be restrained unless the court is satisfied that the applicant is likely to establish a case at trial for a more permanent prohibition.[87] The following account of the English law of prior restraint must be read in the light of these principles.

(i) Criminal matters

There is no procedure in English criminal law for a court to order the publication of a book, article, or piece of information to be restrained unless publication would prejudice the administration of justice (see Chapter 17, below). The general rule is that injunctions will not issue to restrain a threatened breach of the criminal law. Unless the publication would constitute a civil wrong, for which the civil remedy of injunction might be available, courts must wait for the allegedly criminal publication to take place and then try the publisher or distributor for the offence. However, there are certain circumstances where an injunction might be available. The Attorney-General can always seek an injunction to restrain the commission of a public wrong, either of his own motion or at the relation of a member of the public (a 'relator action'). This is an exercise of a prerogative power, flowing from the Crown's duty to protect the public interest as *parens patriae*. A local authority may also bring an action for an

---

82　[1976] AC 16, PC.

83　297 US 233 (1936).

84　460 US 575 (1983). See Barendt, *Freedom of Speech*, 123.

85　Human Rights Act 1998, s. 12(4). Further restrictions apply where journalistic, literary, or artistic material is involved. These are considered in subsequent chapters.

86　Human Rights Act 1998, s. 12(2).

87　Ibid., s. 12(3). For this reason, the applicants in *Douglas v. Hello! Ltd*. [2001] 2 WLR 992, CA, failed to obtain an interim injunction restraining unauthorized publication of photographs of their wedding celebration in *Hello!* magazine when they had already agreed to publication of official photographs in *OK!* magazine.

injunction under section 222 of the Local Government Act 1972. Finally, a private citizen may bring an action in respect of a public wrong if it causes him special damage, or if he has a special interest in its suppression.[88] However, this is of limited importance, as the courts regard the the relator procedure as somewhat anomalous, and actions by others are expensive (both private citizens and local authorities may have to undertake to compensate the defendants for loss or damage which they suffer as a result of the injunction if the plaintiffs lose at trial, in addition to the potential liability to indemnify them for their costs).

(ii) Civil-law principles

There are three main civil-law grounds on which a person may be liable to sanctions for imparting information or ideas: the tort of defamation, the equitable duty of confidentiality, and contempt of court. It is relatively unusual in this country to obtain an injunction restraining publication of allegedly defamatory material before trial, at least where the defendant intends to justify the alleged libel. In relation to breach of confidence, however, the law is much more willing to grant interlocutory injunctions, because refusing to do so would permit the confidence to be disclosed, and the purpose of the action thwarted. For this reason, the government has in recent years made increasing use of the law of breach of confidence when trying to combat revelations. This is considered below. In relation to contempt of court, the courts have fairly extensive powers to restrain or postpone publications. These are exercised in the public interest, rather than the interest of the state, and are considered in Chapter 17 below.

13.3 FREEDOM OF EXPRESSION IN ENGLISH LAW

English law recognizes that people are generally free to express themselves and to impart information in any way they please, in the same way that they are free to do anything else, except in so far as that freedom is restricted by particular legal constraints, mediated by the right under ECHR Article 10. There are four special cases in which a positive right to free expression operates, and a further positive right to freedom of information which resonates with the right to receive and impart information under Article 10(1).

(1) PROCEEDINGS IN PARLIAMENT

Members of the House of Commons and the House of Lords are free to say anything in Parliament without being called to account in the courts for what they say.[89] This absolute privilege attaching to parliamentary proceedings was one of the demands

---

[88] D. Feldman, 'Injunctions and the Criminal Law' (1979) 42 *MLR* 369–388.

[89] J. A. G. Griffith and M. Ryle, *Parliament: Functions, Practice and Procedures* (London: Sweet & Maxwell, 1989), 86–90.

made by MPs in the petition presented to the new King William and Queen Mary on their accession in 1688, and was incorporated in the Bill of Rights 1689, Article IX of which provided 'that the freedom of speech and debate or proceedings in Parliament ought not to be impeached or questioned in any court or place out of Parliament'. It frees members from the fear of prosecution by the government, or civil actions, in respect of expressions of opinion or statements of fact in Parliament. Furthermore, any attempt by outside bodies to discipline MPs for views expressed in Parliament, or their voting behaviour, is a breach of privilege. Examples include attempts by trade unions which sponsor Labour MPs to pressurize them or penalize them when they do not toe the union line.[90] (Abuse of the privilege can be dealt with only by the Committee of Privileges of the House concerned, which may impose and enforce penalties in cases where they consider it to be appropriate. In the House of Commons, this role is performed by the Committee on Standards and Privileges established under Standing Order 149.)

The privilege is now subject to one definite, and one possible, limitation relevant to issues of human rights. The first relates to defamation actions. Before the Defamation Act 1996, the rule which protected members of both Houses from being sued in respect of their speeches in Parliament also in effect prevented them from suing people who cast aspersions on their conduct as members. If the member sued for defamation, the defendant would have been unable to seek to establish the truth of the defamatory statement, as that would have involved questioning or impeaching proceedings in Parliament contrary to Article IX of the Bill of Rights. If the gravamen of the defamatory statement related to things said or done in the performance of a member's duties in the House, this would have made it impossible for the defendant to justify the defamation. A fair trial would have been impossible, and the courts would grant a stay of the action.[91] As a result, an action brought by Neil Hamilton MP against the *Guardian* newspaper over allegations that he had accepted payments from Mohammed Al Fayed in exchange for asking questions in the House of Commons was stayed.[92]

Section 13 of the Defamation Act 1996, introduced to the Bill in response to the staying of the Hamilton libel action, now provides that a person can waive the protection of Article IX of the Bill of Rights (and any legal rule having equivalent effect) so far as the rule prevents his conduct in relation to proceedings in Parliament from being impeached or questioned, where that person's conduct in relation to proceedings in Parliament is in issue in defamation proceedings. This allowed Mr. Hamilton to apply successfully for the stay to be lifted, although he subsequently discontinued his action against the *Guardian*. In 1997 Mr. Al Fayed repeated the allegations against Mr. Hamilton in a televised interview. Subsequently a report on the affair by the Parliamentary Commissioner for Standards, Sir Gordon Downey, to the House of Commons Committee on Standards and Privileges, led to a report from the

---

[90] For examples, see Griffith and Ryle, *Parliament*, 96–8.

[91] *Prebble v. Television New Zealand Ltd.* [1995] 1 AC 321, [1994] 3 All ER 407, PC (where a stay was denied because the main burden of the defamatory allegations related to actions of government Ministers outside Parliament).

[92] *Hamilton v. Guardian Newspapers Ltd.*, 21 July 1995, unreported, May J.

Committee severely criticizing Mr. Hamilton's conduct. The report was approved by the House of Commons. Mr. Al Fayed then applied to dismiss the defamation action as an abuse of the process of the court, or stay it on the ground that parliamentary privilege would make it impossible to try the case fairly. The House of Lords held that a person who has waived the protection of parliamentary privilege for the purposes of a defamation action under section 13 of the 1996 Act could be cross-examined about his own parliamentary conduct without it breaching parliamentary privilege. A fair trial of the action was therefore possible, and was not an abuse of process or a breach of privilege despite the fact that it would involve the plaintiff in challenging the conclusions of a House of Commons Select Committee in a report approved by the House.[93]

Secondly, by virtue of section 3 of the Human Rights Act 1998, Article IX of the Bill of Rights must now be read and given effect by courts in a manner compatible with Convention rights. Those rights should also guide decisions of each House relating to parliamentary privilege: although the Houses do not act unlawfully if they behave in a manner incompatible with a Convention right, the UK may be held in Strasbourg to have violated the right under the ECHR in international law. This should be borne in mind when considering whether either House should permit a person (whether or not a member) to make statements or disclose information under the cloak of parliamentary privilege when that would violate the Convention right of a third party to protection against physical attack or invasion of privacy.

There is statutory protection for those who publish papers printed by order of the Houses or under their authority.[94] This means that House of Commons and House of Lords papers, and their publishers, are immune from criminal and civil proceedings. Reporters who are making a fair and accurate report of proceedings in Parliament, while not covered by parliamentary privilege, have qualified privilege against actions for defamation; this is lost if the publication is actuated by malice.

An important side effect of freedom-of-speech provisions in Parliament is the protection offered to the views of MPs' constituents, expressed through the medium of petitions.[95] These are presented by a member on behalf of the constituent concerned, either publicly on the floor of the House of Commons (immediately before the adjournment is moved, or at the start of business on a Friday) or privately (being placed in the petition bag situated behind the Speaker's chair). If presented publicly, they may be read out. They are published in full in the daily issue of the 'Votes and Proceedings' of the House of Commons. Petitions were very important in the nineteenth century, particularly those leading up to the electoral reform of 1832. Since 1839, there has been no debate on petitions (save in exceptional circumstances when standing orders are suspended), but they may be used to make political points, such

---

[93] *Hamilton v. Al Fayed* [2000] 2 WLR 609, [2000] 2 All ER 224, HL, affirming on different grounds the decision of the CA [1999] 1 WLR 1569, [1999] 3 All ER 317.

[94] Parliamentary Papers Act 1840, reversing the common-law rule in *Stockdale v. Hansard* (1837) 9 A. & E. 1. See, on the history, E. Stockdale, 'The Unnecessary Crisis: The Background to the Parliamentary Papers Act 1840' [1990] *PL* 30–49, and on the modern use of the law, P. M. Leopold, 'The Parliamentary Papers Act 1840 and its Application Today' [1990] *PL* 183–206.

[95] See Griffith and Ryle, *Parliament* 267–8, 383–4.

as the existence of widespread support for, or opposition to, a policy or piece of legislation, and they sometimes elicit observations by the responsible Minister. Although petitions no longer carry the force which they once had—Sir Ivor Jennings wrote that 'under the modern procedure the right of petitioning is of no use whatever'[96]—they retain importance as a way in which constituents can make their representatives aware of their views (the figures on petitions show a dramatic leap in the numbers presented during the middle and late 1980s,[97] when the government had a huge parliamentary majority and were embarking on some very unpopular policies), and as one of the symbols reminding MPs that they represent constituents, not merely parties.

(2) PETITIONING THE MONARCH

The Bill of Rights 1689 proclaimed: 'That it is the right of the subjects to petition the King and commitments and prosecutions for such petitioning are illegal'. This safeguarded the right to bring grievances before the monarch and, by extension, Ministers of the Crown, seeking redress. The preparation of a petition was sometimes used as an occasion for political agitation, and was regarded by the government with grave suspicion at times when they thought that the state was under threat. For example, during the French Revolution and Napoleonic Wars the government took action to prevent meetings to prepare petitions from being used for revolutionary purposes. In 1795, Pitt's government introduced, and Parliament passed, legislation making a meeting of more than fifty people 'for the purpose or on the pretext of considering of or preparing any petition, complaint, remonstrance, or declaration, or other address to the King, or to both houses, or either house of parliament, for alteration of matters established in church or state', into an unlawful assembly unless notice had been given.[98] Through the nineteenth century, after the last Seditious Meetings Act, that of 1817, lapsed, petitions to the Crown were far less important than petitions to Parliament, and they are now of only historical importance.

(3) STATUTORY RIGHTS TO PUBLIC ASSISTANCE IN EXPRESSING VIEWS

Certain Acts impose duties on organizations or people to facilitate free expression in certain circumstances. There is the right of parliamentary candidates to use rooms on school or local authority premises for election meetings free of charge at reasonable times between the date of receipt of the election writ and the day preceding polling day. Similar provisions apply to candidates in local government elections.[99] Any person who acts or incites others to act in a disorderly way at such a meeting, for the purpose of preventing the transaction of the business of the meeting, and fails to give

---

[96] I. Jennings, *Parliament*, 2nd edn. (Cambridge: Cambridge University Press, 1970), 28.

[97] Figures given in Griffith and Ryle, *Parliament*, 268, show a jump from numbers between 20 and 30 per session to 957 in 1984–85, falling to 108 in 1986–87, and rising again to 356 in 1987–88.

[98] Seditious Meetings Act 1795, s. 1.

[99] Representation of the People Act 1983, ss. 95 and 96, as amended by the Representation of the People Act 1985, Sch. 4,

his name and address when asked to do so by a constable at the request of the chairman of the meeting, commits an offence.[100]

Before parliamentary and European Assembly elections, candidates are allowed to send one free postal communication to each elector, or to have one unaddressed communication delivered free to each registered delivery point in the constituency.[101] Such communications must, however, comply with the general law, for example that relating to race relations and incitement to racial hatred, which puts a constraint on the material which can be sent out by extremist political parties.[102]

By convention, the broadcasting bodies allow parties to use the medium for party political broadcasts.[103] The Political Parties, Elections and Referendums Act 2000, section 37 makes it unlawful for a broadcaster to permit a party to make a political broadcast unless the party is registered with the Electoral Commission under that Act. The duty of political impartiality, imposed on independent companies by the Broadcasting Act 1990, is observed by obliging the Independent Television Commission to impose conditions on holders of broadcasting licences requiring the broadcasters to observe rules, to be made by the Commission, governing party political broadcasts. The Governors of the BBC have a similar obligation of impartiality under its Charter, and regard themselves as being under an obligation to include such broadcasts. From 1947, a Committee on Political Broadcasting allocated air time between the parties, but the Committee did not meet after 1983. Thereafter, the main parties in Parliament were allocated five ten-minute broadcasting slots during election campaigns, with other broadcasts at significant points during the year.

Limiting broadcasting opportunities to those parties which had seats in the previous Parliament caused some problems and allegations of unfairness, particularly during election campaigns. In particular, it disadvantaged political parties which had no MPs, including single-issue parties, even if they command a significant amount of support in the country. In the 1997 general election campaign, broadcasters each allowed one broadcast to each of the smaller parties fielding candidates, with additional broadcasts being allocated on the basis of past electoral support for parties fielding at least fifty candidates. In a challenge by the Referendum Party, a new party unable to show past electoral support, it was held that this was neither irrational nor a violation of the broadcasters' duty of impartiality, since impartiality does not necessarily demand equality of treatment.[104] Impartiality must usually be assessed over the whole range of a broadcaster's output rather than within the context of an individual programme,[105] but if the impact of a programme is likely to be considerable (such as a *Panorama* programme devoted to an extended interview with the leader of one party), and there are no plans to broadcast balancing material before the poll, the courts will restrain the broadcast.[106]

---

[100] Representation of the People Act 1983, s. 97.

[101] Ibid.

[102] See generally H. F. Rawlings, *Law and the Electoral Process* (London: Sweet & Maxwell, 1988), 181–9.

[103] A. E. Boyle, 'Political Broadcasting, Fairness and Administrative Law' [1986] *PL* 562–96; E. Barendt and L. Hitchens, *Media Law: Cases and Materials* (Harlow: Longman, 2000), 150–161.

[104] *R. v. British Broadcasting Corporation and another, ex parte Referendum Party* [1997] EMLR 605, DC.

[105] *Scottish National Party v. Scottish Television plc and another*, 1998 SLT 1395, OH.

[106] *Houston v. British Broadcasting Corporation*, 1995 SLT 1305.

Since 1997, the broadcasters have made decisions on the basis of representations directly from the parties. In 1998, the broadcasters proposed that party political broadcasts should cease, because the parties had other good and sufficient channels for making their views known to the public.[107] The parties rejected this suggestion. During the 2001 general election campaign, shorter (five-minute) broadcasts were made available to parties which were fielding candidates but had no representation in Parliament. Section 11 of the Political Parties, Elections and Referendums Act 2000 amends sections 36 and 107 of the Broadcasting Act 1990 to require the Independent Television Commission, when making rules about political broadcasting, to have regard to the views of the Electoral Commission established under the 2000 Act.

In one Scottish case, a Communist candidate challenged the advantage of major parties in access to broadcasting by arguing that the cost of the broadcasts to the broadcasting organizations should be divided up between the candidates who bene-fited from them. If this had been done, it would have resulted in the Conservative candidate in one constituency, the former prime Minister Sir Alec Douglas Home, having exceeded his permitted election expenditure. An election petition alleging that Sir Alec's election was therefore void failed, however, on the ground that expenditure was attributable to a candidate only if it was the intention of the person or body incurring the expenditure to assist the election chances of that candidate.[108] This works both ways: when an organization (such as a trade union) not fielding candidates campaigns against government policy, the cost of the campaign does not count against the permitted total of election expenses of opposition candidates.[109] The Representa-tion of the People Act 1983, section 75 makes it an offence for someone other than a candidate to spend more than £5 on campaigns to advance or prevent the election of a candidate.[109a] In *Bowman v. United Kingdom*,[109b] the European Court of Human Rights held that this effectively prevented an anti-abortion campaigner from producing material to encourage voters to support pro-life, anti-abortion candidates at an elec-tion. It interfered with the campaigner's freedom of expression in a disproportionate way, and violated his right under ECHR Article 10. The Political Parties, Elections and Referendums Act 2000, Part VI, now provides that a person or body may give notice to the Commission established under the Act and become a 'recognized third party' entitled to far more generous spending limits set out in Part II of Schedule 10 to the Act, in exchange for controls over donations to the recognized third party to ensure that the process is safeguarded against improper financial influence.[109c]

This does not deal with the root of the problem, which is the inequality of access to

---

[107] British Broadcasting Corporation, Independent Television Commission, Radio Authority, and S4C Authority, *Consultation Paper on the Reform of Party Political Broadcasting* (London, 1998).

[108] *Grieve v. Douglas-Home*, 1965 SC 315.

[109] *Walker v. UNISON*, 1995 SLT 1226, on Representation of the People Act 1983, s. 75.

[109a] See *DPP v. Luft* [1977] AC 962, HL

[109b] Eur. Ct. HR, Judgment of 19 February 1998, RJD 1998–I, 26 EHRR 1. See R. Ryder, '*Bowman v. United Kingdom*' (1998) 3 J. of Civil Liberties 115–26; H. Davis, '*Bowman v. United Kingdom* Case for the Human Rights Act?' [1998] *PL* 592.

[109c] On the Political Parties, Elections and Referendums Act 2000, see O. Gray, 'What's in a Name? Political Parties, Lists and Candidates in the UK' [2001] *PL* 245–55; K. D. Ewing, 'Transparency, Accountability and Equality: The Political Parties, Elections and Referendums Act 2000' [2001] *PL* 542–70.

the media of information and persuasion. The current arrangements are intrinsically conservative, making life difficult for new parties. The matter is not free from controls under international and domestic law. The European Commission of Human Rights has ruled that, while there is no right to access to the media under Article 10 of the European Convention on Human Rights, the selective barring of one party might amount to a breach of Article 10, either alone or in combination with the anti-discrimination provisions of Article 14.[110] In Scotland, in *Wilson v. IBA*,[111] in the run up to the referendum on Scottish devolution under the Scotland Act 1978, an interim interdict was granted to prevent the independent broadcasters from carrying a series of planned party political broadcasts which would have had the effect of giving three times as much air time to one side of the debate as to the other.

This is particularly easy to establish when the debate revolves round a single issue, with a simple yes–no choice. It is more complicated when there is an election with candidates from many parties standing. Despite a single instance, noted above, in which a court prohibited the broadcast of a current affairs programme (rather than a party political broadcast) before an election,[112] the courts are understandably unwilling to land themselves with the politically delicate task of allocating air time.[113]

(4) EDUCATIONAL INSTITUTIONS

Duties to facilitate free speech (though not other forms of expression) are imposed on the governing bodies maintained by, or substantially dependent on assistance from, the higher education funding councils or the further education funding councils (including colleges of education). First, governing bodies of such further and higher education establishments are required to 'take such steps as are reasonably practicable to secure that any students' union for students at the establishment operates in a fair and democratic manner . . . '[114] The governing body are responsible for ensuring that appointment to major union offices is by secret ballot in which all members are entitled to vote, and must satisfy themselves that the elections are fairly and properly conducted. The arrangements made for these purposes are to be set out in a code of practice.[115] The requirements of democracy imply a duty on the governing body to secure freedom of speech in the course of the elections.

Secondly, such governing bodies are required to take 'such steps as are reasonably practicable to ensure that freedom of speech within the law is secured for members, students and employees of the establishment and for visiting speakers'.[116] This duty was imposed after a number of incidents in the mid-1980s in which visiting speakers at universities and colleges, particularly members of the Conservative government

---

[110] *X. and Association of Z. v. United Kingdom*, App. No. 4515/70, 38 CD 86 (Eur. Comm. HR, 1972).

[111] 1979 SC 351.

[112] *Houston v. British Broadcasting Corporation*, 1995 SLT 1305.

[113] *R. v. Broadcasting Complaints Commission, ex parte Owen* [1985] QB 1153, [1985] 2 All ER 522, DC. See generally Rawlings, *Law and the Electoral Process*, 151–62; Boyle, 'Political Broadcasting' (see n. 103).

[114] Education Act 1994, s. 22(1).

[115] Ibid., s. 22(2)(d) and (e), (3).

[116] Education (No. 2) Act 1986, s. 43(1).

and other visiting speakers or staff with Conservative sympathies, were heckled or threatened and the governing bodies of the institutions had decided to ban the meetings or suspend the staff in order to prevent violence. The duty is expressed to include, in particular, 'the duty to ensure, so far as is reasonably practicable, that the use of any premises of the establishment is not denied to any individual or body of persons on any ground connected with—(a) the beliefs or views of that individual or of any member of that body; or (b) the policy or objectives of that body'.[117] A code of practice is to be issued and kept up to date by the governing body, setting out the procedures to be followed and standards of conduct to be observed in relation to the organization and conduct of meetings,[118] and every person and body concerned in the government of the establishment is under a duty to take such steps as are reasonably practicable to ensure that the code is complied with, including the institution of disciplinary measures where appropiate.[119]

The statute provides for no specific sanction or remedy supporting the duty, so it seems to be enforceable only if a person with a sufficient interest in the matter applies for mandamus. In *R. v. University of Liverpool, ex parte Caesar-Gordon*,[120] the Divisional Court had to consider the way in which governing bodies should balance the interest in freedom of speech against wider public order considerations. The University of Liverpool Conservative Association had applied to the University Guild of Undergraduates for permission to hold a meeting to be addressed by a diplomat representing the apartheid regime in South Africa. The Guild feared an anti-apartheid demonstration on campus, and the local police were worried about the effect which the meeting would have on people in nearby Toxteth, with its large population of black and Asian residents. The Guild initially granted provisional permission for the meeting subject to various conditions, some of which related to the maintenance of order. For example, the meeting was to be by invitation only, and was not to be advertised. After members of the University administration had met members of the Merseyside Police Force, the University Registrar wrote to the chairman of the Conservative Association, Mr. Caesar-Gordon, withdrawing permission to hold the meeting on the ground that it was no longer reasonably practicable to ensure that good order would be maintained. The University's Vice-Chancellor upheld the decision.

The applicant sought judicial review. He accepted that the University could properly take account of the risk of disorder on or affecting its premises, or affecting its property, students, or members elsewhere, but he argued that the University could not lawfully take account of the risk of disorder affecting other people. Furthermore, he claimed that the Guild's conditions (notably those restricting publicity and restricting entry to holders of valid student or staff cards) were *ultra vires* because they restricted freedom of speech contrary to section 43. Watkins LJ, giving the judgment of the Divisional Court, held that the duty to take 'such steps as are reasonably practicable to ensure that freedom of speech within the law is assured' under section 43(1) is a

---

[117] Education (No. 2) Act 1986, s. 43(2).
[118] Ibid., s. 43(3) appropriate.
[119] Ibid., s. 43(4).
[120] [1991] 1 QB 124, [1990] 3 All ER 821, DC.

qualified duty. The University must issue a code of practice to be followed by members of the University in connection with activities on its premises. The duty on the University under section 43 is therefore local to the University and its premises. It was not thought to have been Parliament's intention to impose the intolerable burden on universities of taking into consideration persons and places outside its control.[121] It was therefore *ultra vires* for the university to take account of the risk of disorder elsewhere, and the court granted a declaration to that effect. Matters relating to public disorder elsewhere were the concern of the police, who could consider whether to exercise their powers under the Public Order Act 1986 or at common law to ban or impose conditions on the meeting.

On the other hand, the court upheld the lawfulness of some quite substantial conditions which the University had imposed when it was thought that the meeting would take place. These included banning publicity until the morning of the meeting, requiring that those attending should be able to produce a valid student or staff card, and reserving the right to charge the Conservative Association for the cost of security at the meeting. The court decided that these conditions could reasonably have been considered 'necessary in the interests of free speech and good order in the event of the meeting taking place'. Accordingly they were not *ultra vires* section 43. Educational institutions therefore have considerable leeway in relation to the conditions which they can impose, as long as the conditions (i) are reasonably considered necessary to uphold free speech and good order against attempts at disruption in the event of the meeting taking place, and (ii) relate to the people and premises under the institution's control, rather than a risk of disorder elsewhere which is not the institution's responsibility. The discretion to charge organizers of meetings for the cost of security is a particularly important protection for educational institutions, which often find their budgets inadequate to meet basic educational needs and are understandably reluctant to sink money into policing operations.

(5) INFORMATION ABOUT GOVERNMENT: THE FREEDOM OF INFORMATION ACT 2000

The close link between access to information and the ability to safeguard one's welfare and identity is reflected in the development by the European Court of Human Rights of a right to certain information as an aspect of the right to respect for private and family life and the home under ECHR Article 8 (already noted in Chapters 9 and 12, above). Access to information also contributes to worthwhile freedom of expression, and particularly to the maintenance of a democratically accountable system of government. This is why the freedom to receive and impart information is part of the right to freedom of expression under ECHR Article 10(1), and the right to seek information is part of the equivalent right under ICCPR Article 19(2) (although the European Court of Human Rights has been slow in developing a freedom-of-

---

[121] [1990] 3 All ER at 826.

information jurisprudence under ECHR Article 10).[122] As Sir Anthony Mason has pointed out, the general law has long respected freedom of information by limiting the law of copyright and breach of confidence to allow disclosures of information in response to particular public interests.[123] Under Community law, there is a principle of transparency which requires that any discretion to withhold information relating to the work of Community institutions from the public should be properly considered and exercised, in the light of the principle of proportionality.[123a]

However, until recently English law, unlike that in many other countries, has not included a right of access to government-held information. Instead, the principle has been that no information about or held by government should be released unless the government decides to make it available. A long-running campaign for change, led by the Campaign for Freedom of Information, led to a number of Freedom of Information Bills being introduced to Parliament as private members' bills. They all foundered on the rocks of governmental and civil-service opposition. The Conservative governments of the 1980s and 1990s were beset by allegations that secrecy was being used to cover up impropriety or inefficiency in the public service. The government of Mr. John Major introduced a Code of Practice on Access to Government Information in 1994, but it lacked legal force, was full of loopholes, and had little impact on the availability of information. Only in 1997 did a government, the incoming Labour government, arrive which was committed to legislating on the subject.[124] A White Paper[125] was published in December 1997, basing proposals on the following premise:

'Unnecessary secrecy in government leads to arrogance in governance and defective decision-making. The perception of excessive secrecy has become a corrosive influence in the decline of public confidence in government. Moreover, the climate of public opinion has changed: people expect much greater openness and accountability from government than they used to.'[126]

The proposals in the White Paper represented a significant liberalization in the control of governmental information.[127] Unfortunately, the proposals became the subject of a wrangle within the government. The Minister originally responsible for the liberal proposals, Dr. David Clark (the Chancellor of the Duchy of Lancaster), became

---

[122] See Sir Stephen Sedley, 'Information as a Human Right', in Beatson and Cripps (eds.), *Freedom of Expression and Freedom of Information*, 239–48.

[123] Sir Anthony Mason, 'The Relationship between Freedom of Expression and Freedom of Information', in Beatson and Cripps (eds.), *Freedom of Expression and Freedom of Information*, ch. 13 at 235–6.

[123a] See, e.g. Case T-194/94, *Carvel and Guardian Newspapers Ltd. v. Council* [1995] ECR II–2765, CFI; Case T-105/95, *WWF UK v. Commission* [1997] ECR II–313, CFI.

[124] On the history of the subject, and the genesis and likely effect of the Freedom of Information Act 2000, see P. Birkinshaw and A. Parkin, 'Freedom of Information', in R. Blackburn and R. Plant (eds.), *Constitutional Reform: The Labour Government's Constitutional Reform Agenda* (London: Longman, 1999), 173–201; R. Austin, 'Freedom of Information: The Constitutional Impact', in J. Jowell and D. Oliver (eds.), *The Changing Constitution*, 4th edn. (Oxford: Oxford University Press, 2000), 319–71.

[125] Chancellor of the Duchy of Lancaster, *Your Right to Know: The Government's Proposals for a Freedom of Information Act*, Cm. 3818 (London: TSO, 1997).

[126] Ibid., para. 1.1.

[127] For an assessment, see S. Palmer, 'Freedom of Information—Principles and Problems: A Comparative Analysis of the Australian and Proposed UK Systems', in University of Cambridge Centre for Public Law (ed.), *Constitutional Reform in the UK: Practice and Principles* (Oxford: Hart Publishing, 1998), 147–58.

the first Minister to be dismissed in a reshuffle, and responsibility for freedom of information legislation passed to the Home Office, where the Home Secretary (Mr. Jack Straw) appeared to be far less willing (or to be dominated by officials who were far less willing) to strip away the special protection for government information which had protected central government against rigorous scrutiny.

In these circumstances, it is not surprising that there was a further delay in introducing the Freedom of Information Bill, or that the Bill as finally introduced in November 1999 disappointed many people because of the scope of the exemptions from duties of disclosure and the relative ease with which conditions for withholding information from the public could be met. Some of these losses were clawed back during the passage of the Bill, and the Act which emerged at least established the principles that openness is to be the general rule, restrictions on access to information need to be justified according to justiciable standards, and enforcement procedures are to be provided. The main features of the Act are as follows.

(i) The general duty of public authorities

The Act imposes a duty on public authorities to respond to requests for information. A person who, in writing, requests specified information from a public authority is entitled to be informed in writing whether the public authority holds the information ('the duty to confirm or deny'), and, if it does, to have the information communicated to him within twenty working days (unless a fee is due and has not been paid).[128] Despite the title of the Act, public authorities have no duty to be proactive in releasing information unless they are under a legal obligation to do so at common law or under another statute. The person requesting the information may be required to pay a fee set by regulations made by the Secretary of State, and if the estimated cost of complying with a request exceeds an 'appropriate limit' (also set by regulations made by the Secretary of State) the public authority may either refuse the request or charge a higher fee for complying, based on the cost of compliance, according to a formula set out in the regulations.[129] Public authorities subject to the duties under the Act are the bodies listed in Schedule 1 to the Act, including all governmental bodies and various regulatory bodies such as the General Medical Council, together with 'publicly-owned companies' (i.e. government-owned companies).[130] Some of the listed public authorities are subject to the duties under the Act only in respect of certain information. For example, a person providing personal medical or dental services on the National Health Service is a public authority for this purpose only in respect of information relating to the provision of those services, not (for instance) information relating to treatment provided for private patients.[131]

(ii) Exemptions

The main doubts about the efficacy of the arrangements under the Act stem from the exemptions in the legislation. Apart from the right to require payment of a fee, already

---

[128] Freedom of Information Act 2000, ss. 1(1), 8, 10.

[129] Ibid., ss. 9, 12, 13.

[130] Ibid., ss. 3(1), 6. The Secretary of State may amend the list in Sch. 1: s. 4.

[131] Ibid., s. 7 and Sch. 1, Pt. III, para. 45.

mentioned, and the right under section 14 to refuse to comply with a request which is vexatious or which is the same as one that has already been dealt with, a range of types of information is exempted by Part II of the Act. These include:

- information which is accessible to the applicant by other means, or is intended for publication at some (known or unknown) future date (sections 21 and 22);

- information supplied directly or indirectly by, or relating to, security, intelligence and criminal intelligence services and the tribunals dealing with complaints about them, together with other information conclusively certified by a Minister as requiring exemption in order to safeguard national security (sections 23, 24, and 25);

- information disclosure of which would, or would be likely to, prejudice defence, or the capability, effectiveness or security of relevant armed forces (section 26);

- information disclosure of which would, or would be likely to, prejudice relations with another state, international organization, or court, or the UK's interests abroad (section 27) or relations with administrations in other parts of the UK (section 28);

- information disclosure of which would, or would be likely to, prejudice the economic interests of the UK or the financial interests of any administration in the UK;

- information relating to an investigation by a public authority which might lead to criminal proceedings (section 30);

- information which would be likely to prejudice the prevention or detection of crime, the administration of justice, immigration controls, etc. (section 31), or court records (section 32);

- information disclosure of which would be likely to prejudice the audit functions of public authorities discharging such functions (section 33);

- information which must be exempted in order to avoid an infringement of the privileges of Parliament (section 34);

- information held by a government department or the National Assembly for Wales relating to the formulation of government policy, ministerial communications, advice by the Law Officers, or the operation of a ministerial private office (section 35), or which would be likely to prejudice the maintenance of collective ministerial responsibility, the work of the executive committee of the Northern Ireland Assembly, or the work of the National Assembly for Wales; or which would be likely to inhibit the provision of advice or exchange of views for the purposes of deliberation, or (widest of all) 'would otherwise prejudice, or would be likely otherwise to prejudice, the effective conduct of public affairs' (section 36);

- information relating to communications with members of the Royal Family or relating to the conferring by the Crown of any honour or dignity (section 37);

- information which, if disclosed, would be likely to endanger anyone's physical or mental health, or endanger an individual's safety (section 38);

- environmental information which the authority holding it is obliged to make available to the public, or has a statutory exemption from being made available (section 39);
- information covered by the Data Protection Act 1998, together with certain other personal information (section 40);
- information provided to the authority in confidence, disclosure of which would be an actionable breach of confidence (section 41);
- information subject to legal professional privilege (section 42);
- trade secrets, or information disclosure of which would be likely to prejudice any person's commercial interests (section 43);[131a]
- information disclosure of which is prohibited under any enactment, would be incompatible with a European Community obligation, or would constitute a contempt of court (section 44).

This means that the general entitlement set out in section 1 of the Act is heavily qualified by public and governmental interests of which the government is itself sometimes to be the judge, as well as being subordinated to private interests in respect of commerce, confidentiality, and personal data. Much public information continues to be available, if at all, only at the discretion of the authorities concerned.

(iii) Enforcement and regulation

The Lord Chancellor is required by section 45 to issue a Code of Practice guiding public authorities on desirable practices and procedures under the Act. Under section 47, the Information Commissioner (who is also responsible for data protection) has the task of promoting good practice by public authorities, informing and advising the public, and assessing an authority's practices (with its consent). The Commissioner is also the arbiter of most claims by public authorities to exemptions. If a public authority decides that the information sought is covered by an exemption, or that for any other reason there is no duty of disclosure, it must generally provide a written statement to that effect, it would have the effect of revealing the information in question.[132] The person who made the requests can then complain to the Commissioner, who has power under section 51 to require the authority to provide information so that the Commissioner can decide whether the claim to exemption is justified. If the Commissioner decides that the authority has failed to comply with its duties under the Act, she can issue a decision or enforcement notice requiring the authority to take appropriate action under section 52. The authority usually has to comply, on pain of court proceedings under section 53. However, a government department, the National Assembly for Wales, or another authority designated by a Secretary of State, can evade compliance by way of a certificate, issued by a Secretary of State under section 53, stating that the Secretary of State has formed the view on reasonable grounds that there has been no failure to comply with the duty in question. In addition, either the

131a See M. McDonagh, 'FOI and Confidentiality of Commercial Information' [2001] PL 256–67.
132 Ibid., s. 17.

public authority or the applicant may appeal under Part V of the Act to the Tribunal
established under the Act against a notice served by the Commissioner, or against a
Secretary of State's national security certificate. In a case not involving a certificate,
either party can appeal to the High Court on a point of law against a decision of the
Tribunal.

(iv) Assessment

The Act may turn out to work well in relation to public authorities outside central
government. However, the range of exemptions, the low threshold for justifying a
refusal to comply with requests (usually prejudice or likely prejudice, rather than
serious prejudice or the 'substantial harm' test advocated by the 1997 White Paper),
and the powers of Secretaries of State, make it unlikely that the Act will produce a
significantly beneficial effect on central government. This is a disappointment. The
Act marks a retreat from the commitment to openness and accountability in government which marked the Labour Party's manifesto for the 1997 general election campaign and the White Paper published in December 1997. In due course, obligations
imposed on the UK by the EU may force an extension of the duties of openness on
central government, but that day is some time off. In the meantime, there is remarkable unanimity among commentators on the Act's shortcomings. Rodney Austin's
assessment, trenchantly expressed, is typical:

'The extraordinary list of exemptions, many of them subject to no test at all, others only to a
simple prejudice test, matches and potentially exceeds the existing list of exemptions under
the Code of Practice on government Information, which the White Paper criticized as
containing excessively wide exemptions. This is no accident. The Act's purpose in broadening the range of exemptions and weakening or removing altogether the White Paper's
substantial harm test, is to remove as much material as possible from the scope of the
enforceable right of access and place it within the scope of the discretionary access provisions, under which the Minister has the final say and cannot be overruled by the Information Commissioner. This is no longer a Freedom of Information Act but a regime for open
government only by consent of government Ministers.'[133]

Its value may be enhanced slightly, in areas where the information impacts on Convention rights, by the need to read and give effect to its provisions interpreted so far as
possible in a manner compatible with Convention rights by virtue of section 3 of the
Human Rights Act 1998. But the real gain in relation to central government accountability, beyond symbolism, is likely to be very small. All one can say in favour of the
Act is that it represents a small and extremely tentative first step towards making real
openness in government the norm. As Dr. Stephanie Palmer wrote of the Bill in 2000
before its enactment, 'Freedom of information is a democratic imperative and this Bill
may be just another step on the long road toward establishing a genuinely open
government'.[134]

[133] Austin, 'Freedom of Information: The Constitutional Impact', at 371.
[134] Palmer, 'Freedom of Information: The New Proposals' at 266.

13.4 LIMITATIONS AND CONDITIONS ON FREEDOM OF EXPRESSION

A number of provisions are designed to give effect to the responsibilities which, as the international instruments note, freedom of expression carries with it. The law of defamation protects people's reputation against untrue or unfair attacks. It mainly affects the press, broadcasters, and publishers, and is considered in Chapter 14, below. Other rules which seek to prevent the irresponsible exercise of free speech include rules to protect people against unfair pressure to adopt or change opinions, or to prevent people from using a privileged position to peddle their ideas from a more advantageous position than is available to competitors. This involves a restriction on the free exchange of ideas, and a derogation from the general principle in favour of free expression derived from John Stuart Mill. However, it has often been thought to be permissible in order to prevent people who have positions which give them special authority from abusing their position by seeking to impose their opinions on others who are vulnerable to suggestion. The resulting limitations on freedom of expression represent a form of paternalism, achieved by imposing obligations (particularly on educators) to present balanced accounts of controversial matters to those under their charge.

(1) RESTRICTING FREEDOM OF EXPRESSION IN EDUCATION

The best example of this type of restriction was originally introduced by the Education (No. 2) Act 1986, and is now contained in the Education Act 1996. It attempts to regulate the discussion and teaching of political opinions in schools. Section 406(1)(b) of the 1996 Act requires local education authorities (LEAs), governing bodies, and head teachers of maintained schools to forbid the promotion of partisan political views in the teaching of any subject in the school. The obligation could be enforced against any recalcitrant LEA, governing body, or head teacher, by mandamus in an application for judicial review. Presumably the effect on a teacher who ignores such a prohibition would be that he would be liable to disciplinary proceedings by the LEA. One worrying feature of the provision is its poor drafting. The phrase 'partisan political views' is of uncertain width. It may be limited to expressions of views concerning matters of party politics, whereby a teacher (or other contributor to class discussion, including a pupil, as the Act applies to the whole process of teaching, not merely to that part of lessons in which the teacher is speaking) expresses a preference for the opinions or policies of one recognized political party. However, if the section is so limited it is very badly expressed. A more natural reading of the phrase would interpret it as covering any partisan view (that is, an expression of a preference for one view rather than another, where opinions are divided) on any political issue (that is, an issue concerning the organization, constitution, or government of the state).

'Promotion' seems most appropriately to apply to taking steps which actively encourage others to adopt the same views, rather than giving an account of one's own position when asked to do so. If that is correct, this provision does not excessively limit a teacher's freedom of expression within the class. It seems that a teacher who is asked for his political view on a particular matter could properly answer the question, as this would arguably not amount to promoting the views but only to expressing them. Indeed, it would often be counterproductive to prevent a teacher from explaining the political views which underlie his account of a topic, as the explanation of a teacher's viewpoint can help students to evaluate it. This is particularly likely to be the case in lessons covering the humanities, civics, or social studies. Naturally, the provision does not prevent teachers from pursuing party politics outside teaching time.

Nevertheless, when explaining his political position the teacher may be required by the LEA, governing body, or head teacher, to make sure that students also understand that there are other possible views, and what those are. This requirement may arise because section 407 of the Act requires LEAs, governing bodies, and head teachers, to 'take such steps as are reasonably practicable' to ensure that pupils are offered a balanced presentation of opposing views where political issues are brought to their attention at school or while taking part in extra-curricular activities provided or organized for registered pupils by or on behalf of the school. This means that standing instructions or codes of practice, with possible disciplinary consequences, may demand balance in class, as well as in the school's policy in relation to visiting speakers or visits to outside meetings and discussion groups. At the same time, because the legislation leaves a reasonable amount of discretion in the hands of LEAs, governors, and head teachers as to the manner in which they carry out their obliga-tions, the potentially draconian effects of the Act may turn out to be limited. If problems arose, and a complaint were made to the LEA, the governors would find it difficult to know how to deal with it, as the guide issued to school governors by what is now the Department of Education and Skills makes no mention of the governors' responsibilities under these provisions.[135]

The silence on this subject may suggest that the problem is less common than one might have supposed from the fact that the government felt that legislation was required. There have so far been no reports of the legislation causing any problems to teachers, and it is more than likely that the vast majority of teachers of all political persuasions have always behaved, and continue to behave, according to the standards of professionalism and integrity of which the legislation is merely a par-tial codification. The only problems appear to have been caused by the government itself. In 1991, the government produced what it called a *Parent's Charter*, which has subsequently been updated, explaining the changes which the government had introduced and intended to introduce to schools, and outlining the rights and obligations of educators and parents in respect of children's education. Mr. Kenneth Clarke, then Secretary of State for Education, encouraged head teachers to distribute copies of this document to parents. A number of authorities, including Richmond upon Thames London Borough (controlled by the Liberal Democrat Party), instructed head teachers not to distribute copies, on the ground that there was a

---

[135] Department for Education and Employment, *A Guide to the Law for School Governors* (London: DfEE, January 2001 issue).

serious risk that the *Charter* was 'promoting partisan political views', in that it set out the Conservative Party policy on education, which was, in certain respects, a matter of contention between political parties. If this were so, it would have been unlawful for the material to be distributed at school without (at the very least) distributing further material at the same time which balanced it by putting the competing views of other parties, under what is now section 407 of the 1996 Act. Nevertheless, many authorities had already distributed the material, a sign of the way in which provisions such as these are effective only if someone has a special awareness of them and a particular interest (political or otherwise) in implementing them.

Essentially, the motivation behind the legislation seems to have been to prevent the use of schools for partisan political purposes of which the government disapproved, but not for partisan purposes of which they approved. The legislation, in practice, fails to guarantee the neutrality between visions of the good which is a part of the liberal thinking on which, as noted in Chapter 1 above, civil liberties are based. It is regrettable, but not surprising, that the incoming Labour government has, since 1997, failed to repeal these provisions.

A further example of double standards is that the requirements of the 1996 Act apply only to maintained schools (including community and foundation special schools), and not to independent schools. The ostensible reason for this was that it was part of the efforts of central government to prevent public money, collected from people of a variety of political persuasions, being used to promote narrow, factional, political standpoints. The fact that the legislation imposes no obligation on the governors and head teachers of independent schools suggests that the government was less concerned to restrict the indoctrination of pupils with the conservative beliefs which predominate in the independent sector of education than to control the socialist views which were thought to dominate certain parts of the teaching profession in the maintained sector. On the other hand, the exclusion of independent schools from the Act may flow from respect for the property rights of owners of independent schools, and for the right of those parents who can afford to do so to buy an education for their children which accords with the parents' political, religious, or other conscientiously held, opinions, rather than from overt political bias on the part of the government.

Whatever the shortcomings of the legislation may be as it applies to teachers, their lot under the Act is better than that of junior pupils. Section 406(1)(a) of the Education Act 1996 requires LEAs, governing bodies, and head teachers of maintained schools to forbid registered junior pupils (i.e. those under the age of twelve) at the schools to pursue partisan political activities. Despite some slight ambiguity, there can be little serious doubt that the words of the subsection, 'the pursuit of partisan political activities by any of those registered pupils at a maintained school who are junior pupils', were intended to cover pursuit of such activities anywhere by registered pupils *of* the school, rather than merely while they are on school premises. This impression is borne out by comparison with the similar wording in paragraph (b) of section 406(1), which is clearly intended to cover extra-curricular activities whether conducted on school premises or elsewhere.[136] Any attempt to enforce such a

---

[136] In 1991, the Central Office of Information, *School Governors: The School Curriculum—Briefing Booklet 1*, 6–7, appeared to interpret this provision as imposing an obligation on governors to ensure that junior

prohibition, or to punish a pupil for breaching it, would constitute an extraordinary restriction on pupils' political liberty and freedom of expression. This is particularly serious in view of the potentially wide meaning of 'partisan political activities', similar to that of 'partisan political views' mentioned above in relation to section 406(1)(b). It would clearly breach the rights to freedom of thought and expression under Articles 9 and 10 of the European Convention on Human Rights.

Lest it should be thought that these rights are available only to adults, and not to junior pupils, it must be borne in mind that in the United Nations Convention on the Rights of the Child (1989)—which the UK ratified in 1991—Article 13(1) guarantees to children the right of freedom of expression, and Article 13(2) permits such restrictions to be imposed on the right 'as are provided by law and are necessary: (a) for respect of the rights or reputations of others; or (b) for the protection of national security or of public order (*ordre public*), or of public health or morals'. The restriction represented by section 406(1)(a) of the 1986 Act could not by any stretch of the imagination fall within, or be a reasonably proportionate means of achieving, such a justifiable objective. The provision is regularly breached by head teachers and governors who fail to take action against the young children of politicians who accompany or are photographed with their parents for campaigning purposes. It should be repealed. If it is thought necessary to prevent children from being exploited for political purposes, for the sake of their moral welfare, this should be done by a far more restricted provision which takes account of the age and understanding of the child, and the circumstances surrounding the activity.

A less objectionable constraint on teachers' freedom of expression is contained in section 403(1) of the Education Act 1996, which requires local education authorities, governing bodies, and head teachers of maintained schools 'to secure that where sex education is given to any registered pupils at a maintained school, it is given in such a manner as to encourage those pupils to have due regard to moral considerations and the value of family life'. Necessary and proportionate restrictions on freedom of expression to protect morals are authorized by ECHR Article 10(2), and the European Court of Human Rights has accepted, in its caselaw under ECHR Article 14, that states are entitled to seek to advance family life over other social arrangements as long as their mode of doing so does not interfere disproportionately with the rights and freedoms of people affected.[137] As parents are entitled by section 405 to exempt their children from receiving sex education at school, except so far as it is comprised in the National Curriculum, and pupils are free to seek sex education outside school, the interference is unlikely to be regarded as disproportionate, although it may present difficulties for some teachers. A related difficulty is presented, in schools controlled by local education authorities, by the prohibition on promoting homosexuality in maintained schools, considered below.

pupils 'are not involved in partisan political activity either on the school premises *or organized elsewhere by any member of staff acting in his or her capacity as such*' (italics added). This would be a sensible way of interpreting the section, but, it is submitted, is not open on the plain words of the statute. If it reflects the effect which the Department intended that the section should produce, the section was badly drafted.

[137] See Ch. 3, above.

(2) FREEDOM OF EXPRESSION AND CENTRAL GOVERNMENT CIVIL SERVANTS

Apart from the Official Secrets Act 1989 and the equitable doctrine of confidentiality, which are outlined in Chapter 15, sections 1 and 2, below, the rights of civil servants to participate in political activity and to express themselves publicly are not constrained by law. Instead, they are regulated by well-understood conventions, attitudes, and rules, given expression in what used to be called Estacode, became the Civil Service Pay and Conditions of Service Code, and is now the Civil Service Management Code.[138] Breach of these rules is a disciplinary offence for civil servants. In relation to their political activities, the Code follows the recommendations in a 1978 report.[139] Certain political activities by some types of civil servants are subject to restriction. For the purposes of these rules, civil servants are divided into three groups.[140]

First, there are politically free civil servants. These are people who are not part of the machinery of policy making and advising government: civil servants who are not of office grade and industrial civil servants. They are permitted to undertake any form of political activity at national or local level. Secondly, most clerical and executive officers below the rank of principal equivalent do not do politically sensitive work in advising Ministers or forming policies, or speaking on behalf of government or meeting the public. They are permitted to take part in any political activity at the local or national level, short of becoming a candidate for Parliament or the European Assembly. Candidacy for those bodies is likely to involve overt political partisanship which could compromise the appearance of political neutrality of a civil servant's department, so the candidate must resign from the Civil Service before standing.

Thirdly, there are higher grade civil servants and trainees, who are liable to be involved in advising Ministers, those who speak for the government to the public and outside bodies, and those lower grade clerical and executive officers who deal with the public day to day in tax and social security offices. These are in a 'politically restricted' category. This means that they are not permitted to be candidates for Parliament or the European Assembly; to hold national office in political parties; to speak publicly on matters of national political controversy; to express views on such matters in letters to the press, books, articles, or leaflets; or to canvass on behalf of candidates in national or European Assembly elections, or for political parties. At the same time, those in the politically restricted category who are not speaking for the government in public or facing members of the public as part of their normal work may be permitted to undertake local political activity: candidature for, or co-option to, local authorities; holding local office in political parties; speaking publicly on matters of local political controversy; expressing views on local matters in the press, etc.; and canvassing on

---

[138] The Code was promulgated in April 1996 under the Civil Service Order in Council 1995.

[139] *Report of the Committee on the Political Activities of Civil Servants*, Cmnd. 7057 (London: HMSO, 1978).

[140] For a full account and discussion, see G. S. Morris, 'Political Activities of Public Servants and Freedom of Expression', in Loveland (ed.), *Importing the First Amendment*, 99–122. Employees of the two Houses of Parliament are subject to an equivalent regime under their contracts of employment.

behalf of candidates for election to local authorities, or for local political organizations.

The freedom of those in the second and third categories is dependent on approval from the civil servant's department; permission is unlikely to be granted to people who are working closely with a Minister in a private office or policy division, or on matters which are acutely politically sensitive or affected by national security considerations. Even if permission to take part in political activities is granted, civil servants are expected to avoid embarrassing Ministers or departments, and to express themselves with moderation, and in theory (although this is virtually impossible to achieve in practice) they are to avoid committing themselves so strongly to one party 'as to inhibit or appear to inhibit loyal and effective service to Ministers of another party'.[141]

These restrictions are probably justifiable in terms of ECHR Article 10. The European Court of Human Rights has accepted in a number of cases that states are sometimes entitled to restrict the political activity of civil servants, or to exclude people from the civil service by reason of their political activity and commitments. Restrictions may legitimately protect the right of people in a country to an effective political democracy, one of the goals to which the ECHR is directed. A functioning democracy may involve maintaining a politically neutral civil service.[142] Depoliticizing the public service is particularly important where there is a historically well-founded fear that public servants will either favour or discriminate against people of particular political persuasions,[143] but may be generally desirable in order to secure fair and impartial support and advice for people participating in democratic government, whatever their views.[144] Where a state is engaged in an ideological contest with other states, as was the case in Germany during the Cold War, or with forces within the state, as in post-Communist Hungary, excluding adherents to the opposing ideology from the public service also serves the interest in national security and public safety.[145] These considerations may justify restricting both freedom of expression under ECHR Article 10 and freedom to join political organizations under ECHR Article 11, as long as any restriction goes no further than necessary to achieve the objective and does not deprive the person of the essence of the right. The UK's restrictions on public servants appear to be proportionate, because they are carefully graduated according to the political and social sensitivity of people's roles within the public service. There is no equivalent of Germany's dismissal of a schoolteacher who wished to participate actively in politics on behalf of the German Communist Party, which was held to be disproportionate in *Vogt v. Germany*,[146] or of the blanket prohibition on Canadian public servants, whatever their role, engaging in work for or against

---

[141] *Civil Service Management Code*, para. 4.4.13. The rules as a whole are contained in section 4.4 of the Code.

[142] *Vogt v. Germany*, Eur. Ct. HR, Series A, No. 323, Judgment of 26 September 1995, 21 EHRR 205.

[143] *Rekvényi v. Hungary*, Eur. Ct. HR, App. No. 25390/94, Judgment of 20 May 1999.

[144] *Ahmed and others v. United Kingdom*, Eur. Ct. HR, App. No. 22954/93, Judgment of 2 September 1998.

[145] See; e.g. *Glasenapp v. Germany*, Eur. Ct. HR, Series A, No. 104, Judgment of 28 August 1986, 9 EHRR 25; *Rekvényi v. Hungary*, Eur. Ct. HR, App. No. 25390/94, Judgment of 20 May 1999, at paras. 39, 41.

[146] Eur. Ct. HR, Series A, No. 323, Judgment of 26 September 1995, 21 EHRR 205.

a candidate or political party, which the Supreme Court of Canada held to be over-inclusive and an unjustifiable interference with freedom of expression under the Canadian Charter of Rights and Freedoms.[147]

There are further restrictions, not directly concerned with freedom of expression but rather with the related right to freedom of association, in respect of public-service employees in jobs which are concerned with national security. Apart from the restrictions on party political activity noted above, the government announced in January 1984 that it had given an order which unilaterally altered the conditions of service of employees at the Government Communications Headquarters (GCHQ) in Cheltenham, restricting freedom of association by banning member-ship of trade unions. This was a move to prevent the work of GCHQ being disrupted by industrial action. It was challenged in an application for judicial review of the order. Glidewell J held that the government had breached the unions' legitimate expectation that they would be consulted before any changes to the conditions of service were introduced. This decision was reversed by the Court of Appeal. The House of Lords held that the unions had a legitimate expectation of consultation, and that it had been breached, but decided that the national-security implications justified the breach, and upheld the ban.[148] Although it is arguable that the House gave excessive weight to an affidavit filed by Sir Robert Armstrong, the Cabinet Secretary, claiming that consultation would itself have threatened national security, the European Commission of Human Rights subsequently decided that the order was justifiable under the national-security exception to Article 11 of the Convention.[149] Shortly after the 1997 general election, the new Labour government announced on 15 May 1997 that employees at GCHQ were to be given the right to join independent trade unions, and on 10 June 1997 the Foreign Secretary, Mr. Robin Cooke, was able to tell the House of Commons that management and unions were shortly to start negotiations to provide safeguards against disruption.[150]

Apart from party political and trade union activity, there are restrictions on the freedom of civil servants to give information about their work to the press or to Members of Parliament. The Freedom of Information Act 2000 does little to break down a deeply rooted elitism of those in government, and an obsessive secrecy, which, as Peter Hennessy has written, is 'built into the calcium of a British policy-maker's bones', a carry-over into government of the essential privateness of English life.[151] Apart from the coaching manual on *Talking about the Office*,[152] which is really about how to *avoid* saying anything significant about the office at social gatherings, there are

---

[147] *Osborne v. Canada (Treasury Board)* [1991] 2 SCR 69, SC Canada.

[148] *Council of Civil Service Unions v. Minister for the Civil Service* [1985] AC 374, [1984] 3 All ER 935, HL.

[149] *Council of Civil Service Unions v. United Kingdom*, 20 DR 228 (1987); 10 EHRR 269. See further K. D. Ewing and C. A. Gearty, *Freedom under Thatcher* (Oxford: Clarendon Press, 1990), 130–6.

[150] House of Commons, *Official Report*, 10 June 1997, vol. 313, col. 929.

[151] Hennessy, *Whitehall*, 346–7. For a study of this ethos, see D. Vincent, *The Culture of Secrecy: Britain 1832–1998* (Oxford: Oxford University Press, 1998).

[152] Classified as 'restricted', this cannot be consulted by the public. It is cited in Hennessy, *Whitehall*, 357–8.

detailed rules restricting information which can be given to Parliamentary Select Committees, in answer to Parliamentary questions, or to individual MPs.[153] The restrictions on talking to Select Committees, contained in the 'Osmotherly rules',[154] include an injunction to every official against appearing before any Select Committee without the Minister's approval, unless the Committee issues a formal order for his attendance. When before the Committee, the official must comply with ministerial instructions as to how to answer questions. While being as helpful as possible to the Committee, the official must refuse to divulge information where necessary in the interests of good government and national security, which is said to encompass advice to Ministers, questions concerning politically controversial matters, communications between departments on policy matters, communications between Ministers, and anything which might tend to show the level in the department at which any decision was taken.

This is inconsistent with the purpose of the Select Committees, which were designed in 1979 to make government more accountable to Parliament for its activities. Members of Parliament cannot hope to hold government effectively to account unless they can find out what it is doing. The people best able to give that information are civil servants, and the Osmotherly memorandum, in keeping with the ethos of the civil service, denies to Parliament some of the best evidence concerning the running of government. It also makes it possible for Ministers to mislead the House of Commons, or to deny it the information which is its life blood, with relative impunity, subject only to the risk of the truth being leaked by a rogue civil servant.

In these circumstances, leaks can have a useful 'whistle-blowing' function, putting a stop to abuse of power. They have, on occasion, caught out Ministers. When Mr. Michael Heseltine MP, then Secretary of State for Defence, refused in May 1983 to supply information to Mr. Tam Dalyell MP about the sinking of the Argentinian cruiser *General Belgrano* during the Falklands campaign, Mr. Clive Ponting, then a civil servant in the Ministry of Defence, disclosed the information secretly. He was discovered, and prosecuted unsuccessfully under the Official Secrets Act 1911, section 2 (since repealed). He argued at his trial that the disclosure was in the interest of the state, providing him with a defence under section 2, because he had disclosed the material in pursuit of a duty which the civil service owes to Parliament. This claim was rejected by the trial judge, McCowan J, who held that the civil servant's duty was to the Minister, that the interests of the state were what the government of the day said they were, and that it was not open to a civil servant, a court, or a jury to override the government's view.[155] However, the jury, influenced perhaps by the clever campaign waged by Mr. Ponting and his advisers in and outside the court, and the lack of

---

[153] J. Michael, *The Politics of Secrecy* (Harmondsworth: Penguin, 1982); G. Marshall, 'Ministers, Civil Servants, and Open Government', in C. Harlow (ed.), *Public Law and Politics* (London: Sweet & Maxwell, 1986), 80–90.

[154] *Memorandum of Guidance for Officials Appearing before Select Committees* of 16 May 1980, General Notice GEN80/38, drafted by an assistant secretary in the Civil Service Department, Mr. E. B. C. Osmotherly, and known by his name: Hennessy, *Whitehall*, 361–3.

[155] *R. v. Ponting* [1985] Crim. LR 318.

sensitivity to public opinion which the government had displayed, acquitted despite the judge's ruling.[156]

This did not make the civil service or the government believe in the value of freedom of information. The official reaction, predictably, was to reassert the absolute importance of secrecy. First, a tough statement of the civil servant's responsibilities was promulgated by Sir Robert Armstrong, the Cabinet Secretary.[157] He stressed that the responsibility of the civil service was exclusively to the government of the day, not to the public or Parliament. This went beyond the prevailing orthodoxy, according to which civil servants were servants of the Crown and nation, and not of politicians.[158] Armstrong went on to remind civil servants that the Minister, not the civil service, is responsible to Parliament for the conduct of the department's affairs, and that they have a duty of lifelong obligation to keep the confidences to which they become privy in the course of their duties. Secondly, when the Official Secrets Act 1989 was drafted, the duty of lifelong confidence of Crown servants in respect of matters relating to security and intelligence, defence, international relations, crime, and special investigation powers, was backed up by criminal sanctions in sections 1 to 4. Thirdly, provisions based on the Armstrong memorandum and the 1989 Act were included in the Civil Service Pay and Conditions Code when the Code was revised in the light of the 1989 Act, and now have a place in the Civil Service Management Code.

This closes the door to unauthorized leaks which reveal improper behaviour in government or the civil or security services, although it is still open to Ministers to leak without much fear of prosecution. It leaves the civil servant with problems, however. What is he to do if asked by a Minister or superior officer to do something which he believes to be unlawful? Armstrong exhorted the civil servant to take the matter to the permanent head of the department. What if the civil servant faces a fundamental issue of conscience? Such crises are to be discussed with a superior officer, or the permanent head of the department (who, presumably, can be relied on to advise against revealing anything publicly). There is a right to appeal to the head of the Home Civil Service,[159] although a head who follows the Armstrong line is unlikely to sympathize with a civil servant who finds it hard to square secrecy with his conscience. More usefully, perhaps, many whistle-blowing employees, including most employees of the Crown and contractors,[160] now have a measure of legal protection against dismissal or victimization by their employer if they make 'protected disclosures'. This protection arises under Part IVA of the Employment Rights Act 1996, inserted into the Act by the Public Interest Disclosure Act 1998, originating in a

---

[156] P. Birkinshaw, *Freedom of Information: The Law, the Practice and the Ideal* (London: Weidenfeld & Nicolson, 1988), 81; C. Ponting, '*R. v. Ponting*' (1987) 14 *J. of Law and Soc.* 366–72; R. M. Thomas, 'The British Official Secrets Acts 1911–1939 and the Ponting Case' [1986] Crim. LR 491–510.

[157] *The Duties and Responsibilities of Civil Servants in Relation to Ministers*, set out in a Written Answer of 26 February 1985, 74 HC Debs., cols. 128–30.

[158] Hennessy, *Whitehall*, 346.

[159] Bailey, Harris, and Jones, *Civil Liberties Cases and Materials*, 429; according to the authors, the appeal procedure has not yet been used.

[160] Employment Rights Act 1996, s. 43K. Police officers, members of the security and intelligence services, and members of the armed forces are not covered: ibid., ss. 191–3.

private member's Bill introduced to the House of Commons by Richard Shepherd MP and steered through the House of Lords by Lord Borrie.[161] A protected disclosure is a 'qualifying disclosure' made by a worker in specified circumstances.[162] A qualifying disclosure is one which, in the reasonable belief of the worker making it, tends to show:

- that a criminal offence has been, is being or is likely to be committed;
- that someone has failed, is failing or is likely to fail to comply with a legal obligation;
- that a miscarriage of justice has occurred, is occurring or is likely to occur;
- that the health and safety of an individual has been, is being or is likely to be endangered;
- that the environment has been, is being or is likely to be damaged; or
- that information tending to reveal one of the above events has been, is being or is likely to be deliberately concealed.[163]

People making such disclosures are protected if they make them:

- in good faith to their employers or to someone else who has legal responsibility;[164]
- in the course of obtaining legal advice;[165]
- in the case of someone employed by an individual or body appointed by a Minister of the Crown, in good faith to a Minister;[166]
- in good faith to a person prescribed by an order made by the Secretary of State for these purposes, in the reasonable belief that the relevant failure falls within the order and that the information and any allegations are substantially true;[167]
- to any other person, in good faith and not for personal gain, reasonably believing that the information and any allegations are substantially true, in circumstances which make it reasonable to make the disclosure, and the worker reasonably believes that he will be subjected to a detriment by the employer if the disclosure is made to him, or that the disclosure to a prescribed person under an order made by the Secretary of State will lead to the concealment or destruction of evidence, or that the worker has already made a disclosure to the employer or prescribed person. In such a case, the reasonableness of making the disclosure falls to be assessed with particular reference to the identity of the person to

---

[161] See Y. Cripps, 'The Public Interest Disclosure Act 1997', in J. Beatson and Y. Cripps (eds.), *Freedom of Expression and Freedom of Information: Essays in Honour of Sir David Williams* (Oxford: Oxford University Press, 2000), 275–87.
[162] Employment Rights Act 1998, s. 43A.
[163] Ibid., s. 43B(1).
[164] Ibid., s. 43C.
[165] Ibid., s. 43D.
[166] Ibid., s. 43E.
[167] Ibid., s. 43F.

whom the disclosure is made, the seriousness of the alleged failure, whether it is continuing or likely to occur in the future, and whether the disclosure breaches an obligation of confidentiality.[168]

A disclosure may also be made to anyone if it relates to a failure of an exceptionally serious nature, the worker makes it in good faith and not for personal gain, reasonably believing that the information and allegations are true, and in all the circumstances of the case it is reasonable for him to make that disclosure, having regard particularly to the identity of the person to whom the disclosure is made.[169]

If the disclosure is protected, several consequences follow. First, any contractual obligation of confidentiality between the worker and his employer is void in so far as it purports to prevent the disclosure.[170] Secondly, a worker has the right not to be subjected to any detriment by the employer on the ground that he made the disclosure[171] (although it does not protect the worker against being victimized or ostracized by other potential employers). Thirdly, dismissing the employee on account of the disclosure is actionable as an unfair dismissal.[172]

(3) POLITICAL ACTIVITY BY LOCAL GOVERNMENT EMPLOYEES

Whereas in central government, the code of behaviour for civil servants limits their political activities in well-understood ways on a semi-consensual basis, the political freedom of local-government employees has been a more contentious matter in recent years. In 1989 the Conservative government, concerned about political activities undertaken by Mr. Derek Hatton, a Labour councillor in Liverpool while on the payroll of another council, introduced legislation to curb what they saw as an abuse. The Local Government and Housing Act 1989 identified certain politically sensitive posts, and effectively excluded their holders from representative political activity.[173] The Act created a category of 'politically restricted posts'. Politically restricted posts fall broadly into three categories. First, there are the chief officers, such as the chief executive and those in charge of specific areas of the authority's work, their deputies, the monitoring officer,[174] and people appointed to assist elected members of particular political groups with their work as members. Such posts involve advising elected members on policy, and are not thought to be suitable to be held by anyone who has committed political affiliations.[175] Next, there are two groups of posts which the local authority is required to specify. First, there are jobs with salaries above a sum fixed by the Secretary of State. These people are, presumably, particularly influential, and it is

---

[168] Ibid., s. 43G.

[169] Ibid., s. 43H.

[170] Ibid., s. 43J.

[171] Ibid., s. 47B.

[172] Ibid., s. 103A.

[173] See Morris, 'Political Activities of Public Servants' at 104–10; G. Morris, 'Public Employment and the Human Rights Act 1998' [2001] PL 442–9.

[174] This is a person who must be appointed under s. 5 to monitor the legality of the activities of the council, its committees, sub-committees, officers, etc.

[175] Local Government and Housing Act 1989, s. 2(1).

thought to be important to avoid political bias. Secondly, there are people who, on a regular basis, advise the authority or its committees, sub-committees, and joint committees, or speak on behalf of the authority to journalists and broadcasters (the information or press officers).[176] The advisory and public-representation roles, respectively, of people in these posts are thought to require an appearance of political neutrality. Teachers, who are employed by education authorities but do not regularly advise or represent the authorities, are excluded from the category of politically restricted posts.[177]

Holders of these posts are disqualified from becoming elected members of local authorities or of the House of Commons.[178] Furthermore, the terms and conditions of their employment are deemed to contain provisions laid down centrally by the Secretary of State for the Environment by regulation.[179] The regulations make it a breach of a person's contract of employment to stand as a candidate for election to the European Parliament, the UK Parliament, the devolved assemblies, or any local authority; to act as an agent, or canvass, for a candidate; or to hold office or be a committee member in a political party or branch. People holding politically restricted posts are not permitted to address the public or a section of the public with the 'apparent intention of affecting public support for a political party', or to allow their written or artistic work or work edited by them to be published if it 'appears to be intended to affect public support for a political party'.[180] As Professor Gillian Morris points out:

'the scope of restriction is potentially very extensive, particularly as only "apparent" rather than actual intention need be shown. It is notable that, despite ministerial assurances during the legislation's parliamentary passage that it would not inhibit trade union activity, no provision was made to this effect (in contrast to the Civil Service Management Code, which specifically exempts this).'[181]

These restrictions understandably precipitated an outcry from local-government officers who saw them as a serious infringement of their democratic rights. NALGO, the local-government officers' union, produced a circular, *Will YOU be banned in 1990?*, describing the legislation as 'among the most draconian attempts to remove the civil and political rights of council officers'. A person who is affected may apply for exemption from political restriction to an official appointed by the Secretary of State under section 3 of the 1989 Act, but this is hardly a satisfactory protection for the right to participate in the government of one's country or locality. Even if exemption is granted, the Act limited the amount of paid leave which a person could have from an authority in order to act as an elected member (other than chairman) of another. The professional standards of most local government officers are sufficiently well developed to know how far they can go without compromising their positions as

---

[176] Local Government and Housing Act 1989, s. 2(1), (2), (3).
[177] Ibid., s. 2(10).
[178] Local Government and Housing Act 1989, s. 1(1), (2).
[179] Ibid., s. 1(5).
[180] Local Government Officers (Political Restrictions) Regulations 1990, SI 1889, No. 851, as amended.
[181] Morris, 'Political Activities of Public Servants' at 106 (footnotes omitted).

advisers. The legislation looks like a sledgehammer taken to crack a nut of relatively limited significance. None the less, an application for judicial review failed,[182] and a challenge to the legislation in Strasbourg on the ground that it violated ECHR Articles 10 and 11 was unsuccessful. In *Ahmed and others v. United Kingdom*[183] the European Court of Human Rights held, by a six–three majority which reversed the decision of the Commission, that the restrictions could be seen as proportionate to a real need to of bolster the political neutrality of the public service which was critical to the performance of its functions. According to the government, only about two per cent of the 2.3 million local government officers were in restricted posts. The dissenting judges, Messrs. Spielmann, Pekkanen, and van Dijk, preferred the view of the Canadian Supreme Court in *Osborne v. Canada (Treasury Board)*[184] that the desirability of political neutrality in public servants could not justify denying them all opportunity to participate in the democratic politics of the state.

In principle, there is a real risk that the effect of the legislation is to take away the whole essence of the rights to freedom of political expression and political association from the 46,000 or so people in restricted posts, making the rights illusory for them. Particularly worrying is the fact that the legislation operated to change the contract of employment retrospectively for those employees who were already in post at the time it came into effect. The majority of the Court in *Ahmed* may have been overly influenced by the notion of the margin of appreciation allowed to states to assess proportionality in the light of local conditions. If a case of this kind were to be litigated in the UK under the Human Rights Act 1998, national courts might be able to adopt a more rigorous approach to assessing proportionality than the majority of the Strasbourg Court in *Ahmed*. It is far from clear that the legislation has been drafted with as much careful attention to the actual needs of democratic government at local level as appears to have been given to equivalent restrictions on central-government civil servants. The restrictions on local-government employees seem to interfere with their rights more than is absolutely necessary for the legitimate purpose of securing an impartial service to the democratic process. At any rate, regulations which went further would almost certainly violate ECHR Articles 10 and 11 and so would be invalid by virtue of section 6 of the Human Rights Act 1998. As it stands, the power to control people's political activity in this way is a dangerous one to leave in the hands of central government, exercisable by statutory instrument with only limited opportunities for parliamentary oversight. It is regrettable that the Labour government, despite indicating that they would review the necessity for the restrictions introduced by their Conservative predecessors, have so far taken no action.

---

[182] *R. v. Secretary of State for the Environment, ex parte NALGO and others* (1993) 5 Admin. LR 785, DC and CA.

[183] Eur. Ct. HR, App. No. 22954/93, Judgment of 2 September 1998. See G. S. Morris, 'The Political Activities of Local Government Workers and the European Convention on Human Rights' [1999] *PL* 211–9.

[184] [1991] 2 SCR 69, SC Canada.

111

(4) PUBLICITY BY LOCAL AUTHORITIES

Other examples of taking a sledgehammer to crack a nut are the attempt to stop local authorities from using ratepayers' money to promote political objectives (in the Local Government Act 1986), or promoting homosexuality or teaching which presents its acceptability as a 'pretended family relationship' (in the Local Government Act 1988, section 28, inserting section 2A into the Local Government Act 1986). This legislation was introduced by and passed under the auspices of the Conservative government led by Mrs. Thatcher, and it would be hard to acquit the government of attempting to suppress the expression of views opposed to their own on political and moral matters.[185] The Labour government's attempts to repeal section 2A have so far been thwarted by opposition in the House of Lords.

(5) PUBLICITY BY CENTRAL GOVERNMENT

It has been said that there is a prerogative power, of which central government can take advantage, to publish information to citizens. This was used to justify the campaign in favour of membership of the European Communities in the period leading up to the referendum on accession.[186] In view of the reluctance of government to permit access to information in this country, noted in section (2) above,[187] one would expect this to be a little used power. However, a great deal of publicity is produced on behalf of the government, and its promulgation has recently become politically contentious. Few would object to public information campaigns designed to encourage people to take up their entitlements to state benefits, or to educate us about HIV and AIDS. However, there is a grey area where it becomes hard to distinguish between the public information purpose and the party political purpose behind publications such as the *Citizen's Charter*.

There is no legal regulation of the nature and content of government publicity. There is a degree of self-regulation, under the Central government Convention on Publicity and Advertising.[188] These conventions are not intended to be legally binding. It is possible that a decision to publish might be struck down in judicial review proceedings. There is authority for saying that government publicity can be reviewed by the courts if the advice which it contains is illegal, or if it is published in bad faith or for an improper purpose (particularly if it breaches the conventions which set out

---

[185] For thorough analysis of the law relating to local government publicity, see C. Willmore, *Letting People Know: Local Government Publicity and the Law*, 2nd edn. (London: Association of Metropolitan Authorities, 1988). Early experience of the 1986 Act suggested that it was having little impact, because most local authorities assumed that, as the legislation had been aimed at 'loony left' councils, it did not affect them, while those councils which might have been worried about it generally either found ways round it or decided to carry on as before and wait to see whether they would be challenged (few were). H. F. Rawlings and C. J. Willmore, 'Propaganda on the Rates? Local Authority Publicity and the Local Government Act 1986', paper presented to the Third Bristol Colloquium on Law and Politics, May 1988.

[186] *Jenkins v. Attorney-General, The Times*, 13 August 1971.

[187] See also N. S. Marsh, 'Public Access to Government-Held Information in the UK: Attempts at Reform', in N. S. Marsh (ed.), *Public Access to Government-Held Information* (London: Stevens, 1987), 248–91.

[188] C. R. Munro, 'Government Advertising and Publicity' [1990] *PL* 1–9.

the extent of the proper purposes).[189] Nevertheless, this is somewhat speculative, as no application for review of government publicity has so far been successful. In any case, the constraints on central government are far less severe than those which central government has seen fit to impose on local government by statute. Presumably this is because central government (or the party in power) is more likely to approve of its own publicity than of local government publicity which may be pushing a message inconsistent with that which central government wishes the public to believe.

13.5 CONCLUSION

Freedom of expression, as a general principle, is well established in English law, particularly since it was enshrined in national law by the Human Rights Act 1998. However, in order to understand its true scope, and to protect against the gradual restriction of the freedom which can easily result when what appear to be good prudential or utilitarian reasons are offered for limiting the freedoms of a few people in particular situations, we need to look at the areas in which the main battles over freedom of expression are now fought. The main problems in English law concern the position of the media, and certain systematic restrictions which the law places on the exercise of free expression. The multiplicity of ends which are served by maintaining free expression raise questions about the type and extent of restraints which are justifiable. These matters form the subject of the next five chapters.

[189] *R. v. Secretary of State for Social Security, ex parte Greenwich LBC, The Times,* 17 May 1989, DC, discussed by Munro, 'Government Advertising and Publicity', 1–9.

14

MEDIA FREEDOM

This chapter examines the role of, and forms of control over, the media of mass communication, in the context of legal treatment of the freedom to receive and impart information and ideas. Starting with an outline of the background to the subject, the chapter goes on to consider controls over ownership of the media and the content of communications, and the extent of protection for freedom of expression by the media in English law, including the limiting effect of the law of defamation. Section 4 is devoted to certain special legal protections given to journalists in English law, and a conclusion is offered in section 5.

14.1 BACKGROUND

(1) RELATIONSHIP TO FREEDOM OF EXPRESSION

There is an obvious connection between press freedom and freedom of speech. Like speech, the press is a medium for broadcasting information and opinion. It is therefore important on a number of grounds.[1] First, as a tool of self-expression it is a significant instrument of personal autonomy. Secondly, as a channel of communication it helps to allow the political discourse which is necessary in any country which aspires to democracy. As Lord Steyn has said:

'Freedom of speech is the lifeblood of democracy. The free flow of information and ideas informs political debate. It is a safety valve: people are more ready to accept decisions that go against them if they can, in principle, seek to influence them. It acts as a brake on the abuse of power by public officials. It facilitates the exposure of errors in the governance and administration of justice of the country . . .'[2]

This is why the First Amendment to the Constitution of the USA protects press freedom, although in the USA the law is currently being used in ways which threaten the ability of journalists to gather information about the powerful.[3] Thirdly, it helps to

---

[1] See J. Lichtenberg, 'Foundations and Limits of Freedom of the Press', in J. Lichtenberg (ed.), *Democracy and the Mass Media* (Cambridge: Cambridge University Press, 1990), 102–35.

[2] *R. v. Secretary of State for the Home Department, ex parte Simms* [2000] 2 AC 115 at 126.

[3] D. A. Schulz, 'Newsgathering as Protected Activity', in J. Beatson and Y. Cripps (eds.), *Freedom of Expression and Freedom of Information: Essays in Honour of Sir David Williams* (Oxford: Oxford University Press,

provide one of the essential conditions for scholarship, making possible the exchange and evaluation of theories, explanations, and discoveries. Fourthly, it helps to promulgate a society's cultural values, and, where they are in flux, facilitates the debate about them, advancing the development and survival of civilization. Fifthly, free media can contribute to the implementation of both consumer choice and public policy by providing channels for communicating commercial information and governmental advice or information. For all these reasons, the rights to communicate and to receive information and ideas are guaranteed by Article 10 of the European Convention on Human Rights (ECHR), which now forms part of English law by virtue of the Human Rights Act 1998, and by Article 19 of the International Covenant on Civil and Political Rights (ICCPR).

As noted in Chapter 13, ECHR Article 10 permits the state to regulate the broadcast media by way of a licensing regime; but the boundaries between media and the ability to control transmissions are both collapsing. As a government White Paper put it in December 2000:

'Many people brought up in a world in which there were only a few broadcasting channels feel bewildered by the explosion of choice. The boundaries of industries are blurring: telecommunications companies want to become broadcasters, while broadcasters increasingly are moving into e-commerce, and Internet Service Providers are offering television channels.'[4]

This makes it impossible for any country to control the media of communication. The growth of communication across frontiers by satellite, telephone lines, and the internet has necessitated an international approach to regulation, and 'a framework for these increasingly convergent industries that combines different ingredients'.[5]

To some extent, an individual state can control what is sent and received within its borders. Broadcasters and internet service providers (ISPs) based within the jurisdiction can be licensed and regulated, and signals from elsewhere can be monitored and jammed. This occurred in the UK when pornographic material broadcast via satellite by a broadcaster, Red Hot Television, based in the Netherlands was blocked. But such unilateral regulation is often ineffective, particularly in regulating material sent via the internet. It is also associated with economic inefficiencies. For the provider, having to comply with different rules in each state increases the complexity and cost of the operation. For the receiver, choice is likely to be reduced, as providers may maximize the reach of their broadcasts by making all programmes comply with the most restrictive rules in any of their target states. Allowing the most restrictive state to dictate what is received in other states endangers freedom of expression, and also threatens the European single market in the communication and entertainment industries.

2000), 139–160; C. R. Sunstein, 'Free Speech Now', in G. R. Stone, R. A. Epstein, and C. R. Sunstein (eds.), *The Bill of Rights in the Modern State* (Chicago: University of Chicago Press, 1992), 255–316.

[4] Department of Trade and Industry and Department of Culture, Media and Sport, *A New Future for Telecommunications*, Cm. 5010 (London: The Stationery Office, 2000), 9, para. 1.1.20.

[5] Ibid., 11, para. 1.3.1.

There are therefore powerful reasons for having international agreements governing the regulation of the media of communication.[6] In Europe, there are three main
sources of international or supranational law on this subject. First, ECHR Article 10
provides a minimum standard of freedom of expression which media regulation must
respect. Secondly, the Council of Europe's Member States concluded the European
Convention on Transfrontier Television in 1989. It entered into force in 1993, and has
now been ratified by just over half the Member States of the Council of Europe. The
Convention's object is 'to facilitate, among the Parties, the transfrontier transmission
and retransmission of television programme services' (Article 1).[7] Article 4 requires
states to guarantee freedom of reception and not to restrict the retransmission
of programmes which meet the standards set out. Each state is to ensure that
programmes broadcast within its jurisdiction meet the standards (Article 5). There
is thus a regime of mutual recognition of states' judgments as to a programme's
compliance with the standards.

The standards in the Transfrontier Television Convention are partly designed to
uphold human dignity and fundamental rights. Article 7 requires broadcasters to
ensure that programmes are not indecent. They must not contain pornography,
give undue prominence to violence, or be likely to incite to racial hatred. Programmes otherwise likely to impair the physical, mental, or moral development of
children or adolescents must not be scheduled for reception at times when such
people are likely to watch them (a task made more difficult by differences between
time zones and the advent of the programmable video recorder). Broadcasters are
to ensure that news programmes present facts and events fairly and encourage the
free formation of opinions. As a particular aspect of fairness, Article 8 requires
states from which programmes are transmitted to ensure that everyone has the
opportunity 'to exercise a right of reply or seek other comparable legal or administrative remedies' relating to programmes, and to ensure that the right can be
effectively exercised. Other provisions aim to uphold a minimal level of programme
quality by (*inter alia*) limiting the proportion of time devoted to advertising and
ensuring that it is fair and honest, and not misleading, subliminal, surreptitious, or
harmful to children (Articles 11 to 16). Article 9 exhorts states to prevent a broadcaster obtaining exclusive rights to cover a public event of high public interest
(including sporting events of high national importance) and thereby effectively
depriving a large part of the public in one state or more of the opportunity to
follow it on television. In the UK, this responsibility is discharged by the ITC,
which is entitled to seek to ensure that broadcasters do not acquire exclusive rights
to cover events of importance to other countries (such as World Cup soccer
matches in which the Danish national team is competing) if a large part of the
potential Danish audience would thereby be deprived of the opportunity to watch
them.[8] Finally, Article 10 aims to promote European programme making and

---

[6] E. Barendt, *Broadcasting Law: A Comparative Study* (Oxford: Clarendon Press, 1993), 213–22.

[7] For discussion, see Barendt, *Broadcasting Law*, 222–9.

[8] *R. v. Independent Television Commission, ex parte TV Danmark 1 Ltd.* [2001] UKHL 42, [2001] WLR
1604, HL.

protect European cultures against foreign (particularly American) domination. It requires states to ensure, 'where practicable and by appropriate means, that broadcasters reserve for European works a majority proportion of their transmission time, excluding the time appointed to news, sports events, games, advertising and teletext services'. States are to seek to support European production, and to endeavour co-operatively to avoid endangering the pluralism of the press and the development of the cinema industries.

The third source of international and supranational law is the European Community. While the Transfrontier Television Convention was being negotiated, the European Community was drafting a Directive to govern broadcasting between Member States ('the Television Directive'). This was made in 1989, and was amended in 1997.[9] As amended, Article 2 gives jurisdiction to Member States to license and regulate broadcasters established within that state, or using a frequency granted by, a satellite capacity appertaining to, or a satellite up-link situated in that state. Decisions of the Member State with jurisdiction are to be recognized by other Member States. Article 2a prevents a Member State from restricting retransmissions on its territory of transmissions from other Member States unless the broadcaster concerned has 'manifestly, seriously and gravely' infringed the substantive standards laid down in the Directive on at least two earlier occasions in the preceding twelve months, and consultations with the transmitting Member State and the Commission have failed to produce an amicable settlement within fifteen days.

The substantive standards are similar to those contained in the Transfrontier Television Convention. Article 22 requires Member States to take appropriate measures to ensure that programmes are not such as 'might seriously impair the physical, mental or moral development of minors', and particularly must not involve pornography or gratuitous violence, and that programmes which might impair the physical, mental, or moral development of minors to a lesser degree or in other ways are broadcast in a way or at a time that ensures that minors 'will not normally hear or see such broadcasts'. Article 22a provides that Member States are to 'ensure that broadcasts do not contain any incitement to hatred on grounds of race, sex, religion or nationality'. Article 23 of the Directive provides that anyone whose 'legitimate interests, in particular reputation and good name, have been damaged by an assertion of incorrect facts in a television programme must have a right of reply or equivalent remedies'. Member States are to ensure that the right is not hindered by unreasonable terms or conditions, and that the reply is transmitted within a reasonable time and 'in a manner appropriate to the broadcast to which the request refers'. These requirements highlight the difference of ethos between Europe and the USA on free-speech matters. In the USA, an attempt to compel a newspaper to provide a right of reply was held to

---

[9] Council Directive 89/552/EEC of 3 October 1989 on the co-ordination of certain provisions laid down by law, regulation, or administrative action in Member States concerning the pursuit of television broadcasting activities [1989] OJ L298/23; Directive 97/36/EC of the European Parliament and of the Council of 30 June 1997 [1997] OJ L202/60. For discussion, see P. Keller, 'The New Television Without Frontiers Directive' (1997/ 8) 3 *Yearbook of Media and Entertainment Law* 177–95; D. Goldberg, T. Prosser, and S. Verhulst, *EC Media Law and Policy* (London: Longman, 1998), 56–75. E. Barendt and L. Hitchens, *Media Law: Cases and Materials* (Harlow: Longman, 2000), ch. 5.

violate the First Amendment's guarantee of press freedom,[10] and legislation against hate-speech has been held to be impermissibly content-based.[11] While the constitutionality of sanctions for broadcasting indecent language in mid-afternoon was upheld on the ground of the special scarcity of broadcasting spectra and their unique accessibility to children,[12] legislation to outlaw the transmission of indecent material via the internet was more recently held to be unconstitutionally content-based,[13] and the Supreme Court has held that the Federal Communications Commission may not require broadcasters to segregate programming which 'depicts sexual . . . activities or organs in a patently offensive manner' into a special channel, and then to block viewer access until particular viewers request access. Although the object was to protect children against exposure to inappropriate programmes, the mechanism for doing it imposed excessive burdens on viewers wanting to exercise First Amendment rights, and was not sufficiently narrowly tailored to achieving its legitimate objective.[13a]

Article 4 of the Directive, like Article 10 of the Transfrontier Television Convention, seeks to protect the European programme and cinema production industries and European cultures by requiring broadcasters to reserve a majority proportion of transmission time (excluding news, sports events, games, advertising, teletext services, and teleshopping) for European works, and ten per cent of transmission time for works by independent European producers. This provision is controversial, because of doubts about its practical effectiveness, its legality under the EC Treaty, and its compatibility with ECHR Article 10 and international free-trade law.[14] It is interesting, however, to note that the constitutional right to freedom of speech and of the press under the First Amendment to the Constitution of the USA, often interpreted as permitting almost no interference with the programming freedom of broadcasters, has been held to allow Congress to require cable operators to use some channels for carrying local commercial and public service television channels. The requirement was held to be constitutional as long as the legislation did not specify the content of the programmes, and could be shown to further a substantial state interest in maintaining pluralism of information sources, an aim compatible with First Amendment objectives.[15]

[10] *Miami Herald Publishing Co. v. Tornillo* 418 US 241 (1974), US SC.

[11] *R. A. V. v. City of St Paul, Minnesota* 120 L. Ed. 2d 305 (1992), US SC. On the issues involved, see D. Goldberg, 'Protecting Wider Purposes: Hate Speech, Communication, and the International Community', in R. Cohen-Almagor (ed.), *Liberal Democracy and the Limits of Tolerance* (Ann Arbor, Mich.: University of Michigan Press, 2000), 251–74.

[12] *FCC v. Pacifica Foundation* 438 US 726 (1978), US SC.

[13] *Reno (Attorney-General of the United States) v. American Civil Liberties Union* 521 US 844 (1997), US SC. See D. W. Vick, 'The Internet and the First Amendment' (1998) 61 *MLR* 414–21; M. Blakeney and F. Macmillan, 'Freedom of Speech in Cyberia' (1999) 4 *Yearbook of Copyright and Media Law* 78–103.

[13a] *Denver Area Educational Telecommunications Consortium, Inc. v. Federal Communications Commission* 116 S. Ct. 2374, 135 L. Ed. 2d 888 (1996), SC of US.

[14] For discussion, see B. de Witte, 'The European Content Requirement in the EC Television Directive—Five Years After' (1995) 1 *Yearbook of Media and Entertainment Law* 101–27.

[15] *Turner Broadcasting System, Inc. v. FCC* 114 S. Ct. 2445 (1994); *Turner Broadcasting System, Inc. v. FCC (No. 2)* 117 S. Ct. 1174 (1997); E. Barendt, 'The First Amendment and the Media', in I. Loveland (ed.), *Importing the First Amendment: Freedom of Speech and Expression in Britain, Europe and the USA* (Oxford: Hart Publishing, 1998), 29–50 at 36 ff.

From all these sources, certain general principles emerge as centrally important to media freedom. First, ready access to sources of information and ideas is important, and the media of communication are essential for that. Secondly, pluralism is important. The European Court of Human Rights has held that it violates ECHR Article 10 for a state to licence a single, state-controlled monopoly broadcaster in its jurisdiction.[16] To some extent, this varies between jurisdictions, depending on the social and economic circumstances in a country. In small or poor societies where the market could not support more than one supplier of services, an exclusive licence for one operator to provide telecommunications may be necessary in order to secure people's ability to have access to communications.[16a] However, in Europe this is not the position. Monopoly licensing both disproportionately interferes with other broadcasters' access to the market, and deprives people of multiple sources of information and ideas. The government's White Paper in 2000 commits the government to maintaining public service broadcasting free at point of use, funded by licence-fees and advertising revenues, alongside the growing number of subscription or pay-per-view channels, to ensure that viewers are not excluded from democratically and culturally important media and to counter-balance fears of a growing concentration of media ownership.[17] Thirdly, it is important that at least some parts of the media should be independent of the state, and that state interference, particularly with regard to the content of communications, should be subject to legal controls on principles conformable to human rights.

These principles and provisions form the main elements of the framework of international and supranational law within which rights with regard to the media operate in England and Wales. Apart from the ECHR, they relate to broadcasting, particularly television. Our account of media freedoms in England and Wales starts on the lower level of technology at which freedom of the press was first established.

(2) HISTORY: PRESS LICENSING

The press has developed a special meaning and a particular significance over and above that attaching to freedom of speech. The invention of the printing press, and more particularly its introduction to England by William Caxton in 1477, vastly increased the capacity of books and pamphlets—especially political ones—to reach people of all sorts. This made it a powerful medium for instruction, but also for opposition to the established order. The Roman Catholic Church had quickly responded to the use of the printing-press on mainland Europe by printing its own books and banning others which were deemed to be incompatible with orthodox

---

[16] *Informationsverein Lentia v. Austria*, Eur. Ct. HR, Series A, No. 276, Judgment of 24 November 1993, 17 EHRR 93; E. Barendt, 'Freedom of Speech in an Era of Mass Communication', in P. B. H. Birks (ed.), *Pressing Problems in the Law Vol. 1: Criminal Justice and Human Rights* (Oxford: Oxford University Press, 1995), 109–116; Craufurd Smith, *Broadcasting Law and Fundamental Rights* 138–9, 174–83.

[16a] *Cp. Cable and Wireless (Dominica) Ltd. v. Marpin Telecoms and Broadcasting Co. Ltd.* [2001] 1 WLR 1123, PC.

[17] Department of Trade and Industry and Department of Culture, Media and Sport, *A New Future for Communications*, 48–51, paras. 5.3.1–5.3.12.

teaching. In England, the government did the same. Printing presses were too power-ful to be unregulated. The regulation took two forms (in addition to the criminal law of sedition which might apply to speech as well as printed matter): presses had to be licensed in order to be used legally, and publications had to be licensed, with the payment of a tax on each. Unlicensed presses or publications might be seized, and the printers and publishers were liable to severe penalties.[18]

This continued into the eighteenth century, when the government accidentally allowed the Licensing Acts to lapse. This caused considerable embarrassment in the litigation surrounding issue 45 of *The North Briton*: the Secretary of State had issued warrants under legislation which turned out to be no longer in force, making the subsequent seizure of persons and property by the King's Messengers unlawful.[19] Governments continued to be rightly wary of the power of mass communication, however. A small but important part of the work of writers and printers was political. The capacity of publishers to scrutinize the workings of government and Parliament, to criticize them, and to suggest alternative policies, could significantly affect the standing of a government. This might lead to public disorder or even, it might be feared, revolution. As the electorate became increasingly large and literate during the nineteenth century, the press might sway voters and influence the results of elections. For good or ill, the press was a powerful instrument for achieving popular political consciousness and operating electoral democracy.

(3) REACTIONS TO THREATS TO PRESS FREEDOM

Reactions to governments' overuse of powers to control the press varied. There was civil disobedience in countries, like England, where constitutional means of protect-ing press freedom were out of reach. Where upheavals led to new constitutional orders, these would often include special protection for press freedom, as in the First Amendment to the Constitution of the USA in 1789–91, or section 2 of Canada's Constitution Act 1982, declaring it to be one of the fundamental freedoms of every-one. Such provisions may make it necessary for courts to hold a law to be unconsti-tutional if, for example, it stifles freedom to criticize the government, by imposing criminal penalties on people who make or publish false statements likely to under-mine public confidence in the conduct of public affairs.[20]

In England in recent years, there has been a gradual development of constitutional protection for press or media freedom under the influence of the European Conven-tion on Human Rights and, now, the Human Rights Act 1998. The courts and Parlia-ment have slowly come to recognize that there is a special public interest in press freedom, and legislative steps have been taken to protect it. How successful these have been will have to be assessed in due course. But the importance of mass communica-tion can be used to support an argument for regulation of the industry, as well as

---

[18] S. J. Lewis, 'An Instrument of the New Constitution: the Origins of the General Warrant' (1986) 7 *J. of Legal Hist.* 256–72.

[19] S. J. Lewis, 'The Relationship between Bureaucracy and Law: The Fall and Rise of the General Warrant', unpublished LL.M. dissertation, University of Bristol, 1984.

[20] See *Hector v. A.-G. of Antigua and Barbuda* [1990] 2 AC 312, [1990] 2 All ER 103, PC.

arguments for freedom from interference. For example, it is important to prevent the channels of communication from being dominated by a narrow range of ideas. Balance is important, and this inevitably entails some external interference with the editorial freedom of publishers. Much press law is concerned with the attempt to permit enough intervention (and the right kind of intervention) to maintain freedom of communication, without permitting so much that it stifles that which is to be protected.

14.2 REGULATION OF THE MEDIA[21]

The right of the printed media to be free of direct government controls was won in the eighteenth century in Britain. When new methods of communication were invented in the twentieth century—radio, television, satellite, and cable broadcasting—the balance between regulating the industry to protect quality and independence and threatening that independence by over-regulating it became particularly important, and was among the factors which led to regulation of the electronic media in ways no longer contemplated for the printed media.[22] At the same time, concern has built up about the lack of responsibility on the part of some journalists, editors, and newspaper proprietors, and this might eventually lead to increased regulation of newspapers in the future.

(1) NEWSPAPERS: OWNERSHIP AND CONTROL

Although the printed word has long been substantially protected against governmental control, even in the field of newspaper ownership some regulation is needed to prevent a small group of people gaining a stranglehold over the communications industry, and using their proprietorial muscle to influence editorial policy. Left to themselves, market forces might put a few newspaper proprietors in a position to censor the flow of information (or disinformation) to the public, and deny any outlet to some legitimate political and social opinions. To assist freedom of the press and the free flow of information and ideas, state action is needed to avoid oligopolistic control over the press by commercial magnates who are, by virtue of their interests, unlikely to be sympathetic to left-of-centre political and social ideas.

Because the newspaper industry, unlike broadcasting, is no longer licensed in the UK, the controls over concentration of ownership are no more (and no less) strong than those which apply in relation to other industries. The Director-General of Fair Trading and the Competition Commission have a role in preventing anti-competitive

---

[21] See generally G. Robertson and A. Nicol, *Media Law: The Rights of Journalists and Broadcasters*, 3rd edn. (London: Penguin, 1992), chs 13 and 15; T. Gibbons, *Regulating the Media*, 2nd edn. (London: Sweet & Maxwell, 1998).

[22] See generally R. Craufurd Smith, *Broadcasting Law and Fundamental Rights* (Oxford: Clarendon Press, 1997), ch. 1.

concentrations of power under sections 58 and 59 of the Fair Trading Act 1973,[23] as does the European Commission under Community law. The public interest in the freedom of the press is a consideration which weighs with them, and it is an area of competition law which is highly contentious. However, the field is only incidentally related to civil liberties law, and this volume will not deal with it in any detail.

In principle, subject to the restraint of competition law, all are free to set up in business as publishers so long as they do not contravene any law. Printing presses need no longer be officially licensed. Generally speaking, therefore, the ability to publish printed material depends only on ability to pay for materials, distribution, and so on. Publishing is, in theory, regulated by market pressures rather than by government. In practice, in this as in other spheres, the operation of a publishing market in the UK has tended to lead to an oligopoly. The costs of establishing a publishing business are very high; newcomers need to be well capitalized in order to have a chance of success. Nowhere is this more true than in relation to mass circulation newpapers, which are controlled by a few powerful publishers. Of recent attempts by outsiders to break into the daily newspaper market, only the *Independent* has succeeded in establishing itself.

Proprietors of newspapers tend to exercise editorial control on political grounds. Two consequences follow from this. First, while the right to publish is in theory available to all, it is restricted by access to capital. As in relation to other rights, inequalities of resources make the freedom to publish a liberty of unequal worth. To some minor degree, the effects of this are contained by granting public money to registered political parties participating in elections and referendums, to support their campaigns. Under the Political Parties, Elections and Referendums Act 2000, the amounts of money involved can be substantial, but they offer relatively little help to parties between elections, or to campaigners who are not affiliated to a registered party. Secondly, the market orientation of the industry leads to inequality of access to publication. Writers whose views are unpopular with the owners and editors of mass circulation newspapers have less opportunity to bring their writing before the public than people whose views are in tune with those of the press barons. In political terms, this means that the capitalist right is likely to be advantaged over the socialist left in access to the press, and that the newspaper industry, taken as a whole, is liable to be less effective in scrutinizing a right-wing, economically liberal government than a left-wing, socialist one. This can have the effect of skewing the market-place of ideas within which the system of electoral democracy operates.

Whether this is seen as a problem will depend on one's political and economic preferences. From one viewpoint, the practical and symbolic value of a free press is undermined if it is subject to market forces. These admit opinions to be valuable only to the extent to which they can be shown to enjoy *economic* support in the market. On this view, freedom of speech should be no more privileged against unfavourable market conditions than any other consumer preference. However, such a view can be challenged on two grounds.

---

[23] See Gibbons, *Regulating the Media*, 2nd edn., 207–11; Barendt and Hitchens, *Media Law*, 243–7; R. Whish, *Competition Law*, 3rd edn. (London: Butterworths, 1993), 675 ff; Robertson and Nicol, *Media Law*, 502–7.

First, it can be argued that attempting to subject freedom of speech or of the press to free-market liberalism is self-defeating. In order to make liberalism work as a political system, the necessary conditions for its operation must be in place. These include respect for individual autonomy and freedom to publish ideas. By subjecting the latter freedom to market forces, free-market capitalism treats the conditions for liberalism as being of contingent rather than intrinsic importance. This, it might be said, is an incoherent position for market capitalists to adopt, since a measure of individual freedom is a prerequisite for capitalism itself. But this argument is flawed. Free-market capitalism may thrive on individual freedom, but it is not predicated on the observance of the full range of individual rights. It demands respect for economic rights, particularly those needed in order to make trading possible, but it does not necessitate liberal political freedoms or respect for non-economic aspects of personal autonomy. Capitalism can flourish in countries which are far from being politically liberal or respecting individual autonomy as a fundamental value. Japan provides an example of such a country. Indeed, there may be circumstances in which free speech threatens capitalist market freedoms, for example by advocating a move to a more controlled economy.

A second, more promising, defence of freedom of the press is based in values operating at a higher level than those of the market economy. Why, one can ask, is the market economy worth preserving? Utilitarian capitalists would reply that it is the most efficient means of maximizing aggregate social wealth. This is a controversial claim. It is non-falsifiable (i.e. not capable of being disproved), and therefore has a limited claim to truth-value. Liberal capitalists, by contrast, will argue that markets give the best opportunity for people to explore and exploit their abilities, formulating and giving effect to a plan for life. This makes the market a forum in which people can express their autonomy. There are, however, other spheres of personal autonomy, and it is by no means clear that these are less worthwhile than those which can be realized through the market. Subjecting the availability of all expressions of autonomy to the market fails to remain neutral between socially acceptable types of life plan. It places special value on those which require a market, and undervalues others which demand restrictions on the freedom of the market in order to make it more equal rather than more free. Liberalism requires that different visions of the good should be equally respected as long as they do not undermine society or inflict harm. For liberal capitalists, then, as opposed to utilitarian ones, there should be little difficulty in accepting that it may be necessary to restrain the free operation of the market economy in order to advance non-economic visions of the good.

In short, political liberalism requires a degree of control over the operation of markets in order to protect liberal values against market-expressed preferences. However, the extent to which such control is desirable or acceptable will depend on the view which individuals or society as a whole take of the relative weights attaching to different freedoms. Where newspaper proprietors have bought or built up their newspapers as businesses, limiting their editorial freedom is a potential restriction of their freedom of expression (forcing them to publish expressions with which they disagree or of which they disapprove, for example in order to provide political balance) and is also an interference with their freedom to use their property in the way which seems best to them. In a capitalist economy, it is plausible to expect economic liberals to regard it as improper—a form of disguised taxation—to force a proprietor to fund a publication in order to give publicity to ideas or information which the proprietor would rather not see published. Even those who favour freedom of expression might not be prepared to support it under circumstances in which its exercise conflicts with freedom of property.

The most obvious practical implications of this relate to the vexed question of rights of reply. At present, there is no obligation on newspapers to allow space for people to reply to stories or opinions which have been published about them. The more responsible newspapers will publish corrections where errors have been made, and publish letters from people replying to articles, but other newspapers have in the past been less scrupulous. The Press Complaints Commission Code of Practice, originally adopted in 1991 in response to agitation, in and out of Parliament, for legislation requiring newspapers to give space to members of the public for replies to allegations made in earlier issues and revised several times since, includes three significant provisions. Paragraph 1(ii) provides that significant inaccuracies, misleading statements, and distorted reports should be corrected promptly and with due prominence. Paragraph 1(iii) requires that an apology should be published whenever appropriate. Paragraph 2 provides: 'A fair opportunity for reply to inaccuracies should be given to individuals or organisations when reasonably called for'. This does not suggest that there should be a right to reply to expressions of opinion or to misleading presentations of accurate facts, and it leaves it to the editor in the first instance to decide whether a request for an opportunity to reply is 'reasonable'. Paragraph 1(iv) provides: 'Newspapers, while free to be partisan, should distinguish clearly between comment, conjecture and fact'.

The Code of Practice was a response to complaints that some newspapers have fabricated news items, misrepresented people's opinions, or behaved improperly while gathering information, and to the suggestion in the Calcutt Report that there might be legislation if the industry failed to behave more responsibly in future. But, as paragraph 3 makes clear, the aim is to secure respect for rights to reputation or privacy, rather than an attempt to enforce access to the media for a range of views, or balanced political reporting. Newspapers are property, and it would be seen as a violation of the proprietors' rights, both of ownership and of free expression, to insist that they pay to support the propagation of views with which they disagree. Proprietors are free to be fair and balanced if they want to be (although among national dailies only the *Independent* has an official editorial policy which is politically non-aligned), but they will not be compelled to behave as if they were a public-service undertaking using state money.

If there is a desire to use newspapers to secure access to means of publication for all points of view, it will be necessary to dilute the proprietorial element in newspaper ownership. This might be managed, for example, by providing a state subsidy to cover the cost of producing a proportion of the news and comment parts of the newspaper (excluding commercial advertising space), and requiring that proportion to be devoted to opposing viewpoints for the sake of balance. However, as yet no government has seen fit to act so as to limit the freedom of newpaper proprietors. Political parties which rely on the press to stir up public support would be taking a major risk if they tried to force such an arrangement on proprietors.

(2) CONTROL OVER CONTENT AND INVESTIGATIVE METHODS: NEWSPAPERS

The existing British system of controls over newpapers relies largely on self-regulation, and its effectiveness is questionable. The press has proved resistant to proposals to give people rights of reply when they feel that they have been libelled or misrepresented, and has been very slow to put in place any structures for establishing and enforcing standards of professional integrity, truthfulness, and responsibility among journalists and editors. The free market in newspaper sales has encouraged the less responsible editors and proprietors to allow anything as long as it sells newspapers. Self-regulation by the industry's own appointed watchdogs had little effect on editorial behaviour generally, and in some newspapers abuses abounded.[24] The law has not been able to do much to keep them in check: after one of the grosser abuses of taste, in which a photographer without consent took a picture of a dangerously ill television actor and a newspaper published it, the Court of Appeal lamented the lack of a remedy against the press (represented on this occasion by the *Sunday Sport*) for infringement of privacy.[25] The Press Council, a body for self-regulation by the industry, saw its main role as protecting press freedom, and was largely ineffective in imposing standards. Only in 1990, after a report by a Committee chaired by Mr. (now Sir) David Calcutt QC,[26] did the newspaper industry establish procedures to clean up their practices.[27]

The Newspaper Publishers' Association and the Newspaper Society, representing proprietors of national and local newspapers, put in place a Code of Practice setting out professional and ethical standards for journalists and editors, worked out by a committee of newspaper editors. Next, they established a Press Complaints Commission to adjudicate on complaints about breaches of the Code, to replace the Press Council. The Commission has adopted revised Codes, most recently in 1997, but the work of drafting has been carried out by a committee consisting entirely of editors, without direct lay input. The Commission can censure newspapers or journalists, and can tell (but not compel) editors to publish adjudications. It has no power to require a newspaper to publish a correction or give a right of reply to an aggrieved person, no procedure for mediating to resolve disputes, and no power to award compensation or impose penalties (despite the view of the last Conservative government[28] that the

[24] Gibbons, *Regulating the Media*, 158–66.
[25] *Kaye v. Robertson* [1991] FSR 62, CA. See Ch. 9 above; R. Wacks, *Privacy and Press Freedom* (London: Blackstone Press, 1995).
[26] Home Office, *Report of the Committee on Privacy and Related Matters*, Cm. 1102 (London: HMSO, 1990).
[27] C. R. Munro, 'Press Freedom—How the Beast was Tamed' (1991) 54 *MLR* 104–11.
[28] National Heritage Committee, Report, *Privacy and Media Intrusion* (HC 294 of 1993), para. 75; Department of National Heritage, *Government Response to National Heritage Committee, Privacy and Media Intrusion*, Cm. 2918 (London: HMSO, 1995), para. 2.14(v).

industry should establish a fund to compensate people for unjustifiable invasion of privacy). The main procedural difference between the Commission and the old Press Council, from the complainant's point of view, is that the Press Council would not consider complaints if the complainant was contemplating legal action, whereas the Commission will not require the complainant to give up the legal right to seek damages or other remedies before it will investigate the complaint.

The Press Complaints Commission has a strong press element in its membership, although editors no longer[29] form a majority of its members: as well as Lord Wakeham, its chairman,[30] eight of its other fifteen members come from outside the industry. The seven editors of national and local newspapers and magazines who make up the balance of the membership is intended to achieve two goals: first, to ensure that the Commission understands how newspapers work; secondly, to make its adjudications acceptable to journalists. It is thought that people within the industry will be more likely to accept and adapt to criticisms from a peer group than attacks from an outside body. To a large extent this seems to work, although there have been some cases in which tabloid newspapers have rejected the Commission's adjudications and have gone so far as to re-publish the material which gave rise to the complaint.[31] The work of the Commission has been aided by the appointment, by individual newspapers, of readers' complaints ombudsmen. These do not investigate complaints themselves—that is left to the editorial staff—but they keep an eye on standards of behaviour on the paper, watch the process by which complaints are handled, and publish regular reports in the newspaper about their findings. Complaints to the courts about decisions of the PCC have had little success. Courts regard the PCC as doing a non-technical job, and are reluctant to subject it to judicial review in a case where there is no obvious benefit to be gained. For example, in *R. v. Press Complaints Commission, ex parte Stewart-Brady*[31a] the Court of Appeal held that the PCC had been entitled to decide that publication of a picture of Ian Brady, obtained by long-lens photography while he was a patient at Ashworth Special Hospital, accompanying an article about conditions in which he was being held which was in the public interest, was not worthy of censure, even if it had violated the Code. The PCC was not required first to decide whether or not the taking and publication of the photograph had violated the Code; there would have been no benefit in doing so.

When the Calcutt Committee reported in June 1990, it accepted that statutory regulation would be less than ideal, but recommended that the performance of the press and its self-regulatory organ, the Press Complaints Commission, should be kept under review to see whether they observed standards which would make statutory

---

[29] Originally ten of the fifteen members (other than the lay Chairman) were editors, and the industry provided a majority of members of the Commission which appointed members of the Press Complaints Commission.

[30] Lord Wakeham, formerly a Conservative Cabinet Minister, succeeded Lord MacGregor, the first Chairman, on 1 January 1995.

[31] Sir David Calcutt QC, *Review of Press Self-Regulation*, Cm. 2135 (London: HMSO, 1993), paras. 4.25–4.28 and 4.41.

[31a] [1997] EMLR 185, CA.

regulation unnecessary. By the time Sir David Calcutt reported in January 1993 on his review of the operation of the Commission,[32] there was evidence of further invasion of privacy by the press and of a half-hearted response by the Commission. Personal information, obtained by unlawful entry, secret surveillance, or bugging devices, and amounting to invasions of privacy, had been published concerning the private lives of public figures (including Mr. Paddy Ashdown, leader of the Liberal Democrats, Mr. David Mellor, the Minister then responsible for the review of press self-regulation, the Duchess of York, and the Prince and Princess of Wales), without effective action by the Commission. Private individuals who had suffered similar invasions of privacy had, in some cases, not complained to the Commission, either through ignorance of its existence or because they feared that further publicity would follow, and a number of those who had complained were dissatisfied with the way in which the complaints were handled.[33]

Sir David concluded that self-regulation had not worked, and recommended that a package of measures, originally examined by the Privacy Committee in 1990, should now be implemented. Chief among these was the establishment of a statutory Press Complaints Tribunal with jurisdiction over all newspapers, journals, and magazines. It would be chaired by a judge or senior lawyer, and would have power to order a publisher to print an apology in a form, edition, and position specified by the tribunal. It would also be empowered to award compensation and impose fines.[34] Alongside this, Sir David recommended the imposition of criminal sanctions and civil liability on anyone who unlawfully entered private property, or placed a surveillance device there, or took a photograph or recorded the voice of anyone, intending to obtain personal information with a view to its publication. There would be a defence if the act was done to prevent, detect, or expose a crime or other seriously anti-social conduct, to protect public health or safety, to prevent the public being misled by a public statement or action of the person concerned, or if it was done under lawful authority. He also recommended that the government should give further consideration to the introduction of a tort of infringement of privacy.[35]

The main recommendations of the Review, involving statutory regulation of the press, were rejected by a report of the House of Commons National Heritage Committee,[36] and subsequently both Conservative and Labour governments have declined to introduce legislation. The quiescent approach of governments is partly attributable to the political parties' reliance on the press, but was also the result of changes to the structure of the Press Complaints Commission giving majority weight to members from outside the industry, and the greater assertiveness of Lord Wakeham's chairmanship when he succeeded Lord MacGregor in 1995, particularly in relation to privacy.[37] None the less, the system continues to suffer from a credibility gap.

[32] Calcutt, *Review of Press Self-Regulation*, above.

[33] Ibid., chs 4 and 5.

[34] Ibid., paras 6.17–6.22.

[35] Ibid., ch. 7.

[36] National Heritage Committee, Report, *Privacy and Media Intrusion* (HC 294 of 1993). See Barendt and Hitchens, *Media Law*, 37–44.

[37] On the privacy case law of the PCC under Lord MacGregor's chairmanship, see L. Blom-Cooper and

There can be no doubt that the best solution would be for the press to adopt standards of responsible, professional behaviour, and to police them. Editors and journalists are concerned to be seen by the public as professionals, with a code of ethics and a sense of public responsibility. Unfortunately, they seem to want that public regard without the shackles which normally accompany it. One of the features which distinguishes professions from other groupings is that the former have criteria and procedures for admission to membership, and disciplinary procedures and measures (including the withdrawal of the right to practise), which are designed to impose and uphold standards of ethics and responsibility which protect those with whom the professional has to deal. Until journalism adopts a professional organization of this sort, its claim to be free of regulation in the public interest will always be suspect.

For structural reasons, however, it would be difficult and perhaps impossible to make such a professional body work. Professionals are typically not employed by a single client. Many journalists and all editors, on the other hand, are tied to the proprietor of the newspaper, magazine, or journal on which they work. The proprietor's main aim is profit, and, being the person who pays the piper, will not unnaturally expect to call the tune.[38] The standards and procedures of a professional body of dependent journalists could hardly hope to stand up against such economic power. Regrettable as it is, if society is serious about reining in abuses of press freedom, it might ultimately have no alternative to a Calcutt-style package of measures, at least while the press industry continues to be controlled by an oligopoly of proprietors. The problem is unlikely to be alleviated if the government carries through its plan to 'consider a lighter touch approach for newspaper mergers'.[39] If, on the other hand, society wants to protect the press against statutory incursions on its freedom, it will have to accept the inevitable abuses as the price of the benefits.

(3) REASONS FOR REGULATING THE BROADCASTING MEDIA

The broadcast forms of mass communication were, and are, carefully regulated. There are five interrelated reasons for this. First, governments realized the potential of channels of mass communication for contributing to democracy or undermining it. They hoped to foster a public service ethos in broadcasting, so that it would be a medium for educating and improving the population.[40] This was important to some early broadcasters, notably Lord Reith, the first Director-General of the BBC, as well as to government. Secondly, in order to do this it was necessary to keep the media of mass communications from having programme policy dictated entirely by market forces. A strong public sector and regulation of the independent sector, when one started to

---

L. R. Pruitt, 'Privacy Jurisprudence of the Press Complaints Commission' (1994) 23 *Anglo-Am. L. Rev.* 135; E. Barendt, 'Privacy and the Press' (1995) 1 *Yearbook of Media and Entertainment Law* 23–41 at 37f. For more recent assessments, see Gibbons, *Regulating the Media*, 2nd edn., 82–90, 282–4; Barendt and Hitchens, *Media Law*, 55–65, 404–12.

[38]   See T. Gibbons, 'Freedom of the Press: Ownership and Editorial Values' [1992] *PL* 279–99.

[39]   Department of Trade and Industry and Department of Culture, Media and Sport, *A New Future for Communications*, 45, para. 4.11.

[40]   Gibbons, *Regulating the Media*, 2nd edn., 55–64.

operate, were called for. Initially, the novelty and cost of broadcasting technology helped to discourage press barons from entering the broadcasting arena, and made it easier to ensure that the powerful new means of communication did not fall into the wrong hands. (This was similar to the early history of printing, when presses were expensive and skilled printers scarce.)[41] The government continues to regard this as a proper role for public service broadcasting now that scarcity of broadcasting spectra is no longer a serious constraint on the industry.[42]

Thirdly, when commercial broadcasters appeared on the scene, and a regulatory scheme was being developed for them, it was thought to be important to preserve a diversity of ideas by preventing oligopolistic concentrations of power in the hands of a few, usually rich and conservative, media magnates, and to ensure that licences were granted only to people who could be expected not to abuse the privilege. The need to preserve propriety has been a motivating factor in the regulation of commercial broadcasting over much of the world. In Australia, for example, the Australian Broadcasting Tribunal can refuse a licence to anyone who is shown not to be a fit and proper person to hold one. The same is true of the Independent Television Commission and the Radio Authority in the UK.[43] In 1998, the Radio Authority withdrew licences to operate local radio stations on this ground from companies in which the majority shareholder had been convicted of rape and indecent assault.[44]

Fourthly, government hoped to ensure that civilized standards were maintained, to uphold social values. Accordingly, the Royal Charter and Licence Agreement of the BBC has always set standards which have to be observed in relation to good taste, decency, protecting children, political impartiality, and so on.[45] The same standards are set for the independent broadcasting services by the Broadcasting Act 1990, section 6. It is the responsibility of the Governors of the BBC, under its Charter, and of the Independent Television Commission under section 7 of the 1990 Act, to produce a code giving guidance to programme-makers on the standards to be observed in order to preserve good taste and decency, especially in relation to children's viewing, to avoid offending the feelings of the public, and to control the portrayal of violence. The ITC last revised its programme code in 1998.[46] Two further codes of practice are provided by the Broadcasting Standards Commission (BSC), which has responsibility under the Broadcasting Act 1996 for monitoring programmes, considering complaints about them, publishing its views on programmes after they have been broadcast, and considering complaints from people about unjust or unfair treatment in radio or television programmes broadcast by either the BBC or independent

[41] See J. R. Hale, *Renaissance Europe 1480–1520* (London: Collins, 1971), 188–9.

[42] Department of Trade and Industry and Department of Culture, Media and Sport, *A New Future for Communications*, 49–51, paras. 5.3.9–5.3.12.

[43] Broadcasting Act 1990, s. 3(3).

[44] Radio Authority, News Release 28/98 of 9 April 1998, *Radio Authority Agrees Transfer of Licences Held by Owen Oyston*.

[45] See now *Royal Charter for the Continuance of the British Broadcasting Corporation*, Cm. 3248 (London: HMSO, 1996); Department of National Heritage, *Copy of the Agreement Dated the 25th Day of January 1996 between Her Majesty's Secretary of State for National Heritage and the British Broadcasting Corporation*, Cm. 3152 (London: HMSO, 1996). The current Licence Agreement runs for ten years.

[46] Barendt and Hitchens, *Media Law*, 119–33.

companies, and about invasions of privacy. The Code on Standards and the Code on Fairness and Privacy are administered by separate panels, reflecting the original division of functions between separate bodies (a Broadcasting Standards Council and a Broadcasting Complaints Commission) under the 1990 Act. The BSC has no power to order the companies to give a right of reply or to broadcast a correction or apology, but can only publicize its findings.[47] In failing to provide an effective and enforceable right of reply, the legislation appears to fall short of the UK's obligations under both the Council of European Convention on Transfrontier Television and the EC Television Directive, noted above.

Fifthly, wavelengths for broadcasting were limited. This purely technical consideration sharply distinguishes broadcasting from newspapers, and justifies a higher level of regulation. In theory, if not in practice, there is nothing to prevent any number of newspapers being published simultaneously. The only controlling mechanism needed is that of market forces. This is not true of broadcasting. Some control over the allocation of wavelengths is needed in order to ensure that there are sufficient for all legitimate broadcasters. In the USA, the shortage of broadcasting wavelengths was held to justify limiting the First Amendment rights of broadcasters, allowing the Federal Communications Commission (FCC) to exercise a rulemaking and regulatory function over broadcasting,[48] although the growth of methods of communication and the convergence of technologies means that the justification may no longer apply.

A form of regulation designed to cater for the technical problems of available wavelengths in crowded airwaves, and to enable some control to be imposed over quality and propriety of programmes which can now easily be beamed across frontiers, is the European Convention on Transfrontier Television, which twenty-three European states have now signed.

In two cases, the European Court of Human Rights has had to consider the relationship between restrictions imposed on trans-border broadcasting and the guarantee of freedom of expression under the European Convention on Human Rights. This is a problem which could simply not have been foreseen when the ECHR was drafted, so some creative interpretation has been necessary in order to make it compatible with technological developments. Article 10(1) of the Convention recognizes the right of states to impose licensing systems on broadcasting, television, and cinema enterprises, and Article 10(2) allows interference with freedom of expression to be justified in certain circumstances. In the first case, *Groppera Radio AG and others v. Switzerland*,[49] the Swiss Federal Council adopted an Ordinance in 1983 which prohibited Swiss cable companies, which needed a licence to rebroadcast programmes, from rebroadcasting programmes from transmitters which did not comply with the relevant international agreements on telecommunications and radio. A cable co-operative, which had been receiving and rebroadcasting programmes from an Italian transmitter, was ordered to stop doing so, and was unsuccessful in its attempts to challenge the order in the Swiss Federal Court. When the case reached Strasbourg, the European

---

[47] Gibbons, *Regulating the Media*, 2nd edn., 264–74.
[48] *National Broadcasting Co. v. United States* (1943) 319 US 190.
[49] Eur. Ct. HR, Series A, vol. 173, Judgment of 28 March 1990.

Commission of Human Rights by a narrow majority held that there had been an interference with the rights of the co-operative and the owners of the Italian transmitter (Groppera Radio AG), and that this could not be justified under Article 10(2). The case was referred to the Court, which agreed that there had been an interference contrary to Article 10(1). However, by sixteen votes to three the Court decided that the interference was justifiable under Article 10(2). The order had had two aims which were compatible with the Convention: compliance with and enforcement of the international arrangements on telecommunications (the prevention of disorder is an object which extends to disorder in the ether as well as on the ground), and the protection of the rights of others (the licensees who were complying with the order). Furthermore, the order was within the margin of appreciation left to states in deciding whether the order was necessary in a democratic society. Although Groppera argued that it was not a Swiss company, and therefore should not be subject to damage from Swiss law, it was reasonable (having regard to the international nature of broadcasting) for the Swiss authorities to treat Groppera, which had been transmitting into Switzerland from just over the Italian–Swiss border, as being in reality a Swiss station transmitting to Switzerland, which had positioned itself outside Switzerland solely in order to evade the controls imposed, consistently with the Convention, on Swiss enterprises.

This shows a readiness on the part of the Court to take account of the international nature of (particularly) satellite broadcasting, and to interpret the Convention in the light of the purpose of other international covenants designed to enable governments of states to regulate the material reaching their countries for rebroadcasting, so long as the principles applied are in accord with those in Article 10(2).

The second case, however, shows the limits of the margin of appreciation. In *Autronic AG v. Switzerland*,[50] the Swiss regulatory authority, the Post and Telecommunications Authority, had in 1982 refused to grant Autronic a licence to show at an exhibition a Soviet television programme received directly from a Soviet telecommunications satellite, on the ground that it could not grant authorization unless the Soviet authorities had given their express agreement to the rebroadcast. The Federal Court refused to entertain an application for a public-law appeal, on the ground that Autronic had no direct economic interest which was worth protecting. In this case, the European Court of Human Rights, in agreement with the Commission, held that there had been a violation of Article 10, which could not be justified under Article 10(2). Although the objects pursued were legitimate (preventing disorder in broadcasting, and preventing the disclosure of confidential information), the refusal of permission was not necessary in a democratic society, because the programme had not contained confidential information, it had been intended for public consumption in the Soviet Union, and it had been transmitted by the Soviets via the satellite in uncoded form. Accordingly, the refusal of permission fell outside the margin of appreciation allowed to states. As a result of the ruling, Swiss law was amended to bring it into line with the Convention.[51]

[50] Eur. Ct. HR, Series A, vol. 178, Judgment of 22 May 1990.
[51] Committee of Ministers, Resolution DH (91) 26, adopted on 18 October 1991, appendix.

These decisions illustrate four features of the way the ECHR applies to broadcasting. First, the right to freedom of expression under Article 10(1) applies to 'everyone'—companies and other agencies with legal personality as well as natural persons. Secondly, it is legitimate for the state to limit freedom of expression by broadcasters and telecommunicators so far as is necessary to give effect to a licensing system, subject to the manner of the restrictions being compatible with Article 10(2). Thirdly, one of the legitimate objects of a system of control is to give effect to international treaties on broadcasting, in order to preserve the international order relating to this field of activity. Fourthly, in deciding how best to do this, states have a margin of appreciation which, as usual under Article 10, is substantial but not unconfined. In particular, as the Court held in *Informationsverein Lentia v. Austria*,[52] the demands of pluralism make it extremely difficult, if not impossible, for a state to justify a licensing regime which allows only a single state-controlled broadcaster to transmit programmes.[53]

A further legitimate object of national regulation is to protect the intellectual property rights of programme-makers and broadcasters. It is permissible, on this ground, for organizations to prevent people from getting access to programmes without paying appropriate licence fees. One way of preventing this is to encode programme transmissions, and to restrict access to decoders to people who pay the fee. In the UK, this has been held to be a legitimate way of enforcing rights under the Copyright, Designs and Patents Act 1988, section 298.[54]

For these political, cultural, and technical reasons, communication over the airwaves is subject to regulation of a sort which it would have been unthinkable to apply to printed publications at any time after the late eighteenth century, save in time of war. It is, however, important to limit the control which politicians in or out of government can exercise over this important medium of communication. The need to preserve the accessibility of the broadcasting media to a diversity of opinions, and to protect it against totalitarian control, assumed constitutional significance in countries with constitutions which guarantee the right to free expression, and which rely on the courts to prevent the concentration of control and powers of censorship in the hands of politicians. Professor Barendt has pointed out that the controlling role of the courts is evident in countries such as post-war Italy and the Federal Republic of Germany. Under such constitutions, the constitutional courts were able to play a part in the development of broadcasting regulation, ensuring that central government intervention in broadcasting policy was not excessive, that governmental discretion was cabined, that private broadcasting stations, when permitted, were regulated to ensure freedom of expression, and that free expression on public services was secured.[55] The responsibility placed in the hands of judges in these countries illustrates the relativity

---

[52] Eur. Ct. HR, Series A, No. 276, Judgment of 24 November 1993, 17 EHRR 93.

[53] Craufurd Smith, *Broadcasting Law and Fundamental Rights*, chs. 6 and 7.

[54] *BBC Enterprises Ltd. v. Hi-Tech Xtravision Ltd.* [1991] 2 AC 327, [1991] 3 All ER 257, HL.

[55] E. Barendt, 'The Influence of the German and Italian Constitutional Courts on their National Broadcasting Systems' [1991] *PL* 93–115; E. Barendt, *Broadcasting Law*, chs 1 and 2. Privatization of broadcasting in France is among the matters discussed by T. Prosser, 'Golden Shares: Industrial Policy by Stealth' [1988] *PL* 413–31 at 422; see also Decision 88–248 of 17 January 1989 of the *Conseil constitutionnel*.

of questions of legitimacy. It makes no sense to ask whether it is legitimate in a democracy for judges to exercise such authority over the structure of broadcasting, until one knows more about the circumstances in which the democracy came into being, the resulting constitutional ethos, and the alternative to giving control to the judges. The issue is not simply whether the exercise of power by judges is legitimate, but whether it is more legitimate than the exercise of similar powers by (for example) politicians. The answer to the latter question depends on how much one feels entitled to trust politicians, given the country's recent history.

(4) REGULATING CONTROL OVER BROADCASTING ORGANIZATIONS

In the field of television franchises, the current system (much criticized in the light of the first round of franchise allocations in 1991) is for the Independent Television Commission, a body largely independent of government, to allocate licences on a regional basis to the highest bidder in a silent auction, subject to being satisfied that the highest bidder would be capable of maintaining an adequate range and quality of programmes.[56] There are restrictions on the people who are to be allowed to hold franchises: they must satisfy the Commission that they are 'fit and proper' people for the job, and the Commission is to try as far as possible to ensure that the franchise holder is a national of a Member State of the European Community, and is not a political or religious body or an advertising agency. In addition, the Commission is to avoid, as far as possible, allowing control of interests in the franchise holders from becoming concentrated in too few hands, or falling into the hands of people who hold controlling interests in newspapers. This anti-monopolistic approach is designed to maintain whatever scope there may be for expression of a variety of views through the media. At the same time, interfering with the licence of a broadcasting body during its currency may violate rights both to property and to freedom of expression, and would need to be carefully justified.[57]

The BBC is controlled by its Governors, with cash controls imposed by government by way of its power to set the licence fee from which the BBC derives the lion's share of its income.[58] As the Governors are appointed by government, this leaves them open to suspicion that they are subject to political pressure and patronage. It is hard to regulate a service in the public interest (as seen by government) without impinging on its political independence.[59]

(5) CONTROL OVER CONTENT: BROADCASTING

By comparison with the *laissez-faire* attitude of successive modern governments to newspaper proprietors, the modern media—broadcasting of wireless and television

---

[56] Broadcasting Act 1990, s. 2(2)(b).
[57] See, e.g. *Cable and Wireless (Dominica) Ltd. v. Marpin Telecoms and Broadcasting Co. Ltd.*, [2001] 1 WLR 1123, PC.
[58] Wireless Telegraphy Act 1949, ss. 1 and 2.
[59] See Gibbons, *Regulating the Media*, 2nd edn., 35–54.

programmes by radio, satellite, and cable, and the distribution of video recordings—
are heavily regulated. Many of these matters, including controls in the interests of
state security, are examined in the chapters which follow. It must be borne in mind,
however, that we are dealing with complementary rights: those of broadcasters to
exercise their freedom to express themselves and to impart information and ideas, and
those of listeners and viewers to exercise their right to receive information and ideas
and, if invited, to participate in the process of communication via telephone link-up,
e-mail, etc. Indeed, the rights of receivers of programmes impose certain duties (social
and moral more usually than legal) on broadcasters. As a result, an attempt by state
authorities to prevent a programme or item being broadcast, or to remove a particularly disfavoured broadcaster's access to the airwaves, is likely to violate the rights of
listeners and viewers as well as those of the programme-makers.[60] Here, we should
note five matters. In New Zealand, Sir Robin Cooke (now Lord Cooke of Thorndon)
has suggested that a right to have access to the media might be built on the right to
freedom of expression.[60a]

(i) The requirement of balance

The BBC, under its Charter and Licence and Agreement, and the independent broadcasters, under section 6(1)(b) and (c) of the Broadcasting Act 1990, are obliged to
ensure that news is purveyed with due accuracy and impartiality, and that matters of
political or industrial controversy, or concerned with current public policy, are treated
with due impartiality. Independent television companies are bound by rules setting
out what is required by the impartiality requirement, promulgated by the Independent Television Commission in its Code of Practice.[61] Expressions of partisan views are
permitted, but opposed viewpoints should also be given sufficient prominence for any
bias to be balanced out over the whole of the programme or series of programmes.
The Commission is to exert itself to ensure that the personal views of licence holders
and broadcasters on matters of political or industrial controversy, or which relate to
current public policy, are not expressed on the air.[62] This is designed to prevent the
proprietors of broadcasting stations from using the airwaves in the partisan way in
which newspaper proprietors are allowed to use the columns of their newspapers.

    The impartiality requirement imposes restrictions on the right to free expression of
proprietors and operators of independent broadcasting services which would not be
acceptable if applied to privately owned newspapers. Both here and in the USA, this
has in the past been justified by reference to the special features of broadcasting: its
pervasiveness and the limited number of broadcasting outlets. The tension between
the rights of broadcasters and those of people wanting to be broadcast, and the
influence of models of the market in ideas on the solution to it, can be illustrated by

---

[60] See, e.g. *Fernando v. Sri Lanka Broadcasting Corporation* (1996) 1 BHRC 104, SC of Sri Lanka; *Benjamin
v. Minister of Information and Broadcasting* [2001] 1 WLR 1040, PC.
[60a] See *TV3 Network Ltd. v. Eveready New Zealand Ltd.* [1993] 3 NZLR 435, CA of NZ, at 441 *per* Sir Robin
Cooke P.
[61] Broadcasting Act 1990, s. 6(3), (5). Similar provisions are made in respect of the Independent Radio
Authority under Part III of the Act.
[62] Ibid., s. 6(5).

looking at the position in the USA, where the argument takes place in the context of First Amendment right to freedom of speech. Insisting on impartiality and balance within programmes helps to secure access to the media for a wide variety of viewpoints. This was formalized in the USA as a recognized limitation on the First Amendment rights of broadcasters. The regulatory body, the Federal Communications Commission (FCC), developed a principle in 1949 requiring the broadcasters to give fair coverage to each side of the argument on any public issue (the 'fairness doctrine').[63] The Supreme Court later held this restriction to be compatible with the First Amendment, as it served to advance the free speech rights of those who might otherwise be denied access to an important forum for expressing their views: in effect, the regulation bolstered the market-place of ideas in a setting where the market was imperfect, in that opportunities for access to it were artificially limited.[64] However, if market conditions changed, allowing a wider range of broadcasting outlets, the court accepted that the position might be reconsidered.[65] The doctrine, in its application to private broadcasters, became a contentious political football: the Reagan administration considered that the market had changed its character, with many more broadcasting stations available than in 1949, and agitated for the abolition of the doctrine. Congress failed to respond, so in 1989 the FCC itself reversed the doctrine, holding it now to be a breach of the First Amendment rights of broadcasters. Congress has attempted unsuccessfully to reintroduce the doctrine by legislation.[66]

In the UK, the number of channels is still far below that in the USA, and it remains plausible to argue that access to the media is best maintained by way of an impartiality requirement. Although there has never been a mechanical requirement of equal time being allocated to both sides of an argument on television, there was a judicial suggestion that the impartiality requirement might be breached where one side of an argument received three times as much air time as the other. *Wilson v. IBA*[67] concerned television broadcasts by political parties in the period of campaigning leading to the referendum in Scotland on Scottish devolution under the Scotland Act 1978. Because of the attitudes taken by the various parties, the broadcasts on the issue planned by the independent companies would have given three times as much time to proponents of a 'No' vote as to advocates for a 'Yes' vote. The court granted an interim interdict to restrain the IBA from permitting the broadcasts pending trial of the action, on the ground that there was an arguable case of a breach of the impartiality requirement in the legislation governing independent television broadcasting. As noted in Chapter 13, however, this has not been held to require that equal (or indeed any) time be allotted to competing candidates in elections,[68] unlike the position in the USA, where Congress has legislated to provide that, where one political candidate receives time on the air, others must be allowed equal time.[69]

---

[63] 13 FCC 1246 (1949).

[64] *Red Lion Broadcasting Co. v. FCC* 395 US 367 (1969).

[65] *FCC v. League of Women Voters of California* 468 US 364 (1984) at 377–8 nn. 11 and 12.

[66] L. Fisher, *American Constitutional Law* (New York: McGraw-Hill, 1990), 549.

[67] 1979 SC 351.

[68] *Grieve v. Douglas Home*, 1965 SC 315; *R. v. Broadcasting Complaints Commission, ex parte Owen* [1985] QB 1153, [1985] 2 All ER 522, DC.

[69] 47 USC, s. 315(a) (1982).

Fairness and impartiality requirements, while superficially attractive as ways of securing access to a limited market, are both difficult to apply and morally questionable. It is difficult to form an objective view about the presence of bias or partiality in presentation over a period. There are regular complaints that broadcasters are politically biased. All political parties appear to feel that they have been denied a fair crack of the whip in terms of time allocated to them, or attitudes of interviewers and reporters. It is always hard to know how far such claims are justified, and how far they merely represent politicians' hypersensitivity. The government is particularly likely to feel aggrieved about the substance of reporting, since one of the jobs of reporters and interviewers is to probe and challenge official versions of events. The impartiality requirement is not a complete solution to this. Furthermore, insisting on impartiality involves regulation of content of expression which is ideologically questionable, in that it assumes that all expression is in some sense equally valuable. This view was questioned in Chapter 13 above. It sometimes has a moral cost, in terms of truth and free expression. As Baker has written: 'Balance may often be good. But it is not the philosophy of a first amendment that protects liberty and dissent. And sometimes it is misguided. Sometimes, some positions are just wrong'.[70] Nevertheless, it is not necessarily true, as Baker suggests, that the consequence will tend to be bland, with reporters adopting middle-of-the-road positions on divisive issues. It may have the effect of putting the position of each side clearly before the other, with a net gain to the quality of the democratic decision-making process on the issue.

In the UK, the matter of impartiality is not usually subject to judicial decision (as noted in Chapter 13, above). Instead, the Codes of Practice produced by the ITC and the BBC hold sway, and the Broadcasting Standards Commission can adjudicate on complaints about unfairness.

(ii) The complaints jurisdiction of the Broadcasting Standards Commission

Under the Broadcasting Act 1996, this took over the functions of the Broadcasting Complaints Commission under the 1990 Act.[71] It has statutory responsibility for considering and adjudicating on complaints of partiality, unjust or unfair treatment of people in programmes, and of unwarranted invasions of privacy. The panel dealing with these complaints consists of people who are unconnected with broadcasting, but are appointed by the government. The BSC can entertain complaints about any licensed broadcaster, but must not consider a complaint if it is being ventilated by way of litigation in the UK.[72] It has jurisdiction to consider complaints about unfairness in the treatment of political parties, but has a discretion as to whether to investigate a complaint. It is not required to do so if it would thereby be involved in going beyond an assessment of whether a particular broadcast was fair to the complainant, and into

[70] C. E. Baker, *Human Liberty and Freedom of Speech* (New York and Oxford: Oxford University Press, 1989), 260.

[71] On the work of the Broadcasting Complaints Commission, see T. Gibbons, 'The Role of the Broadcasting Complaints Commission: Current Practice and Future Prospects' (1995) 1 *Yearbook of Media and Entertainment Law* 129–59.

[72] Broadcasting Act 1996, s. 114(2)(a), (b).

a consideration of the political fairness of broad editorial policies.[73] In practice, the courts have turned the discretion to refuse to entertain a complaint if the complainant is not the victim of the alleged unfairness, or has no direct interest in the subject-matter of the complaint,[74] into a duty to refuse to entertain such complaints.[75] The Commission accepts that programmes must not be required to be bland, that interviewers must challenge the assertions and views of those whom they interview in order to make the process useful, and fairness must be judged on the basis of an overview of the entire programme, not by picking out small parts of it. Nevertheless, it is open to the criticism that it displays too much indulgence to miscreants who are under investigation, limiting the scope for public-interest investigations by broadcasters.[76] The Commission has no power to force a broadcasting body to alter a programme or policy, or to order an apology or right of reply, but can require broadcasters to announce the results of adjudications, and to make corrections where necessary.[77] Despite this, broadcasters have become increasingly inclined to challenge its decisions by taking judicial review proceedings, particularly where they consider that it has overstepped its proper powers and illegitimately sought to limit broadcasters' investigations. For example, in *R. v. Broadcasting Standards Commission, ex parte British Broadcasting Corporation*[78] the BBC challenged the BSC's decision that the BBC had committed an unjustified invasion of privacy in clandestinely filming staff working at a branch of the Dixons retail chain. The Court of Appeal held that the company had standing to complain of an invasion of its privacy, and that privacy interests could subsist in shop premises despite their being open to the public. The decision of the BSC was therefore within its powers. Of more general importance is the statement by Lord Woolf MR that the courts would henceforth be slow to call in question the standards applied by the BSC when performing its statutory function of striking a balance between the rights of broadcasters and the rights and interests of others. Only where it is clear that the findings of the BSC are entirely unjustifiable, or based on an entirely untenable interpretation of the word 'privacy' or 'fairness', would the courts intervene.[79]

(iii) The role of the Governors of the BBC, the ITC, and the BSC in matters of taste

Under the Codes of Practice issued by the BBC and the ITC, there are guidelines on the types of programmes which should not be broadcast (e.g. films rated R18 by the British Board of Film Classification), and times when they should be broadcast so as to avoid an excessive risk of causing offence or harming children who might be

---

[73] *R. v. Broadcasting Complaints Commission, ex parte Owen* [1985] QB 1153, [1985] 2 All ER 522, DC.

[74] Broadcasting Act 1996, ss. 111(7), 130(1).

[75] *R. v. Broadcasting Complaints Commission, ex parte British Broadcasting Corporation* [1994] EMLR 497; *R. v. Broadcasting Complaints Commission, ex parte British Broadcasting Corporation* [1995] EMLR 241.

[76] For examples of its work, see Barendt and Hitchens, *Media Law*, 138–50.

[77] Broadcasting Act 1990, Part V; Gibbons, *Regulating the Media*, 149–55.

[78] [2000] 3 WLR 1327, [2000] 3 All ER 989, CA.

[79] [2000] 3 WLR at 1331–3 *per* Lord Woolf MR, although Hale LJ at 1338–9 and Lord Mustill at 1340 expressed themselves in narrower terms. Lord Woolf MR was applying the approach taken in *R. v. Broadcasting Complaints Commission, ex parte Granada Television Ltd.* [1995] EMLR 163, CA.

watching. The Governors of the BBC have a potential role as censors of all programmes to be broadcast. Before the Broadcasting Act 1990, the Governors of the IBA
exercised a similar role, forced on them against their wills by a decision of the Court
of Appeal.[80] This led to accusations that political appointees with no experience of
programme making were becoming too closely involved in editorial and programme-
making decisions.[81] As regards the independent sector, this threat has been partly
removed by the Broadcasting Act 1990. Section 11(3) makes it clear that there is never
to be an obligation on the ITC to watch programmes in advance of their broadcast,
reversing the effect of the earlier Court of Appeal decision; and there has clearly never
been a legal obligation on the BBC Governors to act as programme censors. On the
other hand, it would probably not be unlawful for them to do so, going beyond a
monitoring role.

Matters of portrayal of violence, sexual conduct, and taste and decency, also fall
within the jurisdiction of the BSC.[82] This body has no power to force a broadcasting
body to alter a programme or to order an apology or right of reply. These matters
are essentially left to the good sense and sensitivity of the broadcasters themselves,
reflecting the caution which is rightly shown over interfering with editorial freedom.

(iv) Reform of the regulatory system

To facilitate the development of a flexible but coherent approach to regulating a
number of converging industries, the government has set out plans to legislate to
bring together the regulation of all forms of television and radio broadcasting, telecommunications, and radio communications under a single independent regulator.
The Office of Communications (OFCOM) would perform functions currently exercised by the BSC, ITC, RA, Oftel, and the Radiocommunications Agency. The Board of
Governors of the BBC and the Welsh Authority, Sianel Pedwar Cymru (S4C) would
continue to be responsible, with some modifications, for the output of their respective
organizations. The new body, OFCOM, is to be a corporate body whose main objectives will be protecting the interests of consumers in the choice, price, and quality of
service and value for money; maintaining high quality of content, a wide range of
programming, and plurality of viewpoints and types of programmes; and maintaining accepted community standards in content, balancing freedom of expression
against the need to protect against potentially offensive or harmful material, want of
fairness, and invasions of privacy.[83]

OFCOM will have enforcement powers similar to those of Oftel and the ITC,
including powers to levy penalties and powers in respect of competition which will
operate concurrently with the Office of Fair Trading.[84] However, the government
envisages a type of subsidiarity principle operating: where appropriate, sectors of the

---

[80] *Attorney-General ex rel. McWhirter v. IBA* [1973] 1 QB 629, CA.

[81] *Report of the Committee on the Future of Broadcasting* (Chairman: Lord Annan), Cmnd. 6753 (1977);
Robertson, *Freedom, Individual and Law*, 236–40.

[82] Broadcasting Act 1990, Part VI; Gibbons, *Regulating the Media*, 155–8.

[83] Department of Trade and Industry and Department of Culture, Media and Sport, *A New Future for
Communications*, 78–9, paras. 8.3.1, 8.5.1–8.6.

[84] Ibid., 81, para. 8.9.1.

industry will be self-regulators or will have joint regulatory responsibility with OFCOM, rather than surrendering to OFCOM control over the detailed standards and requirements to govern them. Regulatory regimes will be framed in terms of services delivered rather than particular technologies, making technical innovation more straightforward, and will normally be concerned only with the interests of consumers.[85]

At the time of writing, little progress has been made in implementing in detail the plans published in the White Paper in December 2000. An Office of Telecommunications Bill was introduced to Parliament soon after the 2001 general election to establish OFCOM, without detailed powers, to shadow the existing regulators until the details of its role have been worked out with the assistance of OFCOM in consultation with existing regulators. Further developments are awaited.

(v) The Home Secretary's 'veto' power

The Home Secretary has power to issue a notice ordering the holder of a broadcasting licence to broadcast any announcement specified in the notice, or to refrain from broadcasting any matter, or classes of matter, specified in the notice. Before requiring an announcement to be broadcast, he must be satisfied that it is expedient in connection with his functions as Secretary of State. There is no such condition in connection with veto power.[86] These provisions put great power into the hands of a government Minister. They could be used to stifle political reporting, and have indeed been used in 1927 and 1955 in short-lived attempts to prevent controversial broadcasts or undermine the role of Parliament as the nation's debating chamber on political matters. Yet the veto power has been used only five times, and has not been employed for party political advantage. It is likely that a notice issued for party advantage would be subject to judicial review on the grounds of irrationality and improper purposes.

At present, no notice is in force. The most recent one was made by the Home Secretary in 1988 to prevent statements by members of the IRA being broadcast in the voice of the spokesmen themselves, as part of the drive to limit the terrorists' access to publicity. It led to an unsuccessful application for judicial review in *R. v. Secretary of State for the Home Department, ex parte Brind*.[87] In Ireland, a rather more extensive ban was imposed on the media in relation to reporting on terrorist organizations, and the European Commission of Human Rights held an application to Strasbourg to be inadmissible in *Purcell v. Ireland*.[88] In the UK, the notice was revoked in 1994 when the security position in Northern Ireland began to improve.

(vi) Informal pressure

One reason why it has rarely been necessary for Home Secretaries to invoke their formal veto powers is the ease with which informal pressure can be brought to bear.

[85] Ibid., 82–3, paras. 8.11.1–8.11.4.
[86] These obligations are imposed on the BBC by article 8 of its Licence and Agreement, Cm. 3152 (1996), and on the independent licence holders under the Broadcasting Act 1990, s. 10(1), (3). The licence holders may, but need not, announce that the notice has been issued: s. 10(2), (4).
[87] [1991] 1 AC 696, [1991] 1 All ER 720, HL.
[88] Application No. 15404/89, Decision of 16 April 1991.

There has been considerable pressure applied by the Conservatives during the 1980s. This has often happened in respect of the reporting of incidents involving the security forces in Northern Ireland, or carrying out duties elsewhere combating terrorism. The Conservative Party has made it clear that its members consider that the media, or elements within them, are biased against the armed forces and the security forces. To give but one example, in 1988 Sir Geoffrey Howe, then Foreign Secretary, attempted to persuade the Chairman of the IBA, Lord Thomson of Monifieth, to postpone showing *Death on the Rock* (a programme about the killing of three IRA terrorists by British security forces in Gibraltar) until after the conclusion of the inquest on the three in Gibraltar. The Foreign Secretary suggested that the broadcast might prejudice the result of the inquest, or lead to contamination of evidence, causing witnesses to change their stories.[89] This approach was rejected by the IBA, and the programme was broadcast, but an orchestrated campaign followed from the government and the Conservative Party alleging bias by the IBA. An independent report largely exonerated the producers and programme makers, and concluded:[90] 'Whatever view is taken of the state of public opinion and the legitimacy of government intervention, the making and screening of *Death on the Rock* proved that freedom of expression can prevail in the most extensive, and the most immediate, of all the means of mass communication'.

There has also been a steady pressure applied by political parties to the broadcasting authorities over alleged political bias in reporting the news and making current affairs programmes. Thinly veiled threats that the BBC would suffer when its licence was due for renewal in 1996 were made before the 1992 general election campaign. Happily, they did not appear to have cowed broadcasters; at any rate, the Conservative Party claimed to have noticed evidence of bias against it in the reporting of the campaign, and the media were not noticeably less critical of the Conservative government during the 1997 general election campaign, or of the Labour government during that of 2001.

(6) ADVERTISING

Commercial advertising is subject to regulation to maintain honesty and decency. Non-broadcast advertising is subject to industry self-regulation via the Advertising Standards Authority, while broadcast advertisements are regulated by the ITC and the Radio Authority (RA) under the Broadcasting Act 1990.[91] The Advertising Standards Authority has twelve members, at least half of whom are unconnected with the advertising industry. It adjudicates on complaints about advertisements, and the industry voluntarily refuses to publish advertisements which have been held to violate the British Codes of Advertising Practice and Sales Promotion, which apply to all advertising other than political advertisements.[91a] These Codes require, among other things,

---

[89] Lord Windlesham and Richard Rampton QC, *The Windlesham/Rampton Report on Death on the Rock* (London: Faber & Faber, 1989), ch. 11.

[90] Ibid., 145.

[91] On the regulation of advertising generally, see Barendt and Hitchens, *Media Law*, ch. 6.

[91a] Barendt and Hitchens, *Media Law: Cases and Materials*, 200–14.

that advertisements should be legal, decent, honest, and truthful, and that all claims must be supported by evidence held by the advertiser. Advertisements should not mislead readers through inaccuracy, ambiguity, exaggeration, omission, or in any other way, and should not unfairly attack or discredit other businesses or their products. The Authority has been treated as having expertise in assessing the ordinary meaning of advertisements, so courts will be slow to quash its determinations on the ground of irrationality. For example, in *R. v. Advertising Standards Authority, ex parte International Fund for Animal Welfare*[91b] an animal welfare organization pubished an advertisement claiming that a particular supermarket chain, by selling Canadian salmon, was encouraging the clubbing to death of Canadian seals. The company complained to the Authority, which upheld the complaint on the ground that the advertisement unfairly discredited the supermarket by implying that the supermarket company and its chairman were implicated in the killing of seals. On an application by the campaigners for judicial review of the Authority's decision, the court deferred to the expertise of the Authority in deciding on the true meaning of an advertisement, and whether the impact of a headline had been sufficiently diluted by accompanying text. It could not be said that no reasonable authority could have reached their conclusion, so it was not irrational for the purposes of judicial review.

The right to advertise is an aspect of the right to freedom of expression under ECHR Article 10(1), so restrictions on advertising must meet the conditions for justifying an interference with the freedom under Article 10(2).[92] Under the Human Rights Act 1998, restrictions on freedom of expression resulting from the application of the Codes of Practice would normally be justifiable under ECHR Article 10(2) if they are proportionate to the legitimate aim of protecting the reputations of those attacked and the right of readers to accurate information and the fair presentation of ideas. Treating commercial expression as a human right, particularly when it is exercised by or on behalf of an artificial person such as a company, is controversial, and it may be easier to justify interfering with such expression than with communications directed to public interests, as long as people are not denied the opportunity to bring their goods or services to the attention of potential customers. A test is likely to come if the Tobacco Advertising and Promotion Bill, outlawing advertising to the general public of tobacco and tobacco products and sponsorship of events by tobacco producers, becomes law. The government introduced the Bill to Parliament in the 2000–01 session, but it fell when Parliament was prorogued before the general election in 2001. The Queen's Speech in June 2001 contained no commitment to reintroduce it immediately, but a similar Bill was introduced to the House of Lords by the Liberal Democrat peer, Lord Clement-Jones, in July 2001, just before the summer recess. Supporters of the Bill are likely to argue that it is a proportionate response to a pressing social need to discourage smoking in order to safeguard health, and so is justifiable under ECHR Article 10(2). In principle, and subject to the particular terms

---

[91b] Unreported, 11 November 1997, Dyson J (available from Lexis).

[92] *Markt intern Verlag v. Germany*, Eur. Ct. HR, Series A, No. 165, Judgment of 20 November 1989, 12 EHRR 161; *Casado Coca v. Spain*, Eur. Ct. HR, Series A, No. 285-A, Judgment of 24 February 1994, 18 EHRR 1.

of the Bill in question, this appears to be a tenable view. On the other hand, the Supreme Court of Canada held that a ban on tobacco advertising was disproportionate and unconstitutional, violating the right to free speech under the Canadian Charter of Rights and Freedoms, in *R. J. R.-MacDonald v. Attorney-General of Canada*.[93]

The right to free speech in the USA protects commercial advertising even more strongly. In *44 Liquourmart, Inc. v. Rhode Island*,[93a] state legislation sought to impose a ban on advertising liquor otherwise than at the place of sale. The Supreme Court held that the ban was unconstitutional. It was well established that commercial speech could be regulated to advance a substantial governmental interest, as long as the regulation directly advances that interest and is no more extensive than necessary to serve the interest.[93b]

Preventing untruthful and misleading messages about lawful products and services, in order to ensure that consumers received accurate information, is a substantial state interest. However, a total ban on advertising other than at the point of sale effectively suppressed speech by reference to its content. Commercial speech does not fall into the category of 'law-value' speech which can be regulated in order to prevent consequential or secondary harms. The ban therefore had to be reviewed with special care, being accepted only if the speech is deceptive or is related to some unlawful activity. The ban was not shown to advance a legitimate state interest (manipulation of the market to discourage liquor purchases not being a legitimate interest for First Amendment purposes) and was in any case more extensive than necessary in order to serve the interest. A similar conclusion was reached in respect of restrictions on advertising non-smoking tobacco products and cigars, for example banning such advertisements within 1,000 feet of a school, in *Lorillard Tobacco Co. v. Reilly, Attorney General of Massachusetts*[93c] the Supreme Court accepted that there was sufficient evidence to show that the provisions served a substantial state interest, but held that they restricted commercial speech more than necessary to achieve that interest.

It will be interesting to see whether courts in the UK and Strasbourg are as willing as the Supreme Court of the USA to give strong protection to the operation of the free market against interference with truthful and non-misleading advertising.

Political advertising is an indivisible aspect of free speech in the USA under the First Amendment to the Constitution,[94] but has always been treated with greater suspicion in the UK and Australia. There is a feeling that allowing political interest groups to buy publicity gives an advantage to the wealthy in the democratic process. Where the money is provided for political parties by commercial organizations or individuals, there is a risk that they will have a disproportionate influence on governmental policy if their preferred candidates are elected. For this reason, spending on

---

[93] [1995] 3 SCR 199, SC of Canada.

[93a] 116 S. Ct. 1495, 134 L. Ed. 2d 711 (1996), US Sup. Ct.

[93b] *Central Hudson Gas & Electricity Corporation v. Public Services Commission* 447 US 557 (1980).

[93c] Judgment delivered 28 June 2001, to be reported (2001) 533 US.

[94] *Buckley v. Valeo* 424 US 1 (1976). See D. Tucker, 'Representation-Reinforcing Review: Arguments about Political Advertising in Australia and the United States', in T. Campbell and W. Sadurski (eds.), *Freedom of Communication* (Aldershot: Dartmouth, 1994), 161–77.

political election campaigns is restricted in the UK,[95] and political advertising on television and radio is absolutely prohibited.[96] Despite these legitimate concerns, the High Court of Australia in 1992 struck down legislation designed to restrict political advertising in the run-up to elections and referendums. In the process, the High Court built on an implied constitutional right to freedom of communication on governmental matters which was held to restrict the power of the Commonwealth Parliament to enact such legislation, risking accusations of acting anti-democratically and of turning freedom of expression into a commercial right.[97]

The UK's highly restrictive approach to political advertising has been widely drawn and even more widely interpreted. The Broadcasting Act 1990 requires the ITC and the RA to 'do all that they can to secure' the prohibition of 'any advertisement which is inserted by or on behalf of any body whose objects are wholly or mainly of a political nature' and of 'any advertisement which is directed towards any political end'.[98] The courts have interpreted 'political' as having the same meaning as under the fourth head of the categorization of charities adopted in *Income Tax Special Purposes Commissioners v. Pemsel,*[99] namely 'other purposes beneficial to the community', from which any trust for any political object is excluded. For this purpose, securing a change in the law anywhere in the world is regarded as political. Thus in *McGovern v. Attorney General,*[100] Slade J had held that a trust established to advance the objects of Amnesty International, which included the abolition of the death penalty, was incapable of enjoying charitable status. In *R. v. Radio Authority, ex parte Bull*[101] the Court of Appeal held that it was open to the RA to adopt the same approach when deciding whether a person or organization should be allowed to purchase advertising time on the radio. The court regarded the definition of 'political' as fixed for all purposes, despite the different policy considerations relating to charities and radio advertising respectively. With respect, this is unsatisfactory, as it denies a means of campaigning against the law of a country which has failed to implement basic human rights and humanitarian values which bind it in international law. It shields governments in the UK and elsewhere from criticism, so it is perhaps not surprising that the government favours its retention.[102]

The Court of Appeal in the same case decided that an organization has 'mainly'

---

[95] See now Political Parties, Elections and Referendums Act 2000, Parts V and VI.

[96] Broadcasting Act 1990, ss. 8 (television broadcasting), 92 (radio).

[97] *Australian Capital Television Pty. Co. Ltd. v. Commonwealth* (1992) 177 CLR 106, HC Aust. See D. Z. Cass, 'Through the Looking Glass: The High Court of Australia and the Right to Political Speech', in Campbell and Sadurski (eds.), *Freedom of Communication* 179–98; E. Barendt, 'Importing United States Free Speech Jurisprudence?', ibid., 57–75.

[98] Broadcasting Act 1990, ss. 8(1), (2) (ITC) and 92(1), (2) (RA).

[99] [1891] AC 531, HL.

[100] [1982] Ch. 321.

[101] [1998] QB 294, [1997] 2 All ER 561, CA. See J. Stevens and D. Feldman, 'Broadcasting Advertisements by Bodies with Political Objects, Judicial Review, and the Influence of Charities Law' [1997] *PL* 615–622; B. M. Sheldrick, 'Judicial Review and Judicial Reticence: The Protection of Political Expression under the Common Law' (1998) 3 *J. of Civil Liberties* 191–205.

[102] *Government's Response to the Report of the Neill Committee, The Funding of Political Parties in the UK,* Cm. 4413 (July 1999); Department of Trade and Industry and Department of Culture, Media and Sport, *A New Future for Communications,* 63, paras. 6.6.3–6.6.5.

political objects only if at least 75 per cent of its objects are political. Although surprised that the RA had felt able to conclude that Amnesty's objectives were mainly political, the court was willing to defer to their judgment on the basis that they were a lay, non-expert body doing a difficult job. The court encouraged Amnesty to make a further application to the RA which could be considered in the light of the court's judgment on the meaning of 'mainly'. This led to permission being granted, and avoided the delay which might have been caused had the Court of Appeal decided in favour of Amnesty and the RA appealed to the House of Lords. However, deference to a body like the RA in relation to its *vires* cannot be justified, having the capacity to undermine much of administrative law (not to mention the Rule of Law) and, in that case, an important aspect of freedom of political expression.

(7) SELF-REGULATION AND THE D NOTICE SYSTEM[103]

One of the ways in which the press displays its sense of responsibility towards the state is its participation in a system of informal regulation of the content of publications in the interests of defence. The Defence Press and Broadcasting Committee (DPBC) is a joint committee of the Ministry of Defence, publishers, and broadcasters, which offers advice on proposed publications and broadcasts.

The Committee is concerned with damage to national security. Specifically, the DPBC reviews whether the publication or broadcast contains information which falls into categories which the government considers it necessary to keep secret. If it concludes that a publication threatens national security within one of its areas of concern, it suggests changes. If the advice is not accepted, it may issue a D notice to the editor, publisher, or broadcasting body. There is one D notice, in a standard form, for each area of the Committee's responsibility as defined (fairly broadly) by the Ministry of Defence. At present, there are eight categories of D notice: (1) defence plans, operational capability, state of readiness, and training; (2) defence equipment; (3) nuclear weapons and equipment; (4) radio and radar transmissions; (5) cyphers and communications; (6) British security and intelligence services; (7) war precautions and civil defence; (8) photography, etc. of defence establishments and installations.

The DPBC works in two main ways. In the first, a publisher or broadcaster approaches the Committee, through its secretary (who is normally a senior officer in the armed forces, currently a rear admiral) and asks whether the Committee feels that any changes are needed in the publication to avoid damaging the national interest. The second method is for contact to be initiated by the secretary to the Committee, who receives information from publishers and others—including reading the *Publisher* magazine—about forthcoming books and programmes. When he hears of a publication or programme which, he thinks, might fall within one of the categories of material with which the committee is concerned, he may write to the publisher or broadcaster, saying that it is possible that the publication may contain information within the scope of one of the categories and offering to advise on whether it does so

---

[103] D. Fairley, 'D Notices, Official Secrets and the Law' (1990) 10 *Oxford J. of Legal Studies* 430–40.

if the broadcaster or publisher wishes to supply a copy of the book. The tone of the letter is helpful and businesslike. There are no threats. Where the publisher is one who does not normally participate in the D notice system, copies of the relevant D notice and of the *General Introduction to the D Notice System*[104] are enclosed.

Participation in the process is entirely voluntary, as are any changes which are made in the text or programme as a result of the Committee's advice (which is only advice: it has no legal force). The Committee will not give a security clearance; it has no power to do so. If it considers that a programme or publication does not threaten national security, the Secretary writes to inform the publisher, editor, or broadcaster that he does not consider that any change is necessary to avoid potential prejudice to national security.

The fact that the Committee's advice has no legal force has both an up side and a down side from the point of view of a publisher, editor, or broadcaster. The positive aspect is that the editor commits no criminal offence or tort merely by virtue of publishing in defiance of advice from the Committee. As the whole process is voluntary, and the press and broadcasters are strongly represented on the Committee (albeit heavily dependent on advice from the Ministry of Defence and service members) it is a form of self-regulation. The negative side of this is that a notification that no advice is considered necessary does not assure the editor, broadcaster, or publisher that the publication will not attract civil or criminal sanctions. This is made clear in the Committee's *General Introduction to the D Notice System*, paragraph 8 of which states:

'There is no direct relationship between the D Notice system and the Official Secrets Acts. Nothing in the D Notice system relieves an editor of his responsibilities under the Acts, though D Notices have a useful function in reminding editors that publication of the information which they protect could contravene the provisions of the Act.'

The D notices therefore have a warning function, but the fact that no D notice has been issued, or advice given, does not exonerate an editor. The Committee does not perform a judicial function, and is a consultative, negotiating body between the Ministry and the press and broadcasting media. Nevertheless, there is a substantial overlap between the Acts and the D notices. For example, D notice No. 6, *British Security and Intelligence Services*, after stating that the security and intelligence services must work as far as possible in conditions of secrecy (a proposition which many would dispute), asserts that the publication of detailed information about their activities or methods, or the disclosure of identities, is likely to prejudice present and past operations, and make day-to-day work more difficult. It goes on to request (this is, after all, a voluntary system) that nothing should be published without reference to the secretary about, *inter alia*, specific operations, how operational methods are applied, identities of service employees and their families (although the name and personal details concerning the new Director of MI5 were released, in a remarkable moment of openness, in December 1991), the addresses and telephone numbers of the services,

---

[104] This is a very informative document; the text is reproduced in S. H. Bailey, D. J. Harris, and B. L. Jones, *Civil Liberties Cases and Materials*, 3rd edn. (London: Butterworths, 1991), 431–2.

organizational structures, numerical strengths, training, and technical advances. The list of matters covered is so extensive that it would be surprising if many matters were excluded which could possibly be caught by the Official Secrets Acts.

Similarly, the D notice system confers no defence on participants against actions by the government for restraint of publication, or account of profits, on the ground of breach of confidence. When in 1987 the BBC was planning to broadcast a radio series, *My Country Right or Wrong*, exploring aspects of national security in the light of the *Spycatcher* litigation, the producer sought advice from the secretary of DPBC, who indicated that no advice was necessary. Despite this, the government sought, and obtained, injunctions restraining the BBC from broadcasting the series on the ground of breach of confidence.[105] Although the injunctions were subsequently lifted when the government acknowledged that the programmes were no threat to security, the BBC was subjected to a great deal of expense and trouble, and the programmes were long delayed, some being broadcast only in 1991 by Channel 4, the BBC having apparently got cold feet.

This lack of fit between the advice (or lack of it) given, and D notices issued (or not), by the Secretary and the Committee on the one hand, and the actions of government in pursuing legal remedies to restrain or penalize publication on the other, has brought the D notice system into some disrepute. Editors and publishers wonder what benefit they obtain from seeking and complying with advice from the Committee. The secretary has been reported as saying that his advice concerns a threat to national security, not whether there is a breach of confidence. This is undoubtedly true. If one wanted advice on the latter point, one would be unlikely to seek it from a rear admiral at the Ministry of Defence, or a committee made up of publishers and defence officials. On the other hand, it would be useful if the Committee could speak for the Department, instead of representing a compromise between different interest groups. It would then be able to advise an editor whether the Department intended to take legal proceedings in the event of the broadcast or publication going ahead. What is unhelpful in the present scheme is not that the Committee and its secretary do not give legal advice, but that they cannot give advice about the way in which the Department intends to exercise its discretion to bring proceedings. Without such a power, the advice is likely to be of limited value to the publishing and broadcasting community, and is most useful to the Department in frightening off a certain number of possibly lawful publications behind closed doors, without the need for or benefit of a judicial hearing.[106] The collaborative, consultative nature of the D notice system, intended as its great virtue, is threatening to undermine it because of the limited value of the advice which it can give.

---

[105] See Fairley, 'D Notices', above.

[106] In relation to the newspaper publication of extracts from Anthony Cavendish's *Inside Intelligence* (privately printed in 1987), in respect of which the Secretary had given a 'no advice' intimation, the government's action for breach of confidence failed. However, the publishers were taken all the way to the House of Lords, and would probably have lost had the government's claim been based on the contents rather than the class of material into which the publication fell: *Lord Advocate v. The Scotsman Publications Ltd.* [1990] 1 AC 812, [1989] 2 All ER 852, HL.

14.3 THE EXTENT OF PROTECTION FOR MEDIA FREEDOMS

Originally, freedom of the press related only to freedom to set up a printing press and to publish without prior restraint by the state. To some extent, echoes of this minimalist approach continued to resonate in judicial pronouncements in England and Wales until the passing of the Human Rights Act 1998. For example, in *British Steel Corporation v. Granada Television Ltd.*[107] Lord Wilberforce said: 'Freedom of the press imports, generally, freedom to publish without precensorship, subject always to the laws relating to libel, official secrets, sedition and other recognised inhibitions'. This was an unduly narrow view, which reflected the failure of the UK to provide protection for freedom of expression, and the consequential freedom of judges and Parliament to limit press freedom more or less as they choose.

In the USA, where the First Amendment gives constitutional status to press freedom, and in the law of the ECHR, media freedom has a far wider connotation. It is understood to mean the rights of writers, publishers, and broadcasters to conduct their activities and purvey information and ideas, and to be protected when their scrutiny of government offends it. It means, also, the right of the public to a press which is independent of domination by government and private interests alike. However, it is still essentially a negative rather than positive right. In other words, it limits the range of circumstances and ways in which it is legitimate for public authorities to interfere with free expression. It usually places no obligation on the state to make available the facilities and materials which people need in order to take advantage of the freedom.[108]

There are, then, two distinct aspects to freedom of the media today so far as they bear on civil liberties and human rights: first, the extent of rights to obtain and communicate information and publish opinions; secondly, the scope of protections for journalists, publishers, and others against attack by government and others. Each of these is now coloured by ECHR Article 10,[109] and its incorporation in English law by the Human Rights Act 1998.

This section examines the extent to which the right to freedom of expression, as elaborated in Article 10(1), is protected in English law, concentrating on rights to receive and impart information.

[107] [1981] 1 All ER 417 at 455.

[108] Dr. Marshall points out that Art. 125 of the 1936 USSR Constitution did undertake to provide such materials and facilities, although this provision had limited practical operation: G. Marshall, 'Press Freedom and Free Speech Theory' [1992] *PL* at 40. On positive rights in England and Wales, see Ch. 13, section 3, above.

[109] Art. 10 provides: '1. Everyone has the right to freedom of expression. This right shall include freedom to hold opinions and to receive and impart information and ideas without interference by public authority and regardless of frontiers. This article shall not prevent States from requiring the licensing of broadcasting, television or cinema enterprises. 2. The exercise of these freedoms, since it carries with it duties and responsibilities, may be subject to such formalities, conditions, restrictions or penalties as are prescribed by law and are necessary in a democratic society, in the interests of national security, territorial integrity or public safety, for the prevention of disorder or crime, for the protection of health or morals, for the protection of the reputation or rights of others, for preventing the disclosure of information received in confidence, or for maintaining the authority and impartiality of the judiciary'.

(1) FREEDOM TO RECEIVE INFORMATION AND IDEAS WITHOUT INTERFERENCE BY
PUBLIC AUTHORITY AND REGARDLESS OF FRONTIERS

Obtaining information is an essential part of the job of any investigative journalist, political commentator, or scholar, and is therefore an important incident of freedom of expression whatever rationale for the freedom is adopted. The general rule in English law is that a person is free to receive any information whatsoever, although there may be restrictions on the use which can be made of some types of information. Until the Official Secrets Act 1911, section 2 was repealed by the Official Secrets Act 1989, it was an offence for a person to receive certain types of secret material and information. Now, by contrast, a person who merely receives material commits no offence although it may be an offence under section 1(2) of the Official Secrets Act 1920 or under the 1989 Act to disclose or refuse to return the material. (The effects of the 1989 Act are explained in Chapter 15, below.)

Nevertheless, there remain substantial limitations on freedom of access to information. The main one is the ingrained secrecy which afflicts the civil service, and much of the rest of the British establishment, and which works to the advantage of governments by insulating them to some extent against the uncomfortable, albeit democratically important, experience of public scrutiny.[110] This attitude is not easy to reconcile with a functioning democracy. As noted in Chapter 13, above, the Freedom of Information Act 2000 is hedged about with so many exceptions that it does not mark a significant advance, in practical terms, on the Croham Directive of 1977, in which the head of the home Civil Service recommended that the 'working assumption' should be that all background material to decisions will be published, or the Code of Practice put in place by the government of John Major in the early 1990s.

There remain restrictions on the availability of public records. The Public Records Act 1958 restricts the public availability of administrative or departmental records belonging to the monarch in the UK or elsewhere, in right of HM government, including records of or held by any government department in the UK (other than registers of births, deaths, marriages, and adoptions), offices, commissions, and other bodies or establishments under HM government in the UK.[111] Such records are preserved only if selected for permanent preservation, and are then not made available until, at the earliest, thirty years after 1 January in the year following the year in which the record was made. When the person making the selection considers that records which have been selected for preservation contain information which was obtained from members of the public under such conditions that it might constitute a breach of good faith to make the records available, the Lord Chancellor has an uncontrolled discretion to attach conditions to public access or to deny public access altogether for a further period. In addition, the government can sometimes make use of the law of breach of confidence to limit disclosure of information.

[110] C. Ponting, *Secrecy in Britain* (Oxford: Basil Blackwell, 1990), ch. 4; D. Vincent, *The Culture of Secrecy: Britain 1832–1998* (Oxford: Oxford University Press, 1998), 248–328.
[111] Public Record Act 1958, Sch. 1, para. 2(1). The Act does not apply to departments or bodies wholly or mainly concerned with Scottish affairs: ibid., para. 2(2).

(2) FREEDOM TO IMPART INFORMATION AND IDEAS WITHOUT INTERFERENCE BY PUBLIC AUTHORITY AND REGARDLESS OF FRONTIERS: THE LAW OF DEFAMATION

In principle, this freedom exists so far as it is not limited by law. Like other freedoms, it is residual. The issue, therefore, is the extent of the restrictions on the liberty in English law. A number of the most significant of these restrictions are discussed in Chapters 15 to 17, below. However, here it is appropriate to deal with one which is particularly important to the media, because of its pervasive implications for news reporting and the chilling effect on free expression of the financial consequences: the tort of defamation.[112]

The law of defamation operates to protect reputation, a legitimate ground, recognized under ECHR Article 10(2), for restricting freedom of expression. A publication which lowers a person in the opinion of right-thinking people is defamatory, infringes the right to reputation, and attracts an award of damages. Most legal persons, including corporate bodies, have a right to reputation, and so can normally sue in respect of statements which defame the corporation (as distinct from its officers). However, in 1993 the House of Lords held, in *Derbyshire County Council v. Times Newspapers Ltd.*, that governmental bodies such as local authorities are not entitled to sue for defamation, because there is an overriding public interest in a democracy in uninhibited criticism of the organs of government.[113] This decision finally addressed criticism by Tony Weir as long ago as 1972 of the previous rule,[114] and the Faulks Committee's recommendation that the right of public authorities to sue should be restricted.[115] Nevertheless, individual politicians and office holders may sue in respect of allegations of corruption or incompetence, and (as noted in Chapter 13) section 13 of the Defamation Act 1996 allows MPs to waive parliamentary privilege to enable them to sue for allegations about the performance of their parliamentary activities.

The threat of an action may inhibit free comment. Public figures, who depend for their livelihoods on publicity, may obtain substantial damages when the publicity is bad rather than good, unless the newspaper can establish a defence. In the late 1980s, juries began to show a tendency to award extraordinarily large sums in damages to public figures in libel actions. In 1987, Jeffrey (later Lord) Archer was awarded £500,000 for an allegation in the *Daily Star* that he had had sex with a prostitute (in July 2001 he was convicted of having committed perjury and perverted the course of justice during the 1987 trial, and was sentenced to four years' imprisonment). Mrs. Sutcliffe, the former wife of the Yorkshire Ripper, was awarded £600,000, reduced by a settlement between the parties to £60,000 following a successful appeal on quantum.[116] This had such a potentially chilling effect on newspaper editors and book

---

[112] C. Duncan and B. Neill, *Defamation*, 2nd edn. (London: Butterworths, 1983); E. Barendt, *Freedom of Speech* (Oxford: Clarendon Press, 1987), ch. 6; Robertson and Nicol, *Media Law*, ch. 2.

[113] [1993] AC 534, [1993] 1 All ER 1011, HL.

[114] J. A. Weir, 'Local Authority v. Critical Ratepayer—A Suit in Defamation' [1972A] *CLJ* 238.

[115] *Report of the Committee on Defamation* (Chairman: Mr. Justice Faulks), Cmnd. 5909 (1975), paras. 332*ff*.

[116] *Sutcliffe v. Pressdram Ltd.* [1991] 1 QB 153, [1990] 1 All ER 269, CA.

publishers that the threat or award of huge damages was held to be a disproportionate infringement of the right to freedom of expression under ECHR Article 10 when Lord Aldington was awarded damages of £1,500,000 against Count Tolstoy Miloslavsky in respect of allegations about the former's conduct during World War II.[117]

By this time, the English courts had woken up to the danger, and had begun to exercise some control over jury awards. When Esther Rantzen, the instigator of Child-line, was awarded £250,000 for a libel concerning an alleged cover-up in relation to an informant's offence, the Court of Appeal decided that it was excessive, and reduced it to £100,000, intimating that judges could legitimately give guidance to juries on reasonable levels of awards.[118] In *John v. MGN Ltd.*,[119] the Court of Appeal for the first time accepted that juries in defamation actions could be told, for purposes of comparison, typical levels of damages for pain and suffering caused by different kinds of physical injuries. Elton Hercules John, the singer and song-writer, had been the victim of untrue, offensive, and defamatory newspaper stories which had been published recklessly. The jury had awarded compensatory damages of £75,000 and exemplary damages of £275,000. The Court of Appeal, referring to the *Tolstoy Miloslavsky* case, reduced the awards to £25,000 and £50,000 respectively. More recently, the Court of Appeal has gone further, reversing a jury's findings of fact to exonerate a defendant newspaper in connection with an action over allegations relating to match-fixing in soccer. It has also upheld a judge's conclusion that criticism of the historical methods of David Irving, the right-wing historian of Germany's Third Reich, were justified, and that the historian had distorted historical facts. All this helps to discourage people from resorting to the courts to seek windfall compensation for real or imagined injuries.[120]

However, there are risks which may discourage publication in the public interest. Even where the newspaper knows or believes that the report is true, or that a comment is fair, it might be unwilling to risk trying to prove it. It can very difficult to establish an allegation on the balance of probabilities. Informants may be unwill-ing to be identified or testify (a special rule protects newpapers against orders to disclose their sources in defamation actions), and they might not be believed against the word of the public figure in court. Furthermore, if a newspaper tries to establish the truth of its allegations and fails, the attempt is likely to aggravate the damages.

In the USA, by contrast, the Supreme Court has long held that the First Amend-ment to the Constitution, which prohibits any abridgement of freedom of the press, restricts liability for defaming public figures to situations in which the defamer can be shown to have acted maliciously.[121] The decision reflected the 'profound national commitment to the principle that debate on public issues should be uninhibited,

---

[117] *Tolstoy Miloslavsky v. United Kingdom*, Eur. Ct. HR, Series A, No. 316-B, Judgment of 13 July 1995, 20 EHRR 442.

[118] *Rantzen v. Mirror Group Newspapers (1986) Ltd.* [1994] QB 670, [1993] 4 All ER 975, CA.

[119] [1997] QB 586, [1996] 2 All ER 35, CA. See J. Scott-Bayfield and J. Swann, 'Libel Damages: The Beginning of the End?' (1999) 4 *Yearbook of Copyright and Media Law* 104–23.

[120] *Irving v. Penguin Books and Lipstadt*, unreported, 20 July 2001, CA.

[121] *New York Times v. Sullivan* 376 US 254 (1964).

robust and wide open, and that it may well include vehement, caustic, and sometimes sharply unpleasant attacks on government and national and public officials'.[122]

This difference in approach is instructive, because it shows how complex is the exercise of balancing the rights which conflict when setting the scope of liability for defamation. It is obvious that freedom of expression is to be balanced against rights to reputation; that is clearly recognized in Article 10(2) of the European Convention on Human Rights. But the special rule in the USA requiring public figures to prove malice appears to show that freedom of expression has greater weight, and the right to a personal reputation lesser weight, when the expression concerns public figures than when it is about private citizens. Two factors contribute to this. There is a significant public interest in the behaviour of those who hold or seek public office. Democracy requires that the electorate should have full information about candidates for office. One might wonder why this should lead to a restriction of defamation liability where it is open to a defendant to justify a publication on the ground that it is true. However, the difficulty of establishing that a statement is true, and the risk that fear of defamation actions might inhibit people from publishing the truth about public figures, could justify a special restriction on liability. The argument is based on rule-utilitarian principles (calculating the benefits and harms of applying a general rule rather than looking only at the consequences of a particular act or omission): a rule which facilitates the free flow of opinions and information is likely to be less harmful than other rules. But there is another factor which runs parallel with that. Those who hold themselves out as public officials or potential leaders seek publicity, and it can plausibly be thought that they should accept the risk of damage arising from innocently mistaken publicity, though not malicious falsehoods. After all, politicians can benefit from inaccurately complimentary reports, so they should take the rough with the smooth and bear the risk that some reports will be misleadingly, but innocently, derogatory. This, however, is not a view which holds sway in the UK, where politicians are seen by the law (though not always by themselves) as merely ordinary citizens going about their everyday business.

This has the potential to stifle public debate and inhibit investigative journalism, and offers well known people a way to make some easy money (only the well off can usually afford to sue for defamation, as legal aid is not available). The extent of the chilling effect of potential liability for defamation is unclear. The only systematic study of it in Britain indicates that potential liability looms large in the thinking of editors, and can sometimes lead them to withdraw stories or give way to complaints about allegations which are reliable and in the public interest. The impact of uncertainty is greatest in broadcast media, which are subject to intrusive regulation apart from the law of defamation, and among regional newspapers and small publishers whose budgets and profit margins allow little, if any, risks to be taken.[123]

---

[122] Ibid. at 270 *per* Brennan J. The Supreme Court of India has taken a similar line, applying *New York Times v. Sullivan* when holding that prior restraint of defamatory publications is not available where the alleged defamation relates to a public official: *Rajagopal v. State of Tamil Nadu* [1995] 3 LRC 566, SC of India.

[123] E. Barendt, L. Lustgarten, K. Norrie, and H. Stephenson, *Libel and the Media: The Chilling Effect* (Oxford: Clarendon Press, 1997), especially ch. 9.

English law provides some ways of alleviating the risk, although they sometimes have the effect of increasing uncertainty. First, there is a marked reluctance to grant injunctions restraining publication pending trial of the action. English courts will not usually grant an interlocutory injunction to restrain publication of an alleged libel if the defendant is asserting qualified privilege for the publication, or intends to argue at trial that the allegation is true, because of the importance of leaving free speech unfettered until it is clear that an allegation is untrue and has infringed the claimant's rights.[124] This means that issuing a libel writ does not automatically lead to prior restraint of further discussion of the matter. Under the Human Rights Act 1998, prior restraint must not be granted in such cases if the defendant is neither present nor represented, unless the applicant has taken all reasonable steps to notify the defendant (usually an easy thing to do in media cases) or there are compelling reasons for not notifying the defendant (which will hardly ever be the case in a defamation action). Nor will prior restraint be granted unless the court is satisfied that the applicant is likely to establish a case for a permanent injunction at trial. The court must take account of the extent of any public interest in publication, and the extent to which the material has, or is about to, become available to the public, having particular regard to the importance of the right to freedom of expression and to the defendant's compliance with any relevant code of practice, such as the PCC Code.[125]

However, an injunction may still be granted in special circumstances. One is where further publication would give rise to a substantial risk of serious prejudice to the trial of the action. Publication then would be a contempt of court attracting strict liability,[126] and the court will grant an injunction restraining it. As libel actions are regularly tried before a jury, there is likely to be a substantial risk of prejudice if the allegations are repeated in, for example, a mass circulation popular newspaper, but the degree of risk and the seriousness of the prejudice will be affected by the likely time lag between the publication and the expected commencement of the trial of the action.[127] Another situation in which prior restraint may be allowed is where the defendant can be shown to be proposing, dishonestly and maliciously, to publish the material knowing that it is untrue.[128]

English law also provides certain defences against liability which help to mitigate the chilling effect of the law of defamation. These include (i) justification; (ii) absolute privilege; (iii) qualified privilege; and (iv) fair comment on a matter of public interest.

(i) Truth, or justification

At common law, a defendant is allowed to 'justify' (that is, assert the truth of) the defamatory statement. If it is shown to be true, the claimant cannot obtain damages,

---

[124] *Bonnard v. Perryman* [1891] 2 Ch. 269, CA, at 284–5 *per* Lord Coleridge CJ.

[125] Human Rights Act 1998, s. 12(2),(3),(4).

[126] Contempt of Court Act 1981, s. 2; see below, Ch. 17.

[127] *Attorney-General v. News Group Newspapers Ltd.* [1987] QB 1, [1986] 2 All ER 833, CA (allegations about Mr. Ian Botham's behaviour while on an England cricket tour to New Zealand; eleven-month delay between publication and likely trial made it inappropriate to grant injunction).

[128] *Quartz Hill Consolidated Mining Co. v. Beall* (1882) Ch. D 501, CA; *Harakas v. Baltic Mercantile and Shipping Exchange Ltd.* [1982] 1 WLR 958, [1982] 2 All ER 701, CA.

because he has no right to a reputation which is better than he deserves. This is a defence in relation to defamatory factual claims. By contrast, in some Australian states (New South Wales, Queensland, and Tasmania, as well as the Australian Capital Territory) truth is no defence unless, as well as being true, the publication is for the public benefit (in Queensland, Tasmania, and the ACT) or related to a matter of public interest (in New South Wales).[129] Furthermore, courts in Australia, while respecting rights to freedom of speech and publication,[130] tend to be slightly less reluctant than those in England to grant injunctions restraining publication of alleged libels pending trial.[131] There are historical reasons for this: when the country was a penal colony, the law of libel was designed to prevent people raking up a convict's past, perhaps long after he had served his sentence and become a respectable member of society. The defamation action there protects the right to a fresh start, or to protect recent reputation against the past. However, the effect has been that, in law, the right to a fresh start for convicted criminals who have served their sentences, a private interest, outweighs the public interest in freedom of information about public figures. For example, it made it easier for Sir Joh Bjelke-Petersen, the former premier of Queensland, to suppress publication of information concerning corruption and incompetence in the government of Queensland, until it was finally brought into the open by a Royal Commission of Inquiry (the Fitzgerald Inquiry).[132]

In the era of the Human Rights Act 1998, the Australian comparison points up an important issue about the defence of justification. A defamatory statement, even if true, can do a great deal of harm to its subject. The common law in England and Wales takes the view that a person has no right to an undeservedly good reputation, even if the events casting doubt on it occurred many years ago. Yet there are privacy interests, protected by ECHR Article 8, which may be affected, as well as the interest in reputation which does not rank as a fundamental or human right under the ECHR. While truth is a defence to an action for defamation, it is no defence to an action for breach of confidence, unless there is a public interest in revealing that truth at that time to the target audience. In view of the expansion of breach of confidence towards the point where it will provide a remedy for invasion of privacy more generally, as discussed in Chapters 9 and 11 above, it is at least possible that English law is moving closer to the position in New South Wales, Queensland, Tasmania, and the Australian Capital Territory, albeit by a different route.

(ii) Absolute privilege

Absolute privilege (i.e. protection against liability, even if the person making a publication is acting maliciously, recklessly, or negligently) attaches to statements made in the course of proceedings in Parliament under Article IX of the Bill of Rights 1689, although (as noted in Chapter 13) section 13 of the Defamation Act 1996 allows a

---

[129] See R. P. Balkin and J. L. R. Davis, *Law of Torts*, 2nd edn. (Sydney: Butterworths, 1996), 543–4, 548–9.

[130] *Church of Scientology of California Inc. v. Readers' Digest Services Pty. Ltd.* [1980] 1 NSWLR 344.

[131] See *National Mutual Life Association of Australasia Ltd. v. GTV Corporation Pty. Ltd.* [1989] VR 747; *Chappell v. TCN Channel Nine Pty. Ltd.* (1988) 14 NSWLR 153; Balkin and Davis, *Law of Torts*, 620–1.

[132] *Report of a Commission of Inquiry Pursuant to Orders in Council* (Brisbane: Queensland Government Printer, 1989).

member of either House in certain circumstances to waive the privilege for the purpose of bringing libel proceedings, and at common law to statements by judges, parties, counsel, and witnesses in the course of judicial proceedings. Fair and accurate reports of proceedings before courts in the UK, the European Court of Justice, the European Court of Human Rights, and any international criminal tribunal (such as the international tribunal on war crimes in the former Yugoslavia) are absolutely privileged.[133]

(iii) Qualified privilege

There are several qualified privileges at common law and under statute.

(a) **Qualified privilege at common law.** At common law, the privileges are 'qualified' rather than absolute, in that a defendant loses the benefit of them if shown to have acted with malice, i.e. not believing that the statement was true, being reckless as to whether it was true or false, or pursuing an improper purpose.[133a] Qualified privilege at common law protects the media against liability for defamatory statements made in pursuit of a legal, moral, or social duty. Traditionally this applied to disclosures in the course of private relationships: providing confidential references by request; making disclosures of suspected impropriety to employers, or to the controlling bodies of professions or clubs; and so on. This did not generally protect the press, as they could not usually show a sufficiently close community of interest with the members of the public to whom the information was being disclosed. The English approach contrasted with that in the USA, where (as noted above) newspapers benefit from the constitutional right to freedom of speech and freedom of the press under the First Amendment in order to promote frank and robust debate, particularly on political issues. American public figures cannot succeed in an action for defamation unless they show that the defamatory material was published maliciously, so they cannot use defamation law to gag press criticism.[134] A similar approach was adopted in India.[135]

In Australia in 1994, the High Court developed a slightly different rule out of the recently recognized implied constitutional right to freedom of communication on political and governmental matters. In two cases, the court decided that there was a qualified privilege against defamation liability in respect of publications relating to government and politics, as long as the people publishing them were not aware that the relevant statements were false, were not reckless as to whether they were true or false, and had published reasonably. The reasonableness of publication takes account of such matters as whether the defendant took reasonable care in the circumstances to verify the statements before publishing.[136] The court's approach was reaffirmed in *Lange v. Australian Broadcasting Corporation*.[137] The Supreme Court of South

---

133 Defamation Act 1996, s. 14.

133a See P. Mitchell, 'Malice in Qualified Privilege' [1999] *PL* 328–40

134 See, e.g. *New York Times Co. v. Sullivan* (1964) 376 US 254.

135 *Rajagopal (R.) v. State of Tamil Nadu* [1994] 6 SCC 632, SC of India.

136 *Theophanous v. Herald & Weekly Times Ltd.* (1994) 182 CLR 104, HC of Aust.; *Stephens v. Western Australia Newspapers Ltd.* (1994) 182 CLR 211, HC of Aust. See Balkin and Davis, *Law of Torts*, 2nd edn., 577–9.

137 (1997) 189 CLR 520, HC of Aust.

Africa has adopted a similar approach in a private-law, non-constitutional context.[138]

Among the press, there was a good deal of support for developing a defence of qualified privilege along either American or Australian lines, to give added protection to the media for investigative work in relation to political activities and issues. Some commentators were enthusiastically of the same mind,[139] while others were more cautious, stressing the different constitutional and social contexts within which the American and Australian rules developed and operated.[140] For example, the European Court of Human Rights has regularly held that the press performs a vital function as a public watchdog which needs to be carefully protected under ECHR Article 10, having duty to impart information and ideas which it is the right of members of the public to receive. At the same time, the Court has allowed media freedom to be restricted to protect people's reputations and legitimate public interests.[141] The legitimacy of protecting reputation, provided for expressly in ECHR Article 10(2), excludes an American-style limitation on defamation actions by public figures: those who push themselves into the public eye do not necessarily thereby waive their right to a reputation.[142] The duties and responsibilities, which Article 10(2) mentions as lying on those who exercise freedom of expression, include a duty to take reasonable steps to check the reliability of information which could harm someone, before publishing it. (A corollary of this is that the law must permit the defendant in defamation proceedings to defend himself on the ground that reasonable steps were taken to establish the veracity of the statements, and (if appropriate) that they were in fact true.)[143]

In *Reynolds v. Times Newspapers Ltd.*[144] the House of Lords rejected an argument for a blanket qualified privilege for all publications on political and governmental matters, such as had been accepted by the High Court of Australia. Nevertheless, it accepted in appropriate circumstances the qualified privilege existing at common law

[138] *National Media Ltd. v. Bogoshi* 1998 (4) SA 1196.

[139] See, e.g. I. Loveland, 'A Free Trade in Ideas and Outcomes', in I. Loveland (ed.), *Importing the First Amendment: Freedom of Speech and Expression in Britain, Europe and the USA* (Oxford: Hart Publishing, 1998), 1–21; I. Loveland, *Political Libels* (Oxford: Hart Publishing, 2000), chs 7, 9, and 10.

[140] E. Barendt, 'Importing the United States Free Speech Jurisprudence?', in T. Campbell and W. Sadurski (eds.), *Freedom of Communication* (Aldershot: Dartmouth, 1994), 57–75; Sir Stephen Sedley, 'The First Amendment: A Case for Import Controls?', in Loveland (ed.), *Importing the First Amendment*, 23–7.

[141] See, e.g. *Oberschlick v. Austria*, Eur. Ct. HR, Series A, No. 204, Judgment of 23 May 1991, 19 EHRR 389; *Castells v. Spain*, Eur. Ct. HR, Series A, No. 236, Judgment of 23 April 1992, 14 EHRR 445, at para. 43; *Jersild v. Denmark*, Eur. Ct. HR, Series A, No. 298, Judgment of 23 September 1994, 19 EHRR 1 at para. 31; and the discussion of the scope of rights under Art. 10 in Ch. 13, above.

[142] The public-figure defence was also rejected by the Supreme Court of Canada, in a non-political case: *Hill v. Church of Scientology of Toronto* (1995) 126 DLR (4th) 129.

[143] See, e.g. *Thorgeirson v. Iceland*, Eur. Ct. HR, Series A, No. 239, Judgment of 25 June 1992, 14 EHRR 843; *Fressoz and Roire v. France*, Eur. Ct. HR, App. No. 29183/95, Judgment of 21 January 1999, 31 EHRR 2 at para. 54; *Bladet Tromsø and Stensaas v. Norway*, Eur. Ct. HR, App. No. 21980/93, Judgment of 20 May 1999; *Nilsen and Johnsen v. Norway*, Eur. Ct. HR, App. No. 23118/93, Judgment of 25 November 1999, 30 EHRR 878; and see further *News Verlag GmbH v. Austria*, Eur. Ct. HR, App. No. 31457/96, Judgment of 11 January 2000.

[144] [1999] 3 WLR 1010, HL. On this case, and Australian and New Zealand defamation litigation concerning a former New Zealand Premier, see K. Williams, 'Defaming Politicians: The Not So Common Law' (2000) 63 *MLR* 748–56.

could apply to media publications, expressly recognizing for the first time in English defamation law that the interest of the public in receiving information about political matters entails a correlative duty on the press to publish it. Furthermore, the privilege potentially extends to information about political matters in other countries: the plaintiff in *Reynolds* was the former Irish Taoiseach and leader of the Fianna Fáil party, who claimed damages in respect of an article in the British mainland edition of the *Sunday Times*. Allegations about his behaviour were of public concern in the UK because he had been closely associated with the Northern Ireland peace process. However, the privilege, as it now applies to the media, is hedged about with restrictions. In order to benefit from it, a defendant must establish that it was in the public interest to publish the material. Whether this is so will depend on a number of factors, including the seriousness of the allegation, the nature of the information, the extent to which it is a subject of public concern, the reliability of the source of the information, the steps taken to verify it, the urgency of the matter, whether the claimant has been invited to comment on it, whether the article contained at least the gist of the claimant's response, the tone of the article (including whether it distinguishes between facts, allegations, and conclusions drawn from facts), and the timing and other circumstances of the publication.[145]

This approach has the merit of allowing media freedom and the right to receive and impart information to be given considerable weight, while preventing any one factor from being determinative. Thus, for example, a journalist might be able to establish that proper steps were taken to verify a story without revealing the name of the original source (if it is desired to keep the source secret). There can be little doubt that the defence of qualified privilege now provides the media with a defence which is capable of meeting the requirements of ECHR Article 10, and allowing the public to receive information about questionable behaviour by people generally, whether or not it relates to politics.

On the other hand, the flexibility carries with it significant uncertainty. This can impose two sorts of costs, apart from those intrinsic to news-gathering and promulgation. First, it requires the media to expend considerable time and care in deciding whether to run a completed story, taking account of an assessment of the risk of legal liability. These costs were considerable, even before the decision in *Reynolds*, particularly in national newspapers and the broadcasting media.[146] Secondly, the uncertainty about the level of risk may lead to stories which are in the public interest not being published, particularly in parts of the media which are risk-averse (such as broadcasting and regional newspapers) or when organizations known to be willing and able to maintain actions for defamation (such as the Police Federation) might become involved.[147] Yet there is in principle no reason why the media should be exempt from the obligation which the law normally imposes on people to take reasonable care when doing things in the line of business which are likely to damage others.[148]

---

[145] [1999] 3 WLR 1010 at 1027 *per* Lord Nicholls of Birkenhead.
[146] E. Barendt, L. Lustgarten, K. Norrie, and H. Stephenson, *Libel and the Media: The Chilling Effect* (Oxford: Clarendon Press, 1997), chs 3 and 5.
[147] Ibid., chs 4 and 5.
[148] See *Lange v. Atkinson* [1998] 3 NZLR 424 at 477 *per* Tipping J.

(b) **Qualified privilege under statute.** Section 15 of the Defamation Act 1996 (replacing section 7 of the Defamation Act 1952) confers qualified privilege on publications listed in Schedule 1 to the Act. In each case, an aggrieved party can defeat the privilege by proving that the publication was with malice. The privileged publications fall into two groups.

For the first group of publications, listed in Part I of the Schedule, the privilege is subject only to the proof of malice. They comprise:

- fair and accurate reports of proceedings in public of a legislature, or before a court, or of a person appointed by a government or legislature to hold a public inquiry, anywhere in the world;[149]

- a fair and accurate copy of or extract from any register or other document required by law to be open to public inspection, or from matter published by or on the authority of a government or legislature or by an international organization or international conference, anywhere in the world;[150]

- any notice or advertisement published by, or on the authority of, a court, or of a judge or officer of a court, anywhere in the world.[151]

Items falling within the second group of publications are privileged unless the claimant shows either (i) that the material was published with malice;[152] or (ii) that, after the publication, the defendant was requested to publish in a suitable manner a letter or statement by way of explanation or contradiction, and refused or neglected to do so.[153] Publications privileged on this basis, under Part II of Schedule 1 to the 1996 Act, comprise:

- a fair and accurate copy of, or extract from, a notice or other matter issued for the information of the public by or on behalf of the European Parliament or European Commission, or the legislature of or an authority performing governmental functions in an EU Member State, or an international organization or international conference;[154]

- a fair and accurate copy of, or extract from, a document made available by the European Court of Justice, or by a court in any EU Member State, or by a judge or officer of such a court;[155]

- a fair and accurate report of proceedings at a public meeting or sitting in the UK of a local authority (or one of its committees), justices of the peace acting in a non-judicial capacity, an inquiry appointed by government or under statute, and any other statutory body;[156]

- a fair and accurate report of proceedings at any public meeting (i.e. a meeting

---

[149] Defamation Act 1996, Sch. 1, paras. 1–3.
[150] Ibid., Sch. 1, paras. 4, 5, 7, 8.
[151] Ibid., Sch. 1 para. 6.
[152] Ibid., s. 15(1).
[153] Ibid., s. 15(2).
[154] Ibid., Sch. 1, para. 9.
[155] Ibid., Sch. 1, para. 10.
[156] Ibid., Sch. 1, para. 11.

held bona fide and lawfully for a lawful purpose and for the furtherance or discussion of a matter of public concern, whether admission to the meeting is general or restricted) in an EU Member State,[157] a category which includes all press conferences, and also protects written or printed press releases, even if not read out at the press conference.[158]

These defences represent a statutory balance between the interests of the press and public in the flow of information and ideas and the countervailing interests of public and private bodies which gives appropriate priority to the right to freedom of expression and is compatible with the requirements of ECHR Article 10. They foster public accountability and recognize the position of the press as a fourth estate, having a constitutional role as a channel of information between state officials and citizens.

(iv) Fair comment

This defence arises where the defendant can show that the publication consisted of fair comment, in good faith, on a matter of public interest. This is different from justification, in that it applies to expressions of opinion, not assertions of fact. To be fair, the opinion must be honestly held, and must be one which could fairly be held on the basis of any underlying facts which the defendant is able to prove, although it does not depend on proof of all the facts relied on.[159] None the less, the facts on which comment is based must be contained within the publication or broadcast in which the comment is made, in order to enable the reader, viewer, or listener to evaluate it. A letter in the correspondence column of a newspaper making defamatory comments could not be fair comment when the facts on which it was based had been published in an article published in an earlier issue of the newspaper.[160] The defence finds its rationale, in freedom of speech terms, in the value of fostering public debate with robust and robustly expressed views, rather than in the advancement of truth. To some extent, however, these two aims overlap, since one of the reasons for encouraging free debate is the hope that it will maximize the chance of finding the correct or best answer to problems. This aspiration is not advanced when the comment is dissociated from the facts and analysis giving rise to it.

(v) Innocent publication

Section 1 of the Defamation Act 1996 allows a defence where the defendant can show that he was not the author, editor, or publisher of the defamatory statement complained of, took reasonable care in relation to the publication, and did not know and had no reason to believe that what he did caused or contributed to the publication of the statement. This assists people like bookshop owners and internet service providers, who technically publish material when they sell a book or allow material to be

[157] Defamation Act 1996, Sch. 1, para. 12.
[158] *McCartan Turkington Breen (A Firm) v. Times Newspapers Ltd.* [2000] 3 WLR 1670, HL (NI), decided on provisions in the Defamation Act (Northern Ireland) 1955 which are for relevant purposes identical to those in para. 12 of Sch. 1 to the Defamation Act 1996.
[159] Defamation Act 1952, s. 6.
[160] *Telnikoff v. Matusevitch* [1992] 2 AC 343, HL.

posted on websites which they operate, but have no practical way of knowing what is in all the books or on all the sites. Such people are still liable, however, if they are informed of a defamatory statement in their stock or on their websites and take no effective action to remove the book or item.[161]

(vi) Offer of amends

A publisher has a defence if he offers to publish a suitable correction and sufficient apology in a reasonable manner and to pay such compensation as may be agreed between the parties or, in the absence of agreement, assessed by a court.[162] If the claimant rejects the offer, he can succeed in an action for defamation only if he proves that the publisher of the defamatory statement knew or had reason to believe that the statement was false before publishing it.[163] If the claimant accepts the offer of amends, there is no cause of action in defamation, although the claimant can sue if necessary to enforce the agreement. This is likely to be a useful way of resolving a large number of disputes where the publisher accepts that the publication was unjustified, and the claimant is more concerned to correct the mistake than to pursue a risky court action for the chance of large damages.

14.4 PROTECTIONS FOR THE MEDIA

Apart from the general protection of ECHR Article 10 and section 12 of the Human Rights Act 1998, already considered, there are three specific kinds of shield which English law offers the press against interference with their function of informing people about matters of legitimate public interest. First, there is the common-law exception from restraint of breaches of confidence. Secondly, there is statutory exemption from revealing sources in certain situations under the Contempt of Court Act 1981, section 10. Thirdly, there are special provisions in the Police and Criminal Evidence Act 1984 which purport to offer some protection against the grant of warrants to search for evidence amongst journalists' papers, and impose conditions on the circumstances in which journalists will be required to produce or grant access to material for the purpose of a criminal investigation.

(1) PUBLIC-INTEREST EXCEPTION TO DUTIES OF CONFIDENCE[164]

As explained in Chapter 11, a breach of confidence may be justified where there is a public interest in disclosure which outweighs the public interest in maintaining the confidence. This enables the media to publish, in certain circumstances, confidential material which shows that someone has been acting contrary to the public interest.

---

[161] *Godfrey v. Demon Internet Ltd.* [2000] 3 WLR 1020.
[162] Defamation Act 1996, s. 2.
[163] Ibid., s. 4.
[164] Robertson and Nicol, *Media Law*, 142–5.

The clearest example of this was provided in *Lion Laboratories Ltd. v. Evans*,[165] where the material published showed that a model of the Lion Intoximeter, a machine for measuring the alcohol levels in breath specimens, was unreliable. People were being convicted of drink-drive offences on the basis of evidence provided by these machines. It was held that the fact that the information was confidential to the manufacturer did not prevent publication, because it was in the public interest for it to be widely known in order to prevent unjust convictions. It was not necessary that the evidence should reveal criminality or even wrongdoing on the part of the person to whom the duty of confidence was owed. The issue is whether there is a genuine public interest in publication which is weightier than that in maintaining the confidence. This is an example of the courts allowing the press to exercise a role as scrutineers, on behalf of the public, over the conduct of business which protects the public.

In 1989 Professor Wacks described that case as the high-water mark of the public-interest justification for breach.[166] It is possible that the growing acceptance (both at common law and under the Human Rights Act 1998 through the caselaw of the European Court of Human Rights) of the media as a public-interest sector, with duties to inform the public at large, coupled with a loss of confidence in the ability of both private and public sectors to maintain high standards of probity, will make such cases more common. Nevertheless, there are limits to the public-interest exception to the duty of confidence. The main one is that publication must be the most appropriate way of proceeding. If the material appears to reveal criminal conduct, it will usually be more appropriate to make the material available to the police, so that they may investigate without having the matter prejudiced by publicity, than to spread it across the country in newspapers and broadcasts. For this reason, the publication of recordings of telephone conversations with a leading jockey, which were said to suggest that races were being fixed, was restrained in *Francome v. Mirror Group Newspapers Ltd.*[167] However, if the matter raises questions of genuine public interest, as where conversations appear to reveal serious miscarriages of justice and widespread police malpractice, it will not be inappropriate to retail the information to the public at large as well as drawing it to the attention of the authorities.[168] Knowing that such matters are receiving public attention is a powerful inducement to the authorities to investigate them thoroughly and make the results of the inquiry publicly available.

The duty of confidence protects private information more extensively than public information. However, the distinction between public and private information is not easy to draw. For example, information passed between partners during marriage might seem to be a classic example of private, or personal, information. For this reason, the Duke of Argyll was restrained, after the dissolution of his marriage to the Duchess of Argyll, from publishing, in a daily newspaper, details of the Duchess's behaviour during their marriage.[169] Yet in a very similar case, *Lennon v. News Group*

---

[165] [1985] QB 526, [1984] 2 All ER 417, CA.
[166] R. Wacks, *Personal Information: Privacy and the Law* (Oxford: Clarendon Press, 1989), 111 n. 233.
[167] [1984] 1 WLR 892, [1984] 2 All ER 408, CA.
[168] *Cork v. McVicar*, The Times, 1 November 1984.
[169] *Duchess of Argyll v. Duke of Argyll* [1967] 1 Ch. 302.

Newspapers Ltd.[170] the Court of Appeal refused to restrain publication by the ex-wife of John Lennon, the former Beatle, of intimate details of their relationship. It was said that Mr. Lennon had forfeited the protection of the courts for the privacy of the marriage relationship because he had himself courted publicity about his married life and had published details of the relationship for gain. This goes too far. One should be able to publicize some aspects of one's family life with the consent of one's partner, yet continue to assert the privacy of other facets of it against one's partner's attempt at unilateral exposure, unless disclosure significantly advances a strong public interest. Nevertheless, a willingness to have pictures of an event affecting one's family life, such as a wedding, published by one popular magazine will inevitably weaken a claim to confidentiality and privacy when another magazine wants to publish other, unauthorized, photographs of the same event.[171]

(2) KEEPING SOURCES SECRET: CONTEMPT OF COURT ACT 1981, SECTION 10

Obtaining information is an essential part of the job of journalists. The press, however free of formal constraints it might be, would have nothing to publish if journalists could not obtain information. As noted above, the absence of a general right to freedom of information in the UK makes journalists, like police officers, rely on informants, often from inside the organizations which the journalists are investigating. If it is accepted as being in the public interest to inform the public about certain matters, those who supply information may be acting in the public interest, yet be breaching civil duties of confidence and even the criminal law (particularly where governmental information is concerned, which is likely to be protected by the Official Secrets Act 1989). If the public-interest role of journalists is to flourish, it is important that their informants should not be discouraged from providing information, lest the flow of information to the public should dry up. The press therefore has a long and, on the whole, honourable tradition of refusing to divulge the identity of sources.

However, the common law recognized no privilege for journalists to set against the ordinary legal obligations which affect other people. They had no right to refuse to reveal their sources,[172] and could therefore be imprisoned and fined for contempt of court if they refused to comply with an order to reveal sources. The court had a discretion as to whether to make such an order, or to allow questions which might lead to a source being identified, and in exercising the discretion would balance the general public interests which might be served by requiring disclosure against the particular public interest in safeguarding the flow of information by allowing journalists to honour undertakings as to anonymity given to sources.[173] In *Attorney-General*

---

[170] [1978] FSR 573, CA.

[171] *Douglas v. Hello! Ltd.* [2001] 2 WLR 992, [2001] 2 All ER 289, CA.

[172] There is a limited exception in the form of the 'newspaper rule' in defamation: newspapers which are defendants in defamation actions cannot be forced to reveal the name of the source of the information on which they base the stories of which the claimants complain. For doubts about the scope of the rule, see *Georgius v. Delegates of Oxford University Press* [1949] 1 KB 729, [1949] 1 All ER 342. For the position in Australia, see *John Fairfax & Sons Ltd. v. Cojuangco* (1988) 165 CLR 364, HC of Australia.

[173] *British Steel Corporation v. Granada Television Ltd.* [1981] AC 1096, [1981] 1 All ER 417, HL. See A. Boyle, 'Freedom of Expression as a Public Interest in English Law' [1982] PL 574–612.

v. Mulholland, Attorney-General v. Foster,[174] journalists refused to answer questions which would have involved naming their sources during the inquiry conducted in 1963 by Viscount Radcliffe into the circumstances surrounding the operation of the Vassall spy ring. In contempt proceedings under section 1(2) of the Tribunals of Inquiry (Evidence) Act 1921, the High Court and the Court of Appeal rejected the journalists' claim to be entitled to keep their sources secret.[175] The journalists went to prison, and gained a degree of notoriety and a reputation for keeping confidences.

The experience of the USA shows that adopting a constitutional right to freedom of the press does not necessarily confer any incidental right to protect sources. There, too, constitutional law sets the value of the rule of law against the interests in press freedom and investigative journalism. In *Branzburg v. Hayes*[176] the Supreme Court by a majority held that the First Amendment protection for press freedom did not entitle journalists to refuse to testify before a grand jury about their description, used in published articles, of (in one case) how two men had made hashish from marijuana, and (in the other) about the Black Panthers (a militant organization suspected of involvement in crime). The interest in detecting crime overrode the journalist's interest in protecting the anonymity of his news sources: as White J, writing for the majority, put it, 'The crimes of news sources are no less reprehensible and threatening to the public interest when witnessed by a reporter than when they are not'. There is a public interest in the ability of the press to gather information, but providing information to the public is not a function of the press alone:

'The informative function asserted by representatives of the organised press . . . is also performed by lecturers, political pollsters, novelists, academic researchers and dramatists. Almost any author may quite accurately assert that he is contributing to the flow of information to the public, that he relies on confidential sources of information, and that those sources will be silenced if he is forced to make disclosures before a grand jury.'

Accordingly, suggestions that journalists are uniquely in need of a First Amendment privilege against disclosing information were considered to be unfounded. While the argument of the majority is probably exaggerated—journalists remain the most significant and regular purveyor of information to most people—the majority considered that claims that coerced disclosure would discourage people from providing information, or cause the flow of information to the public to dry up, or enable the police to turn journalists into an investigative arm of the state, were too speculative to override the interest in the detection of crime, particularly as grand juries can, and often do, sit in private.

However, public and legislative disquiet about the moral dilemmas which the decisions presented led to legislation to give some protection to journalists. In America, statutory 'shield laws' for journalists existed in some states before *Branzburg v. Hayes*, and more were enacted by states and Congress in response to the decision. In this country, it took nearly twenty years after the cases arising from the Vassall inquiry before a statute attempted to deal with the matter.

[174] [1963] 2 QB 477, CA.
[175] *A.-G. v. Mulholland; A.-G. v. Foster* [1963] 2 QB 477, CA. See also *A.-G. v. Clough* [1963] 1 QB 773.
[176] 408 US 665 (1972).

The opportunity came when the law of contempt fell to be considered by Parliament in the light of the report of the Phillimore Committee on Contempt of Court and the Law Commission's report on offences of interfering with the course of justice. Section 10 of the Contempt of Court Act 1981 provides:

'No court may require a person to disclose, nor is any person guilty of contempt for refusing to disclose, the source of information contained in a publication for which he is responsible, unless it be established to the satisfaction of the court that disclosure is necessary in the interests of justice or national security or for the prevention of disorder or crime.'

The section attempts to strike a balance between, on the one hand, the public interest in journalists and other authors being able to secure information by assuring their sources of anonymity and freedom from reprisal, and, on the other hand, competing public interests. It provides for the interest in freedom of information to be overridden only in order to secure the public interests in justice, national security, and prevention of disorder or crime, and then only if it is *necessary* to override the source's anonymity in order to secure one of the specified objectives. The exceptions were drafted to be consistent with ECHR Article 10(2), and are capable of being applied in a compatible manner, although (as we will see) the courts have only recently begun to do so consistently.

It has been accepted that the privilege is capable of applying to material obtained for the purposes of publication, even if it has not yet been included in a publication, since to hold otherwise would thwart the purpose of the Act in protecting the anonymity of sources of information.[177] The Act indicates a general policy which is applicable by analogy in cases other than court proceedings.[178] Unless the case falls within one of the exceptions, the section rules out both orders directly requiring naming of a source and orders to do anything which might indirectly enable the source to be identified, even if the effect is to make it impossible for someone to obtain recovery of goods in an action for conversion; the section therefore had to be considered when deciding whether to order a newspaper to return to the Ministry of Defence a leaked document, the property of the Ministry, which had marks on it which would have enabled security staff to identify the person who had passed the document to a journalist of the newspaper.[179] Even if a case falls within one of the exceptions, the court retains a discretion to refuse to order disclosure. Before the Human Rights Act 1998, it was said that it would rarely be appropriate to exercise the discretion in that way unless (for example) disclosure is necessary for the prevention of crime, but the crime is a very minor one, or disclosure would put the

---

[177] *X. Ltd. v. Morgan-Grampian (Publishers) Ltd.* [1991] 1 AC 1, [1990] 2 All ER 1.

[178] *Re an Inquiry Under the Company Securities (Insider Dealing) Act 1985* [1988] AC 660, [1988] 1 All ER 203, HL.

[179] *Secretary of State for Defence v. Guardian Newspapers Ltd.* [1985] AC 339 at 349–50, [1984] 3 All ER 601 at 606–7 *per* Lord Diplock, considering the relationship between s. 10 of the 1981 Act and the judge's discretion to order return of goods under s. 3(3) of the Torts (Interference with Goods) Act 1977. The paper was returned. A civil servant, Miss Sarah Tisdall, was subsequently prosecuted for an offence under s. 2 of the Official Secrets Act 1911 (now repealed and replaced by the Official Secrets Act 1989).

journalist's life at risk.[180] Now, the discretion must be exercised in accordance with the right to freedom of expression under ECHR Article 10. In practice, this will make little difference, because the scope of the exceptions is interpreted in the light of Article 10, so the Article is unlikely to produce much effect at the discretionary stage once the exceptions have been held to apply.

Initially, courts interpreted the exceptions widely, depriving the section of much of its effect[181] until a decision of the European Court of Human Rights in *Goodwin v. United Kingdom*[182] forced a rethink. An early case in the House of Lords, *Re an Inquiry Under the Company Securities (Insider Dealing) Act 1985*,[183] set the tone. Inspectors were appointed under the Financial Services Act 1986 to investigate suspicions of insider dealing by means of leaks of price-sensitive information from government departments. A journalist, Jeremy Warner, refused to answer questions which would have forced him to divulge his sources, arguing that section 10 of the Contempt of Court Act 1981 gave him a 'reasonable excuse' for his refusal.[184] For the inspectors, it was argued that the case fell within the exception to the privilege under section 10, disclosure being 'necessary . . . for the prevention of . . . crime'. The House of Lords rejected the journalist's arguments that disclosure would not be necessary unless the inspectors showed that there was no other way of obtaining the information, and that 'prevention of crime' did not extend to discovering who had committed a crime in the past. 'Necessary' was held to have a meaning somewhere between 'indispensable' (which would be a stronger word than necessary) and 'useful or expedient' (which would be too weak).[185] If the objectives to be achieved were particularly important, something rather closer to the 'useful' end of the scale than the 'indispensable' end might suffice; it was for the judges to decide what it might mean in the context of each case. The 'prevention of crime' encompassed anything calculated to deter or control crime generally, rather than being limited to the prevention of a particular suspected crime. The detection of leaks fell into that category, since leaks of price-sensitive information made insider dealing possible. There was no need to identify any particular offence which the information might enable them to bring home to an offender, so long as they could point to a type of crime (insider dealing) which there was a pressing social need to control.

Not surprisingly, the national security exception was also broadly interpreted. In *Secretary of State for Defence v. Guardian Newspapers Ltd.*[186] a majority of the House of Lords (Lords Diplock, Roskill, and Bridge) decided that a civil servant remaining in post, having already leaked a secret document, gave rise to a threat to national security, and it was necessary to track that person down in order to prevent possible future

---

[180] *Re an Inquiry Under the Company Security (Insider Dealing) Act 1985* [1988] AC 660 at 703, [1988] 1 All ER 203 at 208 *per* Lord Griffiths.

[181] See S. Palmer, 'Protecting Journalists' Sources: Section 10, Contempt of Court Act 1981' [1992] *PL* 61–72.

[182] Eur. Ct. HR, Judgment of 27 March 1996, RJD 1996-II, 22 EHRR 123.

[183] [1988] AC 660, [1988] 1 All ER 203, HL.

[184] Financial Services Act 1986, ss. 177, 178.

[185] In *Secretary of State for Defence v. Guardian Newspapers Ltd.* [1985] AC 339, [1984] 3 All ER 601, HL, 'necessary' was interpreted somewhat similarly.

[186] [1985] AC 339, [1984] 3 All ER 601, HL.

threats. Lord Fraser and Lord Scarman dissented, on the ground that there was only sketchy evidence before the court that the source of the leak would be likely to be in a position to repeat the leak or that a threat to national security (as opposed to a breach of confidence) would result in any case. By contrast, the majority refused to subject the government's assertions about national security to any rigorous examination. Indeed, Lord Bridge said in a later case that the court will virtually always decide that disclosure is necessary where national security or the prevention of crime are involved.[187] This is not a proposition which could be maintained in the face of the obligation to scrutinize asserted justifications for interfering with freedom to impart and receive information, imposed on courts by ECHR Article 10(2) and sections 3 and 6 of the Human Rights Act 1998.

It seemed at first that courts might interpret the 'necessary in the interests of justice' exception more narrowly. Lord Diplock construed 'justice' as referring to 'the administration of justice in the course of legal proceedings in a court of law, or, by reason of the extended definition of "court" in section 19 of the Act of 1981 before a tribunal or body exercising the judicial power of the state'.[188] In another case,[189] the judges refused to make an order that the source be named, holding that it would not 'necessary' to override the statutory public interest in not revealing sources unless there was no other way in which the applicant's rights could reasonably be protected.

In *X. Ltd. v. Morgan-Grampian (Publishers) Ltd.*,[190] Lord Bridge, with whom the other members of the House of Lords agreed, gave a more expansive meaning to the term 'necessary in the interests of justice', covering any situation where disclosure was necessary to enable a person to exercise a legal right to avert a legal wrong, whether or not it proved necessary to resort to legal proceedings:

'Thus, to take a very obvious example, if an employer of a large staff is suffering grave damage from the activities of an unidentified disloyal servant, it is undoubtedly in the interests of justice that he should be able to identify him in order to terminate his contract of employment, notwithstanding that no legal proceedings may be necessary to achieve that end.'

However, before disclosure can be said to be *necessary* in the interests of justice, a claimant will have to show that the interests are so preponderantly strong as to override the public interest in protecting sources recognized by the section. Whereas this was readily assumed in relation to preventing crime and maintaining national security, the 'interests of justice' exception required the court to undertake a serious balancing exercise. Lord Oliver had earlier said, 'Necessity is a relative concept and the degree of need before an act or measure can be said to be "necessary", although not, clearly, a question which is to be answered without reference to some objective

---

[187] *X. Ltd. v. Morgan-Grampian (Publishers) Ltd.* [1991] 1 AC 1 at 43, [1990] 2 All ER 1 at 8–9.

[188] *Secretary of State for Defence v. Guardian Newspapers Ltd.* [1985] AC 339 at 350, [1984] 3 All ER 601 at 607.

[189] *Maxwell v. Pressdram Ltd.* [1987] 1 WLR 298, [1987] 1 All ER 656, CA.

[190] [1991] AC 1 at 43, [1990] 2 All ER 1 at 9.

standards, must, in the end, be and remain a matter of judgment'.[191] In the *Morgan-Grampian* case, he said:[192]

'It means "really needed" and it involves not so much a discretion as a value judgment. But the formation of a value judgment may, and, indeed, nearly always will, involve the consideration of factors which will be equally relevant to the exercise of a discretion. Moreover, there is nothing in the section which dictates that the judgment regarding whether disclosure is "really needed" is to be conducted without reference to the prohibition which the section has imposed. The true question, in my opinion, is not "is the information needed in order to serve the interests of justice?" but "are the interests of justice in this case so pressing as to require the absolute ban on disclosure to be overridden?"'

It would thus be necessary to consider in the round all the features of cases under the 'interests of justice' head, including the seriousness of the implications for the applicant (is he seeking to protect his very livelihood or merely a minor property interest?), the magnitude of the legitimate public interest in the information which the source has provided, and (perhaps curiously) the manner in which the source obtained the material, since it will require a very strong public interest in disclosure to justify protecting a source who has committed an illegitimate act, such as a serious breach of confidence or theft.[193]

Despite these encouraging signs that courts were prepared to conduct a serious balancing exercise, the decision in that case went against the journalist. The protection for sources under section 10 of the 1981 Act remained precarious, for two reasons. First, the way in which the source had acted received excessive weight. Any source within an organization is likely to have committed a breach of confidence at least. A source who behaves with perfect legality and propriety would have little reason to insist on the anonymity which it is the policy of section 10 to protect. Secondly, once the journalist's protection is acknowledged to be subject to an element of judicial discretion, it will be very rare for an appeal court to upset the decision of a first-instance judge that disclosure is necessary. The question will be whether the first-instance judge had material on which it could reasonably be concluded that the interests of justice required disclosure.[194] If that were correct, a journalist's right to withhold disclosure under section 10, which Lord Scarman in the *Guardian* case thought might come to be properly regarded as a constitutional right,[195] would be built on the shifting sands of judicial value judgments.

This is one of the areas in which the European Court of Human Rights has come to the aid of English judges, re-establishing foundations for the constitutional right foreseen by Lord Scarman. The journalist in the *Morgan-Grampian* case, Mr.

[191] *Re an Inquiry Under the Company Securities (Insider Dealing) Act 1985* [1988] AC 660 at 708–9, [1988] 1 All ER 203 at 212.

[192] [1991] 1 AC at 53, [1990] 2 All ER at 16.

[193] [1991] 1 AC at 44, [1990] 2 All ER at 9–10 *per* Lord Bridge.

[194] *X. Ltd. v. Morgan-Grampian (Publishers) Ltd.* [1991] 1 AC at 54, [1990] 2 All ER at 17 *per* Lord Oliver. Lord Bridge was rather more positive: see 44, 10.

[195] *Secretary of State for Defence v. Guardian Newspapers Ltd.* [1985] AC at 361, [1984] 3 All ER at 615.

Goodwin, applied to the European Court of Human Rights,[196] arguing that the right to protect sources was an element in freedom of expression and the right to receive and impart information, and that the interpretation of section 10 violated his rights under ECHR Article 10. The Court accepted that rights under ECHR Article 10(1) encompassed a right to protect sources. This was essential to allow the media to perform their the important role in a democratic society of scrutinizing the activities of governmental bodies and others and informing the public so that people could be held to account. The majority of the Court went on to hold that the English courts, when balancing the various interests in play under section 10 of the 1981 Act, had failed to give sufficient weight to the public interest in maintaining the confidence of sources to allow the media to obtain information for the purposes of journalism, and had given too much weight to the interests of the individual litigant. The order to disclose the identity of the source had therefore been a disproportionate interference with, and a violation of, rights under ECHR Article 10.

The terms of section 10 of the Contempt of Court Act 1981 are sufficiently flexible to allow it to be given effect in a manner compatible with ECHR Article 10. Under the Human Rights Act 1998, sections 2 and 3, there is an obligation to give effect to it in that way so far as possible, taking account of the decision of the European Court of Human Rights in the *Goodwin* case. Courts now have a statutory obligation to conduct a real balancing exercise, giving due weight to the right identified in the *Goodwin* case and the constitutional importance of upholding it unless there are particularly pressing reasons for overriding it. This applies to the national-security and prevention-of-crime exceptions as well as the interests-of-justice exception under section 10.

In the period leading up to the coming into force of the Human Rights Act 1998, the courts were already taking account of the *Goodwin* decision, subtly reinterpreting both section 10 and the House of Lords' decisions on it to fashion an approach which was responsive to the judgment of the European Court of Human Rights. In *Camelot Group Ltd. v. Centaur Communications Ltd.*,[197] before the enactment of the Human Rights Act 1998, the Court of Appeal noted that the dissenting opinions in the *Goodwin* case showed that the application of agreed principles to particular facts could lead to divergent assessments of the appropriate balance between competing interests and rights. The Court upheld an order for disclosure of the source of a leak of draft accounts from the offices of the operator of the National Lottery which had exposed it to widespread criticism, giving overriding weight to a supposed public (rather than private) interest in allowing the company to find and remove a disloyal employee. However, other cases decided at about the same time or later take a somewhat different approach. In *Saunders v. Punch Ltd., t/a Liberty Publishing*[198] the magazine had published a story indicating that they had access to records of meetings between Ernest Saunders and Department of Trade inspectors, which were covered by legal professional privilege. Mr. Saunders was awarded an injunction restraining further

---

[196] *Goodwin v. United Kingdom*, Eur. Ct. HR, Judgment of 27 March 1996, RJD 1996-II, 22 EHRR 123.
[197] [1999] QB 124, [1998] 1 All ER 251, CA.
[198] [1998] 1 WLR 986, [1998] 1 All ER 234.

publication of such material, but Lindsay J refused to order *Punch* to disclose the identity of the source of the material. Lindsay J noted that the European Court of Human Rights in *Goodwin* had thought it significant to consider the residual risk of damage to through further dissemination of confidential information when weighing the various interests. The risk of further damage to Mr. Saunders had been adequately controlled by the order restraining further publication, so even the public importance of upholding legal professional privilege could not override the statutory privilege under section 10 of the Contempt of Court Act 1981, having regard to the decision in *Goodwin*. In *John v. Express Newspapers*,[199] a strong Court of Appeal, presided over by Lord Woolf CJ, quashed an order for disclosure of the identity of the source of draft counsel's opinion, improperly taken from the barrister's chambers and passed to a journalist. The confidentiality of legal advice is a matter of great public interest, but it did not override the statutory privilege, having regard to the decision in *Goodwin*, for two main reasons. First, it was a single incident, and there was no reason to suppose that it posed a threat to lawyer-client confidentiality more generally or that there was a real risk of further leaks. Secondly, no attempt had been made within the chambers to investigate the source of the leak. It could not be said to be necessary to order a journalist to disclose the source until all other reasonable steps had been taken to try to identify the source by other means.

This clearly shows that the courts were responding to the demands of ECHR Article 10 even before the Human Rights Act 1998 came into force. The Court of Appeal in *John v. Express Newspapers* approved the approach of Lindsay J in *Saunders v. Punch Ltd*. Although the *Camelot* case was not disapproved, there is a sense of greater willingness to assess critically a litigant's claim that it is necessary in the interests of justice to order disclosure of the identity of a journalist's source. The new approach to the balancing of interests will inevitably be strengthened by the impact of the Human Rights Act 1998; in particular, one can expect it to be applied to applications by public authorities for disclosure at least as rigorously as to private litigants. This does not mean that disclosure will never be ordered. If there is a real risk of further disclosures, they would do serious damage to extremely important public interests or private rights, and all other reasonable means of preventing them have been tried unsuccessfully, disclosure may be ordered in what would be an exceptional case. Thus in *Ashworth Hospital Authority v. MGN Ltd*.[200] the Court of Appeal ordered the owners of the *Daily Mirror* to disclose the identity of an intermediary who was thought to have received confidential patient records relating to a patient, Ian Brady (one of the Moors murderers) detained at Ashworth Special Hospital, from a source at the hospital, and who alone was thought to know the identity of the source. The court noted that all other methods of discovering the source had failed, that there was a continuing risk of leaks, and that patient confidentiality was a vitally important right and interest in a democratic society. After considering *Goodwin*, the court concluded that this was an exceptional case in which the privilege under section 10 of the Contempt of Court Act 1981 was legitimately outweighed by other factors. The new approach is balanced and

---

[199] [2000] 1 WLR 1931, [2000] 3 All ER 257, CA.
[200] [2001] 1 WLR 515, CA.

gives appropriate weight to all factors and rights, and shows that *Goodwin* has provided a sounder approach to section 10 than was previously in use.

(3) PROTECTION FOR JOURNALISTIC MATERIAL IN CRIMINAL INVESTIGATIONS[201]

Journalists often receive or seek out information, or take photographs or films, which might be useful to police investigating criminal offences. At common law in England and Wales, there has never been a recognized privilege for journalists against being required to surrender their notes, films, etc. in either civil[202] or criminal proceedings. Thus there was no legal bar to a search warrant being issued (usually by a magistrate) to search for evidence in newspaper offices, on an *ex parte* application by the police. Any limitation depended on the good sense of the police and the discretion (rarely if ever exercised) of magistrates. A similar position obtained in Canada, where search warrants were available, although judges have exhorted those issuing warrants to give particularly careful consideration to such applications.[203] The same was true in the USA, where the freedom of the press under the First Amendment to the Constitution did not offer newspapers any higher protection against searches than was available to all under the Fourth Amendment. If the Fourth Amendment's requirement for a warrant was satisfied, the police could constitutionally search for evidence, without prior warning or an *inter partes* hearing, even the premises of third parties who were not suspected of being implicated in the offence. This was settled by the Supreme Court in *Zurcher v. Stanford Daily*.[204]

In the USA, the decision in *Zurcher* was greeted with widespread public condemnation. In 1980, Congress passed legislation[205] which replaced the warrant procedure whereby investigators, who wanted access to material as evidence of crime which was held by innocent third parties, were able to apply *ex parte* for a search warrant giving them freedom to enter premises and rummage through records. Instead, investigators now have to apply for a subpoena requiring the production of specified material. There is, if necessary, an *inter partes* hearing in which the third party can adduce arguments against the order, either in principle or as to its scope. The third party is not then at peril of a search of its premises. The federal legislation protects the press against state and federal investigators, to extend the scope of First Amendment rights, and protects other innocent third parties against federal investigators only (although some states have enacted similar legislation).

In England and Wales, too, legislation has given some procedural protection to the interests of the media and those who are informed by them. The judgment of the European Court of Human Rights in *Goodwin v. United Kingdom*[206] shows that ECHR

---

[201] See generally D. Feldman, 'Press Freedom and Police Access to Journalistic Material' (1995) 1 *Yearbook of Media and Entertainment Law* 43–80; R. Costigan, 'Fleet Street Blues: Police Seizure of Journalists' Material' [1996] Crim. LR 231–9.

[202] *Senior v. Holdsworth, ex parte Independent Television News* [1976] 1 QB 23, [1975] 2 All ER 1009, CA: no privilege, but summons set aside on grounds that the order had been drawn in excessively wide terms.

[203] *Re Pacific Press Ltd. and R.* (1977) 37 CCC (2d) 487.

[204] 436 US 547 (1978).

[205] 94 Stat. 1879 (1980).

[206] Eur. Ct. HR, Judgment of 27 March 1996, RJD 1996-II, 22 EHRR 123.

Article 10 entails a privilege for journalists against being forced to reveal their sources, and that there must be a procedure in criminal as in civil cases for authoritatively weighing that right against countervailing public interests to ensure that it is overridden only in compelling circumstances and for a legitimate purpose. In English law, the arrangement is generally governed by the Police and Criminal Evidence Act 1984 (PACE), which gives a partial shield to 'journalistic material' against enforced disclosure in criminal investigations. Under sections 11 and 14, all 'journalistic material' became either excluded material (if it is held in confidence and consists of documents or other records)[207] or special procedure material (if it is not held in confidence, or is in any other form).[208] The effect of this was that no search warrant could be granted in respect of such material unless the highly restrictive conditions on the grant of warrants under Schedule 1, paragraph 12, were met.[209] In relation to most investigations, the police now have to apply for an order for access or production rather than a warrant, and the procedure requires notice of the application to be given to the person holding the material, who can argue at an *inter partes* hearing before a circuit judge that the access conditions are not met.[210] There are three exceptions:

- cases where a warrant can properly be issued under Schedule 1, paragraph 12 of PACE;

- investigations into terrorist offences and drug-trafficking offences, where a circuit judge may make an order for access to or production of material or issue a warrant *ex parte* even in respect of excluded material, without the need to comply with the special conditions under Schedule 1, paragraph 12, of the 1984 Act;[211]

- before the Human Rights Act 1998 came into force, it was held that warrants issued in Scotland, where the procedures for protecting journalistic material do not apply, and backed for execution in England and Wales,[212] allowed the police to evade the protection normally available in England and Wales under PACE.[213] This may sometimes fail to secure the protection for journalists' sources required by ECHR Article 10. In such cases, an officer exercising his discretion to execute a warrant in that way would now be acting unlawfully under section 6 of the Human Rights Act 1998.

So far as press freedom is concerned, two questions must be addressed. First, what types of material does 'journalistic material' include? Secondly, when will it be in the

---

[207] PACE 1984, s. 11(1)(c).

[208] Ibid., s. 14(1)(b).

[209] Ibid., s. 9.

[210] For discussion of the availability of orders in respect of excluded and special procedure material generally, see above, Ch. 11. This section concentrates on aspects which are special to journalistic material.

[211] Drug Trafficking Act 1994, ss. 55 (orders for access or production) and 56 (search warrant); Terrorism Act 2000, Sch. 5, paras. 5–10 (orders for access or production) and 11–12 (search warrants). Under the latter Act, a police officer of the rank of superintendent or above may authorize a search if satisfied that the case is one of great urgency and immediate action is necessary: Sch. 5, para. 15.

[212] Summary Jurisdiction (Process) Act 1881, s. 4.

[213] *R. v. Manchester Stipendiary Magistrate, ex parte Granada Television Ltd.* [2001] 1 AC 300, [2000] 1 All ER 135, HL.

public interest to require disclosure of journalistic material under Schedule 1 to the 1984 Act?

(i) What is journalistic material?

'Journalistic material' is defined as material acquired or created for the purposes of journalism which is in the possession of a person who himself acquired or created it for that purpose.[214] Thus a journalist's notes of an interview are journalistic material; so is material gathered from anyone for the purpose of writing a newspaper article, even if the person supplying it did not himself acquire or create it for journalistic purposes; so is a photograph taken with a view to possible publication. In all these cases, it does not matter whether or not the material is, in the end, used in print. The test is whether (a) the person who created or acquired it did so for the purposes of journalism, and (b) the person now in possession intends to use it for those purposes. A photograph which is taken by a press photographer and passed to the editor of a newspaper with a view to publication is therefore journalistic material in the hands of the editor.

The classification does not depend on the person who created, acquired, or is now in possession of the material being a journalist by profession. It depends only on people having the relevant intention or purpose, not on their status or calling. What, then, are the purposes of journalism?[215] They can be summarized as being the provision for the public, or a section of the public, of reliable, published information on current events, with informed comment where appropriate or desired. It may cover publication in newspapers, magazines, or through the broadcast media. It is not clear whether it includes publication in book form; this is not the classical form of journalism, in which material is published within a very short time of the events to which it relates.[216] If the book is to be published reasonably soon after the events, there is no reason why the principle should not apply to material compiled for it. The time element is flexible, in any case, and must be a matter of degree, because although investigative journalism is undoubtedly journalism an investigation may last years before the results are published. There seems to be no reason to exclude publications in the form of dramatized documentaries, as long as they are sufficiently topical. However, it goes too far to say that journalism 'includes any form of publication':[217] it certainly would not apply to most novels, nor to many works of scholarship in the fields of history, law, science, nor to most plays other than (perhaps) dramatized documentaries. All these forms of publication are likely to lack the necessary quality of topicality. They may make news, but will usually not themselves be journalistic.

---

[214] PACE, s. 13(1), (2).

[215] For full discussion, see D. Feldman, *The Law Relating to Entry, Search and Seizure* (London: Butterworths, 1986), 104–6.

[216] At common law, it was unclear whether the so-called 'newspaper rule', under which newspapers being sued for libel could not be forced to disclose the sources of the information on which the libel was based, applied to books as well as periodicals: see *Georgius v. Delegates of Oxford University Press* [1949] 1 KB 729, [1949] 1 All ER 342.

[217] This is the view expressed by M. Zander, *The Police and Criminal Evidence Act 1984*, 3rd edn. (London: Sweet & Maxwell, 1995), 41.

(ii) Where does the public interest lie in respect of disclosure?

The effect of material being journalistic is that disclosure will not be ordered, nor a warrant granted, unless one of the sets of access conditions is satisfied.[218] The most important aspect of these for press freedom relates to special procedure material, which is, in this context, journalistic material which does not consist of documents held in confidence. These can be sought under the 'first set of access conditions', i.e. those under Schedule 1, paragraph 2, in cases where before the 1984 Act no search warrant could have been obtained, because there was no provision for granting warrants in respect of the offences. For this purpose, it is necessary to show (*inter alia*) that the public interest would be served by an order requiring access to the material (this is not necessary under the second set of access conditions, which apply where, before the 1984 Act, a search warrant could have been granted). The caselaw under the Act before the Human Rights Act 1998 came into force made it seem likely that the public interest would nearly always be served by requiring access where it is likely (in the words of paragraph 2 of Schedule 1 to the 1984 Act) to be relevant evidence of, or of substantial value to an investigation relating to, a serious arrestable offence. This applied particularly to film of riots or other serious offences, whether broadcast or not. For the media it was argued that allowing the police to take evidence in this way would compromise the impartiality of the press, who would be seen as agents of the police, and would be subject to increased risk of violence next time they went into an area where rioting was occurring. This argument was never accepted, for two reasons. First, journalists and camera crews would be protected by the fact that the photographs were being handed over pursuant to a court order rather than voluntarily. Secondly, judges thought it unlikely that the press would be more likely to be subjected to violence on account the risk of rioters being identified following an order for production of unpublished film or photographs, than because of the risk, which always existed, that the pictures would actually be broadcast or published and the rioters identified as a result.[219] Any added risk was outweighed by the weighty public interest in clearing innocent suspects of crime and identifying the guilty.[220]

The importance accorded to the detection of crime should, however, not be treated as being absolute. If it were absolute, the requirement to consider the public interest would be redundant, as adding nothing to the other access conditions. In addition, there would be a danger of violating the rights of media under ECHR Article 10 in a case where the order had a chilling effect on the gathering, imparting, and receiving of information about current affairs. To give effect to the evident intention of Parliament in enacting PACE and, in cases where ECHR Article 10(1) is engaged, the Human

---

[218] For discussion of the access conditions, see above, section 10.3(2).

[219] *Cp.* the *dictum* of Lord Denning MR in *Senior v. Holdsworth, ex parte ITN Ltd.* [1976] 1 QB 23, CA, relating to a witness summons in respect of unbroadcast news material, applied in the cases under PACE. See Feldman, 'Press Freedom' at 61–6.

[220] See, e.g. *Chief Constable of Avon and Somerset v. Bristol United Press, Independent*, 4 November 1986, Bristol Crown Court (Stuart-Smith J); *R. v. Bristol Crown Court, ex parte Bristol Press & Picture Agency Ltd.* (1986) 85 Cr. App. R. 190, DC. Protection is procedural only: see *R. v. Crown Court at Middlesex Guildhall, ex parte Salinger* [1993] QB 564, [1993] 2 All ER 310, DC. For a New Zealand comparison, see *Television New Zealand Ltd. v. Police* [1995] 2 LRC 808 on applications to obtain film shot by broadcasters, and *R. v. Pratt* [1994] 1 LRC 333 on the use in criminal trials of evidence obtained by such means.

Rights Act 1998, the types of consideration which were identified by Lord Bridge in relation to the Contempt of Court Act 1981, section 10, in *Morgan-Grampian*[221] should properly be equally applicable under the first set of access conditions under Schedule 1 to the 1984 Act. Regrettably, the approach of the courts to the cases so far reported cannot, on a true reading of paragraph 2 of Schedule 1, be sustained. It is to be hoped that it will soon be possible for higher courts to examine the matter afresh.

14.5 CONCLUSION

There has long been a good deal of rhetoric about the importance of a free press as a channel of information to the public on matters of public interest, and a certain amount of support for the idea that this requires journalists' sources to be protected against being unmasked in at least some circumstances. In the first edition of this book it was suggested that the practical impact of the ideas has been limited. Since 1993, changes have begun to occur. More sophisticated caselaw from Strasbourg, and a heightened sensitivity in constitutional courts to the constitutional importance of the media in democratic societies, have led to media freedom being accorded a higher priority. This is clearest in the area of defamation law, but the effects are being felt more widely. The government is committed to a lighter touch in the regulation of the media. The Human Rights Act 1998 and the decision of the European Court of Human Rights in *Goodwin v. United Kingdom* have made freedom of communication and the protection of journalists' sources into a fundamental element in the constitution. Section 12 of the 1998 Act puts freedom of expression at the heart of decisions about remedies, particularly where literary, artistic, and journalistic material are involved. In due course this may begin to affect the approach to allowing police access to journalistic material.

As Lord Scarman said in the *Guardian Newspapers* case in 1984, in relation to the journalist's privilege against disclosure of sources under the Contempt of Court Act 1981, section 10:

'Counsel for the Guardian described the section as introducing in the law "a constitutional right". There being no written constitution, his words will sound strange to some. But they may more accurately prophesy the direction in which English law has to move under the compulsions to which it is now subject than many are yet prepared to accept. The section, it important to note in this connection, bears a striking resemblance to the way in which many of the articles of the European Convention for the Protection of Fundamental Rights and Freedoms ... are framed: namely a general rule subject to carefully drawn and limited exceptions which are required to be established, in case of dispute, to the satisfaction of the European Court of Human Rights.'[222]

More generally, there is a risk that government intervention to maintain standards will degenerate into political pressure in relation to programme making, using threats

---

[221] [1991] 1 AC at 44, [1990] 2 All ER at 9–10, considered above.
[222] [1985] AC at 361, [1984] 3 All ER at 615.

or carping criticism. This seems to have happened in 1988, in the furore surrounding the broadcast of *Death on the Rock*. There is a temptation for even the fairest minded government to use pressure against those who have the job of exposing its behaviour to public scrutiny. There is correspondingly a need for all concerned to continue to be vigilant and strong-minded to ensure that this independence is not whittled away by legal assaults, political intimidation, and behind-the-scenes pressure.

15

RESTRICTING EXPRESSION TO PROTECT THE SECURITY OF THE STATE

The law has to find a way of accommodating the democratic demand for open government within governmental claims that certain public functions (notably security and international relations) cannot be effectively performed in the glare of publicity. The rules should recognize that government, as a public agency, has legitimate concerns which are different from those of ordinary citizens. At the same time they should ensure that governmental bodies do not exploit their special constitutional position in circumstances where it is not in the public interest for them to do so. This chapter examines how English law seeks such an accommodation in relation to restraints imposed on freedom of expression in the interests of the security of the state: prior restraint through use of the doctrine of breach of confidence, and subsequent restraint through imposing criminal penalties under the Official Secrets Acts, and for seditious libel and related offences. In order to clarify the complex relationship between prior restraint by the civil law and subsequent restraint by the criminal law, section 15.1 sketches some of the background. After that, prior restraint by means of the law of breach of confidence is considered in section 15.2, and the remaining sections look at various criminal offences which penalize certain communications after they have occurred.

15.1 BACKGROUND

(1) THREE BACKGROUND ELEMENTS

Three matters, noted above in Chapters 13 and 14, form the backdrop to the discussion of state interest restrictions on free expression.

(i) The ethos of secrecy

In recent years, statutes have given some legal support to openness in government. Such developments may be bolstered by rights to receive or have access to information under Articles 8 and 10 of the European Convention on Human Rights (ECHR) and the duty of public authorities to comply with them under section 6 of the Human Rights Act 1998. But compared with the USA or Australia, the government of the UK remains a private affair, taking place behind a veil, a corner of which may sometimes be lifted to allow limited parliamentary scrutiny. The secretive ethos of the civil service is reinforced by statutes such as the Official Secrets Act 1989, and by the civil services pay and conditions code.[1] Secrecy has also to some extent been bolstered by the tendency of judges, when issues come before the courts, to consider that the government is uniquely well placed to assess where the national interest lies. This is, to some extent, correct: the secrecy which surrounds government ensures that other bodies, which might possibly claim a say in making such choices, are starved of information.

This shows itself in pre-trial civil procedure. Public bodies (and others) can assert a public interest in maintaining the confidentiality of information, sources, or documents, as a ground for resisting discovery of documents.[2] The common law recognizes that a certain degree of secrecy is inevitably necessary in government and the public service, in order to enable public bodies to do their jobs and to encourage frank discussion within government of issues which arise for decision. The judges therefore allow claims to public-interest immunity from discovery in the course of litigation. A claim may be based either on the class of documents of which the particular documents are members, or on the contents of the particular documents. Examples of classes of documents which the public interest may require the Crown and other public bodies to refuse to disclose include Cabinet minutes and any documents brought into existence for the purpose of framing high-level government policy, including papers written by relatively junior officials;[3] minutes of discussions between heads of departments;[4] and papers brought into existence for the purpose of preparing submissions to Cabinet.[5] Other material may be the subject of a 'contents' claim, for instance if disclosure would be likely to impede the body in carrying out the purpose for which it was brought into existence.[6]

Nevertheless, the protection offered by public-interest immunity is not absolute. It applies only if, and so long as, the public interest in preventing harm to the nation or the public service outweighs the public interest in making the information available for the purpose of the due administration of justice.[7] In some cases, some judges have displayed a healthy scepticism when faced by claims that disclosure of documents would inhibit frank advice and exchanges of view amongst Ministers or between Ministers and civil servants,[8] or by assertions that the return of leaked documents was

---

[1] See G. Drewry and T. Butcher, *The Civil Service Today* (Oxford: Basil Blackwell, 1991), 131–3; D. Vincent, *The Culture of Secrecy* (Oxford: Oxford University Press, 1998), 248–310.

[2] *Burmah Oil Co. Ltd. v. Bank of England* [1980] AC 1090, [1979] 3 All ER 700, HL; *Air Canada v. Secretary of State for Trade* [1983] 2 AC 394, [1983] 1 All ER 910, HL.

[3] *Conway v. Rimmer* [1968] AC 910, HL, at 952 *per* Lord Reid; *Sankey v. Whitlam* (1978) 142 CLR 1, HC of Australia.

[4] *Australian National Airlines Commission v. The Commonwealth* (1975) 132 CLR 582, HC of Australia, at 591.

[5] *Lanyon Pty. Ltd. v. The Commonwealth* (1974) 129 CLR 650, HC of Australia.

[6] *Neilson v. Laugharne* [1981] QB 736, CA; *Makanjuola v. Commissioner of Police of the Metropolis* (1989) [1992] 3 All ER 617, CA; *Halford v. Sharples* [1992] 3 All ER 624, CA.

[7] *Conway v. Rimmer* [1968] AC 910 at 940, [1968] 1 All ER 874 at 880, *per* Lord Reid.

[8] *Conway v. Rimmer* [1968] AC 910, [1968] 1 All ER 874, HL. Similar vigilance was evident in *Williams v. Home Office* [1981] 1 All ER 1151.

necessary in the interests of national security.[9] In the past, judges were also ready to inspect documents in respect of which a class claim to immunity was made, and exercise their own judgment as to the balance between the competing public interests.[10] Subsequently, British judges became less critical of expansive claims to privilege,[11] and unwilling to look behind a Minister's certificate asserting that disclosure of particular documents would give rise to a threat to national security. The certificate became, in effect, conclusive evidence of the facts which it stated.[12] Where national security was said to be involved, the judges were very unlikely to probe behind ministerial assessments.[13]

Some cases have placed a further obstacle in the way of obtaining disclosure in the UK, because the courts will not embark on the balancing exercise, which the limits on public-interest immunity appear to require, unless the party seeking disclosure can at least show 'that the documents are very likely to contain material which would give substantial support to his contention on an issue which arises in the case, and that without them he might be "deprived of the means of . . . proper presentation" of his case'.[14] This is intended to prevent fishing expeditions among public papers, and to take account of the difficulty which our judges feel in assessing the sensitivity of different classes of documents, but it places a considerable burden on the party seeking discovery, who must have a clear idea about what he is likely to find before he has a chance of looking at it, and must convince the court that it will substantially assist him.[15] Judges have refused to order production of material likely to contain information which is already in the public domain, on the ground that the party already has access to it and will not be substantially assisted by discovery in that regard.[16]

However, the House of Lords made it clear in *R. v. Chief Constable of the West Midlands Police, ex parte Wiley*[17] that the immunity from disclosure is not to be extended in such a way as to defeat its purposes. Class claims need to be specially justified: for example, in *Ex parte Wiley* it was held that there was no general immunity for all papers (including witness statements) collected during a police disciplinary

---

[9] See Lord Fraser of Tullybelton and Lord Scarman, dissenting, in *Secretary of State for Defence v. Guardian Newspapers Ltd.* [1985] AC 339, [1984] 3 All ER 601, HL.

[10] *Campbell v. Tameside MBC* [1982] QB 1065, [1982] 2 All ER 781, CA.

[11] See the majority speeches in *Secretary of State for Defence v. Guardian Newspapers Ltd.* [1985] AC 339, [1984] 3 All ER 601, HL; Ch. 13, section 4(2), above.

[12] *Balfour v. Foreign and Commonwealth Office* [1994] 1 WLR 681, [1994] 2 All ER 588, CA.

[13] See, e.g. *Council of Civil Service Unions v. Minister for the Civil Service* [1985] AC 374, [1984] 3 All ER 935, HL.

[14] *Air Canada v. Secretary of State for Trade (No. 2)* [1983] 2 AC 394 at 435, [1983] 1 All ER 910 at 917, *per* Lord Fraser of Tullybelton, quoting Lord Radcliffe in *Glasgow Corporation v. Central Land Board*, 1956 SC (HL) 1 at 18. This formulation represents the view of the majority (Lords Fraser, Wilberforce, and Edmund-Davies). Lords Scarman and Templeman adopted a slightly less restrictive approach, allowing inspection where disclosure might assist either party or the court in dealing with the issues, but they concurred in the result on the facts of the case.

[15] See, e.g. *Bookbinder v. Tebbit (No. 2)* [1992] 1 WLR 217.

[16] *Air Canada v. Secretary of State for Trade (No. 2)* [1983] 2 AC 394, [1983] 1 All ER 910, HL.

[17] [1995] 1 AC 274, [1994] 3 All ER 420, HL.

investigation, although it was later held[18] that investigating officers' working papers and final reports were covered as a class. The House of Lords in *Ex parte Wiley* held that immunity does not prevent the use of material, but only its disclosure. Where material is relevant, the presumption is that it should be disclosed, and the person holding it must be satisfied that a sufficiently strong public interest outweighs the normal public interest in the proper administration of justice before non-disclosure will be justified. The immunity should not be used to frustrate or disadvantage the people (for example, witnesses or police informants) for whose benefit the immunity was developed.[19]

The decision in *Ex parte Wiley* is a sign that judicial attitudes to claims to public-interest immunity are changing. If they are, it will be a response to at least two stimuli. First, as Professor David Vincent has written, 'Withholding information became at once a claim to probity and a demand for deference. It implied a sense of responsibility which arose from and defined a position of moral authority'.[20] There has been a loss of faith in the ability or willingness of state agencies to maintain that sense of responsibility and morality consistently. In 1992, when directors of a manufacturing company, Matrix Churchill, were prosecuted for supplying parts of armaments to Iraq in breach of export controls, Judge Smedley, the trial judge, refused to grant immunity from disclosure of information which the prosecution had claimed on the basis of several ministerial certificates. The defendants claimed to have been acting with the knowledge and approval of the authorities. The judge refused to allow the prosecution to withhold information about the relationship between the authorities and the defendants, and the prosecution collapsed. A subsequent inquiry into the affair by Sir Richard Scott revealed that Ministers were not always exercising as much careful judgment as would have been desirable before issuing public interest immunity certificates.[21] The government subsequently announced that Ministers would make claims to public interest immunity only if they believed that the disclosure of a particular document 'will cause real damage or harm to the public interest'.[22] This implied that a less demanding standard had previously been applied. The announcement of the new policy is welcome, but has no legal status.[23] Secondly, the Human Rights Act 1998 requires courts, as public authorities, to act compatibly with Convention rights (unless compelled by primary legislation to behave otherwise). The European Court of Human Rights has held that conclusive certificates signed by a Minister may violate the right of a party to a fair trial under ECHR Article 6(1) if it effectively prevents the party from litigating in support of a legal

---

[18] *Taylor v. Anderton (Police Complaints Authority intervening)* [1995] 1 WLR 447, [1995] 2 All ER 420, CA.

[19] *Savage v. Chief Constable of Hampshire Constabulary* [1997] 1 WLR 1061, [1997] 2 All ER 631, CA.

[20] Vincent, *Culture of Secrecy*, 15.

[21] Sir Richard Scott, *Return to an Address of the Honourable the House of Commons dated 15th February 1996 for the report of the Inquiry into the export of Defence Equipment and Dual-use Goods to Iraq and Related Prosecutions*, HC 115 (London: HMSO, 1996), 5 vols. and index; A. Tomkins, *The Constitution after Scott: Government Unwrapped* (Oxford: Clarendon Press, 1998), especially ch. 5.

[22] House of Commons Official Report, 6th Series, 18 December 1996, vol. 287, col. 949, Sir Nicholas Lyell A-G. The real damage test is intended to equate to substantial harm: see Sir Nicholas Lyell at col. 951.

[23] For penetrating analysis, see G. Ganz, 'Volte-Face on Public Interest Immunity' (1997) 60 *MLR* 552–8.

right.[24] The content of the duty of a court under Article 6(1) is flexible, but the need to consult ECHR standards, including pressing social need and proportionality, will inevitably lead to a more critical attitude being adopted to some public-interest immunity claims.

The effect may be to move English law closer to the Australian approach. The High Court of Australia insists that whenever a claim to public interest immunity is raised the court, and nobody else, is responsible for deciding whether, on balance, the public interest favours disclosure of the documents. In order to do this, the court must always privately examine the documents in question, even if the papers relate to Cabinet discussions, national policy, or investigations by the security service, ASIO.[25] If the court decides that parts of a document should be kept secret, it will still order disclosure if the document can be sealed or otherwise packaged in such a way as to allow disclosure of the non-secret parts while maintaining the secrecy of those parts which deserve protection.[26] If the document has been published already, the claim to immunity from disclosure will be rejected,[27] not (as in the UK) strengthened. The greater confidence of the Australian judges in assessing the public interest in secrecy, and their less deferential attitude to government as compared with their English counterparts, are aspects of Australia's open approach to government in general, which contrasts starkly with the ethos in the UK.

(ii) The special evil of prior restraint

Libertarians traditionally view prior restraint of expressions of opinion and information as being a more serious infringement of liberties than subsequent imposition of penalties. This view is persuasive if one considers that the value of liberty—in this case, freedom of expression and communication—lies in its tendency to advance personal autonomy, in the sense of the freedom to make one's own choices. Where the law imposes a penalty on someone who expresses himself in a certain way, but takes no prior, preventive steps to coerce him to keep quiet, he retains the freedom to make his choice for himself. The risk of suffering the penalty will be one factor which he will take into account in deciding whether or not to speak out, but he may decide that the risk is outweighed by the importance to him or to others of what he wants to say. Forcing him to remain silent removes from him that freedom, and fails to respect his autonomy. On the other hand, if one adopts an instrumental view of the justification for maintaining individual liberty, one can take the view that the end which justifies criminalizing certain types of expression might well be better served by denying people the ability to choose to flout the law. Using criminal law to punish publications can have a chilling effect on freedom of expression and demands substantial justification. If one takes the view that the appropriate criteria for recognizing and restricting liberties are social and teleological—that is, directed to achieving an ulterior purpose,

---

[24] *Tinnelly and McElduff v. United Kingdom*, Eur. Ct. HR, App. No. 20390/92, Judgment of 10 July 1998, 27 EHRR 249.

[25] *Sankey v. Whitlam* (1978) 142 CLR 1; *Alister v. R.* (1984) 154 CLR 404 (Gibbs CJ, Murphy and Brennan JJ; Wilson and Dawson JJ dissented).

[26] *Sankey v. Whitlam* (1978) 142 CLR 1 was such a case.

[27] Ibid. at 45, *per* Gibbs ACJ.

such as a vision of the ideal society—rather than being individual- and autonomy-related,[28] it is far from clear that the liberal preference for any restraints on expression to be subsequent rather than prior is rational. Each type of restraint needs to be justified on similar grounds and to the same standards laid down in ECHR Article 10(2).

Nevertheless, section 12 of the Human Rights Act 1998, requiring courts to have particular regard to the importance of the right to freedom of expression under ECHR Article 10 when considering whether to grant any relief which might affect it, also contains special provisions relating to prior restraint. No pre-publication restraint is allowed before trial 'unless the court is satisfied that the applicant is likely to establish that publication should not be allowed'.[29] Whether before trial or at trial, where proceedings relate to material which is claimed to be, or which appears to the court to be,[30] journalistic, literary, or artistic material, the court must have particular regard to:

- the extent to which the material has, or is about to, become available to the public;
- the extent to which it is or would be in the public interest for the material to be published; and
- any relevant privacy code, such as those issued by bodies like the Press Complaints Commission, the Independent Television Commission, and the Broadcasting Standards Commission,

as well as to the importance of freedom of expression.[31]

(iii) Criteria for justifying interferences with freedom of expression under the European Convention on Human Rights and the Human Rights Act 1998

The right to receive and impart ideas and information under ECHR Article 10(1) can justifiably be interfered with in the interests of national security under Article 10(2), on condition that (*inter alia*) the interferences are in accordance with a procedure prescribed by law and are necessary in a democratic society for the purpose of protecting national security. To meet these criteria, the steps taken must be intended to answer a pressing social need, must be grounded in domestic law in a form which makes them sufficiently accessible to people who are subject to the laws and sufficiently clear to enable those people to understand their likely effects with reasonable certainty, and must be proportionate to the legitimate objectives pursued. A law

---

[28] See Ch. 1 above.

[29] Human Rights Act 1998, s. 12(3).

[30] These appear to be alternatives: it appears that a court must take account of these matters whenever a party claims that the material is journalistic, literary, or artistic, even if the court disagrees, and also when the court thinks that the material falls into those categories, even if no party has made such a claim. This sensibly prevents the courts being the ultimate arbiter of what is journalistic, literary, or artistic, and is consistent with the caselaw of the European Court of Human Rights. See *News Verlag GmbH v. Austria*, Eur. Ct. HR, App. No. 31457/96, Judgment of 11 January 2000 at paras. 37–40; S. Grosz, J. Beatson QC, and P. Duffy QC, *Human Rights: The 1998 Act and the Convention* (London: Sweet & Maxwell, 2000), 102–3.

[31] Human Rights Act 1998, s. 12(4).

imposing criminal sanctions on conduct may be a more effective constraint on behaviour if it is clear and its operation predictable than if the law is unpublished or uncertain. A restrictive law, even if is complies with these requirements, therefore has potentially extensive effects on free expression, and needs to be subjected to careful review in the light of the proportionality requirement.

(2) USING CRIMINAL LAW TO PROTECT NATIONAL SECURITY

The approach of successive British governments to the problem of restraining speech or disclosures which may threaten the security of the state traditionally relied primarily on the criminal law. Fear of German espionage operations in 1911 led to a panic measure, the Official Secrets Act 1911, which replaced earlier official secrets legislation[32] with a series of provisions which included some so broad in their scope that they would have been laughable had they not been so draconian. The legislation was rushed through Parliament with unseemly haste. Parts of the Act remain in force today. Section 1 was originally thought to be a straightforward anti-espionage provision: the side note read 'Penalties for spying'; but it was capable of being used, and later was used, against people who entered prohibited places such as RAF airfields to campaign against nuclear weapons, interfering in any way with security as defined by the government of the day even if they had no such intention, and indeed thought that their campaign would enhance national security.[33] Section 7 makes it an offence to harbour spies or to fail to report them when they have met on one's premises. These measures present few problems from a civil liberties standpoint, since the threat to the state from such activities would normally be thought to justify the restrictions.

Section 2 of the 1911 Act, however, has been replaced by the Official Secrets Act 1989. The old section 2 represented a very extensive restriction on open government and press freedom, to the point where, for several decades, debates about freedom of information and national security in the UK came to be conducted largely in terms of competing proposals for its reform. As the 1989 Act was the result of these debates, we must say something about the old section 2. It was an extraordinary provision. Headed 'Wrongful communication, etc., of information', a phrase in which the 'etc.' was more important than the 'communication', the section made it an offence for anyone who holds or had held office under the Crown, or was a government contractor, or had been employed under such a person, to communicate without authority any sketch, plan, model, article, note, document, or information relating to or used in a prohibited place, or which has been entrusted to the person in confidence or obtained in contravention of the Act, unless communicating it to a person to whom it was his duty in the interest of the state to communicate it. Finally, it was an offence willingly to receive such an article knowing, or having reasonable ground to believe, that it was being communicated in contravention of the Act.

Although in its original form section 2 was by no means narrow in scope, it was subsequently extended by the Official Secrets Acts 1920 and 1939. In its widened

---

[32] The long title of the 1911 Act was: 'An Act to re-enact the Official Secrets Act 1889, with Amendments.'
[33] *Chandler v. DPP* [1964] AC 763, [1962] 3 All ER 142, HL.

form, it covered secret official code words and passwords, and made it an offence for a person in possession of the information, etc. to use it for the benefit of any foreign power (whether or not an enemy), to use it in any way prejudicial to the safety or interests of the state, to communicate it directly or indirectly to a foreign power or in any other manner prejudicial to the safety or interests of the state, or to fail to comply with any direction issued with lawful authority regarding the return or disposal of the item. It was also made an offence to retain it contrary to the person's duty to fail to take reasonable care of it.

The provision was subject to criticism on a number of grounds. First, it was thought to be overinclusive: the detailed descriptions of material or information which was restricted were effectively made redundant by the inclusion of anything held by a person 'which has been entrusted in confidence to him by any person holding office under His Majesty or which he has obtained *or to which he has had access owing to his position as a person* who holds or has held office under His Majesty . . . '.[34] The words in italics covered any information, whether confidential or not, which came into the possession of a civil servant or other person holding office under the Crown in the course of his duties. This included such matters as the number of cups of tea served in a government department. Many prosecutions under section 2 were not concerned with national security at all, but involved people who had misused information about people obtained from police or departmental records.[35] Where information was considered to be confidential, the person receiving it would have his consciousness of his obligations reinforced by being required to sign a piece of paper stating that he had been told the nature of the information and understood that he was subject to the provisions of the Official Secrets Acts 1911–39, either in relation to that particular piece of information (for example, where the person was neither a person holding office under the Crown nor a government con-tractor) or in respect of all information coming to him in the course of his duties.[36] Where any information, however innocuous, about government might be subject to the Act, it weakened the moral authority of the Act over all information, including that which was potentially damaging to the state. While it is true that such informa-tion might be used by the intelligence service of a foreign power as a way of testing the credibility of informants who claim to have access to the inner reaches of government, it would be an exaggeration to say that divulging such information in itself represents a significant threat to the safety of the state.

Secondly, the criminal provisions in section 2 were anomalous in that the only *mens rea* which the prosecution was required to prove was an intention to communicate or receive the material. It was not necessary to prove that the defendant knew what the material was, or that it was likely to harm the interests of the state.

Thirdly, the width of the section made it possible for the government to stifle the flow of information to those, such as MPs, who had a legitimate use for it in

---

[34] Official Secrets Act 1911, s. 2(1), as amended; emphasis added.

[35] D. Hooper, *Official Secrets: The Use and Abuse of the Act* (London: Secker & Warburg, 1987), App. 1, 243–73, provides a very useful summary of seventy-three selected prosecutions brought under s. 2 of the 1911 Act.

[36] This procedure was popularly but misleadingly known as 'signing the Official Secrets Act'. The text of the declaration is reproduced in Hooper, *Official Secrets*, 276.

performing their constitutional function as scrutineers of government activity. Even the limited defence that the defendant was under an obligation to communicate the material in the interests of the state was restricted severely by the interpretation placed on it by McCowan J in *R. v. Ponting*.[37] The defendant had been a senior civil servant in the Ministry of Defence who believed that the government had been misleading Parliament over the circumstances in which an Argentine battle cruiser, the *General Belgrano*, had been sunk during the Falklands war. He had sent documents concerning the sinking to Mr. Tam Dalyell MP, who had been trying to uncover the facts. Nobody suggested that the disclosure had affected national security. For Mr. Ponting it was argued that it was his duty, in the interest of the state, to communicate the documents to an MP, because civil servants had a constitutional duty to Parliament to facilitate the discharge of its functions. The prosecution asserted, and McCowan J accepted, that the interests of the state were to be defined by the government of the day, and for practical purposes were identical with the interests of the government of the day. The judge relied on speeches in a House of Lords decision on section 1 of the Act,[38] but those speeches had established a rebuttable presumption that the implementation of government policy was in the interests of the state, rather than an irrebuttable presumption that whatever the government wanted was in the interests of the state.

In fact, successive governments have made selective use of secrecy obligations, authorizing disclosure, usually on a non-attributable basis, of information they wanted to be made public,[39] and prosecuting when a disclosure disadvantaged them politically. Mr. Ponting and his advisers had exploited this, inside and outside the court, in a highly effective public-relations exercise.[40] Despite McCowan J's direction, the jury acquitted Mr. Ponting, probably reflecting public contempt for the government's attempt to conflate its own narrow political interest with the state's interest.

The jury's decision sounded the death knell for section 2, notwithstanding the effort by the Cabinet Secretary after the case to restate the principles governing a civil servant's obligations in a way which excluded any constitutional responsibility to Parliament, or indeed to anyone other than the government of the day.[41] It was widely accepted that section 2 had to be replaced, and attention turned to deciding the best approach to drafting a new provision. However, the debate was not taking place in isolation from wider security issues. It reached a climax at a time when the processes for maintaining secrecy and stifling whistle-blowing were under intense media and judicial examination in relation to the proposed serialization of the book *Spycatcher* by Mr. Peter Wright, a former MI5 officer. This focused attention on the legal arrangements available for prior restraint, and the way in which the law balanced the public interest in knowing how the state is run against the interest asserted by state organs in keeping their activities secret.

[37] [1985] Crim. LR 318.

[38] *Chandler v. DPP* [1964] AC 763, [1962] 3 All ER 142, HL.

[39] Something of this sort happened in the Westland affair: see Hooper, *Official Secrets*, ch. 16, and R. Austin, 'The Westland Affair: Open Government by Error' (1986) 39 *Current Legal Problems* 269–82.

[40] Hooper, *Official Secrets*, ch. 12; C. Ponting, 'R. v. Ponting' (1987) 14 *J. Law and Soc.* 366–72; R. Thomas, 'The British Official Secrets Act 1911–1939 and the Ponting Case' [1986] Crim. LR 491–510; G. Drewry, 'The Ponting Case: Leaking in the Public Interest' [1985] *PL* 203–12.

[41] See Ch. 13, above.

(3) CIVIL LAW AND PRIOR RESTRAINT OF BREACHES OF SECRECY

From the government's point of view, it is always preferable to prevent disclosures rather than punish the perpetrators after the damage has been done. If public interests are really under threat, prior restraint is a more efficient way of upholding them than subsequent restraint. It is a feature of the criminal law that it does not normally provide for the prior restraint of communications. Injunctions will normally not issue to prevent breaches of the criminal law, although it is open to the Attorney-General, as guardian of the public interest in maintaining compliance with the criminal law, to commence an action for an injunction, either on the relation of a member of the public or of his own motion, if he deems it to be in the public interest.[42] But when seeking to uphold governmental secrecy by restraining threatened disclosures, it would not always have been sufficient for the Attorney-General to rely on prospective breaches of the Official Secrets Acts 1911–39, because the courts might not regard the case as falling within the types of situations in which such discretionary remedies could properly be granted, stated by Lord Wilberforce as follows:[43]

'It is an exceptional power confined, in practice, to cases where an offence is frequently repeated in disregard of a, usually, inadequate penalty (see *Attorney-General (on the relation of Manchester Corporation) v. Harris*)[44] or to cases of emergency (see *Attorney-General v. Chaudry*).'[45]

In 1975, government lawyers hit on a ground for seeking an injunction restraining publication which did not require them to show that these conditions were satisfied. When the literary executors of Richard Crossman, a former Labour Cabinet Minister, were preparing his diaries for publication, the Attorney-General sought to restrain publication on the ground that the diaries revealed details of discussions within Cabinet which were protected by a duty of confidence owed by every Cabinet Minister to his colleagues.[46] The advantage of an application for an injunction to restrain a breach of confidence is that in governmental matters it is usually relatively easy to establish the existence of a duty of confidence, as the whole system of government is dominated by the idea that almost everything is confidential. The doctrine of breach of confidence had been developed in private-law contexts, protecting business and privacy interests, as noted in Chapter 11, above. If adopted in a public-law setting, it would have had the effect of casting the workings of government into yet deeper shadow. This would have appealed only to members of the government and to civil servants and members of the security services.

---

[42] J. Ll. J. Edwards, *The Law Officers of the Crown* (London: Sweet & Maxwell, 1964), 286–93; *Gouriet v. Union of Post Office Workers* [1978] AC 435, [1977] 3 All ER 70, HL; D. Feldman, 'Injunctions and the Criminal Law' (1979) 42 *MLR* 369–88; J. Ll. J. Edwards, *The Attorney General, Politics and the Public Interest* (London: Sweet & Maxwell, 1984), 129–45. The similar power of local authorities under the Local Government Act 1972, s. 222, extends only to cases in which an authority is acting in the interests of inhabitants of its area, and so is not normally appropriate to protecting the national interest as a whole: B. Hough, 'Local Authorities as Guardians of the Public Interest' [1992] *PL* 130–49 at 139–43.

[43] *Gouriet v. Union of Post Office Workers* [1978] AC 435 at 481, [1977] 3 All ER at 83 *per* Lord Wilberforce.

[44] [1961] 1 QB 74.

[45] [1971] 3 All ER 938.

[46] *Attorney-General v. Jonathan Cape Ltd.* [1976] QB 752, [1975] 3 All ER 484.

In the event, Lord Widgery CJ admitted breach of confidence to the public-law sphere, but subject to a major qualification: before it could be invoked by government, the government would have to demonstrate that a public interest required that the publication in question be restrained. This interest would then be weighed against any favouring publication. This imposed a double burden on the Attorney-General: first, to show that the material in question was held in confidence; secondly, a burden not carried by private claimants in breach of confidence actions, to show a public interest in maintaining the confidence. Lord Widgery adopted this approach from the judgments of the US Supreme Court in *New York Times Co. v. United States*,[47] where by a six to three majority the court had, on a balance-of-interest analysis, rejected an attempt by the US administration to enjoin publication by the *New York Times* of a classified document, *History of US Decision-Making Process on Viet Nam Policy* (the so-called 'Pentagon Papers'). The administration had argued that publication would damage national security, but this claim was not accepted by the majority, partly because of the largely historical significance of the material. The approach was also influential in limiting the scope of 'executive privilege', asserted by President Nixon in the course of the Watergate scandal.[48]

In the case of the Crossman diaries, there was little dispute about the confidential nature of Cabinet discussions. Each member of the Cabinet is bound by the convention of collective Cabinet responsibility, one element in which is an expectation that the course of discussion in Cabinet will not be disclosed.[49] However, the Attorney-General failed to discharge the burden of showing that there was an indefinitely continuing, overriding public interest in maintaining the secrecy of Cabinet discussions. The governmental interest in maintaining confidence had to be balanced against the public interest in free expression, particularly, in a democracy, freedom to impart information about the way in which government is conducted. Lord Widgery CJ accepted that the balance favoured enforcing the confidence up to a point, but held that the public interest in protecting confidences in public law did not operate indefinitely. In 1975, the events and issues covered by the first volume of the diaries lay ten years or more in the past, so Lord Widgery decided that publication would not interfere with free and frank discussion in the current Cabinet. Against this, Dr. Geoffrey Marshall has argued persuasively that, when laying down a legal principle concerning the publication of details of Cabinet discussions, the question should have been whether knowing that today's discussion might be published in ten years would inhibit today's Ministers, not whether publishing a ten-year-old discussion would prejudice today's discussions.[50] This is a criticism of the way in which Lord Widgery weighed the relevant interests. It does not affect the fundamental principle which Lord Widgery laid down, namely that the obligation of secrecy on Cabinet Ministers is neither absolute nor of infinite duration, and that the extent of the obligation depends on a balance of public interests which is to be settled by the courts. An

---

[47] 403 US 713 (1971).
[48] *United States v. Nixon* 418 US 683 (1974).
[49] G. Marshall, *Constitutional Conventions* (Oxford: Clarendon Press, 1986), 58–61.
[50] Marshall, *Constitutional Conventions*, at 60.

attempt to induce Ministers voluntarily to accept restrictions on what may be published, based on the *Report of the Radcliffe Committee of Privy Councillors on Ministerial Memoirs*,[51] appears to have been successful. Many Cabinet Ministers have since brought out their own memoirs and diaries, in the process adding greatly to people's understanding of the way in which British Cabinet government works.

The general approach of the Supreme Court of the USA in the Pentagon Papers case and of Lord Widgery CJ in the Crossman Diaries case was developed further by Mason J in the High Court of Australia in *Commonwealth of Australia v. John Fairfax & Sons Ltd*.[52] The federal government attempted to use the doctrine of breach of confidence to restrain publication of a book, *Documents on Australian Defence and Foreign Policy 1968–75*, containing previously unpublished communications between the Australian and Indonesian governments and their diplomats. The relationship between Australia and Indonesia was politically sensitive, because of a division of opinion in Australia concerning the appropriate response to Indonesian claims over East Timor. The government ultimately succeeded on the ground that publication would breach their copyright in the material, but did not succeed on the issue of breach of confidence. The government argued that the material was confidential, as it was not 'public property and public knowledge'.[53] It had probably been leaked by a public servant in breach of his or her duty, and the publishers knew that the documents were classified and that the government had not authorized publication. Mason J refused an interim injunction on this ground, because, when a government seeks to invoke confidentiality protection for governmental information, the court must ask itself what detriment the public interest, rather than the government or the governing party, suffers from an unauthorized disclosure.

'The equitable principle has been fashioned to protect the personal, private and proprietary interests of the citizen, not to protect the very different interests of the executive government. It acts, or is supposed to act, not according to standards of private interest, but in the public interest. This is not to say that Equity will not protect information in the hands of the government, but it is to say that when Equity protects government information it will look at the matter through different spectacles . . . It is unacceptable, in our democratic society, that there should be a restraint on the publication of information relating to government when the only vice of that information is that it enables the public to discuss, review and criticize government action. Accordingly, the court will determine the government's claim to confidentiality by reference to the public interest. Unless disclosure is likely to injure the public interest, it will not be protected.'[54]

This places the public interest in open government and accountability in a democracy at the centre of any consideration of a governmental claim to confidentiality. In that case, Mason J decided that those interests outweighed the interest asserted by the

---

[51] Cmnd. 6386 (1976). The Committee was set up to consider the position in the light of the Crossman Diaries case.

[52] (1980) 147 CLR 39, HC of Australia.

[53] This generous definition of confidentiality was derived from Lord Greene MR in *Saltman Engineering Co. Ltd. v. Campbell Engineering Co. Ltd.* (1948) [1963] 3 All ER 413, CA, at 415.

[54] (1980) 147 CLR 39 at 51–2, *per* Mason J.

government in maintaining trust and a free flow of information between governments when conducting international affairs, not least because the book had already achieved some currency and the continued circulation of the information which it contained could not be prevented by restraining publication of further copies.

Unlike the Pentagon Papers and *John Fairfax* cases, the *Crossman Diaries* case raised no issue of national security or international relations, but Lord Widgery said, *obiter*, that 'the court must have power to deal with publication which threatens national security'.[55] When the doctrine of breach of confidence was invoked in England in support of a national-security interest, the government ultimately failed to show either that the material in question was still secret, or that there was a continuing interest in secrecy which overrode that in publication. This decision, in the *Spycatcher* case,[56] is considered further in the next section.

The decision in the *Spycatcher* case made the prospects for using the civil law of breach of confidence to control leaks of government information look much less rosy, and the government turned its attention back to subsequent restraint and the use of the criminal law. Proposals for reform of the Official Secrets Acts 1911–39, replacing the blanket provisions of section 2 of the 1911 Act with more narrowly drawn and carefully directed categories of secret information and material, had been made regularly—for example, by the Franks Committee[57] in 1972. A Protection of Official Information Bill, introduced in 1979 by the Conservative government, was withdrawn. In the absence of further government-sponsored legislation, there were various attempts by back-benchers to introduce an amending bill. The last of these was a Protection of Official Information Bill, introduced by Mr. Richard Shepherd MP during the 1987–88 session. It was defeated when the government took the highly unusual step of issuing a three-line whip to compel its supporters in the Commons to vote against a private member's bill introduced by one of its own back-benchers. Eventually, the government came forward with its own proposals in a White Paper,[58] translated into legislation as the Official Secrets Act 1989. This at last repealed and replaced the discredited section 2 of the 1911 Act.[59] Instead of a blanket prohibition on disclosure of all types of information, the 1989 Act specified the types of material which are to be protected by the criminal law and the kinds of people subject to criminal sanctions for making disclosures. The main features of the 1989 Act are explained in section 3 below.

This brief survey of the background to the legal treatment of the security interests of the state can best be concluded by drawing attention to bring out three features of the problem of legally restricting freedom to impart and receive information in order to protect national security. First, national security is difficult to define. It used to be given a relatively narrow meaning, if the role of the security service (MI5), as described in 1952 by Sir David Maxwell Fyfe (then Home Secretary) in a memorandum to the Director-General, is any guide: 'the defence of the realm as a whole

---

55 *Attorney General v. Jonathan Cape Ltd.* [1976] QB 752 at 769, [1975] 3 All ER 484 at 495.
56 *Attorney-General v. Guardian Newspapers (No. 2)* [1990] 1 AC 109, [1988] 3 All ER 545, HL.
57 *Report of the Franks Committee on Section 2 of the Official Secrets Act 1911*, Cmnd. 5104 (1972).
58 Home Office, *Reform of Section 2 of the Official Secrets Act 1911*, Cm. 408 (1988).
59 P. Birkinshaw, *Reforming the Secret State* (Hull: Hull University Press, 1990).

from external and internal dangers arising from attempts at espionage and sabotage and from the actions of persons and organisations whether directed from within or without the country which may be judged subversive to the state'. This was a wide and politically charged formulation: subversion is a weasel word, and, as experience elsewhere in the world has shown, what is honest political opposition to one person can easily be regarded as subversion by a government or security service.[60] Evidence suggests that the security service exploited the idea of subversion during the 1950s and 1960s to launch operations motivated by right-wing political bias against trade unions, the Labour Party, and liberal or civil liberties groups.

The duties of MI5 were placed on a statutory footing by the Security Service Act 1989, and they have subsequently been extended by amendments. Section 1(2) and (4)[61] defines its functions considerably more widely than Maxwell Fyfe did:[62] 'the protection of national security and, in particular, its protection against threats from espionage, terrorism and sabotage, from the activities of agents of foreign powers and *from actions intended to overthrow or undermine parliamentary democracy by political, industrial or violent means*' (italics added), and 'to act in support of the activities of police forces, the National Criminal Intelligence Service, the National Crime Squad, and other law enforcement agencies in the prevention and detection of serious crime'. Concentrating on the protection of national security, the notion of subversion is absent from the formulation. None the less, the suggestion, in the words italicized in this passage, that national security requires that parliamentary democracy (itself a problematic term) should not be undermined by political means, is ominous. It seems to be over-inclusive, threatening repression of the non-violent expression of a brand of political thought. It is a throw-back to the eighteenth century, when a non-violent attack on any institution or official of the state was liable to be stigmatized as a seditious libel.[63] It is at least arguable that one of the important principles of modern parliamentary democracy is that it should be permissible to put before the electorate any political creed, including advocating non-parliamentary processes of democracy or even anarchy, so long as it is done peaceably and in a time, place, and manner which is not likely to give rise to public disorder or racial hatred.

Secondly, there is a problematical relationship between the public interest, national security (which is just one aspect of the public interest, but may sometimes be accorded overriding weight), and the interests of the government (which in a system dominated by party politics are largely partisan, rather than being the interests of either the nation or the public). The sensitivity of this relationship is illustrated by cases which gave the appearance that the criminal law was being used in an attempt to prevent political embarrassment to the government.[64] (The attempts backfired.) It

---

[60] A different formulation is offered by L. Lustgarten and I. Leigh, *In from the Cold: National Security and Parliamentary Democracy* (Oxford: Clarendon Press, 1994), ch. 1.

[61] Subs. (4) was inserted by the Security Service Act 1996 and amended by the Police Act 1997.

[62] For full discussion of the national security aspects of this legislation, see I. Leigh and L. Lustgarten, 'The Security Service Act 1989' (1989) 52 *MLR* 801–36; Lustgarten and Leigh, *In From the Cold*, ch. 14.

[63] See section 4(2), below.

[64] Besides the *Ponting* case, see, e.g. the account of the trial in 1971 of Mr. Jonathan Aitken, then a journalist, under the Official Secrets Act 1911, s. 2: J. Aitken, *Officially Secret* (London: Weidenfeld & Nicolson, 1971). Mr. Aitken became an MP, and following the May 1992 general election became Minister for Defence

becomes still more sensitive if, as suggested above in relation to the Security Service Act 1989, the protection of national security is held to take on a substantive political content, requiring officials to discriminate against certain types of political belief.

The third characteristic is the complex interaction of civil and criminal law. Governments have used each in turn, or both together, in order to maintain a system in which secrecy is normal practice. It is possible that there may in the future be cross-pollination between the standards in security matters laid down by the two systems. When the *Spycatcher* case was before the courts, Scott J pointed out that it was open to Parliament to provide guidelines for the relative weightings of different public interests in civil proceedings to restrain publication of state secrets, but that, as Parliament had not done so, the judges had to use their own judgment.[65] Later, in *Lord Advocate v. The Scotsman Publications Ltd.*,[66] the government applied unsuccessfully in civil proceedings for an interim interdict preventing a Scottish newspaper from publishing extracts from the memoirs of a former officer of MI6, the secret intelligence service. By this time, the Official Secrets Act 1989 had been passed, but had not yet been brought into force. In the House of Lords, Lord Templeman based his rejection of the government's claim on his view that the 1989 Act, creating criminal offences, provided guidance as to the circumstances in which restraint of expression is necessary in a democratic society. Noting that third parties who disclose material passed to them in breach of the Act do not commit an offence unless their disclosure is damaging to the state, Lord Templeman said:

'In my opinion the civil jurisdiction of the courts of this country to grant an injunction restraining a breach of confidence at the suit of the Crown should not, in principle, be exercised in a manner different from or more severe than any appropriate restriction which Parliament has imposed in the 1989 Act and which, if breached, will create a criminal offence under that Act.'[67]

This is a welcome assertion of an important liberal principle in relation to freedom of expression: namely that prior restraint is, at least, no less objectionable than subsequent restraint by criminal sanctions, and should therefore be no more extensive in its operation. A similar approach may be implicit in the speeches of Lord Keith, with whom Lord Griffiths and Lord Goff agreed, and Lord Jauncey. They held that the government was not entitled to the interim interdict because disclosure would cause no damage to national security. However, they did not employ or endorse Lord Templeman's explicit linking of the civil-law principles to the criminal law; indeed, Lord Jauncey was the only other Law Lord who even mentioned the 1989 Act. The

---

Procurement. He later lost a libel action over allegations that he had received favours in connection with his parliamentary functions, and was sentenced to 18 months' imprisonment for attempting to pervert the course of justice in the libel proceedings. He became religious while in prison, and undertook study for a degree in theology. At the time of writing, David Shayler faces prosecution for revealing information and making allegations about the workings of the security and intelligence services based on his experience when he was a member.

65 [1990] 1 AC 109 at 144, [1988] 3 All ER 545 at 570.
66 [1990] 1 AC 812, [1989] 2 All ER 852, HL.
67 [1990] 1 AC at 824, [1989] 2 All ER at 859.

authority for saying that the link exists, and that prior restraint is not to extend beyond the reach of the criminal law, is therefore by no means unequivocal.

15.2 CIVIL PROCEEDINGS TO RESTRAIN PUBLICATION, NATIONAL SECURITY, AND THE PUBLIC INTEREST: BREACH OF CONFIDENCE, *SPYCATCHER*, AND ITS IMPLICATIONS[68]

The efficiency, from the government's point of view, of stifling information or opinion before it can do harm falls to be balanced against the public interest in the flow of information and the exchange of opinion necessary to a functioning democracy. The conflict between these interests was seen in stark form in the litigation which surrounded the attempts by a number of newspapers to serialize or report on a book, *Spycatcher*, by Peter Wright, who had been a scientific officer in the counter-espionage branch of the security service, MI5, from 1955 to 1973, and had been on the personal staff of the Director-General of MI5 as adviser on counter-espionage from 1973 until he retired in 1976. The book, completed and in the hands of Australian publishers in 1985, contained an account of Mr. Wright's work for MI5. It included accounts of buggings and burglaries, including an attempt to bug the suit occupied by Mr. Kruschev at Claridges when he was on an official visit to the UK; an allegation that Sir Roger Hollis, a previous Director-General of MI5, had been a double agent employed by the USSR; and various allegations concerning (*inter alia*) a plan to assassinate President Nasser, and a conspiracy by some officers to discredit Mr. Harold Wilson and destabilize his government.

Whether or not these accounts were true (and official inquiries failed to find convincing evidence to support the allegations concerning Sir Roger Hollis and the conspiracy against the Wilson government), the information and allegations were stale. They related to a period preceding Mr. Wright's retirement, and had nearly all been published before by other writers without any legal action being taken against them. Nevertheless, the government considered that publication had to be stopped as a matter of principle, because Mr. Wright, having been a member of the security service, was under a lifelong duty of secrecy in respect of matters which came to his attention in the course of his duties. It was said to be in the public interest to prevent disclosures by members and former members of the security and intelligence services, for two main reasons. First (irrespective of the content of any disclosure), the confidence and morale of the services depended on maintaining absolute trust that their discussions, policies, and actions would not be disclosed by colleagues and former colleagues. Secondly, good international relations, and particularly co-operation and sharing of information with the intelligence and security services of friendly powers, depended on being able to ensure that confidences would not be breached by officers.

---

[68] See generally F. Gurry, *Breach of Confidence* (Oxford: Clarendon Press, 1985); R. Wacks, *Personal Information: Privacy and the Law* (Oxford: Clarendon Press, 1989), ch. 3; Robertson and Nicol, *Media Law*, 3rd edn., 172–96.

In order to prevent a breach of this trust, the government invoked the law of breach of confidence.[69]

The government's first step was to sue the Australian publishers in New South Wales for an injunction restraining publication, or, failing that, an account of profits.[70] Before the hearing, two English newspapers, the *Observer* and the *Guardian*, obtained details of the allegations made in Mr. Wright's manuscript, and published them in June 1986, together with a description of the nature of the pending New South Wales proceedings. The Attorney-General obtained injunctions in England restraining those newspapers from further publication of the allegations, and interim injunctions to preserve the confidentiality of the material pending trial of the action. In the form in which the interim injunctions were upheld by a majority of the House of Lords, they restrained not only publication of extracts from the *Spycatcher* manuscript, but also publication of reports on the Australian proceedings.[71] In contempt proceedings, it was subsequently held that the injunctions against the *Observer* and the *Guardian* also bound other newspapers which had notice of them.[72] Nevertheless, news of the allegations continued to leak out in the UK and abroad. The New South Wales application failed.[73]

Meanwhile, the editor of the *Sunday Times*, having heard that *Spycatcher* was to be published shortly in the USA, negotiated a serialization with the American publishers, and obtained from them a copy of the manuscript. On 12 July 1987, the day before the book was published in the USA, the *Sunday Times* published extracts from the manuscript in the UK. By now, the government seemed engaged in a futile attempt to stop people from discovering that which they already knew. Sir Nicolas Browne-Wilkinson V-C discharged the English interim injunctions, accepting that they could no longer serve their main purpose in preserving the alleged confidentiality of the information in *Spycatcher* pending trial, but his decision was reversed by the Court of Appeal, and on appeal their decision was upheld by a majority of the House of Lords.[74] At the end of 1987, the full trial of the government's action started, leading eventually to the discharge of the injunctions, but the award of an account of profits against Times Newspapers.[75] In the course of this litigation, the courts went a substantial way

---

[69] Scott J was later to point out that the government's claim was not strictly based on a duty of confidence, as it encompassed secret material unearthed by Mr. Wright's own efforts, without being confided to him, and also all information, whether confidential or not, which Mr. Wright acquired in his capacity as a member of MI5: [1990] 1 AC at 144, [1988] 3 All ER at 571. Nevertheless, it was accepted that the principles of breach of confidence were applicable by analogy, subject to any special extensions or restrictions necessitated by the public-law nature of the case.

[70] For an account of the history of the proceedings and of the allegations published in *Spycatcher*, see the judgment of Scott J in *A.-G. v. Guardian Newspapers (No. 2)* [1990] 1 AC at 120–38, [1988] 3 All ER at 552–66.

[71] *A.-G. v. Guardian Newspapers Ltd.* [1987] 1 WLR 1248, [1987] All ER 316, HL.

[72] *A.-G. v. Newspaper Publishing plc* [1988] Ch. 333, [1987] 3 All ER 276, CA; *A.-G. v. Times Newspapers Ltd.* [1992] 1 AC 191, [1991] 2 All ER 398, HL.

[73] *A.-G. v. Heinemann Publishers Australia Pty Ltd.* (1987) 8 NSWLR 341, affirmed CA of NSW (1987) 10 NSWLR 86, and HC of Australia (1988) 165 CLR 30.

[74] *A.-G. v. Guardian Newspapers Ltd.* [1987] 1 WLR 1248, [1987] 3 All ER 316 (Lords Brandon, Templeman, and Ackner; Lords Bridge and Oliver dissented).

[75] *A.-G. v. Guardian Newspapers Ltd. (No. 2)* [1990] 1 AC 109, [1988] 3 All ER 545, HL.

towards settling the scope and enforceability of duties of confidence in respect of information about, or held by, the state.

The English and Scottish caselaw on prior restraint for national-security purposes must now be read in the light of the right under ECHR Article 10 and the Human Rights Act 1998 to receive and impart information and ideas. In 1991 the European Court of Human Rights unanimously decided that the courts in the UK had violated the rights of newspapers under ECHR Article 10 in the *Spycatcher* litigation by continuing the pre-trial injunctions after the material had entered the public domain in the USA.[76] The Court held that the law on interim injunctions had been sufficiently clear to be said to be 'prescribed by law', as the criteria for granting interim injunctions had been well established in the common law.[77] It also held that the aim of the injunctions, to maintain the authority of the judiciary by preserving the subject matter of the action, was legitimate within Article 10(2).[78] However, the question remained whether the interference was 'necessary in a democratic society' for those purposes. This required the Court to consider four factors:

(1) Freedom of expression constitutes one of the essential foundations of democratic society, and is as applicable to offensive, shocking, or disturbing ideas as to inoffensive ones.[79]

(2) This was particularly important in relation to the press, which has the responsibility for imparting information and ideas to a public which has the right to receive them.

(3) 'Necessary' implies the existence of a pressing social need, as the Court had earlier held in the *Sunday Times* case.[80]

(4) The Court had to apply the principle of proportionality to the measures adopted, to see whether they were proportionate to the aim pursued, and whether the reasons supporting them were relevant and sufficient.

Applying these considerations, the Court held by a majority of fourteen to ten that the injunctions had originally been justified, having regard to the margin of appreciation allowed to the English courts in assessing the exigencies of the case. However, the Court held unanimously that the situation changed radically once the book *Spycatcher* was published in the USA in July 1987. At that point, confidentiality was destroyed, and the desire to maintain the authority of the court by preventing further prejudice to the Attorney-General's claim did not constitute a sufficient reason for the purposes of Article 10(2), because the substance of the Attorney-General's interest, the confidentiality of the matters canvassed in *Spycatcher*, had already been destroyed. The majority decision of the House of Lords in *Attorney-General v. Guardian*

---

[76] *The Observer and The Guardian v. United Kingdom*, Eur. Ct. HR, Series A, No. 216, Judgment of 26 November 1991, 14 EHRR 153; *The Sunday Times v. United Kingdom (No. 2)*, Eur. Ct. HR, Series A, No. 217, Judgment of 26 November 1991, 14 EHRR 229.

[77] See *American Cyanamid Co. v. Ethicon Ltd.* [1975] AC 396, [1975] 1 All ER 504, HL.

[78] Protecting the position of parties to an action forms a legitimate element in maintaining the authority and impartiality of the judiciary: *Sunday Times v. United Kingdom* (1979) 2 EHRR 245.

[79] *Lingens v. Austria*, Eur. Ct. HR, Series A, No. 103, Judgment of 8 July 1986, 8 EHRR 407.

[80] Eur. Ct. HR, Series A, No. 3, Judgment of 26 April 1979, 2 EHRR 245.

Newspapers Ltd. on 30 July 1987 to continue the injunctions had probably served no useful purpose, and had prevented the press from exercising its right and duty to purvey information, which was already available, on a matter of legitimate public concern. Accordingly, the interference with press freedom represented by the injunctions was no longer 'necessary in a democratic society' after 30 July 1987. Lord Bridge's prophecy that the government would 'face inevitable condemnation and humiliation by the European Court of Human Rights' thus proved accurate.[81]

Ten judges, in partly dissenting judgments, held that the interim injunctions had offended against the principle of necessity in the period between their first granting on 11 July 1986 and 30 July 1987. Judge Morenilla argued that the appropriate standard to adopt in a case of prior restraint would be that of the US Supreme Court in cases such as *Nebraska Press Association v. Stuart*,[82] admitting such restraint only where disclosure would be sure to result in direct, immediate, and irreparable damage to the nation or its people.[83] However, such an approach might make it unnecessarily difficult for plaintiffs to protect their legitimate interests in obtaining a fair trial of their actions (in accordance with rights guaranteed under Article 6 of the Convention) in cases where the alleged wrong consists of a threatened, wrongful disclosure. The judgment of the majority of the European Court of Human Rights strikes a reasonable balance between the rights of the press and the interests of the justice system in maintaining confidentiality pending final hearing of the case. In addition, as noted in section 15.1 above, section 12 of the Human Rights Act 1998 imposes further constraints on the power of courts to grant interim and final remedies which affect the rights under Article 10.

In the light of these principles, the remainder of this section examines the conditions for prior restraint of threatened breaches of confidence, and other remedies available to government.

(1) CONDITIONS FOR PRIOR RESTRAINT FOR BREACH OF CONFIDENCE

(i) The nature of breach of confidence in public law

As noted in Chapter 11 above, breach of confidence is a civil wrong capable of imposing sanctions on publication of information (though not mere opinion). Remedies are available where information is confidential and the defendant obtained it in circumstances which imposed on him a duty to maintain the confidentiality of the information. Duties of confidence may either arise under contracts, or be imposed by equity. In considering the applicability of duties of confidence to government information in *Attorney-General v. Jonathan Cape Ltd.*,[84] Lord Widgery CJ had recognized that actions for breach of confidence have the potential to interfere substantially with the capacity of MPs, the press, and the public to scrutinize and evaluate government. Since there is a public interest in a democracy in being able to evaluate and debate

[81] *A.-G. v. Guardian Newspapers* [1987] 1 WLR at 1286, [1987] 3 All ER at 347.
[82] 427 US 593 (1976).
[83] (1991) 14 EHRR at 220.
[84] [1976] QB 752, [1975] 3 All ER 484.

government organization and policies, he subjected the duties of confidentiality in respect of information about government to certain limits. The most significant limits are the following:

1. Government cannot assert a duty of confidence in respect of information about its activities unless it can demonstrate a clear public interest in maintaining secrecy, which in practice means showing that damage would flow from disclosure. Private claimants are usually assumed to have legitimate grounds for wanting to protect confidential information. By contrast, because the government carries on its activities solely for the public benefit, it is assumed to have no legitimate private interests to protest. Governmental bodies must therefore satisfy the court both that the material is confidential and that it is in the general public interest to keep it secret.

2. Disclosure of a confidence will not be restrained if it can be shown that there is a public interest in revealing it which outweighs the public interest in keeping it secret. As in private law, a person is not bound by a duty of confidence to keep secret iniquitous behaviour or other matters if it is in the public interest that they should be investigated or exposed. However, a person wishing to take advantage of the iniquity defence must show that the allegation appears to be based on substantial grounds, and that any disclosure was made to a person and in a manner appropriate to the matter in question.

'Even if the balance comes down in favour of publication, it does not follow that publication should be to the world through the media. In certain circumstances the public interest may be better served by a limited form of publication perhaps to the police or some other authority who can follow up a suspicion that wrongdoing may lurk beneath the cloak of confidence.'[85]

3. To justify prior restraint, the defendant must normally be present or represented at the hearing, and the court must be satisfied that the applicant is likely to establish at trial that publication should not be allowed, having particular regard to the importance of freedom of expression, the extent to which the material has, or is about to, become available to the public, and the extent to which it is or would be in the public interest for the material to be published.[86] This means that the material must usually retain its confidential quality at the time of the litigation, although it remains possible that a defendant who appears to have acted unlawfully (such as Mr. Wright in the *Spycatcher* case, or the newspapers which entered into agreements with him) might be restrained from publishing what another person or media organization coming by the information innocently would be allowed to publish. The existence of a defendant's legal duty of secrecy puts him in a special position, analogous to that of a fiduciary, for the purpose of the equitable remedy of account of profits, as a majority of the House of Lords held in relation to the former spy George Blake in *Attorney-General v. Blake (Jonathan Cape Ltd., third party)*,[87] decided just over two months before the Human Rights Act 1998 came into force. It remains to be seen whether liability to be

---

[85] A.-G. v. *Guardian Newspapers Ltd. (No. 2)* [1988] 3 All ER at 649 *per* Lord Griffiths. See also *Francome v. Mirror Group Newspapers* [1984] 1 WLR 892, [1984] 2 All ER 408, CA.
[86] Human Rights Act 1998, s. 12.
[87] [2000] 3 WLR 625, HL.

restrained from publishing also depends on the identity of the particular defendant now the 1998 Act is in force.

The public interest in national security goes beyond keeping secrets. It extends to maintaining the efficiency of the defence and security services generally. The effect of knowing that a member or former member of the service could disclose information without sanction might undermine the sense of obligation felt by other members or former members, or simply damage morale, and so indirectly threaten the efficiency of the service. This risk may give rise to a public interest in preventing disclosure. In the interlocutory proceedings in *Attorney-General v. Guardian Newspapers Ltd.*,[88] Lord Templeman and Lord Ackner thought it appropriate to grant an interim injunction to protect the public interest in the proper functioning of the security service. Sir Robert Armstrong, the Cabinet Secretary, had said that there was a risk that morale would be harmed by allowing disclosures by former officers. In *Attorney-General v. Guardian Newspapers Ltd. (No. 2)*[89] Lord Griffiths, noting that Article 10(2) of the European Convention on Human Rights accepts that it may be justifiable to restrict freedom of expression in order to protect national security,[90] treated the national-security implications as quite separate from confidentiality:

'The worldwide publication of *Spycatcher* disposes of the Attorney General's claim based on confidential information, but the claim based on national security remains to be examined. If I had thought that further publication would so damage the morale of the security service that they could not operate efficiently I would have been prepared to grant the injunction in the interests of national security. Of course, I think no such thing.'[91]

If correct, this would mean that publication of non-confidential information by third parties could be restrained if that were necessary to maintain staff morale at an efficient level. However, maintenance of morale is the responsibility of MI5 managers, not courts of Equity. As Lord Goff said:

'In our civil law there is, so far as I am aware, no ground for restricting publication of information relating to national security other than breach of confidence. Information relating to national security is, of its very nature, *prima facie* confidential. . . . [A]ny such publication, if threatened, can therefore be restrained by injunction as a threatened breach of confidence, subject of course to the usual limitations on the duty of confidence. One of these is that information is no longer confidential once it has entered the public domain; once information relating to national security has entered the public domain, I find it difficult to see on what basis further disclosure of such information can be restrained.'[92]

The fact that a disclosure may affect the efficiency of the security service is only one element (though an important one) in the balance of interests which affects the availability of remedies for breach of confidence. It is not an independent head of claim. It will, as Lord Griffiths said, have relatively little weight in relation to a decision

---

[88] [1987] 1 WLR 1248, [1987] 3 All ER 316, HL.
[89] [1990] 1 AC 109, [1988] 3 All ER 545, HL.
[90] [1990] 1 AC at 273, [1988] 3 All ER at 652.
[91] [1990] 1 AC at 275, [1988] 3 All ER at 654.
[92] [1990] 1 AC at 291, [1988] 3 All ER at 666.

whether or not to restrain a publication, but may have more weight when deciding whether to make an order for an account of profits by a former member of the security or intelligence services who has profited from disclosures in breach of a contractual obligation of secrecy, as the House of Lords held by a majority in *Attorney-General v. Blake (Jonathan Cape Ltd., third party)*.[93]

(ii) Weighing the interests: the difference between interlocutory and final hearings

At common law, the weight given to relevant interests varied, depending on whether the proceedings were interlocutory or final. Before trial, courts applied the 'balance of convenience' test which governs interim injunctions generally, without making special allowance for the importance of freedom of expression. Under that test, laid down in *American Cyanamid Co. v. Ethicon*,[94] the court had to balance (a) the plaintiff's need, if successful at trial, to be protected against injury which could not be adequately compensated by an award of damages at trial, against (b) the defendant's need, if successful at trial, to be protected against injury, which could not be adequately compensated under the plaintiff's undertaking in damages, resulting from having been restrained from exercising his rights pending trial. Accordingly, the court had first to decide whether there was a serious issue to be tried (the plaintiff did not need to show a strong prima-facie case, or a likelihood of succeeding at trial). If there was, the court asked whether damages would adequately compensate the plaintiff if successful at trial. In cases concerning national security, damages would never adequately compensate the government. On the other hand, it would not be possible for the defendant to rely on being compensated if successful, as the courts would not require the Crown to give an undertaking in damages when applying for an interim injunction.[95] When the merits were evenly balanced, the court would grant the injunction to preserve the *status quo*. An interim injunction was likely to be granted to restrain publication of information that remained confidential pending trial of the action, because there is a public interest in ensuring that wrongdoers are not able to destroy the plaintiff's cause of action in advance of its enforcement. Restraining a publication pending trial is only a temporary interference with freedom of expression and communication, and is thought to be easier to justify than the permanent ban imposed by a final injunction.

The effect of these principles in national-security and breach-of-confidence cases was that where the government asserted that some damage to security will be done by a breach of a duty of confidence, and there was a serious issue to be tried, the court would virtually always grant an interim injunction, safeguarding the government's interest pending a full hearing of the case, regardless of the court's view of the likely result of the trial, for on an interlocutory application the court is not well placed to assess the strength of the evidence. Only where the government accepted that there

---

[93] [2000] 3 WLR 625 at 641 *per* Lord Nicholls of Birkenhead, 644 *per* Lord Goff of Chieveley and Lord Browne-Wilkinson, 647 *per* Lord Steyn. Lord Hobhouse of Woodborough dissented.

[94] [1975] AC 396, [1975] 1 All ER 504, HL.

[95] *F. Hoffmann-La Roche & Co. AG v. Secretary of State for Trade and Industry* [1975] AC 295, [1974] 2 All ER 1128, HL.

would be no further detriment to the public interest from publication would an interim injunction be refused. For example, in *Lord Advocate v. The Scotsman Publications Ltd.*,[96] the Lord Advocate was refused an interim interdict restraining the publishers of a newspaper from publishing a serialization of the memoirs of *Inside Intelligence* by Anthony Cavendish, a former MI6 officer, which book had already been privately distributed, a copy coming innocently into the hands of the newspaper. The government denied that further publication would harm national security, but argued that publication should be restrained to enforce the lifelong duty of confidentiality attaching to officers of the security and intelligence services. The House of Lords decided that, while it would have been appropriate to restrain the initial publication by Mr. Cavendish, no public interest would be served by restraining the further publication by an innocent third party where no damage would result.

At the hearing of the action, the position was very different. The public interest in the due administration of justice, which justified the interim injunction, usually ceased to be a relevant consideration, and the case for a permanent interference with free expression stood or fell on its own merits. This meant that the grounds for granting an interim injunction were very different from those for granting a final injunction. This was well illustrated by the *Spycatcher* litigation, in which very wide injunctions were granted at the interim stage, even preventing public libraries from purchasing the book (although not from taking the newspapers),[97] but no injunction was granted at trial. Now, however, section 12 of the Human Rights Act 1998, outlined above, has the effect of removing such cases from the scope of the balance-of-convenience test, bringing the test for pre-trial restraint much closer to that which applies at trial. There, the position both at common law and under ECHR Article 10 is and has always been similar to that adopted by Lord Widgery CJ in the *Jonathan Cape* case and by Mason J in the *John Fairfax* case. In *Attorney-General v. Guardian Newspapers Ltd. (No. 2)* the House of Lords unanimously held that the publicity given abroad to the publication of Peter Wright's allegations, together with their previous publication by other authors, had effectively undermined the confidentiality of the material. In view of the worldwide publicity for Mr. Wright's allegations, it could not be in the public interest for the public in the UK to be prevented from learning what everyone else in the world already had the opportunity of knowing. They also held, by a four to one majority, that any damage which the articles published in the *Guardian* and the *Observer* in 1986, reporting the progress of the litigation in New South Wales, might have done to the public interest in national security was outweighed by the public interest in the freedom of the press to report court action. In the House of Lords, Lord Goff said:[98]

'. . . the articles were very short: they gave little detail of the allegations; a number of the allegations had been made before; and in so far as the articles went beyond what had previously been published, I do not consider that the judge erred in holding that, in the

---

[96] [1990] 1 AC 812, [1989] 2 All ER 852, HL (Sc.).

[97] A.-G. v. Observer Ltd.; Re an application by Derbyshire County Council [1988] 1 All ER 385.

[98] [1990] 1 AC at 290, [1988] 3 All ER at 665.

circumstances, the claim to an injunction was not proportionate to the legitimate aim pursued.'

The House refused an injunction permanently restraining the *Guardian* and the *Observer*, or anyone else, from publishing extracts from or reviewing or commenting on the book, because the material in it was by then in the public domain. Furthermore, the House refused an injunction against future publication of material derived from Mr. Wright. Even the *Sunday Times* was to be free to publish.

All the judges accepted that Mr. Wright, as a former member of MI5, was *prima facie* subject to a lifelong duty of confidentiality in respect of matters which came to his attention in the course of his service. Several of them considered, *obiter*, that he or his publishers would have been restrained by injunction from any further publication, had they been within the jurisdiction of the English courts, even after widespread publicity for the allegations. However, they differed as to the reasons for this. Scott J, all the judges in the Court of Appeal, and Lord Griffiths and Lord Jauncey in the House of Lords, considered that a person should be unable to relieve himself of an obligation of confidence by his own wrongful act of publication, regardless of any other obligations which might arise therefrom. Lord Brightman and Lord Goff considered that even Mr. Wright's obligation of confidence ceased once the information was published and so lost its confidential character (albeit by Mr. Wright's own wrongful act). They and Lord Keith thought that the sole reason for preventing a person in Mr. Wright's position from further publications of old revelations would be to prevent him or his publishers from profiting by their own wrongs. In other words, any injunction would be punitive rather than protective; it would not advance any legitimate national-security interest, but might be available to prevent unjust enrichment or a breach of copyright. The aim of preventing people from making an illicit profit by breach of duty can legitimately be pursued even after the information has been disclosed by others. The question for a court of equity is not merely whether the information remains secret, but whether the particular defendant is subject to an obligation not to take a benefit from disclosing it. For this reason, the government has a remedy by way of account of profits where anyone has profited by breaching the duty of non-disclosure, and it may be proper to use the two remedies—injunction and account—against different people at different times.

In view of the judges' conclusion that no damage would be caused to the public interests advanced by the government to justify an injunction, because of the widespread publicity already given to Mr. Wright's allegations, it was unnecessary to consider the iniquity defence advanced by the newspapers. Nevertheless, it was considered. Scott J drew a distinction between matters such as the adequacy of the system for securing accountability of the security service, which were matters of legitimate public debate but could not justify reporting unauthorized disclosures about the operation of the service, and matters such as the attempt to assassinate President Nasser or destabilize the Wilson government, which involved iniquity of a high order such that it was in the pubic interest to inform the public. 'The press has a legitimate role in disclosing scandals in government'.[99] It is the purpose of the duty of con-

---

[99] [1990] 1 AC at 167, [1988] 3 All ER at 588.

fidence in this sphere to facilitate the efficiency of the security service, not to prevent the government of the day from being exposed to embarrassment or pressure.[100] In the House of Lords, it was suggested that it would be in the public interest for their recipient to air allegations only if (in the words of Lord Goff) 'following such investigations as are reasonably open to the recipient, and having regard to all the circumstances of the case, the allegation in question can reasonably be regarded as being a credible allegation from an apparently reliable source'.[101] This would seem to be satisfied in the case of Mr. Wright, a former MI5 officer whose evidence had been accepted by other writers on the security service in the past. The seriousness of the allegations would also probably have justified publishing them in the news media, rather than referring them to the police or a member of Parliament. On the other hand, it could not justify publishing the details of other MI5 operations contained in the remainder of *Spycatcher*, nor could it justify publishing extracts from those other parts of the book which could not claim to be serving a legitimate public interest.

(4) OTHER REMEDIES AVAILABLE TO THE GOVERNMENT

There is no general power at common law to grant an injunction freezing or seizing assets in order to prevent a person from benefitting from his or her wrongful acts. This was established in *Attorney-General v. Blake (Jonathan Cape Ltd., third party)*,[102] when the House of Lords, overruling the Court of Appeal, refused to grant such an injunction to the Attorney-General in respect of royalties owed to the former spy George Blake from sales of his memoirs. It was accepted that the publication of the memoirs probably breached section 1 of the Official Secrets Act 1989 (examined below), but the statutory power to confiscate proceeds of crime depended on a conviction, and Mr. Blake was outside the jurisdiction and unlikely ever to return to it. The common law and Equity could not develop powers of expropriation where the ground was fully occupied by statute.

On the other hand, the courts can grant the equitable remedy of an account of profits, which can have an equivalent effect. The action for an account of profits is distinct from an action for an injunction to restrain publication. The former does not chill free expression; it merely makes it unprofitable. Even in the USA, with the tenderness which American courts display for freedom of speech under the First Amendment, national-security concerns may limit even constitutionally guaranteed rights. In *Snepp v. United States*[103] a former CIA agent published a book on the Vietnam war which contained no classified information, in contravention of a contractual undertaking not to publish such material without first obtaining security clearance. The Supreme Court made him account for his profits to the government, holding that the contractual term did not violate Snepp's First Amendment rights, and accepting that the government had an interest because publishing non-classified

---

[100] [1990] 1 AC at 167, [1988] 3 All ER at 589.
[101] [1990] 1 AC at 283, [1988] 3 All ER at 660.
[102] [2000] 3 WLR 625, HL.
[103] 444 US 507 (1980), US Supreme Court.

material might facilitate the identification of other agents and endanger lives or channels of information in ways neither the author nor the court could foresee. There are good reasons for permitting publication in the public interest, but there are few good reasons for allowing people who make themselves a party to wrongdoing to profit from their actions. In the *Spycatcher* case, the government were granted an order against the publishers of the *Sunday Times* for an account of profits accruing from its publication of extracts from Mr. Wright's memoirs on 12 July 1986, the day before *Spycatcher* was published in the USA. The publication had detrimentally affected the government's interest because at that stage there had been no such publication elsewhere as would destroy the confidentiality of the material, and the publishers of the *Sunday Times*, by entering into a licensing agreement with the American publishers, had effectively put themselves in the shoes of Mr. Wright and were infected by his breach of trust. This is in line with a policy of the law and a subsidiary purpose of the law of breach of confidence, that of ensuring that people do not profit from their wrongful appropriation of confidential information.

In *Attorney-General v. Blake (Jonathan Cape Ltd., third party)*, the remedy of an account of profits was granted against a former double-agent who had worked for MI6 and had later published his memoirs. He had a contractual obligation of secrecy, but no equitable duty, because the information in the book was no longer confidential at the time when he submitted it for publication. A majority of the House of Lords considered that his undertaking on joining the service gave rise to something closely akin to a fiduciary obligation, and that an account of profits could be awarded as a remedy for breach of contract, and not only for equitable wrongs, if, in an exceptional case, normal remedies such as damages, injunction, and specific performance were inadequate to compensate for the damage done by disclosures. In that case, it was said that damages limited to the loss suffered by the Crown would be an inadequate remedy. Had he been within the jurisdiction, it would have been appropriate to grant a permanent injunction against the author of the book because of his obligation of secrecy, notwithstanding the fact that nothing in it was now confidential. That being so, an account of profits could be ordered to prevent him from profiting further from his notorious and egregious faithlessness, as in the *Snepp* case in the USA. It lies outside the scope of this book to assess the quality of the reasoning in relation to the law of contractual damages and unjust enrichment, but in his dissenting speech Lord Hobhouse of Woodborough argued persuasively that the majority had opened a Pandora's box in awarding, in effect, non-compensatory damages for breach of contract in order to give effect to a penal policy, allowing a hard case to give rise to a departure from principle.[104]

Apart from an account of profits, the government may be able to restrain publication if they hold the copyright in the material. This was the ground on which the Australian government succeeded in obtaining an interim injunction restraining publication of documents relating to the East Timor crisis in *Commonwealth of Australia v. Fairfax & Sons Ltd.*[105] This remedy is useful only where the recipient of the material

---

[104] [2000] 3 WLR at 653.
[105] (1980) 147 CLR 39, HC of Australia.

plans to reproduce it in whole or part, as in the *John Fairfax* case. It is not clear that it would have availed the government in the *Spycatcher* case or in *Lord Advocate v. The Scotsman Publications Ltd.*, as the publications in those cases consisted of an original account of events, incorporating confidential information, rather than a reproduction of copyright material. In these cases, Wright and Cavendish respectively held the legal copyright.[106] However, in the final *Spycatcher* hearing several of the judges thought that the legal copyright might be held under a constructive trust for the benefit of the government, giving them an equitable copyright, because of the author's breach of confidence.[107] The government nevertheless disclaimed any reliance on equitable copyright, perhaps, as Lord Donaldson MR suggested, because the newspapers could still have relied on a 'fair dealing' defence under section 6 of the Copyright Act 1956 (now the Copyright, Designs and Patents Act 1988, section 30) to justify their reports on the book.[108]

15.3 NATIONAL SECURITY AND THE CRIME OF IMPARTING INFORMATION: THE OFFICIAL SECRETS ACT 1989[109]

The failure of the government to obtain a permanent injunction in the *Spycatcher* case made it clear that securing prior restraint of publications concerning government was likely to be less easy than the government would have liked, even if it was not to be as difficult as in the USA. The government realized that it was likely to be forced back on the criminal law, and subsequent restraint, in order to influence editorial decisions about publication of governmental confidences. However, as noted in section 1 above, the main statute providing criminal penalties for unauthorized disclosures and receipts of information, section 2 of the Official Secrets Act 1911 as amended, was by then a discredited instrument. The government's response, eventually, was the Official Secrets Act 1989, which swept away section 2 of the 1911 Act, replacing it with a series of more specific prohibitions on disclosure. In most cases, these related to classes of information in which there is an understandable public interest in confidentiality, concerning the security and intelligence services, defence, international relations, and criminal investigation. It is no longer an offence to be the recipient of unsolicited information from a person who is infringing the Act. There is also a general defence,

---

[106] A suggestion that authors guilty of turpitude lose copyright is unsustainable. The better view is that the authors had the legal copyright, but that, because of their behaviour, no court of equity would grant them remedies to enforce it; see Lord Jauncey of Tullichettle [1990] 1 AC at 294, [1988] 3 All ER at 668; Y. Cripps, 'Breaches of Copyright and Confidence: The Spycatcher Effect' [1989] *PL* 13–20.

[107] See [1990] 1 AC, [1988] 3 All ER, at 140, 567, respectively (Scott J.); 194–5, 608–9 (Lord Donaldson MR); 211, 621 (Dillon LJ); 266, 647 (Lord Brightman); 276, 654 (Lord Griffiths); and 288, 664 (Lord Goff).

[108] [1990] 1 AC at 288, [1988] 3 All ER at 608–9. See also *Attorney-General v. Blake (Jonathan Cape Ltd., third party)* [1996] 3 All ER 903 at 908 *per* Sir Richard Scott V-C [1998] Ch. 439, [1998] 1 All ER 833, CA. The issue had dropped away before the case reached the House of Lords.

[109] K. D. Ewing and C. A. Gearty, *Freedom under Thatcher* (Oxford: Clarendon Press, 1990), 189–208; Robertson and Nicol, *Media Law*, 3rd edn., 418–28; Lustgarten and Leigh, *In from the Cold*, 228–45.

applying to all offences under the Act, where a person who has made a disclosure proves that at the time of the alleged offence he believed that he had lawful authority to make the disclosure and had no reasonable cause to believe otherwise.[110]

In some ways, therefore, this is a liberalizing measure, and it was introduced by the government on that basis. Nevertheless, in one respect it is possible that all the offences under the Act have the capacity to violate the right to freedom of expression under ECHR Article 10 in certain cases. It is not a defence for a defendant to plead that the disclosure was for the public good or served a recognized public interest. Such a defence was, in theory, available under the 1911 Act, although its scope was uncertain: see section 15.1 above. A public-interest defence is also available in civil proceedings: see section 15.2 above. It seems anomalous that under all provisions of the 1989 Act criminal liability may be imposed in circumstances when no injunction could have been obtained to restrain publication. It is arguable that convicting people who act in the public interest to bring official inefficiency or malpractice to public attention is not 'necessary in a democratic society' within the meaning of ECHR Article 10(2), particularly as the other channels for ventilating such concerns are not well developed.

There are other concerns about specific offences, particularly in relation to section 1 of the Act. Under section 1, a person who is or has been a member of the security service (MI5) or intelligence service (MI6), or has been notified in writing by a Minister that he is subject to the provisions of the section (this can happen to anyone who, in the Minister's opinion, is undertaking work which is or includes work connected with the security or intelligence services and is of such a nature that the interests of national security require that he should be subject to the provision), is guilty of an offence if, without lawful authority,[111] he discloses any information, document, or other article relating to security or intelligence which is or has been in his possession by virtue of his position or in the course of his work while the notification was in force. There is a defence if the person can show that he did not know, and had no reason to believe, that the information, etc., related to the security or intelligence services.

The offence clearly interferes with the freedom of members and former members of the security and intelligence services to impart information. There is no reason why they should not be able to assert that right under ECHR Article 10, which is available to members of the armed forces and civil servants who are securely in post,[112] and members of the security and intelligence services are in an analogous position, although in their cases the state may find it easier to justify interfering with the rights under ECHR Article 10(2) in many circumstances. To justify the interference, it must be shown to be necessary in a democratic society, i.e. a proportionate response to a pressing social need to pursue a legitimate aim under Article 10(2), and compatible with the values underpinning a liberal democracy. Securing accountability of public

---

[110]   Official Secrets Act 1989, s. 7(4). See also s. 8(2).

[111]   'Lawful authority' is defined by s. 7.

[112]   *Vereinigung Demokratische Soldaten Österreich and Gubi v. Austria*, Eur. Ct. HR, Series A, No. 302, Judgment of 19 December 1994, 20 EHRR 56; *Vereiniging Weekblad Bluf! v. The Netherlands*, Eur. Ct. HR, Series A, No. 306-A, Judgment of 9 February 1995, 20 EHRR 189; *Vogt v. Germany*, Eur. Ct. HR, Series A, No. 323, Judgment of 26 September 1995, 21 EHRR 205.

officials is essential in a liberal democracy, and information about their activities is necessary for democracy. Section 1 of the 1989 Act fails to respect the values of liberal democracy or guarantee the principle of proportionality in cases where a disclosure causes no significant damage to national security or is justified by a legitimate democratic interest in securing the accountability of public authorities. Not only does the section not require the prosecution to show that the disclosure was in any way damaging; it prevents the defendant from showing that it was not damaging, or that there was a legitimate public interest in receiving the information. In some, perhaps many, cases the prosecution probably could show that a disclosure caused serious damage and that penalizing it was proportionate to a pressing social need, but section 1 effectively removes those questions entirely from the trial. This cannot be shown to represent a legitimate balance between the competing rights and interests.

The section makes it a criminal offence for members or former members of the security and intelligence services ever to reveal anything which came into their possession by virtue of their position, even if it is no longer confidential—indeed, is already well known—and could be published without civil or criminal liability by any newspaper in the country. This is the position faced, at the time of writing, by Mr. David Shayler, a former member of MI5 whose revelations (or purported revelations) about the working methods of the service led to his being charged under section 1 of the 1989 Act.[112a] The government failed in its attempt to have him extradited from France when the French court decided that section 1 created a political, and hence non-extraditable, offence. He subsequently returned voluntarily, and is arguing that he should be permitted to raise a public interest defence by virtue of ECHR Article 10 and the Human Rights Act 1998, notwithstanding the absence of such a defence from the express terms of section 1. The case will provide an indication of the potential of the 1998 Act to impose principles of necessity and proportionality in security matters.

Section 2 provides that anyone who is or has been a Crown servant or contractor,[113] even if not covered by section 1, commits an offence if without lawful authority he makes a *damaging* disclosure of information, a document, or other article relating to defence[114] which was in his possession by virtue of his position.[115] A damaging disclosure is one which *either*:

(a) damages the ability of any part of the armed forces to carry out their tasks, or leads to loss of life or injury to members of those forces or serious damage to the equipment or installations of the forces; *or*

(b) otherwise endangers the interests of the UK abroad, seriously obstructs the promotion or protection by the UK of those interests, or endangers the lives of British citizens abroad; *or*

(c) is of such a nature that it would be likely to have any of those consequences.[116]

[112a] K. Best, 'The Control of Official Information: Implications of the Shayler Affair' (2001) 6 *J. of Civil Liberties* 18–34.

[113] These terms are defined by s. 12.

[114] This is widely defined: see Official Secrets Act 1989, s. 2(4).

[115] Ibid., s. 2(1).

[116] Official Secrets Act 1989, s. 2(2).

It is a defence for the person concerned to prove that he did not know, and had no reasonable cause to believe, that the information, etc. related to defence or that its disclosure would be damaging.[117] This defence is ambiguously worded. It is not clear whether there are actually two defences (*either* that the defendant did not know and had no reasonable cause to believe that the material related to defence, *or* did not know or have reasonable cause to believe that its disclosure would be damaging) or only one, with the accused carrying the burden of a two-part test (the 'or' in the middle being conjunctive rather than disjunctive). In principle, an ambiguity in a criminal statute should be resolved in favour of the defendant, particularly as the purpose of the 1989 Act was avowedly to replace and cut down the very wide criminal liability imposed under section 2 of the Official Secrets Act 1911. However, a court might take the view that it is not unreasonable to penalize behaviour which the accused has reason to believe would be damaging, even if he does not know that it is. The section will probably be held to be compatible with ECHR Article 10(2) on that ground, although the problem arising from the lack of a public-interest disclosure defence remains.

Further penal provisions apply, by virtue of section 3 of the 1989 Act, to Crown servants and government contractors who make damaging disclosures of material relating to international relations, or any confidential material obtained from another state or international organization, which he has by virtue of his position.[118] Here, a 'damaging' disclosure is one which endangers the interests of the UK abroad, which seriously obstructs the promotion or protection of those interests, which endangers the lives of British citizens abroad, or which, if unauthorized, would be likely to have any of those effects.[119] The mere fact that material is confidential and obtained from another state or international organization may (but will not necessarily) be enough to establish that unauthorized disclosure might have those effects.[120] There is a defence if the accused proves that at the time of the alleged offence he did not know, and had no reasonable cause to believe, that the information, etc. was of a type covered by the section, or that its disclosure would be damaging.[121] The interpretation of this subsection raises difficulties similar to those which arise in relation to the defence under section 2.

Section 4 of the 1989 Act goes on to criminalize disclosure without lawful authority, by a person who is or has been a Crown servant or contractor, of information concerning criminal intelligence and investigations, which is or has been in his possession by virtue of his position.[122] The section applies to two types of information, documents, or other articles. First, there are items disclosure of which has, or is likely to have, the effect of resulting in the commission of an offence, facilitating an escape from legal custody or prejudicing the safekeeping of people in custody, or impeding prevention or detection of offences or the apprehension of suspects.[123] Secondly, it applies to information etc. gathered, or relating to the obtaining of information, by means of, an interception of communications authorized by a warrant issued under

---

[117] Official Secrets Act 1989, s. 2(3). [118] Ibid., s. 3(1). [119] Ibid., s. 3(2).
[120] Ibid., s. 3(3). [121] Ibid., s. 3(4). [122] Ibid., s. 4(1).
[123] Ibid., s. 4(2).

Part I of the Regulation of Investigatory Powers Act 2000, or action taken under a warrant issued under the Security Service Act 1989, section 3.[124] There are two defences under this section. The first, a general defence, is available to any defendant who can prove that at the time of the alleged offence he did not know, and had no reasonable cause to believe, that the section applied to the information, etc. in question.[125] The other defence applies only to a person charged with an offence in respect of a disclosure which is alleged to have actually resulted in the commission of an offence, the facilitation of an escape or an act prejudicing the safekeeping of people in custody, or the impeding of the prevention or detection of offenders or the apprehension of suspects. This defence is available if the accused can prove that at the time of the alleged offence he did not know, and had no reasonable cause to believe, that the disclosure would have any of those effects.[126]

In section 5, the 1989 Act deals with third parties who come into possession of material which has been disclosed by others. It provides that, when information, a document, or other article protected by sections 1, 2, 3, or 4 of the Act:

(i)   comes into a person's possession as a result of an unauthorized disclosure (whether to him or to someone else) by a Crown servant or government contractor; or

(ii) is entrusted to a person by a Crown servant or government contractor on terms requiring it to be held in confidence or in circumstances in which the servant or contractor could reasonably expect it to be so held; or

(iii) is disclosed without lawful authority to any person by a person entrusted with the information, etc. under (ii) above,[127]

a person is guilty of an offence under section 5 (as long as the disclosure does not constitute an offence under any of sections 1 to 4) if:

(a)   he discloses it without lawful authority; *and*

(b)   he knows or has reasonable cause to believe that it is protected against disclosure by sections 1 to 4, and that it came into his possession in one of the ways mentioned above;[128] *and*

(c)   the disclosure is damaging within the meaning of section 1, 2, or 3; *and*

(d)   the person knows or has reasonable cause to believe that it is damaging.[129]

The effect of this section is that a third party who comes into possession of information or material by way of a chain, any part of which consists of an unauthorized disclosure, may be guilty of a section 5 offence if he further discloses it. However, he commits no offence in disclosing the information or material unless the disclosure by him is damaging and he knows or has reasonable cause to believe that it is. This makes

---

[124] Ibid., s. 4(3) as amended by Regulation of Investigatory Powers Act 2000, Sch. 4, para. 5.
[125] Ibid., s. 4(5).
[126] Ibid., s. 4(4).
[127] Ibid., s. 5(1).
[128] Ibid., s. 5(2), (5).
[129] Ibid., s. 5(3).

the extent of any previous publication relevant, importing considerations similar to those which apply to breach of confidence under *Attorney-General v. Guardian Newspapers Ltd. (No. 2)*,[130] and adding to them a *mens rea* requirement. On facts similar to those relating to *Spycatcher*, it means that the newspapers would not be liable under section 5 for publishing Mr. Wright's allegations once publicity elsewhere for them had inflicted all the possible damage. Before that, the newspapers would have been liable, if they knew or had reasonable cause to believe that the disclosure was damaging, and would have had no public-interest defence.

Other acts which constitute criminal offences under the Act are:

(a) disclosure without lawful authority of ay information, document, or other article which the confider knows, or has reasonable cause to believe, came into his possession as a result of an offence of spying contrary to section 1 of the Official Secrets Act 1911;[131] or

(b) disclosure without lawful authority of any information, document, or other article which relates to security, intelligence, defence, or international relations, and which was communicated in confidence to another state or an international organization by or on behalf of the UK, and which has been disclosed to any person without the authority of the state or a member of the organization concerned, where the disclosure by the accused was damaging and the accused knew or had reasonable cause to suspect that the disclosure would be damaging;[132]

(c) Crown servants, including a person in whose case a notification under section 1(1) is in force, retaining documents or articles contrary to their official duty, or government contractors failing to comply with official directions for their return or disposal, or Crown servants or government contractors failing to take reasonable care to prevent unauthorized disclosure of documents or other articles which they have in their possession by virtue of their positions and which it would be an offence under the Act to disclose.[133]

Viewed as a liberalizing measure, the 1989 Act is something of a disappointment. While more certain and specific than section 2 of the 1911 Act which it superseded, the 1989 Act continues to make it difficult to obtain information about the workings of government and those who are, in name at any rate, our servants. It reflects a governmental ethos which is profoundly suspicious of outsiders, resistant to accountability, and antipathetic to the idea of freedom of information. The defences do not protect the rights of subjects. They do not protect the public interest, save in cases where the government's view of the public interest is the correct one. It is, in this context, extremely worrying to remember that in Sir Robert Armstrong's memorandum to civil servants following the Clive Ponting case, and in the trial judge's direction to the jury in the *Ponting* case itself, it was said that the interests of the state

---

[130] [1990] 1 AC 109, [1988] 3 All ER 545.
[131] Official Secrets Act 1989, s. 5(6).
[132] Ibid., s. 6(1).
[133] Ibid., s. 8.

are synonymous with its interests as defined by the government for the time being. This meant that there was, in theory, no room for a defendant to argue under the old section 2 that it was in the interests of the state to leak information to the elected representatives of the people, in order to counteract suspected mendacity or incompetence on the part of the government or its servants. Under the 1989 Act, the prosecution is not even nominally required to show that the unauthorized disclosure was damaging to the interests of the state. Nor is there any defence of public good (as under the obscenity legislation) or public interest (as in civil actions for breach of confidence). There is a real risk that the legislation will be used in ways which violate the Convention right under ECHR Article 10, unless courts robustly interpret the Act in order to achieve compatibility, reading in whole defences if necessary in reliance on their interpretative obligation under section 3 of the Human Rights Act 1998. If (as seems likely) judges feel unable to take this step, the legislation may operate incompatibly with the needs of a liberal democracy, denying people the information needed for the democratic process to operate as those in the best position to provide it reliably are put *in terrorem* by the threat of severe criminal sanctions.

15.4 CRIMINAL SPEECH, OPINION, AND DISAFFECTION: SEDITION AND RELATED OFFENCES[134]

This section deals with the criminal law which applies to those who attempt to undermine the state directly.

(1) TREASON AND TREASON FELONY[135]

Since feudal times, actions which constitute a breach of the subject's obligation of allegiance to his lord the monarch have been punishable with death, as treasons. As defined and extended by statute, such actions include compassing or imagining the death of the King, the Queen, or their eldest son and heir, within or without the realm; violating the King's companion, the King's eldest daughter before her marriage, or the wife of the King's eldest son and heir; levying war against the King or being adherent to the King's enemies in the realm, or giving them aid or comfort anywhere,[136] or killing the King's justices when in the performance of their offices.[137] Any person who

---

[134] See M. Supperstone, *Brownlie's Law of Public Order and National Security*, 2nd edn. (London: Butterworths, 1981), ch. 11.

[135] J. C. Smith and Brian Hogan, *Criminal Law*, 6th edn. (London: Butterworths, 1988), 827–33. This discussion is omitted from the 7th edn.

[136] *R. v. Casement* [1917] 1 KB 98, CCA.

[137] Treason Act 1351, 25 Edw. III, stat. 5, c. 2; Treason Act 1795, s. 1. See also Treason Act 1842, s. 2, which introduced a lesser penalty than that for high treason in the case of people who (among other activities) point or shoot firearms at the monarch. This Act was passed following two such incidents while Queen Victoria was driving in public in 1842. An earlier attempt had been made on the Queen's life by an insane youth, Edward Oxford, in 1840.

owes a duty of allegiance by reason of being under the protection of the Crown can be guilty of treason. In *R. v. Joyce*, the House of Lords held that an alien who had been in the UK, and so under the protection of the Crown, remained under its protection when he went abroad with a British passport which he had obtained by deception. His broadcasts (as 'Lord Haw-Haw') from Germany during the Second World War, designed to undermine British morale and assist the German war effort, were therefore treasonable.[138] This can be seen as a particularly vindictive extension of the law of treason to permit the execution of an alien for expressions uttered abroad which had been a thorn in the flesh of the government during the war; it is inconceivable that the passport would have been held to give Joyce any enforceable rights against the Crown, yet it was enough to hang him.

Related offences extend criminal liability to words and publications. Under the Treason Felony Act 1848, section 3, anyone owing a duty of allegiance to the Crown who anywhere compasses, imagines, invents, devises, or intends (a) to deprive or depose the Queen from her titles, or (b) to levy war against the Queen in the UK in order to compel her to change her policies (in effect, her government's policies), or (c) to put force or constraint on, or intimidate or overawe, Parliament or either House thereof, or (d) to move or stir any foreigner to invade the UK or any of the Queen's dominions, is guilty of treason felony, and this offence may be committed either by acts or by words, writing, or other publication.

This offence has the potential to stifle debate about the future of the monarchy, and proposals to replace it with a republic. In tune with the policy of the government in 1848, when popular revolutions were occurring all over Europe and monarchies were under threat from violent uprisings, it is not in keeping with a mature and reasonably stable twenty-first-century democracy. In October 2000, when the Human Rights Act 1998 came into force, a national newspaper, the *Guardian*, launched a campaign for a republic, and challenged the Attorney-General to prosecute the editor for treason or treason felony. The Attorney-General, Lord Williams of Mostyn, declined to prosecute. In 2001, the *Guardian* pursued the matter further, seeking a declaration of incompatibility under section 4 of the Human Rights Act 1998 in respect of the Act of Settlement 1700, arguing that section 3 of that Act, requiring the monarch to be a communicant of the Church of England, is incompatible with the the right to freedom of religion and the right to be free of discrimination on the ground of religion in the enjoyment of other Convention rights under ECHR Articles 9 and 14. The application was unsuccessful, because the applicants could not claim to be victims of the incompatibility. The *Guardian* and its editor would have had a stronger claim to a declaration of incompatibility in respect of the Treason Felony Act 1848, section 3, on the ground that it violates their right to freedom of expression under ECHR Article 10. As noted in Chapter 2 above, a person may be a victim of a violation if they are liable to prosecution, even if there is an administrative policy of not prosecuting for the offence in question.

The creation of the offence of treason felony reflects a move in political theory away from identifying the state with the monarch: the formulation of the crime recognizes

---

[138] [1946] AC 347, [1946] 1 All ER 186, HL.

the significance to the state of institutions other than the monarchy, which by the time of Queen Victoria had waned in practical importance. Attempts to stir up dissatisfaction with the policies of the government of the day were, in effect, attempts to undermine the established institutions of the state, in times when there was little democracy and the forces of public opinion were not regarded with any respect. The criminal law addressed this objective through the law of sedition.

(2) SEDITION

Words and publications play an important role in stirring up discontent and violent opposition to the established order, and ever since medieval times steps have been taken to criminalize attempts to undermine the state by means of scurrilous publications, particularly in times of unrest when insurrection has been threatened or feared. By the end of the eighteenth century, the crime of seditious libel at common law was backed up by statutes which (for example) made meetings of more than fifty people, to make speeches or raise petitions critical of the established institutions of the state, into unlawful assemblies unless advertised in advance according to statutory requirements as to notice. These statutes were most often passed in times of war, and the latest of them, the Seditious Meetings Act 1817 (passed amid fear of Jacobinism and foreign invasion in the aftermath of the Napoleonic wars) remained in force, although long unused, until at last repealed by the Public Order Act 1986, in line with a recommendation from the Law Commission.[139]

At common law, the main weapon in the government's armoury is the crime, rarely invoked in the last century, of seditious libel. This originally covered any attack on any institution of the state.[140] One commentator has described the original crime as being committed whenever anyone published 'a speech or writing with intent to bring into hatred or contempt, or excite hostility towards, the Crown, government, Parliament, and administration of justice, or with the aim of inducing reform by unlawful means or of promoting class warfare'.[141] This reflects the historical use of sedition to stifle criticism of government policy,[142] potentially including all democratic debate and party-political activity, as it encompassed almost any political opposition to the government of the day.[143] As we shall see, the modern law is a good deal more restricted than this, and takes account of a more enlightened view of the value of political opposition to government, which made it less acceptable for governments to use the law to stifle opposition. At the same time, procedural changes introduced by Fox's Libel Act 1792, which required a jury, rather than the judge, to decide whether statements were defamatory, made it easier for defendants to canvass political issues before juries.

---

[139] Law Commission Report No. 123, *Criminal Law: Offences Relating to Public Order* (London: HMSO, 1983), 86–7, paras. 8.4–8.5, especially n. 7; Public Order Act 1986, s. 40(3) and Sch. 3.

[140] *R. v. Burns* (1886) 16 Cox CC 355.

[141] This formulation is by E. Barendt, *Freedom of Speech* (Oxford: Clarendon Press, 1987), 153.

[142] Sir James Fitzjames Stephen, *A History of the Criminal Law of England* (London: Macmillan, 1883, 3 vols.), ii. 299–376.

[143] *Hector v. A.-G. of Antigua and Barbuda* [1990] 2 AC 312, [1990] 3 All ER 103, PC.

This made prosecutions for seditious libel less attractive to government. Instead, attention turned from defamation to public-order concerns.[144] Accordingly, more recent cases have stressed that the speaker or publisher must intend to provoke violence aimed at disturbing the government by force in order to be liable to conviction,[145] although a more flexible approach was adopted in the mid-1920s when members of the Communist Party of Great Britain were prosecuted for sedition in respect of articles and speeches advancing a political programme opposed to that of the government and advocating strike action.[146] Today, the *actus reus* consists of publishing or speaking words which have a tendency to incite public disorder involving physical violence, having regard to the likely effect of the words on ordinary people and on the audience which is addressed.[147] According to Professor Sir John Smith and Professor Brian Hogan, 'words are seditious (i) if they are likely to incite ordinary men whether likely to incite the audience actually addressed or not; or (ii) if, though not likely to incite ordinary men, they are likely to incite the audience actually addressed'.[148] This appears to be a fair account of the cases, as long as (i) is read subject to a proviso that if, in the context in which the words are spoken or published, it is highly unlikely that any intemperate people will be present and no disorder results, the words are not to be regarded as seditious. It follows that in England and Wales the crime of seditious libel has a public-order aspect, and is probably now not incompatible with ECHR Article 10.

The *mens rea* of sedition is in doubt, for two reasons. First, there has been a certain element of uncertainty, now largely laid to rest, as to whether the prosecution must prove specific intent to produce disorder, or whether it suffices to establish basic intent. Sir James Fitzjames Stephen, the nineteenth-century codifier and historian of the criminal law, at different times gave two inconsistent answers to this question. In his *Digest of the Criminal Law of England*, he required only deliberateness in publishing or speaking words which had a seditious tendency. The intention to produce public disorder was inferred from that act.[149] This is inconsistent with general principles of criminal law, but is in line with the approach to *mens rea* taken in other types of criminal libel, such as blasphemous libel.[150] However, Stephen adopted a different view in his *History of the Criminal Law*,[151] where he takes the view that a requirement of specific intent—an intention to produce public disorders—had become part of the

---

[144] See M. Lobban, 'From Seditious Libel to Unlawful Assembly: Peterloo and the Changing Face of Political Crime c.1770–1820' (1990) 10 *Oxford J. of Legal Studies* 307–52.

[145] Barendt, *Freedom of Speech*, 155, refers to *R. v. Aldred* (1909) 22 Cox CC 1 at 4 *per* Coleridge J, and the note by E. C. S. Wade, 'Seditious Libel and the Press' (1948) 64 *LQR* 203 on *R. v. Caunt* (unreported, Birkett J); *Boucher v. R.* [1951] 2 DLR 369, Supreme Court of Canada. See also *Hector v. A.-G. of Antigua and Barbuda* [1990] 2 AC 312, [1990] 3 All ER 103, PC.

[146] See K. D. Ewing and C. A. Gearty, *The Struggle for Civil Liberties: Political Freedom and the Rule of Law in Britain, 1914–1945* (Oxford: Oxford University Press, 2000), ch. 3, especially 136–51.

[147] See *R. v. Aldred* (1909) 22 Cox CC 1, especially at 3, 4, *per* Coleridge J; *R. v. Burns* (1886) 16 Cox CC 355, at 365 *per* Cave J.

[148] J. C. Smith and B. Hogan, *Criminal Law*, 7th edn. (London: Butterworths, 1992), 751.

[149] Sir James Fitzjames Stephen, *A Digest of the Criminal Law*, 4th edn. (London: Sweet & Maxwell, 1887), art. 94. See now Criminal Law Act 1967, s. 8.

[150] See. Ch. 16 below.

[151] ii. 359.

mens rea by virtue of the Libel Act 1792. It is this later view which appears to have been adopted in more recent English decisions. In *R. v. Burns*,[152] Cave J told the jury that there must be a distinct intention, going beyond mere recklessness, to produce disturbances, in order to establish the necessary *mens rea*. Similarly in *R. v. Caunt*,[153] where a newspaper editor was prosecuted in respect of an article which was alleged to create a risk of disorder because of its anti-Semitic bias, Birkett J instructed the jury that the prosecution had to prove that the defendant intended to provoke such disorder, and the jury acquitted.

Secondly, there is doubt about the matters as to which the requisite intention must be directed. Classically, seditious libel was concerned with words calculated or intended to stir up violent opposition to the institutions of the state.[154] More recently, however, it has been said to extend to words which are intended, not to obstruct established authority by violence, but to set sections or classes of the community at each other's throats. This makes safeguarding harmonious relations between sections of Her Majesty's subjects as much the purpose of sedition law as preventing violent insurrection against the state. In *R. v. Caunt*, above, Birkett J told the jury that words intended to stir up hatred of Jews could be seditious. The essence of this manifestation of the offence was creating division and disaffection between classes of Her Majesty's subjects, creating conditions for violence. The prosecution did not need to show that the speech or publication actually led to violence, or was likely to lead directly to violence.

The need for such an extension is not clear. In recent years, this aspect of the offence has been largely superseded by public-order legislation, including the statutory crime of inciting racial hatred.[155] Seditious libel is now often represented as a sledge-hammer to be used against nuts. However, the statutory crime of inciting racial hatred does not protect purely religious, rather than racial, groups.[156] For this reason, in 1989 Muslims campaigning against Salman Rushdie's book, *The Satanic Verses*, attempted to prosecute the author and publishers for seditious libel, arguing that the book's representation of Islam created hostility between Her Majesty's Muslim and non-Muslim subjects, in that it provoked widespread violence and threats of violence between Muslims and others by vilifying Islam and ridiculing its prophets and adherents. In *R. v. Chief Metropolitan Magistrate, ex parte Choudhury*[157] the applicant applied for summonses accusing the defendants of (among other things) seditious libel by distributing the book. The magistrate refused to issue the summonses, and the applicant applied for judicial review of the refusal.

The court adopted the formulation of the *mens rea* in *Boucher v. R.*,[158] in which the

---

[152] (1886) 16 Cox CC 355 at 364.

[153] Unreported, 1947; see Wade (1948) 64 *LQR* 203.

[154] See Lord Cockburn, *Examination of Trials for Sedition in Scotland* (Edinburgh: D. Douglas, 1888), i. 8.

[155] Race Relations Act 1976, s. 70, as substituted by the Public Order Act 1986 (see Ch. 18, below); Public Order Act 1986, ss. 4, 5. See also Anti-terrorism, Crime and Security Bill 2001, Part 5, on incitement to religious hatred.

[156] See *Mandla v. Dowell Lee* [1983] 2 AC 548, [1983] 1 All ER 1062, HL; below, ch. 18.

[157] [1991] 1 QB 429, [1991] 1 All ER 306, DC. See M. Tregilgas-Davey, 'Ex parte Choudhury: An Opportunity Missed' (1991) 54 *MLR* 294–9.

[158] [1951] 2 DLR 369.

Supreme Court of Canada held that a pamphlet, published in Quebec by a Jehovah's Witness, about the animosity of officials and Roman Catholic clergy towards Jehovah's Witnesses, would not constitute a seditious libel, whether or not it was intended to stir up feelings of ill will and hostility between classes of subjects. The Divisional Court in *Ex parte Choudhury* held that seditious libel is founded on: 'an intention to incite to violence or to create public disturbance or disorder against His Majesty or the institutions of government. Proof of an intention to promote feelings of ill will and hostility between different classes of subjects does not alone establish a seditious intention'.[159] The violence, disturbance, or defiance must be 'for the purpose of disturbing constituted authority', which means 'some person or body holding public office or discharging some public function of the state'.[160] The Divisional Court decided that there was no evidence that Mr. Rushdie or his publishers had had the requisite intention, and so held that there was no possibility that a prosecution could succeed. The application for judicial review of the magistrate's decision was therefore dismissed.

If the Divisional Court decision on this point is correct, Birkett J in *Caunt* was wrong to extend the reach of the crime to catch those inciting racial hatred or class violence. It leaves a lacuna in the law, in that the criminal law offers no protection against those who spawn religious hostility unless they fall within one of the statutory public-order offences, at least until Part 5 of the Anti-terrorism, Crime and Security Bill 2001 is passed and comes into force. At the same time, the formulation in *Ex parte Choudhury* potentially gives seditious libel a wider reach than previously thought, in that it may be committed if there is an intention to disturb by violence the operation of a person or body holding no public office if performing public functions. This would compel courts to perform a functional analysis of the activities of the state and of the person or body concerned, perhaps allowing a person to be prosecuted for seditious libel who had incited the overthrow of an organization delivering public services, such as the National Health Service. This overcomes the difficulty which might be caused by the lack of any developed conception of 'the state' in the constitutional law of the UK.

From a civil liberties standpoint, anything which expands the scope of the crime of seditious libel in any way is to be deprecated. It is properly for Parliament, not the courts, to impose restrictions on freedom of expression, whether in the interests of the state or of social harmony. The willingness of Parliament to take steps in the Public Order Act 1986, and the limits to those steps, should make judges hesitate before creating new inroads into freedom of speech which are not authorized by statute. The decision in *Ex parte Choudhury* to limit the *mens rea* of the offence to a specific intention to 'incite to violence or to create public disturbance or disorder against His Majesty or the institutions of government'[161] is to be welcomed. Conversely, the extension to protect people performing public state functions but not holding public office, is to be regretted. Even now, the scope of the offence remains uncertain, as in modern times it has so far been the subject of decisions of a fairly low level of

---

[159] [1991] 1 QB at 453, [1991] 1 All ER 306 at 323, Watkins LJ.
[160] Ibid.
[161] Ibid.

authority. It is by no means impossible that those who inspired riots against the government's plans to introduce the Community Charge in 1988 and 1989 might have been guilty of seditious libel, apart from any other public-order offences with which they were charged. The uncertainty surrounding the scope of the offence makes it particularly objectionable as a restriction on expression, since people potentially held *in terrorem* may be afraid to exercise political rights guaranteed under Articles 9, 10, and 11 of the European Convention on Human Rights. The potential is present, despite the fact that the charge is rarely laid and still more rarely successfully prosecuted: the European Court of Human Rights has held that a person may be a victim of a law which breaches the Convention even if he has never personally been charged or threatened with proceedings under that law, and the state organs have announced an intention of not invoking legal procedures to enforce the law.[162] If democratic freedom depends on people remaining ignorant of, or refusing to be intimidated by, the law, and the good sense of the government in refusing to enforce it, one might regard it as being on insecure foundations.

Nevertheless, the general effect of developments over the last 200 years has been that the potential of the law of seditious libel to stifle criticism of government and political debate, evident in practice and as a matter of legal theory until the nineteenth century, is not great. Even before the nineteenth century, there were always people ready to ignore the law in order to assert rights and contest what they saw as abuse of power. Having citizens who are willing to challenge the law in the interest of a higher value, and being prepared to tolerate such behaviour, are, perhaps, the distinctive characteristics of a free society. In practice, the law of seditious libel has rarely been invoked, and those prosecutions which have taken place have tended to lead to acquittals at the hands of juries.

This pattern is replicated in the USA, where the commitment to free speech and a free press enshrined in the First Amendment to the Constitution in 1791 did not prevent the Congress from passing the Sedition Act of 1798 less than ten years later, amid fears that the USA might be sucked into the war between Britain and France. The Act made it criminal to 'write, print, utter or publish' false, scandalous, and malicious writings against the government, Congress, or President, or 'to bring them, or either of them, into contempt or disrepute; or to excite against them, or either of them, the hatred of the good people of the United States, or to stir up sedition'. The object of the Act was to silence opposition to the government. It was unsuccessful: heated debate continued, despite prosecutions. President John Adams was defeated in the presidential election of 1800, and Thomas Jefferson, the new president, pardoned all who had been convicted under the Act. Although the constitutionality of the Act was never tested, it came to be regarded by Congress as unconstitutional. A leading authority on the First Amendment, Leonard Levy, has shown that, although in theory the law of sedition as it operated both under British rule and under the Sedition Act 1798 should have significantly constrained free political expression, in practice tough, uncompromising criticism of government normally flourished.[163] The First

---

[162] *Johnston v. Ireland*, Eur. Ct. HR, Series A, No. 122, Judgment of 18 December 1986, 9 EHHR 203.

[163] L. W. Levy, *Emergence of a Free Press* (New York: Oxford University Press, 1985), especially at p. x.

Amendment reflected the dominant ethos of the society as regards free expression; the law of sedition was, for most people most of the time, an irrelevance.

(3) INCITEMENT TO DISAFFECTION[164]

The Incitement to Mutiny Act 1797, which made it an offence to endeavour, maliciously and advisedly, to seduce any member of the armed forces away from his duty to and allegiance to Her Majesty or induce him to commit an act of mutiny,[165] was repealed in 1998,[166] only twenty-one years after the Law Commission had recommended its repeal.[167]

The Incitement to Disaffection Act 1934 was specially passed to deter Communist propaganda amongst members of the armed forces.[168] Section 1 makes it an offence for a person maliciously and advisedly to endeavour to seduce 'any member of His Majesty's forces from his duty or allegiance to His Majesty'. This provision is somewhat wider than the equivalent term in the 1797 Act: under the 1934 Act, a defendant can be punished for seducing a member of the forces from his duty, even if he does not also seduce him from his allegiance to the Crown. Under section 2(1), it is an offence to have in one's possession or under one's control 'any document of such a nature that the dissemination of copies thereof among members of His Majesty's forces would constitute' an offence under section 1, with the intention to commit, aid, abet, counsel, or procure, the commission of such an offence. The consent of the DPP is required before anyone may be prosecuted for these offences (section 3(2)), and in truth there have been few prosecutions. The most recent was the trial in 1975 of fourteen pacifists who had distributed leaflets to troops explaining how they could register conscientious objections to serving in Northern Ireland, or, if they were not excused, desert. This ended in an acquittal which led the Attorney-General, Mr. Sam Silkin, to express his regret that the prosecution had been brought.[169] Nevertheless, the Act remains in place, if not now currently in use.

A significantly more widely drawn provision in the Police Act 1996 makes it an offence to cause, attempt to cause, or do any act calculated to cause, disaffection amongst members of any police force, or to induce, attempt to induce, or do any act calculated to induce, any member of a police force to withhold his services.[170] These

---

[164] D. G. T. Williams, *Keeping the Peace—The Police and Public Order* (London: Hutchinson, 1967), 179–92.

[165] It was a response to unfounded fears that the naval mutinies at the Spithead and the Nore had been incited by supporters of the revolutionary regime in France, and were intended to provoke open rebellion in Britain. See G. E. Manwaring and B. Dobrée, *The Floating Republic* (London: Geoffrey Bles, 1935). The Act was used during the early part of the twentieth century against members of the Communist Party of Great Britain who tried to persuade members of the armed forces not to act against strikers: Ewing and Gearty, *Struggle for Civil Liberties*, 118–27.

[166] Statute Law (Repeals) Act 1998, s. 1(1) and Sch. 1, Part I. Group 2.

[167] Law Commission Working Paper No. 72, (2nd Programme, Item XVI), *Codification of the Criminal Law: Treason, Sedition and Allied Offences* (London: HMSO, 1977), para. 94.

[168] C. Townshend, *Making the Peace: Public Order and Public Security in Modern Britain* (Oxford: Oxford University Press, 1993), 98–104; Ewing and Gearty, *Struggle for Civil Liberties*, 243–52.

[169] See G. Robertson, *Freedom, the Individual and the Law*, 175–6.

[170] Police Act 1996, s. 91.

provisions, which date back to 1919, were originally aimed at people intent on undermining public order and social stability,[171] but, as Robertson has pointed out, are now in disuse, perhaps because the commonest offenders today are probably officials of the Police Federation when advocating industrial action in pursuit of claims for improved wages, resources, and working conditions for police officers.[172]

All these conditions interfere with freedom of expression under ECHR Article 10. In cases where there is a real risk to public order or the rights and freedoms of others, the interference with freedom of expression is likely to be justifiable under ECHR Article 10(2). In other cases, however, there is a risk of an incompatibility, and the provisions should be read restrictively (as authorized by section 3 of the Human Rights Act 1998) in order to avoid an incompatibility.

15.5 CONCLUSION

The security of the state and its institutions is an important public interest. Yet the law which buttresses those institutions is inevitably viewed with suspicion by democrats and civil libertarians, as a threat to state security can too easily be asserted by those in power to justify restricting a wide range of freedoms in ways which protect the interests of the governing party rather than the public. At present, the external threat to the state from the activities of the USSR has disintegrated, extremist influences over domestic movements such as the trade unions appear to be in abeyance, and even the random, sometimes deadly, but generally fairly limited activities of Irish republican paramilitaries and international terrorists are limited in scale. Furthermore, in the 1990s the Scott report revealed behaviour on the part of government and various state agencies which undermined their claim to be reliably responsible and ethical in their use of power. It is not surprising that governmental demands for secrecy provoke scepticism. The Human Rights Act 1998, together with the caselaw of the European Court of Human Rights under ECHR Article 10 has altered the legal landscape and may gradually provide a principled foundation for a more balanced approach to questions of national security and freedom of expression on the part of both courts and other public authorities.

[171] Police Act 1919, s. 3; Williams, *Keeping the Peace*, 192–7.
[172] G. Robertson, *Freedom, the Individual and the Law*, 6th edn. (Harmondsworth: Penguin, 1989), 176.

16

RESTRICTING EXPRESSION TO PROTECT MIXED PUBLIC AND PRIVATE INTERESTS: BLASPHEMY, OBSCENITY, AND INDECENCY

This chapter examines a number of criminal offences and regulatory mechanisms which have the effect of abridging freedom of expression and of the press in order to protect individuals, and (on some views) the public in general, against harm of different kinds. For adherents to the harm principle as expounded by John Stuart Mill, the harm flowing from permitting free speech normally takes the form of hurt feelings and injured sensitivities, which are either not classified as harms justifying restriction of speech or are outweighed by the benefit which accrues from permitting free intercourse of ideas. However, this is controversial, because many people regard some effects of at least some expression as being significantly harmful to individuals, groups, or society as a whole in a variety of important ways. First, people who challenge, ridicule, or outrage a society's core values may be accused of undermining the bonds holding the society together, making it more difficult to maintain co-operation and social harmony. Secondly, some forms of expression offend the moral and religious sensibilities of sections of the community. Societies which allow such offence are said to show a lack of respect for those groups. Thirdly, such disrespect is sometimes said to constitute unequal treatment of the affected groups, amounting to a type of degradation which is intrinsically objectionable. Fourthly, the expression in question is said to reflect and reinforce patterns of discrimination and domination in society, harming individuals or groups by making unequal treatment of them appear morally unproblematic. Finally, it is sometimes argued that allowing certain types of unacceptable behaviour to be presented to people makes it more likely that they will indulge in the behaviour, damaging others through violence or discrimination.

Proponents of these different viewpoints argue for restrictions on expression for reasons which sometimes conflict. The first ground relies on a model of society which is essentially homogeneous. It is unlikely to appeal to those who advance the third and fourth propositions, who assume that society is essentially plural and heterogeneous, from religious, cultural, ethnic, or ethical perspectives, and see respect for those differences as important for the development of social goods such as equality and harmony. The second proposition could allow the boundaries of acceptable expression to be set by the least tolerant members of society who object not only to what they themselves hear or see, but also to the knowledge that other people have access to things of which they disapprove. Acceding to such claims would be incompatible with the first, third, and fourth propositions, and with a commitment to freedom of expression as a human right or fundamental freedom. The fifth proposition is distinctive, in that it presents an empirical claim about the causal relationship between expressive utterances and people's behaviour which is in theory (if not always in practice) capable of being tested scientifically.

This chapter explores related areas of law which form battlegrounds for these ideas: blasphemy, obscenity, and indecency of various kinds. Proponents of each of the five propositions are active in these areas, contending both with the general principle of freedom of expression (and sometimes respect for private life), and with each other. If one can bear in mind the distinctions between them, it will be easier to analyze and evaluate the law clearly and fairly.

Freedom of expression provides the background to this discussion, but it is a field in which Article 10 of the European Convention on Human Rights (ECHR) and the Human Rights Act 1998 may prove to offer relatively little to help. The caselaw of the European Court of Human Rights has done little to clarify the boundaries of acceptable limitation of freedom of blasphemous and indecent expression, for three reasons. First, ECHR Article 10(2) allows the state to justify interfering with expression for (*inter alia*) the prevention of disorder and the protection of morals or the rights of others. Article 19(3) of the International Covenant on Civil and Political Rights (ICCPR) is broadly similar in these respects. Both provisions allow significant scope for limiting expression, as long as any restriction is prescribed by law and proportionate to a pressing social need to advance the legitimate aim.

Secondly, the European Court of Human Rights in its caselaw has tended to accept that people have a right to be free from offence of different kinds, particularly (in the context of blasphemy) offence to their religious beliefs, protected by ECHR Article 9. In *Otto-Preminger-Institut v. Austria*[1] the applicant, a private association promoting creativity in the audio-visual media, challenged a decision to seize and forfeit a film, *Das Liebeskonzil*, which had been scheduled for showing at its cinema. The film was a satirical tragedy, set in Heaven, which according to the applicant's information bulleting caricatured 'trivial imagery and absurdities of the Christian creed' and investigated 'the relationship between religious beliefs and worldly mechanisms of oppression'. The prosecutor argued that the film aroused 'justified indignation' and disparaged 'an object of veneration of a church or religious community established within the country' and 'a dogma, a lawful custom or a lawful institution of such a church or religious community', contrary to section 188 of the Austrian Penal Code. The Innsbruck Court of Appeal, in upholding the seizure and forfeiture, held that indignation was justified under section 188 only if the film could be said to offend the religious feelings of an average person with normal religious sensitivity. The European Court of Human Rights decided that this was a legitimate aim for

---

[1] Eur. Ct. HR, Series A, No. 295-A, Judgment of 20 September 1994, 19 EHRR 34, at paras. 47–48. See D. Pannick, 'Religious Feelings and the European Court' [1995] *PL* 7–10; A. Sherlock, 'Freedom of Expression: How Far Should it Go?' (1995) 20 *EL Rev.* 329–37.

906 CIVIL LIBERTIES AND HUMAN RIGHTS

restricting freedom of expression. The Court's statement of principle merits quotation in full.

'47. . . . Those who choose to exercise the freedom to manifest their religion, irrespective of whether they do so as members of a religious majority or a minority, cannot reasonably expect to be exempt from all criticism. They must tolerate and accept the denial by others of their religious beliefs and even the propagation by others of doctrines hostile to their faith. However, the manner in which religious beliefs and doctrines are opposed or denied is a matter which may engage the responsibility of the state, notably in its responsibility to ensure the peaceful enjoyment of the right guaranteed under Article 9 to the holders of those beliefs and doctrines. Indeed, in extreme cases the effect of particular methods of opposing or denying religious beliefs can be such as to inhibit those who hold such beliefs from exercising their freedom to hold and express them.

In the *Kokkinakis* judgment[2] the Court held, in the context of Article 9, that a state may legitimately consider it necessary to take measures aimed at repressing certain forms of conduct, including the imparting of information and ideas, judged incompatible with with the respect for the freedom of thought, conscience and religion of others . . . The respect for the religious feelings of believers as guaranteed by Article 9 can legitimately be thought to have been violated by provocative portrayals of objects of religious veneration; and such portrayals can be regarded as malicious violation of the spirit of tolerance, which must also be a feature of democratic society. The Convention is to be read as a whole and therefore the interpretation and application of Article 10 in the present case must be in harmony with the logic of the Convention . . .

48. The measures complained of were based on section 188 of the Austrian Penal Code, which is intended to suppress behaviour directed against objects of religious veneration that is likely to cause "justified indignation". It follows that their purpose was to protect the right of citizens not to be insulted in their religious feelings by the public expression of views of other persons. Considering also the terms in which the decisions of the Austrian courts were phrased, the Court accepts that the impugned measures pursued a legitimate aim under Article 10 § 2, namely "the protection of the rights of others".'

This prevents Article 10 from exercising much control over the solutions adopted by a public authority faced by the kinds of arguments outlined above. Indeed, the Court's approach is potentially dangerous, as it could sometimes serve simply to legitimize, rather than to test rigorously, a regime of stringent censorship.

Thirdly, when assessing whether there is a pressing social need to restrict expression under ECHR Article 10(2) in order to enforce respect for people's Article 9 rights or to protect morals, and in considering the proportionality of any response, the Court has allowed states a significant margin of appreciation. The margin is far wider than the Court has allowed in relation to other kinds of speech, such as political expression, or other legitimate aims, such as the protection of reputation or maintaining the authority of the judiciary. There is no uniform conception throughout Europe of the content and significance of either morals or religion, so the Court is content to delegate to national authorities, within certain fairly imprecise limits, the responsibility for assessing when it is necessary to interfere with freedom of expression on these

[2] *Kokkinakis v. Greece*, Eur. Ct. HR, Series A, No. 260-A, Judgment of 25 May 1993, 17 EHRR 397, at para. 48.

grounds and how best to do so. 'By reason of their direct and continuous contact with the vital forces of their countries, state authorities are in principle in a better position than the international judge to give an opinion on the exact content of these require-ments as well as on the "necessity" of a "restriction" or "penalty" intended to meet them'.[3] The margin of appreciation doctrine does not apply to national courts under the Human Rights Act 1998, for reasons explained in Chapter 2, above, but its impact in Strasbourg makes the caselaw of the European Court of Human Rights less helpful than it might otherwise be in guiding national courts through the complexities and conflicts which beset these matters.

This chapter examines the way in which English law has sought to come to terms with these problems. Blasphemous libel is examined first; then, the foundations of liability for indecency and obscenity; common-law offences of indecency and obscenity; statutory offences; and, finally, controls by way of licensing and regulation.

16.1 BLASPHEMOUS LIBEL: STATE AND RELIGION

Blasphemous libel is extremely difficult to define,[4] although the European Court of Human Rights has decided that it is not so uncertain as to breach the legal certainty requirement of ECHR Article 10(2) that a restriction on expression be 'prescribed by law'.[5] It can be said, as a rough guide, that matter is blasphemous if it denies the truth of Christian doctrine,[6] or of the Bible,[7] or vilifies God or Jesus, in terms of wanton and unnecessary profanity which are likely to shock and outrage the feelings of ordinary Christians.[8] The fact that the prohibition is somewhat uncertain in scope, and protects only Christian sensibilities, led the Irish Supreme Court to hold in *Corway v. Independent Newspapers (Ireland) Ltd.*[8a] that the offence is too uncertain in its definition to be compatible with the Irish Constitution. It is far from clear that such a restriction on freedom of expression can be justified within a framework of liberal philosophy. Even if one accepts (as do some liberals, including Joel Feinberg[9] in his work on the moral limits of the criminal law) that offence is a form of harm, and that conduct or expression which provokes sufficiently grave offence can justifiably be criminalized, there is the problem, left over from the days when blasphemy protected

---

[3] *Handyside v. United Kingdom*, Eur. Ct. HR, Series A, No. 24, Judgment of 12 December 1976, 1 EHRR 737, at para. 48. See also *Otto-Preminger-Institut*, above, at para. 50.

[4] St. John A Robilliard, *Religion and the Law: Religious Liberty in Modern English Law* (Manchester: Manchester University Press, 1984), ch. 2; A. Bradney, *Religions, Rights and Laws* (Leicester: Leicester University Press, 1993), 82–5.

[5] *Wingrove v. United Kingdom*, Eur. Ct. HR, Judgment of 25 November 1996, RJD 1996-V, 24 EHRR 1, at paras. 42–3.

[6] *R. v. Taylor* (1676) 1 Vent. 293.

[7] *R. v. Hetherington* (1840) 4 St. Tr. (NS) 563.

[8] *R. v. Lemon* [1979] AC 617, [1979] 1 All ER 898, HL, especially *per* Lord Russell of Killowen and Lord Scarman.

[8a] [2000] ILRM 426.

[9] J. Feinburg, *Offense to Others* (New York: Oxford University Press, 1985), 54.

state interests, that it protects only the state religion, and so fails to protect adequately other religious, and non-religious, beliefs.

Blasphemous libel was originally an offshoot of the ecclesiastical offence of heresy, and was at first triable only in church courts. The state first took an interest in enforcing sound religious doctrine when uprisings inspired by heretical religious movements threatened the stability of the state. Statutes against heresy were passed under King Henry IV and King Henry V, aimed principally at the Lollards.[10] In the early sixteenth century, the rise of Protestantism and the significance of the link between the position of the secular prince as a protector of the church, and the position of the church as protector and guarantor of the legitimacy of the prince, gave the secular arm a particular interest in stamping out challenges to established religions. In England, the Court of High Commission seems to have treated various forms of expression (sedition and blasphemy among them) as criminal libels,[11] and in 1539 the Act of the Six Articles imposed ordinary criminal liability on people who denied orthodox doctrine, for example by denying transubstantiation.[12] During the seventeenth century the position became very uncertain. Under the Protectorate, section 35 of the Instrument of Government 1653 encouraged sound doctrine, but under section 36 nobody was to be compelled to the public profession of Christianity by penalties or otherwise. Although Jews were readmitted to the country and permitted to worship, savage attacks were launched against Quakers, and their leaders George Fox, James Nayler, Francis Howgill, and William Dewsbury were sentenced for blasphemy by Parliament and suffered horrible punishments.[13]

After the Restoration, greater religious tolerance became normal, but religious affiliation was an important consideration in the choice of William, Prince of Orange and his wife Mary to succeed the Catholic King James II in 1688 (even today the monarch must be a communicant of the Church of England).[14] The Court of King's Bench began to treat criminal libels, including blasphemies, which had earlier been dealt with by the Court of High Commission, as misdemeanours at common law.[15] An early example of such a case, containing a classic statement of the elements of the offence as then understood, was *R. v. Taylor*.[16] Hale CJ directed the jury that calling religion a cheat, as the defendant had done in that case, was an attack on Christianity, the constitutionally established religion of the state, and that, since the state religion was one of the buttresses of the legitimacy of the state and the law, 'to reproach the Christian religion is to speak in subversion of the law'. For this reason (if it be a

[10] Stat. 5 Ric. II, c. 5 (1382); Stat. 2 Hen. IV, c. 15 (1401), *De heretico comburendo*, under which heresy was indictable, but triable in the ecclesiastical courts; Stat. 2 Hen. V, c. 7 (1414); Sir James Fitzjames Stephen, *History of the Criminal Law* (London: Macmillan, 1883), II. 448–57.

[11] On the work of the Council, Court of High Commission, and Star Chamber, see Sir William Holdsworth, *A History of English Law* (London: Methuen, 1924), v. 208*ff*.

[12] Stat. 31 Hen. VIII, c. 14.

[13] The history is described by Leonard W. Levy, *Constitutional Opinions: Aspects of the Bill of Rights* (New York: Oxford University Press, 1986), 40–71.

[14] Act of Settlement 1700, Stat. 12 & 13 Will. III, c. 2, ss. 2 and 3. This provision appears to be incompatible with ICCPR Art. 26, and, if the UK ever ratifies ECHR Protocol No. 12, would also breach the UK's international obligations thereunder.

[15] Stephen, *History of Criminal Law*, ii. 470.

[16] (1676) 1 Vent. 293, 86 ER 189.

reason) it was held to be justifiable for the civil courts to exercise jurisdiction in respect of blasphemy alongside that of the ecclesiastical courts, which had a more obvious interest than the state's in punishing (for example) clergymen who joked about the biblical miracles.[17] Blasphemy as a crime, then, was concerned more with the protection of the state than with the protection of religion *per se*, and was an offence more akin to seditious libel than to outraging public decency. Blasphemous libel thus grew up as a means of protecting the state religion against attack at a time when the legitimacy of the state was intimately bound up with respect for the state religion, and the religious beliefs of the monarch were central to the legitimacy of his claim to the throne. The criminal law was protecting state interests rather than the sensibilities of citizens. Religion remains a powerful cultural influence on individuals, officials, legislators, and judges in many countries. This is often reflected in constitutional arrangements. For example, Article 44.1.2 of the 1937 Constitution of Ireland (repealed in 1972 by the referendum which approved the Fifth Amendment to the Constitution Bill) did this, recognizing 'the special position of the Holy Catholic Apostolic and Roman Church as the guardian of the Faith professed by the great majority of the citizens'. Some other named (and some unnamed) religious denominations were also 'recognized'.[18] This had certain consequences for the law of charities, for the ability of the bodies named to hold property, for privilege between priest and penitent, and for the law of standing in legal proceedings. Interestingly, the repeal of these constitutional provisions has not made the state, or the judges' interpretations of the Constitution, less Catholic. In the Preamble, the people of Eire adopt the Constitution 'In the name of the Most Holy Trinity, from Whom is all authority and to Whom, as our final end, all actions both of men and States must be referred, . . . Humbly acknowledging all our obligations to our Divine Lord, Jesus Christ . . . '. In *Norris v. Attorney-General*[19] the Supreme Court held that this required the courts to view a claim by a homosexual, that his personal freedom under the Constitution had been improperly abridged by laws against homosexual practices, in the light of Christian teaching which generally disapproved of homosexuality. Similarly in *Attorney-General (at the relation of Society for the Protection of the Unborn Child (Ireland) Ltd.) v. Open Door Counselling Ltd.*[20] an appeal to Christian doctrine was made to help to justify an injunction against the provision of advice about contraception and abortion. The ultimate constitutional authority is the will of the people, who have power to amend the Constitution notwithstanding any principles of natural law or canon law,[21] but Christian values remain a privileged part of the normative matrix on

---

[17] *R. v. Woolston* (1729) 1 Barn. KB 162, 94 ER 112.

[18] Article 44.1.3 of the 1937 Constitution, recognizing the Church of Ireland, the Presbyterian Church in Ireland, the Methodist Church in Ireland, the Religious Society of Friends in Ireland, 'as well as the Jewish Congregations and the other religious denominations existing in Ireland at the date of the coming into operation of this Constitution'. The final clause potentially reopened the debate about the nature of a religious denomination.

[19] [1984] IR 36.

[20] [1988] IR 593.

[21] *Re Article 26 and the Regulation of Information (Services outside the State for the Termination of Pregnancies) Bill 1995* [1995] 1 IR 1, SC of Ireland. See G. F. White, 'Natural Law and the Constitution' (1996) 14 *Irish Law Times* 8.

which society and the Constitution are based.[22] Yet even under this Constitution, blasphemous libel was held to be too uncertain a crime to pass muster.[22a]

In the USA, immigrants over the centuries have often been escaping religious persecution in Europe, not because they thought that religion was unimportant, but because it was fundamental to their lives. Respect for religious pluralism is supported by the First Amendment, which guarantees freedom of religion and forbids Congress to establish any religion. Legislatures and presidents regarded spiritual belief as being sufficiently important as an antidote to the materialist beliefs of the USSR, and more recently for its own sake, to justify promoting religious belief. Since 1956, the national motto has been 'In God we trust'.[23] Although it has been said that this has no theological significance such as to breach the First Amendment,[24] the Supreme Court had earlier held that it is permissible for a public (i.e. state-funded) school to release students for religious education elsewhere during school time at the request of parents, since (according to Douglas J, writing for the majority in a 6–3 majority decision) this allows schools to respect the religious nature of American society.[25] The view that religion is important (even if individuals should have a free choice between religions) has influenced the US Supreme Court in upholding the constitutionality of tax exemptions for religious purposes.[26] Nevertheless, the court has consistently refused to allow religion to be forced on people, or to give any protected status to religion. Compulsory acts of religious worship by students in public schools have been held to contravene the establishment clause of the First Amendment.[27] A law which imposes a penalty, or requires a licence, for expressing anti-religious views, including virulent criticism of a religion, is unconstitutional.[28] A law which prevents public-school teachers from teaching the theory of evolution, on the ground that it is inconsistent with the Book of Genesis, is unconstitutional, because, as Fortas J put it, delivering the judgment of the Supreme Court in *Epperson v. Arkansas*:[29] 'The First Amendment mandates governmental neutrality between religion and religion, and between religion and non-religion'. As early as 1872, in *Watson v. Jones*,[30] the Supreme Court had affirmed that, in the USA, 'The law knows no heresy, and is committed to the support of no dogma, the establishment of no sect'. Under such a Constitution, there is no room for a law criminalizing blasphemy, save on public-order grounds.

The law of blasphemy as it exists today in England is premised on the special status of religious belief over non-religious belief, a position hard to justify in a philosophically plural society, and on the special position of the Anglican Church within the state.

---

[22] N. Browne, 'Church and State in Modern Ireland', in T. Murphy and P. Twomey (eds.), *Ireland's Evolving Constitution 1937–97: Collected Essays* (Oxford: Hart Publishing, 1998), 41–50.

[22a] See p. 907 above.

[23] 36 USC s. 186 (1956).

[24] *Aronow v. US* 432 F.2d 242 (1970) (USCA, 9th Cir.).

[25] *Zorach v. Clauson* 343 US 306 (1952).

[26] *Walz v. Tax Commission* 397 US 664 (1970).

[27] *Engel v. Vitale* 370 US 421 (1962); *Lee v. Weisman* 112 S. Ct. 2649 (1992).

[28] *Cantwell v. Connecticut* 310 US 296 (1940).

[29] 393 US 97 (1968) at 103–4. See also *Torcaso v. Watkins* 367 US 488 (1961), holding unconstitutional a requirement that public officials should swear an oath affirming belief in God.

[30] 13 Wall. 679 (1872) at 728, 20 L. Ed. 666 at 676, *per* Miller J delivering the judgment of the court.

However, the legitimacy of the modern British state today relies more on popular consent, based on its record of respect for democracy or freedom, than on the Church of England. This has made it necessary to find another justification for retaining the offence. Blasphemous libel remains a common-law offence, but is now generally regarded as protecting the religious sensibilities of individual believers, rather than the state. Nevertheless, the link with the state and its established religion lives on as a factor limiting the scope of the offence, long after the reason for it has passed away. Even today, only attacks on Christianity, and (as forms of Christianity vary) on the established form (the Church of England), may amount to criminal blasphemy at common law. That, indeed, was what Alderson B told the jury in *R. v. Gathercole*:[31]

'. . . a person may, without being liable to prosecution for it, attack Judaism, or Mahomed-anism, or even any sect of the Christian Religion (save the established religion of the country); and the only reason why the latter is in a different situation from the others is, because it is the form established by law, and is therefore a part of the constitution of the country.'

Thus, but for the historical circumstance of Henry VIII's decision to part company with the Church of Rome, Roman Catholicism might still have been the religion enjoying a special position in the state, and only attacks on that denomination would have constituted blasphemy at common law.

This was comprehensible when English society was substantially homogeneous in its religious beliefs. Yet even in 1815, it has been said, there were more dissenters than communicants of the Church of England in Wales and some parts of England; Presby-terianism was the strongest denomination in Scotland; and there was a growing minority of Roman Catholics.[32] As the rationalist movement grew in strength, and immigration (Roman Catholic, Jewish, and, as the twentieth century progressed, Mus-lim, among other religions) mushroomed, the idea that the legitimacy of the state's laws rested on the established church might have appeared to make the laws less, rather than more, secure. There would therefore have been good reasons for abolish-ing the crime of blasphemy altogether, as a field in which the state no longer had the necessary interest to justify criminalizing expression. However, in *Bowman v. Secular Society*,[33] the House of Lords, while holding that a bequest to a society which aimed to propagate atheism was not illegal, felt unable to take the responsibility for overturning the crime of blasphemous libel, which would have involved judicial legislation over-ruling centuries of precedents. More recently, the Law Commission has unanimously recommended that the offence should be abolished, but could not agree on what, if anything, should replace it.[34]

---

[31] (1838) 2 Lew. CC 237 at 254, 168 ER 1140 at 1145.
[32] Sir Llewellyn Woodward, *The Age of Reform 1815–1870*, 2nd edn. (Oxford: Clarendon Press, 1962), 502. See also E. P. Thompson, *The Making of the English Working Class* (Harmondsworth: Penguin, 1968), 28–58; C. Hibbert, *The English: A Social History 1066–1945* (London: Grafton Books, 1987), 640–3.
[33] [1917] AC 406, HL.
[34] Law Commission Report No. 145, *Offences against Religion and Public Worship* (London: HMSO, 1985). See I. Bryan, 'Suffering Offence: the Place, Function and Future of the Blasphemy Laws Revisited' (1999) 4 *J. of Civil Liberties* 332–62.

If the offence is to be retained with the protection of religious sensibilities as its rationale, in a multi-ethnic, multi-cultural society, where there is a need to maintain social harmony between major sections of society, each of which takes its religion seriously, this would naturally tend to lead to a recognition that the law of blasphemy should protect an ever wider range of religious beliefs. But, although in *Bowman v. Secular Society*[35] Lord Sumner described as 'strange' Alderson B's direction in *Gathercole* that a statement was blasphemous only if it attacked the established denomination of the Christian religion, no court has felt able to take even that relatively small step away from centuries of authority.

In *R. v. Chief Metropolitan Magistrate, ex parte Choudhury*,[36] the applicant, a Muslim, had sought a summons charging Salman Rushdie with blasphemous libel in respect of the publication of the book *The Satanic Verses*, on the ground that the book blasphemed against (*inter alia*) God (Allah), the Prophet Abraham and his son Ishmael, Muhammad (Pbuh) the Holy Prophet of Islam, his wives and companions, and the religion of Islam. The magistrate refused to issue the summons, on the ground that the crime of blasphemy protects only Christian beliefs. The applicant applied for judicial review of this decision. The Divisional Court, after an exhaustive review of the matter, held that the limitation to Christian beliefs was settled law, and that it was outside its powers to extend the offence to religions other than Christianity. Even had it not been so bound, the court considered that it would not have been willing to initiate an extension to other religions. There were three reasons for this. First, the judges did not feel able to delimit the meaning of 'religion' sufficiently clearly to give a clear idea of the scope of the new offence. Secondly, the creation or widening of an offence at common law, although possible in theory, risked contravening the prohibition in the European Convention on Human Rights, Article 7, on retrospectively criminalizing actions or omissions. Thirdly, it would have been inappropriate judicial behaviour where there was no settled agreement (and had been none for over hundred years)[37] on whether it was appropriate to extend or abolish the offence, a lack of consensus illustrated by the powerful division of opinion in the Law Commission's report on the subject. We are therefore left with an offence which protects directly only the religious sensibilities of communicants of the Church of England, although it incidentally protects adherents to other religions so far as their beliefs overlap with central tenets of Anglican belief.

How wide is the protection offered to this select group of religionists? Although *R. v. Taylor*[38] might suggest that any aspersion on the Church of England would be criminally blasphemous, this is not the case. Admittedly, a wide range of material is protected against aspersion. For example, an attack on the Old Testament is impliedly an attack on Christianity, since Christian theology regards the Old and New Testaments as intimately connected, the Old forming the basis for the New, so that an attack on the Old Testament threatens to undermine the New Testament.[39] However,

---

[35] [1917] AC at 459.
[36] [1991] QB 429, [1991] 1 All ER 306, DC.
[37] See C. S. Kenny, 'The Evolution of the Law of Blasphemy' (1922) 1 *CLJ* 127–42.
[38] (1676) 1 Vent. 293.
[39] *R. v. Hetherington* (1840) 4 St. Tr. (NS) 563, especially at 596 *per* Lord Denman CJ.

much depends on the manner of the attack and the state of mind of the attacker. There must be an intention to subvert the established church, and, as Watkins LJ has observed, this must be achieved by means of 'scurrilous vilification'.[40] Discussion and differences of opinion are tolerated, so long as they are carried on 'in a sober and temperate and decent style' as opposed to cases where 'the tone and spirit is that of offence, and insult, and ridicule, which leaves the judgment really not free to act, and, therefore, cannot be truly called an appeal to the judgment, but an appeal to the wild and improper feelings of the human mind . . . '.[41] For a conviction, there must have been an attack of the latter sort on the established church's religion, scriptures, or sacred persons or objects.

In practice, however, this distinction between appeals to judgment and appeals to raw feelings, based in nineteenth-century rationalism, is difficult to maintain. Literary forms using rhetorical devices such as metaphor rather than reason to deliver their message can cross the boundary from the permissible to the impermissible. In *R. v. Lemon*[42] a jury decided that suggestions that Jesus had contemplated or enjoyed homosexual acts with the apostles, contained in a poem by Professor James Kirkup about a homosexual who had been converted to Christianity and published in *Gay News*, a magazine aimed at homosexuals, amounted to a blasphemous libel. It did not avail the author or publishers to argue that the purpose of the poem was to suggest that God's love is capable of encompassing an infinite range of people and practices. The jury was entitled to look at the medium rather than the message.

In fact, the *actus reus* of the crime of blasphemy has been expressed in so many different ways that it is hard to know what conduct is or is not caught by it. For example, in *R. v. Lemon* Lord Diplock spoke of publications which 'shock and arouse resentment among believing Christians', while Lord Scarman approved a definition of the offence as covering any publication 'which contains any contemptuous, reviling, scurrilous or ludicrous matter relating to God, Jesus Christ, or the Bible, or the formularies of the Church of England as by law established'.[43] It will be immediately evident that these formulations are not identical. The differences between formulations of the *actus reus* resulted from differences of opinion about the proper orientation and objective of the crime of blasphemy. The increasingly pluralistic nature of religious beliefs (or lack of them) in society undermined the idea that attacks on Christianity are more likely than attacks on other religions to 'shake the fabric of society generally' or subvert the law.[44] Another possible approach was to treat

[40] *R. v. Chief Metropolitan Magistrate, ex parte Choudhury* [1991] 1 QB 429 at 442–3, [1991] 1 All ER 306 at 314, DC.

[41] *R. v. Hetherington* (1840) 4 St. Tr. (NS) 563 at 590 *per* Lord Denman CJ.

[42] [1979] AC 617, [1979] 1 All ER 898, HL.

[43] [1979] AC 617, [1979] 1 All ER 898, at 632, 900–1, *per* Lord Diplock, and 658–9, 921–2, *per* Lord Scarman, quoting *Stephen's Digest of the Criminal Law*, 9th edn. (London: Macmillan, 1950), art. 214.

[44] *Cp.* Lord Sumner in *Bowman v. Secular Society Ltd.* [1917] AC 406 at 459–60. In *R. v. Lemon* [1979] AC 617 at 658–9, [1979] 1 All ER at 921–2, Lord Scarman accepted that the crime of blasphemy 'belongs to a group of criminal offences designed to safeguard the internal tranquillity of the kingdom', and went on to advocate legislative intervention to extend its protection to the religious feelings of all religions as the best means of achieving that objective, in the mean time maintaining the protection given to Christians under common law.

blasphemy as a simple public-order offence, made criminal because intemperate attacks on Christianity are likely to cause a breach of the peace. But the idea that a threat of a breach of the peace was an essential element of blasphemy was rejected in *Bowman v. Secular Society Ltd.*, since 'to insult a Jew's religion is not less likely to provoke a fight than to insult an Episcopalian'.[45] Accordingly, blasphemy is now viewed as an offence aimed at saving Anglicans from suffering a sense of outrage at attacks on their religion. This object of protecting religious sensibility enabled the Court of Appeal to uphold a conviction where a publication described Jesus entering Jerusalem 'like a circus clown on the back of two donkeys'.[46] It would seem that either Anglicans are thought to be extremely sensitive, or a very low level of offensiveness will suffice. Similarly, a poem giving a homosexual viewpoint on the spectacle of the crucifixion of Jesus was held to be blasphemous in *R. v. Lemon*,[47] although it was a serious attempt to put forward the view that God's love is capable of embracing all forms of human love, not only heterosexual attachments.

The position of English law is squarely based on preventing offence to a class of believers—those in the Christian traditions—from the presentation of views which are incompatible with their deeply held convictions. It used to be possible to bolster the argument from offence by invoking the bonds holding society together, by arguing that orthodox Christian doctrine (which varies somewhat between the various Christian traditions) was the foundation of English society. It is now much more difficult to maintain this, both because of the steady loss of practising support for mainstream Judaeo-Christian religious denominations and because of the growing following for other religious and philosophical positions. One might have expected ECHR Article 10 to have provided limits on the extent to which those grounds could justify imposing legal penalties on blasphemers, but so far both the European Court of Human Rights and national authorities have failed to provide a lead in this area. After the *Lemon* case, the publishers of *Gay News* failed to persuade the European Commission of Human Rights that they had suffered a violation of their rights,[48] and (as noted above) the Court in *Otto-Preminger-Institut v. Austria*[49] decided that the right to be free from offence to normal religious sensibilities was one of the rights which states could legitimately protect by restricting freedom of expression through criminal law and seizure of material.

The privileged position of orthodox religious beliefs was extended to the field of film censorship in Britain in 1989, when the British Board of Film Classification (BBFC) refused a certificate for the sale or distribution of an eighteen-minute video, *Visions of Ecstasy*, on the ground that it was blasphemous.[50] The video portrayed a

[45] Lord Sumner in *Bowman v. Secular Society Ltd.* at 459–60. *Cp.* the mistaken remark by Avory J when directing the jury in *R. v. Gott* (1922) 16 Cr. App. R. 87 at 89.

[46] *R. v. Gott* (1922) 16 Cr. App. R. 87, CCA.

[47] [1979] AC 617, [1979] 1 All ER 898, HL.

[48] *Gay News v. United Kingdom*, Eur. Comm. HR, Application No. 8710/79, Report of 7 May 1982, 28 DR 77, 5 EHRR 123, Eur. Commn. HR.

[49] Eur. Ct. HR, Series A, No. 295-A, Judgment of 20 September 1994, 19 EHRR 34.

[50] The BBFC was empowered to refuse a certificate to criminal material, and blasphemy falls within that category.

nun, identified in the cast-list with St Theresa of Avila, and depicted her as having homoerotic dreams, as well as what a journalist called 'her well-documented unsaintly visions of Christ',[51] featuring a vision of erotic activity with the figure of Jesus crucified. The video was no doubt in poor taste and of limited artistic merit. The BBFC decided that the video was blasphemous because of the erotic manner in which the subject-matter was approached, without religious or historical context. The three members in the majority on the five-member Video Appeals Committee (VAC) agreed, concluding that the video lacked seriousness, historical accuracy, or religious content. The video concentrated on St Theresa expressing her devotion in purely carnal terms, instead of showing her battling with her sexuality. The majority mixed artistic judgment (lack of seriousness) with concern for accurate representation of Christian hagiography (failure to show the saint contending with her human weakness) and religious sensibility (offence caused to believers by showing religious devotion expressed in carnal terms) to censor a lack of seriousness in dealing with certain topics of religious significance to some people.[52] The decision protected a certain group of Christians, who were unlikely to have seen the video itself, 'from self-induced discomfort *at the thought* that some other adult would be able to view it without being shocked'.[53]

The producer of *Visions of Ecstasy*, Mr. Nigel Wingrove, complained to the European Commission of Human Rights, alleging a violation of his freedom of expression under ECHR Article 10. The Commission ruled in his favour by a majority of fourteen votes to two.[54] The Court, however, decided by seven votes to two that the interference with freedom of expression was justifiable.[55] Following the Court's *Otto-Preminger-Institut* decision, the refusal of a certificate pursued a legitimate aim, namely the protection of the rights of others to be guarded from 'the treatment of a religious subject in such a manner 'as to be calculated (that is, bound, not intended) "to outrage those who have an understanding of, sympathy towards and support for the Christian story and ethic, because of the contemptuous, reviling, insulting, scurrilous or ludicrous tone, style and spirit in which the subject is presented"'.[56] The majority of the Court decided that the refusal of a certificate fell within the state's margin of appreciation, which was wider in the field of morals and religion than in respect of political speech. The Court bore in mind that English law of blasphemy contained a high threshold of profanation which had to be crossed before a work became criminal; that the law did not ban all critical discussion of religion, but was concerned with the manner in which it was discussed; that the decisions of the BBFC and VAC had been reached after careful consideration of all the relevant matters, and that the video could easily have been reproduced to reach a wide audience. That being

---

[51] R. Wynne-Jones, 'Celestial Orgasm that Went Too Far', *Independent on Sunday*, 24 March 1996, 5.

[52] For an acute critique, see C. Unsworth, 'Blasphemy, Cultural Divergence and Legal Relativism' (1995) 58 *MLR* 658–77.

[53] G. Robertson, *Freedom, the Individual and the Law*, 7th edn. (Harmondsworth: Penguin, 1993), 254. The author was counsel for the film's producer when the case went to Strasbourg. See further Unsworth, *op. cit.*, n. 52.

[54] *Wingrove v. United Kingdom*, Eur. Commn. HR, App. No. 17419/90, Report of 10 January 1995.

[55] *Wingrove v. United Kingdom*, Eur. Ct. HR, Judgment of 25 November 1996, RJD 1996-V, 24 EHRR 1.

[56] Ibid. at para. 48, quoting from the reasoning of the BBFC.

so, a complete ban on the video was understandable.[57] The potential impact of the judgment was drawn out in the separate, concurring opinion of Judge Pettiti, who pointed out that the judgment should have been framed in terms of protecting philosophical convictions as well as religious beliefs, as respect for both is guaranteed under ECHR Article 9. Judge De Meyer, dissenting, saw the case as an unacceptable example of prior restraint, going further than could be justified. He questioned the necessity for blasphemy law, considering that the strength of a believer's own belief is the best defence against blasphemy, while Judge Lohmus, also dissenting, thought it told against the necessity for blasphemy laws that they protected only Christians.

The refusal of a certificate to *Visions of Ecstasy* was not a great loss to western culture, but it was important in demonstrating that the Court at the time, unlike the Commission, was willing to allow protection for expression under ECHR Article 10 to become variable as between countries and communication media, and to allow states to censor expression in order to protect the sensitivities of people of any religion or, potentially, philosophical conviction. It is hard to justify treating such beliefs more tenderly than others.

We can now turn from the *actus reus* of blasphemy to its *mens rea*. The intention required to constitute the *mens rea* has been expressed as 'an intention to publish material which in the opinion of the jury is likely to shock and arouse resentment among believing Christians'.[58] It is not necessary that the accused should be shown to have intended to shock or arouse resentment, or even to have been indifferent as to whether shock or resentment resulted from his actions.[59] This approach has been followed by analogy in relation to the offence of outraging public decency, discussed below, in section 16.3(2). However, it compounds an unsatisfactory state of affairs in which a common-law crime, carrying an unlimited penalty, has an uncertain purpose, an uncertain *actus reus*, and minimal *mens rea* requirements.

The English law of blasphemy, it seems to be generally agreed, is in need of reform. Unfortunately, there is no agreement about the nature of the necessary reform. In essence, there are only two options: the abolition of the offence, and its extension (with, perhaps, modifications) to cover insults to all or most religions. Each of these options has its supporters. As noted above, Lord Scarman in *Lemon*[60] supported the idea of generalizing the protection of religious susceptibilities, but felt that only Parliament could take that step.[61] The Law Commission, on the other hand, unanimously recommended abolishing the common-law offence, and, although a minority favoured introducing a statutory provision which would protect religious sensibilities, the majority of the Commission recommended that religious beliefs should not have

[57] *Wingrove v. United Kingdom*, Eur. Ct. HR, Judgment of 25 November 1996, RJD 1996-V, 24 EHRR 1 at paras. 58, 60–64.

[58] *R. v. Lemon* [1979] AC 617 at 632, [1979] 1 All ER 898 at 900–1, *per* Lord Diplock.

[59] The *mens rea* requirement is therefore less demanding than that laid down in *R. v. Ramsay and Foote* (1883) 15 Cox CC 231, where Lord Coleridge CJ at 236 approved a formulation which demanded either malicious or wilful intention to pervert, insult, or mislead, or a state of indifference to the interests of society.

[60] *R. v. Lemon* [1979] AC 617, [1979] 1 All ER 898, HL.

[61] Lord Scarman later retreated from this suggestion, preferring to concentrate on the public-order consequences of attacks on religions, although he remained of the view that people's religious beliefs should be protected: Unsworth, 'Blasphemy, Cultural Divergence and Legal Relativism', above, at 673–4.

more extensive protection than other types of beliefs.[62] This view treats the matter simply as a public-order issue: insults to any religion would be punishable if (and only if) they threatened to provoke public-order offences, or constituted some other specific criminal offence. There have been several attempts to introduce legislation to achieve this, but so far all have been unsuccessful.[63]

Those who advocate creating a wider offence, which would protect adherents of all religions against having their religious sensibilities outraged, treat the sensibilities of those who believe in religion as a special interest, more significant than people's interests in (for example) philosophy, politics, art, music, and football, none of which are specially protected against outrage by the criminal law. There is some philosophical support for such a weighting of interests. Joseph Raz and John Finnis each give special status to religious beliefs. For Raz, freedom of religion is primarily a social good, because, in addition to the fact that it may form a central tenet of a person's chosen path through life, it is worthy of protection on the ground that it is seen as a socially useful phenomenon.[64] For Finnis, religion is a self-evident good, because people seek an understanding, for its own sake, of their relationship with the forces which created the universe.[65] Michael Perry has argued that a legal system which becomes detached from fundamental spiritual values loses an important part of its point and legitimacy.[66] However, while these theories demand protection for freedom of religious belief and practice, it is by no means clear that they entail laws imposing criminal sanctions on anyone who offends another's religious sensibilities. Indeed, it is possible that such a law might itself threaten the religious freedom of members of religions whose innocent expressions of belief might outrage members of other religions which are fundamentally intolerant of the beliefs of others. The law might also threaten the right of people to express atheist beliefs or agnosticism, both philosophical positions which express a position in relation to the creative forces of the universe no less than, though different from, orthodox religious positions.

As well as offering only questionable support for a law of blasphemy, Raz's argument for the importance of religious freedom might in some circumstances justify a restriction of that freedom. If the value of religious freedom is primarily social, as Raz suggests, then it would seem to follow that society is justified in restricting the freedom to pursue those religions which, so far from upholding social morality, strike at

---

[62] Law Commission, Report No. 145, *Offences against Religion*.

[63] Mr. Tony Benn MP introduced a Blasphemy (Abolition) Bill to the House of Commons as a private member's bill in 1989, and Lord Avebury introduced a similar bill to the House of Lords in 1995. Both were denied a second reading. During the passage through the House of Lords of the Criminal Justice and Public Order Bill in 1994, Lord Lester of Herne Hill QC proposed but later withdrew amendments which would have abolished blasphemy and introduced a crime of inciting religious hatred, and the Bishop of Oxford proposed and pressed to a division an amendment to introduce a crime of inciting religious hatred to operate alongside the existing offence of blasphemy: see House of Lords, *Official Report*, vol. 555, cols. 1890–1909, 16 June 1994; vol. 556, cols. 1737–52, 12 July 1994.

[64] J. Raz, *The Morality of Freedom* (Oxford: Clarendon Press, 1986), 251–2.

[65] J. Finnis, *Natural Law and Natural Rights* (Oxford: Clarendon Press, 1980), 89–90.

[66] M. Perry, *Religion and Politics: Constitutional and Moral Perspectives* (New York: Oxford University Press, 1997); G. F. Whyte, 'Some Reflections on the Role of Religion in the Constitutional Order', in Murphy and Twomey (eds.), *Ireland's Evolving Constitution*, 51–63.

CIVIL LIBERTIES AND HUMAN RIGHTS

the root of established social values. For example, it is arguable that the Muslim attack on Salman Rushdie, far from deserving the support of an extended law of blasphemy, would have justified active legal steps against those Muslims who threatened to commit heinous criminal offences against Rushdie. The *fatwah*, a sentence of death which would not be recognized in any British court, was, as a matter of English law, an incitement to murder. Any religion which supports or requires such action strikes at the root of the ideals of the rule of law and the sanctity of life on which (among other things) liberal society is based. A society which is so liberal that it turns a blind eye to such threats has gone beyond liberalism into a form of relativism in which it fails to stand up for the rights and freedoms which it purports to hold as fundamental. It is, indeed, licence rather than liberalism, and represents an open invitation to those who would undermine liberty of conscience and toleration in the name of respect for religion.

The problem here is that the rights to freedom of religion and of expression are of rather similar weight, and it is not easy to say which should prevail.[67] The Human Rights Act 1998 embodies rather than reduces perplexity. Section 12(4) requires courts to have particular regard to the importance of the Convention right to freedom of expression when considering whether to grant any relief which might affect it. Section 13(1) requires a court to have particular regard to the importance of the Convention right to freedom of thought, conscience, and religion when determining any question which might affect the exercise of the right by a religious organization or its members. If the question of the compatibility of the law of blasphemy with ECHR Article 10 arises in an English court, sections 12 and 13 will not provide much help. The problem is further exacerbated by the vastly different perspectives and world views of the protagonists, which prevents them from conceiving of the issue, or even reading the book, in sufficiently similar ways to allow for constructive discussion.[68]

It is therefore perhaps not surprising that the European Commission of Human Rights has decided that, while a state has a discretion to penalize scurrilous attacks on religious beliefs which are deeply held among its citizens,[69] the right to freedom of religion under Article 9 of the European Convention does not compel freedom for adherents of any religion to bring legal proceedings in respect of such scurrilous abuse.[70] Although it has sometimes been argued that the existing English law of blasphemy breaches Article 14 of the Convention, as it discriminates against non-Christians,[71] the text of Article 14 outlaws discrimination on the ground of (*inter alia*) religion only in respect of 'the rights and freedoms set forth in this Convention'. Once it has been decided that the right to freedom of religion does not encompass a right to

---

[67] S. Poulter, *Ethnicity, Law and Human Rights* (Oxford: Clarendon Press, 1998), 101–4.

[68] For illuminating discussion, see Bradney, *Religions, Rights and Laws*, 85–91.

[69] *Gay News Ltd. v. United Kingdom*, Eur. Comm. HR, Application No. 8710/79, Report of 7 May 1982; 28 DR 77, 5 EHRR 123.

[70] *Choudhury v. United Kingdom*, Application No. 17439/90, Decision of 8 March 1991 (1991) 12 *Human Rights LJ* 172.

[71] E.g. by S. Poulter, 'Towards Legislative Reform of the Blasphemy and Racial Hatred Laws' [1991] *PL* 371–85 at 375.

have criminal sanctions imposed for scurrilous attacks on tenets of a religion, it is hard to see how a domestic law which imposes such sanctions differentially can be said to breach Article 14. It is no answer to point out that a restriction, justifiable under another Article, on a right which is, in fact, recognized in the Convention, may contravene Article 14 if imposed in a discriminatory way:[72] there is no warrant for extending such a principle to cases in which an applicant is asserting a right which is not recognized within the Convention. A stronger argument could, however, be made on the basis of the ICCPR Article 26, which provides that all are entitled to the equal protection of the law, which must provide effective protection against discrimination on the ground of (*inter alia*) religion. The question would appear to turn on the issue of whether the different treatment of groups is based on reasonable and objective criteria, a matter on which opinions might differ.[73] ICCPR Article 20(2) requires states to outlaw 'advocacy of national, racial or religious hatred that constitutes incitement to discrimination, hostility or violence'. The Strasbourg Court has regarded this as legitimizing some controls over the dissemination of racist political views,[74] but it says nothing about expression which members of a religious group consider to reflect hostility to their beliefs, but which does not advocate hatred. International human rights law is, therefore, unhelpful on the form which any new law should take.

It is clear that any criminal offence which replaces blasphemy would need to cover all religious beliefs if it were to be acceptable in a pluralist society such as modern Britain.[75] At the same time, there is a widespread liberal mistrust of criminal laws which seek to penalize expressions of opinions merely on the ground that some people find the opinions, or the manner in which they are expressed, objectionable.[76] A possible compromise would treat a person's religious beliefs as special interests for the purposes of the criminal law in the same way that a person's membership of a racial group is treated as a special interest. That would lead to legislation which would criminalize attacks on religious beliefs to the same extent as attacks on racial groups. Such a proposal has been advanced by Sebastian Poulter.[77] This would impose sanctions on behaviour which met the same criterion as are set out in Part III of the Public Order Act 1986, namely an intention to stir up hatred against a racial (or, in this case, religious) group.[78] Such hatred affects religious groups in much the same way as it affects racial groups, and should be subjected to the same criminal-law regime.

---

[72] This is Poulter's argument, 'Towards Legislative Reform', at 372, relying on *Grundrath v. Federal Republic of Germany* (1967) *Yearbook of the European Convention of Human Rights* 626 at 678; *Belgian Linguistics Case (No. 2)* Eur. Ct. HR, Series A, No. 6, Judgment of 23 July 1968, at paras. 7–9; 1 EHRR 252 at 283–4.

[73] See *Annual Report of the Human Rights Committee*, 1987, UN Doc. A/42/40, 139.

[74] So long as the restriction is proportionate to the legitimate aim: *Jersild v. Denmark*, Eur. Ct. HR, Series A, No. 298, Judgment of 23 September 1994, 19 EHRR 1.

[75] See, e.g. Report of the Archbishop of Canterbury's Working Group, *Offences against Religion and Public Worship*, General Synod Misc. 286 of 1988.

[76] J. Feinberg, *Offense to Others* (New York: Oxford University Press, 1985), accepts that offensiveness is an evil, even when not harmful (i.e. against anyone's interests), but argues that criminalization is justified only if the offence is wrongful (i.e. interferes with rights) and profound.

[77] Poulter, 'Towards Legislative Reform', at 377–85.

[78] This would have been the effect of an amendment to the Public Order and Criminal Justice Bill 1994 proposed by Lord Lester of Herne Hill QC, but later withdrawn: see n. 63 above.

Indeed, some religious groups[79] (though not Christians or, perhaps, Muslims) are also racial groups within the meaning of the current legislation. The Anti-terrorism, Crime and Security Bill 2001, Part 5, adopts this approach.

On this model, it would be an offence to use threatening, abusive, or insulting words or behaviour, or to display any written material which is threatening, abusive, or insulting, with the intention of stirring up hatred against a racial or religious group, or whereby such hatred is likely to be stirred up. It would be hard to object to such legislation on principled grounds; indeed, it is possible that such behaviour would in the past have constituted seditious libel (though not blasphemy) when directed against a religious group such as Anglo-Jewry.[80] The legislation does not automatically outlaw outrage to sensibilities. If one feels that the risk of such outrage is necessarily concomitant with having sensibilities, and that it should not attract criminal sanctions, this will not be a serious concern. Those who are not of this view would perhaps see some justification for widening the scope of the offence to make the use of threatening, abusive, or insulting words, behaviour, or written material a criminal offence if it is intended to outrage the feelings of a significant number of members of a racial or religious group.[81] However, many would be likely to see such an extension of the criminal law as an unacceptable infringement of freedom of expression, in the absence of a clear and imminent risk that public disorder would result from the words, behaviour, or display of written material. To punish mere offensiveness strikes at the heart of liberal democracy, based as it is on a willingness to tolerate offence in order to preserve the greater good of free expression, which 'is applicable not only to "information" or "ideas" that are favourably received or regarded as inoffensive or as a matter of indifference, but also to those that offend, shock or disturb the state or any sector of the population'.[82]

The Bill protects religious groups, defined by reference to the presence or absence of religious belief. It therefore protects atheists and agnostics. But religion is not defined. It will be left for judges and juries to interpret.[83] Would it encompass devil worship, scientology, and polytheism? One difficulty is how to reach a consensus on what constitutes a religion, a matter on which even theologians disagree. In the UK, the predominant constitutional position of the Anglican Church is reflected in a wide range of institutions, notably the monarchy and the role of bishops in the House of Lords. Tax exemptions are also available in the UK for bodies which pursue religious purposes, and so fall within the definition of a charity.[84] However, this presents the Charity Commissioners and the courts with difficult problems in deciding what constitutes a religion. In *R. v. Registrar General, ex parte Segerdal*[85] the Court of Appeal

---

[79] E.g. Jews and Sikhs are covered by existing legislation, as they constitute ethnic groups as well as religious ones: *Mandla v. Dowell Lee* [1983] 2 AC 548, [1983] 1 All ER 1062, HL.

[80] Robilliard, *Religion and the Law*, 8–10.

[81] This is Dr. Poulter's proposal, 'Towards Legislative Reform', at 378; note his proposed redraft of the Public Order Act 1986, s. 18(1).

[82] *Handyside v. United Kingdom*, Eur. Ct. HR, Series A, No. 24, Judgment of 7 December 1976, 1 EHRR 737, at para. 49.

[83] Dr. Poulter's preference is for leaving this to the judges: 'Towards Legislative Reform', 379–80.

[84] Robilliard, *Religion and the Law*, ch. 4.

[85] (1970) 2 QB 697, (1970) 3 All ER 886, CA.

held that a chapel used by the Church of Scientology was not a 'place of meeting for religious worship' entitled to relief from rates, because with a few exceptions (including Buddhism) religious worship involves doing reverence to a deity. The court decided that scientology is a philosophy rather than a religion. It follows that neither Freemasonry[86] nor the South Place Ethical Society[87] are charitable as being for the advancement of religion, because their activities do not sufficiently display the characteristics of 'submission to the object worshipped, veneration of that object, praise, thanksgiving, prayer, or intercession'.[88]

However, the distinction between religions and other forms of philosophy presents insuperable problems. Buddhism is not theistic, but is commonly regarded as a religion. The English courts treat Buddhism as an exception to the general rule, but this makes it hard to find a principled ground for excluding scientology from the category of religions. By contrast, the High Court of Australia has decided that religions are not necessarily theistic, and that scientology qualifies as a religion for the purposes of tax relief.[89] In the USA, the Supreme Court has also adopted a non-theistic view of religion, allowing exemption from conscription on the ground of religious conviction to one who holds a 'sincere and meaningful belief, which occupies in the life of its possessor a place parallel to that filled by the God of those admittedly qualifying for the exemption on the grounds of religion'.[90] Instead of attempting a definition, it would be preferable (but perhaps not much easier) to approach the issue from a policy orientation, by asking whether the particular philosophy or creed benefits society morally in a way which merits special legal privileges. One would then have a range of privileges for specifically recognized religious groups, without the need to agree a definition of religion. Alternatively, one might extend the protection to all philosophical beliefs, whether grounded in religion or not.

The *mens rea* for the offence under Part 5 of the Bill is intention to use threatening, abusive or insulting words or behaviour, or recklessness as to whether they would be so regarded, coupled with intention or negligence as to whether religious hatred would be stirred up by them. The relationship between the offence and blasphemy is unclear. Once it has been agreed to treat attacks on religion as a public order matter, the justification for retaining the offence of blasphemy, with its uncertain and selective protection for some religious sensibilities,[91] becomes increasingly tenuous.

---

[86] *United Grand Lodge of Ancient, Free and Accepted Masons of England v. Holborn Borough Council* (1957) 1 WLR 1080, (1957) 3 All ER 281, CA.

[87] *In re South Place Ethical Society; Barralet v. A.-G.* (1980) 1 WLR 1565, (1980) 3 All ER 918.

[88] *R. v. Registrar General, ex parte Segerdal* (1970) 2 QB 697 at 709, (1970) 3 All ER 886 at 892, *per* Buckley LJ.

[89] *Church of the New Faith v. Commissioner for Pay-Roll Tax* (1983) 154 CLR 120.

[90] *United States v. Seeger*, 380 US 163 (1965) at 176 *per* Clark J, writing for the court.

[91] See R. Abel, *Speech and Respect* (London: Stevens & Sons, 1994), 11–29, 123–52.

16.2 FOUNDATIONS OF THE LAW OF DECENCY: PUBLIC MORALITY

AND PRIVATE SENSIBILITY

Expression of a sort which might contravene accepted standards of social morality is potentially subject to restrictions of three types in English law. First, there are various statutory and common-law offences for which people may be prosecuted. Secondly, there are provisions restricting access to material, and requiring outlets selling the material to be licensed and regulated. Thirdly, there are provisions allowing seizure and forfeiture of immoral goods in certain circumstances, without the need for anyone to be shown to have committed any offence. The law is in a confused state. It has developed over the centuries since the invention of printing. Common-law rules and statutory rules, laws controlling indecency and laws controlling obscenity, exist side by side.[92] Because of the confusion about standards, innocent family photographs may be liable to be seized under warrant if the police decide that photographs of one's children pursuing normal activities, such as playing in the bath, are indecent. In 1993, Mr. Ron Oliver, a well respected portrait photographer frequently commissioned by well-off parents to photograph their children, had 20,000 images seized by police and held indefinitely without being charged with an offence, although it was later said that only three of the images had even been suspected of being indecent. Apart from the threat of prosecution, this made it impossible for him to practise in the UK, and forced him to move to the Netherlands.[92a] In 1998, a book of photographs by the distinguished homosexual photographic artist Robert Mapplethorpe was seized by police from the library of the University of Central England, but the University put up a spirited resistance and legal action against it was discontinued. The confused state of the law makes it possible for society and the police to demonize and then pursue people of whose images they disapprove. The different aspects of the law have different purposes. In particular, there is a difference between the law on obscene publications and the law on indecency.

Obscenity, as defined by statute in England and Wales, is criminalized to protect those who come to it willingly against moral harm—depravity and corruption—which the obscene article is held to threaten.[93] This crime therefore does not protect people's right to keep their sensitivities free from outrage, but instead either guards their moral integrity in a wholly paternalistic way, doing what is considered best for them whether or not they want it, or protects some public interest in maintaining moral standards in a way which overrides personal freedoms and desires. For this reason, it presents particular difficulties for those who seek to justify or formulate obscenity law in accordance with a civil libertarian philosophy.

Offences dealing with indecency, by contrast, aim to protect people's sensibilities.[94]

---

[92] G. Robertson, *Obscenity: An Account of Censorship Laws and their Enforcement in England and Wales* (London: Weidenfeld & Nicolson, 1979), chs 1 and 2.

[92a] See *The Independent Magazine*, 4 September 1993; *The Observer: Uncensored*, Part 2, 17 April 1994.

[93] Smith and Hogan, *Criminal Law*, 7th edn., 730–42; G. Robertson and A. Nicol, *Media Law*, 3rd edn. (London: Penguin, 1992), 106–38.

[94] Robertson and Nicol, *Media Law*, 3rd edn., 147–60.

The moral justification for regulating or criminalizing indecent expression is therefore essentially the same as the modern moral justification for criminalizing assaults on religious convictions. It is also subject to a similar objection. Although the indecency laws appear to apply to all forms of indecency, and are not, like blasphemy, limited to protecting the feelings of a particular religious or philosophical creed, the definition of indecency is heavily influenced by cultural and ethnic factors. Things may be indecent to a devout Muslim or Orthodox Jew which would not be indecent in the eyes of a communicant of the Church of England. A vicar might have regarded some things as indecent fifty years ago which would not be regarded in that light by a modern vicar. The fact that indecency is a cultural construction means that the law of indecency is likely to protect a limited range of notions of decency. If the law stops short at protecting a common core of sensitivities, it will be attacked by those whose sensitivities, deeply felt but not shared with others, are left unprotected. If it goes further, it will be attacked by those of the dominant culture who feel that their freedom of expression is being abridged unjustifiably.

It is not clear whether the objective of the law is, or should be, to put a stop to pornography, and, if so, why; to prevent pornography from falling into the wrong hands; to maintain standards of morality, and, if so, whose; to stop people from being upset by public displays; or to achieve some combination of those objects. Were it acceptable to criminalize or contain all conduct or expression which the dominant members of society found offensive or immoral, it would seriously restrict the range of discussion of ethical and political issues, since many expressions of opinion will be found offensive by those who disagree either with the opinion or with the way in which it is expressed.

This section examines the foundations for such laws against a background of liberal theory. On this view, tolerating offensive conduct and speech is one of the prices to be paid for a reasonably free and open society. Alternatively, free-speech theory can be regarded as a forum for debate, in which societies develop their intellectual attitudes. A bias in favour of toleration can best be developed and systematized in cases concerning relatively innocuous forms of offensiveness, and, once established, can then be applied and extended in relation to other, potentially more upsetting, offences.[95] In a pluralist society there is unlikely to be agreement about moral standards, and in a liberal society it is a commonplace assumption that choice between moral values is primarily a matter for individuals. There is a widely, but not universally, accepted view in Britain of the limits of the criminal law. The job of the law, and particularly criminal law, is to exclude from the range of individual choice those acts which are incompatible with the maintenance of society and the safety and rights of its members. It is no part of its job to seek to uphold the preferences of one part of society over those of another part, save in limited circumstances: namely, when the preferences of some members of society cause harm, rather than mere inconvenience or offence, to others. Since being articulated by John Stuart Mill in *On Liberty*, published in 1859, the 'harm principle' has been adopted as a basis for philosophical discussion, and for the recommendations

---

[95] L. C. Bollinger, *The Tolerant Society: Freedom of Speech and Extremist Speech in America* (Oxford and New York: Clarendon Press, 1986), esp. 137–40.

of the Home Office Departmental Committee on Obscenity and Film Censorship, chaired by Professor Bernard Williams (the Williams Committee).[96]

However, there is considerable variation between people's views of what constitutes 'harm' for this purpose. Some people, impressed by the wide range of interferences with rights which would become permissible if harm is given an extended meaning, restrict it to harm which is objectively verifiable according to established scientific criteria. They therefore look for physical or psychological harm which constitutes a condition or syndrome recognized by competent medical or social scientific opinion. On this basis, the Williams Committee took the view in 1979 that the burden of establishing harm lay on those who seek to justify interference with liberty of expression, and that those people had failed to discharge the burden of showing a causative link between reading or watching pornography and committing criminal or anti-social acts.[97] This was consistent with the conclusion of the Commission on Obscenity and Pornography in 1970 in the USA.[98] However, there is growing evidence that people who commit crimes of violence, especially sexual violence, are likely to have been influenced by pornographic or violent books, magazines, pictures, and films, even if there is as yet limited evidence as to the likelihood of exposure to that material causing people to go on to commit such offences.[99]

Others, instead of concentrating on material harm, are prepared to take account of moral, social, or ideological harm. This is less easy to establish on objective criteria than the former kind of harm.[100] It is more impressionistic, and allows people to propose interferences with liberty on the strength of assertions of social or moral harm which cannot be scientifically tested. The main difference between Professor H. L. A. Hart and Sir Patrick (later Lord) Devlin, in relation to the proper relationship of morals to law, did not concern whether harm should be the basis for legal interference with liberty of expression. They agreed that it should, but disagreed about the type of harm which should be regarded as significant. Hart favoured reliance on personal harm, following the line traceable to John Stuart Mill, while Devlin considered that attacks on any basic moral standards threatened, and so caused harm to, society as a whole, weakening the bonds which hold it together, even if no identifiable individual suffered immediate and identifiable personal harm. Accordingly, Devlin was prepared

[96] Ch. 1 above; *Report of the Committee on Obscenity and Film Censorship* (Chairman: Professor Bernard Williams), Cmnd. 7772 (London: HMSO, 1979), hereafter 'Williams Committee Report'.

[97] Williams Committee Report, ch. 6, para. 10.8, and (for a summary of the research) App. 5.

[98] *Report of the Commission on Obscenity and Pornography* (Washington, DC: Government Printing Office, 1970).

[99] For useful analyses of empirical evidence, see E. F. Einsiedel, 'The Experimental Research Evidence: Effects of Pornography on the "Average Individual"', in C. Itzin (ed.), *Pornography: Women, Violence and Civil Liberties* (New York: Oxford University Press, 1992), 248–83 (based on a survey of published research up to 1986); J. Weaver, 'The Social Science and Psychological Research Evidence: Perceptual and Behavioural Consequences of Exposure to Pornography', ibid., 284–309; D. E. H. Russell, 'Pornography and Rape: A Causal Model', ibid., 310–49.

[100] This is not to say that assessing psychological harm does not depend on judgment. Clearly it does. The difference, however, lies in the fact that psychiatric diagnosis proceeds on the basis of criteria which are agreed in advance by those who do the job, and which rely on observable symptoms or manifestations of abnormality, so that diagnosis is testable and falsifiable. This is not true of most other forms of harm.

to contemplate the criminal law enforcing a wider range of moral demands than was Hart.[101]

The moral basis of society is important, but it is probably impossible to establish which moral standards are basic to the survival of any society and which are merely peripheral. It would be unsafe to allow indiscriminate criminalization of all immoral conduct or expression, both because of the uncertain scope of morality in a pluralist society and because the resulting interference with freedom would be likely to cause social and economic stagnation. At the same time, people sometimes suffer offence which is of such a type, and so intense, as to be experienced subjectively as a form of harm which may be as wounding as physical harm. When this happens, it is understandable that there are demands for the cause to be repressed by law. These demands are ultimately political demands, rather than moral or legal ones, and have to be addressed by members of society in the context of a debate about the type of society in which they wish to live.

In 1979, the Williams Committee, adopting a physical or psychological harm test and deciding that the link between pornography and such harm had not been proved, made a number of recommendations which, if implemented, would have gone some way towards clarifying the law, if not making it more socially acceptable than it was before. The Committee recommended that there should be no constraints on the written word, however explicit or offensive, or on written words which were accompanied by inoffensive illustrations. This is a far-reaching proposal. Even the US Supreme Court has not granted First Amendment protection to all written matter. Books can be banned in the USA if they are obscene: that is, appealing to prurient interest as judged by contemporary community standards; depicting or describing, in a patently offensive way, sexual conduct which has been specifically defined by the relevant law; and lacking in serious literary, artistic, political, or scientific value.[102] Child pornography may be banned in the USA,[103] and children and young people under the age of seventeen may be denied access to material which would not be regarded as obscene in adult hands.[104] It is perhaps not surprising that the government in the UK was unwilling to make pornography more readily available in the UK than in the USA in order to achieve some kind of principled consistency in the law.

Taking the view that pictures are more harmful than words, the Committee recommended that it should be a criminal offence to trade in or import paedophilic photographic material which portrays indecent activity involving people under the age of sixteen, or sadistic photographs in which physical harm appears to have been inflicted on people in a sexual context. Other pictorial pornography which portrays,

---

[101] Sir Patrick Devlin, *The Enforcement of Morals* (Oxford: Oxford University Press, 1965), ch. 1; H. L. A. Hart, *Law, Liberty, and Morality* (Oxford: Oxford University Press, 1963). For further discussion, see Joel Feinberg's attempt to distinguish between offensive and harmful conduct, and to explain the justification for putting up with at least some offensive conduct, in *Offense to Others*; P. R. Macmillan, *Censorship and Public Morality* (Aldershot: Gower, 1983), 105–26; H. L. A. Hart, 'Between Utility and Rights', 39 *Columbia LR* 828–46.

[102] *Miller v. California* 413 US 15 (1973).

[103] *New York v. Ferber* 458 US 747 (1982). Using children under sixteen in pornographic films and photographs is a federal crime.

[104] *Ginsberg v. New York* 390 US 629 (1968); *Virginia v. Booksellers Association* 484 US 383 (1988).

deals with, or relates to violence, cruelty, or horror, faecal or urinary functions, sexual functions, or genitalia, should be restricted if its unrestricted availability is offensive to reasonable people by reason of the manner in which those matters are portrayed or dealt with. The Committee recommended that such material should be available only to people over the age of eighteen, either by mail order or in shops which admit only those aged eighteen and over, exhibit warnings of the type of material sold, and do not display pornographic material in a way which allows it to be visible from the street. The idea was to keep the material out of the way of people who might be offended or harmed by it, such as children and people encountering it unawares.

The restriction of these controls to material dealing with defined matters would have given some objectivity to the notion of offensiveness. However, although the Williams Committee had managed to achieve unanimity among its members, its report was attacked from all directions. The newly elected Conservative government was not prepared to relax restrictions on written matter. In this, they were supported by an odd alliance of the moral conservatives, liberals, and feminists, who are opposed to pornography for different reasons.[105] We will examine some of these in a moment. The Williams Committee's proposals to restrict access to offensive material was more favourably received. Legislation to some extent modelled on the proposals has been passed, and is explained in section 16.5 below. Generally, however, the notion of restricting sexually offensive material is problematic, for two reasons.

First, the standard of offensiveness can be criticized as being unacceptably indeterminate standard for the law governing the availability of public expression.[106] The implication of this is liberal in a traditional sense: any interference with freedom must be aimed at meeting a pressing social need and should be circumscribed in sufficiently clear terms to enable people to know what the law is, and plan their activities accordingly. This standard is laid down in the caselaw of the European Court of Human Rights as a condition for the justifiability of interferences with freedom of expression under Article 10(2) of the Convention in order to protect morals.

Secondly, restricting, but not banning, offensive matter can be seen as based on a misconception about the type and significance of the harm which pornography works. Feminist theorists have argued that pornography causes a kind of social harm distinct both from any causal relationship between access to pornography and crime or offence, and from any damage it does to the shared values of the community. Instead, they suggest that all pornographic representations (or, at any rate, all pornographic representations of heterosexual activity) harm all women. The harm is done by degrading women, presenting them as dominated by men in a context in which such domination is thought to be regarded as natural and even enjoyable. Women may, as Catharine MacKinnon has written, be entirely dehumanized in pornography,

---

[105] A. W. B. Simpson, *Pornography and Politics: A Look Back to the Williams Committee* (London: Waterlow, 1983), chs 3 and 5. The book is a re-evaluation of the report and of its political reception by a distinguished legal scholar who was a member of the Committee.

[106] For a critique of the principle of offensiveness, see Barendt, *Freedom of Speech*, 272–9. For a more fully worked out model of the type of offensiveness which might justify a liberal in interfering with free expression, see Feinberg, *Offense to Others*.

becoming merely recipients of treatment by men.[107] MacKinnon, and Andrea Dworkin, argue that sexual explicitness in the representation of this sort of relationship, combined with sexual arousal in the viewer or reader, cause or reinforce attitudes of men towards women, and of women towards themselves (particularly if they find the pornography arousing), which tend to encourage male domination in all areas of life.[108] Pornography is seen as a form of discrimination against women disempowering them and tending to silence them politically, and it merits banning as such.[109] It has also been suggested that there is a link between pornography and racism, both trading on stereotypes of women and oppressed minorities and exploiting the needs of the poor and their weak bargaining position to facilitate the cheap production of pornographic photographs and films.[110] Attempts to ban pornography on the ground that it constitutes a particular representation of the relationship between the sexes have failed in the USA (indeed, in a sense were self-defeating), because they necessarily imply that pornographers are advancing a political perspective, and this will tend to bring them within the protection of the First Amendment.[111]

MacKinnon's and Dworkin's attempts to politicize pornography as violence against women faces a further problem. It assumes that all pornography is the same. In reality, there are many varieties, reflecting many different types of sexual activity. It is only possible to argue convincingly that all pornography is violence against women if one imposes a definition which artificially limits pornography to material which represents sadistic heterosexual or lesbian activity. Other types of pornography may represent violence against entities other than women (dogs, pigs, children, men), but is it objectionable (if one believes it is) because it reflects violent and dominating attitudes in the relationships between the parties, or because it may be in some way harmful, or because it is revolting? To insist on the equation $P = V$ (where P is pornography and V is violence against women) wrongly treats pornography 'as one indivisible phenomenon', as Professor Simpson observed. One can accept that this is the commonest form of pornography, so it is unfair to suggest, as Simpson does, 'it is hard to believe that some feminist writers have ever seen any'.[112] Yet the feminist analysis, once accepted, leaves open the question as to the appropriate criterion for action against other types of explicit and offensive appeals to prurient sexual interest. It also leaves open the question whether the blunt instrument of legal control is the best way of rectifying the problem.[113]

---

[107] C. MacKinnon, *Feminism Unmodified: Discourses on Life and Law* (London: Harvard University Press, 1987), 176.

[108] MacKinnon, *Feminism Unmodified*, 147; A. Dworkin, *Pornography: Men Possessing Women* (London: The Women's Press, 1981).

[109] See R. Langton, 'Speech Act and Unspeakable Acts', in T. Campbell and W. Sadurski (eds.), *Freedom of Communication* (Aldershot: Dartmouth, 1994), 95–129; B. Gaze, 'Theories of Free Speech, Pornography and Sexual Equality', ibid., 131–59. The relatively unusual form of pornography which represents women dominating men would presumably be regarded as equally discriminatory and violent, although in a different direction, and so equally merit banning.

[110] A. Forna, 'Pornography and Racism: Sexualizing Oppression and Inciting Hatred', in Itzin (ed.), *Pornography*, 102–12.

[111] *Hudnut v. American Booksellers Association, Inc.* 771 F.2d 323 (1986) US 7th Cir., affd. 475 US 1001.

[112] Simpson, *Pornography and Politics*, 71.

[113] See Abel, *Speech and Respect*, 4–8, 123–52.

A variant on the radical feminist view, influenced by the post-modernist school of literary and social criticism, argues that nothing is intrinsically pornographic, but that a representation of activities becomes pornographic because of the conventional ways in which the representation is viewed. Material can be defined as pornographic only in terms of the way in which people read or view it, but material which is seen as pornographic may affect the way in which life is viewed if women come to be seen as being, in general and without reference to specific contexts, sexually arousing. This tends to make the social rules which shape attitudes into the centre of attention, and does not attempt to homogenize pornography. It thus avoids some of the problems which face the more radical feminist critique of pornography, but as a corollary places relatively little reliance on the capacity of law to change the social rules which dictate how images are understood, and so tends to discourage legal action against pornography.[114]

In the UK, the Williams Committee's reliance on the harm principle left greater room for control of pornography by treating the rationale for control as being to protect people against harmful material, or material which is so offensive that the offence caused constitutes a harm, rather than suggesting that the reason for controlling pornography might be that it carries an unacceptable political message. But the idea of harm or offensiveness as a root justification for restricting people's freedom is always controversial, and may allow the most sensitive or the most vulnerable to dictate the behaviour of the rest of society, in political matters as well as morality or decency.

If it is arguable that rejecting or modifying Mill's harm principle threatens to open the way to intolerance and more or less arbitrary interference with freedom of expression, it is equally arguable that unqualified adoption of Mill's approach undermines rights. For example, Ronald Dworkin describes the Williams Committee's strategy as combining a free-market approach derived from Mill with a 'slippery slope' argument which evaluates types of expression by reference to the effect they might have, directly or indirectly, on some social goal, rather than by reference to rights. This, he argues, fails to respect people's right to equal moral independence, because it makes people's rights to express themselves in certain ways, or to have access to certain types of expression, subject to other people's mere preferences. It creates the potential for the entire structure of rights to be overwhelmed on utilitarian principles. If one regards the constitution as being based on respect for rights, therefore, the Williams Committee's strategy can be seen as threatening the basic structure of the constitution.[115]

Despite the fact that both Ronald Dworkin and feminist theorists such as Andrea Dworkin and Catharine MacKinnon are opposed to the approach of the Williams Committee, their reasons are very different. Ronald Dworkin's arguments confront the feminist approach as much as that of the Williams Committee. Any attempt to control publications on the basis of offensiveness, either of their content or of the background of rules or power relations which they reflect, to people who are not likely to have to read or view them, will tend to be hard to justify on individual rights

---

[114] For discussion, see C. Smart, *Feminism and the Power of Law* (London: Routledge, 1989), ch. 6.

[115] R. Dworkin, *A Matter of Principle* (Oxford: Clarendon Press, 1986), ch. 17, especially 336–5.

grounds. The question is whether rights ought to be restricted to achieve some wider social purpose. The answer to this question is essentially a matter of social and political choice. That the line will be drawn in different places by different societies is recognized by the European Court of Human Rights. In its caselaw under Article 10(2) of the European Convention on Human Rights and Fundamental Freedoms, the Court has accepted that the steps necessary in a democratic society for the protection of morals will depend on the type of morality to which a country is committed. It is not part of the Court's job to lay down moral standards for societies, so the Court will allow a substantial 'margin of appreciation' to states in deciding what moral standards they should enforce.[116] However, once a society has settled on a view of morality, the Court will examine, under Article 10(2), whether the means adopted to give effect to that moral vision are prescribed by law and necessary in a democratic society.

16.3 COMMON-LAW OFFENCES OF INDECENCY
AND OBSCENITY[117]

At common law, there are several offences of indecency and obscenity.[118] The offence of obscene libel has now fallen into disuse, replaced by the Obscene Publications Acts 1959 and 1964 and other statutory provisions governing broadcasting, theatre, and cinema. Although the common-law offence was not formally abolished, there is now a statutory bar to prosecuting anyone for a common-law offence involving publication of any matter 'where it is of the essence of the offence that the matter is obscene'.[119] However, this does not prevent a person being prosecuted for a common-law offence the essence of which is indecency or immorality not amounting to obscenity. Nor does it preclude prosecution for common-law offences which depend, not on publication, but on an agreement to publish. Accordingly, the offences of outraging public decency, conspiracy to outrage public decency, and conspiracy to corrupt public morals, all remain crimes at common law.[120]

---

[116] *Handyside v. United Kingdom*, Eur. Ct. HR, Series A, No. 24, Judgment of 7 December 1976, 1 EHRR 737; *Müller v. Switzerland*, Eur. Ct. HR, Series A, No. 133, Judgment of 24 May 1988, 13 EHRR 212. The law on obscenity in Switzerland was changed following the *Müller* case: see the reasons given for striking a subsequent case out of the Court's list in *Scherer v. Switerland*, Eur. Ct. HR, Series A, No. 287, Judgment of 25 March 1994, 5 HRCD 61. An appeal to the freedom to provide services in EC law under Article 59 of the Treaty of Rome, to prevent an Irish court holding that providing information about abortions was unlawful, failed in *The Society for the Protection of Unborn Children Ireland Ltd. v. Grogan* [1991] 3 CMLR 849, ECJ.

[117] Law Commission, Working Paper No. 57, *Codification of the Criminal Law: Conspiracies Related to Morals and Decency* (London: HMSO, 1974); Law Commission, Report No. 76, *Criminal Law: Report on Conspiracy and Criminal Law Reform* (London: HMSO, 1976), 72–125.

[118] On the emergence of the concept of obscenity in English law, see Macmillan, *Censorship*, ch. 1.

[119] Obscene Publications Act 1959, s. 2(4).

[120] *Shaw v. DPP* [1962] AC 220, [1961] 2 All ER 446, HL; *Knuller v. DPP* [1973] AC 435, [1972] 2 All ER 898, HL; *R. v. Gibson* [1990] 2 QB 619, [1991] 1 All ER 439, CA.

(1) CONSPIRACY TO CORRUPT PUBLIC MORALS

The crime of conspiracy to corrupt public morals consists of an agreement between two or more people to do any act which, if completed, would be likely to have the effect of undermining morality. It is unique among remaining offences of conspiracy, in that the conspiracy is criminal whereas the completed act, carried out by a single person, would not necessarily be criminal: there is no offence of corrupting public morals *per se*, although often the circumstances may give rise to the offence of outraging public decency or an offence under the Obscene Publications Act 1959. However, on the facts of *Shaw* (see below) it was by no means clear that the *Directory* would have satisfied the conditions for the statutory offence. Because the criminality of corrupting morals is held to arise from the conspiracy rather than the corrupting act itself, even the completed act can be charged only as a conspiracy.

For example, in the leading case, *Shaw v. Director of Public Prosecutions*,[121] the defendants were compilers and publishers of *The Ladies Directory*, a publication in which prostitutes advertised and gave details of the services which they offered. For the prosecution, it was argued that providing, in one place, a directory of that sort would make it easier for people who were so inclined to indulge their lusts. Although prostitution is always present in society, facilitating access to it in that way was said to increase the likelihood that people would resort to prostitutes. This, it was said, threatened to undermine significant moral values concerning sex and family life. Accordingly, the agreement between the defendants to publish the *Directory* amounted to a conspiracy to corrupt public morals. This argument was accepted by the trial judge, the Court of Appeal, and a majority of the House of Lords, which decided that the offence was available at common law by reason of the judges' role in taking steps to protect society against threats to its moral foundations. This is an argument which has much in common with that advanced by Devlin for permitting the criminalization of certain types of immoral conduct.

Lord Reid, who dissented in *Shaw*, thought that the majority was indulging in judicial legislation, and that it was the job of Parliament, not the courts, to alter the law to extend the bounds of criminal liability. This was particularly the case where the allegation against the defendants was of a conspiracy to cause moral harm to society, rather than physical or psychological harm to individuals. This approach, relying on the desirability of extensions to the criminal law in morally contentious fields being carried out by a democratically accountable body, is much closer to being an application of the harm principle of J. S. Mill and H. L. A. Hart than to Devlin.

In so far as the law on the subject before *Shaw* gave little indication to potential publishers of either the crime's existence at common law or its scope, the imposition of criminal liability on the defendants in that case might well have contravened Article 7 of the European Convention on Human Rights: '1. No one shall be held guilty of any criminal offence on account of any act or omission which did not constitute a criminal offence under national or international law at the time when it was committed . . .'. However, after *Shaw*, what was then a novel extension of common-law criminal liability is reasonably well settled law, so much so that Lord Reid felt bound to accept

---

[121] [1962] AC 220, [1961] 2 All ER 446, HL.

the authority of *Shaw* in a subsequent case.[122] It would therefore not be possible to use Article 7 to impugn any conviction on this charge on facts arising after the decision in *Shaw*. The Criminal Justice and Police Act 2001, section 46, has now created a special offence committed by a person who places an advertisement relating to prostitution on, or in the immediate vicinity of, a public telephone with the intention that it should come to the attention of any other person or people. This was a response to the proliferation of cards, posters, and leaflets placed on and around public telephones by or on behalf of prostitutes or their pimps, especially in London, to drum up custom.

Another issue remains, however: namely, whether or not the imposition of liability for such a publication could breach Article 10's guarantee of protection to freedom of expression. The guarantee covers commercial expression, such as advertising,[123] as well as literary, scholarly, or current-affairs material. It is, therefore, necessary to consider whether the restriction imposed by the offence of conspiring to corrupt public morals is justified under ECHR Article 10(2). Considering that the European Court of Human Rights does not require common-law offences concerned with morality to be defined in completely unambiguous terms as long as there is a sufficient level of objectivity and reasonable predictability in their operation, the offence probably meets the test of legal certainty contained in the phrase 'prescribed by law'. It also seems, in principle, to pursue a legitimate aim, namely to protect morals, under Article 10(2). In view of the wide margin of appreciation allowed to states in deciding what is necessary in order to protect morals, it is likely that the Court would hold that this common-law offence is capable of being justified under Article 10(2). However, the margin of appreciation does not apply in municipal law. Under section 6(1) of the Human Rights Act 1998, the courts which developed and now apply the common-law offences act unlawfully if they impose a penalty for a criminal offence in circumstances where the imposition is incompatible with ECHR Article 10, which for this purpose must be interpreted without regard to the margin of appreciation. There is a significant chance that it might be difficult, in modern English conditions, to persuade right-thinking judges that criminalizing at least some of the conduct which has in the past fallen within the purview of the offence is either demanded by a pressing social need or is proportionate to any legitimate aim. One may venture to suggest that the facts on which the conviction in *Shaw* was based would no longer justify the imposition of criminal sanctions (if, indeed, they ever really did).

(2) OUTRAGING PUBLIC DECENCY AND CONSPIRING TO OUTRAGE
PUBLIC DECENCY

The common-law offence of outraging public decency is committed by anyone who says or does or exhibits in public anything which outrages public decency, whether or

---

[122] *Knuller (Publishing Printing and Promotions) Ltd. v. DPP* [1973] AC 435, [1972] 2 All ER 898, HL.

[123] *Barthold v. Federal Republic of Germany*, Eur. Ct. HR, Series A, vol. 90, Judgment of 25 March 1985, 7 EHRR 383; *Markt intern Verlag v. Germany*, Eur. Ct. HR, Series A, No. 165, Judgment of 20 November 1989, 12 EHRR 161.

not it is obscene.[124] An event takes place in public if it is in a place to which the public have access (such as a public lavatory) where at least two people must have been able to witness it,[125] or in private premises where there was a real possibility that at least two members of the general public might witness it.[126] It is possible that events in a private place where all participants have consented to the activities, and so are not likely to be outraged, would not ground a conviction.[127] The argument for this qualification is particularly strong now the courts are subject to a duty under section 6 of the Human Rights Act 1998 and ECHR Article 8 to act compatibly with the right to respect for private life when applying common-law offences.

There is a difference of some significance for legal purposes between indecency and obscenity. Both indecency and obscenity, as the words are ordinarily used, relate to standards of propriety. They are seen as standing at different points on a continuum of impropriety.[128] Indecency might be described as a breach of propriety which is seriously offensive (otherwise it would not be necessary to criminalize it) but not grossly or outrageously offensive. Obscenity, in its common usage, is a good deal more offensive than indecency. However, as Lord Sands said in *McGowan v. Langmuir*:[129]

'It is easier to illustrate than define, and I illustrate it thus. For a male bather to enter the water nude in the presence of ladies would be indecent, but it would not necessarily be obscene. But if he directed the attention of a lady to a certain member of his body his conduct would certainly be obscene.'

It has been said that 'an indecent article is not necessarily obscene, whereas an obscene article almost certainly must be indecent'.[130]

However, the distinction is somewhat complicated by the statutory meaning given to 'obscene' by, and for the purposes of, the Obscene Publications Act 1959. This Act was framed to penalize conduct by reference to the harm principle, rather than to impose sanctions on all moral improprieties so as to protect people's sensibilities. By section 1(1), an article is deemed to be obscene if its effect as a whole is such as to tend to deprave and corrupt people likely to read, see, or hear it. The statute thus centres its attention on likely victims, and demands an assessment of the harm which such people would suffer. By contrast, indecency has been held to be a quality of articles or

---

[124] *R. v. Gibson* [1990] 2 QB 619, [1991] 1 All ER 439, CA, applying *dicta* in *Shaw v. DPP* [1962] AC 220 at 281 and 292, [1961] 2 All ER 446 at 460 and 467, *per* Lord Reid and Lord Morris of Borth-y-Gest respectively; *Knuller (Publishing Printing and Promotions) Ltd. v. DPP* [1973] AC 435 at 493, [1972] 2 All ER 898 at 935, *per* Lord Simon of Glaisdale.

[125] *R. v. Mayling* (1963) 47 Cr. App. R. 102, CA.

[126] *R. v. Walker* [1996] 1 Cr. App. R. 111, [1995] Crim. LR 826, CA (man convicted in respect of act allegedly done towards ten-year-old girl in defendant's own home; requirement of publicity not met; conviction quashed).

[127] In *R. v. Church*, unreported, Southwark Crown Court, 29 March 1996, a jury acquitted people concerned in running a club where fetishists gathered and entertainment took place on a charge of outraging public decency. Undercover police officers in fetishist costumes had infiltrated the club, but could presumably be taken to have consented to, and so not to be members of the public who were likely to be outraged by, the performance. See *Independent*, 30 March 1996, 3.

[128] *R. v. Stanley* [1965] 2 QB 327, [1965] 1 All ER 1035, CCA, especially at 333, 1038 *per* Lord Parker CJ.

[129] 1931 JC 10, at 13, a Scottish decision followed by the English Court of Criminal Appeal in *R. v. Stanley* (see n. 128).

[130] *R. v. Stanley* [1965] 2 QB at 333 *per* Lord Parker CJ.

actions, judged objectively and without reference to the intentions of the author or the damage (if any) done to observers.[131] The question, in relation to indecency, is whether a person's sense of decency would be outraged by what occurred, not whether anyone would be depraved, debauched, or corrupted.[132] Accordingly, in *R. v. May*[133] it was held that the defendant, a schoolmaster, had been properly convicted after he had asked pupils to order him to perform acts of an explicitly sexual nature, despite there being no evidence that the pupils themselves were offended, depraved, or outraged; they may, indeed, have derived a degree of malicious amusement from the exhibition.

The offence extends to cover all forms of outrage to decency, not merely outrages to sexual decency. For example, in *R. v. Gibson*[134] it was held to encompass displaying for sale, in a gallery open to the public, two ear-rings, each said to have been made out of a freeze-dried human foetus of three or four months' gestation, attached to the ear of a model's head by means of a ring fitting tapped into the skull of the foetus. It is not necessary to provide evidence that anyone's feelings were in fact outraged,[135] nor that the defendant did anything to draw anyone's attention particularly to the indecent act or article.[136] However, there must be an act which is objectively indecent. It will not suffice to obtain a conviction merely that the accused did something with an indecent intent, or did something which can reasonably be interpreted as an act preparatory to an act of indecency, such as leaving notes in public places suggesting a time and place for a rendezvous for purposes which might be, but were not stated to be, indecent.[137] It was held in *Gibson* that the defendants had done enough to meet this requirement: the maker of the ear-rings, Mr. Gibson, had actively sought publicity, making it known that the ear-rings were made of human foetuses, while the proprietor of the gallery, Mr. Sylveire, had invited the public into the gallery knowing that the ear-rings were there. This was sufficient to show that the act of displaying the foetuses was a public one for the purposes of the common-law offence.

Several aspects of the offence make it possible that, without adjustment, its application might violate defendants' Convention rights, so that the courts would act unlawfully by reason of section 6 of the Human Rights Act 1998 if they failed to make an appropriate adjustment to the common-law rules. The offence is capable of interfering with freedom of expression under ECHR Article 10 and, if (contrary to the suggestion above) it applies to events in private, with the right to respect for private life under ECHR Article 8. The notion of public decency is so vague as to call in question the capacity of the offence to satisfy the test of legal certainty, failing which any interference with the rights would be unjustifiable, not being 'prescribed by law'

---

[131] *R. v. Graham-Kerr* [1988] 1 WLR 1098, 88 Cr. App. R. 302, CA (prosecution under Protection of Children Act 1981, s. 1(1)(a)); *Kosmos Publications v. DPP* [1975] Crim. LR 345, DC (prosecution under Post Office Act 1953, s. 11).

[132] *Cf. Knuller v. DPP* [1973] AC at 468, [1972] 2 All ER at 913, *per* Lord Morris of Borth-y-Gest.

[133] (1989) 91 Cr. App. R. 157, CA.

[134] [1990] 2 QB 619, [1991] 1 All ER 439, CA, discussed by M. Childs, 'Outraging Public Decency: The Offence of Offensiveness' [1991] *PL* 20–9.

[135] *R. v. May* (1989) 91 Cr. App. R. 157, CA.

[136] *R. v. Gibson* [1990] 2 QB 619, [1991] 1 All ER 439, CA; *R. v. Lunderbech* [1991] Crim. LR 784, CA.

[137] *R. v. Graham-Kerr* [1988] 1 WLR 1098, CA; *R. v. Rowley* [1991] Crim. LR 785, CA.

or 'in accordance with the law' for the purposes of ECHR Article 10(2) or 8(2). In 1976, the Law Commission recommended that the common-law offence of outraging public decency should be abolished, because of the vagueness of the definition of the offence.[138] *Gibson's* case illustrates some of this vagueness. There are certain questions concerning the *actus reus* of the crime of outraging public decency which are unanswered after *Gibson*. They mainly concern the cause of the outrage. Did it lie in the fact that the ear-rings were made from human foetuses? Would the offence have been made out if the ear-rings had merely looked like human foetuses but been modelled realistically in clay or plastic? Is the source of the outrage to decency one's revulsion at the idea of human beings (albeit at an early stage of development) being treated in that way, or in the spectacle of something in the form of a human child being used for a frivolous purpose? If the former, did the outrage flow from the fact that people were told that they were made from human foetuses? Would the offence have been made out if the ear-rings had really been made from plastic, but people had been told that they were real foetuses as a publicity gimmick? If the essence of the outrage flowed from the use of human foetuses, would Gibson have been properly convicted had the ear-rings been made of animal foetuses, or of human material removed from a live person during surgery? Would the offence be committed by a person who made jewellery from an embryo of (say) one month's gestation, instead of three or four months, if people would not be able to recognize the one month embryo as a distinctively human form?

None of these questions can be answered with confidence. However, if it is correct that the essence of the offence lies in the outraging of people's sense of decency, what people are led to believe about an exhibit would seem to be at least as important as what it really is. That being so, a person may be convicted of the offence for doing something which other people wrongly but reasonably believe to constitute a form of action which, if it happened, would outrage their sense of decency. Such an offence is wider than could conceivably serve a worthwhile social purpose. The European Commission of Human Rights has accepted the view of the UK government that the offence operates sufficiently foreseeably because it is 'concerned with more offensive material which engenders such revulsion, disgust and outrage that it is irrelevant whether its consequence is actually to undermine public morals'.[139] But this is simplistic. To take another example, in 1991 a popular outcry followed revulsion when a rather gory colour photograph of a newly born naked baby was plastered over advertising hoardings to promote (with stunning inappropriateness) the wares of a clothing retailer, Benetton. Could the publishers of the advertisements have been charged with outraging public decency on any of the bases suggested above? Would a prosecution have served any socially useful purpose?

Even if the formulation of the offence passes the legal certainty test, it may be difficult to establish, on the facts of some cases, that the imposition of criminal sanctions is a response to a pressing social need for action in pursuit of a legitimate aim under Article 10(2) or 8(2), or is proportionate to the end to be achieved. Unlike

---

[138] Law Commission, *Criminal Law*.
[139] *S. and G. v. United Kingdom*, Eur. Commn. HR, Application No. 17634, Decision of 2 September 1991.

conspiracy to corrupt public morals, the offences of outraging public decency and conspiring to outrage public decency do not purport to protect morals. Indeed, one of the planks on which the Court of Appeal's decision in *Gibson* rested was the submission of counsel for the prosecution 'that the object of the common law offence is to protect the public from suffering feelings of outrage'.[140] It is clear from the caselaw of the European Court of Human Rights that there is a major difference between protecting sensibilities from outrage and protecting morals: the freedom of expression guaranteed by Article 10(1) covers all expression, including that which is provocative, shocking, or disturbing to many people.[141] That being so, it is hard to see how the existence of a crime could be justified when its very essence consists of shocking people without harming morals. One can go further. The effect of an outrage to public decency (unlike a conspiracy to corrupt public morals) is not so much to undermine morality as to reinforce it, since those whose sense of decency is outraged are likely to end up having their values reinforced by the experience.

The crimes of outraging public decency and conspiring to outrage public decency would seem in general to be difficult to reconcile with ECHR Article 10. The European Commission of Human Rights in September 1991 ruled inadmissible an application made by the defendants in *Gibson*, effectively holding the common-law offence to be within the permitted purpose of upholding public morality purpose under Article 10(2).[142] That may possibly be true of the way in which the offence was used on the particular facts of that case (although it is curious that the Commission reached its decision on this point after accepting the government's submission, noted above, that in the offence of outraging public decency it was irrelevant whether the activity in question actually undermined public morals). There was a plausible argument that moral standards were in issue there. But in many cases, no moral issue may arise. The Commission was heavily influenced by the wide margin of appreciation accorded states in setting the bounds of public morality in their territories. Nevertheless, it should not be lightly assumed that the use of the common-law charge is justifiable under Article 10(2) in all the cases to which it potentially applies. If it were used in a way which did not involve considerations of morality, as opposed to mere decency, justification under Article 10(2) would be far more difficult. Furthermore, the margin of appreciation applies to relationships between international courts and national authorities, and would not be relevant to a case in a national court governed by the Human Rights Act 1998. The offence needs to be significantly refined if it is to survive challenge under the 1998 Act.

Several aspects of the offence heighten this need. First, many cases in which defendants might be charged with the common-law offence will overlap with statutory offences. Unlike the statutory obscenity offence under the 1959 Act, there is no defence of public good under the common law. Secondly, being an offence of indecency rather than obscenity, it is apparently not necessary (or, indeed, relevant) that the defendant should intend to outrage public decency, or even be aware that it

---

[140] [1990] 2 QB at 627, [1991] 1 All ER at 445 *per* Lord Lane CJ.

[141] E.g. *Oberschlick v. Austria*, Eur. Ct. HR, Judgment of 23 May 1991.

[142] *S. and G. v. United Kingdom*, Eur. Commn. HR, Application No. 17634, Decision of 2 September 1991.

might be outraged. All that is needed by way of *mens rea* is for the defendant to have done something deliberately, and for that something to have been of a quality which, objectively, outraged public decency. Any other approach, said the Court of Appeal in *Gibson*, would make it possible for a defendant to escape liability by the very baseness of his own standards.[143] In any case, the court took the view that intention to outrage decency would virtually always be inferred (even without the legal presumption, abolished by the Criminal Justice Act 1967, section 8, that people intend the natural and probable consequences of their acts) once outrage is established to the satisfaction of the jury.[144] However, there might be situations in which it would be impossible to make the inference, for example where a defendant suffered from a mental disability which, without constituting insanity under the *McNaghten* rules, made it difficult for him to appreciate the way in which his actions would be viewed by others. It would be unfortunate to stigmatize such people as criminals.

The Court of Appeal attempted to justify these peculiarities of the common-law offence in *R. v. Gibson*[145] on the ground that offences under section 1 of the 1959 Act are 'factually and morally distinct' from outraging public decency at common law.[146] Two separate reasons have been offered for this. First, the latter do not necessarily involve the former, and so prosecutions for them are not precluded by section 2(4) of the 1959 Act. At first sight it is not easy to see why the Obscene Publications Act 1959 should not be applied to a case such as *Gibson*. Although, in principle, there is a clear distinction between outraging decency and corrupting morals, in particular cases there may be an overlap, especially if, as suggested above, 'an obscene article almost certainly must be indecent'.[147] As obscenity is not restricted to sexual matters (as will be seen below), it is hard to see why, on the facts of *Gibson*, it should have been thought to be inappropriate to apply the test for obscenity to the case. This would have enabled the defendants to avail themselves of the defence of public good under section 4 of the 1959 Act.

Secondly, there is a technical legal distinction between the statutory offence, the gravamen of which consists of the completed publication and its consequences, and a common-law conspiracy to corrupt public morals (or outrage public decency), in which the *actus reus* is the agreement to act rather than the act itself and its consequences.[148] This gives rise to the strange position in which a person who is charged with an inchoate crime is denied defences which would have been available had the completed crime been charged. In the wake of *Shaw v. Director of Public Prosecutions*[149] a number of MPs sought, and the Solicitor General gave, assurances[150] that the prosecuting authorities would not seek to use the common-law crimes of conspiracy to corrupt public morals and conspiracy to outrage public decency in cases where

---

[143] [1990] 2 QB at 627, [1991] 1 All ER at 445.

[144] [1990] 2 QB at 629, [1991] 1 All ER at 447 *per* Lord Lane CJ.

[145] [1990] 2 QB 619, [1991] 1 All ER 439, CA.

[146] [1990] 2 QB at 624, [1991] 1 All ER at 443 *per* Lord Lane CJ.

[147] *R. v. Stanley* [1965] 2 QB 327 at 333, [1965] 1 All ER 1035 at 1038 *per* Lord Parker CJ.

[148] *Shaw v. DPP* [1962] AC 220 at 268 *per* Viscount Simonds, 290 *per* Lord Tucker, 291 *per* Lord Morris of Borth-y-Gest.

[149] [1962] AC 220, [1961] 2 All ER 446, HL.

[150] 695 HC Debs. 1212 (3 June 1964); 698 HC Debs. 315–16 (7 July 1964).

doing so would effectively deprive defendants of protections for liberty of speech given by the Obscene Publications Acts 1959 and 1964. This was intended to allay a fear that the liberalizing purpose of the 1959 Act would otherwise be frustrated.[151] However, in the light of the decision of the Court of Appeal in *Gibson* this risk seems to have re-emerged.

Lord Lane CJ suggested that 'in this type of case . . . it is unlikely that a defence of public good could possibly arise'.[152] However, this is highly questionable once one accepts that social comment on matters of public concern may be made otherwise than by verbal means. The defendants might, for instance, have wanted to argue that the use of human foetuses was an ironic technique, attempting to shock observers into realizing the cheapness of human life and the lack of protection offered to unborn children. The display of the ear-rings might have been presented as a political comment on the failure of the legislature to give adequate protection to embryos which are produced by *in vitro* methods of fertilization. It would by no means be inevitable that a jury would have been unimpressed by the public-good defence, and it is unfortunate that a defendant with such a potential defence should be prevented from putting it before the jury merely because the prosecution elects to charge an alternative offence. *Gibson* appears to be an example of a case in which the defendants' rights were abridged by an exercise of the prosecutor's discretion. Under the Human Rights Act 1998, the appearance of arbitrariness would weigh heavily in favour of a conclusion that a conviction was disproportionate in a case where it was even arguable that a public-good defence might have been run before a jury under the 1959 Act.

Taken together with the assurance given to the House of Commons in 1964 that the common-law offences would not be used to deprive defendants of the benefit of the public-good defence, the human-rights implications of the conspiracy to outrage and outraging public decency offences gives rise to serious doubts about the appropriateness of charging any form of writing or representation with the common-law offence unless the defendant agrees in advance that the public-good defence would be inappropriate. It is strange that a defence of public good should be available where the accused is alleged to have published an obscene article which threatens the actual harm of inducing depravity or corruption, but not where it is alleged that he has merely offended against public decency. The strangeness is amplified by the fact that a person convicted on indictment of the common-law indecency offence is subject to an unlimited term of imprisonment, whereas a person convicted on indictment of the supposedly more serious obscenity offence faces a maximum term of three years' imprisonment.[153] The possibility of overlap between the common-law and statutory offences has been long understood by prosecutors, as the assurances given by the law officers in 1964 show. Furthermore, there is an anomaly in prosecuting a display of ear-rings at common law when a film showing the making or display of the ear-rings would have to have been prosecuted, if at all, under the Obscene Publications Act 1959, with the public-good defence being available. This results from the provision,

---

[151] See *Knuller v. DPP* [1973] AC at p. 456, [1972] 2 All ER at 903–4 *per* Lord Reid.

[152] [1990] 2 QB at 625, [1991] 1 All ER at 444.

[153] Obscene Publications Act 1959, s. 2(1). In each case, the defendant is also liable to an unlimited fine.

inserted into the 1959 Act, preventing prosecution of film exhibitions for the common-law offence where it is of the essence of the offence that the exhibition was 'obscene, indecent, offensive, disgusting, or injurious to morality'.[154] The accident that wider words were used when this provision was introduced in respect of film exhibitions in 1977 than were used in section 2(4) in 1964 does not provide a principled argument for maintaining the anomaly. There is no reason to treat films differently from other displays, or to treat the completed offence of outraging public decency differently from a conspiracy to commit the offence.

A further consideration relates to penalties. The maximum penalty for a statutory offence is limited by the statute; the common law offence exposes defendants to an unlimited penalty. It is anomalous to allow prosecutors and sentencers to evade the limitations imposed by Parliament by electing to charge the common-law offence.

For these reasons, as well as those relating to human rights discussed above, the proper approach would be to enact the 1976 recommendations of the Law Commission and abolish the common-law offence.

16.4 THE STATUTORY OBSCENITY AND INDECENCY OFFENCES

(1) THE OBSCENE PUBLICATIONS ACTS 1959 AND 1964

Under the Obscene Publications Act 1959, section 2, as amended, it is an offence to publish any obscene article, whether or not for gain, or to have possession of an obscene article for publication for gain.[155] The Act catches any obscene article containing or embodying matter to be read or looked at or both, any sound record, and any film or other record of a picture or pictures.[156] The Act thus covers compact discs, video cassettes,[157] television and sound broadcasts,[158] and computerized or electronically stored images, as well as more conventional articles. It also catches any article from which the images, etc. are intended to be reproduced or manufactured,[159] such as photographic negatives or casts; possession of such articles is deemed to be possession of an article for publication for gain if the articles to be produced or

---

[154] Obscene Publications Act, s. 4A, as inserted by the Criminal Law Act 1977 and amended by the Cinemas Act 1985.

[155] Obscene Publications Act 1959, s. 2(1), as amended by Obscene Publications Act 1964, s. 1(1). A person is deemed to 'have' an article for publication for gain if, with a view to such publication, he has the article in his ownership, possession, or control: Obscene Publications Act 1964, s. 1(2). The offence may therefore be committed by someone who owns articles which are actually in the possession of another person, or who is in control of articles which are owned by and in the possession of someone else. In Scotland, see Civic Government (Scotland) Act 1982, s. 51.

[156] Obscene Publications Act 1959, s. 1(2).

[157] *Attorney-General's Reference (No. 5 of 1980)* [1980] 3 All ER 816, CA.

[158] Obscene Publications Act 1959, s. 1(4), (5), (6), inserted by Broadcasting Act 1990, s. 162(1)(b). Previously, television and sound broadcasts were exempted by a proviso to s. 1(3) of the 1959 Act, which was repealed by s. 162(1)(a), s. 203(3) of and Sch. 21 to the 1990 Act.

[159] Obscene Publications Act 1964, s. 2(1).

manufactured from them are intended for publication for gain.[160] There is, however, a defence for the person in possession if he can prove that he had not examined the article and had no reasonable cause to suspect that it was of a type which might make him liable to be convicted under section 2 of the 1959 Act.[161]

Publication is widely defined:[162] it includes distribution, circulation, selling, letting on hire, offering for sale or for letting on hire, giving, lending, or (where the article contains or embodies matter to be looked at or a record) showing, playing, or projecting. This is sufficiently wide to encompass displays in galleries and studios, and cable television. Although broadcasting has been brought within the scope of the legislation by the Broadcasting Act 1990, the separate regulatory framework described in Chapter 14 above should normally prevent material which has any chance of infringing the 1959 Act from being broadcast. Where the matter consists of electronically stored data, any transmission of them, for example over the Internet, is a publication.

Section 3 of the 1959 Act provides search, seizure, and forfeiture powers. It permits a justice of the peace, on an information laid by the Director of Public Prosecutions or a constable,[163] to issue a warrant authorizing search of any premises, stall, or vehicle if he or she is satisfied that there is reasonable ground for suspecting that obscene articles are kept there for publication for gain, and seizure of any offending articles found, with any documents relating to a trade or business carried on there.[164] If a person is charged with and convicted of having the obscene articles for gain, contrary to section 2, the court which convicts him must order forfeiture of the articles.[165] Where nobody is proceeded against under section 2, or the accused is acquitted, the articles seized, if not returned to the occupier, are to be brought before a justice of the peace, who may summon the occupier to show cause why the articles should not be forfeited. If satisfied, after a hearing (in which the occupier, owner, author, or other person through whose hands the articles passed are to be heard if they appear), that the articles are obscene and were kept for publication for gain, the court must then order forfeiture of the articles.[166]

The test of obscenity is that the effect of an article, taken as a whole,[167] must be such

---

[160] Ibid., s. 2(2). See *R. v. Taylor (Alan)* [1995] 1 Cr. App. R. 131, CA.

[161] Ibid., s. 1(3)(a).

[162] Obscene Publications Act 1959, s. 1(3) as amended.

[163] Criminal Justice Act 1967, s. 25. This provision was intended to prevent repetition of the incident when the DPP decided not to prosecute the publishers of *Last Exit to Brooklyn*, but private individuals none the less brought forfeiture proceedings under s. 3 of the 1959 Act without requiring a conviction. The forfeiture proceedings succeeded, and the DPP consequently felt bound to institute a prosecution of the publishers, which ultimately failed: *R. v. Calder & Boyars Ltd.* [1969] 1 QB 151, [1968] 3 All ER 644, CA.

[164] Obscene Publications Act 1959, s. 3(1), (2).

[165] Obscene Publications Act 1964, s. 1(4).

[166] Obscene Publications Act 1959, s. 3(3), as amended by Criminal Law Act 1977; s. 3(4). Where the seized items consist of film of a width of at least 16 mm, in respect of which a prosecution could be instituted only by the DPP (see s. 2(3A)), forfeiture proceedings in the absence of a conviction may be brought only if the warrant was issued on an information laid by or on behalf of the DPP: s. 3(3A), added by Criminal Law Act 1977, s. 53.

[167] If the article is made up of several separate articles, each of these may be examined separately: ibid., s. 1(1). Thus each item in a magazine containing several articles or short stories, or a collection of essays, falls to be individually assessed: *R. v. Anderson* [1972] 1 QB 304 at 312, [1971] 3 All ER 1152 at 1158 *per* Lord Widgery CJ. On the application of this to films, see *R. v. Goring* [1999] Crim. LR 670, CA, and the commentary by D. C. Ormerod, ibid., at 671–2.

as to tend to deprave and corrupt persons who are likely, having regard to all relevant circumstances, to read, see, or hear the matter contained or embodied in it.[168] This test is based on the harm principle, although the harm contemplated is of a sort which is peculiarly hard to pin down.[169] (An Obscenity Bill, introduced to Parliament in 1999, would have replaced the test with a list of subjects and treatments which were criminal regardless of their effects, but the bill did not make progress.) What constitutes being depraved and corrupted? The judges have, on the whole, not attempted much in the way of guidance, beyond making it clear that articles which are objectively filthy, lewd, repulsive, or indecent according to community standards are not necessarily obscene within the meaning of the Act.[170] The US Supreme Court's approach to the First Amendment offers far less protection to free speech than is provided by the 1959 Act in England and Wales. It seems that the First Amendment is interpreted as permitting the control of works which in England would be regarded as indecent but not obscene. The test in the USA is whether the material would be found by an average reader, applying contemporary community standards, to appeal to prurient interest, depicting or describing sexual conduct in a patently offensive way, without serious literary, artistic, political, or scientific value.[171] The reference to community standards (which are not applied to the assessment of a work's literary, artistic, political, or scientific value, which is regarded as constant)[172] is related to what we would regard as indecency, and assumes that local rather than national community standards are to be applied.[173]

The English test for obscenity is in one way more demanding. To tend to deprave and corrupt people, material must degrade the reader or viewer. This need not be manifested in the shape of a change in behaviour; indeed, one may encourage people to commit improper behaviour without corrupting or depraving them. Corruption is an affliction of the mind and emotions, which may but need not be evidenced by behaviour.[174] But in another way, the test for a tendency to deprave or corrupt is very uncertain. What is this corruption, and what should juries look for when deciding whether material has a tendency to induce it? A tendency to arouse erotic feelings, or feelings of sexual arousal, cannot in itself be depraving or corrupting, since such feelings are normal in everyday life and may even be necessary for the propagation of the species. Perhaps the best explanation is that an article depraves and corrupts a person only if it results in a suspension or destruction of the moral standards which that person applies self-critically. In other words, pornography is obscene, within the English definition, if it makes it possible for a person to contemplate doing, seeing, or hearing something with less feeling of guilt than previously would have been

[168] Obscene Publications Act 1959, s. 1(1). See Robertson, *Obscenity*, ch. 3.

[169] The test was adapted from the common-law obscenity test: *R. v. Hicklin* (1868) LR 3 QB 360; Macmillan, *Censorship and Public Morality*, 5–12; Robertson, *Obscenity*, 29–30.

[170] E.g. *R. v. Anderson* [1972] 1 QB 304, [1971] 3 All ER 1152, CA. On the approach to deciding whether an article is obscene, and the proper direction for a judge to give to the jury, see *R. v. O'Sullivan* [1995] 1 Cr. App. R. 455; *R. v. Elliott* (1996) 1 Cr. App R. 69, (1996) Crim. LR 264, CA.

[171] *Miller v. California* 413 US 15 (1973).

[172] *Pope v. Illinois* 481 US 497 (1988).

[173] *Jacobellis v. Ohio* 378 US 184 (1964) at 200 *per* Warren CJ (dissenting). In the same case, Stewart J said that, while he could not define obscenity, he knew it when he saw it (at 197).

[174] *DPP v. Whyte* [1972] AC 849, [1972] 3 All ER 12, HL.

engendered. Obscenity blunts one's self-critical moral faculties. This is consistent with the principle that a book which produces in its likely readers an aversion to the behaviour described is not obscene, the so-called 'aversion theory'.[175] It ought to follow that psychological evidence will be admitted as to the likely effect of material on the average reader, but in fact such evidence is admissible only in relation to the effect on special groups, such as children, whose reactions might be outside the experience of the jury.[176]

People may be depraved or corrupted by all sorts of things. Most prosecutions centre on sexual matters, but it seems to be accepted by the courts that violence is capable of depraving and corrupting people,[177] and there is statutory authority for supposing that crime, cruelty, and other 'incidents of a repulsive and horrible nature' may be corrupting, at any rate to children.[178] Moral and spiritual corruption, the undermining of moral values, is the evil at which the offence is directed. An article or book which glorifies, or incites people to indulge in, drug abuse can be considered likely to deprave and corrupt, and so is capable of being obscene.[179] The depravity or corruption may, but need not necessarily, be manifested in outward behaviour.[180]

The courts have taken the view that moral depravity and corruption is a matter of degree. People may be more or less depraved or corrupted; a person may therefore be corrupted more than once,[181] so that selling pornographic material to 'dirty old men' is likely to deprave and corrupt them still further, and constitutes an offence under the Acts.[182] The material which may deprave and corrupt people will depend, to some extent, on the age and suggestibility of the audience likely to come in contact with it. Material may be liable to corrupt young children which would not have that effect on adults. The test is whether it is likely to deprave or corrupt 'persons who are likely, having regard to all the relevant circumstances, to read, see or hear the matter contained or embodied in it'.[183] Not all such people need be likely to be depraved or

---

[175] *R. v. Anderson* [1972] 1 QB 304, [1971] 3 All ER 1152, CA.

[176] *DPP v. A & BC Chewing Gum Ltd.* [1968] 1 QB 159, [1967] 2 All ER 504, DC; *R. v. Calder & Boyars* [1969] 1 QB 151, [1968] 3 All ER 644, CA.

[177] *DPP v. A & BC Chewing Gum Ltd.* [1968] 1 QB 159, [1967] 2 All ER 504, DC (picture cards depicting scenes of violence, distributed free with packets of chewing gum).

[178] Children and Young Persons (Harmful Publications) Act 1955, s. 1.

[179] *John Calder (Publications) Ltd. v. Powell* [1965] 1 QB 509, [1965] 1 All ER 159, DC; *R. v. Skirving* [1985] QB 819, [1985] 2 All ER 705, CA. On the other hand, it has been said that prosecution policy is to use the law mainly against hard-core pornography, especially that which depicts unorthodox sexual activity. 'DPP officials have their lines to draw, and they draw them fairly consistently at the male groin: nudity is now acceptable and even artistic, but to erect a penis is to provoke a prosecution'. G. Robertson, *Freedom, the Individual and the Law* (Harmondsworth: Penguin, 1989), 190.

[180] *DPP v. Whyte* [1972] AC 849, [1972] 3 All ER 12, HL. Some judges consider that their experience in criminal and matrimonial cases confirms that obscene articles do, sometimes, provoke changes in patterns of conduct: see, e.g. *R. v. Holloway* (1982) 4 Cr. App. R. (S) 128, CA, at 131 *per* Lawton LJ. However, the Williams Committee decided that the causal link between pornography and anti-social conduct had not been established on the basis of the scientific evidence.

[181] *R. v. Shaw* [1962] AC 220, [1961] 1 All ER 330, CA (the case went to the House of Lords on another point: [1962] AC 220, [1961] 2 All ER 446, HL).

[182] *DPP v. Whyte* [1972] AC 849, [1979] 3 All ER 12, HL.

[183] Obscene Publications Act 1959, s. 1(1).

corrupted, nor a majority of them, but it has been held necessary that a substantial proportion be likely to be so affected in order to ground a conviction.[184]

There is therefore the potential for the legislation to restrict freedom of expression considerably. The potential interference with freedom of expression is, however, mitigated in two ways. First, there is the legal defence of public good under the legislation, which allows publication of an article to be justified even though it is obscene. Secondly, there is a bureaucratic safeguard provided in the role of the Director of Public Prosecutions, who has regard to the wider public interest when deciding whether or not to institute or take over forfeiture proceedings or criminal prosecutions. These will be considered separately.

(i) The defence of public good

Unlike the common law and Scottish law,[185] section 4 of the 1959 Act provides that a person is not to be convicted of an offence against section 2, and no forfeiture order is to be made, in respect of any article (other than a moving picture film or soundtrack) if it is proved that the publication 'is justified as being for the public good on the ground that it is in the interests of science, literature, art or learning, or of other objects of general concern'.[186] Obscene moving picture films and soundtracks are allowed a more limited justification. Publication of these is justified if proved to be 'in the public good on the ground that it is in the interests of drama, opera, ballet or any other art, or of literature or learning'.[187] In other words, the interests of science and 'other objects of general concern', such as news journalism on current affairs, do not serve to justify a film unless it also serves the interests of literature, learning, or art.

Since the provision offers justification to articles which are obscene, it is not surprising that the courts have tended to interpret the scope of section 4 fairly narrowly. They have generally limited it to explorations of matters falling within the words of the section on a literal interpretation (so that sex education for children was held not to be within 'learning', a noun signifying the fruits of scholarship rather than the correlative of teaching)[188] or which clearly relate to the public good. For example, in relation to the concluding words of section 4(1), they have recognized that sociological or ethical merit may justify publishing an obscene book, because of the potential benefit for society as a whole in having social and ethical matters canvassed.[189]

---

[184] *R. v. Calder & Boyars Ltd.* [1969] 1 QB 151, [1968] 3 All ER 644, CA, especially at 168, 648 *per* Salmon LJ; *DPP v. Whyte* [1972] AC 849, [1972] 3 All ER 12, HL, especially at 870, 25 *per* Lord Cross of Chelsea.

[185] There is no statutory defence of public good under the Civic Government (Scotland) Act 1982, s. 51, but a defence may exist at common law for literary, scientific, artistic, and philosophical works which are appropriate for study by serious scholars. See *Galletly v. Laird*, 1953 SLT 67; K. D. Ewing and W. Finnie, *Civil Liberties in Scotland: Cases and Materials*, 2nd edn. (Edinburgh: W. Green & Son, 1988), 309.

[186] Obscene Publications Act 1959, s. 4(1).

[187] Ibid., s. 4(1A), added by Criminal Law Act 1977, s. 53.

[188] *Attorney-General's Reference (No. 3 of 1977)* [1978] 1 WLR 1123, [1978] 3 All ER 1166, CA. Accordingly, the trial judge had been wrong to admit expert testimony on the educational merits of such material. It might, perhaps, still be arguable that sex education is a matter of 'general concern'.

[189] *R. v. Calder & Boyars Ltd.* [1969] 1 QB 151, [1968] 3 All ER 644, CA, on *Last Exit to Brooklyn*.

Similarly, religious merits were considered in the *Lady Chatterley's Lover* trial.[190] On the other hand, although some pornography may serve a therapeutic end, enabling people to relieve their sexual tensions harmlessly who might otherwise suffer psychological illness or indulge in anti-social and, perhaps, criminal acts towards others, the judges have held that the therapeutic value of obscene articles for some members of the public is not 'in the interests of . . . other objects of general concern'.[191]

The ultimate arbiter of the public good under this provision is the jury, but evidence of expert opinion is permitted in order to give guidance on the literary or other merit of a publication, presumably because jurors are not necessarily equipped to make judgments about the artistic, literary, or other qualities of publications.[192] Thus the Bishop of Woolwich was among the many eminent people who gave evidence on behalf of *Lady Chatterley's Lover* in 1960, and Professor Ronald Dworkin gave evidence on behalf of the publishers of *Inside Linda Lovelace*, described by a leading authority as '[t]he last, and undoubtedly the worst, "serious" book to be prosecuted',[193] in 1976.

If the jury concludes that the article has some literary, scientific, artistic, or other relevant form of merit, they must then decide whether or not it is for the public good. This requires the jury to perform a balancing exercise. Jurors must ask themselves whether the good flowing from the merits identified by the defendant outweigh the public harm which flows from the risk of people being depraved and corrupted by the article. Of relevance will be the number of those likely to be depraved and corrupted, the strength of the tendency to deprave and corrupt, and the depth of the likely depravity of corruption; these will be balanced against the strength of the relevant merits of the article.[194] As Geoffrey Robertson points out,[195] there is a certain sense of absurdity in deciding that it is for the public good for an article to be published despite the fact that it will deprave and corrupt a significant number of people. However, to argue that this makes the test meaningless goes too far. Many of the decisions which people have to make in life, and a very high proportion of the decisions which have to be made in government, require apparently incommensurable goods and harms to be weighed against each other. The acquittals of publishers of books such as *Inside Linda Lovelace* and *Last Exit to Brooklyn* shows that the jury, performing for this purpose a function in balancing goods and harms which can

---

[190] *R. v. Penguin Books*, 1960, Central Criminal Court, unreported. See C. H. Rolph, *The Trial of Lady Chatterley* (Harmondsworth: Penguin, 1961); B. Levin, *The Pendulum Years: Britain and the Sixties* (London: Pan Books, 1972), 280–92.

[191] *R. v. Metropolitan Police Commissioner, ex parte Blackburn* [1973] QB 241, [1973] 1 All ER 324, CA, at 250, 329 *per* Lord Denning MR; *DPP v. Jordan* [1977] AC 699, [1976] 3 All ER 775, HL.

[192] Obscene Publications Act 1959, s. 4(2). However, the experts must confine their evidence to the merits of the article. They are not normally allowed to guide the jury as to whether the article is obscene or not. The latter issue lies entirely within the jury's commonsense judgment (*R. v. Calder & Boyars Ltd.* [1969] 1 QB 151, CA; *R. v. Anderson* [1972] 1 QB 304, CA) unless the people who are said to be in danger of being depraved or corrupted have special characteristics which might lie outside the experience of members of the jury, such as young children (*DPP v. A & BC Chewing Gum Ltd.* [1968] 1 QB 159, CA, as explained in *Anderson* at 313 *per* Lord Widgery CJ).

[193] Robertson, *Freedom, Individual and Law*, 189.

[194] *R. v. Calder & Boyars Ltd.* [1969] 1 QB 151 at 171, [1968] 3 All ER 644 at 649–50, *per* Salmon LJ.

[195] *Freedom, Individual and Law*, 191–2.

properly be regarded as governmental, is not often overwhelmed by the absurdity of what they are asked to do. It is true that, when separate proceedings are brought against each distributor of an article, rather than bringing one prosecution against the producer, different juries may reach inconsistent decisions. But this should not blind us to the fact that the prospect of having to satisfy a jury on a matter such as this provides a useful check on the over-enthusiasm of would-be prosecutors, and may even offer a positive protection to freedom of expression.[196]

(ii) Bureacratic controls: prosecution policy

This second means of mitigating the effects of interference with freedom of expression relies on the ability of the Director of Public Prosecutions to impose some reasonableness and consistency on the types of cases in which proceedings are brought. Thus proceedings in respect of commercial (16 mm) films may be instituted only with the consent of the Director of Public Prosecutions.[197] However, other prosecutions may be brought by any citizen, subject to the power of the Director of Public Prosecutions to take over the conduct of the case and offer no evidence, or the power of the Attorney-General to intervene and enter a *nolle prosequi*. Furthermore, any constable may obtain a warrant to seize articles under section 3 of the 1959 Act, bring them before a justice of the peace, and (except in the case of 16 mm films) apply for forfeiture. Another way of evading the control of the Director of Public Prosecutions has been used in the past. This involved the police in visiting booksellers and inviting them to sign disclaimers in respect of allegedly obscene articles, which would then be carried away and destroyed without any court proceedings. From the points of view of both booksellers and police this saved a great deal of trouble and formality. However, it helped to put the booksellers at the mercy of corrupt police officers,[198] and was criticized by the *Report of the Parliamentary Select Committee on Obscene Publications*.[199] The object of requiring all seized goods to be taken before a justice of the peace, under section 3 of the 1959 Act, was to root out this practice, but it continued, perhaps because the police thought that taking articles which the owner had disclaimed did not constitute a seizure, and attracted further criticism from the Court of Appeal in *R. v. Metropolitan Police Commissioner, ex parte Blackburn (No. 3)*.[200] However, even when the Director of Public Prosecutions is involved and the statutory procedures are being followed, there are ways in which the public interest in art, literature, science, and other worthwhile undertakings may be subverted through the use of section 3 itself.

The power to order forfeiture without a conviction is objectionable because it deprives the publishers of the opportunity to deploy the public-good defence before a jury, as trial by jury is available only in criminal proceedings. In the summary forfeiture proceedings, a bench of magistrates (or a District Judge (Magistrates' Courts))

---

[196] For a more sceptical view of the role of juries, see P. Darbishire, 'The Lamp that Shows that Freedom Lives: Is It Worth the Candle?' [1991] Crim. LR 740–52.

[197] Obscene Publications Act 1959, s. 2(3A), added by Criminal Law Act 1977, s. 53.

[198] Sir Robert Mark, *In the Office of Constable* (London: Collins, 1978), 173–4, 263 ff.

[199] HC 123–1 of 1957–58.

[200] [1973] QB 241 at 252–4.

decides on the applicability of the public-good defence. The notion of public good relies heavily on community standards and perceptions, and should be applied by a cross-section of the community. A jury is more likely to constitute such a cross-section than a magistrates' court. In 1964, during the passage of the bill which became the Obscene Publications Act 1964, Mr. Roy Jenkins MP proposed an amendment which would have guaranteed to publishers a right to elect for jury trial in respect of any book in relation to which they intended to raise a defence of public good. The amendment was widely supported, following a disgraceful incident in which the publishers of Cleland's *Fanny Hill* had been denied jury trial because, according to the Director of Public Prosecutions, they had behaved so responsibly that a criminal prosecution would have been oppressive.[201] As Robertson comments, 'The DPP's attitude was catch-22: a responsible publisher could never, by definition, obtain a fair trial—this right was reserved for those who acted irresponsibly'.[202] To head off the amendment, the Solicitor General gave an undertaking on behalf of the law officers that the ordinary policy of the DPP would be to prosecute rather than use section 3 proceedings whenever the publisher indicates an intention to continue to publish the work regardless of the result of the forfeiture proceedings, in circumstances which would constitute a criminal offence.[203] However, this turned out not to offer much protection to publishers. Prosecutors have sometimes been unwilling to find out what publishers' intentions are, so the publisher has to be alert and knowledgeable in order to take advantage of the undertaking. There are several examples of abuse of section 3.[204] The law in this area gives excessive discretion to the police, the DPP, and to justices of the peace. It should be changed to require the publisher of articles to be served with notice of proceedings for forfeiture which are taken following seizure of articles from a wholesaler or retailer, and to allow the publishers a statutory right to elect for trial by jury where they want to advance a public-good defence.

Although the offences under the Obscene Publications Act 1959 and 1964 are the most significant restrictions on free expression in the name of morality, there are numerous other statutory offences concerning indecency and obscenity, some of which affect freedom of expression. The main ones are briefly outlined here.

(2) THE CHILDREN AND YOUNG PERSONS (HARMFUL PUBLICATIONS) ACT 1955

This was enacted in reaction to a spate of horror comics. It set out to penalize anyone who prints, publishes, sells, or lets on hire a book, magazine, or similar work, which is of a kind likely to fall into the hands of children or young persons, and which consists wholly or mainly of cartoon stories portraying commission of crimes, acts of violence or cruelty, or incidents of a repulsive or horrible nature, in such a way that the work as a whole would tend to corrupt a child or young person into whose hands it might

[201] See Levin, *Pendulum Years*, 297–9, on the proceedings against the bookseller of John Cleland's *Fanny Hill*.
[202] Robertson, *Obscenity*, 106.
[203] HC Deb., 7 July 1964, col. 302, Sir Peter Rawlinson S-G.
[204] Robertson, *Obscenity*, 106–8; Robertson, *Freedom, Individual and Law*, 193; *Olympia Press v. Hollis* [1974] 1 All ER 108.

fall.[205] There is no defence of public good. On the other hand, all prosecutions require the consent of the Attorney-General.[206] In view of the range of comics which would need to be the subject of proceedings if this legislation were taken seriously, it is not surprising that it has rarely if ever been invoked. Legislation such as this might, however, come into its own if the law on obscenity were to be reformed so as to remove restrictions on what might be published to adults. As the Williams Committee recognized, pornography has different effects on people of different ages, and it would be justifiable on grounds of paternalism to protect children and young people from some kinds of publication, even if paternalist arguments were held insufficient to justify criminalizing sale to adults.

(3) THE INDECENT DISPLAYS (CONTROL) ACT 1981

This applies to Scotland as well as England and Wales. It is justified by similar, though not identical, arguments to those invoked in support of the offences under the Obscene Publications Acts 1959–64. Section 1(1) makes it an offence to display publicly[207] any indecent matter.[208] This both protects young people from being offended or corrupted (an argument from paternalism), and saves adults from being the unwilling observers of things which they would have chosen to avoid (an argument from autonomy).

(4) THE THEATRES ACT 1968

In the case of the theatre, following the ending of the routine censorship of plays which had been one of the responsibilities of the Lord Chamberlain, the Theatres Act 1968, section 2, provides that it is an offence to present or direct a public[209] performance of a play which is obscene,[210] the definition of obscenity being (*mutatis mutandis*) similar to that under the Obscene Publications Act 1959. A public-good defence is provided by section 3. It is also an offence to present or direct a public performance of a play involving the use of threatening, abusive, or insulting words or behaviour, with intent to provoke a breach of the peace or where it is likely, taking the performance as a whole, that a breach of the peace is likely to be occasioned.[211] The

---

[205] Children and Young Persons (Harmful Publications) Act 1955, ss. 1, 2(1).

[206] Ibid., s. 2(2).

[207] Under s. 1(2) and 1(3), matter is publicly displayed if it is displayed in, or so as to be visible from, any public place, i.e. any place to which the public have access at the time, except (i) a place for which people have to pay for entry, where the payment includes a payment for the display, and (ii) a shop or part of a shop which cannot be reached without passing an adequate warning notice (the required terms of which are set out in s. 1(6)), and to which people under eighteen are not admitted.

[208] This does not apply to theatres or cinemas, or to broadcast or cable programmes, all of which have their own regulatory schemes. Nor does it apply to displays in museums, or to displays by or on the authority of the Crown or a local authority, in buildings occupied by them: Indecent Displays (Control) Act 1981, s. 1(4).

[209] See Theatres Act 1968, s. 7.

[210] See Robertson, *Media Law*, 3rd edn., 138–47.

[211] Theatres Act 1968, s. 6.

Attorney-General's consent is needed for prosecutions under the Theatres Act 1968. Finally, it is an offence to present or direct a public performance of a play intending thereby to stir up racial hatred or where, having regard to all the circumstances, racial hatred is likely to be stirred up.[212]

(5) THE POST OFFICE ACT 1953, SECTION 11

This makes it an offence to send any obscene or indecent article, whether in the form of writing, pictures, or in any other form, through the post. The important element here is the objective quality of the article, not its effect on the recipient. Thus an article may be indecent, in that it is repulsive, filthy, lewd, or loathsome, even if it would not have been obscene within the meaning of the Obscene Publications Act 1959.[213]

(6) INDECENT PHOTOGRAPHS OF CHILDREN

Taking, or permitting to be taken, an indecent photograph of a child[214] is an offence; so is showing or distributing such a photograph, or having one in one's possession with a view to its distribution or showing, or publishing an advertisement for such a photograph.[215] There are search, seizure, and forfeiture provisions[216] to much the same effect as those in section 3 of the Obscene Publications Act 1959. The impetus for these provisions was provided by the discovery of paedophile pornography rings, which gave rise to concern about the exploitation of children. The provisions are capable of interfering with freedom of expression, but would appear to be justifiable under ECHR Article 10(2) by reference to the protection of morals, and the protection of the rights of others, since indecent photographs of children require children to pose for them, and the object of the legislation is to 'protect children from exploitation and degradation' and from 'damage . . . when he or she is posed or pictured indecently' by eliminating the trade in photographs.[217] It is also an offence to have possession of such a photograph without intending to show or distribute it.

There is a defence to these charges if the accused has a legitimate reason for possessing it. It is for the defendant to convince the jury that he or she had a legitimate reason. If, for instance, the defendant claims to have been conducting legitimate research, it will be necessary to show that the research was genuine, and necessitated

[212] Public Order Act 1986, s. 20.

[213] *R. v. Anderson* [1972] QB 304, [1971] 3 All ER 1152, CA; *Kosmos Publications v. DPP* [1975] Crim. LR 345, DC.

[214] For this purpose, 'child' means a person under the age of 16, not the more usual 14. The matter is one of impression, and does not require either knowledge on the part of the defendant or expert evidence that the age of the subjects is under 16: *R. v. Land* [1999] QB 65, [1998] 1 All ER 403, CA.

[215] Protection of Children Act 1978, s. 1. 'Photograph' includes the negative of the picture, and also film and video recordings and data stored on a computer disc or by other electronic means, which are capable of being converted into a photograph: s. 7, as interpreted in *R. v. Fellows* [1997] 2 All ER 548, CA, and provided expressly by amendment by Criminal Justice and Public Order Act 1994, s. 84(3). See C. Manchester, 'More About Computer Pornography' [1996] Crim. LR 645.

[216] Protection of Children Act 1978, ss. 4, 5.

[217] *R. v. Land* [1999] QB 65, [1998] 1 All ER 403, CA at 407 *per* Judge LJ.

the possession, etc. of the pictures.[218] It is also a defence to a charge of possession for the defendant to show that he had not seen the photograph and neither knew nor had cause to suspect that it was indecent, or had received it unsolicited and had not kept it for an unreasonable time. Knowledge is therefore essential; where a computer automatically stores photographs from an internet site without the operator's knowledge, the operator is not guilty of possession.[219] This offence involves an interference with rights under ECHR Article 8 rather than Article 10, but would seem to be justifiable on similar grounds, protecting children's right to be free of exploitation and degradation by eliminating the trade in such photographs. Unfortunately, the law was brought into a measure of disrepute by heavy-footed police actions against people who had or displayed photographs of their children partially clothed or naked in poses which were natural and not indecent in any way. In these cases, the police (and also some commercial developers and printers of films who informed the police about supposedly 'suspect' photographs) defeated the purpose of the legislation by casting suspicion on people's entirely innocent recording of happy family events, inhibiting their normal relationships with their children and inflicting considerable upset on both parents and children.

In the early 1990s, concern was caused by the development of computerized methods of adjusting or creating pictures. Digital technology made it possible to create what appeared to be photographic representations of children in indecent poses, but were in reality combinations of parts taken from innocent photographs, adapted using a computer graphics program. It was thought by the Conservative government to be objectionable that people should be able to make and retain such pictures. This was seriously muddled thinking. The purpose of the 1978 and 1988 Acts was to protect children from exploitation and degradation, not to penalize people for possession of pictures which, however objectionable, had been made without subjecting anyone to exploitation or degradation. None the less, the Criminal Justice and Public Order Act 1994 amended the 1978 and 1988 Acts to put making,[220] possession, and distribution of indecent 'pseudo-photographs' of children in the same position as the taking, possession, and distribution of indecent photographs of them.[221] A 'pseudo-photograph' is defined as 'any image, whether made by computer graphics or otherwise, which appears to be a photograph'.[222] A pseudo-photograph is to be treated as being of a child if it conveys the impression, or predominant impression, that the person shown is a child, even if the figure has some of the physical characteristics of an adult.[223]

[218] *Atkins v. DPP* [2000] 1 WLR 1427, [2000] 2 All ER 425 DC.

[219] Criminal Justice Act 1988, s. 160; *Atkins v. DPP* [2000] 1 WLR 1427, [2000] 2 All ER 425 DC.

[220] A person who downloads, stores, copies, or prints a picture in electronic form 'makes' it for this purpose, even if he has done nothing to create an original image: *R. v. Bowden (Jonathan)* [2000] 2 WLR 1083, [2000] 2 All ER 418, CA; *Atkins v. DPP* [2000] 1 WLR 1427, [2000] 2 All ER 425 DC.

[221] C. Manchester, 'Criminal Justice and Public Order Act 1994: Obscenity, Pornography and Videos' [1995] Crim. LR 123–31 at 123–6.

[222] Protection of Children Act 1978, s. 1(7) and Criminal Justice Act 1988, s. 160(1), as amended by Criminal Justice and Public Order Act 1994, s. 84(1), (2), (3), (4). Parts of two photographs, one of an adult in an indecent position and a decent one of a child, taped together so that they can be manipulated to give a crude impression of a child in an indecent position, is not a pseudo-photograph within the meaning of the legislation: *Atkins v. DPP* [2000] 1 WLR 1427, [2000] 2 All ER 425 DC.

[223] Protection of Children Act 1978, s. 1(8), inserted by Criminal Justice and Public Order Act 1994, s. 84(3).

The 1994 amendments appear to have been a knee-jerk reaction from a government which had lost sight of the real and legitimate purpose of the 1978 Act. Criminalizing distribution and possession of indecent pseudo-photographs of children on the face of it do nothing to protect children, and are merely concerned to enforce a particular form of sexual morality by preventing people making or sharing a particular kind of picture which gives them sexual pleasure and can be manufactured without exploiting or harming anyone. The confusion about the purpose of the legislation has human-rights implications: penalizing a person for possessing such pseudo-photographs interferes with the right to respect for private life. The interference may be justified, but only if it represents a proportionate response to a pressing social need to pursue a legitimate aim under ECHR Article 8(2). In *R. v. Bowden (Jonathan)*,[224] decided before the Human Rights Act 1998 came into force the Court of Appeal took the view that the criminal provisions were not inconsistent with ECHR Article 8, as the interference was necessary for the protection of health or morals or for the protection of the rights and freedoms of others. However, the court did not analyze or provide argument for this proposition, which is questionable. As pseudo-photographs do no harm to children, the criminal provisions do not seem to protect the rights and freedom of children. If the purpose is to prevent paedophiles having their lust inflamed, which might lead to attacks on children, one is entitled to ask for evidence that the photographs have that effect, rather than (for example) assuaging paedophiles' sexual drives so that they feel no need to exploit or attack children. If the purpose is to stop distributors profiting from immoral or indecent material, it might be justifiable as protecting morals, but it would not then be necessary to criminalize possession of pseudo-photographs which a person has created for himself. It seems most likely that the object is to stop people from getting enjoyment from pictures of which others disapprove, and to save those others the discomfort of feeling that people out there might be looking at that sort of thing. This is sheer moralism, and is hard to justify on criteria of pressing social need and proportionality of response.

(7) IMPORT CONTROLS

Customs legislation forbids the importation of indecent or obscene articles.[225] Forbidden articles are liable to forfeiture.[226] This is a potential restriction on the right to receive and impart information and ideas regardless of frontiers, under ECHR Article 10(1). However, where the effect of the legislation is to subject importers

---

[224] [2000] 2 WLR 1083, CA, at 1089–90.

[225] Customs Consolidation Act 1876, s. 42.

[226] Customs and Excise Management Act 1979, s. 49. In forfeiture proceedings, the public-good defence is not available. It has been suggested that this breaches EC law where the importation is from a Member State of the EC, but this has been rejected by the courts: *R. v. Bow Street Metropolitan Stipendiary Magistrate, ex parte Noncyp Ltd.* [1990] 1 QB 123, where Woolf LJ in the Divisional Court suggested at 132 that none the less it would be a judicially reviewable abuse of power for a Customs officer to seize and forfeit goods which, in previous criminal proceedings, had been held to be justifiable under the public-good defence in the Obscene Publications Act 1959, s. 4. In the Court of Appeal, however, Glidewell LJ at 145–6 doubted whether an application for judicial review in such circumstances would succeed.

from other Member States of the European Community to restrictions which do not apply to UK producers, it conflicts with, and is overridden by, Article 28 (previously Article 30) of the EC Treaty, because it constitutes a quantitative restriction on imports. Under Article 30 (previously Article 36), it is permissible to control imports on grounds of (*inter alia*) public morality, but only if the prohibition or restriction do not 'constitute a means of arbitrary discrimination or a disguised restriction on trade between Member States'. Banning obscene articles, while a breach of Article 28 (previously Article 30), is justified under Article 30 (previously Article 36), because such articles would be liable to lead to forfeiture and criminal prosecutions if marketed by UK nationals,[227] under the Obscene Publications Act 1959. However, banning imports of articles which are indecent but not obscene will not be justified under Article 30 (previously Article 36), because such goods are not generally illegal in this country. Accordingly, an importer of obscene books does not have a defence under Article 30 (previously Article 36),[228] but an importer of merely indecent items does.[229] In response to this, instead of changing the law to treat imports from European Community Member States differently from imports from elsewhere, there has been an administrative policy of not seizing or prosecuting in respect of imports of merely indecent goods.

(8) INDECENT DETAILS OF LEGAL PROCEEDINGS

It is an offence to print or publish, or cause or procure to be printed or published, certain matters in relation to any judicial proceedings. In particular, it is unlawful to print, etc. any indecent matter, or indecent medical, surgical, or psychological details, if the publication would be calculated to injure public morals.[230] In context, it is clear that, if the matter is indecent, the issue is the likely effect on public morals, not the intention of the publisher or printer. This criminalizes a type of publication relating to judicial proceedings which would not be punishable as a contempt of court (see Chapter 17, below) because it neither interferes with the administration of justice nor amounts to breach of a court order.

There is also a blanket prohibition on publishing more than the barest information relating to matrimonial matters, although it is not clear whether this is to protect the privacy of the parties, to avoid public morals being harmed by titillating details, or both. In relation to proceedings for the dissolution or annulment of marriage, judicial separation, overseas adoption, or declarations as to parentage or legitimacy, and

---

[227] The question is whether there is a legal market in the items in the UK. The answer may vary between different parts of the UK, because of the different legal systems operating in Scotland, N. Ireland, and England. The court will take an overall view to see whether the item is, broadly speaking, marketable legally over the country. See Case 34/79, *R. v. Henn* [1981] AC 850, [1980] 2 All ER 166, ECJ and HL; *R. v. Bow Street Metropolitan Stipendiary Magistrate, ex parte Noncyp Ltd.* [1990] 1 QB 123, CA.

[228] Case 34/79, *R. v. Henn* [1980] AC 850, [1980] 2 All ER 166, CJEC and HL.

[229] Case 121/85, *Conegate Ltd. v. HM Customs and Excise* [1987] QB 254, [1986] 2 All ER 688, CJEC and Kennedy J (importation of life-size, inflatable, rubber dolls). See further *Wright v. Commissioners of Customs and Excise* [1999] 1 Cr. App. R. 69, DC.

[230] Judicial Proceedings (Regulation of Reports) Act 1926, s. 1(1)(a).

proceedings concerning maintenance orders,[231] the only details which may be published[232] are: the names, addresses, and occupations of parties and witnesses; a concise statement of charges, defences, and counter-charges (but not the evidence led in support or rebuttal of them); submissions on points of law, and the court's decisions on them; and the judge's summing up to jury and the jury's findings (if the case is heard before a jury), the judgment of the court, and any observations made by the judge in giving judgment. Even these truncated details are permitted only so far as they do not include indecent matter which would be calculated to injure public morals.[233]

There is no public-good defence, but there is an exception from liability in relation to law reports and publications of a technical character intended for circulation among members of the legal and medical professions.[234] In other cases, an administrative safeguard is provided by the proviso that, in England and Wales, no prosecution for these offences may be commenced without the Attorney-General's sanction.[235]

Although criminal liability is imposed, there is no express provision for a court to make an order restraining publication. Normally, courts will not enjoin the commission of criminal offences, but a party who would suffer special damage from publication of details which would constitute a criminal offence may be able to obtain an injunction restraining reports. Although it will rarely be proper to grant such an injunction, one was granted restraining a party to divorce proceedings from reporting details of allegations made in the proceedings which were not supported by evidence at the hearing.[236] The special damage, in that case, arose from a potential combination of interference with privacy and injury to reputation.

16.5 REGULATION AND LICENSING

The regulation of the broadcasting and cable programme media is considered in Chapter 14, above. This section notes the regulatory schemes for three other conduits of expression: cinema, video recordings, and sex shops.

---

[231] Ibid., s. 1(1)(b); Family Law Act 1986, Part III and s. 56, replacing Matrimonial Causes Act 1973, s. 45; Family Law Act 1996, Part II; Magistrates' Courts Act 1980, s. 71, as amended. See *Moynihan v. Moynihan* [1997] 1 FLR 59. See C. J. Miller, *Contempt of Court*, 3rd edn. (Oxford: Oxford University Press, 2000), 479–81.

[232] In relation to proceedings in magistrates' courts, similar restrictions apply to reports in newspapers and periodicals of domestic proceedings. They seem not to apply to reports in broadcast and cable programmes. See Magistrates' Courts Act 1980, s. 71. 'Domestic proceedings' are defined in s. 65.

[233] Judicial Proceedings (Regulation of Reports) Act 1926, s. 1(1)(b); Domestic and Appellate Proceedings (Restriction of Publicity) Act 1968, s. 2(3), as amended by Matrimonial Causes Act 1973, s. 45, Family Law Act 1986, s. 68, and Family Law Reform Act 1987, s. 33.

[234] Judicial Proceedings (Regulation of Reports) Act 1926, s. 1(4); Magistrates' Courts Act 1980, s. 71(5).

[235] Judicial Proceedings (Regulation of Reports) Act 1926, s. 1(3); Magistrates' Courts Act 1980, s. 71(4).

[236] *Duchess of Argyll v. Duke of Argyll* [1967] 2 Ch. 302, [1965] 1 All ER 611.

(1) CINEMA

Premises require a licence before they can be used for the purpose of film exhibitions.[237] Licensing is the responsibility of the district council (or, in London, the borough council) for the area concerned. The authority has a very wide discretion as to the people to whom, and the terms on which, they grant licences, and may impose special conditions when the exhibition is organized wholly or mainly for children.[238] Pursuant to this, they may, and customarily do, decide which films may and may not be shown, and provide for age limits for admission to particular films. Although authorities usually follow the recommendation of the British Board of Film Classification[239] in respect of individual films, they need not do so, and have sometimes refused licences to show films to which the Board has granted a certificate, or given licences to films refused a certificate by the Board.[240] There is a right of appeal to the Crown Court against a refusal of a licence or against a condition which the authority has imposed.[241]

(2) VIDEO RECORDINGS

In the Video Recordings Act 1984, a scheme was introduced to regulate the supply, for reward or in the course or furtherance of a business, of video recordings.[242] The authority designated by the Home Secretary to act as regulator under the legislation is the British Board of Film Classification (BBFC).[243] The Board has the job of deciding whether to issue classification certificates to video recordings, and, if so, how to classify them.[244] The criteria applied by the BBFC were originally set out in a note from the Home Secretary, but are now on a statutory footing. The BBFC is to determine the suitability of a video work for a particular certificate, having special regard (among other relevant factors) to the following:

- the harm that may be caused to individual viewers who are likely to see it, including children, if a certificate of a particular class is given; and

- the manner in which the work deals with criminal behaviour, illegal drugs, violent behaviour or incidents (including behaviour which inflicts or would be likely to inflict injury), horrific behaviour or incidents, and human sexual activity.[245]

---

[237] Cinemas Act 1985, s. 1(1). 'Film exhibition' means any moving picture show other than a simultaneous television broadcast: s. 21(1). See generally Robertson and Nicol, *Media Law*, 3rd edn., 564–72; S. H. Bailey, D. J. Harris, and B. L. Jones, *Civil Liberties Cases and Materials*, 4th edn. (London: Butterworths, 1995), 323–31.

[238] Cinemas Act 1985, ss. 1(2), (3) and 2(2).

[239] On the constitution and work of the Board, a self-regulatory body first established by the film industry in 1912, see Robertson and Nicol, *Media Law*, 3rd edn., 566–9, 583–93.

[240] See *R. v. Greater London Council, ex parte Blackburn* [1976] 1 WLR 550, [1976] 3 All ER 184, CA.

[241] Cinemas Act 1985, s. 16.

[242] Video Recordings Act 1984, s. 3.

[243] On the work of the Board in relation to video recordings, see Robertson and Nicol, *Media Law*, 3rd edn., 575–83.

[244] Video Recordings Act 1984, s. 4.

[245] Video Recordings Act 1984, s. 4A, inserted by Criminal Justice and Public Order Act 1994, s. 90.

The category of criminal behaviour was the basis for refusing a certificate in 1989 (before the statutory criteria were in place) to *Visions of Ecstasy*, discussed in section 16.2 above.

It is an offence to supply a video recording, or to have a video recording in one's possession for the purposes of supply, if it has not been granted a classification certificate, unless it is an exempted work.[246] It is also an offence to supply a video recording in breach of the terms on which a classification certificate has been issued.[247] The classification certificate may provide that the recording is not to be supplied other than in a licensed sex shop, and it is an offence to supply such a recording in any other place.[248] This legislation was introduced in the wake of concern that 'video nasties' were falling into the hands of children, and being watched by them. It is an aspect of paternalistic concern for children's welfare. Although it is still open to a parent to hire or buy a recording for which a classification certificate has been issued, the adult then has the responsibility for safeguarding his or her children.

The principle of parental responsibility was reinforced in 2000 by the Video Appeals Committee (VAC), which reversed a decision of the BBFC to refuse an R18 certificate to seven hard-core pornographic videos. The VAC took the view that it would be wrong to ban videos unless they were likely to cause more than insignificant harm to children and young people, interpreting section 4A(1) of the Video Recordings Act 1984 in the light of the obligations imposed on the state by ECHR Article 10. The VAC concluded that the BBFC had not established that significant harm to children and young people was likely. The empirical evidence about the effect of pornography on children and young people was said to be equivocal, and in any case not many children and young people were likely to have an opportunity to watch the videos. This upset the BBFC, as it represented a major shift of classification policy. The BBFC applied for judicial review of the VAC's decision. In *R. v. Video Appeals Committee of the British Board of Film Censors, ex parte British Board of Film Censors*,[248a] Hooper J decided that the VAC had correctly interpreted section 4A(1) of the Video Recordings Act 1984 in the light of ECHR Article 10, and accepted that the VAC had been entitled to find the risk of harm insignificant on the basis of the evidence presented to it. The validity of the VAC's decision was therefore upheld. As a result, the BBFC rewrote its guidelines. expanding the range of permissible material in videos. This is a welcome approach from the standpoint of free speech, although it has been pointed out that concern for the welfare of children might justify giving more

---

[246] Ibid., ss. 9 and 10. 'Exempted works' (defined in s. 2) are those which are designed to inform, educate, or instruct; are concerned with sport, religion, or music; or are video games. However, recordings which depict, to any significant extent, human sexual activity, associated acts of force, or restraint; mutilation or torture of, or other acts of gross violence towards, humans or animals; or human genital organs or excretory functions, are not exempted works. Nor are recordings exempted works which are designed to any significant extent to stimulate or encourage human sexual activity, associated acts of force or restraint, or mutilation, torture, or other acts of gross violence in relation to humans or animals.

[247] Video Recordings Act 1984, s. 11. Companies are liable for the acts of their employees and agents: *Tesco Stores Ltd. v. Brent London Borough Council* [1993] 1 WLR 1037, [1993] 2 All ER 718, DC.

[248] Ibid., s. 12. On the meaning of 'licensed sex shop', see below.

[248a] *The Times*, 7 June 2000.

weight to less scientific, more anecdotal evidence about the effect of pornography on children.[248b]

(3) SEX SHOPS

Concern that towns and cities were being affected by a proliferation of shops retailing articles and books of an explicitly sexual nature, and a feeling that each locality should be able to decide whether and to what extent it was desirable to control such shops in the light of the character of the area, led to the enactment of section 2 of the Local Government (Miscellaneous Provisions) Act 1982. This enables any district council, or (in London) borough council or the Common Council of the City of London, to resolve that a licensing scheme for sex establishments under Schedule 3 shall come into force in its area. If a licensing scheme is in force, the council decides how many (if any) sex shops there are to be in its area and where they may be situated, and licenses the operators. It is an offence knowingly to operate a sex shop without a licence in an area in which a licensing scheme is in force. The effect of the Act has been to drive sex establishments out of some areas entirely, although the major proprietors fought a gallant but largely unavailing rearguard action through the courts.[249] In consequence, the outlets for the distribution of sex articles and the showing of sex films are increasingly concentrated in relatively few areas.[250]

16.6 CONCLUSION

Mystery and confusion surrounds the law in the fields covered by this chapter. Difficulties exist on two levels. First, at the deeper, philosophical level, there is no agreement about the ends which the law is intended to serve. It is not clear whether it protects social or individual interests; whether it is concerned to prevent offence or to impose a moral standard; whether it is soundly based in any philosophy, and if so whether that philosophy enjoys general agreement and is compatible with liberal values of freedom of choice and action. The only recent attempt in the UK to develop a coherent legal strategy to deal with obscenity and indecency law on the basis of an agreed philosophical position, the Williams Committee Report based on the harm principle, has largely been ignored by legislators, and has been attacked both as justifying a utilitarian interference with rights and as undervaluing intuitively significant values: a gut reaction against certain forms of expression may be right and socially important.

Even liberals committed to personal and political freedom may find their values

---

[248b] S. Edwards, 'The Video Appeals Committee and the Standard of Legal Pornography' [2001] Crim. LR 305–11.

[249] See, e.g. *Quietlynn Ltd. v. Southend Borough Council* [1991] QB 454, [1990] 3 All ER 207, CJEC.

[250] For a full account of the background and the legislation, see C. Manchester, *Sex Shops and the Law* (Aldershot: Gower, 1986).

leading them in several directions at once. In relation to blasphemy, freedom to express religious beliefs may interfere with other people's freedom to hold and express different beliefs, and may offend people even if it does not interfere with their freedom of conscience. Pornographic and indecent expression raises still more acute difficulties. If one believes in a free market in ideas, with values being controlled by the choices of purchasers, people should be free to produce and market most types of material for which there is a market. On the other hand, someone who follows Raz, treating moral autonomy as demanding a combination of a reasonable range of available options and the mental ability to choose between them,[251] may regard material which depraves and corrupts people as interfering significantly with one's ability to exercise free and rational choice (if one accepts the validity of the idea of personal or moral corruption). On this view, it is justifiable to interfere with people's freedom to publish or read obscene works, in order to protect their own or other people's autonomy. One's view of freedom of expression in these fields therefore depends not merely on whether or not one is a liberal, but on what sort of liberal one is.

This has an impact on the second, practical level at which the law operates. The substance of the law reflects all the oddities and inconsistencies of the conflicting ideals and ideologies which have given rise to it. Blasphemy law is recognized as being consistent with no known philosophy, but there has until now been no political will to change it. The complex relationship between the common law offences of indecency and corruption of public morality on the one hand and the Obscene Publications Act on the other exemplifies yet further confusion, to some extent made inevitable by the way in which, as in relation to blasphemy, the law is forced to accommodate standards and beliefs left over from an earlier stage in its development. The earlier ideas may be no worse than those current today, but they are likely to be hard to reconcile with them.

At some stage, Parliament will have to decide comprehensively what it wants to ban and why. One powerful incentive to embark on the process, although not a necessary precondition to it, would be the enactment of a domestic bill of rights requiring respect for freedom of expression. Until the attempt is made, and it will be a painful nettle for politicians to grasp, judges will have to make the best they can of an unsatisfactory body of law, perhaps aided a little—but probably not very much—by the Human Rights Act 1998 and the ECHR.

[251] Raz, *Morality of Freedom*, 425.

17

RESTRICTING EXPRESSION TO FURTHER A PUBLIC INTEREST: CONTEMPT OF COURT

This chapter examines a variety of restrictions, all criminal or quasi-criminal in form, which are directed to securing the integrity of the system of justice in the public interest. The rules interfere in various ways with the freedom of expression of parties to proceedings, witnesses, lawyers, and journalists who report the proceedings. They also affect the right of members of the public to receive information about legal proceedings and pending litigation. Under the Human Rights Act 1998, section 6, courts and tribunals must act compatibly with Convention rights unless compelled by primary legislation to act otherwise. In the area of contempt of court, the courts generally have a wide range of powers, which must be exercised in accordance with Article 10 of the European Convention on Human Rights (ECHR).

Restrictions on freedom of expression (including the right to receive and impart information and ideas) may be justified under ECHR Article 10(2) if they are pre-scribed by law and are necessary in a democratic society to advance one of a limited number of legitimate aims, including 'the protection of the reputation or rights of others . . . or for maintaining the authority and impartiality of the judiciary'. We will examine the decisions as they become relevant to particular aspects of the law of contempt. At the outset, we should note the view of the European Court of Human Rights, expressed at various times and in different contexts, that restrictions on freedom of expression may properly be imposed for these purposes having the effect of restricting what can be said to or about judges, litigants, and the evidence and arguments in cases, as long as the restrictions are a proportionate response to a pressing social need, and their application is supported by relevant and sufficient reasons.

Generally speaking, both the law of contempt and the law of the Convention recognize the public interest in open justice,[1] and in permitting fair and accurate contemporaneous reporting of legal proceedings.[2] At times, however, these interests come into conflict with other rights and interests. The most important of these is the

---

[1] *Scott v. Scott* [1913] AC 417, HL; *Axen v. Germany*, Eur. Ct. HR, Series A, No. 72, Judgment of 8 December 1983, 6 EHRR 195.

[2] E.g. Administration of Justice Act 1960, s. 12(1), recognizing the general principle while authorizing certain restrictions; Contempt of Court Act 1981, s. 4; *Sunday Times v. United Kingdom*, Eur. Ct. HR, Series A, No. 30, Judgment of 26 April 1979, 2 EHRR 245.

right of litigants to a fair hearing in public before an impartial tribunal under ECHR Article 6(1). The right to an independent and impartial tribunal under Article 6(1) is absolute; unlike the general concept of a 'fair trial', it does not admit any balancing of interests.[3] But the ECHR does not entirely guarantee a right to a public trial to litigants, or the right of the press and public to attend trials. Article 6(1) of the Convention provides, in part:

'Judgment shall be pronounced publicly but the press and public may be excluded from all or part of the trial in the interests of morals, public order, or national security in a democratic society, where the interests of juveniles or the protection of the private life of the parties so require, or to the extent strictly necessary in the opinion of the court in special circumstances where publicity would prejudice the interests of justice.'

As the *Report of the Committee on Contempt of Court* observed in 1974, although contempt is not a standard criminal charge, and in Scotland is not a criminal offence at all, 'it would be contrary to the spirit of the Convention if contempt procedure, both in England and Wales and in Scotland, did not comply with Article 6'.[4] The Committee went on to argue that most of the law of contempt complied with the requirements of Article 6. This is not surprising, since the exceptions from the right to a public hearing under Article 6, which are mirrored in the International Covenant on Civil and Political Rights, Article 14(1), go beyond anything available in English law, and, as Professor Sir James Fawcett observed, 'are so large and loosely expressed as to cover almost any denial of public hearing'.[5] Broadly speaking, and with limited exceptions, English law allows interference with public trials and with free reporting of and public comment on the judicial system only where they would interfere with the interests of justice. None the less, there are some areas in which the wide powers granted to judges in English law may be exercised in a manner which violates Convention rights.

The parties' right to a fair trial can justify restricting reports about pending or current proceedings. Other reporting restrictions may be justified by the rights of witnesses and others (especially children) to respect for private life, or to protect them against threats to the right to life. The European Court of Human Rights has also said that the state has a legitimate interest in protecting the reputation of judges in order to uphold the authority of the judiciary, and in ensuring that unjustified criticism of the judiciary does not undermine public confidence in the impartial operation of the system of justice.[6]

The conflict between these interests is universal, but the constitutional context in which it falls to be resolved varies from place to place, and affects the balance between the opposing interests. In the USA, the Constitution permits fewer restrictions on the openness of justice and freedom to comment on it. There is a constitutional guarantee

---

[3] *Millar v. Procurator Fiscal, Elgin,* unreported, DRA No. 5 of 2000, Judgment of 24 July 2001, PC.

[4] Cmnd. 5794 (1974) para. 18.

[5] J. E. S. Fawcett, *The Application of the European Convention on Human Rights,* 2nd edn. (Oxford: Clarendon Press, 1987), 160.

[6] *Barfod v. Denmark,* Eur. Ct. HR, Series A, No. 149, Judgment of 22 February 1989, 13 EHRR 493; *Prager and Oberschlick v. Austria,* Eur. Ct. HR, Series A, No. 313, Judgment of 26 April 1995, 21 EHRR 1.

of a right to a public trial in criminal prosecutions under the Sixth Amendment, but this right belongs only to the accused, and accordingly can sometimes be waived by the accused in respect of pre-trial hearings, in order to avoid adverse publicity which might make a fair trial impossible.[7] On the other hand, the general public has a right, implied in the First Amendment, to attend criminal trials, and this right has been held to promote a number of public interests: in particular, public trials allow an independent check on the fairness of judicial procedure, educate the public in an aspect of civic organization, help to maintain public trust in the judicial system, and satisfy the desire to see justice done. Accordingly, a defendant cannot choose to have the trial itself closed to the public.[8] The same applies to the part of the hearing in which potential jurors are examined before a jury is empanelled.[9] The press is *prima facie* entitled under the First Amendment to report on offences and on the progress of all stages of investigations and proceedings. An order for prior restraint of such reports is permissible only where publication of details would create a clear and present danger that publicity would impair the defendant's right to a fair trial by an impartial jury. Even if there is such a danger, a blanket ban on reporting will not be justified unless the court is satisfied that alternative measures would be incapable of protecting the defendant's rights.[10]

Such restrictions as are permitted in England and Wales are enforced chiefly through the instrumentality of the law of contempt of court, and the power of the courts in certain circumstances to order restrictions on or postponement of reports of cases or the details of evidence. These form the subject of this chapter. Contempt is considered first, and then orders imposing restrictions on reporting and more general prior restraints are examined.

17.1 THE NATURE OF CONTEMPT OF COURT[11]

The law has always taken steps to enforce respect for its procedures and to protect them against abuse.[12] Punishment for contempt of court is part of the armoury which the courts have deployed for these purposes. Contempt of court has been defined as an act or omission calculated to interfere with the due administration of justice.[13] It restricts freedom of expression in a number of ways. First, the types of criminal

---

[7] *Gannett Co. v. Pasquale* 443 US 368 (1979).

[8] *Richmond Newspapers, Inc. v. Virginia* 448 US 555 (1980).

[9] *Press-Enterprise Co. v. Superior Court of California* 464 US 501 (1984).

[10] *Nebraska Press Association v. Stuart* 427 US 539 (1976).

[11] See generally C. J. Miller, *Contempt of Court*, 3rd edn. (Oxford: Oxford University Press, 2000); David Eady and A. T. H. Smith, *Arlidge, Eady and Smith on Contempt* (London: Sweet & Maxwell, 2000); N. Lowe and B. Sufrin, *Borrie and Lowe: The Law of Contempt*, 3rd edn. (London: Butterworth, 1995); E. Barendt, *Freedom of Speech* (Oxford: Clarendon Press, 1987), ch. 8.

[12] For the background to this, see R. L. Goldfarb, *The Contempt Power* (New York: Columbia University Press, 1963), 1–100; R. Dhavan, 'Contempt of Court and the Phillimore Committee Report' (1976) 5 *Anglo-American LR* 186–253.

[13] *Helmore v. Smith* (1886) 35 Ch. D. 436 at 455 *per* Bowen LJ.

contempt[14] known as 'contempt in the face of the court' and 'scandalizing the court' are capable of restricting both the conduct of people before the court, and people's freedom to comment elsewhere on proceedings. Secondly, the head of criminal contempt which consists of prejudicing proceedings, which may attract strict liability (subject to the provisions of the Contempt of Court Act 1981, considered below), can restrict pre-trial comment and reporting of the trial itself. Thirdly, since breach of an undertaking to the court or of an order made by the court is a civil contempt, any such undertaking or order which requires that matters be not published will restrict freedom to publish information or opinions or to receive them, on pain of punishment. The second and third types of contempt are particularly likely to be committed by the press and broadcasting media.

The scope for the law of contempt to restrict the right to freedom of expression is, therefore, substantial. This section attempts to explain the current state of English law in the light of the Human Rights Act 1998 and the ECHR. It would be hard to justify the law of contempt under the very general terms of Article 19 of the Universal Declaration of Human Rights, which gives unqualified recognition to the right to freedom of expression. There is more scope for the law of contempt under Article 19(2) and (3) of the International Covenant on Civil and Political Rights (ICCPR), which permits restrictions of freedom of expression only if they are provided by law and necessary (a) for the protection of the rights and reputations of others, or (b) for the protection of national security or of public order (*ordre public*), or of public health or morals. Protection of the rights of others would justify restricting expression which would prejudice a litigant's right to a fair hearing under ICCPR Article 14(1), but would not justify restrictions on comments about the behaviour of judges which are imposed solely in order to uphold the dignity of the judiciary.

The ECHR leaves more scope for the law of contempt in all its aspects. This is not surprising, as the UK would have been unlikely to agree to an instrument which required it to abolish a substantial part of contempt law. Article 10(1) of the ECHR guarantees freedom of expression, but Article 10(2) permits that freedom to be interfered with under certain circumstances 'for the protection of the reputation or rights of others, . . . or for maintaining the authority and impartiality of the judiciary'. This has been held to permit restrictions which protect the interests of litigants in having a fair trial of their claims,[15] but it also allows more extensive restrictions to protect judicial dignity and reputation. However, in order to be justifiable within Article 10(2) of the Convention, restrictions of this sort must be:

(a) prescribed by law, a requirement which the law of contempt has so far been held to satisfy; and

---

[14] Criminal contempts are regarded as a sufficiently serious attack on the administration of justice to deserve punishment. Civil contempts, such as non-compliance with a court order, are those which the court punishes in order to coerce the contemnor into complying. On the distinction, its consequences, and options for reform, see Miller, *Contempt of Court*, 3–5 and 43–69.

[15] *Sunday Times v. United Kingdom*, Eur. Ct. HR, Series A, No. 30, Judgment of 26 April 1979, 2 EHRR 245; *Observer and Guardian v. United Kingdom*, Eur. Ct. HR, Series A, No. 216, Judgment of 26 November 1991, 14 EHRR 153.

(b) necessary in a democratic society for a legitimate purpose under that paragraph, which means that the restriction must be a response to a pressing social
need and must be proportionate to its purpose.[16]

The discussion of the law in this section is divided up as follows. First, the meaning of
'court' for contempt purposes is examined and then common-law criminal contempts: contempt in the face of the court; scandalizing the court; prejudicing or
impeding proceedings; contempt by prejudgment. The rest of the section deals with
strict liability for contempts by way of publication, under the Contempt of Court Act
1981: strict liability under the Contempt of Court Act 1981; the time when proceedings become active; circumstances in which there is a substantial risk of serious
prejudice to proceedings; the section 5 defence, where prejudice is incidental to a
discussion in good faith of matters of public interest; and the defence of ignorance
under section 3.

(1) WHAT IS A COURT?

A preliminary matter which arises is the notion of the 'court', contempt of which is
penalized. Judicial activities are today carried on by a wide variety of courts, tribunals,
and other bodies, and the public interest in safeguarding the administration of justice
extends, more or less compellingly, to all of them. However, if penalties are to be
imposed for contempt of court, it is important, in the interests of certainty, to know
what bodies are covered by the rules. In the leading case on the matter, *Attorney-
General v. British Broadcasting Corporation*,[17] the House of Lords had to consider a
programme about the activities of the Exclusive Brethren, a religious sect. The programme criticized the sect, and argued that its meeting rooms were not places of
public religious worship within the meaning of the General Rate Act 1967, section 39,
and were therefore ineligible for exemption from liability for rates. The Attorney-
General, seeking an injunction to restrain the broadcast, argued that this programme
would prejudice the determination of this issue at a pending hearing by a local
valuation court. The BBC argued that the local valuation court was not an inferior
court for the purpose of the contempt jurisdiction.

The Divisional Court and Court of Appeal held that the local valuation court was a
court for this purpose. However, on appeal to the House of Lords it was held that the
nomenclature attached to a body was not decisive, and that a local valuation court was
not a court of law such as to attract the protection of the law of contempt. Viscount
Dilhorne thought that, where Parliament had not called a body a court, it could not be
a court, although where Parliament had called a body a court, it might still not be a
court of law for contempt purposes. The other Law Lords did not give even that
limited overriding power to the name conferred by Parliament on a body. Lords
Scarman and Fraser distinguished between bodies discharging judicial functions in
the exercise of the judicial power of the state (to which the law of contempt applied)

---

[16] *Sunday Times v. United Kingdom*, Eur. Ct. HR, Series A, No. 30, Judgment of 26 April 1979, 12 EHRR
245.
[17] [1981] AC 303, [1980] 3 All ER 161, HL.

and other decision-making bodies, particularly those discharging administrative functions (which were not covered by the law of contempt).[18] They made the substance of the body's functions central to its classification, as did Viscount Dilhorne in relation to bodies which were called courts. Lord Salmon argued against extending the law of contempt even to tribunals exercising the judicial power of the state, on the ground that extending the law of contempt restricted freedom of speech and freedom of the press. Lord Edmund-Davies thought that none of the features of judicial or administrative bodies respectively was decisive as to the correct classification of a particular body, and preferred to leave Parliament to widen the scope of the law of contempt if it thought that to be appropriate. Applying the general approach of Lord Scarman and Lord Fraser in particular, courts have subsequently held that industrial tribunals (now known as employment tribunals) are courts for contempt purposes, because they act judicially and exercise the judicial power of the state.[19]

The same test was adopted in relation to statutory contempt of court by the drafters of the Contempt of Court Act 1981 (below), which provides that for its purposes the term 'court' 'includes any tribunal or body exercising the judicial power of the state'.[20] This adoption of the judicial power test, however, gives little help to those who had to decide on the classification of various types of body, and it is perhaps fair to conclude that the range of bodies which can be protected by the contempt jurisdiction is best resolved as a matter of policy rather than technicality.[21] This was certainly the approach in *P. v. Liverpool Daily Post and Echo Newspapers plc*,[22] where the House of Lords held that a mental health review tribunal was a court for contempt purposes. Among other grounds for reaching this decision, Lord Bridge[23] (with whom the other Law Lords agreed) approved the reasoning of Lord Donaldson MR in the Court of Appeal on this point.[24] Lord Donaldson had pointed out that the tribunal had been set up under the Mental Health Act 1983, enacted in part to bring English law into line with the requirements of ECHR Article 5(4). That paragraph requires that people deprived of their liberty by arrest or detention are to be entitled to have the lawfulness of their detention 'decided speedily by a court', and to have their release ordered if the detention is held to be unlawful. Before 1982, English law had not provided such a

---

[18] Note that an administrative body may be under a duty to act judicially, i.e. fairly and without bias, in some of its activities. This is true, e.g. of licensing bodies, and of those who have the responsibility for determining applications for warrants to search premises or arrest people. Nevertheless, this does not make those functions judicial. See *Shell Co. of Australia Ltd. v. Federal Commissioner of Taxation* [1931] AC 275, PC, at 296–7 *per* Viscount Sankey LC; D. Feldman, *The Law Relating to Entry, Search and Seizure* (London: Butterworths, 1986), 73–4; *Love v. A.-G. of New South Wales* (1990) 169 CLR 307, especially at 322, HC of Australia.

[19] *Peach Grey & Co. (A Firm) v. Sommers* [1995] 2 All ER 513, DC.

[20] Contempt of Court Act 1981, s. 19.

[21] See N. V. Lowe and H. F. Rawlings, 'Tribunals and the Laws Protecting the Administration of Justice' [1982] *PL* 418–50.

[22] [1991] 2 AC 370, reported *sub nom. Pickering v. Liverpool Daily Post and Echo Newspapers plc* [1991] 1 All ER 622, HL.

[23] [1991] 2 AC at 417, [1991] 1 All ER at 630.

[24] [1991] 2 AC 370, [1990] 1 All ER 335, CA.

procedure in relation to mental patients detained pursuant to a restriction order (an order which may be imposed by a criminal court where a person is convicted of an offence and is made the subject of a hospital order). Accordingly, in *X. v. United Kingdom*[25] the European Court of Human Rights had held that the UK was in breach of the Convention in this regard. The Mental Health (Amendment) Act 1982 therefore gave the mental health review tribunals power to determine whether the legal criteria for detention were met in relation to patients detained under restriction orders made by other courts, and to order the release of patients unlawfully detained.[26] Lord Donaldson continued:[27]

'If such a tribunal is not a "court" for all purposes, the Human Rights Convention is not being complied with, since there is no indication that "court" in the convention has any different meaning from that which it bears in English law. However, I have no doubt that in law a mental health review tribunal is a court. Contrary to what is stated in [*Attorney-General v. Associated Newspapers Group plc*],[28] it did not inherit an executive function. It was given a new and quite different function.'

Farquharson LJ set out the factors which influenced him to hold that the tribunal was a court:[29]

'The tribunals are independent of the state; they do not exercise a purely administrative function; they are required to act judicially and make their findings on the basis of the evidence submitted to them; they can administer an oath to the witnesses called before them; they have, and have had since their introduction in 1959, the power to release, conditionally or otherwise, patients detained under the Mental Health Acts, and since 1982 patients subject to a restriction order under section 65 of the 1959 Act or section 41 of the 1983 Act. Decisions of such consequence affecting the release from detention of patients who are subject to hospital orders made by the criminal courts of the country come within the description of "any tribunal ... exercising the judicial power of the state."'

The correct approach, therefore, is to see whether the tribunal in question is making decisions which dispose of claims to or disputes over entitlements on the basis of legal criteria, exercising the judicial power of the state rather than an administrative or private jurisdiction, and to ask whether there are any indications in the circumstances surrounding the establishment of the tribunal that it ought to be regarded as a court rather than an administrative body. On this basis the Professional Conduct Committee of the General Medical Council, a tribunal deciding disciplinary cases against doctors, has been held not to be a court for this purpose. Although it exercised statutory powers and followed court-like procedures laid down in subordinate

---

[25] Eur. Ct. HR, Series A, No. 46, Judgment of 5 November 1981, 4 EHRR 188.

[26] The relevant law has since been consolidated in the Mental Health Act 1983 as amended, and in rules made thereunder. See Ch. 7 above.

[27] [1991] 2 AC at 381, [1990] 1 All ER 335 at 341.

[28] [1989] 1 WLR 322, [1989] 1 All ER 604, DC, holding that a mental health review tribunal was not a court for the purpose of contempt proceedings. This decision was not followed by the Court of Appeal in the *Liverpool Daily Post and Echo* case, and was overruled by the House of Lords.

[29] [1991] 2 AC at 395, [1990] 1 All ER at 352.

legislation, it was a regulatory body of a professional organization operating independently of the state, not part of the judicial arm of the state.[30]

(2) CONTEMPT IN THE FACE OF THE COURT[31]

Contempt in the face of the court is committed by anyone who, in court, interferes with the proceedings, abuses the process of the court, or threatens, insults, or interferes with the judge, any witness, a juror, or a party. It includes refusal by a witness to answer questions, an assault on the judge, or casting aspersions on a juror. It encompasses demonstrations in court.[32] It has also been held, in some Australian cases, to cover demonstrations outside courts, at least where potential jurors are given leaflets which seek to encourage them to be sceptical about the value and accuracy of evidence to be given by some of the witnesses.[33] Accusations by counsel that the judge has acted unjudicially may, if sufficiently scurrilous, amount to contempt. While it may be painful for people in court to have to moderate their language and behaviour, it is essential for the smooth functioning of the justice system that courts should be able to regulate their procedure and protect it by summary action against attempts[34] at disruption. There is a resulting restriction of freedom of expression, but the restriction is insubstantial and is fully justified by the need to maintain the authority of the judicial process, as long as the steps taken are proportionate.

Potentially, a more significant threat to liberty lies in the fact that it is open to the trial judge in the case in respect of which the contempt is committed to institute summary action against the contemnor, summoning him, accusing him, judging him, and sentencing him.[35] Until 1960 there was no right of appeal against the judge's decision, but an appeal to the Court of Appeal was eventually provided by the Administration of Justice Act 1960, section 13. This power of a court to act of its own motion is rarely exercised. The usual course is for the Attorney-General or a party aggrieved by the contempt to bring a motion before the High Court to commit the alleged contemnor to prison for contempt, proving the charge in the usual way before an impartial tribunal.[36] However, the summary procedure remains available, and seems to contravene both the right to be tried by an independent and impartial tribunal under ECHR Article 6(1), and the right to have adequate time and facilities for the preparation of a defence and the right to legal assistance under ECHR Article 6(3)(b) and (c). In *Balogh v. Crown Court at St Albans*,[37] the Court of Appeal laid down some guidelines for the use of the summary power. Mr. Balogh had stolen a

---

[30] *General Medical Council v. British Broadcasting Corporation* [1998] 1 WLR 1573, [1998] 3 All ER 426, CA.

[31] Miller, *Contempt of Court*, 3rd edn., 139–205.

[32] *Morris v. Crown Office* [1970] 2 QB 114, [1970] 1 All ER 1079, CA.

[33] *Registrar, Court of Appeal v. Collins* [1982] 1 NSWLR 682, CA of NSW; *Prothonotary v. Collins* (1985) 2 NSWLR 549, SC of NSW.

[34] On attempts to commit contempt, see *Balogh v. Crown Court at St Albans* [1975] QB 73, [1974] 3 All ER 283, CA.

[35] *R. v. Almon* (1765) Wilm. 243 at 254 *per* Wilmot CJ.

[36] RSC Ord. 52.

[37] [1975] QB 73, [1974] 3 All ER 283, CA.

cylinder of laughing gas (nitrous oxide) and had found out which ventilation duct led from the roof of the Crown Court into the courtroom. Balogh had intended to introduce the gas into a courtroom where a pornography trial was in progress, via the ventilation duct, next-door to one presided over by Mr. Justice Melford Stephenson, a judge not given to levity in the discharge of his judicial duties. The police found the gas cylinder in his brief-case before he had an opportunity of carrying out the plan. Melford Stephenson J, the senior judge, summarily sentenced him to six months' imprisonment for contempt of court. Balogh appealed. He succeeded on the ground that he had not committed contempt, or even attempted to commit it, his acts being merely preparatory to the completed offence. Lord Denning MR (with whom Stephenson and Lawton LJJ agreed) said that summary punishment should be imposed only in cases where there was sufficient urgency to warrant it, for example where the contemnor is interfering with witnesses or jurors. In other cases, such as *Balogh*, where there is no urgent need to protect the administration of justice, the judge should invite counsel to represent the accused, with a remand in custody if necessary. But Lord Denning did not entirely disapprove of the judge's actions. 'The judge acted with a firmness which became him. As it happened, he went too far. That is no reproach to him. It only shows the wisdom of having an appeal'.[38]

Such judicial ambivalence towards the use of a power of summary punishment which infringes the Convention is a good reason for abolishing the power. Another good reason is that its exercise may violate the contemnor's right to a fair trial before an impartial tribunal. There is little doubt that the risk of long-term committal for contempt makes it a criminal charge for the purposes of ECHR Article 6. Where the contempt occurred in court while it was in session, the judge will often have been a victim, and usually a witness, of the alleged contempt, and is unlikely to be regarded as impartial for Article 6 purposes. In such cases, the judge should never hear the case. If the contempt took the form of intimidating a witness, or attempting to influence a juror, so as to put a person or the fair conduct of the trial at risk, the judge will often be justified in taking the initial step of remanding the alleged contemnor in custody pending a bail application to, or hearing before, another judge. Anything less would fail to take seriously the rights of other participants in the trial. But it is likely to violate ECHR Article 6 if the judge who witnesses or is a victim of the contempt conducts the full hearing of the contempt charge or decides the sentence.

Sometimes the judge is neither victim nor witness. For example, in *R. v. McLeod*[39] a defendant confronted a prosecution witness outside the courtroom after the court had risen for the day, abusing her and accusing her in colourful language of lying. The matter was reported to the judge, who the next day conducted a hearing to determine whether the defendant was guilty of contempt. He found the contempt to be proved, and sentenced the contemnor to two months' imprisonment. In these circumstances, the judge did not violate ECHR Article 6(1) by hearing the case and deciding sentence, although there was a risk of failing to respect the procedural guarantees of

---

[38] [1975] QB at 86–7, [1974] 3 All ER at 290.

[39] Unreported, 29 November 2000, CA; judgment available on the internet at www.courtservice.gov.uk/judgements.

Article 6(3) in a case where there was a dispute as to what had happened. The judge took the victim through her evidence, but inquisitorial behaviour by a court does not violate Article 6 as long as it does not compromise the fairness of the hearing. In that case, the conduct of the case was fair, and the decision and sentence were upheld on appeal. However, the decision does not give a green light to judges hearing cases in which they are either a victim or a witness. The fact that an appeal is available is unlikely to avoid such a hearing violating ECHR Article 6, particularly if the contemnor loses his liberty and is in prison pending the appeal.

The potential clash with the standards of the Convention was recognized by the Phillimore Committee as long ago as 1974. The Committee recommended that legal aid should be made available to people accused of contempt in the face of the court, and that they should be allowed to be legally represented. Subject to that, it recommended that the summary procedure should be retained, on account of the advantages of speed, and the judge's personal knowledge of the circumstances of the contempt which might lead to greater leniency than an independent judge would feel able to permit.[40] This modest change would not go far enough to meet the UK's obligations under Article 6 in a case of contempt within the sight of, or aimed at, the judge who hears the contempt case. There are other ways of protecting parties and witnesses while deferring the case to be heard before another judge with appropriate procedural safeguards. Great care is needed in the exercise of the jurisdiction.[41]

(3) SCANDALIZING THE COURT

Scandalizing the court potentially represents a far more extensive incursion on freedom of expression. It has been defined as: 'Any act done or writing published calculated to bring a Court or a judge of the Court into contempt, or to lower his authority ... '.[42] This appears to be a very broad *actus reus*, and taken at face value would threaten a good deal of the critical commentary on judicial decisions which may be found in respectable law journals. However, it is qualified to take account of three matters: (a) the fact that the law of contempt protects the administration of justice rather than the feelings of judges; (b) the need for open justice to be scrutinized; and (c) the right of citizens to comment on matters of public concern. As Lord Atkin said in *Ambard v. Attorney-General for Trinidad and Tobago*:[43]

' ... no wrong is committed by any member of the public who exercises the ordinary right of criticising in good faith in private or public the public act done in the seat of justice. The path of criticism is a public way: the wrong headed are permitted to err therein: provided that members of the public abstain from imputing improper motives to those taking part in

---

[40] *Report of the Committee on Contempt of Court*, Cmnd. 5794, paras. 30–1.

[41] *DPP v. Channel Four Television Co. Ltd.* [1993] 2 All ER 517, DC; *In re M. (A Minor) (Contempt of Court: Committal of Court's Own Motion)* [1999] Fam. 263, [1999] 2 All ER 56, CA.

[42] *R. v. Gray* [1900] 2 QB 36 at 40 *per* Lord Russell CJ. The decision came not long after Lord Morris, in *McLeod v. St Aubyn* [1899] AC 549 at 561, PC, had opined that this head of contempt was obsolete in England. The article which was in issue in *Gray* (reproduced in part in the report of the case in 82 LT 534) is probably among the most vitriolic attacks on overweening judicial self-importance in English literature.

[43] [1936] AC 322 at 335, [1936] 1 All ER 704 at 709, PC.

the administration of justice, and are genuinely exercising a right of criticism and not acting in malice or attempting to impair the administration of justice, they are immune. Justice is not a cloistered virtue: she must be allowed to suffer the scrutiny and respectful even though outspoken comments of ordinary men.'

The critic in that case committed no contempt by drawing attention to the human element in sentencing, which can lead to inconsistency between sentences for similar offences. But critics must not impute improper motives to judges or others, nor act in malice, nor attempt to impair the administration of justice (for example, by bringing the judicial system into disrepute).

This ban on imputing improper motives to judges might be thought to be unobjectionable. For example, in a case like *Badry v. Director of Public Prosecutions of Mauritius*,[44] where a person asserted that a claim for compensation by an injured worker was dismissed by the Supreme Court because the judge was influenced by the fact that the defendant was an important commercial concern in the area, the asser-tion could be understood as tending to undermine both the finality and authority of the decision in that particular piece of litigation, and the moral authority of the court generally. The Privy Council decided that it constituted a contempt. Yet it is not clear why there should be a blanket ban on such assertions. The law of contempt should take account of the public interest in the performance of the courts being publicly aired and discussed, and it is unrealistic to suppose, as Lord Atkin apparently assumed in *Ambard*, that it would always be wrong to impute improper motives to a judge. In the UK, we are fortunate in the general level of rectitude among our judges. However, there is no guarantee that this will always be the case, or that it is true of all common-law jurisdictions. There is a public interest in people being able to air serious misgiv-ings about the quality of judges, whether these derive from apparent weaknesses in their reasoning abilities or from suspected corruption or bias.

For this reason, the High Court of Australia held early in its existence that it was not necessarily a contempt to impute lack of impartiality to a judge. In *R. v. Nichols*,[45] Mr. Justice Higgins had stopped counsel from criticizing the government. A newspaper commented that the judge was a political judge, who had been appointed to the bench only because he was a servant of a particular political party. The High Court held that this did not constitute a contempt of court. Griffiths CJ, delivering the unanimous judgment of the court, pointed out that public confidence in the judges depends on their behaviour, and that the press has a role in maintaining judicial standards by way of open and critical public scrutiny of judicial performance, in the public interest. He said:[46]

' . . . I think that, if any judge of this Court or of any other Court were to make a public utterance of such a character as to be likely to impair the confidence of the public, or of suitors or any class of suitors in the impartiality of the court in any matter likely to be brought before it, any public comment on such an utterance, if it were a fair comment, would, so far from being a contempt of court, be for the public benefit, and would be

---

[44] [1983] 2 AC 297, [1982] 3 All ER 973, PC.
[45] (1911) 12 CLR 280.
[46] Ibid. at 286.

entitled to similar protection to that which comment upon matters of public interest is entitled under the law of libel.'

The same approach has subsequently been followed in Australia and New Zealand,[47] and an eminent Australian commentator has described it as a qualification, 'at least as far as Australasian law is concerned', of Lord Atkin's statement in *Ambard*.[48] In New South Wales, the judges seem to have become increasingly relaxed in the face of criticism. When the President of the Builder's Labourers' Federation (then a powerful trade union) gave a television interview outside a court, saying that the verdict in the case which he had just watched (in which protesters against a tour of Australia by the South African rugby union team had been convicted of malicious damage to property for damaging the goalposts at the Sydney Cricket Ground where rugby football is played in winter) was a miscarriage of justice which illustrated the extent of racism in Australian society, it was held to be no contempt. The judges chose to interpret his words as an attack on society, not on the judges.[49]

It is true that the position in the UK would be rather different if our judges follow the *Ambard* formulation of the contempt rule, but it would not necessarily be an unjustifiable interference with freedom of expression under ECHR Article 10 to penalize someone for accusing a judge of bias or incompetence. In the few cases to come before the European Court in which the state has restricted penalized journalists in order to uphold the authority of the judiciary against such attacks, the Court has been surprisingly supportive of the restrictions. In *Barfod v. Denmark*,[50] two of the three members of the High Court of Greenland were lay judges who were employed by a council which was a party to a case before the court. When the council won by a two-to-one majority, an article was published suggesting that the two employees of the council had formed the majority, and that they had done their duty by their employer. The author was penalized, and the European Court of Human Rights held that it was a justifiable interference with freedom of expression. The state had a legitimate interest in protecting the reputation of its judges, in order to uphold the authority of the judiciary without which public confidence in courts as the proper forum for deciding legal disputes would be undermined, and with it any possibility of a litigant being able to enjoy the benefits of winning a case after a hearing publicly recognized as being fair.

The decision in *Barfod* is bizarre to an English lawyer who would regard it as entirely improper, and a flagrant breach of the rules of natural justice, for a judge, magistrate, or juror to hear a case in which his employer is a party. It is clear from a subsequent case, *Prager and Oberschlick v. Austria*,[51] that the Court recognizes that there is a strong public interest in a democracy in ensuring that allegations of impropriety on the part of judges are aired and properly investigated. In that, it was held that the state had been entitled to penalize authors for allegations about the

---

[47] See, e.g. *R. v. Fletcher; ex parte Kisch* (1935) 52 CLR 248; *A.-G. for New South Wales v. Mundey* [1972] 2 NSWLR 887; *Solicitor-General v. Radio Avon Ltd.* [1978] 1 NZLR 225, at 230–1.

[48] G. A. Flick, *Civil Liberties in Australia* (Sydney: Law Book Co., 1981), 131.

[49] *A.-G. for New South Wales v. Mundey* [1972] 2 NSWLR 887.

[50] Eur. Ct. HR, Series A, No. 149, Judgment of 22 February 1989, 13 EHRR 493.

[51] Eur. Ct. HR, Series A, No. 313, Judgment of 26 April 1995, 21 EHRR 1.

behaviour of judges in Vienna when the authors had failed either to substantiate the claims at their trials or to show that the articles amounted to fair comment. The general principle seems to be that a state may penalize mere insults or allegations of judicial impropriety which strike at the legitimacy of the state's judicial process, but the interference with freedom of expression will be disproportionate, and hence not necessary in a democratic society, if the author is not allowed to establish the truth of the allegations or the fairness of any comment, or if the penalty is out of proportion to the seriousness of the offence.

One of the problems with laying down worldwide, or even pan-European, principles to govern an offence of scandalizing the court is that it is hard to know in advance what will be needed to uphold the authority of the judiciary in any jurisdiction. The effect of criticism on the due administration of justice may vary between societies, and in any society its effects may vary from time to time. For example, in small communities, where everyone knows the judges personally and the authority of the courts may depend more on personal than institutional authority, an attack on the judge may seriously undermine respect for law.[52] This may be why the European Court of Human Rights in *Barfod* was so accommodating to the state of Denmark: the population of Greenland is small, and the authority of the judiciary could easily be undermined by personal attacks. In larger societies, the law is more impersonal, its authority is less affected by the idiosyncrasies of its individual personnel, and the approach adopted in the USA seems particularly attractive. There, the First Amendment to the Constitution, protecting freedom of speech and of the press, has been held to permit criticism, even if not altogether in good taste, unless it constitutes a clear and present danger to the administration of justice. '[A]n enforced silence, however limited solely in the name of preserving the dignity of the bench, would probably engender resentment, suspicion, and contempt much more than it would enhance respect . . . '[53]

The political and constitutional structure of a society will also affect the position of the courts. If the constitution demands a separation of power between the executive and an independent judiciary, as one of the pillars of the rule of law, any direct attack on a judge by a member of the executive will threaten to undermine that independence and the associated constitutional principles. Where, as in the Canadian case *Re Borowski*,[54] the alleged contemnor is a government Minister who not only accuses a judge of basing a decision on political views (something which has often been said of English judges by the media and legal commentators in sensitive cases) but also threatens to remove the judge from office, the law of contempt is protecting an important constitutional principle which goes beyond safeguarding the dignity or authority of the courts and the adminsitration of justice against vulgar abuse. The

---

[52] See K. Patchett, 'Small is Different?', in G. Hand and J. McBride (eds.), *Droit sans frontières: Essays in honour of L. Neville Brown* (Birmingham: Holdsworth Club, 1991), 43–52. Western legal processes grafted on to a small society may still rely for their authority on charismatic forms of domination.

[53] *Bridges v. California, Times-Mirror Co. v. California* 314 US 252 (1941) at 270–1 *per* Black J. Even allegations of judicial bias in pending proceedings have been held not to constitute contempt: *Pennekamp v. Florida* 328 US 331 (1946). See further Barendt, *Freedom of Speech*, 218–23.

[54] (1971) 19 DLR (3d) 537.

public interest in maintaining respect for law may require different forms of contempt law in each type of society. Even in Australia, there is a strange ambivalence to the crime of contempt by scandalizing the court. While the High Court was following a substantial tradition in *Nichols* when it asserted the importance of public criticism in keeping judges up to the mark,[55] and allowed allegations of bias to be made against judges if they amounted to fair comment, it had been held to be a contempt to accuse a judge of behaving in a thoroughly unjudicial way.[56] It seems that, in Australia, the rhetoric of fair comment has turned into practice, superseding the earlier practice of suppressing criticism.

In England, it has been said that 'if reasonable argument or expostulation is offered against any judicial act as contrary to law or public good, no Court could or would treat that as a contempt of Court'.[57] These considerations demand protection for the reasoned opinions of commentators, even if outspoken or even intemperate. It was on this ground that the Court of Appeal held that Mr. Quintin Hogg, QC, MP, PC, who later became Lord Hailsham LC, was not guilty of contempt for publishing an article in *Punch* magazine vehemently criticizing a decision of the Court of Appeal (which he wrongly attributed to the Divisional Court). The court had said that the police might in some circumstances be acting unlawfully if they turned a blind eye to the operation of illegal gambling clubs in Soho.[58] Mr. Hogg argued that the police should not be blamed for the persistence of such clubs when the fault lay with the legislation and the courts (including the Court of Appeal), which (he wrote) had interpreted the legislation in unrealistic, contradictory, and erroneous decisions, which made it very difficult to obtain convictions and so made it unreasonable to expect the police to prosecute. He suggested that the Court of Appeal should apologize to the police for the trouble and expense to which they were put by the decisions of the courts. Mr. Raymond Blackburn, the applicant in the earlier proceedings against the police, invited the Court of Appeal to commit Mr. Hogg for contempt. The court decided, however, that it would be wrong to invoke the contempt jurisdiction in order to shelter itself from criticism, even erroneous criticism. It was anyone's right to comment rumbustiously on judicial decisions, so long as it was done in good faith, without intending contempt, and kept within the bounds of reasonable courtesy (although, according to Salmon LJ, it need not necessarily observe the canons of good taste). The decisions of the courts must be left to look after themselves; their judgments must be their own vindication; and the judges ought not to allow themselves to be deflected from duly administering justice by criticism.[59]

In the light of this, it is hard to know what the bounds of the offence are. If it is a contempt to cast doubt on the impartiality of a judge, as *Badry* accepts, what is the

---

[55] *In re Syme; ex parte The Daily Telegraph Newspaper Co.* (1879) 5 VLR (L) 291, especially at 296, SC Victoria; *In the matter of 'The Evening News'* (1880) 1 NSWLR 211 at 239, *per* Sir James Martin CJ.

[56] *In the matter of 'The Evening News'* (1880) 1 NSWLR 211. See Flick, *Civil Liberties*, 128; *R. v. Dunbabin, ex parte Williams* (1935) 53 CLR 434.

[57] *R. v. Gray* [1900] 2 QB 36 at 40 *per* Lord Russell CJ.

[58] *R. v. Commissioner of Police of the Metropolis, ex parte Blackburn* [1968] 2 QB 118, CA.

[59] *R. v. Commissioner of Police of the Metropolis, ex parte Blackburn (No. 2)* [1968] 2 QB 150, [1968] 2 All ER 319, CA.

position of people who argue that judges exhibit traits and preferences in their judgments which are the result of institutional conditioning over a long period? For example, if one suggests that the judges (or certain judges) are predominantly conservative in their politics, or lack sympathy with the objectives and methods of collective bargaining and industrial action by trade unions, is this a contempt of court? There are, perhaps, two possible answers.

The first answer would be that the proposition amounts to a contempt only if it implies that judges act unjudicially, by ignoring or twisting relevant legal rules or principles to give effect to their personal preferences in their judgments. It would, therefore, not be a contempt to suggest that the rules and principles which the judges are required to administer embody such attitudes, and that these attitudes happen to coincide with the judges' own; nor would it be a contempt to assert that judges have political views, unless the further claim were made that the judges' decisions are entirely determined by those views rather than by the law. This turns on the interpretation of an utterance in the light of a nice distinction between judicial attitudes, legal values, and the causative link between those attitudes and values and the results of particular cases, which may well not have been present in the mind of the author. Although it may be possible for the courts to use the distinction to acquit rather than convict for contempt in doubtful cases, it may equally be employed to the opposite end.[60]

Alternatively, it might be said that the answer depends on the stability and structure of particular societies. If the independence of the judicial system is firmly established in a given society, its integrity, and the due administration of justice, will not be undermined (and might well be enhanced) by allowing robust and vigorous criticism of its decisions. On the other hand, in societies where the judges' independence of the executive is weak or threatened, or the fair administration of justice is threatened by public unrest or mob rule, there may be stronger grounds for restricting some types of criticism of the judges, particularly those which encourage the executive or others to disregard court decisions and interfere with proceedings. There may, therefore, be a core of good sense in the apparently patronizing and possibly racist comment by Lord Morris, in *McLeod v. St Aubyn*,[61] that 'in small colonies, consisting principally of coloured populations, the enforcement in proper cases of committal for contempt of Court for attacks on the Court may be absolutely necessary to preserve in such a community the dignity of and respect for the Court'.

Uncertainty about the essential nature of the offence of contempt by scandalizing the court raises a further issue about its justification under ECHR Article 10(2). It is likely that the law is sufficiently accessible, certain, and predictable to be prescribed by law as that term has been interpreted by the European Court of Human Rights:[62] at least it is probably not so unforeseeable in its effect as to fall foul of this requirement. But is it a response to a pressing social need, in the conditions current in English

---

[60] Contrast *A.-G. for New South Wales v. Mundey* [1972] 2 NSWLR 887 with the Canadian approach in *Re Borowski* (1971) 19 DLR (3d) 537, or that of the Privy Council sitting on appeal from Mauritius in *Badry v. DPP of Mauritius* [1983] 2 AC 297, [1982] 3 All ER 973.

[61] [1899] AC 549, PC, at 561.

[62] *Sunday Times v. United Kingdom*, Eur. Ct. HR, Series A, No. 30, Judgment of 26 April 1979, 2 EHRR 245.

society? It is hard to see any pressing social need which demands general protection for the judges against public comment. Even given the sensitivity of the European Court of Human Rights to local needs, it is hard to see how the law on scandalizing could be said to be proportionate to the aim pursued. Not only is it counter-democratic, but it is also highly unlikely to achieve its purpose: in modern English conditions, the more thoroughly expression is suppressed, the more it is likely to fuel, rather than allay, suspicions about the conduct and attitudes of the judges. The English courts may have to deal with this question under the Human Rights Act 1998, where the doctrine of the margin of appreciation, which the European Court of Human Rights invokes in deferring to national judgments of need and proportionality, will not be applicable.[63] It is noteworthy that in Canada it has been held that the law of contempt by scandalizing the court is incompatible with the guarantee of freedom of expression and the press under section 2(b) of the Canadian Charter of Rights and Freedoms, and is not a permissible limit of that right under section 1 of the Charter because the law is disproportionate to any legitimate purpose which it might serve.[64]

The risk that the law offends against the Convention right to freedom of expression under the Human Rights Act 1998, as the right would be interpreted by an English court, should concentrate minds on reform. The Phillimore Committee wondered whether the offence of scandalizing the court should be entirely abolished, but eventually recommended that it should be narrowed substantially. The Committee thought that the law of contempt is there essentially to protect the integrity of the legal process and to prevent prejudice in particular cases. It should not be used against people who criticize judges, or publish vituperative comments, unless they create a risk of serious prejudice to some particular, identifiable proceedings.[65] This would bring the law back into line with the Convention's requirements, because it would ensure that criminal sanctions could be imposed only in cases where they would be proportionate to the legitimate objective of maintaining the authority of the judiciary in a democratic society, but no action has so far been taken to implement the proposal. On the other hand, a further recommendation would, if implemented, create further difficulties in relation to the Convention. The Committee recommended that there should be a new statutory offence of publishing material which imputes improper or corrupt behaviour to judges, in the performance of their judicial functions, with intent to impair confidence in the administration of justice.[66] They suggested a defence if the allegation is both true and for the public benefit.[67] Such a defence would be needed if the interference with freedom of expression were to be proportionate to a legitimate aim in a democratic society, as required under Article 10(2) of the Convention.

The Law Commission later considered the matter. It thought that the test for intent to impair confidence in the administration of justice would probably be unworkable,

---

[63] See Ch. 2 above.
[64] *R. v. Kopyto* (1987) 47 DLR (4th) 213, Ontario CA.
[65] *Report of the Committee on Contempt of Court*, Cmnd. 5794 (London: HMSO, 1974), paras. 161–2.
[66] Ibid., para. 164.
[67] Ibid., paras. 166–7.

and disliked the idea that liability could ever be imposed for making a true allegation of judicial impropriety. It therefore recommended that it should be an offence to publish or distribute false matter, which imputes corrupt judicial conduct to any judge, tribunal, or member of a tribunal, knowing it to be false or being reckless whether it is false, with the intent that it should be taken as true.[68] This would have given adequate protection to the reputation of the judicial service, while allowing robust criticism, investigative journalism, and satire, leaving other attacks on judges to the law of defamation. However, no action has been taken to implement any of these proposals. The matter might have to be addressed by the judges, developing common law in accordance with their duty to comply with Convention rights under section 6 of the Human Rights Act 1998.

(4) PREJUDICING OR IMPEDING PROCEEDINGS

The main objects of the contempt power are to guarantee access to judicial decision-making and to safeguard the fairness of legal processes for intending litigants. Interfering with a party, witness, or juror, by any means, is a criminal contempt at common law, and is punished in order to maintain the integrity of the legal system and its ability to determine fairly all cases which come before it. Thus a prison governor was guilty of contempt of court when he stopped an inmate's letter attempting to initiate proceedings to have the governor committed for contempt of court in relation to an earlier interception, and it seems that intercepting a letter to a solicitor giving instructions about pending litigation would also be a contempt if, without legal authority (such as valid Prison Rules), it impeded the prisoner's ability to pursue legal proceedings.[69]

Sometimes a publication can have the effect of impeding access to justice, and when it does so it may constitute a contempt. In *Attorney-General v. Hislop*[70] the editor of the periodical *Private Eye* was being sued for libel by Mrs. Sonia Sutcliffe in respect of allegations that she had known that her husband, Peter Sutcliffe, had been the notorious mass murderer, the 'Yorkshire Ripper', and had lied to the police in order to provide him with a false alibi. The defence included a plea of justification. The editor then published further articles, repeating the allegations. After Mrs. Sutcliffe had won

---

[68] Law Commission Report No. 96, *Offences Relating to Interference with the Course of Justice* (London: HMSO, 1979), para. 3.70.

[69] *Raymond v. Honey* [1983] 1 AC 1, [1982] 1 All ER 756, HL. In New Zealand, it has been accepted that freedom of expression can legitimately be curtailed temporarily in order to secure a fair trial: *Gisborne v. Solicitor-General* [1995] 4 LRC 730, CA of NZ. In Australia, it has been said that the implied constitutional right to communicate on matters of political and governmental interest cannot prevent the court from temporarily restraining publication of material which would prejudice a defendant's chance of receiving a fair trial on criminal charges, even if the material publication of which is restrained is concerned with fixing horse races, while the criminal charges relate to alleged drug offences and money laundering. *John Fairfax Publications Pty. Ltd. v. Doe* (1995) 130 ALR 488, CA of NSW. For a balanced assessment of the law of contempt as it applies to the press, and of the issue of trial by newspaper in particular, see A. T. H. Smith, 'Free Press and Fair Trial: Challenges and Change', in J. Beatson and Y. Cripps (eds.), *Freedom of Expression and Freedom of Information: Essays in Honour of Sir David Williams* (Oxford: Oxford University Press, 2000), 123–38.

[70] [1991] 1 QB 514, [1991] 1 All ER 911, CA.

the libel action, the Attorney-General instituted proceedings against the editor, alleging that he had committed a contempt of court. The judge found that in publishing the articles the editor had intended to deter Mrs. Sutcliffe from pursuing her libel action, rather than to prejudice jurors. He went on to decide that there was no real or substantial risk of the trial being impeded or prejudiced, and so no contempt. The Attorney-General appealed to the Court of Appeal, which reversed the decision and fined the editor and the publishers £10,000 each. By publishing libels, intending to deter another party to litigation from pursuing her claim, they had given rise to a substantial risk that the course of justice would be impeded, as it was likely that a litigant might be put off. There is, said the judges, a real difference between bringing home to another party the strength of one's own case, and publishing material which holds that party up to public obloquy and scurrilous abuse. The former is permissible, but the latter is a contempt, because it is likely to impede justice, as had been accepted by all the members of the House of Lords in *Attorney-General v. Times Newspapers Ltd.* (the Thalidomide case).

This is a particular problem in relation to actions for defamation. The general rule is that the court will not grant an interlocutory injunction restraining repetition of an alleged libel which the defendant intends to justify, because until it is clear that an allegation is untrue the public interest in free speech outweighs the private interests of the possibly unwronged claimant.[71] Yet if publication is likely to be a contempt, an injunction may be granted. It is hard to imagine a case in which republishing the allegations could avoid either prejudicing jurors or impeding justice by deterring the claimant from having his day in court, unless (as in *Attorney-General v. News Group Newspapers Ltd.*)[72] the action is certain to proceed and the trial is unlikely to take place soon enough for the effect of the republication to be likely to continue until then.

The common law offence of contempt by prejudicing or impeding proceedings was a strict liability offence of wide scope. However, the Contempt of Court Act 1981, section 6(c), while preserving common-law liability under this head of contempt, did so only 'in respect of conduct *intended* to impede or prejudice the administration of justice' (italics added). The common-law offence is therefore no longer one of strict liability. Indeed, it has been held that it is now a crime of specific intent, rather than basic or general intent. Following the recommendations of the Phillimore Committee,[73] Lord Donaldson MR said:[74]

'I am quite satisfied that . . . what is "saved" [by section 6(c) of the 1981 Act] is the power of the court to commit for contempt where the conduct complained of is specifically intended

---

[71] *Bonnard v. Perryman* [1891] 2 Ch. 269.

[72] [1987] QB 1, [1986] 2 All ER 833, CA, where the Court of Appeal discharged an injunction which had previously been granted restraining newspaper publishers from repeating allegations concerning the behaviour of Mr. Ian Botham, an England cricketer, while on tour in New Zealand. The allegations were the subject of libel actions against those who had originally published them, but the trial was likely to be delayed for at least ten months.

[73] *Report of the Committee on Contempt of Court*, Cmnd. 5794 (1974), discussed by Dhavan, 'Contempt of Court and Phillimore', 186–253.

[74] *A.-G. v. Newspaper Publishing plc* [1988] Ch. 333 at 374–5, [1987] 3 All ER 276 at 303–4.

to impede or prejudice the administration of justice. Such an intent need not be expressly avowed or admitted, but can be inferred from all the circumstances, including the foresee-ability of the the the consequences of the conduct.'

The surrounding circumstances may include the interest of the alleged contemnor in the case in issue, as where a newspaper's editor published allegations about somebody, intending to sponsor a private prosecution against that person in respect of the allegations contained in the publication.[75] Similarly, where a news-paper editor published extracts from *Spycatcher*, knowing that proceedings were in progress against another newspaper to preserve rights of confidentiality in respect of the material and knowing that publication would help to compromise the duty of confidence owed by the other newspapers' publishers, the court could infer that the publication was intended to prejudice the administration of justice.[76] This aspect of the contempt power enables the court to safeguard the integrity of its procedures, but may (as in the *Spycatcher* case) have the effect of extending the effect of an injunction far beyond the people to whom the injunction is addressed. This is, in principle, a cause for concern, as the third parties who are liable to be punished for contempt for breaching the injunction would not have been able to appear before the court to oppose the grant of the injunction. It is particularly unfortunate in the context of *Spycatcher*, where the interim injunction in question had been granted to preserve any remaining confidentiality attaching to matters dealt with in the book: as the House of Lords later decided that different people, and different newspapers, may be differently affected by the competing public interests, it is conceivable that newspaper X may be liable to punishment for contempt for breaching an injunction addressed to another newspaper, Y, in cir-cumstances which would not have justified the grant of an injunction had one been sought directly against newspaper X. Such an extension of the effect of injunctions beyond their proper limits by the procedural sidewind of contempt proceedings against a third party should not be permitted. If extended protection is required for claimants, it should be achieved through injunctions of express general application, where all know where they stand and will have standing to apply to discharge the injunction.[77]

It is possible that this deliberate contempt of court by publication at common law may, in two respects, cast the net of liability more widely than under the Contempt of Court Act 1981. First, although at common law the publication no longer attracts strict liability, the *actus reus* of the common law offence may be wider than that for statutory contempts. Whereas the 1981 Act applies only where proceedings are active, as we shall see in sections (6) and (7) below, it is possible that common-law contempt by prejudicing or impeding proceedings applies to publications even before any pro-ceedings are active or pending. Secondly, common-law contempt is not limited to the types of publications contemplated by the Contempt of Court Act 1981, which is limited to those which create a substantial risk that active proceedings will be

---

[75] A.-G. v. News Group Newspapers plc [1989] QB 110, [1988] 2 All ER 906, DC.
[76] A.-G. v. Times Newspapers Ltd. [1992] 1 AC 191, [1991] 2 All ER 398, HL.
[77] Cp. the comments by C. J. Miller in All ER Rev. 1991, 65–6.

seriously impeded or prejudiced. The common law offence covers other types of conduct as well, such as bringing improper pressure to bear on a party to litigation to discontinue it.[78] This widening, if it is upheld, may impose a significant fetter on the ability of journalists and others to uncover and publicize wrongdoing, and to pursue the alleged wrongdoers. The extra scope of the interference with investigative journalism, and the reasons which prompted the extension, can be seen from the two cases in which it has so far been discussed.

In *Attorney-General v. News Group Newspapers plc*,[79] a newspaper, the *Sun*, had launched a campaign seeking the prosecution of a doctor who, it was alleged, had raped an eight-year-old girl who had been staying with his family at the time. The county prosecuting solicitor, acting on counsel's advice, and the Director of Public Prosecutions, both decided that there was insufficient evidence to prosecute. The newspaper decided to try to bring the suspected man to justice, and agreed with the girl's mother to give financial support for a private prosecution. This was widely publicized. In addition, after Geoffrey Dickens MP had named the doctor in the House of Commons under cover of parliamentary privilege, the newspaper published the doctor's name, and also published interviews with the girl's relations accusing the doctor of being 'a beast and a swine', and printing statements from potential witnesses which seemed to incriminate the doctor and prejudge the issues in any forthcoming prosecution. Up to this time, no proceedings were active within the meaning of the Contempt of Court Act 1981. Seven weeks later, a private prosecution was commenced against the doctor when an information was laid. In due course, the doctor was acquitted at trial.

After the acquittal, the Attorney-General brought proceedings for contempt of court against the owners of the *Sun*, News Group Newspapers plc. For the Attorney-General, it was argued that a person could be liable for common-law contempt not only when proceedings were 'pending' (i.e. had already been commenced) but also when they were 'imminent' (i.e. before they had been commenced).[80] This was because '[i]t is possible very effectually to poison the fountain of justice before it begins to flow'.[81] Although at the time of the publications no proceedings were pending, it was argued that they were 'imminent', because the publishers intended that the private prosecution should be commenced as soon as possible, and were actively pursuing that goal. The Divisional Court accepted this argument.[82] Although 'imminence' is a vague and uncertain term, it applies when there is 'a likelihood or a real risk that they will be instituted in the near future and when there is a real risk that the kind of publication as here would interfere with the course of justice'.[83] On this basis, contempt liability for intentionally prejudicing or impeding the course of justice might apply to publications about a suspect during the progress of a police investi-

---

[78] *A.-G. v. Times Newspapers Ltd.* [1974] AC 273, [1973] 3 All ER 54, HL; *A.-G. v. Hislop* [1991] 1 All ER 911, CA.

[79] [1989] QB 110, [1988] 2 All ER 906, DC.

[80] Miller, *Contempt of Court*, 3rd edn., 258–66.

[81] *R. v. Parke* [1903] 2 KB 432 at 438 *per* Wills J.

[82] [1989] QB at 135, [1988] 2 All ER at 921.

[83] *A.-G. v. News Group Newspapers plc* [1989] QB 110 at 132, [1988] 2 All ER 906 at 919 *per* Watkins LJ.

gation or a manhunt, unless there was likely to be a long delay before trial to mitigate the risk of prejudice.

But counsel for the Attorney-General went further. He argued, and the Divisional Court accepted,[84] that there was no authority precluding liability for contempt even before proceedings are imminent. The overriding principle is that the administration of justice must be protected. This may require punishment of acts occurring after the conclusion of proceedings, as where someone seeks to penalize a witness for having given evidence,[85] and may equally require sanctions to be imposed in respect of conduct occurring before proceedings are imminent.[86]

The apparent width of this restriction on press freedom is somewhat modified by the meaning given to 'intention' for the purpose of the common law offence: a publisher would not be liable unless he knew that proceedings were likely to follow soon enough to make prejudice likely, and intended that to happen. Nevertheless, the extension of liability was challenged in a subsequent case, *Attorney-General v. Sport Newspapers Ltd.*,[87] and divided the judges. Here, the police were trying to trace a fifteen-year-old girl who had disappeared. They issued to the press a description of a man whom they wanted to contact. The editor of *The Sport* published a front-page story describing the man as a vicious rapist and sex monster, revealing previous convictions for rape and indecent assault. In due course the suspect was arrested, charged, and convicted of murder. Subsequently the Attorney-General brought contempt proceedings against the publishers. The Divisional Court held that the editor and publishers had not had the necessary intention to prejudice or impede the course of justice. However, the judges also expressed views about the period of time affected by the common law of contempt.

Bingham LJ accepted that the *News Group Newspapers* case had marked a novel extension of liability for contempt beyond the time when proceedings were pending or imminent. He recognized that this made the ambit of the contempt power wider in England and Wales than in Scotland or Australia, where it is limited to preventing prejudice following the commencement of proceedings by arrest or charge.[88] However, he felt that it would be wrong to depart from such a clear and recent decision. By contrast, Hodgson J. was impressed by the difficulties which the decision posed for investigative journalists who publish damning information about malefactors, in the hope that legal action will be taken to stop them in the public interest. In such circumstances, legal proceedings would be contemplated, and the journalist, editor, or publisher might well be liable to committal for contempt. This position would be tolerable only if the law were regularly not enforced. He felt that prosecutions for perverting the course of justice would suffice to deal with the most serious cases, and the law of contempt ought not to be extended to cases where a charge of perverting the course of justice would be inappropriate. Accordingly, he would have

[84] [1989] QB at 132–5, [1988] 2 All ER at 919–21.
[85] A.-G. v. Butterworth [1963] 1 QB 696, [1962] 3 All ER 326, CA.
[86] Ibid., at 725, 332 respectively per Donovan LJ.
[87] [1991] 1 WLR 1194, [1992] 1 All ER 503, DC.
[88] James v. Robinson (1963) 109 CLR 593, HC of Aust.; Hall v. Associated Newspapers Ltd. 1979 JC 1, High Ct. of Justiciary.

declined to follow the *News Group Newspapers* decision had it been necessary to do so.

It is submitted that the law of contempt ought not to be extended in ways which make its scope more uncertain than it already is, or which subject people to the risk of committal for contempt by prejudicing proceedings when they do not know whether or when those proceedings are likely to follow. However, as long as the offence is one of specific intent, the need for intention rather than recklessness will limit liability to cases where the likelihood of proceedings is known to the alleged contemnor. Where, as in Hodgson J's example, an investigative journalist hopes that the revelations in an article or broadcast will precipitate the commencement of proceedings, but does not himself intend to commence them, it is submitted that the requisite *mens rea* would not be present. Alternatively, the prospect of proceedings would be so speculative at the time of publication that the *actus reus*, involving likelihood of prejudice, would not be made out. It will behove journalists to check on whether proceedings are contemplated before they publish, but, if none are contemplated, the journalist need not normally be deterred by worries about contempt liability, even under the extended *News Group Newspapers* test. For the same reasons, it would seem that this extension to the law of contempt, while an interference with freedom of expression under ECHR Article 10(1), would be justifiable as being prescribed by law and necessary in a democratic society for the maintenance of the authority of the judiciary and the protection of the rights of litigants, under Article 10(2).

Reform by statute would be welcome. The Phillimore Committee on Contempt of Court and the Law Commission both recommended that this head of contempt should be replaced by statutory offences to penalize only those interferences which take the form of violence, threats of violence, blackmail, or bribery.[89] This would make it clearer what type of tactical behaviour is impermissible in relation to an opponent in litigation. In doing so, it would remove a certain amount of uncertainty as to the types of behaviour which constitute contempt, and relieve the danger that people might be liable for behaving towards each other in ways which would normally be lawful but which become unlawful because of the circumstance that one of them is a party in active litigation. However, as yet, no action has been taken on the Law Commission's recommendations.

(5) CONTEMPT BY PREJUDGMENT

One of the major considerations in this area is that people who are parties to litigation of any sort should be entitled both to have the matters in issue decided by the court, and to have the decision of the court accepted as final. Any action which prevents people from having their day in court, or interferes with the fairness of the proceedings by way of pre-trial publicity, or creates widespread public prejudice against a party, may be a contempt of court, and it is important for journalists, broadcasters, and publishers to moderate their reporting to take account of this. The law of contempt thus tempers press freedom to a significant degree.

---

[89] *Report on Contempt of Court*; Law Commission, *Interference with the Course of Justice.*

At common law, a comment which prejudged the result of a trial or hearing, or which created a real risk that the course or result of civil or criminal proceedings would be impeded or prejudiced, was a strict liability form of contempt. It was not necessary to show that the contemnor intended to prejudice the proceedings, nor was it necessary for the comment to be widely disseminated (although, as a matter of fact, it was usually the media which were prosecuted for this offence). The sensitivity of the courts to any attempt to prejudge matters was shown by *Attorney-General v. Times Newspapers Ltd.*[90] In that case, people who had been born suffering from physical deformities, allegedly as a result of their mothers having consumed a drug, Thalidomide, for morning sickness during pregnancy, sued the manufacturers, Distillers, for compensation. The preparation for the litigation dragged on over many years, and, in an apparent attempt to build up public pressure on Distillers to settle, the *Sunday Times* ran an article which examined the evidence and effectively concluded that the drug had caused the deformities and that Distillers had been negligent in marketing it. This was held by the House of Lords to amount to contempt by prejudging the issues with which the trial court would have had to deal. There was no real likelihood of the judges being biased as a result of reading the article, but the prejudgment rule was designed to uphold the authority of the court and prevent trial by media, irrespective of any actual bias.

In *Attorney-General v. Times Newspapers Ltd.*[91] opinions in the House of Lords differed as to whether it was a contempt for a person to hold a litigant up to public obloquy or to exert pressure on a party to litigation to settle or not to insist on enforcing his or her full legal rights. They discussed, *obiter*, an article in the *Sunday Times*, which was not the subject of proceedings, in which Distillers, the defendant company, had been criticized for the way in which it was contesting the litigation, and which implied that this was a case in which the company should refrain from insisting on its strict legal rights. Two members of the House (Lords Diplock and Simon of Glaisdale) thought that a person who put a party under any pressure, or held it up to public obloquy, to dissuade it from exercising its constitutional right to have allegations against it decided by a judge, was guilty of contempt.[92] However, Lord Reid took the view that it was perfectly proper for people to use their economic power for moral purposes:[93]

'Why would it be contrary to public policy to seek by fair comment to dissuade Shylock from proceeding with his action? Surely it could not be wrong for the officious bystander to draw his attention to the risk that, if he goes on, decent people will cease to trade with him. Or suppose that his best customer ceased to trade with him when he heard of his lawsuit.

[90] [1974] AC 273, [1973] 3 All ER 54, HL.

[91] Ibid.

[92] The view that litigation concerns only the parties, and other people should not be permitted to exert their economic or other power in an attempt to support one party, has a long history. It dates back to attempts between the thirteenth and the sixteenth centuries to control the mischief of maintenance, which threatened to undermine the enforcement of the common law. King Henry VII gave his new court, the Court of Star Chamber, jurisdiction over maintenance cases in 1487 (3 H. VII, c. 1), and is usually credited with eradicating maintenance through the Statute of Liveries 1504 (19 H. VII, c. 14), although Henry VIII again found it necessary to prohibit the practice in an Act of 1540 (32 H. VIII, c. 9, s. 3).

[93] [1974] AC 273 at 295–6, [1973] 3 All ER 54 at 61.

That could not be contempt of court. Would it become contempt if, when asked by Shylock why he was sending no more business his way, he told him the reason? Nothing would be more likely to influence Shylock to discontinue his action. It might become widely known that such pressure was being brought to bear. Would that make any difference? And though widely known must the local press keep silent about it?'

This series of rhetorical questions highlights the difficulty of finding a principle which prohibits illegitimate use of economic or moral power for personal gain, while excluding from liability those activities which would normally be regarded as permissible if not morally laudable. Lord Reid had taken the view that fair and temperate criticism of a party was permissible, although unfair or intemperate criticism would be a contempt.[94] On this basis, Lords Reid and Cross of Chelsea decided that the article which consisted of a fair and balanced account of the evidence would not have been a contempt.[95] On the other hand, for Lords Diplock and Simon, fair and temperate criticism of a party might have the effect of holding it up to public obloquy, and so constitute a strict-liability contempt.

The prejudgment test was heavily criticized by the Phillimore Committee on Contempt of Court, on the ground that, while it is desirable to prevent trial by media, judicious comment and expressions of opinion are not in a watertight category and shade into prejudgment, especially when the person expressing the opinion is regarded by readers as authoritative or the views (however tentative) are expressed persuasively. The line drawn by the majority of the House of Lords, between balanced comment which is permissible and prejudgment which is not, was therefore hard to draw, and was an unsatisfactory basis for an offence of strict liability which imposed a substantial limitation on freedom of expression and freedom of the press.[96] The matter was the subject of an application to the European Commission of Human Rights, and eventually came before the European Court of Human Rights.[97] The Court held that the law of contempt represented a restriction on freedom of expression guaranteed under Article 10(1) of the European Convention on Human Rights. The Court went on to consider whether the restriction could be justified under Article 10(2). It decided that the restriction was imposed for a legitimate purpose and was 'prescribed by law', because the prejudgment rule applied by the House of Lords had been known about beforehand. While its precise scope had not been entirely clear, any rule of law has a 'penumbra of doubt' surrounding its 'core of certainty',[98] and the prejudgment rule was not unreasonably uncertain for a common-law rule. Nevertheless, the Court decided by a narrow majority (eleven judges to nine) that the restriction was not justified under Article 10(2), because it went further than was 'necessary in a democratic society . . . for maintaining the authority and impartiality of the

---

[94] [1974] AC at 297–8.

[95] See [1974] AC at 326 *per* Lord Cross.

[96] *Report on Contempt of Court*, para. 111. The Committee proposed that strict liability should be imposed only where a publication creates a risk that the course of justice would be seriously impeded or prejudiced. This formed the basis of section 2(2) of the Contempt of Court Act 1981, with the additional requirement that the risk should be 'substantial'.

[97] *Sunday Times* case, Eur. Ct. of HR, Series A, vol. 30, Judgment of 26 April 1979; (1979) 2 EHRR 245.

[98] H. L. A. Hart, *The Concept of Law* (Oxford: Clarendon Press, 1961), 119.

judiciary'. Although a state has to be allowed some discretion in deciding what is necessary for a given purpose in its form of democratic society, this so-called 'margin of appreciation' is not unlimited. A rule which protects the authority of the judiciary is justifiable, as long as it protects the right to a fair trial (in general, rather than in any particular case). The Court later held in *Worm v. Austria*[99] that a rule criminalizing a published prejudgment of the result of a criminal trial is permissible where the article was expressed in unbalanced terms and there was a probability that the publication would influence the judges, particularly lay judges, and jeopardize the impartiality of the court. Where there is no probability that the court will be prejudiced by the prejudgment, as in the *Sunday Times* case, the prejudgment rule is a disproportionate interference with freedom of expression, because the House of Lords held that it prohibited publication of an article which, on the facts, was expressed in moderate terms, gave a balanced account of the evidence and arguments, and was on a matter of undisputed public concern. The principle of freedom of expression is subject to exceptions, but these rest, on the whole, on public interests rather than matters of principle, and must be interpreted narrowly. Such an interference could not, in the Court's view, be seen as necessary in a democratic society.

(6) STRICT LIABILITY FOR CONTEMPT: THE CONTEMPT OF COURT ACT 1981

The decision of the European Court of Human Rights in the *Sunday Times* case was one of the important spurs to legislative reform. The Contempt of Court Act 1981 limited the applicability of strict liability for contempt of court to 'publications'[100] addressed to the public or a section of the public.[101] These publications are contempts for the purposes of the strict-liability rule only if proceedings are active at the time of publication,[102] and the publication creates a substantial risk that the course of justice in the proceedings in question will be seriously impeded or prejudiced.[103]

[99] Eur. Ct. HR, App. No. 22714/93, Judgment of 29 August 1997, 25 EHRR 454, at paras. 44–50.

[100] '... for this purpose "publication" includes any speech, writing, broadcast, [cable programme] or other communication in whatever form, which is addressed to the public at large or any section of the public'. Contempt of Court Act 1981, s.2(1); words in brackets added by Cable and Broadcasting Act 1984, Sch. 5, para. 39(1). Although the word 'includes' makes it possible that this is not an exhaustive definition of 'publication', the context makes it reasonably clear that it is intended to mark the outer limits of the meaning of the term, and is comprehensive and exhaustive: *Secretary of State for Defence v. Guardian Newspapers Ltd.* [1985] AC 339 at 348, [1984] 3 All ER 601 at 606, HL, *per* Lord Diplock. The intention is, as the Phillimore Committee recommended (*Report*, para. 77), to ensure so far as possible that the strict liability offence is limited to those in the business of publishing, with appropriate safeguards, and that other people are liable in contempt for what they say and do only if their conduct is deliberately prejudicial or obstructive: see Miller, *Contempt of Court*, 3rd edn., 212.

[101] The possibility of contempt by publication to a section of the public was a dilution of the Phillimore Committee's recommendation, but seems justified in the light of the risk of prejudice by press conference. It would, for example, very properly have made possible contempt proceedings for what Miller, *Contempt of Court*, 3rd edn., 267, calls 'the extraordinary behaviour of the police in calling a congratulatory news conference' after the arrest of Peter Sutcliffe, the 'Yorkshire Ripper', in 1981. No action was taken, but both the officers concerned and virtually the whole newspaper industry could have been liable for the intense prejudice caused to Sutcliffe's chance of a fair trial. See the Press Council report on the affair, *Conduct in the Sutcliffe Case* (London: Press Council, 1983).

[102] Contempt of Court Act 1981, s.2(3).

[103] Ibid., s.2(2).

(7) WHEN ARE PROCEEDINGS ACTIVE?

The times when proceedings are 'active' are defined in Schedule 1 to the Act. First-instance criminal proceedings are active from the earliest moment when an initial step is taken.[104] The initial steps are: arrest without warrant; the issue (grant in Scotland) of a warrant for arrest; the issue of a summons to appear, or, in Scotland, the grant of a warrant to cite; the service of an indictment or other document specifying the charge; and an oral charge (except in Scotland).[105] The proceedings remain active until criminal proceedings are concluded by: acquittal or sentence; any other verdict, finding, order, or decision (such as a finding of no case to answer, or a decision that the prosecution amounts to an abuse of process) which puts an end to them; discontinuance by the prosecution;[106] or operation of law, as where twelve months elapse after the issue of an arrest warrant without an arrest being made,[107] or a time limit for prosecution expires.[108] One implication of this is that public discussion of a person's involvement in high-profile suspected wrongdoing may be curtailed where anyone is arrested for an offence in connection with the matter, even if the arrestee is subsequently released on bail and no criminal proceedings are ever brought.

First-instance civil proceedings become active from the time when arrangements for the hearing are made (in England and Wales, when the case is set down for trial if provision is made for this under Rules of the Supreme Court, or, in other cases, when the date for the trial or hearing is fixed), or (where no previous arrangements have been made) when the hearing begins.[109] They remain active until they are disposed of, discontinued, or withdrawn.[110] Appellate proceedings (which include applications for judicial review)[111] are active (where leave is required) from the time of the application for leave to appeal or apply for review. Where no leave is required, they are active from the moment when notice of appeal or of an application for review is given, or when the originating process is commenced (for example, an originating summons or writ). The proceedings remain active until they are disposed of, abandoned, discontinued, or withdrawn.[112] Where, in criminal proceedings, an appeal results in the case being remitted to the court below, or in a new trial or *venire de novo* being ordered, the further proceedings are treated as active from the moment the appellate proceedings conclude.[113]

[104] Ibid., s. 2(4) and Sch. 1, para. 3.
[105] Ibid., Sch. 1, para. 4.
[106] This may be effected by withdrawal of the charge or by entering a *nolle prosequi*; by discontinuance under the Prosecution of Offences Act 1985, s. 23; by express abandonment or being deserted *simpliciter* (in Scotland); or (in England, Wales, and Northern Ireland) where proceedings are commenced by arrest without warrant, by releasing the person, without charge, otherwise than on bail. See Contempt of Court Act 1981, Sch. 1, para. 7, as amended by Prosecution of Offences Act 1985, Sch. 1, para. 4.
[107] Contempt of Court Act 1981, Sch. 1, para. 11.
[108] Ibid., Sch. 1, para. 5.
[109] Ibid., Sch. 1, paras. 12, 13. For Scotland, see para. 14.
[110] Ibid., Sch. 1, para. 12, which also provides that each interlocutory hearing and (in the county court) pre-trial review is to be treated as a separate proceeding for this purpose.
[111] Ibid., Sch. 1, para. 2.
[112] Ibid., Sch. 1, para. 15.
[113] Ibid., Sch. 1, para. 16. The same applies in Scotland where the appellate court grants authority to bring a new prosecution: ibid.

(8) WHEN IS THERE A SUBSTANTIAL RISK THAT THE PROCEEDINGS IN QUESTION
WILL BE SERIOUSLY IMPEDED OR PREJUDICED?

The scope of the strict liability offence under section 2 of the Contempt of Court Act
1981 is not self-evident. The terms in which the section is couched are vague, and may
be interpreted either expansively or narrowly. The most authoritative guidance was
provided when the section was considered by the House of Lords in *Attorney-General
v. English*.[114] The defendants were the editor and owners of the *Daily Mail*, which had
published an article by Mr. Malcolm Muggeridge endorsing the position of a handicapped, pro-life parliamentary candidate who opposed action (or inaction) by doctors and nurses to allow certain handicapped babies to die if they judged that the
babies' lives would be intolerable in the event of survival. In the course of the article,
Mr. Muggeridge had asserted that it would be very unlikely that a baby without arms
(such as the candidate had been) would have been allowed to survive today: 'Someone
would surely have recommended letting her die of starvation, or otherwise disposing
of her'. Unfortunately for all concerned, the article was published during the trial of
Dr. Leonard Arthur, a consultant paediatrician, for the alleged murder of a Down's
syndrome baby under just such circumstances.[115] The trial was attracting wide publicity, and the article was widely discussed. Although the article did not refer to Dr.
Arthur or the trial, the Attorney-General took the view that it might have prejudiced
Dr. Arthur's chance of a fair trial. When the trial was over (Dr. Arthur was acquitted),
the Attorney-General brought contempt proceedings against the newspaper's editor
and owners. It was accepted that they had not intended to prejudice the trial, but
counsel for the Attorney-General relied on the strict liability rule under section 2 of
the 1981 Act.

The Divisional Court held that the publication had been a contempt, and the
defendants appealed to the House of Lords. Lord Diplock, with whom the other Law
Lords concurred, agreed with the Divisional Court that the article fell within the
terms of section 2(2), although he went on to hold that the publication was protected
under section 5 (see below). The fact that Dr. Arthur had subsequently been acquitted
was irrelevant, because the risk is to be assessed at the time when the publication
occurred, in order to deter any prejudicial publication, rather than with the benefit
of hindsight. Nevertheless, the approach taken by Lord Diplock to the meaning of
section 2(2) suggested that it would not have a particularly liberalizing effect on the
law of contempt. Lord Diplock held that the adjective 'substantial', when applied
(somewhat inappropriately) to the noun 'risk', serves only to exclude remote risks. It
does not provide any more demanding measure of the seriousness of the risk
involved.[116] Lord Diplock declined to paraphrase serious impediment or prejudice to
the course of justice in the proceedings, for the purpose of interpreting section 2(2).
The word 'serious', he pointed out, refers to the impediment or prejudice, not to the
degree of risk. One has to look at the possible consequences of the publication. If it

---

[114] [1983] 1 AC 116, [1982] 2 All ER 903, HL.
[115] For discussion, see I. Kennedy, *Treat Me Right: Essays in Medical Law and Ethics* (Oxford: Clarendon
Press, 1991), 154–74; above, Ch. 4.
[116] [1983] 1 AC at 142, [1982] 2 All ER at 918–19.

might lead to the outcome of the trial being influenced, or to the jury being discharged,[117] it would be a serious impediment or prejudice.

On this view, the widely quoted statement by the (then) Secretary of State for Northern Ireland, during the trial of three alleged terrorist plotters (the 'Winchester Three') who had exercised the right to remain silent under questioning, that the right to silence was to be restricted in Northern Ireland because only those with no innocent explanation need to make use of the right, might have amounted to a strict-liability contempt under section 2. The three were convicted, but their convictions were later quashed on appeal because of the possible influence of the statement on the jury.[118] However, as the Secretary of State was speaking in the course of his duties, proposing a change in the law in Northern Ireland, the prosecution would probably have failed to discharge the burden imposed by section 5 of the Act of showing that the publication was not a discussion in good faith of public affairs or other matters of public interest, or that the risk of impediment or prejudice to the proceedings was more than merely incidental to such a discussion (see pages 986–7 below).

However, in the light of subsequent decisions it would be wrong to dismiss the 'substantial risk' and 'serious impediment or prejudice' requirements as insignificant hurdles for the prosecution under section 2(2). The courts have given increasing weight to the right and duty of the press to report matters of public interest at common law, under ECHR Article 10, and (now) under the Human Rights Act 1998. When assessing whether a publication created a substantial risk of serious prejudice, the court is prepared to credit jurors with reasonable independence of mind and judgment, and with the will and ability to follow a judge's proper direction at the end of a trial which, by its nature, focuses the jurors' attention on the evidence presented in court rather than on extraneous publications. A report in a local or regional newspaper or news bulletin will be unlikely to cause serious prejudice if a trial is taking place in a different region, while a report in a national news bulletin or national newspaper would be more likely to cause such prejudice.[119] As Lord Donaldson MR has said:[120]

' . . . "substantial" as a qualification of "risk" does not have the meaning of "weighty," but rather means "not insubstantial" or "not minimal." The "risk" part of the test will usually be of importance in the context of the width of the publication. To declare in a speech at a public meeting in Cornwall that a man about to be tried in Durham is guilty of the offence charged and has many previous convictions for the same offence may well carry no substantial risk of affecting his trial, but, if it occurred, the prejudice would be most serious. By contrast, a nationwide television broadcast at peak viewing time of some far more innocuous statement would certainly involve a substantial risk of having some effect on a trial anywhere in the country and the sole effective question would arise under the "seriousness" limb of the test.'

---

[117] It does not matter that the trial actually continued. The question is whether there was a substantial risk of it being retarded, slowed down, delayed, or hindered: *A.-G. v. BBC, Independent*, 3 January 1992, DC.

[118] *R. v. McCann* (1990) 92 Cr. App. R. 239, CA.

[119] *A.-G. v. Independent Television News Ltd. and others* [1995] 2 All ER 370, DC.

[120] *A.-G. v. News Group Newspapers Ltd.* [1987] QB 1 at 15, [1986] 2 All ER 833 at 841, CA.

Neither the inaccuracy of a statement in a newspaper, nor the fact that it might be a libel on a party to proceedings, will necessarily give rise to a substantial risk of serious prejudice if one believes that jurors, magistrates, or judges have the sophistication to recognize that much of what is printed in newspapers is unreliable.[121] Furthermore, where publications have appeared some time before the trial, the court has regard to the evanescent quality of most news reports, which are relatively quickly forgotten (particularly as to the detail) by most people. A long lapse of time between the report and the trial will make it less likely that potential jurors will recall the report so as to create a serious risk of prejudice to the administration of justice at trial.[122] This makes it clear the provisions of section 2(2) limit the scope of the old, common-law, strict liability rule as expounded in the *Times Newspapers* case in a more than cosmetic way: the media should not take it on themselves to assess the strength of evidence against a defendant,[123] but the fact that a publication prejudges or prejudices the merits of a case will not of itself make the publisher liable, unless either the publication gives rise to a substantial risk of serious prejudice or impediment to the course of justice in the proceedings (the statutory strict liability offence), or the publisher was deliberately interfering with the course of justice, for example by threatening witnesses or a party (the common-law offence, demanding *mens rea*). If the publications create no new prejudice, over and above that which already existed, it may be difficult to convict.[124]

Not only must the risk be substantial; that risk must also relate to serious impediment or prejudice in order to discharge the burden of establishing liability under section 2(2). This is a question of fact. 'Proximity in time between the publication and the proceedings would probably have a greater bearing on the risk limb than on the seriousness limb, but could go to both'.[125] The test of serious impediment or prejudice overlaps with the circumstances in which a court will stay proceedings, temporarily or permanently, because a publication before or during the trial has caused prejudice to

---

[121] *A.-G. v. Times Newspapers Ltd. and others, The Times,* 12 February 1983, DC. For a similar view before the 1981 Act, see *R. v. Kray* (1969) 53 Cr. App. R. 412 at 414 *per* Lawton J. However, in *A.-G. v. BBC, Independent,* 3 January 1992, DC, the fact that a news report concerning a trial was 'literally strewn with error' seems to have disposed the court towards holding it to be a contempt, although technically the accuracy or otherwise of the report is irrelevant to s. 2, being relevant only to the defence under s. 4(1) once it has been decided that the publication is caught by the strict-liability rule under s. 2. Are judges' expectations of the BBC so high that they are disappointed when its reporters prove to have feet of clay? Probably not.

[122] *A.-G. v. News Group Newspapers Ltd.* [1987] QB 1, [1986] 2 All ER 833, CA (repetition of allegations subject of libel action not within s. 2 of the 1981 Act where there would be a delay of at least ten months between republication and trial); *A.-G. v. Independent Television News Ltd. and others* [1995] 2 All ER 370, DC (man arrested for murder of police officer in Yorkshire; reports revealing that he was an escaped IRA prisoner serving a life sentence for a terrorist murder; trial starting nine months later; single television broadcast, not repeated, unlikely to have caused more than an insubstantial risk of serious prejudice nine months later); *A.-G. v. Unger* [1998] 1 Cr. App. R. 308, CA (newspaper published pictures of defendant in theft case apparently taking money hidden in a refrigerator, describing her as the thief and reporting a confession she allegedly made to a reporter; potential for serious prejudice, but no substantial risk that it would have survived the likely nine-month delay before a jury trial).

[123] *A.-G. v. Unger* [1998] 1 Cr. App. R. 308, CA, at 316 *per* Simon Brown LJ.

[124] *A.-G. v. MGN Ltd. and others* [1997] 1 All ER 456, DC.

[125] *A.-G. v. News Group Newspapers Ltd.* [1987] QB 1 at 15, [1986] 2 All ER 833 at 841, CA, *per* Lord Donaldson MR. See generally Miller, *Contempt of Court,* 3rd edn., 232–5.

one of the parties.[126] A trial judge's decision to discharge a jury and stay proceedings whether temporarily or permanently, because of prejudice created by a publication, is evidence that the publication has given rise to a serious impediment to the administration of justice. As long as the trial judge acted properly in granting the stay, it is arguable that the publisher should always be liable for contempt unless one of the statutory defences in sections 3 and 5 applies. Simon Brown LJ took this view in *Attorney-General v. Birmingham Post and Mail Ltd.*[127] when he said that the degree of prejudice needed under section 2 is less than that needed either to grant a stay or to ground an appeal against conviction. It is sufficient if a publication which brings about a situation in which it is seriously arguable that the trial should be stayed is sufficient.[128] In that case, an article linking the murder for which eight defendants were on trial with the drug wars in Birmingham, and linking the defendants with the gangs involved in those battles, had caused the trial judge to discharge the jury and order a new trial which started ten days later. The article was held to amount to a strict-liability contempt.

Two rather different views emerged in *Attorney-General v. Guardian Newspapers Ltd.*,[129] a case arising out of a newspaper article during the trial of a man accused of stealing body parts from the Royal College of Surgeons for use in his artworks. The article cast aspersions on the defendant, suggesting that his interest was linked to sexual perversion. Although the article was highly prejudicial, only one juror had seen it, and the trial was allowed to proceed. In contempt proceedings, Collins J accepted that a degree prejudice justifying a stay or appeal against conviction, or creating a seriously arguable ground of appeal, would be serious prejudice for the purpose of section 2, but would not have accepted a lower level of prejudice as grounding strict liability for contempt.[130] Sedley LJ went further, suggesting that a publisher ought not to be guilty of strict-liability contempt unless an appeal against a conviction would have succeeded on the ground that the publication caused such prejudice as to make the conviction unsafe.[131] This has the attraction of facilitating consistency of approach between decisions about prejudice in different fora and giving a high level of protection to media freedom under ECHR Article 10. But it might make it difficult to deter the media from publishing or broadcasting prejudicial reports if they are prepared to risk arguing that the reports would not have given rise to successful appeals. This is a particular risk if the Court of Appeal (Criminal Division) concentrates increasingly on the safety of the conviction rather than the procedural propriety of the trial when deciding whether to allow appeals against conviction.[132] It would be wrong to weaken unduly a safeguard for a defendant's right to a fair trial by an impartial tribunal under ECHR Article 6, or to tolerate trial by media.

Can a publication which, without being intended to do so, exerts pressure on

---

[126] Miller, *Contempt of Court*, 3rd edn., 235–9.

[127] [1999] 1 WLR 361 at 369–70, 371, [1998] 4 All ER 49 at 57, 59.

[128] [1999] 1 WLR at 374, [1998] 4 All ER at 62 *per* Thomas J.

[129] [1999] EMLR 904, DC.

[130] Ibid. at 915.

[131] Ibid. at 924–5. In the event, both judges considered that there had been a risk of serious prejudice in that case, but acquitted the newspaper because Sedley LJ thought that the risk had not been substantial.

[132] Miller, *Contempt of Court*, 3rd edn., 239.

parties to proceedings to negotiate a settlement or discontinue the proceedings, be said to impede proceedings seriously so as to give rise to strict liability for contempt?[133] Under the Contempt of Court Act 1981, a comment which is not made to the public or a section of the public will not attract strict liability. If it is made to the public or a section of the public, it will attract strict liability only if there is a substantial risk that the course of justice will be seriously impeded or prejudiced.

(9) THE 'DISCUSSION OF PUBLIC AFFAIRS' AND 'FAIR REPORT OF LEGAL PROCEEDINGS' EXCEPTIONS TO THE STRICT LIABILITY OFFENCE

Section 5 of the Act provides that a discussion in good faith of public affairs or other matters of public interest is not subject to the strict-liability rule if the risk of impediment or prejudice to active legal proceedings is merely incidental to the discussion.[134] This is a significant safeguard for freedom of expression under ECHR Article 10. As noted above, the House of Lords in *Attorney-General v. English* held that the publication of Mr. Malcolm Muggeridge's article on the treatment of handicapped babies fell within section 2(2) of the Act, but exempted the publishers from strict liability because of the effect of section 5. In *English*, it was not disputed that the article had been published in good faith as a contribution to a continuing public debate on a matter of general public interest, namely the morality of mercy killing, and the treatment of hopelessly handicapped neonates in particular. Lord Diplock therefore held that it was for the Attorney-General to show that the risk of prejudice to Dr. Arthur's trial which resulted from publication had not been 'merely incidental' to the discussion. The Divisional Court had treated certain parts of the article as unnecessary to the argument, and as casting imputations on doctors generally. However, as Lord Diplock said, the test is whether the risk of prejudice was merely incidental to the discussion, not whether the article could have been written without the potentially prejudicial parts. He contrasted the article with the articles on Thalidomide which had been in issue in the *Times Newspapers* case. The Thalidomide articles had been directed to the litigation against Distillers, but Mr. Muggeridge's article had made no mention of Dr. Arthur's trial. Some risk of prejudice to the trial was probably incidental to any meaningful discussion of the pro-life candidate's election programme, and the risk which materialized was, on the facts, properly to be regarded as 'merely incidental' to it.[135] Lord Diplock appears to be balancing a fairly wide interpretation of section 2(2) with a relatively stringent standard which the prosecution must discharge under section 5, but there are clear limits to the scope of the section 5 exception. The main one is that an article or programme which sets out to expose the behaviour of a particular person, who is a party to active proceedings, will constitute a strict-liability contempt, as the prejudice will (as in the *Times Newspapers* case concerning Distillers) be the direct result of the main thrust of the article, rather than

---

[133] If it were intended to have that effect, it would be a common-law contempt: *A.-G. v. Hislop* [1991] 1 QB 514, [1991] 1 All ER 911, CA.
[134] Ibid., s.5.
[135] [1983] 1 AC at 143–4, [1982] 2 All ER at 919–20.

an incidental effect of a discussion of some other matter of general public importance.[136]

A similarly liberal interpretation of section 5 is evident in *Attorney-General v. Times Newspapers and others*.[137] This was a series of proceedings for contempt against different newspapers for their reporting of and commenting on the case of Michael Fagan, who was arrested for intruding into the Queen's bedroom in Buckingham Palace. In proceedings against the *Mail on Sunday*, which before Mr. Fagan's trial had published an article by Lady Falkender casting seriously prejudicial slurs on the defendant's character and alleged a homosexual liaison between Mr. Fagan and a member of the Queen's bodyguard, it was held that the article satisfied the test in section 2(2), but was exempted from strict liability by section 5. This was said to be because the article formed part of the discussion of the Queen's safety, a matter of legitimate public concern. This sensitivity towards freedom of public discussion on matters of public interest contrasts markedly with the attitude of the courts in certain other cases (notably the *Spycatcher* cases, considered in Chapter 15). This might give rise to a suspicion that the press are freer to 'discuss' parties to litigation who do not enjoy the sympathy of the courts than they are to 'discuss' the affairs of those parties who are regarded as more 'respectable' (for want of a better adjective). On the other hand, where a judge made an order postponing reporting of a case under section 4(2) of the Contempt of Court Act 1981 (see below), and a journalist wrote an article mentioning the case in the course of complaining about the frequency with which judges made such orders, the Divisional Court held that the article was protected by section 5, as any risk of prejudice was incidental to fair comment.[138]

The Act provides a further exception in section 4, which exempts from strict liability all fair and accurate reports, in good faith, of legal proceedings held in public, although the court in question may in certain circumstances order that publication be postponed, or that certain details exempt from disclosure in court be not published.[139] The section 4 exception mirrors one which was previously available at common law.

(10) IGNORANCE AS A DEFENCE UNDER THE 1981 ACT

In addition to the above elements which the prosecution must establish in order to bring home strict liability on a publisher, the Act provides for one defence in regard to which the burden of proof lies on the defendant. The publisher or distributor is not strictly liable if, having taken all reasonable care, he does not know and has no reason to suspect that proceedings are active, or that the publication contains the sort of material which might give rise to strict liability under section 2.[140]

---

[136] *A.-G. v. TVS Television Ltd.*, *The Times*, 7 July 1989, DC.

[137] *The Times*, 12 February 1983, DC.

[138] *A.-G. v. Guardian Newspapers Ltd. (No. 3)* [1992] 1 WLR 874, [1992] 3 All ER 38, DC. The risk of prejudice was in any case not thought to be a real or practical prospect.

[139] Contempt of Court Act 1981, ss. 4, 11. See below, pp. 1001–4.

[140] Contempt of Court Act 1981, s. 3.

17.2 ORDERS RESTRICTING OR POSTPONING REPORTING

Generally speaking, in the light of the public interest in open justice,[141] trials are open and anyone may observe them and report on them. Magistrates, judges, and jurors, sitting in public, are not entitled to adopt a practice of keeping their names secret for the purposes of preserving their privacy.[142] They perform a public function, and it is a valuable check on their behaviour that their identities should be known. However, there are limits to the principle of openness where justice cannot be done effectively in public.[143] This leads to a number of restrictions on freedom to report court proceedings, which include:

(a) restrictions on reporting certain cases heard in private;

(b) orders postponing the reporting of matter which might prejudice the fairness of proceedings;

(c) restrictions on reporting names in cases involving children, rape trials, and blackmail cases;

(d) restrictions on reporting material disclosed on discovery.

Breaches of these orders or rules constitute criminal contempt of court and are punishable as such. In this section, the various heads will be examined in turn.

(1) HEARINGS IN PRIVATE

As part of their inherent power to regulate their own proceedings to ensure that justice can be done, all courts have a discretion to sit in private, but the normal principle is that the power should be exercised only in exceptional cases where justice could not be done while sitting in public.[144]

An application for a hearing to be held in camera must be supported by convincing evidence which shows why it is necessary to exclude the public to protect national security or witnesses or other people from a real risk of harm. This applies whether the application is made by a prosecutor, a defendant, or a party to civil litigation.[144a] Even when hearings are conducted in chambers there is a presumption that public access should be allowed, because of the importance of public hearings in deterring abuse of power and improper behaviour.[144b] There are often good reasons for conducting hearings relating to child-care in private, and even to make orders restraining

---

[141] *Scott v. Scott* [1913] AC 417, HL.

[142] *R. v. Felixstowe Justices, ex parte Leigh* [1987] QB 582, [1987] 1 All ER 551, DC.

[143] *Scott v. Scott* [1913] AC 417, HL.

[144] *Scott v. Scott* [1913] AC 417; *R. v. Chancellor of Chichester Consistory Court, ex parte News Group Newspapers Ltd.*, *Independent*, 10 September 1991, DC; *R. v. Dover Justices, ex parte Dover District Council and another*, *Independent*, 21 October 1991, DC. The courts in England and Wales do not take the principle of open justice to the point of admitting television cameras, for fear of sensationalizing trials and putting undue pressure on witnesses, jurors, and parties. See Andrea Biondi, 'TV Cameras Access into the Courtroom: A Comparative Note' (1996) 2 *Yearbook of Media and Entertainment Law* 133–50.

[144a] *Ex parte Guardian Newspapers Ltd.* [1999] 1 WLR 2130, CA.

[144b] *Hodgson v. Imperial Tobacco Ltd.* [1998] 1 WLR 1056, [1998] 2 All ER 673, CA.

parties and witnesses from speaking about the proceedings outside the court, to protect the child against harmful publicity. This does not violate the right to a fair and public hearing under ECHR Article 6, and so far as it interferes with freedom of expression it is justifiable under ECHR Article 10(2). In relation to Article 6, the European Court of Human Rights held in *B. v. United Kingdom* and *P. v. United Kingdom*[144c] that it was permissible to hold proceedings in private for the legitimate purposes listed in Article 6(1), including 'where the interests of juveniles or the protection of the private life of the parties so require, or to the extent strictly necessary in the opinion of the court in special circumstances where publicity would prejudice the interests of justice'. Hearings in chambers encouraged parties and witnesses to express themselves candidly on highly personal issues without fear of public curiosity, thus protecting the best interests of the children. Normally, however, the open-justice principle is supreme.

The general principle applies even in non-judicial proceedings. In *R. (Wagstaff) v. Secretary of State for Health; R. (Associated Newspapers Ltd. and others) v. Secretary of State for Health*[145] it was held that it was unreasonable[146] for a Minister, establishing a statutory inquiry established to inquire into a matter of great public concern, to decide that the inquiry should not sit in public. The inquiry related to the death of a great number of patients of a doctor, Harold Shipman, who had already been convicted of murdering fifteen patients. The decision had to be taken in the light of the right of relations of the patients and of the press to receive and impart information. As the matter raised questions of considerable public interest, it would be proper for an inquiry to sit in private only if that could be shown to be required by a pressing social need. No such need had been established. The same principle applies *a fortiori* to judicial hearings.

There are cases in which the pressing social need for privacy can be established. For example, it would be ridiculous to expect the hearing of an application for an injunction to restrain a breach of confidence to be heard in open court where the effect would be to allow publication of the information which it is the purpose of the proceedings to keep confidential.[147] Nevertheless, restrictions on public access to, and proper reporting of, the administration of justice have to be evaluated in relation to the criteria in ECHR Article 10.

Some statutes expressly provide for matters to be dealt with in private. These include the Official Secrets Act 1920, section 8(4), and certain matters relating to children.[148] However, where there is no mandatory, statutory requirement that proceedings be held in private, the discretion should be sparingly exercised. The effect of

---

[144c] Eur. Ct. HR, Apps. Nos. 36337/97 and 35974/97, Judgment of 24 April 2001; *The Times*, 15 May 2001, by a five-to-two majority.

[145] [2001] 1 WLR 292, DC.

[146] It should have been held to be unlawful in the sense of being *ultra vires*, as under the Human Rights Act 1998, s. 6, violation of ECHR Art. 8 goes to the legality of the exercise of a discretion rather than its rationality.

[147] Law Commission, Report No. 110, *Breach of Confidence*, Cmnd. 8388 (London: HMSO, 1981), para. 4.110.

[148] Adoption Act 1976, s. 64; Magistrates' Courts Act 1980, s. 69(2) as amended by Children Act 1989, s. 97; Family Proceedings Courts (Children Act 1989) Rules 1991, SI 1991, No. 1395, r. 16(7); *In re P.-B. (A Minor) (Child Cases: Hearings in Open Court)* [1997] 1 All ER 58, CA.

excluding the public, including journalists, goes beyond a restriction of the public interest in freedom of information and expression on matters of public interest. It represents a move away from the ideal of justice being administered under public scrutiny. Because of this, it is a course of last resort, and normally more restrained steps should be employed, such as allowing people to observe proceedings but making orders restricting publicity.

Generally, the courts are sensible of the importance of justice being seen to be done, and they will not permit privacy to be imposed merely to save witnesses or defendants the embarrassment of giving evidence as to intimate details of their private lives, if these are a necessary element in the pursuit of justice.[149] However, a good deal of latitude is allowed to judges and magistrates as long as they direct themselves properly on the relevant principles of law. This, combined with the reluctance of reviewing courts to intervene as long as the first-instance judges or magistrates had some material on which to base their decision, sometimes fosters suspicions that the power is used by magistrates who sympathize with defendants, in order to spare them embarrassment, rather than in the interests of justice.[150] It may be hard to distinguish between a desire to avoid embarrassment and the needs of justice. For example, it has been held that a judge is entitled to exclude the press where there is some indication (albeit not very substantial) that witnesses would be so distressed at having to discuss intimate details in public that they would be unable to give full evidence.[151] However, it is not likely that this would survive scrutiny under the 'pressing social need' test in relation to showing that a restriction of freedom of expression is necessary in a democratic society under ECHR Article 10(1), or the parties' right to a public hearing under ECHR Article 6, unless it could be shown to be necessary to exclude the public in order to achieve justice. The question is whether exclusion of the press and public is necessary, not whether it makes life easier.

When cases are heard in private, for reasons of justice, national security, or otherwise, reporting of the proceedings is governed by the Administration of Justice Act 1960, section 12. This provides that publishing information relating to proceedings before a court, judge, or tribunal sitting in private (including a hearing in camera or in chambers) is not, in itself, to be a contempt of court save in specified cases.[152] The cases in which it will be a contempt of court to publish any information about the proceedings are:[153]

(a) where proceedings relate to the wardship or adoption of an infant, or relate wholly or mainly to the guardianship, custody, maintenance or upbringing of, or access to, an infant;

---

[149] R. v. Chancellor of Chichester Consistory Court, ex parte News Group Newspapers Ltd., Independent, 10 September 1991, DC, per Mann LJ.

[150] See, e.g. R. v. Reigate Justices, ex parte Argus Newspapers Ltd. (1983) 147 JP 385, DC; R. v. Malvern Justice, ex parte Evans [1988] QB 540, [1988] 1 All ER 371, DC.

[151] R. v. Chancellor of Chichester Consistory Court, ex parte News Group Newspapers Ltd., Independent, 10 September 1991, DC.

[152] Administration of Justice Act 1960, s. 12(1), (3). On the meaning of 'court', see P. v. Liverpool Daily Post and Echo Newspapers plc [1991] 2 AC 370, [1991] 1 All ER 622, HL, discussed above.

[153] Administration of Justice Act 1960, s. 12(1).

(b) where proceedings are brought under what is now Part VII of the Mental Health Act 1983, whereby judges deal with matters which previously came within the judges in lunacy acting on behalf of the Crown as *parens patriae*, or under any provision of the Mental Health Act 1983 authorizing an application or reference to be made to a mental health review tribunal or a county court;

(c) where the court sits in private for reasons of national security during that part of the proceedings about which the information is published;

(d) where the information relates to a secret process, discovery, or invention which is in issue in the proceedings;

(e) where the court, acting within its powers, expressly prohibits the publication of all information relating to the proceedings, or of information of the particular description which is published.

The above provisions apply to information relating to the proceedings, and make it *prima facie* a contempt to publish such information in those circumstances,[154] although the section preserves any defences which a person accused of contempt would normally have, so a breach of section 12(1) is not automatically and conclusively a contempt.[155] It has been said, in relation to wardship proceedings, that 'information relating to proceedings' in section 12 covers 'information which the person giving it believes to be protected by the cloak of secrecy provided by the court. "Proceedings" must include such matters as statements of evidence, reports, accounts of interviews and such like, which are prepared for use in court once the wardship proceedings have been properly set on foot'.[156] The existence of the proceedings is therefore not secret. Furthermore, it is permissible to publish the text of the judgment, or a summary of the whole or part of it, unless the court, acting within its powers, expressly prohibits such publication.[157] Thus not all information about proceedings is information 'relating to' them for the purposes of section 12. The test, as expressed rather imprecisely in the *Liverpool Daily Post and Echo* case, is whether the information in question is 'within the mischief which the cloak of privacy in relation to the substance of the proceedings is designed to guard against', or 'information

---

[154] *P. v. Liverpool Daily Post and Echo Newspapers plc* [1991] 2 AC 370 at 416, [1991] 1 All ER 622 at 629, *per* Lord Bridge.

[155] Administration of Justice Act 1960, s. 12(4), as explained in *Re F. (A Minor) (Publication of Information)* [1977] Fam. 58, [1977] 1 All ER 114, CA, at 99, 130–1 respectively *per* Scarman LJ, approved in *P. v. Liverpool Daily Post and Echo Newspapers plc* [1991] 2 AC at 421, [1991] 1 All ER at 633, *per* Lord Bridge. Subs. (4) is not altogether unambiguous, and an alternative interpretation (rejected in the above cases) would be that paragraphs (a)–(e) of subs. (1) provide an exhaustive list of the cases in which publication of information relating to proceedings is capable of being a contempt of court. See Miller, *Contempt of Court*, 2nd edn., 349.

[156] *Re F. (A Minor) (Publication of Information)*, [1977] Fam. at 105, [1977] 1 All ER at 135 *per* Geoffrey Lane LJ.

[157] Administration of Justice Act 1960, s. 12(2). This assumes that there is power in the court to order that the judgment be not reported. The power may exist at common law, but is probably limited to cases in which publishing the judgment would interfere with interests of the sort set out in paras. (a) to (d) of subs (1). Where there is to be publication of the judgment in such cases, the names or other sensitive details may be disguised to protect the anonymity of the vulnerable parties.

about the proceedings which ought to be kept secret'.[158] If the judge thinks that it is appropriate to prevent publication of information which might not be considered by an outsider to be private or to relate to the substance of the proceedings, the way to do it is to make an express prohibition, if the power to do so exists, so bringing the case within section 12(1)(e). Even where there is an embargo on publication of information, it is not necessarily permanent, as information may lose its confidential quality with the passage of time.[159] The implications of each paragraph (a) to (e) will now be considered.

Under paragraph (a), it follows from the above that publishing the fact that wardship proceedings are taking place, or have taken place, in respect of an identified minor, would not be a contempt. Nor is it a contempt to publish the name and address of a ward unless there has been an express order not to publish.[160] In deciding whether to grant an injunction restraining publication in cases going beyond the strict terms of section 12(1)(a), the High Court is exericising an inherent jurisdiction originating in the Crown's role as *parens patriae*. It has to strike a balance between protecting the ward's privacy and the right of free publication. Where there is such a contest between the interests of the child and the freedom of the press, the courts will hesitate to interfere with press freedom to publish. The courts have to weigh up the competing interests. In this balancing exercise, the guarantee of freedom of expression under Article 10 of the European Convention on Human Rights will be given substantial weight, and it follows that the welfare of the child is not the paramount consideration in this type of case, which concerns freedom of publication rather than matters directly related to the care of the child.[161] In *In re Z. (A Minor) (Identification: Restriction on Publication)*[161a] the Court of Appeal rationalized the principles on which judges will decide whether to exercise the High Court's inherent jurisdiction to protect minors from the risk of harm through publication. The power will not be exercised where the child is not already under the court's protective jurisdiction and the publication is only incidentally about the child. On the other hand, the jurisdiction will be exercised where the publication is directed to the child, or some aspect of the welfare or upbringing of the child, and the circumstances are such that the publicity would be inimical to the child's welfare. If an issue relating to upbringing is being determined, the child's welfare is paramount, and where there is likely to be harm to the child from publicity, for example by allowing the child to know about matters better unknown by him or her, publication will be restrained. Where the issue before the court does not relate to upbringing, the welfare of the child must be balanced

---

[158] *P. v. Liverpool Daily Post and Echo Newspapers plc* [1991] 2 AC at 422–3, [1991] 1 All ER at 634, *per* Lord Bridge.

[159] *Re F. (A Minor) (Publication of Information)* [1977] Fam. at 107, [1977] 1 All ER at 137, *per* Geoffrey Lane LJ.

[160] *Re L. (A Minor) (Wardship: Freedom of Publication)* [1988] 1 All ER 418, concerning a newspaper article, with photograph, about a minor, who had been made a ward of court, and the funeral of members of her family who had died in the ferry disaster at Zeebrugge; *Re W. (Wardship: Publication of Information)* [1989] 1 FLR 246, concerning the publication of the names of children affected by the controversy surrounding the diagnosis of children as having suffered sexual abuse in Cleveland.

[161] *Re W. (A Minor) (Wardship: Freedom of Publication)* [1992] 1 All ER 794, CA.

[161a] [1997] Fam. 1, [1995] 4 All ER 961, CA.

against freedom of the press. Courts must now take account of the rights to freedom of expression and respect for private life, respectively under ECHR Articles 10 and 8. Any restriction of either to benefit the other must be justifiable by reference to the conditions set out in Articles 8(2) and 10(2). In practice, the restrictions will almost always be for a legitimate purpose, and the question will come down to an assessment of where the balance between competing social needs, and the proportionality of the impact of a granting or refusing a restriction on each right.

The freedom of the press is likely to prevail where the press is acting in the public interest, for example when it is publishing the results of an investigation into a matter affecting the public, or is informing the public about the way in which a local authority exercises its child-care powers. It will normally be possible to satisfy the public interest in favour of publication without identifying the ward to people other than those who already know the facts; any restriction on publication should be no wider than necessary in order to protect the ward from the risk of harassment.[162] For example, where a child in care was transferred to the custody of his father who was a male-to-female transsexual, it was a matter of public interest which the press were entitled to report; but neither the press nor the father (who had become something of a celebrity campaigner for transsexuals after appearing on a television programme about transsexualism) was entitled to do anything that would reveal the identity of the child, who was likely to suffer harm from publicity. The general issues are matters of public interest, but the identities of those involved are merely matters of public curiosity which could not outweigh the interests of the child.[162a] It may also be desirable to relax restrictions on identifying children in order to harness the assistance of the media in tracking down a child who has run away or been abducted.[162b] If the proposed publication is likely to upset the ward but refers to relatives of the ward rather than the ward herself or wardship proceedings, it is unlikely that an injunction will be granted. People will not normally be spared embarrassment unrelated to their children merely because the children have been made wards of court.[163]

Where the balance requires it, an order may be made which allows some information to be published but requires other information to be suppressed where that is necessary for the ward's welfare. For example, it may be desirable to protect the ward against intrusion, as in *Re C. (A Minor) (Wardship: Medical Treatment) (No. 2)*,[164]

---

[162] *Re M. and N. (Minors) (Wardship: Freedom of Information)* [1990] Fam. 211, [1990] 1 All ER 205, CA; *Re W. (A Minor) (Wardship: Freedom of Publication)* [1992] 1 All ER 794, CA.

[162a] *In re H.-S. (Minors) (Protection of Identity)* [1994] 1 WLR 1141, [1994] 3 All ER 390, CA. See also *In re W. (A Minor) (Wardship: Restrictions on Publication)* [1992] 1 WLR 100, [1992] 1 All ER 794, CA (male teenage ward fostered with male homosexual couple; injunction restraining all publications which might lead to identification of ward discharged to allow identification of local authority concerned; the great public interest involved in the case led the court to decide that the teenager would have to accept the risk of publicity).

[162b] See, *e.g. Kelly v. British Broadcasting Corporation* [2001] Fam. 59, [2001] 2 WLR 253 *per* Munby J.

[163] *Re X. (A Minor) (Wardship: Restriction of Publication)* [1975] Fam. 47, [1975] 1 All ER 697; *In re R. (Wardship: Restriction on Publication)* [1994] Fam. 254, [1994] 3 All ER 658, CA (limits on restriction on reporting of criminal proceedings in which father was charged with abducting ward). *Cp. X County Council v. A.* [1984] 1 WLR 1422, [1985] 1 All ER 53.

[164] [1990] Fam. 39, [1989] 2 All ER 791, CA.

concerning a ward whose medical condition and proposed treatment had been the subject of proceedings which had attracted a good deal of publicity.[165] Because the intrusions of the press could have adversely affected the quality of the care which the ward could be given, and might discourage parents of similarly placed minors from allowing their children to become wards of court, an injunction was granted prohibiting soliciting or publication of information identifying the ward, her parents, the hospital where she was being treated, or anyone concerned in her care, notwithstanding the fact that the ward's condition was such that she would not be personally conscious of any interference with her privacy. In the same way, in *Re M. and N. (Minors) (Wardship: Publication of Information)*[166] the Court of Appeal granted an injunction which, while allowing publication of information about the way in which the local-authority social services department had allegedly acted in taking two children into care, prohibited publication of information which might enable the children in the case to be identified.

But if the court considers that the case raises a matter of genuine public interest, it will not restrain publication. Such a case arose in *Re W. (A Minor) (Wardship: Freedom of Publication)*,[167] where a local authority had placed a ward, who had previously suffered homosexual abuse, with a male homosexual couple as foster parents. The council's policy was said to raise public-interest questions which it would be proper for newspapers to ventilate, so long as care was taken as far as possible to avoid details which might identify the ward in question (and it was accepted that it might not be possible entirely to avoid this). The right to freedom of expression operates even more strongly where a programme deals with a matter of public interest, and any risk that the child will be identified is incidental to the theme of the programme. In *In re Central Independent Television plc*[168] a broadcaster was planning to transmit a programme about an operation conducted by a police Obscene Publications Squad leading to the arrest and conviction of a man for indecency with young boys. The man's former wife objected that showing the father on film might have enabled their young daughter, a ward of court, to be identified. The film was not concerned with her upbringing, and any risk of identification of the child was wholly incidental to the subject of the programme, so the Court of Appeal refused to order the man's face to be obscured in any film in which he appeared. Hoffmann LJ in particular took the view that any interference with freedom of expression had to be strongly justified, and the courts should not create new exceptions going beyond those created by statute. On the other hand, a newspaper's private interest in contesting a libel action will not entitle it to have access to wardship files, where there is no wider public interest to protect.[169]

Where an injunction is granted, it must be done in express terms, which must

---

[165] *Re C. (A Minor) (Wardship: Medical Treatment)* [1990] Fam. 26, [1989] 2 All ER 782, CA, discussed in Ch. 4 above.
[166] [1991] Fam. 211, [1990] 1 All ER 205, CA.
[167] [1992] 1 All ER 794, CA.
[168] [1994] Fam. 192, [1994] 3 All ER 641, CA.
[169] *Re X., Y., and Z. (Minors) (Wardship: Disclosure of Documents)* [1992] 2 All ER 595.

clearly identify the people who are bound by it,[170] the boundaries of the restraint,[171] and must be no wider than necessary in the circumstances to protect the welfare of the child.[172]

Under paragraph (b) it is permissible to publish the fact that the court or tribunal is sitting to hear an application from a named patient, because (according to the House of Lords in *P. v. Liverpool Daily Post and Echo Newspapers plc*)[173] it was the purpose of the legislation to protect the privacy of medical considerations, and the fact that a particular patient had (as in that case) applied to be released is not within the cloak of privacy protected by the Act. It followed in the *Liverpool Daily Post and Echo* case that the newspaper was also permitted to publish the result of the application, although not the tribunal's reasons, which would fall within the protected area of privacy.

Paragraphs (c) and (d) speak for themselves. Under paragraph (e), it remains a contempt to disobey an express *intra vires* order by the court or tribunal prohibiting the publication of all information relating to the proceedings (this term having the meaning explained above) or information of a particular description. The order must be express, and the description of the matters not to be published must be clear, as seen above in relation to paragraph (a).

(2) RESTRICTIONS ON REPORTING INFORMATION CONCERNING HEARINGS HELD IN PUBLIC

There are several restrictions which affect reporting of hearings held in public. Besides the provisions of the Judicial Proceedings (Regulation of Reports) Act 1926,[174] there are provisions which allow people to remain anonymous, and provisions permitting details of cases to be suppressed at certain stages in the litigation. The main ones are as follows.

(i) Sexual offences

From the moment when a person makes an allegation or complaint of a sexual offence,[175] it is an offence to publish or broadcast matter likely to lead to the identification of the complainant during the complainant's lifetime.[176] It is similarly an offence to publish such matter when someone has been accused of such an offence.[177]

---

[170] An order in respect of a ward can be made against the world, but will not bind those who have no notice of it: *X County Council v. A.* [1984] 1 WLR 1422 at 1426, [1985] 1 All ER 53 at 56 *per* Balcombe J; *Re L. (A Minor) (Wardship: Freedom of Publication)* [1988] 1 All ER 418 at 421 *per* Booth J.

[171] *Re L. (A Minor) (Wardship: Freedom of Publication)* [1988] 2 All ER at 423 *per* Booth J.

[172] *Re M. and another (Minors) (Wardship: Freedom of Publication)* [1990] Fam. at 225, [1990] 1 All ER 205 at 211 *per* Butler-Sloss LJ.

[173] [1991] 2 AC 370, [1991] 1 All ER 622, HL.

[174] See Ch. 16 above; Miller, *Contempt of Court*, 3rd edn., 479–81.

[175] The offences covered are listed in Sexual Offences (Amendment) Act 1992, s. 2, as amended by Youth Justice and Criminal Evidence Act 1999, s. 48 and Sch. 2, para. 7.

[176] Sexual Offences (Amendment) Act 1992, s. 1(1), as amended by Youth Justice and Criminal Evidence Act 1999, s. 48 and Sch. 2, para. 7.

[177] Sexual Offences (Amendment) Act 1992, ss. 1(2), 6(3), as amended by Youth Justice and Criminal Evidence Act 1999, s. 48 and Sch. 2, para. 7.

There used to be a power for a judge of the Crown Court to permit such a publication or broadcast in the interests of the administration of justice, for example in order to encourage potential witnesses to come forward, but that provision has been repealed.[178] There might be cases in which this would create difficulties in relation to the right to a fair trial under ECHR Article 6, as well as a danger of violating ECHR Article 10. These risks are reduced by section 3 of the Sexual Offences (Amendment) Act 1992, allowing a trial judge to remove or restrict the prohibition on identifying the complainant if the judge is satisfied that it imposes a substantial and unreasonable restriction on reporting, and that it is in the public interest to remove or relax it.[179]

(ii) Children

There are some automatic restrictions on reporting criminal investigations and proceedings involving to children and young persons. In addition, courts have power to restrict reports of cases which could identify children under certain circumstances.

Whenever a criminal investigation has begun in respect of an alleged offence, the identity of anyone involved in the offence is automatically protected if he is under the age of eighteen. Unless and until there are proceedings in court in respect of the offence, the protection is conferred by section 44(2) of the Youth Justice and Criminal Evidence Act 1999, making it an offence to publish matter likely to lead members of the public to identify the young person as someone involved in the offence. This includes the person's name, address, school or other educational establishment, or place or work, and any picture of him.[180] The protection extends to children and young persons who are the alleged or suspected offenders, and can be extended to victims or witnesses by an order made by statutory instrument by the Secretary of State.[181] A court may dispense with the restriction if satisfied that it is in the interests of justice to do so, after having regard to the welfare of the child or young person concerned.[182] When court proceedings begin, other than in a youth court or on an appeal from a youth court,[183] equivalent protection is provided by section 45 of the Youth Justice and Criminal Evidence Act 1999. The automatic protection extends to defendants and witnesses, but not victims, who are under eighteen.[184] At this stage, however, the judge has a further dispensing power if satisfied that the anonymity rule imposes a substantial and unreasonable restriction on reporting the proceedings and it is in the public interests of justice to remove or relax it. The court must have regard

---

[178] Sexual Offences (Amendment) Act 1976, s. 4, as amended by Criminal Justice Act 1988, s. 158, repealed by Youth Justice and Criminal Evidence Act 1999, s. 48 and Sch. 2, para. 4.

[179] In addition, under s. 5 of the 1992 Act the complainant, if over sixteen, can consent in writing to being identified.

[180] Youth Justice and Criminal Evidence Act 1999, s. 44(6).

[181] Ibid., s. 44(4), (5).

[182] Ibid., s. 44(7), (8).

[183] In relation to such proceedings, protection is provided by Children and Young Persons Act 1933, s. 49: see Youth Justice and Criminal Evidence Act 1999, s. 45(2).

[184] Ibid., s. 45(7).

to the welfare of the child, and must not relax or remove the restriction merely because the proceedings are ended.[185]

Where the case is heard in or on appeal from a youth court, broadly similar, automatic, protection operates, in this case for the benefit of the alleged wrongdoer, witnesses, and victims who are under eighteen, under section 49 of the Children and Young Persons Act 1933, as amended. In this situation, however, the power to dispense with anonymity applies where the judge is satisfied that it will avoid injustice to the child or young person, where he is unlawfully at large after being charged with or convicted of specified offences,[186] or it is in the public interest to dispense with anonymity in relation to a particular offender[187] (sometimes used to identify social troublemakers who have been repeatedly before the courts but have not changed their behaviour).

Under the Children and Young Persons Act 1933, section 39(1) as amended, a court may, in any proceedings, direct that no media report of the proceedings 'shall reveal the name, address, or school, or include any particulars calculated to lead to the identification, of any child' concerned in the proceedings as a party, witness, or subject of the proceedings. The court may also direct that no picture shall be published 'except in so far (if at all) as may be permitted by the direction of the court'. The order must be made in that form. It is not permissible for the court to identify the particulars which would be calculated to lead to the child's identification, apart from the name, address, or school of the child. They must be left to the good sense and caution of the journalists and editors.[188] Journalists therefore have to be aware of the risks involved in publishing details not covered by the order. If, for example, defendants charged with indecently assaulting a child are members of a small, closely knit community, publishing the names of the the defendants might well make the child identifiable. In such a case, the court often gives advice to the media, which is virtually always respected. But even if no advice is offered, Glidewell LJ has said:

'If the inevitable effect of making an order is that it is apparent that some details, including for instance the names of defendants, may not be published because publication would breach the order, that is the practical application of the order: it is not a part of the terms of the order itself.'[189]

Reporters and editors therefore need to exercise considerable care and judgment in deciding what features of a case may be reported when a court has made an order under section 39.

When an order is made under section 39, it is open to a judge to discharge it. Where

---

[185] Ibid., s. 45(4)–(6). On the factors to be taken into account, see *R. v. Central Criminal Court, ex parte W.* [2001] Cr. App. R. 7, CA; and on the position before the 1999 Act, see *R. v. Lee* [1993] 1 WLR 103, [1993] 2 All ER 170, CA; *R. v. Leicester Crown Court, ex parte S. (A Minor) (Note)* [1993] 1 WLR 111, [1992] 2 All ER 659, DC.

[186] Children and Young Persons Act 1933, s. 49(5).

[187] Ibid., s. 49(4A), inserted by Crime (Sentences) Act 1997, s. 45.

[188] *R. v. Crown Court at Southwark, ex parte Godwin* [1992] QB 190, [1991] 3 All ER 818, CA.

[189] Ibid. at 197, 823 respectively.

one judge has made an order and another discharges it, the latter must give reasons for doing so, and the reasons are open to review by the High Court on an application for judicial review. Judges should bear in mind the harm to children which may result, so that a heavy responsibility is borne by a judge who withdraws the protection of an order. In *R. v. Crown Court at Leicester, ex parte S. (A Minor)*[190] the Divisional Court quashed a decision by a judge to revoke a section 39 order in respect of a twelve-year-old boy who had pleaded guilty to arson. On the boy's first appearance before the Crown Court, the judge had made an order that he be not identified. A different judge, passing sentence later, decided to revoke the order because of 'exceptional circumstances', without saying what these circumstances were. This convinced the Divisional Court that the second judge had exercised his discretion without taking account of relevant matters, or that the decision to revoke the order was wholly unreasonable within the meaning of *Associated Provincial Picture Houses Ltd. v. Wednesbury Corporation.*[191] While a judge who relies on exceptional circumstances must be able to explain what they are, there is no statutory requirement for the circumstances to be exceptional before an anonymity order is discharged. The judge must carefully balance the competing interests and act with 'great care, caution and circumspection',[192] but in appropriate cases may lift an order, for example where the child or young person has committed really serious offences, will be detained for a long period and so would not benefit from anonymity during that time, and the interests of the community in knowing about the offences outweigh the interests of the offender.[193]

(iii) Other cases of anonymity for witnesses

At common law, there is a power to order that witnesses should be given anonymity, being identified only by letter (e.g. 'Mr. Y'). This power is exercisable in the wider interests of the civil and criminal process, apart from the need to do justice to the parties in the particular case.[194] Examples of the use of the power include cases where it is necessary to protect victims of alleged blackmail, in order, first, to avoid a situation in which the stories which they had been paying to keep private would become public through the prosecution of the alleged blackmailer, and, secondly, to avoid discouraging other blackmail victims from seeking legal relief. In *R. v. Socialist Worker Printers and Publishers Ltd., ex parte Attorney-General*[195] the *Socialist Worker* newspaper published the names of two alleged blackmail victims who had been giving evidence against Miss Janie Jones, despite an order of the trial judge that the witnesses should be known as Mr. Y and Mr. Z. The editor of the newspaper, Mr. Paul Foot, apparently felt that this was an example of tenderness towards members of the establishment rather than a genuine attempt to further the cause of justice. The publication of the names of the witnesses was held to be a contempt, being both an affront to the

---

190 [1992] 2 All ER 659, DC.
191 [1948] 1 KB 223, [1947] 2 All ER 680, CA.
192 *McKerry v. Teesside and Wear Valley Justices, The Times,* 29 February 2000.
193 *R. v. Lee* [1993] 2 All ER 170, CA; *R. v. Central Criminal Court, ex parte Simpkins* [1999] 1 FLR 480, DC.
194 Miller, *Contempt of Court,* 3rd edn., 486–96.
195 [1975] QB 637, [1975] 1 All ER 142, DC.

court's authority and an act likely to interfere with the course of justice by inhibiting blackmail victims from giving evidence in the future.

Another example of a case where a court might exercise the power to permit witnesses to remain anonymous, particularly in cases which involve sensitive security matters, is where the witness is a member of the security or intelligence services, and for reasons of national security or safety it would be contrary to the public interest to allow the name to be given. If anonymity were not ordered in such cases, the prosecution might well not call the witness. This could easily lead to the withdrawal or collapse of that prosecution, and a reluctance to prosecute in future cases where members of the security or intelligence service would have to give evidence. Similarly, in all cases where a witness is at risk of physical reprisals which might cause death, their right to life is a factor which requires the most anxious scrutiny: if anonymity will reduce the risk, it should normally be granted.[196]

There are limits to this power. It is not to be used merely to avoid embarrassment to a party to proceedings who faces allegations which might damage his professional reputation.[197] Furthermore, the purpose of the order is to protect the administration of justice, not to uphold confidentiality. In *Birmingham Post and Mail Ltd. v. Birmingham City Council*,[198] a stipendiary magistrate had granted an order *ex parte* to the local authority allowing a patient suffering from tuberculosis to be compulsorily removed to hospital.[199] At the same time, the magistrate had made an order to protect the anonymity of the patient. A local newspaper appealed against the anonymity order. The Divisional Court allowed the appeal, holding that the order should have been limited in time. Legal proceedings ceased once the hospital order had become final and unchallengeable, and thereafter no interest of justice remained which the anonymity order could protect. There was no jurisdiction to restrict publications to protect confidentiality unrelated to the interests of justice.

It is fairly clear from the leading House of Lords decision that there must be an order or direction from the judge before publication of the name will be a contempt. A request will not suffice. What is more, even if there has been an order, it will not be a contempt to publish the name if the witness himself, in the course of evidence, gives away his identity or makes it possible to identify him. *Attorney-General v. Leveller Magazine Ltd.*[200] concerned committal proceedings in relation to an alleged breach of the Official Secrets Acts. A witness, 'Colonel B', was granted anonymity for reasons of national security. In the course of his evidence, however, he let the cat out of the bag by mentioning that his promotion had been reported in the *Wire*, the magazine of the Royal Corps of Signals. Two magazines, the *Leveller* and *Peace News*, followed up this lead, identified him from the item in the *Wire*, and published details of his name and

---

[196] *R. v. Lord Saville of Newdigate, ex parte A.* [2000] 1 WLR 1855, [1999] 4 All ER 860, CA (quashing decision of tribunal sitting as the Bloody Sunday Inquiry to deny soldiers anonymity when they gave evidence); B. Hadfield, 'R. v. Lord Saville of Newdigate, ex p. Anonymous Soldiers: What Is the Purpose of a Tribunal of Inquiry?' [1999] *PL* 663–81.

[197] *R. v. Legal Aid Board, ex parte Kaim Todner (A Firm)* [1999] QB 966, [1998] 3 All ER 541, CA.

[198] *Independent*, 25 November 1993, DC.

[199] The hospital order was made under the Public Health (Control of Disease) Act 1984, s. 37.

[200] [1979] AC 440, [1979] 1 All ER 745, HL. For discussion of the implications, especially in terrorism trials in Northern Ireland, see G. Marcus, 'Secret Witnesses' [1990] *PL* 207–23.

career. The House of Lords held that this was not a contempt, since Colonel B had himself given away his identity.

This result does not seem strange at first sight: it would be odd to go to great lengths to protect information which has already passed into the public domain, especially if it was revealed by the person who was intended to benefit from the order, however unfortunate it may be that it should have been disclosed. Nevertheless, on further examination the picture is not quite so clear. Two matters should be considered. First, the damage to prosecution policy in future cases is not alleviated by the fact that the witness himself gave the game away in the present case. Secondly, letting slip a clue to the identity of the witness in court may not cause serious damage to the public interest if people in court do not realize how it may be used to identify the witness, and journalists do not report the connection between the slip and extraneous evidence of identity to people who understand its significance. In a case like *Leveller Magazine*, publishing the results of the researches which were prompted by Colonel B's slip in court could easily have done substantial damage to the public interest beyond anything which the slip in itself caused. This risk would further discourage prosecutors in further cases from calling witnesses such as Colonel B, and injure the interests of justice.

In *Leveller*, therefore, even after the witness let slip the clue to his identity, the continuance of the order might have been in the wider interests of justice. If it is in the interests of justice to make an anonymity order in the first place, the same interests of justice may require that the information should be kept confidential, whatever the witness might accidentally let slip under the pressure of giving evidence. It is strange to allow the long-term interests of justice to be subject to the accidental slip of a witness's tongue.

Viewed from this angle, the result of the *Leveller* case suggests a degree of confusion between two different objectives: the protection of the course of justice, and the protection of privacy and confidentiality. The latter aim is principally a matter for the witness, and it would be understandable to say that it is up to the witness to protect his interests as best he may, or waive his protection. The former aim, by contrast, is a public-interest objective, and the court should be able to restrain publications which could harm that interest, so long as the risk is well established rather than speculative, and the harm would be substantial. Courts must be willing to scrutinize critically claims that anonymity is necessary in the interests of justice.

The confusion between public and private interests contributes to another doubt which survives the *Leveller* decision, concerning the scope of any order. At common law, an order was effective as regards the course of proceedings, but there was doubt in the House of Lords as to whether or not the order could prohibit people, including those not in court to hear the ruling, from using the witness's name outside the court, gagging reporting. Orders as to publication may bind people who are not before the court so long as they know of the order and act with the intention of prejudicing the course of justice in the proceedings in question, as the *Spycatcher* saga demonstrated.[201] However, it is not clear whether an order is similarly binding when made to

---

[201] *A.-G. v. Times Newspapers Ltd.* [1992] 1 AC 191, [1991] 2 All ER 398, HL.

protect interests which go beyond the integrity of the particular proceedings in which the order is made. In the *Leveller* case, the question did not directly arise. Viscount Dilhorne and Lord Edmund-Davies, *obiter*, took the view that there was no common-law power to make an order with such extended effects, and Lord Diplock expressly left the question open.

The matter is to some extent clarified by the Contempt of Court Act 1981, section 11. This does not grant a power to make an anonymity order during proceedings, but provides that, where a power exists to allow 'a name or other matter to be withheld from the public in proceedings before the court', the court is to have power to give directions 'prohibiting the publication of that name or matter in connection with the proceedings'. These directions may be 'such . . . as appear to the court to be necessary' to achieve the purpose for which the name or other matter is being withheld in the proceedings. This does not alter the effect of the *Leveller* case, because, being parasitic on a power to order anonymity in court, the power to give directions regarding publication fails once the name is mentioned in court and anonymity is lost.[202] However, it does make it clear that in certain circumstances, having made an order regulating procedure in the court, the court may make a further order to prohibit or delay publication of the interdicted details, and the latter order will be valid if (and only if) the former was. Section 11 provides that the order must be 'in connection with the proceedings', so it could not extend to prohibiting comment on the behaviour of a person apart from his role as a witness.[203] The circumstances justifying an order prohibiting publication under section 11 must be related to the proceedings. It is not enough that the witness fears that an ex-wife will be able to track him down and molest him if publicity draws attention to his whereabouts.[204]

(iv) Substantial risk of prejudice to the administration of justice

Under the Contempt of Court Act 1981, section 4(2), there is power to order postponement (rather than permanent prohibition) of any report of proceedings or part of proceedings where it appears to the court to be necessary in order to avoid a substantial risk of prejudice to the administration of justice in those proceedings, or in any other pending or imminent proceedings. The court may order postponement of reports for such period as it thinks necessary for that purpose.[205] It is therefore important that the terms of the order should be clear.[206]

This power applies in a wider range of circumstances than would give rise to strict liability for contempt of court: the latter requires that the substantial risk relates to

---

[202] *R. v. Arundel Justices, ex parte Westminster Press Ltd.* [1986] 1 WLR 676, [1985] 2 All ER 390, DC.

[203] See Miller, *Contempt of Court*, 3rd edn., 491. On the form of orders under s. 11, see *Practice Note*, [1982] 1 All ER 1475, and *Practice Direction: Contempt: Reporting Restrictions* [1983] 1 WLR 1475, [1983] 1 All ER 64.

[204] *R. v. Evesham Justices, ex parte McDonagh* [1988] QB 553, [1988] 1 All ER 371, DC.

[205] A similar power existed at common law before the 1981 Act. See, generally, Miller, *Contempt of Court*, 3rd edn., 512–21; I. Cram, 'Section 4(2) Postponement Orders: Media Reports of Court Proceedings under the Contempt of Court Act 1981' (1996) 2 *Yearbook of Media and Entertainment Law* 111–32. For a study of the operation of the powers under ss. 4 and 11, see C. Walker, I. Cram, and D. Brogarth, 'The Reporting of Crown Court Proceedings and the Contempt of Court Act 1981' (1992) 55 *MLR* 647–69.

[206] See *Practice Direction* [1982] 1 WLR 1475, [1983] 1 All ER 64.

serious prejudice to the administration of justice, whereas a substantial risk of *any* prejudice will justify the court in using its power under section 4(2). Because of this, there is a question over the effect of breaching an order. Since the subsection does not provide that breach is automatically to be treated as a contempt of court, it is arguable that it is not a contempt unless (under section 2(2) of the Act) it is shown that either (a) the publication gave rise to a substantial risk of serious prejudice, and was not part of a discussion in good faith of public affairs or other matters of public interest, in which the risk of impediment or prejudice to legal proceedings is merely incidental to the discussion, as required by section 5 of the 1981 Act, or (b) it would have amounted to a common-law contempt because of the contemnor's intention to prejudice proceedings, as in the *Spycatcher* cases. This restrictive view of contempt liability for breaching a court order was accepted by the Court of Appeal in *Attorney-General v. Guardian Newspapers Ltd.*[207]

However, in *R. v. Horsham Justices, ex parte Farquharson*[208] a majority of the Court of Appeal (Shaw and Ackner LJJ, Lord Denning MR dissenting) had previously held that section 4(1) impliedly created a new head of strict liability contempt, as the rule protecting fair and accurate reports, made contemporaneously and in good faith, was made subject to the other provisions of section 4, including section 4(2).[209] Curiously, the decision in *Ex parte Farquharson* appears not to have been cited to the court in *Guardian Newspapers*, so the next court facing the issue will be free to choose between the conflicting decisions of the Court of Appeal, with the possibility of holding that the later decision, reached without reference to the earlier, was *per incuriam*. In principle, the *Guardian Newspapers* decision, and Lord Denning's dissenting judgment in *Ex parte Farquharson*, are preferable. It is unsatisfactory for a journalist (or anyone else) to be convicted of contempt for publishing in breach of an order which is ultra vires the judge who made it. Nevertheless, there is authority (albeit unsatisfactory on civil liberties grounds, and arguably inconsistent with other authorities) for saying that a conviction for contempt may be founded on a refusal to comply with a possibly invalid order, unless and until the order has been quashed on appeal or in judicial review proceedings.[210] This represents a direct assault on the principle of legality, which requires that penalties should not be imposed for an act which was not unlawful according to the law in force at the time when it was committed. It probably cannot stand with decisions of the House of Lords holding that it is open to a defendant in a criminal case to rely by way of defence on the invalidity of the order or by-law.[211] Under the Human Rights Act 1998, imposing a penalty on the basis of an invalid order purporting to postpone publication would engage the right to freedom of expression under ECHR Article 10(1), and would be difficult if not impossible to

---

[207] [1992] 3 All ER 38, CA.

[208] [1982] QB 762, [1982] 2 All ER 269, CA.

[209] See generally Miller, *Contempt of Court*, 2nd edn., 332–8.

[210] *DPP v. Channel Four Television Co.* [1993] 2 All ER 517, DC.

[211] *R. v. Wicks* [1998] AC 98, [1997] 2 All ER 801, HL; *Boddington v. British Transport Police* [1999] 2 AC 143, [1998] 2 All ER 203, HL. In Australia, it has been held that if a court makes an order, or accepts an undertaking, without power to do so, the order or undertaking is of no effect, so disobedience to it is not contempt: *United Telecasters Sydney Ltd. v. Hardy* (1991) 23 NSWLR 323, CA of NSW.

justify under Article 10(2) because the restriction would not have been 'prescribed by law', having no adequate legal foundation under English law. It might also give rise to a claim that imposing a penalty for infringing an invalid order violated the right under ECHR Article 7.[212]

In order to give rise to the requisite risk of substantial prejudice, the nature of the proceedings has to be considered. Judges will be expected to be able to avoid being prejudiced by newspaper reports, so the risk of inducing bias in the tribunal will not justify an order where the proceedings which may be prejudiced are trials before judges alone. Even where juries are likely to be involved, the courts give credit to the ability of jurors to be guided by the evidence given in court, rather than what they read in newspapers.[213] It is also proper to give credit to the reporters for having the sense and awareness to avoid prejudice. For example, in the trial of Ernest Saunders on charges arising out of his conduct during the attempt by Guinness plc to take over Distillers, the issues and charges were so complex that the judge ordered the indictment to be severed, so that the accused would be tried separately on different counts which arose out of interconnected facts. The judge, Henry J, refused to make an order under section 4 in respect of the first trial, trusting that the reporting would be fair and accurate and published with a view to preserving the fairness of the second trial. He also expected the media to put in place suitable internal disciplines to secure the standard of reporting and the fairness of the second trial. The Court of Appeal held that the exercise of the discretion raised no issue of law, no wrong principles having been applied.[214] Everything will depend on the circumstances. Where several defendants are to be tried separately on similar charges, it may be appropriate to prohibit reports of information arising at the first trial which would identify defendants in subsequent trials, in order to avoid prejudicing their trials, while allowing all other aspects of the first trial to be reported.[215] However, in an appropriate case there is power, for example, to postpone reports of evidence given at 'old style' committal proceedings, where evidence is given and cross-examination takes place, because of the risk of prejudice to the trial.[216]

Even if reports would give rise to a substantial risk of prejudice, the court must consider under section 4(2) whether it is necessary to postpone reporting. The question of necessity has tended in practice to be bound up with the court's general discretion to refuse an order even where substantial prejudice is likely. The discretion-necessity assessment has to take account of the public interest in reports of

[212] 'No one shall be held guilty of any criminal offence on account of any act or omission which did not constitute a criminal offence under national or international law at the time when it was committed'. It would be interesting to see how a court would respond were it to be argued that it is open to the state to create a criminal offence of acting in disregard of an unlawful order.

[213] R. v. Kray (1969) 53 Cr. App. R. 412 at 414 per Lawton J; R. v. Horsham Justices, ex parte Farquharson [1982] QB 762 at 794–5, [1982] 2 All ER 269 at 287 per Lord Denning MR; A.-G. v. Times Newspapers, The Times, 12 February 1983 (concerning reports about Michael Fagan, who had effected an entry to the Queen's bedroom).

[214] R. v. Saunders [1990] Crim. LR 597, CA.

[215] Ex parte Daily Telegraph plc [1993] 2 All ER 973, CA; Ex parte The Telegraph Group plc [2001] 1 WLR 1983, CA.

[216] R. v. Horsham Justices, ex parte Farquharson [1982] QB 762, [1982] 2 All ER 269, CA; R. v. Beck, ex parte Daily Telegraph plc [1993] 2 All ER 177, CA.

proceedings. Where a case raises issues of considerable public importance, such as the reasons for a long delay in investigating allegations of child abuse by social workers, the court may well conclude that it is not necessary to postpone reporting, because the public interest in discovering what went wrong outweighs the prejudice that might result.[217] When making this assessment, the court has a discretion to hear submissions from representatives of the media.[218]

(v) Committal and other pre-trial proceedings

Apart from section 4(2) of the Contempt of Court Act, and predating it, the Criminal Justice Act 1967, section 3, later replaced by the Magistrates' Courts Act 1980, section 8, provides that the only details or committal proceedings which may be reported are normally: the identity of the court and the names of the examining justices; names, addresses, and occupations of parties and witnesses; ages of the accused and witnesses; the offences with which the accused is charged, or a summary of them; names of counsel and solicitors; any decision disposing of the case or committing the accused for trial; the charges (if any) on which the accused is committed; where proceedings are adjourned, the date and place to which they are adjourned; arrangements for bail; and whether legal aid was granted.[219]

Normally, therefore, the reports of committal proceedings are sketchy, in order not to prejudice any subsequent jury trial. However, the accused may want to have details widely reported, perhaps feeling that a fuller report would serve to bring the proceedings to the notice of potential witnesses in his behalf, or would counter adverse publicity preceding charge. The section therefore allows an accused to apply to have reporting restrictions lifted. On such an application, the justices must make an order lifting restrictions, unless the accused has one or more co-accused, one of whom objects. Where there is such an objection, the justices must hear representations from the accused, and may order that restrictions be lifted only if they are satisfied that it is in the interests of justice to do so.[220]

In other cases to be tried on indictment, there are restrictions on reporting of preparatory hearings.[221] Most significantly, perhaps, where a pre-trial hearing takes place it is an offence to report any aspect of the proceedings or of any rulings made at it. This is important, because the judge at a pre-trial hearing can make decisions about admissibility of evidence or applications for anonymity for a witness, for example,

---

[217] *R. v. Beck, ex parte Daily Telegraph* [1993] 2 All ER 177, CA (successive trial of same defendants on different charges; postponement refused); *M.G.N. Pension Trustees Ltd. v. Bank of America National Trust and Savings Association* [1995] 2 All ER 355 (civil action relating to Mirror Group pension fund scandal; criminal proceedings pending; judge in civil action refusing postponement of reporting of that action, as mere evidence and allegations unlikely to be particularly prejudicial, and any prejudice outweighed by public interest in issues; possible postponement of publication of reporting of judgment in civil case left open).

[218] *R. v. Clerkenwell Magistrates' Court, ex parte Daily Telegraph plc* [1993] 2 All ER 183, DC.

[219] Magistrates' Courts Act 1980, s. 8(4).

[220] Ibid., s. 8(2), (2A), inserted by the Criminal Justice (Amendment) Act 1981, s. 1(2). See *R. v. Horsham Justices, ex parte Farquharson* [1982] QB 762, [1982] 2 All ER 269, CA and *R. v. Leeds Justices, ex parte Sykes* [1983] 1 WLR 132, [1983] 1 All ER 460, DC, on the burden on an accused seeking to have the objections of a co-accused to reporting overridden.

[221] Criminal Procedure and Investigations Act 1996, ss. 37, 38.

which are binding at trial.[222] The automatic application of the restriction without any need for a balancing of rights and interests might be held to violate rights under ECHR Article 10. A judge may lift the restriction on reporting if satisfied that it is in the interests of justice to do so, although this may cause problems where there are multiple defendants with conflicting interests who may rely on their right under ECHR Article 6 to a fair trial.[223] It will be interesting to see how well the process can be operated within the requirements of the Human Right Act 1998.

The relationship between section 8 of the Magistrates' Courts Act 1980 and the Contempt of Court Act 1981 is slightly complicated. Breach of the prohibition on reporting under the 1980 Act is a statutory offence, attracting a fine.[224] It is not a contempt of court unless there was an intention to prejudice proceedings (common-law contempt) or the case falls within section 2(2) of the 1981 Act (strict liability). Furthermore, it seems that under the 1980 Act the court cannot take account of the interests of parties in other cases; if justices think it appropriate to restrict reporting in order to protect such interests, they must make an order under section 4 (or, in some cases, section 11) of the Contempt of Court Act 1981. The two powers therefore co-exist side by side, dealing with different problems.[225]

(vi) Serious fraud: transfer of proceedings

Similar provision to that contained in section 8 of the Magistrates' Courts Act 1980 is made in respect of the Crown Court in relation to serious fraud offences. The Criminal Justice Act 1987, section 11, makes it an offence to report applications to the Crown Court for dismissal of charges and preparatory hearings where a serious fraud offence has been transferred from a magistrates' court to the Crown Court.

(vii) Restrictions on reporting material disclosed on disclosure

A final discretion to prohibit publication of material read or referred to in open court concerns material handed over during the process of discovery of documents. Such material is made available by each side only for the purposes of the litigation, and is received by the other side subject to an implied undertaking that it will be used only for that litigation. Any other use normally requires the leave of the court. In *Home Office v. Harman*,[226] the House of Lords held that it was a contempt for Miss Harman, a solicitor representing a prisoner in an action against the Home Office,[227] to show to a journalist documents which had been handed over by the Home Office pursuant to an order for discovery.[228] The relevant parts had been read aloud in open court;

---

[222] Ibid., ss. 39–42.

[223] See I. Cram, 'Automatic Reporting Restrictions in Criminal Proceedings and Article 10 of the ECHR' [1998] *EHRL Rev.* 742–53.

[224] Magistrates' Court Act 1980, s. 8(5). Proceedings in England and Wales for this offence may be commenced only by or with the consent of the Attorney-General: ibid., s. 8(6).

[225] *R. v. Horsham Justices, ex parte Farquharson* [1982] QB 762, [1982] 2 All ER 269, CA. See Miller, *Contempt of Court*, 2nd edn., 320–5.

[226] [1983] 1 AC 280, [1982] 1 All ER 532, HL.

[227] Miss Harman then worked for the National Council of Civil Liberties. She later entered Parliament, and was appointed Solicitor General after the general election in May 2001.

[228] See *Williams v. Home Office* [1981] 1 All ER 1151.

nevertheless, it was a breach of the implied undertaking, and so a contempt, to show them to a journalist for the purposes of journalism. Lord Diplock categorized the issue as narrow and technical, and denied that it gave rise to any human rights issues. Lord Scarman, dissenting, and expressing opinions which he shared with Lord Simon of Glaisdale (who had died after hearing argument but before delivering his speech in the appeal), held that the information was in the public domain, and argued that a restriction on publishing such information was a breach of the principles of open justice, press freedom, and ECHR Article 10. The effect of the majority decision was, as one commentator wrote, that litigants faced 'an obligation uncertain in scope and indefinite in duration'.[229]

Miss Harman petitioned the European Commission on Human Rights, which held her application to be admissible.[230] A friendly settlement followed, which involved (*inter alia*) a change to the Rules of the Supreme Court.[231] Rule 31.22(1) of the Civil Procedure Rules (CPR) now provides that a party to whom a document has been disclosed may use it only for the purpose of the proceedings in which it was disclosed, except where:

- the document has been read or referred to at a public hearing;
- the court gives permission; or
- the party who disclosed the document and the owner of the document agree to the different use.

However, the Rule leaves the court a discretion to make an order restricting or prohibiting the use of the disclosed document even when it has been read or referred to at a public hearing.[232] Under the Human Rights Act 1998, section 6, a court acts unlawfully if it fails to act in a manner compatible with ECHR Article 10 when exercising the discretion.

In criminal cases as in civil proceedings, there is an implied undertaking at common law not to use material disclosed to the defence otherwise than for the purpose of the case in which it is disclosed,[233] which applies under statute to disclosures made pursuant to the Criminal Procedure and Investigations Act 1996.[234]

---

[229] I. Eagles, 'Disclosure of Material Obtained on Discovery' (1984) 47 *MLR* 284–302, at 297. For comment on the Court of Appeal judgments, see N. V. Lowe, 'Discovering Contempt' (1982) 1 *CJQ* 10–17.

[230] Application No. 10038/82, *Harman v. United Kingdom*, Eur. Commn. HR, Decision of 11 May 1984, 38 DR 53.

[231] Application No. 10038/82, *Harman v. United Kingdom*, Eur. Commn. HR, Report of 15 May 1986, 46 DR 57.

[232] CPR r. 31.22(2). On the conflicting interests in play, see *SmithKline Beecham Biologicals SA v. Connaught Laboratories Inc.* [1999] 4 All ER 498, CA. Under CPR r. 31.22(3), any party or the owner of the document may apply for such an order. On unauthorized use of material obtained from inspecting the court file, see *Dobson v. Hastings* [1992] Ch. 394, [1992] 2 All ER 94.

[233] *Taylor v. Director of the Serious Fraud Office* [1999] 2 AC 177, [1998] 4 All ER 801, HL.

[234] Criminal Procedure and Investigations Act 1996, ss. 17, 18.

17.3 CONCLUSION

The law of contempt of court can adversely affect rights, particularly rights in respect of free expression, in the interests of the administration of justice, particularly the right of litigants to a fair trial. Care is needed to restrict the contempt law to its proper ambit. Contempt and free expression are not always in opposition to each other. The law of contempt is designed to protect the integrity and fairness of the legal process. Free expression may have the same purpose, and restricting free expression, while perhaps being fair to the parties in individual cases, is liable to weaken the quality of justice as a whole if pressed too far. Like the quality of government, the quality of justice and public confidence in it depend on rigorous public scrutiny and, where necessary, sharply critical commentary, particularly after recent revelations of miscarriages of justice. There is no real justification for the offence of scandalizing the court in the context of a large and developed democratic society where the authority of the judiciary depends on institutional factors rather than matters personal to individual judges. Furthermore, there is a risk that the rules on contempt by prejudicing proceedings may be abused by people who want to silence discussion or revelation which might be in the public interest. There is at least a suspicion that the government was using the law in this way in the *Spycatcher* affair, discussed in Chapter 15 above. Even where no contempt proceedings are brought, the threat that they might be available may put the press and broadcasting media in fear of penalty, and might be a means of bringing pressure to bear illegitimately on editorial judgment.

The prior restraints imposed on publicity in order to maintain the prospects of a fair trial, particularly by way of court orders in criminal cases and those involving juveniles, are generally well policed by the judges. They have the potential to stifle the openness of justice, but that may be considered a necessary price to pay for the protection of other interests. Until the press as a whole is in a position to impose and enforce standards of professional ethics and responsibility, some legal controls will be necessary, and it is important to ensure that neither the legal rules which restrict free expression nor their application should be over-inclusive.

18

PROTEST AND PUBLIC ORDER

The freedom to assemble and protest is important in a democracy, and is valued (whether as an individual right or a collective one) by many people and groups who want to exercise it for their own purposes, which often conflict with those of others.[1] Its value as a form of self-expression lies in its role in developing personality, giving effect to choices as autonomous individuals, and allowing people to participate in the political process (particularly when they lack ready access to other media for communicating with the public).[2] At a communal level, the freedom maximizes the available choice of opinion and policy, thereby improving the chances of finding the best possible policy or most accurate account of the world. At the level of the democratic state, it is important because the public expression of dissent keeps government responsive to public opinion and discourages officials from behaving improperly by making it clear that government is being vigilantly watched and evaluated. But freedom of assembly and protest, like other freedoms, has costs. It must be weighed in each context against citizens' interests in privacy, freedom of movement, and freedom from physical attack or abuse.[3] It is therefore understandable that the structure of rights to protest should be rather different from that of rights of assembly and association and freedom from arbitrary interference with liberty.

In every society there is a tension between the desire of citizens to be free from annoyance and disorder and their wish to be free to bring to the attention of their fellow citizens matters which they consider to be important. The way in which any legal system resolves the tension, and the balance which it strikes between the competing interests, is indicative of the attitude of that society towards the relative value of different sorts of freedom. A society which tolerates a good deal of annoyance or disorder so as to encourage the greatest possible freedom of expression, particularly political expression, is likely to be one in which the public, political activities of citizens are regarded as making a useful contribution to the health of a democratic system. The citizens will enjoy a right, if not an obligation, to participate in political debate, and to try to persuade other people to their point of view. The problem is that this inevitably collides with other people's right to be free of that sort of persuasion,

---

[1] See E. Barendt, 'Freedom of Assembly', in J. Beatson and Y. Cripps (eds.), *Freedom of Expression and Freedom of Information: Essays in Honour of Sir David Williams* (Oxford: Oxford University Press, 2000), 161–76.

[2] D. G. T. Williams, *Keeping the Peace: The Police and Public Order* (London: Hutchinson, 1967), especially at 10, 130–1.

[3] F. Schauer, *Free Speech: A Philosophical Inquiry* (Cambridge: Cambridge University Press, 1982), 203 ff; E. Barendt, *Freedom of Speech* (Oxford: Clarendon Press, 1987), 193–9.

and of its accompanying annoyance and even offence. The job of the lawmakers is to decide when the interests of society in being free of unwanted persuasion or disorder outweigh the interest in free expression of opinions and persuasion.

This may happen in two types of situation: first, where the manner of the expression or the substance of the message infringes some other interest which is so weighty that no restriction of it should be allowed; secondly, where the infringed interest is not that important, but the manner of expression or the substance of the message impinges on it to an extent which is disproportionate to the benefit which would be gained by allowing the expression. An extreme example of the former would be a person killing another in order to publicize a political programme (the classic form of political terrorism); the latter might (according to one's viewpoint) be thought to be exemplified by the use of a large number of people in an industrial dispute picketing premises to prevent others from going to work.

This chapter examines the problem in the context of public order. The first section outlines the basis for rights to protest and looks at some values of fundamental importance in this area of English law. Historically, the field has been dominated by principles which limited rather than protected freedom of assembly: the desirability of maintaining public order and the Queen's peace, respect for rights of property, and respect for the discretion and judgment of the police. Since 2 October 2000, by virtue of the Human Rights Act 1998, these have to be subjected to the rights to freedom of belief, expression, and freedom of peaceful assembly and association under Articles 9, 10, and 11 of the European Court of Human Rights (ECHR), interpreted taking account of the caselaw of the European Commission and Court of Human Rights.[4] There is also a growing sense of the social importance of public space. Nevertheless, because of the historical shape of the law of assembly, much of the chapter is devoted to restrictions on freedom of public expression and assembly, assessed in the light of the Human Rights Act 1998. Section 18.2 examines statutory public order offences. Sections 18.3 and 18.4 are concerned with powers to regulate and control public meetings and processions in the interests of order. The fifth section examines the role of bail conditions and binding over in maintaining order and restricting freedom of expression and protest. Some conclusions are drawn in the final section.

18.1 FUNDAMENTAL RIGHTS AND VALUES IN THE LAW OF ASSEMBLY AND PROTEST

(1) HUMAN RIGHTS: FREEDOM OF EXPRESSION AND PEACEFUL ASSEMBLY

We start from the fundamental freedoms and human rights under the ECHR which form part of English law by virtue of the Human Rights Act 1998, section 1 and

---

[4] For recent analyses, see H. Fenwick, *Civil Rights: New Labour, Freedom and the Human Rights Act* (London: Longman, 2000), 112–70; N. Whitty, T. Murphy, and S. Livingstone, *Civil Liberties Law: The Human Rights Act Era* (London: Butterworths, 2001), ch. 2.

Schedule 1. The reader will by now be very familiar with freedom of expression as guaranteed under ECHR Article 10. In the field of public protest, this is supplemented by ECHR Article 11, which provides:

'1.   Everyone has the right to freedom of peaceful assembly and to freedom of association with others, including the right to form and join trade unions for the protection of his interests.

2.   No restrictions shall be placed on the exercise of these rights other than such as are prescribed by law and are necessary in a democratic society in the interests of national security or public safety, for the prevention of disorder or crime, for the protection of health or morals or for the protection of the rights and freedoms of others. This Article shall not prevent the imposition of lawful restrictions on the exercise of these rights by members of the armed forces, of the police or of the administration of the state.'

Articles 21 and 22 of the International Covenant on Civil and Political Rights (ICCPR) contain provisions to similar effect.[5]

ECHR Article 11 has the potential to influence the future development of public-order law in England and Wales in important ways. Three aspects of Article 11, as it has been interpreted by the European Court of Human Rights, are particularly significant.

First, the right to freedom of peaceful assembly must now be recognized as being of central importance in a functioning democracy, whether exercised in private or in public, and whether the assembly is moving or stationery.[6] Those who wish to restrict or interfere with a peaceful assembly accordingly carry a significant burden of providing legal justification. Instead of a presumption in favour of order, there is now a presumption in favour of freedom of peaceful assembly. As the European Court of Human Rights has said, freedom of peaceful assembly 'is of such importance that it cannot be restricted, even for an *avocat*, so long as the person concerned does not himself commit any reprehensible act on such an occasion'.[7] The justification for an interference must take the form with which we are familiar from ECHR Article 10.

- Any restriction must be 'prescribed by law' as that phrase has been interpreted by the European Court of Human Rights, importing a dual test of lawfulness under national law and legal certainty assessed under the principles of public international law. A restriction may be lawful under English law, yet fail the 'prescribed by law' test if, for example, the criterion for imposing a restriction is insufficiently clear and objective to allow people to be reasonably clear about their obligations. This led the Court to decide in *Hashman and Harrup v. United Kingdom*,[8] that binding over people to be of good behaviour after a protest

---

[5] For an assessment of the law in the UK against the standards of the ICCPR, see T. Murphy, 'Freedom of Assembly', in D. Harris and S. Joseph (eds.), *The International Covenant on Civil and Political Rights and UK Law* (Oxford: Clarendon Press, 1995), 439–64.

[6] *Rassemblement Jurassien and Unité Jurasienne v. Switzerland*, Eur. Commn. HR, App. No. 8191/78, 17 DR 93 (1980); *Christians against Racism and Fascism v. United Kingdom*, Eur. Commn. HR, App. No. 8440/78, 21 DR 138 (1981); *Ezelin v. France*, Eur. Ct. HR, Series A, No. 202, Judgment of 26 April 1991, 14 EHRR 362.

[7] *Ezelin v. France*, Eur. Ct. HR, Series A, No. 202, Judgment of 26 April 1991, 14 EHRR 362, at para. 53.

[8] Eur. Ct. HR, App. No. 25594/94, Judgment of 25 November 1999.

against hunting did not give sufficient guidance as to the behaviour required of them to make the restriction on freedom of expression 'prescribed by law', whereas binding over to keep the peace (as interpreted by English courts)[9] and prohibiting conduct causing 'a breach of the peace likely to cause annoyance' (as interpreted by Austrian courts)[10] embodied standards sufficiently objective and precise to pass the test of being 'prescribed by law'.

- The interference must be shown to pursue one of the legitimate aims listed in ECHR Article 11(2).

- The restriction must be necessary in a democratic society in support of that aim. That is, it must be a proportionate response to a pressing social need. Restrictions which interfere with the right more than necessary to achieve the purpose, or applied without regard to the peacefulness of an assembly and the importance of the right, will be incompatible with Article 11. There was a violation of this Article, together with Article 10, where the police arrested demonstrators and a court sought to bind them over in circumstances where there had been no immediate threat to property, life, or limb.[11]

Secondly, the right under ECHR Article 11(1) is not only a negative one of the 'freedom from interference' kind. It imposes positive obligations on public authorities to take reasonable steps to enable people to exercise the right, providing protection against counter-demonstrators if necessary. As the Court wrote in *Plattform 'Ärzte für das Leben' v. Austria*:[12]

'A demonstration may annoy or give offence to persons opposed to the ideas or claims that it is seeking to promote. The participants must, however, be able to hold the demonstration without having to fear that they will be subjected to physical violence by their opponents; such a fear would be liable to deter associations or other groups from openly expressing their opinions on highly controversial issues affecting the community. In a democracy the right to counter-demonstrate cannot extend to inhibiting the exercise of the right to demonstrate. Genuine, effective freedom of peaceful assembly cannot, therefore, be reduced to a mere duty on the part of the state not to interfere: a purely negative conception would not be compatible with the object and purpose of Article 11. Like Article 8, Article 11 sometimes requires positive measures to be taken, even in the sphere of relations between individuals, if need be . . . '

That case concerned a demonstration by anti-abortion campaigners. The issue was whether the demonstrators had received sufficient protection against pro-abortion counter-demonstrators. On the facts, it was held that the police had taken sufficient action to protect the anti-abortion campaigners:

'While it is the duty of Contracting States to take reasonable and appropriate measures to enable lawful demonstrations to proceed peacefully, they cannot guarantee this absolutely and they have a wide discretion in the choice of the means to be used . . . In this area the

---

9 *Steel and others v. United Kingdom*, Eur. Ct. HR, Judgment of 23 September 1998, RJD 1998-VII.
10 *Chorherr v. Austria*, Eur. Ct. HR, Series A, No. 266-B, Judgment of 25 August 1993, 17 EHRR 358.
11 *Steel and others v. United Kingdom*, Eur. Ct. HR, Judgment of 23 September 1998, RJD 1998-VII.
12 Eur. Ct. HR, Series A, No. 139, Judgment of 21 June 1988, 13 EHRR 204, at para. 38.

obligation they enter into under Article 11 of the Convention is an obligation as to measures to be taken and not as to results to be achieved.'[13]

Thirdly, Article 11 protects people against being victimized by public authorities and professional regulators on account of their participation in public, collective expressions of political views. Where a lawyer was subjected to professional disciplinary proceedings after taking part in a political demonstration, it violated his right to freedom of peaceful assembly.[14] The strictly limited exceptions (which must be narrowly construed[15]) for members of the armed forces, police, and public administrators do not imply any restriction for others.

This requires an important change of spirit in public-order law in England and Wales. In the past, although statutes and judicial decisions have recognized that the expression of views and information is in the public interest, the law tended to operate in terms of powers and duties rather than rights in public-law matters (as already noted in the context of other rights and liberties). Freedom of assembly, when it existed, was incidental to rights developed for other purposes (such as the right to pass and repass on the highway), and was severely limited by the powers and duties of police and others to preserve the peace, enforce the criminal law, and safeguard the interests of non-protesters.[16] It was a very different picture from that in the USA, where the First Amendment to the Constitution often protects verbal and non-verbal forms of political protest from legal prohibition, even if it causes very considerable offence.[17] Thus burning the national flag, the Stars and Stripes, has been held to be protected as symbolic speech. The Supreme Court has held attempts by states and Congress to legislate for the criminalization of flag burning to be unconstitutional. This has outraged conservatives and patriots, and has led to moves to introduce a constitutional amendment which would except flag burning from the protection of the First Amendment. So far, the legislative proposals have failed to achieve the necessary two-thirds majority support in each House of Congress, showing the substantial impact of which constitutional protection for free expression is capable.[18] In this country, even under the Human Rights Act 1998 and ECHR Articles 10 and 11, protection for protest is far less absolute. A balancing of interests will often be required.

[13] Eur. Ct. HR, Series A, No. 139, Judgment of 21 June 1988, 13 EHRR 204, at para. 34.

[14] *Ezelin v. France*, Eur. Ct. HR, Series A, No. 202, Judgment of 26 April 1991, 14 EHRR 362.

[15] *Vogt v. Germany*, Eur. Ct. HR, Series A, No. 323, Judgment of 26 September 1995, 21 EHRR 205; *United Communist Party of Turkey and others v. Turkey*, Eur. Ct. HR, Judgment of 30 January 1998, RJD 1998-I, 26 EHRR 121; A. Mowbray, 'The Role of the European Court of Human Rights in the Promotion of Democracy' [1999] *PL* 703–25 at 710–13. It is noteworthy that under the ICCPR, the limitation of the rights of the police and members of the armed forces applies only in relation to the freedom of association and the right to form and join a trade union (ICCPR Art. 22), not to freedom of peaceful assembly (ICCPR Art. 21).

[16] See D. Feldman, 'Protest and Tolerance: Legal Values and the Control of Public-Order Policing', in R. Cohen-Almagor (ed.), *Liberal Democracy and the Limits of Tolerance: Essays in Honor and Memory of Yitzhak Rabin* (Ann Arbor, Mich.: University of Michigan Press, 2000), 43–69 at 45–7; Murphy, 'Freedom of Assembly', above.

[17] *Stromberg v. California* 283 US 359 (1931), invalidating a California law against displaying red flags; *Thornhill v. Alabama* 310 US 88, (1940), invalidating an anti-picketing law which had been interpreted as preventing a single picket from carrying a placard outside a factory.

[18] *Texas v. Johnson* 109 S. Ct. 2533 (1989); *Eichman v. United States* 110 S. Ct. 2404 (1990); M. Dry, 'Flag Burning and the Constitution' [1990] *Supreme Court Review* 69–103.

In the context of protest (unlike the position in relation to some other freedoms) it would be misleading to assume that the central principle is that people are free to do anything which they have not been lawfully forbidden to do. Protest, like expression, is an activity which makes more demands on others than does freedom from arbitrary arrest or detention. The latter demands only self-restraint from others. Rights to free expression and protest, by contrast, require (if they are to be effectively used) some form of communication with others, and so presuppose that the freedom of other people from annoyance is to be restricted at least so far as necessary to allow the protester to impart the nature of the protest and invite people to join in protest or discussion. It highlights a tension at the core of liberalism between the value of freeing people from interference with their personal autonomy and space, and demanding tolerance from people so all can enjoy a measure of freedom. Classical liberalism would permit people and groups to buy or hire a private hall to ventilate their grievances or policies (if they can afford to do so) but would not allow them to force their opinions on non-consenting adults. The European Court of Human Rights has held that the right to freedom of association under ECHR Article 11 is infringed when people's freedom to choose when and with whom they do not wish to associate is seriously interfered with, either by imposing severe sanctions on them for refusing to associate (as where people lost their jobs for refusal to join a particular union under a closed-shop agreement) or by restricting people's range of choices so that they have no real choice.[19]

But in the context of freedom to protest, this is a weak form of liberalism, because it restricts freedom to that which the least tolerant will tolerate. The question is how far one gives the same weight to a right to be free of annoyance as to freedom of peaceful (i.e. non-violent) assembly to demonstrate in a cause. The right to protest implies a duty to provide opportunities for people to be protested at, but the right to be free from annoyance and unwanted invasions of privacy suggests that the right to protest must be balanced by a negative right to choose whether or not one wants to be the object of protest. These competing rights must be balanced, as Lord Scarman pointed out in his report on the Red Lion Square disorders.[20]

(2) PUBLIC AND PRIVATE PROPERTY AND AVAILABILITY OF FORUMS FOR ASSEMBLY AND PROTEST

Further problems arise over the location of protests. There are few recognized public places for protesting. Most protests occur on public streets, but some happen on private property. Do private-property owners have any duty to allow their property to be used as a forum for protest? In the USA, the public streets have been progressively

---

[19] *Young, James, and Webster v. United Kingdom*, Eur. Ct. HR, Series A, No. 44, Judgment of 13 August 1981, 4 EHRR 38. See Barendt, *Freedom of Speech* (Oxford: Clarendon Press, 1987), ch. 10.

[20] Sir Leslie Scarman, *Report on the Red Lion Square Disorders of 15 June 1974*, Cmnd. 5919 (London: HMSO, 1975). On the ECHR caselaw on public protest and its likely impact on English law, see H. Fenwick and G. Phillipson, 'Public Protest, the Human Rights Act and Judicial Responses to Political Expression' [2000] *PL* 627–50; D. Mead, 'The Human Rights Act: A Panacea for Peaceful Public Protest?' (1998) 3 *J. of Civil Liberties* 206–23.

supplanted by privately owned shopping malls as the main places where the public gather and shop. This has led to a shortage of spaces in which protests can be made so as to reach a large number of members of the public effectively. In such circumstances, there is a natural desire to carry the protest into the private shopping malls, and the right to protest comes into conflict with the private interests of property owners in their property and privacy, which are likely to prevail unless the right to protest on private property is protected by a statute or state Constitution which is compatible with the property owner's rights under the state and Federal Constitutions.[21]

If the right to assemble is to be preserved and protected, steps need to be taken to limit the extent to which the process of privatizing public space, by enclosing it and excluding unwelcome visitors, can remove opportunities for putting one's point of view to fellow citizens. The problem is particularly acute in England and Wales, where all land is owned by somebody and is subject to the private law of land ownership, which usually give near-absolute powers of exclusion to landowners, even when they are public authorities who hold land in the public interest. Two responses are possible. One approach is to subject land held by public authorities to public-law duties, so that a public-authority landowner would be unable to exclude anyone from their land without a reason that would stand scrutiny under administrative law principles. This was happening to some extent before the Human Rights Act 1998 came into force. Decisions required public authorities to act within their powers, for proper purposes, and rationally when deciding not to allow people to enter land or to carry on particular activities there. Thus Barnet London Borough Council acted beyond its powers when it purported to impose on the organizing committee of the East Finchley Community Festival a condition that no political organization would be permitted to attend the festival. The condition was *ultra vires* because it was inconsistent with the purpose for which the council held the land as a pleasure ground under the Public Health Act 1864, section 164. An attempt to stop people with political objects from using it was a use of the power of the council for an improper purpose. It was also discriminatory. Furthermore, as the committee would have found it impossible to meet the condition, it effectively negated the licence to which it was attached.[22] Leicester City Council acted unlawfully in refusing to allow a rugby club to use its training facilities unless the club stopped its members from playing in South Africa, a condition which the club had no power to fulfil.[23] A restriction on the use by stag-hunters of land owned and managed by Somerset County Council was quashed on the ground that the council had not adequately considered the competing considerations when coming to a decision as to whether a ban would benefit the area.[24] A parent's implied licence to enter the premises of her child's school, operated by the local education authority, cannot be revoked without

---

[21] *PruneYard Shopping Center v. Robbins* 447 US 74 (1980).

[22] *R. v. London Borough of Barnet, ex parte Johnson* (1990) 89 LGR 581, CA, affirming (1989) 88 LGR 73, DC.

[23] *Wheeler v. Leicester City Council* [1985] AC 1054, [1985] 2 All ER 1106, HL.

[24] *R. v. Somerset County Council, ex parte Fewings* [1995] 1 WLR 1037, [1995] 3 All ER 20, CA, affirming on different grounds Laws J, [1995] 1 All ER 513.

first giving her an opportunity to make representations, because the relationship between the parent, the authority, and the head teacher is governed by public law principles.[25] Under the Human Rights Act 1998, a public authority landowner will act unlawfully (contrary to section 6 of the Act) if it excludes people from its land or imposes conditions on the use of land in a manner incompatible with the rights to freedom of expression and freedom of peaceful assembly under ECHR Articles 10 and 11. Furthermore, people are entitled to express themselves when lawfully using land owned by a public authority. Where the surface of a road is vested in a highway authority, people have a right to assemble on land adjoining the highway in a peaceful and non-obstructive manner to protest, as that is to be regarded as a legitimate incident of the right to pass and re-pass on the highway.[26] What is emerging slowly is a notion of the public forum, and its development is likely to be accelerated by the application to public authorities of ECHR Articles 10 and 11 under the Human Rights Act 1998.

The effect thus achieved is gradually coming closer to that in the USA and Canada.[27] In the USA, the Supreme Court has held that the public have First Amendment rights to free speech on state-owned property to which there is a traditional right of public access ('public forums'), such as roads and parks. Any restriction must be imposed for compelling reasons in support of a substantial state interest, must be narrowly drawn, and must not discriminate by reference to the ideas communicated. On other state-owned property, to which there is no traditional right of access ('non-public forums'), the state can restrict communication by reference to its content as long as the restriction is reasonable and does not discriminate by reference to the viewpoint expressed.[28] On privately owned forums, the owner can restrict speech; indeed, forcing people to allow their property to be used to carry communications of which they disapprove would violate their First Amendment rights.[29]

In Canada, the Supreme Court has held that public authorities cannot exclude people from using state-owned property for communicating with others as long as that use is compatible with the purpose for which the public authority uses the property. That use has priority over freedom to communicate, but so far as the two can co-exist (and on that question the court largely deferred to the judgment of the public authority) the authority may subject freedom of expression only to 'such reasonable limits prescribed by law as can be demonstrably justified in a free and democratic society'.[30] There appears to be no right under the Constitution Act 1982 to be provided with a forum at public expense.[31]

---

[25] *Wandsworth London Borough Council v. A.* [2000] 1 WLR 1246, CA.

[26] *DPP v. Jones (Margaret)* [1999] 2 AC 240, [1999] 2 All ER 257, HL.

[27] See R. Moon, *The Constitutional Protection of Freedom of Expression* (Toronto: University of Toronto Press, 2000), 148–71.

[28] *Arkansas Educational Television Commission v. Forbes* 118 S. Ct. 1633 (1998), SC of USA.

[29] *Hudgens v. NLRB* 424 US 507 (1976), SC of USA.

[30] *The Queen in Right of Canada v. Committee for the Commonwealth of Canada* (1991) 77 DLR (4th) 385, SC of Canada. The quotation is from the Constitution Act 1982 (Canada), Part I, s. 1.

[31] *Native Women's Association of Canada v. Canada* [1994] 3 SCR 627, SC of Canada.

This public-law approach offers an opportunity for people to gather and express themselves, but only as long as there are adequate spaces in public ownership in the vicinity free of disabling constraints. An alternative approach is to impose limitations on the freedom of private landowners to exclude people from, or control activities on, their land. There is a long history of doing this, in order to allow other people to live their lives in a dignified and convenient way. Easements in land law serve this purpose, as do rights of way and rights of common, which are imposed on landowners for the common good by means of fictions, such as treating use of a claimed right for twenty years as evidence of use as of right from time immemorial, or of a lost modern grant or presumed dedication to public use.[32] The theoretical foundations for such incursions on private property are twofold: first, the idea that property carries with it responsibilities; secondly, the recognition that property rights are given by law for the public good, and can legitimately be limited by the state for the public good (just as property can be taxed for the public good) giving rise to rights which Professor Kevin Gray has called 'equitable property', exercisable by members of the community for the advancement of their rights, welfare, and dignity.[33] It would be possible to extend this to such places as private shopping centres, although there are indications that legal tribunals (both national and international) are reluctant as yet to take this to the lengths of requiring private landowners to admit people or permit conduct against their will.[34]

(3) PREVENTION OF DISORDER

More worrying, however, than the slowness of the development towards judicial recognition of rights of public access and expression is a movement in the opposite direction in the legislature. Since the early 1990s, Parliament has enacted legislation which has sought to exclude people—individuals or groups—from public areas. Sometimes this is done as a public-order measure, as in the case of several restrictions on freedom of access and protest under the Criminal Justice and Public Order Act 1994. At other times it is said to be to protect children from coming to harm in dangerous places at night or to combat rowdy behaviour in public (as in the case of child curfew orders under the Crime and Disorder Act 1998 and powers to combat public drinking under the Criminal Justice and Police Act 2001), or to protect sections of the community against alleged troublemakers (for example by making anti-social behaviour orders under the Crime and Disorder Act 1998). The overall effect is to exclude people from making use of the relatively few genuinely public places still

[32] See R. v. Oxfordshire County Council, ex parte Sunningwell Parish Council [2000] AC 335, [1999] 3 All ER 385, HL; D. Feldman, 'Property and Public Protest', in F. Meisel and P. J. Cook (eds.), Property and Protection, Legal Rights and Restrictions: Essays in Honour of Brian W. Harvey (Oxford: Hart Publishing, 2000), 31–59 at 38ff.

[33] K. Gray, 'Equitable Property' (1994) 47(2) CLP 157–214. See also K. Gray, 'Property in Thin Air' (1991) 50 CLJ 252–307; Moon, Freedom of Expression, 171–5.

[34] CIN Properties Ltd. v. Rawlins [1995] 2 EGLR 130, CA; Mark Anderson and others v. United Kingdom, Eur. Commn. HR, App. No. 336889/97, [1998] EHRLR Rev. 218 (admissibility decision). Both decisions are subjected to searching criticism, with more wide-ranging argument, by K. Gray and S. F. Gray, 'Civil Rights, Civil Wrongs and Quasi-Public Space' [1999] EHRLR Rev. 46–102.

available, and to discourage or prohibit the exercise of freedom of assembly.[35] The Human Rights Act 1998 will affect these conflicting forces, but the maintenance of public order at present retains its place as a central value in this field of law.

A certain level of order is essential for the exercise of freedoms, their protection under the rule of law, and the operation of a liberal economy. A desire for order, not as an end in itself but as a means to allowing the fullest possible exercise of freedoms, is not, therefore, inherently repressive. Its importance to liberty can perhaps be fully understood only by those who have lived in societies where it was absent. Liberal critics of the balance which English law strikes between freedom of protest and public order have usually objected to the degree of order which the law demands, the indeterminacy of the rules for regulating protest, or the extent of official discretion in administering the rules.[36] Indeterminacy undermines liberty by making its scope uncertain, expanding the discretionary power of the police, and easing the constraints on state power which the rule of law demands. The critics do not usually say that there should be *no* constraints on rights of protest. As explained above, one effect of the Human Rights Act 1998 should be to reduce the level of indeterminacy in the law, and to subject official discretion to more rigorous legal scrutiny and justification than has hitherto been demanded.

(4) THE QUEEN'S PEACE AND PUBLIC ORDER

(i) What is the Queen's Peace?

The fundamental concept in public-order law in England has historically been (and to a lesser extent remains) the Queen's (or King's) Peace. This started as a special case of the 'peace' which attached to all dwelling places and churches, and was extended from the environs of the royal court across the country, first when the medieval kings took the main thoroughfares under their protection, later by grants of protection to individual royal servants and traders, and finally (this was common by the fourteenth century) when the royal justices allowed litigants to bring certain matters (such as trespass) within the jurisdiction of royal courts by pleading that wrongs had been done *vi et armis* or *contra pacem domini Regis*.[37] Such pleas were soon treated as being non-traversable, so that the jurisdiction of the royal courts could not be contested in cases of violence. This aided the Crown in its battle for legal authority with manorial and other local courts, and also helped to extend a uniform criminal and land law across the country.[38]

[35] A. von Hirsch and C. Shearing, 'Exclusion from Public Space', in A. von Hirsch, D. Garland, and A. Wakefield (eds.), *Ethical and Social Perspectives on Situational Crime Prevention* (Oxford: Hart Publishing, 2000), 77–96.

[36] See, e.g. J. Baxter, 'Policing and the Rule of Law', in J. Baxter and L. Koffman (eds.), *Police: The Constitution and the Community* (Abingdon: Professional Books, 1985), 38–61; P. Hewitt, *The Abuse of Power: Civil Liberties in the UK* (Oxford: Martin Robertson, 1982), ch. 5.

[37] S. F. C. Milsom, *Historical Foundations of the Common Law*, 2nd edn. (London: Butterworths, 1981), 286–90.

[38] See J. K. Weber, 'The King's Peace: A Comparative Study' (1989) 10 *J. of Legal Hist.* 135–60; Sir Carleton Kemp Allen, *The Queen's Peace* (London: Stevens & Son, 1953), 23–66; F. Pollock, *Oxford Lectures and Other Discourses* (London: Macmillan, 1890), 65–90; D. Feldman, 'The King's Peace, the Royal Prerogative and Public Order: The Roots and Early Development of Binding Over Powers' [1988] *CLJ* 101–28 at 103 ff.

Despite the modern connotation of the term 'peace', in law it has never been concerned with absence of noise. It rather functions in contradistinction to 'war': peace is a freedom from violence or the threat of violence. As the basis of public-order law, the centrality of 'peace' expresses the idea that people should be free to act as they choose so long as they do not cause violence. It has long been the duty of public officials (Keepers of the Peace, then Justices of the Peace, and constables) to preserve the peace, meaning to prevent or end anything which involves or threatens to provoke violence against citizens. But this duty has not been limited to public officials. All citizens have a duty to preserve the peace, albeit a duty of imperfect obligation on the part of ordinary citizens, as only constables suffer sanctions for failing to take appropriate action to prevent or end a breach of the peace. As early as the tenth century they were organized for that purpose (among others) in the *frith-borh* under ordinances of King Edgar (AD 959–75) and King Ethelred (978–1016),[39] and it has never since been doubted that officials who perform peace-keeping roles are doing their duty as citizens (albeit with special additional responsibilities) rather than doing something special as agents of the state. Thus in *Albert v. Lavin*[40] Mr. Albert had been trying to jump the queue at a bus stop when PC Lavin, off duty and out of uniform, decided that this was likely to lead to a breach of the peace and restrained him. Albert, not believing that Lavin was a constable, punched Lavin and was charged with assaulting a constable in the execution of his duty. The case was argued before magistrates and in the Divisional Court on the footing that the issue was whether Albert would have a defence if, as the magistrates found, he had honestly but unreasonably believed that Lavin was not a constable. In the House of Lords, the Law Lords pointed out that Albert would not have been entitled to resist anyone who was performing the citizen's duty of restraining an actual or reasonably apprehended breach of the peace. It therefore did not matter what Albert had believed or whether the belief had been reasonable: Lavin was in fact a constable, and had been in the execution of his duty as constable and citizen whatever Albert had believed. This is the clearest illustration of the duty of all citizens to preserve the 'peace'.

The 'peace' therefore has great potential for allowing people to contain other people's scope for protest and other sorts of behaviour which affect the public. Because of its elasticity, the Law Commission recommended that the concept 'breach of the peace' should no longer be used as part of the definition of criminal offences,[41] and this was accepted when the Public Order Act 1986 was drafted. However, unlike the criminal offences, the peace-keeping powers and duties of citizens and constables have not been regulated or replaced by statute. This makes it important to establish what constitutes a breach of the peace, and the extent of powers to deal with breaches.

(ii) What is a breach of the peace?

The meaning of 'breach of the peace' has been the subject of judicial disagreement, but the clear balance of authority favours the view that a breach of the peace consists

---

[39] See Stubbs, *Select Charters*, 9th edn., ed. H. W. C. Davis (Oxford: Oxford University Press, 1913), 83–5.
[40] [1982] AC 546, [1981] 3 All ER 878, HL.
[41] Law Commission No. 123, *Criminal Law: Offences Relating to Public Order* (London: HMSO, 1983), 7–8.

of violence or the threat of violence. It was on this basis that the European Court of Human Rights held in *Steel and others v. United Kingdom*[42] that the standard set by the concept of a breach of the peace was sufficiently certain and predictable in operation for the restrictions imposed in its name to be 'prescribed by law' for the purposes of ECHR Articles 10(2) and 11(2). Thus not every disturbance, even if in public, constitutes a breach of the peace. In *R. v. Howell*,[43] Watkins LJ said that there must be a positive act which harms a person or damages his messuage[44] in his presence, or which is likely to cause such harm or puts someone in fear of such harm being done. The act need not be unlawful in itself, but must give rise to a real risk of violence.[45] The interest of individuals and the Crown in suppressing violence against the person is self-evident. Attacks on or crimes against property generally do not breach the peace. The extension to attacks on dwellings in the occupiers' presence probably arises from the attendant likelihood that such an attack will be met with violence from the occupiers.[46] There must be a real risk of violence in order to give rise to a likelihood of a breach of the peace: a mere possibility is insufficient.[47]

In *R. v. Chief Constable of Devon and Cornwall Constabulary, ex parte Central Electricity Generating Board*,[48] Lord Denning MR suggested that breach of the peace might be considerably wider than this. He said: 'There is a breach of the peace whenever a person who is lawfully carrying out his work is unlawfully and physically prevented by another from doing it'.[49] However, he seems to have been saying not that a breach of the peace is automatic in such circumstances, but rather that, because the workers are entitled to use self-help, including reasonable force, in order to overcome the obstruction to their lawful pursuits,[50] any obstruction could give the police a reasonable apprehension of a breach of the peace, in the sense of violence.[51] At any rate, the case must now be interpreted in this way in order to make it compatible with ECHR Articles 10 and 11, as interpreted by the European Court of Human Rights in *Steel*, above, and with subsequent English caselaw.[52] The threat of violence against the person, or messuage in the presence of the occupier, remains essential to constitute a breach of the peace in England and Wales and to trigger the powers and duties which attach to it, so (for example) a person masturbating in a public lavatory where nobody

[42] Eur. Ct. HR, Judgment of 23 September 1998, RJD 1998-VII.

[43] [1982] QB 416, [1981] 3 All ER 383, CA, discussed by A. T. H. Smith, 'Breaching the Peace and Disturbing the Quiet' [1982] *PL* 212–18.

[44] 'Originally, the portion of land intended to be occupied, or actually occupied, as a site for a dwelling-house and its appurtenances. In modern legal language, a dwelling-house with its outbuildings and curtilage and the adjacent land assigned to its use'. *Oxford English Dictionary.*

[45] See *R. v. Morpeth Ward Justices, ex parte Ward and others* [1996] Crim. LR 497, DC.

[46] See *Ingle v. Bell* (1836) 1 W. & W. 516; *Cohen v. Huskisson* (1837) 2 M. & W. 477; *R. v. Bright* (1830) 4 C. & P. 387; *R. v. Howell* [1982] QB at 426, [1981] 3 All ER at 388 *per* Watkins LJ.

[47] *Percy v. DPP* [1995] 1 WLR 1382, [1995] 3 All ER 124, DC.

[48] [1982] QB 458, [1981] 3 All ER 826, CA.

[49] [1982] QB at 471, [1981] 3 All ER at 832.

[50] *Holmes v. Bagge* (1853) 1 E. & B. 782 at 786–7, 118 ER 629 at 631, *per* Lord Campbell CJ.

[51] See also Lawton LJ [1982] QB at 473, [1981] 3 All ER at 834, and Templeman LJ at 478, 839.

[52] *Percy v. DPP* [1995] 1 WLR 1382, [1995] 3 All ER 124, DC. For discussion of the possible indeterminacy of powers 'breach of the peace', see D. Nicolson, 'The European Convention on Human Rights and Arrest for Breach of the Peace' [1996] Crim. LR 764–74.

else was likely to see and nobody catching him unawares would be likely to be moved to violence is not conduct likely to cause a breach of the peace.[53]

A breach of the peace can occur on private premises, whether or not it affects anyone outside the premises. Its essence is violence, not public violence.[54] The preventive powers in respect of breaches of the peace, discussed below, therefore include power to enter private premises if necessary for the purpose.

The violence (actual or threatened) must be unlawful if it is to give rise to a breach of the peace.[55] Reasonable force used to expel a trespasser is not unlawful, and so is not a breach of the peace, although unlawful resistance by the trespasser may amount to a breach of the peace. In the context of the *Central Electricity Generating Board* case, there would have been no breach of the peace had the Board's employees simply carried trespassing protesters away from the Board's land without resistance. This can become complicated, however, where the person trespassing is claiming to be attempting to prevent a breach of the peace. In *McBean v. Parker*, a constable was trespassing on property occupied by the defendant, who used reasonable force in order to remove him. The constable claimed that the use of force against him constituted a breach of the peace, so that at this point he was entitled to remain on the premises and arrest the defendant in order to end the breach. The Divisional Court held that the force, being lawful, could not give rise to a breach of the peace. It would seem that, if excessive force were used in similar circumstances, the force, being unlawful, would give rise to a charge of assault against the defendant, and that would amount to a breach of the peace. However, it would be odd if a constable could assert a power to remain on premises to restrain a breach of the peace constituted by the adoption of unlawful means to achieve his lawful removal from the premises, when the simplest and most effective way of ending the breach would have been for the trespassing constable to depart. One solution to this conundrum would be to apply administrative-law principles to the constable's exercise of discretion: on *Wednesbury*[56] principles, it is arguable that the behaviour of the constable in seeking to remain on the premises, even in the face of excessive force, would be a wholly unreasonable way of trying to achieve his proper purpose of ending the breach of the peace. Furthermore, if it occurs on domestic premises, the constable's action may be a disproportionate interference with the right to respect for the home under ECHR Article 8(2), and so violate the right.[57]

(iii) What powers exist to prevent or stop breaches of the peace?[58]

The duty to prevent or stop breaches of the peace carries with it a number of powers. These are:

---

[53] *Parkin v. Norman, Valentine v. Lilley* [1983] QB 92, [1982] 2 All ER 583, a decision on s. 5 of the Public Order Act 1936 (now repealed).

[54] *McConnell v. Chief Constable of Greater Manchester Police* [1990] 1 WLR 364, [1990] 1 All ER 423, CA; *McQuade v. Chief Constable of Humberside Police, The Times*, 3 September 2001, CA.

[55] *McBean v. Parker* [1983] Crim. LR 399, 147 JP 205, DC.

[56] *Associated Provincial Picture Houses Ltd. v. Wednesbury Corporation* [1948] 1 KB 223, [1947] 2 All ER 680, CA. The principles of irrationality are applicable to the exercise of discretion by police officers: *Holgate-Mohammed v. Duke* [1984] AC 437, [1984] 1 All ER 1054, HL.

[57] *McLeod v. United Kingdom*, Eur. Ct. HR, Judgment of 23 September 1998, 27 EHRR 493.

[58] See D. G. T. Williams, *Keeping the Peace: The Police and Public Order* (London: Hutchinson, 1967), ch. 5.

- a power to take steps short of arrest to defuse the situation;
- a power to arrest and detain;
- a power to enter or remain on private premises for the purpose.

This section will concentrate on the first two powers; the last of them is considered in section 18.3, below. There are two main issues: first, the extent of the powers and the circumstances in which they can lawfully be used; secondly, the target of the power, or the person against whom it is deployed. The latter is particularly significant where demonstrators manifest beliefs or advance opinions which are unpopular with their audience, and are likely to provoke a hostile response. Should the police attempt to restrain the hostile members of the audience, or seek to prevent the demonstrators from doing anything to provoke a violent response? Restraining the hostile audience denies people the chance to silence people through violence and upholds the rule of law. Restraining peaceful speakers or assemblies may be easier, and a more efficient use of police resources, but at a high social cost.

(a) **The common-law background.** At common law, a peace officer (and, presumably, anyone else) may be justified in committing what would otherwise be a trespass to person and property. For example, in *Humphries v. Connor*[59] a policeman was held to be justified in removing an orange lily, symbol of the Protestant Unionists in Northern Ireland, from a woman who was wearing it while walking through the Catholic nationalist area of Swanlinbar and thereby provoking the local inhabitants to threaten violence. Similarly in *O'Kelly v. Harvey*[60] a magistrate was justified in laying a hand on a man while dispersing a meeting of the Catholic Land League which was being threatened with violent disruption by Fermanagh Orangemen. In the past it did not matter whether the steps were taken against the person threatening violence or those threatened. The main priority was to end the risk of reasonably apprehended violence by any means which were reasonable and necessary.

The police were allowed considerable leeway in deciding what was reasonable and necessary, and when anticipated violence could reasonably be regarded as imminent. For example, in *Moss v. McLachlan*,[61] the police during the miners' strike stopped miners some miles from a colliery where there had been violent disturbances. The police feared that the miners were on their way to reinforce the pickets at the pit, contributing to a risk of further violence. They instructed the miners to turn back, and arrested those who refused. The Divisional Court held that this was sufficiently proximate in time and place to the disturbances to be a lawful exercise of the power to give instructions and take other steps to prevent a breach of the peace. The decision allowed the police a degree of flexibility in the management of an explosive situation. It would make the job of the police unreasonably difficult to insist that the police should have to allow large numbers of people to gather at the expected trouble spot before taking steps to relieve the situation. But the flexibility was too wide. Such police

[59] (1864) 17 Ir. CLR 1.
[60] (1883) 15 Cox CC 435.
[61] [1984] IRLR 76, DC.

action in creating an exclusion zone around trouble spots interfered with people's freedom of movement under ICCPR Article 12 as well as their freedom to assemble and protest. The larger the exclusion zone, the greater the level of interference, and the more likely it is that innocent people will be seriously inconvenienced. There were many cases (which were not litigated) in which the police exceeded their powers by stopping people so far away from the scene of trouble that it could not even arguably have been a proper exercise of their power or a reasonable exercise of their discretion. For example, at one stage in March 1984 Kent miners (and all who looked like miners) were stopped at the Dartford Tunnel if the police thought that they were heading towards the Nottinghamshire, Durham, or Yorkshire collieries. This had the effect of confining those people to the southernmost counties of England for the duration of the dispute. The Human Rights Act 1998 now requires the police to exercise their discretion in a proportionate manner when its exercise interferes with rights under ECHR Articles 10(1) and 11(1). Officers (and people who are affected by assemblies and protests) will need to exercise a great deal more tolerance of protestors' rights of passage than was evident in *Moss v. McLachlan* if their efforts to avert disruption are not to be regarded as a disproportionate and, therefore, unlawful exercise of state power.

The same applies to the use by the police of their powers at common law to ban or re-locate a meeting or march or form of expression. The problem is particularly acute where there is, or is likely to be, a hostile audience. If the organizer of an assembly or a speaker refuses to cancel or end the assembly, or to move a meeting or to reroute a procession, when there is a reasonable apprehension that opponents will cause a breach of the peace, the police must decide whether to invoke the power to prevent a breach of the peace in support of an instruction to the organizer to stop or move the assembly. In *Duncan v. Jones*,[62] it was held that a constable had been entitled to tell a speaker to move a meeting from one street to another in order to avoid a breach of the peace being fomented by political opponents. But if anybody could stifle the expression of views by threatening violence, freedom of expression and freedom of protest would be worth little. The *dictum* of O'Brien J in *R. v. Londonderry Justices*[63] makes a good deal of sense from a human-rights standpoint: 'If danger arises from the exercise of lawful rights resulting in a breach of the peace, the remedy is the presence of sufficient force to prevent the result, not the legal condemnation of those who exercise those rights'. This seems at first sight to gain support from *Beatty v. Gillbanks*,[64] where the Divisional Court quashed binding over orders made against members of a Salvation Army parade when their noisy but peaceable procession through Weston-super-Mare had been disrupted by a noisy and belligerent crowd (the Skeleton Army) which disliked the Salvation Army's religious proselytizing and its opposition to alcohol. However, the support is more apparent than real. The magistrates had made the binding over orders on the basis of finding that the Salvation

---

[62] [1936] 1 KB 218, DC.

[63] (1891) 28 LR Ir. 440 at 450.

[64] (1882) 9 QBD 308. For the history of the events from which the case stemmed, see D. G. T. Williams, 'The Principle of *Beatty v. Gillbanks*: a Reappraisal', in A. N. Doob and E. L. Greenspan (eds.), *Perspectives in Criminal Law* (Aurora, Ont.: Canada Law Book, 1985), 105–25.

Army had been guilty of unlawful assembly at common law. The Divisional Court held that this finding was incorrect, and that it would not be right to bind over a person who had committed no offence.[65] But binding over after an event is different from assessing the legality of decisions made by the police under the pressure of fast-moving events. Furthermore, the police have a duty to prevent reasonably apprehended and imminent breaches of the peace, and failure to obey instructions reasonably directed to that end constitutes the offence of obstructing a constable in the execution of his duty.[66] That being so, the decision in *Beatty v. Gillbanks* tells us nothing about how the very wide discretion to act preventively in apprehension of a breach of the peace should be exercised.[67]

Protecting a person's right to protest or express opinions, against those who seek to disrupt their demonstration, sometimes affects the rights of others who are acting lawfully, or calls for a heavy commitment of police resources. It makes sense to allow police decision-makers to limit freedom of expression and freedom of peaceful assembly if it would interfere with rights (including the right to carry on lawful activities) to an unacceptable extent, or the cost of safeguarding the freedom to protest while preserving public order would be disproportionately greater than the cost to freedom which would result from preventing the protest or public expression from taking place. Although this represents a limitation on freedom of expression and freedom of peaceful assembly, it does not necessarily breach the rights guaranteed under international law by ECHR Articles 10 and 11. The European Court of Human Rights held, in *Plattform 'Ärzte für das Leben' v. Austria*,[68] that there is no absolute obligation on the state under Article 11 to ensure that a demonstration which is lawful is unimpeded by counter-demonstrators. There is an obligation to take reasonable and appropriate steps to allow the peaceful demonstration to proceed, as the right to counter-demonstrate must not be allowed to inhibit the exercise of the right to demonstrate. Nevertheless, in international law under the ECHR the state has a wide discretion as to the measures to be adopted, and if the steps fail because of violence the state will not necessarily have breached the demonstrators' rights. The police would be entitled to restrict the freedom of the demonstrators, so long as the restrictions met the criteria laid down in Article 11(2).

The problem is deciding when an expressive assembly interferes with other people to an unacceptable degree, and how to respond if it does. It requires an exercise of judgment balancing rights of different kinds and public interests in the light of available resources. Ideally, a way will be found of allowing people to demonstrate without

[65] Later cases have shown that this was mistaken, binding over orders may be made against witnesses, acquitted defendants, or people who happen to be present in court, as a preventive measure without the need to prove that they have committed or threatened any offence. For discussion, see Law Commission, Working Paper No. 103, *Criminal Law: Binding Over—The Issues* (London: HMSO, 1987); below, section 18.5(2).

[66] *Duncan v. Jones* [1936] 1 KB 218, DC.

[67] See *R. v. Chief Constable of Sussex, ex parte International Trader's Ferry Ltd.* [1999] 1 All ER 129, HL, at 142 *per* Lord Slynn, with whom Lords Nolan and Hope agreed at 146, 159. For discussion of these problems, see W. Birtles, 'The Common Law Power of the Police to Control Public Meetings' (1973) 36 *MLR* 587–99; D. G. Barnum, 'Freedom of Assembly and the Hostile Audience in Anglo-American Law' (1981) 29 *Am. J. Comp. Law* 59–96; Smith, *Offences against Public Order* 12–20.

[68] Eur. Ct. HR, Series A, No. 139, Judgment of 21 June 1988, 13 EHRR 204, at paras. 32–4.

preventing others from going about their lawful activities. However, this is difficult if the demonstration is protesting about those activities. Examples include demonstrations against experiments on animals, directed towards scientists; against hunting or fishing, intended to disrupt the activities of hunters and fisherfolk; or against exportation of live animals, attempting to block the lorries in which animals are being transported. Other things being equal, there is much to be said for the balancing of interests and rights expressed by Sachs LJ in *R. v. Caird*,[69] a case of common-law riot and unlawful assembly, as follows:

'Any suggestion that a section of the community strongly holding one set of views is justified in banding together to disrupt the lawful activities of a section that does not hold the same views so strongly or which holds different views cannot be tolerated and must unhesitatingly be rejected by the courts.'

As a matter of law, this made perfect sense when all rights and freedoms were treated as having essentially similar weight. For example, in *R. v. Coventry City Council, ex parte Phoenix Aviation*[70] animal welfare protestors were disrupting exports of livestock. The Divisional Court was asked to decide on the legality of (*inter alia*) the decision of harbour boards to accept or turn away live animal traffic. Simon Brown LJ considered that even harbour boards had power to refuse to accept business of a particular type, they could not lawfully exercise it merely to avoid the risk of protest. He said:

'Tempting though it may sometimes be for public authorities to yield too readily to threats of disruption, they must expect the courts to review any such decision with particular rigour ... We confirm that it will indeed be for the chief constable to decide upon the measures necessary and that all concerned should co-operate fully with him. Given the obvious importance of Dover to the national economy, both the police and the board may now be expected to use all their extensive powers to ensure that the port is not too severely disrupted in future. We note with approval too this statement from the commander of the Plymouth police quoted in one of the many newspaper articles exhibited by the city council: "It is our legal obligation to make sure that this lawful trade can continue while allowing those who want to demonstrate in a law abiding way to do so." That rightly recognizes the importance also of the right of lawful demonstration which nothing in this judgment must be taken to qualify.'[71]

This did not help the police or port authorities to decide how to deal with clashes between competing rights and interests. It deferred to their decisions, unless they acted wholly unreasonably or for patently inappropriate reasons, or violated Community law (then the only form of 'higher law' in the UK). Subject to that, the police owed no substantive duty to do anything concrete for or to any of the parties to the clash.

The dilemma facing the police, and the relative powerlessness of law to provide guidance to them in the exercise of their discretion, became clear in *R. v. Chief*

[69] (1970) 54 Cr. App. R. 499 at 506.
[70] [1995] 3 All ER 37, DC.
[71] Ibid. at 62–4.

Constable of Sussex, ex parte International Trader's Ferry Ltd.[72] People protesting about live animal exports blocked the road to Shoreham Harbour in Sussex and tried to prevent animals from being taken to the port for export to mainland Europe. The police were unable to provide sufficient personnel to keep the road passable for lorries five days a week. Trade was disrupted. International Trader's Ferry Ltd. (ITF) applied for an order requiring the Chief Constable to control the demonstrations in such a way as to allow lorries to enter and leave the port on a regular basis. The House of Lords held that the Chief Constable's decision was not *Wednesbury* unreasonable. The refusal to give full protection to ITF against protestors was within the range of permissible decisions. Relevant factors included the Chief Constable's limited financial resources, and doubt over what (if any) additional resources the Home Office might make available. Diverting officers from ordinary duties to Shoreham Harbour would have compromised the protection and law enforcement that could be offered to residents in other parts of Sussex. The company could have used other ports (albeit at increased cost), rather than seeking a large expenditure of public money in support of its lawful, but not uncontroversial, commercial activities. For these reasons, the decision to provide only limited policing at Shoreham Harbour was within the Chief Constable's discretion, although as Lord Cooke of Thorndon acknowledged, it was 'a defeat for the rule of law and a victory for mob rule ... It is not a question of the rights of peaceable protesters against the rights of a lawful trader. It is the lawless elements acting on the side of the protesters who have won the day'.[73] Their Lordships distinguished *R. v. Coventry City Council, ex parte Phoenix Aviation* as applying only where a public authority (whether Harbour Board, council, or police force) attempted to impose a complete ban on transportation in connection with a lawful activity. The House accepted that, short of a ban, public authorities and the police in particular had a very wide discretion as to what to do in the face of a threat of mass protest and violence against a lawful activity. The interests of all residents in the area, not merely those of the protesters and the commercial undertaking adversely affected by them, had to be borne in mind, together with the responsibilities of the police in other fields and the constraints of personnel and financial management. This meant that English administrative law largely failed to regard either protestors or other people carrying on their lawful activities as being entitled to expect support from the police. The law did not impose worthwhile legal accountability on the police in respect of the exercise of their discretion.

However, some legal constraints on police discretion were potentially available under Community law. ITF argued that the failure of the police to enforce access to the harbour was a measure having equivalent effect to a quantitative restriction on imports, contrary to Article 34 (now Article 29) of the EC Treaty. In the House of Lords, Lord Hoffmann held that the duty under Article 34 could not be directly

---

[72] [1999] 2 AC 418, [1999] 1 All ER 129, HL. For an illuminating discussion of the case, see C. Barnard and I. Hare, 'Police Discretion and the Rule of Law: Economic Community Rights versus Civil Rights' (2000) 63 *MLR* 581–95.

[73] [1999] 1 All ER at 158.

enforceable against the Chief Constable at the suit of a private litigant, because the obligation would be uncertain in scope and the Chief Constable (unlike a government) could not be assumed to command all the resources of the state. But in any case, the House unanimously decided that an interference with imports, if there had been one, could be justified on the ground of public policy under Article 36 (now Article 30) of the EC Treaty, the purpose being to secure adequate policing for the rest of Sussex and the measure (a limitation of the major police presence at Shoreham Harbour to two days per week) was proportionate to that aim. The factors relevant to the justification of a quantitative restriction on imports were similar to those relevant to the reasonableness or unreasonableness of the decision in English administrative law. Neither under English administrative law nor under Community law was the Chief Constable under a duty to protect ITF's business, its drivers, and its directors. It was for the police to balance the right of *lawful* demonstration, the importance of upholding the rule of law, the interest in restricting otherwise lawful demonstrations if they interfere to an intolerable extent with the lawful activities (including commercial activities) of others, the importance of various activities to the national economy, and the cost to the taxpayer.[74] In the result, ITF went into liquidation, and the managing director and his family were subjected to a long-running campaign of harassment at his home as well as at work.

(b) **Recent decisions at common law, and the impact of the Human Rights Act 1998.** The *International Trader's Ferry* case shows that the police are entitled to consider both resource constraints and the significance of any freedoms which are in play when deciding how to perform their duty to preserve the peace, even if innocent people suffer considerable loss as a result. But the police are not free to disregard rights and freedoms in the face of resource constraints. Before the Human Rights Act 1998 came fully into force, it was becoming clear that there were significant limits to the range of legally acceptable responses when the police were caught between speakers and a hostile audience, or between demonstrators and those against whom they were demonstrating. As early as 1975, Lord Denning MR said in *Hubbard v. Pitt*[75] that the law jealously protected the right to free expression and public protest if conducted lawfully. In the same spirit, recent decisions have provided clearer guidance to the police than was available previously as to the factors to be taken into account when exercising their common-law powers to restrict protest in circumstances which engage the rights to freedom of belief and expression. If the protestors' behaviour is unlawful and likely to give rise to violence initiated by a third party, the police are entitled to stop the protestors' behaviour. However, if the protestors are behaving lawfully but their lawful behaviour interferes with someone else's freedom to pursue another lawful activity, the police may interfere with the protestors' activity only if it could properly be said that it would naturally provoke

---

[74] See *Harris v. Sheffield United Football Club Ltd.* [1987] QB 77, CA, at 95 *per* Balcombe LJ; *R. v. Chief Constable of Sussex, ex parte International Trader's Ferry Ltd.* [1999] 2 AC 418, [1999] 1 All ER 129, HL.

[75] [1976] QB 142, [1975] 3 All ER 1, CA. See also Sir Leslie Scarman, *Red Lion Square Disorders*, Cmnd. 5919, 2.

others to violence by unreasonably interfering with their lawful activities.[76] The new approach, focusing on the reasonableness of the behaviour of all parties, brought the law governing the exercise of the common-law powers of the police closer to that governing binding over to keep the peace. The position of the common law was converging on a point closer to that adopted in *Beatty v. Gillbanks* than to that adopted in *Duncan v. Jones*.

Thus in *Nicol and Selvanayagam v. Director of Public Prosecutions*[77] Simon Brown LJ said that lawful demonstrations could properly be said naturally to provoke violence in others only if the demonstrators are interfering with the rights or freedoms of third parties in an unreasonable way, and the third parties would not be regarded as acting unreasonably in resorting to unlawful violence in response. In that case, animal-rights protestors had attempted to disrupt an angling competition by throwing sticks into the water and at fishing lines. The Divisional Court considered that this had gone beyond reasonable behaviour, so the police had been entitled to decide that a reasonable angler might have responded violently.

On the other hand, although attempting to persuade anglers to stop without disrupting the competition would presumably have been a reasonable exercise of the protestors' rights under ECHR Articles 9, 10, and 11. Even before the Human Rights Act 1998 came into force, those Convention rights provided a framework for considering the reasonableness of action, as *Redmond-Bate v. Director of Public Prosecutions*[78] demonstrates. Members of a fundamentalist Christian group stood on the steps of Wakefield Cathedral and preached at passers-by. An audience of about 100 people gathered, some of whom showed hostility towards the preachers. A constable, fearing a breach of the peace, asked the preachers to desist, and arrested them when they refused. One of them was convicted of wilfully obstructing the constable in the execution of his duty. On appeal by case stated, the Divisional Court quashed the conviction. The facts found by the trial court did not support the conclusion that the constable's apprehension of violence was reasonable. Mere noise and disorder among the audience did not make the apprehension reasonable. Furthermore, even if the apprehension had been reasonable, the constable should have considered whether preventive action should be directed against the preachers or the hostile members of the audience. As the preachers were not interfering with the rights of the audience under English law, and were not acting unreasonably, any violence directed against them would have been unreasonable, and the constable should have directed any preventive action towards the potentially unreasonably violent members of the audience. Sedley LJ pointed to the significance of the rights to manifest a belief, to express opinions, and to assemble peacefully, under ECHR Articles 9, 10, and 11. Echoing sentiments often expressed by the European Court of Human Rights, he reminded us that, 'Free speech includes not only the inoffensive but the irritating, the contentious,

---

[76] This formulation is based on that of Professor Sir John Smith in the commentary on *R. v. Morpeth Ward Justices, ex parte Ward and others* (1992) 95 Cr. App. R. 215, DC, [1992] Crim. LR 499, approved in *Nicol and Selvanayagam v. DPP* [1996] Crim. LR 318, DC.

[77] [1996] Crim. LR 318, DC. For commentaries, see ibid., 319 (Professor Sir John Smith), and (1996) 1 *J. of Civil Liberties* 75–80 (anon.).

[78] (1999) 7 BHRC 375, DC. See the commentary at [1999] Crim. LR 998 (Professor D. J. Birch).

the heretical, the unwelcome and the provocative provided it does not tend to provoke violence'.

The importance of these considerations is now, of course, enhanced by the Human Rights Act 1998, which requires the police to justify any interference with freedom of expression and of peaceful assembly under the terms of ECHR Articles 9(2), 10(2), and 11(2) using the concepts of legitimate aim, pressing social need and proportionality, rather than unreasonableness, as the test of the lawfulness of police action. In some respects, the decision in *Redmond-Bate* provides stronger protection for freedom of expression and assembly than the European Court of Human Rights has so far provided. As noted above, the caselaw of the Strasbourg Court allows states to recognize a right to be free of having opinions which outrage one's own beliefs expressed in one's presence or within one's jurisdiction. The decision in *Redmond-Bate* makes it clear that English common law recognizes no such right (except in established fields of public decency and blasphemy examined in Chapter 16, above), so protecting people's sensitivities cannot be brought within the 'protection of the rights and freedoms of others' as a legitimate aim for an interference with rights under ECHR Article 9, 10, or 11 in English law under the Human Rights Act 1998.

On the other hand, the law may still allow a constable to stop a peaceful speaker to take account of the level of risk and the physical support available to the constable when deciding how to proceed when there is a real threat of imminent violence from a large and hostile audience reacting to a provocative speaker. In *Humphries v. Connor*,[79] in relation to dispersing a crowd, Hayes J, noting that the best way of preventing a breach of the peace will usually be to remove the provocation, continued: 'when a person deliberately refuses to acquiesce in such removal, after warning to do so, I think the constable is authorised to do everything necessary and proper to enforce it. . . . But whether the act which he did was or was not, under all the circumstances, *necessary* to preserve the peace, is for the jury to decide'.[80]

This objective necessity test has the advantage of being closely in line with the doctrine of proportionality. It may require the constable to bear the burden of proving that there was no other practicable way of resolving the problem, or at least that other methods were considered and discarded for good reasons, so far as was possible in the exigencies of the situation facing the constable.[81] A less demanding test (in theory, although there is probably little practical difference in most cases) is that the constable should reasonably believe it to be necessary. It is compatible with a test of proportionality, since a course of action which is reasonably believed to be necessary would rarely, if ever, properly be regarded as disproportionate. The test of reasonable belief in necessity was approved in *O'Kelly v. Harvey*.[82] Law LC in the Court of Appeal in Ireland said that he thought that it had been 'substantially decided' in *Humphries v. Connor* that: 'if the defendant believed and had just grounds for believing that the

---

[79] (1864) 17 Ir. CLR 1.

[80] Ibid. at 8; emphasis in original.

[81] *Cp.* however the House of Lords' less demanding interpretation of 'necessary' in *Re an inquiry under the Company Securities (Insider Dealing) Act 1985* [1988] AC 660, [1988] 1 All ER 203, HL.

[82] (1883) 15 Cox CC 435 at 445–6.

peace could only be preserved by withdrawing the plaintiff and his friends from the attack with which they were threatened, it was I think the duty of the defendant to take that course'.

In view of the presumption in favour of protecting people who are acting lawfully from being prevented from expressing their views, or holding meetings, merely because of violent opposition from other groups, it would be perfectly sensible to adopt the *O'Kelly v. Harvey* test (belief on reasonable grounds that it is necessary to interfere with freedom) to justify action against the innocent party, but to leave the police free to act against the troublemaker subject only to a test for unreasonableness. It seems unlikely that the law would require a constable single-handedly to take on a large and violent crowd if the risk of violence could more safely be averted by removing the speaker. From a practical point of view, the constable must retain a discretion to stop a speaker in exceptional circumstances. A reasonable speaker's behaviour becomes less reasonable if he refuses to comply with a request designed to prevent a breach of the peace, although it remains important to ensure that a speaker's or demonstrator's freedom is not interfered with more than is reasonably necessary to prevent a breach of the peace. The difference between this and the approach adopted in *Duncan v. Jones* is that the courts will now sanction such an interference with the speaker only in exceptional circumstances, when there is a pressing need to safeguard people, including the speaker, from violence which could not otherwise reasonably be contained.

Through the combination of common-law developments and the impact of the Human Rights Act 1998, many earlier decisions on police discretion with regard to breaches of the peace would now probably be decided differently. It might now be regarded as unreasonable, in the absence of special circumstances, for the police to interfere with a person who is doing something lawful in order to forestall an unreasonably violent response by an opponent. Under ECHR Articles 9 and 10, removing a symbol of a religious belief or political opinion needs to be justified, and removing it from someone who is behaving peaceably is likely to be a disproportionate interference with freedom to manifest a religion or express a political opinion, and so unlawful under section 6 of the Human Rights Act 1998, unless it is the only practicable way of averting violence. In the same way, the authorities can probably no longer properly use the power to prevent a breach of the peace to put a large exclusion area round the site of an anticipated confrontation (although, as we shall see, some statutory powers have a similar effect). Both at common law and under the ECHR and the Human Rights Act 1998, there is a general presumption in favour of protecting the exercise of free expression in public and in private.[83]

This means that police discretion is being gradually restricted by law. The police previously faced few legal difficulties when keeping the peace, although there were formidable practical and policy problems. Legal issues have become more pressing since the law recognized a group of special rights or freedoms with greater weight than others, demanding special justification when police action interferes with or fails

[83] *Steel and others v. United Kingdom*, Eur. Ct. HR, Judgment of 23 September 1998, RJD 1998-VII.

to protect them. The difficulties, for courts as well as police officers, are further exacerbated when (as in the *International Trader's Ferry* case):

'different legal orders to which they are subject require them to prioritise varying activities in an inconsistent manner ... From the perspective of civil and political rights, which is essentially that of the European Convention and the Human Rights Act, the commercial activity of the exporters is of less value than the opposition to the trade mounted as a matter of principle by the protesters; yet from the perspective of economic rights, essentially that of the European Community legal order, ITF's commercial activity was entitled to the highest degree of legal protection because it involved conduct at the core of that guaranteed by the Treaty.'[84]

The freedom to engage in lawful activities such as hunting or experimenting may be of a lower status than a human right to a fundamental freedom, such as freedom of religion or belief, expression, or peaceful assembly, guaranteed under the ECHR and the Human Rights Act 1998. Interference with the latter freedoms needs special justification. It is no longer proper for courts simply to leave the matter to the discretion of public authorities, such as the police or port authorities. The judges must be willing to make their own judgments about the grounds of justification for interfering with Convention rights, ensuring also that the police deal even-handedly with people and avoid discriminating in ways that would violate municipal or Community anti-discrimination law or ECHR Article 14 taken together with a Convention right (on which see Chapter 3, above). This necessarily forces decision-makers (police and judges alike) to address political and moral considerations.[85] If the police favour one viewpoint over another, it causes special problems. During the miners' strike in 1984–85, large numbers of striking miners protesting about their grievances confronted police and miners who wanted to go to work. The confrontations between the strikers and the police, and between the strikers and the non-strikers, gave rise to a great deal of ill feeling and provoked many breaches of the peace. It would have been simple, cheap, and have required few resources, for the police to have provided a small force to monitor the situation and stop the non-strikers from attempting to go to work. Although there was nothing inherently unlawful in the non-strikers' actions, and it was not unreasonable for them to want to work, restraining them would have been the most efficient way to minimize the chances of a breach of the peace, since the concentration of force required to escort the non-strikers through picket lines, and the high feelings engendered, made it very likely that non-strikers, by attempting to go to work, would provoke a breach of the peace. However, in their discretion, and probably encouraged by the government (which had its own political reasons for wanting to ensure that the strike failed), the police summoned massive reinforcements from forces across the country, through the mutual assistance arrangements co-ordinated by the National Reporting Centre at New Scotland Yard. They then insisted on escorting the non-strikers to work, despite the resulting breaches of the peace. There was no similar political will to

---

[84] Barnard and Hare, 'Police Discretion and the Rule of Law' at 594 (footnote omitted).

[85] D. Galligan, 'Preserving Public Protest: The Legal Approach', in L. Gostin (ed.), *Civil Liberties in Conflict* (London: Routledge, 1988), 39–64.

allow the lorries to get through to Shoreham Harbour in the *International Trader's Ferry* case.

This illustrates the fact that the weighting of the costs and benefits of various courses of action to prevent threatened breaches of the peace is neither a scientific nor an apolitical matter.[86] This is most obvious in the context of parades in Northern Ireland, where the Royal Ulster Constabulary (RUC) had to make decisions about controlling parades through hostile territory, particularly when Protestant, unionist organizations sought to parade through Catholic, nationalist areas. The problem came to a head in July 1996, when the unionists wanted to march in uniform, fifes playing and drums beating, through an area inhabited by Catholic republican nationalists. The Chief Constable of the RUC used his powers under the Public Order (Northern Ireland) Order 1987 to re-route unionist marches away from a Catholic nationalist area, infuriating unionists. Violence flared, and the Chief Constable decided to permit the march to take place a few days later on its planned route, alienating Catholics. Protestant crowds refused to disperse after the march, and violence ensued which spread to other parts of the province. The RUC had managed to alienate both communities, each of which regarded it as having favoured the other side, and at the same time had given an impression of unprincipled vacillation.

Following the events of July 1996, an independent inquiry was established under the chairmanship of Dr. (later Sir) Peter North to review what had occurred and to make recommendations. The Report[87] stressed the need for accommodation to be achieved by discussion and mediation at local level whenever possible, to avoid the imposition of a resolution to conflicts over parades. Nevertheless, the Report accepted that it would be necessary to impose solutions where no accommodation could be reached. To save the police from having to make political decisions which balanced the interests of different groups, the Report recommended that an independent Parades Commission should be established, both to facilitate local accommodations by education and mediation and to take decisions in the light of seven fundamental principles (including the needs to be responsible in the way rights are exercised, and to take account of the way actions would be perceived by others) when agreement proved impossible. The Parades Commission has since been established to perform this function, but its decisions have proved as controversial as those of the police.

---

[86] For discussion of policing methods in relation to industrial disputes, see R. Geary, *Policing Industrial Disputes 1893 to 1985* (London: Methuen, 1985); R. de Friend and S. Uglow, 'Policing Industrial Disputes', in J. Baxter and L. Koffman (eds.), *Police: The Constitution and the Community*, (Abingdon: Professional Books, 1985), 62–71. On tactics and equipment, see P. A. J. Waddington, *The Strong Arm of the Law* (Oxford: Clarendon Press, 1991). For provocative views on aspects of the miners' strike of 1984–85, see B. Fine and R. Millar (eds.), *Policing the Miners' Strike* (London: Lawrence and Wishart, 1985), especially the essays by M. Kettle, 'The National Reporting Centre and the 1984 Miners' Strike', at 23–33, and N. Blake, 'Picketing, Justice and the Law' at 101–19.

[87] *Report: Independent Review of Parades and Marches 1997* (Belfast: Stationery Office, 1997). I have discussed the implications of the Report and of the review team's working methods in 'Achieving Transparency and Accountability in Public-Order Decision-Making: Evaluating the North Report on Parades in Northern Ireland', a paper presented to the meeting of the Public Law Section of the Society of Public Teachers of Law, Birmingham, 5–6 April 1997.

Professor Denis Galligan's argument that a substantial amount of discretion is inevitably needed in public-order policing and policy-making, and that the way forward is to seek ways of making decision-makers publicly accountable for those of their decisions which have political implications,[88] is therefore convincing. The Human Rights Act 1998 is one way of enhancing principled accountability through law.

(c) Are there unacceptable views, or only unacceptable ways of expressing them?
There may be circumstances in which the views expressed, or the manner of expressing them, is regarded as being so reprehensible that they do not deserve protection. Even in the USA, where freedom of religion, speech, and peaceable assembly are constitutionally guaranteed by the First Amendment, it has been held that, while there are no limits to the forms of opinion which must be tolerated, there are limits to the tolerable manner of expression.[89] In this country, where there is no constitutional protection for free expression, there are fewer restrictions on police, courts, or Parliament treating certain opinions as unworthy of protection. However, there is generally a sensitivity to the risk inherent in banning types of opinion. Even the Public Order Act 1936, a panic measure rushed through Parliament in response to violent fascist demonstrations, while permitting orders to be made banning processions, did not allow particular organizations to be singled out. Banning orders could be made only in respect of 'all public processions or . . . any class of public procession so specified'.[90] This avoided discrimination between opinions, but with the incidental result that in the wake of the Brixton riots in 1981 a ban prevented the CND[91] and various groups of Boy Scouts from holding parades. The same position obtains under the Public Order Act 1986, section 13(1), (4), which has replaced section 3 of the 1936 Act. One effect of the Human Rights Act 1998, section 6 is that the police now act unlawfully (by virtue of the combined effect of ECHR Articles 10, 11, and 14) if they use their common-law powers to prevent breaches of the peace in a discriminatory way, so that it is more difficult for proponents of some views to exercise their freedom of expression than for proponents of other views. Previously, we relied almost entirely on the good sense and balance of the police to avoid discriminatory use of common-law powers.[92]

The presumption in favour of freedoms of belief, expression, and peaceful assembly does not entail an entirely level playing-field between different viewpoints. As noted above, there is an obligation under ICCPR Article 20 to prohibit certain kinds of expression. In addition, ECHR Article 17 (which forms part of the Convention rights in English law under the Human Rights Act 1998) makes it clear that nobody can rely on ECHR Articles 9, 10, and 11 in support of an activity or act 'aimed at the destruction of any of the rights set forth herein or at their limitation to a greater extent than

---

[88] Galligan, 'Preserving Public Protest', at 45–9.

[89] See L. Fisher, *American Constitutional Law* (New York: McGraw-Hill, 1990), ch. 10.

[90] Public Order Act 1936, s. 3(2), (3) (now repealed: see Public Order Act 1986).

[91] *Kent v. Metropolitan Police Commissioner, The Times,* 15 May 1981, DC.

[92] See Williams, *Keeping the Peace,* ch. 5; S. H. Bailey, D. J. Harris, and B. L. Jones, *Civil Liberties: Cases and Materials,* 3rd edn. (London: Butterworths, 1991), 146–9.

is provided for in the Convention'. This may justify the state in restricting behaviour which prevents, or seeks to discourage, people from exercising Convention rights. There may be good reasons for restricting expression, particularly in public, of viewpoints which denigrate or intimidate people, either individually or by reference to the groups to which they belong. This matter is considered below, in relation to expression stirring up racial hatred in particular. Here, we can note that these are matters which the police are entitled to take into account in deciding how, and against whom, to exercise their powers in respect of breaches of the peace.

(4) WHEN, WHERE, AND HOW CAN POWERS IN RESPECT OF BREACHES OF THE PEACE BE EXERCISED?

Before a power can be exercised to prevent a breach of the peace, there must be either

(a) a breach of the peace in progress, or

(b) a reasonable apprehension of an imminent breach of the peace.

Where the power is exercised in an anticipatory way, the court in the past examined the constable's assessment of the risk to see whether it is honest and reasonable,[93] but deferred to the view of the constable on the spot where there was any doubt about it, taking account of the need for constables to form a view quickly and act on it.[94] The low level of review is illustrated by *Duncan v. Jones*,[95] where the court held that the magistrates had been entitled to conclude that there was a reasonable apprehension that a breach of the peace would result from a meeting organized in July 1934 to protest against the Incitement to Disaffection Bill, because disturbances had followed a similar meeting organized in May 1933. On this basis, the police could have imposed restrictive conditions on any meeting of any organization (or indeed on any football match) if a previous meeting or match had led to a breach of the peace. This gave too much power to the police to stifle public protest and many other sorts of activity without parliamentary authority, or adequate public accountability (legal or political), for their actions.

Fortunately, more recent cases, influenced in part by the ECHR, show a heightened judicial awareness of the need for courts to decide for themselves whether the facts as known to a constable at the time of an incident made it reasonable to conclude that there was a real likelihood of imminent violence.[96] The requirement of imminence has been held to mean that the exercise of the power must be sufficiently close both to the time and to the scene of the breach. In addition, under the Human Rights Act 1998 the steps taken by the police to avert the danger, if they interfere with the right to manifest a belief, express an opinion, or peacefully assemble, must be justifiable under ECHR Article 9(2), 10(2), or 11(2) respectively. It must be possible to show that the

[93] *O'Kelly v. Harvey* (1883) 15 Cox CC 435.
[94] *G. v. Chief Superintendent of Police, Stroud* (1986) 86 Cr. App. R. 92, DC.
[95] [1936] 1 KB 218, DC.
[96] *R. v. Howell* [1982] QB 416, [1981] 3 All ER 383, CA; *Lewis v. Chief Constable of Greater Manchester, Independent*, 23 October 1991, CA; *Redmond-Bate v. DPP* (1999) 7 BHRC 375, DC.

police action was directed to achieving a legitimate aim (such as the protection of public order or the rights and freedoms of others), and were necessary in a democratic society (i.e. a proportionate response to a pressing social need to act) for that purpose. As suggested earlier, this may lead to cases such as *Moss v. McLachlan*,[97] where the police were held to have been justified in considering that a risk of violence was sufficiently imminent to justify stopping supporters of the strikers some miles from the site of protests, being decided differently today.

Another aspect of police tactics calling for careful consideration under the 1998 Act is the degree of force deployed in response to a threat of public disorder. The scenes of violence which attended the miners' strike in 1984–85 and other industrial disputes and urban riots during the 1970s and 1980s showed that insensitive policing and over-reaction by the police were significant causes, albeit not the only causes, of major violence associated with demonstrations of various kinds. Lord Scarman's reports on two such incidents[98] led to a rethinking of police tactics and the principles of public-order policing. Training of officers in crowd control is now more systematic than it used to be, using methods and guidelines established by the police themselves in standing orders and training manuals or by the Home Office in circulars,[99] but neither Parliament nor courts systematically review the content of these kinds of quasi-legislation or their implementation in particular situations,[100] not least because the content of the training manual on public order policing has been held to be protected by public interest immunity from disclosure.[101] Now the tactics of the police will come under scrutiny by reference to human-rights standards. Deaths caused by police action will have to be justified under ECHR Article 2 (see Chapter 4 above), and injuries of any severity may give rise to claims under ECHR Article 3 (see Chapter 5 above). Both provisions give rise to positive obligations on the state to ensure (*inter alia*) that the use of force is properly controlled, that there is an effective and timely investigation of allegations that people have been unlawfully deprived of their lives or subjected to inhuman or degrading treatment, and that those responsible can be brought to justice. It is likely the police will have to be more open about their tactics

---

[97] [1984] IRLR 76, DC.

[98] Sir Leslie Scarman, *Report on the Red Lion Square Disorders of 15 June 1974*, Cmnd. 5919 (London: HMSO, 1975); Lord Scarman, *The Brixton Disorders 10–12 April 1981*, Cmnd. 8427 (London: HMSO, 1981).

[99] For discussion, see R. Geary, *Policing Industrial Disputes 1893–1985* (London: Methuen, 1985); R. de Friend and S. Uglow, 'Policing Industrial Disputes', in J. Baxter and L. Koffman (eds.), *Police: The Constitution and the Community* (Abingdon: Professional Books, 1985), 62–71; S. McCabe and P. Wallington (with J. Alderson, L. Gostin, and C. Mason), *The Police, Public Order and Civil Liberties: Legacies of the Miners' Strike* (London: Routledge, 1988), ch. 6; G. Northam, *Shooting in the Dark: Riot Police in Britain* (London: Faber, 1988); P. A. J. Waddington, *The Strong Arm of the Law: Armed and Public Order Policing* (Oxford: Clarendon Press, 1991), ch. 6; P. A. J. Waddington, *Liberty and Order* (London: UCL Press, 1994); M. King, *Public Order Policing: Contemporary Perspectives on Strategy and Tactics* (Leicester: Perpetuity, 1995).

[100] In *R. v. Wiltshire Constabulary, ex parte Taylor*, DC (Kennedy J), 25 February 1992, unreported (text available on Lexis) the court refused judicial review of a circular concerning the use of a power to direct travellers to leave premises under the Public Order Act 1986, s. 39.

[101] *Goodwin v. Chief Constable of Lancashire Constabulary*, The Times, 3 November 1992; full text available from Lexis. It is possible that the decision might now be different in the light of *R. v. Chief Constable of West Midlands Police, ex parte Wiley* [1995] 1 AC 274, [1994] 3 All ER 420, HL, and the Freedom of Information Act 2000.

and rules of engagement in order to satisfy investigators and courts that the command-and-control requirements have been met. In addition, where police tactics interfere with freedoms to manifest belief, express opinions, or assemble peacefully under ECHR Articles 9, 10, and 11, their use will have to be shown to be a proportionate response to a pressing social need to advance a legitimate aim (such as protecting public order or the rights and freedoms of others) in order to be justifiable and hence lawful under the Human Rights Act 1998. It does not resolve all the problems in this area, but it advances the rule of law by providing a coherent set of legal principles by which police action of different kinds and in very varied circumstances are to be evaluated.

(5) PRESERVING THE PEACE AND THE POLICE ACT 1996, SECTION 89

It is an offence to assault a constable in the execution of his duty, or a person assisting a constable in the execution of that duty.[102] It is also an offence to resist or wilfully obstruct a constable in the execution of his duty, or a person assisting the constable in the execution of that duty.[103] Although the offence of wilful obstruction does not carry with it a power to arrest suspected offenders without warrant, it is regularly used to criminalize otherwise lawful behaviour in ways that interfere with freedom of expression and assembly. A constable who reasonably apprehends an imminent breach of the peace may direct someone to desist from a lawful activity (such as moving together round a city centre, or speaking or preaching in public) in order to reduce the risk of violence. If the person knowingly refuses to comply with the direction without a lawful excuse, he commits the offence of wilfully obstructing the constable in the execution of his duty to prevent a breach of the peace. This was established in *Duncan v. Jones*.[104] Mrs. Duncan had been planning to speak in the street opposite a training centre for unemployed workers. The police reasonably (as the courts later found) anticipated that her speech might precipitate a breach of the peace, and told Mrs. Duncan that she was to hold her meeting in another street about 175 yards away. She refused, and began to speak. She was arrested (presumably to prevent a breach of the peace), and was later charged under a forerunner of what is now section 89(2) of the Police Act 1996. The magistrates convicted her. The Divisional Court upheld the decision on the ground that the police had been acting in the execution of their duty in trying to prevent a reasonably apprehended breach of the peace, and had been obstructed by Mrs. Duncan's refusal to comply with the steps which the police thought necessary to avert the apprehended breach of the peace.

Even in 1936 the decision was unsatisfactory. The evidence that a breach of the peace was imminent was hardly adequate. The legislation had in the past been regarded as being concerned with physical obstruction, not verbal disobedience, and had not been intended by its drafters to be used to support public-order

[102] Police Act 1996, s. 89(1).
[103] Ibid., s. 89(2).
[104] [1936] 1 KB 218, DC.

powers.[105] But there was, and remains, a more fundamental objection, particularly at a time when human rights are a developed part of English law. The offence presents the police with a means of criminalizing non-compliance with instructions about public speech and protest. It makes it possible for the police to turn public speech into a potential criminal offence on an *ad hoc* basis, whenever a constable reasonably apprehends a breach of the peace, merely by telling the speaker to stop. Today, the courts must take account of two developments. First, at common law there is now a preference for requiring the police to protect lawful and reasonable behaviour against unreasonable and unlawful interference where practicable.[106] Secondly, the Human Rights Act 1998, section 6, makes it unlawful for a constable to act incompatibly with a Convention right unless required to do so by primary legislation. An interference with, for example, freedom of expression under ECHR Article 10(1) is lawful only if it is prescribed by law and necessary in a democratic society (i.e. a proportionate response to a pressing social need) for one of a limited number of purposes, including the protection of public order. The legality of the constable's action thus depends now not only on the reasonableness of the assessment that a breach of the peace is imminent, but also on the proportionality of the constable's response to the risk so far as it interferes with the Convention right.

18.2 CRIMINALIZING PUBLIC DISORDER UNDER STATUTE

(1) BACKGROUND

Parliament has utilized three means to control public disorder. First, it has created criminal offences and attached powers of arrest to them. Secondly, it has created statutory regulatory powers to control the routes and other incidents of processions and the terms on which meetings may be held. Thirdly, it has granted powers to restrict the movement of potential trouble-makers, bar vulnerable people from trouble-spots, and ban activities such as public drinking which often precipitate disorder. In doing so, Parliament has had to decide what types of behaviour are absolutely unacceptable, and what behaviour is acceptable if confined within limits. It has also had to settle the limits which are acceptable in the light of the need to maintain the conditions necessary for democracy. Finally, it has had to decide how much of the day-to-day operation of the system of regulation and control, including making decisions which (as noted above in relation to breach of the peace powers) have substantial policy implications, should be within the discretion of police officers and others, and how that discretion should be circumscribed.

---

[105] T. C. Daintith, 'Disobeying a Policeman: A Fresh Look at *Duncan v. Jones*' [1966] *PL* 248–61; Supperstone, *Brownlie's Law of Public Order and National Security*, 2nd edn., 111–14; A. T. H. Smith, *Offences against Public Order including the Public Order Act 1986* (London: Sweet & Maxwell, 1987), 174–6; Barendt, *Freedom of Speech*, 208.

[106] *Redmond-Bate v. DPP* (1999) 7 BHRC 375, DC, discussed above in the context of the use of common-law powers to prevent breaches of the peace.

Until the passing of the Public Order Act 1986, the criminal offences relating to public order were a mixture of old common-law crimes (riot, rout, affray, unlawful assembly, and public nuisance), and statutory offences to control picketing and the provocative display of uniforms and of armed force. The common-law offences were of considerable antiquity. They belonged to an age before government was legitimized by democratic activity; public gatherings and public protest were seen as a threat to good government.[107] Yet sometimes protest was a necessary pressure-valve allowing political outsiders to relieve their feelings and impress their concerns on their governors. Although often stigmatized as a criminal rabble, protestors were frequently respectable members of society who lacked any other effective way of making the political elite take their complaints seriously.[108] (This remains evident in many modern protests in the UK, such as the riots against the Community Charge or 'Poll Tax' in the late 1980s and environmental and animal welfare demonstrations in the 1990s.[109]) Those in power recognized this, and were surprisingly tolerant of illegal activities as a necessary safety-valve for political grievances.[110] When legislation gave powers to restrict protest in a way which went beyond what was regarded as the just level of repressive force, many members of English society resisted it as being out of tune with their social expectations.[111] To cope with the tension between social acceptance (if not approval) of protest on the one hand and legal powers to repress it on the other, governments developed a sense of the just proportion between a threat to order and the proper level of force in response to it. Criminal law was used to allow the state to crack down on opposition when, and to the extent that, it seemed politic to do so. It is only relatively recently that governments have lost sight of the fact that vigorous and sometimes violent public demonstrations are a long-standing and central, if occasional, part of English political life.

The common law developed a series of offences designed to allow the desired flexibility to prosecuting authorities. The most serious was riot, essentially a gathering of three or more people (fewer, probably, than would be needed to form a riot in

[107] C. Hill, *Liberty against the Law: Some Seventeenth-Century Controversies* (London: Allan Lane/Penguin Books, 1996), especially chs 2, 20, 21.

[108] J. Guy, *Tudor England* (Oxford: Oxford University Press, 1988), 209: the Devon and Cornwall rebellion in 1549 was led by people 'from just outside the governing class', while the leaders of the East Anglian revolt 'were just outside the magisterial orbit'.

[109] See G. Rudé, *The Crowd in History: A Study of Popular Disturbances in France and England, 1730–1848*, revised edn. (London: Lawrence and Wishart, 1981), 59–62, and chs 5, 10, and 12; D. J. V. Jones, *Rebecca's Children: a Study of Rural Society, Crime, and Protest* (Oxford: Clarendon Press, 1989), *passim*; and D. Butler, A. Adonis, and T. Travers, *Failure in British Government: The Politics of the Poll Tax* (Oxford: Oxford University Press, 1994), ch. 7.

[110] This could be seen, both by the elite and the disenfranchised, as weakness. See Guy, *Tudor England*, 211 on the Protector Somerset's response to the popular risings of 1549: 'Somerset's vacillation gave rebels both occasion and boldness to strike'; P. Williams, *The Later Tudors: England 1547–1603* (Oxford: Oxford University Press, 1995), 51–6; B. L. Beer, *Rebellion and Riot: Popular Disorder in England during the Reign of Edward VI* (Kent, Ohio, 1982), 38–139. But it could also help to maintain the balance of consent essential to social order. On ambivalence towards later disturbances, see, e.g. J. Walter, 'Grain Riots and Popular Attitudes to the Law: Maldon and the Crisis of 1629', in J. Brewer and J. Styles (eds.), *An Ungovernable People: The English and their Law in the Seventeenth and Eighteenth Centuries* (London: Hutchinson, 1983), ch. 2.

[111] C. Townshend, *Making the Peace: Public Order and Public Security in Modern Britain* (Oxford: Oxford University Press, 1993), ch. 2.

popular or journalistic usage of the word) giving effect to a common purpose, displaying force or violence in such a way as to alarm a person of reasonable firmness and courage, and intending to use force if necessary against anyone who opposes them.[112] Rout was essentially an attempted riot.[113] Unlawful assembly was an offence of uncertain scope,[114] but the Law Commission adopted, as a working definition, an assembly of at least three people with a common purpose either to commit a crime of violence or to achieve any object in such a way as to cause reasonable people to apprehend a breach of the peace.[115] Lord Hailsham LC described it as 'only an inchoate riot'.[116] Affray was unlawful fighting by at least one person (who might be fighting unlawfully even if the other fighter was lawfully trying to restrain him) in a public place, or on private premises where an innocent person was present, in such a way that the bystander was, or might reasonably be expected to have been, terrified.[117]

Alongside these common-law crimes were various statutory offences, of which the most used was section 5 of the Public Order Act 1936 (as amended), forbidding threatening, abusive, or insulting words, behaviour, or visible displays, in a public place or at a public meeting, with intent to provoke a breach of the peace or whereby a breach of the peace was likely to be occasioned (some local legislation was to a similar effect). This section and related local legislation was used by the police as a catch-all provision, taking in any behaviour which did not clearly fall within the common law offences. Section 5 was used very much more broadly than its framers had expected: it had been introduced hurriedly and rushed through Parliament in 1936 as part of a package of measures aimed at quasi-military fascist groups which were terrorizing people with uniforms, military training, and public meetings and marches. Once passed, however, the section was used indiscriminately by police against people making a nuisance of themselves in public toilets, jumping on elasticated ropes from bridges, and doing a variety of other things which the police felt should be unlawful.

The regulatory mechanism in section 3 of the Public Order Act 1936 allowed a chief police officer to seek an order from a local authority with the Home Secretary's consent (in the City of London, from the Home Secretary alone) banning processions or a class of processions for a period not exceeding three months. It also allowed the chief police officer to impose such conditions on the procession as he thought necessary to preserve public order (subject to certain limitations). The power to ban processions, which had generally been used very sparingly (although there was a spate of banning orders in the wake of the riots in inner-city areas in 1981), left too much discretion in the hands of the police to apply for bans (or, indeed, to impose conditions) where there was no real risk of substantial disorder, and the power to dictate conditions as to a route could make the procession an ineffective way of publicizing a

---

[112] *R. v. Caird* (1970) 54 Cr. App. R. 499, CA.

[113] See *Redford v. Birley* (1822) 1 St. Tr. (NS) 1071 at cols. 1211, 1214.

[114] For full discussion, see Law Commission Working Paper No. 82 (London: HMSO, 1982), ch. 2.

[115] Law Com. No. 123, *Criminal Law: Offences Relating to Public Order* (London: HMSO, 1983), para. 5.2, adopting the formulation of J. C. Smith and B. Hogan, *Criminal Law*, 4th edn. (London: Butterworths, 1978), 750.

[116] *Kamara v. DPP* [1974] AC 104 at 116.

[117] *Button v. DPP* [1966] AC 591, HL; *Taylor v. DPP* [1973] AC 964, HL.

grievance or appealing to the public. At the same time, the police were seeking legislation nationally to impose on the organizers of marches an obligation to give notice of processions so that appropriate measures could be planned to preserve order. Such obligations already applied locally under various local Acts. The greater the risk of major disorder, the stronger grew the acceptance of the need for such notice requirements, and the 1981 riots were influential in this regard. Lord Scarman, generally regarded as a libertarian in civil liberties matters, had opposed the general imposition of notice requirements in his report on the Red Lion Square disorders in 1975, but in his report on the Brixton riots of 1981 he changed his mind, deciding that a need for notice had been shown to exist.[118]

All this prompted a major re-examination of public-order law. The common-law offences were thought to be obscure and outdated; there was disquiet about the operation of the Public Order Act 1936; and the relationship between the common-law and statutory offences was in need of clarification. The statutory offences themselves, and the powers of the police under statute, were thought to need revision. The Law Commission, as part of its programme of codifying the criminal law, took on the responsibility for reviewing the common-law offences. The Home Office, responding to a critical report of the House of Commons Home Affairs Select Committee in the 1979–80 session, published a Green Paper on the 1936 Act in 1980.[119] Eventually, after much debate, proposals for legislative reform were turned into the Public Order Act 1986. However, one major area which was omitted from both the reviews and the reforms was that of powers to prevent breaches of the peace. This major source of power therefore remains on a common-law footing, as noted above.

Subsequently, during the 1990s, successive Conservative and Labour governments successfully introduced Bills to Parliament to create new public-order offences and to extend the powers of the police, local authorities, and courts to regulate access to and behaviour in public places. The legislation took the form of a series of *ad hoc* reactions to what were perceived as pressing social problems. The Criminal Justice and Public Order Act 1994 included measures in response to New Age travellers parking vehicles on private land and refusing to leave, damaging property and often insulting the landowners; powers to combat animal rights campaigners who were trying to disrupt hunts; and provisions to deal with the increasingly popular phenomenon of 'raves' on disused premises. A series of Acts increased powers to control the movements of football hooligans and suspected hooligans, as outlined in Chapter 8, above. The Protection from Harassment Act 1997 was enacted in response to concern about stalkers, but has a far wider application, enhanced by provisions in the Criminal Justice and Police Act 2001 for controlling harassment of people at their homes for political purposes. The Crime and Disorder Act 1998 introduced anti-social behaviour orders, allowing courts to restrict the movement and behaviour of people who appear to have been acting in an anti-social manner, even if they had not been

---

[118] Compare *Red Lion Square Disorders*, paras. 128–9, with *The Brixton Disorders*, paras. 7.45–9.

[119] Home Affairs Committee, *Fifth Report: The Law Relating to Public Order*, HC 756 of 1979–80; *Review of the Public Order Act 1936 and Related Legislation*, Cmnd. 7891 (London: HMSO, 1980); Law Commission Report No. 123, *Criminal Law: Offences Relating to Public Order* (London: HMSO, 1983).

convicted of any offence, originally in order to protect people against so-called 'neighbours from hell'. The 1998 Act also introduced child safety orders, allowing courts to restrict the activity of trouble-making children under the age of ten, and child curfew orders by which councils (and later police forces) could bar children under ten (later raised to sixteen) from specified public places at night.[119a] The Criminal Justice and Police Act 2001 includes powers in sections 12 to 16 to ban the consumption of alcohol in public places, to combat what the government stigmatized as a 'yob culture' based around drunken behaviour after consumption of liquor.

Although most of this legislation was enacted for apparently non-political purposes, it can be used to restrict people's opportunity to express political and other views in public, and to gain access to public spaces on which people without extensive private land depend to assemble with their friends and acquaintances for other purposes. It falls to be examined in the light of the right to respect for private life under ECHR Article 8 and the right to freedom of movement under ICCPR Article 12, as well as the rights to manifest beliefs, express opinions, and assemble peacefully under ECHR Articles 9, 10, and 11.

(2) THE PUBLIC ORDER ACT 1986 AND THE CRIMINAL JUSTICE AND PUBLIC ORDER ACT 1994: CRIMINAL OFFENCES OF PUBLIC DISORDER[120]

The Public Order Act 1986 abolished the common law offences of riot, rout, unlawful assembly, and affray,[121] and the offences under section 5 of the 1936 Act. In their place, Part I of the Act introduces five statutory crimes, following the Law Commission's recommendations. In decreasing order of seriousness, these are riot (section 1), violent disorder (section 2), affray (section 3), causing fear of or provoking violence (section 4), and causing harassment, alarm, or distress (section 5). In addition, there is an offence of intentionally causing harassment, alarm, or distress (section 4A, added by the Criminal Justice and Public Order Act 1994), and one of aggravated trespass, aimed originally at hunt saboteurs, under section 68 of the Criminal Justice and Public Order Act 1994. As these offences may be committed either in public or in private places, and offences under sections 1 and 2 may be committed even if nobody

---

[119a] Anti-social behaviour orders are made in civil, not criminal, proceedings, and are concerned with protection of the public, not punishment, and so can be made without complying with the requirements of ECHR Article 6(2) re criminal charges or criminal standard of proof: *R. (McCann) v. Crown Court at Manchester* [2001] 1 WLR 358, DC, affirmed [2001] 1 WLR 1084, CA. The same applies to sex offender orders: *B. v. Avon and Somerset Constabulary* [2001] 1 WLR 340, applied in *McCann*. For the same reason, hearsay evidence is admissible on applications for anti-social behaviour orders: *Clingham v. Kensington and Chelsea LBC, The Times*, 20 February 2001, DC. On the Crime and Disorder Act 1998, the approach to children in public places, and child safety orders, see C. Piper, 'The Crime and Disorder Act 1998: Child and Community "Safety"' (1999) 62 *MLR* 397–408.

[120] A. T. H. Smith, 'The Public Order Act 1986 Part I: The New Offences' [1987] Crim. LR 156–67; A. T. H. Smith, *Offences against Public Order*, chs 3–7; A. T. H. Smith, 'The Public Order Elements' [1995] Crim. LR 19–27.

[121] Public Order Act 1986, s. 9(1). In the remainder of the present section, all section numbers refer to the Public Order Act 1986 unless otherwise specified.

else is present.[122] The words 'public order' in the short titles of the 1986 and 1994 Acts are a misnomer: these offences are aimed at private as well as public disorder on private as well as public land.

(i) Riot

Riot, the most violent offence, is triable only on indictment and carries a maximum penalty of ten years' imprisonment and an unlimited fine.[123] A person commits this offence if:

(a) he is one of twelve or more people present together, who

(b) together use or threaten unlawful violence[124]

(c) for a common purpose,[125] and

(d) the person uses violence, either intending to be violent or being aware that his own conduct may be violent,[126] and

(e) the violence is such as would cause a hypothetical person of reasonable firmness, were one present at the scene, to fear for his personal safety.[127]

This provision increased the number of people required for riot from three to twelve, turning it into a small-crowd offence rather than a small group offence. It also clarified the *mens rea* of the offence. Elements (a) to (c) have been said to provide the context in which the offence can take place, while elements (d) and (e) specify the actual offence. In other words, the offence is committed by people who actually use violence, or who aid and abet it by encouraging or assisting those using it. A mere onlooker in the crowd does not commit an offence under the section.[128]

(ii) Violent disorder

Violent disorder is committed by members of a violent small group or crowd who do not (necessarily) have a common purpose. It is triable either summarily (maximum sentence: six months' imprisonment and fine not exceeding the statutory maximum) or on indictment (five years' imprisonment and unlimited fine).[129] A person is guilty of violent disorder if:

(a) he is one of three or more people present together, who

---

[122] See ss. 1(4), (5); 2(3), (4); 3(4), (5); 4(2); 5(2).

[123] S. 1(6).

[124] They need not all satisfy the *mens rea* requirements: s. 6(7).

[125] The common purpose may be inferred from conduct: s. 1(3). It need not be very specific—a common purpose to use unlawful violence in celebrating an England soccer victory over Egypt suffices: *R. v. Jefferson and others* [1994] 1 All ER 270, CA.

[126] Public Order Act 1986, s. 6(1). Intoxication caused by any means does not negative *mens rea* if a sober person would have realized that his conduct may be violent, unless the defendant shows either (a) that the intoxication was not self-induced, or (b) that it was caused solely by the taking or administration of a substance in the course of medical treatment: s. 6(5), (6).

[127] S. 1(1).

[128] *R. v. Tyler* (1992) 96 Cr. App. R. 332, CA; *R. v. Jefferson and others* [1994] 1 All ER 270, CA.

[129] S. 2(7).

(b) use or threaten violence (not necessarily simultaneously),[130] either intending to do so or being aware that their conduct may be violent or threaten violence,[131]

(c) in such a way that (taking their conduct together) it would cause a hypothetical person of reasonable firmness, were one present at the scene, to fear for his personal safety.[132]

A person can be guilty of the offence by aiding and abetting it.[133] However, because of element (b), if only three people were present and all are charged with the offence, and one is acquitted on the ground that he did not actually use violence, the other two must also be acquitted. The fact that the third person was aiding and abetting the other two cannot make the three of them, or any of them, guilty of the offence, even if the other two were using violence together.[134] If the evidence is that other people, who have not been charged, were involved in the violence as well, then it will be possible to convict the accused as long as it is proved beyond reasonable doubt that at least three people, including the accused, were using violence unlawfully.[135] A defendant can plead self-defence on the basis of a genuine (although not necessarily accurate) belief that he was about to be attacked and was defending himself.[136]

(iii) Affray

Affray is committed by a person who:

(a) uses or threatens (by conduct, not mere words: see section 3(3))[137] unlawful violence towards another person, where

(b) his conduct, together with that of anyone else who is using or threatening unlawful violence, would cause a hypothetical third person of reasonable firmness (not the person against whom the violence was originally directed[138]) to fear for his personal safety.

Behaviour which gives rise to a general fear of violence, without being directed towards a specific person or people, does not constitute affray, however threatening it may seem. In *I. v. Director of Public Prosecutions*[139] the House of Lords unanimously quashed the convictions of several defendants who had been carrying petrol bombs in public, because they had not used them to threaten anyone directly. In the leading speech, Lord Hutton drew attention to the provenance of the statutory offence in a

---

[130] They need not all satisfy the *mens rea* requirements: s. 6(7).

[131] S. 6(2). 'Threat' is therefore an objectively, rather than subjectively, judged phenomenon. See also s. 6(5), (6).

[132] S. 2.

[133] *R. v. Jefferson and others* [1994] 1 All ER 270, CA.

[134] *R. v. McGuigan and Cameron* [1991] Crim. LR 719, CA. See also *R. v. Fleming and Robinson* [1989] Crim. LR 658, *R. v. Mahroof* [1989] Crim. LR 72.

[135] *R. v. Worton* [1990] Crim. LR 124, CA (the appeal was allowed on other grounds).

[136] *R. v. Hughes* [1995] Crim. LR 956, CA.

[137] As for violent disorder, the test of 'threatening' is objective, not subjective: s. 6(2).

[138] *R. v. Sanchez* (1996) 160 JP 321, CA; *R. v. Thind* [1999] Crim. LR 842, CA.

[139] [2001] 2 WLR 765, HL.

common law crime of unlawful fighting. The element of direct confrontation was held to be a requirement of the statutory offence as well. This accentuates the importance of ensuring that the jury knows exactly what facts the prosecution relies on, particularly in cases involving a sequence of events in different places.[140]

The offence is triable summarily, with the same sentence as for violent disorder, or on indictment, with a maximum prison term of three years. This means that affray, unlike riot and violent disorder, is not an arrestable offence, and so cannot be a serious arrestable offence, within the meaning of the Police and Criminal Evidence Act 1984. A power to arrest without warrant is conferred on a constable by section 3(6), probably unnecessarily, since affray will virtually always give rise to a breach of the peace giving a common-law power of arrest to anyone. The arrest power under the Act is more limited than the common-law power, as it applies only where a constable reasonably suspects that the arrestee is committing the offence, not where he reasonably apprehends that a breach of the peace is about to occur.

(iv) Causing fear of, or provoking, violence

Causing fear of, or provoking, violence is an offence committed by a person who behaves in certain ways towards someone else, who must actually be present. A person is guilty if:[141]

(a) he (i) uses threatening, abusive, or insulting words or behaviour, or (ii) distributes or displays to another person any writing, sign, or other visible representation which is threatening, abusive, or insulting,

(b) in a public place, or in a private place (unless the words, behaviour, etc., are used or displayed inside a dwelling and the person to whom they are addressed is within the same or another dwelling),

(c) he intends the words, behaviour, writing, sign, etc. to be threatening, abusive, or insulting, or is aware that they may be threatening, abusive, or insulting,[142] and

(d) he intends, or the conduct is likely, (i) to cause the other person to believe that immediate unlawful violence will be used against him or anyone else by any person,[143] or (ii) to provoke the immediate use of unlawful violence by that person or another.[144]

The offence covers part of the ground previously covered by section 5 of the Public Order Act 1936. Under that section, it was an offence if the words or behaviour were

---

[140] See *R. v. Smith (Christopher)* [1997] 1 Cr. App. R. 14, CA.

[141] S. 4.

[142] S. 6(3). Note also s. 6(5), (6).

[143] Where a letter threatens a bombing campaign against the recipient, it is open to the trial court to conclude that it is likely to cause the recipient to believe that immediate unlawful violence will be used if the letter does not say when the bombing will begin: *DPP v. Ramos* [2000] Crim. LR 768, DC (a not entirely satisfactory decision, as the court appears to have been confused about what the prosecution had to prove, and spoke of the recipient's actual state of mind as well as the recipient's likely belief).

[144] Only one offence is created by s. 4, but it may be committed in a number of different ways. See *Wynn v. DPP*, *Independent*, 4 May 1992, DC.

objectively threatening, abusive, or insulting and were either intended or likely to occasion a breach of the peace. Under the new Act, there must be a subjective recognition of the nature of the words or behaviour, and a fear of violence engendered in an identified person. The elements of the old section 5 which are not covered by the offence of causing fear of or provoking violence are incorporated in the less serious offence of causing harassment, alarm, or distress, which is outlined below.

The offence of causing fear of, or provoking, violence is triable summarily, with a maximum sentence of six months' imprisonment and a fine not exceeding level 5 on the standard scale. It is therefore not an arrestable offence, but a constable is given power to arrest without warrant anyone he reasonably suspects is committing the offence. Again, this is a narrower power than the concurrent common-law power to restrain a reasonably apprehended breach of the peace, which will often be available.

(v) Causing harassment, alarm, or distress

Causing harassment, alarm, or distress is an offence punishable only by a fine not exceeding level 3 on the standard scale. It penalizes anyone who:

(a) (i) uses threatening, abusive, or insulting words or behaviour, or disorderly behaviour, or (ii) displays any writing, sign, or other visible representation which is threatening, abusive, or insulting,[145]

(b) in a public place (or in a private place unless the words, behaviour, etc. are used or displayed inside a dwelling and the person to whom they are addressed is within the same or another dwelling),

(c) within the sight of another person, who must be a real rather than a hypothetical person for this purpose,

(d) who is likely to be caused harassment, alarm, or distress thereby,[146] if

(e) the defendant intends the words, behaviour, writing, etc., to be threatening, abusive, or insulting, or is aware that it may be, or intends or is aware that his behaviour shall or may be disorderly.[147]

The test of awareness and intention is subjective, so the prosecution must show that the accused is aware of the threatening, abusive, or insulting nature of the display, etc. If the defendant is not aware of the fact that those seeing a display of, for example, an aborted foetus might think it threatening, abusive, or insulting, he cannot be convicted.[148] This offence covers part of the field previously dealt with by section 5 of the old 1936 Act, but is wider than the old Act, because the new provision does not require that the conduct is likely to occasion a breach of the peace, and it goes beyond the sort of behaviour which is aimed at bystanders, being threatening, abusive, or insulting. Instead, it criminalizes merely 'disorderly behaviour', a term wide enough

---

[145] Note that a person who is part of a crowd of people committing this offence may be guilty as an aider and abettor, even if the person himself was not doing anything specified by the section: see *DPP v. Fidler* [1992] 1 WLR 91, DC, and the commentary by Professor J. C. Smith, [1992] Crim. LR at 63.

[146] Public Order Act 1986, s. 5(1), (2).

[147] Ibid., s. 6(4); note also s. 6(5), (6).

[148] *DPP v. Clarke, Lewis, O'Connell and O'Keefe* [1992] Crim. LR 60, DC.

to include horseplay, or running exuberantly along a footpath. There need be no violent or physically disorderly behaviour. In *Chambers and Edwards v. Director of Public Prosecutions*,[149] people protesting against the building of a road had interfered with the work of a surveyor on the site by standing or putting placards in the path of the infra-red beam from his theodolite, preventing him from using it. The Divisional Court decided that this amounted to disorderly behaviour, and could constitute the offence as it caused harassment to the surveyor, making him annoyed. This stretches the meaning of disorderly behaviour a long way beyond the general Saturday-night closing-time yobbishness at which the section was aimed, but the court was not deterred by this, or by the fact that it gives rise to an overlap with the offence of aggravated trespass under section 68 of the Criminal Justice and Public Order Act 1994.

However, the rigour of this is slightly modified by giving the accused a defence if he can discharge the burden of proving (on the balance of probabilities) that either:

(a) he had no reason to believe that there was anyone within hearing or sight who was likely to be caused harassment, alarm, or distress; or

(b) where he was in a dwelling, he had no reason to believe that the words, behaviour, writing, etc., would be heard or seen by anyone outside that or another dwelling; or

(c) that his conduct was reasonable.[150]

Under defence (a), the defendant who can show that he did not believe, subjectively, that a display could have the effect of causing harassment, alarm, or distress to others present would be entitled to be acquitted.[151] This means that people, particularly when demonstrating about emotive issues such as abortion, have some protection against the over-sensitivity of others. However, once the effect on observers has been pointed out to a demonstrator, the use of the same display in future is unlikely to attract the defence, since he will no longer be able to say that he had no reason to believe that it was likely to cause harassment, alarm, or distress. Under defence (c), the reasonableness of a display is to be judged objectively. Accordingly, courts were entitled to find that it was not objectively reasonable for anti-abortion campaigners to display a picture of an aborted foetus when demonstrating outside a clinic where abortions were performed,[152] and that it was unreasonable for them to cause severe distress to staff and patients by preventing them from entering the clinic to exercise their lawful rights,[153] even if the campaigners honestly believed that illegal abortions were being performed on the premises. This interferes with freedom of expression. Under the Human Rights Act 1998, it is hard to imagine that criminalizing the use of a picture of an aborted foetus would be justifiable under ECHR Article 10(2). It is hard

---

[149] [1995] Crim. LR 896, DC.

[150] S. 5(3).

[151] *DPP v. Clarke, Lewis, O'Connell and O'Keefe* [1992] Crim. LR 60, DC.

[152] See n. 151.

[153] *Morrow, Geach and Thomas v. DPP, Secretary of State for Health and British Pregnancy Advisory Service intervening* [1994] Crim. LR 58, DC, where a defence that reasonable force was being used to prevent a crime under Criminal Law Act 1967, s. 3, also failed.

to separate the message expressed (abortion harms unborn children) from the graphic means used to convey it: both should be protected if used for a serious purpose. On the other hand, it would be legitimate to stop people preventing staff and patients gaining access to the clinic. It will be interesting to see how rigorously the courts use ECHR Article 10(2) to give substance to the word 'reasonable' in the 1986 Act and so offer real and predictable protection to free expression against charges under the Act. In the USA, where First Amendment rights are particularly strongly protected, the time, place, and manner of protestors' activities can be restricted to allow staff and patients to enter clinics, but the restrictions must be narrowly tailored to that purpose.[154] It is likely that scrutiny of public-order cases under the Human Rights Act 1998 will develop in the same direction.

As there need be no threat of violence or breach of the peace to constitute the offence, the power to arrest without warrant for this offence is heavily circumscribed. A constable may arrest without warrant only where the suspect has engaged in 'offensive conduct' (defined as conduct the constable reasonably suspects to be an offence under section 5), the constable has warned him to stop, and the suspect engages in further offensive conduct (which may or may not be of the same type as that which provoked the original warning) immediately or shortly after the warning.[155] The warning need not be given in any set or formal terms. A court will look at the substance of the conversation, and, if it was clear that the constable would arrest the defendant if the behaviour recurred, it will suffice.[156]

This offence, and its related arrest power, have equivalents in other jurisdictions. In Scotland, the common-law offence of breach of the peace is said to encompass any conduct which may reasonably be expected to cause any person to be alarmed, upset, or annoyed, or to provoke a disturbance, or which is likely to lead to such consequences if allowed to continue.[157] In New Zealand there are equivalent statutory provisions. However, any such offence is subject to two objections.

First, it makes criminal a very wide and unpredictable range of types of behaviour. The object of the prohibition on disorderly conduct was to target hooliganism, particularly drunken hooliganism, in public, and it seems to have been assumed that there would be fairly general agreement about what constituted disorderly conduct. However, one may doubt whether this is so. Disorderly conduct is a relative notion, and depends heavily on context. Where one expects high standards of conduct, any non-conforming behaviour may be thought disorderly. Behaviour which would be thought disorderly in a street or a bar, such as abusive shouting, might not be disorderly in a place where expected standards of conduct are less genteel, such as the floor of the House of Commons or a rugby-club dinner. There is a danger that conduct will be stigmatized as criminal not because of its intrinsic nature, or the expectations of the people in the area where it occurs, but because the police and, at

---

[154] *Masden v. Women's Health Center, Inc.* 512 US 753 (1994), US Supreme Court.
[155] S.5(4), (5).
[156] *Groom v. DPP* [1991] Crim. LR 713, DC.
[157] *Wilson v. Brown*, 1982 SCCR 49; K. D. Ewing and W. Finnie, *Civil Liberties in Scotland: Cases and Materials*, 2nd edn. (Edinburgh: W. Green & Son, 1988), 412–14.

the hearing, the magistrates disapprove of the expected standards of conduct and wish that higher (or different) standards obtained. In terms of civil liberties and the rule of law, it is unacceptable to make the imposition of criminal sanctions depend on uncertain and variable standards.

Secondly, quite apart from the discretion given to the police, Crown Prosecution Service, and magistrates, the arrest power may appear less concerned with preventing harassment, alarm, or distress to citizens than with bolstering the authority of the constable. The event which triggers the arrest is not the original unlawful act but the disobedience to a constable. Generally, there is (probably) no power to arrest for obstructing a constable in the execution of his duty unless the obstruction also amounts to an arrestable offence, another offence carrying a power to arrest without warrant, or a breach of the peace, although conduct which does not amount to any offence may lead to an arrest if a person is reasonably suspected of an earlier offence and the later conduct satisfies the general arrest conditions under section 25 of the Police and Criminal Evidence Act 1984 (see Chapter 6 above). Here, however, the challenge to the authority of the constable, which results where a suspect wants to push his luck or show off to friends by disobeying the constable, may lead to an arrest. Perhaps it is a justification that, because of the definition of 'offensive conduct' in section 5(5), the arrest might avoid further harassment, alarm, or distress to bystanders. Yet this will not necessarily be the case, as it has been held in *Director of Public Prosecutions v. Orum*[158] that an offence under section 5(1) may be committed even where the only person likely to be caused harassment, alarm, or distress is a police officer. Although at trial a court would have to consider whether the conduct, etc. would actually have been likely to cause harassment, alarm, or distress (rather than weariness and boredom) to the constable, given that constables soon become familiar with many impolite forms of behaviour,[159] the constable himself might not be in the best position to make that assessment in the heat of the moment before deciding to make an arrest. In addition, where the 'offensive conduct' relied on is 'disorderly conduct', it raises again all the uncertainties and disagreements which may surround the meaning of the latter term.

(vi) Intentionally causing harassment, alarm, or distress

Intentionally causing harassment, alarm, or distress is an offence by section 4A, inserted into the 1986 Act to allow a heavier sentence to be passed on people who cause harassment, alarm, or distress intentionally than on those who do not intend the result. It is punishable by up to six months' imprisonment or a fine not exceeding level 5 on the standard scale. The offence is committed by anyone who:

(a) (i) uses threatening, abusive, or insulting words or behaviour, or disorderly behaviour, or (ii) displays any writing, sign, or other visible representation which is threatening, abusive, or insulting,

---

[158] [1989] 1 WLR 88, [1988] 3 All ER 449, DC.

[159] For discussion of this familiarity in a different context, see *Cheeseman v. DPP* [1992] QB 83, [1991] 3 All ER 54, DC.

(b) in a public place (or in a private place unless the words, behaviour, etc. are used or displayed inside a dwelling and the person to whom they are addressed is within the same or another dwelling),

(c) with intent to cause harassment, alarm, or distress to a person, if

(d) he actually causes harassment, alarm, or distress to that person or another person.[160]

Unlike the offence under section 4, the act causing the harassment, alarm, or distress need not take place within the sight of anyone, so the offence can be committed where the distress, etc. is caused when the event is reported to the victim by someone else. The restriction of freedom of expression represented by this provision is usually justifiable under ECHR Article 10(2) as a proportionate measure to protect the rights and freedoms of others, since the offender's intention must be to cause one of the kinds of harm listed in section 4A, rather than the harm being an incidental effect of speech or action undertaken for another reason as under section 4. There is a power to arrest without warrant for the section 4A offence.

(vii) Aggravated trespass

Aggravated trespass is an offence created by the Criminal Justice and Public Order Act 1994, originally to deter hunt saboteurs from disrupting lawful hunting, but with a wider application. Section 68 of the 1994 Act makes it an offence to trespass on land in the open air and there to do anything which is intended to intimidate people who are engaging or about to engage in a lawful activity on the land so as to deter any of them from engaging in that activity, or intended to obstruct or disrupt such activity.[161] For this purpose, activity is lawful if the people engaging in it are not committing an offence or trespassing.[162] A constable may arrest without warrant anyone whom he reasonably suspects is committing an offence.[163] Alternatively, section 69 permits the senior police officer at the scene to direct anyone he reasonably believes is committing, has committed, or is about to commit an offence under section 68 to leave the land. The senior officer present may also give a direction to leave land to two or more people who he reasonably believes are there with a common purpose of intimidating people to deter them from engaging in a lawful activity. Failing to leave as soon as practicable after such a direction has been given, or returning subsequently, is an offence, in respect of which the police have a power to arrest without warrant.

For the purpose of section 68, 'land' includes footpaths, bridleways, byways open to all traffic and roads used as public paths, but does not include other roads or highways.[164] Protestors may be trespassers on public footpaths and bridleways if they unreasonably obstruct the path, for example by blocking the lawful passage of hunters or their dogs. The effect of these provisions is not significantly different from the

---

160 Public Order Act 1986, s. 4A(1), (2).
161 Criminal Justice and Public Order Act 1994, s. 68(1).
162 Ibid., s. 68(2).
163 Ibid., s. 68(4).
164 Criminal Justice and Public Order Act 1994, ss. 68(5), 61(9).

common-law powers of the police when acting to prevent a current or reasonably anticipated and imminent breach of the peace. The main advantages of the statutory provisions are that the scope of the power and the circumstances in which it can be used are clearly set out, and the power is backed by tailor-made statutory criminal offences and powers of arrest. The main disadvantage is that section 68 allows no defence of reasonable excuse. A strict application of the section would therefore risk violating rights under ECHR Articles 9, 10, and 11, as the section appears to leave no room for the police or courts to consider whether the restriction of the rights of the protestor are, in the circumstances, proportionate to a pressing social need, or even whether the protestor was acting reasonably. It would be difficult to imply such a limitation into the section in reliance on the interpretative duty under the Human Rights Act 1998, section 3, to read and give effect to legislation in a manner compatible with Convention rights so far as it is possible to do so: the presence of a 'reasonable excuse' defence to a charge of failing to leave land under section 69 makes it clear that the omission of the defence from section 68 was conscious and intentional.

Compatibility with the Convention rights will therefore often depend on the police and Crown Prosecution Service exercising their discretions over directions, arrests, and prosecutions to ensure that the legislation is not given effect in an incompatible manner. So far as they have a discretion under the sections, they act unlawfully by virtue of section 6(1) of the Human Rights Act 1998 if they use their powers in a manner which is incompatible with a Convention right, so there is some scope for courts to control the use made of sections 68 and 69. In the early stages of the operation of the sections, they were used predominantly against environmental anti-road protestors; in hunting protests, they played a small part alongside a strategy of negotiations between police, hunters, and protestors.[165] Their impact was generally not great, but they offered the police the flexibility and discretion which was the hallmark of public-order law in England before the Human Rights Act 1998.

(viii) Racial hatred

A further public order offence is created by section 18 of the 1986 Act,[166] namely the use of words or behaviour, or display of written material, intended or likely to stir up racial hatred contrary to section 18. This is a public-order offence only in the loosest sense, since it can be committed in private premises, and need not lead to any (or any immediate) disorder. A person is guilty of an offence under section 18 if:

(a) he (i) uses threatening, abusive, or insulting words or behaviour, or (ii) displays any written material (but not other types of representation) which is threatening, abusive, or insulting,[167]

(b) in (i) a public place, or (ii) in private unless it is inside a dwelling and the

---

[165] T. Bucke and Z. James, *Trespass and Protest: Policing under the Criminal Justice and Public Order Act 1994*, Home Office Research Study 190 (London: Home Office, 1998), ch. 4.

[166] Part 5 of the Anti-terrorism, Crime and Security Bill 2001 would, if passed, extend the offence to include stirring up religious hatred.

[167] There is an exception if this is solely for the purpose of being included in a broadcast or cable-service programme: s. 18(6). Broadcasts and cable programmes are dealt with under s. 22.

words, etc. are not heard or seen except by people in that or another dwelling, and

(c) he intends thereby to stir up racial hatred or racial hatred is likely to be stirred up thereby.[168]

This goes beyond being a race relations offence, however, because under section 18 stirring up racial hatred is unlawful only if it is done by means of threatening, abusive, or insulting words, etc. Where this happens in public, it gives rise to a risk of violent reaction which justifies criminal sanctions. However, people may be guilty if they use the words, etc. in private places (other than dwellings) where everyone present agrees with the sentiments expressed. Presumably, the justification for criminalizing this sort of behaviour is that those present may be encouraged to convert their hatred into concrete action later. However, it is unusual for words or behaviour to constitute an offence in the absence of an immediate threat to somebody else. Any attempt to give practical expression to hatred outside is likely to constitute an offence, so it is particularly draconian to impose liability at the pre-attempt stage on words or conduct which might not even amount to an incitement to commit any offence. Fortunately the section has been very rarely invoked. The Attorney-General's consent is needed for any prosecution,[169] and everyone concerned with law enforcement is conscious that a prosecution might be counter-productive in terms of public sympathy. Not only does a trial (whether summary or on indictment) give a bigot a privileged platform for his views with plenty of free publicity, but the defendant will be able to claim the moral high ground by concentrating on the inroads which section 18 makes on freedom of expression, freedom of association, and rights of privacy. No less importantly, the sentence (up to two years' imprisonment and an unlimited fine after a conviction on indictment, or up to six months and a fine not exceeding the statutory maximum in the magistrates' court)[170] may make the defendant appear to be a martyr.

Section 18 criminalizes incitement to racial hatred. Incitement to hatred on other grounds is not criminal unless it amounts to a separate offence (although the Anti-terrorism, Crime and Security Bill 2001, if passed, would make incitement to religious hatred an offence). 'Racial hatred' is defined as: 'hatred against a group of persons in Great Britain defined by reference to colour, race, nationality (including citizenship), or ethnic or national origins'.[171] This uses the same extended definition of 'racial' as was used in the Race Relations Act 1976, and it will be interpreted in the same way as it has been under that Act.[172] Courts have so far given no guidance on the meaning of 'hatred'. It seems to cover the stirring up of naked ill feeling, but not to encompass messages which affront the dignity or sensitivities of members of the racial groups or their sympathizers. It is also unclear what is meant by 'stir up' hatred. The phrase

---

[168] S. 18(1), (2). To establish the necessary *mens rea*, the prosecution must show that the defendant intended to stir up racial hatred, or intended the words, etc. to be, or was aware that they might be, threatening, abusive, or insulting: s. 18(5).

[169] S. 27(1).

[170] S. 27(3).

[171] Public Order Act 1986, s. 17.

[172] See Ch. 3, above.

seems different from 'incite' or 'instigate', as it would include stirring up hatred which already exists. A racist preaching to other racists could be stirring up their hatred, encouraging them to give it free rein, if he expressed their existing shared feelings in a sufficiently provocative way. It seems likely, therefore, that political programmes which advocate forced emigration of certain ethnic groups would not automatically stir up racial hatred, but the manner of their expression might do so. The provisions have not often led to successful prosecutions, although there are occasional, high-profile cases such as the conviction of the eighty-year-old Dowager Lady Birdwood in 1994 on charges arising from her anti-Jewish booklet *The Longest Hatred*, one of many such publications for which she had been responsible.

The provisions of section 18 are supplemented by a special offence, under the Football (Offences) Act 1991, of engaging or taking part in chanting of an indecent or racialist nature, either alone or in concert with others, at a designated football match (which are mainly Football League and Premiership matches).[173] This was Parliament's response to a growing phenomenon of abuse directed towards black and foreign players.

These offences directly interfere with freedom to express a particular viewpoint. This is a questionable use of state power, and needs special justification, for all the reasons developed in Chapter 13, above. In fact, such offences are subject to two diametrically opposed critiques. The first, which is easier to deal with, can be described as the American critique: because of the reasons for valuing freedom of speech, any restriction of a particular viewpoint is intrinsically dangerous. Under the First Amendment to the Constitution of the USA, the time, place, and manner of speech may be regulated to protect a pressing state interest, but any legislative restriction on freedom of speech must be neutral between viewpoints and as to the content of expression. A rule which interferes with speech by reference to its content is unconstitutional, even if the proscribed content is objectionable and racist. In *R.A.V. v. City of St Paul, Minnesota*,[174] the petitioner had allegedly been one of a party which had taped together two chair legs to make a crude cross, and had then burnt it, employing classic Ku Klux Klan symbolism, on a black family's lawn. He had been charged under the Bias-Motivated Crime Ordinance of the City of St Paul, Minnesota, which prohibited the display of a symbol which one 'knows or has reason to know arouses anger, alarm or resentment in others on the basis of race, color, creed, religion, or gender'. The Supreme Court accepted the interpretation of the Ordinance by the Supreme Court of Minnesota, which held that it was restricted to 'fighting words', so the Ordinance was not constitutionally overbroad. Nevertheless, the majority held that the Ordinance was facially invalid, because it outlawed expressive behaviour by reference to its content: only fighting words relating to race, colour, creed, religion, or gender were prohibited. People wishing to use fighting words in relation to those subjects were at a disadvantage compared to people wishing to use fighting words against (for example) trades unions or homosexuals. As the minority judges argued, this seems to lead to a potential paradox, in that a limitation on freedom of speech

---

[173] Football (Offences) Act 1991, s. 3, as amended by Football (Offences and Disorder) Act 1999, s. 9.
[174] *R. A. V. v. City of St Paul, Minnesota* 120 L. Ed. 2d 305 (1992), US Supreme Court.

was struck down under the First Amendment for prohibiting, not too much speech, but too little: it appears to create a doctrine under which restrictions on speech can be struck down for 'underbreadth' rather than overbreadth. (In *R.A.V.*, the minority were prepared to strike down the Ordinance on the basis of overbreadth, because it extended to behaviour which merely arouses anger, alarm, or resentment, rather than being limited to conduct which inflicts injury or tends to incite immediate violence, as demanded by *Chaplinsky v. New Hampshire*.[175] Even the majority relied, as an alternative ground of decision, on the tendency for the Ordinance to be implemented in a discriminatory way, being applied to anti-black advocates rather than advocates against discrimination.)

By identifying viewpoint-based discrimination in the control of speech as specially problematic, the US Supreme Court makes an important point. Viewpoint-based controls are the stuff of totalitarianism. But it does not follow that any content-based restriction is necessarily unjustifiable. As Professor Christopher McCrudden has argued, some values are sufficiently strong to counterbalance the danger of totalitarianism flowing from non-neutral restrictions, particularly where the nature of the proscribed speech adds little to the market-place of ideas or the political process. Indeed, he argues that some values, particularly equality, positively demand non-neutral controls over speech: racist speech should be controlled.[176]

The argument can be supported from international law,[177] and from the constitutional law of other countries, including Canada, where legal controls over racist expression have been upheld as justifiable interferences with freedom of speech under the Canadian Charter of Rights and Freedoms.[178] The American approach is based on an idea of equality, but in the sense of equal treatment of different viewpoints rather than different people or peoples. It underestimates the significance of the harm which racist speech occasions to already underprivileged groups, entrenching their exclusion from mainstream participation in society. Equality as a value may not offer the solution to the problem, because there are enough forms of equality leading to different results to defy analysis. A commitment to desirable outcomes and the avoidance of harm, taking account of a wider range of psychological and communal harms than the US approach recognizes, may be the way to deal with it. Some ideas are unacceptable because of the damaging results they produce. The expression of those ideas

---

[175] 315 US 568 (1942), US Supreme Court.

[176] C. McCrudden, 'Freedom of Speech and Racial Equality', in P. Birks (ed.), *Pressing Problems in the Law Volume 1: Criminal Justice and Human Rights* (Oxford: Oxford University Press, 1995), 125–48. The present section of this book owes a great deal to the critique of the equivalent section in the first edition which Professor McCrudden offered in that paper, and to the discussion in A. Halpin, *Rights and Law: Analysis and Theory* (Oxford: Hart Publishing, 1997), especially at 122.

[177] See ICCPR Art. 20, International Convention on the Elimination of All Forms of Racial Discrimination, Art. 4, and the decision of the European Court of Human Rights in *Jersild v. Denmark*, Series A, No. 298 (1994).

[178] *R. v. Keegstra* [1990] 3 SCR 697, SC Canada; *R. v. Andrews* [1990] SCR 870, SC Canada; *Canada (Human Rights Commission) v. Taylor* [1990] 3 SCR 892, SC Canada. For discussion see Moon, *Freedom of Expression*, 126–47. For comparison with the US caselaw, see James Weinstein, 'An American's View of the Canadian Hate Speech Decisions', in W. J. Waluchow (ed.), *Free Expression: Essays in Law and Philosophy* (Oxford: Clarendon Press, 1994), 175–221.

should be banned in a civilized society which treats its citizens as equally important, and as more important than abstract ideas. No theorem allows one to calculate which ideas those are. It will vary between societies and ages, and the debate about it should be conducted in good faith through the political process.[179]

On this basis, a stronger critique of the approach taken in section 18 of the Public Order Act 1986 may be that its proscription of racist speech is too limited, rather than too intrusive. There may be good arguments for prohibiting certain types of expression which incite discrimination on grounds of sex, religion, and perhaps other things. Prohibiting sexual harassment can be seen as an example of such a development. Another example would be outlawing Holocaust denial, a view of history which is both unsustainable on the evidence and perceived by those who suffered in the Holocaust as an attack on them more subtle and less deadly than the Holocaust itself but just as determined. If it is correct to see Holocaust denial as an attack on Jews, Gypsies, homosexuals, and other groups traditionally marginalized in western societies, it could be an acceptable restriction on speech.[180]

English law has recently begun to treat racist motivation as an aggravating factor in certain offences against the person and public order offences.[181] It is not always easy to establish the necessary motivation, but the Court of Appeal has held that a defendant who called his victim a 'stupid African bitch' could be treated as being racially motivated, despite himself being a West Indian who viewed himself as an African and did not regard being called African as insulting.[182] At one level, treating racist motivation as aggravating a crime penalizes people's opinions, and risks violating the right to hold opinions under ECHR Article 10(1). However, the better view is that the criminal law penalizes the act of assault, and the motivation of the offender is simply a factor affecting the sentence. This is the approach taken in the USA to such provisions.[183] But if a person's opinion were to be the ground of liability to criminal sanctions, rather than merely a factor relevant to sentence for an offence defined without reference to the defendant's opinions, it would certainly engage the right to hold opinions under ECHR Article 10(1) and ICCPR Article 19(1). While the interference with the right might be justifiable under ECHR Article 10(2) for the purposes of the Human Rights Act 1998, it would not be justifiable under ICCPR Article 19, which permits no interference with the right to hold, rather than express, opinions.

[179] For fuller development of the ideas sketched here, see D. Feldman, 'Content Neutrality', in I. Loveland (ed.), *Importing the First Amendment: Freedom of Expression in American, English and European Law* (Oxford: Hart Publishing, 1998), 139–71.

[180] See D. McGoldrick and T. O'Donnell, 'Hate-Speech Laws: Consistency with National and International Human Rights Law' (1998) 18 *LS* 453–85; J. Cooper and A. Marshall Williams, 'Hate Speech, Holocaust Denial and International Human Rights Law' [1999] *EHRLR* 593–613; G. Bindman, 'Outlawing Holocaust Denial' (1997) 147 *NLJ* 466–8; Institute for Jewish Policy Research, *Combating Holocaust Denial through Law in the UK* (London: IJPR, 2000, accessible by the Internet at http://www.jpr.org.uk/publications/reports/civil_society_/No_3_200/index.htm).

[181] Crime and Disorder Act 1998, ss. 28–32; F. Brennan, 'Racially Motivated Crime: the Response of the Criminal Justice System' [1999] Crim. LR 17–28; M. Malik, '"Racist crime": Racially Aggravated Offences in the Crime and Disorder Act 1998 Part II' (1999) 62 *MLR* 409–24.

[182] *R. v. White (Anthony)* [2001] 1 WLR 1352, CA.

[183] *Barclay v. Florida* 463 US 939 (1983), US Supreme Court; *Wisconsin v. Mitchell* 124 L. Ed. 2d 436 (1992), US Supreme Court.

The UK's obligations in international law under the ICCPR should influence the approach English courts would take to interpreting ECHR Article 10 in those circumstances, making the task of justifying such legislation under ECHR Article 10 and the Human Rights Act extremely difficult.

(3) WATCHING AND BESETTING[184] AND HARASSMENT[185]

Two sets of provisions create criminal offences to protect people from harassment of many kinds. The first is section 7 of the Conspiracy and Protection of Property Act 1875, directed against intimidation by trades unions in the course of disputes. It makes it an offence for a person, wrongfully and without legal authority, persistently to follow another from place to place, to watch or beset a person's house or place of work, or to follow him, with two or more other persons, in a disorderly manner in or through a street or road, with a view to compelling the person to do or abstain from doing any act which the victim has a legal right to do or refrain from doing. This offence has been deployed against pickets in industrial disputes, but has recently been used against demonstrators in support of political causes such as abortion law reform. In *Director of Public Prosecutions v. Fidler*,[186] where demonstrators chanted outside a clinic where lawful abortions were performed, the prosecutor suggested that the offence was committed where people tried to dissuade people from going in to have pregnancies terminated. The Divisional Court held that persuasion, and obtaining or communicating information, did not amount to compulsion within the meaning of section 7, even if verbal abuse was used and shocking pictures of aborted foetuses were displayed. As there was no evidence that anyone had been prevented from performing or undergoing a termination, the charge under section 7 was held to have been rightly dismissed by the justices.

This is an essential limitation on the scope of section 7. Were it not so limited, it could be used to stifle free expression in public on matters of public concern, and to criminalize the behaviour of people exercising their right to protest.

The second set of provisions protects against harassment on a far wider front, protecting people's privacy (including their right not to be put under pressure in public places) and psychological welfare as well as their freedom to work and associated economic rights. We have seen above how sections 4, 4A, and 5 of the Public Order Act 1986 and section 68 of the Criminal Justice and Public Order Act 1994 protect people against harassment in public or quasi-public spaces. In addition, the Protection from Harassment Act 1997 creates two further offences.[187] The more serious one is committed by a person who undertakes a course of conduct which causes someone to fear, on at least two occasions, that violence will be used against him, where the accused knows or ought to know that the course of conduct will cause such

---

[184] Smith, *Offences against Public Order*, 213–18.

[185] Bob Hepple QC, 'Freedom of Expression and the Problem of Harassment', in Beatson and Cripps (eds.), *Freedom of Expression and Freedom of Information*, 177–96.

[186] [1992] 1 WLR 91, DC.

[187] See N. Addison and T. Lawson-Cruttenden, *Harassment Law and Practice* (London: Blackstone, 1998), ch. 3.

fear on each of the occasions. A person ought to know that such fear will be caused if a reasonable person, in possession of the same information, would think that the course of conduct would cause such fear.[188] Unlike the offence putting a person in fear of violence under section 4 of the Public Order Act 1986, the fear under section 4 of the 1997 Act need not be of immediate violence. On the other hand there must be a course of conduct relating to at least two occasions under the 1997 Act, whereas a single occasion suffices under the 1986 Act. The wide scope of the 1997 Act is shown by the defences contained in section 4(3) for a person who shows that he was pursuing the course of conduct for the purpose of preventing or detecting crime, or under any enactment or rule of law or to comply with a condition imposed under any enactment, or was reasonable for the protection of any person or for the protection of any person's property. The defence must be established in relation to the whole course of conduct, not individual occasions, if it is to succeed. There is no more general defence for reasonable conduct or for protestors: the assumption is that conduct of this kind can never be reasonable, and that assumption is fair. A person convicted of the offence is liable to imprisonment for up to five years and a fine not exceeding the statutory maximum.

The less serious offence, under sections 1 and 2 of the 1997 Act, is punishable by up to six months' imprisonment or a fine not exceeding level 5 on the standard scale. It is committed by anyone who pursues a course of conduct[189] which amounts to harassment of another, and which the accused knows or ought to know[190] amounts to harassment.[191] A course of conduct must involve conduct on at least two occasions if it is to amount to harassment.[192] The Act does not define harassment, except to say that it includes alarming the victim or causing him distress.[193] The offence is arrestable under the Police and Criminal Evidence Act 1984. There is a defence where the accused shows that the course of conduct as a whole was pursued for the purpose of preventing or detecting crime, or under any enactment or rule of law or to comply with a condition imposed under any enactment. Because of the obvious potential impact of the offence on legitimate protests of various kinds, there is a further defence for an accused who shows that in the circumstances the course of conduct was reasonable.[194] Reasonableness is partly a question of fact, but by virtue of sections 3 and 6 of the Human Rights Act 1998 (the obligations to read and give effect to legislation in a manner compatible with Convention rights so far as possible, and to comply with Convention rights unless compelled by primary legislation to act otherwise) it will have to be interpreted in such a way as to protect protestors and others from violation of their rights to freedom to manifest belief, freedom of expression and freedom of peaceful assembly under ECHR Articles 9, 10, and 11, importing the considerations of pressing social need and proportionality canvassed earlier in this chapter. On

---

[188] Protection from Harassment Act 1997, s. 4(1), (2).
[189] Conduct includes speech: Protection from Harassment Act 1997, s. 7(4).
[190] The test is what a reasonable person with the same information would think.
[191] Protection from Harassment Act 1997, ss. 1, 2.
[192] Ibid., s. 7(3).
[193] Ibid., s. 7(2).
[194] Ibid., s. 1(3).

conviction, a court may make an order restraining the offender from further courses of conduct harassing the victim or causing a fear of violence; breach of a restraining order is a criminal offence.[195]

Besides the criminal proceedings, a civil court may grant damages to a victim of unlawful harassment under the Act, and an injunction to restrain further harassment.[196] In an early case on the Act in the context of the long-running campaign by animal-rights campaigners against treatment of experimental animals at the laboratories of Huntingdon Life Sciences Ltd., Eady J discharged an interim injunction granted *ex parte* restraining the British Union for the Abolition of Vivisection (BUAV) from participating in a course of conduct amounting to harassment of the company, or going within fifty yards of the homes of employees of Huntingdon Life Sciences, or entering the company's premises. He held that an interim injunction required it to be shown that the plaintiffs had at least an arguable case to advance at trial, and decided that there was no evidence of BUAV involvement. The decision makes it clear that plaintiffs who apply for injunctions, particularly *ex parte*, have a responsibility to ensure that all relevant information is put fairly before the judge. Eady J also held that BUAV, as an unincorporated association or members' club, could not fairly be made a defendant in proceedings merely because some of its members might have attended a protest. Finally, he said that Parliament had not intended to suppress discussion of matters of public interest, or 'the rights of political protest and public demonstration which are so much part of our democratic tradition'.[197] All these comments are now reinforced, as a matter of law, by the introduction to English law of the rights under ECHR Articles 9, 10, and 11, and the special provisions in section 12 of the Human Rights Act 1998 restricting *ex parte* injunctions in cases where the Convention right to freedom of expression would be affected (discussed in Chapter 14, above).

(4) OBSTRUCTING THE HIGHWAY AND PUBLIC NUISANCE[198]

The control of processions is a very difficult matter, because of the variables which have to be taken into account. These include the number of people processing, which may be unpredictable, the reaction of others to the procession, the traffic implications, and the availability of police resources to ensure that contingencies are provided for. If things go wrong, the police tend to suffer public criticism. This sometimes makes police officers very cautious, particularly where a procession is to take place in support of a cause which is likely to attract a counter-demonstration. The problems facing officers who have to try to keep two rival groups apart are unenviable, and can be seen regularly at soccer matches as well as political demonstrations.

The general principles of law governing processions are relatively straightforward.

---

[195] Protection from Harassment Act 1997, s. 5.

[196] Ibid., s. 3.

[197] *Huntingdon Life Sciences Ltd. v. Curtin and others*, 28 November 1997, QBD. See the commentary by K. Kerrigan, (1998) 3 *J. Civil Liberties* 37–44.

[198] Supperstone, *Brownlie's Law of Public Order*, 2nd edn., 42–50; Smith, *Offences Against Public Order*, ch. 11; Ewing and Finnie, *Civil Liberties in Scotland*, 365–8, 388–94.

All land, including a highway, is owned by someone, so one starts from the private law of land ownership and trespass to land. What is the scope of the implied permission given to users of highways? If a person exceeds the bounds of the permission, he is acting unlawfully, as all members of the House of Lords made clear in *Director of Public Prosecutions v. Jones (Margaret).*[199] On the highway, it has long been established that anyone has a *prima facie* right to pass and repass along it, and to do things necessarily incidental to passage, including stopping for a rest or to make repairs.[200] This applies to people who are part of processions and demonstrations as to anyone else. In *Jones,* a decision with important implications for the right of peaceful assembly, the majority (Lord Irvine of Lairg LC, Lord Clyde, and Lord Hutton) decided that a gathering on the verge of a highway to protest about the closure of Stonehenge was not intrinsically a trespass, because (*per* Lord Irvine LC and Lord Clyde) the permission actually or impliedly given by occupiers of the soil to users of the highway either already went beyond passing, repassing, and activities necessarily incidental thereto, or (*per* Lord Hutton) should henceforth be treated as extending beyond them. Assemblies on the highway to register a protest are a traditional activity, and the law would not prohibit such commonplace and well accepted usages as long as the behaviour of those involved was reasonable (having regard to the size and duration of the assembly, the behaviour of the participants, and degree of obstruction caused to other users of the highway). Lord Slynn of Hadley and Lord Hope of Craighead dissented on this point. They distinguished toleration of demonstrations and other activities commonly undertaken on highways from a legal right to engage in them,[201] and considered that constructing a right of peaceful assembly on the highway interfered with the rights of occupiers in a way which was undesirable and unsupported by authority.

This approach of the dissenting Law Lords is closely in line with traditional, English private-property law, concentrating on the rights of the landowner rather than those of the public. The majority, by contrast, were prepared to restrict private property rights in the interest of protecting a right to assemble peacefully to demonstrate support for a viewpoint. This has implications for private land ownership, because the principles enunciated by the majority apply to footpaths and bridleways across private land as to roads. The decision may therefore restrict the right of private landowners to exclude people from their land, although (as Lords Irvine and Hutton held[202]) the tribunal of fact might form a different view as to the reasonableness of an assembly taking place on wholly private land from that of an assembly on a road.

The majority reached their conclusion without directly applying the Convention rights, since the decision predated the coming into force of the Human Rights Act

---

[199] [1999] 2 AC 240, [1999] 2 WLR 625, [1999] 2 All ER 257, HL. See B. Fitzpatrick and N. Taylor, 'Trespassers *Might* Be Prosecuted: The European Convention and Restrictions on the Right to Assemble' [1998] *EHRLR* 292–305.

[200] See, e.g. *Harrison v. Duke of Rutland* [1893] 1 QB 142; *Hickman v. Maisey* [1900] 1 QB 753; for Scotland, *McAra v. Edinburgh Magistrates,* 1913 SC 1059.

[201] [1999] 2 WLR at 639 *per* Lord Slynn; see to the same effect Lord Hope at 647.

[202] [1999] 2 WLR at 633, 666.

1998. Nevertheless, had it been necessary to refer to the European Convention on Human Rights Lord Irvine and perhaps Lord Clyde[203] would have held that undue restrictions on rights of the public on highways would have threatened the right to freedom of peaceful assembly under ECHR Article 11, and there is no doubt that the 1998 Act reinforces the grounds for the decision by the majority.

The test of reasonableness was already in use to determine criminal liability of those who obstruct a highway. By virtue of both statute and common law, people have no right to stop on the highway unreasonably. Any wilful obstruction of free passage along a highway without lawful authority or excuse is an offence under the Highways Act 1980, section 137. 'Wilful' here means intentional, in the sense of deliberate.[204] There need not be an intention to obstruct the highway, as long as the deliberate act or omission of the defendant objectively viewed has the effect of obstructing it.[205] A partial obstruction of the highway will suffice, but only if it is an unreasonable use of the highway:[206] it is accepted that some degree of obstruction is inevitable when doing normal things like parking a car temporarily, or making repairs, so legitimate activities which do not block the road become unlawful only if the degree of disruption to other road users or the period for which they continue make them unreasonable.[207] Thus in *North Yorkshire County Council v. Lee and others (No. 2)*,[208] Hooper J held that parking a caravan permanently in a lay-by on the A59, to support people campaigning against US military activity at RAF Menwith Hill in Yorkshire, went beyond a reasonable user of the highway, but was sympathetic to the view that parking a trailer or small caravan during the day in a safe place, and removing it at night, would be reasonable.

Obstructing the highway also constitutes a public nuisance at common law if it is unreasonable.[209] The highway authority is responsible for seeing that the highway is kept free for passage. This applies to the police as to other road users:[210] a road block is therefore unlawful unless within the statutory powers granted by, for example, the Police and Criminal Evidence Act 1984, section 4. This means that, while a moving

---

[203] [1999] 2 WLR at 634–5 *per* Lord Irvine, 654 *per* Lord Clyde.

[204] *Arrowsmith v. Jenkins* [1963] 2 QB 561, [1963] 2 All ER 210, DC.

[205] *Cooper v. Commissioner of Police of the Metropolis* (1985) 82 Cr. App. R. 238, DC.

[206] *Homer v. Cadman* (1886) 16 Cox CC 51.

[207] See, e.g. *Carey v. Chief Constable of Avon and Somerset* 1995] RTR 405, CA (coach adapted for use as a dwelling parked for a long period on a road); *North Yorkshire County Council v. Lee and others*, 22 June 1998, High Court at Leeds, unreported (peace camp on a lay-by on the A59 near the US Air Force base at RAF Menwith Hill in Yorkshire. I am grateful to Sir Anthony Hooper for supplying me with a copy of his judgment).

[208] 14 June 1999, High Court at Leeds, unreported. I am once again grateful to Sir Anthony Hooper for supplying me with a copy of his judgment.

[209] *R. v. Clark (No. 2)* [1964] 2 QB 315, [1963] 3 All ER 884, CCA: a demonstration by an anti-nuclear-weapons group in London, blocking several streets, not necessarily unreasonable.

[210] The Highways Act 1980 has been held not to bind the Crown, however. It was held that a road may therefore be narrowed in order to facilitate repairs to a Ministry of Defence establishment without the need for any application for permission from the Highways Authority: *Lord Advocate v. Dumbarton DC* [1990] 2 AC 580, [1990] 1 All ER 1, HL. However, this decision seems to rest on an over-wide view of the bodies which constitute the Crown, and on a contested view of the extent of the 'shield of the Crown' doctrine which has been rejected in Australia and is inconsistent with previous Scottish decisions.

procession is *prima facie* lawful, sitting down in the middle of the road to block the traffic is likely to be regarded as unreasonable, and so unlawful, as a means of protest both at common law and under statute, at any rate if the protestors remain there for an extended period.

Lawful authority or excuse takes account of the reasonableness of the activity or inactivity which causes the obstruction. As campaigning depends on bringing matters to the attention of the public, at least where one wants to do more than preach to the converted, streets are cheap and convenient places to make one's views known. With the increasing importance of broadcasting as a means of imparting information and opinions, the public demonstration, leafleting, or picketing might have been expected to decline in importance, but access to broadcasting remains difficult for most people, access to the newspapers depends on editorial and proprietorial discretion (see Chapter 14 above), and special difficulties in obtaining publicity attach to campaigners for local or unpopular causes. Because of this, public demonstrations remain important ways of raising public consciousness of a cause or issue. It is perhaps true, as Sir Robert Mark suggested in the mid-1970s, that: 'Political demonstrations seem to give satisfaction in the main to those taking part. The public as a whole are usually not interested unless affected by inconvenience or aroused by disorder or violence'.[211] However, it is equally true that the satisfaction of participants derives in part from the knowledge that they are taking a rare opportunity to put their views across to others. This is why, as Sir Robert went on to note, 'the right to hold them is much valued and jealously preserved'.[212]

It is therefore not true to say that all unauthorized obstructions to the highway are unlawful. The reasonableness of the obstructer's behaviour, considering the scale of the obstruction and the object in view, must be taken into account, and if the obstruction is reasonable in the circumstances it will provide a lawful excuse under section 137 of the Highways Act 1980.[213] A very minor obstruction may be excused under the *de minimis* principle.[214] Nevertheless, the reasonableness of the protesters' behaviour provides at best an uncertain defence to a prosecution, as it is dependent on the magistrates' view as to reasonableness. This may vary according to the ethos of particular benches, or perhaps the political or other causes which the protesters espoused. The common law rules on public nuisance and trespass have thus been brought into line with the statutory rules on obstructing the highway. Since *Director of Public Prosecutions v. Jones* in 1999 there has been at least a presumptive freedom in English law to use a highway for peaceful assembly and protest, subject to conditions designed to protect public order and the rights and freedoms of other users. Although the flexibility of the test of reasonableness makes the true scope of the freedom somewhat

---

[211] Sir Robert Mark, QPM, 'The Metropolitan Police and Political Demonstrations', *Report of the Commissioner of Police of the Metropolis for the Year 1974*, App. 8, at para. 13 (quoted in Bailey, Harris, and Jones, *Civil Liberties*, 3rd edn., 148–9).

[212] Mark, 'Metropolitan Police', para. 13.

[213] *Nagy v. Weston* [1965] 1 WLR 280, [1965] 1 All ER 78, DC; *Hirst and Agu v. Chief Constable of West Yorkshire* (1986) 85 Cr. App. R. 143, DC.

[214] *Putnam v. Colvin* [1984] RTR 150, where, however, the obstruction (more than thirty plant pots containing shrubs) was not thought to be within the *de minimis* principle.

uncertain, the terms of ECHR Articles 10(2) and 11(2) should ensure that any interference with the freedom is necessary and proportionate.[215]

18.3 POWERS TO REGULATE PROCESSIONS AND ASSEMBLIES IN PUBLIC PLACES[216]

There are various prior restraints on processions and assemblies in public places. Sometimes, private individuals who suffer harm from a procession or assembly in a public place can obtain injunctions to stop the harm. This is particularly common in relation to picketing. Where the picket was outside an estate agent's office, by people protesting at the effect on the character of Islington of property owners moving in from elsewhere (the so-called gentrification of Islington), an interlocutory injunction was granted to restrain the picket, pending hearing of the estate agent's action for a private nuisance allegedly caused by the protesters in watching and besetting the premises.[217] In *Burris v. Azadani*[218] the Court of Appeal held that courts had power under the common law to grant an interim injunction restraining harassment if the applicant has invoked the protection of the court in support of his legitimate interests, the defendant has no legitimate interests that would be compromised by granting the order, and the balance of convenience favours granting an order. The same principles apply following the enactment of the Protection from Harassment Act 1997,[219] with the additional requirement that any injunction must be compatible with the duties of the court under the Human Rights Act 1998, particularly section 12 and ECHR Articles 10 and 11.

When picketing forms part of industrial action, the pickets' unions are protected against actions in tort only so long as their members attend only at their own place of work.[220] Injunctions may be granted against the union if pickets attend elsewhere.[221] Major industrial action can cause intimidation of non-striking workers, and produce interference with their right to work which goes beyond peaceful attempts to persuade them to strike.[222] To cater for such cases, there is a Code of Practice on Picketing, which, although not legally binding, represents good practice and may be taken into

---

[215] For discussion, see G. Clayton, 'Reclaiming Public Ground: The Right to Peaceful Assembly' (2000) 63 *MLR* 252–60; Feldman, 'Property and Public Protest', at 51–8.

[216] A. L. Goodhart, 'Public Meetings and Processions' (1937) 6 *CLJ* 161–74; D. G. T. Williams, 'Processions, Assemblies and the Freedom of the Individual' [1987] Crim. LR 167–79; Smith, *Offences against Public Order*, ch. 8.

[217] *Hubbard v. Pitt* [1976] QB 142, [1975] 3 All ER 1, CA.

[218] [1995] 1 WLR 1372, [1995] 4 All ER 802, CA.

[219] *Huntingdon Life Sciences Ltd. v. Curtin and others*, 28 November 1997, QBD. See the commentary by K. Kerrigan, (1998) 3 *J. Civil Liberties* 37–44.

[220] Trade Union and Labour Relations (Consolidation) Act 1992, s. 220.

[221] *Thomas v. National Union of Mineworkers (South Wales Area)* [1986] Ch. 20, [1985] 2 All ER 1; *News Group Newspapers Ltd. v. Society of Graphical and Allied Trades 1982* [1986] IRLR 337.

[222] This was recognized by NCCL, *Civil Liberties and the Miners' Dispute: First Report of the Independent Inquiry* (London: NCCL, 1984), 6, 10.

account by courts when it becomes relevant.[223] Although the number of pickets is not limited by statute,[224] the Code describes excessive numbers of pickets as the main cause of violence and disorder on picket lines, which may get out of control, leading to arrests and prosecutions.[225] The Code advises that people demonstrating support for the industrial action should do so well away from the picket line, normally leaving a maximum of six pickets to persuade people not to enter the premises.[226]

It is not the job of the police to enforce industrial relations law, although there were suspicions during the miners' dispute and the action against News International in Wapping that they were doing so. The police are conscious of the importance for their authority and effectiveness of appearing neutral in maintaining public peace and upholding the law when faced by problems arising out of industrial or political action. Nevertheless, as Paul Wiles has written, during the 1980s 'the police's claim to objectivity, as upholders of the rule of law, was undermined because the law in question was seen by many trade unionists as partial'.[227] In relation to both industrial and other demonstrations and meetings, the police have extensive powers, independently of industrial relations law, to prevent obstructions of the highway, including a power to arrest an obstructer whether or not there is any imminent risk of a breach of the peace.[228] The remainder of this section deals with these powers, treating powers in respect of processions and those in respect of other assemblies separately.

(1) PROCESSIONS ON HIGHWAYS

The police have all the usual common-law powers to prevent breaches of the peace. This means that they can give directions as to the route of the procession in order to avoid trouble which emerges during the course of the procession, and arrest people if necessary to prevent the occurrence, continuance, or recurrence of a breach of the peace which is in progress or is reasonably apprehended as being imminent.[229] However, as the powers can be exercised only when the breach of the peace is imminent in time and place, they cannot be used to ban a procession or to impose conditions on the organizers in advance. This makes them of limited value as aids to planning. The Public Order Act 1986, Part II, passed in the wake of the disorders and riots of 1981, has therefore conferred additional powers on the police and imposed certain duties on people who organize public processions. 'Public procession' means any procession in a public place, and 'public place' is defined in turn as meaning any highway (or, in Scotland, a road within the meaning of the Roads (Scotland) Act 1984), and any place

---

[223] Trade Union and Labour Relations (Consolidation) Act 1992, ss. 203–7.

[224] Trade Union and Labour Relations Act 1974, s. 15 as substituted.

[225] Code of Practice, para. 29.

[226] Ibid., paras. 30, 31. See generally B. Perrins, *Harvey on Industrial Relations and Employment Law* (London: Butterworths, 1992), binder 2, division N, s. 18.

[227] P. Wiles, 'Law, Order and the State', in C. Graham and T. Prosser (eds.), *Waiving the Rules: The Constitution under Thatcherism* (Milton Keynes: Open University Press, 1988), 153–73 at 163.

[228] Police and Criminal Evidence Act 1984, s. 25; see particularly s. 25(3)(d)(v).

[229] See B. Hough, 'Common Law Restrictions on Commercial and Political Users of the Highway' (1999) 4 *J. Civil Liberties* 206–29; above, section 18.1(3).

to which the public has access at the material time, as of right or by virtue of express or implied permission, on payment or otherwise.[230] It does not include, for this purpose, land to which people can obtain access as trespassers. 'Procession' is not defined in the Act. In a case under the Public Order Act 1936 Lord Denning MR defined 'public procession' as 'the act of a body of persons marching along in orderly succession'.[231] It is important that the people be acting in concert. An orderly crowd moving along Oxford Street at sale time is not a procession.

(i) Notice of processions

The legislation requires written notice to be given of any proposed public procession which is intended to demonstrate support for or opposition to the views or actions of any person or persons, or to publicize a cause or campaign, or to mark or commemorate any event. This is wide enough to encompass religious and charitable fundraising processions as well as political ones.[232] The notice must be delivered to a police station in the police area where the procession is to start or (if it starts in Scotland) in the area where it will first enter England.[233] The notice must reach the police station at least six clear days before the date when the procession is intended to be held, either by recorded delivery or by hand.[234] If it is not reasonably practicable for it to be delivered six clear days in advance, it must be delivered by hand as soon as is reasonably practicable.[235] It must specify the intended date, starting time, and route of the procession, and give the name and address of at least one of the people proposing to organize it.[236]

Each organizer of a procession commits an offence, punishable by a fine, if the procession takes place without notice being given, or does not comply with the date, time, or route specified in the notice, unless he can prove either (a) that he did not know of, and had no reason to suspect, the failure to satisfy the requirements or comply with the specified details in the notice, or (b) that any difference in the date, time, or route arose from circumstances beyond his control or from something done with the agreement, or under the direction, of a police officer.[237] The defence allows an organizer to comply with the request of a constable at the scene to change the route or time, for example in order to avoid a breach of the peace.

The only processions of the kind mentioned above for which notice is not required are (a) those commonly or customarily held in that police area, and (b) funeral processions organized by a funeral director acting in the ordinary course of his business. The latter exception can be important, as (particularly in the case of violent deaths of political activists, or the funerals of people killed in clashes with the police) the funeral procession may be a focus of anger and emotion as well as displaying

---

[230] S. 16.

[231] *Kent v. Metropolitan Police Commissioner, The Times*, 13 May 1981, CA.

[232] S. 11(1).

[233] S. 11(1), (4).

[234] S. 11(5), which excludes the operation of s. 7 of the Interpretation Act 1978, so that notice sent by post is not deemed either to be served when posted or to have been delivered in the ordinary course of the post.

[235] S. 11(6).

[236] S. 11(3).

[237] S. 11(7), (8), (9).

respect for the dead. However, although written notice of such processions is not required under section 11, the police have power to impose conditions on them under section 12 or, in extreme cases, to make a banning order under section 13.

(ii) Imposing conditions on processions

The power to impose conditions on public processions under the Public Order Act 1986, section 12, is bestowed on the chief officer of police beforehand, and on the senior officer at the scene once people have begun to assemble.[238] It can be exercised if the officer reasonably believes, having regard to the time, place, and route of the procession, that either (a) it may result in serious public disorder, serious damage to property, or serious disruption to the life of the community, or (b) the organizers' purpose is to intimidate others with a view to compelling them not to do or omit something which they have a right to do or omit.[239] The conditions take the form of directions to the organizers, and may be such as appear to the officer to be necessary to prevent the anticipated disorder, damage, disruption, or intimidation. Section 12(1) provides that they may include, but are not limited to, conditions as to the route of the procession, or prohibiting it from entering any specified public place. Conditions which are so demanding that they amount in effect to a ban are an improper use of the power, and so are unlawful on ordinary public-law principles.[240]

Anyone who organizes or takes part in a public procession who knowingly fails to comply with a condition, or who incites another not to comply, is guilty of an offence, but organizers and participants, other than those inciting people not to comply, have a defence if they can prove that the failure to comply arose from circumstances beyond their control.[241]

This impliedly presents organizers with further duties: they are responsible, at least in large measure, for ensuring that the procession goes where it is supposed to go. They must exert their persuasiveness and authority to ensure that people not only attend, but that they behave while they are processing. Organizers normally appoint stewards to do this. This should ease the job of the police. In the 1980 Green Paper, the Home Office floated but ultimately rejected the idea that organizers of demonstrations should be made to pay for the policing necessary to prevent disorder at them. It was felt that this would be likely to make it impossible for anyone who lacked very substantial amounts of money to organize a lawful demonstration, removing one of the chief advantages for those who do not have access to the media or money to pay for an advertising campaign. It would also impose a burden on organizers of processions to pay for the policing of counter-demonstrations by people seeking unlawfully to disrupt their lawful procession.[242] The Act, by making the organizers responsible

---

[238] S. 12(2). In Scotland, the power only applies at the scene once people have begun to assemble: s. 12(11).

[239] S. 12(1).

[240] See *DPP v. Baillie* [1995] Crim. LR 426, DC, a decision on the analogous power in respect of assemblies under s. 14 of the Act.

[241] S. 12(4), (5), (6). Organizers and inciters face up to three months' imprisonment and a fine; others face a fine: s. 12(8), (9), (10). This is separate from the offence of wilfully obstructing a constable in the execution of his duty, contrary to s. 89 of the Police Act 1996.

[242] Cmnd. 7891, paras. 64–5.

for ensuring that, so far as possible, the details contained in their notice and any conditions imposed by the police are complied with, helps to reduce the burden on the police without making it financially impossible for ordinary people to mount processions. Certain policing operations are paid for by their beneficiaries: for example, soccer clubs can be required to pay for the policing of home matches where substantial numbers of police are needed inside the ground, as this constitutes a 'special police service' for which the police are entitled to charge.[243] However, policing a public demonstration is not such a service, as it is intended to protect the public at large rather than prevent disorder on the private premises of a commercial enterprise.

The discretion which the Act accords to the police, particularly in relation to the nature of any conditions, is staggeringly wide. Even under the power to ban processions under section 3 of the Public Order Act 1936 (now repealed and replaced) it was held that an *intra vires* exercise of the officer's discretion was reviewable by the courts only if the applicant could show that there had been no reasonable ground on which a banning order could have been made.[244] On the wording of section 12 of the 1986 Act, it would seem that the officer would have to be able to show reasonable grounds for believing that disorder, etc. might result from the march, but his judgment about the conditions necessary to prevent such disorder is well nigh unreviewable. Furthermore, the discretion is wider than that which used to apply under section 3(1) of the 1936 Act, which prevented conditions being imposed to restrict the display of flags, banners, or emblems unless the restrictions were reasonably necessary to prevent a breach of the peace. This discretion imposes a prior restraint on freedom of expression and protest. The terms of the statute itself do not provide narrowly drawn, reasonable, objective, and definite standards to guide the exercise of the discretion, so the provision would be regarded as unconstitutional on its face under the First Amendment to the US Constitution.[245] However, the exercise of the discretion is now subject to Convention rights under English law: by virtue of the Human Rights Act 1998, section 6, discretionary police action which is incompatible with a Convention right is unlawful. ECHR Articles 10(2) and 11(2) allow proportionate restrictions on freedom of expression and peaceful assembly to protect the rights and freedoms of others, and the decision of the European Court of Human Rights in *Jersild v. Denmark*[246] shows that a restriction is permitted in order to protect people against the corrosive effects of racist speech. The same may be true of other forms of hate-speech. It is therefore legitimate to require the officer exercising the discretion to consider the probable reaction of other groups to the views expressed by the procession. There is a danger that people whose views are unpopular with bottle-throwers will have a more restricted freedom than those whose views are popular, or unpopular only with people who are too civilized or apathetic to initiate a fracas over them. Such a content-based prior

[243] Police Act 1996, s.25(1); *Harris v. Sheffield Utd. Football Club Ltd.* [1988] QB 77, [1987] 2 All ER 838, CA.

[244] *Kent v. Commissioner of Police of the Metropolis*, The Times, 15 May 1981, CA.

[245] *Cantwell v. Connecticut* 310 US 296 (1940); *Niemotko v. Maryland* 340 US 286 (1951); *Freedman v. Maryland* 380 US 51 (1965); *Shuttlesworth v. Birmingham* 394 US 147 (1969).

[246] Eur. Ct. HR, Series A, No. 298, Judgment of 23 September 1994, 19 EHRR 1.

restraint on freedom of expression in a public forum would, in the USA, be regarded as an unconstitutional interference with First Amendment rights.[247] In modern English law, it is likely that the duty on public authorities to take reasonable steps to safeguard the right to assemble peacefully under ECHR Article 11[248] and the developing common-law presumption in favour of protecting peaceful speakers or demonstrators against hostile reactions[249] will alleviate this risk in practice.

The discretion to lay down conditions may be sometimes be partially justified on the ground that conditions are, in principle, less of a restriction on public expression and democratic activity than a complete ban. However, sometimes a condition as to the route to be taken, or timing, may seriously affect the impact of the procession. For example, as the Green Paper on *The Public Order Act and Related Legislation*[250] pointed out, there may be circumstances in which a march to a foreign embassy is planned to protest against a country's policy on, for example, torture or capital punishment. The point of the march would be to make the country's diplomats aware of the strength of public feelings, so that they can inform their government. The point would be partly, if not wholly, lost if the procession had to be routed away from the embassy.

Constables in uniform have power to arrest without warrant anyone whom they reasonably suspect to be committing a section 12 offence.[251] This is apart from the common-law power which they have to arrest in order to restrain conduct likely to provoke a breach of the peace.

(iii) Prohibiting processions

If the power to impose conditions is questionable on human rights and civil liberties principles, a power to ban processions entirely is *a fortiori* objectionable. Nevertheless, section 13 of the 1986 Act (which replaced section 3(3) and (4) of the 1936 Act) provides a power to prohibit public processions, or a class of public processions, entirely. This comes into operation where the chief officer of police reasonably believes that the powers to impose conditions on a public procession under section 12 will be insufficient to prevent serious public disorder resulting from public processions held in a district or part of a district, because of the particular circumstances existing in that district or part.[252]

Outside London[253] the chief officer cannot make an order himself. He is under a duty (he is not exercising a discretionary power) to apply to the council for an order prohibiting the holding of all public processions, or a specified class of them, in the district or part of the district concerned, for a specified period not exceeding three months. The council may then make an order (though it has a discretion), with the

---

[247] *Forsyth County v. Nationalist Movement* 60 USLW 4597, 120 LEd 2d 101 (1992).

[248] See *Plattform 'Ärzte für das Leben' v. Austria*, Eur. Ct. HR, Series A, No. 139, Judgment of 21 June 1988, 13 EHRR 204.

[249] See, e.g. *Redmond-Bate v. DPP* (1999) 7 BHRC 375, DC.

[250] Cmnd. 7891, 1980, para. 68.

[251] S. 12(7).

[252] S. 13(1).

[253] S. 13(3).

consent of the Home Secretary, either in the terms requested in the chief officer's application or with such amendments to those terms as the Home Secretary is prepared to approve.[254]

In London, the Commissioner of Police of the Metropolis, or (in the City) the Commissioner of Police for the City of London, may make a similar order with the consent of the Home Secretary.[255] This special treatment is the result of several peculiarities in the position of London. First, as the capital city, it attracts far more demonstrations than other places. Traditional gathering places for public assembly, protest, and demonstration, such as Trafalgar Square and Speaker's Corner at Hyde Park, are within its area. This presents special policing problems. Secondly, the Metropolitan Police and City of London Police are responsible for order and security at Westminster and Whitehall, in the environs of Parliament and government, and for foreign embassies. This again presents special problems. Thirdly, the metropolis has no single council or pair of councils covering the entire Metropolitan Police area which acts as a police authority. (Even when there was a Greater London Council, before 1986, it did not operate as a police authority.) The London boroughs are fragmented, and as processions can easily move between boroughs it would be cumbersome to have to obtain orders from large numbers of borough councils, which might make differing political judgments. As the Home Secretary is accountable to Parliament, and as the police authority for London is in a good position to know about the political and policing considerations, the Act bypasses the London borough councils and makes the Commissioner responsible for banning orders, subject to the Home Secretary's approval. In the past, except in the year or so immediately following the Brixton riots in 1981, the power to make orders has been sparingly used, in London as elsewhere.[256]

This three-stage process (chief officer of police, local authority, and Home Secretary)[257] is required because the decision to ban processions combines policing and political considerations. The police must make an assessment of the risks arising from a procession, and to decide on the basis of intelligence and experience, both generally and of local conditions, whether any risk can be avoided by imposing conditions under section 12. If a risk of serious public disorder exists and, in the chief officer's reasonable belief, cannot be avoided by imposing conditions, a further question arises: does the risk outweigh the value of allowing people to express themselves publicly, by any means which are not intrinsically unlawful, in a democracy? This question is essentially one calling for political judgment. One might argue that it is properly left to authorities which are democratically accountable: the council, elected locally and knowing local conditions, and the Home Secretary, accountable to Parliament for the maintenance of both order and democracy. On the other hand, there could be good reasons for distancing politically partisan people from the decision-making process, particularly in polarized societies. Northern Ireland provides an example of this.

---

[254] S. 13(2).

[255] S. 13(4). Orders may be revoked or varied by further orders made in the same way: s. 13(5).

[256] Bailey, Harris, and Jones, *Civil Liberties*, 4th edn., 200–3.

[257] Two-stage process in London—Commissioner of Police of the Metropolis or Commissioner of Police for the City of London, and Home Secretary—s. 13(4).

There, the independent Parades Commission took statutory responsibility for regulating parades under the Public Processions (Northern Ireland) Act 1998. The idea was to de-politicize decisions about parades, but in a society as divided as that in Northern Ireland the Commission, while independent of government and police, has had difficulty in persuading the unionist and nationalist communities that it is genuinely unbiased. The model might have a better chance of working effectively in mainland Britain.

The power to prohibit operates in a much narrower band of circumstances than the power to impose conditions: it does not apply to circumstances giving rise to a risk of serious damage to property, serious disruption to the life of the community, or intimidation, unless the chief officer reasonably believes that they will result in serious public disorder. Of course, this may well be the case, but the chief officer must consider the likelihood and seriousness of the disorder which will result. A minor scuffle, or series of them, will not qualify as serious public disorder; nor, it is submitted, will serious disruption to community life which is not accompanied by violence. Unlike the position under section 12, it is not a sufficient condition for banning processions under section 13 that the chief officer reasonably believes that serious public disorder *may* result. Under section 13, he must reasonably believe that imposing conditions *will* not be sufficient to prevent serious public disorder resulting. The more demanding standards under section 13(1) are necessary for two reasons: first, because a ban normally stifles free expression more completely than imposing conditions; secondly, because, in order to avoid discrimination against processions by particular groups or opinions, section 13(1) does not permit the banning of a single procession. Instead, the chief officer of police must apply to the council for an order prohibiting all public processions, or a specified class of processions, in the district or part of a district concerned, for a specified period not exceeding three months. The repercussions of applying for an order may therefore go well beyond the particular procession.

The Act, in section 13(6), provides that the order must, if not made in writing, be recorded in writing as soon as practicable after being made. The Act does not provide for it to be publicized in any way, but it will normally be contained in a press release and publicized widely. Its effectiveness depends on it being known to all who might be planning processions in the area. It is an offence for anyone to organize, take part in, or incite another to take part in a public procession which he knows to be prohibited by a section 13 order,[258] and a constable in uniform may arrest without warrant anyone whom he reasonably suspects to be committing any such offence.[259]

In London, the Commissioners of the Metropolitan Police and City of London Police have a further power, under the Metropolitan Police Act 1839, section 52, to

'make regulations . . . for preventing obstruction of the streets and thoroughfares within the metropolitan police district, in all times of public processions, public rejoicings, or illuminations, and also to give directions to constables for keeping order and for preventing any obstruction of the thoroughfares in the immediate neighbourhood of her Majesty's palaces

[258] S. 13(7), (8), (9).
[259] S. 13(10).

and the public offices, the High Court of Parliament, the courts of law and equity, the police courts, the theatres, and other places of public resort . . .'

This authorizes regulations, which have been made by way of Sessional Orders, controlling processions in the vicinity of Westminster. However, the regulations must be concerned with preventing obstructions to the highway or (at common law) breaches of the peace. If they are not directed to those objects, they will be wider than necessary, and (if not severable) will be *ultra vires*. In *Papworth v. Coventry*,[260] a person protesting against the Vietnam war taking part in a well-ordered and peaceable vigil in Downing Street, which did not cause an obstruction of the highway, was charged with failing to comply with a section 52 direction (contrary to section 54(9)) which had purported to ban all assemblies and processions in the Westminster area during the parliamentary session. He was convicted at summary trial, but had his conviction quashed on appeal, because there had been no disorder or obstruction. The scope of the directions, and the manner of their enforcement, must (on ordinary principles of administrative law) be within the objects contemplated by the enabling legislation.

(2) POWERS TO REGULATE OTHER ASSEMBLIES IN PUBLICLY OWNED PLACES

Public places are not *res nullius*. They are actually vested in and the property of some body. For example, beaches are vested in the Crown or the local authority;[261] Hyde Park, with its famous Corner, is vested in the Crown;[262] highways, including Trafalgar Square, a traditional venue for meetings, are vested in the Crown or local authorities, subject to a right of members of the public to pass and repass on them.[263] Meetings in Trafalgar Square are controlled by the Secretary of State for Transport, the Environment and the Regions under powers conferred by statutory instrument which were held to be compatible, in principle, with ECHR Article 11 in *Rai, Allmond and 'Negotiate Now!' v. United Kingdom*.[264]

There have long been regulations covering the use of specific public places.[265] These regulations are subject to judicial review if they are outside the powers conferred by the enabling legislation. For example, in *Director of Public Prosecutions v. Hutchinson*[266] a protester at the airbase at Greenham Common had been convicted of entering without permission the area enclosed by the perimeter fence of the base, contrary to By-law 2(b) of the RAF Greenham Common By-laws 1985, made under section 14(1) of the Military Lands Act 1892. This subsection contained a proviso that rights of common were not to be prejudicially affected. By-law 2(b) contained no

---

[260] [1967] 1 WLR 663, [1967] 2 All ER 41, DC.

[261] *New South Wales v. Commonwealth (Seas and Submerged Land Case)* (1975) 135 CLR 337; *Llandudno Urban District Council v. Woods* [1899] 2 Ch. 705; *Brighton Corporation v. Packham* (1908) 72 JP 318.

[262] *Bailey v. Williamson* (1873) LR 8 QB 118, DC. See Royal and Other Parks and Gardens Regulations 1977, SI 1977, No. 217.

[263] *R. v. Graham and Burns* (1888) 16 Cox CC 420; *Ex parte Lewis* (1888) 21 QBD 191, DC.

[264] App. No. 25522/94, Eur. Commn. HR, Decision of 6 April 1995 (inadmissible).

[265] See Supperstone, *Brownlie's Law of Public Order*, 35–8; Williams, *Keeping the Peace*, 72–86.

[266] [1990] 2 AC 783, [1990] 2 All ER 836, HL.

saving for rights of the commoners on Greenham Common, so the House of Lords held that it was *ultra vires*. As the by-law was held not to be severable, the House quashed the defendant's conviction, although she was not herself a commoner.[267] Where an *intra vires* regulation is in force, a local authority may obtain an injunction to restrain threatened breaches. For example, in *Burnley BC v. England*[268] the council had passed a by-law banning dogs from certain parks. Protesting dog owners planned a procession with their dogs through one of the parks, as a political statement and act of civil disobedience in support of what they conceived to be their civil liberties. The council obtained interim and final injunctions to restrain the march.

Apart from specific regulations, the use of a highway for an assembly may be a public nuisance and a contravention of section 137 of the Highways Act 1980 if passage along the highway is obstructed unreasonably, as discussed above. If an obstruction is held to be unreasonable, the police have a discretion as to how to use their powers to deal with it. The fact that other meetings have been held at the same place in the past will not prevent the next one from being prosecuted as an obstruction. Thus in *Arrowsmith v. Jenkins*[269] the Divisional Court upheld the conviction of Pat Arrowsmith for obstructing the highway on a road where she had previously held other meetings to make speeches protesting against nuclear arms. The meeting had largely blocked the road, and had made it difficult for a fire engine to get through. Although Ms. Arrowsmith had co-operated with the police by making announcements asking people in the crowd to clear the road, it was held that she had caused the highway to be obstructed and had been rightly convicted.

Alongside the duty to keep the highway clear, the organizers of meetings on highways and elsewhere face two sets of powers. The common law powers to prevent reasonably apprehended breaches of the peace, discussed above, apply to meetings as they do to processions. In addition, a special power to ban 'trespassory assemblies' is contained in section 14A of the Public Order Act 1986, inserted by the Criminal Justice and Public Order Act 1994. A trespassory assembly is an assembly of twenty or more people on land to which the public has no right of access or only a limited right of access, without or in excess of the limits of the occupier's permission.[270] A council may make an order, on the application of a Chief Constable and with the consent of the Home Secretary, prohibiting trespassory assemblies within a specified area not exceeding a radius of five miles, during a specified period not exceeding four days.[271] The Chief Constable may apply to the council for an order if he reasonably believes that an assembly:

- is intended to be held on land to which the public have no right of access or only a limited right of access;

---

[267] It was later held that a police officer could rely on the invalid by-law as a defence to an action for false imprisonment: *Percy v. Hall* [1997] QB 924, [1996] 4 All ER 523, CA, although the decision may now need to be reconsidered in the light of the right under ECHR Art. 5(5) to compensation for unlawful detention.

[268] (1977) 76 LGR 393 (interlocutory injunction); (1978) 77 LGR 227 (permanent injunction).

[269] [1963] 2 QB 561, [1963] 2 All ER 210, DC.

[270] Public Order Act 1986, s. 14A(5).

[271] Ibid., s. 14A(2), (6).

- is likely to be held without the occupier's permission or in excess of any such permission; and

- may result in serious disruption to the life of the community, or in significant damage to the land or a building or monument on it if the land, building or monument is of historical, architectural, archaeological or scientific importance.[272]

Within the area covered by an order, a constable in uniform may stop and re-direct a person he reasonably believes to be on his way to a prohibited trespassory assembly.[273] It is an offence to organize or take part in a prohibited trespassory assembly, or to incite another person to do so.[274]

These provisions could have a decidedly chilling effect on free expression, and could be used in circumstances which would not fall within the legitimate purposes for interfering with freedom of expression under ECHR Article 10(2). The risk is much reduced by two factors. First, the Human Rights Act 1998, section 6 makes it unlawful for a public authority to make or confirm an order if it would be incompatible with a Convention right, so the requirements of Article 10(2) are added to the preconditions for making an order expressed in section 14A. Secondly, the decision of the House of Lords in *Director of Public Prosecutions v. Jones (Margaret)*[275] significantly limits the impact of the orders. The Chief Constable of Wiltshire was concerned that there might be violent demonstrations at Stonehenge to mark the tenth anniversary of the so-called 'Battle of the Beanfield' when New Age protestors and the police had clashed over the enclosure of Stonehenge. The Chief Constable applied to Salisbury City Council for an order banning trespassory assemblies within four miles of Stonehenge for four days. The order was duly made, with the Home Secretary's approval. On the last day at 6.45 p.m., the senior officer at the scene claimed to have counted twenty-one people on the grass verge of the main A344 highway by the fence surrounding Stonehenge (although it was never entirely clear whether they all belonged to the small group who were there to demonstrate). He asked people to leave, but three people refused. They were arrested and two were later convicted by a magistrates' court of the offence of participating in a trespassory assembly, although they had been on a public highway and it was accepted that their behaviour was peaceful and did not threaten a breach of the peace or obstruct the highway. The Crown Court allowed their appeal, but the conviction was reinstated by the Divisional Court, which held, in effect, that a lawful assembly became trespassory by virtue of the banning order. The House of Lords allowed the defendants' appeal by a three–two majority, but were unanimous in making it clear that the trespassory nature of the anticipated assembly is a necessary precondition for the making of an order, not a result of it. This is the unavoidable result of the manner in which the provisions were drafted, and has the curious and not altogether satisfactory effect of making criminal liability depend on complex and disputed questions of private law. None the less, it is a welcome

---

[272] Public Order Act 1986, s. 14A(1). On the procedure in London, see s. 14A(3), (4).
[273] Ibid., s. 14C.
[274] Ibid., s. 14B(1)–(3).
[275] [1999] 2 AC 240, [1999] 2 WLR 625, [1999] 2 All ER 257, HL.

example of judicial reluctance to see public authorities given arbitrary power to criminalize otherwise lawful assemblies.[276]

A further set of powers which organizers of public assemblies face is contained in the Public Order Act 1986, section 14(1). This permits the chief officer of police or senior officer at the site of the meeting[277] to give directions imposing certain conditions on the assembly. Such directions may be given only if both the following conditions apply

(1) The meeting is a public assembly within the meaning of the Act. A public assembly consists of twenty or more people[278] in a public place (any highway or any place to which the public, or any section of the public, has access as of right or by virtue of any express or implied conditions, on payment or otherwise).[279] This means that most cricket or football matches with two teams of eleven, plus officials, are public assemblies, and the emotions engendered amongst supporters and players regularly give rise to public-order problems. On the other hand, the premises of clubs which have a genuine system for scrutinizing applications for membership are normally excluded, as their members do not constitute a 'section of the public'.[280] People who enter private land as trespassers are not within the definition of a public assembly, and separate powers are provided in sections 61, 63, and 77 of the Criminal Justice and Public Order Act 1994 to allow the police to direct trespassers to leave land.[281]

(2) The officer reasonably believes that, having regard to the place or time of the assembly and the circumstances in which it is to be held (or being held), *either* it may result in serious public disorder, serious damage to property, or serious disruption to the life of the community, *or* the purpose of the organizers is to intimidate others with a view to compelling them to refrain from doing something which they have a right to do, or to do something which they have a right not to do.

---

[276] See Clayton, 'Reclaiming Public Ground'; Feldman, 'Property and Public Protest' at 51–9.

[277] Public Order Act 1986, s. 14(2). The chief officer may delegate the power to a deputy or assistant chief constable (in London, an assistant commissioner): s. 15.

[278] Crowds are made up of individuals, and it is not always easy to say whether a particular individual is part of the crowd so as to count towards the total of twenty. This caused difficulties in finding the facts under s. 14B in *Jones (Margaret)*, above, and under s. 14 in *Broadwith v. Chief Constable of Thames Valley Police Authority* [2000] Crim. LR 924, DC.

[279] Public Order Act 1986, s. 16. The place may be indoors or out of doors. These provisions remove doubts which arose under the earlier legislation as to whether or not a railway platform or football-ground terrace, to which access was available on purchase of a ticket or payment of an entrance fee, was a public place.

[280] *Charter v. Race Relations Board* [1973] AC 868, [1973] 1 All ER 512, HL. The effect of the case has been restricted for the purposes of race relations law by the Race Relations Act 1976, s. 25, but the case remains good persuasive authority on the meaning of 'section of the public' in statutes. The grounds of football clubs which operate a membership scheme, and admit only members (as Luton Town FC did for some time), may come within this exception.

[281] The powers originated in s. 39 of the Public Order Act 1986, now repealed, which was aimed mainly at hippy convoys who caused a national stir by ensconcing themselves on farmers' land in Wiltshire and the surrounding areas during the passage of the Public Order Bill, wishing to celebrate the summer solstice at Stonehenge, a desire blocked by English Heritage, which controls the site of Stonehenge.

These criteria have been considered above in relation to section 12 of the 1986 Act.

The directions may be given to the organizers of or participants in a public assembly. They may include such conditions as appear to the officer to be necessary to prevent the anticipated serious public disorder, damage, disruption, or intimidation, but the conditions may relate only to the place at which the assembly may be held or may continue, its maximum duration, or the maximum number of people who may attend. This gives the officer a very wide discretion, couched in subjective language. It can be reviewed on ordinary public law principles if the power appears to have been used for an improper purpose. For example, if the conditions imposed amount virtually to a ban, they will be unlawful.[282] The exercise of the discretion is also reviewable for compatibility with Convention rights: under section 6 of the Human Rights Act 1998, incompatible conditions are unlawful, so the power must not be used to interfere in a disproportionate way with freedom of expression or peaceful assembly under ECHR Articles 10 and 11.

When given in advance by the chief officer or his delegate, the directions must be given in writing,[283] which will help to avoid misunderstandings. It is an offence for an organizer or participant knowingly to fail to comply with a valid direction, unless the accused can show that the failure arose from circumstances beyond his control. This might occur, for example, where a limit on the number of participants is exceeded when the meeting is invaded by a rival group; but in such circumstances it would probably be necessary for the organizer to show that he had taken reasonable steps to prevent gatecrashers, for example by positioning stewards in adequate numbers for normal purposes. A constable in uniform may arrest without warrant anyone whom he reasonably suspects of committing such an offence.[284]

A related power to deal with harassment of people in their homes by protestors is created by the Criminal Justice and Police Act 2001, section 42, which allows a constable at the scene to give directions to people to prevent harassment of, or alarm or distress to, a resident if:

- the person to whom the direction is given is outside or in the vicinity of the resident's dwelling;
- the constable reasonably believes that the person is there to persuade someone not to do something he is entitled to do, or to do something he or she is under no obligation to do; and
- the constable reasonably believes that the presence of the person, alone or together with others who are there, amounts to or is likely to result in the harassment of the resident, or is likely to cause alarm or distress to the resident.

A person who knowingly contravenes such a direction is guilty of an offence, and the constable may arrest without warrant anyone he reasonably suspects of committing such an offence. The power was created in the wake of protests about treatment of

---

[282] *DPP v. Baillie* [1995] Crim. LR 426, DC.
[283] S. 14(3).
[284] Ibid., s. 14(5), (6), (7).

animals by Huntingdon Life Sciences Ltd. where the protestors picketed the homes of the company's employees. It is narrowly drawn to protect the right of the employees and their families to respect for their private and family lives and homes, to which they are entitled under ECHR Article 8, and if operated sensibly should not constitute an improper or disproportionate interference with protestors' rights under ECHR Articles 10 and 11.

The statutory powers to give directions are wider than that available at common law, as they can be exercised well before any breach of the peace is imminent, unlike the power to prevent a breach of the peace, and in advance of any obstruction to a highway, unlike the exercise of power which was in question in *Arrowsmith v. Jenkins.* They are also exercisable in order to avoid consequences, such as serious disruption to the life of the community, which might not amount to a breach of the peace. Although there is no requirement for organizers of a public assembly (in contrast with a public procession) to give notice of it to the police, in practice the police usually hear in advance about any large assemblies which are being planned, and organizers themselves often consult with police about public-order issues arising from the planned assembly.

On the other hand, once a public assembly is in progress it is hard to see what advantage the statutory powers offer. They go no further than the power in respect of a breach of the peace, except with regard to disruption to community life which does not amount to a breach of the peace (admittedly rather hard to envisage), and are not apt to impose conditions relating to dress or the display of banners or other indications of political or religious adherence, and so are somewhat narrower than the common law power upheld in *Humphries v. Connor.*[285] Perhaps the enactment of section 14 reflects a certain concern as to the propriety of relying on heavily criticized common law decisions for a power to interfere in the assemblies of people pursuing lawful purposes in apparently lawful ways.

18.4 REGULATION OF ASSEMBLIES IN PRIVATE PREMISES

(1) RIGHTS TO MEET IN PRIVATE

State intervention in a private assembly held on private premises potentially interferes with several sets of rights. It may infringe rights to privacy and property, and (according to the purpose of the assembly) to freedom of expression, religion, or philosophical conviction. Accordingly the powers of state agencies in respect of such assemblies is limited. Where there is a sufficient element of publicity in the surrounding circumstances, Parliament has allowed the police or others a regulatory role, as in relation to public processions and assemblies discussed above. There is also power to remove trespassers from private land,[286] to ban trespassory assemblies on private land

---

[285] (1864) 17 Ir. CLR 1.
[286] Criminal Justice and Public Order Act 1994, ss. 61, 63, 77.

(discussed above), and to stop the consumption of alcohol in designated public places, which may include private land to which the public have access.[287]

Generally, however, the state has eschewed power to regulate private meetings held in private with the occupier's consent. This has two sets of implications. First, it means that landowners cannot usually be forced to allow, or prevented from allowing, their property to be used in any particular way. This is similar to the position in the USA, where action taken by a landowner to interfere unreasonably with freedom of speech on his property will not normally be restrained by the courts under the First Amendment to the US Constitution.[288]

Secondly, where the landowner is a public authority or performing a public function, there are few prospects of compelling the authority to allow its property to be used by the public. In the USA, it would be constitutionally improper for a public authority to discriminate in the access which it allowed to different groups for meetings. In the UK, there are certain situations in which people have a right to use public premises for meetings in the course of election campaigns (see Chapter 13, above). Courts will sometimes constrain the behaviour of public-authority landowners to ensure that their allocation of the property, or use of it, conforms to public-law principles.[289] However, this has never yet been used to impose an obligation on an authority to allow its property to be used for meetings unless there is a statutory requirement, as in the case of election meetings, or a contract, in which case the authority's discretion to change its mind and prevent a meeting by an extreme right-wing political party is subject to the ordinary law of contract.[290] This may change in the light of the positive obligation of public authorities to protect the exercise of the right of freedom of peaceful assembly under ECHR Article 11, coupled with the right to use a footpath across private land for assembling peacefully as long as it is done reasonably and does not obstruct the path.[291]

(2) CRIMINAL OFFENCES

Certain types of meeting receive special protection from the criminal law. These are meetings which are thought to be for the public benefit in some way. For example, it is an offence to act in a disorderly manner at a lawful public meeting for the purpose of preventing the transaction of business, and a constable who reasonably suspects a person of committing the offence can ask for his name and address.[292] A refusal, or giving a false name or address, constitutes an offence.[293] If the person refuses, or the

---

[287] Criminal Justice and Police Act 2001, s. 12.

[288] *Hudgens v. NLRB* 424 US 507 (1976), overruling *Amalgamated Food Employees Union v. Logan Valley Plaza* 391 US 308 (1968).

[289] *Wheeler v. Leicester City Council* [1985] AC 1054, [1985] 2 All ER 1106, HL. See generally Feldman, 'Property and Public Protest' at 42–6.

[290] *Verrall v. Great Yarmouth Borough Council* [1981] QB 202, [1980] 1 All ER 839, CA. See also *Webster v. Newham London Borough Council, The Times*, 22 November 1980, CA.

[291] *DPP v. Jones (Margaret)* [1999] 2 AC 240, [1999] 2 All ER 257, HL.

[292] Public Meetings Act 1908, s. 1(1).

[293] Ibid., s. 1(3), added by Public Order Act 1936, s. 6.

constable has reason to suspect that a false name or address has been given, the person may be arrested.[294] It is an offence to commit riotous, violent, or indecent behaviour in places of worship,[295] or to use force to prevent a Minister from celebrating divine service.[296] However, generally meetings are subject to the ordinary criminal and civil law.

(3) ENTRY BY THE POLICE TO GATHERINGS ON PRIVATE PREMISES

The only power which has been clearly asserted in relation to private meetings is a common law power to enter, or remain on, private premises in order to stop or prevent a breach of the peace. As noted above, breaches of the peace are regarded as matters in which there is a sufficient public interest to justify an extension of police powers even into private houses. The police may therefore enter or remain on premises to stop a breach of the peace which is in progress, or to conduct a fresh pursuit of a person who has just been causing a breach of the peace. They may also stay for long enough to ensure that the breach is not likely to recur. However, they may not enter premises to arrest a person for a breach of the peace once it has ended and the risk of repetition has abated.[297]

Less clearly established is an anticipatory power to enter private meetings in order to prevent an apprehended breach of the peace. The scope of this power is uncertain, having its origin in unreserved judgments in a decision of the Divisional Court in *Thomas v. Sawkins*.[298] That case was one of several arising from the social and political unrest of the 1930s, and concerned a meeting at a private hall in Glamorgan in 1934 to protest against the Incitement to Disaffection Bill, then before Parliament, and to demand that the Chief Constable of Glamorgan be dismissed. This was one of several meetings addressed by Alun Thomas, which the police had attended despite being asked to leave. The magistrates found as a fact that, at previous meetings, seditious speeches had been made, the Chief Constable had been vilified, and breaches of the peace had followed. In the instant case, the police again decided to attend, and the magistrates found that the police had reasonable grounds for apprehending that there would again be 'seditious speeches . . . and/or incitements to violence and/or breaches of the peace' at the meeting. The organizers invited the public to attend the meeting. The police officers who arrived at the meeting were refused admission, but entered regardless. They were then twice asked to leave by Alun Thomas. When they refused to do so, Thomas said that they would be ejected, but, when he tried to eject Inspector

---

[294] Police and Criminal Evidence Act 1984, s. 25; see Ch. 5 above.

[295] Ecclesiastical Courts Jurisdiction Act 1860, s. 2. Breach of the Peace of the Church (*ciricfrith*) has been a serious offence since the early 7th cent. at latest: Laws of Ethelbert (AD 601–4), c. 1.

[296] Offences against the Person Act 1861, s. 36. See St. John A. Robilliard, *Religion and the Law: Religious Liberty in Modern English Law* (Manchester: Manchester University Press, 1984), 15–19.

[297] *R. v. Marsden* (1868) LR 1 CCR 131; *Robson v. Hallett* [1967] 2 QB 939, [1967] 2 All ER 407, DC; *McConnell v. Chief Constable of Greater Manchester Police* [1990] 1 WLR 364, [1990] 1 All ER 423, CA. See generally D. Feldman, *The Law Relating to Entry, Search and Seizure* (London: Butterworths, 1986), 321–3.

[298] [1935] 2 KB 249. For discussion and criticism, see A. L. Goodhart, 'Thomas v. Sawkins: A Constitutional Innovation' (1936) 6 *CLJ* 22–30; D. G. T. Williams, *Keeping the Peace*, ch. 6, especially at 142–4; Feldman, *Entry, Search and Seizure*, 323–31.

Parry, Sergeant Sawkins pushed Thomas's arm away. The police stayed, but Thomas later prosecuted Sergeant Sawkins for assault and battery. The matter turned on whether the officers had had a right to remain. If they had not, Thomas had been entitled to use reasonable force to remove them after revoking any implied licence to enter the hall, and the use of force to resist ejection had been unlawful. If the police had a legal right to remain, the attempt at ejection was unlawful, and the sergeant had been entitled to use reasonable force to repulse the attempt. The magistrates decided that the police had been entitled to remain in order to prevent reasonably appre-hended sedition, breach of the peace, or incitement to violence, and acquitted the sergeant. Thomas appealed by case stated.

Three unreserved judgments dismissing the appeal were delivered in the Divisional Court. Lord Hewart CJ gave a judgment, which is unsatisfactorily reported,[299] in which he spoke of a preventive power and duty of the police to enter premises where a constable has reasonable ground for believing that an offence is imminent or is likely to be committed. This formulation, as it stands, is unsatisfactory in two respects. First, it goes beyond the prevention of breaches of the peace, appearing to encompass any offence. However, the judgment must be read in the context of the findings of the magistrates, which were expressly referred to by Lord Hewart when he spoke of 'such reasonable grounds of apprehension as the justices have found here'. That apprehen-sion related to sedition, breach of the peace, and (which is the same thing) incitement to violence. All the offences consisted of, or entailed, breaches of the peace or the threat of one. That being so, the term 'offence' as used by Lord Hewart must, it is submitted, be understood as applying only to breaches of the peace which, as noted above, infringe a recognized public interest and give rise to special powers and duties of police acting, as Lord Hewart said, *ex virtute officii*. This is particularly important today, after Parliament has established a legislative balance between the competing interests involved in these cases. In the Police and Criminal Evidence Act 1984, sec-tions 17, 18, and 32, Parliament has provided a code of police entry powers in respect of criminal offences, and abolished other powers of entry in respect of offences not involving breaches of the peace in section 17(5). Secondly, Lord Hewart's formulation appears to allow entry before the offence is imminent. However, this cannot stand with later decisions, notably that of the Court of Appeal (Criminal Division) in *R. v. Howell*,[300] to the effect that powers and duties arise only when the breach of the peace is imminent.

Noting that the prosecutor's case depended on the policemen being trespassers, Lord Hewart remarked that it seemed 'somewhat remarkable to speak of trespass when members of the public who happened to be police officers attend, after a public invitation, a public meeting which is to discuss as one part of its business the dismissal of the chief constable of the county'. In other words, the police were to be regarded as members of the public who had been invited to attend, as they had a legitimate interest in the matter under consideration. But this argument fails, because on the

---

[299] Note the differences between the report at 33 LGR 330, presumably compiled from the contem-poraneous shorthand note, and that at [1935] KB 249, presumably revised by Lord Hewart subsequently.
[300] [1982] QB 416, [1981] 3 All ER 383, CA.

facts found by the magistrates any licence issued to the officers had been revoked by the organizers. The question, therefore, was whether the officers had had any independent right to remain, such as might override the withdrawal of their licence. That right could come only from the duty to prevent a reasonably apprehended and imminent breach of the peace.

Avory J therefore rightly concentrated on the question whether on the facts of the case the organizers could effectively withdraw the invitation from the officers, and he decided that they could not. He restricted his decision to the prevention of breach of the peace or sedition at widely publicized meetings to which the general public had been invited. Lawrence J limited his decision firmly to the facts of the case, and so may be thought to have adopted a formulation of the entry power even narrower than that of Avory J. The preventive or anticipatory power of the police to enter should, it is submitted, therefore be seen as restricted to cases where a meeting has been advertised, the public are invited, and the police have reasonable grounds for apprehending that a breach of the peace (or offences involving breaches of the peace, such as sedition and inciting violence) will occur at the meeting if the police are not present. In this form, the power is, as Avory J pointed out, analogous to the power to bind over to keep the peace when no breach is imminent. It would not allow the police to enter private premises to attend a meeting of a private group against the organizers' wishes.

However, even when so limited the power is controversial. Before the decision in *Thomas v. Sawkins*, the official line had been that no such anticipatory power to enter private premises existed at common law.[301] Only ten weeks before the events which gave rise to *Thomas v. Sawkins*, the Home Secretary had told the House of Commons that the police had no such power.[302] The presence of the police may be successful in preventing a breach of the peace, but one will never know: as in *Thomas v. Sawkins* itself, where there was no violence or disorder at the event, it is impossible to tell whether a breach would have occurred without the police presence. In addition, there is a risk that the presence of the police will stifle debate and free expression. On the facts of *Thomas v. Sawkins* itself, this amounted to a probability: the presence of more than thirty officers by the time the meeting started, with batons drawn on entry, looks more like a crude attempt to suppress expressions of public opinion about the Chief Constable. This makes Lord Hewart's comment, 'It goes without saying that the powers and duties of the police are directed, not to the interests of the police, but to the protection and welfare of the public', look disingenuous. But it is perhaps not unreasonable to allow the police unrestricted access to meetings to which the public has been invited if there is a reasonably apprehended risk of a breach of the peace, as the presence of members of the general public creates a special public interest in maintaining order which, if the meeting were restricted to a private group, could properly be the responsibility of the organizers.

For these reasons it has been argued that the power of entry should be restricted to

---

[301] See *Report of the Departmental Committee on the Duties of the Police with Respect to the Preservation of Order at Public Meetings*, Cd. 4673 (London: HMSO, 1909) at 6.

[302] Sir John Gilmour, 14 June 1934, 290 HC Debs. (5th Series), col. 1968, in connection with the policing of violence at a fascist meeting at Olympia a week earlier.

public meetings, and should not extend to a private meeting in private premises.[303] However, the Court of Appeal rejected the argument in *McLeod v. Commissioner of Police of the Metropolis*,[304] where it was held that a constable was entitled to enter a person's home to make sure that there was no breach of the peace while lawyers for the occupier's ex-husband were improperly executing a court order. The decision made it clear that English law was inadequate to ensure that the police acted in a proportionate manner, interfering with the right to respect for the home no more than necessary, so it was not surprising that the European Court of Human Rights subsequently held in *McLeod v. United Kingdom*[305] that the entry of the constable and his remaining on the premises against the will of the occupier had violated her rights under ECHR Article 8. It will be interesting to see how the application of Article 8, alongside Articles 9, 10, and 11, in English law by way of the Human Rights Act 1998 will affect the courts' view of the obligations of constables in this field.

(4) AN ENTRY POWER IN RESPECT OF PRIVATE PREMISES WITHOUT PUBLIC MEETINGS?

The question next arises whether the power extends beyond public meetings. There are cases where it has been held that the police have an anticipatory power to enter private premises to prevent reasonably apprehended domestic violence. This was one of the grounds of decision in *McGowan v. Chief Constable of Kingston upon Hull*,[306] in which a man had forcibly seized a child from his former cohabitant in order to lure her back. She went to the house with two constables, who entered with her in reliance first on her invitation and secondly on their reasonable apprehension that a breach of the peace might imminently occur. The man assaulted the constables, and was convicted of assaulting them in the execution of their duty. On appeal, it was held that they had been in the execution of their duty, being lawfully on the premises both because of the woman's invitation[307] and because of the reasonable apprehension of a breach of the peace. However, it seems from the report in *The Times* that the defendant might have conceded that the police had a right to enter initially, and *Thomas v. Sawkins* was not considered by the court, so the decision is of limited value. When *Thomas v. Sawkins* was considered by the Court of Appeal in a domestic setting, in *McLeod v. Commissioner of Police of the Metropolis*,[308] the decision to apply it to allow preventive entry to a home cannot be said to have been argued with any great rigour. As noted above, the European Court of Human Rights subsequently decided that the use of the power in the circumstances of *McLeod*'s case was disproportionate, and violated the right to respect for the home under ECHR Article 8. The police and the courts will have to take account of that under the Human Rights Act 1998, section 6, the police as a public authority act unlawfully if they use discretionary powers in a

---

[303] Feldman, *Entry, Search and Seizure*, 324–5.

[304] [1994] 4 All ER 553, CA, at 560 *per* Neill LJ, noted at (1995) 111 *LQR* 562–5 (D. Feldman).

[305] Eur. Ct. HR, (1999) 27 EHRR 493.

[306] [1968] Crim. LR 34, *The Times*, 21 October, 1967, DC. The report in *The Times* is fuller.

[307] For criticism, see Feldman, *Entry, Search and Seizure* at 31.

[308] [1994] 4 All ER 553, CA.

manner which is incompatible with ECHR Article 8. It is high time the extension of *Thomas v. Sawkins*, an unsatisfactory decision in its original context, to domestic matters was ended. Before *McGowan*'s case, Parliament had already created a power to obtain a warrant to enter and search premises where children are reasonably believed to be at risk, and another to make arrests without a warrant in certain cases.[309] Once an imminent breach of the peace is reasonably apprehended, or is in progress, a constable can enter or remain on land in order to suppress it.[310] This should be a sufficient power. It is anomalous for the courts to invent powers of entry in situations beyond those where Parliament has seen fit to act. The decision of the European Court of Human Rights should be the last nail in the coffin of this regrettable line of authority.

18.5 RESTRICTING PROTEST AND FREE EXPRESSION BY BAIL CONDITIONS AND BINDING OVER

The discussion so far has been about general norms which are used to enable the authorities to regulate public protest in order to prevent disorder, or to criminalize types of behaviour. However, there are certain procedures which allow courts to attempt to control in some detail the behaviour of particular people who are thought to be especially likely to break the law or cause breaches of the peace. Sometimes this follows conviction and forms part of the sentence of the court. For example, national and international banning orders can be made to stop convicted or suspected football hooligans attending matches, as noted in Chapter 8 above. Another sentence which can limit a defendant's freedom short of imprisonment is the conditional discharge. This can affect the ability of convicted people to take part in protests and public assemblies.

That carries the risk that the sentencing power could be used for political rather than penological purposes. However, those subject to the order will at least have been convicted of an offence to which the sentence relates. Far more worrying is the use of coercive powers against people who have not been convicted of any offence, for the purpose of preventing their participation in public protest.[311] There are two procedures which may have this effect: attaching conditions to a grant of bail, and binding over. These are considered below. It is important to bear in mind that the power to impose bail conditions or bind a person over is now always subject to the demands of ECHR Articles 9, 10, and 11 as a result of the Human Rights Act 1998.

---

[309] Children and Young Persons Act 1933, s. 40. See now Children Act 1989, ss. 44, 45; Police and Criminal Evidence Act 1984, s. 17; Chs 5, 9 above.

[310] *Robson v. Hallett* [1967] 2 QB 939, [1967] 2 All ER 407, DC; *R. v. Lamb* [1990] Crim. LR 58, DC.

[311] Other powers to restrict freedom of action or movement, such as anti-social behaviour orders, child safety orders, and child curfew schemes, under the Crime and Disorder Act 1998 as amended, are important interferences with civil liberties and human rights, but usually present relatively little threat to the ability to participate in protests.

(1) BAIL CONDITIONS

Under the Bail Act 1976 people accused of criminal offences have, *prima facie*, a right to bail pending trial, which may be withheld only if there are 'substantial grounds' for believing that the accused might fail to surrender to custody, commit offences while on bail, or interfere with witnesses.[312] However, when granting bail there is power to attach to a grant of bail

'such requirements as appear to the court to be necessary to secure that:

> (a) [the defendant] surrenders to custody,
>
> (b) he does not commit an offence while on bail,
>
> (c) he does not interfere with witnesses or otherwise obstruct the course of justice . . . ,
>
> (d) he makes himself available for the purpose of enabling inquiries or a report to be made to assist the court in dealing with him for the offence . . .'[313]

This is often used to require people with no fixed address to reside at a bail hostel, or to observe a curfew, or not to leave the country, pending trial. During the miners' strike of 1984–85, magistrates' courts dealing with striking miners, who had been charged with offences arising out of the strike, commonly attached a more unusual condition to grants of bail, namely that the defendants were 'not to visit any premises or place for the purpose of picketing or demonstrating in connection with the current trade dispute . . . other than peacefully to picket or demonstrate at his current place of employment'. The effect was to make the defendants, from pits where the miners had voted to strike, liable to be remanded in custody if they picketed at pits where workers had voted to continue to work. The condition was said to be necessary to prevent the commission of further offences while on bail, but the defendants claimed that it had been routinely imposed on all defendants without regard to the particular circumstances of individual defendants, and without inquiry to discover whether there were substantial grounds for believing that the conditions were necessary for the purposes set out above.

In *R. v. Mansfield Justices, ex parte Sharkey*,[314] the lawfulness of the condition was challenged in conjoined applications for judicial review by nine protesters who had been bailed subject to the condition. It was held that the statutory requirement for substantial grounds when refusing bail could not be implied into the provisions dealing with the less draconian step of imposing conditions on the grant of bail. No formal evidence is required at bail hearings,[315] and the court refused to impose an obligation to look for substantial grounds for believing that offences would be committed without the imposition of a condition. The only basis for reviewing the decisions was that of *Wednesbury* unreasonableness, including failure to take account of relevant considerations. Although the court felt that the procedure adopted in

---

[312] Bail Act 1976, Sch. 1, Part I, para. 2.
[313] Ibid., s. 3(6).
[314] [1985] QB 613, [1985] 1 All ER 193, DC.
[315] *Re Moles* [1981] Crim. LR 170, DC.

Mansfield Magistrates' Court could easily give the appearance of group rather than individual justice, with eight people in the dock having their applications simultaneously dealt with and the clerk merely attaching stick-on slips, with the condition already typed out, to the bail form, the court was not prepared to find that there were not reasonable grounds for imposing the conditions. It was held that the magistrates were entitled to look beyond the circumstances and record of individual defendants, and take account of the general situation in which large numbers of striking miners were gathering at non-striking pits in Nottinghamshire and conducting picketing by intimidation. Under those circumstances, it was reasonable for the magistrates to accede to police requests for the condition to be imposed, as there was a clear risk of defendants contributing to further offences of intimidation (including assault, which does not necessarily involve a battery, and offences under section 5 of the Public Order Act 1936, now replaced by the Public Order Act 1986, sections 4 and 5) if the conditions were not imposed.

Indeed, in the case of the only defendant in relation to whom irrelevant considerations appeared to have been taken into account (a Mr. Fellows), the court refused relief because, on a rehearing, any properly instructed bench of magistrates 'could not fail to impose the same or a similar condition on any grant of bail'.[316] This amounted to a direction to magistrates to impose the condition, rather than a decision that it was not unreasonable for them to have done so, despite the affidavit of the chairman of the magistrates in that case, stating that in the majority of cases his bench had granted unconditional bail.

It seems, therefore, to be lawful to use bail conditions to regulate the behaviour of accused protesters pending trial if there is a risk of further offences in which they might be tempted to participate, even though the defendant has not yet been convicted of any offence. In the context of public protest and industrial action, this represents a major interference with freedoms of movement, expression, and protest. Under the Human Rights Act 1998 the power to impose bail conditions must be exercised in a way which does not impose a disproportionate restriction on freedom of expression and peaceful assembly, but proportionality may not help those seeking bail very much. Where there is no prospect of a speedy trial, the interference may last for a considerable length of time. Admittedly the condition imposed in these cases did not prevent the defendants from protesting, but only prevented them from doing so at pits other than their own and in ways which were not peaceable. Although at first sight this seems to be a major restriction of the condition, respecting the defendants' political and industrial right to protest in support of their side in the dispute, in context the concession is far less impressive. The dispute was a national one, and was in part a dispute not simply between the National Union of Mineworkers and the National Coal Board but between striking members of the NUM and those who had disregarded the union's call for a national strike (many of the non-strikers went on to form a separate union, the Union of Democratic Mineworkers). Preventing miners from pits where the strike was being observed from picketing pits where work was continuing treated the dispute as a series of local strikes rather than the national strike

---

[316] [1985] QB at 629–30, [1985] 1 All ER at 204.

which it had in reality become, and interfered with the NUM's attempt to picket working miners. Nevertheless, perhaps it can be said that the risk of further participation in potentially unlawful activity by the defendants brought the case within the terms of section 3(6) of the Bail Act 1976. The issue, on this view, is whether or not the magistrates took proper account of the defendants' political rights when exercising their discretion to frame and impose the condition.

(2) BINDING OVER[317]

There are procedures whereby a person can be required to undertake to keep the peace or be of good behaviour, on pain of forfeiting a sum of money (a 'recognizance') in the event that he is proved to have committed anti-social behaviour (which need not be unlawful) or a breach of the peace. This is known as binding over: the person is 'bound over' to keep the peace or be of good behaviour. There are several forms of binding over. It is available as part of the sentence imposed on a convicted offender,[318] or it can be used as a type of deferred sentence[319] or bail condition.[320] More controversially, it can be imposed by magistrates of their own motion on acquitted defendants,[321] witnesses, or anyone who happens to be before the court, if the bench considers that the person has caused or given rise to a likelihood of a breach of the peace in the past and there is a risk of a breach of the peace in the future.[322] It may also be imposed in proceedings brought in order to obtain such an order, commenced by complaint in the magistrates' court, often against people arrested in connection with breaches of the peace.[323] The person to be bound over is required by the court to enter into a recognizance, and may be required to provide sureties. A recognizance is a conditional debt, owed to the Crown, which becomes due if the person breaches the undertaking within a specified time. Although it is a civil obligation, and is in theory undertaken voluntarily (a binding over order cannot be made if the person to be bound over does not agree to it), the court can imprison a person for up to six months for refusing to be bound over.

The undertaking entered into may be in either or both of two forms: an undertaking to keep the peace generally; or an undertaking to be of good behaviour towards a

---

[317] See generally D. G. T. Williams, *Keeping the Peace*, ch. 4; A. D. Grunis, 'Binding Over to Keep the Peace and be of Good Behaviour in England and Canada' [1976] *PL* 16–41, arguing for abolition; Law Commission, Working Paper No 103, *Criminal Law: Binding Over—the Issues* (London: HMSO, 1987); Law Commission, Report No. 222, *Binding Over*, Cm. 2439 (London: HMSO, 1994).

[318] There is some doubt as to whether it can be the only sentence imposed: see the discussion in Law Commission, *Criminal Law: Binding Over*, 16–18.

[319] Binding over to come up for judgment in the Crown Court: *R. v. Spratling* [1911] 1 KB 77; Powers of Criminal Courts Act 1973, s. 1(7); Supreme Court Act 1981, s. 79(2).

[320] *R. v. Aubrey-Fletcher, ex parte Thompson* [1969] 1 WLR 872.

[321] *Wilson v. Skeock* (1949) 65 TLR 418; *R. v. South West London Magistrates' Court, ex parte Brown* [1974] Crim. LR 313, DC; *R. v. Woking Justices, ex parte Gossage* [1973] QB 448, [1973] 2 All ER 621, DC; *R. v. Inner London Crown Court, ex parte Benjamin* [1987] Crim. LR 417, DC.

[322] This power arises from common law and the Justices of the Peace Act 1361. See D. Feldman, 'The King's Peace, the Royal Prerogative and Public Order: The Roots and Early Development of Binding Over Powers' [1988] *CLJ* 101–28.

[323] Magistrates' Courts Act 1980, s. 115(1).

particular person. It forms a convenient way of dealing with certain types of disputes between neighbours or cohabitants, but was developed primarily to provide a way of discouraging public disturbances caused by people who were, and later people who were not, of good repute. The use of the power as a preventive weapon in respect of public disorder thus has a long history, going back well before 1361, and in this century has been regularly used in relation to political activists. However, used in this way, the order may have the effect of debarring a person from conducting legitimate political activities. It therefore falls to be assessed by reference to the tests set out in ECHR Article 10(2).

When the Law Commission reported on binding over in 1994, it concluded that the standards of behaviour which are applied in deciding whether there has been a breach of the order are unacceptably vague and uncertain, and that the informality made it likely that they were incompatible with the ECHR. The Commission recommended that all binding-over powers should be abolished without replacement, and published a draft Bill to achieve it.[324] So far, no action has been taken on the report. In the meantime, the European Court of Human Rights has examined the compatibility of both binding over to keep the peace and binding over to be of good behaviour with Article 10 in the context of public protests.

In *Steel and others v. United Kingdom*,[325] the Court held that the elements of a breach of the peace, with its requirement for violence or the threat of violence, constitute a standard which is reasonably objective, certain, and predictable. A person bound over to keep the peace can be tolerably sure of what is expected of him. It meets the requirement of being 'prescribed by law' under Article 10(2), and will be a justifiable interference with freedom of expression to protect public order and the rights of others as long as it is imposed only in circumstances where it is proportionate to the legitimate objective.

By contrast, the Court decided in *Hashman and Harrup v. United Kingdom*[326] that a requirement that a person is of good behaviour, or does not act *contra bonos mores*, is insufficiently precise and objective to allow the person to be reasonably sure what conduct will lead to liability. The interference with freedom of expression was therefore not prescribed by law within the meaning of that term in Article 10(2), and so was not justifiable. It puts too much power in the hands of magistrates to decide, *ex post facto*, whether a person has behaved in a way which justifies estreating his recognizance. This, as Professor Glanville Williams has argued, threatens an extraordinary breach of rule-of-law standards,[327] and, as Patricia Hewitt notes, allows arbitrary judicial interference with freedom of peaceful assembly and other freedoms.[328]

---

[324] Law Commission, Report No. 222, *Binding Over*, Cm. 2439 (London: HMSO, 1994).

[325] Eur. Ct. HR, Judgment of 23 September 1998, RJD 1998-VII.

[326] Eur. Ct. HR, App. No. 25594/94, Judgment of 25 November 1999.

[327] Glanville Williams, 'Preventive Justice and the Rule of Law' (1953) 16 *MLR* 417–27; Glanville Williams, *Criminal Law: The General Part*, 2nd edn. (London: Stevens, 1961), 719.

[328] P. Hewitt, *The Abuse of Power*, 125. See also Williams, *Keeping the Peace*, 87 ff; A. Sherr, *Freedom of Protest, Public Order and the Law* (Oxford: Blackwell, 1989), 121–4; G. Robertson, *Freedom, the Individual and the Law*, 77–8.

The Divisional Court held in 1984, in *R. v. Central Criminal Court, ex parte Boulding*,[329] that binding over powers must not be used in such a way as to deter a person, through fear of the consequences, from exercising rights of free speech within the law. Unfortunately, they often had that effect. The European Court of Human Rights has now held that all orders binding people over to be of good behaviour violate Article 10, and the Law Commission has recommended the abolition of all binding-over powers. In *R. v. Morpeth Ward JJ, ex parte Ward*,[330] the Divisional Court upheld a binding over order against protesters who had invaded a private field to try to interfere with a pheasant shoot. The court held that it was not necessary to show that a breach of the peace had occurred, but only that there be risk that the protesters' behaviour would cause a breach of the peace in the future. Brooke J considered that, on the facts of the case, 'provocative disorderly behaviour which is likely to have the natural consequence of causing violence, even if only to the persons of the provokers, is capable of being treated as conduct likely to cause a breach of the peace'. There is an evident risk that the bellicose tendencies of one's opponents may be invoked to justify a prior restraint on one's own freedom to protest and express political ideas. The only difference between this case and the case of the Salvationists in *Beatty v. Gillbanks*, presumably, is that the Salvationists, despite behaving in a noisy and provocative way, were not regarded as being disorderly. It is dangerous to allow a judge's or magistrate's perception of disorderliness to become a criterion for rationing freedom of expression and protest. The power to bind over was somewhat limited in *Nicol and Selvanayagam*[331] to cases where the person bound over was acting unlawfully, or was acting unreasonably and it would have been reasonable (although not necessarily lawful) for someone to respond violently. But the problem remains that under the Human Rights Act 1998 it seems that any court which binds someone over to be of good behaviour, and so restricts their freedom of speech and protest, is likely to be acting in violation of ECHR Article 10 and thus acting unlawfully. The power to bind over to be of good behaviour will have to fall into disuse and should be abolished, while consideration should be given to abolishing binding over to keep the peace as well, as recommended by the Law Commission.

18.6 CONCLUSION

At the end of this long chapter, the conclusion can be kept short. After a history of allowing and even encouraging significant infringements of rights to free expression and peaceful assembly, the courts have recently begun to redress the balance, recognizing that people should not be liable to have their freedom routinely restricted merely because they use it in a way that offends others. A small but important step has been taken towards securing highways as places where people can assemble and protest,

---

[329] [1984] 1 QB 813, [1984] 1 All ER 766, DC.
[330] [1992] Crim. LR 497, *sub. nom. R. v. Morpeth Ward JJ, ex parte Joseland* [1992] *NLJ Rep.* 312, DC.
[331] [1996] Crim. LR 318, DC.

under conditions which will have to be assessed in the light of the newly incorporated requirements of the ECHR under the Human Rights Act 1998, which also offers an enhanced standard of judicial review of administrative and policing decisions which interfere with freedom of expression and assembly. It will be interesting to see what impact this has in practice. Meanwhile, one can only hope that Parliament will resist the temptation to introduce legislation to destroy the green shoots of a politically active and tolerant society.

19

HUMAN RIGHTS, LIBERTY, AND POLITICAL WILL

This chapter is not a conclusion, either in name or in substance. It would be impossible to have a true conclusion for a book on civil liberties and human rights, because the subject is in a state of constant, dynamic development, although it is not always easy to see the direction in which it is moving. The range of rights is elastic, and the circumstances in which they can come into play are infinite; any worthwhile conclusion would be no more than the beginning of a new exploration in different directions, and a conclusion which seeks to close off the subject is worse than useless. Nevertheless, it is perhaps worthwhile, at the end of a book which has ranged over a wide variety of matters, to bring together some of the main themes which have emerged from the previous eighteen chapters.

(1) THE PRIMACY OF NEGATIVE RIGHTS

The rights which we have are on the whole negative, based on the classic liberal doctrine that it is the main job of government to establish the conditions for freedom and to refrain from interfering with people further than necessary to achieve that end. Although in Chapter 1 it was argued that the distribution of liberty to all would be useless to some unless steps were taken to ensure that all beneficiaries of rights were in a position to use their freedoms constructively, the state action required for the implementation of public programmes for this purpose is subject to political control. It will be clear from the sections of the book dealing with dignity (Chapter 3) and rights to life and physical integrity (Chapters 4 and 5), requiring rights to health care and decent living conditions, that the extent to which it is helpful or realistic to express aspirations for such state action in terms of social or economic rights is limited. The implementation of such rights, like the advancement of any social interest which requires positive action or expenditure on the part of the state, is mediated through the political system, is subject to considerable executive discretion, and is likely to be a less weighty consideration than budgetary constraints and the need to maintain international competitiveness, particularly in times of recession. The move from recognizing the importance of rights to ensuring that everyone has an equal opportunity to benefit from them is only just beginning. The drive to secure the equal worth of individual rights, by way of rights in social programmes and anti-discrimination legislation, is barely under way yet, but is likely to be encouraged by the growing influence of social rights in the legal and political orders of the European

Union (illustrated by the EU Charter of Rights) and of the Council of Europe's European Social Charter. This, ultimately, is a matter of political commitment; it will be interesting to observe its progress.

(2) THE SUBSTANTIAL BUT LIMITED SIGNIFICANCE OF FUNDAMENTAL FREEDOMS AND HUMAN RIGHTS

Since the first edition of this book was published in 1993, the UK has acquired a distinctive type of bill of rights. It is based on the European Convention on Human Rights (ECHR), introduced to national law by the Human Rights Act 1998 and the devolution statutes for Scotland, Wales, and Northern Ireland, enhanced by the Data Protection Act 1998 (influenced heavily by European Community and Council of Europe instruments) and, potentially, by the Freedom of Information Act 2000. The rights are not entrenched against repeal or amendment by Parliament, and courts cannot strike down incompatible primary legislation. Nevertheless, like the New Zealand Bill of Rights Act 1990, which initially appeared an unpromising piece of legislation, the UK's rights are likely to have a substantial impact on the law, and, over time, on the ways administrators, politicians, and lawyers think. The lack of entrenchment is not necessarily a serious weakness, particularly as there is a strong legal obligation to interpret legislation in a manner compatible with Convention rights so far as it is possible to do so.

Examination of the role of the European Court and Commission of Human Rights, and the sidelong glances we have taken at the work of the Court of Justice of the European Community, the United States Supreme Court, and judges elsewhere, show that the enactment of a justiciable and constitutionally entrenched Bill of Rights can be a powerful political and legal weapon in the hands of those who are in danger of having their rights systematically infringed or abrogated. Nevertheless, useful as it may be, such legislation has been seen to be an incomplete answer to the demands of individuals and groups. Bills of Rights are only as extensive as the rights which they identify and protect, and only as powerful as the politicians who draft them and are bound by them and the judges who enforce them wish them to be. Any failure of will on the part of any of these people will leave the citizens unprotected.

Just as one can exaggerate the value of entrenchment of rights and judicial power to strike down primary legislation, one can too easily forget how important it is for the acceptance of a bill of rights that it should operate in a manner that fits a state's constitutional theory and practices. The UK's constitution at this stage in its development could not comfortably have accommodated a bill of rights modelled on the constitutions of Canada or the USA. Politics and practical government are central to the constitution of the UK; abstract values are new kids on the block. Politicians, administrators, other public officials, and ordinary citizens must share responsibility for protecting rights with judges and lawyers, whether under a bill of rights or without one. Special parliamentary procedures for scrutinizing legislation, and freedom of information legislation to open up government to the public gaze, are just as important in developing the system in a rights-conscious way. Parliamentarians have a particularly heavy responsibility, because they carry the burden of scrutinizing

CIVIL LIBERTIES AND HUMAN RIGHTS

legislation which, in our system, can so easily violate rights. But the ethos of rights must be accepted more generally. It must influence private or privatized bodies supplying goods and services to the public: gas and electricity supply companies, for example, control people's happiness and their abilities to achieve goals and advance plans at least as effectively as government departments or agencies.

(3) THE NEED FOR POLITICIANS AND OTHERS TO BELIEVE IN RIGHTS, AND TO RECOGNIZE THE RESPONSIBILITIES WHICH GO WITH THEM

In order to protect rights, politicians must think them important. This is true both of rights which would impose positive obligations on the state, as in the case of social and economic-equality-related rights, and of classical, liberal individualist rights to freedom from state interference. If the political will to respect rights is absent or in abeyance, the rights will not long flourish. This is no less true in democratic countries than others. Indeed, there is a particular danger that governments which are subject to electoral accountability will be too ready to restrict the rights of unpopular groups in order to be seen to be active in relation to some perceived problem which is exercising the electorate. Chapters 6, 10, and 11 showed the results of a clash between commitment to rights and a government's determination to be seen to be tackling crime: there is a risk of either a gradual erosion of rights, or of a wholesale restriction (as in relation to the right to silence in the criminal process, or access to confidential information under the Drug Trafficking Act 1994 and the Regulation of Investigatory Powers Act 2000). In such cases, rights cease to enjoy primacy, and are liable to be traded off against more pragmatic, albeit often important, considerations. The Human Rights Act 1998 can only ensure that the impact on rights is properly considered. The political and implementation processes must ensure that they are respected in practice.

But oversight is critically important, whether it is carried out by judges, non-governmental organizations or parliamentary committees (or, preferably, by all of them and others besides). Left to itself, the domestic political process is likely to tend towards devaluing rights and over-emphasizing order. This was illustrated in relation to the position of disadvantaged groups in prisons and mental hospitals in Chapter 7, in relation to immigration in Chapter 8, and with reference to public order law in Chapter 18. The signs so far are promising. The judges have made a start on implementing the Human Rights Act 1998. Whitehall was generally well prepared, and Westminster seems to be starting to catch up, although the pressure to respond to international terrorism is testing Parliament's commitment to human rights. A remarkable change has come about in the legal professions. Before 1998, few solicitors had any human-rights expertise, and even among those with experience of making applications to Strasbourg not many described themselves as specialists on human-rights law.[1] Now there are few solicitors' practices which do not profess at least competence, if not expertise, in the law of the ECHR, and there are several specialist sets of barristers' chambers specializing in human-rights matters.

---

[1] G. Chambers, *Practising Human Rights: UK Lawyers and the European Convention on Human Rights*, The Law Society Research and Policy Planning Unit Research Study No. 28 (London: The Law Society, 1998).

Ordinary citizens too must internalize the values of individual and group rights, because democracy can be reconciled with respect for rights only if the people who participate in political decision-making, however remotely, exercise their powers in the light of people's rights. For this, education is essential, and the state needs to facilitate it by making available the resources and opportunities for all students to receive a grounding in civil liberties and rights and their personal, constitutional, and political importance.[2] Rights which are essential to the democratic process are particularly in need of protection against erosion, as noted for example in Chapters 14, 15, and 18.

However, if liberties are to retain the support of politicians and others, and if rights are to be regarded as politically respectable and morally compelling values, those who claim them must exercise them responsibly. Claims to freedom lie ill in the mouths of those who refuse to formulate or comply with standards protecting people against abuse. To reject accountability not only undermines the reputation of the people who abuse freedoms, but may also be held to justify curtailing the freedoms themselves, with a consequential loss to all. This risk seems to be particularly acute in relation to press freedom. The desire to exercise freedom unaccompanied by the trammels of self-critical social responsibility is a tendency from which adults, as well as young children, have to be weaned. If those of us who enjoy freedom of the press do not appear to treat it seriously and responsibly, it should come as no surprise if politicians and others regard our actions as devaluing the freedom, and come to consider that it is legitimate to restrict it. The representatives of the press undermine the strength of their own case by indulging in a form of brinkmanship with government which makes it look as if they are prepared to put press freedom substantially at risk.

This is a topical example of a responsibility which attaches to all rights. Those who exercise rights enjoy them by the consent of others, and must be careful not to abuse their liberty by using the freedom in ways which deny others their rights or threaten the society by whose authority the rights are granted, and whose continued tolerance is needed if they are to be enjoyed. Rights will inevitably sometimes conflict, and the bounds of each will have to be established by political or legal decision. At other times it may be permissible to flout other people's rights as part of a campaign of civil disobedience in order to achieve some greater social good. But in all such cases, a liberal citizen will respect freedom, and will permit its restriction or infringement only to achieve a goal which can be justified within a framework of liberal theory, and then only to the smallest extent necessary to achieve the goal.

(4) THE IMPORTANCE OF REMEDIES

The range and type of remedies is important. We saw how constraints in legal remedies may restrict the value of legal rights. For example, in relation to the police many rights are protected by administrative review, disciplinary proceedings, or a court's duty or discretion to exclude evidence at trial. Where substantial remedies are not provided, rights are not likely to be taken seriously. Increased attention to remedies in

---

[2] See C. Palley, *The UK and Human Rights* (London: Sweet & Maxwell, 1991), especially ch. 4.

public law generally[3] has led to a number of more specialist studies, and, in relation to the police, an influential text, devoted entirely to remedies for police misbehaviour, has gone into a second edition.[4] The development of legal remedies into new fields has begun to produce significant gains for some of the most vulnerable people in society, including prisoners and patients, as explained in Chapters 5 and 7, and under the Human Rights Act 1998 the trend is beginning to accelerate. Provision of remedies is central to commitment to rights, and, if judicial remedies are to be restricted, other remedies must be provided and made to work effectively if rights are not to be compromised. In this context, attention will undoubtedly focus on the performance of special Commissioners established to oversee areas where national security is at stake, and on the special tribunals set up to adjudicate on complaints.

The attempt by government to lay down standards and give effect to them by way of a Citizen's Charter, with a range of Charters dealing with specialized areas of administration and service delivery, has probably not satisfied the expectations Mr. Major had of it when he initiated it as Prime Minister. The work of independent bodies such as the Equal Opportunities Commission, the Commission for Racial Equality, and the Disability Rights Commission, has been enhanced, although they still face structural problems which make it hard for them to function as effectively as would be desirable. Nevertheless, they offer a way of merging a collective approach to remedying injustice with an individualist one, and provide a model which could be developed usefully in the future. The next step may be the establishment of a Human Rights Commission for England and Wales, following in the footsteps of the Human Rights Commission established for Northern Ireland under the Northern Ireland Act 1998; a similar commission is already under consideration in Scotland.

(5) THE CONTINUING CHALLENGE

If this book has a concluding message, it is that the future of civil liberties and human rights is at least as important as the present, and more important than the past. The UK has, on the whole, a respectable (although not unblemished) record for maintaining and exporting respect for rights and liberties. The Human Rights Act 1998 undoubtedly gives it a boost. However, the continuation of that record is not guaranteed. As experience elsewhere in the world shows, the belief in the importance of equal liberties, and of achieving equal value of liberty for all, is hard to maintain, particularly in adverse social and economic circumstances. The danger that standards will be allowed to slip, or that our achievements in the field of rights will be outstripped by developments elsewhere, is always present. Since 1997, the UK has experienced a significant amount of constitutional reform, which has improved our chance of meeting the danger successfully, but the present system for protecting rights against ill-judged legislative action remains somewhat unreliable; this book alone offers numerous examples of the resulting law. Any method of safeguarding our rights, let alone improving them, requires us to review them constantly, to debate them

---

[3] P. Birkinshaw, *Grievances, Remedies and the State*, 2nd edn. (London: Sweet & Maxwell, 1994).
[4] R. Clayton and H. Tomlinson, *Civil Actions Against the Police*, 2nd edn. (London: Sweet & Maxwell, 1992).

rigorously, and to protect them forcefully when they are challenged. The words of John Philpott Curran are as true now as on 10 July 1790, when he first uttered them in connection with the right of election of the Lord Mayor of Dublin: 'The condition upon which God hath given liberty to man is eternal vigilance; which condition if he break, servitude is at once the consequence of his crime, and the punishment of his guilt'. Or as Nelson Mandela has written more recently of his and his country's walk along the road to freedom:

' . . . I have discovered the secret that after climbing a great hill, one only finds that there are many more hills to climb. I have taken a moment here to rest, to steal a view of the glorious vista that surrounds me, to look back on the distance I have come. But I can rest only for a moment, for with freedom come responsibilities, and I dare not linger, for my long walk is not yet ended.'[5]

The challenge is to plan for the future with ideals but without complacency, and to have faith in democratic processes without ignoring the capacity of any political system to subvert the liberty on which it is founded.

[5] N. Mandela, *Long Walk to Freedom* (London: Abacus, 1995), 751.

SELECT BIBLIOGRAPHY

The purpose of this bibliography is to indicate some starting-points for further reading on specific topics. The literature on civil liberties and human rights has expanded exponentially over the last ten years; no one person can possibly now be familiar with anything approaching the whole range of material which is available. What follows is highly selective, and concentrates mainly on printed books rather than other sources. More detailed references to useful material on particular topics is contained in the footnotes, and will not be replicated here.

A. LAW REPORTS

Several specialist series of law reports will be found to be useful. The *European Human Rights Reports* provide more or less full-text reports of selected judgments and decisions on admissibility by the European Court of Human Rights. The *International Human Rights Reports* provide texts emerging from the United Nations human-rights institutions, including the Human Rights Committee. A wide range of materials, including selected treaties and decisions on human-rights cases, can be found in the *Human Rights Law Journal*.

Comparative human-rights lawyers will find much valuable caselaw from national courts worldwide in *Butterworths Human Rights Cases*, although the high price of this series puts it beyond the reach of most individuals and many law libraries. Another useful source of decisions of national courts within the British Commonwealth on human-rights issues is to be found in the *Law Reports of the Commonwealth*.

Within the UK, most important decisions of courts are reported in the various series of generalist law reports. For those who want reports of relevant judgments from the courts of each jurisdiction within the UK brought together within a single, specialist series, including some judgments not fully reported elsewhere, the *Human Rights Reports—UK Cases* is beginning to represent a useful resource.

In addition, the internet is providing an increasingly valuable source of caselaw, nationally and internationally.

B. PERIODICALS

Important material may be found in a number of specialist and not-so-specialist journals. On international human-rights law, useful periodicals include the *Human Rights Law Journal*, the *International and Comparative Law Quarterly*, and the *British Year Book of International Law*. From a European perspective, valuable articles and regular discussions of recent developments will be found in the *European Law Review*, the *European Human Rights Law Review*, and *European Public Law*, as well as the *British Yearbook of European Law*. Significant articles on the impact of human-rights law on the various jurisdictions of the UK can be found in generalist journals, including the *Northern Ireland Legal Quarterly*, and in more specialized periodicals such as *Public Law*, the *European Human Rights Law Review*, and the *Journal of Civil Liberties* (all of which include sections on recent developments). Specialist periodicals, such as the *Yearbook of Copyright and Media Law* and the *International Journal of Refugee Law*, often contain significant material on specific topics.

C. GENERAL WORKS ON HUMAN RIGHTS AND CIVIL LIBERTIES

Among the best short introductions to the idea of human rights and their operation in international law are Paul Sieghart, *The Lawful Rights of Mankind: An Introduction to the International Legal Code of Human Rights* (Oxford: Oxford University Press, 1986), which has dated very little and can be read and enjoyed by anyone; and Scott Davidson, *Human Rights* (Buckingham: Open University Press, 1993), a book designed to introduce human rights to people with some knowledge of law, including suggestions for further reading on each topic. For a more detailed treatment, A. H. Robertson and J. G. Merrills, *Human Rights in the World: An Introduction to the Study of the International Protection of Human Rights*, 4th edn. (Manchester: Manchester University Press, 1996) is clear, well-organized and informative. A useful book of text and materials is Rebecca M. M. Wallace (assisted by Kenneth Dale-Risk), *International Human Rights: Text and Materials* (London: Sweet & Maxwell, 2001). Henry J. Steiner and Philip Alston, *International Human Rights in Context: Law, Politics, Morals*, 2nd edn. (Oxford: Oxford University Press, 2000), illuminates the operation of human rights by showing how they influence, and are in turn affected by, the development of international law, the maintenance of international relations, and national politics. All these books can be broadly categorized as being in favour of human rights, while being aware of their limitations. For those who seek an accessible counter-argument, Tom Campbell, Keith Ewing, and Adam Tomkins (eds.), *Sceptical Essays on Human Rights* (Oxford: Oxford University Press, 2001) contains a more systematically sceptical set of essays, looking at the shortcomings of human rights both in theory and in practice from a number of perspectives without being unreservedly hostile.

For a wide-ranging and very detailed book on the law of human rights, going well beyond the European Convention on Human Rights and including a wealth of comparative material, Richard Clayton and Hugh Tomlinson, *The Law of Human Rights* (Oxford: Oxford University Press, 2000), in two volumes (the second being a collection of national and international human-rights texts with 2001 supplement), provide an important point of reference. Lord Lester of Herne Hill QC and David Pannick QC, *Human Rights Law and Practice* (London: Butterworths, 1999, with supplement) is full of the authors' accumulated wisdom and experience as leading practitioners in the field. Both are aimed mainly at legal practitioners, and are priced accordingly, but parts of the book by Clayton and Tomlinson have been reprinted at a more affordable price in paperback as *Fair Trial Rights* and *Privacy and Freedom of Expression* (both Oxford: Oxford University Press, 2001).

There are many books covering the European Convention on Human Rights. Brian Simpson, *Human Rights and the End of Empire: Britain and the Genesis of the European Convention* (Oxford: Oxford University Press, 2001) is likely to be the leading account for some time to come of the origins of the Convention and the part played by the UK in its drafting. The best detailed treatments in English of the Convention as an international legal instrument are probably D. J. Harris, M. O'Boyle, and C. Warbrick, *Law of the European Convention on Human Rights* (London: Butterworths, 1995; new edition expected shortly), and P. van Dijk and G. J. H. van Hoof, *Theory and Practice of the European Convention on Human Rights*, 3rd edn. (The Hague: Kluwer, 1998). Excellent accounts at a less detailed level are Francis G. Jacobs and Robin C. A. White, *The European Convention on Human Rights* (Oxford: Clarendon Press, 1996), and A. H. Robertson and J. G. Merrills, *Human Rights in Europe: A Study of the European Convention on Human Rights*, 3rd edn. (Manchester: Manchester University Press, 1993); while Mark W. Janis, Richard Kay, and Anthony Bradley, *European Human Rights Law: Text and Materials*, 2nd edn. (Oxford: Oxford

University Press, 2000) provide materials alongside discussion. Brice Dickson (ed.), *Human Rights and the European Convention: The Effects of the Convention on the UK and Ireland* (London: Sweet & Maxwell, 1997) offers general assessments.

There is a growing body of literature on ways of making human rights derived from treaties work effectively in national law. David Kinley, *The European Convention on Human Rights: Compliance without Incorporation* (Aldershot: Dartmouth, 1993) was influential in arguing for the importance of parliamentary mechanisms to secure compliance with Convention rights. Philip Alston (ed.), *Promoting Human Rights through Bills of Rights: Comparative Perspectives* (Oxford: Oxford University Press, 1999) contains valuable essays on different methods of protecting rights in general, and some particular rights, in national legal systems. Several books provide studies of the impact of the Convention on other European countries, which may be increasingly important in the UK for understanding the process of making the Convention part of national law: see for example C. A. Gearty (ed.), *European Civil Liberties and the European Convention on Human Rights* (The Hague: Martinus Nijhoff, 1997); Robert Blackburn and Jorg Polakiewicz (eds.), *Fundamental Rights in Europe: the ECHR and its Member States, 1950–2000* (Oxford: Oxford University Press, 2001).

For an introduction to the development of an ethos of human rights in and through Community law, see Lammy Betten and Nicholas Grief, *EU Law and Human Rights* (London: Longman, 1998). Philip Alston, Mara Bustelo, and James Heenan (eds.), *The EU and Human Rights* (Oxford: Oxford University Press, 1999), contains a wide range of important essays offering acute discussions of the past developments and potential for the future from a variety of perspectives.

Books on civil liberties in the UK have tended to become rather dated since the implementation of the Human Rights Act 1998. For a stimulating history of civil liberties in the first half of the twentieth century, see K. D. Ewing and C. A. Gearty, *The Struggle for Civil Liberties: Political Freedom and the Rule of Law in Britain, 1914–1945* (Oxford: Oxford University Press, 2000). S. H. Bailey, D. J. Harris, and B. L. Jones, *Civil Liberties Cases and Materials*, 4th edn. (London: Butterworths, 1995) remains an outstanding volume, and a new edition, to appear shortly, will bring it fully up to date. Among text books, Helen Fenwick, *Civil Rights: New Labour, Freedom and the Human Rights Act* (Harlow: Longman, 2000) provides a stimulating analysis of many recent developments, as does Noel Whitty, Thérèse Murphy, and Stephen Livingstone, *Civil Liberties Law: The Human Rights Act Era* (London: Butterworths, 2001). Edwin Shorts and Claire de Than, *Human Rights Law in the UK* (London: Sweet & Maxwell, 2001) is useful on the structure of protection for civil liberties in the light of the Human Rights Act 1998, with additional material available via the internet.

D. WORKS ON THE HUMAN RIGHTS ACT 1998

Francesca Krug, *Values for a Godless Age* (Harmondsworth: Penguin, 2000) is a readable account of the purposes of the Human Rights Act 1998 in fostering the development of a culture of rights in the UK, together with an accessible analysis of the values that the Act enshrines. A useful and well organized selection of extracts from the parliamentary debates on the Human Rights Bill is provided by Jonathan Cooper and Adrian Marshall-Williams (eds.), *Legislating for Human Rights: The Parliamentary Debates on the Human Rights Bill* (Oxford: Hart Publishing, 2000). In addition, there are many articles on the Act and its genesis.

Going into more legal detail, a number of

books deal with the Act alongside the European Convention on Human Rights, combining national and international law. Some are organized on a subject-by-subject basis, while others are organized right-by-right. One of the best short treatments is that by John Wadham and Helen Mountfield, *Blackstone's Guide to the Human Rights Act 1998*, 2nd edn. (London: Blackstone, 2001). Of the more detailed accounts, Keir Starmer, *European Human Rights Law: The Human Rights Act 1998 and the European Convention on Human Rights* (London: Legal Action Group, 1999) is excellent and very reasonably priced, while good books aimed more at the practitioner, and priced accordingly, include Stephen Grosz, Jack Beatson QC, and Peter Duffy QC, *Human Rights: The 1998 Act and the European Convention* (London: Sweet & Maxwell, 2000), alongside Clayton and Tomlinson, *The Law of Human Rights*, and Lester and Pannick, *Human Rights Law and Practice*, already mentioned.

E. Works on particular topics in international law and English law

The values which underpin human rights have been very extensively discussed over many decades. Here we can do no more than suggest useful starting points for anyone wanting to explore the literature.

A basic problem for exponents of human-rights law is to find the appropriate balance between the interests of the community and the rights of individuals. For a stimulating discussion of the difficulties inherent in this process and the implications for the theory and practice of human rights, see Aileen McHarg, 'Reconciling Human Rights and the Public Interest: Conceptual Problems and Doctrinal Uncertainty in the Jurisprudence of the European Court of Human Rights' (1999) 62 *MLR* 671–96.

The values which human rights advance include autonomy, dignity, and equality. On autonomy, see Gerald Dworkin, *The Theory and Practice of Autonomy* (Cambridge: Cambridge University Press, 1988) and Thomas E. Hill, *Autonomy and Self-Respect* (Cambridge: Cambridge University Press, 1991). For discussion of dignity, see David Feldman, 'Human Dignity as a Legal Value' [1999] *PL* 682–702 and [2000] *PL* 61–76. An excellent philosophical investigation of equality is provided by Peter Westen, *Speaking of Equality: An Analysis of the Rhetorical Force of Equality in Moral and Legal Discourse* (Princeton, NJ: Princeton University Press, 1991).

To see how the theory of equality relates to anti-discrimination law, a good starting point is Christopher McCrudden, 'Introduction', in Christopher McCrudden (ed.), *Anti-Discrimination Law* (Aldershot: Dartmouth, 1991), xi–xxxi, a book which also reprints interesting essays on the subject which are not otherwise readily accessible. For general coverage of anti-discrimination law, see Richard Townshend-Smith, *Discrimination Law: Text, Cases and Materials* (London: Cavendish, 1998). Sex discrimination, which is heavily influenced by Community law, receives authoritative treatment in Sandra Fredman, *Women and the Law* (Oxford: Clarendon Press, 1997) and Evelyn Ellis, *European Community Sex Equality Law*, 2nd edn. (Oxford: Clarendon Press, 1998), although this is a field in which accounts are being constantly overtaken by new developments. Comparative treatment of the law governing sexual orientation is to be found in Robert Wintemute, *Sexual Orientation and Human Rights: The United States Constitution, the European Convention, and the Canadian Charter* (Oxford: Clarendon Press, 1995; paperback edition with updating introduction, 1997). On race discrimination in Europe, see the lectures collected in Sandra Fredman (ed.), *Discrimination and Human Rights: The Case of Racism* (Oxford: Oxford University Press, 2001). Sebastian Poulter, *Ethnicity, Law and Human Rights* (Oxford: Clarendon Press, 1998) is a perceptive monograph on the treatment of ethnicity in English law in the light of international standards. For an assessment of the confused state of the law on discrimination generally, see Bob Hepple QC, Mary Coussey, and Tufyal Choudhury, *Equality: A New Framework. Report of the Independent Review of the Enforcement of UK Anti-Discrimination Law* (Oxford: Hart Publishing, 2000).

There are a number of authoritative treatments of aspects of particular rights in national and international law. Ian Kennedy and Andrew Grubb (eds.), *Principles of Medical Law*, with cumulative supplements (Oxford: Oxford University Press, 2000), provides excellent discussions of medicolegal aspects of the right to life and the right to be free of inhuman and degrading treatment, while John Seymour, *Childbirth and the Law* (Oxford: Oxford University Press, 2000) is a thought-provoking guide to issues of autonomy and conflicts between the interests and rights of mother and child during childbirth. Malcolm D. Evans and Rod Morgan, *Preventing Torture: A Study of the European Convention for the Prevention of Torture and Inhuman or Degrading Treatment or Punishment* (Oxford: Clarendon Press, 1998), is a comprehensive account of its subject, with particular reference to the work of the European Committee for the Prevention of Torture.

The international law governing the treatment and rights of prisoners, including but going well beyond discussion of torture, inhuman and degrading treatment, and capital and corporal punishment, is examined with learning, experience, and humanity by Sir Nigel Rodley, *The Treatment of Prisoners under International Law*, 2nd edn. (Oxford: Oxford University Press, 1999).

The right to liberty depends on the structure of remedies for arbitrary or unlawful detention. The most up-to-date and illuminating comparative examination of this, and more besides, is provided by David Clark and Gerard McCoy QC, *The Most Fundamental Human Right: Habeas Corpus in the Commonwealth* (Oxford: Oxford University Press, 2000).

Freedom of movement into and within the state is less well protected in the legal systems of the UK than in international law. For the international law position on internal movement, see Chaloka Beyani, *Human Rights Standards and the Free Movement of People within States* (Oxford: Oxford University Press, 2000). On immigration in national law, see Ian Macdonald QC and Frances Webber, *Macdonald's Immigration Law and Practice*, 5th edn. (London: Butterworths, 2001).

Freedom of religion and belief in international law are well covered by Malcolm D. Evans, *Religious Liberty and International Law in Europe* (Cambridge: Cambridge University Press, 1997), and (with a slightly narrower focus) Carolyn Evans, *Freedom of Religion under the European Convention on Human Rights* (Oxford: Oxford University Press, 2001). On national law, see St. John Robilliard, *Religion and the Law: Religious Liberty in Modern English Law* (Manchester: Manchester University Press, 1984); A. Bradney, *Religions, Rights and Laws* (Leicester: Leicester University Press, 1993); Sebastian Poulter, *Ethnicity, Law and Human Rights* (above); and Carolyn Hamilton, *Family, Law and Religion* (London: Sweet & Maxwell, 1995).

Books abound on freedom of expression, information, and the media. Good starting points include Eric Barendt, *Freedom of Speech* (Oxford: Clarendon Press, 1987), which is now somewhat dated but still valuable, and will be refreshed by the new edition which is in preparation; Eric Barendt, *Broadcasting Law: A Comparative Study* (Oxford: Clarendon Press, 1993); Eric Barendt and Lesley Hitchens, *Media Law: Cases and Materials* (Harlow: Longman, 2000); Rachael Craufurd Smith, *Broadcasting Law and Fundamental Rights* (Oxford:

Clarendon Press, 1997); Thomas Gibbons, *Regulating the Media*, 2nd edn. (London: Sweet & Maxwell, 1998); and Patrick Birkinshaw, *Freedom of Information*, 3rd edn. (London: Butterworths, 2001). Grounds for interfering with freedom of expression also have books to themselves. National security is examined by David Vincent, *The Culture of Secrecy: Britain 1832–1998* (Oxford: Oxford University Press, 1998), while Laurence Lustgarten and Ian Leigh, *In from the Cold: National Security and Parliamentary Democracy* (Oxford: Clarendon Press, 1994) is still valuable although needing to be brought up to date. The law of contempt of court is well served by the magisterial monograph by C. J. Miller, *Contempt of Court*, 3rd edn. (Oxford: Clarendon Press, 2000), and David Eady and A. T. H. Smith, *Arlidge, Eady and Smith on Contempt* (London: Sweet & Maxwell, 2000). Nigel Lowe and Brenda Sufrin, *Borrie and Lowe: The Law of Contempt*, 3rd edn. (London: Butterworth, 1995) still has value, although it is now somewhat out of date. For a stimulating collection of essays on particular aspects of the general area, see Jack Beatson and Yvonne Cripps, *Freedom of Expression and Freedom of Information: Essays in Honour of Sir David Williams* (Oxford: Oxford University Press, 2000).

Books on the current law of freedom of assembly and protest have been largely outstripped by recent developments. See Kevin Gray, 'Equitable Property' (1994) 47(2) *CLP* 157–214. See also Kevin Gray, 'Property in Thin Air' (1991) 50 *CLJ* 252–307; Kevin Gray and Susan Francis Gray, 'Civil Rights, Civil Wrongs and Quasi-Public Space' [1999] *EHRLR* 46–102; Christopher McCrudden, 'Freedom of Speech and Racial Equality', in Peter Birks (ed.), *Pressing Problems in the Law Volume 1: Criminal Justice and Human Rights* (Oxford: Oxford University Press, 1995), 125–48; David Feldman, 'Content Neutrality', in Ian Loveland (ed.), *Importing the First Amendment: Freedom of Expression in American, English and European Law* (Oxford: Hart Publishing, 1998), 139–71; David Feldman, 'Protest and Tolerance: Legal Values and the Control of Public-Order Policing', in Raphael Cohen-Almagor (ed.), *Liberal Democracy and the Limits of Tolerance: Essays in Honour and Memory of Yitzhak Rabin* (Ann Arbor, Mich.: University of Michigan Press, 2000), 43–69; David Feldman, 'Property and Public Protest', in F. Meisel and P. J. Cook (eds.), *Property and Protection, Legal Rights and Restrictions: Essays in Honour of Brian W. Harvey* (Oxford: Hart Publishing, 2000), 31–59.

Human rights in the law relating to children are well covered by Geraldine Van Bueren, *The International Law on the Rights of the Child* (The Hague: Martinus Nijhoff, 1998), and, in relation to English law, Jane Fortin, *Children's Rights and the Developing Law* (London: Butterworths, 1998, with internet-based up-dates).

INDEX